# The Craft of the Country Cook

# The Craft of the Country Cook

*From A-Z: over 1,000 recipes & food ideas*

by

## Pat Katz

A Cloudburst Press Book
Hartley & Marks, Publishers

*A Cloudburst Press Book*

Published in the U.S.A. by
Hartley & Marks, Inc.
P.O. Box 147
Point Roberts, WA 98281

Published in Canada by
Hartley & Marks, Ltd.
3663 W. Broadway
Vancouver, B.C. V6R 2B8

*Cover art*: Detail from "The Kitchen," watercolor from
the series *A Home*, by Carl Larsson. By permission of the
National museum, Stockholm. *Photograph*: Statens Konstmuseer.

*Illustrators*: Sharyn Yuen; Robert English

*Library of Congress Cataloging-in-Publication Data*

Katz, Pat, 1934–
Craft of the country cook.

1. Cookery,   I. Title
TX715.K194   1988        641.5        88-2671
ISBN 0-88179-014-1
ISBN 0-88179-015-1 (pbk.)


Designed and typeset by The Typeworks
Manufactured in the United States of America
Smythe-sewn and printed on acid-free paper
1st Printing, 1988

# INTRODUCTION

I would very much like you to meet this, my book, without delay or lengthy preamble. I ask, therefore, that you simply leaf through its one hundred and seventy-seven sections, each about a different food or food handling procedure, and introduce yourself. Find a topic that interests you, and (if I have done a good job), you will gain a better over-all understanding of that food or procedure, and have, as well, clear, useful directions for relevant techniques such as storage and preparation. I also hope that the recipes and ideas included in every food section will lead to a healthier, more imaginative enjoyment of all that you eat.

My other great hope is that this book will be a help to all my readers—to my family, who, for the ten years plus of its construction, so cheerfully ate, and then discussed alphabetical meals ("A" ingredients one month, "B" ingredients the next), to old friends whose unflagging interest, encouragement, and generous sharing of knowledge helped me more than they probably know, and to all those friends in spirit whom I may never meet in person, who also seek a better understanding of their food, and a closer involvement with its cultivation, collection, and preparation.

I want to express my appreciation to COUNTRYSIDE magazine and all of its readers, for the invaluable experience and advice I received over the many years I wrote its "Country Kitchen" column. I wish also to thank my editor, Sue Tauber, for her painstaking, word-by-word evaluations and criticisms of a very long and sometimes clumsy manuscript.

PAT KATZ

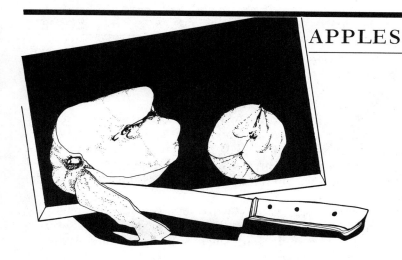

IT IS HARD TO IMAGINE A FOOD MORE VERSATILE THAN THE APPLE. IT IS everyone's favorite for eating raw, for making sauce and juice, and for drying. Apples are as delicious in salads or in cooked meat and vegetable dishes as they are when made into desserts. A winter's supply of apples stored in several ways, some in a root cellar or other cool place, some canned, and some dried, guarantees a healthful diet as well as a varied and pleasant one. The doctor that stays away when an apple is eaten every day might easily be increased to three who stay away every day, one for eating a raw apple, one for a glass of apple juice or dish of applesauce, and one for a handful of dried apple rings.

There are apple varieties numbering in the thousands, among them early and late varieties, and special varieties for particular regions and climatic conditions with additional variations in size, color, flavor and texture of the fruit. Those who plant their own apple trees can choose heirloom varieties, or apples known for their special flavors and textures, rather than the standard commercial varieties. Also many wild or untended apple trees are worthwhile for the excellent juice and sauce that can be made from their fruit.

## HANDLING APPLES

Apples should not be picked until they are at the peak of ripeness. It is also important to pick them carefully without bruising them or damaging the fruiting spur, the small branch from which the apple grows. Bruised apples and windfalls should be used without delay, since they spoil quickly. Methods of storage and preparation depend to a large extent on the apples' variety. Early varieties do not keep well in cold storage and are usually canned or dried. Late varieties will keep for months in cold storage and are also good for canning and drying. The ways of cooking and canning apples will depend on their various textures and flavors. Some varieties break down when cooked, making them very good for applesauce, but unsuitable where a

---

### STORAGE

**Canning**  *Chunks or Slices* (For varieties that hold shape when cooked.) Drop several cups into boiling juice, syrup, or water. Cook 5 min., lift out with strainer, fill jars. Repeat with more apples. (Optional: put whole spices in jars.) Add boiling cooking liquid, ½ in. headroom. Process boiling water bath. Pints: 15 min. Quarts: 20 min.

**Baked**  Core, put 1 teaspoon honey, dash cinnamon in each apple. Bake to half done (see below). Pack in jars, add boiling juice or syrup, ½ in. headroom. Process boiling water bath. Pints or quarts: 20 min. Refer to CANNING section. Also see CANNING APPLESAUCE, *Apple Cider Butter,* and CANNING CIDER, below, and PICKLING CRABAPPLES, in the PICKLING section.

**Cold Storage**  See KEEPING APPLES IN COLD STORAGE, below.

**Drying**  (Superb flavor!) Peel, core, slice. Spread on trays or thread on string and hang. Dry until leathery, so no moisture shows when broken and squeezed. For making fruit leather from sauce, refer to DRYING section.

**Freezing**  (Least practical method. Texture poor when thawed, but acceptable if cooked.) *Chunks or Slices* Sprinkle with ½ teaspoon ascorbic acid powder diluted in 3 tablespoons water, or pack in liquid. Refer to FREEZING section, for LIQUIDS IN WHICH TO FREEZE FRUITS.

---

3 MEDIUM APPLES = ABOUT 1 POUND = ABOUT 1½ CUPS APPLESAUCE;  1 BUSHEL APPLES = 16–20 QUARTS APPLESAUCE OR 2–3 GALLONS CIDER

chunky texture is wanted. Very tart apples are outstanding for cooking, but mouth-puckering eaten raw. Very sweet or bland apples taste best in mixtures with tart fruits. (Refer to COMBINING SWEET AND TART FRUITS, in the FRUITS section.)

Apples are very often sprayed with chemicals to prevent damage from insects and disease, and in some areas it is difficult to grow useable apples without sprays. This makes unsprayed, homegrown apples and wild apples especially precious, but all apples—even sprayed ones—are worth using. (Refer to INSECTICIDES IN FRUIT, in the FRUITS section.)

*Crabapples* Any apple variety with very small fruits might be called a crabapple, but the name is generally associated with flowering ornamentals, or wild varieties with small, sour, sometimes astringent fruits. Though sour crabapples can be used in all the same ways as sour apples, it is easiest to make juice from them, because they can then be cooked without peeling, coring, or removing stems. Some ornamental crabapple fruits are so bland as to be almost tasteless. These are good pickled whole, or when cooked with strong flavored fruits; by themselves they are not very useful.

## APPLES IN COLD STORAGE

Only fall maturing varieties of apples keep well in cold storage. Early apples can be refrigerated from one to several weeks, but no longer. Different varieties of fall and winter apples keep for different lengths of time. Some must be used by January while others will keep until May.

Long storage apples must be perfect, without blemishes or bruises, and with their stems left on. The ideal conditions for storing apples are 32°F, with high humidity. In a root cellar or in similar conditions, apples keep well in open containers. If to be kept in a cool, dry place, they should be individually wrapped in newspaper, or packed in a closed container to retain moisture. The traditional container is an old style milk can, but a box lined with a plastic bag with a few holes cut in it can be used just as well. Some other materials that work as packing are dry leaves, straw, and shredded paper.

Loose apples should not be stored in the same area as cabbage, cabbage family vegetables, turnips, or potatoes. The apples may absorb vegetable odors, and their moisture and gases may cause potatoes to sprout. It is nice to have a quite separate storage area for fruits, but if that is not possible, apples should always be packed in a dry material, as described.

When time for careful packing is limited, or a special storage space not available, most fall maturing apples will keep 2 months or so in any cool place, such as an unheated bedroom. It is important that the temperature remain above freezing. Those apples not quickly used can be preserved in other ways when time permits.

Stored apples should be checked periodically for spoilage. If the proverbial bad apple is not removed, it very definitely will spoil the whole barrel or bagful. When first stored, they do not have to be checked very often, but toward the end of their storage life they should be checked every week or two. (Refer to COLD STORAGE OF FRUITS, in the COLD STORAGE section.)

## APPLESAUCE

There is almost no limit to the amount of applesauce a family can use in a year. It is very good plain, and goes with everything from pancakes and pork chops to yogurt. It can be used in baking, in desserts such as fruit gelatines and ice creams, and dried to make fruit leather. It is the perfect way to use imperfect apples and windfalls, or wild apples, that need trimming to remove wormy or damaged places.

Any variety of apple can be made into sauce. Some make delicious sauce with nothing added at all, others taste best if perked up with lemon juice, or sweetened with honey or another sweetener. Traditional spices, such as cinnamon and cloves, herb seeds such as fennel and caraway, lemon or orange peel, and other flavorings can be added to taste. Delicious sauces can also be made by combining apples with other fruits.

Applesauce can be prepared with a variety of textures as well as flavors. It can have a smooth, purée-like texture, a coarse, or a chunky texture. Smooth applesauce is easiest to make, since the apples do not have to be peeled or cored, but many people prefer a chunky or coarse applesauce.

*Smooth Applesauce* Wash apples and cut them in quarters or eighths, trimming away bad spots. Do not peel or core. Put the pieces in a pot with enough water to almost but not quite cover them. Bring to a boil, stirring occasionally to cook them evenly. When very soft, purée and remove skins and seeds with a food mill or strainer. (Refer to the KITCHEN UTENSILS section.) If the sauce is too thin it can be simmered uncovered in a heavy pot over low heat to concentrate it. Stir often to prevent sticking and burning. It can be canned as soon as it is thick enough to suit family tastes.

*Chunky Applesauce* Prepare apples by peeling, coring, and cutting in quarters or eighths. (Peeling is optional, but texture of the peels in the sauce can be bothersome. (See USING PEELS AND CORES below.) An apple peeler and corer makes that job quick and easy. To prevent darkening, the apple pieces can be sprinkled with lemon juice as they are prepared, but this is not necessary if they are to be cooked at once.

Put the apples in a pot, and cover about ¾ of them with water. (More can be added later, if necessary. As stored apples become dryer they need more cooking water than freshly picked apples.) Cook until they are very soft. Textures differ according to variety; some break

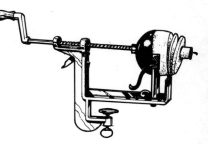

*Apple peeler/corer*

down completely and some remain in large pieces. Either way tastes good. The sauce can be canned as soon as the apples are cooked through.

*Canning Applesauce*   Stir boiling hot applesauce for an even thickness and ladle into canning jars, allowing ½ inch headroom. Process in a boiling water bath, for 10 minutes for both pints and quarts. (Refer to the CANNING section.)

*Apple Butter*   Applesauce is easily made into apple butter by cooking it with sweetening and spices until very thick. (Refer to MAKING JAMS AND FRUIT BUTTERS, in the JAM AND JELLY section.) To make it without sweetening see *Apple Cider Butter,* below.

## APPLE CIDER

Apple cider is the juice of raw apples made by grinding or crushing apples to break down their cell walls and then pressing to extract juice. It is called sweet cider when fresh, and hard cider after it begins to ferment. Apple "juice" is strained from cooked apples or it is cider that has been strained to clarify it and heated to keep it sweet. (Refer to the FRUITS section.)

Making apple cider is a traditional fall activity for many households. It is an excellent way to use windfalls and bruised or imperfect apples, but the cider must be made soon after the apples are gathered. Even one spoiled or moldy apple can ruin the flavor of a whole batch of cider. Wash apples before making cider, especially if they have been recently sprayed, but there is no need to remove stems, peels or cores. A blend of sweet and sour apples makes especially good cider.

It is possible to make small amounts of cider by cutting up apples, grinding them in a meat grinder, then pressing them in a fruit press. (Refer to the KITCHEN UTENSILS section.) It is even possible to crush apples with a mallet, tie the mash in a cloth bag and squeeze or press to extract juice. Extractors for making carrot juice will extract small amounts of cider, but heavier equipment is needed if cider is to be made by the gallon. Homestead sized cider presses are widely available, and advertized in magazines and catalogs featuring country items. They have two parts: one that grinds the apples and one that presses them. It is important that the grinder does a good job at reducing the apples to pulp. If coarse apple pieces are left, not all of the cider can be squeezed. Pulp from a bushel of apples should yield 3 gallons of cider compared to about 2 gallons when coarsely ground. After pressing, cider is usually strained through a sieve.

Fresh cider stays sweet for only a day or two at room temperature. If refrigerated immediately, it will stay sweet for a week or more. Many people like cider best when it is just beginning to ferment and has a light fizziness. When completely fermented it becomes cider vinegar. (Refer to the VINEGAR section.)

The pulp left from pressing cider is called pomace, and can be used to make pectin. (See USING PEELS AND CORES, below. Also, refer to the PECTIN section.)

***Canning or Freezing Cider*** Cider can be heated to a boil and canned like any fruit juice, but the flavor stays fresher if it is canned like grape juice (p. 634). Though freezing also preserves the fresh flavor, finding freezer space can be a problem. A frozen concentrate can be made (refer to CONCENTRATED JUICE in the FREEZING section), but this is time consuming and impractical for large quantities.

***Cider Syrup*** For an intensely sweet syrup, boil cider in an open kettle until reduced to about ¼ its original volume. This can be canned by the open kettle method. (Refer to the CANNING section.)

Cider syrup can be used to sweeten and flavor baked goods, fruit desserts, and in other foods where a fruit flavor is welcome. It is also good served with pancakes or waffles. For "ciderade", mix a few tablespoons of syrup with ice water.

***Hard Cider*** One way to "make" hard cider is to keep a watch on cider as it ferments, and drink it while it is bubbly and alcoholic, before it can turn to vinegar. It takes special attention to hold cider at the alcoholic stage. Adding extra sweetening to increase its alcoholic content is one possibility. (Refer to the WINE section.)

Old recipes often call for the addition of raisins or grapes, as in these nineteenth century directions for Crab Cider, from *Housekeeping in Old Virginia*:

"To a thirty-gallon cask put one bushel clean picked grapes. Fill up with sweet cider, just from the press—crab preferred. Draw off in March, and it is fit for use. Add brandy, as much as you think best."

## USING APPLE PEELS AND CORES

Most of the vitamins and minerals in apples are in or right under the skin, while both skins and cores are rich in pectin and flavor. There is, therefore, ample reason to save and use them. As the pomace, or pulp, left from pressing apples for cider is composed largely of peels and cores, it is also valuable.

There are many warnings against eating apple seeds because of their cyanide content. They *can* be dangerous if eaten in large quantities, but swallowing an occasional seed or using peels and cores in the ways described here is absolutely harmless. The leftover seeds and other solids are always strained off and eventually discarded.

The most basic way to use peels and cores is for making juice. Cover them with water, bring to a boil, and cook until the apple parts are soft. Strain through cloth. This juice can be used as a drink or made into jelly or pectin. The juice from pomace is blander than the juice from unpressed peels and cores. This makes it ideal for pectin, but not so good for beverages or jellies unless other flavors are added.

(Refer to the JAM AND JELLY and PECTIN sections.) To make vinegar from fresh peels and cores refer to the VINEGAR FROM MASHED FRUIT, TRIMMINGS OR CULLS, in the VINEGAR section.

Apple peels and cores can be dried and stored for later use. They are spread out on trays and dried in a food dryer, or any warm, airy place. They can then be reconstituted with water and used in any of the above ways, or for APPLE TEA AND APPLE BEER (see APPLE IDEAS, below).

## APPLE RECIPES

(In the days before fast transportation and supermarkets people used only what they had, and thanks to the apples' good storage qualities, they had lots of them all winter long. As a result, apple recipes of every imaginable kind abound. The recipes given here feature apples in vegetable dishes and in other non-sweet combinations, rather than in familiar sweet desserts.)

### *Apple and Onion Bake* (Makes 6—8 side servings.)

*6 medium-sized tart apples, cored and sliced medium thick*
*1 large onion, sliced medium thick, separated into rings*
*2 tablespoons (about) butter*
*pepper, salt, optional*
*½ cup dry bread crumbs*

Lay half of the apple slices in a medium-sized buttered baking dish and add a layer of half of the onions. Dot with butter, and sprinkle with seasonings, if desired. Add another layer of apples and one of the onions. Repeat seasonings, cover with bread crumbs, and dot with butter. Pour ¼ cup water over all, cover with a lid or with aluminum foil, and bake in a moderate oven, about 375°F for 1 hour, or until the apples are done. Remove the lid for the last 15 minutes.

**Apple, Onion, and Tomato Savory** Slice several fresh tomatoes and place them in alternating layers with the apples and onions. (Canned tomatoes can also be used.) Omit water and bake as above.

### *Braised Apples and Cabbage* (Makes 6—8 side servings.)

*4 tablespoons bacon fat, chicken fat, or oil*
*1 tablespoon honey or 2 tablespoons sugar*
*1 small onion, finely chopped*
*4 cups tart apples, cored and sliced thin*
*4 cups cabbage, finely shredded*
*2 tablespoons vinegar*
*½ teaspoon caraway seed*
*2 teaspoons (or to taste) cayenne pepper*
*salt, optional*

Heat the fat or oil in a large, heavy frying pan. Add sweetening and stir. If using sugar, let it brown slightly. Add the onion and fry over low heat until it is limp. Add the apples, cabbage, vinegar, caraway, pepper, and salt, if desired. Stir to combine ingredients, and cook over moderate heat, stirring occasionally until the cabbage and apples are done (usually about 20 minutes). If the mixture becomes very dry or starts to stick add a few tablespoons of water. This combination, rich because of the fat, is best as a cold weather dish.

## *Apple Carrot Tzimmes*          (Makes 6–8 side servings.)

| | |
|---|---|
| 4 apples, cut in chunks and cored | ½ cup orange juice |
| carrots, sliced, an equal volume | 2 teaspoons honey |
| 1 tablespoon whole grain barley | ½ teaspoon nutmeg |
| 2 tablespoons butter, or other fat | ½ teaspoon cinnamon |

Put all ingredients in a sauce pan, cover, and simmer over low heat for 1½ to 2 hours. Stir occasionally and add a few tablespoons of water if it dries out. Spicy, flavorful, and excellent with plainly cooked meats.

## *Creamed Apple Soup*          (Makes 5–6 medium bowls.)

| | |
|---|---|
| 1 quart applesauce | ¼ teaspoon cloves |
| 3–4 tablespoons lemon juice, or vinegar | ½ teaspoon cinnamon |
| honey, optional (Omit if applesauce is sweetened.) | ½ cup raisins, or other dried fruit. (Chop if pieces are large and pre-soak if necessary.) |
| 1 teaspoon rosemary | ½ cup cream |

Heat the applesauce with 2 cups of water or enough water to thin it to a soup consistency. Add lemon juice or vinegar and honey, adjusting these for a sweet and sour flavor. Amounts will depend on the flavor of the applesauce. Add the rosemary, cloves, cinnamon, and raisins or dried fruit. Include soaking water if there is any. Simmer about 10 minutes to blend flavors. Just before serving stir in the cream.

## *Baked Apples with a Choice of Fillings*     (Makes 6–10 servings.)

| | |
|---|---|
| 6 large, or 8 to 10 medium apples | ½ cup (about) orange juice, other fruit juice, or water |
| 1½–2 cups filling (Use one of the fillings described below or improvise with whatever is on hand.) | |

A variety of apple that holds its shape when cooked is best, but baked apples taste very good even when they fall apart.

Core the apples starting at the stem end. Do not cut through the bottom. Peel away about a ½ inch ring of skin around the core hole.

---

### APPLE IDEAS

**Apple Muffins, Pancakes, Baked Goodies** Raw apples chopped, sliced or grated are as versatile for baking as raisins. For a dozen apple muffins, add 1 cup of chopped raw apple to the dry ingredients and put a round slice of apple on top of the batter for each muffin. Just before baking a drizzle of honey and dash of spice can be added as a finishing touch. With pancake batter either dip in sliced apple rings and fry, or add chopped or grated apple to the batter. Try chopped or grated apple in any baked goods that go well with a fruit flavor, such as oatmeal cookies.

**Apple Desserts with Herb Seeds** Instead of the usual spices used to flavor apple desserts, try crushed or powdered herb seeds. Anise, fennel, caraway, coriander, or dill are all very good. (Refer to the HERB SEEDS section.)

**Apple Slump** For this old-fashioned dessert, heat sweetened applesauce in a wide pot with a tight lid. Add one of the above herb seeds for flavor if desired. Prepare dumplings according to any favorite recipe and cook them in the applesauce. Sweeten only the sauce, not the dumplings.

**Baked Apple Sauce** For a particularly delicious apple sauce, bake whole apples without peeling or coring them. When they are soft scrape the sauce away from the peels and cores.

**APPLE IDEAS,** *cont.*

**Apple Tea and Apple Beer**

Dry some apple peels and store them in a jar. To make tea, pour 1 or 2 cups boiling water over a handful of peels and let steep for a few minutes, as for herb tea. Other flavorings, such as mint leaves or rose hips, can be included. For apple beer, begin as for making tea, but let sit at room temperature for about 2 days, then strain and drink. The flavor is "applely" and sometimes a little fizzy.

**OTHER RECIPES FEATURING APPLES**

**Recipes With Apple Cider**

This will help keep the apple from bursting. The hole for stuffing can be enlarged by scraping out extra pulp with a small spoon. The pulp can either be added to the filling, or put in the pan around the apples to make a sauce.

Stuff the apples, mounding up any extra filling on top. Set them close together in a baking dish and pour the orange juice or other liquid around them. The amount of liquid can be increased if apple pulp is put in the pan around the apples, or if extra juice is liked. Bake in a moderate oven, about 375°F, for 40 to 60 minutes, or until the apples are soft when poked with a fork. If preferred, they can be kept moist by basting with the pan juices.

Most baked apples are good eaten either warm or cold. A little milk or cream goes well with most variations.

*Bread Crumb Filling*   Mix 1½ cups bread crumbs with ¼ to ½ cup chopped nuts, seeds, or shredded coconut. Perhaps add a handful of raisins or other dried fruit. Flavor with spices like cinnamon and nutmeg, and add grated lemon or orange rind to taste. For sweetening add honey, maple syrup, or molasses. Mix well and moisten with fruit juice or water. Stuff into the apples. Put a dab of butter on top.

*Date Nut Filling*   Scoop extra pulp out of the centers of the apples, and mix with ¾ cup chopped dates, and ½ cup chopped nuts or sunflower seeds. Fill the apples, and sprinkle with cinnamon or cloves if desired.

*Date Cheese Filling*   Mix ¾ cup chopped dates with ¾ cup dry cheese cut in small cubes and fill the apples. Cheddar works well.

*Rum Raisin Filling*   Soak about 1 cup of raisins in enough rum to cover them for several hours or until the raisins are plump. Fill the apples (they do not have to be very full), and add a little of the leftover soaking rum to each one. If desired, sprinkle with honey or brown sugar, and grated lemon peel. Cover for the first 20 minutes and finish baking uncovered. Another variation would be to use a different liquor, such as white wine, and another kind of dried fruit.

*Sausage Filling*   Mince a tablespoon of onion, and a clove of garlic (optional). Fry until transparent in a teaspoon of oil or butter. Add about ½ pound breakfast sausage broken in pieces. Fry gently until it is cooked through. Stuff the apples, and if desired, sweeten with a little honey or brown sugar. They should be eaten while warm or hot, and make a splendid holiday breakfast.

*Apple Cider Butter*                                            (Makes 3–4 pints)

*1 gallon cider*                              cinnamon, optional
*3 quarts apple, cored, peeled and cut*
*   in small pieces*

Put the cider in a large kettle and boil down to about 2 quarts. Skim off foam as it forms. Add the apple pieces and continue cooking, stirring frequently until thickened. This may take up to an hour. Add cinnamon, if desired. Pour into containers and seal as for open kettle canning. (Refer to the CANNING section.)

Large quantities of this butter can be made in one batch. The only limitation is the size of the kettle. In the past it was sometimes made outdoors in a copper kettle using as much as 25 gallons of cider at a time.

***Cider Butter Leather***    Fruit leather made by drying this butter comes out rich and sweet, almost like candy. (Refer to DRYING FRUIT, in the DRYING section.)

# APRICOTS

S WEET, FRESH TREE RIPENED APRICOTS ARE TREATS UNKNOWN TO many people. The ripe fruit does not keep long or ship well, so to enjoy them at their peak, one has to live where apricots grow, or raise one's own. The best apricot growing areas are in the western half of the United States and Canada. Elsewhere it is best to buy dried apricots. They rank with raisins and prunes as superior snack foods, and are good in all kinds of cooked mixtures as well. The apricot's flavor is quite intense and gives a special zing to foods even when added in small amounts. In pastry or cookie fillings, poultry stuffings, and sauces for meat, apricots provide the touch that makes a dish memorable.

As apricots are high in vitamin A, and contain respectable amounts of other vitamins and minerals, they are a valuable fruit from every point of view.

## HANDLING APRICOTS

After apricots are picked sugar no longer forms, so they must be left on the tree until fully ripe. Though they change color if picked green, they will never lose their astringence. When very ripe they become soft, tending to fall apart with cooking, but their fine flavor remains intact. For canning it is best to pick them just before they get soft. For juice or puree, soft apricots are excellent. If they become overripe, however, they may lose acidity, and it is then necessary to add lemon juice or vinegar when canning them.

Apricots for drying are sometimes picked while firm because the dried fruit has a better shape, but they are sweeter if left on the tree until soft and ready to drop. If there is grass under the tree they can be gathered after they drop. Soft apricots will flatten into thin pieces when dried.

Apricots from wild or volunteer trees may have wiry fibers around the pits. The best way to remove them is to cook the fruits, and put

## STORAGE

**Canning**   Leave whole or pit. Blanching and peeling optional.

**Hot Pack** (Preferred, except for varieties that fall apart easily.) Simmer 2–3 min. in boiling syrup, juice or water. Drain, pack. (Optional: 1–2 pits per jar for flavor.) Add boiling cooking liquid, ½ in. headroom. Process boiling water bath. Pints: 20 min. Quarts: 25 min.

**Raw Pack** Fill jars, add boiling syrup, juice or water, ½ in. headroom. Process boiling water bath. Pints: 25 min. Quarts: 30 min. Refer to CANNING section. Also see CANNING FRUIT JUICE AND SAUCE, in the FRUITS section, and *Apricot Chutney*, below. Caution: if overripe, add 2 teaspoons lemon juice per pint, 4 teaspoons per quart.

**Drying**   Arrange halves cut side up. Dry until leathery. To use like raisins, dry chopped pieces. Excellent for fruit leather. (Refer to DRYING section.)

**Freezing**   Blanch 30 seconds in boiling water to prevent tough skins. Remove pits. Optional: Sprinkle with ascorbic acid solution or lemon juice. Pack in liquid. Refer to FREEZING section.

2–2½ POUNDS FRESH APRICOTS = I QUART CANNED OR I–I½ QUARTS FROZEN; 5 POUNDS FRESH = ABOUT I POUND DRIED; I BUSHEL = 20 TO 24 QUARTS CANNED

them through a food mill or strainer to make a smooth purée or juice. It is necessary to add pectin to apricots when making most kinds of preserves. (Refer to the PECTIN section.)

***Apricot Pits and Kernels*** The kernels inside apricot pits have a strong almond smell and taste, and have been used in small amounts to flavor other foods. Since these kernels also contain a cyanide compound, eating them in large numbers is dangerous. There is no harm in putting 1 or 2 pits in a jar when canning apricots, nor in canning whole, unpitted apricots, since the pits are eventually discarded. However, recipes are questionable if they call for shelling these pits for chopping into jams or other mixtures.

It is possible to remove the cyanide from shelled apricot kernels by soaking them in many changes of warm (about 140°F) water over a period of 24 hours. They should taste free of any bitterness and will then be safe to use like almonds. Apricots, plums, cherries, peaches, and almonds are closely related botanically and all have almond flavored kernels, but apricot kernels are used most often because the pits are easier to shell and have bigger kernels. Commercial macaroon paste has also been made from apricot kernels, and oil is extracted from the kernels of all of these fruits for various uses.

## APRICOT RECIPES

***Apricot Dumplings*** (Makes 10–15 dumplings.)

| | |
|---|---|
| *2 cups flour, preferably wholewheat* | *¼ cup (about) honey* |
| *½ cup shortening or butter* | *cinnamon to taste* |
| *1 egg, lightly beaten* | *10–15 apricots, whole, unpitted* |
| *water* | *1 tablespoon (about) butter* |
| | *milk to glaze tops, optional* |

Make pastry dough by putting the flour in a bowl and cutting the shortening or butter into it. Work in the egg and several spoons of cold water to make a stiff dough. Knead just enough to form a ball, cover, and refrigerate for half an hour, or until chilled. Roll out the dough on a floured board and cut into squares about 4 by 4 inches. Adjust this size to suit the size of the apricots.

Mix honey and cinnamon and roll each apricot in it until well coated. Set an apricot on a square of dough and put on a small dab of butter. Wet the edges of the dough with a finger dipped in water. Shape the dough around each apricot and press to seal it. The dumplings can be made round, or the corners of the dough can be brought together on top of the apricot and pressed to the shape of a fat "four cornered" hat.

Put the dumplings on an ungreased baking sheet, prick each once or twice with a fork, and brush the tops with milk, if desired. Bake in a moderately hot oven, 375°F for 25 to 30 minutes.

These dumplings are an interesting and delicious alternative to richer pastries. They are especially good eaten warm.

---

**APRICOT IDEAS**

**Apricot Nectar Treats**
Apricot nectar is a purée that is thin enough to drink. If a good supply is canned, many special treats are insured. It can be made into frozen apricot desserts (refer to the ICE CREAM SHERBET AND POPSICLES section), or made into apricot gelatine (refer to the GELATINE section).

**Apricot Nectar Milkshake**
Mix 1 cup nectar, 1 cup milk, and 2 scoops preferred ice cream. Or make a blender concoction with apricot nectar, yogurt, an ice cube, and maybe a banana to sweeten and thicken it.

*Persian Lamb
and Apricot Stew*     (Makes about 6 dinner servings.)

| | |
|---|---|
| 4 tablespoons butter | pepper and salt, to taste |
| 1 medium onion, chopped fine | 2 rounded tablespoons raisins |
| 1 pound lean lamb, cut in small cubes | 1 cup dried apricot halves water |
| ½ teaspoon cinnamon | 2 cups raw rice |

Heat the butter in a pot and sauté the onion in it until it is soft. Add the lamb and brown it lightly over moderate heat. Season with cinnamon, pepper, and a little salt, then add the raisins and apricots and stir together for a minute or two. Add water to cover all ingredients. Simmer covered over low heat for 1½ hours, or until the lamb is tender. The mixture should be like a stew. If too juicy, simmer uncovered for a few minutes to reduce liquid.

Meanwhile, heat the rice in a separate pot, using about 3½ cups water, and cook covered until the water is absorbed. When both stew and rice are done, alternate them in a large heavy pot, beginning and ending with rice. Cover and cook over very low heat for 20 minutes. If there is a chance of the bottom burning use an insulated pad under the pot. A cloth can be stretched over the pot under the lid to absorb steam and make the rice lighter.

*Apricot Sourdough
Baked Skillet Bread*     (Makes 6–8 medium portions.)

| | |
|---|---|
| 1½ cups flour (Whole wheat or mixtures with cornmeal, millet flour or other flours.) | 1 cup dried apricots; halved if small, quartered if large |
| ½–1 teaspoon baking soda | 1½ cups (about) sourdough starter |
| 2 tablespoons oil or fat, melted | milk or water, optional |

Grease or oil an 8 or 9 inch cast iron skillet and put over very low heat to warm up while mixing the bread dough.

Mix or sift the flour with the baking soda. The amount of soda depends on the sourness of the sourdough. If very sour, a full teaspoon is needed. Work in the oil or melted fat, mix in the apricots, then add enough sourdough to make a fairly stiff batter. If the sourdough is thick it may be necessary to work a little milk or water into the batter. Spread the batter in the warm skillet. Cover loosely. A pan or bowl turned upside down can be used. Cook on top of the stove over low heat for 20 minuts. Preheat the oven to 350°F. Remove the lid, and bake for 30 minutes or until lightly browned. Cool the loaf on a rack.

This bread is somewhat dense with exceptional flavor, and good used like cornbread and other quickbreads.

**APRICOT IDEAS,** *cont.*

**Baked Apricots**   Preheat the oven to 300°F. Arrange pitted apricots in a shallow, buttered baking dish. They can be 2 or 3 layers deep. Drizzle with honey or vanilla sugar (sugar that has had a vanilla bean enclosed with it). Bake until the apricots are soft, 30 to 40 minutes. For a delightful breakfast version of this dish, set the apricots on buttered slices of bread on an oiled baking sheet, sweeten and bake.

Plums and peaches are also good baked in these ways. Plums bake a little faster and peaches a little slower than apricots.

**Sautéed Apricots**   Slice an onion and a green pepper and sauté them for 5 minutes or so in a little butter, bacon fat, or oil. Add fresh apricot halves, and sauté slowly till they are soft. Serve as a side dish with meats.

**Apricot Nut Sauce**   Mix dried apricots with whole or chopped nuts of any kind, cover with water, and soak for about 2 days. This makes a delicious, rich sauce. For a favorite Middle Eastern combination, soak dried apricots with a few prunes and raisins, halved almonds, and either pistachio nuts or pine nuts. Rose water (refer to the ROSE section) is usually added for more flavor.

A quick version can be made by pouring boiling water over the dried apricot and nut mixtures, and soaking for a few hours. However, the long soaking gives the richest flavor. Sherry or another liquor may be used instead of water for a festive touch.

### Apricot Chutney                                    (Makes 3–4 pints.)

3 pounds apricots, pitted and
    quartered
1 ½ cups (about) vinegar
1 cup (about) honey, or 1 ½ cups
    sugar
1 ½ cups onions, chopped
1 sweet pepper, chopped, optional
1 cup raisins, or other dried fruit,
    chopped if pieces are large

1–2 cloves garlic, minced,
    optional
small piece ginger root, minced,
    optional
1–2 teaspoons mixed spices
    (Such as cinnamon, cloves,
    allspice.)
1 teaspoon cayenne or other hot
    pepper, or to taste

Mix all ingredients in a kettle and bring to a simmer, stirring several times. Taste and adjust amounts of vinegar and sweetener. Simmer uncovered until the apricots are soft and the chutney has thickened, usually about 30 minutes.

Ladle into canning jars, and process 10 minutes in a boiling water bath. (Refer to the CANNING section.)

The flavor of the chutney improves after it sits for a month or two. It goes well with curries and wherever chutneys are enjoyed.

**Fruit Chutney**   Most fresh fruits in season can be used instead of apricots. Plums or peaches are good. Seasonings can be adjusted to taste. Mixtures of fruits can also be used.

# ARTICHOKES

GLOBE ARTICHOKES, ALSO CALLED BURR ARTICHOKES, ARE THE UNopened flower buds of a plant in the thistle family. They are interesting vegetables to cook and fun to eat, but are difficult to grow in most places. They are perennials, ordinarily requiring a long growing season, with a mild winter and a cool summer. The California coast suits them perfectly. However, they should become more common in other areas in the future, thanks to a newly developed annual variety that can be grown in home gardens where the growing season is fairly long.

**Cardoon and Wild Thistles**   Cardoon is closely related to artichokes. It has been raised since early Roman times for its stalk and the midribs of its leaves, which are peeled, then cooked as a vegetable. Wild thistle stalks and leaf midribs, when big enough, are eaten in the same way. The roots and very young leaves of both plants can also be eaten, and it is possible to extract a rennet for making cheese from the flowers of some species. (Refer to RENNET FROM PLANTS, in the RENNET section.)

Wild thistles of one kind or another grow almost everywhere, and are a good survival food because they are easily recognized at any time of the year. Cardoon seeds for garden plantings are listed among the herb seeds in many seed catalogs. (The Jerusalem artichoke is an entirely different plant, not related to artichokes or thistles.)

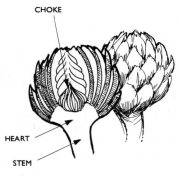

Artichoke

---

**STORAGE,** *cont.*

**Freezing** Trim off outer leaves, tips, or remove all, leaving hearts. Blanch 7 min. in boiling water. Optional: Add lemon juice to water or dip hearts in lemon juice. Refer to FREEZING section.

---

## HANDLING ARTICHOKES

Artichokes should be cut with 1 to 1½ inches of stem, while the buds are still compact, with closed tightly leaves or bracts. An artichoke's size does not necessarily reflect its age or maturity. The top bud on a plant is usually the largest, and the side buds become smaller the lower down they grow on the plant. Only the fleshy bases of the leaves, the hearts, and the stems can be eaten when fully formed buds are cut from a mature plant. However, the buds can be cut early, before the choke develops, and then all parts are edible, except perhaps the sharp tips of the outer leaves.

The cut surfaces of artichokes, cardoon, or wild thistle discolor quickly when exposed to air, so prepare them just before cooking, or else sprinkle them with lemon juice or another acidic liquid. Whole artichokes can take anywhere from 20 to 60 minutes to cook depending on their size and maturity. Poke with a fork to test for doneness.

If just the hearts are wanted for a recipe, the leaves can be steamed separately until tender, and the fleshy parts at their base used in salads or other mixtures. To clean artichokes, hold them by the stems and swish them up and down in cold water.

## ARTICHOKE RECIPES

### *Steamed Artichokes*

1 celery stalk with leaves, cut into several pieces
1 small onion, sliced, or 1 clove garlic, crushed
1–2 bay leaves
1 thin slice lemon, with rind

2 tablespoons lemon juice or white wine
water
1 medium artichoke for 1 serving, or 1 large for 2
mayonnaise, or melted butter

Put the celery, onion or garlic, bay leaves, lemon slice, and lemon juice or wine in a large enameled or stainless steel pot. Add about an inch of water. Cover, and heat while preparing the artichokes, so they can go in without delay.

Clean the artichokes and trim the stems to about 1 inch. Pull off small, tough outer leaves. Set the artichokes stem side down in the pot on top of the seasonings. Cover, and steam until artichokes are tender, 30 to 60 minutes depending on size and age. Test by poking with a fork. Add a little extra water if necessary.

Serve each person with artichoke and a small dish with a spoons of mayonnaise or melted butter in it for dipping. The leaves can then be pulled off one by one, dipped, and the tender part scraped off with the teeth. When most of the leaves are off, the inedible center and choke should be cut out, so that the heart and stem can be enjoyed.

Eating artichokes is fun when they are served in this way, and they make a good first course for almost any meal.

### Italian Stuffed Artichokes, from Lecce

(Makes 5–8 side servings.)

8–10 small artichokes
1½ cups fine bread crumbs
1 small tomato, mashed with a fork, or 3 tablespoons canned tomato
2 tablespoons canned tuna fish, drained

1 tablespoon capers, or pickled nasturtium buds (Refer to PICKLED NASTURTIUM BUDS in the HERBS section.)
1 tablespoon parsley, minced
pepper, to taste
water
1 egg, lightly beaten
3 tablespoons (about) oil, preferably olive

Trim the artichokes' stems to about 1 inch and pull off any tough outer leaves. Cut off the tops of the leaves at about 1 inch above the heart. If the artichokes are young enough the choke can be eaten, but if it is prickly, scoop it out with a small spoon or apple corer. Hold each artichoke by the stem and hit the flat top lightly against a board to spread out and soften the leaves.

Combine the bread crumbs, tomato, tuna fish, capers, parsley, and pepper. Knead together with the fingers, adding a little water for a slightly doughy mass. Press this stuffing firmly into the artichoke leaves, and flatten on top. It should not fall out when the artichoke is held upside down by the stem.

Heat the oil in a pot wide enough to hold the artichokes in one layer. Holding each artichoke by the stem, dip the stuffed part in the beaten egg, then set stuffed side down in the pot. It is tricky to get them into the pot without losing the stuffing, but it can be done. Add ½ to 1 cup water, cover the pot, and simmer over low heat until the artichokes are tender and the water is absorbed (20 to 40 minutes depending on the artichokes). If necessary, the lid can be removed for a few minutes to let water evaporate. A painstaking recipe, but well worth the trouble.

---

### ARTICHOKE IDEAS

**Artichoke in Salads**  Add cooked and sliced or chopped artichoke to salads of all kinds. It adds a special touch to tossed green salads, and goes well with egg, potato, shellfish, or chicken salads. In a salad is a good way to use leaves when preparing artichoke hearts alone for another recipe. (To prepare the leaves, steam them and scrape or cut off the tender part at the base of each.)

**Creamed Artichoke, Wild Thistle, or Cardoon Stalks** Slice or chop the cooked vegetable. Mix into a cream sauce (refer to MILK RECIPES in the MILK section), or creamed mushrooms (refer to MUSHROOM RECIPES in the MUSHROOMS section), and serve with mashed potatoes, rice, or on toast.

**Fried Artichokes**  Slice tender, young artichokes, roll in seasoned flour or dip in batter, and sauté in oil or fat until browned on both sides. If the artichokes are not very tender, pre-cook them first. Baby artichoke buds, 1 to 1½ inches, can be fried whole in deep fat. When drained, sprinkle with pepper (salt optional), and arrange on a platter for an unusual hors d'oeuvre.

**Artichoke Leaves with Dips** Arrange cooked artichoke leaves on a platter around a vegetable dip. A garlic flavored dip is especially good.

### Pickled Artichoke Hearts, Middle Eastern Style

(Makes 1½ – 2 quarts.)

½ cup lemon juice (from 3 – 4 lemons)
lemon peels

12 artichokes
½ cup corn oil or other salad oil
salt, optional

Put lemon juice (and salt, if desired) in a bowl. Trim stems, leaves, and chokes from the artichokes, leaving the hearts. If these are large, cut them in half. Take each heart and rub it with a squeezed out lemon rind, then place it in the lemon juice. When all the hearts are ready, take them out of the juice and arrange them in a lidded glass jar. Add the oil to the lemon juice and beat with a fork until well combined. Pour over the hearts in the jar, adding more oil if not completely covered. Seal with a tight lid for at least a month before eating. They will keep indefinitely in a cool place.

### Wild Thistle or Cardoon Stew

(Makes 6 – 8 side servings.)

1½ cups beef stock, or other soup stock
2 cups wild thistle or cardoon stalks, peeled and cut in bite sized pieces
1 green pepper, in medium slices

several small carrots, or 1 large, in medium slices
½ cup mushrooms, in medium slices
2 – 3 scallions, or 1 onion, in medium slices
pepper, salt, optional

Heat the stock to a boil in a sauce pan. Add all of the vegetables, cover, and simmer about 30 minutes, or until the vegetables are tender. Add seasonings if desired.

**OTHER RECIPES WITH ARTICHOKES**

Artichoke Soup, p.18
Recipes, and Ideas for Vegetables, p.669

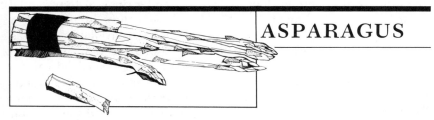

# ASPARAGUS

THERE IS NO OTHER VEGETABLE LIKE ASPARAGUS. IT HAS ITS OWN special look and taste, and its own special season. When the first spears push their way up in the garden, it is proof that spring has truly begun. These first spears are a delight to eat, and are also known as a spring tonic, good for the kidneys and bladder.

Asparagus is the first vegetable of spring because, in temperate climates, it is the only perennial vegetable maintained in home gardens. An established asparagus bed is an asset yielding dividends for many years. Starting one is like planting a tree; the hope and promise of good things to come are planted with it.

**STORAGE**

**Canning** *Whole Spears* Trim to jar length. (Optional: Cook trimmings in the water used for blanching and filling jars to add flavor.) Blanch 3 min. in boiling water. Pack upright in jars, add boiling blanching water, ½ in. headroom. Process 240°F, 11 pounds pressure. Pints: 25 min. Quarts: 30 min. *Cut Pieces* Blanch 2 – 3 min., pack, add boiling blanching water, ½ in. headroom. Process as for spears. Refer to CANNING section.

**STORAGE,** *cont.*

**Drying**  Chop or slice thin. Dry until hard. Excellent for soup (recipe below). Refer to the DRYING section.

**Freezing**  Use whole spears or cut in pieces. Blanch 2 min. if slender, 3 to 4 min. if medium, or thick. If using rigid containers, alternate spear and stem ends for better fit. Quality retained 8–12 months. Refer to FREEZING section.

3–4 POUNDS = 1 QUART CANNED OR 1½–2 QUARTS FROZEN

Asparagus grows wild in many places, and in spite of more than 2,000 years of cultivation, there is little difference between the wild and domesticated plants. Knowing where wild asparagus grows is almost as good as having a patch in the back yard. One folk name for asparagus is sparrowgrass.

## HANDLING ASPARAGUS

Asparagus should be harvested before tops begin to open, or "feather out". Flavor is still good, though, even when they are slightly open. The spears should be cut or broken off at ground level, or just below. Breaking is preferred because there is less risk of damaging nearby underground spears. Morning is the best time for harvesting, as the stalks tend to dry out and toughen later in the day. It is important to refrigerate asparagus soon after it is harvested, because sitting at room temperature will also dry and toughen it.

The outside of the bottom of an asparagus stalk is too tough and stringy to eat. If the stalks are to be eaten by hand, the tough part can be used as a handle. Otherwise, the outer layer of the bottom of the stalk should be peeled off, leaving only the tender white inner part. Another alternative is to cut off the bottoms to be cooked for soup stock or the liquid for canning asparagus. The bottoms can also be peeled, chopped, and added raw to salads, or cooked in soups. If asparagus was grown in sandy soil there may be sand under the scales on the stalks. The easiest way to get rid of it is to scrape off the scales.

Steaming is the best cooking method for asparagus. The spears can be set upright in a tall pot with 1 or 2 inches of boiling water (which cooks the tougher bottoms longer than the tender tips), or they can be laid on a rack and steamed. For steaming upright they can be tied in a bundle to hold them in position. If a tall pot is not available, a coffee pot might be used, or a double boiler with the top section turned upside down over the bottom section for a lid. Or a domed lid can be shaped with aluminum foil to fit on a regular pot. Whenever practical, sort asparagus so as to cook spears of the same diameter together. Their cooking time will vary from 8 to 15 minutes, depending on thickness. When done, the spears should still be bright in color, and somewhat firm in texture.

## ASPARAGUS RECIPES

### *Dutch Egg and Butter Sauced Asparagus*                           (For 2–3 pounds asparagus.)

3 tablespoons butter
2 hard-boiled eggs
nutmeg, to taste

salt, optional
asparagus spears

Warm 2 tablespoons of butter until almost melted. Stir in the other tablespoon of butter to make a creamy texture. Mash the eggs into the butter with a fork until they are finely minced. Add the seasonings.

Steam the asparagus spears until just tender, and serve them with the sauce.

### Asparagus Stir-fried with Meat

(Makes 8–10 Chinese side servings; 4–6 western style.)

1 pound pork, chicken, rabbit, or other light meat
2 tablespoons soy sauce
1 tablespoon sherry, or ¼ teaspoon vinegar

1 teaspoon honey or other sweetening
1½ pounds asparagus
3 tablespoons oil

Slice the meat as thinly as possible and cut into 1 inch squares. Mix 1 tablespoon of the soy sauce with the sherry or vinegar, and the honey. Put in the meat, and let soak while preparing the asparagus.

Peel the tough bottoms of the stalks. Cut at an angle into ¼ inch thick oval slices, which are about an inch long. The tip of the spear can be left as one small piece.

Heat the oil in a wok or heavy frying pan until very hot. Add the meat and stir-fry till its pinkness is gone, about 1 minute. Add the asparagus and the other tablespoon of soy sauce. Stir fry over high heat until the asparagus is cooked but still bright and crisp, about 3 minutes. (Refer to the STIR-FRYING section.) When stir-fried, asparagus is mild, almost sweet flavored, and not typically asparagusy.

### Asparagus Soup

(Makes 6–8 medium bowls.)

4 tablespoons butter
2 cups potatoes, cubed
½ cup onions, chopped
1–2 cloves garlic, minced
4 cups milk, soup stock, or asparagus cooking water (Any mixture of these is excellent.)

1–2 pounds asparagus, chopped; or ½ cup dried asparagus, soaked a few minutes in water
1 cup light cream, optional
salt, optional
fresh herbs, minced (Parsley, mint, chervil, or tarragon are some good choices.)

Heat the butter in a soup pot. Add the potatoes, onions, and garlic, and sauté until the onion is limp. Add the milk, soup stock, or cooking water made from tough asparagus trimmings. Cook about 30 minutes, then purée with a blender or food mill.

Return the soup to the pot and reheat it. Add the asparagus. Include the soaking water if using dried asparagus. Simmer about 10 minutes, or until the asparagus is done. Add cream, if desired, and sprinkle with herbs just before serving. If reheating after cream is added, do not let it boil. The prospect of enjoying this soup through the winter months is reason enough for drying as much asparagus as possible when it is in season.

---

### ASPARAGUS IDEAS

**Asparagus Salads**  Sliced raw asparagus, including the peeled white bottoms of the stalks, is very flavorful in all kinds of salads. The raw spears are good to munch just like carrot or celery sticks. (For some delicious dips, refer to the following recipes: FRESH CHEESE DIPS, p. 144; *Guacamole*, p. 293; *Indonesian Peanut Sauce*, p. 459; *Spanish Parsley Sauce*, p. 451; WHIPPED TOMATO CREAM, p. 642.)

Cooked, chilled asparagus spears also make a nice salad arranged on lettuce leaves with the *Nut Butter Salad Dressing* from the SALADS section.

**Asparagus Steamed with New Potatoes**  When steaming asparagus upright in a tall pot, cook small new potatoes in the pot around the bottoms of the stalks. The asparagus and new potatoes go very well together with a little butter.

**Baked Asparagus**  Steam asparagus until just barely tender, then spread in a shallow, oiled or buttered baking dish. Sprinkle with melted butter or olive oil, grated cheese, and pepper, and season with lemon juice and nutmeg if desired. Bake only a few minutes to heat through and brown lightly.

**Asparagus Instead of Bamboo Shoots, Stir-fried**  Slice asparagus spears about ¼ inch thick diagonally, and use them for stir-frying instead of bamboo shoots. They cook in the same amount of time, and go well with Chinese seasonings.

***Celery or Artichoke Soup***   Instead of asparagus make the soup with chopped celery, or the fleshy parts of artichoke, pre-cooked and chopped. For celery soup, omit garlic. Minced dill leaves make an outstanding garnish. For artichoke soup use soup stock, rather than milk or cooking water. A little lemon juice can be included. Artichoke soup is good either hot or cold.

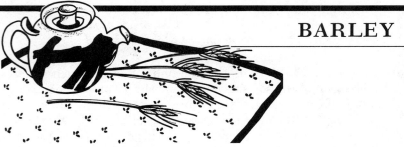

# BARLEY

B ARLEY WAS, AS FAR AS ANYONE KNOWS, THE FIRST GRAIN EVER cultivated. It is also the grain with the most sharply differentiated varieties, including some that will grow where no other grain can survive. Barley is a basic food for people living in drastically different climates, from the most northern part of Norway, and the hot, semidesert regions of Africa, to the Himalayas at altitudes up to 15,000 feet. In these places whole barley and barley meal are cooked for cereal or into puddings, and barley flour is made into flat bread. In less remote parts of the world, a large part of the barley raised for human use goes into the malting and brewing of beer. Barley is also raised for animal feed and, in some places, is as important as feed corn.

## HANDLING BARLEY

Barley is harvested like wheat, except that unlike wheat, most varieties have tight hulls. This presents a problem for those who want to raise a small amount for family use. The familiar, store-bought pearled barley has been mechanically polished to remove the hull and part of the bran layer, but there is no mechanism available for polishing small quantities of grain. There are, however, some home methods that can be tried. (Refer to HARVESTING GRAIN, and HULLING DIFFICULT GRAINS in the GRAINS section. For making barley meal or grits, and barley flour, refer to GRINDING GRAINS, in the GRAINS section.) Unhulled barley can be roasted, or malted, as described below.

***Parched or Roasted Barley***   Barley has an especially good flavor when it is parched or browned in a low oven, or in a dry pan on top of the stove. Both whole barley and barley flour can be browned, but as the flour scorches easily, it is best to stir it constantly in a heavy pan on top of the stove where it can be watched. Whole barley's flavor is best when roasted with the hulls on. Spread it out in a shallow layer in a pan in a low oven, and stir or shake it often so it browns evenly. It can be lightly browned for a mild flavor, or roasted until quite dark for a strong flavor, but it should not char or burn. For a coffee-like drink made with barley, refer to HOT DRINKS in the BEVERAGES section. For barley tonic, water, and tea, see BARLEY RECIPES, below. Dark roasted barley can be ground to make a rich flour that adds flavor in baking. It can be used to give pumpernickel bread its typical color and flavor. The dark roasting weakens the hulls so that they are not noticeable in the flour.

*Malted Barley*   Malting is the process of sprouting and then drying a cereal grain. When the grain germinates, an imporant enzyme, diastase, is developed. Diastase is helpful in the making of bread, and necessary for making beer. Barley is the best grain for malting, but rye, wheat, and rice can also be used. The barley must be unhulled. (Pearled barley is not viable.)

To malt barley, soak it in water for 2 to 4 days in a moderately warm place. After draining, keep it moist and at a temperature near 65°F. (Refer to the SPROUTS section.) The traditional way to sprout barley is to pile it on a clean floor, sprinkling it as necessary with warm water. To control its temperature, the barley is piled higher when it gets too cool, and spread out when it gets too hot. In a week or so, the sprout should grow to the right length—⅔ the length of the kernel. It can be seen inside the hull, though it will not have pushed out yet. The root will also be growing and may be as long as 1 inch, but it is the sprout's size that must be watched.

When the sprout is the right length, growth is stopped by drying the barley. This drying temperature is important. If dried at 120°F or less, all enzyme activity is retained. With temperatures between 120 and 140°F the malt has more flavor, but some enzyme activity is lost. The temperature must never go over 140°F, where enzyme activity stops completely. After it is dried the malted barley can be stored indefinitely in sealed containers in a cool, dry place.

For baking, the malted barley is ground to a flour, while for making beer it is usually crushed or cracked. Commercial malt flavored syrups and powders are made by evaporating strained mashes of malted grains and water. This process cannot be duplicated at home.

*Beer from Barley Malt*   Brewing one's own beer, starting with growing barley, is an art that is rarely practiced today. It takes extraordinary care and skill, along with the right equipment, to make good, home brewed beer. Everything has an impact, from the variety of barley and the way it is grown, to the quality of the water and yeast, and the steps of the malting and brewing processes. Refer to the end of the GRAINS section for books which describe making beer from home-grown barley.

By comparison, it is easy to make beer at home using a commercial extract for brewing. Directions are readily available for the use of these extracts.

# BARLEY RECIPES

### Finnish Barley Pudding                (Makes 6–8 side servings.)

| | |
|---|---|
| 1 ¼ cups barley | 6 cups milk (Raw milk gives |
| 4 cups water | the best flavor.) |
| | 5 tablespoons butter |

Soak the barley in 4 cups of water for several hours, or overnight. Cook in the soaking water at a simmer until the barley swells and has absorbed most of the water. Heat the milk almost to a boil, and pour it slowly into the barley, stirring constantly. Simmer over very low heat for 30 minutes more, stirring often. The mixture should thicken like a pudding. To prevent scorching the milk, this is best done in a double boiler, or by using an insulated pad under the pot.

Butter a baking dish and pour in the barley mixture. Dot with butter all over the top. Bake in a very slow oven, about 250°F, for 2 hours, or until the top is golden brown.

Use this pudding for a light lunch or supper, or as a side dish with the main meal.

### Barley Flour Potato Cookies                (Makes 24–30 small cookies.)

| | |
|---|---|
| 2 eggs, lightly beaten | 1 ⅓ cups barley flour (Lightly |
| 1 cup mashed potatoes, unseasoned | roasted is good.) |
| ¼ cup butter or other fat, melted | 1 teaspoon baking powder |
| ½ cup honey, or ¾ cup molasses | ½ cup raisins or other dried |
| | fruit, chopped if necessary, |
| | optional |

Mix together the eggs, potato, butter, and honey. Sift or mix the barley flour and baking powder, then, if using them, add the raisins or other dried fruit. Mix the wet and dry ingredients, and drop by small spoonfuls onto a greased baking sheet. Bake in a moderate, 350°F, oven for about 15 minutes, or until the cookies are lightly browned and firm to the touch. These hearty, old style cookies are excellent home made from scratch.

**Buckwheat or Other Whole Grain Potato Cookies**  Use buckwheat flour or another whole grain flour instead of barley flour for these cookies. This is a good recipe for any unusual kinds of home ground flour.

### Barley Tonic                                        (Makes about 8 cups.)

(In the past barley tonic was recommended for invalids, especially if feverish, but it can be enjoyed any time.)

| | |
|---|---|
| ⅓ cup barley, preferably unhulled | ¼ cup figs, chopped |
| (It can be lightly roasted.) | small piece ginger or licorice |
| ¼ cup raisins | root, optional |

---

## BARLEY IDEAS

### Barley to Replace Rice
Pearled barley is outstanding when prepared like brown rice. (Refer to RICE RECIPES in the RICE section.) Barley will take as long to cook as the slower cooking kinds of brown rice. It has a nicely chewy texture, and a good flavor. A combination of 1 part barley and 3 parts rice may be enjoyed by those who find barley too chewy by itself.

### Barley Grits with Meals
Coarsely ground barley makes an excellent hot cereal that is good with meals instead of mashed potatoes or hominy grits. It is also a good breakfast cereal.

### Using Leftover Cooked Barley
Nothing is handier for making a quick soup than pre-cooked barley. Just heat soup stock or vegetable juice with the barley and add a finely chopped onion, or grated or finely chopped vegetables of any kind. The vegetables will cook in about a minute and the soup will be ready. For a heartier soup, other leftovers such as chopped cooked vegetables or meat can be added.

Leftover cooked barley is also good in many kinds of casseroles and mixed dishes, and can even be included in salads. Try it in fruit salad for an interesting change of pace.

Simmer the barley in 2 quarts of water for an hour. Add the raisins and figs, and simmer another hour. If using it, add the licorice root just a minute or two before taking the pot off of the stove. Strain and chill. Drink full strength if liked, or dilute for a longer drink.

**Barley Water**　Cook the barley in water for 1½ hours, omitting raisins, figs, ginger or licorice. Sweeten with a little honey, if desired.

**Korean Barley Tea**　Roast unhulled barley until quite dark. Use 1 tablespoon for every 2 to 3 cups of water, and simmer as for Barley Water. This favorite Korean beverage is enjoyed cold in summer and hot in winter.

---

| OTHER RECIPES WITH BARLEY |
|---|

Basic Flatbread, p. 64
Beans and Barley, p. 26
Black Pudding, English Style, and Goose Blood Pudding, p. 54
Chinese Style Lung Soup, p. 398
Goose Legs with Barley and Beans, p. 309
Kale Soup, Scottish Style, p. 365
Roast Beverages (with unhulled, or malted barley), p. 44
Welsh Mutton Soup, p. 381
Whole Grain Ideas, p. 314

# BEANS, DRY

"BEANS FOR DINNER!"—NOT A FANCIFUL PRONOUNCEMENT, BUT CERtainly a comfortable one. A pot of beans always means a satisfying meal, and is the epitome of solid dependability in food.

Dried beans of various kinds are eaten with appreciation everywhere in the world. Beans have always been important for winter diets because they are easy to grow and harvest and keep so well. Gardeners can easily raise a year's supply without special skills, equipment, or storage facilities. Beans are also a worthwhile source of protein. If eaten with grains or dairy products, they equal meat in protein value.

There are many many varieties of beans, including some native to America and some with origins in other parts of the world. They are distinguished by different colors, sizes, and shapes, by their cooking characteristics, and by the areas in which they grow well. With the exception of soybeans, they are all similar in composition and nutritional value. Because soybeans are higher in protein and fat, and lower in carbohydrates, they must be handled differently. (Refer to the SOYBEANS section.)

## DRIED BEAN VARIETIES

**Adsuki Beans**　These small, reddish black beans are grown primarily in Asian countries, and require a fairly long growing season. More easily digested than many other kinds of beans, they also have a unique flavor. They are often cooked in combination with rice.

**Black-eyed Peas or Cowpeas**　Despite their names these are beans, not peas. There are several other local names for them in the southern United States where they are popular. Good both when freshly shelled or when dried, they are especially enjoyable in mixtures with other vegetables.

| STORAGE |
|---|

**Canning**　(For pre-cooked convenience.) Soak. Use *Basic Beans, Traditional Method,* under RECIPES below, and boil 30 min., or soak with QUICK METHOD and bring to boil. Drain, pack, add the boiling cooking water, 1 in. headroom. Process 240°F, 11 pounds pressure. Pints: 1 hour, 15 min. Quarts: 1 hour, 30 min. Refer to the CANNING section, and also CANNING BAKED BEANS, under RECIPES, below.

**Storage**　Will keep indefinitely at any temperature, but high quality retained longer if stored below 50°F.

**Drying**　See HANDLING DRIED BEANS, below.

1 POUND DRY = 1½–2½ CUPS
DRY = 6 OR MORE CUPS COOKED

*Broad, Fava, Horse, or Windsor Beans*   These names all refer to one kind of bean, commonly grown in Europe. They like cool weather, and so are cultivated like peas. They are eaten both freshly shelled or dried. The large seeded types originated in the Mediterranean area, while the small seeded ones are from the Middle East.

*Garbanzo Beans, or Chick Peas*   The round, rather bumpy shape of these beans is distinctive, as is their nutty flavor and somewhat firm texture. They are very well suited for use as snacks and as additions to salads. There are many delicious, special recipes for these beans, such as *Hummus*. (Refer to the RECIPES in the SEEDS section.)

*Kidney, French, and other Common Garden Beans*   There are many bean varieties of this general type. They originated in Central and South America, and are the beans now most commonly grown in North America. Among them are the fresh green or snap home garden beans, and also many of the dried beans.

*Lentils*   Though these small, flattened beans grow in tiny pods with only 1 or 2 seeds per pods, one plant may produce 100 to 150 pods. They are grown extensively in Europe, Asia, and northern Africa, but are not common in American gardens, probably because they require more space than other beans. They are a cool season crop, cultivated like peas. Lentils are quick cooking, and much appreciated for soups and stews.

*Lima Beans*   There are many kinds of lima beans, with a variety of sizes and colors. Some are called "butterbeans," because of their smooth, soft, buttery texture. All limas are good when used both freshly shelled, or dried.

*Mung Beans*   These small, round, greenish beans are most familiar when used for sprouting. (Refer to the SPROUTS section.) However, they are also good when cooked like lentils in soups or stews. They grow best in warm climates.

*Scarlet or White Runner Beans*   These large, coarse podded beans are native to the tropical parts of Central and South America. Scarlet runners are often grown as ornamentals because of their showy red flowers. Both kinds of runner beans can be used dried, freshly shelled, and as green beans, if the pods are picked very young. The cooked, dried beans make a fine soup, and add interest to salads and mixed dishes because of their large size.

## HANDLING DRIED BEANS

*Drying and Shelling*   During dry weather, some varieties of beans can be left on the plant until the pods are completely dry and brittle. Some varieties split open and "spill the beans" when completely dry, and so must be picked in time. Mature beans left out too long in damp weather may sprout or mold while still in the pods.

Beans can be harvested as soon as the pods become thin, limp, and start to lose color. At this stage the whole plant can be pulled, and hung upside down in a dry, airy place, like an attic, until the pods are completely dry. Or the pods can be picked and spread out in a single layer to finish drying. Though one can shell the beans immediately and then finish drying them, this is usually more work than shelling the brittle pods.

Small quantities of dry beans are easily shelled by hand. A family bean-shelling and story-telling evening make the chore a pleasant one. Larger quantities can be shelled by threshing and winnowing after the pods are dry and brittle. To do so, put the pods, or the entire plant, in a sack or large cloth bag, and tramp on it, or hit it with a mallet or baseball bat until all the beans have been knocked out of the pods. Pull out any large stalks, then winnow by pouring beans from one container to another in a brisk wind to blow away pieces of pod. Another alternative is to shake the beans on hardware cloth, or a screening with the right size mesh to let only the beans fall through.

***Storing Dried Beans*** To exclude rodents and insects beans should be stored in a tightly closed sturdy container. Problems with weevils can be prevented by pasteurizing the beans before storage to kill insect eggs. Spread the beans on trays and put them in a 175°F oven for 10 to 15 minutes. Cool, then store. Beans cannot be sprouted after pasteurization. A dried hot pepper can be placed in each container to repel insects.

Dried beans should be sorted before use to remove any small rocks or clumps of dirt mixed with them. Beans that float will not germinate and may have insect damage. There is no harm in eating the floaters, but the damaged ones may be unattractive. Though dried beans keep indefinitely, it is best to use them within a year. As they get older they need a longer soaking and cooking time, and beans stored for several years may never get soft, no matter how long they are cooked.

***Preventing Gas*** When eating beans, some people are made very uncomfortable by the formation of gas in the digestive tract. For those who are bothered, there are several different ways to minimize the problem:

• Cook beans together with seaweed. The seaweed's flavor goes well with beans, and it is especially effective in reducing problems with gas. For convenience, kelp powder can be used to season bean recipes. (Refer to the SEAWEED section for a special recipe.)

• Eat beans together with generous amounts of raw or cooked green vegetables. Other folk remedies are seasoning with ginger, or serving with vinegar, or olive oil.

• Discard beans' soaking water, and cook them in fresh water. Some water soluble nutrients will be lost, but this method works well enough to make the loss acceptable.

# DRIED BEAN RECIPES

### Basic Beans

1 part dry beans

3 – 4 parts pure, soft water (Hard or mineralized water, or "off" tastes, such as chlorine or sulphur, give beans a poor flavor.)

Optional additional ingredients: ham bone, or piece of salt pork

vegetable seasonings, chopped (May include all or any of these: onion, carrot, celery, green pepper, garlic.)

oil, butter, or other fat

herbs (For example, parsley, bay leaf, savory, or others.)

tomatoes, fresh or canned

black or red pepper

salt

Two methods for soaking and cooking beans follow. (A third alternative, pressure cooking, can be used if manufacturer's directions are carefully followed to avoid a clogged vent. However, the texture of some varieties will be poor, especially if skins are tough.) For the very best flavor and texture the traditional method is recommended.

**Traditional Method**    Soak the beans in water overnight or until their size is at least doubled. (Optional: drain and add fresh water to cover.) Bring to a boil, then reduce heat and simmer very slowly until the beans are tender. This may take 2 hours, or it may take all day! Both soaking and cooking times will depend on the beans' variety, its growing conditions, and its time in storage.

**Quick Method**    Bring the beans to a boil in water, and simmer 2 minutes. Remove from heat, cover, and let stand 1 hour or until the beans have doubled in size. (Optional: drain and add fresh water to cover.) Simmer until the beans are tender.

If using a ham bone or salt pork, add it when the beans begin to cook. Vegetable seasonings and herbs can go in near the beginning of the cooking time if a blend of flavors is desired, or near the end of the cooking time if distinctive flavors and textures are preferred. If neither ham nor salt pork is used, chopped vegetables can be sautéed in oil or fat before they are added. Tomatoes should be added towards the end of the cooking time, as their acids may keep beans from getting soft. If salt is used it should also be added towards the end because it toughens the skins of some kinds of beans.

### Garlicky Bean Soup                             (Makes 8 – 10 medium bowls.)

1 pound (1½ – 2½ cups) dry beans

4 or more cloves garlic, minced

4 tablespoons bacon fat, oil, or butter

1 cup parsley, minced

2 – 3 tablespoons powdered seaweed, dried seaweed, or pieces soaked in water, optional

pepper, salt, optional

3 – 4 slices bacon, fried crisp and crumbled, optional

water

Soak the beans, and simmer them until soft in about 2½ quarts of water.

Drain and set aside a cup of whole beans. Purée the rest with the cooking water, in a food mill or blender, and return to the soup pot. If too thick, dilute with water to a good consistency.

In a frying pan, sauté the garlic in fat or oil over low heat until golden. Add to the soup along with the reserved beans, parsley, seaweed, and desired seasonings. Heat and simmer 5 to 10 minutes. When serving, sprinkle the bacon on each bowl of soup.

***Beans and Greens Soup***   Omit parsley or reduce to only a few tablespoons, then add 2 to 3 cups cooked chopped spinach or other cooked greens.

### *Shaker Style Baked Beans*      (Makes 8–12 dinner servings.)

| | |
|---|---|
| *4 cups dry beans* (Preferably navy beans or another small, baking bean.) | *½ cup molasses, or maple syrup* |
| | *2 teaspoons dry mustard* |
| | *½ cup catsup, or tomato sauce* |
| *1 peeled onion* | *1 teaspoon salt, or to taste* |
| *½ cup butter* | |

Soak the beans in 3 to 4 quarts water overnight. Drain, then cook in fresh water to cover until almost tender. To test for doneness take out a few beans in a spoon and blow on them. If the skin cracks or wrinkles they are ready. Drain the beans, and save the cooking water.

Butter a bean pot or deep casserole with a lid, and put the onion in it. Add the drained beans. Mix the hot bean cooking water with the remaining butter, molasses, or syrup, salt, mustard, and catsup or tomato sauce. Stir until the butter is melted, then pour over the beans, cover, and bake in a very low oven, 275°F, for 3 hours or longer. For the last half hour, uncover and let the beans brown on top. The excellence of these slowly baked beans cannot be duplicated by any short cut method.

***Baked Beans with Salt Pork***   Omit butter and salt. Cut about ¼ pound salt pork into thick slices, and put them in the bottom of the bean pot with the onion. Bake as above. The salt pork will gradually rise through the beans, seasoning them along the way.

***Canning Baked Beans***   (About 6 pints) Precook the beans as above, or use the Quick Method, p. 24, and pack the drained beans in jars. Leave 1 inch headroom if making the version with butter. If using salt pork, fill the jars only ¾ full, and put a 1 inch cube on top of the beans in the pint jars, a larger piece in the quarts. Make a sauce, using the bean cooking water and butter, sweetener, mustard, and catsup, as above, for *Shaker Style Baked Beans*. Grate the onion and add it. Heat the sauce to a boil, and pour it into the jars, dividing it equally. If necessary add boiling water to fill, allowing 1 inch headroom. Process at 240°F, 11 pounds pressure. Pints: 1 hour 20 minutes; quarts: 1 hour 35 minutes. (Refer to the CANNING section.)

### Red Beans and Rice

(Makes 8–12 dinner servings.)

2 cups dried red or kidney beans
2 tablespoons oil
1 medium onion, chopped in medium
    pieces
2 cloves garlic, minced
½ pound fresh sausage, cut in bite-
    sized pieces (Preferably Spanish
    or Italian style.)

1 cup tomato sauce
1 bay leaf
1 teaspoon cumin
pepper, salt, optional
1½ cups raw rice

Soak and cook the beans until tender as for *Basic Beans,* above.

Heat the oil in a large pot or Dutch oven, and sauté the onion and garlic in it until the onion is limp. Add the sausage and stir until it browns. Next, add the cooked beans with their cooking water, the tomato sauce, bay leaf, cumin and other seasonings, then stir in the rice. If the mixture is dry, add about a cup of water, or as much as is needed to be absorbed by the rice while it cooks. Heat to a boil, cover, and simmer without stirring until the rice is done, 30 to 40 minutes for brown rice. A typically Caribbean and delicious combination of flavors.

**Beans and Barley**   Use barley instead of rice. Add about one cup more water and cook for 1 hour, or until the barley is tender.

### Black-eyed Peas and Peppers

(Makes 8–12 side servings.)

1 pound dried black-eyed peas or
    other small beans
1 clove garlic, halved
6 tablespoons (about) oil
3 cloves garlic, crushed
3 medium onions, chopped in me-
    dium pieces

4 green peppers, chopped in me-
    dium pieces
½ teaspoon sage
2 bay leaves, crumbled
3 tablespoons (about) cider
    vinegar
pepper, salt, optional

Soak and cook beans until tender, as for *Basic Beans,* above, adding the halved clove of garlic before cooking. Use a minimum of water, as the beans should be fairly dry when done. Keep hot till ready to serve.

Heat the oil in a large frying pan, then add the garlic, onions, green peppers, sage, and bay leaves. Sauté until the vegetables are tender. Add vinegar, and desired seasonings to make a flavorful sauce.

Put the black-eyed peas in a serving dish, pour the vegetable mixture over them, and serve.

### Texas Chili Beans

(Makes 6–8 dinner servings.)

½ pound kidney, pinto, or similar
    beans
2 pounds lean stewing beef or other
    red meat, cut in small cubes
2 tablespoons oil

1 cup onions, chopped in me-
    dium pieces
1 green pepper, chopped in me-
    dium pieces
1 clove garlic, minced

---

### DRY BEAN IDEAS

**Cooking Beans Ahead**   Precooked beans are useful for numerous recipes and for adding to soups, salads, casseroles, and mixed vegetable dishes. So it is an excellent idea, when cooking beans for one dish, to prepare an extra amount. This can then be refrigerated for a week or more to be used as needed.

**Hot Beans with Raw Vegetables**   Heat plain cooked beans and, just before serving, mix with fresh chopped tomatoes and other raw, chopped or grated garden vegetables. Grated carrot, summer squash, and chopped leafy greens all go well with the tomato and beans. Minced parsley and other fresh herbs, such as chives, basil, or summer savory, can be sprinkled on top. Black-eyed peas are especially good prepared in this way.

3 cups tomato sauce, or stewed
   tomatoes
2 jalapeño peppers, minced (fresh,
   pickled, or canned), or other hot
   pepper, to taste

1½ tablespoons chili powder
½ teaspoon oregano
½ teaspoon cumin

Soak and cook beans until tender as for *Basic Beans*, above.

Brown the meat in oil in a Dutch oven or other heavy pot. Add the onions, green pepper and garlic, and fry another 5 minutes. Add tomatoes, hot peppers, chili powder, oregano, and cumin. Cover and simmer until the meat is tender, about 1½ hours. Lastly, add the cooked beans and simmer another 30 minutes. If the mixture appears to be too runny, drain the beans before adding them, or cook uncovered so extra water evaporates.

These chili beans are delicious with rice or on toast.

**Chili Bean Pie**   Use Texas Chili Beans as the filling for TAMALE PIE. (Refer to the *Tamale* recipe, in the CORN, DRY section.)

### *Lebanese Beans and Rice Soup*       (Makes 12–15 medium bowls.)

1 cup chick peas or garbanzos
½ cup black beans
1 cup lentils
1 cup rice
½ cup oil, preferably olive

½ cup onions, minced
1 teaspoon salt, or to taste
½ teaspoon caraway seeds, optional

Soak the chick peas and black beans in water overnight. In the morning add the lentils and more water if necessary. Bring to a boil, then simmer uncovered until all three kinds of beans are tender. This will take 3 to 4 hours, or more, depending on the beans' age and variety.

When the beans are done, add the rice. Adjust the amount of water for the desired thickness. The soup can be almost as thick as stew or quite thin. Simmer until the rice is done, about 30 minutes.

Meanwhile heat the oil, and gently sauté the onions in it until they are golden. Add salt and caraway seeds if desired, and stir the mixture into the soup. Let sit covered 5 to 10 minutes, then serve.

### *Korean Bean Pancakes*       (Makes 6–10 side servings.)

2 cups dried beans (Usually mung
   beans, but others are also
   good.)
Optional additional ingredients:
   ½ pound pork, shredded and
   stir-fried (Refer to STIR-
   FRYING section.)

1 medium leek, minced
2 cloves garlic, minced
1 teaspoon fresh ginger root,
   minced
1–2 tablespoons oil for frying
soy sauce

---

**DRY BEAN IDEAS,** *cont.*

**Beans with Noodles or Grains**
Mix hot cooked beans with hot cooked, drained noodles or grain of any kind. Use an equal amount of each. Season to taste. Some good seasonings are: butter, pepper, grated Parmesan cheese, or minced parsley and garlic.

Green noodles (refer to GREEN NOODLES in the NOODLES RECIPES section) look and taste outstanding when mixed with white beans. In the South black-eyed peas are mixed with rice, and seasoned with bacon fat, to make a dish called "Hopping John."

**Bean Porridge**   Heat cooked beans with enough soup stock or vegetable cooking water to cover them generously. For 1½ to 2 quarts of this mixture, moisten ½ cup cornmeal with water (which prevents lumping) and stir it in. Leftover cooked beef, pork, game, or other meat, chopped in small pieces can be added as well. Cook about 30 minutes, stirring often.

This makes a thick, hearty porridge that was once popular in New England. It was made in large quantities in winter to be set out in pots to freeze. Then a pot could be taken along when working in the woods and heated over a camp fire for a quick, hot meal.

**Bean Patties and Loaves**
Mashed cooked beans, and most thick bean mixtures can be seasoned, and shaped into patties or loaves for frying or baking. A beaten egg, breadcrumbs, tomato sauce, or catsup, minced parsley and onion, or a variety of other seasonings can be added. Loaves can be baked with strips of bacon on top, if desired. Usually it takes 45 to 60 minutes in a moderate, 350°F oven, to bake a loaf with beans in it.

Soak the beans in water overnight or until they have doubled in size. Grind in a blender with just enough soaking water for the blender to function. Or grind in a food chopper, with enough soaking water to make the consistency of a thick batter. Mix in any of the optional ingredients, if desired.

Heat a griddle or a heavy frying pan and oil lightly. Drop on tablespoonfuls of the batter, and allow to brown slowly on each side. Sprinkle soy sauce over the pancakes, or dip them in soy sauce as they are eaten. These bean pancakes have a surprisingly delicious, crispy texture.

### *Portuguese Bean Tarts*                    (Makes 12 small tarts.)

| | |
|---|---|
| 2½ cups cooked beans (any kind), unseasoned | 6 egg yolks, or 2 whole eggs, well beaten |
| 1 cup honey | pastry dough from about 2 cups of flour (Any standard recipe using about 2 cups of flour.) |
| 4 tablespoons almonds, ground or finely grated (Or other nuts, or sunflower seeds.) | chopped nuts, optional |

Drain the beans and force them through a sieve, or food mill. Liquify the honey over very low heat, or in a double boiler, then mix in the bean paste. Cook gently, stirring, for 3 or 4 minutes. Now add the ground nuts or seeds, and continue to cook, stirring until the mixture starts to bubble. Quickly remove from heat, and cool to lukewarm. Mix in the beaten egg, and heat, stirring constantly till the mixture thickens. Let cool while preparing the pastry.

Roll out the pastry dough on a floured surface, making it as thin as possible. Cut 12 circles about 3 inches in diameter, using a large cookie cutter or jar lid. (The ring from a wide mouth canning jar is just right.) Line small tart pans or the cups of muffin tins with the pastry. Fill with the bean mixture and sprinkle with nuts. Bake in a hot, 400°F oven for 15 to 20 minutes.

*Maple Bean Tarts*   Use maple syrup instead of honey for a special flavor.

Green, snap, and wax beans used to be called "string beans" because of strings along their seams that had to be removed, but most modern varieties are stringless so the name has fallen into disuse. Tender young bean pods, by any name, remain a favorite vegetable, the kind nobody talks about yet everyone likes. Garden favorites because they grow well everywhere, they taste especially good when cooked immediately after they are picked.

The tender young bean pods are the first good tasting stage. Later on, the pods can be picked and shelled for the fresh, tender beans inside. These are generally known as fresh or green shelled beans, to differentiate them from mature, dried beans. Though it is possible to eat most varieties of beans in all stages of development, they are usually bred for a particular use, for which they are most productive and best tasting. For descriptions of some distinctive varieties refer to the BEANS, DRIED section.

## HANDLING FRESH BEANS

***Tender Young Bean Pods*** Besides green and wax or yellow there is also a purple podded bean, and all are good treated in the same ways, regardless of the pod's color or shape. Pods should be picked when they are almost full size, but before the shapes of the beans inside show clearly. They should snap crisply when broken. If the tips at the stem end are tough, they can be broken off. Any strings along the seams of the pods will come off with the tips.

Beans can be cooked whole, sliced, or broken into bite sized pieces. Breaking is preferred because it prevents the tiny, developing beans in the pods from falling out. While whole beans or pieces can be prepared by steaming them their flavor is often better if they are boiled briefly in plenty of water. This is because most steamers do not cook the beans quickly enough. A special way to slice raw beans is lengthwise in the French style. This helps to tenderize pods that are a little tough. Different styles of bean slicers or "frenchers" are sold in many stores and mail order catalogs. Stir-fried frenched beans are particularly good.

***Fresh Shelled Beans*** For shelling when fresh, pods should be picked after the shape of the bean shows clearly, but before they become limp or dry. It is good to test shell a few beans to see if they are ready, before picking a large batch. Small manual or electric bean and pea shellers are available that make quick work of shelling fresh (but not dried) beans or peas. These shellers are carried by many seed and garden supply catalogs.

Some excellent varieties of beans for shelling fresh are: black-eyed peas, broad beans, lima beans, and soybeans. (Refer to HARVESTING AND SHELLING GREEN SOYBEANS, in the SOYBEANS section.)

## STORAGE

**Canning** *Green, Snap, or Wax* Trim, cut to uniform size.

**Hot Pack** Boil 5 min. Pack. Add boiling cooking water, ½ in. headroom. Process 240°F, 11 pounds pressure. Pints: 20 min. Quarts: 25 min.

**Raw Pack** Pack tightly, add boiling water, ½ in. headroom. Process as for hot pack. *Fresh Shelled Limas, Butter beans, or Others*

**Hot Pack** Boil 3 min. Pack loosely, add boiling cooking water, 1 in. headroom. Process 240°F, 11 pounds pressure. Pints: 40 min. Quarts: 50 min. Add 10 min. for very large beans.

**Cold Pack** Pack loosely, do not press or shake, add boiling water, 1 in. headroom. Process as for hot pack. Refer to CANNING section, and *Dilly Green Beans*, in recipe section, below.

**Drying** (But canning or freezing is preferred.) *Green, Snap, or Wax* Optional: Steam cook 15–20 min. Spread on trays. Or raw, string on a thread and hang. Dry in shade until leathery. (These, called "Leather Britches," need long soaking and cooking to tenderize.) *Fresh Shelled* Pre-cook, dry until hard. Refer to DRYING section.

**Freezing** *Green, Snap, or Wax* Trim, cut to uniform size. Blanch in boiling water 3 min. *Fresh Shelled* Blanch in boiling water, 1–2 min. if small, 3 min. if medium, 4 min. if large. Refer to FREEZING section.

1½–2 POUNDS GREEN, SNAP, OR WAX = 1 QUART COOKED; 4–5 POUNDS UNSHELLED = 1 QUART SHELLED AND COOKED

# FRESH BEAN RECIPES

### Three Bean Salad                        (Makes 8–10 side servings.)

3 cups snap beans, cooked (Half green, half yellow or wax make a pleasant combination.)

1 ½ cups fresh, shelled beans, cooked (Limas, green soybeans, or any others are good. If unavailable, use more snap and dried beans.)

1 ½ cups cooked, dried beans, drained (Half kidney, or another dark bean, and half chick peas or garbanzos are good.)

2–3 tablespoons scallion or onion, chopped

3 tablespoons fresh parsley, minced

2 tablespoons fresh dill leaves, minced, or 1 teaspoon seeds, crushed

1 green pepper, chopped small, optional

6 tablespoons (about) vinegar

6 tablespoons (about) oil

cayenne or black pepper, to taste

salt, optional

Combine all ingredients. Taste, and adjust proportions of vinegar, oil, and other seasonings. Another way to make this salad is to combine the beans, whirl all the other ingredients in the blender until smooth, and pour this dressing over the beans.

Let the salad marinate at least a ½ hour before serving. Several hours is better, and the salad still tastes very good the second day.

**Sauerkraut Bean Salad**   Add about 2 cups well drained sauerkraut to the salad. The amount of oil and seasonings can be increased.

### Stir-fried Snap Beans                    (Makes 8–10 side servings.)

3 tablespoons chicken fat, vegetable oil, or lard

1 ½ pounds snap beans, broken in 1 inch pieces, or French style

¾ cup soup stock, or water

salt, optional

Heat a wok or heavy frying pan and add the fat or oil. When quite hot, add the beans and stir-fry 1 minute. Add the stock or water, cover, and cook about 3 minutes, or until the beans are bright in color. Uncover and cook for 3 to 6 minutes, or till just tender, stirring often. The liquid should evaporate almost completely. Serve immediately. (Refer to the STIR-FRYING section for detailed directions.) These are a very good vegetable side dish with any meal, Western or Chinese.

### Savory Snap Bean Stew                    (Makes 6–8 side servings.)

2 medium onions, sliced thin

1 clove garlic, minced, optional

hot pepper, minced, optional

3 tablespoons butter

2 cups tomatoes, canned or fresh, chopped

½ teaspoon savory, sage, or oregano, or herbs to taste

parsley, minced, optional

salt, if desired

4 cups snap beans, fresh, frozen, or canned

Sauté the onions, garlic, and hot pepper in 2 tablespoons of the butter until the onions are limp. Add the tomatoes and herbs (except parsley), and simmer uncovered for 15 to 20 minutes, stirring several times. Add the snap beans, and cook until tender. If canned beans are used, the drained canning liquid can be added with the tomatoes, and cooked over fairly high heat until the sauce thickens. Just before serving add the parsley, and the other tablespoon of butter. Good alone with bread or rice, or as a side dish with dinner.

**Savory Broccoli Stew** Use chopped broccoli instead of snap beans in this recipe.

## Buttery Beans Casserole  (Makes 5–6 dinner servings.)

| | |
|---|---|
| 2 cups fresh or canned shelled beans (Green limas, butterbeans, or any others.) | pepper, to taste |
| | 1 onion, minced |
| 2 cups soup stock or water (Omit for canned beans.) | ½ cup mild cheese, grated, optional |
| 2 tablespoons (about) butter, or other fat | ½ cup nuts, chopped, or sunflower seeds, whole |
| 1–3 teaspoons soy sauce | breadcrumbs, or rolled oats |

Cook the beans in the soup stock or water until they are tender. (If using canned beans, they only need heating.) Drain the beans, saving the liquid. Add a tablespoon of butter or fat to the liquid, stir until it melts, and add soy sauce and pepper.

Butter a casserole dish, and make a layer of a third of the beans. Sprinkle with half of the onion, cheese and nuts, and pour over part of the cooking liquid. Add another third of the beans, the rest of the onion, cheese and nuts, and more of the cooking liquid. Finish with the rest of the beans and liquid, then sprinkle generously with breadcrumbs or rolled oats. Dot with butter and bake at 350°F for about 35 minutes. This makes an excellent, high protein side dish. For a main course, amounts can be doubled.

## Succotash  (Makes about 4 cups.)

Many bean and corn mixtures are called "succotash." It is an Amerindian dish whose name comes from the Narragansett word "misiskquatash" (made with kidney beans, corn, and bear fat). Most modern versions are made with fresh shelled beans.

| | |
|---|---|
| 2 cups fresh, or canned shelled beans | pepper, to taste |
| salt pork, small slice, optional | ¼ cup cream |
| 2 cups whole kernel corn | salt, if desired (and if not using |
| 1 tablespoon butter | salt pork) |

---

### FRESH BEAN IDEAS

**Snap Beans as Dried Beans** If snap beans become tough before they can be picked, leave them to mature completely, and harvest them as dried beans. (Refer to the BEANS, DRIED section.) They can also be used as fresh shelled beans, but snap bean varieties tend to make better dried beans than fresh shelled beans.

**Green and Wax Beans in Salads** Tender green beans, or wax beans, add a nice flavor when chopped raw into salads. They are also very good simply eaten whole as a raw snack, or served with dips. For an attractive display, arrange fresh green beans with wax beans and purple podded beans.

**Fresh Beans with Nuts** Sauté chopped nuts such as cashews, raw peanuts, or cooked chestnuts, in butter until lightly browned, then toss them with hot, cooked snap or shelled beans. If desired, season with pepper, and a sprinkling of minced, fresh herbs, such as savory, basil, chives, or parsley.

**Barbecued Bean Bundles** Cook whole snap beans until just barely tender. When cool enough to handle, group them in bundles of 5 or 6 beans. Then wrap a slice of bacon around each, and pin together with a toothpick. Broil, turning several times until the bacon is cooked. Sprinkle with pepper, or serve with barbecue sauce if desired. These look as good as they taste.

Put the beans in a sauce pan with the salt pork, cover with water, and cook until tender. Time will vary with the type of beans. Add the corn, butter and pepper, and cook until the corn is tender. If there is extra liquid, drain it off. (It can be saved for soup or other cooking.) Add the cream and remove from heat. Season with salt, if desired.

**Tomato Succotash**   When adding corn, also add a chopped fresh tomato or 1 cup stewed tomatoes. Omit the cream. Other vegetables such as chopped onion, green pepper, okra or celery can also be included.

### Dilly Green Beans                    (Makes 6 pints canned pickles.)

6 cloves garlic
6 small heads of fresh dill or 2
    tablespoons dill seeds
6 slices of raw hot pepper, or 1 ½
    teaspoons hot pepper flakes (or add
    to taste)

3 quarts (about 3 pounds) green
    beans
3 ½ cups vinegar (White is best
    for appearance, but cider
    gives excellent flavor.)
3 ½ cups water
½ teaspoon salt, optional

Put a clove of garlic, a dill head, or 1 teaspoon seed, and a piece of hot pepper or ¼ teaspoon flakes in each pint jar. Break the tips off the green beans, if preferred, and pack them whole into the jars, leaving ¼ inch headroom. Bring the vinegar, water, and salt if desired, to a boil, then pour boiling hot over the beans, leaving ¼ inch headroom. Process in a boiling water bath, for 10 minutes whether in pints or quarts. (Refer to the CANNING section.)

**Dilly Okra, Asparagus, or Brussels Sprouts**   Instead of beans, use tender young okra pods, or asparagus spears trimmed to jar length, and process in exactly the same way. Brussels sprouts should be steamed until just tender before they are packed in jars. Use pints only, and process in a boiling water bath for 15 minutes.

## STORAGE

**Canning**   *Chunks* (Tougher cuts best.) Remove bone, fat. Cut into large chunks, 1 to each straight-sided jar, or uniform small chunks. (Optional: Brown under broiler or in a little oil.) Then stew or bake in enough water to prevent sticking until medium done. Put large chunk, or loosely packed small chunks in each jar. Boil and add defatted cooking juice, add boiling water,

# BEEF

BEEF IS THE MEAT OF MATURE CATTLE; STEERS, HEIFERS, COWS, OR bulls. The meat of immature cattle is veal or baby beef. (Refer to the VEAL section.) Beef is North America's most popular meat. Some people eat it every day and many more would if they could afford it. For modern homesteaders, however, beef is less important than the meat of smaller animals requiring less space, less time to mature, and less equipment and experience to butcher.

As grazing animals, cattle can live entirely on pasture, fodder crops, silage, and crop residues. Raised on feeds of this kind they are practical meat animals, but when fattened on large amounts of grain their meat becomes much more expensive. It also becomes less nutritious because of the amount of fat incorporated into it. If questionable feed additives, such as antibiotics and hormones are used as well, beef is not a praiseworthy food. (Refer to the MEAT section.)

Home raised lean beef that is mostly grass fed is excellent to eat as well as practical to raise. By comparison, most commercial beef tastes watery and flavorless with a texture approaching mushiness.

## HANDLING BEEF

Butchering beef is a big job because of the size and weight of the animals, 600 to 1000 pounds for steers or heifers and more for older animals. Though the basic procedures are the same as for the smaller animals, such as lamb (refer to the LAMB section), some special equipment and the help of an experienced person are almost essential. Detailed directions are available in government agricultural publications and bulletins, and from the references at the end of the LAMB section.

Every part of a beef carcass is useful. The saying that "Every part of a pig can be used except the squeal," could just as well be said about a cow, "except the moo." For uses of special parts, and directions for cleaning and preparing, refer to the chart on p. 486 in the PORK section. Organ meats and other specialties are handled in much the same way no matter what animal they are from. Parts never mentioned in a modern context have had their uses in less affluent times and places. The bladders of beef animals, for instance, were washed and dried for storage, and then used by dipping them in water and wrapping them around jars of pickles or other foods to seal them. Smoked cow's udder was not unknown as a specialty. Beef carcass parts are often listed as coming from an ox, such as ox tail, ox cheek, and ox muzzle.

Lean, home raised beef is ideal for stews, pot roasts, soups, and chopped meat. When an older animal, such as a cull from a dairy herd, is butchered, the whole carcass is used in these ways. Steaks and roasts from young animals can also be superior, as long as their leanness is taken into account when they are prepared. Refer to the MEAT section for cooking methods.

## BEEF RECIPES

(Beef recipes of every kind abound, but for home-raised, grass-fed beef, stews are among the best.)

---

**STORAGE,** *cont.*

if needed; 1 in. headroom. Process 240°F, 11 pounds pressure. Pints: 1 hr. 15 min. Quarts: 1 hr. 30 min. *Lean Chopped Meat* (Better frozen.) Shape into meat balls, or patties the diameter of jars. Bake, 325°F oven, in shallow pans, to medium done. Pack, boil and add defatted cooking juice, add boiling broth or water if needed; 1 in. headroom. Process as for chunks. (To can other cuts, and for other packing methods, refer to CANNING section.) Also refer to REFERENCES at end of CANNING section for more ways to can beef and CANNING CORNED BEEF, below.

**Cold Storage**   Refer to AGING MEAT, in MEAT section.

**Drying**   Excellent for very lean beef. Refer to DRYING MEAT, in DRYING section.

**Freezing**   Cut and trim as desired for eventual cooking. Wrap well. (Refer to FREEZING section.)

**Salt Curing**   See *Corned Beef* and DRIED CHIP BEEF, below.

1 POUND GROUND BEEF = ABOUT 2 CUPS.

### Pot Au Feu

(There are many versions of this French style stew, which can make from 8–20 dinner servings.)

| | |
|---|---|
| 3–4 pounds stewing beef, in one piece | 1 teaspoon thyme |
| 6 leeks | 3 cloves |
| 2 stalks celery | 12 peppercorns |
| 1 stewing chicken, or 1 pound giblets | 1 large clove garlic |
| 1 bay leaf | 3 onions, quartered |
| 1 bunch parsley, coarsely chopped | 4 carrots, cut in large pieces |
| | 2 parsnips, cut in large pieces |
| | salt, optional |

Put the beef in a large pot, and add water to cover. Bring slowly to a boil. Skim off the scum as it rises. When the pot boils, add a cup of cold water and skim again. Tie the leeks and celery together in a bundle with string, and drop them in the pot. Let them cook for 20 minutes or until tender, then remove them. (Save for a salad or vegetable side dish.) Add the chicken or giblets. If using a chicken, it can be left whole or cut in pieces. Add the bay leaf, parsley, thyme, cloves, peppercorns, garlic, and salt, if desired. Cover and simmer over very low heat for several hours. If either beef or chicken should become tender while the other is still tough, remove the tender one and continue cooking the other. About 30 minutes before the pot is done add the onions, carrots and parsnips.

There are several different ways to serve *Pot au feu*. Either the beef or the chicken can be set aside for dinner the next day. Some of the broth can be made into a gravy for the meat and vegetables, and the rest of the broth, which is delicious, can be saved for soup. Alternatively, the meats, vegetables and broth can be served together in bowls, like a hearty soup.

### Sukiyaki Homestead Style     (Makes 8–12 dinner servings.)

| | |
|---|---|
| 2 pounds beef (Flank steak or another lean moderately tender cut.) | 2 tablespoons (about) honey, or sugar |
| 1 large onion | ½ cup (about) soup stock |
| 3–4 large or 10–12 small scallions (Or another onion.) | Optional additional ingredients: |
| ½ pound spinach, or other greens |    mushrooms, sliced ¼ inch thick |
| 1½ (about) pounds seasonal vegetables (Good choices are snow peas, carrots, green beans, broccoli, celery, leeks.) |    bamboo shoots (canned), sliced ¼ inch thick |
| 1–2 tablespoons oil, lard, or piece of suet |    bean thread noodles, soaked and drained |
| 3 tablespoons (about) soy sauce |    tofu, cut in 1 inch cubes (Refer to TOFU section.) |

The sukiyaki ingredients should be prepared ahead, and arranged on platters ready to cook.

Slice the beef across the grain, about ¼ inch thick, then cut into 1 or 2 inch squares or rectangles. Slice the onion ¼ inch thick and separate into rings. Cut the scallions into 2 or 3 inch lengths. Separate spinach or greens into individual leaves and tear or cut large leaves into several smaller pieces. Slice other vegetables ¼ inch thick, or as necessary to make pieces that will cook in 10 to 15 minutes. Carrots and celery can be sliced diagonally to make larger pieces.

Often sukiyaki is cooked at the table in an electric frying pan or in a large frying pan on a hot plate. Heat the frying pan and coat it with oil or fat, or rub with the suet. Lay half of the meat in the pan and put the onions and slower cooking vegetables such as carrots, green beans, or broccoli on it. Add half of the soy sauce, half of the honey or sugar, and half of the soup stock. Then add half of the scallions and any other quick cooking vegetables such as snow peas. Pile half of the spinach or other greens loosely on top. They act as a lid, holding in the steam.

Let the sukiyaki cook over fairly high heat undisturbed for 3 or 4 minutes, or until the spinach or greens start to wilt. Then stir gently turning any ingredients that seem to need it. Taste the juice and adjust amounts of soy sauce and sweetener. Add more stock it if boils away. Let simmer until ingredients are just tender, about 10 minutes. Serve with rice.

The traditional family way to eat sukiyaki cooked at the table is for people to help themselves, using chop sticks to pick out what they want.

When part of the first batch of sukiyaki has been eaten the cook should push the remaining part to one side of the pan, then put the rest of the raw ingredients in the cleared space, starting with the meat and adding the vegetables, stock and seasonings, as before. While the second batch is cooking, everyone can continue to eat the first batch.

***Chicken or Venison Sukiyaki*** Bone and slice chicken, or slice a tender cut of venison, and use instead of beef with the above recipe.

## Corned Beef

(For more about salting meat refer to the SALT CURING section.)

25 *pounds beef* (Brisket, plate, or chuck.)
2 *pounds plain or pickling salt*
4 – 5 *cloves garlic, optional*
1 *pound honey or sugar*
1 *ounce saltpeter*
2 *tablespoons pickling spices, optional*
*water*

Cut the beef into 1½ to 2 inch thick slabs, 5 or 6 inches square. Rub salt into each piece of meat. Spread a layer of salt on the bottom of a large (about 5 gallon) crock or other non-porous container. Pack the meat closely, but do not force it in. Add a thin layer of salt after every 2 layers of meat. End with salt, using the full 2 pounds. If the corned beef is to be stored in brine rather than canned, add another cup of salt. If using pickling spices or garlic, or both, sprinkle them here and there between layers. Let the salt packed meat stand in a cool place (between freezing and 45°F) for 24 hours.

Boil and cool 1 gallon of water. Dissolve the honey or sugar and saltpeter in the water, then pour it over the beef. There should be enough liquid to make the pack of meat loosen and start to float. Add more boiled, cooled water, if necessary. Weigh down the meat to keep every bit of it under the liquid and cover the crock. (Refer to the KITCHEN UTENSILS section for how to use crocks.) To cure, store in a cool place, between freezing and 45°F, for 4 to 6 weeks.

If the brine around the corned beef becomes thick or ropy (which may happen if the temperature gets too high), take the corned beef out and wash it in warm water. Discard the old brine, then wash the crock and scald it with boiling water. Re-pack the meat, and cover it with a fresh brine made of a gallon of boiled then cooled water, 1½ pounds salt, and the same proportions of sweetener and saltpeter originally used.

***Canning Corned Beef***   After the corned beef has finished curing, freshen it by soaking in cold water for several hours. Drain, then cut the meat to fit canning jars. Cover with fresh water and heat just to a boil. Taste the water, and if it is too salty, drain, add fresh water, and heat again. Pack the hot pieces of corned beef in jars and add boiling cooking water, leaving 1 inch headroom. Process at 240°F (11 pounds pressure at sea level on a dial gauge or 10 pounds for a weighted gauge). Pints: 1 hour, 15 minutes; quarts: 1 hour, 30 minutes. (Refer to the CANNING section.)

***Cooking Crock Stored Corned Beef***   Remove the desired amount of corned beef from the crock (rearranging the remainder to be sure it is held under the brine). Rinse the meat, and soak in cold water for several hours or overnight, in a cold place, to freshen. Drain, cover with fresh water, and bring to a boil. If still too salty, drain, then heat again in fresh water. Simmer over low heat until the meat is tender, 2 to 4 hours depending on size and toughness. Unless it is served hot, it should be refrigerated once cooked.

***Corned Beef Boiled Dinner***   Freshen and cook corned beef as described above. About an hour before it is done, add potatoes, carrots, turnips, onions, or any other preferred vegetables. Cabbage wedges can be added for the last 15 minutes of cooking, or they can be cooked separately and arranged around the corned beef on a serving platter.

***Corned Chevon, Lamb, or Venison***   Salt cure any of these meats in the same way as corned beef. Lamb cuts most often used are the breast and shank. When corned, all of these meats are quite strongly flavored and may not be to everyone's taste. If preferred, they can be

---

## BEEF IDEAS

**Beef Salad**   Slice leftover cooked beef, and marinate it in an oil and vinegar salad dressing for several hours. Arrange the meat on a bed of lettuce or other greens. Add sliced tomatoes, cucumbers, sliced hard boiled eggs, or other favorite salad ingredients. A garnish of minced parsley, chives, or other fresh herbs makes a pleasant addition.

**Beef Tea**   Cover small pieces of lean, raw beef with cold water, and let stand 1 hour at room temperature. Heat slowly over low heat to a boil and strain. Season if wished. All of the flavor will be in the tea, and the meat almost tasteless.

This is an old beverage once thought to be beneficial for invalids, but it makes an enjoyable, strength-giving drink for anyone. Minced chives, parsley, or other herbs can be added, if desired.

**Lean Beef Steak Fried with Onions**   Home raised beef is very good lightly fried with onions and green peppers.

smoked like the DRIED CHIP BEEF below. They need only 24 to 36 hours of smoking.

**Salt Cured Tongue** The tongues of most animals can be salt cured following the directions for corning beef, but curing times must be adjusted. Beef tongues should stay in the brine for 25 to 30 days, calf tongues, 12 to 14 days, pig tongues, 10 days, and lamb tongues, 8 days. Cured tongues can be washed, drained, and lightly smoked. Small tongues require only a few hours of smoking and large ones take about 12 hours. After smoking, store in a dry cool place, or refrigerate and use within a few months.

**Dried Chip Beef** Salt cure beef as for corned beef, except increase the sweetener to 1¼ pounds. Lean cuts are best. After the beef has cured from 4 to 6 weeks, wash it well, and hang it in a cool, dry, airy place for 24 hours. Then cool smoke it at 100 to 120°F for 70 to 80 hours. (Refer to the SMOKING section.) Wrap in moisture proof paper and hang in a cool place, or refrigerate for storage. Storage temperatures must be below 45°F.

Dried chip beef is sliced paper thin before it is used. It is often cooked in a white sauce, like the ones described under MILK RECIPES in the MILK section.

*Plymouth Succotash*
(An Early American stew.)   (Makes 6–10 dinner servings.)

| | |
|---|---|
| 1 cup dry navy or other small beans | 2 medium potatoes |
| 1 pound (about) corned beef | ½ small rutabaga |
| salt pork, small piece, optional | 3 cups cooked hominy or whole |
| 1½ pounds (about) stewing chicken, | kernel corn, pre-cooked |
| cut in serving pieces | |

Soak the beans overnight, and cook until tender. Then purée them with their cooking water in a blender or food mill.

Meanwhile, soak the corned beef for several hours in cold water, or as necessary to freshen. Put it in a pot with the chicken and just enough fresh water to cover, and simmer until tender, from 2 to 3 hours. Add the potatoes and rutabaga when the meat is about half done, cook them until tender, then remove and slice them. When the meats are done, add the bean purée, hominy or corn, and the vegetable slices. Reheat to serve. The corned beef can be removed, sliced, and returned to the pot.

**OTHER RECIPES FEATURING BEEF**

Barbecued Slices of Beef, Chinese Style, p. 380
Beef and Winter Radish (or Turnip) Soup, p. 506
Broccoli Stir-fried with Beef, p. 77
Chinese Smoked Beef, p. 572
Farmer's Meat Loaf, p. 396
Old Fashioned Mincemeat, p. 409
Other Basic Meat Preparations, p. 410
Quebec Pork Ragout, p. 489
Raw Garlic and Parsley Relish (with steaks), p. 296
Red Flannel Hash, p. 494
Sausage recipes with beef, p. 551
Turnip (or Carrot) Tzimmes, p. 658

# BEETS

## STORAGE

**Canning** Sort for size. Cook (see instructions below) until skins slip. Trim, peel. Pack whole, sliced or diced. Add fresh boiling water, ½ in. headroom. Process 240°F, 11 pounds pressure. Pints: 30 min. Quarts: 35 min. (Refer to CANNING section, and *Pickled Beets,* below.) *Beet Greens* Refer to CANNING SPINACH, in the SPINACH section.

**Cold Storage** Root cellar ideal. Do not wash or trim roots, leave 1–2 in. of tops. Pack in damp sand or other damp material. Late varieties keep all winter. Late varieties keep all winter. Refer to COLD STORAGE section.

**Drying** (Excellent) Optional: Pre-cook till tender. Slice thin, or grate coarsely. Dry to very tough or brittle. Refer to DRYING section, and DRIED VEGETABLE PICKLES in PICKLING section, and cooking directions, below. *Beet Greens* Refer to DRYING SPINACH in the SPINACH section.

**Freezing** (Large beets' flavor better with other storage methods.) Pre-cook till tender. Trim, peel, slice or dice, if desired. Refer to FREEZING section. *Beet Greens* Refer to FREEZING SPINACH in the SPINACH section.

2½–3 POUNDS, TOPS REMOVED = 1 QUART COOKED.

B EETS ARE, IN A SENSE, SUBJECT TO DISCRIMINATION BECAUSE OF their color—the redness that is so penetrating that everything they touch turns "red as a beet." The first consideration, when combining beets with other foods, is apt to be how the mixture will look, rather than how it will taste. If beets only kept their color to themselves, they would be as versatile as carrots or potatoes! Their pleasant, sweet taste and firm texture would be welcome wherever vegetables mix. However, facts are facts and beets dye red. If one or two are added to a dish, its name may be changed to suit its new color. Thus "Hash" with added beets becomes "Red Flannel Hash," and beets are valued some of the time just because they color other foods. (Refer to the FOOD COLORING section.)

Beet greens as well as roots are valuable. Beet plants were grown as greens for many centuries before the fleshy rooted varieties were developed. The greens taste very much like their close relative, Swiss chard, and can be used in the same ways. (Refer to the SWISS CHARD section, HANDLING and RECIPES.)

## HANDLING BEETS

Beets can be pulled at any age. Baby beets, ranging from large marble to golf ball size, are tender and sweet, delicious raw as well as cooked. Medium sized beets can be used whole or sliced. Fully-grown, fall-maturing beets will keep for months in a root cellar retaining their sweet, delicate flavor. Though they sometimes develop woody cores, these are easily pulled out after the beets are cooked. Cut cooked beets in half to see if their center rings are fibrous or tough. If so, remove them.

***Cooking Raw Beets*** When beets are cooked by themselves, it is important not to cut into them until after they are done. If cut, flavor and color leach out into the cooking or steaming water. If the beets are to be made into soup or a mixed stew the leaching will not matter. To prepare beets for cooking, cut the tops off an inch or two above the crown. Do not cut the tap root or rootlets. Rinse well without scraping or damaging the beet's skin. Then steam or boil until tender. This can take from 30 minutes to more than an hour depending on the size of the beets.

Beet cooking water is very often thrown away, but it should not be. It has nutritional value, and according to some, it is a blood builder. (Why not, considering its color?!) When possible, use beet cooking water in beet recipes, or include it in soup, or in vegetable drinks.

***Cooking Dried Beets*** Put dried beets in a sauce pan and cover with water. Let soak 15 minutes, or a little longer if pieces are large. Heat to a simmer and cook till tender, usually 15 to 30 minutes. These can be used in any of the recipes in this section. (Also refer to DRIED VEG-ETABLE PICKLES, in the PICKLING section.)

## BEET RECIPES

### *Beet Salad*        (Makes 6—8 side servings.)

2 cups beets, cooked and sliced
1 onion, sliced and separated into
   rings, optional
½ teaspoon dry mustard
¼ teaspoon powdered cloves
½ teaspoon salt, optional

6 tablespoons vinegar
6 tablespoons oil
1 clove garlic, optional
dill or fennel leaves for garnish,
   optional

Arrange the beet slices and onion rings in a dish. Mix the mustard, cloves, and salt with a few drops of vinegar to moisten them, then mix with the rest of the vinegar and oil. The garlic can be added whole to the salad and removed before serving, or it can be minced and added to the dressing. Pour the dressing over the beets and onions. Let marinate several hours before serving. This is an especially good beet salad which also tastes good the second day. Garnish with dill or fennel just before serving.

### *Piquant Red Beet Aspic*        (Makes 6—8 side servings.)

2 cups beet cooking water
2 tablespoons powdered gelatine
⅓—½ cup vinegar
3 tablespoons (about) honey or other
   sweetening
2 cups cooked beets, diced
1½ cups scallions, or sweet onions,
   minced

1½ cups celery, minced, optional
2 teaspoons horseradish, grated,
   optional
½ cup cucumber or other relish,
   optional (Refer to the recipe
   in CUCUMBER section.)

If there is not enough cooking water left from cooking the beets, add plain water to make 2 cups. Soak the gelatine in about ½ cup of the cold cooking water until it swells. Heat the rest of the liquid until warm, and add the gelatine mixture. Stir until dissolved. Remove from heat, add the vinegar and honey, and stir to combine completely.

Taste, and adjust amounts of vinegar and honey to make a piquant, sweet and sour flavor.

Add the beets and scallions or onions. Add celery, horseradish, or relish if used. Pour into one large mold or 6 to 8 cup-sized molds. Refrigerate until set. Unmold to serve.

### Cold Borscht                              (Makes 6–8 bowls.)

*1½ quarts beet cooking water and*      *1–2 eggs, beaten*
*    plain water*                           *sour cream, or yogurt*
*1 cup beets, cooked and grated*      *3–4 hot boiled potatoes, option-*
*1 small onion, grated*                   *al* (About ½ medium potato
*juice of 1 lemon*                      *per serving.*)
*2–3 tablespoons honey*

Combine the beet water, beets, onion, lemon juice, and honey in a soup pot. Heat and simmer for 30 minutes. Taste, and adjust proportions of lemon juice and honey if desired. Let cool 5 to 10 minutes. In a separate bowl, mix 2 or 3 tablespoons of the borscht into the eggs, then mix in several more tablespoons. (This heats the egg gradually so that it does not curdle.) Stir the egg mixture gradually into the rest of the borscht. Chill completely. It will keep a week or longer when refrigerated.

Float a spoonful of sour cream or yogurt on each bowl of soup when serving it. If desired a chunk of hot potato can be put in each bowl before the borscht is added. This deep red, sweet and sour soup is perfect when the weather is hot. (When it is cold, try the *Hot Borscht*, below.)

### Old Time Hot Borscht                     (Makes 8–12 bowls.)

*6–8 medium beets*                      *1½ quarts beef or pork stock*
*¼ cup vinegar* (Red wine vinegar is     *2 cups fresh or canned tomatoes,*
*    best.*)                               *chopped*
*3 tablespoons* (about) *bacon fat, or*     *1 bay leaf*
*    butter*                            *½ teaspoon thyme*
*1 cup onion, minced*                 *pepper, and salt, optional*
*1 clove garlic, minced*               *1 or more cups leftover cooked*
*1½ cups cabbage, shredded*        *meat, chopped, optional*
*1 cup carrots, coarsely grated, or cut*   *sour cream, or yogurt, optional*
*    julienne style*
*½ cup celery, thinly sliced, optional*

The day before the soup is wanted, cook the beets in water to cover. Drain, saving the cooking water. (Or the beets can be cooked in the pot when the soup stock is made, and removed when done.) Grate the beets or cut them julienne style. Mix about ½ cup beets with the vinegar, and soak overnight.

---

## BEET IDEAS

**Baked Beets** Whole beets, untrimmed except for tops, are very good oven baked like potatoes, and served with butter. Large beets may take as long as 3 hours to bake, so put them in early.

Trimmed and peeled beets can be baked in the pan with roasting meat, but will change the color of the meat and other vegetables if allowed to touch them.

**Polish Style Beets for Roast Meats** Grate about 3 cups of cooked beets, and make a sauce for them as follows: Sauté a minced, medium sized onion in 3 tablespoons butter or other fat till limp. Stir in 2 tablespoons flour, and continue stirring till the flour browns lightly. Add either 1 cup meat broth or defatted pan drippings mixed with water. When thickened to a sauce, add the beets and 1 or 2 cloves of crushed garlic. Simmer a few minutes more. Just before serving flavor with several tablespoons lemon juice or wine vinegar.

Very good served with roast or pot roasted meat, especially dark flavorful meats like mutton, venison, and other game.

**Raw Beets in Salads** Small amounts of grated or very thinly sliced raw beet are delicious in many kinds of salads. They can also be used as a colorful garnish on cottage cheese or potato salads.

The next day, heat the fat or butter in a soup pot, and gently sauté the onion, garlic, cabbage, carrots, and celery in it until they are limp. Add the soup stock, tomatoes, bay leaf, thyme, pepper, and salt. Add the beets and any beet cooking water, but continue to reserve the beet and vinegar mixture. Heat to a boil, and simmer about 30 minutes. Add the leftover meat.

Just before serving add the beet and vinegar mixture, and adjust seasonings, if necessary. Sour cream or yogurt can be added to each bowl of soup.

---

### Pickled Beets　　　　　　　　　　　　　　　　(4 pints, canned.)

(A good way to store beets for those who prefer not to use a pressure canner.)

| | |
|---|---|
| 4 pints cooked beets, small whole or sliced | 4 slices onion |
| 1 cup beet cooking water | 8−12 whole cloves |
| 3 cups vinegar | 4 pieces of celery stalk |
| ¼ cup honey, or to taste, optional | dill or caraway seeds |

Heat the beet cooking water, vinegar, and honey to a boil in a saucepan. Meanwhile put a slice of onion, 2−3 cloves, a piece of celery and a few dill or caraway seeds in each jar. Add beets to fill the jars without jamming them in too tightly. Pour in the boiling vinegar mixture, leaving ½ inch headroom. Process in a boiling water bath, 30 minutes for both pints and quarts. (Refer to the CANNING section.) This recipe is healthier than most pickled beet recipes, with no salt and little or no honey.

**Pickling Juice Soup**　Mix 1 part juice from pickled beets with 3 to 4 parts yogurt or buttermilk. Add fresh minced dill leaves, scallions, or other fresh herbs. Grated horseradish is also good. Chopped cucumber or other chopped vegetables can be included. Chill before serving.

---

**BEET IDEAS,** *cont.*

**Stuffed Beet Salad**　Cook medium or large beets and scoop out their centers with a spoon to make a hollow for stuffing. Cut a slice off the bottoms so that they sit firmly. Chop up the beet centers with onion, celery, and cooked leftover vegetables such as peas or green beans. Moisten with mayonnaise or the *Yogurt Dressing for Vegetable Salads* in the YOGURT section, and stuff the beets. They look very nice arranged on lettuce leaves. Plain sliced beets are also good with these dressings.

**Beet and Horseradish Relish**　Mix 1 part grated cooked beet and 1 part grated raw horseradish, or other preferred proportions. Add as much vinegar as the mixture will absorb. Some people like to add a little honey also. This keeps refrigerated for about a month.

---

### OTHER RECIPES WITH BEETS

Dandelion Beet Salad, p. 219
Dried Vegetable Pickles, p. 480
Eggs or Beets Marinated in Pickle Liquid, p. 480
Elizabethan Stuffed Fish, p. 268
Rainbow Noodles, p. 431
Recipes, and Ideas for Swiss Chard (using beet greens), p. 626
Red Flannel Hash, p. 494
Roast Beverages, p. 44

---

# BEVERAGES

Beverages are important foods psychologically, and should be nutritionally worthwhile, or at the very least not harmful. Drinking a cup of something hot, or a glass of something cold is a pleasant way to take a break, visit with friends, or just relax for a while. It is unfortunate that so many popular beverages, advertized to be appealing in these ways, have so little other value. Carbonated beverages are largely sugar and chemicals, or, in the case of diet soda, just chemicals. "Fruit" drinks designed to please children are very often made with just sugar, water, and artificial color and flavor, with vitamin C added. The vitamin does not make up for the poor quality of the drink. The harmful effects of the caffeine in coffee, tea, and some kinds of soda are well known. Chocolate drinks contain a stimulant that is very similar to caffeine, and large amounts of sugar, as well. Alcoholic beverages are controversial for other reasons, but most would agree that they are not the thing for a midday "beverage break."

So, what is a good beverage? Fresh, good-tasting water is one. Some others are fruit and vegetable juices, herb teas, roast beverages made from roots, grains and seeds, broth, and milk based drinks of many kinds.

## WATER

The taste of water is extremely important. No one enjoys a drink that tastes of chlorine or sulphur, and the taste of hard or highly mineralized water is seldom good. Beverages and other foods containing a large proportion of water are greatly affected by water quality. Frozen juice concentrates, tea, soup, bread, and dry beans are examples of foods that taste their best only when made with pure, soft water. Fermented foods like sauerkraut, vinegar, wine, and sourdough also require pure water. The presence of chlorine stops fermentation, while the presence of minerals such as calcium salts interferes with it.

If pure, good tasting water does not come from the tap, it is worth some effort to find a source for beverages and cooking. Water filtering systems often help. Water softening systems using chemicals are not good for drinking and cooking water, because they add excess sodium to the diet, and may cause changes in the flavor and texture of cooked foods. Some people buy bottled spring water for drinking and cooking, while others collect rain water. Rain water should always be collected in the open, and not from a dusty roof. The container should be put out after it has rained for an hour and cleaned dust out of the air. In rural areas, another possibility is to find someone with good spring or well water who is willing to share.

## HOT DRINKS

No doubt the most familiar hot drinks of all are tea and coffee, but there are good home-grown and homemade alternatives for both. Teas made from home dried herbs and other dried ingredients are excellent, and the possible variations are endless. (Refer to RECIPES in the HERBS section.) Coffee-like beverages can be made from roasted roots, grains, and seeds of many kinds, and blends of these can be made to suit personal tastes.

***Roasting Roots, Grains, and Seeds for Beverages*** Many kinds of foods have a definite, coffee-like flavor and aroma if they are roasted until very dark. Coffee itself is, after all nothing but roasted seeds. Roasted chicory and dandelion roots have a bitter quality which some like and others find too strong. Roasted grains have a smoother flavor, but are too mild for some tastes. There are many seeds with good roasted flavors and aromas (see the list below, FOODS TO ROAST FOR BEVERAGES), which can be tried separately or in blends.

Roots will roast more evenly if they are sliced to a uniform thickness when raw. They can be dried till hard in a food dryer before they are roasted, or they can be dried in a very low oven (150°F), for several hours, and then the heat increased to roast them. Most grains and seeds are dry enough for roasting without preliminary drying, but can also be handled like roots, if necessary.

Spread roots, grains, and seeds to be roasted in shallow layers in pans, and put them in a low oven, 200 to 300°F. If more than one kind of root, grain, or seed is to be roasted at the same time, put each in a separate pan, as they will need different lengths of time. It can take one or several hours, depending on thickness, on other characteristics of the food, and on the degree of darkness of the roast. As they roast, the foods should be turned or stirred several times so that they brown evenly. Break open roots and large seeds to see how they are coming, as the centers tend to darken faster than the outsides. They are usually done when the centers are very dark brown or black. A way to save fuel is to put the foods in an oven that has just been turned off after cooking something else. When the oven has cooled, they can be set aside, and then put in again after the next use. This can be repeated until they are dark enough.

The roasted foods can be ground in a grain mill, meat grinder, or in small amounts in a blender or food processor. They are generally ground to the coarseness of coffee, but can be ground finer. (If ground into flour, small amounts can be added to baked goods to flavor and darken them.) It is also possible to roast pre-ground meals or flours in a heavy, dry frying pan on top of the stove. If grinding is difficult, roasted grains and seeds can be used whole, but the beverages will take an hour or more of brewing.

**Brewing Roast Beverages** Roasted and ground roots like chicory can be brewed in a regular coffee pot, but grains and seeds tend to swell and clog the pot. Generally it is best to steep roast beverages as for tea, or to simmer them in a sauce pan over very low heat for 10 to 15 minutes. They can be kept warm on a wood stove for hours and still taste good.

About a teaspoon of "ground roast" is needed per cup of water, and brewing can begin in cold or in hot water. If the grounds do not settle out by themselves, the drink can be strained into the cup. Milk, cream, and sweetening can be added to taste. Molasses is especially good with roast beverages.

## FOODS TO ROAST FOR BEVERAGES

| *Roots* | *Grains* | *Seeds* |
|---|---|---|
| Beet | Barley, unhulled | Acorns, debittered (in |
| Carrot | Barley Malt (in | WILD FOODS |
| Chicory | BARLEY section) | section) |
| Comfrey | Corn | Asparagus berries |
| Dandelion | Rye | Chestnuts |
| Parsnip | Sorghum | Dry Beans |
| | Wheat | Dry Peas |
| | | Kentucky Coffee |
| | | Tree seeds |
| | | Okra seeds |
| | | Persimmon seeds |
| | | Soybeans, soaked |
| | | overnight and |
| | | drained |
| | | Sunflower seeds with |
| | | shells, or shells |
| | | only |

*Others*
Stale whole grain bread, crumbs, or slices
Bran moistened with diluted syrup

*Some Favorite Roasted Blends*   (Mix after roasting.)
1 part chicory or dandelion root, and 1 part any grain
1 part chicory, 1 part carrot or another bland root, and 1 part any grain
1 part rye, and 1 part beet
1 part comfrey, and 1 part chicory
1 part soybean, 2 parts rye, and 2 parts barley

## COLD DRINKS

Plain fruit and vegetable juices make excellent cold drinks, but in hot weather a lighter drink may be preferred. Unsweetened "fruitades" or those made with a minimum of sweetening are very refreshing. If made with too much sugar they become heavy and cloying rather than refreshing. Lemonade is the best known, but any strong flavored fruit juice can be diluted and slightly sweetened. Rhubarbade, grapeade, berryade, and wild fruitade are some possibilities. Adding a few spoons of a strong syrup (like the CIDER SYRUP in the APPLES section) to a glass of cold water makes a refreshing cold drink, too.

*Homemade Carbonated Beverages*   Some people make carbonated beverages or "soda pop" at home, but if they use commercial flavored extracts they are not very nutritious because of their high sugar content. Their only advantage over the commercial drinks is that the cost is less.

The basic procedure for making carbonated beverages is like the first steps for making wine. (Refer to the WINE section.) Yeast is used to ferment a sweet liquid just until it is fizzy, and the drink is bottled before most of the sugar changes to alcohol. Bottles, caps, and a bottle capper like those used in bottling beer are necessary for making soda pop.

## BEVERAGE RECIPES

The following old time recipe for root beer shows how to make a carbonated beverage at home.

*Root Beer*      (From *In The Kitchen*, by Elizabeth S. Miller, 1875.)

"Take a handful of yellow dock-roots (be sure to get the long and pointed green leaf without the red streaks), a handful of dandelion roots, and one of sarsaparilla roots, and a small branch of the spruce tree; tie them in a bag, and boil half an hour in three quarts of water, and then take out the bag and pour the liquid in a crock [and cover as described in the WINE section]; if too strong, add water; sweeten with sugar or molasses, and when cool add a pint of yeast and let it ferment, skimming it occasionally. It will be fit to use in a day or two, and must then be bottled and securely corked."

Yellow dock is also called curled dock. If sarsaparilla roots are not available, sassafrass roots can be tried. For liquid yeast refer to the RECIPES in the YEAST section, or use 1 tablespoon dry yeast; for fermenting in a crock refer to FERMENTATION, in the WINE section.

### *Fresh Berryade*

*ripe, soft berries* (Strawberries, raspberries, mulberries or blackberries are all delicious.)

*honey, or maple, syrup, optional, to taste*

Crush the berries with a potato masher or a wooden mallet, adding a little water if they are dry. Let them sit for 15 or 20 minutes, then strain the juice through a cloth, squeezing to get as much liquid as possible. Sweeten the juice if desired and refrigerate. It will keep about a week. Or it can be frozen as ice cubes for longer storage.

To make a glass of berryade, mix several spoonfuls of the juice with a glass of cold water.

(The leftover pulp from the berries can be mixed with water, then strained again for a mild, immediate drink.)

### *Gingerade*                              (Makes 4—8 glasses.)

*1 tablespoon ginger root, crushed or minced, or 1 teaspoon powdered ginger*
*1 lemon peel, grated or thinly sliced*

*juice of 1 lemon*
*honey or other sweetener, to taste*
*1 quart water*

Boil the water and pour it over the ginger and lemon peel. Let steep 30 minutes. Strain and chill. Then, add the lemon juice and honey. If the flavor is too strong, add more water, if weak, add more lemon juice.

### *Fruit Punch*    (Makes 10–14 glasses.)

3 cups mixed fruit juice (1 part orange or pineapple and 1 part cherry or berry juice are delicious.)
2 cups regular tea, cooled
4 cups mint tea, or other herb tea, cooled

lemon juice, optional
honey, optional
(Fresh or frozen fruit, sliced if necessary, can be added. Frozen strawberries are very good.)

Mix the fruit juice and both kinds of tea, then add lemon juice and honey to taste. Pour over ice cubes in a punch bowl and float fresh or frozen fruit in it, if desired. Colorful as well as delightfully refreshing.

# BIRDS, SMALL

SMALL BIRDS FOR THE TABLE HAVE ALWAYS HAD A SPECIAL APPEAL. Through the ages all kinds of small, wild birds have been hunted, trapped, and netted, and eaten with gusto. Squab (very young pigeons) are among the few small birds raised domestically for meat. Preparing them or any small birds seems to bring out the dramatic in the cook. They are stuffed with an oyster or truffle, seasoned with exotic herbs and wine, adorned with grapes and other fresh fruits, and surrounded by delicate greens. None could be fancier, however, than this early American recipe for pigeons in a mould, from *In The Kitchen*, by Elizabeth S. Miller, 1875.

"Pick a pair of pigeons [squab], and make them look as well as possible by singeing, washing, and cleaning the heads thoroughly; be very particular with the feet also, clipping the nails close to the claws; rub them in the inside with a little pepper, salt, and chopped celery; skewer them in a sitting position in the dripping-pan, with the feet under, keeping the heads up as if the birds were alive; this may be done by means of a thread kept around the neck while roasting.

"Have ready a savory jelly [gelatine], and pour it an inch deep in the mould designed for the pigeons; let this harden, while the rest of the jelly is kept soft, just thick enough to pour and fill in closely. See that no gravy adheres to the birds; place them in the mould side by side, with the heads down, and a sprig of myrtle in each bill; [upside down so that they are right side up when unmoulded] then fill with the jelly which should come three inches above the feet. Make this dish twenty-four hours before using and keep it on ice."

## COMMONLY COOKED SMALL BIRDS

(There are also many other very small birds used for food in different countries throughout the world. These include snipe, plover, rails, and reed birds in general, as well as thrushes, larks, and even robins.)

***Cornish Game Hens***    These small, plump birds are the Cornish breed of chicken butchered when 6 weeks old. This is a practical time to butcher, since the birds make very fast growth up to 6 weeks, and then mature more slowly than other chickens. Though tender and good when roasted, they are not as interesting and special in flavor as other small birds.

***Doves and Wild Pigeons***    Mourning doves are best known and most often hunted, but other kinds of doves and pigeons are just as good to eat. Their breasts are plump with dark, flavorful meat. Sometimes these birds are simply cut open and the breasts alone taken out, but they will be more moist and juicy if they are plucked, leaving the skin covering the meat during the cooking.

***Grouse***    All species of grouse make excellent eating. Ruffed grouse, sometimes called partridge, is the best known species in the eastern half of North America. These are larger than quail and smaller than pheasants. Ptarmigans are another relatively small grouse found mostly in arctic and northern areas. Some kinds of grouse, such as prairie chickens, are as large as domestic chickens, but they can be cooked like the smaller grouse and other small birds.

***Quail, Partridge, and Pheasants***    While the best known of these are Bobwhite quail, Chukar and Hungarian partridge, and Ring-necked pheasants, other species are just as good to eat. These birds are often raised on game farms, but there are also places where they can be hunted in the wild. Game farm birds are milder in flavor than the wild ones. Quail and partridge are small and rather time consuming to pluck compared to larger birds, but plucking makes them nicer for cooking. Though pheasants are larger, they are very good cooked in the same ways as the smaller birds.

***Squab***    It is practical to raise squab for homestead meat if the adult pigeons can be left to forage for some of their own feed. If they must be confined, their purchased feed will make the meat expensive. Squab are butchered at less than a month old, just before they are ready to leave their nests. They are very tender and delicate at this age, and do not need long cooking.

***Starlings***    The four and twenty blackbirds baked in the pie in the nursery rhyme may well have been starlings, as they have often been eaten. If trapped in large numbers, they make a very good meal. Generally, they are cut open, the breasts taken out, and the rest of the bird discarded, which makes cleaning them quick and easy. The breasts can be simmered in water until tender, and then baked in a pie (see GAME MEAT PIE, below), or used in other recipes. This is a good way to make some use of a bird that is a pest otherwise.

*Woodcock* This little game bird has dark, distinctively flavored meat. It is best plucked rather than skinned in spite of its small size. Though the breast alone can be plucked and removed, the slight amount of meat on the rest of the bird has a fine flavor. Woodcock is often served rare.

## HANDLING SMALL BIRDS

Shooting is the usual way to kill game birds. Squab and birds that have been trapped, snared, or netted are killed by wringing (dislocating) their necks. This is easily done by hand with a quick pulling and twisting motion. Larger birds can be killed like chickens. (Refer to the CHICKEN section.) Bleeding is not emphasized for small birds, and many prefer the flavor of the meat with the blood still in it.

Plucking small birds is preferred, though skinning is faster. It is best to pluck them dry, while they are still warm. As the skin is delicate and easily torn, the feathers must be pulled out with small pinches, in the same direction that they grow. Pin hairs and down can be singed off. If the birds are cold, they can be dipped briefly in moderately hot water but this must be done carefully to avoid damaging or cooking the skin. Game birds are often cut open and cleaned in the field, then plucked later on at home. (Refer to PLUCKING CHICKENS, in the CHICKEN section.)

Small birds are drawn or cleaned exactly like chickens, saving the liver, gizzard, and heart which, though small, all taste good. The birds can also be cut open along the backbone instead of the abdomen to clean them. Sometimes the entrails of very tiny birds are not removed, but are cooked with the meat. When the birds are done, the entrails may be taken out, chopped or puréed, and used in a sauce to go with the meat. The flavor is pleasantly like giblets. The crop must be removed, however, even if the head is left on.

There are as many ways to cook small birds as any other animal. They can be roasted, broiled, fried, braised, stewed, and made into soup. Breasts are often cooked separately, since they contain most of the meat. The legs, wings, backs, and necks can then be made into a delicious soup. Cooking times vary from about 20 minutes for roasting or broiling a tender young bird, to several hours for stewing tough, older birds. To judge a bird's toughness refer to DETERMINING THE ANIMAL'S AGE, in the WILD FOODS section.

## SMALL BIRD RECIPES

***Small Birds Baked
in Grape Leaves***

(One per serving, more or less,
depending on the bird's size.)

**SMALL BIRD IDEAS**

| | |
|---|---|
| *quail, doves, grouse, or other small birds* | *sprigs of parsley* |
| *butter* | *bay leaf, crushed* |
| *pepper* | *grape leaves* (About 2 for a quail, more for larger birds.) |
| *sprigs of fresh thyme or dried thyme* | |

Rub the skins of the birds with butter, and in each cavity put a dab of butter, a sprinkling of pepper, a sprig of fresh or pinch of dried thyme, a sprig of parsley, and a tiny pinch of bay leaf. Wrap each bird with grape leaves, and set the birds close together in a buttered baking dish, tucking in the leaves so that they will not come unwrapped. Cover tightly with a lid or aluminum foil, and bake in a moderate, 350°F oven until tender. This may take 2 hours or more if the birds are tough.

**Stuffed, Roasted Small Birds**   Use squab, Cornish game hens, or tender, young birds. They can be stuffed with CELERY BREADCRUMB STUFFING (refer to the CELERY section), or another favorite stuffing. A hard boiled egg in each bird is a stuffing suggested in one early American cookbook. After wrapping with grape leaves, wrap a strip of bacon, or of fresh pork fat around each bird and fasten with toothpicks. The pork fat is preferable, since it will not dominate the flavor as bacon might. Roast on a rack over a dripping pan, in a 350°F oven, for about 40 minutes or until tender. The pan juices can be defatted and poured over the birds, or made into gravy.

***Birds Fried in Honey***

(From an old Malayan recipe.)

(Makes 6–8 servings.)

| | |
|---|---|
| *6–8 small, tender birds* (Or a frying chicken, cut in pieces.) | *¼ cup (about) honey* |
| *2 teaspoons (about) anise seeds, bruised or crushed* | *¼ cup (about) oil* |
| *1 teaspoon (about) salt* | *black pepper* (Preferably freshly ground.) |

If the birds are very small, leave them whole. If they are to be one serving each, cut them open along the backbone and flatten them, so they can be fried easily.

Rub the birds all over with salt and anise seeds. Warm the honey to thin it, and coat the birds well with it. Heat the oil very hot in a heavy frying pan, and fry the birds in it, turning them often, until they are tender and very dark brown in color. Sprinkle with pepper and serve.

The birds are sticky and sputtery to handle, but the results are exquisite.

**Spit Roasted Small Birds**
Wrap bacon or strips of fresh pork fat around whole tender birds and tie it in place. Thread the birds on a spit and roast slowly, turning often, until well browned and done. They can also be broiled or grilled over charcoal.

**Birds Roasted in a Brown Paper Bag**   This method avoids the drying effect of regular roasting. Rub a brown paper bag thoroughly with fat of any kind. It is best to use a cooking bag, if one can be found. Otherwise make sure the bag does not touch the meat, as it may add a bad taste. The birds can be stuffed, if desired. Place them on a small rack with a pan or aluminum foil underneath to catch drippings. Set the whole arrangement inside the paper bag and tie it shut, making sure there is air space around the birds in the bag. Roast as usual in a moderate oven. The birds will brown inside the bag, staying moist and juicy at the same time. The paper bag will not burn as long as it is not too close to a heating element.

**Crushed Birds**   This is an old way to prepare very small reed birds, from *Housekeeping in Old Virginia*, 1879.

"Pick, open, and carefully wash one dozen or more birds. Place them between the folds of a towel, and with a rolling-pin mash the bones quite flat. Season with salt and a little cayenne and black pepper. Either fry or broil on gridiron made for broiling oysters. This must be done over a clear fire. When done, season, put a lump of butter on each bird and serve hot."

**OTHER RECIPES
WITH SMALL BIRDS**

Kitchen Smoked Poultry, p.572
Small Birds Baked with Sauer-
  kraut, p.237
Pigeons in a Mould, p.46

## *Bird and Oyster Pie*   (Makes 8–12 dinner servings.)

| | |
|---|---|
| 8–10 *doves, other small birds, or a large, dark meated bird, cut in pieces* | 2 *slices bacon, chopped medium pepper, to taste* |
| 1½ *cups celery, chopped* | 3 *tablespoons (about) flour* |
| 1 *onion, chopped medium* | 1–2 *dozen oysters* |
| | 2 *pastry crusts (for a large pie)* |

Put the birds, celery, onion, bacon, and pepper in a pot, and add water to just cover the ingredients. Bring to a boil, then simmer, covered, until the meat is tender. This could take 30 minutes for a tender bird and 2 hours or so for a tough one. When done, remove the birds from the pot with a slotted spoon and set them aside. Mix the flour with a little water to moisten it and then stir in some of the hot juice from the pot. Stir this into the pot and cook, stirring, until thickened as for gravy. Taste and adjust seasonings if necessary.

Drain the oysters and stuff one or more into each bird. Add any extra oysters and liquid to the gravy in the pot. (If a large bird has been cut in pieces put all of the oysters in the gravy.)

Line a deep pie dish or shallow baking dish with the pastry. If wished it can be baked for 10 minutes in a hot oven to set it. Arrange the birds in the dish and pour the gravy over them. Cover with the top crust, prick or cut a small hole in the center, and bake in a 350°F oven for 30 minutes or until nicely browned. An early American favorite, and extravagantly good.

*Game Meat Pie*   Omit Oysters. Use any kind of game meat. Mixtures are good when there is not enough of one kind of meat to fill the pie. Squirrel, rabbit, or different kinds of birds can be used. Chunks of carrot or other vegetables can be included. Or the meat can be cooked leftovers and the gravy can be made from soup stock. For a special, elegant touch, sauté whole small mushrooms or thick slices of mushroom in butter and arrange them in the pie with the meat.

**STORAGE**

**Canning**   (Seeds of some varieties may become too prominent when cooked.) Mix 2 tablespoons warm honey with each quart berries. Let stand 2 hours or until juice collects. Heat to a boil, fill jars, ½ in. headroom. Process boiling water bath. Pints: 10 min. Quarts: 15 min. (Or may pack raw as for RASP-BERRIES.) Refer to CANNING section, CANNING FRUIT JUICE AND SAUCE in the FRUITS section, and BLACKBERRY CORDIAL, below.

# BLACKBERRIES

BLACKBERRIES ARE PROLIFIC WHEN THEY GROW IN A PLACE THAT suits them. A vigorous patch of wild blackberries can easily yield as much as a family can eat fresh, with plenty left for making juice and other good things for the winter. If there are wild blackberries nearby there is usually no need to cultivate them, though the price may be a few scratches from picking them.

As there are thousands of overlapping varieties of blackberries, both wild and cultivated, it would be confusing to try to pinpoint a particular one. They may differ in size, flavor, seediness and thorniness, but most varieties taste good and can be used in the same ways. A local, wild berry affectionately called "sow tits," may be as big, juicy and flavorful as the properly named varieties, like loganberries and boysenberries.

## HANDLING BLACKBERRIES

Pick blackberries when the dew has evaporated on a dry day. Avoid picking after heavy rains because the berries are more watery then and less sweet. Long sleeves, long pants and a hat are a help when picking in a tangled thorny patch. Berries too high to reach can be brough closer by gently lowering the stem with a curved walking stick.

Fully ripe blackberries come off the plant readily, and can be picked more quickly than most other kinds of berries. Tightly attached berries should be left to ripen another day or two. As blackberries bruise easily they should be handled gently, and put in shallow containers so that the weight of the top berries will not crush the ones on the bottom. After they are picked they should not sit out in the sun, or they will lose color and sweetness. If the berries are gathered cleanly, washing them may not be necessary. (Refer to GATHERING SOFT BERRIES, in the WILD FOODS section.) If they must be washed, do it quickly, just before they are used. Blackberries will keep only a day or two in the refrigerator.

***Seediness in Blackberries*** The seeds in fresh blackberries are not troublesome, but in most wild blackberries and some cultivated varieties they become more prominent after cooking or freezing and may be disliked. They can easily be removed by pushing the fresh berries through the fine screen of a food mill or other strainer. The seedless purée can be made into jam, ice cream, or fruit desserts. If some contrast in texture is preferred a mixture of purée and whole berries can be used.

## BLACKBERRY RECIPES

***Blackberry Pudding***                   (Makes 8–12 servings.)

| | |
|---|---|
| ½ cup butter or shortening, softened if necessary | 4 eggs, separated |
| ¾ cup honey or maple syrup, or 1 cup brown sugar | 2 cups whole grain flour |
| | 1 quart blackberries, fresh or frozen |

Mix the butter or shortening with the sweetening, beat until smooth, and beat in the egg yolks. Beat the egg whites until stiff, and add them alternately with the flour. That is, stir in some of the beaten egg whites, some of the flour, then more egg whites and more flour, until both are used up. Gently stir in the blackberries. Put the batter in a buttered baking dish and bake in a moderate oven, about

350°F, for 1½ hours or until cooked through and browned on top.

This pudding is good warm or cold. Milk or cream, or one of the pudding sauces among the recipes in the STEAM COOKING section can be served with it.

### Blackberry Roll                                          (Makes 6–8 servings.)

*biscuit dough made with about 2*
*cups flour* (CREAM BISCUITS, in
the CREAM *section are very*
*good.*)
*2 cups blackberries, fresh or frozen*
(A mixture of seedless purée
and whole berries works well.)

*honey or other sweetening, to*
*taste*
*cinnamon to taste*
*butter, melted, optional*

Pat or roll out the biscuit dough to make a square. The dough should be about ½ inch thick. Spread the blackberries over the dough and dribble the sweetening over them. Sprinkle with cinnamon. Roll up like a jelly roll and place seam side down on a greased baking sheet. The top can be brushed with melted butter, if desired. Bake in a hot oven, 375 to 400°F, for 30 minutes or until browned. Simply beautiful, and beautifully simple!

**Berry or Cherry Roll** Use other kinds of berries or pitted cherries instead of blackberries.

### Blackberry Wine                                          (Makes about 1 gallon.)

(For detailed wine making instructions refer to the WINE section.)

*3 quarts water*
*2 quarts ripe blackberries*
*wine yeast* (follow package directions) *or 1 teaspoon dry baking*
*yeast*

*2–4 cups sugar or 1–2 cups*
*honey*

Bring 3 quarts of water to a full boil and pour it over the blackberries. If the fruit seems sour add half of the sweetener. (Sweetening is not necessary at this stage if the berries are very sweet.) Cool to lukewarm, then add the yeast. Put in a crock or other non-corrosive container, cover, and keep in a warm place. After 4 to 5 days, or when vigorous bubbling subsides, strain through a cloth. Add 2 cups sugar or 1 cup honey. (If honey is used, heat it enough to pasteurize it and then cool before adding it.) Put the mixture in a gallon jug with a fermentation lock and let sit about 3 months or until fermentation stops. Siphon into bottles, seal and let age 3 months.

THE BLOOD OF ANY HEALTHY MEAT ANIMAL OR BIRD IS GOOD FOOD. Sometimes it is not considered a food because of religious prohibitions, or because of prejudice based, perhaps, on the bad connotations of words like bloodthirsty and bloodsucker. Perhaps, also, the repeated exhortations to bleed slaughtered animals completely have made it seem that the blood itself is a bad thing. Complete bleeding is necessary if meat is to keep well and look its best, but the blood can be collected and used. And even the rule about bleeding completely is not universal. For some kinds of cooking, small birds and poultry are considered more flavorful if the blood stays in the meat rather than draining away, and there are ways to make use of bloody meat when necessary. (Refer to BLOODY OR BRUISED MEAT, in the MEAT section.)

Blood has been used for food in more ways and in more places than most people would believe. Blood sausage, also called blood pudding, is made in many different parts of the world. Many cuisines include recipes using blood in soups and stews. The fanciest recipes for small animals and poultry often call for blood to thicken the sauce that goes with the meat. In Europe, chunks of coagulated blood are sold in some markets. The Masai in Africa are not the only people to have taken small amounts of blood from living animals to use for food. It was an ancient practice in Scotland, and probably many other places, to take blood from farm cattle to use as food. It has been humorously described as a way to equalize cattles' and their owners' circumstances. The cattle could eat grass and provide themselves with a sufficient supply of blood. Their owners could not eat grass and had very little else they could eat to keep sufficient blood in themselves, so they used a "lancet" to make a division of the "all-essential fluid." (This was recounted in Hugh Miller's *My Schools and Schoolmasters,* 1852.)

Chances are that modern homesteaders will be content to use the blood of slaughtered animals only. There is certainly no point in wasting the blood when an animal is killed. It is higher in food value than many other parts of the animal and there are some very good tasting ways to prepare it.

## HANDLING BLOOD

The blood of any meat animal, large or small, can be collected and used. Blood from pigs and cows is often mentioned because there is so much of it, but blood from lambs, goats, rabbits, chickens, geese, and other poultry is also worth collecting. The different kinds are interchangeable in recipes.

***Collecting Blood*** Blood used for food should come directly from the

| STORAGE |
| --- |
| **Freezing** (Usually made into sausage and then frozen.) Pour into containers, or wrap if coagulated. Quality retained several months. Refer to FREEZING section. |

jugular vein, not from the animal's nose or mouth. Large animals have to be positioned so that a pan or bucket can be put under the neck when the vein is cut. One way to catch the blood of poultry and small animals is to set a large funnel in a container, and as soon as the head is cut off to hold the neck down into the funnel for the short time that it bleeds.

Liquid blood rather than coagulated blood is required in many recipes. To prevent coagulation the blood must be stirred while it cools. When the amount is large a clean hand is often used, but a wooden spoon will do as well. Any fibers that wrap around the hand or the spoon should be discarded. When blood is collected from a large animal a few tablespoons of vinegar are usually put in the container to help stop coagulation, but the constant stirring is most important. If desired, a few drops of vinegar can be added when blood is collected from a bird or small animal. When cool the blood should be strained and refrigerated. It will keep for a day or two in the refrigerator.

There are several ways to use coagulated blood. It can be ground and made into sausage, or it can be cut into pieces and added to gravy, stew or soup just like small pieces of cooked meat.

## BLOOD RECIPES

### Black Pudding, English Style            (Makes 3–4 quarts.)

*1 quart skimmed milk*
*½ pound bread, cut in cubes*
   (Preferably whole grain.)
*1 quart blood* (Usually hog's blood.)
*2 cups cooked rice* (Preferably
   brown.)
*2 cups cooked barley*

*1 pound fat, minced or grated*
   (Usually suet from beef.)
*½ cup (about) oatmeal* (Ground
   whole oats or rolled oats
   whirled in a blender.)
*dried mint to taste*
*pepper, salt, to taste*

Warm the milk to take the chill off, and pour it over the bread. Let soak a few minutes. Add the blood, rice, barley, and fat. Mix well. Now add enough oatmeal to make a mixture that is moist, but not too wet. Season with mint, pepper, and salt. Pack in greased loaf pans, and bake in a moderate oven, 350°F, for about 1 hour or until cooked through. Let cool.

A good way to use this for breakfast or dinner is to slice the loaf and fry the slices until lightly browned on both sides. To freeze slices, refer to SPECIAL FREEZING TECHNIQUES, in the FREEZING section.

### Goose Blood Pudding    Adjust quantities in the ingredients above according to the amount of blood taken from the goose. Stuff the mixture into the neck skin of the goose and simmer in goose broth. (Refer to STUFFING GOOSE NECK SKINS, in the GOOSE section.)

For a Scottish style stuffing, mix the blood with about 2 cups uncooked barley grits, fat, and seasonings. Omit all other ingredients.
Fresh herbs such as chives or scallions can be added.

## *J. Zastrow's Blood Sausage*

(Makes several loaves, depending
on the size of the hog's head.)

| | |
|---|---|
| ½ hog's head | ¼ teaspoon cloves |
| 1 large loaf homemade bread, sliced or cubed | 1 teaspoon allspice |
| ¼ cup honey or ½ cup sugar | 2 teaspoons salt |
| 2 teaspoons cinnamon | ¼ cup flour |
| | 1 quart hog's blood, strained |

Soak the hog's head in salted water for a few hours. Remove the
eyes, skin, and snout and scrub clean. Cook in fresh water to cover
until the meat is tender. Strain off the broth and skim to remove excess fat. Put the bread in the broth to soak. If the head is cooked a
day ahead, warm the broth before adding the bread. Take the meat
off the bone and grind it with a meat grinder.

Add the sweetening, cinnamon, cloves, allspice, salt, and flour to
the broth and bread mixture and mix well. Then mix in the ground
meat and blood. Pour into greased loaf pans and bake 1 hour at
300°F, or until it sets, somewhat like custard. Let cool.

To serve, slice and warm the slices in a frying pan. This sausage
keeps a few days to a week in the refrigerator, or it can be frozen like
BLOOD PUDDING, above.

## *Boudin* (Creole style blood sausage)

(Makes about 4 pounds.)

| | |
|---|---|
| 2 pounds bread crumbs (Preferably whole grain.) | 4 sprigs thyme, chopped, or 1 teaspoon dried thyme |
| 6–10 hot chili peppers, or other hot peppers, to taste | 2 teaspoons salt |
| ¼ cup (about) milk | 1 quart blood, strained |
| 1 pound onions, chopped | oil, or ½ pound (about) ground pork fat, optional |
| oil or lard (for sautéeing) | 2–4 yards sausage casings, hog or sheep (Refer to SAUSAGE CASINGS in the SAUSAGE section.) |
| 1 bunch parsley, chopped | |
| 3 stalks celery, chopped | |

Soak the bread crumbs in water for a few minutes, then squeeze
dry. After removing seeds from the peppers, chop them, and soak
them in milk. Sauté the onions gently in oil or lard until they are
limp. Combine the bread crumbs, peppers with milk, and fried
onions. Add the parsley, celery, thyme, salt, and blood. Grind the
mixture with a meat grinder to an even texture. If desired, a bit of
sausage can be fried and tasted for seasonings. It should be quite hot
and peppery. Additional seasonings must be mixed in thoroughly. If
the mixture is too dry to push through the funnel into sausage casing

a little oil or pork fat can be worked in to soften it. Or a ½ pound of pork fat can be chopped and then ground with the other ingredients to begin with.

Stuff the sausage casings and tie them off to make 3 or 4 inch links. (Refer to STUFFING SAUSAGE, in the SAUSAGE section.) Prick each link once or twice with a needle to prevent bursting. Put the sausages in a cloth bag and tie shut. The bag protects them and makes them easier to handle while cooking. Heat a big pot of water *almost* to a boil and put in the bag of sausages. Cover and simmer for 30 minutes. Do not let the water boil. Take out the sausages and prick one to make sure they are done. No blood should ooze out. If it does they must be cooked a little longer.

Broil or fry the boudin for serving. They can be frozen for long storage, and will keep from 4 to 6 months.

---

# BLUEBERRIES

UNTIL THE TWENTIETH CENTURY THERE WERE NO CULTIVATED BLUE-berries. Wild blueberries were, and still are, an important fruit in these regions of North America with the necessary moist acid soil. American Indians and early settlers picked huge quantities and dried them for winter. Today wild blueberries are more apt to be canned or frozen, but are as popular as ever. Wild berries generally have more flavor than cultivated ones, and their small, firm shape makes them better for baking.

There are several related species that are called blueberries or huckleberries, or, in some places, bilberries, wortleberries or cowberries. The names are used differently in different locations. A species called blueberry in one place might be called huckleberry in another, but the confusion is not important, since all are edible and can be used in the same ways. Whatever the name they use, for eating fresh, most people like the softer, dusty-blue berries better than the black, shiny kinds with the hard seeds.

***Garden Huckleberries*** Seeds for garden huckleberries are sold in some catalogs. They are an annual, unrelated to blueberries, producing fruit in one season. The raw berries do not have a very good flavor, but are acceptable cooked. Their flavor is best after light frosts.

## HANDLING BLUEBERRIES

The full flavor and sweetness of blueberries develops several days to a week after they turn blue. They are ripe if they fall off the bush

---

### STORAGE

**Canning** This method is best for whole berries to use in baking: Put 2–3 quarts in square of cheesecloth, hold corners, dip in boiling water until spots of juice show, about 30 seconds. Dip in cold water, drain, pack, ½ in. headroom. Do not add water or sweetener. Process boiling water bath. Pints: 15 min. Quarts: 20 min. Refer to CANNING section. Also see CANNING FRUIT JUICE AND SAUCE, in FRUITS section and *Blueberry Marmalade,* below.

Note: Overly ripe berries may lack acid. Add 2 teaspoons lemon juice per pint, 4 teaspoons per quart.

**Cold Storage** Small, dry wild berries keep 3–4 weeks refrigerated in tightly closed containers. If soft, cultivated berries keep 1–2 weeks.

**Drying** Optional: Blanch briefly to crack skins and speed drying. Spread on trays, dry until hard. Refer to DRYING section.

**Freezing** Excellent packed plain. Small wild berries stay separated, so pour directly into batter without thawing. Refer to FREEZING section.

5–8 CUPS FRESH = I QUART CANNED OR COOKED

when touched. Commercially sold blueberries are often picked too soon, which accounts for some of their lack of flavor. If gathered carefully from a clean spot, blueberries should not need washing. They can immediately be put into containers, and refrigerated or frozen, or spread on trays for drying. At times it may be easier to gather berries by shaking them onto a cloth or plastic sheet, and remove the debris afterwards. (Refer to GATHERING FRUIT FROM TREES AND BUSHES, at the beginning of the WILD FOODS section.)

**BLUEBERRY IDEAS**

**Dried Blueberries in Meat Stews**   Stew beef or other red meat with onions, then add dried blueberries about 30 minutes before it is done. This is a favorite American Indian combination.

**Blueberries with Breakfast Cereal**   Blueberries are good with cold cereal and superb with hot cereal. Stir fresh, frozen, or canned blueberries into hot cereal just before it is served. Add milk and a sprinkle of nutmeg and enjoy.

**Blender Blue Shakes and Puddings**   Blend several cups of fresh, canned, or frozen (and thawed as necessary for blender use) blueberries at low speed, gradually adding enough chopped dates or figs to sweeten and thicken the mixture. For shakes add milk or yogurt, and an ice cube, if desired. Puddings can be further thickened and flavored by blending in 1 or 2 tablespoons sunflower seeds or nuts. Chill pudding in a bowl, or in individual dishes for a firmer texture.

## BLUEBERRY RECIPES

### *Fresh Blueberry Salad*                       (Makes 6–10 servings.)

2½ cups blueberries
2 cups cooked, cold rice, or other cooked grain
½ cup chopped nuts, or ⅓ cup sunflower seeds
½ cup dry, unsweetened coconut, optional

*Yogurt Fruit Salad Dressing* (Refer to recipe in the YOGURT section.)
*toasted wheat germ for garnish, optional*

Combine the blueberries, nuts or sunflower seeds, and coconut, then fold in the salad dressing. Sprinkle with wheat germ if desired.

This salad is good eaten for breakfast, as well as lunch and dinner, and it tastes as delicious the second day as the first.

*Fruit Rice Salad*   Use chopped apple, peach, orange, or another fruit instead of blueberries to make this salad.

### *Blueberry Marmalade*                       (Makes about 3 half-pint jars.)

4–6 tablespoons orange or lemon peel, coarsely grated or thinly sliced
1¾ cups honey or maple syrup

½ cup homemade pectin, optional (Refer to the PECTIN section.)
5 cups blueberries
½ teaspoon nutmeg

If the orange or lemon peel is too strong or bitter in flavor, boil it for 10 minutes in plenty of water and drain.

Heat the sweetening, orange or lemon peel, and pectin to a boil in a deep pot. (Pectin is necessary for a firm set, but the flavor and texture are good without it.) Watch the pot if using honey because it may foam up suddenly. Add the blueberries and nutmeg, and cook uncovered, about 20 minutes or until the marmalade thickens somewhat. Pour into jars and seal. (Refer to the JAM AND JELLY section.)

*Raspberry Marmalade*   Use raspberries instead of blueberries. Instead of nutmeg try using cinnamon or a tiny pinch of cloves.

**OTHER RECIPES WITH BLUEBERRIES**

Berry Roll, p.52
Fruit Doughboys, p.196
Pemmican (with dried blueberries), p.231
Recipes, and Ideas for Fruit, p.290
Sourdough Hot Cakes, p.582
Sourdough Muffins, p.583

## STORAGE

**Canning** See CANNING SOUP STOCK (made from bones) in SOUP section.

**Freezing** Saw into convenient sizes. Refer to SPECIAL FREEZING TECHNIQUES in FREEZING section. Freeze before wrapping or wrap individually so 1 or 2 can be used at a time. Quality retained 12 months.

## BONE AND BONE MARROW IDEAS

**Bones for Flavoring** Cook a few pieces of bone with the meat when stewing or braising. The bones will add nutritional value and flavor. Brown the bone with the meat when browning is called for. It is handy to have bones in the freezer, packed so they can be removed a few at a time.

**Broiled Marrow Bones** Saw the leg bones of a large animal into 3 or 4 inch lengths and split them in half lengthwise with a meat cleaver. Set them, split side up in a pan, and broil until the marrow is bubbly. Sprinkle with pepper and salt, if desired. Served with a salad these make an elegant lunch.

**Using Marrow Fat** Take the marrow from the leg bones of any large, mature animal and use it like suet in steamed puddings. Or chop it with scallions, or shallots and parsley, or other fresh herbs, and spread it on grilled steaks after they have been turned once. North American Indians cook marrow from buffalo bones and mix it with ground sunflower seeds before eating it. In Mexico marrow is sometimes used in dough for making a flatbread like tortilla.

BONE IS A PROMINENT PART OF EVERY BUTCHERED ANIMAL. IT IS also a valuable part and should not automatically be considered a waste product. Though the bones of poultry and small animals do generally find their way into the soup pot, when a large animal is butchered, there are so many bones all at once that some are usually thrown out. The pile of leftover bones is particularly awesome when the meat of a large animal is deboned for grinding, but even then there are ways to use them. They can be made into a concentrated stock for soup or gelatine, and canned or frozen for later use. (Refer to the SOUP and GELATINE sections.) It is worth the effort because of the stock's nutritional value, particularly its calcium content, and because of the delicious homemade flavor.

*Bones as a Calcium Source* Calcium is an extremely important nutrient often lacking in people's diets, and bones contain large quantities of it. There are basically two ways to take advantage of the calcium in bones. One is to eat bones directly by gnawing or chewing the soft ones. (Fish like sardines that are canned with the bones in are a good source of calcium because they can be eaten bones and all.) The other way is to cook bones in water with an added acidic ingredient like vinegar or tomato. The acid dissolves the calcium from the bones into the liquid or stock. Pickled meats and fish made by cooking bones and flesh in a strong vinegar solution are particularly high in calcium. A single serving of pickled pig's feet has been known to contain as much calcium as 3 quarts of milk! The calcium content of all soups, stews and other dishes made with bones can be increased by adding tomato or a little vinegar or lemon juice as cooking begins.

People who cannot, or do not, drink milk or eat dairy products should pay particular attention to bones as a source of calcium, as such rich sources are hard to come by.

## HANDLING BONES

The meat and other more perishable parts of an animal's carcass should be dealt with before the bones are used, as trimmed bones will keep a week or more in a cold place. They should not be washed, because contact with water makes them spoil faster. Bones give more flavor and nutritional value to the water they are cooked in if they are first cracked or sawed in small pieces. (Refer to SOUP STOCK, at the beginning of the SOUP section.)

*Marrow Bones* Marrow is the soft material inside the bones. All bones have some marrow, but only the long leg bones of large animals contain enough to use separately. The marrow bones called for in recipes are usually the leg bones of veal or beef. In the bones of veal and other young animals the marrow is red because it is blood-forming tissue. In the bones of beef and other adult animals it is yellow and contains a lot of fat. Usually veal marrow bones are cooked with the marrow still in the bone, while beef marrow is taken out of the bone and used in the same ways as suet.

## BONE RECIPE

### Marrow Bones, Italian Style (Osso Bucco)

(Makes 6–8 servings.)

3 tablespoons olive oil
2–3 pounds marrow bones (veal preferred), *cut in 2 inch long cross sections*
1 small onion, minced
1 small carrot, minced

1 tablespoon flour
1 large fresh tomato, chopped, or 1 cup tomato sauce
pepper, salt, optional
parsley, for garnish
small squares or triangles of toast

Heat the oil in a deep, heavy frying pan with a lid. Fry the marrow bones, onion, and carrot in the oil over medium heat. Turn often and baste with the juice that collects in the pan. When the bones and onion are lightly browned, stir in the flour. Add the tomato, and pepper and salt, if desired. Cover and simmer over very low heat for 30 minutes. Lift out the bones and put them in a serving dish. Skim the fat off of the sauce, and strain, if liked. Pour the sauce over the bones, garnish with parsley, and serve with toast. Dip the marrow and sauce out of the center of the bone with a small spoon and eat it, or spread on the toast. Osso bucco is often served as the first course of a big dinner, but it is also very good for lunch or supper.

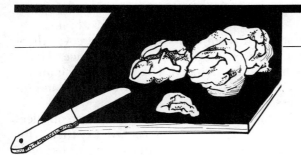

## BRAINS

DOES EATING BRAINS MAKE A PERSON SMARTER? SOME PEOPLE believe so. Some also believe that people take on the intelligence of the animal whose brains they have eaten. These interesting notions should not influence anyone either towards or away from eating brains. It is instead their delicate flavor and texture, and their high protein content that make them a memorable food, worth enjoying as

---

### BONE IDEAS, *cont.*

**Bones for Fertilizer**  All bones not eaten by people, pets, or livestock can go into the compost pile or garden. Bones break down faster in the soil if they have been cooked to remove fat, so leftover soup bones are especially valuable. Where cooked bones can be crushed or ground they can be used instead of commercial bone meal.

### OTHER BASIC PREPARATIONS WITH BONES

Jelled Stock, p.298
Soup Stock (with bones), p.576

### STORAGE

**Freezing**  Prepare ready to cook, wrap well. Quality retained about 4 months. Refer to FREEZING section.

#### AVERAGE SIZES

BEEF BRAINS: ¾ POUND;   VEAL BRAINS: ½ POUND;   PORK OR LAMB BRAINS: 3–4 OUNCES

often as possible. Such a special food as brains should never be over-looked or forgotten when meat animals are butchered.

## HANDLING BRAINS

The brains of all mammals are edible, even those of small animals like rabbits, but it takes patience to collect enough of these to make a meal. The brains of cows, calves, lambs, goats, pigs, and big game animals like deer are all excellent. They taste very much alike and can be prepared in the same ways, regardless of an animal's age.

As brains do not keep well, they should be prepared or frozen as soon after the animal is slaughtered as possible. Removing the brains from the animal's head the day after it is slaughtered is acceptable, as long as the head is kept in a cool place. The brains will then keep an-other day or two in the refrigerator. If pre-cooked, they can be refrigerated for several more days. For how to remove the brains refer to PREPARING LARGE ANIMAL'S HEADS, in the HEADS section.

If the brains are bloody, they can be soaked in cool water for a few minutes to an hour to draw out the blood. Covering the brains is a thin membrane with tiny blood vessels running through it. If promi-nent, it should be pulled off either after pre-cooking or before cook-ing. Where it is very thin and hardly noticeable, it will not interfere with the taste, and can be left intact.

*Pre-cooking Brains*    It is customary to pre-cook brains in water con-taining a little vinegar, or in soup stock. This firms the brains and makes them easier to handle. If this step is omitted from a recipe, cooking time should be increased by 10 to 15 minutes.

When soup is made from parts of an animal's head the brains can be pre-cooked in the same pot. Tie them in a piece of cheesecloth and put them in the pot when the water is simmering, just below a boil. Let them simmer 15 to 30 minutes, depending on their size. Then lift them out and let them cool. Remove membranes if necessary, and they are ready to use in any recipe calling for pre-cooked brains.

To pre-cook brains alone, put them in a sauce pan and cover them with cold water and a tablespoon of vinegar or lemon juice. Herbs such as bay leaf and thyme can be included. Heat to a boil, simmer a minute or two, then let them cool in the cooking water. Drain and re-move membranes if necessary.

The texture of brains remains soft and moist even after consider-able cooking. They can be pre-cooked, then cooked together with other ingredients, and then reheated without drying out. They will only gradually become firmer.

Brains and sweetbreads are prepared in the same ways and can be used interchangeably in most recipes. If amounts of either are insuffi-cient for a meal they can be combined to make one dish. (Refer to the SWEETBREADS section.)

---

### BRAIN IDEAS

**Sautéed Brains**    Slice the brains about ½ inch thick. They can be pre-cooked or raw, but if raw they must be handled very gently. Dust the slices with flour seasoned with pepper, and salt, if desired, and sauté gently in but-ter to brown on both sides. A little minced parsley and garlic can be sautéed with them. If they are raw, allow about 20 minutes cooking time, 10 minutes on each side. Serve hot with a wedge of lemon.

These are also good on toast. For a sauce, heat 1 to 2 table-spoons of wine vinegar in the pan in which the brains were cooked, and pour immediately over the brains on toast.

# BRAIN RECIPES

*Baked Brains and Spinach*     (Makes 6–8 dinner servings.)

| | |
|---|---|
| 1 pound spinach (or other greens) fresh or frozen | pepper, to taste |
| 3–4 tablespoons butter | salt, optional |
| 1 tablespoon flour | 1 large or 2 small brains (about |
| 1 cup (about) milk | 1 pound), pre-cooked as described above |
| | bread crumbs |

Cook fresh spinach just long enough to wilt it, using no more water than what is left on the leaves after washing. If frozen, heat in a minimum of water until thawed. Chop small.

Heat 2 tablespoons of the butter in a pan and add the spinach. Cook uncovered for 5 minutes, stirring often. Put the flour in a measuring cup, with a few tablespoons of milk and mix until well blended. Then add enough milk to make 1 cup. Add this to the spinach, and cook over very low heat, stirring constantly, until thickened. Season with pepper, and salt, if desired.

Slice the brains and lay them in a shallow, buttered baking dish, or deep pie dish. Pour over the creamed spinach, sprinkle with bread crumbs, and dot the top with thin shavings of butter. Bake in a hot, 400°F oven until browned and bubbly, about 20 minutes. A very delicious combination.

*Brain Balls in Soup*     (Makes 8–12 bowls.)

| | |
|---|---|
| brains, 1 large or several small, pre-cooked | ¼ teaspoon nutmeg, or to taste |
| dry, fine bread crumbs (Use amount equal to quantity of brains.) | pepper, salt, optional |
| | 1–2 eggs, lightly beaten |
| sprig parsley, minced | fat or butter for sautéeing |
| ¼ teaspoon sage, or to taste | 2 quarts (about) HEAD SOUP, p.329, or any clear soup broth |

If using the head from which the brains came for the soup, the brains can be pre-cooked in the same pot.

Mash the cooked brains with a fork, and mix in bread crumbs to make a dough stiff enough to hold its shape. Season with parsley, sage, nutmeg, pepper, and salt, if desired. Mix in the egg, making sure all ingredients are blended evenly. Shape into small, marble-sized balls, and sauté them in fat or butter until lightly browned on all sides. As the soup is served, put several brain balls in each bowl.

***Brain Hors d'oeuvres***  Instead of putting the brain balls in soup, put a toothpick in each and serve immediately, while they are hot.

---

**BRAIN IDEAS,** *cont.*

**Marinated Brains**  Cut pre-cooked and cooled brains into small cubes and marinate them for several hours in an oil and vinegar salad dressing. A dressing of 1 part lemon juice to 3 parts olive oil, with minced fresh herbs such as parsley, chives, or dill is very good. Capers or minced green olives can be included. For a salad, serve on a bed of lettuce, watercress, or other greens.

**Creamed Brains**  Pre-cook and chop the brains and add them to a cream sauce. Nutmeg is a good seasoning. When the mixture is heated, take it off the stove and stir in a teaspoon or so of sherry or lemon juice. Garnish with minced parsley, if liked. Good served with rice, noodles, or on toast.

**Brains and Eggs**  Heat butter in a frying pan and add pieces of raw or pre-cooked brains. Over low heat stir and mash the brains with a fork as they cook. When they become dry and fluffy looking, which takes about 10 minutes, increase the heat, add slightly beaten eggs, and scramble as usual.

---

**OTHER RECIPES WITH BRAINS**

Brown Butter Sauce (for brains), p.87
Recipes, and Ideas for Sweetbreads, p.622
Roast Lamb's or Kid's Heads, p.328
Son-of-a-Bitch Stew, p.666

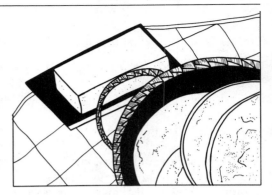

EVERYBODY LIKES QUICK BREADS. THE FAMILY COOK LIKES THEM because they are quick and convenient to make. Many can be mixed, baked, and put on the table in less than an hour. Anyone concerned with nutrition likes them because it is so easy to use healthful ingredients in them. They can exemplify the complete carbohydrate food high in protein, vitamins, minerals, and fiber. Those who eat quick breads like them because they taste so good, and are always a special treat, no matter how often they are made.

Quick breads include muffins, biscuits, dumplings, fruit and nut loaves, and other baked goods leavened with baking powder and baking soda. (Refer to the LEAVENS section.) Here in these pages they also include unleavened flatbreads.

*Flatbreads*  Unleavened flatbread is the least complicated, most basic kind of bread. A simple flour and water dough is patted or rolled into think circles and baked quickly on top of the stove. The sheets of bread are pliable when done and handy to use as scoops or holders for other foods. In some parts of the world the basic breads are such flatbreads as tortillas (Mexico) and chapatis (India). Flatbreads are also popular in Scandinavian countries, in the Middle East, and in many other places.

Anyone interested in a practical, versatile, and delicious kind of bread should try making flatbreads. Many kinds of flour besides wheat flour can be used since they do not depend on a reaction between flour and a leaven. It is not necessary to heat the oven since they cook on top of the stove, and flatbreads go well with all kinds of foods, from fancy dips to plain soups and stews. They are even good simply buttered, for breakfast.

## HANDLING QUICK BREADS

The usual quick bread recipe calls for all purpose white flour, with often a high proportion of white sugar, as well. The nutritional value of this kind of recipe is greatly improved if whole wheat flour or one of the following flour combinations is used instead of white flour, and the sweetening is limited as suggested below. It may be necessary when converting recipes in this way to adjust the proportions of liquid to dry ingredients so that the batter will be the right consistency. The moisture content of different flours can vary from batch to batch, throwing off standard proportions.

One hundred percent whole wheat flour can always be substituted for white flour in a recipe, but this would always result in a dominantly whole wheat taste. By using different flour combinations, a variety of flavors are possible. (Refer to GRINDING GRAINS, in the GRAINS section.)

## FLOUR COMBINATIONS FOR QUICK BREADS

For every 2 cups of white flour substitute:
   1 cup unbleached while flour or whole wheat flour
   1 cup finely ground whole grain flour (For example, rye, buckwheat, corn, barley, rice, or millet.)
   ¼ cup wheat germ, optional.
Or for every 2 cups of white flour substitute:
   1 cup unbleached white flour or whole wheat flour
   ¾ cup whole grain flour (See possibilities listed above.)
   ¼ cup soy flour or other bean or pea flour.
Or for every 2 cups of white flour substitute:
   1¼ cups unbleached white flour
   ¼ cup soy flour, or other bean or pea flour
   ¾ cup wheat germ. (Raw wheat germ blends in more completely, but toasted adds more flavor. Add either after the flour is sifted.)
Several tablespoons of nutritional yeast can be included in any combination for its nutritional value.

## LIMITING SUGAR IN QUICK BREADS

For every 2 cups of flour in *muffins, cornbreads,* or other *baked goods* in which a touch of sweetness if preferred, add no more than:
   1 to 2 tablespoons honey, molasses, sorghum, maple syrup, or other sweetener.
For every 2 cups of flour in *fruit* and *nut breads* and *other sweet baked goods,* use no more than:
   ½ cup honey, molasses, or other sweetener.
Or, with sweet dried fruits like raisins, prunes, figs, etc., no more than:
   ¼ cup honey, molasses, or other sweetener.
Or omit other sweeteners and add instead:
   1 to 2 mashed bananas.

# QUICK BREAD RECIPES

(At altitudes above 5000 feet refer to LEAVENS section.)

### *Vegetable or Fruit Quick Bread*   (Makes 2 small or 1 large loaf.)

*3 eggs, slightly beaten*
*1 cup vegetable oil*
*¾ cup honey, or other sweetening*
*2 cups raw vegetables or fruit, grated*
  (For example, zucchini or other
  summer squash, carrot,
  rutabaga, parsnip, apple,
  quince, hard pears, or combinations of these.)
*1 tablespoon grated orange or lemon*
  *peel, or vanilla, optional*

*3 cups flour* (Whole wheat or a
  combination of flours.)
*3 tablespoons dark roasted flour,*
  *optional* (Refer to ROASTING
  ROOTS in BEVERAGES sec-
  tion.)
*3 teaspoons cinnamon or other*
  *spices, optional*
*1 tablespoon baking powder*
*¾ cup chopped nuts or seeds, op-*
  *tional*

Combine the eggs, oil, sweetening, grated vegetables or fruit, and orange or lemon peel, or vanilla. Sift or mix the flour, roasted flour, cinnamon, and baking powder, and add to the wet ingredients. Stir in the nuts or seeds. Grease and flour two small loaf pans, or a large shallow baking dish. Pour in the batter and bake in a 350°F oven for 50 to 60 minutes, or until done when tested with a toothpick. Turn out of the pan and cool on a rack.

The moist texture and nutty flavor of this bread are best the second or third day after baking.

### *Basic Flatbread*        (Makes 10–15 small, or 6–8 larger rounds.)

*1 cup water*
*½ teaspoon salt, optional*
*1–2 tablespoons oil, or melted fat*

*2–3 cups flour* (Whole wheat,
  or a combination of flours.)

Mix the water, salt, and oil or fat in a bowl. Add the flour slowly, working in enough to make a soft dough that kneads easily. Knead 5 to 10 minutes, using more flour as necessary to prevent sticking. The dough should remain soft enough to roll out easily. For the best texture, cover the dough and let it rest for about 2 hours. The rest can be shortened, for convenience, omitted, or extended to overnight in a cool place.

For small flatbreads, about 6 inches in diameter, shape the dough into a long cylinder and cut or pinch off pieces the size of a walnut. This yields 10 to 15 pieces. But bigger pieces can also be used for larger flatbreads.

Flatten each piece of dough by hand, then roll it out into a thin round sheet. Bake on a hot, dry griddle or large frying pan, or bake directly on the clean top of a wood burning cookstove or wood heater. The cooking surface must be hot enough to cook each side of the bread in 1 or 2 minutes. Bubbles and brown spots should form as it cooks. Some flatbreads will puff up like an inflating ball, then flatten again after they are done, leaving a pocket that can be filled.

Wheat flour flatbreads are more likely to form pockets than other flours. To encourage big bubbles to form into pockets, press down on them with a spatula as soon as the bread is turned. Flatbread tastes very good whether the bubbles are small or large.

To keep the flatbreads moist and pliable, have ready a damp cloth folded on a plate. As each one is taken off the stove put it inside the cloth. Set the stack of wrapped bread in a warm place if they are to be eaten soon. If not, they can be cooled in the cloth, then put in a plastic bag, cloth and all, and kept in the refrigerator.

To reheat the flatbreads put them, still wrapped in their damp cloth, in a warm oven for a few minutes. If they should dry out, sprinkle each one with a little water, stack, wrap in a damp cloth and then heat. Flatbreads can also be eaten cold.

Making flatbread is easier than it sounds. It takes longer to explain how than to make them. With practice a rhythm develops in which 2 or 3 flatbreads are cooking, another 2 or 3 are waiting to cook, and more are being rolled out, in between turning and stacking the cooked ones.

Flatbreads go well with vegetable stews, such as *Ratatouille* (in the EGGPLANT section), *Raita* made with yogurt (in the YOGURT section), and the *Herb Butter* in the BUTTER section.

See OTHER RECIPES FOR QUICK BREADS, for tortillas, millet chapatis, and oatcakes.

---

## OTHER RECIPES FOR QUICK BREADS

Apple Muffins, Pancakes, Baked Goodies, p.7
Whipped Cream (or Sour Cream) Biscuits, p.209
Essene Bread, p.596
Ham or Bacon Biscuits, p.325
Little Dumplings, p.379
Millet (or Herb or Barley) Chapatis, p.419
Oatcakes, p.441
Recipes, and Ideas for Crackers, p.204
Recipes for Sourdough, p.582
Recipes with Cornmeal, p.195
Rye Drops, p.529
Sorghum Sourdough Muffins, p.575
Tortillas, p.194
Whole grain Boston Brown Bread, p.611

---

# BREAD, YEAST

---

THE ABILITY TO MAKE GOOD YEAST BREAD HAS BECOME A STATUS symbol of sorts. People yearn to learn. This learning begins with following directions, but it takes practice to make perfect bread. With practice comes a sense of when the bread dough is right, when it has been kneaded enough, and when it has risen long enough. It is a little like learning to swim. Instruction helps, but the feeling of swimming cannot be taught. It comes with trying again and again until the breakthrough when one's body feels how to swim without thinking about it. Once bread baking is "felt" it is never forgotten. From then on that person can make good yeast breads of every type, using any method.

Throughout the world, there are quite a variety of methods for making bread, and thousands of variations in ingredients, and shapes and sizes of loaves. The essential ingredients are simply flour, water and yeast. Some excellent peasant style bread is made with just these ingredients, nothing else, not even salt. Unsalted bread, like unsalted

## STORAGE

**Drying** See USING DRIED BREAD, below.
**Freezing** Bake, cool, wrap. Quality retained, loaves: 6–12 months; rolls: 2–4 months. (Thawed bread dries out quickly. Use without delay.) *Unbaked Dough* Use double amount yeast. Shape small loaves. Freeze, then wrap. Rises while thawing in warm place in about 4 hours. Quality retained 2–4 weeks. Refer to FREEZING section.

rice, goes well with flavorful or spicy, highly seasoned foods. Such a simple bread has traditionally been the basic carbohydrate food in many people's diets. If made with whole grain flour it deserves to be called "the staff of life." Commercial bread made in North America usually contains salt, sweetening, fat, and milk, along with flour and yeast. Made with white flour and rich ingredients, it might kindly be called "the fluff of life" or, unkindly, "the scourge of life." It is certainly not the staff of life.

## HANDLING YEAST BREADS

### *Ingredients*

***Bread Flour***   A proportion of the flour in virtually all breads made with yeast is wheat. Wheat is the only grain containing enough of the protein gluten to make bread light. When bread dough from high gluten flour is kneaded, it develops the elastic quality that is necessary to trap and hold the gas bubbles given off by the yeast. The trapped bubbles expand the dough and make it rise, then baking sets the dough in its expanded state, resulting in a light textured bread.

Because hard winter wheat contains more gluten than other varieties it is preferred for making bread. Bread made with other kinds of wheat also rises, but not quite as well. Rye flour contains some gluten, but not enough to make light bread on its own. Other flours will not rise at all, but can be used in small amounts along with wheat to add their own flavor. A light bread can be made with half or more than half rye flour, but no more than ¼ part of other kinds of flour can be used. As the proportion of non-wheat flour increases the bread becomes heavier and moister—not necessarily a disadvantage. Many heavy moist breads, with their full, rich flavors, are delicious.

Whole wheat flour is ideal for routine bread baking because of its nutritional excellence and good flavor. However, it is nice, once in a while, to make special breads that are finer in texture and less intense in flavor than whole wheat. For these, unbleached white flour can be used. Its nutritional content can be bolstered by adding wheat germ and perhaps a small amount of soy flour, or a mixture of unbleached and whole wheat flours can be used. Some health food stores sell bread flour with part of the bran removed, making it less coarse than 100% whole wheat. Though sometimes called "unbleached" it is not as light as conventional unbleached white flour.

The proportions of flour to liquid given in bread recipes must not be taken too literally, because flour varies in moisture content and in the amount of liquid it will absorb. The proportions are right when the dough feels right, no matter what the recipe says.

***Liquids for Making Bread***   Water and milk are the liquids used most often in bread. Some others that work well without appreciably changing the flavor are: potato cooking water, sweet whey from making cheese or tofu (refer to the WHEY section) and maple sap. Others with stronger flavors are: vegetable cooking water, clear soup stock, beer, and fruit or vegetable juices. A slight acidity in the liquid seems to make the bread rise better.

Bread made with water has a crisp or chewy crust and a clean, grainy flavor. Pure, good tasting water is important for good bread. Bread made with milk has a soft crust and a more cake-like texture. The milk can be whole or skim, or powdered milk can be used and mixed with the flour. Raw milk is pasteurized or scalded before it is added, to stop enzyme action while the bread is rising.

*Bread Yeast*    The dry baking yeast sold in stores everywhere is the most practical form to use. Some believe, however, that moist yeast cakes or homemade yeast gives bread a better texture, because it rises more slowly. (Refer to the YEAST section.) Dry yeast keeps for months if refrigerated in a sealed container, but eventually it does lose its liveliness. It is important to notice the date on the package when buying small amounts. When buying in bulk, go to a place with a steady turnover so the yeast is always fresh. Bulk yeast is much cheaper than the small foil packets sold in some place.

Yeast becomes livelier when a small amount of sugar or other sweetener is added to the bread dough. About a teaspoon of barley malt (refer to directions in the BARLEY section) has the same effect, but good bread can be made without the addition of either. If too much yeast is used or temperatures are above 85°F while the bread rises, it may cause the bread to rise too fast, giving it poor flavor or a yeasty taste. A small amount of salt in bread dough also keeps yeast from working too fast.

## TRADITIONAL METHODS FOR MIXING BREAD DOUGH

The following three dough mixing methods all achieve the same goal—a kneadable dough. The dough must be stiff enough to hold together in a ball, and soft enough to be pushed around and shaped easily.

*Measuring Liquids First*    Most American breads are mixed in this way, so it is the method learned by most beginners. The liquid is first heated to lukewarm and measured into a large mixing bowl. Ingredients such as salt, sugar, and fat are added along with the dissolved yeast, and the flour is then mixed in gradually. Mixing is begun with a spoon. When the dough becomes stiff enough, the hands can be used. How much flour to add is judged by the texture of the dough. It should not be too stiff, since more flour is worked in when the bread is kneaded on a floured surface.

*The Sponge Method*    This is the best method to use when making bread with a large proportion of either whole wheat or rye flour. It gives the bread a lighter, less crumbly texture.

The sponge is a thin batter made of lukewarm liquid, yeast, flour, and sometimes other ingredients. It is made ahead and left to sit in a warm place until it becomes light and bubbly. This may take 1 or 2 hours, or the sponge can be made in the evening and left at room temperature overnight. To make the bread dough, flour and other ingredients are worked into the sponge until it is stiff enough for kneading. The *100% Whole Wheat Bread* and *Mrs. Voboril's Old Fashioned Rye Bread* under RECIPES below, both use the sponge method.

*Measuring Flour First*    This method has been used for centuries for some kinds of breads, but beginners will find it harder to manage than the other two methods. A mixing bowl is not necessary, though convenient.

The flour is measured, often by weight, and put in a mixing bowl or piled on a flat work surface. A well or hollow is made in the center of the flour and the dissolved yeast, warmed liquid, and other ingredients are poured in. Mixing is started by stirring only in the center well, and then gradually moving out to draw in more and more flour until all of the flour is incorporated. If the dough is too stiff it may be necessary to sprinkle water over it and work it in, but this is a difficult procedure. If the dough is too soft more flour can easily be added, so it is better to err with too much liquid than too little. The *Syrian Bread*, under RECIPES below, is mixed in this way.

## KNEADING BREAD DOUGH

Bread dough must be kneaded to develop the gluten and give it the elasticity needed for a light, non-crumbly loaf. Some recipes do omit this step, but the resultant bread does not have the characteristic cohesive texture of the best yeast breads. If kneading is too much of a chore, there are modern electric dough mixers and old fashioned manual ones that can do the job. However, hand kneading is a pleasant, satisfying activity if done the right way under comfortable circumstances. It is a pity to miss the magic feeling of a lumpy, floppy, sometimes sticky glob of dough, as it becomes a smooth, bouncy, alive-feeling shape in one's hands.

The dough should be kneaded on a work surface low enough to lean over comfortably. The whole weight of the body and not just the arm muscles can then be used to push against the dough. The work surface should be floured and the dough put on it in as much of a ball as possible. Kneading begins by pushing the dough, folding it in, pushing, turning, folding, and so on, over and over again in a rhythmical way. Only the amount of flour necessary to prevent sticking should be kneaded in. If the dough gets too dry and stiff the bread will be heavy and crumbly. Towards the end of the kneading not more than a thin sprinkling of flour should be used.

Kneading may take anywhere from 5 to 15 minutes depending on the type of bread and the mixing method. However, it is almost impossible to knead too much by hand. A well kneaded dough will have a bouncy resilient feeling. It will bounce back if poked with a finger, and sometimes little air bubbles or blisters will show on its surface. All of these characteristics are most pronounced when white flour is

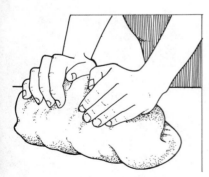

Use heels and palms of hands, keeping dough together in a ball.

used, but they are also there with whole wheat. If in doubt, knead for a few more mintues. Keep the dough in one round shape as much as possible as kneading comes to an end.

## THE WRONG AND RIGHT WAY TO GO ABOUT KNEADING BREAD

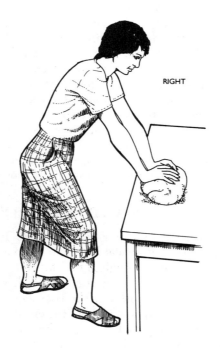

WRONG

RIGHT

Jerky movements tiring to maintain.

Squeezing motion of fingers which breaks ball of dough apart.

High counter requiring use of arm and shoulder muscles only, making a tedious job of it.

Relaxing rhythmical movement of pushing, turning, and folding the dough.

Low work surface so that body weight can be used to push down on dough, leaning over the dough with each push.

## LETTING BREAD DOUGH RISE

Dough can be shaped into loaves immediately after it is kneaded, allowed to rise, and then baked, but the texture will be better if it rises once in the bowl, and again after the loaves are shaped. Some kinds of bread are best if allowed to rise two or more times before being shaped into loaves.

To prepare the dough for rising shape it into a smooth ball, put it in a large, oiled bowl or other container, and turn it once so that oil coats it completely. (There must be space in the bowl for the dough to double in size.) Lay a damp cloth over all, and keep at room temperature, or a little warmer as it rises. If the climate is dry it is a good idea to lay plastic over the damp cloth to prevent drying. Temperatures between 70 and 85°F are best for rising. Above 85°F it rises too fast, hurting the quality of the bread. At cooler temperatures the dough rises very slowly, though usually the bread is still successful. Modern dry yeasts can tolerate a greater range of temperatures than the old fashioned kinds.

Instructions are usually to let bread dough rise until it has doubled in bulk, but some whole grain breads will not rise that much, while some light breads will rise more. To test if the dough has risen as much as it can, dent it with two fingers. If the dent remains, the dough is ready for the next step. If the dent slowly fills in, it can rise a little more. It is important to let dough rise completely the first time, while loaves rising for the second or third time can be put in the oven before they are completely raised. If a dough rises too much, it will fall by itself and not rise again. Bread dough that cannot be shaped into loaves when ready should be punched down, shaped into a ball, and left to rise again. At high altitudes bread dough rises faster and must be watched especially closely.

## SHAPING BREAD DOUGH

Bread dough can be shaped to fit any size pan, or formed into round or cylindrical loaves, or into a variety of odd shapes. The trick when shaping dough is to fold, roll, or push it so that the top remains a smooth, unbroken surface, with seams or rough spots on the underside. A smooth surface is especially important for those free standing loaves expected to hold their shape while rising.

For loaves to fit regular bread pans, make a flattened square of dough the same length as the pan. Fold or roll tightly, then set in the greased pan seam side down. This same shape can be set on a greased baking sheet for a free standing loaf. For a round loaf, make a somewhat flattened circle of dough. Choose the smoothest side for the outer surface and shape into a ball, tucking in or bunching up the rim of the circle, to put the rough spot on the bottom of the ball of dough, with the outside as tight and smooth as possible. Small, round rolls can be formed in the same way. If free standing loaves flatten or spread out too much it may be because the dough was too soft or because the bread was left to rise too long. It works well to put free standing loaves in the oven when they are only partly raised, usually 20 to 30 minutes after they are shaped. They will finish rising in the oven without spreading unduly.

## BAKING AND STORING BREAD

Bread is done when it is browned and has pulled slightly away from the sides of the pans. Loaves should be taken out of the pans and set on a rack to cool as soon as they come out of the oven. Bread sliced immediately often seems too moist or underdone, but it is usually fine after it has cooled for a few minutes. It must be completely cooled before it is wrapped or stored, so that moisture will not condense inside the wrapping, making spoilage more likely.

Well made bread keeps about a week at room temperature, and an old-fashioned bread box with a few ventilation holes is ideal for storing it. Bread keeps longest in the refrigerator, but tastes best at room temperature. Unsliced stale bread can be freshened by sprinkling the crust with water and putting it in a moderate oven until it dries. A serrated knife is best for slicing bread.

***Using Dried Bread*** One of the best ways to save extra bread, or make use of bread that is getting stale, is to dry it. Dried slices of bread or dry bread crumbs will keep indefinitely in airtight containers. Some kinds of dried bread slices are good eaten like crackers, and others are good in soup or salads. (Refer to TOAST CRACKERS, in the CRACKERS section, and FRISELLI in the TOMATOES section.) There are so many uses for dry bread crumbs that it is impossible to list them, but if they are handy they will be used.

Slices of bread can be dried in a food dryer or in a very low oven. They should become completely hard and brittle, though not browned. To make crumbs from the dried bread, roll over it with a rolling pin, or, if very hard, grind it with a meat grinder or grain mill. In most recipes calling for fresh bread crumbs, dry crumbs can be soaked briefly in water or another liquid and then used.

## BREAD RECIPES

### 100% *Whole Wheat Bread*   (Makes 4 loaves.)

2 tablespoons molasses, or honey
2 tablespoons butter, or lard (Do not use oil; it makes the bread heavy.)
1 teaspoon salt, optional
6 cups hot water, milk, or other liquid

12–14 cups whole wheat bread flour
1 tablespoon dry yeast, dissolved in ½ cup lukewarm water

Put the molasses or honey, butter or lard, and salt in a large mixing bowl. Add the hot water or milk, and stir until the butter or lard is melted. Stir in 3 or 4 cups of flour—enough to cool the mixture to lukewarm. Stir in the dissolved yeast, and then add about 2 more cups of flour, or enough to make a medium batter. This is the sponge. Cover and let rise at room temperature or a little warmer until it is light and bubbly, usually about an hour.

Work in the rest of the flour—enough to make the dough kneadable. Turn out on a floured surface and knead about 10 minutes or until a smooth elastic ball is formed. Put the dough in a bowl, cover, and let rise until double in bulk, about 1 hour.

Now turn the dough out onto a lightly floured board and shape into

---

**BREAD DOUGH IDEAS**

**The Same Dough, Different Ways** When making bread, separate a piece of dough from the main batch and use it in any of the following ways. A light resilient dough is best. Use the dough after it has risen once.

**Rolls, Bread Sticks, Pretzels** Form dough in small shapes and bake on greased baking sheets. Rolls can be round, flattened like hamburger buns, or flat triangular pieces rolled up to make crescents. Cloverleaf rolls can be made by putting three small balls of dough in each cup of greased muffin tins. For bread sticks, strips of dough can be rolled into long, snake-like strands. For pretzels, curve each strand into the shape of a loose knot. Any of these can be glazed by brushing them with milk or an egg and water mixture. A sprinkling of sesame or poppy seeds is nice, too. Baking time is about 20 minutes for rolls, 10 minutes for thin bread sticks and pretzels.

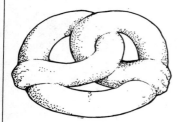

*Pretzel*

**Biscuits** Knead a stiffly beaten egg white and 4 tablespoons softened butter into a piece of bread dough equal to about 2 cups. Though this is messy as kneading begins, it blends together in a couple of minutes. Roll out ½ inch thick and cut into biscuit rounds. Lay on a greased baking sheet, prick each several times with a fork and let rise about 15 minutes. Bake in a hot, 400°F oven until lightly browned, 10 to 15 minutes.

**Dumplings** Shape bread dough into small balls, cover with a cloth, and let them rise on a floured surface. Gently set them on top of a simmering stew, cover tightly, and cook over very low heat for about 40 minutes without lifting the lid.

**Fried Bread Puffs** Have light, raised bread dough ready. Heat fat for deep frying. Gently pinch off about 1 inch globs of dough and slide or drop them into the

4 loaves. Put in greased pans and let rise until almost doubled again, about 40 minutes. Bake at 350°F for 50 to 60 minutes, or until lightly browned. Cool on racks.

***Brown Bread*** For the flour use half unbleached white flour and half whole wheat. Optional: Add about 1 cup of wheat germ and ½ cup soy flour. If desired, the sponge step can be omitted and all the ingredients mixed and kneaded immediately.

***Raisin Bread*** Work about 2 cups of raisins into the dough for either 100% whole wheat or brown bread. If wished raisins can be worked into 2 loaves of bread when they are shaped and the other two can be left plain. To do this, flatten the dough, sprinkle with raisins, fold over, flatten again and sprinkle with more raisins. Continue in the same way until enough have been added. For an unusual touch, try a caraway seed topping. (Refer to CARAWAY, in the HERB SEEDS section.)

### Mrs. Voboril's Old Fashioned Rye Bread

(Makes 4 small or 2 large loaves.)

"This is the rye bread my mother used to make in 1908, and we have been making it since." Mrs. Voboril

In the evening make a sponge, using:

| | |
|---|---|
| *4 cups potato cooking water* | *1 teaspoon or more caraway seed* |
| *1 tablespoon dry yeast* | *4 cups (about) pure rye flour* |

Mix the potato water and yeast and let sit 15 minutes. Add the seeds and rye flour. Make a batter thick enough to drop from the spoon in a clump. It should not pour. Let sit overnight in a large bowl or crock. It should rise a lot during the night and be flat again in the morning.

In the morning add:

| | |
|---|---|
| *½ cup lard, or other fat* | *1 teaspoon salt, or to taste* |
| *¼ cup sugar, or 2 tablespoons honey* | *unbleached white flour or whole wheat flour* |

Mix the lard, sugar or honey and salt with the sponge, then work in enough flour to make a stiff dough. Knead for about 15 minutes, adding more flour as necessary to keep the dough from sticking. Put the dough in a large, greased bowl, cover with a damp cloth, and let rise until doubled. Punch down and form 4 small or 2 large loaves. Put in greased loaf pans or shape into free standing loaves and set on greased baking sheets. Let rise again until almost doubled, 45 to 60 minutes. Brush with cold water and let sit 15 minutes. Bake at 375°F for 35 to 40 minutes, or until lightly browned. Cool on wire racks. For soft crusts, brush with lard when the bread is set on the racks and cover with a dish towel while it cools.

***Sourdough Rye*** When making the sponge in the evening omit caraway seeds and yeast, and add about 1 cup lively sourdough starter. (Refer to the SOURDOUGH section.) In the morning remove

1 cup dough to save for the continuing sourdough starter. Then add the caraway seeds. If the sponge is not active, dissolve yeast in a little warm water and add it. Then finish the bread as above. If no yeast is added, allow more time for the dough to rise.

***Pumpernickle*** When making the sponge in the evening add 1 cup unseasoned mashed potatoes to the potato cooking water. Omit caraway seeds. In the morning, omit lard or fat. Add ¼ cup molasses instead of sugar or honey. Before adding wheat flour to the sponge, add ½ cup cornmeal, ¼ cup dark roasted flour, optional (refer to ROASTING ROOTS, GRAINS, AND SEEDS, in the BEVERAGES section), and 2 more cups rye flour. Then add whole wheat flour, and finish the bread as above. If desired, a sourdough version can also be made.

This pumpernickle is very good shaped into small, round or cylindrical loaves, and set on ungreased baking sheets that are sprinkled with cornmeal. Increase the baking time to about 1¼ hours or as necessary. This bread will be dense and should be sliced thinly.

### *Challah or Braided Egg Bread, Jewish Style*   (Makes 2 loaves.)

| | |
|---|---|
| 1 tablespoon honey, or sugar | 8 cups (about) unbleached white |
| 1 teaspoon salt, optional | flour |
| 2 tablespoons vegetable oil | ½ cup wheat germ, optional |
| 1 tablespoon dry yeast | 1 egg yolk, mixed with 1 |
| 2 eggs plus 1 egg white, slightly | tablespoon water |
| beaten (If plentiful, as many as | poppy seeds, for sprinkling on top |
| 4 eggs can be used.) | |

Put the honey, or sugar, salt, and vegetable oil in a bowl, and pour 2 cups of hot water over them. Very hot tap water can be used. Stir to dissolve honey and salt. Cool to lukewarm, then sprinkle in the yeast. Let stand 5 minutes, or until the yeast dissolves. Add the slightly beaten eggs, then work in the flour and wheat germ. Add enough flour to make a medium stiff dough. Knead on a floured board until elastic, 5 to 10 minutes. Put in an oiled bowl and turn to coat all surfaces with oil. Cover and let rise until doubled, about 1 hour. Turn out on a floured surface, punch down the dough gently and shape into loaves. Traditionally the loaves are braided as follows:

Divide the dough in half for the two loaves. Pinch the dough for one loaf into 4 equal pieces. For the base of the loaf, roll 3 of the pieces into strands 12 to 14 inches long. Then braid them. They may be easiest to braid starting from the middle and going to one end, then braiding backwards from the middle to the other end. Set this braided loaf on an oiled baking sheet. For the additional small braid, divide the other piece of dough into 3 equal parts and roll them into thin strands 10 to 12 inches long. Braid them and set to run down the middle of the larger braid. Repeat to make the second braided loaf. (The small braid is sometimes omitted, but is very decorative.)

Brush the bread with the egg yolk and water mixture, and sprinkle

### BREAD DOUGH IDEAS, *cont.*

fat. One way to do this is to pick up strands of dough with the thumb and two fingers of one hand and pinch or cut off pieces with the other hand. Fry several pieces at a time, allowing about 3 minutes for them to puff up and brown. Turn over if necessary to brown both sides. Drain them on paper and eat fresh and hot. Or roll them first in carob powder, finely ground nuts, sugar, to eat like donuts. They are scrumptious hot, and also good cold.

**Stove Top English Muffins** Roll out bread dough on a floured surface to about ½ inch thick, and cut large circles with a cookie cutter, or a tuna fish can with both ends removed. Cover the muffins with a cloth, and let rise until doubled. Heat an ungreased griddle or large heavy frying pan over low heat. Lift the muffins with a spatula and slide them onto the griddle. Slowly brown them on one side, then turn to brown the other. They should take about 30 minutes, 10 to 15 minutes each side. The lighter the bread dough, the better these taste.

**Brother Johnathan** This is an old time dessert, sweetened only with honey or maple syrup when it is served. Put 1½ to 2 inches of sliced apples in the bottom of a deep pot with a tight lid. Add about ½ cup water, or just

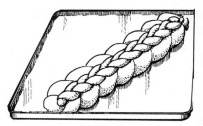

*Braided challah before the dough rises.*

enough to keep the apples from sticking. Shape a piece of bread dough about ¾ inch thick to fit inside the pot, and set this on the apples. Leave at least 2 inches of space above the dough to give it room to rise. Cover the pot, put on medium heat, and bring to a boil. Then reduce heat and simmer for 45 minutes. Do not open the pot until the end of this cooking time, then check to be sure it is done.

To serve the Brother Johnathan, set a platter on top of the pot, and turn both upside down, so the bread is on bottom and the apples on top. Very good eaten warm with milk and honey, or another sweetening. For reheating, cover with aluminum foil and steam for half an hour. Other fruits such as pitted cherries can be used instead of apples. The amount of water added must be adjusted to the wetness or dryness of the fruit.

**Baked Fruit Pudding**  Butter a casserole or baking dish, and put in a layer of canned, pitted or deseeded fruit, with its juice. Apricots, plums, peaches, cherries, and apples are all very good. For thickening, mix in a small amount of tapioca, cornstarch, or flour, and, if desired, honey. Such spices as cinnamon or nutmeg can be added. Shape a thin circle of bread dough to fit over the top of the fruit in the baking dish. Set the dough on the fruit for a moment, then turn it over to glaze the top with juice. Let rise about 30 minutes, and bake in a moderate oven for 30 to 40 minutes or until browned, with bubbles of juice showing around the edges. For a sweet topping, dots of butter and dribbles of honey can be added just before the pudding goes in the oven. Very good warm or cold, with milk or cream.

generously with poppy seeds. Let rise about 30 minutes, or until the loaves are expanding, but before they are doubled. Bake in a 375°F oven for 40 minutes or until nicely browned.

*Rolls*  Shape challah dough into rolls instead of loaves. These bake in about 25 minutes.

*French Toast*  Challah that is 4 or 5 days old makes superb French toast. Soak slices in a mixture of milk and egg and fry slowly in butter until lightly browned on both sides.

### Herb Bread (Makes 2 loaves.)

*1 ½ cups milk, lukewarm* (Scald if raw, then cool to lukewarm.)
*4 tablespoons butter, or shortening*
*4 tablespoons honey, or sugar*
*½ teaspoon salt, optional*
*7 cups (about) flour* (Half whole wheat with half unbleached white is good.)
*2 tablespoons dry yeast, dissolved in ½ cup lukewarm water*
*½ cup wheat germ, optional*
*4 teaspoons celery seed, or caraway seed*
*2 teaspoons ground sage*
*1 teaspoon nutmeg*
*2 eggs, beaten*
*1 egg white, optional*
*sesame seed, optional, for sprinkling on top*

Mix the milk, butter or shortening, honey or sugar, and salt in a large bowl. When the butter or shortening has softened, add 3 cups of the flour and beat until smooth. Add the wheat germ, celery or caraway seed, sage, nutmeg, and eggs, then beat again until well mixed. Work in enough flour to make a moderately soft dough. Turn out on a floured surface and let rest 10 minutes, then knead until smooth and elastic, 5 to 10 minutes. Put the ball of dough in an oiled bowl and turn to coat all sides. Cover and let rise until doubled, about 1 hour. Punch down and let rest 10 minutes. Shape into 2 round loaves, and set on greased baking sheets. For a glazed top, brush the loaves with slightly beaten egg white. Sprinkle with sesame seeds.

Let rise about 30 minutes or until almost doubled and bake in a 400°F oven for 35 minutes, or until browned.

### Syrian Bread (Makes 12 flat round loaves.)

*1 tablespoon dry yeast*
*½ teaspoon sugar, or honey*
*5 pounds flour* (Half whole wheat with half unbleached white is good.)
*1 cup wheat germ, optional*
*1 teaspoon salt, optional*
*1 tablespoon crushed mahleb, optional* (Refer to CHERRY PITS, in the CHERRY section.)
*1 tablespoon oil*

Mix the yeast and the sugar or honey with 1 cup of lukewarm water and let sit until bubbly, 5 to 10 minutes. Mix the flour, wheat germ, salt and mahleb in a large bowl. Make a well in the center of the flour and pour in the yeast mixture, oil, and 4½ cups of lukewarm water. Start mixing with a large spoon, stirring first in the center well and gradually moving out to bring in more flour. When it becomes difficult to stir, begin working in flour with clean hands. If necessary, add a little more lukewarm water to make a kneadable dough. Turn out on a floured surface and knead 10 to 15 minutes, or until the dough is smooth and elastic. Put the ball of dough in an oiled bowl and turn it over to coat all sides with oil. Cover with a damp cloth and let rise until double in bulk, about 1 hour.

Turn out the dough on a floured surface, punch down, and divide into 12 pieces. Shape the pieces into balls, the size of large oranges. Set them on the floured surface, cover with a cloth and let rise 30 minutes. Then gently flatten each ball by hand to make a large pancake shape about ¼ inch thick. Put as many loaves as possible on lightly greased baking sheets. Leave the rest on a floured surface, cover with cloth, and let rise again for about 30 minutes. By the time the last loaves are being shaped the first ones should be ready to bake.

Heat the oven very hot, 450 to 475°F. Bake the loaves about 5 minutes, or until lightly browned. They will puff up like an inflating ball, then flatten again as they cool. If the bread does not puff up the oven may not be hot enough. With some ovens it helps to turn on the broiler for a minute or two while each batch is baking. If necessary, the loaves can be turned for a minute to brown the bottoms. This bread tastes good whether the loaves puff up or not, but it is more fun if they do! If the bread did not puff up to make a pocket, one can be cut open instead.

When one batch of bread is done put it on racks to cool, then gently slide more loaves onto the pans to bake.

Syrian bread is traditionally torn in pieces for eating, rather than cut. A half or a quarter of a loaf can be filled with salad, SHISH KEBAB (in LAMB section), or cooked, well-seasoned beans, to make a sandwich middle eastern style.

---

### OTHER YEAST BREAD RECIPES

Cranberry Anadama Bread, p. 206
Sourdough Bread, p. 584

### OTHER RECIPES WITH YEAST BREAD DOUGH

Bread Dough Crackers, p.204
Cabbage Pie or Pirog, p.94
Friselli, p.642
Hamantaschen or Three Cornered Hats, p.563
Sauerkraut Onion Rolls or Loaf, p.545

### RECIPES FEATURING BREAD OR BREAD CRUMBS

Bread Pudding, p.418
Celery Bread Crumb Stuffing, p.124
Dad's Graveyard Stew, p.417
Garlic Bread, p.296
Layered Bread and Fruit Pudding, p.292
Mulberry Bread Pudding, p.421
Roast Beverages, p.44
Steamed Suet Pudding, p.611
Tomato Bread Salad, p.642

---

# BROCCOLI

Broccoli is a relatively new vegetable in the new world, and an old one in the old world. It has become popular in North America only in the last thirty to fifty years, but has been cultivated in Italy since the time of the ancient Romans. Large headed broccolis are favored in North America, while sprouting varieties are preferred in Mediterranean and Asian countries. Sprouting broccoli is very leafy and tender with small buds. It is cooked like other leafy greens.

Broccoli and cauliflower are closely related members of the cabbage

### STORAGE

**Canning**  Not recommended. (It becomes strong tasting and discolored.)

**Cold Storage**  Heads keep about 2 weeks if refrigerated. Whole plants pulled just before hard frost keep 4–5 weeks in a root cellar.

**Drying**  Slice uniformly thin. Steam 10 min. or till cooked through. Dry until brittle. Refer to DRYING section.

### STORAGE, *cont.*

**Freezing** (Preferred storage method.) Prepare (see below). Slice stalks and florets no thicker than 1½ in., or chop coarsely, then blanch. Steam chunks: 5 min. Boil: 3 min. If chopped, steam 1 to 2 min. Refer to FREEZING section.

2–3 POUNDS FRESH = 1 QUART FROZEN

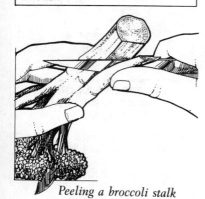

*Peeling a broccoli stalk*

### BROCCOLI IDEAS

**Broccoli in Salads** Raw broccoli is good added to most kinds of salads. The peeled stalks are especially fine because their flavor is a little milder than the tops. They can be cut into rectangles to eat like carrot sticks, or slices can be marinated in an oil and vinegar dressing for several hours to make a special broccoli stalk salad. Leftover cooked broccoli is very good in salads, especially vegetable salads and aspics.

**Broccoli and Beans** Add chopped broccoli or chunks of broccoli to lentils or other cooked dry beans about 20 minutes before serving time. The broccoli should not cook much longer than that because its flavor will grow too strong. The *Lebanese Beans and Rice Soup* recipe in the BEANS, DRY section is very good with broccoli added.

**Broccoli Soup** Heat a broth or soup stock, add chopped broccoli,

family. Though their heads, or buds, look alike except for color, their flavor and texture are quite different, and they taste best with different kinds of seasonings. The green vegetable taste of broccoli calls for the same seasonings that suit leafy greens, green beans, and other green vegetables, for example, onions, garlic, vinegar, tomato, olive oil or crumbled crisp bacon. Cauliflower, with its milder flavor and crisper texture, goes better with the kinds of seasonings used with potatoes. Broccoli is far richer in vitamins and minerals, especially vitamin A, than cauliflower.

## HANDLING BROCCOLI

Heads of broccoli should be cut after the buds are fully formed, but before they start to open. The stalk and small leaves should be used along with the head, since they are equally good to eat. If the plant is left growing after the central head is cut, it will produce many smaller buds for later harvest. These, too, should be cut or broken off before they begin to open.

The inner parts of thick broccoli stalks are very tender and delicious when they are peeled. They are good raw or cooked with the florets. To peel the tough stalks, cut away a strip at the base of the stalk and pull until it comes off. So that both are done at the same time when cooking them together, peeled stalks should be cut in chunks the same size as the florets.

*De-bugging Broccoli* Various little bugs and worms like to hide themselves in broccoli heads. The standard method for driving them out is soaking in salt water for ½ to 1 hour. This works, but it is too drastic a step to take against such small problems. More harm is done by the soaking, which removes water soluble nutrients and adds unwanted salt, than could possibly be caused by the eating of an occasional harmless bug. However, it is not necessary to resign oneself to eating bugs with one's broccoli. If the broccoli is swished vigorously in a pan of cold water after it is cut or broken into separate florets, most bugs and worms will be dislodged. A second rinsing will do the rest. With broccoli that is to be blanched in boiling water for freezing, any bugs and worms will sink or float off after they are killed.

## BROCCOLI RECIPES

### Broccoli California Style
(Makes 6–8 side servings.)

| | |
|---|---|
| 1 large head broccoli | 1 clove garlic, peeled |
| 3–4 tablespoons oil | slice of hot pepper, optional |
| 1 onion, minced | |

Peal the stalk of the broccoli and chop it with the florets into pieces a little smaller than bite size.

Heat the oil in a heavy pan that has a lid. Add the onion, garlic, and hot pepper, and sauté gently until the onion is translucent. Remove the garlic and pepper. (If a stronger flavor is preferred, the garlic and pepper can be minced and left in the pan.) Add the broccoli, and stir to coat with oil. Add 2 to 3 tablespoons of water, cover, and simmer until the broccoli is just barely tender, about 10 minutes. Stir once or twice while it cooks. A vegetable dish that can easily become the featured part of the meal, outshining ordinary meat and potato accompaniments.

### Broccoli Stir-fried with Beef, Chinese Style

(Makes 8–10 side servings.)

| | |
|---|---|
| ½ pound lean beef, very thinly sliced | 3–4 tablespoons oil or lard |
| 2 teaspoons soy sauce | ½ cup soup stock or water |
| ¼ teaspoon honey or sugar | 1 tablespoon cornstarch mixed |
| 1 large head broccoli |    with 3 tablespoons water |

Slice the beef ¼ inch thick or less, then cut in rectangles about 1 by 2 inches. Mix the slices with the soy sauce and honey or sugar and let sit while preparing the broccoli.

Cut the head off the broccoli and break it into bite-sized florets. Peel the stalks, and slice diagonally, about ¼ inch thick.

Heat a wok or heavy frying pan until quite hot and add half of the oil or lard. Add the beef and stir-fry until it just starts to brown, about 2 minutes. Take out the beef. Add the rest of the oil and stir-fry the broccoli in it for about 1 minute or until it brightens in color. Add the stock or water, cover, and cook 3 to 4 minutes over medium heat. Now uncover, return the beef to the pan and stir-fry until it is reheated. Add the cornstarch with water, and stir until thickened. (Refer to the STIR-FRYING section.)

## BRUSSELS SPROUTS

ARE BRUSSELS SPROUTS A GENTLE, REAL-WORLD VERSION OF AN improbable science fiction creature? What else could have one neck with dozens of heads, grow in the garden, and taste delicious? This cabbage family plant, which originated somewhere in Europe—

**BROCCOLI IDEAS,** *cont.*

and cook about 5 minutes. It tastes best just barely tender. Soy sauce is a tasty seasoning for this soup. This is a good way to use the small batches of side shoots from broccoli plants.

**Broccoli with Herbs, Roman Style** Do as the ancient Romans did and embellish broccoli with any combination of their favorite herbs: savory, mint, lovage or celery leaves, coriander leaves, scallion or a small onion or leek, and cumin seeds. Steam the broccoli florets and peeled stalks until tender, then put them in a saucepan with a little olive oil and wine or wine vinegar. Add a generous amount minced herbs (crush cumin seeds if using them) and heat for 2 or 3 minutes to blend flavors.

### OTHER RECIPES WITH BROCCOLI

Broiled Tomatoes with Cheese and Broccoli, p. 641
Recipes, and Ideas for Vegetables, p. 669
Savory Broccoli Stew, p. 31
Stir-fried Nuts and Green Vegetables, p. 438
Yogurt Horseradish Sauce for Vegetables, p. 708

### STORAGE

**Canning** Poor. Watery, soggy, and generally unpleasant, except when pickled. See DILLY BRUSSELS SPROUTS variation of DILLY BEAN PICKLES in BEANS, FRESH section.

**Cold Storage** Dig plants before hard frost, holding damp soil around roots. Keep about 2 months in root cellar or similar conditions. Budded sprouts often mature in storage.

**Drying** Slice ½ in. thick. Steam 10 min. or till tender. Dry until crisp. Refer to DRYING section.

<table>
<tr><td>

---

**STORAGE**, *cont.*

---

**Freezing** Blanch in steam or boiling water. Small: 3 min.; medium: 4 min; large: 5 min. Refer to FREEZING section.

**Live Storage** Mulch well in garden. Will keep most of the winter where weather is not too severe.

ABOUT 2 POUNDS FRESH = I QUART COOKED.

---

</td></tr>
</table>

possibly in Belgium as the name suggests—needs cool weather and some frosts to do well. Where growing conditions are right it is a pleasure to have in the garden. It does not take too much space, is very productive over a long period of time, is easy to harvest, usually continues into early winter after other vegetables have disappeared. Brussels sprouts are also a pleasure in the kitchen. They have the elegance and flavor of a fancy gourmet vegetable, no matter how simply they are cooked or how often they are served.

## HANDLING BRUSSELS SPROUTS

The lowest sprouts on the stalk are harvested first. They tend to be smaller and looser leafed than sprouts that form later, but they are still very good. Picking them encourages more sprouts to form. Each sprout is simply twisted to break it off from the stalk. Brussels sprouts need very little preparation. The base of the sprout is trimmed, if necessary, and wilted leaves are pulled off. When sprouts are large, sometimes a cross is cut in the base to make them cook evenly throughout.

After all the sprouts have been harvested, the tops of the plants can be eaten. The inner rosettes of leaves at the top are very tender, with the typical Brussels sprouts flavor. They cook very quickly, and are good served like cabbage or other leafy greens. If wished, the stalks can be peeled like broccoli stalks, to cook or eat raw. The lower leaves of Brussels sprout plants can be picked early in the season while they are tender and cooked as greens.

## BRUSSELS SPROUTS RECIPES

### Brussels Sprouts with Chestnuts    (Makes 6–8 side servings.)

| | |
|---|---|
| 3–4 cups Brussels sprouts | ½ pound chestnuts, cooked and |
| 4 tablespoons butter | peeled (They can be whole |
| | or chopped.) |
| | pepper, salt, optional |

Steam the sprouts until just tender, 8 to 15 minutes depending on size.

Heat the butter in a pan and add the sprouts and chestnuts. Cook uncovered over medium heat, stirring often, for about 5 minutes. They are delicious without extra seasoning, but salt and pepper can be added if wished. A holiday classic!

### Brussels Sprouts with Nuts
Sauté chopped nuts in the butter until lightly browned before adding the hot cooked sprouts. Cashews, raw peanuts, or almonds go especially well. For a more elegant version, make the NUTTY LEMON BUTTER SAUCE recipe in the BUTTER section, and serve the sprouts in it.

<table>
<tr><td>

---

**BRUSSELS SPROUTS
IDEAS**

---

**Baked Sprouts** Cook Brussels sprouts until almost tender. They can be cooked in chicken stock or other soup stock if desired, or use leftover sprouts. Butter a shallow baking dish and put the sprouts in it. Add several spoons of soup stock, cooking water, or water. Sprinkle with grated cheese or breadcrumbs, and dots of butter. Bake about 15 minutes in a hot oven.

**Brussels Tops Chowder** Cut the tender rosettes from the tops of Brussels sprout plants after all of the sprouts have been harvested. Cook them in 1 or 2 cups boiling soup stock or water until limp, about 5 minutes. Drain, reserving the cooking liquid, and chop the tops. Make a white or cream sauce (refer to the MILK section), and add the reserved liquid to make it thin enough for chowder. Season with celery seeds or other herbs, to taste. Add the chopped tops just before serving. Slices of hard boiled eggs or cubes of whole wheat toast can be floated on the soup as a garnish. The sprouts themselves can also be used to make this chowder.

---

</td></tr>
</table>

### *Brussels Sprouts with Egg Lemon Sauce* (Makes 6–8 side servings.)

2 pounds Brussels sprouts
1 tablespoon butter
2 egg yolks

2 tablespoons lemon juice
cayenne pepper, to taste

Put the Brussels sprouts and butter in a sauce pan with a minimum of water, about 1 inch. Cook, covered, until just barely tender, or 8 to 10 minutes. Stir once or twice.

Meanwhile beat the egg yolks in a deep bowl that is large enough to hold the sprouts. When the yolks are thick beat in the lemon juice. When the sprouts are done, drain, reserving the liquid. Beat 2 tablespoons of the liquid into the egg mixture. Then stir in the hot sprouts to coat them with the sauce. They must be kept very hot so that the egg yolk thickens as it comes in contact with them.

**OTHER RECIPES WITH BRUSSELS SPROUTS**

Brussels Sprouts Brown Soup, p. 95
Dilly Brussels Sprouts Pickles, p. 32
Nutty Lemon Butter Sauce (for Brussels Sprouts), p. 87
Recipes, and Ideas for Vegetables, p. 669
Sweet Potato Nests for Green Vegetables, p. 624
Yogurt Horseradish Sauce for Vegetables, p. 708

# BUCKWHEAT

**B**UCKWHEAT IS GRAIN THAT IS NOT A GRAIN. IT IS HARVESTED, prepared, and eaten like a grain, but does not grow like one. Most grains are grasses. Buckwheat is a somewhat bushy plant with many small white flowers that are followed by three sided seeds. It is closely related to smartweed and can claim rhubarb as a more distant relative.

While buckwheat is not as productive as most grain crops, it does have its advantages. Practical to plant on a small scale because easy to harvest by hand, it will grow in poor soil, in hilly locations, and will choke out weeds as it grows. It is an excellent honey plant for anyone who keeps bees. It is also nutritious, containing more useable protein than most grains, and it tastes good. Buckwheat specialties are enjoyed everywhere. Kasha made from toasted buckwheat groats is important in Russia and middle European countries. Buckwheat noodles are a delicacy in Japan. Buckwheat pancakes were a winter breakfast staple in many early American homes, and are still many people's favorite kind of pancake.

## HANDLING BUCKWHEAT

The seeds of buckwheat plants do not mature evenly. Those growing low on the plant are earlier than those near the top. Usually buckwheat is harvested late, after frost has killed the plant, and the loss of early seeds is ignored. However, those who grow their own can shake some of these early seeds into a container when they are mature and enjoy a few meals of buckwheat before the main harvest.

Small patches of buckwheat can be cut with a scythe, then

**STORAGE**

Refer to STORING GRAIN, in the GRAINS section.

threshed and winnowed by hand. Buckwheat seeds are covered with thin hulls which are difficult to remove. The methods suggested under HULLING DIFFICULT GRAINS, in the GRAINS section, can be tried, or the seeds can be ground, hulls and all, to make flour. If the buckwheat is first dried thoroughly, or roasted, the hulls may shatter into pieces big enough to sift out after grinding. Early American pancakes were often made from unhulled buckwheat flour. (Refer to the GRAINS section for harvesting and grinding instructions.) Buckwheat can also be sprouted. (Refer to the SPROUTS section.)

Buckwheat groats are whole, hulled buckwheat seeds. Grits are coarsely ground hulled seeds. Buckwheat flour is a heavy or dense kind of flour with a distinctive flavor. Since buckwheat seeds are soft, small quantities of flour are easily made in a blender.

**Toasted Buckwheat Groats or Grits** Groats and grits are often toasted in a low oven until lightly browned, which gives them a special, nutty flavor. Toasted buckwheat groats are sometimes called "kasha" even before being made into that special dish. (See the recipe, below.)

For toasting, spread the groats or grits in a shallow pan in a low oven, about 300°F, for 10 minutes, or until lightly browned. Stir or shake once or twice to brown them evenly. Toasted buckwheat can be ground to make a special flour with a toasted flavor.

## BUCKWHEAT RECIPES

### Buckwheat Cakes

(These are the kind of pancakes some families used to eat every morning from November 1st to April 1st. The recipe is quoted from *In The Kitchen,* by Elizabeth S. Miller, 1875.)

*"One quart of buckwheat flour*
*One gill [½ cup] of wheat flour*
*One quart less one gill [3½ cups]*
   *warm water*

*One gill of yeast* [Use 1 tablespoon dry yeast dissolved in ½ cup water.]
*Two teaspoonfuls of salt* [Best reduced to ¼ – ½ teaspoon.]

Mix the batter at night in order to have the cakes for breakfast; if very light, an hour before they are required stir the batter down and let it rise again. Bake the cakes on a smooth, nicely-greased griddle, and send them to the table the moment they are baked, piled regularly in the centre of the plate, and every one *right side up with care;* for although they may be well-baked on both sides, the lower side never has the beautiful, brown lace-like appearance which makes a good buckwheat cake so attractive. If some of the batter is left from the baking it will serve as yeast for the next making; put it away in a cool place, but not where it will freeze; bring it out at night, add buckwheat, etc., and leave it to rise. With a little care, no fresh yeast will be necessary during the entire winter.

These cakes may be raised with baking powder, but the batter should be thinner than when mixed with yeast. A gill [½ cup] of oatmeal may be used in addition to the wheat."

## Kasha                                    (Makes 6−8 servings.)

*1 ½ cups toasted buckwheat groats or grits*

*1 egg*

*3 cups soup stock, meat juices and water, or plain water*

*paprika, to taste, optional*

*salt, optional*

*yogurt, optional*

Stir the buckwheat with the raw egg until well mixed. Every groat or grit should be sticky with egg. Heat a frying pan or heavy sauce pan. Do *not* grease it. Add the buckwheat and egg and stir constantly over medium heat until the buckwheat dries out and separates into individual groats or grits again.

Meanwhile heat the liquid. Add it to the buckwheat when it is ready, put in seasonings, and simmer, covered, until the buckwheat is tender and the liquid absorbed, about 20 minutes. The egg improves the texture of the buckwheat; without egg it cooks to a mush.

Kasha made with chicken stock is often served with chicken, and when made with beef juices or stock it is served with pot roast. Yogurt can be served on the side with the kasha, so that each person can take some and mix it in to suit himself.

**Kasha with Vegetables and for Stuffing** Sauté chopped vegetables in butter or bacon fat and add them to the kasha after cooking as above. Some vegetables that go well are onions, leeks, celery, green pepper, parsley, and mushrooms. Kasha with vegetables makes a flavorful stuffing for chicken and other poultry, and for veal breast, and other meats. It is also a good stuffing for such vegetables as green peppers or tomatoes.

**Kasha Dumplings** Make noodle dough (refer to the NOODLES section), roll it thin, and cut into 2 inch squares. Make kasha or kasha with vegetables, as above, and put a spoonful on a square of noodle dough. Dip a finger in water and run it around the square to dampen the edges. Set another square of dough on top and press the edges together to seal them. Drop the dumplings in boiling water, then cook for about 5 minutes. Drain and serve immediately with butter, or let cool and then fry them until crisp and brown on both sides.

---

### BUCKWHEAT IDEAS

**Buckwheat Instead of Bread Crumbs** When making meat loaves, patties, or meat balls use cooked buckwheat groats or kasha instead of bread crumbs. The flavor is excellent. Cooked buckwheat is also very good in vegetable loaves and patties. Try it in the *Versatile Vegetable Loaf* recipe, in the VEGETABLES section.

**Buckwheat Noodles** Use 1 part buckwheat flour and 1 part wheat flour when making noodles, p. 429. Though they do not taste like the buckwheat noodles made in Japan, they are quite good.

**Buckwheat Salad** Prepare extra when making *Kasha*, above, and add it to green salads. It is especially good in mixtures with chopped raw vegetables like cabbage, broccoli, or green beans. It is also good instead of bulghur wheat in the recipe for *Tabbouleh, a Middle Eastern Salad* in the WHEAT section.

---

### OTHER RECIPES WITH BUCKWHEAT

Buckwheat Potato Cookies, p. 20
Ideas for Grain, p. 314
Recipes for Sourdough, p. 582
Scrapple, p. 329

## STORAGE

**Cold Storage**  See STORING BUTTER, below.

**Freezing**  Butter from pasteurized cream is best. Pack in containers or wrap well. Quality retained 5–6 months. Thaw in refrigerator. Refer to FREEZING section.

**Salt Curing**  See SALT CURING BUTTER, below.

1 GALLON MEDIUM THICK CREAM (30% BUTTERFAT) = ABOUT 3 POUNDS BUTTER; 1 POUND BUTTER = ABOUT 1¾ CUPS CLARIFIED (SEE BELOW) ½ POUND BUTTER = 1 CUP

NOBODY KNOWS WHEN THE FIRST BUTTER WAS MADE, BUT IT MUST have been soon after the first bovine animal was milked. In any case butter is, and always has been, a very important food in northern Europe and in the parts of the world colonized by northern Europeans, including North America.

Butter is composed of butterfat, water, and a small amount of milk solids. It usually contains some vitamin A and D, and some calcium and phosphorous, but its main food value is as a fat. Some fat is necessary in a well balanced diet to provide energy and heat. Butter made from the milk of a home raised dairy animal is a good source of pure, additive-free fat, and is healthful as long as it is eaten in small or balanced amounts. It would be nutritionally sensible for a family with a dairy animal to skim their milk for drinking and eat the butter made from the cream. However, there would be too much fat in the diet if the family fed its skim milk to a pig, ate the butter, and drank whole milk. It would be downright excessive if they then slaughtered the pig and ate lots of lard and fatty pork as well!

### HANDLING BUTTER

Cream for making butter comes most often from cows, because the milk separates easily, but cream from goats can be used just as well. (Refer to the MILK section for how to separate cream from milk.) Goat butter is white rather than yellow, and according to some tastes, is not "buttery" in flavor. Cream from animals other than cows and goats can also be used to make butter. In India a large amount of butter is made using water buffalo cream. Ghee is made from it for use as a cooking fat. (See CLARIFIED BUTTER, OR GHEE, below.)

### MAKING BUTTER

Cream for making butter can be either sweet or sour, as long as it's flavor is good. Sweet cream must be fresh, without "off" flavors and sour or ripened cream must have a pleasant, tart taste. Traditional farm butter is made from soured cream because it churns more easily and keeps better. Also the resulting buttermilk has a better flavor.

Medium thick cream, about 30% butterfat, is best. Cream that is too thick or too thin is more difficult to churn. Other variations in the cream caused by differences among dairy animals, changes in feed, and so on, will also influence butter making and flavor. Cream from an animal near the end of her lactation is often difficult to churn.

***Sweet Cream for Butter*** Always pasteurize sweet cream before using it to make butter. Pasteurization will prevent a goaty or cheesy taste in butter made from goat's milk. (Refer to PASTEURIZING MILK, in the MILK section.)

***Souring or Ripening Cream for Butter*** Cream can be soured with a culture in the same way as milk. If using a yogurt culture, follow directions for making yogurt. (Refer to the YOGURT section.) Or a buttermilk culture can be used, as for making *Cultured Buttermilk,* below.

When cream only becomes available in small quantities at a time, it can be cultured and refrigerated until enough has collected to make butter. Cultured sour cream keeps about 2 weeks in the refrigerator, if undisturbed. One batch should not be mixed with another until ready to churn. If yogurt is made regularly in small containers, it is easy to add the yogurt culture to a container of cream and incubate it along with the milk.

***Butter Coloring*** Coloring is often used to make goat butter yellow, and to give cow butter more color in winter when lack of green feed makes it pale. An artificial butter coloring is sold by dairy supply stores and catalogs. But it is possible to make natural colorings from carrots, pot marigolds, or calendula, as was done in the past. (Refer to YELLOW coloring, in the FOOD COLORING section.) When coloring is used, it is added to the cream before churning begins.

***Churning Cream for Butter*** Churning is the process of stirring or agitating cream until it separates into butter and buttermilk. Small amounts of butter can be made with an egg beater, by shaking cream in a glass jar, or by putting it in an electric mixer or blender set at the slowest speed. For making large amounts of butter regularly, a butter churn is a necessity. There are many different styles and sizes of churns in both hand turned and electric models. It is also possible to make a simple churn following plans from books and magazine articles.

Cream should be cool as churning begins, about 60°F in summer and 65°F in winter. If it is too warm the butter will come too quickly

*A butter churn*

with a soft and greasy texture—and there will be less of it. The churn, or other container should be filled only ⅓ to ½ full, leaving room for the cream to expand as it is agitated. The best butter results when churning is done at a slow, steady rate, taking 30–40 minutes to come. In some circumstances churning can take an hour or so, but the butter will eventually come.

When butter is made in a closed container as when shaking it in a glass jar, the container should be opened every few minutes to let gases escape.

## BUTTER COMES MORE SLOWLY IF:

- The cream is too cold, too thin, or too thick.
- The cream is sweet, rather than sour or ripened.
- The churn is too full so that the cream is not agitated evenly.
- The cream is from a dairy animal at the end of her lactation.

(Changes in feed and individual differences in dairy animals can also affect the speed with which the butter comes.)

***Draining and Washing Butter***   When it is about to separate into butter and buttermilk there is an obvious change in the texture of the cream. It becomes rough textured, and then small grains of butter show up which begin to clump together into larger pieces of butter. The butter is easiest to drain and wash if churning is stopped when it is in pea-sized pieces. Drain off and save the buttermilk. Use a strainer to catch bits of butter, unless the design of the churn makes a strainer unnecessary. The easiest way to wash butter is to pour cool water into the churn with it, agitate a few times, and pour off the water. This must be repeated several times, until the rinse water runs off clear. If it is not possible to wash the butter in the churn, it can be put in another container. Be sure to pour off the water through a strainer to catch loose bits of butter.

***Working and Shaping Butter***   After it is washed, butter is worked to press out droplets of water, and improve its texture. For salted butter, the salt is worked in at the same time. Standard proportions are 1 tablespoon salt to a pound of butter, but light salting, ¼ to 1 teaspoon salt per pound, is preferred by many people. Butter is also very good unsalted, but may not keep quite as well in cold storage.

Special devices called butter workers were often used for making farm butter, but the job is easily done in a bowl with a wooden paddle, spoon, or a rubber spatula. The butter should be gathered into a lump or ball, pressed to flatten it, then folded or gathered into a ball again, pressed again, and so on. The dribbles of water pressed out of it should be drained off. When no more water comes out working should stop. Over-working can make the butter greasy.

When it is done, press the butter into containers, or make balls or other shapes for wrapping. If available, special butter molds can be used. Glass containers are better than plastic ones because air and odors can penetrate plastic. Butter must be well wrapped for cold storage or for freezing.

## STORING BUTTER

Butter made from pasteurized sweet cream or from cultured sour cream keeps better than butter from raw cream, and salted butter keeps its flavor longer than unsalted butter. If kept in the refrigerator or other cold place butter is useable up to 2 months, but after the first 2 weeks its flavor gradually deteriorates. If left too long it becomes rancid and must be discarded. When possible it is best to freeze butter for long storage. Butter can also be salt cured to preserve it, or clarified to use as a cooking fat. (Though clarified butter keeps well, it is not good for use as a spread.) Instructions for both processes follow.

***Clarified Butter, or Ghee*** When it is clarified, butter is heated to remove water and milk solids, leaving almost pure butterfat. It is excellent as a cooking fat because it can be heated to high temperatures without burning.

Unsalted butter should be used, and results are best if a pound or more is processed at one time. Melt the butter in a heavy pot over low, even heat. If necessary use an insulating pad under the pot. Keep the melted butter at a slow simmer until bubbling from the evaporating moisture stops, and milk solids start to settle or stick to the sides of the pan. The sediment may brown lightly, but must not burn, as that would spoil the ghee. Cooking will take 30 to 40 minutes, or longer if more than 2 pounds of butter are to be clarified.

Take the clarified butter off the stove and let it sit until the clear liquid can be poured off. It can be strained through a light cloth, if wished. Store in closed containers in a cool place. It will keep several months or longer.

Some instructions say to clarify butter by simply melting it and waiting for the milk solids to settle. However, long cooking drives off moisture, producing a clarified butter that is good for long storage. It is done in this way in India. If completely purified, ghee keeps as long as a year at room temperature, but it is best to refrigerate homemade ghee or keep it in a cool place to be used within 3 or 4 months. When making ghee at home, it is difficult to be sure that it is pure enough for warm storage. If cooked too little it may still contain traces of moisture or impurities, while cooking it a little longer to make sure it is done may cause it to brown and change flavor. Fortunately this browned flavor is very good with vegetables, noodles, fish, and other foods. (See the recipe for BROWN BUTTER SAUCE, below.) Pure clarified butter has also been used like lard for perserving other foods. (Refer to the MEAT section for instructions.)

The ghee made in India from water buffalo butter has a milder flavor than ghee from cow's butter, so the latter is sometimes diluted with lard or oil when used in recipes for Indian foods.

***Salt Curing Butter*** Most old cookbooks include directions for preserving butter in salt, since that was a common way to store it in the days before mechanical refrigeration. It is not recommended where other storage methods are available. (Refer to the SALT CURING section for pros and cons.)

Put rolls or balls of salted butter in a crock. Sometimes each one is wrapped in cloth so that they stay separated and keep their shape. They should not be packed tightly because there must be room for brine between them. Make the brine by boiling 6 quarts of water, 1 quart plain or pickling salt, 1 ounce saltpeter and 2 ounces sugar. Cool till completely cold and pour over the butter. Use a weight to hold the butter under the brine. (Refer to the paragraphs about crocks in the KITCHEN UTENSILS section.)

## BUTTERMILK

True buttermilk is the liquid separated from butter when cream is churned. The "buttermilk" sold in stores is a cultured milk with no connection at all to the making of butter. Churned buttermilk will vary depending on the cream from which it comes. When sour or ripened cream is used the buttermilk has a delicious, lively, tart flavor. When sweet cream is used the buttermilk has a bland, flat taste. It can be used like skim milk in cooking, but is not very good as a beverage, unless it has been cultured. (See the recipe for *Cultured Buttermilk,* below.)

References to buttermilk in recipes or as a beverage always imply a tart or sour flavored kind. Buttermilk from churned sour cream and cultured buttermilk can be used interchangeably, except when cultured buttermilk is called for as a starter for making cheese or other cultured milk products. In this case, churned buttermilk cannot be used as a starter.

## BUTTER RECIPES

***Lemon Butter***                                                                    (Makes about ⅓ cup.)

4 tablespoons butter
1–4 teaspoons lemon juice
paprika or cayenne, to taste

salt, *optional* (Omit if butter is salted.)
1 tablespoon parsley, finely minced, optional

Soften the butter at room temperature for a spread, or melt it if a sauce is wanted. Work in lemon, adjusting the amount according to the way it will be used. If it is to be put on the table for people to help themselves, 1 teaspoon may be enough. If it is to be tossed with a strong flavored vegetable, or poured over fish, use more lemon juice.

*Nutty Lemon Butter Sauce* Melt butter in a small pan, and in it brown 3 or 4 tablespoons slivered almonds or other nuts or seeds. Shelled pumpkin or sunflower seeds can be used. Add seasonings to taste as above. A teaspoon of cognac or another liquor can be included. This sauce is delicious with Brussels sprouts, green beans, and other vegetables.

*Brown Butter Sauce* Melt butter and cook over very low heat until it browns lightly. Add seasonings as above. This is excellent with brains, fish and other bland foods.

## Herb Butter                                    (Makes about 1 cup.)

½ cup unsalted butter
squeeze of lemon juice, optional
6–8 tablespoons fresh herbs, finely
   minced (A combination of any
   of the following is very good:
   Parsley, chives, scallions, shallots, tarragon, watercress,

chervil, dill leaves, celery leaves, savory, basil, thyme, marjoram, mint, finely grated horseradish, garlic crushed with a garlic press, grated lemon rind, finely chopped raw spinach leaves, or green pepper.)

Soften the butter at room temperature, and work in the lemon juice and herbs. Shape it into a long roll on a sheet of waxed paper or other wrapping. Wrap well and refrigerate until firm. Cut slices or pats. A pat of herb butter is good on vegetables, including potatoes, carrots, asparagus and many others. It also goes well with fish and some meats, and can be used for making sandwiches instead of plain butter.

Refrigerated herb butter keeps its flavor for a few days to a week. If it is to be frozen for longer storage, garlic should not be used.

## Cultured Buttermilk

1 quart skim milk, or bland buttermilk from churned sweet cream

¼ to ½ cup cultured buttermilk
   (From the store, or from a
   previous batch.)

If the milk is raw, heat it to scald or pasteurize it. If using buttermilk it should be made from pasteurized sweet cream.

Have the milk or buttermilk lukewarm, about 85°F. Stir in the cultured buttermilk, cover, and let sit in a warm room until the mixture coagulates. If it is held at about 70°F this will take about 16 hours. Stir the buttermilk until smooth before using it. It keeps a week to 10 days refrigerated.

### BUTTER IDEAS

**Whipped Butter** Hold ¼ pound butter at room temperature until softened. Put in a blender with ¼ cup water, also at room temperature. Blend until whipped and smooth. This should be made in small batches as it is best not refrigerated for too long. Makes the butter light textured and easy to spread thinly, even when cold.

**Butter Extended with Milk and Gelatine** Put 1 pound of butter in a bowl and let sit at room temperature until softened. Soak ¼ cup gelatine in 2 cups of milk for about 5 minutes, then stir it over very low heat, until the gelatine dissolves. Gradually beat this into the butter, until all bubbles disappear. Pour into molds and chill. Use as a spread. This cannot be used in cooking.

**Butter Extended with Lard** Melt 1 part pure lard, preferably home rendered, and mix with 1 part room softened butter. This old time way to make butter go farther is excellent for cooking.

**Butter Extended with Oil** Put ¼ pound softened butter, ¼ cup water, and ¼ cup light, bland vegetable oil in a blender or food processor. Mix well. Store in closed container in the refrigerator. This is preferred by many as a spread because it is considered more nutritious than butter, with its lower cholesterol content.

### OTHER RECIPES FEATURING BUTTER

Coral Butter, p.568
Strawberry Butter, p.617

### OTHER RECIPES FEATURING BUTTERMILK

Pickling Juice Soup, p.41
Buttermilk Sherbet, p.357
Watercress Soup, p.678
Yogurt Chiffon Gelatine, p.303
Yogurt Drinks, p.708

## Buttermilk Cheese

*churned buttermilk*　　　　　　　　　*cream, or butter and salt, optional*

Heat the buttermilk slowly to 100°F or a little warmer and hold it there, stirring every so often until the curd sinks. Let cool, overnight if wished, then pour off the whey. Put the curd in a cloth bag, and hang it to drain for several hours. When drained well enough, the curd should stick together if pressed. Work in a little cream, or butter and salt if preferred. Can be eaten immediately like cottage cheese, or pressed in a cheese press for 24 hours. (Refer to the cheese press instructions in the CHEESE, AGED section.)

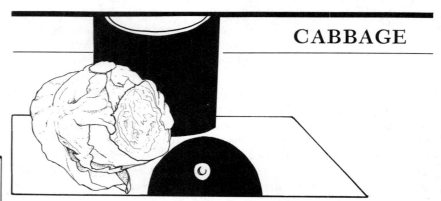

# CABBAGE

CABBAGE IS THE "HEAD" AND MOST IMPORTANT VEGETABLE OF the cabbage family. Usually it is a green head, but it can also be a red head or a Savoy curly head. Its nearest relatives are: kale and collards—the leafy greens; broccoli and cauliflower—the buds; kohlrabi—the bulbous stem; and Brussels sprouts—a lot of little heads. All of these vegetables have the same ancestor, the sea cabbage, a small wild plant that grows in some coastal areas of England and Europe. Head cabbage is grown in temperate zones throughout the world, and has always had special value as a winter vegetable because it stores so well. Sauerkraut is also a winter staple. (Refer to the SAUERKRAUT section.)

Since cabbage is eaten in so many places, there are many different approaches to preparing it. Homesteaders who want to depend on cabbage as a major winter vegetable have a rich heritage of recipes and ideas to draw upon, and can look forward to eating it often without getting tired of it.

## HANDLING CABBAGE

Cabbage is best if it has matured in cool weather. When spring cabbage is harvested early, it is tender and delicate in flavor and ex-

### STORAGE

**Canning** (Possible but not recommended because of strong taste and mushy texture, unless pickled.) Refer to CANNING SAUERKRAUT in SAUERKRAUT section. See also *Spiced Pickled Cabbage for Canning,* below.

**Cold Storage** See STORING WINTER CABBAGE, below. See also KEEPING SAUERKRAUT IN COLD STORAGE in SAUERKRAUT section.

**Drying** Shred coarsely, or slice thinly. Steam blanch 8–10 min. (optional). Dry till ribs are tough, leafy parts crumble. Refer to DRYING FOODS section.

**Freezing** Shred, chop, or cut in wedges. Blanch in boiling water. Shredded or chopped: 1½ min. Wedges: 3 min. Or blanch leaves for stuffing, see below. Refer to FREEZING section.

I POUND = I QUART SHREDDED RAW

cellent for salads, but if it is left in the garden after hot weather arrives it is apt to taste bitter or strong. Fall cabbages can be harvested whenever they are big and firm enough to be useful. Cabbage for storage is best left in the garden until just before the first hard freeze. Light frosts will not hurt it and even seem to improve the flavor.

When the cabbage is pulled or cut, remove only the toughest outer leaves. Keep as many green leaves as possible, as they contain more vitamins and minerals than the white inner leaves. If necessary, wash the cabbage before preparing it, but do not soak it. Soaking removes water soluble nutrients. Usually, the tight inner part of the head does not need washing.

For quick slicing tools, refer to SLICERS AND GRATERS in the KITCHEN UTENSILS section.

***Storing Winter Cabbage*** Any kind of cabbage will keep several weeks in a cool place like the refrigerator. Fall and winter varieties will keep 2 or 3 months under the right conditions. After long storage they do lose some of their color, flavor, and nutritional value, but they are still one of the best, most useful green vegetables to keep in cold storage.

Cabbage keeps very well in root cellars and in most outdoor storage arrangements such as mounds, pits, and insulated areas in outbuildings. Ideal conditions are 32°F with a fairly high humidity, but some variation is tolerated. Cabbages should be protected from temperatures below 30°F. Though they will keep in storage areas such as basements and unheated rooms, they give off a strong odor that can penetrate throughout a house, so most people prefer outdoor storage. The odor can be minimized if cabbages are wrapped in newspaper or packed in sand, leaves, or peat moss.

There are two ways to harvest cabbages for storage. One is to pull up the whole plant, leaving the stalk for a handle; the other is to cut off the head at its base. In either case, pull off loose outer leaves so that the head is fairly compact. Cut heads are then wrapped in several layers of newspaper or packed in damp sand, dry leaves, damp peat moss, or a similar material. They are then ready for the cold storage area.

Cabbages with stalks are either hung upside down in root cellars, or packed upside down in hay, straw, or dry leaves, and put in outdoor storage pits, mounds, or other protected areas. Sometimes cabbages for hanging in root cellars are hung first at room temperature for a few days to "paper over," where the outer leaves dry to a paperlike texture and protect the inside of the head.

Though it is possible to keep cabbage with less time and attention than required by these methods, some spoilage is likely. One such traditional method was to simply pull cabbages and pile them in a windrow in the field without any trimming or careful stacking. A layer of hay 2 or 3 feet thick was thrown on top. In the winter when they were dug out they would often be frozen, but if used immediately they would still be good.

If stored cabbage should start to go bad because of a warm spell or any other reason, it can be saved by making sauerkraut, or by freezing, or drying.

***Moisture Content***   The moisture content of cabbage varies considerably with the growing season and the way it was stored. A high moisture content means no extra liquid will be needed when making sauerkraut. It also means the cabbage will not fry or sauté well, because it will stew in its own juices. Before frying cabbage, recipes sometimes recommend sprinkling chopped or shredded cabbage with salt, letting it sit for a while, and then squeezing it to remove moisture. This step is unnecessary when cabbage is already somewhat dry. Since stored winter cabbage tends to get drier with time, it is excellent for frying or sautéeing. If recipes requiring this step are prepared only in winter, the use of salt can be avoided entirely. (In stir-frying the moisture content does not matter, as the quick, high heat seals moisture in.)

***Preventing Strong Odors or Digestive Upsets***   Cabbage is sometimes avoided because of its reputation for giving off strong smells while cooking, or for causing gas and stomach upsets. These problems are due more to the cooking method than the cabbage itself. When cabbage is overcooked in a lot of water at high temperatures its sulfur compounds break down, causing odors and digestive upsets. But if it is steamed, or stewed in a minimum of water at moderate temperatures for 10 to 15 minutes, or only until it is tender, these problems will not develop. Cabbage cooked by baking, sautéeing, or stir-frying is problem free. Preparations containing liquids, like soups and stews, can be troublesome, especially when reheated, and cabbage is not a good choice for use in soup stock. However, it is good when added to soups or stews just a few minutes before serving.

# CABBAGE RECIPES

### *Coleslaw (Cold Slaw)*                    (Makes 6–8 medium servings.)

*1 small cabbage, shredded* (May be green or red, or some of each.)
*1 cup coleslaw dressing* (See recipes below.)
Optional, and add according to taste:
*scallions, chives, or onion, minced*
*dill leaves, parsley, or other herbs, minced*
*carrot or other vegetables, grated*
*apple or pear, grated or chopped*
*pinch of herb seeds (celery, dill, anise, caraway)*

Combine the cabbage and optional ingredients. Mix with the coleslaw dressing, and chill for about an hour before serving.

Coleslaw keeps better than most salads, and usually still tastes good after a day in the refrigerator.

## Basic Coleslaw Dressing

(Makes about 1 cup.)

1 cup mayonnaise, yogurt, or sweet
or sour cream (Half mayonnaise
and half yogurt is good.)
1–2 tablespoons vinegar, or lemon
juice

1 teaspoon prepared mustard, or
¼ teaspoon dry mustard
¼ teaspoon honey, or sugar
¼ teaspoon salt, optional
dash pepper (black or red)
1 tablespoon catsup or tomato
paste, optional

Combine all ingredients thoroughly, then taste and adjust seasonings.

## Old Fashioned Coleslaw Dressing

(Makes about 1 cup.)

¼ cup vinegar
¼ cup water
2 eggs, slightly beaten
1 tablespoon butter, or other fat

1–2 teaspoons honey, or sugar
½ teaspoon celery seed, optional
½ teaspoon salt, optional

Use a small double boiler, or a bowl set in a pan of boiling water. (One old cookbook suggests using a bowl that fits into the top of a teakettle.) Mix the vinegar and water and add them to the beaten eggs. Then add the butter, honey or sugar, celery seeds, and salt. Stir constantly over boiling water until the mixture thickens. Let this dressing cool completely before mixing with the slaw.

## Hot Slaw

(Makes 6–8 side servings.)

1 small cabbage or part of a larger
cabbage, chopped or shredded
4 tablespoons butter, or bacon fat
¾ cup vinegar

¼ cup water
dash cayenne pepper
1 clove garlic, mashed or minced
fine, optional

Put the cabbage in a heat proof container. Heat the butter or fat, vinegar, water, pepper, and garlic to a full boil. Pour boiling hot over the cabbage and cover immediately. Let sit 5 to 10 minutes, and serve as a vegetable side dish.

Leftovers should be reheated only enough to melt the butter or bacon fat and warm the mixture.

## Colcannon (Scottish)

(Makes 6–8 dinner servings.)

4–5 medium potatoes, cubed
2 carrots, cut in pieces, optional
1 turnip, or piece of rutabaga, cubed,
optional

1 small cabbage or part of a
larger cabbage, shredded
2 tablespoons butter
1 tablespoon soy sauce
pepper, salt, optional

Cook the potatoes, carrots and turnip together in as little water as possible. When they are tender (20 to 30 minutes), mash them with a potato masher. Meanwhile cook the cabbage in another pot until just tender (10 to 15 minutes). Drain the cabbage and stir it into the mashed potato mixture. If it is dry, add cabbage liquid. Season with the butter, soy sauce, and pepper and salt. Serve hot. Colcannon is made from vegetables most commonly stored in root cellars, and so is eminently practical in winter. It has, as well, an exceptionally enticing flavor.

*Kale or Collards Colcannon*   Cook and chop kale or collard greens and use in this mixture instead of cabbage.

*Rumbledethumps*   (Scottish and English) Make colcannon using only the potatoes and cabbage. Season the mixture with a small minced or grated onion, pepper, and salt. Put it into a greased baking dish and sprinkle grated cheese on top. Bake in a hot oven until the cheese is melted and bubbly. Leftover colcannon can also be baked in this way.

*Cabbage Chops*   (India) Make colcannon using only the potatoes and cabbage. Season with a little minced onion, ½ teaspoon paprika, 1 teaspoon turmeric, and 1 teaspoon minced fresh ginger root, if available. Make small, flattened cakes or patties and sauté in oil or fat until browned on both sides. (Leftover Scottish colcannon can also be fried as patties. Mix in an egg if desired.)

*Cauliflower Chops*   Cook and chop cauliflower and use instead of cabbage to make "chops."

### *How to Stuff Cabbage Rolls*          (For about 6 medium servings.)

*1 medium cabbage*                    *1 stuffing recipe* (From recipes below.)

Cut the core out of the cabbage head and set it, core side down, on a rack over boiling water. Cover and steam about 10 minutes, or until the outer leaves are pliable. Separate and remove the leaves without tearing them. After several layers are removed, return the cabbage to the steamer for another few minutes to soften more leaves. About 12 pliable leaves are needed. If the heavy midrib remains stiff it can be pared down to the same thickness as the rest of the leaf. Very large leaves can sometimes be cut in half, the midrib removed, and then used to make two cabbage rolls.

To stuff the rolls, lay a narrow mound of stuffing across the stem end of the leaf, fold over the stem end, then fold in the two sides, and roll, starting from the stem (rib) end, to make a neat package. To divide the stuffing evenly, lay out all 12 leaves and put stuffing on each before rolling them. Set the rolls seam side down to cook, and they will not unroll. Cook as described in the stuffing recipes that follow.

*Steps for stuffing a cabbage leaf*

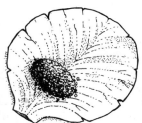  

Put several spoons of stuffing near the stem end of the leaf. Make a longish mound.

Roll the rib end of the leaf over the stuffing. Then fold over the sides.

Roll from rib end, making a neat package. The thin part of the leaf is on the outside.

## Creole Cabbage Stuffing      (Makes 6 medium servings—12 rolls.)

1 tablespoon lard, or other fat
2 onions, chopped small
1 pound sausage (Chaurice is the Creole sausage, but any fresh, highly seasoned variety is good.)
2 tablespoons ham or lean bacon, minced
1 cup cabbage (about), minced

1 clove garlic, minced
1 tomato, chopped, or ¼ cup stewed tomatoes or tomato sauce
1 bay leaf
1 teaspoon fresh, or ½ teaspoon dried thyme
2 tablespoons parsley, minced
hot red pepper, to taste

Heat the lard in a frying pan. Add the onion and sauté until lightly browned. Remove sausage from casings if necessary, and add to pan, with the ham, cabbage, and garlic. Stir to break the sausage into small pieces and fry about 5 minutes. Add the tomato, thyme, parsley and red pepper. Simmer uncovered for 10 minutes or until thickened enough for stuffing. Remove the bay leaf. Cool the mixture till it can be handled, then make cabbage rolls as described above.

Put the rolls seam side down in a single layer in a large frying pan with a lid, or in a large pot. Add several tablespoons of water, cover, and simmer 30 minutes. Good served plain or with a cream sauce, and rice or noodles.

## Sweet and Sour Jewish Style Cabbage Stuffing      (Makes 6 medium servings—12 rolls.)

1 pound lean ground beef
1 small onion, minced
½ cup cooked rice
pepper, salt, to taste

2 cups stewed tomatoes
2 tablespoons vinegar
2 tablespoons honey, or sugar

---

### CABBAGE IDEAS

**Cabbage Seasonings** Cabbage is particularly good with herb seeds. Anise, dill, and caraway seeds, and juniper berries are especially complementary. Tart flavors such as tomato, sour apple, or a splash of vinegar also go well. Cured meats like ham, bacon, sausage, or corned beef are other favorites with cabbage.

**Cabbage Instead of Lettuce** Young tender raw cabbage is as versatile as lettuce in salads. It is good in every combination from tossed green salads to aspics. Small, rounded cabbage leaves are very nice for holding a serving of a hearty potato or egg salad. Wedges of cabbage are good with any kind of dressing. Mature winter cabbage is best in salads if it is chopped small or shredded before it is added.

**Cabbage and Fish Salad** Flake leftover cooked fish and mix with shredded or finely chopped raw cabbage. Add other shredded or chopped salad vegetables to taste, and moisten with mayonnaise. Sprinkle with paprika if desired.

**Stir-fried Cabbage** Shredded or thinly sliced cabbage is very good in many stir-fried mixtures. To stir-fry alone, heat lard, chicken fat, or oil very hot. If wished, stir in minced garlic. Add the cabbage and stir-fry 1 minute or until it brightens in color. Add several tablespoons of soup stock or water, cover, and cook 3 to 5 minutes or until the cabbage is just tender. Pepper, salt, or other seasonings are optional. (Refer to the STIR-FRYING section.)

**Baked Cabbage** Grease a baking dish and put pre-cooked, chopped or shredded cabbage in it. Leftover cabbage or frozen and thawed cabbage can be used, if desired. Add a little light cream, soup stock, or water. Sprinkle the top with breadcrumbs, grated cheese, and dots of butter. Bake in a hot oven until browned on top, about 20 minutes.

**Creamed Cabbage** Cook shredded or chopped cabbage until just tender, and drain if necessary. Make a cream sauce. (Refer to recipe in the MILK section.) Just before serving mix the hot cabbage with the hot cream sauce. This mixture can be baked in the same way as BAKED CABBAGE, above. Seasonings such as dill leaves or seeds, celery leaves or seeds, and onion or garlic are good.

**Cabbage Pie, or Pirog** Roll out bread dough and line a deep pie dish with it. Roll out dough to use for an upper crust also. To make the filling sauté chopped cabbage and a chopped onion in butter. If moisture collects in the pan add a tablespoon of flour. Add several chopped, hard boiled eggs to the sautéed cabbage. Season to taste with paprika, pepper, dill or caraway, and salt if desired, to taste. Fill the pie, seal the upper crust, let rise a few minutes, and bake in a moderate, 375°F oven about 30 minutes, or until browned. For a pirog, roll out bread dough in a rectangular shape. Make a long mound of the filling, and fold or roll the dough to cover it. Set seam side down on a lightly greased baking sheet. Bake about 30 minutes, in a moderate oven.

Mix the ground beef, onion, rice, pepper, and salt. Use to make cabbage rolls as described above. Put the rolls in a pot seam side down. They can be several layers deep. Add the tomatoes, vinegar, and sweetening. Simmer gently, without stirring, for 30 to 40 minutes. Shake the pot several times to blend ingredients. When about half done, taste and, if necessary, adjust amounts of vinegar and sweetening for the sweet and sour flavor.

These rolls are improved when reheated on the second day. Delicious with bread, potatoes, or any starchy food that will soak up the juice.

### Hungarian Style Cabbage Stuffing  (Makes 6 medium servings—12 rolls.)

| | |
|---|---|
| ¼ cup raw rice | ½ teaspoon salt, optional |
| 1 pound lean ground pork | 2 tablespoons lard, or other fat |
| ½ pound lean ground beef, optional | 2 tablespoons flour |
| 2 cloves garlic, crushed | 1 quart sauerkraut, drained |
| 2 medium onions, minced | ½ cup tomato juice, or soup stock |
| 1 egg | ½ pound ham, cut in small pieces |
| ½ teaspoon pepper | ½ cup sour cream, optional |
| 2 tablespoons paprika | |

Cook the rice until about half done, 10 to 20 minutes, and drain. Mix with the pork, beef, garlic, half of the onions, egg, pepper, paprika, and salt. Make the rolls as described above. Roll loosely to allow the stuffing to expand. (Make extra rolls rather than packing them too tightly.)

In a large, deep frying pan or pot large enough to fit rolls in one layer, sauté the other half of the onions until golden. Stir in the flour, blending completely. Stir in the sauerkraut, tomato juice or stock, and ham. There should be about enough liquid to cover ingredients. If not, add water or soup stock or the juice from the sauerkraut. Bring to a boil, cover, and simmer over low heat for 5 minutes. Then make hollows in the sauerkraut mixture with a spoon and set the cabbage rolls into them. Cover, and simmer over very low heat for 1 hour. If desired, spread sour cream over the top just before serving.

***Unstuffed Cabbage Casserole*** Blanch chopped or shredded cabbage until limp, or use frozen and thawed cabbage. Make layers in a greased casserole or baking dish, alternating the cabbage and one of the above stuffing mixtures. Add a little tomato juice or other liquid, and bake covered in a moderate, 350°F oven about 40 minutes.

## Scandinavian Brown Cabbage Soup (Makes 6–8 medium bowls.)

*1 medium cabbage, shredded* (One with low moisture content is best.)
*¼ cup butter*
*2 tablespoons honey, or brown sugar*

*1 quart soup stock* (Beef stock is excellent.)
*½ teaspoon pepper*
*½ teaspoon allspice*
*salt, optional*

Melt the butter in a soup pot, add the cabbage and fry it over medium heat, stirring frequently, until it is browned, about 15 to 20 minutes. The cabbage will shrink and get limp before it browns. When ready, stir in the sweetening. Add the stock, pepper, allspice, and salt. Bring to a boil and simmer 10 to 15 minutes. Noodles or the LITTLE DUMPLINGS, in the LAMB AND MUTTON section, can be cooked in the soup to make a hearty dish.

This soup is best the first day, as it tends to get strong in flavor after reheating.

**Brussels Sprouts Brown Soup** Use chopped Brussels sprouts, or the center part of the tops of the Brussels sprouts plants instead of cabbage. The Brussels sprouts will cook faster than the cabbage.

## Spiced Pickled Cabbage for Canning (Makes 4–6 quarts.)

*2 small cabbages, or 6 to 8 quarts finely shredded* (Red cabbage is best.)
*⅓ cup plain or pickling salt* (Refer to the PICKLING section.)
*¼ cup mustard seed*
*2 quarts vinegar* (Wine vinegar is very nice.)

*½ cup honey or 1 cup brown sugar*
*¼ cup pickling spices* (Or a mixture of whole cloves, mace, allspice, peppercorns, celery seed, and stick cinnamon.)

In a large bowl, sprinkle layers of cabbage with salt. Mix well and let sit 24 hours in a cool place. Drain and set out in the sun on a rack for 2 or 3 hours, or put in a cloth bag and hang over the sink for about 6 hours. The cabbage should become quite dry in this time. Mix the mustard seed with the cabbage, and pack in clean canning jars, leaving ½ inch headroom.

Meanwhile, heat the vinegar, sweetening, and spices to a boil and cook 5 minutes. Let cool, then strain to remove the spices. (If preferred, a spice bag can be used.) Pour the vinegar mixture over the cabbage in the jars, dividing it evenly between them. Run a knife around the perimeter of the jar to remove bubbles. If necessary add plain vinegar to fill the jars, leaving ¼ inch headroom. Adjust the lids and process in a boiling water bath, 15 minutes for pints, 20 minutes for quarts. Since the jars start out cool, place them in warm, not boiling water. Start to time when water boils. (Refer to the CANNING section for further directions.)

This pickle can also be packed in tightly closed containers and stored in a cool place without cooking or canning. It will keep 1–2 months.

***Spiced Red Cabbage with Chestnuts and Raisins***    Drain the liquid from 1 pint of *Spiced Pickled Red Cabbage*. (The pickling liquid is delicious for pickling eggs. Refer to the EGG section.) In a saucepan combine the cabbage with 1 cup cooked chestnuts, ¼ cup raisins and 1 cup water. Mix 1 tablespoon flour with ¼ cup water and add. Heat, stirring often, until the sauce has thickened. Serve hot. It is very good with pork chops or roast pork.

Note: For sauerkraut directions, refer to MAKING SAUERKRAUT, in the SAUERKRAUT section.

# CANNING

THE CANNING PROCESS WAS INVENTED WHEN THE FRENCH GOVernment offered a prize to the inventor of a practical method for food preservation. Nicolas Appert won the prize in 1810 when he invented a way of sealing food in glass containers and cooking them in boiling water. That process is essentially the same as modern boiling water bath canning. The heat of the cooking destroys enzymes and microorganisms that would cause food spoilage, and the airtight vacuum seal prevents recontamination from exposure to air.

Since then, years of research and experience have established exact requirements for home canning most foods. When modern canning instructions are followed carefully, safe, high quality canned foods are assured.

## REQUIREMENTS FOR CANNING HIGH- AND LOW-ACID FOODS

The most important fact to know about canning is that high- and low-acid foods have different canning requirements. Acidic foods, those with a pH of 4.6 or below, including most fruits, tomatoes, and pickles, are safe to can at 212°F (100°C), or at boiling temperature. Low-acid foods, those with a pH above 4.6, including vegetables, meat, and fish, must be canned in a pressure canner so as to maintain a temperature of 240°F (121°C). The reason for the difference is that the toxins that cause botulism poisoning cannot develop in acidic foods, but can develop in low-acid foods unless very high temperatures are used when processing them. (See BOTULISM POISONING, below.)

Most foods fall clearly into either the high-acid or low-acid group, but there are some borderline cases. All home canning guides clearly state which foods are acidic enough for boiling water bath canning, and which require pressure canning. Where there is doubt about a food, such as low-acid tomatoes, lemon juice or citric acid can be added to increase acidity. (Refer to the STORAGE directions for each food section for the necessary quantities and precautions.)

Many people find it practical to can only acidic foods, such as fruit, tomatoes, sauerkraut, relish, and pickles. Often, vegetables and meat are frozen, or perhaps dried, or salt cured. This eliminates the need for a pressure canner and the more painstaking processing it requires.

**_Botulism Poisoning_** The bacteria that cause botulism poisoning are confusing because they are quite harmless in some circumstances, and highly dangerous in others. _Botulinum spores_ are widely distributed in the environment, are not toxic themselves, and ordinarily do not cause any trouble. However, under certain circumstances the spores germinate and multiply to produce a highly poisonous toxin. In stored foods, these spores must either be prevented from germinating and producing the toxin, or they must be destroyed.

Botulinum spores are difficult to destroy, and it takes a combination of high temperature (240°F in home canning, usually) and time to kill them. There are, however, many substances and conditions that prevent their germination and growth. Most stored foods are safe because the spores cannot grow in them for one reason or another. They cannot grow when sufficient acid is present, with a pH of 4.6 or lower. Nor can they grow in concentrations of salt above 10%, and of sugar above 50%. Such physical conditions as temperatures below freezing, and dehydration or lack of moisture also prevent growth. The spores will grow in a vacuum, or partial vacuum, where it is moist and warm. Conditions inside a sealed can or jar of a low-acid food are perfect for the germination and growth of the botulinum spores and the production of poison. For this reason the spores must be killed when low-acid foods are canned. This requires heating every bit of the food to a temperature of 240°F, including the inside of food chunks, for an adequate time. The time given for processing each low-acid food in a pressure canner is carefully tested to make absolutely sure this happens.

Poisons produced by the botulinum spores are easier to destroy than the spores themselves, since boiling at 212°F will destroy the poison. This is why canning instructions say to boil home canned, low-acid foods for 15 to 20 minutes before eating them as an extra safety precaution. Remember that the boiling will not affect the spores, and they will still produce toxins if conditions are right—for example, if the food is recanned improperly.

Another dangerous aspect of botulism poisoning is that there may be no obvious signs of spoilage. Sometimes bubbling and foam, a swelled can, a spurt of liquid when the can or jar is opened, or a strange look or smell before or during cooking will indicate trouble, but these signs are not always present. If there are any suspicions that botulism toxins are present, destroy the food so that no person or animal can eat it. *DO NOT* touch or taste it. Burn the food or bury it in a deep hole, or boil it, jar, lids, and all, and then throw it out.

Acidic foods should also be carefully destroyed should they mold, because certain molds raise the pH enough for botulism poisons to develop.

A generation ago in some areas people regularly canned low-acid foods at boiling temperature apparently without botulism problems. Perhaps there were very few botulism bacteria present in those regions, or perhaps those people were just lucky. It is neither safe nor sensible to depend on past records of safety. There is now so much movement of people, food, and soil that the botulinum spores are sure to be present everywhere, whether they once were or not—and considering what is known about botulism—who wants to depend on luck?

However, worries about botulism poisoning should not discourage people from home canning. Actual cases of poisoning are very rare, and huge quantities of food are canned at home every year without any hint of a problem. As long as the danger is understood, and each food is properly processed, canning is an excellent and safe way to preserve low-acid, as well as high-acid, foods.

## CANNING AT HIGH ALTITUDES

The altitude at which food is canned will affect the processing requirements. Because air pressure decreases with higher altitudes, water boils at temperatures below 212°F. At altitudes above 1,000 feet boiling water bath canning is done at a lower temperature, and to compensate, processing times must be increased. Decreased air pressure also affects pressure canner processing, but a temperature of 240°F must still be reached inside the canner. To do so, the canner's pressure is set higher at altitudes over 2,000 feet. Processing times remain the same. The following chart gives adjustments at various altitudes.

*Altitude Adjustments for Boiling Water Bath Canning*

| Feet above sea level | If processing time required is 21 minutes or less add: | If processing time required is 22 minutes or longer, add: |
|---|---|---|
| 1–2,000 | 2 minutes | 4 minutes |
| 2,001–4,000 | 4 minutes | 8 minutes |
| 4,001–6,000 | 6 minutes | 12 minutes |
| 6,001–8,000 | 8 minutes | 16 minutes |

*Altitude Adjustments for Pressure Canning*

| Feet above sea level | When 11 pounds pressure is required at sea level use: |
|---|---|
| 2,000–4,000 | 12 pounds |
| 4,001–6,000 | 13 pounds |
| 6,001–8,000 | 14 pounds |

## CANNING CONTAINERS

Glass jars are the most popular containers for home canning. It is possible to use tin cans, but there are more complications. For information about them, see the references at the end of this section.

Jars made especially for canning are often called "mason" jars, after their inventor, John L. Mason. The commonly used sizes are pints and quarts, but half-pint jars are handy for foods to be used in small amounts. Although half-gallon mason jars are sold, their use is not advised for boiling water bath or pressure canning. They are too big for safe processing, and most canning instructions do not give processing times for them. Pint and quart jars come in standard and wide mouth sizes. The wide mouth jars are best for packing large pieces of food.

One of the nicest things about canning jars is that they are reusable year after year if well cared for. However, they cannot be handled too roughly, and must be protected from drastic temperature changes. (Cold jars may crack if boiling liquids are poured into them, and very hot jars may do so if set on very cold surfaces or in cold drafts.) Another requirement when canning in glass jars is a dark storage place, as exposure to light will gradually reduce the food's quality.

***Canning Lids*** Modern canning lids are usually two-piece, screw band metal lids. The actual lid is a round, flat disc with a rubber-like sealing compound around the edge. This lid can be used only once. The other part is the band, or ring, which screws onto the jar and holds the lid in place during processing and sealing. These rings are reusable as long as they remain free of rust or corrosion, and screw on easily. One or the other of the two lid sizes, regular and wide mouth, will fit most styles and sizes of modern canning jar, regardless of brand.

There may be small variations among the canning lid brands, but they basically all work in the same ways. They must be boiled in water for about 5 minutes to soften their sealing compound before they are set on the filled jar. Follow the directions that come with the jar lids. The rings are then screwed down firmly, but not fully tightened. The lids then have enough give so that air escapes during processing, but they still hold the lid in place so that a vacuum seal forms as the jars cool. One person's idea of firmly tightened may be different from another's, so some leeway in the tightness of the canning lids can be allowed. Very tight lids could cause breakage during processing, or the lids could buckle and not seal, though this is unusual. When the jars have cooled completely the rings should be removed and reused.

Some old style lids, such as zinc ones with porcelain liners, and glass lids on jars with wire bales, are still in use. Both require new rubber rings every time they are used. These lids are only partially sealed before processing, and the final seal is made when the jars are removed from the canner. Directions for using such lids usually come with the rubber rings.

***Recycling Canning Containers*** Using old jars or bottles for canning that originally contained commercially processed foods is condemned in most canning guides. However, many people have successfully made limited use of some of these containers, and the practice is not going to disappear. Instead of dismissing the whole idea, why not explore the circumstances where this has worked and those where it has not?

Only jars that originally contained food should be considered for recycling. But because commercial food jars are not always made as strongly and carefully as regulation canning jars, their use is limited. They should never be used for pressure canning as the stresses are simply too great.

There are two kinds of jars with reuse value. First, there are those jars, especially mayonnaise jars, that will fit to standard canning lids. These have been used quite successfully for boiling water bath canning. They must be pint or quart sizes so that the processing time will be standard. There is the possibility that a jar will crack during canning, or that a lid will not seal properly, but the same thing can happen with regulation canning jars, and must always be watched for. Any jar that fails to seal after one or two tries should be thrown out.

To check a jar for flaws, run a finger around the rim, feeling for irregularities or nicks. Then set the jar upside down on a flat surface, and see if it touches all the way around the rim. Test the canning lid and ring together on the jar to make sure they screw down firmly. Sometimes a ring will fit well by itself, but when screwed down with the lid it will not work. If a jar passes all these tests it can be tried for boiling water bath canning. One experienced user of recycled jars says they are more dependable than the old tinted mason jars that some people still use.

The second kind of commercial jars with some limited reuse value are those whose screw-on lids have a plasticized sealing compound around the rim for making a vacuum seal. These jars can only be used for open kettle canning of very acidic foods, or very sweet foods, such as jams, jellies, pickles, concentrated fruit juices, or maple syrup. They are not safe for boiling water bath canning, because the lids will not necessarily form as effective a seal as regulation canning lids. Also, the shapes and sizes of these jars are too irregular for accurate timing.

Before using these jars for open kettle canning, check the lids and jars carefully. They must both be in perfect shape. The lids should have no scratches, rust, or dents, and the sealing compound around the inside of the rim should be unmarred. Lids that have been pried off the jar cannot be reused.

Always boil the jars and lids before using them. Then follow the directions under OPEN KETTLE CANNING, below. Check the seal after the jars have cooled. Usually the lids will look or feel slightly concave. If the contents are liquid, turn the jar upside down and watch for a stream of bubbles from around the inside jar rim, indicating a faulty seal. Random bubbles are not significant. Do not try the lids, since that would break the seal. Later on, if any signs of mold or other spoilage should appear, throw out the jar and its contents. It is best to reuse this kind of commercial lid only once, although some of them will reseal several times.


## CANNING METHODS

It is very important to use the correct canning method for each kind of food. As described above, all low-acid foods are canned in a pressure canner, while most acidic foods are canned in a boiling water bath canner. Two other canning methods, steam bath canning (not to be confused with pressure canning), and open kettle canning, are also described below. These are used only for canning acidic foods. Another food storage method used for a few very acidic fruits is cold water canning, but it is not really canning in spite of the name. (Refer to COLD WATER CANNING, in the COLD STORAGE section.) The outmoded method called oven canning described in some old cookbooks is never safe to use.

***Boiling Water Bath Canning*** This canning method works by submerging jars of food, ready for processing, in boiling water, and cooking them at a full boil for the required time. It is the preferred method for canning fruit, tomatoes, and pickles.

A deep canning kettle or a large, deep pot with a rack and a lid is necessary. The pot must be deep enough to hold the jars on the rack, 1 or 2 inches of water above them, and about 2 inches of air space to prevent boiling over. A pot for quarts should be 11 to 12 inches deep, and 9 to 10 inches deep for pints. Some commercial canning kettles are not deep enough, so measure before buying. A kettle that is too

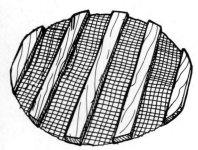

*A hardware cloth rack. Use with wood strips down.*

shallow will probably not seal jars properly. The racks that come with canners are usually basket shaped, with high or folding handles for lifting all the jars at once. A rack can be improvised by placing several old canning lid rings in the pot and setting a round, cake cooling rack on them. A more permanent rack can be cut from hardware cloth (small mesh wire fencing) to fit the pot, then stapled to strips of wood for support. With an improvised rack, a pair of tongs is esssential for lifting jars out of the boiling water. Special canning tongs can be purchased, but some other kinds of tongs may work. Try them ahead of time to make sure. It is also helpful, but not essential, to have a wide mouth funnel for filling jars without getting food on the rims. Other equipment that may be needed will already be in most kitchens.

To begin canning, fill the kettle about half full of water. If the food to be canned is hot packed (see CANNING, STEP BY STEP, below), bring the water to a boil and have extra water boiling as well. If the food is raw packed, have warm water in the kettle. When the jars have been filled and the lids adjusted according to directions, set them in the water on the rack. The jars should not touch each other, or the sides of the kettle. Add enough water of the correct temperature to cover the jar tops by 1 to 2 inches, pouring the water around the jars, not directly onto the lids. Cover and bring to a boil. Begin timing after the water has reached a full boil, and keep the water boiling for the entire processing time. (Adjust the processing time for high altitudes as described on the chart above.) When processing is complete, remove the jars from the kettle and set them in a draft-free place where they will not be disturbed for 12 hours. (See CANNING, STEP BY STEP, below, for details of preparing, packing, and storing.)

***Steam Bath Canning***   This method worked in the same way as boiling water bath canning, except that it used the heat of steam from the boiling water. It is labeled unsafe in modern canning guides because regulation processing times have not been developed. As well, in a home canning situation it is impossible to make sure that the steam reaches and remains at the temperature of boiling water.

***Open Kettle Canning***   Open kettle canning is accomplished by pouring boiling hot food into hot, sterile jars, and sealing them immediately with sterile lids. The method is successful only with very acidic fruit juices, syrup, jam, and jelly. It is not a substitute for most boiling water bath canning, and is discouraged in modern canning guides. There is a possibility of contamination when the food is exposed to the air before sealing, and the lids do not seal well if the food cools too much when the jars are filled. At high altitudes the boiling temperature is lower, making it more difficult to have everything hot enough to seal properly. If jars do not seal, spoilage, such as mold or rotting, may occur, and the food must be discarded.

The advantages of open kettle canning are that it saves time and fuel, and makes it feasible to can one or two jars of fruit juice, syrup, or preserves without setting up a full-scale canning operation. Very acidic fruit juices, maple syrup, and other syrups, and jams and jellies may be canned by the open kettle method or by the more secure boiling water bath method, except for some jelly, whose texture will be damaged by the extra processing.

### Steps for Open Kettle Canning

1 Boil jars and lids at least 5 minutes to soften the sealing compound on the lids. Keep jars and lids at a simmer until they are to be used.

2 Have the liquid to be canned at a boil. Remove only 1 or 2 jars from their boiling water. Fill them immediately almost to the brim with the boiling liquid. If necessary, wipe jar rims with a paper or cloth towel dampened by dipping in boiling water. Remove lids from their boiling water with tongs and seal immediately. Screw lids down firmly.

3 Turn the jars upside down for about 30 seconds, letting the hot liquid reheat the inside of the lid. Let the jars cool, and test for a seal as for any canning procedure.

4 Success depends upon having everything ready, and then working quickly. It is important to fill and seal only 1 or 2 jars at a time so that nothing can cool before it is sealed. Tongs, pot holders, and other equipment should be laid out before beginning.

**Pressure Canning** The only safe way to can low-acid foods is in a steam pressure canner. Only a pressure canner can reach and maintain the required temperature of 240°F. (See REQUIREMENTS FOR CANNING HIGH- AND LOW-ACID FOODS, above.) Pressure cookers that are not designed for canning are not recommended. They are usually too small, and do not heat up and cool off at the same rate as the canners. If one must be used, add 20 minutes at 11 pounds pressure to the required processing time. Large steam pressure canners are expensive, but will last for many years if properly cared for.

Many brands and styles of pressure canners are available. They operate differently, so their enclosed instructions must be followed. Note especially the directions for cleaning the safety valve and petcock openings. A piece of string is normally pulled through them after every use. If the canner has a dial gauge, it *must* be checked every year to ensure its accuracy. The canner's manufacturer, or, in the U.S., a local Agricultural Extension Office, should be able to check it.

Many people prefer to freeze low-acid foods rather than can them. The advantages of canning are that canned foods are stored without electricity and without the fear of power failure or unplugged freezers, and they can be used immediately without thawing.

The basic procedure for pressure canning is as follows. Put several inches of water in the canner. Heat it to a boil if the jars are filled with very hot food, otherwise, just warm the water. Set the filled jars, with their lids adjusted, on the rack in the canner. Follow the directions that came with the canner for all procedures, including closing the lid, venting air, raising pressure to the necessary level, and maintaining it, cooling naturally, opening the vent, and finally removing the cover and the jars.

Most canning at sea level is done at 11 pounds of pressure. If the altitude is above 2,000 feet, adjust the pounds of pressure used according to the high-altitude chart, above, to maintain a temperature of 240°F.

## CANNING, STEP BY STEP

1   PREPARE CANNING LIDS AND JARS   Check each jar to make sure there are no nicks or cracks. Run a finger around the rim to feel for flaws. Inspect lids to make sure they are perfect. Wash and rinse the jars. If necessary for the canning method used, bring them to a boil in a pot of water and leave them in it to stay hot. Follow the package directions for the lids, or wash and boil them for 5 minutes. The lids and jars can be boiled in the same pot and left there till needed.

2   PREPARE FOOD AND FILL JARS   (Information for canning a specific food is given under the Storage heading in each food section. Also included is the feasibility of canning.)

Prepare food just before it is processed, one kettle or canner load at a time.

There are two methods for packing food in jars—raw pack and hot pack. Delicate foods that break or crush easily, such as fresh fruits, are usually raw packed. Dense foods that take a long time to heat through are usually hot packed, and foods that must be cooked in preparation are also hot packed. Some foods can be packed either way.

*Raw Pack*   This method is sometimes called cold pack. Prepare the raw food by washing, trimming, peeling, coring, or cutting as necessary. Pack the pieces of food close together in clean jars. Leave as little space as possible between pieces without crushing or damaging the food. Add hot liquid to fill the jar, unless the food's own juices will fill it. Boiling water, stock, syrup, or a pickling liquid may be used. Leave the required headroom both when packing the food and adding liquid.

*Hot Pack*   Prepare the food as necessary, and cook or partially cook it according to the directions for that food. For foods with a processing time of less than 10 minutes, pack or pour the hot food into jars that have been kept hot after being boiled for 10 minutes. (The water bath canner may be used to do this and the water saved for use in processing.) Pack pieces of food close together without crushing. Add boiling hot cooking liquid or water to fill the jars, if necessary, leaving the required headroom both when packing the food and adding the liquid. It may be easier to ladle foods such as soup and fruit sauces into jars. A wide mouth funnel will facilitate ladling or pouring, and will keep the jar rims clean.

3   REMOVE BUBBLES, CLEAN RIMS, ADJUST LIDS   Run a plastic knife or similar tool, such as a spatula's plastic handle around the inside of the jar between the food and the glass to dislodge bubbles. A shake or light tap on the table will also help settle the food and loosen bubbles. Check the headroom and add more liquid if necessary. Wipe

the jar rim with a damp cloth or paper towel, making sure no food or juice is stuck to the rim. Set the lids in place and tighten according to their package directions. If two-piece screw lids are used, set the flat lid piece on the jar with the sealing compound against the rim. Screw on the ring firmly but do not use full strength to tighten it.

4   PROCESS THE FILLED JARS   Using the method appropriate for the food, process the jars for the required time. (See CANNING METHODS, and chart for altitude adjustments, above.)

5   COOL JARS, CHECK LIDS   Carefully remove the hot jars from the canner, and set them in a draft-free place where they will not be disturbed. After 12 to 24 hours remove the rings from two-piece lids. Check the seal on each jar. Most metal lids will be slightly concave, or sunken in, if they are sealed. If the jars are sticky or have food on the outsides, wash them in warm water, then rinse and dry.

6   STORE IN A COOL DARK DRY PLACE   The ideal storage place for canned goods is dark, dry, and above freezing but below 50°F. High temperatures and exposure to light destroy some of the vitamins in canned food. Light can also bleach out color. Dampness can cause metal lids to rust and lose their seals. If a dark storage area is unavailable, keep the jars in boxes, or wrap or otherwise cover them. If they cannot be kept cool enough, use canned goods before hot summer weather sets in. In winter, store them away from heat sources, but also prevent freezing, as this may cause the seal to break.

Properly canned and stored foods will keep indefinitely, but they gradually lose quality, so it is best to eat them within a year.

7   USING CANNED FOODS   Check canned foods for signs of spoilage before using. Is the seal loose or broken? Is there mold, gas, slime, or a spurt of liquid when the seal is broken? Does the food smell bad, or look discolored? (This does not apply to fruit that darkens at the top of the jar. See below.) If any of these signs are present, destroy the food as described below.

As a precaution, boil all home-canned, low-acid foods for 15 to 20 minutes before eating them. This is a final insurance against botulism poisoning, since boiling destroys any toxins. Leafy greens, corn, meat, poultry and seafoods need a full 20 minutes of boiling because of their density, but it can usually be incorporated into the normal food preparation. *The food should not be tasted before it has been boiled.* If there is a spurt of liquid when a jar is opened, or an odd smell, or a lot of foaming, when the food is boiled, it should be destroyed. These are also signs of botulism toxin production.

It is important to use the liquid surrounding canned foods, as many of the vitamins and minerals are in it. Liquid from canned vegetables and meats can be used for making soup or in mixed dishes, if it is not otherwise needed.

8   DESTROY SPOILED OR SUSPECT CANNED FOOD   Destroy such food without touching or tasting. It should not be given to animals. This is most important with low-acid canned foods. Spoiled food should be burned, buried deep, or boiled for 20 minutes and discarded.

## CANNING FRUIT

(Also refer to individual fruits, and CANNING FRUIT JUICE AND SAUCE, in the FRUITS section.)

Most fruit is acidic enough for boiling water bath canning. Some tomatoes and fruits may vary in acidity, so it is recommended that 2 tablespoons of lemon juice or ½ teaspoon of citric acid be added to each quart. If such a precaution could be necessary, it is noted in the canning instructions for the individual fruit.

***Sweetening Canned Fruit***    Fruit is commonly canned in a sweetened syrup, but this is not essential. Plain water or unsweetened fruit juice can be used instead. The addition of a sweetener helps to retain the fruit's color and, to some extent, its flavor and texture, but the amounts needed are much less than are usually recommended. Very, very light syrups can be used to good effect.

## LIQUID SYRUP
## FOR CANNING FRUIT

***Fruit Juice***    Any fruit juice with a compatible flavor can be used. Sweet juices go well with tart fruits, and tart juices go well with bland or sweet fruits. (Refer to COMBINING SWEET AND TART FRUITS in the FRUITS section.)

***Pectin***    Thin, homemade pectin can be used as the canning liquid for any fruit, but it is especially good with tart fruits. (Refer to the PECTIN section.)

***Very Light Syrup***    Use 2 to 3 tablespoons honey or sugar per quart of water. Include any juice collected while preparing the fruit. Use the cooking water if the fruit is hot packed.

***Light Syrup***    Use ¼ cup honey or ½ cup sugar per quart of water. Include any juice collected while preparing the fruit. Use the cooking water if the fruit is hot packed.

• Have ready about 1 cup of liquid per pint, or 2 cups per quart of fruit to be canned.

***Darkening and Other Difficulties with Canned Fruit***    The best way to prevent darkening of fruit is to prepare it in small batches, and pack and process it without delay. However, lemon juice or an ascorbic acid solution (1 teaspoon crystalline ascorbic acid in a cup of water) can be used as a dip for fruit pieces, or to sprinkle over peeled or cut sections. Avoid soaking fruit in water because of the loss of water-soluble nutrients.

Darkening of the top fruit in a jar is caused by too much headroom. The fruit will be good to eat if the jar's seal is tight and there are no signs of spoilage. If fruit floats in its jar, it may have been packed too loosely, or in a very heavy syrup, or the fruit may have been very ripe. Floating does not affect the fruit's eating quality, only its appearance. Often fruit that was hot packed looks better in the jar than raw packed fruit.

# CANNING PICKLES

(Also refer to individual pickle recipes.)

Most pickles and relishes are canned in a boiling water bath. They are acidic because vinegar has been used, or acid has been produced during fermentation. (Refer to the PICKLING section.) There is a variation for a few kinds of pickles, however, which should perhaps not be called canning. For this, pack vegetables raw with seasonings, and pour a boiling hot vinegar solution over them. Use at least 1 part vinegar to 1 part water. Then seal the jars, with no further processing, and store in a cool place. The flavor and texture of the raw vegetables are retained. The vegetables should be packed loosely enough to allow room for more liquid than usual. If using regular canning lids, leave the rings on the jars to ensure a tight seal. An example of this method is the *Hot Pepper Pickle* recipe, in the PEPPERS, HOT section.

# CANNING VEGETABLES

(Also refer to individual vegetables.) All vegetables, except tomatoes, must be pressure canned at 240°F. The hot pack method is usually recommended over the raw pack, because air is driven out of the food before processing, resulting in a better product. To save nutrients, the water used to prepare the vegetable should be used as the canning liquid. It is not necessary to add salt when canning vegetables.

Vegetable mixtures should be processed and timed according to the vegetable that requires the most time. Even when tomatoes are included, the mixture must be pressure processed as for the slowest cooking vegetable.

**Canning Leafy Greens** All leafy greens can be canned as for spinach. (Refer to the SPINACH section.) Greens that hold up well after long cooking are the best for canning, but it is generally better to freeze greens if possible. Dandelion greens and many wild greens can be canned, as well as Swiss chard, turnip tops, beet tops, and mustard greens.

# CANNING MEAT

(Also refer to individual meats.) All meat must be processed in a pressure canner. The tougher cuts of lean meat are best for canning, and make good stews, pot roasts, and casseroles. However, any cut of meat can be canned if most of the fat has been trimmed. Fat may give canned meat a strong taste, and it may also damage the sealing compound on some kinds of canning lids.

Meat from large animals (beef, veal, lamb, chevon, pork, and venison) must be boned, trimmed of fat and gristle, and cut to fit the canning jars. A solid piece can be canned, but usually stew sized pieces are used. Canned ground meat is best used in hash meat loaf, or in vegetable mixtures. However, patties, seasoned meatballs, and a few kinds of sausage are sometimes canned. The only variety meat that cans well is tongue.

Most people prefer to freeze meat. Freezing is faster and easier, and the quality is excellent for all cuts. The advantage of canning over freezing is that electricity is not required. In an emergency, frozen meat can be thawed and canned like fresh meat.

Straight sided, wide mouthed canning jars are the best for meat because the pieces can be easily packed and removed. Either hot pack or raw pack is possible for most kinds of plain meat, but raw pack may require heating the meat in the jars to 170°F before they are sealed and processed.

If meat mixtures, such as stews or soups, are canned, process them as for plain meat, unless a specific recipe states otherwise. Most canned meat is processed for the same length of time whether it has been hot or raw packed.

It is not necessary to add salt when canning meat. Salt can be added, if desired, before serving.

*Always* boil home canned meat for 20 minutes before tasting or serving it. (See USING CANNED FOODS, above.)

***Canning Poultry, Rabbit, and Small Game***   Mature stewing poultry, rabbits, and other small animals are better for canning than young, tender fryers. These meats can be canned with the leg bones left in, and the ribs, backbone and breast bone removed. Broth made from these bones can be used as the canning liquid. The skin can be left on poultry if desired. Pieces with skin are usually packed around the outside of the jar, to cushion the meat and protect it from compaction during canning. Skinned pieces are packed in the center.

## CANNING FISH, SHELLFISH AND ROE

Fish, shellfish and roe are the most difficult foods to can safely at home. They are very low in acid, they spoil quickly, and their texture is dense. Additionally, each kind of shellfish and most kinds of fish require individual procedures for safe processing. Freezing, or salt curing and drying is usually preferable. However, people do can them successfully. For directions, see REFERENCES, below.

## CANNING CAUTIONS

• Can fresh, high quality foods only. Mature or fully grown foods can better than young or immature foods because they stand up better during processing.

• Prepare foods cleanly, using clean cutting boards and utensils. Chill foods before preparing them if possible, to slow down spoilage organisms.

• Pay close attention to headroom requirements for canning jars. If there is too little headroom, food can be forced between the lid and jar rim, preventing a seal. If there is too much headroom, space is wasted. A large air space can also prevent a seal.

• Handle hot foods, hot liquids and hot jars carefully, to prevent accidents. Keep children away from the canning area. Tip canner lids away from people when opening, to prevent steam burns. Hold hot jars away from the body when moving them.

• Protect glass jars from drastic temperature changes. Do not pour very hot foods into cold jars. Do not set jars of hot food on a cold metal surface. Set them on padding or a wooden board. Avoid cold drafts against hot jars.

## REFERENCES

Ashbrook, Frank G., *Butchering, Processing and Preservation of Meat,* Van Nostrand Reinhold Company 1955.

*Ball Blue Book,* published by the Ball Corporation, Muncie, Indiana, 47302.

*Conservation Bulletin No. 28, Home Canning of Fishery Products,* published by U.S. Dept. of Interior, Fish and Wildlife Service and other government canning bulletins.

Hertsberg, Ruth, *Putting Food By,* The Stephen Greene Press, 1982.

"Is It Safe to Can In Mayonnaise Jars?", *Organic Gardening,* August, 1983. (A short, but helpful article showing how mayonnaise jars can be safely used.)

*USDA Home and Garden Bulletin No. 8, Home Canning of Fruits and Vegetables,* published by U.S. Dept. of Agriculture.

*USDA Home and Garden Bulletin No. 106, Home Canning of Meat and Poultry,* published by U.S. Dept. of Agriculture.

# CAROB

| **STORAGE** |
| --- |
| **Drying** See DRYING, ROASTING, AND GRINDING CAROB PODS, below. |
| 2 POUNDS WHOLE PODS = ABOUT 2 CUPS POWDER |

THE LARGE SEED PODS OF THE CAROB TREE, SOMETIMES CALLED St. John's bread, are very nutritious. Carob is native to the eastern Mediterranean region where it is a common food. The trees grow best in a mild, fairly dry climate, and low humidity is very important when the pods are maturing. Most North American carob is grown in California.

Trees of the locust species are closely related to carob and also have edible pods. Honey-locust pods taste sweet when nibbled. Both carob and locust pods have been used successfully as livestock feed.

Roasted carob tastes similar to chocolate, and because it is much more nutritious than chocolate it is a popular substitute. It is naturally sweet, with about fifty percent sugar content. It has less fat and more calcium than chocolate, and does not contain the caffein-like stimulants found in chocolate.

# HANDLING CAROB

Carob pods ripen and fall from the tree in October and November. Shake the tree to loosen as many pods as possible and gather them from the ground. The pods must be de-seeded before they are eaten because the seeds have an unpleasantly bitter taste. In North America carob is most often dried, ground, and roasted to make a powder to be used like cocoa, but in Mediterranean countries carob pods are also eaten raw and made into a syrup.

***Drying, Roasting, and Grinding Carob Pods***   Carob pods must be de-seeded before they are dried, but de-seeding the raw pods is difficult and requires twisting them open with a pair of pliers. It is much easier to de-seed the pods if they are first blanched to soften them.

Pour boiling water over them and let them sit 15 minutes, or until they are soft. Drain and cool them, then cut along the seam to remove the seeds. Cutting the seed-free pods into small pieces will make them easier to grind after they are dried. Handling damp pods causes stains, so rubber gloves are usually worn when seeding and cutting.

The pieces of pod can be dried on trays in the sun, in a food dryer, or in a 150°F oven. The dry pieces can be ground before or after roasting. They can also be used unroasted, but most people prefer the roasted flavor, as it tastes more like chocolate.

To oven roast carob, spread it in shallow pans and roast it in a low oven. Check and stir often so that it browns evenly. A light to medium brown roast is best. A very dark roast destroys vitamins and may burn natural sugars, causing a bitter taste.

To grind carob, use a grain mill, blender, or other food grinder. It must be ground to a powder if it is to be used like cocoa. Put the carob through the mill or grinder as often as necessary to pulverize it, then sift to remove coarse bits. Some like to use coarse carob meal as a cereal.

***Carob Powder (or Flour)***    There is considerable variation in carob powders, depending on where the carob was grown and how it was roasted. When purchasing carob powder try several sources to see which tastes best.

Although roasted carob powder's flavor is similar to cocoa, it is cooked differently. It is a substantial food, not just a flavoring, and quite large amounts are used in recipes. Since carob is naturally sweet, only small amounts of other sweeteners are needed, and some people require none at all. As carob is low in fat foods made with it are less rich and filling than chocolate mixtures. However, carob powder does not dissolve as completely in liquids as cocoa, so carob drinks and liquid mixtures should be stirred just before they are used.

When a taste for carob has been acquired it will be savored as delicious in itself, and not merely as a cocoa substitute.

***Carob Syrup***   In some Mediterranean countries a syrup is made from freshly gathered carob pods. The raw pods are broken apart to remove seeds and simmered without boiling until they dissolve and thicken into a syrup. After filtering the syrup is light colored and flavorful, but not chocolaty.

A syrup somewhat like chocolate sauce can be made from roasted carob powder. (See recipe below.)

***Carob Chips and Bars:*** The commercial processes used to make solid carob cannot be duplicated at home. Most commercial carob chips and chunks contain sugar, stabilizers, and emulsifiers, and do not really qualify as healthy foods. But they are still far more nutritious than chocolate.

## CAROB RECIPES

*Carob Syrup*                                    (Makes about 1 cup.)

> 1 cup carob powder
> 1 cup water
> 2 tablespoons butter or oil, optional
>
> ¼ to ½ cup honey, or other sweetener, optional

Combine all ingredients in a sauce pan. Bring slowly to a boil over low heat, stirring constantly. Simmer 8–9 minutes or until the syrup is smooth, stirring often.

This syrup keeps several weeks in the refrigerator, and goes well with puddings, ice cream, and other desserts.

***Carob Milk*** Put a spoonful of carob syrup into a cup of hot or cold milk. Stir well.

*Mom's Carob Squares*                    (Makes 3–4 dozen squares.)

> 3 cups graham cracker crumbs or fine dry bread crumbs
> ½ cup chopped nuts, seeds, or shredded coconut
> ¼ – ½ cup honey or other sweetening (Optional. Not needed if graham crackers are used.)
>
> 1 cup milk (Or undiluted evaporated milk.)
> 1½ cups carob powder
> 1 teaspoon vanilla or powdered orange peel, optional
> powdered milk, optional, to thicken

Mix the crumbs and nuts or seeds in a large bowl. Heat the honey and milk in a sauce pan and stir until they are blended. Do not boil. Remove from heat and stir in the carob (and vanilla or orange peel). Stir until smooth. Mixing in the carob will take considerable stirring. Pour over the crumb mixture and stir well. The texture should be thick and somewhat dry. (If it is too soft, work in enough powdered milk to thicken it.) Butter a shallow dish or pan and spread the mixture in it, pressing down firmly. When cool, cut into squares, or refrigerate first to make it more solid.

Carob squares are excellent on trips. They are nutritious and satisfying without being too rich or heavy. Refrigerate or freeze them for longer storage.

***Peanut Butter Carob Squares*** Reduce milk to ½ cup. Heat 1 cup of peanut butter with the milk and honey and proceed with the recipe.

### CAROB IDEAS

**Carob Powder in Baked Goods** Substitute a few tablespoons of carob powder in baked goods. It adds a pleasantly unusual flavor. Try it in muffins, pancakes, etc. It is very good in the *Vegetable or Fruit Quick Bread* recipe, in the BREAD, QUICK section.

**Carob Powder for Dusting** Use carob powder instead of powdered sugar for dusting or coating foods. It is sweet and tasty. Try it on baked goods, snacks, puddings, and dried fruits.

**Carob Cereal** Add carob powder to grains for either hot or cold cereal. Carob meal or powder is a flavorful ingredient in the *Granola* recipe, in the CEREALS section.

### OTHER RECIPES WITH CAROB

Carob Brownies, p.188
Carob Ice Cream, p.356
Carob Pudding, p.418
Flavored Yogurt, p.706
Honey Confection, p.352
Non-dairy Ice Cream, p.356
Sourdough Carob Cake, p.583

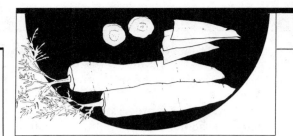

# CARROTS

**Canning**  Leave whole if small. Slice, dice, or cut to matchstick size if large.

**Hot Pack**  Cover with boiling water, bring to boil, drain. Pack, add boiling cooking water, ½ in. headroom. Process 240°F, 11 pounds pressure. Pints: 25 min. Quarts: 30 min.

**Raw Pack**  Pack tightly, 1 in. headroom. Add boiling water, ½ in. headroom. Process as for HOT PACK. Refer to CANNING section.

**Cold Storage**  Root cellar is ideal. In dryer storage place, pack in damp sand or other damp material for cool but dry storage area. Winter varieties keep 6 months. Overwinter in mulched garden row in moderate climate. Refer to COLD STORAGE section.

**Drying**  Steam whole, and cook through, 20—30 min., optional. Slice or shred. Dry until leathery or brittle. Refer to DRYING FOODS section.

**Freezing**  Leave whole if small. Slice, dice, or cut to matchsticks if large. Blanch in boiling water. Whole or large pieces: 5 min.; small pieces: 2—3 min. Refer to FREEZING section.

2½–3 POUNDS WITHOUT TOPS = 1 QUART COOKED;  1 BUSHEL, 50 POUNDS, WITHOUT TOPS = 16–20 QUARTS CANNED OR FROZEN

## CARROT IDEAS

**Carrot Drinks**  Raw carrot juice is a well known tonic, but a special juice extractor is needed for making it. However, many carrot drinks can be made in a blender, with raw chopped carrots or cooked carrot purée. Try blending chopped carrot into apple, pineapple, or orange juice. It adds a nice flavor and golden color. For a sharper taste, add lemon juice. A good cocktail can

CARROTS CAN APPEAR IN EVERY DISH ON THE MENU FROM SOUPS, salads, and main dishes, to desserts. Their sweet flavor and aroma, and their bright orange color make them a welcome food, worldwide. They make a basic seasoning for stews, sauces, and soups everywhere in Europe. They are stir-fried and stewed in China and most other Asian countries, and are a standard item in most North American refrigerators.

White, purple, yellow, and red carrots exist, but orange is the color for which they are known. The orange is caused by their large carotene content. Since carotene becomes Vitamin A when it is digested, orange carrots are especially nutritious. However, to break down their cells and to make the carotene available to the body, carrots must be either cooked, very finely grated, or juiced.

Home-grown fresh carrots taste infinitely better than most store carrots. Carrots keep so well, that unfortunately, most commercial suppliers let them sit for a long time, losing flavor, before selling them. Even the last carrots to come out of the home root cellar in early spring are better than most store carrots. The home gardener who can grow enough carrots to store for a year round supply is lucky, indeed.

## HANDLING CARROTS

Carrots can be harvested whenever they are big enough to use. Many people like the delicate flavor of baby carrots pulled as thinnings. Others prefer the full flavor of larger carrots. It is best to cut off the green tops when the carrots are pulled, as the greens drain vitality and flavor from the roots if left on. Some people use sprigs of carrot greens in salads or cook a few like spinach. There have, however, been occasional reports of stomach upsets as a result.

Harvest carrots for cold storage before heavy frost. Leave ½ to 1 inch of the stem on, but do not otherwise trim or wash them. For immediate use cut off the crown and trim off root hairs. Wash the carrots and scrub with a vegetable brush, if necessary. Do not scrape them unless the skins are in very bad shape, as there are many vitamins in the outside layer. It is possible to blanch carrots in boiling water and easily peel off a very thin skin, but except for looks, there is little reason to do it.

The texture and appearance of carrots can be varied greatly by the way they are cut. Long slim carrot sticks are nice for snacks and with vegetable dips. In salads, carrots are good grated, sliced thinly cross-wise, cut to julienne or matchstick size, and shaved length-wise into curls. Various kinds of vegetable slicers make most of these slicing jobs quick and easy. For cooking, carrots can be left whole, cut in chunks, or cut as for salads. Mashing or puréeing them after cooking is another possibility. Steaming is the most nutritious way to cook whole carrots or large pieces. (Refer to the STEAM COOKING section.)

## CARROT RECIPES

### *Carrot Shred Salad*                    (Makes 4–6 medium servings.)

| | |
|---|---|
| 2 cups (about) carrots, grated | honey, salt for flavoring, if |
| 3 tablespoons fresh herbs, chopped | desired |
|    (Try fennel, dill leaves, | Optional additional ingre- |
|    parsley, chives, or a combina- | dients: |
|    tion.) |    raisins, |
| 5 tablespoons oil |    chopped apple, |
| 1 tablespoon (about) lemon juice, or |    alfalfa sprouts, |
|    2 tablespoons vinegar |    shredded cabbage |

Combine the carrots, herbs, and optional ingredients. Toss with the oil until well coated. Mix the lemon juice or vinegar, with honey and salt, if used, and then mix into the salad. Taste and adjust seasonings, if desired. Chill for an hour or so before serving.

### *Carrot Soup*                          (Makes 6–8 medium bowls.)

| | |
|---|---|
| 2–3 cups carrots, grated or chopped | 5–6 cups soup stock, or water |
| 2 medium onions, chopped | 1 teaspoon dried thyme, or a |
| 6 tablespoons butter |    sprig fresh thyme |
| ¼–½ cup raw rice, or barley | bread cubes, sautéed in butter, |
| |    optional |

In a soup pot, sauté the carrots and onions with the butter. When the onions are limp add the rice or barley, soup stock, and thyme. (The larger amount of rice or barley makes a thicker soup.) Simmer gently for 30 minutes, or until everything is cooked. Purée with a food mill or blender. Reheat to serve, garnishing with bread cubes, if desired.

This soup is also good when served without puréeing.

**Cream of Carrot Soup**  Use only 3 cups of stock or water when cooking the carrot mixture. After the soup is puréed add about 2 cups of milk (or top milk, or evaporated milk for a richer soup). Reheat without boiling.

### *Italian Marinated Carrots*              (Makes about 1 quart.)

| | |
|---|---|
| 2–3 pounds (about 1 quart) carrots, | 3 tablespoons wine vinegar |
|    thickly sliced | 1 teaspoon oregano (Or try |
| 2 cloves garlic, sliced thinly |    thyme, or savory.) |
| ¼ cup olive oil | pepper, salt, optional |

**CARROT IDEAS,** *cont.*

be made by blending carrot and such vegetables as cucumber, green pepper, onion, and celery with tomato juice. Lemon juice or vinegar, a dash of Tabasco sauce and such herbs as parsley and basil also go well.

Puréed cooked carrots can be used instead of raw carrot in any of the above mixtures. In Jamaica a chilled drink is made from puréed carrot, milk, vanilla, and sweetening. A carrot milkshake could be made in this way.

**Grated Carrot Mixtures**
Grated raw carrot goes well with ground meat in meat loaves and patties. It is especially good with ground lamb, as in the *Lamb Meatballs* recipe, in the LAMB section. When added to yeast breads, pancakes, muffins, quick breads, and cakes, grated carrots add moistness and sweetness. It is a favorite in the *Vegetable or Fruit Quick Bread* recipe, in the BREAD, QUICK, section.

**Stir-fried Carrots**  Carrots add color, flavor, and texture to stir-fried mixtures. Cut them to match other ingredients used. Julienne or matchstick size are good for stir-frying with bean sprouts or meat shreds, while thin, cross-wise slices go with meat slices. As carrots take longer to cook than many other ingredients they should be among the first foods added when stir-frying. (Refer to the STIR-FRYING section.)

**Mashed Carrots**  Cook and mash carrots with potatoes or other vegetables. They can also be cooked alone, mashed, and then seasoned as a vegetable side dish. Mashed or puréed carrots can also be substituted for puréed pumpkin in many recipes, including pies, puddings, and ice cream. (Refer to recipes in the SQUASH, WINTER AND PUMPKIN section.)

### CARROT IDEAS, *cont.*

**Carrot for Color** Grated or blenderized carrot will add a golden glow to beverages, puddings, and other desserts, and can be used as a natural food coloring. (Refer to the FOOD COLORING section.)

### OTHER RECIPES FEATURING CARROTS

Apple Carrot Tzimmes, p.7
Bewitched Onion Stew, p.448
Carrot Raita, p.706
Carrot Tzimmes (with meat), p.658
Celery and Carrots in Cider, p.124
Chestnut Carrot Salad, p.151
Glazed Carrots, p.453
Rainbow Noodles, p.431
Recipes, and Ideas for Vegetables, p.669
Roast Beverages, p.44
Vegetable or Fruit Quick Bread, p.64
Vegetable Sherbets, p.357

Steam the carrots until just tender, about 15 minutes. Mix the garlic, oil, vinegar, oregano, pepper, and salt, in a large bowl. Add the hot cooked carrot slices and coat well with the marinade. Taste and adjust seasonings. Let stand 12 hours before serving, stirring once or twice while it sits, and serve with an antipasto or salad, or as a snack.

### Sautéed Carrots from the Balkans (Makes about 6 side servings.)

| | |
|---|---|
| 1½ *pounds (about 2 cups) carrots* | *oil for frying* |
| 2 *tablespoons (about) flour* | 1 *cup yogurt, stirred until* |
| *pepper, salt, optional* | *smooth* |

Cut long carrots in half or as necessary to fit the steamer, and steam until just tender, about 20 minutes. When cool enough, slice them ¼ to ½ inch thick. They can be cut the long way to make 3 or 4 inch slabs. Season the flour with pepper and salt, if desired, and then roll the carrot pieces in it. Sauté in several tablespoons of oil until they are lightly browned. Remove pan from heat and pour in the yogurt. Stir gently. Return to very low heat for a minute or two to thicken the sauce. (Cow's milk yogurt, unlike goat's milk yogurt, curdles when heated, unless very carefully handled. Curdling hurts appearance more than flavor, but it can be prevented. Refer to the *Stabilized Cow's Milk Yogurt* recipe in the YOGURT section.)

# CASSEROLES

Casseroles are combinations of foods baked and served in the same dish. They are often designed as one-dish meals, containing vegetables and meat, cheese or eggs, and a carbohydrate ingredient like noodles, rice, potatoes, or bread crumbs. As they can be made ahead and reheated they are very convenient. Double recipes can also be made, one to use immediately and one to freeze. Just about any garden vegetable can go into a casserole, and so can many kinds of leftovers. Substitutions and additions are the rule, and if one ingredient is not available, substitute something that is. Vegetable casseroles can be expanded by adding leftover meat, sliced, hard-boiled eggs, or cheese, and familiar combinations can be enlivened with a variety of seasonings.

## FREEZING CASSEROLES

There are two basic approaches to freezing casseroles. One is to freeze the finished casserole which only needs thawing and heating

### STORAGE

**Freezing** See FREEZING CASSEROLES, below. Quality retained 4—8 months. Vegetable only mixtures, 8—12 months.

before being served. The other is to freeze vegetable mixtures to be thawed and combined with other ingredients for a casserole.

***Freezing Finished Casseroles*** Most casseroles freeze best if baked before freezing. However, casseroles made largely with pre-cooked ingredients can simply be mixed and frozen for later baking.

It is easiest to freeze casseroles in their baking dishes. Just cool, wrap and freeze them. If a baking dish cannot be spared for long, use disposable aluminum pans, or press aluminum foil smoothly into the dish and grease it well before adding the casserole mixture. Bake as usual, cool, and freeze solid. Then, take the casserole out of the dish with the foil, wrap it, and return to the freezer. To use such a casserole, unwrap it, peel off the foil, and replace in the same baking dish. Baking dishes that can withstand extreme temperature changes can go directly from the freezer to the oven. With other dishes, first thaw the casserole before heating it. If using a microwave oven, follow manufacturers directions when baking or heating casseroles, especially when choosing baking dishes.

Some kinds of casserole mixtures freeze better than others. Mixtures low in fat keep best. Milk mixtures curdle, and hard-boiled egg whites become tough, so these should not be frozen. As bread crumb toppings get soggy, they should only be added after the casserole is thawed. Freezing tends to strengthen the flavor of garlic, so do not use too much of it. However, onions and most herbs tend to lose flavor when frozen.

***Freezing Casserole Vegetable Mixtures*** Freezing vegetable mixtures for later use in casseroles is a versatile approach. The vegetables can then be used in different recipes at different times, as well as alone, as side dishes. Also, vegetable mixtures keep much longer in the freezer—8–12 months, compared to 4–8 months for more complicated, finished dishes.

Prepare the vegetables for freezing by blanching them in tomato juice, soup stock, or another liquid. Then, pack and freeze them in the blanching liquid. In most recipes, a main vegetable like zucchini, eggplant, green beans or okra, is prominent, while smaller amounts of seasoning vegetables, like green pepper, celery, onion, parsley, or other fresh herbs are also used. First, heat about a quart of the liquid to a boil in a large pot, then add chopped seasoning vegetables. When the liquid boils again add about two cups of the main vegetable, sliced or cut as necessary. Cover and cook for the blanching time recommended for freezing that vegetable. Usually this is about the time it takes for the pot to boil again after the vegetable is added. Remove the vegetable with a slotted spoon, sieve, or skimmer, and set aside to cool. Then add another portion of vegetable and blanch, as before. Continue until all of the vegetable has been blanched. Both vegetables and liquid can be left to cool at room temperature, or their container can be set in a pan of ice water for quick cooling. Pack the vegetables in freezer containers, and evenly divide the seasoning vegetables with the liquid among the containers. Leave headroom for expansion in the freezer. Seal, label, and freeze. The label should show the kind of liquid and seasonings used, as well as the main vegetable.

For use, thaw the vegetables enough so that they can be separated and mixed with other ingredients. Casserole recipes are included in the recipe sections for likely ingredients throughout the book.

## BASIC CASSEROLE RECIPES

### Vegetable Pie Casserole          (Makes about 6 medium servings.)

| | |
|---|---|
| *1 quart vegetables, pre-cooked, or frozen and thawed* (Try summer squash, green beans, eggplant, corn, or a combination.) | *1 – 2 eggs, lightly beaten* *herbs, to taste* *pepper, salt, optional* |
| *½ cup vegetable cooking water, vegetable juice, or other liquid* | *1 cup (about) bread crumbs* *butter or oil* *cheese, grated or sliced, optional* |

Butter or oil a shallow casserole or deep pie dish. Spread the vegetables and cooking water or other liquid in it. Pour the egg over, and add seasonings. (Refer to the HERBS section.) Sprinkle thickly with bread crumbs. Dot the top with butter, or spread with cheese. Bake in a moderate oven for 30 minutes, or till the eggs are set and the top lightly browned. Quick, and quite delicious!

### Vegetable-Rice Casserole          (Makes about 6 medium servings.)

| | |
|---|---|
| *1 onion, chopped* *2 tablespoons oil or fat* *2 – 4 cups vegetables, sliced or chopped.* (Some good vegetables are squash, okra, or eggplant.) *1 cup raw rice* | *1½ – 2 cups soup stock, vegetable cooking or soaking water, or other liquid* *herbs, to taste* (Basil, parsley, and savory are good.) *pepper, salt, optional* |

Sauté the onion in the fat until it is limp. Mix with the vegetables, rice, stock or other liquid, and seasonings in a 2 quart casserole. (Refer to the HERBS section.) Adjust the amount of liquid according to the moisture in the vegetables and the type of rice used. Brown rice usually takes a little more liquid than white. Cover and bake in a moderate, 350°F oven, until the rice is cooked, about 1 hour. Towards the end of cooking add water if it is needed. The casserole can be uncovered for the last 15 minutes to brown the top.

This dish may also be simmered on top of the stove, tightly covered. Do not stir while it cooks.

### Layered Invented Casseroles  (For 6 – 10 generous dinner servings.)

In these casseroles use ingredients that are on hand. Try a new combination, invent a fancy name and *remember what went into it*. It may be extraordinarily good and worth repeating.

***Vegetable layers*** Use about one quart of any of the following, or a mixture:

*Frozen vegetables and liquid, thawed*

*Raw vegetables, sliced or chopped*

*Sautéed vegetables, especially onions*

***Protein layer*** Use from one to several cups. Combinations of meat, eggs, or tofu with nuts or seeds and cheese are very good.

*Leftover cooked meat, sliced or chopped*

*Ground meat*

*Ham or bacon, thinly sliced or chopped*

*Cooked fish, leftover or canned*

*Hard-boiled eggs, sliced*

*Nuts, sunflower seeds, or other seeds, chopped if appropriate*

*Cheese, sliced or grated*

*Tofu (soybean curd) sliced (Refer to the TOFU section.)*

***Carbohydrate layer*** Use one quart or more:

*Mashed potatoes*

*Boiled or baked potatoes, sliced*

*Cooked rice, or other cooked grains*

*Cooked noodles, macaroni, or other pasta*

*Leftover cornmeal mush, grits, or millet*

*Cooked dry beans*

*Bread crumbs*

***Liquids*** If other ingredients are fairly dry, add 2–3 cups liquid. If they are quite moist, liquid may not be needed.

*Soup stock*

*Tomatoes: stewed, fresh, or juiced*

*Milk, thin gravy, or a cream sauce. (Refer to RECIPES in the MILK section.)*

### Optional

*Herbs, pepper, salt, butter or other fat*

Grease a 3–4 quart casserole dish (or use two smaller baking dishes, and perhaps freeze one). Make layers of the various ingredients. Add seasonings and liquid as needed. Usually the carbohydrate ingredient is best as the beginning and ending layer. The top can be dotted with butter or sprinkled with cheese. Bake in a moderate oven for 30 to 60 minutes, or until all ingredients are cooked. Cover the casserole for part of the baking time to prevent the top from browning too much.

### Casserole Marinara      (Makes 6–8 generous dinner servings.)

*2 pounds (about) spinach or greens, cooked, drained, chopped*

*1 pound ricotta, or small curd cottage cheese*

*3 eggs, lightly beaten*

*⅓ cup parsley, chopped*

*3–4 cups spaghetti sauce or well seasoned tomato sauce*

*¼ cup Parmesan or Romano cheese, grated, optional*

*1 pound pasta, cooked (Preferably large size macaroni, tubes, or shells.)*

Combine the spinach, ricotta, eggs, parsley, spaghetti or tomato sauce, and cheese. Mix in the cooked pasta, and pour into a large (or two small) oiled baking dish. Bake in a moderate, 350°F oven about 40 minutes or until set. Cover for part of the time if over-browning may occur. Serve with more grated cheese, if desired. An irresistable, Italian style one dish meal.

# CAULIFLOWER

H OW TO WIN NEW FRIENDS AND PLEASE OLD ONES? GIVE THEM cauliflower freshly cut from the garden. The cool greenness of the tight inner leaves contrasting with the whiteness of the compact head of curds is pleasing to the eye, while the crisp texture and mild flavor will please the palate. Who could resist a vegetable that is delightful to eat raw, delectable cooked alone or in mixtures, and good looking, as well?

A cauliflower is a large, compact head of flower buds. The buds are sometimes called curds (because of their white, cheese-like appearance). This member of the cabbage family is not as nutritious as its greener relatives, though it does have a respectable amount of calcium. But it has a mild flavor and crisp texture that is delicious raw or cooked. Cauliflower leaves are also quite good if prepared in the same ways as cabbage.

Cauliflower, which means "flowered cabbage," grows very much like broccoli, though its flavor is quite different. For a comparison, refer to the BROCCOLI section.

## HANDLING CAULIFLOWER

Cut cauliflower heads after they have grown to their full size, but before they start to open or "rice." Leave as many tight leaves clinging to the head as possible. Not only do the leaves have a good flavor but they also contain more nutrients than the white curds. When cauliflower is harvested for fall storage it should be cut together with many of the protective leaves, or else it should be pulled roots and all. Whole plants can be kept by planting the roots in damp sand in the root cellar. According to some reports immature heads stored in this way will grow and fill out during storage.

Avoid soaking cauliflower in salt water, an unhealthy practice often recommended to remove bugs. Instead, rinse thoroughly in a pan of cold water which should remove all of them from the florets. If one escapes notice when a whole trimmed head is rinsed it will come out in the water used for steaming or boiling. (Refer to DE-BUGGING BROCCOLI in the BROCCOLI section.)

---

### STORAGE

**Canning**   Not recommended! It becomes discolored and strongly flavored.

**Cold Storage**   Keeps in root cellar 1–2 months, refrigerated about 1 month. Refer to COLD STORAGE section.

**Drying**   Separate into florets and cut into ½ in. thick slices. Steam 6–8 min. or till cooked through. Dry until tough or brittle. Refer to DRYING FOODS section.

**Freezing**   Break or cut florets into 1 in. thick pieces. Blanch in boiling water 3 min. Refer to FREEZING section.

3 POUNDS = 1 QUART PREPARED
12 POUNDS = 4–6 QUARTS FROZEN

Many recipes call for pre-cooked or partially cooked cauliflower, and steaming is the best way to do this. Florets take from 8 to 15 minutes, and whole heads from 20 to 30 minutes, depending on size. To steam whole heads, set them stem side down in the steamer. To boil whole heads, put them stem side down in about an inch of water. This allows the tougher stem to cook more than the tender curds.

Enjoy cauliflower raw in salads, and with dips, as well as cooked. If only the tops of the florets are used raw, the stalks can be pickled. (See the recipe below.)

## CAULIFLOWER RECIPES

### *Baked Scalloped Cauliflower*                (Makes about 6 side servings.)

| | |
|---|---|
| 1 medium cauliflower, cooked | 1 cup (about) milk |
| 1 cup bread crumbs | 1 egg |
| 2 tablespoons butter, softened | pepper, to taste |

Separate the cauliflower into florets either before or after cooking. Do not overcook. Arrange the florets in a buttered baking dish. Mash the bread crumbs with the butter and enough milk to make a soft paste. The dryness of the crumbs will determine how much milk to use. Very dry crumbs may need to soak in the milk for a few minutes before they will mash. Beat the egg into the paste and season with pepper. Spread the mixture over the cauliflower. Bake in a hot, 425°F oven. Cover for the first 10 minutes, then uncover and bake until the top is browned.

**Scalloped Salsify**   Pre-cook and slice several cups of salsify and prepare as above.

### *Braised Cauliflower from India*                (Makes 6–8 side servings.)

| | |
|---|---|
| 1 large cauliflower, cut into small florets | ½ teaspoon turmeric |
| 2 tablespoons ghee (Refer to BUTTER section.) or 1 tablespoon each butter and oil | 2 teaspoons cumin |
| | ¼ teaspoon paprika, or hot red pepper |
| 2 teaspoons mustard seed | ¼ teaspoon black pepper |
| 2 inch piece fresh ginger root thinly sliced, or ½ teaspoon powder | 1 small tomato, chopped, optional |

Wash the florets and pat them dry with a towel. Heat the ghee or butter and oil in a large frying pan or wok with a tight lid. Add the mustard seed and stir. When the mustard seeds start to pop (like corn) add the ginger root, if using it, and sauté it for 2 to 3 minutes while stirring. Stir in the turmeric. Add the cauliflower and stir till it is evenly yellow. Stir in cumin, paprika or red pepper, black pepper, and powdered ginger, if used. Put on high heat, sprinkle with a

### CAULIFLOWER IDEAS

**Leftover Cauliflower, Baked** Arrange cooked cauliflower in a buttered baking dish. Cover with white sauce or cheese sauce (refer to the MILK section), or sprinkle it with bread crumbs, grated cheese, or both. Bake until it is heated through and the top is browned, about 20 minutes. Add a garnish of parsley when it is served. For a heartier dish, include hard-boiled eggs, cooked ham, or another cooked meat.

**Cauliflower Salads** Raw cauliflower florets or cooked florets that are still somewhat crisp are very good in salads. They can be added to tossed salads or arranged on a bed of lettuce with other ingredients and served with a dressing. Some ingredients that combine well with cauliflower are sliced cooked beets, green peppers or pimiento, chopped scallions, parsley sprigs, olives, cooked shrimp, or other seafoods, and crisp, fried bacon crumbs. Mayonnaise makes a good dressing, or, for a special treat, try the *Guacamole* recipe in the FRUITS section.

### CAULIFLOWER IDEAS,
*cont.*

**Cauliflower Fried in Batter**
Pre-cook cauliflower, or use left-overs that are tender but not soft. Florets or cauliflower sliced into thin wedges can be used. Dip in pancake batter or another favorite batter, or in lightly beaten egg and then in bread crumbs or flour. Fry in a generous amount of oil or other fat in a frying pan or deep fry. Refer to the *Tempura* recipe in the FRUITS section.

**Cauliflower for Stir-frying**
Thinly slice raw cauliflower. It can be cut in squares, rectangles, or matchsticks to go with the other foods used. Stir-fry with the slower cooking ingredients. It will take 3 to 4 minutes to cook. (Refer to the STIR-FRYING section.)

**Cauliflower Spaghetti**  Brown several cloves of minced garlic in oil. Add chopped, raw cauliflower and a tablespoon or two of water. Cover, and cook over low heat until tender, 10 to 15 minutes. Stir and mash with a fork several times as it cooks. Cook and drain spaghetti or other pasta and mix it with the cauliflower. Season to taste with grated cheese, butter and pepper. Serve immediately.

**Cauliflower Greens**  Cook tender cauliflower leaves in the same ways as cabbage. Their flavor is surprisingly pleasant.

### OTHER RECIPES
### WITH CAULIFLOWER

tablespoon of water and cover tightly. As soon as steam builds up in the pan reduce heat and simmer 5 minutes. Uncover, add the tomato, and continue to stir until the moisture has dried up. The cauliflower should still be somewhat crisp in texture. It is fun and a surprise to serve this spicy, bright yellow version of what is usually a bland white vegetable.

### *Chinese Cauliflower Fu-yung*                    (Makes about 6 western style side servings.)

1 cauliflower, broken into small
  florets
½ pound chicken white meat
3 egg whites

1 tablespoon cornstarch
½ teaspoon salt
2 tablespoons lard or oil

Pre-cook florets by steaming them for 10 minutes. Finely grind the chicken meat. In a bowl, mix it with egg whites, starch, salt, and 2 tablespoons of water. Beat with an egg beater until it puffs up. Heat lard or oil in a wok or heavy frying pan until it is quite hot, but not smoking. Add the chicken mixture and stir-fry over high heat for 2 minutes. Add the cauliflower and stir 2 more minutes. Serve immediately. (Refer to the STIR-FRYING section.)

### *Pickled Cauliflower Stalks*                    (Makes 1–1½ quarts.)

(See also MAKING FERMENTED PICKLES, in the PICKLING section.)

1 pound cauliflower stalks
2½ tablespoons plain or pickling salt
1 tablespoon mustard seeds, crushed,
  or ½ teaspoon mustard powder, or
  to taste

½ teaspoon cayenne or other hot
  pepper, or to taste.
3 cups water, boiled and cooled

Cut the cauliflower stalks into 2 to 3 inch long, finger sized sticks, blanch them in boiling water for 30 seconds, then drain. Pack the sticks into a 1½–2 quart size jar. Add salt, mustard, cayenne, and water. The water should cover the stalks completely. Put a clean cloth over the jar mouth, tie it in place or use a rubber band. Keep in a warm place for 2 days. Stir once each day. Then keep in a cool, dry place for about a week, after which the pickles should be fermented and ready to eat. Refrigerated, they will keep for about a month.

   *Pickled Kohlrabi Sticks*  Cut kohlrabi into sticks and pickle in the same way.

# CELERIAC

CELERIAC IS A TYPE OF CELERY GROWN FOR ITS LARGE ROOT. ALSO called knob celery, celery root, or turnip rooted celery, it is a flavorful and practical root vegetable that is generally overlooked. Home gardeners can grow it and store it as easily as carrots, beets, and other root vegetables. It is easier to grow than regular celery and will flourish in a much greater range of soils and climatic conditions.

Celeriac has a pleasant, celery-like flavor that tastes delicious cooked by itself, or mixed with other vegetables and meat. In France and other European countries, it is often served with game meats. Celeriac tops look and taste like celery, but do not form thick stalks. They make an excellent herbal seasoning, and can be used wherever a celery flavoring would be welcome.

## HANDLING CELERIAC

Celeriac reaches about 4 inches in diameter but can be pulled as soon as it is large enough to use. (If it will be stored in the root cellar, it should be pulled in late fall just before the heavy freezes.) After pulling, cut off tops about an inch above the root and shake out as much dirt as possible. Wait to trim it further till just before use. (For using the tops refer to CELERY section.)

Celeriac requires a lot of trimming because the tops and rootlets grow out of a large part of its surface in twisted tangles. The soil works into the creases and cannot be washed out. Parts of the root may have to be peeled, to get it clean.

Celeriac discolors easily, but this does not affect its flavor. Chilling before preparation will slow down discoloration. Or it can be sprinkled with lemon juice, vinegar, or ascorbic acid solution.

Celeriac cooks like any other root vegetable, adding an exceptional flavor to soups and stews. Grated raw celeriac is good in salads.

## CELERIAC RECIPES

### Celeriac Salad

(Makes 6−8 medium servings.)

1 or 2 celeriacs, julienned or grated
  coarsely
3 tablespoons lemon juice or vinegar
1 apple, grated, optional

Mayonnaise, seasoned with
  mustard (Refer to the
  SALADS section for
  recipe.)
parsley for garnish, optional

Cut the celeriac into julienne or matchstick sized strips, or grate it, and sprinkle it immediately with lemon juice or vinegar, or else blanch it. To blanch, add the lemon juice or vinegar to a quart of water, then heat it to a full boil while preparing the celeriac. Add the

## STORAGE

**Cold Storage** Keeps all winter in root cellar or similar conditions. Can be packed in damp sand or other damp material. Refer to COLD STORAGE section.

**Drying** Thinly slice or grate roots. Precooking optional. Dry until hard or brittle. Excellent in soups and stews. Spread leaves and minced stalks on trays. Dry till leaves crumble and stalk bits are hard, for use as an herbal seasoning. Refer to DRYING FOODS section.

**Freezing** Tops only. Refer to FREEZING HERBS in HERBS section.

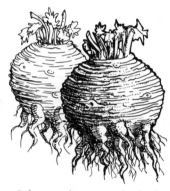

*Celeriac, celery root, or knob celery*

## CELERIAC IDEAS

**Celeriac in Soup Stock** Include whole, trimmed celeriacs in the pot when cooking soup stock. Let simmer 45 minutes to an hour, or till tender. Remove celeriac, drain, and use in any cooked celeriac recipe. The soup stock will be much improved by the celeriac's flavor. (Refer to the SOUP section.)

**Creamed Celeriac** Stir cooked, diced celeriac into the *Cream Sauce* recipe in the MILK section. Minced parsley makes a nice addition. Diced, raw celeriac can be cooked by simmering it in

## CELERIAC IDEAS, *cont.*

milk, and the milk used to make the cream sauce. A thin version, made with puréed celeriac, becomes Cream of Celeriac Soup.

**Cooked Celeriac Salads** Slice cooked celeriac and sprinkle with olive oil, pepper or paprika, minced scallion, and salt. Serve at room temperature. Cooked celeriac is also very good served with French or other salad dressings. Try it with a sprinkling of chopped almonds, or other nuts.

**Baked Celeriac** Trim or peel celeriac as necessary. Cut large ones in half. Oil all surfaces. Bake in a moderate oven as for potatoes, until tender. These are also delicious baked in the pan with roasting meat.

### OTHER RECIPES WITH CELERIAC

Celery Leaves, Celeriac Leaves, and Lovage (as an herb), p. 336
Celery, Celeriac, and Lovage Seeds, p. 347
Vegetable Hot Pot, p. 669
Recipes, and Ideas for Vegetables, p. 669

### STORAGE

**Canning** Cut 1 in. pieces, cover with boiling water, boil 3 min. Drain, pack in jars, add boiling cooking water, 1 in. headroom. Process, 240°F, 11 pounds pressure. Pint: 30 min. Quarts: 35 min. *Celery and Tomato* Boil equal parts celery and fresh chopped tomato 5 min. Pack 1 in. headroom. Process as for celery alone. Refer to CANNING section.

celeriac and bring to a boil again. Drain and spread the celeriac on a towel to cool.

Mix the celeriac, and apple if used, with the mayonnaise. Chill for a few minutes before serving.

### *Sautéed Celeriac* (Makes about 6 side servings.)

2 large celeriacs, in ¾ inch cubes    juice of 1 lemon, or to taste
4 tablespoons oil, preferably olive    pepper, salt, optional

Sauté celeriac in the oil, stirring often, till it is lightly colored. Add water to almost cover it, the lemon juice, and pepper or salt, if desired. Simmer uncovered until the celeriac is tender and the water has nearly evaporated, about 30 minutes.

Serve hot or cold. A good introduction to this distinctive vegetable.

### *Celeriac-Potato Purée* (Makes about 6 side servings.)

1 large celeriac                              parsley or chervil, minced, op-
potato to equal amount of celeriac       tional
2–3 tablespoons cream                    pepper, salt, optional
1 tablespoon (about) butter

Cook the celeriac and potatoes separately until tender, or steam in the same pot. If steaming, test with a fork and remove whichever is done, so one does not overcook while waiting for the other. The celeriac can be cut into several pieces to make it cook faster. Purée the celeriac and potatoes with a food mill or other device. Season with the cream, butter, parsley or chervil, pepper, and salt, if desired. Reheat as necessary.

Very good served with game dishes.

***Jerusalem Artichoke and Potato Purée*** Use equal amounts of Jerusalem artichokes and potatoes and follow this recipe.

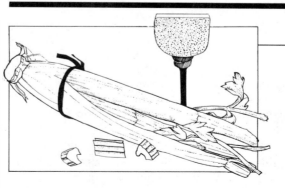

# CELERY

LARGE, FLESHY CELERY STALKS WERE FIRST DEVELOPED IN THE 18TH century. Before that, celery looked like an herb and was used as one. A clump of thin-stemmed, leafy green celery might be grown next to parsley, so that a few sprigs of each could be conveniently picked for flavoring soups, stews, and salads. The leaves of the modern celery plant are often used as a flavoring in cooking, like their early herbal counterpart, while the crisp stalks are a favorite raw vegetable snack and salad ingredient.

The home gardener who can grow thick, crisp celery stalks is fortunate, because it does not grow well everywhere. However, most gardeners can take a hint from the past and grow celery as an herb. Ordinary celery seeds will produce leaves and stems for seasoning, even if thick stalks never form. The tops of celeriac plants, and the leaves of the herb lovage, also provide a celery flavor. Celery seeds are another source of celery flavor. (Refer to the HERBS section.)

## HANDLING CELERY

Harvest celery for immediate use by cutting the root just below the soil surface. (Some root is needed to hold the stalks together.) Do not wash the celery till it is to be used, as it keeps best dry. When celery is harvested for fall storage, pull the plant roots and all, so it can be "replanted" in the storage area.

A few leaves for seasoning can be taken from celery plants as needed. When the main crop is harvested, a supply of leaves can be dried or frozen. Powdered or crumbled dried leaves can be used instead of celery salt when it is called for in recipes, avoiding the salt.

Celery is a good mixer. Raw, it goes with every kind of salad, vegetable dip and stuffing. Cooked, it blends with all kinds of meats and vegetables. In fact, it is so busy mixing and joining, that it is not often featured alone. The following recipes are unusual because celery is the main ingredient.

## CELERY RECIPES

### *Celery Stir-fried with Mushrooms* (Makes about 6– 8 side servings.)

*1 head celery*
*½ pound fresh mushrooms*
*2 tablespoons oil, or lard*

*2 tablespoons soy sauce*
*½ teaspoon honey or sugar*

Trim the celery and slice diagonally into pieces ¼ inch thick. Slice mushrooms ¼ inch thick. Heat the oil or lard in a heavy frying pan or wok. Stir-fry the mushrooms for 1 minute. Add the soy sauce, honey or sugar and then the celery. Stir-fry over high heat for three minutes and serve. (Refer to the STIR-FRYING section.)

---

**STORAGE,** *cont.*

**Cold Storage** Pull with roots in late fall. Replant in damp sand or soil. Will keep most of winter in root cellar or protected outdoor storage area. Refer to COLD STORAGE section.

**Drying** *Stalks* Slice ¼ in. thick. Optional: Steam 4 min. Dry until brittle. *Leaves* Refer to DRYING HERBS, in HERBS section. Stalks and leaves can be powdered to use as seasoning. Refer to DRYING FOODS section.

**Freezing** (Useful in cooked dishes only.) *Stalks* Slice 1 in. pieces or smaller. Blanch 3 min. in boiling water, 4 min. in steam. *Leaves* Refer to FREEZING HERBS, in HERBS section, and FREEZING section.

I POUND TRIMMED = 3 TO 4 CUPS CHOPPED

---

**CELERY IDEAS**

**Celery Stalk Stuffings** Stuff trimmed stalks of celery with any of the following. Children enjoy making their own stuffed stalks. Peanut butter, or other nut butters. Try the SUNFLOWER PEANUT BUTTER idea, in the SUNFLOWER section. Cream cheese, cottage cheese or yogurt cheese, (refer to the YOGURT section). Enhancements such as chopped nuts or minced herbs, and a sprinkle of paprika are fun. (Refer to FRESH CHEESE SEASONINGS at the end of the CHEESE, FRESH section.) Tuna or egg salad mixtures made from finely chopped ingredients. Many sandwich spreads. Try the *Liver Paté/Sandwich Spread*, in the SAUSAGE section.

**Celery and Cabbage Salad**
Slice or chop celery and mix with an equal amount of shredded cabbage. Mix with the *Old Fashioned Coleslaw Dressing* recipe, in the CABBAGE section, or mayonnaise. A little prepared or dry mustard can be added to the dressing. For a special effect, cut large green peppers in half, seed them, and fill them with the salad.

**Creamed Celery**   Cook diced celery in enough milk to cover it. When the celery is tender, drain, and use the milk for the *Cream Sauce* recipe, in the MILK section. Add the cooked celery to the sauce. This is delicious over toast or with bread cubes sautéed in butter. If the celery is puréed and added to the white sauce, a celery-flavored cream sauce results that can be used for creamed chicken or turkey.

**Celery Bread Crumb Stuffing**
Combine 2 parts chopped celery with 3 parts bread crumbs. Season with such herbs as sage, thyme, marjoram, and savory, and onion, pepper, and salt, to taste. Moisten with meat juice or soup stock. Other ingredients like grated carrot or cooked, chopped chestnuts can be included. Use to stuff poultry or vegetables.

## Celery and Carrots in Cider    (Makes about 6 side servings.)

| | |
|---|---|
| outside stalks from a head of celery | pepper, salt, optional |
| 1 pound (about) carrots | parsley, chopped, for garnish |
| 2 ½ cups apple cider, or apple juice | |

Cut both the celery and carrots into 2 inch sections, then slice each section into several sticks. Heat the cider to a boil and add carrots. Simmer for 15 minutes. Add the celery and season lightly with pepper and salt, if desired. The seasoning will get stronger as the cider becomes concentrated. Cook till both the celery and carrots are tender, about 20 more minutes. Remove the vegetables from the pot, and keep them warm in a serving dish. Boil the cider over high heat until it is reduced to about ¼ cup. Pour over the vegetables and serve sprinkled with parsley. Excellent as a side dish with roast meats.

## Celery Casserole    (Makes 6–8 side servings.)

| | |
|---|---|
| 1 large head celery, cut into thin sticks a few inches long | ½ cup cheese, grated (Parmesan is good.) |
| 1 small onion, finely chopped | butter |
| bacon, 2 slices, or a small piece salt pork, finely chopped | |

Cook the celery, onion, and bacon or salt pork in a small amount of water until the celery is just getting tender, about 15 minutes. Drain. (The cooking water can be saved for soup.) Butter a casserole. Spread about a third of the celery mixture in it and sprinkle with a third of the cheese. Add two more layers of celery and cheese. Dot with butter. Bake in a 400°F oven for 8 to 10 minutes.

**Celery and Tomato Casserole**   Pour about ⅓ cup tomato sauce or stewed tomatoes over each layer of celery in the above recipe. (1 cup tomato altogether). If using a canned or frozen mixture of tomatoes and celery, sprinkle the layers with cheese, butter, and bits of crisply fried bacon. Bread crumbs can be sprinkled on top.

## Waldorf Salad    (Makes about 6 medium servings.)

| | |
|---|---|
| 2 cups celery, chopped | ½ – 1 cup Mayonnaise or Yogurt Fruit Salad Dressing (Refer to recipes in the SALADS and YOGURT sections.) |
| 2 cups apple or pear, chopped | |
| ½ – 1 cup walnuts, chopped | |
| ½ cup (about) raisins, or chopped figs, optional | lettuce, optional |

Mix together the celery, apple or pear, walnuts, and raisins or figs. Add enough mayonnaise or salad dressing to moisten well. Arrange on a bed of lettuce if desired. This cool, crisp, and crunchy salad is delightful in the summertime for a light lunch or supper.

### Mrs. Scarlett's Celery Wine

"There is always a waste of the outside pieces of celery: here is a recipe which makes from them an excellent wine, and is also good for those who suffer from rheumatism.

"To each pound of green or outside stalks of celery allow 1 quart of water and boil all until tender. Then strain the liquid off and allow 3 lbs. Demerara sugar and 1 oz. of yeast [about 1 tablespoon dry baking yeast] to each gallon put into the cask. Keep the cask well filled up until all the yeast has worked out, [active fermentation has ceased], and close the bung lightly until the wine is quite still. Then close firmly, leave for a year and bottle off, when it will be ready for use."

*Farmhouse Fare*

(For a more detailed look at wine making refer to the WINE section. To make Celery Mead, use 2½ to 3 pounds of honey instead of sugar per gallon of liquid.) Celery wine and mead have an enjoyable herbal flavor. Commercially sold celery tonic or sodas have a similar taste.

| OTHER RECIPES FEATURING CELERY |
| --- |
| Celery Leaves (as an herb), p. 336 |
| Celery Seeds, p. 347 |
| Celery Soup, p. 18 |
| Herb Teas, p. 341 |
| Herb Vinegar, p. 677 |
| Oxtail Stew, p. 628 |
| Pesto, Herb-Garlic Sauce, p. 340 |
| Recipes, and Ideas for Vegetables, p. 669 |

# CEREALS, BREAKFAST

| STORAGE |
| --- |
| Store thoroughly dry cereal in airtight, insect-proof containers. Most kinds will keep for a year or more in a cool place. |

CEREALS HAVE ALWAYS BEEN THE MAINSTAY OF THE NORTH American breakfast. At one time hot, cooked "mush," such as cornmeal, rolled oats, or cracked wheat, was eaten every morning, but hot cereals have gradually given way in popularity to packaged, ready-to-eat cold cereals.

Ready-to-eat, cold cereals originated in the 19th century among American health food and vegetarian groups. Both C. W. Post and W. K. Kellog got their ideas and their starts in a health sanitarium in Battle Creek, Michigan. In the beginning their products were given fancy packages and big advertising promotions, but they were, at that time, healthful foods. The advertising and packaging techniques have not changed, but the healthfulness of the products has, unfortunately, fallen considerably. Modern ready-to-eat cereals now are loaded with sugars, preservatives, artificial colors, and flavors. Most of those advertised for their nutritional value merely have vitamins added. More recent health food movements have introduced granola, and now heavily sweetened versions of it are found on store shelves everywhere. (Using excessive amounts of honey instead of sugar does not make a cereal nutritious.)

With careful label reading, it is possible to find a few ready-to-eat cereals, especially in natural food stores that have no chemical additives and little or no sugar. The breakfast cereal alternatives are to make cold cereals from scratch or to eat hot cereals.

## HOT CEREALS

Most grains and some other seeds make good, hot breakfast cereals. A few grains can be cooked whole, but most are better if cracked, ground, or rolled. A grain mill or other home grinder allows experimentation with cereals and cereal mixtures. (Refer to GRINDING, in the GRAINS section.) The protein value of most cereals can be increased by adding several spoonfuls of soy grits to a pot of cereal.

Besides the usual cornmeal, rolled oats, and cracked wheat, many other cereal grains and seeds can be home grown and prepared. Some of these are:

*Amaranth Cereal*   (Also refer to the SEEDS section.) Amaranth seeds cook into cereal in about 20 minutes, and have an excellent flavor. The tiny cooked seeds have an unusual texture, somewhat like fish roe, so many people prefer it mixed with other cereals, such as millet.

*Barley Grits* and *Hominy Grits*   (Refer to the BARLEY and CORN sections.) These look and taste very much alike. Most people like them both immediately.

*Buckwheat Groats or Grits*   (Refer to the BUCKWHEAT section.) Whole, husked buckwheat seeds or groats cook quickly into a soft mush. The flavor of toasted groats is usually preferred. For a grainier texture, make the *Kasha* recipe, in the BUCKWHEAT section.

*Millet* and *Grain Sorghum*   (Refer to the MILLET and SORGHUM sections.) Both are flavorful, but the texture can be somewhat gritty or sandy. For a smoother texture, mix with amaranth seeds, sunflower seed meal, flax seeds, or another cereal.

*Rice*   Cooked brown rice makes an excellent breakfast cereal, especially when raisins or other dried fruits are cooked in it. *Congee* (refer to the RICE section) is another way to have rice for breakfast.

*Sunflower Seeds or Meal*   (Refer to the SUNFLOWER section.) Sunflower seeds are surprisingly good cooked as a cereal. They are, however, quite rich and filling alone, so try them mixed with other cereals.

*Bulghur Wheat or Rye*   Because these grains are cooked and dried before being cracked or ground, they make a quick-cooking cereal that retains the whole-grain flavor. Bulghur wheat or rye can be prepared in large batches and kept on hand for a fast breakfast cereal.


## COLD, READY-TO-EAT CEREALS

The puffed, flaked, shredded, and otherwise strangely shaped, packaged cereals cannot be duplicated at home, as they require heavy machinery and complicated technology. There are, however, some cold cereals that can be made at home in large batches, such as the *Grape Nuts* and *Granola,* below.

# BREAKFAST CEREAL RECIPES

### Basic Hot Cooked Cereal

1 part cereal, such as cracked grain, meal, or grits. (Allow about ¼ cup per serving.)

2 – 3 parts liquid (Water, half water and half milk, or sweet whey. Refer to the WHEY section.)

salt, optional

Heat the liquid to a boil and stir in the cereal gradually to prevent lumps. If any lumps do form, beat them quickly with an egg beater or whisk to break them up. Cereals, such as cornmeal, that lump easily can be mixed first with enough cold liquid to moisten them, then added to the rest of the liquid when it boils. Bring the pot of cereal to a boil, then set on low heat, or put in a double boiler. Stir occasionally till done. If necessary, more water can be added during cooking.

The proportions of liquid to cereal and the cooking time depend on the type of cereal, and on personal tastes. Slow-cooking cereals require the most liquid. A short cooking time with less liquid makes a chewier cereal, while long cooking in more liquid makes a soft, creamy gruel, or congee. Cooking times can vary from 10 minutes to an hour or more. People who like the softer, creamier cereals can start them in the evening to be finished the next morning for breakfast.

Salt can be added to the cereal towards the end of the cooking time, as it may harden or prevent the swelling of some cereals if added too soon. Though hot cereal is habitually salted, this is unfortunate, as the unsalted flavor is very good indeed and well worth getting used to.

Hot cereal is usually eaten with cold milk, but is also excellent with yogurt or buttermilk. Other favored additions are butter, honey or maple syrup, and such fresh fruits as bananas or berries. Raisins and other dried fruits can be cooked with the cereal.

For using leftovers, see BREAKFAST CEREAL IDEAS.

### Grape Nuts

(Makes 5 – 6 cups.)

½ cup honey, or other syrup
½ teaspoon salt, optional
2 cups sour milk, buttermilk, yogurt, or sour whey (Refer to the WHEY section.)

2 tablespoons malt powder, or syrup, optional (Refer to MALTED BARLEY, in the BARLEY section.)
6 – 8 cups whole grain flour (Whole wheat, or a mixture with rye are good.)

Combine the sweetening, sour milk, malt, and salt, if desired. Warm slightly if necessary to mix in the honey. Work in enough

**Upside-down Cereal Cups**
Put leftover hot cereal in cup sized molds or muffin tins that have been rinsed with cold water. Let cool till the cereal has set. For breakfast next morning, butter a baking pan and turn the cups out onto it. Put a dab of butter on each. Bake in a moderate oven for 10 to 15 min., or till heated through. When served in individual bowls with milk and sliced banana or other fruits around them they are so attractive and so good that it is worth cooking extra cereal for them.

**Fried Cereal** Break leftover, cooked cereal into pieces, then fry with onions, or put hot cereal in a mold, let cool, and cut into slices for frying. A slice fried with a fried sausage patty on top is fancy enough for Sunday breakfast.

For hearty cereal patties, mash the leftover cereal and mix with grated cheese, minced onion, parsley or any favored herb combinations, an egg, and pepper. Shape into patties and fry.

**Spoon Bread from Leftovers**
Mix 2 cups leftover, cooked cereal with 2 cups milk. Cornmeal or hominy grits are traditional, but other cereals are also good. Separate 2 or 3 eggs, and mix the yolks with the cereal and milk. Add 1 – 2 tablespoons melted butter or ½ cup cream if desired. Season with pepper and salt to taste. Beat the egg whites till stiff and fold them in. Pour into an ungreased baking dish and bake in a hot oven for 40 min. or till set. Serve hot or warm, dishing it out with a spoon, as a side dish with dinner or a main dish for lunch or supper.

## CEREAL IDEAS, cont.

**Leftover Cooked Cereal in Baked Goods** Small amounts of cooked cereal can be worked into yeast bread dough, or added to the batter of some other baked goods. The cereal adds moisture and an interesting texture, but too much is apt to make bread heavy. In the following old recipe the *Oatmeal Gems* act similarly to popovers. To succeed, the oven must be very hot, about 450°F.

*Miss Herrick's Oatmeal Gems, 1889*

"To half a pint of cooked oatmeal add half a pint of thick sour milk, one egg, a tablespoon of melted butter, half a tablespoonful of syrup, half a teaspoonful of sifted soda, and three gills [1½ cups] of flour; beat thoroughly together; fill hot, well-buttered gem-pans [muffin tins are fine], and bake in a quick oven." (From *In the Kitchen*, by Elizabeth S. Miller, 1875.)

**Popped Corn and other Popped Grains for Breakfast** Unseasoned, popped corn with milk makes an unusual breakfast cereal. Hard wheat and some other grains can also be popped for breakfast. However, they remain rather hard and chewy even after popping, and may be better enjoyed as snacks. (Commercial puffed wheat and rice are shot from a big cannon to pop them and cannot be made at home.)

flour (6 to 8 cups) to make a stiff dough. Pat out the dough in a large, shallow, lightly oiled pan to make a layer ¼ to ½ inch thick. Bake in a low, 300°F oven for about an hour or till it is becoming hard. Break the slab into pieces small enough to be fed into a grinder—this is easiest while it is still warm. Before grinding in a grain mill, dry the pieces completely in a food dryer or very low oven. A meat grinder might be able to handle slightly doughy pieces. Grind to a coarse, "grape nuts" texture. Be sure the grape nuts are completely dry before storing in airtight containers. They keep indefinitely, so large quantities—double this recipe, or more—can be made at one time.

These grape nuts are harder than the commercial variety, so they are best soaked in milk or water for 5 to 10 minutes before they are eaten. The flavor is excellent.

### Granola                                        (Makes about 12 cups.)

Granola can be heavy and hard to digest. This version is lighter than most because it uses less oil. Okara (described in ingredients) makes a particularly light and pleasant mixture. If desired, omit the oil and sweetening completely and lightly toast the ingredients.

*12 cups mixed dry ingredients, including any of the following:*
*rolled oats, up to 9 cups*
*okara, up to 9 cups* (The meal left after making soy milk or tofu. Refer to the TOFU section. If a large quantity is used, dry separately before mixing with other ingredients.)
*1 cup or more rolled wheat, rye, or barley*
*up to 1 cup sunflower, sesame, pumpkin, or flax seeds*
*1 cup or more coconut, shredded, unsweetened*
*up to ½ cup soy flour or grits* (Refer to the SOYBEANS section.)

*1 cup or more wheat germ*
*1 cup or more nuts, chopped*
*½—1 cup carob meal or powder* (Refer to the CAROB section.)
*1 cup or more fruit meal* (Refer to the DRYING FOODS section.)
*1 cup honey, maple syrup, or other syrup*
*½ cup vegetable oil* (Preferably not raw or cold pressed oils that require refrigeration to prevent rancidity.)
*1—2 cups raisins, dried apples, or other dried fruit, chopped if necessary*

Mix the dry ingredients thoroughly. Warm the honey or syrup with the oil to blend completely. Pour over the dry ingredients and mix well. Spread about an inch deep in one or two large shallow pans. Bake in a low, 250°F oven till completely dry and lightly browned. Stir often and turn the pans as necessary to brown the granola evenly. It usually takes from 1 to 2 hours, but could take longer if the mixture is too deep in the pans, or if it is very moist.

When cool, mix in the raisins or other dried fruit. Store in airtight containers. Granola will keep for months stored in a place cool enough to keep nuts or other oily ingredients from becoming rancid.

### Muesli

Muesli is a popular breakfast in Germany and other northern European countries, and is a quick, nutritious meal. Since rolled oats and other rolled grains have been steamed before rolling, they are perfectly healthful eaten without further cooking.

*½ - ¾ cup rolled oats, or other rolled grain* (Oats are the most tender.)
*yogurt, milk, or fruit juice, as desired*
*apple, grated or chopped, or other fresh or dried fruit, as desired*
Any of the following to taste:
    *wheat germ*

*nuts or sunflower seeds, chopped, if necessary*
*honey, or other sweetening*
*cinnamon and spices* (Such as nutmeg, or powdered coriander.)

Mix the rolled oats with enough yogurt, milk, or juice to make a fairly wet mixture. Let soak for a few minutes or overnight, for a very soft texture. Add the apple or other fruit, and other ingredients as desired.

**OTHER RECIPES WITH BREAKFAST CEREALS**

Layered Invented Casseroles, p.116
Soaked Grain Cereals, p.315

# CHEESE, AGED

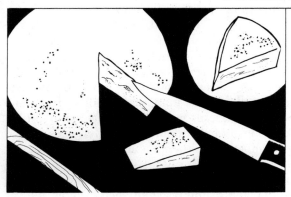

T HE MAKING AND AGING OF CHEESE IS AN ANCIENT PRACTICE— and the traditional way to store extra milk. The first step, making fresh cheese, is a routine activity in most households that keep dairy animals. The additional step of aging, or curing, the cheese requires more interest and dedication. It is both an art and a skill. The combination of intuition and technique that produces consistently good aged cheese must be cultivated, but this should not discourage the home cheese maker. Aging cheese is intrinsically a homestead activity.

The great cheeses of the world were developed rurally, where dairy animals were raised. Modern commercial cheese making can be des-

**STORAGE**

**Cold Storage**  Wrap well to prevent drying. Refrigerate or keep in other cool area. Storage life varies greatly for different types, from 1 mo. to 1 yr. See HOW LONG TO AGE CHEESE, STORING CHEESE WHILE IT AGES, and refer to COLD STORAGE section.

**Freezing**  (Not recommended for most aged cheeses because of damage to texture and loss of flavor. Acceptable for Camembert and similar surface ripened cheeses, and for Parmesan and other hard, grating cheeses.) Cut in about half pound pieces. Wrap well. Quality retained 6–12 mos. Refer to FREEZING section.

I GALLON MILK = ABOUT I POUND AGED CHEESE
¼ POUND CHEESE = ABOUT I CUP GRATED

cribed as a scientific effort to duplicate the conditions and procedures that made particular local farm cheeses so outstanding. Modern home cheese makers may also discover that their own cheeses have uniquely delectable qualities.

The following is a general review of the factors involved in aging cheese. Anyone who wants to become an expert will need a good book or two on the subject as well. (See the REFERENCES at the end of this section. For the basic steps, refer to MAKING FRESH CHEESE in the CHEESE, FRESH section.)

## FACTORS THAT AFFECT AGING OF CHEESE

Cheese undergoes great physical, biological, and chemical changes as it ages. Everything that goes into the cheese and everything that happens to it as it is made and aged affects the final result. Most of the changes and the conditions that cause them can be understood and controlled, but there still remains some mystery. One remarkable and fortuitous change is that, after two months of aging, cheese develops antibiotic properties that kill almost all disease germs that might have been present in the milk.

Some of the factors that affect cheese are—the characteristics of the milk; the acidity, moisture, and fat content of the cheese curd; the shape and size of the cheese; and the number and type of microorganisms in it. Also important are the temperature and humidity of the storage place, and the handling of the cheese's surface, or rind.

***Milk for Cheese***  The quality of the milk drastically affects the cheese. Good-tasting milk from a healthy animal must be used, and cleanliness in handling the milk is essential. Either goat's or cow's milk is fine for most cheeses. Milk from sheep, water buffalo, and a few other animals has also been used. The cheese may vary in taste and texture with different milk, but as long as the milk is fresh and good, the cheese will be good. Cheeses will also be affected by differences between the milk of one animal and another, differences caused by feed and the time of year, and whether the animal is near the beginning or end of her lactation.

Most aged cheeses are made from milk containing some fat. Skim milk cheese tends to be dry and crumbly when aged. Whole milk is most popular for homemade, aged cheeses, but partially skimmed milk or milk with extra cream added is also used.

***Acidity of the Milk***  The acidity level in milk is important for cheese. Old recipes often call for evening milk plus morning milk. The evening milk, sitting all night at 50°F to 60°F, sours slightly, and this added to sweet morning milk gives a good acidity level. Modern recipes usually call for pasteurized milk (in which naturally occuring bacteria have been destroyed) and a culture, usually cultured buttermilk. Freeze dried cultures for making cheese are available by mail order. (See the REFERENCES at the end of this section.) Pasteurized milk plus a culture gives more control, but the old way has produced excellent cheese for centuries, and is still a good method. (For information about raw milk, refer to the MILK section.)

Rennet (refer to the RENNET section) is essential for maintaining the right acidity because it coagulates milk without adding acid. Milk does clabber, or coagulate, by itself, but as it does it becomes too acidic for most cheeses.

The acidity combined with aging gives cheese its sharp taste. A higher level of acidity and longer aging produce a sharper cheese.

***Moisture Content of Cheese***   The moistness of a cheese depends on several things—the amount of whey (moisture) left in the curd after it is cut, the weight with which it is pressed, the heat to which it is subjected, and the amount of salt added. If the curd is cut in small cubes, ¼ to ½ inch, more whey is released and the cheese will be dryer. Larger cubes, ¾ to 1 inch, make a moister cheese. The longer a cheese is pressed and the greater the weight or pressure on it, the dryer it will be. Higher heats and more salt make it dryer, and, with the passage of time as it ages, it gradually becomes dryer. Dry cheese keeps longer and molds less than moist, so it is a little easier to age at home.

The driest cheeses are used for grating. They should keep a year if well wrapped and stored in a cool place. If a homemade cheese turns out drier than intended, use it for grating. If cheese should become so hard that it cannot be grated, try cutting it in small pieces and grinding it.

*Rotary cheese grater*

***Microorganisms in Cheese***   Many types of microorganisms, both helpful and harmful, are attracted to dairy products. The cheese maker adds or encourages the desirable ones and discourages the others. Lactic acid-producing bacteria, which cause milk to become pleasantly sour, are most important. They develop acidity, which discourages the growth of undesirable bacteria, yeasts, and molds. Lactic acid bacteria are present in raw milk, or they can be added in the form of a milk or cheese culture. Undesirable microorganisms are also discouraged by thorough cleanliness in handling the milk and cheese. (Refer to the MILK section.) As it ages, cheese becomes less susceptible to attack by spoilage organisms.

A few special bacteria and molds are available to add to cheeses to give them characteristic tastes or textures. These were originally part of the environment where the cheese was made, and can now be purchased for cheese making. (See the REFERENCES at the end of this section.)

***Cheese Size and Shape***   It is not practical to make cheese for aging with less than a gallon of milk. A gallon makes about a pound of cheese and it is not worth trying to age less. Larger cheeses made from 2 or more gallons of milk usually age better, and there is less waste from the rind.

If the cheese is wrapped with a cloth "bandage" it will be wheel shaped. Otherwise, the shape of a cheese will depend on the mold

used. Many kinds of presses and molds can be made at home that allow pressure on the cheese to be increased gradually by adding more

## TIN CAN CHEESE MOLD AND PRESS

Punch holes in the bottom and
sides of a smooth-sided tin can.
Punch out from inside, and
cheese will not catch. Cut a
wooden follower to fit inside the
can, or if the can is small, use its
lid. Use a jar of something heavy
(water, nails) for a weight.

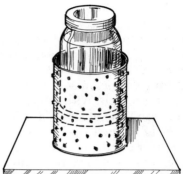

Set dowel sticks solidly in the
bottom board. The top board
slides onto the dowels. Attach the
follower to the top board with
another dowel. Add weight as
needed.

## BANDAGED CHEESE AND PRESS

Wrap cloth bandage securely
around ball of cheese. Pin closed.
Flatten to make a wheel. 4 dowels
will be more solid than 2. Bricks
or a large rock make good
weights.

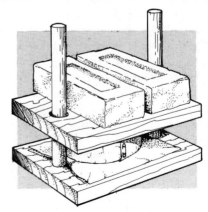

weights. A mold must be large enough to hold the cheese curd, without producing an overly flat or thin cheese after pressing. A few molds and presses are suggested on the previous page. Also refer to the TOFU section, for a wooden mold design.

*Forming the Rind*    After a cheese is pressed, a dry, leathery rind must form to protect it while it ages. The rind helps the cheese retain moisture, and keeps out bacteria and mold. If a cheese has deep cracks or is broken after pressing, a complete rind cannot form, and it must be used fresh. If there are rough or bumpy places on the cheese, they can be trimmed before the rind forms.

Salt helps dry the rind. It can be rubbed in, or the cheese can be soaked in brine. The cheese should then sit on a clean board or cloth covered rack in a cool, airy place that is not too humid, while the rind forms. Turn the cheese every day at first so that the rind can form evenly. Turning also keeps the inside texture even. Olive oil or butter can be rubbed into the rind to help it harden.

In fairly dry climates, the rind protects the cheese quite well, but in humid areas the cheese is apt to mold in spite of the rind. Remove mold by rubbing it with salt, or with a cloth dampened in vinegar. If mold is a continuing problem it is best to wax or paraffin the cheese. This can be done when the initial rind has formed and the surface of the cheese is dry, usually after a week or two of drying.

*Waxing or Paraffining Cheese*    Melt wax or paraffin in a pot large enough to hold the cheese. Beeswax is excellent and, unlike paraffin, can be produced at home. The wax should be deep enough to cover more than half the cheese's surface. A double boiler is the safest container, because wax can catch fire very easily if it touches the stove. Dip one side of the cheese in wax and let it cool. Then hold the waxed side and dip again to cover the rest of the cheese. It may be necessary to repeat the process once or twice more for a smooth coating.

There should be an airtight seal between the cheese and the wax or paraffin. If moisture appears on the cheese under the wax, the cheese rind was not dry enough for waxing. It should air dry for a few days longer.

*How Long to Age Cheese*    The flavor and texture of cheese continues to change as it ages. The cheese is ready whenever it tastes good. That may take only a few weeks, or as long as a year. It is interesting to eat cheeses at different stages and choose when they taste best.

*Storing Cheese While It Ages*    The ideal place to age cheese is a cool, airy room, such as a cellar or pantry. The best temperature is between 40°F and 55°F. The highest acceptable humidity is around 85%. Cheeses have been hung in wells or even under very shady trees to age. These makeshift systems are most successful in climates that are neither very dry nor very damp. A spare refrigerator set above

## AGED CHEESE IDEAS

**Grated Cheese on the Table**
Parmesan and Romano cheese are often set on the table with Italian dishes for people to help themselves. A small, hand turned, rotary grater can be passed around for truly fresh, grated hard cheeses, and they go well with many styles of food besides Italian. Softer cheeses like cheddar can also be grated and set out to be sprinkled on soup, salads, vegetables, casseroles, and bean dishes.

**Cheese in Casseroles** Sliced, diced, or grated cheese is excellent in many casseroles. It can be layered with other ingredients, added to a mixture or sprinkled on top a few minutes before the casserole is done. Cheese added to a vegetable casserole will turn it into a one-dish meal.

**Bread and Cheese Casserole**
Spread slices of bread lightly with prepared mustard. Layer bread and sliced cheese in a buttered baking dish. Beat several eggs with enough milk to barely cover the bread, and pour it over all. Let soak a few minutes, then bake in a moderate oven till set, about 30 min. Let the casserole sit a few minutes before serving.

**Cheese Pancakes or Waffles**
Mix grated cheese into pancake or waffle batter. Serve for breakfast, lunch or supper with meat and vegetables. Try cheese waffles topped with sautéed chicken livers—exceptionally good!

**Cheese and Apples** Almost any combination is good. Serve raw apple slices and cheese for a snack or dessert. Diced or shredded cheese adds zest to many apple desserts. Half a cup is delicious mixed with the apples in an apple pie, and try the *Date Cheese Filling* recipe in the APPLES section.

**Cheese and Pepper Pie** Sauté long strips of green or red sweet

40°F is a good place to age waxed cheeses. When the temperature is too low, cheeses age too slowly, and when it is too high, cheeses tend to mold or sour.

## CHEESE RECIPES

(Aged cheese can also be used in some FRESH CHEESE RECIPES in the next section.)

### *Old English Herbed Cheese Spread*          (Makes about 1 cup.)

*1 cup cheese, grated*
*1–2 tablespoons fresh herbs, very finely minced* (Refer to FINES HERBES, in the HERBS section.)

*3 tablespoons dry sherry, apple cider, or dry, homemade wine* (Refer to the WINE section.)
*1 tablespoon butter*
*3 tablespoons top milk or cream*

Put all the ingredients in a heavy saucepan or the top of a double boiler. Heat gently, stirring constantly until well blended and creamy. Make sure all the cheese has melted and blended. Pack into a small container and chill. Spread on crackers or toast. This makes about a cup of cheese spread, and keeps several weeks refrigerated.

*Hot Cheese Dip* Omit butter and milk or cream. Herbs are optional. If a spicy flavor is wanted, add a tiny pinch of cayenne and a teaspoon of soy sauce. Serve when hot and well blended. To eat, spear cubes of toast on a fork or toothpick and dip in the cheese mixture. This makes a delicious hors d'oeuvre, and a chafing dish will keep the dip hot.

*Cider Rarebit* Omit butter and milk or cream. Herbs are optional. Increase proportions to 2 cups cheese (Swiss is good), and ¾ cup cider. Let the cheese and cider sit for several hours in a saucepan, then heat, pour over toast, and serve immediately. This is enough for 4 to 6 servings. (For a conventional rarebit use the *Cheese Sauce* recipe, in the MILK section, or melt ½ pound cheese in 2 cups milk and season to taste.)

### *Cheese-Onion Quiche*          (Makes about 6 servings.)

*pastry for two 9 inch pie pans, bottom crusts only* (Whole wheat flour is best.)
*3 cups onion, chopped*
*2 tablespoons butter*
*2½ cups cheese, grated*

*fresh hot pepper, minced, or cayenne powder, to taste*
*3 cups milk*
*4–5 eggs, lightly beaten*
*½ teaspoon thyme or other herbs*

Line pie pans with pastry. Sauté the onions in butter till they are limp and translucent, but not browned. Spread half the onions in each pastry shell, then spread half the cheese over the onions. Sprinkle with hot pepper. Mix the milk, eggs, and thyme, and pour over the cheese in each pan. Bake at 350°F till set, usually from 25 to 30 minutes. Let cool a few minutes before serving. Less rich and less salty than many quiche recipes, and an excellent main course for any meal.

*Leftovers Quiche*   Reduce onions to about 1 cup. Use 2 cups of leftover, cooked meat or vegetables in their place. Combinations that include cooked sausage, ham, or bacon, and green vegetables, such as asparagus, zucchini, green pepper, green beans, or broccoli are excellent.

### REFERENCES AND SOURCES FOR CHEESE MAKING

Charles Hansen's Laboratory, 9015 Maple St., Milwaukee, Wis, 53214. Their agent in Canada is the Horan-Lally Company, Ltd., 1146 Aerowood Drive, Mississauga, Ontario, Canada, L4W 1Y5. (This is the primary mail order source of cheese cultures, rennet, and other dairy related supplies. They also have a good free recipe for hard cheese.)

Flake, Lue Dean, *Kitchen Cheese Making,* Stackpole Books, Harrisburg, Pa. (This includes directions for many special kinds of cheeses. Directions are detailed and the results will be the genuine cheese, not just a similar one.)

New England Cheesemaking Supply Co. P. O. Box 85, Ashfield, Mass. 01330. (This is a good mail order source of cheese making supplies. They are also helpful about answering questions.)

---

## CHEESE, FRESH

When milk coagulates, or clabbers, and separates into curds and whey, the curds (solid material) are cheese and the liquid is whey. Simple enough—except that there are many ways to coagulate milk and many ways to separate curds from whey, and many, many ways to handle curds to make a vast variety of cheeses. Fresh cheeses are those made to be eaten immediately, or within a week or two. Cottage cheese is the best known fresh cheese in North America, but there are many others.

---

**AGED CHEESE IDEAS,**
*cont.*

pepper till limp. Line a pie pan with them. Put a thick layer of diced or sliced cheese on the peppers and press firmly into place. Lightly beat several eggs and pour over all. Bake in a moderate oven till eggs are set, 30–40 min. Cut in wedges and serve. For a more pungent flavor sauté one or two Jalapeño peppers with the sweet peppers, or use all hot peppers, and serve very small wedges as hors d'oeuvres.

---

**OTHER RECIPES FEATURING CHEESE**

---

**STORAGE**

**Freezing** (Most fresh cheeses freeze well. An exception is rinsed or store bought cottage cheese, which becomes dry and rubbery. Unrinsed, homemade cottage cheese is acceptable frozen.) Pack loose cheese in containers. Wrap firm pieces. Quality retained 4–6 mos. Refer to FREEZING section.

1 GALLON MILK = ABOUT 1½ QUARTS LOOSE FRESH CHEESE

Most fresh cheeses are so easy to make, that they soon become routine for people who keep dairy animals. Aging, or curing cheese is a more painstaking process. It is best to learn to make fresh cheese before trying to age cheese, so that clabbering (souring, thickening, and separating into curds and whey) becomes familiar. Years ago, curds and whey were often eaten together, as Miss Muffit was doing when the spider sat down beside her. They were enjoyed plain, or with sugar and cream.

This old recipe for Bonny-Clabber shows an earlier way to do things, and the loving care necessary to make curds and whey a delicacy. From *In The Kitchen,* Elizabeth S. Miller, 1875.

## BONNY-CLABBER

"For this dish the milk should sour and thicken quickly; before it has thickened it may be poured in any shallow glass or china dish, and when thick placed on the ice for an hour or two before serving. There is no objection to serving it in the pan, if it be bright and clean, and the bonny-clabber cold. If there is cream on the surface leave it unbroken; a saucer or a shallow ladle may be used for helping it, and when not in use should lie on a plate, not in the bonny-clabber. To be eaten from deep dessert-plates, sprinkled with brown sugar and a little grated nutmeg, with sweet cream poured *around* it, not over the top, hiding the beauty which is half its charm. After the bonny-clabber has been disturbed, whey collects in the bottom of the pan; be careful to avoid it in the second helping."

## MAKING FRESH CHEESE

It is only a small step from clabber to cottage cheese and a wide range of other fresh cheeses. Most kitchens have the equipment necessary for making fresh cheese, with the exception of a dairy thermometer. Milk temperatures have to be carefully controlled during some cheese making steps, so a thermometer is essential. Utensils needed are: a large, stainless steel or enameled pot, or a large crock (aluminum should not be used) that will fit inside a larger pan or pot for a double boiler; a large colander or strainer; and some light cotton cloth or cheesecloth for draining the cheese.

Fresh, good tasting milk is the vital ingredient. Often rennet (refer to the RENNET section) and a starter culture, such as cultured buttermilk, are also called for. Salt is optional in most fresh cheeses, but salted cheese will keep a few days longer.

## WHAT CHEESE MAKERS DO

### Making Fresh Cheese

Test coagulated milk with bent finger to see if it has set firmly enough to show a clean break.

First and second cuts. Hold knife vertically.

Cut curd four ways for cubes of about the same size.

Third cut. Hold knife diagonally.

Fourth cut. Hold knife diagonally.

Warm curds and whey slowly in double boiler arrangement. Use thermometer to control temperature. Stir gently with wooden spoon or clean hand every few minutes.

Drain curds in cloth-lined colander. Or gather cloth at top to make a bag for hanging curds to drain.

### Cottage Cheese

Any sour milk will separate into curds and whey when heated. Some will separate without heat. For centuries, cottagers with dairy animals have used this phenomenon to make cheese and, as a result, there are almost as many versions of cottage cheese as there are, or were, cottages. New versions are still being developed on small homesteads today.

Cottage cheese is almost always made from skim milk. Because cow's milk is easy to skim, it is used more often than goat's milk, which is just as good. (Refer to the CREAM section.) Some ways to start cottage cheese are to use pasteurized milk and a starter culture and let it clabber, or to use pasteurized milk, a starter, and rennet to coagulate the milk. (If milk does not clabber or set as it should refer to YOGURT PROBLEMS, in the YOGURT section.)

When the milk has set, it is usually cut into cubes, heated to firm the curds, and drained. If cutting the curds and heating are omitted, the result will resemble a cream cheese.

### Large Curd Cottage Cheese (With rennet.) (Makes about 1½ quarts.)

*1 gallon skim milk* (May be pasteurized, or dried reconstituted.)
*¼ cup cultured buttermilk or another cheese culture*

*half the amount rennet usually used to coagulate 1 gallon milk (about ⅛ Hansen's tablet)*

Have the milk at room temperature, and mix in the buttermilk or other culture. Using a double boiler, heat the milk very slowly to 90°F. If it is heated too quickly or if it gets too hot, the culture will be killed. Dissolve the rennet tablet in several tablespoons of cold water and mix with the milk. Keep the milk warm, near 90°F but not above, till it coagulates and shows a little whey on the surface. This takes 5 to 6 hours, or longer if the temperature falls too far.

Cut the curd into ½ inch cubes. Slowly heat to between 100 and 115°F. Maintain this temperature for 20 to 30 minutes, or till the curds have become firm. Stir often with a wooden spoon or clean hand. Pour into cloth lined colander to drain. The cloth can be gathered and tied to make a bag for hanging the curds as they drain. Once or twice lift a corner of the cloth to partly turn the curds. When most of the dripping has stopped, turn the cottage cheese into a bowl and salt if desired. The curds can be rinsed, still in the cloth, in a pan of cool water, by swishing them gently and draining them again, but as this cheese is mild it is usually not necessary.

***Quick Cottage Cheese*** Use twice as much rennet as above (¼ Hansen's tablet) to set the milk. It will set in an hour or less. These curds will be bland. A little yogurt or sour cream can be added to perk up the flavor. (Also see VINEGAR CHEESE, below.)

## *Fresh Cheese from Whole Milk*

(Good made with goat's milk.)      (Makes about 1½ quarts.)

1 gallon whole milk
¼ cup cultured buttermilk, or
     yogurt, or other cheese culture

rennet to coagulate 1 gallon milk
     (¼ Hansen's tablet.)
1 teaspoon salt, or to taste, op-
     tional

Have the milk at room temperature and mix in the buttermilk or yogurt. Using a double boiler, slowly heat the milk to 86°F. Dissolve rennet in several tablespoons of cold water and mix thoroughly with the milk. Let stand till a curd forms, in about 30 to 40 minutes. Test with a finger for a clean break. Goat's milk tends to take longer to set than cow's milk.

When the curd is ready, cut it into ½ inch cubes. Heat very slowly in the double boiler to 100°F over 30 to 45 minutes. Stir often with a clean hand or wooden spoon to keep the temperature even throughout the pot, and the curds separate. If any curds are too large, cut them with a small knife. Gradually the curds will become firmer, and when done will have a tendency to stick together. Sometimes goat's milk curds separate into small particles. The cheese will still be good, as long as the curds and whey are separated.

Pour the curds into a cloth lined colander and drain. The cheese can now be handled like cottage cheese in the preceding recipes. However, if it is pressed to make a firm slicing cheese, the flavor improves during the pressing time. Mix salt, if desired, with the curds after most of the whey has drained off. Put the curds in a press lined with cheesecloth or soft cotton cloth. Press for 5 or 6 hours, or overnight, increasing the pressure several times. (Refer to the cheese molds and presses illustrated in the CHEESE, AGED section.)

Refrigerate the cheese and use within a week or so. Slices sprinkled with freshly ground black pepper are superb. This cheese can also be aged or cured to make a hard cheese. (Refer to the CHEESE, AGED section.)

**Round Cheese** Instead of pressing the curds, hang them in their draining cloth after salting. Leave for 24 hours, or up to 2 or 3 days. If the cloth will not come away from the cheese, run warm water over it till it loosens.

**Brined Cheese** Press the cheese for 5 or 6 hours, or overnight, without salting it. Make enough brine to cover the cheese by about an inch, using 4½ tablespoons of plain salt for every quart of water needed. Soak the cheese from 12 to 24 hours. A small cheese requires less time than a large one. Turn the cheese once or twice to ensure that the brine penetrates all sides. Drain for about an hour on a cloth covered rack. Cover and refrigerate. Keeps for a week or more, longer than most fresh cheeses. If made with goat's milk, this cheese is somewhat like Greek feta cheese and can be used in the same ways.

### Cream Cheese                                                  (Makes about ½ pound.)

True cream cheese is made from cream, but cheese with a soft, creamy texture made from whole or even skim milk is also called cream cheese. All creamy cheeses can be used in the same ways. (Two excellent variations are the *Yogurt Cream Cheese* and the *Buttermilk Cheese* recipes, in the YOGURT and BUTTER sections, respectively.)

*1 quart cream*
*2 tablespoons cultured buttermilk or another cheese culture*
*rennet to coagulate 1 quart milk*
*(¼ tablet Junket rennet or a*

crumb of a Hansen's rennet tablet), *optional*
*¼ – ½ teaspoon salt, optional*
(But helps preserve the cheese.)

Have the cream at 60 to 65°F. Mix the buttermilk in thoroughly. Dissolve the rennet in 1 to 2 tablespoons of cold water. Add to the cream and mix it well also. Dip a square of finely woven cloth in boiling water, wring it out, and lay it in a pot or bowl. Pour in the cream. Gather and tie the cloth's corners to make a bag, and hang to drain for 1 to 2 days. To hasten draining, take down the bag several times, open it, and scrape the thick, pasty cheese off the sides of the cloth. Changing the cheese to a new, sterilized cloth once or twice, or tying the bag securely and putting on a light weight, will also speed draining.

When the cream cheese is thick enough, mix in the salt, if desired, and pack into molds or small containers. It will keep up to 2 weeks if salted and refrigerated.

**Whole Milk Cream Cheese**  Follow the above recipe using whole milk or whole milk with cream added, or, for a low fat version, add ½ cup powdered milk to 2 quarts whole milk. (Since the yield is less than with cream, this recipe is usually doubled when using whole milk.) After adding the buttermilk and rennet, let the milk sit till clabbered. Rennet makes it clabber faster, but the texture will be smoother without it. In a warm room and using rennet, the milk will clabber in several hours. In a cooler room (60°F), it may take 12 or more hours. When set, hang and drain as for regular cream cheese.

If fresh milk is not available, 2 quarts reconstituted, powdered milk, 1 large can evaporated milk, and ½ cup buttermilk will make an excellent cream cheese.

### Mozzarella                                      (Usually makes 4 half pound cheeses.)

Mozzarella is one of several kinds of "plastic-curd" cheeses originating in Italy. In making them the curds are kneaded, which expels whey and produces plasticity. Because of their dense texture they keep well in warm climates and are ideal for smoking. Provolone is an aged version of a plastic-curd cheese. Mozzarella is one of the most versatile cheeses to make at home, since it tastes wonderful freshly made, freezes well, and can be used like an aged cheese in cooking, melting readily when heated.

> 2 gallons milk, pasteurized and
>   cooled to 90°F
> 7 tablespoons cultured buttermilk
> 6 tablespoons yogurt
>
> rennet to coagulate 2 gallons
>   milk (½ Hansen's tablet)
>   dissolved in about ½ cup cold
>   water

Start this cheese in the evening. Maintain the milk at 90°F in a double boiler. Mix the buttermilk and yogurt separately with a little of the milk to remove lumps, then blend into the rest of the milk. Add the rennet solution and mix thoroughly. Let sit till the curd sets and breaks clearly when tested with a finger, about 20 to 30 minutes.

Cut the curd into ½ inch cubes as evenly as possible. Maintain at 90°F for 15 minutes, stirring with a clean hand. The curds are fragile because they have not been cooked, so stir very gently, just enough to keep them from matting together. Gently pour the curds into a cloth lined colander. When the whey has drained, the curd should be in one solid piece. Rinse in cold water, then soak in a pan of cold water for 15 minutes. If it is a big batch, cut the curd into several blocks, 4 or 5 inches square. Drain off most of the water, then refrigerate the curds, or keep in a cool, 40°F place. Leave them in a colander or other container that allows drainage. (Commercially, mozzarella curds are shipped to delicatessens at this stage, where the cheese is finished.)

The next day, warm the cheese to room temperature so it will ripen, or become more acidic. After an hour or so, test the cheese for acidity as follows. Cut off a small piece of cheese and cut it into three ½ inch cubes. Heat several cups of water in a sauce pan to 165°F. Put in the cubes and stir for 5 minutes. Remove the cubes and mold them together like modeling clay. Reheat the lump of cheese in the water for a minute, then remove and work or mold it together a little more. After repeating several times, try to pull the curd apart. If it breaks or tears, and clouds the water, it is underripe. Wait an hour or so and test it again. When it pulls into a long rope and can be molded together again, it is ready. It will have a glossy surface and will cloud the water only slightly.

The whole cheese is treated somewhat like the test sample to finish it. Cut it into small cubes and put them in a pan. Heat water to 170°F and pour enough over them, to cover the curds by about 2 inches. Keep a thermometer in the pan and let the temperature drop to 135°F. Press the cubes together, and then knead the cheese, by stretching and pulling it, as if working modelling clay. It should become "plastic" and stretch into long strands. When it does, shape into half pound balls, or make a thick rope, fold it in half, and twist several times to make a decorative oblong cheese. Mozzarella can be dipped in hot water to make a glossy surface, or wrapped in cheese cloth to protect it. To keep the cheese very fresh tasting for up to a week, keep it in a bowl of water in the refrigerator, and change the water every day.

To salt mozzarella for longer keeping, or to prepare it for smoking, soak it in brine for 4 or 5 hours (see BRINED CHEESE, above).

The whey from making mozzarella is perfect for making ricotta because it does not have a chance to develop much acidity.

**Smoked Mozzarella** Mozzarella and many other firm cheeses can be cold smoked for flavor. Salting and smoking both help preserve the cheese by drying it, and discouraging bacteria and insects. Set the cheese on a rack in the smoker, or wrap in cheesecloth and hang it. Keep the temperature below 90°F to prevent sweating of butterfat or melting. Smoke at 60 to 85°F for 4 to 15 hours. (Refer to the SMOKING section.)

### Ricotta

(From ¼ cup to 2 cups, depending on method and ingredients.)

Ricotta is like a very finely curded cottage cheese. It is thought of as a whey cheese, but it is actually the name for a method of precipitating solid material, or curd, out of whey left from making other cheeses. For true whey cheese, refer to the WHEY section. The name ricotta is also applied to ricotta-like cheeses made with milk instead of whey.

The original Italian ricotta is made from sweet, or low-acid, whey, and ricotta curds are precipitated with an acid ingredient, such as vinegar. A type of reverse ricotta can be made by heating sour whey and adding milk or reconstituted powdered milk. The textures will be similar, but the flavor of true ricotta is more delicate.

Ricotta making is often unpredictable, since the whey from different cheese batches varies considerably in acidity. The most successful ricotta makers make the same kind of cheese regularly, so the whey will always be about the same. They can then experiment to learn the best way to handle their whey for ricotta. The following basic recipe uses sweet whey.

*several quarts sweet whey*
*¼ cup milk per quart whey, optional*
   (Whole milk makes a moister
   cheese than skim.)

*acid coagulant, enough to induce*
*curd formation (½ – 3 table-*
*spoons vinegar, lemon or*
*lime juice, or very sour*
*whey.)*

Mix whey and milk, and heat to about 200°F, or till it is almost boiling. Stir in ½ to 3 tablespoons of vinegar, or lemon or lime juice. If sour whey is used, more will probably be needed, depending on its acidity. Add more acid coagulant if nothing happens, and if nothing happens this time ricotta is unlikely to form from this batch of whey.

The ricotta curds should form and rise quickly after the acid has been added. Be ready to skim them off with a skimmer, a small sieve, or a piece of cloth held on two sides and dipped under them. Drain the ricotta in a cloth lined strainer. (Flavor and texture are better when the curds are skimmed off rather than poured into the strainer.) Adding more acidic coagulant may cause a second batch of curds to form. The amount of ricotta will be small compared to the amount of whey, especially when milk has not been added.

Let the ricotta drain till it is cool. If a solid block of cheese is wanted, press it in a mold for a few hours. A tablespoon of buttermilk per 1–2 cups ricotta can be added to ripen the cheese slightly while it is pressed.

**Vinegar Cheese**  Instead of whey, use milk, and coagulate with vinegar. Milk that has been refrigerated several days often works better than absolute fresh milk. Heat the milk to 180°F, remove from stove, add 4 to 5 tablespoons vinegar per gallon of milk, and stir till curds form. Wait 2 or 3 minutes, then skim out curds and drain as for ricotta.

For a Mexican version, queso blanco, mix in chopped pimientos, green chiles, jalapeños, pitted ripe olives, and salt to taste, after the cheese has been drained. Press for 8 to 10 hours to make a firm slicing cheese. Eat within 2 or 3 weeks.

**Powdered Milk Ricotta**  Heat sour whey until almost simmering. Add ¾ to 1 cup reconstituted, powdered milk per quart of whey and stir well. Curds should form as for regular ricotta. Fresh milk can be used instead of powdered.

## FRESH CHEESE RECIPES

### Mozzarella in a Carriage                (Makes 4–6 moderate servings.)

| | |
|---|---|
| ½ cup flour, preferably whole grain | 1–2 eggs |
| dash of pepper | mozzarella cheese, sliced ¼ inch |
| ¼ teaspoon salt, optional | thick |
| water | oil, for frying |

Combine flour, pepper, and salt. Add enough water, several tablespoons at a time, to make a thick batter. Beat in the eggs with a fork to make a smooth, pancake-like batter. Dip the mozzarella slices in the batter and fry in hot oil, turning once to brown both sides. Serve immediately.

These can be enjoyed for breakfast, lunch, or dinner.

**Fresh Cheese, Fried**  Any fresh cheese that is firm enough to be sliced can be fried. Slices can be coated with flour and fried in butter instead of using batter and oil.

## FRESH CHEESE IDEAS

**Seasonings for Fresh Cheese**
Chives in cottage cheese are traditional, but many other herbs and seasonings add interest to fresh soft cheeses. Try minced parsley, dill or fennel leaves, chervil, fresh savory or sage leaves, or other fresh herbs. Herb seeds, such as caraway, dill, and celery, are very good. For a cottage cheese salad, mix in grated onion or minced scallion, minced green pepper, minced celery, and paprika or freshly ground black pepper.

**Fresh Cheese Dips and Spreads** Most smooth textured, homemade, fresh cheeses are delicious as dips and spreads without additional seasonings. (Large curd cottage cheese can be put through a food mill to make it smooth.) Any soft fresh cheese can be substituted for cream cheese in dip and sandwich recipes.

**Fresh Cheese with Hot Potatoes or Pasta** Hot boiled potatoes served with a fresh, soft cheese like cottage cheese or ricotta is a German peasant dish well worth trying. Fresh cheese is also good with baked potatoes, or any hot, just-cooked pasta, especially egg noodles. A sprinkling of pepper, and minced chives, scallions, or onion adds a piquant finishing touch.

**Cream Cheese Ice Cream**
Mix cream cheese with an equal amount of whipped cream, or chilled and whipped canned milk. Flavor with fruit and honey, or with jam, and freeze. This makes a rich, delightful dessert. (Refer to the ICE CREAM section.)

### Fresh Cheese Custard          (Makes 6–8 servings.)

| | |
|---|---|
| 1 pound fine curd cottage cheese, ricotta or other soft, fresh cheese | ¼ cup flour |
| 1 cup yogurt or thick buttermilk | 1 tablespoon lemon or orange peel, grated, or 1 teaspoon vanilla, optional |
| 3 eggs, separated | |
| ½ cup honey, or other sweetening | 1 tablespoon lemon juice, or other tart juice, optional |

Stir together cheese, yogurt or buttermilk, egg yolks, sweetening, and flour. Add citrus or vanilla flavorings, as desired. If the cheese is tart flavored as it sometimes is when homemade, lemon juice is not needed. Beat the egg whites stiff and fold into the cheese mixture. Pour into a baking dish and bake in a moderate oven till set, about 30 to 40 minutes. Test by cutting with a knife, as for custard.

This delectable pudding sometimes separates into two layers, with a custard-like bottom and a cheesecake-like top.

### Papanash
(Cheese dumplings from the Balkans.)          (Makes 4–6 side servings.)

| | |
|---|---|
| ½ pound whole milk Cream Cheese, (recipe above), or similar soft cheese | 1 tablespoon semolina, or cornmeal |
| 1 tablespoon soft butter, optional | 1 cup flour (about), preferably whole grain |
| 1 egg | |

Mix cheese, butter, and egg thoroughly. Add semolina or cornmeal, and work in enough flour to make a fairly stiff dough. Heat a pot of water to simmering and drop teaspoonfuls of dough into the water. Dip the spoon in cold water between spoonfuls to help prevent sticking. When all the dough is in, cover, and simmer 15 minutes. Do not let the water boil hard, or the dumplings will break up.

Lift the papanash out of the water with a slotted spoon or small sieve. Serve hot with butter or sour cream, or sprinkle with breadcrumbs sautéed in butter. They can also be dusted with brown sugar and eaten for dessert.

### Fried Cottage Cheese Patties    (Makes 10–12 medium-sized patties.)

| | |
|---|---|
| 1½ cups cottage cheese, or other soft fresh cheese | ½ teaspoon sage or rosemary or other herbs |
| 1½ cups bread crumbs | 3–4 eggs |
| 1½ cups rolled oats | oil or fat for frying |
| 1 medium onion, minced | tomato sauce, seasoned to taste, optional |
| several sprigs parsley, minced | |

Mix together cottage cheese, bread crumbs, rolled oats, onion, parsley, and herbs. Blend in enough eggs to hold the mixture together. Form patties, and fry to lightly brown both sides. They are delicious served with tomato sauce, or another sauce, such as a cream sauce or a leftover gravy.

These patties freeze well after frying. They make a quick meal taken from the freezer, put in a shallow ungreased baking dish, covered with tomato sauce, and baked in a moderate oven till bubbly, about 20 to 30 minutes.

***Cheese Nut Patties*** Mix 2 cups cottage cheese, 5 to 6 chopped, hard-boiled eggs, ½ cup bread crumbs, ½ cup ground nuts or sunflower seeds, and seasonings to taste. Fry as above. These patties make a good hi-protein main course for a vegetarian meal, but they do not freeze well because the egg whites become tough.

### OTHER RECIPES FEATURING FRESH CHEESE

Casserole Marinara, p.117
Cheesecake, p.708
Cottage Cheese, Cream Cheese, or Sour Cream Gelatines, p.301
Cream Cheese Pie, p.707
Kale (or Green) Cakes, p.365
The Foolproof Omelet, p.249
Persimmon Cheese Balls, p.476
Spinach and Cheese Pie, p.590
Stuffed Pepper Salads, p.473

# CHERRIES

THE SEASON FOR FRESH CHERRIES IS SHORT AND SWEET, SO THE provident person who is lucky enough to have surplus cherries will want to capture some of the sweetness and flavor for other seasons of the year. Canned cherries, dried cherries, cherry juice, cherry preserves, and all the delicacies that can be made from cherries are sure to cheer the dreariest winter day. One only hopes that the dreary days come to an end before the cherries.

Though cherries are usually classed as either sweet or sour, some varieties are inbetween. Sweet cherries are most often enjoyed plain. Even when canned, dried, or frozen, they are delicious plain. It is sour cherries that are best for cooking and making juice. Wild cherries, almost always sour and flavorful, make a fine juice, and are good in mixtures with blander fruits. When they can be picked in large enough amounts, wild cherries are well worth the effort.

## HANDLING CHERRIES

Cherries keep best if picked with stems left on, but people with their own cherry trees may prefer to pick them without stems so as to avoid damage to the trees, fruiting twigs, or to have them ready for

### STORAGE

**Canning** Pit (see below), or prick unpitted with large needle to prevent bursting. Unpitted hold shape best.

**Raw Pack** Shake down in jars, add boiling syrup or other liquid, ½ in. headroom. Process boiling water bath, Pint: 20 min. Quart: 25 min.

**Hot Pack** Heat slowly in pot, add water to prevent sticking if unpitted. Sweetening, optional. When they boil, pack in jars, add boiling water if necessary, ½ in. headroom. Process boiling water bath. Pints: 10 min. Quarts: 15 min. Refer to CANNING section, and CANNING FRUIT JUICE AND SAUCE, in FRUITS section.

**Drying** Pitted (see below) preferred. If not, crack skins in boiling water to speed drying. Dry sweet cherries till leathery, sticky; sour cherries till hard. Or make fruit leather. Refer to DRYING FOODS section.

**Freezing**  Pitted (see below) preferred. (Pits may add almond flavor.) Pack plain, or sweetened, or covered with liquid. (A pectin pack is excellent. Refer to PECTIN section.) Sweet cherries hold color best in liquid or sprinkled with lemon juice. Refer to FREEZING section.

2–2½ POUNDS = I QUART UNPITTED;  I BUSHEL (56 POUNDS) = 22–23 QUARTS UNPITTED

*Cherry pitter*

use without the extra step of removing stems. Cherries picked stemless should be eaten or processed very soon or they will spoil at the spot where the stem was removed.

Sour cherries become sweeter if left on the tree for an extra week or two after they first ripen, but will require protection from birds.

Cherry juice is an excellent, but often overlooked, way to use cherries. The best juice comes from sour cherries. Sweet cherry juice tastes bland and is best mixed with sour cherry juice or another tart juice. (Refer to the FRUITS section.) Cherries are sometimes candied, (refer to *Candied Fruit and Citrus Peel* in the FRUITS section), but dried, sweet cherries are healthier, and can be used in the same ways. Maraschino cherries are heavily processed, not worth the trouble of making at home, and not really even worth eating. Their processing involves a long soak in lime and sulphur dioxide followed by cooking and draining. This makes them white and flavorless, so then they are sweetened, artificially flavored, and dyed red. Instead, use cherry preserves or dried sweet cherries.

***Pitting Cherries***  For many uses cherries must be pitted, and doing large numbers by hand is tedious, at best. Some use the looped end of a clean hair pin or paper clip, pushing it in at the stem end to hook the pit and pull it out. Others find it easiest to slit the cherry with a small knife and pick out the pit. Always work over a bowl to catch the dripping juice. Less juice will drip out if the cherries are chilled before pitting.

Anyone who pits cherries regularly will find it worthwhile to buy a cherry pitter. There are several kinds. The simplest is a small hand held tool that pits one cherry at a time. There is also a fairly inexpensive pitter that clamps onto the table and is turned by hand. It does the job quickly and can also be used to pit canned, black olives.

***Uses for Cherry Pits***  A dilute juice for a fruit drink can be made from cherry pits and the bits of fruit left on them. Cover with water, heat to a boil, then strain off the juice. Chill, sweeten if needed, and use like lemonade.

The kernels inside cherry pits can be used in several ways. In the Middle East the kernels of black cherries, called "mahleb," are crushed and used as a food flavoring. A tablespoon of crushed mahleb added to *Syrian Bread* (recipe in the BREAD, YEAST section) gives a delightful flavor. An American Indian use was to stew black wild cherry kernels together with the fruit, some maple syrup, and some apple cider to be used as sauce for cornmeal or puddings. The kernels of cherries and other stone fruits are sometimes pressed commercially for the oil in them. The leftover press-cake has been used as a stock feed.

Cracking cherry pits for the kernels is like shelling very small nuts. If the pits are crushed with just enough pressure to crack the shells, the kernels can be picked out.

## CHERRY RECIPES

*Sour Cherry-Meat Stew,*                    (Makes about 6
*Middle Eastern Style*                       dinner servings.)

2 pounds stewing lamb, veal, or         2 cups sour cherries, pitted (May
    other meat, in 1 inch cubes              be canned or frozen, un-
4 tablespoons butter                         sweetened.)
1 cup split peas, or other dried peas   1 apple, diced, or ⅓ cup raisins
1 small onion, or 4 scallions,          pepper, salt, optional
    chopped, optional

Lightly brown the meat in butter in a stew pot or Dutch oven. Add peas and enough water to cover them and the meat. If canned cherries are used, drain them, and replace some of the water with juice. Bring to a boil and skim off any scum. Cover and simmer until both meat and peas are done, 1½ to 2 hours. Add a little extra water while cooking if the stew dries out, being careful not to make it too soupy.

Add onions, cherries, apple or raisins, pepper and salt, if desired. Simmer for 30 minutes more to blend flavors. This stew is usually served with rice.

*Cherry Fritters*         (Makes about 6 snack or dessert servings.)

2 eggs                                  1 tablespoon rum, optional
½ cup flour, preferably whole grain    1 cup fat for frying (Half butter
1 tablespoon honey                          and half oil is very good.)
                                        1 pound cherries, with stems on

Mix eggs, flour, honey, and rum together to make a smooth batter. Let sit for about an hour.

Heat the fat in a frying pan until it is quite hot but not smoking. Dip each cherry in the batter and stand it up in the fat. Turn the cherries if necessary to make them brown and crisp on all sides. Blot them on paper towels and serve. They can be sprinkled with powdered sugar or carob powder.

So they will not tip over, the cherries can also be tied, several in a bunch by their stems, and fried together. Then a little batter can be poured around the cherries after they are in the fat. If preferred, simple pancake batter can be used.

---

### CHERRY IDEAS

**Cherries with Maple Syrup or Maple Sugar**  Sour cherries are especially good sweetened with maple syrup or sugar. They can be stewed in a little maple syrup, or in their own juice with maple sugar. The American Indians often used this combination. The *Maple Fruit Preserves* (in the JAM AND JELLY section) are excellent made with sour cherries.

**Cherries Instead of Berries or Currants**  Pitted cherries can replace berries or currants in most recipes. They are also good in most fruit mixtures.

**Cherry Pot Pie or Cobbler**  Put a layer of sweetened, stewed cherries in a baking dish. They may be canned or frozen and thawed. If there is a lot of juice mix in 1 or 2 tablespoons flour or tapioca. Prepare biscuit dough, cut out biscuits, and set them touching each other on top of the cherries. Bake about 30 minutes or until the biscuits are browned.

---

### OTHER RECIPES FEATURING CHERRIES

# CHESTNUTS

## STORAGE

**Cold Storage**  Chestnuts mold quickly in damp root cellars, but need high humidity to prevent drying. If refrigerated in plastic bags with a little dry peat moss, they keep 2–3 months.

**Drying**  See DRYING CHEST-NUTS, below.

**Freezing**  May be frozen in the shell, but space is saved if precooked and peeled (see below). Package in plastic bags or other containers. Quality retained 1 year. Thaw at room temperature, or drop in boiling water and cook approx. 5 min. Also freeze as CHESTNUT PURÉE (see below). Refer to FREEZING section.

1 POUND = ABOUT 1½ CUPS SHELLED

THE LOSS OF THE AMERICAN CHESTNUT TO THE BLIGHT WAS A GREAT loss of valuable food for the people living in its growing regions. Chestnuts are an excellent carbohydrate food. People can and have lived on them. A family with a supply of dried chestnuts in the attic can enjoy chestnut dishes all winter, ranging from salads and vegetable mixtures to soups, stuffings, sandwiches, snacks, and desserts.

Chestnuts are a common food in Korea and some other Asian countries, and in Italy and the Mediterranean area. In some places, they are used as livestock feed. There is hope that the chestnut will again become common in North America. Some blight resistant varieties of Asian and European chestnut trees are being planted in home orchards, particularly the Chinese chestnut, which has about the same range as the peach tree. Researchers are also working to protect the American chestnut from the blight, and some progress has been made towards that goal.

## HANDLING CHESTNUTS

Chestnuts should be gathered about every other day during the fall ripening season. If they lie on the ground long they become moldy or wormy. Shaking the tree may knock more chestnuts down. If the burrs fall to the ground unopened, store them in a cool place until they open, usually within a week. Fresh chestnuts are somewhat astringent, but improve if held at room temperature for a few days. They should then be refrigerated or dried or frozen.

***Peeling Chestnuts***  Chestnuts have an outer shell and an inner skin or pellicle. It is possible to peel raw chestnuts by cutting through the shell with a knife, but it is slow work. The inner skin sticks to the nut and is hard to remove. Peeling is much easier when the nuts are hot, so they are usually cooked by boiling or roasting and peeled before they cool. Cook about 10 minutes in boiling water or roast for 15 to 20 minutes in a moderate oven. The shells should be slit with a knife or pricked with a fork before roasting to prevent bursting. This is not essential when boiling, but many people prefer to do it anyway, as the opening makes a handy place to start peeling.

Remove the chestnuts from the heat a few at a time so they do not cool too much, and cut or pull off the shells as soon as they can be handled. The pellicle or inner skin will come off with the shell, as long as the chestnuts are still very warm.

If whole nutmeats are not important a quick method is to cut the chestnuts in half with a heavy knife. Drop the halves in boiling water and cook until the nutmeats fall from the shells.

***Drying Chestnuts*** Chestnuts will dry in the shell if kept in a dry airy place, such as an attic. If there are mice or other rodents, put the chestnuts in large metal cans that have many small ventilation holes punched in them. After a month or so the meats will shrink to hard lumps inside their shells. They will keep a year or more. The dried nuts can be reconstituted and used like fresh chestnuts, or shelled and ground into flour.

To shell dried chestnuts, cut the shell with a sturdy knife. The inner skin will usually come off when the shell is removed. If it does not, drop the nut in boiling water for a minute to loosen the skin. Shelled dried chestnuts can be reconstituted by soaking several hours or overnight in water, then cooking until soft in the same water. Dried chestnuts can also be soaked and cooked until soft before they are shelled. They are then shelled as for fresh chestnuts.

Another way to dry chestnuts is to cook and peel them fresh (see above), then spread them on racks or trays and dry in a food dryer or other warm, dry place. This works well for small quantities but would probably be too time consuming for a big fall harvest. These dried cooked chestnuts require less soaking and cooking time for reconstitution than the dried raw nuts. They can also be ground for flour.

***Chestnut Flour*** Dry, hard chestnuts grind easily in a grain mill. For some mills it may be necessary to first break the chestnuts into small pieces with a hammer or nutcracker. Some meat grinders, blenders, and food processors will also grind chestnuts.

Chestnut flour can be substituted for some of the wheat flour in recipes for baked goods. To make a purée for recipes that require it, slowly add boiling water to the flour, stirring constantly till the desired thickness is reached. If flour from precooked dried chestnuts is used, the purée can be sweetened for an instant chestnut pudding.

***Roast Chestnuts*** Roast chestnuts are a popular snack all over the world. They are seasonal, since only fresh chestnuts can be roasted. In China, chestnuts are roasted in hot sand. To try this, heat a pan of sand in the oven or on top of the wood stove until it is too hot to touch. Embed some chestnuts in the sand. Do not cut slits in the shells because sand will get in. They can be pricked with a needle, but they do not seem to explode as easily as those roasted on coals. Stir the sand and chestnuts a few times for even cooking. They will be done in about a half hour.

To roast chestnuts on an open fire cut a slit or an X in them, or prick with a fork. Cook in the coals at the edge of a fireplace or on charcoal, turning them often so they do not burn. After a few minutes taste one to see if they are done. Everyone peel their own chestnut, as hot as they can stand handling them. Chestnuts can also be shaken over a fire in a perforated container like an old fashioned corn popper, or set on the surface of a wood burning stove and turned frequently. They will also roast in a pan in the oven in about 20 to 30 minutes.

*Chestnut Purée*   Peel chestnuts (see above), and simmer them in water or soup stock, or in a mixture of half water or soup stock and half milk. Cook over low heat for an hour, or until quite soft. Purée in a food mill or blender. Purée can also be made from flour. See CHESTNUT FLOUR, above.

Chestnut purée is a classic accompaniment to game meats. It is usually seasoned with butter or a little of the meat juice, and served like mashed potatoes. The purée can be reheated in a double boiler or over very low heat. If overheated it will become thick and heavy.

Chestnut purée thinned with soup stock or meat juices makes delicious gravy. If it is very thin, and vegetables are added, it makes a tasty soup.

Desserts can also be made from chestnut purée. Cook the chestnuts in water, or water and milk. The purée sweetened with honey is already a pudding. Other chestnut purée desserts are the *Mix-a-flavor Ice Cream* recipe in the ICE CREAM section, or the *Chestnut Pudding* in the MILK section.

## CHESTNUT RECIPES

Most recipes call for precooked chestnuts. Dried chestnuts that have been reconstituted, or thawed frozen chestnuts are just as good as freshly cooked, peeled chestnuts.

### Chestnuts and Rice                              (Makes 6–8 side servings.)

*2 cups raw rice, preferably brown*          *1 cup chestnuts, cooked and coarsely chopped*

Combine the rice, chestnuts, and about 3 cups of water in a saucepan. Slow cooking brown rice usually takes a little more water than white rice. (Refer to the *Plainly Cooked Rice* recipe, in the RICE section.) Cover, heat to a boil, and simmer without stirring until the rice is tender—20 to 40 minutes depending on the type of rice.

Serve instead of plain rice. The chestnut flavor makes this an excellent accompaniment to meats.

*Chestnut and Rice Patties*   Mix 2 or 3 cups of *Chestnuts and Rice* with ½ cup bread crumbs, 2 eggs, and some minced parsley. Add a tablespoon or two of milk or cream, enough to make the mixture stick together. Season with pepper and salt to taste. Form patties and fry. If the mixture does not hold together well, put spoonfuls into the frying pan and flatten with the back of the spoon. These patties make a nice family lunch, or quantities can be increased to make a main course at dinner.

### Jim's Mother's Chestnut Butter

(When chestnuts could be gathered by the barrelful in the fall,

---

**CHESTNUT IDEAS**

**Stewed Chestnuts with Vegetables or Fruit**   Peeled chestnuts make an excellent side dish when cooked until tender in water or soup stock. They are especially tasty mixed with most cooked green vegetables or with stewed prunes, apples, or other fruits.

**Sautéed Chestnuts**   Heat oil or butter in a frying pan. Toss cooked chestnuts in it for a minute or two just before serving. They take the place of potatoes or rice in a meal, and are delicious mixed with hot, cooked green vegetables. (Refer to the *Brussels Sprouts and Chestnuts* recipe, in the BRUSSELS SPROUTS section, and FRESH BEANS WITH NUTS idea, in the BEANS, FRESH section.)

**Chestnut Stuffing**   Mix cooked, chopped chestnuts into bread crumb stuffing for poultry or meat. This is a traditional stuffing for the holiday turkey. Chestnuts are also good in rice stuffings, and in stuffings with dried fruits such as prunes.

One Italian poultry stuffing combines ½ pound cooked macaroni, 2 diced apples, 1 cup pitted, quartered prunes, 1½ cups cooked, chopped chestnuts, and 1 egg, seasoned with butter, salt, pepper, and oregano.

**Creamed Chestnuts**   Cook chestnuts until very tender and add them to the *Cream Sauce* recipe, in the MILK section. They also add flavor to the CREAMED MUSHROOMS recipe, in the MUSHROOM section, and most creamed vegetable dishes.

chestnut butter sandwiches were an everyday school lunch for many children.)

Peel raw chestnuts and grind in a meat grinder. After the first grinding, salt them lightly, if desired, and put them through the grinder several more times, until the mixture is fairly smooth. Use as a spread for bread. Make small batches at a time, because the butter sours easily. (Cooked chestnuts can also be used, and some may prefer their flavor over that of the raw nuts.)

When fresh chestnuts are no longer available, peel and grind dried chestnuts. Mix the resulting flour with enough butter to make it spreadable. This chestnut butter improves after a day or two as the chestnut flavor becomes stronger.

**Korean Chestnut Balls** Grind cooked, peeled chestnuts as for chestnut butter. Omit salt. Flavor with a little honey or cinnamon and shape into small balls. They are traditionally rolled in chopped pine nuts, but any chopped nuts can be used.

---

### Chestnut Carrot Salad                (Makes 6–8 side servings.)

2 cups chestnuts, cooked, chopping
  optional
2 cups carrots, cooked and sliced or
  diced
½ cup green pepper, chopped,
  optional
¼ cup chives or 1–2 scallions,
  minced

1 cup (about) Old Fashioned
  Coleslaw Dressing made
  without honey or sugar (Refer
  to the CABBAGE section.)
lettuce leaves, optional

Toss the chestnuts, carrots, green pepper, and chives or scallions with the salad dressing. Arrange on lettuce leaves to make a very attractive and delicious salad.

---

### Chestnut Coffee Cake, Italian Style      (Makes 6–8 servings.)

1½ cups chestnut flour
2 tablespoons oil, preferably olive
4 tablespoons raisins

4 tablespoons nuts (Pine nuts
  are traditional, but chopped
  almonds or other nuts are
  also good.)
1 teaspoon fresh rosemary,
  minced, or ¼ teaspoon dried

Combine the chestnut flour and oil, and mix in enough water to make a pourable batter, about 1½ cups. Oil an 8 or 9 inch heavy frying pan or cake pan. Pour in the batter and sprinkle it with raisins, nuts, and rosemary. Bake in a moderate oven, 375°F, about 45 minutes, or until the top is crisp. The natural sweetness of the chestnut flour and raisins, and the unusual rosemary flavor, makes this a memorable treat.

---

### CHESTNUT IDEAS, cont.

**Boiled Chestnut Snacks**
Instead of roasting chestnuts, boil them in their shells in salted water for a few minutes. Let people peel their own chestnuts as soon as they are cool enough to handle. Chestnuts dried in the shell (see DRYING CHESTNUTS, above), can be boiled for a snack in this way, but it takes a long time. If they are soaked in water for several hours, then simmered on a stove for several more hours, they will be very good.

**Chestnuts and Corn** The American Indians made a mixture of chestnuts and corn that was wrapped in green corn shucks and boiled for 2 hours or so. Various mixtures are suggested in different references to native Indian cooking. Whole kernel corn and peeled chestnuts can be ground together, and wrapped and cooked like tamales. (Refer to the *Tamale* recipe, in the CORN, DRY section.) Boiling water can be poured over a mixture of cornmeal and chestnut flour to make a dough that can be wrapped. Cotton cloth, prepared pudding cloths (refer to STEAM COOKING PUDDINGS, in the STEAM COOKING section), or aluminum foil can be substituted for corn shucks if they are not available.

---

### OTHER RECIPES WITH CHESTNUTS

Brussels Sprouts with
    Chestnuts, p.78
Chestnut Pudding, p.418
Fresh Beans with Nuts, p.31
Mix-a-flavor Ice Cream, p.356
Roast Beverages, p.44
Spiced Red Cabbage with
    Chestnuts and Raisins, p.96
Versatile Vegetable Loaf, p.669

CHEVON MEANS MEAT FROM GOATS, IN THE SAME WAY PORK means meat from pigs, and beef means meat from cows. Chevon is not well known in North America because most goats are raised as dairy animals only. Goats are, or have been, an important meat animal in parts of Africa, the Mediterranean area, and the West Indies. Wild goat has also been eaten in various parts of the world. There are, therefore, diverse traditions of preparing chevon that the modern goat keeper can draw upon. Unwanted buck kids and culls from the dairy herd can add a valuable and interesting new dimension to the family meat supply.

## BUTCHERING GOATS

Goats can be butchered at any age. Unweaned kids are a traditional spring delicacy in some places, as are baby lambs. Goats butchered at birth usually weigh around 7 pounds and can be skinned and cleaned like rabbits. (Refer to the RABBIT section.) More often, though, kids are kept till they weigh 15 to 20 pounds. They still have a delicate milk fed flavor, but there is more meat. Kids of this size are often roasted whole over coals. They can also be cut up for stewing, frying or other uses, and cooked like lamb, veal or rabbit. (Refer to recipes in the appropriate sections.) The stomachs of unweaned kids can be made into rennet (refer to the RENNET section), and the variety meats such as heart, liver and kidneys can be used as for any small animal. (Refer to individual sections for these.)

Male goats are often castrated and raised for fall butchering. Follow the same procedures as for butchering lambs. The diagram in the LAMB section shows parts of the animal that can be used. Chevon from these full sized animals has a distinctive flavor, more like venison or other good tasting game meat than like lamb. It is excellent cooked according to venison recipes, or it can be cooked like lamb, mutton, or lean beef. For the meat of old, tough goats, refer to USING TOUGH MEAT, in the MEAT section.

## ROASTING CHEVON OVER COALS

Goat kids of all sizes, from unweaned to large fall butchered kids, can be roasted over coals. The kid is butchered and cleaned as usual, except that the head (with the eyes removed) is sometimes left on. If a whole kid is too large, the loin and hindquarters can be roasted in one piece, and the rest of the kid used in other ways. Small roasts or a single leg can also be cooked over charcoal.

A whole kid is put on a spit or rack 2 or 3 feet above a bed of hot coals. If a spit is used, it goes through the kid from breast to hindquarters. The legs are trussed or tied together, and the front legs may be folded under the body. When stretched out, the front quarters cook more quickly than the hindquarters. The meat should be turned often, at least every half hour. Roasting time varies greatly according to the size of the kid, the degree of doneness desired, and the arrangement of the spit or rack, and fire. A smaller kid usually takes about 2½ to 3 hours, while a large one can take 4 to 8 hours.

A large barbecue pit with a big bed of coals is needed for roasting a whole, fall butchered goat. Roasts or a single leg can be cooked over a portable charcoal broiler, as long as the meat is not too close to the coals.

## CHEVON RECIPES

(Allow about 1 pound dressed weight per serving—less if partly boned.)

### Barbecued Chevon

| | |
|---|---|
| 1 large kid, or a leg or large roast of chevon | oil or butter<br>barbecue sauce as necessary |

For a large whole kid (20–40 pounds, dressed)

| | |
|---|---|
| 1 quart vinegar | ½ cup (about 1 ounce) paprika |
| 1 cup oil | pepper, to taste |
| 2 cups water | 1 large onion, minced |
| ¼ cup soy sauce or 2 tablespoons salt | 2–4 cloves garlic, minced |

For a leg or large roast (5–10 pounds)

| | |
|---|---|
| ½ cup vinegar | 1–2 tablespoons paprika |
| 2 tablespoons oil | pepper to taste |
| ¼ cup water | half a small onion, minced |
| 2 teaspoons soy sauce or 1 teaspoon salt | 1 clove garlic, minced |

Trim fat off the meat and rub it all over with oil. To prepare for roasting, see ROASTING CHEVON OVER COALS, above.

Combine all ingredients for the barbecue sauce. A blender can be used to liquify the onion and garlic so they spread easily. As the meat roasts, baste it often with the sauce. To spread sauce over a whole goat, a swab can be made by wiring bunched-up cloth to a stick. Turn the meat often. The barbecuing will take 2 to 3 hours for a leg or roast, and as much as 8 hours for a whole kid.

**Marinade for Tough Meat** Marinate tough cuts of meat in the barbecue sauce overnight, then simmer meat in the sauce until tender. The meat can also be removed from the marinade, browned in fat to add flavor, and then returned to simmer till tender.

### Barbecued Kid with Rice, West Indies Style
(Makes 10–15 servings.)

1 whole kid, cleaned and prepared
(The amounts given below are
for a dressed 10–15 pound kid.
Adjust for other sizes.)
1 cup vinegar
salt
2 large onions
5 cloves garlic, crushed

1 chili pepper, minced, or hot
red pepper to taste
1 teaspoon nutmeg
2 teaspoons sage
2 teaspoons rosemary
½ cup vegetable oil
4 cups raw rice

Mix the vinegar with 2 or 3 cups water and rinse the kid several times with the solution. Sprinkle lightly with salt and keep in a cool place overnight, then rinse off the salt and dry the kid inside and out.

Mince one of the onions and mix with the garlic, chili pepper, nutmeg, sage, rosemary, and oil. Rub this all over the kid and let sit several hours.

Chop the other onion and boil it with the rice in just enough water to cover, till about half done. Brown rice should cook about 15 minutes, white rice about 8 minutes. Allow to cool.

Pack the rice stuffing lightly into the kid and sew up the opening. (If there is too much rice, finish cooking it separately, and mix with the rice from the kid at serving time.) Put the kid on a spit, tying the legs together. (See ROASTING CHEVON OVER COALS, above.) Set over a bed of coals and roast slowly, turning often. A small kid will be done in about 2 hours. Towards the end of the cooking time, smother the fire a little to give the meat a lightly smoked flavor.

**Barbecued Lamb West Indies Style** Lamb can be used instead of goat, in this recipe.

### Oven Roasted Suckling Kid, Italian Style
(Makes 6–10 dinner servings.)

1 suckling kid, 7–10 pounds after
cleaning
1 lemon
3–4 medium cooking apples
3–4 strips fatty bacon, or pork fat
3–4 cloves
2–3 cloves garlic, sliced

½ teaspoon pepper
½ teaspoon ginger
½ teaspoon salt, optional
oil or butter, melted
apple juice, optional
cream, or flour

Rub the kid inside and out with the lemon juice and peel.

Core the apples and wrap each one with a strip of bacon or pork fat. Push a clove into each apple, and pack them into the kid as a stuffing. Sew up the opening. Make small slits on the sides of the kid and insert garlic slices. Mix together the pepper, ginger, and salt, if desired, and rub the kid with it. Brush oil or melted butter over all.

Roast the kid on a rack over a drip pan in a moderate, 350°F oven. Allow about 15 minutes per pound. If desired, baste frequently with hot apple juice or water. When the meat is done, set it on a serving platter. Strain the pan juices and thicken with cream or a little flour mixed with water to make a gravy. If cream is used, heat without boiling. If flour is used, simmer until the gravy thickens.

**Oven Roasted Suckling Lamb**    Use a suckling lamb instead of a kid in this recipe.

### Sweet and Sour Chevon, South African Style     (Makes about 6 dinner servings.)

2–3 pounds stewing chevon
pepper, salt, optional
small bunch fresh herbs, or 2–3
    teaspoons dried (May include
    rosemary, thyme, sage,
    parsley.)
½ pound (about) spinach or other
    greens
1 tablespoon pork or bacon fat,
    minced
½ teaspoon cloves
½ teaspoon cinnamon
½ teaspoon mace

slice of ginger root, optional
2 cups mixed dried fruit (May
    include raisins, prunes,
    apricots, and other avail-
    able dried fruits.)
1 tablespoon (about) vinegar
honey or brown sugar, to taste,
    optional
apple cider or dry sherry, to
    taste, optional
fresh orange segments and al-
    monds, for garnish, optional

Simmer the chevon in water to cover till tender. It may take from one to several hours, depending on its toughness. Add pepper and salt to taste when the meat is partly cooked. Remove the meat when done and set aside.

Add the herbs and spinach to the cooking broth and bring to a boil. Add the fat, and the cloves, cinnamon, mace, and ginger root. Tie the dried fruit in a cloth bag, leaving room for the fruit to expand. Add to the pot with the vinegar. Simmer for about 30 minutes, or till the fruit has softened and swelled. Return the meat to the pot to reheat it, about 5 minutes. Slice the meat onto a serving dish and arrange the stewed fruit on top. Keep warm while preparing the broth.

Strain the cooking broth and discard the herbs and spinach. Bring the broth to a boil, and add a little brown sugar or honey, and cider or sherry to give a mild sweet and sour flavor. If very sweet dried fruits were used, little, if any, sugar or honey will be needed. More vinegar can be added if the broth is too sweet. Boil vigorously to reduce to a syrup, and pour over the meat and fruit. Decorate with orange segments and almonds before serving, if desired. Rice is a good accompaniment for this delicious dish. Though somewhat complicated to make, the resulting rich blend of flavors is well worth the trouble.

**Sweet and Sour Venison, Beef, or other Stew Meat**    Use any lean, flavorful stewing meat instead of chevon.

### Breaded Chevon Cutlets                              (Makes 6 moderate servings.)

Cutlets are thin, boneless slices of meat, usually from the leg, which are lightly pounded before cooking. Horseshoe shaped slices from the tough lower leg are excellent since pounding tenderizes them. Use the dull side of a knife or a mallet with teeth cut in one side. The pounding should flatten the meat and break up the fibers, but the cutlet should stay in one piece, without holes.

6 small chevon cutlets, lightly
  pounded
1 egg, lightly beaten

½ cup (about) flour, or fine dry
  bread crumbs
pepper and salt, optional
fat, or oil for frying

Season the flour or bread crumbs with pepper and salt, if desired. Dip each cutlet in the beaten egg, and then in the flour or bread crumbs. Fry in fat or oil in a heavy frying pan over medium heat till the cutlets are golden brown, about 5 minutes on each side.

### Breaded Veal, Pork, Chicken or Turkey Breast Cutlets   Cut veal as for chevon cutlets. Trim fat from pork slices to make cutlets. Cut thin slices of raw chicken breast, or turkey breast. If the chicken will not stay together in large slices, small cutlets taste just as good. Pound gently, dip, and fry any of these as for chevon cutlets.

### Jaternice, or Czech Goat Sausage
(From the Meersma family.)                      (Makes 10–12 pounds sausage.)

8 pounds boned chevon
2 pounds raw barley
2–3 onions, quartered
2–3 cloves garlic
2 teaspoons black or red pepper, or to
  taste

1½ teaspoons marjoram
2 teaspoons allspice
2 tablespoons salt, optional
½ teaspoon cloves, optional
½ teaspoon ginger, optional
hog casings, optional

Cook the meat in enough water to cover till tender, about 2 hours. Drain, saving the broth, and set aside to cool. Cook the barley in the broth until soft, 30–40 minutes, adding water if necessary to cover generously. When done, drain off any extra broth and cool.

Cut the cooked meat into pieces and grind it finely in a grinder with the onion. The garlic can be chopped and mixed with the meat before grinding, or crushed with a garlic press and added after grinding. Thoroughly combine the meat, barley, and all seasonings.

Stuff the sausage mixture into hog casings, and twist off at 12 to 15 inch intervals. (It will curve to fit the pan.) (See STUFFING SAUSAGE, in the SAUSAGE section.) Before serving, fry the sausage slowly until browned on all sides. If casings are not used, form the sausage into patties and fry, or fry loose like hash.

This sausage freezes very well because it is almost fat free. It will also keep from a week to 10 days in the refrigerator.

### CHEVON IDEAS

**Ground Chevon**  Ground chevon is as versatile as any other ground meat. Chevon burgers, chevon loaf, and chevon meatballs with spaghetti are all good. Try mixing ground chevon with cooked rice or bread crumbs, ground or minced vegetables such as onion, carrot, and green pepper, with herbs and seasonings to taste. Tomato sauce or an egg can also be added. Make patties or balls for frying, or bake as a meat loaf, or use to stuff green peppers or tomatoes. Also refer to the *Stuffed Peppers, Middle Eastern Style* recipe, in the PEPPERS, SWEET section.

**Stir-fried Chevon**  Chevon that is not overly tough is excellent for stir-frying. It should be thinly sliced or shredded to go with the vegetables used. (Refer to the STIR-FRYING section.)

**Unseasoned Roast Suckling Kid**  Very small, unweaned kids are so delicate in flavor that they are delicious roasted over coals without seasonings. They can be served plain or with melted *Herb Butter*. (Refer to the recipe in the BUTTER section.) A tasty sauce can be made by slicing the kid's liver, heart and kidneys thinly and sautéing them quickly in butter. Add to this a little white wine and the drippings from roasting the kid, if they can be collected. Season to taste with pepper and salt, if desired. Suckling lambs can be roasted in the same way.

***Blood Sausage, Czech Style*** Mix 1 pint liquid blood with the sausage ingredients. (Refer to COLLECTING BLOOD, in the BLOOD section.) After the sausage is stuffed in casings, put them in hot water and simmer without boiling until the blood changes color or darkens. Cool quickly, and store in the freezer. Fry before serving as for regular sausage.

***Venison Sausage, Czech Style*** Use venison instead of chevon. It is equally good.

### OTHER RECIPES WITH CHEVON
Barbecued Chevon Breast, p. 380
Chevon Bologna, p. 554
Corned Chevon, p. 36
Recipes and Other Basic Meat Preparations, p. 408
Roast Kid's Head, p. 328

# CHICKEN

"HENS ARE CONSIDERED DOWN RIGHT STUPID BY SOME. HOWEVER true this may be, there is considerable human nature in a chicken, more character, perhaps, than one would suppose." (H. Armstrong Roberts, *Commercial Poultry Raising,* 1920.)

Chickens have been domesticated for 4,000 years or more. In fact, they have been scratching around dooryards since doors and yards existed. If, in that time, they have gained something from human nature, humans have also gained something from "chicken nature." Chickens and eggs are not only an indispensable part of people's diets the world over, they are also a part of folklore, stories, and language everywhere. The English language abounds with chicken expressions, as anyone knows who has ever "run around like a chicken with its head cut off." It is no wonder that chickens are the first livestock most people obtain when they decide to raise more of their own food. What else could provide eggs and meat, amusement, and be easy to handle and house as well?

The usual homestead flock of chickens consists of laying hens that will become stewing hens, a rooster that will probably end up in the stew or soup pot, and perhaps some cockerels, or young roosters, raised as fryers, broilers, and roasters. These chickens are cooked differently than the usual store-bought chicken for various reasons, including breeding, diet, and age when butchered. Cooking stewing chickens in particular has become almost a lost art. Modern cookbooks have very few recipes for them. While rediscovering ways to cook homestead chickens, there is another discovery to be made—the superior flavor of the old fashioned chicken that forages for greens and bugs as part of its diet.

Some are finding it practical to raise the newly developed meat breeds of chickens, as they grow large very quickly and are ready for butchering at an early age. They can then be frozen to provide a year's supply of broilers, fryers, and roasting chickens. But one thing

### STORAGE

**Canning** Stewing hens are best. Joint, and remove loose fat. (Back, neck, wings usually not canned.) Skin and bone (optional). Pack legs and pieces with skin around sides of jar, skinned breast in center.

**Hot Pack** Simmer meat to medium cooked, in unseasoned broth or water. Pack loosely. Add boiling broth, 1 in. headroom. Process 240°F, 11 pounds pressure. *Bone in* Pint: 1 hr. 5 min. Quart: 1 hr. 15 min. *Boneless* Pint: 1 hr. 15 min. Quart: 1 hr. 30 min.

**Raw Pack** (bone in only) Pack loosely, 1 in. headroom. Add no liquid. Process 240°F, 11 pounds pressure. Pints: 1 hr. 15 min. Quarts: 1 hr. 20 min. Refer to CANNING section. See also CANNING GIBLETS (below).

For canning soup, refer to the NOODLES and SOUP sections.

**Drying** Possible only with all skin and fat removed. Refer to DRYING MEAT, in DRYING FOODS section.

**Freezing** Chickens may be whole, jointed, or otherwise cut. Do not freeze prestuffed. Chill 12 hrs after butchering. Thaw before stuffing or cooking. Quality retained 6–12 mos. Refer to FREEZING section.

that might be questioned is the feed required for these birds. To meet
their fast growth potential, they must be fed specially designed commercial feeds, and a chicken fed only commercial feed will taste only
as good as a store chicken. The flavor and texture of these meat
breeds is improved by feeding supplementary greens, and scraps, but
the result is still not the same as the old time, foraging chicken. Also
in question are the growth stimulants in some commercial feeds
which may be detrimental to human health.

A capon is a rooster castrated when young. It grows into a very
large, tender bird, especially good for roasting. Raising capons is less
common than it once was since it is easier to raise the new meat
breeds. Considerable surgical skill is necessary to successfully castrate
(caponize) birds.

*Guinea Fowl*   These chicken sized birds, though they are wilder
can be raised similarly to chickens. They are butchered like chickens.
Their meat is dark, and lean, but they can be cooked like chicken if
care is taken not to let the meat dry out, or they can be cooked like
game birds. Refer to the BIRDS, SMALL, section.

## BUTCHERING AND PREPARATION

*Killing Chickens*   The time honored way to kill a chicken is to lay
its head on a chopping block and chop it off. This method is quick
and practical for the small flock owner. Other good methods are as
follows. When butchered in larger numbers, chickens are usually
hung by their feet, and a small, strong knife is used to cut the neck
arteries. To accomplish this the chicken's head is held in one hand,
and the knife is pushed into its mouth till the point reaches the junc-
ture of head and neck, cutting through the arteries there. Another
method, often included with this one, involves piercing the chicken's
brain, with the knife in one thrust, causing a muscular contraction
that loosens the feathers. But the surgical accuracy required is beyond
most people's capabilities.

Another practical, though uncommon, way to kill chickens is to
dislocate or break their necks. This method is quick, easy, and foolproof—good for those who have a poor aim with a hatchet. Stand on
firm level ground. Hold the chicken by its feet with its head on the
ground. Lay a broom-handle sized stick over its neck and stand on the
stick to hold it down firmly. Pull up on the chicken's feet till the neck
dislocates; this will be clearly felt. It is also possible to take off a
young chicken's head with a hard pull. This may be disconcerting,
but there will be no doubt that the chicken is dead. After dislocation,
hold the chicken until it stops flapping, or lay it down where it will
not bang into any thing. The movement quickly subsides and is not
nearly as bizarre as a chicken running around after its head has been
cut off. Ducks and other small poultry can also be killed by this
method.

*Quick chicken killing method*

The chicken will be bled properly by dislocating the neck, because when the neck is dislocated the blood collects in the neck area and does not stay in the meat. There is no mess and the clot of blood in the neck can be added to other scraps for animal feed. (See PET OR ANIMAL FEED, below)

If blood is wanted for cooking, cut the head off immediately after it is dislocated. To collect a chicken's blood, immediately place the decapitated chicken neck down in a large funnel set in a container to catch the blood. (Refer to COLLECTING BLOOD, in the BLOOD section.)

***Plucking Chickens*** It is possible to dry-pick a chicken's feathers immediately after it has been killed. However, plucking is easier and faster if the birds are first dunked in hot water to loosen the feathers. The water should be 140°F or slightly warmer. Keep the chicken in it for about 1 minute, turning it over several times, and swishing it up and down, so that the water gets into the feathers all over the bird. Try plucking a few feathers. When they come out easily the chicken is ready. Some directions suggest dunking in hotter water for a shorter time. This does loosen the feathers, but it may also cook the skin slightly so it tears easily. The lower temperature ensures a carcass that looks as good as if it had been dry picked.

Pluck chickens outdoors if possible to avoid the mess from tiny feathers floating in the air. A pad of newspaper is useful to set the wet bird on. Begin by plucking the wing and tail feathers, a few at a time. These will reset and be hard to pull as the chicken cools. Pull the rest of the feathers in small tufts. With a little practice the job goes quickly.

A fully feathered bird is easiest to pluck. Molting chickens, or young chickens with feathers still growing in, are most difficult. After plucking there are sometimes tiny hairs left on the bird. These can be scraped off with the dull side of a table knife, but are usually singed or burned off. To singe the chicken, twist several sheets of newspaper, or a paper bag, and light one end. Hold the chicken in one hand and the burning paper in the other, letting the flames touch all parts of the bird. Be sure the flame is clear so that the skin is not smoked. A chicken can also be singed over the flame of a gas stove.

Sometimes it may be more practical to skin a chicken than to pluck it. The skin and feathers can be easily removed together. The skin is flavorful and also protects the meat as it cooks, so it is a shame to lose it. However, if a chicken has been killed by an animal or car, or the skin is otherwise damaged, skinning may be the best way to salvage usable meat. (It may also be best to skin commercially raised birds to remove fat which retains more of the chemical feed additives than the meat.)

***Drawing Chickens*** Cleaning, or drawing, a chicken is least messy if the bird is killed in the morning before it eats anything. Some people give chickens water only for 24 hours before killing them.

Gather the necessary tools and containers before drawing the

chicken. As well as a sharp knife and a cutting board, have newspaper or a waste container ready. It is also useful to have containers for fat, the liver, gizzard, and heart, a pot for pet food scraps, and a soup pot. Most parts of a chicken can be used. When several chickens are butchered at once, the extra food value is considerable.

Cut off the chicken's head and neck close to the body if not already done. Save the head for soup or pet food. Cut off the feet at the joint and set aside for soup. (See FEET, HEADS, NECKS, AND CHICKEN SOUP, below.) Cut open the abdomen and around the vent, being careful not to cut into the intestines. The abdomen can be either cut from breast bone to vent, or crosswise. Pull out and set aside any pads of fat from under the skin. (See CHICKEN FAT, below.)

Hold the chicken under the wings with one hand and reach into it with the other. Pull out the mass of intestines. The vent area, liver and gizzard should come out with the intestines. If they do not, reach in and pull again. The heart should come out this time as well. Set aside the liver, gizzard and heart (the giblets). (See CHICKEN LIVER and CHICKEN GIZZARD AND HEART, below.) If there are partly formed eggs or yolks, set them aside. (See YOLKS AND PARTLY FORMED EGGS, below.) Parts such as the egg laying canal in hens, the reproductive organs in roosters, lungs, bits of tissue and blood can go into the pet food pot, or they can be used to make soup stock. The intestines usually are buried in the garden or compost pile, but some people do feed them to livestock. (See PET OR ANIMAL FEED, below.)

The crop and the windpipe must also be removed. They are under the neck skin, which may have to be slit to take them out. If the crop is empty, it appears only as a membrane. Both crop and windpipe can go with the pet food. The oil sac at the base of the chicken's tail should be cut out if the chicken is old. Removing it is optional with young chickens. If the oil sac is cut into, it will look like a piece of dark yellow fat. (See page 235.)

Wash the chicken thoroughly inside and out in cold water and refrigerate, unless it will be cooked within a few hours. The chicken can be jointed, or cut up, before or after chilling. If the chicken is left whole, bits of lung or other tissue may remain against the backbone and ribs, but these are not harmful even when cooked with the chicken.

When chickens are to be frozen, they must be chilled in the refrigerator for 12 hours before going in the freezer. If frozen while in a state of rigor mortis, they will be tough when cooked.

***Chicken Liver***   The little sac of green liquid attached to a chicken liver is the gall bladder. It must be cut away from the liver carefully so it does not break, otherwise it gives the liver a strong, bitter taste that makes it unusable except as pet food. Cut a bit of the liver off with the gall bladder if necessary, to keep it intact. Wash the liver

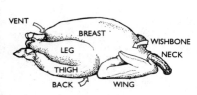

*Parts of a chicken*

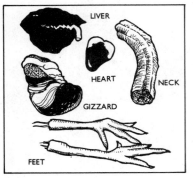

thoroughly in cold water, drain well, and refrigerate until used, or freeze immediately.

Chicken liver can be cooked like other livers, but as it has a unique flavor there are many special recipes for it. When only one chicken liver is available, it is often cooked with the gizzard and heart. Single livers can also be frozen till enough are collected to make a special dish. (Refer to HANDLING LIVER, in the LIVER section, chicken liver recipes, below, and OTHER RECIPES at the end of this section.)

*Chicken Gizzard and Heart*    Gizzards and hearts are almost always cooked together since the heart is too small to be useful alone. To prepare the gizzard, trim it and pull off any fat. Cut the gizzard open. Remove the material in it, pull off its inner lining, then wash thoroughly. Trim the top of the heart, wash, and it also is ready for use.

Gizzards and hearts are usually precooked until tender, for about an hour, in water or soup stock, and then sliced or chopped for use in stuffings, gravies, soups, or casseroles. If the liver is added it will only need about 20 minutes. Gizzards and hearts are good without the liver in most recipes that call for giblets. (See the OTHER RECIPES list at the end of this section.)

Like livers, gizzards and hearts freeze well and can be collected till there are enough for a separate dish.

*Canning Giblets*    Processing is the same for canning chicken livers, gizzards, and hearts, but the flavor is best if livers are canned separately.

Cover the prepared giblets with hot water or unseasoned broth—livers in one pan, gizzards and hearts in another. Simmer till firm and medium done, usually 30 to 40 minutes. The livers will be cooked first. Pack meat in jars (pint jars only so every part reaches processing temperature), leaving 1 inch headroom. If desired, add ¼ to ½ teaspoon salt per jar. Add boiling cooking liquid, 1 inch headroom. Pressure process at 240°F, with 11 pounds of pressure for 75 minutes. (Refer to the CANNING section.)

*Feet, Heads, Necks, and Chicken Soup*    A delicious chicken broth or stock can be made from parts that are usually thrown away. Chicken feet are particularly valuable for soup. They add flavor and gelatine and are easy to prepare, so it is a shame to waste them. Dunk the feet in hot water and peel off their thin, outer skin. If the skin does not slip right off, dunk them again. The outer layer of each toenail will usually also slip off or the whole nail can be cut off. Rinse, and drop the feet into the soup pot. The gelatinous meat can be eaten when tender. The Chinese prepare a special snack from chicken feet. They cut them into 1 inch sections with a cleaver, and cook them in a well seasoned soy sauce mixture. If a number of chickens are butchered at once, their feet can be set aside for making gelatine. (Refer to JELLED STOCK, in the GELATINE section.)

Plucked and washed chicken heads and necks are also good additions to the soup pot. If they are bloody, soak them in cold water for a few minutes. The stock will need skimming when it first boils after the heads are added. If plucking chicken heads seems too tedious, the necks can be used alone. Some old recipe books suggest uses for chicken neck skins and cock's combs. The neck skins, kept tubular, and cut as long as possible, can be stuffed like sausages. (Refer to *Chicken or Turkey Sausage,* in the SAUSAGE section, or use a stuffing recipe for roast chicken.) Cock's combs are recommended as additions to fancy stews, with such ingredients as oysters and sweetbreads. They are soft and bland when cooked.

If a pot of water is set on the stove when chickens are butchered and soup parts are added as they are cleaned, chicken broth will be obtained with very little effort. Two or three cups of water are about right for one chicken. Besides the feet and head or neck, the gizzard and heart can be precooked in the pot. Wing tips, the back, and the bones (if a chicken is boned), can be added. The meat can be picked off the bones when cooked for the soup. When a chicken is stewed to precook it, this can also be done in the soup pot, making a large amount of chicken stock at once. See *Plain Stewed Chicken,* in the RECIPE section below. Any extra stock or soup can be frozen or canned for later use.

A final batch of chicken soup can be made by boiling the carcass of a roast chicken, or leftover bones and scraps from people's plates. The bones and scraps are well sterilized by cooking. (Refer to MAKING SOUP STOCK, in the SOUP section, and the ideas and recipes that follow. Also see OTHER RECIPES at the end of this section.)

**Chicken Fat**   Chicken fat is well worth rendering and saving. A plump hen can give a cup or so of rendered fat that is excellent for frying or stir-frying vegetables. It also makes a good shortening for biscuits and other baked goods, and can be used instead of butter for seasoning many foods.

To render the fat, cut up any large pieces into small ones. Set over very low heat, uncovered, until it melts and becomes clear. Stir a few times to prevent sticking. When any membrane bits have shrivelled and turned light brown, strain the fat into jars. Keep in a cool place. (Refer to RENDERING FAT, in the LARD section.)

**Chicken Fat, Rendered Jewish Style**   Cut the fat from a very fat hen into small pieces. Put in a saucepan with 1 small onion, chopped, a dash of salt, and 1 to 2 tablespoons of water. Cook over very low heat, and render as described above. Chicken fat rendered with onion and salt keeps better than plain rendered fat, lasting for months in the refrigerator.

**Yolks and Partly Formed Eggs**   When hens are butchered, they sometimes contain partly formed eggs and yolks of different sizes. These can be used like regular eggs or yolks, if the membrane covering them is kept intact. One convenient way to prepare them is to cook them in the soup pot for 5 to 10 minutes, till they are hard-boiled. Remove them with a slotted spoon and use as hard-boiled eggs.

If the yolks are to be used raw, puncture the membrane and squeeze the yolk into a bowl. The membranes can go into the soup or pet food pot, along with the clump of tiny new eggs found against the hen's backbone. For egg yolk recipes, refer to OTHER RECIPES at the end of the EGGS section.

*Pet or Animal Food*    An appreciable amount of high protein pet or animal feed can be collected from every chicken butchered. These scraps can be fed raw, but cooking has advantages. They keep longer, many animals prefer them cooked, and any diseases carried by the scraps are wiped out. This last reason is especially important if they will be fed to chickens or other poultry. Usable parts are the blood, lungs, windpipe, crop, the hen's egg laying canal, the rooster's reproductive parts, the head if not wanted for soup, and any other bits of tissue. The intestines are sometimes fed to animals, but they shouldn't be cooked unless empty. They smell foul when cooking.

The leftovers from the soup pot, after the stock has been strained off, can also be used for pet and animal feed. Bones can be cooked on the back of the stove till they are soft enough not to splinter and added.

*Chickens for Stewing*    Most mature hens and roosters are good for stewing but the ideal is a plump, heavy breed hen, butchered to make room for the new pullets. Home raised chickens that have had exercise, and a varied diet including greens, bugs, and kitchen scraps are the most flavorful. Least desirable are the commercial egg producers, such as leghorns, worn out by a year of intensive egg laying till they are neither meaty nor flavorful. The homestead chicken that survives to a tough and scrawny old age is probably best used for making soup. It will have flavor, but the meat will be stringy.

A large stewing chicken will provide two meals for a large family, one of meat and one of soup. For the meat serving, a stew with vegetables and seasonings can be made, or stewing can precook the meat for dozens of uses. See *Plain Stewed Chicken* below, and the recipes following. Stewing chickens are also ideal for canning.

*Chicken Burger*    Stewing chickens can be boned and ground raw. Include the skin and some fat. The bones and attached meat are good for making soup, of course, and extra fat can be rendered. Ground chicken meat can be seasoned and made into patties or meat loaf as with other ground meats. However, take care not to overcook it because it dries out more quickly than most meats. Ground chicken freezes well. (For recipes, refer to *Chicken or Turkey Sausage,* in the SAUSAGE section, and *Chicken Hash,* below.)

*Chickens for Roasting, Broiling, and Frying*    There can be much variation in the cooking characteristics of home raised roasting, broiling, and frying chickens, because of differences in breed, feed, and butchering age. Active young chickens that eat a varied diet are more flavorful, with more firmly textured meat than commercially raised meat chickens. However, some home raised chicken may be less meaty, and the legs especially may be somewhat tougher or more sinewy.

Generally, home raised chickens should be broiled or fried longer, at a lower temperature, than store chickens. Fried chicken that might be slightly tough can be covered and steamed over low heat for 15 or 20 minutes after it is browned. Oven roasted chickens can also be covered for part of the cooking time. Another way to tenderize a roasting chicken is to roast it in a well greased paper bag, like game birds. (Refer to the BIRDS ROASTED IN A BROWN PAPER BAG idea, in the BIRDS, SMALL section.)

Chicken recipes that call for browning the meat, then simmering or baking it in a sauce, are ideal for questionably tender birds. When several chickens are butchered at once, one good method is to cut up the chickens, packaging and freezing by parts. The breasts can then be used in recipes that require tenderness, and the legs used where some steaming or stewing is involved.

## CHICKEN RECIPES

*Homestead Fried Chicken*                    (Makes 4–8 servings, depending on the bird's size.)

| | |
|---|---|
| 1 homestead fryer, cut in pieces | 2–4 tablespoons oil or fat, for |
| flour for dredging, optional | frying |
| pinch of powdered ginger, optional | ¼ cup chicken broth, dry white |
| pepper, salt, to taste | or red wine, or water |

If flour is used, season it with ginger, pepper, and salt, if desired. Shake the chicken with the flour in a paper bag, or roll the pieces in flour on a plate. Heat the oil or fat in a heavy frying pan that has a lid. If necessary, use two pans so that the chicken pieces can all lie flat. Fry the chicken over moderate heat, turning several times until nicely browned all over, about 30 to 40 minutes. Put all the chicken pieces in one pan, if two were used, and add the broth, wine, or water. If flour and seasonings were not used, add pepper and salt now, if desired. Cover and simmer over very low heat for about 20 minutes.

Remove extra fat from the pan juices and serve with the chicken or make into gravy, or, if preferred, the juices can go into soup. To remove fat easily, pour the juices into a tall container. Once the fat rises it can be easily dipped out with a spoon.

*Herbed Homestead Chicken* When the liquid is added to the browned chicken in the above recipe, also add a small onion with a clove stuck in it, a bay leaf, and fresh or dried herbs. One good combination is parsley, thyme, rosemary, and celery leaves. A few tablespoons of minced vegetables, such as carrot and green pepper, can be included.

**Herbed Chicken with Rice**   Together with the herbs in the above variation, add 2 cups of chicken broth and 1 cup of raw rice to the browned chicken. Cover and cook without stirring until the rice is done (15 to 20 minutes for white, 30 to 40 minutes for brown rice).

**Chicken Cacciatori**   Brown the chicken without flouring it. When it is almost done, add a chopped onion, 2 or 3 cloves minced garlic, and any or all of the following, chopped as necessary—mushrooms, green pepper, parsley, and basil or bay leaf. When the onion and garlic are lightly browned, add ½ cup dry red or white wine, or sherry, and 2 cups chopped fresh tomatoes or tomato sauce. Season with pepper, and salt if desired, and simmer uncovered for about 30 minutes. Sometimes peas are added before serving, and cooked just till tender. Turn the chicken several times as it simmers.

---

**Yogurt Marinated Chicken**   (Makes 4–8 servings, depending on the bird's size.)

| | |
|---|---|
| 1 young chicken, jointed | 2 cloves garlic, minced |
| 2 tablespoons lemon juice | ½ teaspoon cardamom powder |
| 1 cup plain yogurt | ½ teaspoon chili powder, or hot |
| small piece fresh ginger root, minced, | red pepper |
| optional | ½ teaspoon cinnamon |

Combine the lemon juice, yogurt, ginger root, garlic, cardamom, chili powder or pepper, and cinnamon. Marinate the chicken pieces in it overnight or all day, turning the chicken several times. Remove the chicken from the marinade and set on a rack in a moderate 375°F oven. Bake till tender, about 30 to 45 minutes. Baste several times with the marinade and turn if necessary for even browning. This marinade gives the meat a very pleasant, tart piquancy.

---

**Plain Precooked Stewed Chicken**   (A way to prepare chicken for many different uses.)

| | |
|---|---|
| 1 stewing chicken, whole or jointed | seasonings, and vegetables, optional |

Put the chicken in a pot and add water. The chicken may be covered with water, but a more concentrated and flavorful broth can be made in a pot with a tight lid. The chicken is then cooked partly with steam. For this method, add water to half cover a whole chicken, or three-quarters of a jointed chicken. For an even more flavorful broth, stew the chicken with the soup parts described under FEET, HEADS, NECKS, AND CHICKEN SOUP, above.

Bring the chicken and water to a boil and skim off any foam that rises. Reduce heat and simmer covered, without boiling, until the meat is tender when tested with a fork. Turn the meat once or twice while it stews to be sure it cooks evenly. Do not let it overcook. It should not fall apart or come off the bone. Cooking time is usually two hours or more, depending on the chicken's toughness. The low simmering temperature keeps the meat juicy. (Refer to USING TOUGH MEAT, in the MEAT section.) Salt is not necessary during stewing, and, if desired, is best added later, when the chicken is about to be served.

Vegetables, such as onion, carrot, and potato, and seasonings can be added about an hour before the chicken is done for a finished stew. If the chicken is not wanted immediately, let it cool in its cooking water to keep it juicy. It is often easiest to cook the chicken a day before it will be needed. When cool, remove the chicken from the broth. The meat can be used in any recipe requiring cooked chicken. It is good sliced for sandwiches, diced for salads, or added to casseroles, stuffings for vegetables, creamed mixtures, soups, and more.

***Chicken Gelatine***   Stew a chicken, making a concentrated broth, as described above. When the chicken is done, remove the meat from the bones and return the bones to the stock. Cook another 2 hours, or till the stock has been reduced by about half. If possible, cook the chicken's feet with the bones. (See FEET, HEADS, NECKS, AND CHICKEN SOUP, above, for preparing feet.) The stock, after straining and chilling, should jell firmly. Use to make gelatines or aspics. The cooked chicken meat can be used in the gelatine or for other dishes. (Refer to JELLED STOCK, in the GELATINE section.)

***Chicken Stewed with Ham or Beef Bones***   For a different flavor in both meat and broth, stew chicken with a ham bone or beef soup bones. Soup made from this broth is especially tasty.

***Roasted or Broiled Stewer***   Stew a chicken till it is almost tender, being very careful not to overcook it. Drain thoroughly and set on a rack over a dripping pan. Bake in a moderate, 350°F oven, or broil, till the skin is well browned. A whole chicken can be stuffed like any roast chicken and baked. If broiled, any favorite seasonings can be used.

***Soy Sauced Chicken***   Precook a chicken by stewing. It can be whole, jointed, or cut in half down the center of the breast and back, as for broiling. Mix together 4 tablespoons of soy sauce, 1 or 2 tablespoons of honey, and a crushed garlic clove. Brush the mixture over all surfaces of the chicken. Brown it in a moderate oven or under the broiler. Turn once or twice and brush with the soy sauce mixture as it browns.

### Chicken and Apple or Rhubarb Stew (Makes 6—10 dinner servings.)

| | |
|---|---|
| 1 stewing chicken, cut in serving pieces | 4 sour apples, quartered or sliced, or 1½ cups rhubarb, chopped |
| 2 carrots, cut in chunks | |
| 2 parsnips, or turnips, cut in chunks | 1 tablespoon honey or sugar |
| 1 small onion, chopped | ½ cup sour cream or yogurt |
| | 2 tablespoons flour |

Put the chicken in a pot and cover with water. Bring to a boil and skim off foam. Cover and simmer slowly till the meat is about half done, usually 1 to 1½ hours. Skim off excess fat with a spoon, if necessary. Add the carrots, parsnips or turnips, and onion. Continue cooking till the chicken and vegetables are tender.

Put the fruit in a separate pot and add enough of the chicken stock to almost cover them. Add the sweetening, and cook till the fruit is soft, about 15 to 20 minutes. Mix together the sour cream or yogurt and flour, and stir in several spoonfuls of the hot fruit liquid. Then combine with the apple or rhubarb mixture and stir well. Simmer this till thickened, about 2 minutes. Add the pieces of chicken and simmer for 5 more minutes. Taste, and adjust seasonings, if necessary. The vegetables that were cooked with the chicken can be added to the stew or served separately, or they can be made into soup with any remaining stock. The fruit makes an interesting sauce alternative to the more familiar tomato flavor.

**Duck and Apple or Rhubarb Stew** Duck can be used instead of chicken. Be sure to skim fat off well before adding vegetables.

### Chick Pea Chicken Stew, Middle Eastern Style (Makes 8—10 servings.)

| | |
|---|---|
| 1 cup chick peas (Also called garbanzos.) | 4 onions, quartered |
| | 2 large potatoes, cubed |
| 1 stewing chicken, cut in serving pieces | pepper, salt, optional |
| | cinnamon to taste, optional |

Soak the chick peas overnight in water, then put them in a big pot with their soaking water. Add the chicken pieces and enough water to just cover the chicken. Bring to a boil, then simmer over low heat for several hours till both the chicken and chick peas are tender. Add the onions, potatoes, cinnamon, pepper, and salt, if desired. Cook till the onions and potatoes are done, about 20 minutes more. Though simple, the bean, onion, and potato mixture is especially hearty and satisfying, and makes one chicken go considerably further than it otherwise would.

**Small Sized Chicken Pieces**
Borrow an idea from the Chinese and cut young chickens in smaller sections, about ½ to ⅓ the size of a jointed section. These pieces will cook faster and go farther, and are perfect for small children. A meat cleaver or poultry shears can be used to cut through bone where necessary. It is best to remove leg bones before cutting since they often produce slivers.

**Chicken Skin Topping for Casseroles and Stuffed Vegetables** When using extra cooked chicken in casseroles, such as those under BASIC CASSEROLE RECIPES, in the CASSEROLE section, lay pieces of chicken skin on top instead of the usual dots of butter or grated cheese. Skin from a stewed chicken will become nicely browned and crisp while the casserole bakes. Pieces of skin can also be used to top stuffed vegetables.

**Chicken Livers with Barbecued Chicken** When charcoal broiling or barbecuing chicken, add an extra treat. Wrap each chicken liver in a slice of bacon and fasten with a toothpick, or thread onto skewers. Broil until the bacon is browned and the liver is cooked through, but do not overcook and dry out the liver. For shish kebab, thread vegetable pieces, such as onion, tomato, and green pepper, between the livers.

**Chinese Chicken Sandwiches** Stew chicken in a soy sauce mixture, according to the recipe for *Chinese Master Sauce for Red Cooking Meat*, in the MEAT section. When the chicken is cool, slice for sandwiches. Alfalfa sprouts go well with these sandwiches. The meat has a delicate flavor that everyone will enjoy.

## Chicken Pie
(Makes 6–8 dinner servings.)

*1 stewing chicken, cooked*
*3 tablespoons chicken fat*
*4 tablespoons flour*
*1½ cups chicken broth*
*½ cup cream or top milk*
*pepper, salt, optional*
*several tablespoons parsley or chervil, minced*

*vegetables stewed with the chicken, optional* (May include thick slices carrot, onion, potato, celery.)
*pastry for a 2 crust pie, or 1 recipe biscuit dough* (May use chicken fat for shortening.)

Pull the chicken meat from the bones in large pieces. Heat the chicken fat in a saucepan or skillet and stir in the flour. Add the chicken broth. Heat, stirring constantly, till it thickens. Stir in the cream or top milk, and season with pepper and salt, if desired. Add the parsley or chervil, chicken meat, and the vegetables, if desired.

If pastry is used, line a deep pie dish or shallow casserole with it. Add the chicken mixture and the top crust, sealing as for pie. If biscuit dough is used, pour the chicken mixture into a casserole or baking pan and set biscuits close together on top. Bake in a hot oven, 425°F, for 25 minutes or till the pie crust or biscuits have browned.

## Chicken Hash
(Makes about 6 servings.)

*meat and skin from 1 chicken, ground raw*
*6 tablespoons chicken fat or butter*
*4 cups cooked potatoes, coarsely chopped*

*1 small onion, ground or minced*
*pinch nutmeg*
*pinch sage*
*3 tablespoons cream*
*pepper, salt, optional*

Using a large heavy frying pan, sauté the chicken meat in half of the chicken fat or butter for 2 or 3 minutes, or till it has lost its pink, raw look. Mix the chicken with the potatoes, onion, nutmeg, sage, cream, pepper, and salt, if desired, in a bowl. Heat the rest of the fat or butter in the frying pan and spread the hash mixture evenly in it. Cook over medium heat till the hash is crusty brown on the bottom. Turn it over, in one piece if possible, and brown the other side. Cooking time is about 15 minutes per side. Cut into wedges to serve. Rich, but crispy, and delicious.

## Mulligatawny Soup
(Makes 10–12 medium bowls.)

*¼ cup chicken fat, or other fat or oil*
*2 sour apples, chopped medium*
*1 onion, chopped medium*
*1 celery stalk with leaves, chopped*
*1 carrot, chopped medium*
*½ green pepper, chopped medium*

*1 teaspoon curry powder*
*1 tablespoon flour*
*1 cup tomatoes or tomato sauce*
*2 cloves*
*pinch mace*
*1 teaspoon honey, or sugar*

¼ teaspoon black or red pepper
2 tablespoons parsley, minced
2 quarts chicken broth

salt, to taste (Omit if broth is salted.)

leftover cooked chicken meat, chopped, optional

Heat the fat in a soup pot and sauté the apples, onion, celery, carrot, and green pepper till they are very lightly browned. Stir in the curry powder and flour. Add the tomatoes, cloves, mace, sweetening, pepper, parsley, chicken broth, and salt, if desired. Simmer for about 45 minutes. The soup can be puréed with a food mill or blender, or served as is. Add chicken meat after puréeing, or about 5 to 10 minutes before serving. Taste and adjust seasonings as desired when the chicken meat is added.

### Chopped Chicken Livers, Jewish Style          (Makes about 1 cup.)

2–3 chicken livers
1 tablespoon chicken fat or butter
1–2 eggs, hard-boiled

1–2 teaspoons scallion or onion, minced
salt, optional

Fry the chicken livers gently over low heat in the fat or butter till they are cooked through, about 10 minutes. Chop the chicken livers and eggs together. When they are minced, add the scallion or onion and continue chopping until thoroughly combined. (The texture is not as good if the mixture is ground or chopped in a high-speed device.) Mix in salt, if desired.

Spread the chopped mixture on crackers, matzohs (a traditional Jewish cracker) or thinly sliced dark bread. These are good as hors d'oeuvres or with soup.

**Giblet Spread**   Along with the livers and eggs, chop 2 to 3 gizzards and hearts that have been cooked until very tender. This mixture can be chopped in a food chopper or by hand. Besides onion, soy sauce and 1 teaspoon catsup or tomato paste can be added for seasoning. Giblets from geese, turkeys, and other poultry can be used.

**Leftover Liver Spread**   Instead of chicken livers, use a slice or two of leftover fried liver of any kind. Chop with the hard-boiled eggs and onion. Add mayonnaise to moisten and let sit an hour or so before serving, for the flavors to blend.

### Baked Chicken Livers

(Makes hors d'oeuvres for 8–12, or about 4 dinner servings.)

1 pound chicken livers
1 cup fine dry bread crumbs
2 teaspoons fresh herbs, minced, or ½ teaspoon dry herbs (Savory, thyme, and parsley are a good combination.)

¼ teaspoon salt, or to taste
¼ cup butter, melted, or rendered chicken fat

Cut each chicken liver in half, unless they are small. Mix together the bread crumbs, herbs, salt, and enough of the butter or fat to moisten the bread crumbs. Roll each piece of liver in the crumb mixture and place on a baking sheet or shallow baking pan. Bake in a moderate, 350°F oven, till cooked through, 20 to 30 minutes.

These can be served as a main course with a sauce, such as the *Creamed Mushrooms* recipe in the MUSHROOMS section, or they can be speared with toothpicks for hors d'oeuvres.

### Chicken Livers in Wine                     (Makes 4–6 dinner servings.)

*½ pound chicken livers, each cut into 2 or 3 pieces*
*flour*
*pepper, to taste*
*2–3 tablespoons butter*

*¼ cup ham, chopped small*
*2–3 tablespoons dry white wine*
*3 tablespoons chicken stock*
*hot cooked rice or noodles*

Shake or toss the chicken liver pieces in flour, seasoned with pepper if desired. Heat the butter in a frying pan till it foams. Add the liver and the ham, and sauté, stirring often, till the liver has browned lightly. Add the wine, then let it bubble up and reduce for about 10 minutes. Add the stock and cook several minutes more.

Pour the livers and sauce over hot cooked rice or noodles in a serving dish and serve immediately. Their flavor is enhanced if the rice or noodles are cooked in chicken stock.

# CHICORY

### STORAGE

**Canning**  *Leafy tops* Handle as for spinach. Refer to SPINACH and CANNING LEAFY GREENS, in CANNING section.

**Cold Storage**  (Preferred method for leafy heads and roots.) *Leafy heads, Endive, Escarole* Pull with roots, tie heads to blanch, replant in sand or soil. Store in root cellar or similar conditions. Keeps 2–3 mos. *Roots* Store in root cellar to keep all winter. Refer to COLD STORAGE section. Also WINTER FORCING OF CHICORY ROOTS, below.

CHICORY, WITH ALL OF ITS DIVERSITY, SHOULD NOT BE OVERLOOKED by the home gardener. Many seed catalogs offer five or six varieties; some for salad greens such as endive, escarole, and radicchio, a red-leafed variety from Italy; and some with large roots for winter forcing, such as witloof chicory, also known as Belgian endive. The greens are much more versatile than lettuce, since most varieties will grow during hot summer weather as well as cool fall and mild winter weather, and they are also good cooked as a pot herb like dandelion greens. For a superb winter salad delicacy, chicory roots can be forced. Witloof chicory produces a tightly packed head of blanched leaves shaped like an oversized cigar, while another forcing variety, *Barbe de Capucin*, has loose pink and white leaves. Another way to use chicory roots is to dry and roast them for a coffee-like beverage.

Wild chicory, which grows abundantly in some regions, can be used similarly to cultivated chicory. Both the leaves and roots, however, have a more bitter flavor. The leaves should be gathered and used in early spring along with dandelion leaves, which they greatly resemble when young. (Refer to the DANDELIONS section.) Wild roots can be forced and are good for drying and roasting, but they must be dug before they produce a flower and seed stalk.

## HANDLING CHICORY

With planning, chicory leaves for salads and cooking can be harvested all year. In spring, there are thinnings, and perhaps shoots from broken root tips remaining in the soil. Varieties such as endive and escarole are usually harvested in summer and fall since they withstand both heat and frosts well. Open-headed varieties are tied closed about 3 weeks before harvest to blanch them, making them crisper, tender and less bitter. Often the outer green leaves are cooked and the inner leaves used for salads. Endive and escarole can be stored longer than most salad greens and enjoyed well into winter. Forced roots also provide chicory leaves in winter, and dried roots can be roasted as a beverage all year. (Refer to BREWING ROAST BEVERAGES, in the BEVERAGES section.)

*Winter Forcing of Chicory Roots*  Forcing simply means providing conditions to start a plant's spring growth early. Most varieties of chicory root will produce a leafy head when forced, as long as they have not yet produced a blossom and seed stock. However, the varieties developed especially for forcing are the most dependable. Generally, only straight, undamaged roots should be forced. Less than perfect roots are best for drying and roasting, or even cooked as a vegetable. Dandelion roots can be forced or roasted in the same way as chicory.

Dig the roots late in the fall, just before hard freezes. Trim the tops to about 1 inch above the crown. The roots can be trimmed to 9 or 10 inches if they are inconveniently long. A practical forcing method for a small planting is to "replant" the roots close together in containers of soil or sand as soon as they are dug and trimmed. Store the containers in a cold place where they will not freeze, such as a root cellar. When wanted for forcing, move them to a warm, dark place. A 60°F room is fine. If the room is lighted, cover the containers with large cardboard boxes, or another covering that will keep out light and allow growing space. Forced chicory grown in light becomes too bitter to enjoy. The soil or sand should be kept barely damp and the containers should have drainage holes, because the roots will rot if they are too wet.

Within 2 to 3 weeks, blanched heads of chicory will grow large enough to use and can be cut. A second growth usually appears after the first cutting. It is not as delicate, but can still be used for salads. The spent roots can then be added to the compost pile, or given to the chickens for mid-winter pecking. If containers of chicory roots are

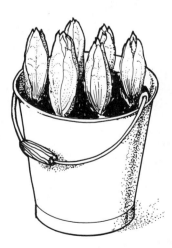

*Winter forced witloof chicory (Belgian endive) ready to harvest.*

brought in from cold storage and forced at regular intervals, this delicacy can be enjoyed all winter.

Forced chicory is so crisp and flavorful raw that it is easy to find ways to use it. It is also tasty cooked, but in winter, when home-grown, raw vegetables are at a premium, it seems a shame to cook it. Recipes for cooking Belgian endive appear in most French and Italian cookbooks.

A simple way to enjoy witloof chicory, or Belgian endive, is to serve one head to each person as a first course. The leaves can be pulled off and eaten one by one. As the center is approached, the leaves become increasingly crisp and delicious, with the most delicate heart leaves to be enjoyed last. A dip or salad dressing can be provided. Belgian endive leaves are also excellent when stuffed like celery. (Refer to stuffing ideas in the CELERY section.)

***Bitterness in Cooked Chicory***   The greatest problem when cooking chicory is its varying degrees of bitterness. In cultivated varieties, especially those with blanched leaves, the bitterness is diminished to a pleasantly sharp flavor. The mildest chicory is usually one harvested in cool weather. Exceedingly bitter greens or roots can be cooked in one or more changes of water, as for some wild foods, but of course vitamins and minerals will be lost. (Refer to REMOVING BITTER TASTES FROM WILD FOODS, in the WILD FOODS section.) Moderate bitterness in cooked greens can be balanced by serving them with lemon juice or vinegar, or by using them in recipes with milk. Recipes for dandelion greens can be used since their greens are very similar. (Refer to the DANDELION section.)

Large, cultivated chicory roots are a tender and quick cooking vegetable, but they also have a characteristic sharp flavor. They are good added to stews and soups in small amounts, but opinions will vary about their flavor when served alone.

## CHICORY RECIPES

### *Italian Braised Chicory*                    (Makes about 6 side servings.)

*1 pound (about) chicory leaves* (The outer green leaves of endive or escarole can be used, saving inner leaves for salad.)
*3 tablespoons oil, preferably olive*
*1 clove garlic, sliced*

*1 teaspoon fresh basil or parsley, minced*
*½ teaspoon fresh mint, minced, or ¼ teaspoon dried*
*½ teaspoon pepper, or to taste*
*½ teaspoon salt, optional*

Wash chicory and shred, not too finely. Place in a saucepan with the oil, garlic, basil or parsley, mint, pepper, and salt, if desired. Cover and simmer over very low heat for about 45 minutes, stirring occasionally. Add a little water if it should become dry. Good served with lemon slices or vinegar.

*Chicory with Pasta*   Prepare chicory as above and toss with hot, cooked spaghetti, or other pasta. Serve immediately with grated parmesan, or other cheese.

*Braised Dandelion Greens*   Use dandelion leaves instead of chicory.

### Hot Chicory and Bacon Salad   (Makes about 6 side servings.)

*1 pound chicory greens, washed and*
   *cut in pieces (Somewhat tough*
   *or bitter greens can be used.)*

*2–3 slices bacon, chopped*
*2–3 tablespoons cider or wine*
   *vinegar*

Have the greens ready in a bowl that will stand heat. Fry the bacon till just crisp. Pour most of the bacon fat over the greens, keeping the bacon in the pan. Return the pan to the heat and add the vinegar. As soon as it bubbles, pour with the bacon over the greens. Toss to combine ingredients and serve immediately.

*Dandelion and Bacon Salad*   Use young, tender dandelion leaves instead of, or mixed with, the chicory leaves.

### Endive and Potato Salad   (Makes about 6 side servings.)

*1 head endive or escarole*
*1 slice garlic, for rubbing bowl*
*2 cups potatoes, cooked and sliced*
*2 or more eggs, hard-boiled*

*juice of 2 lemons, or ¼ cup*
   *vinegar*
*¼ cup salad oil*
*pepper, oregano, to taste*
*salt, optional*

Remove the tough outer leaves of the endive or escarole and save them to use in another recipe. Wash and dry the inner leaves. Rub a salad bowl with the cut side of a garlic clove. Arrange the endive or escarole in the bowl with the potato slices. Slice hard-boiled eggs and arrange decoratively around the bowl. Mix the lemon juice or vinegar, oil, and seasonings for a dressing. Pour over the salad. An attractive arrangement that depends on the high quality of its ingredients for its goodness.

### Gratin of Belgian Endive   (Makes about 6 servings.)

*6 (about) Belgian endives or witloof*
   *chicory*
*2 tablespoons (about) butter*
*pepper, to taste*
*½ cup grated cheese (Such as*
   *Parmesan or Romano.)*

*½ cup fine dry bread crumbs*
*2 tablespoons parsley, minced*
*2 slices bacon, chopped*
*½ cup cream, optional*
*1 lemon, sliced, or cut in wedges*

Trim the endives and rinse quickly, if necessary. Cut them in half lengthwise and pack in a tight, single layer in a heavily buttered, shallow baking dish. Sprinkle with pepper. Mix the cheese, bread crumbs, parsley, and bacon. Make sure bacon pieces are not stuck to-

---

### CHICORY IDEAS

**Chicory with Beef**   Chicory flavor goes very well with beef, and the cooked greens are a good side dish with a roast or pot roast. A few spoonfuls of the beef juices can be poured over the greens before serving. Chopped chicory greens or root add flavor to beef stew, or to soup made with beef stock. Greens should be added about 20 minutes before the stew or soup is done.

**Endive or Escarole with Spinach**   For an excellent tossed salad combine half endive or escarole, and half fresh spinach leaves. Other salad vegetables and herbs can be added, as desired, with an oil and vinegar or other favorite dressing.

---

### OTHER RECIPES WITH CHICORY

Beans and Greens Soup, p.25
Creamed Chicory Greens, p.219
Greens and Rice, p.519
Hot Drinks (roots), p.42
Gumbo Z'Herbes, p.341
Mix and Match Greens, p.688

gether in clumps. Spread the mixture evenly over the endives. Put in a hot oven, about 450°F. After 10 minutes reduce heat to 350°F and bake for 40 minutes more. If desired, pour cream over the endives 20 minutes before they are done. Serve with lemon slices or wedges.

# CHINESE CABBAGE

THE POSSIBILITIES FOR USING CHINESE CABBAGE ARE JUST BEGINning to be understood in western countries. This vegetable is certain to increase in popularity, as it is very productive, grows well in cool weather, and keeps well. Best of all, it lends itself to western cuisine as readily as to Chinese and other East Asian cooking methods. It can be the main ingredient in a tossed salad French or Italian style one day, and appear stir-fried Chinese style the next.

There are scores of varieties of Chinese cabbage. The various names and characteristics can be confusing, due to different translations, and the constant introduction of new varieties. There are, however, several notable types. Best known are the "heading" types, which include michili and wong bok. These form large, oval or cylindrical heads with wide, white stalks and blanched centers. The celery cabbage sold in groceries is of this type, with an especially tall, celery shaped head. The loose leaf types are another group. Many look like Swiss chard, with thick, white stalks and dark green, rounded leaves, but loose feathery leaves and other variations also occur. This group is sometimes called mustard cabbage, and is often listed under "greens" in seed catalogs. Bok choi and pak choi are among this type.

Despite distinctive differences in looks and some difference in taste and texture, all Chinese cabbages can be used in similar ways, and are interchangeable in recipes.

## HANDLING CHINESE CABBAGE

Most varieties of Chinese cabbage have better flavor and texture when harvested in cool weather, in either spring or fall. If harvested in fall before heavy frosts, long keeping varieties can be stored all winter. (Refer to the COLD STORAGE section.) Some varieties also do well in insulated cold frames and cool greenhouses.

Raw Chinese cabbage is delicious in salads. The thick, crisp stalks can be sliced like celery. The leafy parts are like lettuce, with a peppery flavor. Stir-frying is an ideal way to cook Chinese cabbage, or it can be cooked like spinach or mustard greens, if the heavy stalks are allowed extra cooking time. The best method is to place the stalks in the pot or steamer first, with the leafy parts on top.

Chinese cabbage seeds can be used for seasoning in the same way as mustard seeds. They can also be ground for prepared mustard. (Refer to the MUSTARD section.)

## CHINESE CABBAGE RECIPES

### *Chinese Cabbage Yogurt Salad* (Makes about 6 side servings.)

*several cups Chinese cabbage,
    shredded or sliced*
*Yogurt Dressing for Vegetable Salad*
    (Recipe in the YOGURT sec-
    tion.)

*pimiento or paprika, parsley,
    scallion or chives for garnish,
    optional*

Mix the Chinese cabbage with the yogurt dressing and let stand a few minutes. Garnish as desired.

### *Chinese Cabbage Apple Salad* (Makes about 6 side servings.)

*Chinese cabbage, cut in bite sized
    pieces*
*1 apple, chopped, without peeling*

*1–2 tablespoons scallion,
    chives, or sweet onion,
    minced*
*Soy Sauce Dressing* (Recipe in
    the SALADS section.)

Mix all ingredients. May be served immediately, or after flavors have blended for several hours.

### *Stir-fried Chinese Cabbage* (Makes about 6 side servings.)

*2 pounds (about) Chinese cabbage*
*2–3 tablespoons lard, chicken fat, or
    oil*
*1 clove garlic, minced, optional*

*ginger root, small piece fresh,
    minced, optional*
*¼ teaspoon salt, optional*
*¼–½ cup chicken stock or
    water, optional*

Cut the leafy parts of the Chinese cabbage away from the stalks and into about 2 inch pieces. Slice the stalks diagonally into 1 or 1½ inch pieces. Heat the fat or oil in a heavy frying pan or wok till it is quite hot, but not smoking. Add the garlic, ginger root, and salt, if desired, and stir once or twice. Add the Chinese cabbage stalks and stir-fry 2 to 3 minutes. If the stalks are tender and juicy, add the leaves, stir-fry for only about a minute, till they are wilted and bright in color, then serve. No liquid is needed. If the stalks are dry or a little tough, add the chicken stock or water after stir-frying them for about 2 minutes. Cover and cook 2 minutes more. Then add the leaves and stir-fry till wilted and bright colored. If desired, the juices can be thickened by stirring in a tablespoon of cornstarch that has been mixed with a little water. (Refer to the STIR-FRYING section for more about the cooking method.) This dish exemplifies simple, stir-fried excellence.

***Chinese Cabbage and Shrimp, Stir-fried***   Prepare ½ cup fresh shrimp. Cut large shrimp into half inch pieces. Stir-fry the shrimp for 2 to 3 minutes, or till cooked through, and set aside. Stir-fry the Chinese cabbage as described above. After the leaves are done, add the shrimp and stir-fry to reheat them.

To use dried shrimp, boil about ¼ cup of shrimp in ½ cup of chicken stock or water for 5 minutes. Add the shrimp and liquid to the stir-fried stalks. Cover and cook 2 minutes, and add the leaves as usual.

***Stir-fried Mustard Greens***   Cut mustard leaves into about 2 inch pieces without removing the stalks. Stir-fry as described above for 2 to 4 minutes, or till the leaves are wilted and bright colored. If the greens are young and tender, serve immediately. If not, add stock or water and cook, covered, for about 2 minutes.

### *Kimchi (or Kim Chee)*   (A Korean condiment; makes 4–6 cups.)

| | |
|---|---|
| 1½–2 pounds Chinese cabbage | 3 tablespoons plain or pickling salt |
| 1–1½ pounds turnip, rutabaga, or large white winter radish (Or omit this and add an extra pound of Chinese cabbage instead.) | 4–6 cloves garlic, minced |
| | 2 tablespoons fresh ginger root, minced, optional |
| 4–5 scallions | 2 tablespoons cayenne or hot pepper flakes, or to taste (Some like it hotter.) |

Cut the Chinese cabbage in 1 inch slices across the stalks. Cut large turnips, rutabagas, or radishes into sections and slice them thinly across the grain. Slice small turnips or radishes thinly crosswise. Use a vegetable slicer if possible. Slices should be 1 to 2 inches across and very thin. Cut the scallions into 1 inch lengths, including tops. Cut the white part of large scallions in half lengthwise. Combine the vegetables with the salt, garlic, ginger root, and pepper in a large bowl. Toss to mix seasonings evenly. Pack in a crock, large, wide mouth jar, or other non-corrosive, approximately 2 quart container. Weigh it down with a jar of water or other heavy object. (Refer to the KITCHEN UTENSILS section.)

Keep the kimchi at room temperature. If liquid does not rise to cover the vegetables after 12 to 24 hours, add water to cover. After 2

### CHINESE CABBAGE IDEAS

**Chinese Cabbage in Soup**
For a crisp, fresh addition to soup, put a small mound of shredded or sliced Chinese cabbage in each soup bowl. Ladle very hot soup over it. The Chinese cabbage will cook slightly, but retain its freshness, and the soup will be cooled to just the right temperature for eating. (Refer to the SIMPLE SOUP, EAST ASIAN STYLE idea, in the SOUP section.)

Chinese cabbage can also be added to the soup pot just before serving, but if it sits very long, or is reheated, it will become an ordinary vegetable soup without distinctive texture or flavor.

to 3 days the kimchi should ferment and taste lightly pickled, somewhat like sauerkraut. The fermentation time will depend on the room temperature. If cool, it may take a week. When the kimchi tastes fermented it can be packed in small jars and kept in the refrigerator, or a large container can be stored in any cold storage area. It will keep a month or more. (Refer to the PICKLING section for more on fermentation.)

Serve kimchi as a snack, an appetizer, or a relish with meals. The combination of hot, strong flavors is surprisingly pleasant and invigorating. In Korea kimchi is eaten every day, often for breakfast, in one of its many variations.

***Kimchi with Rice*** Mix together 1 cup raw rice, ½ cup kimchi, and, if desired, ¼ cup raw pork or beef cut into shreds. Add about 2 cups of water. More water may be needed if the kimchi is dry, or if slow cooking, brown rice is used. Heat to a boil, reduce heat, and simmer till the rice is done, 20 to 40 minutes depending on the type of rice. Do not stir or uncover unnecessarily during cooking.

***Chinese Cabbage, Salted Japanese Style*** Prepare Chinese cabbage as for kimchi, but mix with salt only, omitting other ingredients. Use 3 to 4 pounds Chinese cabbage to 3 tablespoons salt. Pack and ferment as above. To serve, remove the desired amount of Chinese cabbage from the brine and squeeze dry. It can be rinsed in water before squeezing to remove extra salt. Sprinkle with soy sauce and toasted sesame seeds.

***Fermented Turnip, Rutabaga, or Winter Radish Japanese Style*** Slice as for kimchi. Ferment and serve as for Chinese cabbage, salted Japanese style, above.

---

**OTHER RECIPES WITH CHINESE CABBAGE**

Basic Recipe for Prepared
    Mustard from Seeds, p.427
Braised Chinese Cabbage, p.393
Making Sauerkraut, p.540
Recipes, and Ideas for Lettuce,
    p.392

---

# COLD STORAGE

W HEN MECHANICAL REFRIGERATION WAS DEVELOPED, AND REFRIGERATORS became standard home equipment, most old methods for keeping food cold became obsolete. However, one old method is as practical as ever—using the earth's coolness for storing vegetables. fruits, and other foods. A well designed root cellar is the most sophisticated arrangement, but other possibilities are underground pits, insulated mounds, and simply leaving root vegetables in the ground under a heavy mulch for digging during winter thaws. Use can be made of unheated space, such as an attic, spare room, pantry or basement. If available, a well insulated outbuilding or spare refrigerator are also good storage spaces. The modern gardener or homesteader with an interest in storing home-grown food all year will want to use every method available, whether old or new.

Requirements for cold storage are so variable, depending on climate, the foods to be stored, and individual circumstances, that every-

*The Weed family's root cellar, ca. 1930, Walker Valley, New York.*
Inside view of root cellar. Food for a large family was stored in it.

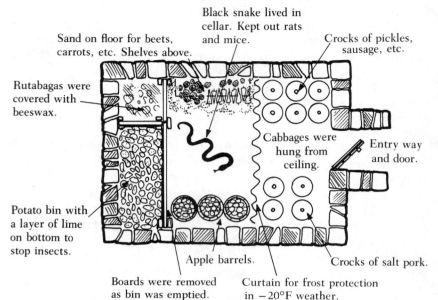

Sand on floor for beets, carrots, etc. Shelves above.

Black snake lived in cellar. Kept out rats and mice.

Crocks of pickles, sausage, etc.

Rutabagas were covered with beeswax.

Cabbages were hung from ceiling.

Entry way and door.

Potato bin with a layer of lime on bottom to stop insects.

Apple barrels.

Crocks of salt pork.

Boards were removed as bin was emptied.

Curtain for frost protection in −20°F weather.

Outside view of cellar before back filling with dirt. The cellar was set into a hillside, and the roof boards covered with hay to keep dirt from falling through. Two to 3 feet of dirt covered the roof. Dirt surrounded the entryway. Every 3 or 4 years the roof was uncovered and replaced.

one has to work out the best methods for themselves. Information on designing and building root cellars and other cold storage structures is available from many sources, including U.S. Department of Agriculture bulletins and state agricultural department publications. The root cellar shown above could be improved with the addition of a ventilation system, but is otherwise as useful as a modern structure. (See the REFERENCES at the end of this section.)

## FACTORS AFFECTING COLD STORAGE OF FOODS

Temperatures above freezing and below 40°F are best for storing most foods, but anything below room temperature will help to delay spoilage. When temperatures drop low enough to freeze foods, special storage techniques are required. (Refer to the FREEZING section.)

The temperature at which various foods will freeze and be damaged also varies. Most root vegetables, onions, and apples will survive a few degrees below freezing without damage, while potatoes are damaged by even slight frost. The foods in the root cellar illustration are arranged with potatoes in the back and less vulnerable foods in the front. If stored foods should be exposed to below freezing temperatures, check them often for the next week or two. They may appear to be all right at first, and then show signs of spoilage later.

Besides temperature, other factors affecting cold storage are humidity, air circulation, and light. Root cellars and similar storage areas provide an even, cold temperature between 32 and 40°F, a high humidity, and darkness. A well designed root cellar has ventilation providing adequate air circulation, but a closed underground pit has very little. Attics and unheated rooms are likely to fluctuate in temperature, but are still useful if the temperature stays above freezing and below room temperature. Humidity is usually lower in unheated rooms than in a root cellar, which is better for some foods. Attics are the driest storage areas available in most houses. Some foods will need protection from light in storage areas with windows. Refrigerators provide an even, cold temperature and darkness, but have no air circulation and low humidity. Humidity is usually lower in frost free refrigerators than in models that need defrosting.

## COLD STORAGE OF ROOT VEGETABLES AND TUBERS

Also refer to specific root vegetables and tubers.

Root vegetables and tubers are among the most practical fresh or raw foods for cold storage. Root cellars are ideal, but these foods also keep well in other cool areas if protected from drying out and freezing. They do best at temperatures between 32 and 40°F with a humidity of 90 to 95%, in darkness and with some air circulation. They will keep all winter under the right conditions.

The best varieties of root vegetables and tubers for storage are those bred for long keeping. Planting must be timed so they mature in fall and can be harvested just before heavy frosts. Dig and handle the roots carefully to avoid injury or bruising. If undue spoilage has been a problem, freshly dug roots can be left in the sun for a few hours to kill bacteria that could cause spoilage. Shake dirt from vegetables but do not wash them before storage. Water is more likely to cause spoilage than dirt. The only trimming needed is to cut off the tops of root vegetables to ½ to 1 inch above the crowns. Be careful not to cut into the root itself, and do not trim rootlets or root hairs. Whole roots and tubers keep best, and large, unblemished roots keep the longest. Sort out small and imperfect roots and store separately for early use.

Carrots layered in sand in a plastic dish pan with drainage holes in the bottom. Will keep in any cool place that will not freeze.

Some packing material or covering is necessary for root vegetables stored in less than ideal conditions. In a good root cellar they keep well simply laid in bins, but packing material may increase storage life there as well. Packing or covering keeps roots moist, provides darkness, and offers some protection from fluctuating temperatures. Damp sand, peat moss, or dry leaves make good packing materials. Other possibilities are wrapping each root in newspaper, or putting small bunches in plastic bags with a few air holes. Rutabagas can be coated with paraffin or wax. Damp sand is excellent if the vegetables will be stored in low humidity. The sand can be lightly sprinkled if necessary. Buckets, bins, plastic pans, and sturdy boxes are good storage containers. They should have drainage holes so moisture cannot collect. Leave the top uncovered, or use a top with holes in it.

Towards the end of their storage life, root vegetables often show signs of growth. Leaves sprout or tiny root hairs may grow. If tops grow on beets or turnips they can be used for greens. Roots lose flavor and food value quickly once they start to grow, and should be used immediately. Extras can be dried or fed to livestock.

***Carrots, Celeriac, Chicory roots, Horseradish, Jerusalem Artichoke, Parsnips, Salsify*** Where winter is not too severe, these vegetables can be left in the garden over the winter. They will stay in excellent condition till spring growth starts, as long as they do not freeze severely, or suffer rodent damage. They should be heavily mulched and their rows or beds well marked, for digging during winter thaws and in early spring. It may be practical to harvest part of a crop in fall for indoor cold storage, and leave part in the garden for early spring use.

Jerusalem artichokes do not keep well after they are dug. They are best left in the ground till needed. Freezing in the ground does not damage them.

## COLD STORAGE OF ABOVE-GROUND VEGETABLES

Also refer to specific vegetables.

Many above-ground vegetables that mature in fall can be stored in a root cellar or similar storage conditions. They may keep only 1 or 2 months or all winter, depending on the vegetable and storage techniques. Cabbage keeps all winter stored in several ways. Cucumbers, cauliflower, kohlrabi, tomatoes, and eggplant keep up to 2 months. A few vegetables require less humidity than in a root cellar. Onions keep best in a cold, dry place, while winter squash and pumpkins prefer a moderately cool, dry place.

***Cauliflower, Celery, Chinese Cabbage, Endive, Escarole, Kale, Kohlrabi, Leeks***  An excellent and simple way to store these vegetables is to pull the whole plant, roots and all, and "replant" them in moist sand or soil. Store in a root cellar or in similar storage. Pull the plants in dry weather, and do not wash them. Check for slugs or other pests and pick off as many as possible by hand. Endive and escarole tops are best tied to make compact heads for close packing, and the tops of leeks cut to the same length.

Where winters are mild, all these vegetables can be heavily mulched in the garden and pulled as needed through the winter.

Leeks packed in sand in a plastic-lined box with drainage holes ready for cold storage.

## COLD STORAGE OF FRUITS

Also refer to specific fruits.

The winter keeping or late varieties of many fruits can be stored in a root cellar or similar conditions. Apples and pears will keep all winter, while citrus fruits, grapes, quinces, and firm, small berries will keep from one to several months. It is necessary, however, to store most fruits separately from vegetables, particularly potatoes, turnips and cabbage family vegetables. The fruits can absorb odors, or give off odors or moisture that harm the vegetables. The root cellar can be divided into separate areas, or the fruits can be kept in closed containers.

Fruit must be checked often for spoilage. It is quite true that one bad apple (or orange or grape) will spoil the whole barrel (or box or bag). If spoiled fruit is found, wipe any mold or wetness off adjacent fruits before repacking.

***Cold Water Canning: Cranberries, Green Gooseberries, Lemons, Limes, Rhubarb, Wild Plums***  These firm and very acidic fruits can be kept raw in cold storage by a process called cold water canning. It is not actually canning, however, since there is no vacuum seal. The cold water is really just a packing material that prevents contact with the air, thereby extending storage life. Fruit must be fresh, raw, and unblemished. Wash in cold water if washing is necessary.

Sterilize jars with lids that seal tightly. They can be any size and can be, but do not have to be, canning jars. Fill the jars with fresh, whole fruit without crushing it. Rhubarb can be cut in any convenient length. Wash a deep pail and scald it with boiling water. Put a jar of fruit in the pail and run cold drinking water into the jar till it overflows and the water is well above the jar top. Put the jar lid on under water and seal tightly. Remove the jar, empty the pail and repeat with the next jar. This procedure drives out air bubbles and seals in the fruit without any air space.

Store the jars in a cool, dark place. The fruit will keep for months if the storage place is cold enough. Just above freezing is ideal. The water will be flavored and can be used with the fruit.

## SUGGESTIONS FOR VEGETABLES AND FRUITS IN COLD STORAGE

• Check stored foods often, especially towards the end of the storage season. Remove spoiled foods and any spoiled material on nearby foods.

• Keep track of the amounts of remaining foods. If there is too much of something, consider preserving it another way while it is still in prime condition. Most of the vegetables and fruits kept in cold storage are also good dried, particularly root vegetables, potatoes, onions, and apples. Canning, pickling, and freezing are other alternatives.

• If stored foods dry out or lose flavor so they are unacceptable for people, feed them to livestock or pets. Some animals will prefer them cooked. There is no need to trim or wash foods for animals. Simply cook it in a big pot of water.

## COLD STORAGE OF FOODS IN CROCKS

Many foods can be packed in crocks or similar non-corrosive containers, covered with pickling liquid, brine, fat, or oil to exclude air, and stored in a cold place for the winter. They should normally be used before warm spring weather arrives. In spite of differences in foods their storage needs are similar. They keep best between freezing and 40°F. Containers should be covered to keep out dust and pests. The food must be well covered by the pickling liquid, brine, fat, or oil because it will spoil if exposed to air. If food tends to float, a weight must be used. (Refer to CROCKS AND CROCK SUBSTITUTES, in the KITCHEN UTENSILS section.) (For some examples of food stored in crocks, refer to PRESERVING MEAT IN LARD, in the MEAT section, and the PICKLING and SAUERKRAUT sections.)

## REFERENCES

Agriculture Canada, Publication 1478/E, "Home storage room for fruits and vegetables," 1978.

Hertzberg, Ruth, *Putting Food By*, The Stephen Greene Press, 1982.

USDA Home & Garden Bulletin No. 119, "Storing Vegetables and Fruits in Basements, Cellars, Outbuildings, and Pits."

Collards or collard greens have the same botanical name as kale, which suggests that the two of them should be as alike as twins. If so, each twin has gone its separate way. Collards are favorite greens in the southeastern United States because they tolerate the summer heat and winter coolness equally well. In mild, somewhat humid climates they are a year-round vegetable. Kale is a northern green, especially beloved in Scotland. (Refer to the KALE section.) These two vegetables can often be interchanged in recipes, but prepared in traditional ways they are markedly different.

Some of the best ways to cook collards come from southern black cooking traditions, but they can be enjoyed as a summer, fall, and early winter vegetable almost everywhere. They have a mild cabbage flavor, and can be cooked like cabbage or any leafy green. They are rich in vitamins A and C and in minerals.

## HANDLING COLLARDS

Collards taste best when picked young from fast growing plants. The leaves should be almost full sized for cooking, but quite small and young for salads. The lowest leaves can be harvested progressively as the plant grows, leaving a tall stalk with a rosette of leaves on top. Eventually, the whole rosette can be harvested.

Since collards in the South can be harvested fresh most of the year, long-term storage is seldom necessary. In the North they can be frozen or dried for winter and spring use, and will keep up to a month in the refrigerator or root cellar.

Collard greens are cooked like spinach, except that they require a longer cooking time, 10 to 20 minutes depending on age and toughness. (Refer to COOKING SPINACH, in the SPINACH section.)

## COLLARD RECIPES

### *Collard and Ham Hock Soup* (Makes 8–12 bowls.)

*1 or 2 ham hocks*
*1 large onion, chopped*
*bunch collard greens (1–2 quarts), coarsely chopped*
*1 tablespoon honey or 2 tablespoons sugar*

Put the ham hocks and onion in a soup pot with about two quarts of water. Boil gently for about an hour, or till the ham is tender. Add the collard greens and sweetening and cook another 30 minutes.

A piece of ham can be put in each soup bowl before serving. A plain, delicious everyday soup from the U.S. South.

---

### STORAGE

**Canning** Possible, but flavor and texture are poor.

**Drying** Cut off stalks. Steam 8–10 min. (optional). Spread in thin layer. Dry until crumbly. Refer to DRYING FOODS section.

**Freezing** Blanch leaves 3 min. in boiling water. Refer to FREEZING section.

---

### COLLARD IDEAS

**Collards and Cured Meats** Collards are delicious flavored with ham, bacon, or salt pork. They can be cooked with a small slice of any of these, or cooked in ham or ham bone stock. Try topping them with bacon fat and crisp, crumbled bacon. Collards are also good substituted for cabbage in the *Corned Beef Boiled Dinner* recipe, in the BEEF section.

**Creamed Collards** Chop collards coarsely and cook as above without seasoning. In a separate pot gently sauté a minced onion in about 2 tablespoons butter or other fat. When the onion is golden, stir in 1 tablespoon flour. Blend well and add 1 cup milk. Stir constantly over low heat or in a double boiler till it thickens to a smooth sauce. Season with pepper and salt, if desired, add the hot, cooked collards, and serve.

**OTHER RECIPES
WITH COLLARDS**

Beans and Greens Soup, p.25
Greens Stuffed Ham, p.325
Gumbo Z'Herbes, p.341
Kale or Collards Colcannon, p.92
Making Sauerkraut, p.540

### Collard Greens, Italian Style                 (Makes about 6 side servings.)

3 tablespoons oil, preferably olive
1 clove garlic, whole
1 cup tomato juice, or sauce
1 cup vegetable stock, or cooking
  water
2 pounds collard greens, coarsely
  chopped

1 medium onion
marjoram or oregano, to taste
pepper, salt, optional
parmesan, or other grated cheese

Heat the olive oil and whole garlic clove in a saucepan. Add tomato juice and vegetable stock or water and bring to a boil, uncovered. Add the collards and whole onion, cover, and cook 10 minutes. Remove the onion and garlic. Season with marjoram or oregano, pepper and salt, if desired. Simmer 20 minutes. Serve sprinkled with cheese.

This can be a first course, or a side dish served in individual bowls.

# COLOSTRUM

COLOSTRUM IS THE FIRST MILK A MAMMAL GIVES AFTER THE BIRTH of young. For the first several days the colostrum is thick and yellowish, and then gradually changes to regular milk. Since colostrum is very important for a newborn's health, it is not usually available for cooking, but people who keep dairy animals will sometimes have extra. It makes a delicious, smooth and creamy custard pudding.

Colostrum is sometimes called firstlings or, in England, beestings.

## HANDLING COLOSTRUM

Colostrum from the second or third day's milking is considered best for cooking. It is often mixed with regular milk in recipes, and has the same effect on milk as eggs. The mixture will thicken or set when cooked. Colostrum from the first few days of milking, mixed half and half with milk, should set well. This effect gradually disappears. When cooking with colostrum, the heat must be kept low. Too high a temperature will make it curdle on the stovetop, or become tough and leathery in the oven.

The following useful suggestions are in Country Recipes, collected by the Farmer's Weekly, England, 1946.

"I always test it [beestings or colostrum] by putting a little on a saucer in the oven. If it sets too "thick", I put a pint of milk to 3 pints of beestings (or in proportion, according to the way it sets), sprinkle a little pudding-spice on top, and add a little sugar. Let it simmer in the oven, but not boil, just as if you were making an egg custard.

I make tarts with it just as one would make egg custard tarts."

**STORAGE**

**Freezing**   Pour in clean, scalded containers. Leave 1–1½ in. headroom. Quality retained 3 mos. Refer to FREEZING section.

Though cream does not rise readily on goat's colostrum, it does so readily on cow's. Cream collected from colostrum can replace cream and eggs in rich desserts.

## COLOSTRUM RECIPE

***Firstlings Custard***          (Makes 4–6 dessert servings.)

   *2 cups colostrum*
   *2 cups milk* (Or adjust proportions
      of colostrum and milk accord-
      ing to the strength of the
      colostrum.)

*¼ cup honey, or other sweeten-*
    *ing to taste*
*nutmeg, optional*

Combine colostrum, milk, and honey, and stir to dissolve the honey. Pour into a baking dish, about 1½ quart size, and sprinkle with nutmeg. Bake in a low, 300°F oven, till set, about 45 minutes to an hour. It is done when a knife cut into it comes out clean. As smooth, rich, and delicious as a custard can be.

# COMFREY

COMFREY IS HIGHLY REGARDED AS A MEDICINAL HERB WITH WELL documented success in speeding the healing of many kinds of sores, bruises, and boils. Early spring comfrey greens are appetizing cooked like spinach, but later in the season their leaves are too fuzzy and their taste too bland and mucilaginous to be appealing. The late greens are improved if chopped small and cooked with other more flavorful ingredients. Comfrey's extraordinary nutritional value makes it worth eating often. It is unusually high in protein and vitamin B12, and is rich in many other vitamins and minerals. The protein and B12 are especially important to vegetarians.

## HANDLING COMFREY

The first spring comfrey leaves make the best greens for cooking or salads. For salads, chop them small to minimize fuzziness and use in

---

### COMFREY IDEAS

**Comfrey as Nutritional Supplement**  Mince fresh comfrey leaves or crumble dried leaves, and add to soups, stews, salads, and casseroles, or anywhere parsley would be added. Their bland flavor is not especially noticed, but the dish's nutritional value is increased.

**Blenderized Comfrey**  Put comfrey leaves in a blender or food processor and liquify with milk, soup stock, vegetable juice or water. Use as the liquid in sauces, gravy or soup, or as a fresh vegetable drink.

**Comfrey as Livestock Feed** Comfrey plants are very productive, so there are usually more greens than a family can eat. Goats, rabbits, and other livestock will enjoy the extras, and benefit nutritionally as well.

---

### OTHER RECIPES WITH COMFREY

Herb Teas, p.341
Mix 'n Match Greens or Fruits, p.688

---

small amounts. Cook the leaves like spinach, using the water that clings to them after washing plus a few extra tablespoons. Comfrey greens are good cooked with other, stronger-flavored greens.

Comfrey leaves that grow after the first harvesting are not as tasty as the first leaves, even if they are young and tender. Cooking these later leaves is more a matter of disguise than of bringing out good qualities. They are best cut fairly small and mixed with stronger flavored ingredients.

It is possible to eat comfrey roots as a vegetable, but they are more enjoyable steeped in milk for a soothing beverage, or dried, roasted, and ground for a coffee-like drink. An effective compress for human or animal bruises, abcesses and boils can be made from the root. Wrap a clean slice of root loosely in gauze or cheesecloth. Mash with a mallet or the flat side of a heavy knife to flatten the compress and free the root juices. Dip the compress in boiling water to sterilize it and apply it to the sore. Leave on overnight if possible, using tape or a cloth binding.

Most herb books list other ways to take advantage of the healing properties of comfrey.

### COMFREY RECIPE

***Sue Weaver's Comfrey Pie***                          (Makes about 6 servings.)

| | |
|---|---|
| *1–2 pounds comfrey, cooked and chopped small* | *1 cup cheese, shredded mushrooms, sliced or chopped,* |
| *1½ cups milk* | *optional* |
| *3 tablespoons butter* | *pepper, to taste* |
| *2–3 eggs, lightly beaten* | *1 single pie crust* |

Mix the comfrey, milk, butter, eggs, cheese, and mushrooms. (The mushrooms can be lightly sautéed in the butter, if desired.) Season with pepper. Line a pie pan with the crust and pour in the comfrey mixture. Bake at 375°F for 30 to 40 minutes, or till the pie is set when tested with a knife.

Serve hot or cold. A slice packed in a lunch box makes a pleasant surprise.

---

# COOKIES

Cookies made from whole natural ingredients can be delicious as well as extraordinarily nutritious. Even conventional cookie recipes can often be adjusted to improve them nutritionally without hurting their taste. Basic improvements are: using whole wheat flour or a combination of flours instead of plain white flour, and reducing the amount of sugar or other sweetening. (Refer to FLOUR COMBINATIONS FOR QUICK BREADS and LIMITING SUGAR IN QUICK BREADS in the BREAD, QUICK section.) When making these improvements, adjust the amount of flour as necessary to make dough of the right thickness.

Healthful cookies are a boon for parents, who no longer have to worry about the snacks their children are eating—and a boon for all snack nibblers, who can enjoy their habit without reservation or recrimination.

## COOKIE RECIPES

These recipes are for cookies with unusual flavorings and high food value.

### *Coasting Cookies* (Makes 3–4 dozen 3 inch cookies.)

*1 cup molasses, sorghum, birch syrup, or other dark syrup*
*2 teaspoons baking soda*
*1 cup butter, softened*
*1 tablespoon coriander seeds, crushed*

*1 tablespoon caraway seeds, crushed*
*1 teaspoon ginger powder*
*About 4 cups whole wheat flour, or a combination* (In BREAD, QUICK section.)

Beat the soda very hard into the molasses or syrup. Blend in the butter, coriander seeds, caraway seeds, and ginger. (The seeds can be crushed in a mortar or whirled for a minute in a blender.) Add enough flour to make a stiff dough. Roll out very thin on a floured board, and cut out cookies. Large circles or other large shapes are nice. Bake on oiled cookie sheets in a hot, 400°F oven until lightly browned, usually 10 minutes. This very old recipe yields intensely flavored, unusually sustaining cookies, especially when birch syrup is used.

### *Grandma Minnie's Onion Cookies* (Makes about 4 dozen medium to large cookies.)

*4 cups whole wheat flour, or a combination* (In BREAD, QUICK section.)
*2 teaspoons baking powder*
*1/3 teaspoon pepper*
*1/2 cup shortening, or butter*

*2 medium onions, minced*
*2–3 tablespoons poppy seeds*
*2 eggs*
*1/2 cup oil*
*1/4 cup water*

Sift the flour, baking powder, and pepper. Cut in the shortening with a pastry cutter or two knives. Add the onions and poppy seeds. Lightly beat the eggs, and mix the oil and water with them. Add to

### COOKIE IDEAS

**Cookie Leather**   Follow the directions for FRUIT LEATHER, in the DRYING section, adding dry ingredients to the fruit purée for a thicker, though still spreadable texture. Use such dry ingredients as sunflower seeds or meal, sesame seeds, pumpkin, seeds, or shredded coconut. Sprouted grains puréed in a blender with a little juice or water or ground in a meat grinder, may also be added. These mixtures can be sweetened to taste, and spices can be added.

the flour mixture and work together with a fork or clean hands. Shape the dough into a ball and roll out flat on a floured board, or on waxed paper, to about ⅛ inch thick. Cut into circles, or any desired shape, and put on ungreased cookie sheets. Bake in a very hot oven, 420°F, for 10 to 15 minutes or until browned. These have a definitely cookie-like character, but can also be eaten like crackers.

### Brownies, Two Versions   (Makes about 3 dozen small squares.)

#### Carob Brownies

| | |
|---|---|
| 1 cup whole wheat flour | ½ cup honey |
| ½ cup carob powder | 2 teaspoons vanilla, optional |
| ½ cup wheat germ | 1 cup nuts, chopped or ½ cup |
| 4 eggs. | sunflower seeds, optional |
| ½ cup oil, or melted butter | |

#### Molasses Brownies

| | |
|---|---|
| 1 cup whole wheat flour | ½ cup oil, or melted butter |
| 1 cup wheat germ | ½ cup molasses |
| 1 teaspoon cinnamon | 1 cup nuts, chopped or ½ cup |
| ¼ teaspoon cloves | sunflower seeds, optional |
| 4 eggs | |

Combine dry ingredients in a mixing bowl. In another bowl beat the eggs slightly, and mix in the oil or butter, sweetening, and vanilla, if used. Stir the egg mixture into the dry ingredients and mix in nuts or seeds. Butter a 9″ x 9″ baking pan, or one of a similar size. Spread the batter in the pan and bake for 25 to 30 minutes in a moderate oven, about 325°F. The brownies are done when their surface is firm to the touch. Cut them into squares as soon as they come from the oven, and let them cool in the pan.

### Fruit Meal or Coconut Cookies   (Makes about 2 dozen small cookies.)

| | |
|---|---|
| 1 cup whole wheat flour, or a combination (In BREAD, QUICK section.) | ¼ cup wheat germ |
| | 1 teaspoon dried citrus fruit peel, powdered, or 1 tablespoon fresh, grated |
| 2 teaspoons baking powder | ⅓ cup oil or melted butter |
| ¾ cup dried FRUIT MEAL (in DRYING section), or dried coconut | ¼ cup honey or maple syrup |

Sift the flour and baking powder. Add the fruit meal or coconut, wheat germ, and citrus peel. Combine the oil or butter, and sweetening. Warm slightly if necessary to mix them. Add to the dry ingredients and mix together to make a stiff dough. Shape the dough into little balls about 1 inch in diameter. Put on an oiled cookie sheet and bake in a moderate over, 350°F, for about 10 minutes, or until lightly browned.

ORN IS NATIVE TO THE AMERICAN CONTINENTS, AND WAS VITAL TO
the survival of most North, Central, and South American Indians. Soon after their arrival in the new world early settlers learned
to grown corn from the Indians, and it helped them survive and
prosper just as it had the Indians. They found corn to be more versatile than other grains, because it could be eaten fresh as a vegetable
or left to dry and stored for later use. It was also easy to harvest by
hand, without special tools. Today, modern homesteaders appreciate
corn and grow it for many of the same reasons.

There are literally hundreds of races and varieties of corn with an
amazing range of characteristics. A corn plant can be as small as two
feet, or as tall as twenty. It can manture in two months or in eleven.
An ear can be the size of a man's thumb or two feet long. The kernels
can be yellow, white, blue, black, brown, and varying shades inbetween. And less spectacular, but most important, there are varieties
suited to a wide range of climates and soils.

The commonly grown modern varieties are distinctly divided between those used dry for cornmeal, hominy, and animal feed, and
sweet corn for eating fresh. Most corn intended for dry use is too
starchy and tough to be enjoyable fresh, while mature, dry sweet corn
is not as flavorful or practical as specialized dry varieties. However, if
sweet corn should pass its prime for eating fresh, it can be used as dry
corn. A few old varieties of corn, such as the blue or black corn from
the southwestern United States and Mexico are good both fresh and
dried.

Fresh corn is discussed in the CORN, SWEET section, which follows this section.

Dry or field corn varieties are grouped according to the kernels'
texture. When the starch is very hard it is called flint corn. Popcorn
is an extremely hard kind of flint corn. Dent corn kernels combine
both hard and soft starch, and the unequal drying causes a dent to
form in the top of each kernel. Another variety, sometimes called
flour corn, has very soft, mealy kernels that are easily ground or
chewed. It is commonly used by South American Indians. Some seed
catalogs carry the different dry corn varieties in small quantities
which is nice for the adventurous home gardener.

## CORN'S NUTRITIONAL VALUE

Corn has a rather poor reputation regarding its nutritional value.
But though it is not exceptionally high in nutrients, it is a valuable
carbohydrate food with some protein, vitamins, and minerals, and
should not be crossed off anyone's food list. The open-pollinated
varieties have higher protein levels than most hybrids. Since corn is
low in lysine, which is one of the essential amino acids in protein

---

**STORAGE**

**Canning** See CANNING
HOMINY, below.

**Drying** See HANDLING CORN
and DRYING HOMINY, below.

¾ CUP DRY CORN = ABOUT I CUP
CORNMEAL; I CUP CORN FOR
POPPING = ABOUT 5 CUPS POPPED

food, high-lysine corn has been developed. Another way to increase protein value is to eat corn with foods that are high in lysine, such as beans. For example, several tablespoons of soy flour added to cornmeal in recipes considerably increases the protein value. The American Indians combined corn with a great variety of vegetables, nuts, and seeds, often by drying and grinding the other food and mixing it with cornmeal. This no doubt enhanced the nutritional value of the corn, as well as producing many interesting flavors.

Yellow corn is preferable to white as it contains more Vitamin A. It is also worth noting that corn, like any other plant, contains more nutrients when grown on good soil and in good growing conditions.

## HANDLING CORN

***Harvesting***    Large plantings of dry corn for human consumption are harvested with the same machinery as dry feed corn for animals. Where good dry feed corn is available, some can simply be appropriated for household use, though it may need sorting to remove pieces of cob, or winnowing to blow off bits of chaff.

When growing a small stand of dry corn, pick the ears when they are fully mature, and dry them in an airy place safe from rodents. One way to dry them is to pull back the husks from each ear, then tie a bunch of ears together by the husks, and drape them over a wire in a protected, airy place. If a tin can lid is strung on each end of the wire mice will not be able to get at the corn.

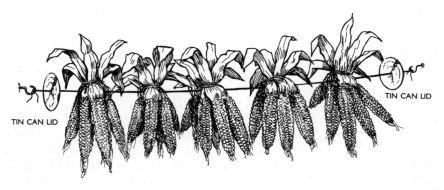

*Drying corn*

***Shelling Kernels***    Corn should be shelled only after it is completely dry. Either the whole cob can be stored and then shelled a few ears at a time, as needed, or the whole crop can be shelled at once. Of course, the shelled kernels take up less space than ears. They are stored like other grains. (Refer to STORING GRAINS, in the GRAINS section.)

To hand shell small amounts of corn, grasp the ear firmly with both hands and twist in opposite directions to dislodge the kernels.

Small hand held shellers can be purchased to make the job easier, or, for larger amounts of corn, there are hand cranked shellers that do about 10 bushels an hour.

***Cornmeal*** Any dry corn can be ground to make cornmeal, including field corn, popcorn, Indian corn, and dry sweet corn. (Refer to GRINDING GRAIN FOR MEAL AND FLOUR, in the GRAINS section.) Taste and texture will vary with the kind of corn used. Corn with softer starch makes a very floury meal. Dent corn makes a somewhat floury meal, while flint corn or popcorn make a grainy meal.

Home ground cornmeal is whole grain and therefore more nutritious than degerminated commercial cornmeal. Whole grain cornmeal works better in recipes than the degerminated kind. This is especially true for recipes that require cooking the cornmeal in water and then using it in other mixtures such as bread dough. When recipes call for water ground or stone ground cornmeal it is whole grain meal that is wanted, so any home ground meal will work no matter what type of mill is used. The difference for cooking seems to lie in the greater thickening power or more cohesive quality of the whole grain cornmeal.

To make a plain cornmeal mush, refer to the *Basic Cooked Cereal* recipe, in the CEREALS section.

***Corn Starch*** Corn starch is pure starch refined from corn, and cannot be made at home. Potato starch, however, can easily be made. It is essentially the same and can be substituted for corn starch in recipes. (Refer to MAKING POTATO STARCH, in the POTATOES section.)

Occasionally in recipes there is confusion between corn flour and corn starch. If small amounts are called for to thicken liquids it is corn starch that is wanted; if larger amounts to serve as a basic flour are required, use a finely ground or floury cornmeal.

***Parched (Browned) Corn*** Two quite different corn preparations are called parched corn. One is dry corn that has been browned in the oven or a heavy dry frying pan. The other is cooked sweet corn that has been dried. (Refer to the CORN, SWEET section.)

Both dry kernels and cornmeal can be parched. Spread the corn in a thin layer in a shallow pan, and roast in a low, 250–300°F oven until browned, but not black. Stir often. Whole kernels will take much longer to parch than meal. To parch corn on top of the stove, put a thin layer of kernels or meal in a heavy, dry frying pan over very low heat, stirring often, until it is browned. Whole kernels will take up to 2 hours; meal will take about half an hour. A wood fueled heating stove can often be used for this kind of parching.

Parched corn brings a pleasant flavor to bread and baked goods. Lightly parched, it makes a flavorful cooked cereal. It is also a common ingredient in coffee-like beverages. (Refer to ROAST BEVERAGES, in the BEVERAGES section.)

***Popcorn*** Popcorn is a very hard variety of flint corn. It pops when moisture trapped in the kernel expands and explodes the kernel as it is heated. Too dry popcorn will not pop properly. Instead it only partly splits with a muffled pop, or scorches without popping at all. When too moist, it makes an especially loud sound, yet the popped kernels are small and tough.

When drying popcorn, test pop some every so often. Then, when it pops perfectly, store it where it will not get any dryer. It can be shelled, and put in air tight containers in a cool place, or the ears can be kept at about 32°F, with a humidity of 85%.

If popcorn becomes too dry it can be moistened by putting it in a jar with a tablespoon of water for every 3 or 4 cups of corn. Close the jar tightly, and shake well twice a day for several days. If it still does not pop well, add a little more water and leave for another few days.

## HOMINY, OR HULLED CORN

The only practical use for dry corn, other than making cornmeal, is making it into hominy. Kernels of dry corn cooked in plain water will have an unpleasantly tough, skin-like hull that interferes with eating them. Hominy is prepared by cooking in a solution of hardwood ashes, lye, or lime to remove the hulls. This treatment also gives the corn the characteristic flavor and texture that many enjoy. The dough for tortillas and tamales is made by grinding hulled corn or hominy. Hominy grits are made by drying and grinding hominy.

Traditional hominy is made from white corn with big kernels. White flint, or the blue, or black varieties of corn are preferred for tortillia dough. However, yellow field corn can be treated to remove hulls, and then used for hominy or tortilla dough. It will have the same flavor.

Hominy or hulled corn loses vitamins during processing, but retains its protein and carbohydrate value. These have been enough to make it a basic life-sustaining food for large groups of people in the southern United States and Mexico. The many hominy dishes, especially tortillas, are popular everywhere.

## MAKING HOMINY

The basic proportions for making hominy are 1 quart dry corn to 1 gallon of any of the following:

*Hardwood Ashes*  Put about 1½ quarts clean hardwood ashes in a big enameled or stainless steel pot. *Do not use aluminum.* Add 5 quarts of water. Boil 15 minutes, then let sit away from the fire until the ashes settle. Pour off the clear water to use—about a gallon. It will feel slippery to the fingers because it is a lye solution.

*Lye*  Buy plain lye—the kind used for making soap, and *make sure* it does not contain aluminum, nitrates, or stabilizers. When using, follow the safety precautions listed on the label. Mix 2 tablespoons of lye into a gallon of cold water, in an enameled or stainless steel pot. This is the solution most often recommended for making hominy.

*Slaked (Hydrated) Lime* (Do not use quicklime, calcium oxide, which is dangerous to handle, or agricultural lime, which does not work.) Mexican grocery stores sell slaked lime for making tortillas, and some other grocery stores sell hydrated lime as a pickling aid. Or buy calcium carbonate from a drug store, or pure calcium hydroxide (builder's lime) from a building supply store. Slaked lime can also be made at home by heating small pieces of limestone till red hot, dropping them in water and stirring till dissolved. Enough limestone must be used to make the water milky white. (The use of snail shells described below is similar.) Use about 4 tablespoons slaked lime mixed in 1 gallon of water.

*Cooking the Corn* Heat the corn in the solution and boil until swelled and the skins ready to slip. To test if it is done, remove and rinse a few kernels, rubbing them to see if the hulls loosen. To prevent changes in flavor or texture, it is best not to leave the hominy in the solution any longer than necessary. The time will vary according to the type of corn and the solution used, but it is usually between 1 and 2 hours. When using lye, the corn can be cooked 30 minutes, then soaked 20 minutes more, or until it is ready.

When the hulls are loosened, drain and rinse the corn in hot water several times. Then rub the kernels between the hands until the hulls come loose. The dark specks at the base of the kernel are usually also rubbed loose. When the hominy is rinsed the hulls will float off. They can plug a sink drain so its best to catch them in a strainer. The hominy must be well rinsed to remove all taste of the hulling solution. Soaking for several hours in 3 or 4 changes of water is sometimes recommended.

Cook the rinsed hominy in fresh water until it is tender and ready to eat. Time will vary for different kinds of corn. Some will just need heating to a boil, and some may need to cook for an hour.

*Canning Hominy* Pressure can only! Pack hot cooked hominy in jars and add boiling hot water, leaving ½ inch headroom. Optional, add ¼ teaspoon salt to pints, ½ teaspoon to quarts. Pressure process at 240°F, 11 pounds pressure. Pints: 60 minutes; quarts: 70 minutes. (Refer to CANNING section.)

*Drying Hominy* Spread cooked hominy on trays or screens. Dry until brittle in a food dryer or very low oven. Soak to reconstitute before cooking. Use like regular hominy.

*Making Grits* Grind dried hominy coarsely to make grits. (Refer to GRINDING GRAIN in the GRAINS section.) Use as a cereal. Grits are good served with butter, like mashed potatoes.

Hominy grits are usually made from white corn, but yellow corn tastes just as good. Grits tasting a lot like hominy can be made by coarsely grinding very hard flint corn or popcorn, or by coarsely grinding barley. Hard corn or barley grits are easier to prepare and more nutritious than hominy grits, since they do not need treating to remove hulls. They can be substituted for hominy grits in recipes.

## TORTILLAS

Tortillas have been Mexico's basic bread since ancient Aztec times, and they are still made in the same ways today. Marian Hengerford, who stayed with an Indian family in Chiapas, Mexico for a while, describes how they made tortillas in a letter to *Countryside* magazine, April, 1976.

"First of all they started with dried-on-the-stalk field corn. The corn was stored in the husk until the day before use, when it was husked and shelled. The corn kernels were put in an earthenware pot over a fire with water barely covering the kernels. The lime was obtained by gathering snails in the rivers and creeks and burning the shells to a powder. This concentrated lime was added, about a handful to a pot of kernels, and boiled until the corn was kind of soft. It did seem similar to making hominy. The Indians said the snail shells made the kernels pop open easier.

The softish kernels were rinsed in woven baskets in running water until the water ran clear. A slight draining occurred as the kernels were carried back to the kitchen in the basket. Only then was the grinding done. The kernels were forced through a grinder once and then the resulting mash was ground again. This gives the basic tortilla dough. The liquid came only from the water that stuck on the kernels after washing. If it was too dry to pat into shape a little water might be added, but not often and not in large quantities."

***Tortilla Dough*** Make hominy ("nixtamal" in Mexico) in any of the ways described above. Grind it twice in a meat grinder to make a workable dough ("masa"). If it is too dry to hold together, work in a little water, but do not let it become sticky. In Mexico, balls of dough are patted out by hand to make thin, round tortillas. Newcomers to the art of tortilla making will find it much easier to flatten the dough between damp cloths. Put an egg sized ball of dough on a damp cloth. Cover with another damp cloth and press with a small board to make a tortilla 4 to 5 inches across and ⅛ inch thick. It takes practice to make perfect tortillas, but they taste good even if oddly shaped. (A tortilla press can also be bought to shape the tortillas more quickly.)

Cook the tortillas on a hot dry griddle or frying pan, for about 2 minutes on each side. They should remain flexible. To keep them warm and a little moist, wrap them in a damp towel, adding tortillas to the stack in the towel as they are cooked.

Tortillas will keep about a week in the refrigerator. Before refrigerating, put waxed paper between each one, wrap a damp cloth around them all, and put them in a plastic bag. Freeze them for long storage. For the freezer put waxed paper or freezer wrap between them and seal them in plastic bags. Tortilla dough is excellent for making the tamales or tamale pie recipe below.

***Masa*** In some areas, stores sell masa harina, a special flour for making tortilla dough. A similar flour can be made at home by grinding dried hominy as finely as possible. (Regular dried corn does not work.) To use this flour, work in warm water till the right consistency is reached; 2 cups masa harina and 1⅓ cups warm water are the usual proportions.

***Tortilla Chips*** Tortilla dough can also be made into flavorful crackers. Work seasonings to taste into the dough. Chilli powder, salt, and a bit of cayenne make a good flavor, but any seasonings, from onion juice to curry powder can be used. Flatten the dough as for tortillas and cut it into squares or triangles. Bake the chips on an oiled cookie sheet, or fry them in a lightly oiled pan until they are crisp.

## DRY CORN RECIPES

All the recipes in this section originated with American Indians or Mexican Indians—the first experts in corn cookery.

### Two Corn Bread (Makes 6–8 servings.)

*1 cup cornmeal*
*½ teaspoon baking soda*
*1 cup cooked sweet corn*
*3 eggs*
*¾ cup milk, buttermilk, or yogurt*
*⅓ cup melted lard or butter, or vegetable oil*

*pepper to taste (A minced jalapeño pepper is good for those who like it hot.)*
*½ cup sharp cheese, grated*
*2 tablespoons bacon fat, butter, or lard*

Mix the cornmeal and soda. (Press the soda through a sieve if it is lumpy.) Add the sweet corn, eggs, milk, lard or butter, pepper, and half of the cheese. Beat together to make a smooth batter.

Meanwhile warm a 1½ quart casserole or heavy 9 inch frying pan, and melt the 2 tablespoons of fat or butter in it. Do not let it get hot enough to burn the fat or butter. Pour in the batter and sprinkle with the rest of the cheese. Bake 40 minutes in a hot, 400°F oven. Cut in wedges to serve.

### North Woods Doughboys (Makes about 6 side servings.)

This particular name comes from an 1875 cookbook, but the recipe represents a very old and basic way to cook cornmeal. The same sort of mixture was called "hoecake" when baked on a hoe over an open fire, and "ashcake" when it was buried to cook in hot ashes at the edge of the fireplace. The ashes were rinsed off just before the cake was eaten. One old recipe suggests putting the ashcake between two cabbage leaves while baking to keep it clean. Other early versions were called "Johnnycake," "corn pone," or just "pone," from "apone," an Indian name for them.

*1 cup cornmeal*
*2 tablespoons soy, or peanut flour,*
　*optional* (Not part of early
　recipes.)
*¼ teaspoon salt, optional*

*1 tablespoon lard, or other fat,*
　*optional*
*2 – 2½ cups boiling water*
*fat or oil, for frying*

Mix the cornmeal, soy or peanut flour, salt, and lard in a heat proof bowl. Pour in boiling water, a little at a time, stirring constantly. Keep adding water until a soft dough is formed. As the water is added the cornmeal thickens and requires more water.

Heat fat or oil in a frying pan, then put in spoonfuls of the dough, flattening them to about ½ inch thick with the spoon. Fry until nicely browned on both sides. (The dough can also be fried as one large, flat cake.) These doughboys are very good fried in the fat of the meat with which they are served. (At camps in the "North Woods," the meat was fried first, then the doughboys, using the same pan.)

***Fruit Doughboys***　Let the cornmeal and water mixture cool. If the dough become stiff mix in a little milk, then mix in about ½ cup blueberries, elderberries, or chopped raw apple. An egg can also be added. Fry as above or shape into flat cakes and bake on an oiled cookie sheet, in a moderate oven.

## DRY CORN IDEAS

(For detailed directions for making the cornmeal mush required in most of these ideas, refer to *Basic Cooked Cereal* in the CEREALS, BREAKFAST section.)

**Cornmeal to Replace Potatoes**
Make cornmeal mush to serve in a mound with a dab of butter in the center instead of mashed potatoes. This goes well with eggs for breakfast, or with meat and vegetables for dinner. Cornmeal mush with yogurt, sour cream, or cheese, is a common dish in Rumania, called mamaliga. Hominy grits are good eaten in the same ways.

**Polenta**　Cooked yellow cornmeal mush is called polenta in Italy, and eaten with tomato sauce and grated cheese instead of pasta. The polenta can be cooked plain, or seasoned with butter and grated cheese. For the latter, stir 2 to 3 tablespoons butter and ½ to 1 cup grated Parmesan type cheese into several cups of hot mash that have almost finished cooking.

**Fried Cornmeal Slices**　Hot cornmeal mush can be poured in a dish cooled, sliced, and fried. It is especially good when cooked with other ingredients to flavor it. The polenta mixture described above is very good fried. To make another good mixture, sauté a little minced garlic, onion, and green pepper, with about ¼ pound ground meat in the cookpot. Add about 2 cups of water or soup stock, ½ cup cornmeal, and any desired seasonings. Cook as for ordinary cornmeal mush.

The cooked cornmeal slices can be dusted with flour before frying if they are sticky. A special, traditional version of fried cornmeal is the *Scrapple* recipe, in the HEADS section.

## *Pozole (Hog and Hominy)*　　　(Makes 6 – 8 dinner servings.)

*2 onions, chopped*
*1 tablespoon oil, or fat*
*2 pounds pork, cubed*
*4 – 6 tablespoons chili powder, or 1*
　*cup red chili pulp*

*1 bay leaf*
*½ teaspoon oregano*
*½ teaspoon salt, optional*
*2 cups hominy*

Fry the onions until limp in the oil or fat. Add the pork and fry, stirring, until the meat changes color. Add the chili, bay leaf, oregano, salt, if desired, and hominy. Add enough hot water to cover the ingredients. Simmer covered until the pork is tender, usually about an hour.

This dish falls between a soup and a stew. Serve it in soup bowls, with dishes of raw radishes, lettuce, chopped onion, hot pepper, and wedges of lemon or lime, so each person can add their own extras.

***Pig's Feet Pozole***　Cut 2 or 3 pig's feet into pieces, and precook with several cloves of garlic in water to cover, for about an hour. Fry onions and add with other ingredients as above. The cubed pork may be omitted or reduced to about 1 pound. The pig's feet make this a richer, more interesting dish.

## *Family Style Tacos*

Depending on the ingredients chosen and the quantities prepared, these tacos can be a lively and satisfying buffet for family and friends, a delicious way to use leftovers, or a light, quick lunch for one.

TORTILLAS (See above.)
cooked beans (Usually red or kidney beans.)
Some or all of the following:
  lettuce, shredded
  fresh tomato, chopped
  onion, chopped
  any kind of ground meat, cooked and crumbled
  cooked leftover pork or chicken, shredded
cheese, shredded (Mild cheddar or American cheese are excellent.)
pickled or fresh jalapeno, or other hot pepper, minced or shredded
Green Tomato Hot Sauce (Recipe in TOMATOES, GREEN section.)
Guacamole (Recipe in FRUITS section.)
FRESH TOMATO SAUCE (In IDEAS in the TOMATOES section.)

Cook the tortillas briefly on each side, on a hot dry, or lightly oiled griddle or frying pan. As they are cooked, wrap them in a damp cloth and keep warm. Mash the beans with a fork, then cook them in an oiled frying pan. Stir often, until they are hot and as dry as stiff mashed potatoes.

Serve the taco ingredients in separate dishes. Everyone then makes their own tacos by folding a tortilla in half, putting in a spoon of beans, and adding other ingredients to taste.

A simple but delicious taco can be made with beans, lettuce, cheese, and hot sauce.

## Tamales                                          (Makes about 20.)

4—5 cups tortilla dough (See instructions above.)
corn husks (Refer to CORN, SWEET section.)
Filling:
  1 onion, minced
  1 clove garlic, minced
  1 tablespoon lard, or oil
2 cups cooked meat, coarsely chopped or shredded (Traditionally pork or chicken, but beef and other meats also taste good.)
½ tablespoon chilli powder
1 very small sprig coriander leaves, minced or ⅛ teaspoon seeds, powdered
hot pepper to taste
1 cup tomatoes, mashed, fresh, or canned sauce

Brown the onions and garlic in the fat. Add the meat, chili powder, coriander, pepper, and tomatoes. Simmer 10 minutes, uncovered.

To shape the tamales lay out large husk leaves, or overlap 2 or 3 smaller leaves. The small leaves can be stuck together with a bit of dough. Flatten a large spoonful of dough to make a rectangular shape on one side of the husk. Put a small spoon of filling on the dough. Roll or fold over the dough side of the husk to enclose the filling and fold the rest of the husk around the tamale. Fold in the ends to make

---

### DRY CORN IDEAS, cont.

**Cornmeal Layers for Casseroles** Pour hot cornmeal mush in an oiled, round casserole. When cool and firm, turn it out, and slice across it to make 2 or 3 round layers. Put the bottom layer back in the casserole, add sauce or filling layered with the cornmeal. (For filling ideas, refer to the CASSEROLES section.)

**Corn with Nuts or Seeds** The American Indians often mixed corn with either chopped or ground nuts and seeds. Cornmeal mush is quite good cooked with chopped nuts or sunflower seeds. Two such recipes are the CHESTNUTS AND CORN, and Corn Mohawk, listed below in OTHER RECIPES.

**Hominy and Beans Stew** Cook hominy and any kind of dry beans separately. Mix them together with some of their cooking water, chopped onion, green pepper, parsley, or other vegetable and herb seasonings. Cook about 30 minutes to blend flavors. This is stew if it is thick and soup if extra water or soup stock is added.

**Hasty Pudding** As the name suggests this is a quick and easy old fashioned dessert. It is simply hot cornmeal mush with a dab of butter, some molasses, maple syrup, or honey, some milk or cream, and a sprinkle of cinnamon and nutmeg.

a neat package. Set the tamales folded side down in a steamer, and steam about 1 hour. Each person unwraps the tamales before eating them. The husks impart flavor but remain too tough to chew.

Homemade tamales are far better than most commercial canned versions.

***Tamale Pie***   Make a double recipe of the tamale filling, adding 1½ cups pitted ripe olives and ½ cup raisins. The meat can be cut in cubes rather than chopped. (Another good filling is the *Texas Chili Beans* recipe, in the BEANS, DRY section.) For the shell use the tortilla dough described above or make thick cornmeal mush, using 2 cups cornmeal, ½ tablespoon chili powder and 6 cups water.

Use about a 3 quart oiled baking dish or Dutch oven, or make 2 smaller pies and freeze one. Line with the cornmeal mush or tortilla dough, saving a small portion for the top. Pour in the filling. Flatten the remaining mush or masa and lay it on top. It does not have to cover perfectly. Bake at 325°F for 1½ hours. If desired, grated or sliced mild cheese can be spread on top about 15 minutes before the pie is done.

### *Old Fashioned Indian Pudding*   (Makes about 6 dessert servings.)

| | |
| --- | --- |
| 4 cups milk | ½ teaspoon powdered ginger |
| ¾ cup cornmeal | ½ teaspoon powdered nutmeg |
| ¾ cup dark molasses | 1 tablespoon butter |

Warm 2 cups of the milk and stir the cornmeal into it. Cook, stirring, till it thickens, 5 to 10 minutes. Take off the stove and add the molasses, ginger, nutmeg, and butter. Stir in 2 cups of cold milk and bake in a low, 300°F, oven till it thickens or sets, about 2 hours.

Simply delicious served warm with cold milk!

# CORN, SWEET

A HUNDRED YEARS AGO WHEN CORN WAS EATEN FRESH IT WAS CALLED green corn, meaning immature corn. Since then a series of newer, sweeter varieties have been developed for eating fresh which quite reasonably are called sweet corn. In fact, the latest varieties are so sweet that some people find them cloying to the taste.

Whatever variety is preferred, sweet corn is a favorite food that everyone can enjoy with one qualification. Although considered a vegetable, it should not replace green vegetables, as it does not contain the same important vitamins and minerals. It is actually a grain and should be considered a carbohydrate in meal planning. So eat it instead of potatoes or bread, and serve green vegetables or salad with it. (Refer to CORN'S NUTRITIONAL VALUE, in the CORN, DRY section.)

## HANDLING SWEET CORN

The prime time for picking sweet corn is rather short lived. If picked too early the kernels are small and lacking in flavor; if picked too late the corn is doughy, or starchy and somewhat tough. Some people can judge ripeness by feeling the ears of corn. When they feel full and give a little when pressed they are ready. Other indications are: silk that is turning brown and dry; tips that are rounded and full; and kernels that yield "milk" when dented with a fingernail. Sweet corn will stay at its best for only a week or two, so eat, can, dry, or freeze it without delay. If it is only a little past its prime it can be used for making the *Corn Relish* or BAKED CORN OFF-THE-COB recipes, below. It can also be left to mature and dry and be used as dry corn.

Standard varieties of sweet corn become less sweet as soon as they are picked, and their sugar begins changing to starch. If the corn cannot be rushed to the kitchen and cooked immediately, it should be refrigerated, or kept in a cold place to slow down this process. It can be husked before refrigeration. New extra sweet varieties hold their sweetness better than older varieties, and their immediate processing is not so important.

Whether sweet corn is canned, dried, or frozen, is largely a matter of convenience, since quality is excellent with all three. Though today canned and frozen corn are most common, in the past huge quantities of sweet corn (sometimes called parched corn) were dried for winter use. When prime quality sweet corn is cooked immediately, and then dried, it tastes just as good as canned or frozen corn. (See RECIPES below.)

***Blanching or Boiling Corn-on-the-Cob*** Ears of corn can be steamed, but unless the steamer holds the heat very well, boiling cooks the corn faster. For best results, bring a large pot of water to a rapid boil. Add only enough ears of corn so they will not be crowded in the pot, and the water quickly returns to a boil. When one batch is done, take it out with tongs, and repeat. The corn will cook in 3 to 10 minutes, depending on the size of the ears.

***Cutting Whole Kernel or Cream Style Corn*** The two ways to cut corn from the cob are whole kernel and cream style. Either style can be frozen, or canned, but for drying corn is cut whole kernel. For canning and some recipes corn is cut raw; for freezing and drying it is precooked.

To cut whole kernels, hold the ear against a cutting board, stalk end down, and slice off the kernels top to bottom with a sharp knife. Cut close to the cob but not into it. For cream style corn slice off only the tips or top halves of the kernels. Next, scrape the cobs with the

### STORAGE

**Canning** Cut from cob. (See below.)

**Whole Kernel Hot Pack** Use 2 cups water per 4 cups kernels. Heat to boil, stirring often. Drain, pack in jars, add boiling cooking water, 1 in. headroom. Process, 240°F, 11 pounds pressure. Pints: 55 min. Quarts: 1 hr. 25 min.

**Whole Kernel Raw Pack** Fill jars loosely, 1 in. headroom. Add boiling water, ½ in headroom. Process as for HOT PACK above.

**Cream Style Hot Pack** (Pints only, too dense for quarts.) Add 2 cups boiling water per 4 cups cream style corn. Heat to boil, stirring to prevent scorching. Fill pints, 1 in. headroom. Process 240°F, 11 pounds pressure, 1 hr. 25 min.

**Cream Style Raw Pack** Fill pints only, 1½ in headroom. Add boiling water, ½ in. headroom. Process 240°F, 11 pounds pressure, 1 hr. 35 min. Refer to CANNING section. Also *Corn Relishes,* below.

**Drying** (Excellent quality!) Cook on cob, cut whole kernels (see below). Spread, dry till brittle. To use, soak several hours or overnight and cook approx. 30 min. Refer to DRYING FOODS section.

**Freezing** *Whole Kernel or Cream Style* Blanch ears 4 min. in boiling water, then cut (see below). *On-the-Cob* (Slim cobs best.) Blanch in boiling water 6—10 min. according to size. Thaw completely before cooking. Refer to FREEZING section.

I BUSHEL WITH HUSKS = 6—10 QUARTS PREPARED; 3—5 POUNDS WITH HUSKS = 6—12 EARS = I QUART PREPARED

*Device for holding corn cob*

back of the knife to force out the milky juice and the hearts of the kernels. Then combine the cut tips and the scrapings. Cream style corn can also be made by grating the corn off the cob with a hand grater.

The special hand held tools that adjust for cutting whole kernel or cream style corn probably save more time when cutting cream style than whole kernel. A knife is quite as efficient for cutting whole kernel corn.

A device for holding the corn can be made by cutting a clean wooden board to fit in a cake pan. Drive a 3 or 4 inch nail completely through the board, then put it in the pan with the nail sticking up. Impale one end of the ear of corn on the nail, hold the other end steady with one hand, and cut off the kernels. The pan catches the cut kernels.

**Using Corn Husks**   Husks from sweet corn or fresh field corn are traditional food wrappings, and too tough to be edible. Though best known as wrappings for tamales, they can also be wrapped around other mixtures. (Refer to CHESTNUTS AND CORN, in the CHESTNUTS section, *Tamales,* in the CORN, DRY section, and *Roast Corn-in-the-Husk* below.)

To remove the husks as whole leaves, cut off the ears of corn at their base just where the kernels begin. The husks can then be unwrapped leaf by leaf. They are sometimes blanched in boiling water before use, or tough or dry husks can be soaked in water to make them pliable.

If fresh husks and silk are not wanted, many animals like eating them. An old time use for dry husks was as a stuffing for pillows and mattresses.

**Using Leftover Corn Cobs**   A lot of flavor is left in the cobs after the corn is removed. Cook them in water to cover for half an hour, then drain off the liquid. Sweet corn cob cooking water is good as a soup base or used instead of water in any corn recipe. Years ago, cooking water from the red cobs of dry field corn was used with pectin and sugar to make corn cob jelly. Dry corn cobs are also used for smoking meat, as kindling for starting fires, and even for making pipes. Fresh corn cobs are used to feed livestock.

## SWEET CORN RECIPES

### Roast Corn-in-the-Husk

Prepare fresh corn ears by pulling off the silk and any loose outer leaves. Bury them in hot ashes or roast them over coals that are not too hot. (To minimize scorching of the kernels over a hot fire, moisten the husks with water.) Roast 20 to 30 minutes depending on the size of the ears and the heat of the ashes or coals. The husks will blacken, but the corn inside will be deliciously cooked. Corn-in-the-husks can also be roasted in a 300°F oven for 30 minutes, and, if husks are thin, aluminum foil wrapping can be added.

For a change from plain butter, pepper, and salt, try eating the corn with the *Herb Butter,* from the BUTTER section. A garlic flavor is good.

**Boiled Corn-in-the-Husk**   Strip off the silk and the outer leaves, leaving a thin layer of inner leaves around each ear. Cook 3 to 10 minutes in boiling water. The husks will add a delicately sweet flavor.

---

### Green Corn Soup                   (Makes about 6 bowls.)

*4 – 6 ears sweet corn, or fresh imma-*
    *ture field corn, or 2 cups frozen or*
    *canned cream style corn*
*water*
*2 cups milk, or light cream*
*1 tablespoon flour*
*1 tablespoon butter, softened*

*dash of pepper*
*1 teaspoon honey or sugar* (Omit
    if corn is very sweet.)
*1 small onion*
*salt, optional*
*popped corn, or unflavored*
    *whipped cream, for garnish,*
    *optional*

If using fresh corn, prepare kernels, cream style, and refrigerate. Cover the cobs with water and boil them for 30 minutes. Drain and save the liquid—about 2 cups. Combine it with the corn from the refrigerator and cook 5 minutes. If using frozen or canned corn, heat it with 1 cup water.

Add the milk or cream to the corn. Mix the flour and butter to a paste, then add to the soup with the pepper, sugar, onion, and salt, if desired. Simmer 10 minutes, remove the onion, and serve. Garnish with popped corn or whipped cream, if desired.

---

### Corn Oysters                 (Makes about 6 side servings.)

*2 cups cream style corn, fresh,*
    *frozen, or canned*
*2 eggs separated*

*pepper, salt, optional*
*¼ cup flour*

Mix the corn with the egg yolks, pepper, and salt. Stir with a fork to blend in the yolks completely, then mix in the flour. Beat the egg whites till stiff and fold them into the batter. Heat a well oiled griddle or frying pan and drop oyster sized tablespoons of batter on it. Brown on both sides and serve hot. These are good both for breakfast with syrup, or for supper with meat and vegetables.

**Dried Corn Fritters**   Soak 1 cup dried sweet corn in 1¼ cups milk till softened—overnight in the refrigerator for breakfast or during the day for supper. Add the other ingredients and cook as for *Corn Oysters,* above, increasing the flour to about 1 cup for a medium thick batter.

---

### SWEET CORN IDEAS

**Corn Omelets**   Cooked sweet corn is delicious in any style omelet. For a fluffy omelet add the corn to well beaten egg yolks and seasonings. Fold in stiffly beaten whites. Cook in a buttered frying pan until the bottom has browned. Fold the omelet and turn out on a heated plate. For a western style omelet, sauté the corn in butter, if desired with sweet peppers and tomato. Then add the lightly beaten eggs. Turn when almost set, or finish like scrambled eggs. Garnish with minced chives or scallions.

**Baked Corn-off-the-Cob**
Sweet corn that has just passed its prime is best for this. Cut the corn from the cob and scrape off the rest. Mix with melted butter, and pepper. Put in a deep layer in a buttered baking dish. Bake in a moderate, 350°F oven until set and crusty brown on top. With salad, this makes a nice lunch, or serve as a side dish with dinner.

**Super Sweet Corn in Desserts**
New super sweet corn varieties can be used to sweeten desserts. Try adding ½ cup corn to recipes for cookies, puddings, custard, or fruit bread. Whole kernel corn will impart a chewy texture while cream style corn blends in more completely. For a smooth mixture the corn can be puréed.

### Corn Mohawk, from H. R. Mills          (Makes 6–8 side servings.)

(The Mohawk Indians made a dish like this with Jack-in-the-Pulpit root instead of onions, making it very hot tasting.)

2 cups dried sweet corn
¼ cup dried sweet peppers (Red and green mixed are nice.)
1 medium onion, chopped
¼ cup black walnuts, ground fine (Other kinds of nuts may be substituted.)
milk
butter, pepper, and salt, to taste

Soak the corn in water to cover for several hours. Add the peppers, onion, and black walnuts. Do not drain the corn, but add enough milk to cover the additional ingredients. Simmer slowly for about an hour, or until tender. Season with butter, pepper, and salt.

**Fresh Corn Mohawk or Succotash**   Instead of dried ingredients use 3–4 cups fresh or frozen whole kernel corn and ½ cup fresh or frozen sweet peppers. Nuts are optional. Cook 15 to 20 minutes. The pepper and onion can first be sautéed in butter. If this is done omit butter as seasoning.

**Corn and Okra**   Add ½ cup dried, sliced okra to the basic *Corn Mohawk* recipe along with the sweet peppers, or add 1 cup fresh or frozen sliced okra to FRESH CORN MOHAWK. Omit milk and add extra water as needed. Nuts are optional. A similar mixture with green shelled beans and tomato is used for the *Succotash* recipes in the BEANS, FRESH and the SOYBEANS sections.

Relishes are the best ways to keep sweet corn that is past its prime for the usual storage methods. The toughened kernels add texture, and the loss of sweetness will not be noticed. The following recipes can be enjoyed side by side, as they are quite different. In addition, relishes are perhaps the most nutritious of the pickles. (Refer to the PICKLING section.)

### OTHER RECIPES WITH SWEET CORN

### Canned Corn Relish, Shaker Style          (Makes 5–6 pints.)

2 cups corn, cut raw from the cob
2 cups onions, chopped small
2 cups ripe tomatoes, chopped small
2 cups cucumbers, chopped small
2 cups cabbage, chopped small
¾ cup honey or 1 cup sugar
1 ½ teaspoons celery seed
1 teaspoon turmeric
1 teaspoon salt, optional
2 cups vinegar

Combine the corn, onions, tomatoes, cucumbers, and cabbage in a large pot. Mix the honey or sugar, celery seed, tumeric, and salt, if desired, with the vinegar, and add to the vegetables. Heat to a boil and simmer, uncovered, about 20 minutes, stirring often. Pour boiling hot into hot canning jars, adjust lids and process 10 minutes in a boiling water bath. (Refer to the CANNING section.)

*Canned Corn Relish, Yankee Style*          (Makes about 5 pints.)

| | |
|---|---|
| 5 cups cooked corn, cut from cob | 1 tablespoon mustard seed |
| ½ cup green pepper, chopped small | 2 teaspoons celery seed |
| ½ cup sweet red pepper, chopped small | ½ teaspoon tumeric |
| | ½ cup honey or ¾ cup sugar |
| 1 cup onion, chopped small | 2 cups vinegar |
| ½ cup celery, chopped small | 1 teaspoon salt, optional |

Mix all ingredients and simmer slowly for 30 minutes, stirring often. Pack boiling hot in hot canning jars, adjust lids and process 10 minutes in a boiling water bath. (Refer to the CANNING section.)

This relish was often eaten as a sandwich spread in the past and is quite good that way.

# CRACKERS

HOMEMADE CRACKERS CAN BE ANY SIZE, SHAPE, AND FLAVOR THAT suits the cook. Making them is recreation for the kitchen adventurer. Young cooks who want a change from making after-school cookies might try their hand at crackers. They are just as easy to make as cookies, and most people like them just as well.

Crackers made from whole grains, with a minimum of salt and fat are very nutritious, unlike many commercial varieties. Made in this way, they tend to be more dense and filling than commercial crackers, as well as being more flavorful.

## MAKING AND STORING CRACKERS

Cracker dough is rolled out like cookie or pie crust doughs and should be like them in texture—soft enough to be worked and stiff enough not to be sticky. Unleavened crackers are best when rolled very thin, paper thin if possible. Cracker dough leavened with baking soda, baking powder, or yeast can be a little thicker, about ⅛ inch thick.

Crackers made with little or no shortening tend to puff up like little inflated balls when baked. To prevent this, prick each cracker 4 or 5 times with a fork before baking. Most varieties bake quickly in a very hot, 400–425°F oven. Take them out of the oven when they are just barely beginning to brown. If too brown a burnt flavor will penetrate them. If they are not crisp after they have cooled, they can be dried in a 200–250°F oven, or in a food dryer. (Or they can be returned to the oven after it has been turned off and is cooling.) They must dry completely if they are to be stored for very long.

Store crackers in airtight containers so that they will not absorb moisture and become soggy. If jar or can lids do not seal completely, a layer of waxed paper can be laid over the mouth of the container and pressed or screwed down tightly with the lid.

Some crackers will keep for many months, but those made with butter can be kept only about a month because the butter eventually gives a rancid taste.

Crackers that have lost crispness can be restored by drying them for a few minutes in a very low oven or food dryer.

## CRACKER RECIPES

### Water Wafers                    (Makes about 12 dozen small crackers.)

*2 cups whole grain flour* (May be whole wheat, rye, cornmeal, or a mixture of these and other flours.)
*1 cup soy flour, optional, for protein content*

*1−2 teaspoons herb seeds, optional* (Such as celery, poppy, caraway.)
*¼ teaspoon salt, optional*
*1−2 tablespoons grated onion or onion juice, optional*
*1 cup (about) boiling water*

Mix the flour, soy flour, herb seeds, salt, if desired, and onion. Add boiling water little by little, stirring constantly until a stiff dough is formed. Let cool a few minutes and roll out as thinly as possible on a floured board. Roll less than ⅛ inch thick. (When very thin these have something of the character of potato chips.) Cut in any shape desired. For circles use a thin lipped glass or a cookie cutter. Cut squares, rectangles, or triangles with a table knife. Place crackers close together (they can touch) on oiled cookie sheets. Prick with a fork to prevent curling or swelling up like inflated balls. However, these will taste just as good, and may even be preferred by some.

Bake in a hot, 400°F oven until lightly browned, about 10 minutes. Cool on a rack. If, after taking them from the oven, they are still somewhat moist, dry them in a very low oven or food dryer till they are crisp. Or they can be returned to the oven while it cools.

These wafers will keep for months in an airtight container.

### Cooked Cereal Crackers
Mix flour and any desired seasonings into leftover cooked cereal to make a workable dough. It is easiest to knead in the flour by hand. Roll out and bake as above. The cereals will add interesting textures and flavors to crackers.

### Cream Crisps                    (Makes about 12 dozen small crackers.)

*2 cups whole grain flour* (Or a combination from the BREAD, QUICK section.)
*¼ teaspoon salt, optional*

*1 cup (about) cream* (Light or heavy cream.)
*1 egg yolk or whole egg, and sesame or other seeds for tops, optional*

## CRACKER IDEAS

**Bread Dough Crackers** Yeast bread dough can be rolled thin, cut in small shapes, and baked for crackers. The thinner the dough is rolled the better. Before baking, these crackers can be sprinkled very lightly with coarse salt, or brushed with egg and sprinkled with seeds.

For herb crackers, use the dough for the *Herb Bread* recipe, in the BREAD, YEAST section, or work dried herbs or minced, fresh herbs into any bread dough.

**Biscuit Dough Crackers** To make crackers from biscuit dough, roll the dough thin, cut in small shapes, and bake on ungreased cookie sheets in a hot, 400°F oven until lightly browned. The dough for the *Cream Biscuits* recipe, in the CREAM section can be used.

**Toast Crackers** Cut thin slices of bread and dry them out in a very low, 200−250°F oven without browning them very much. This may take 30 minutes to an hour. When crisp they resemble zwieback or melba toast. They are very good with soup, and small pieces are good in tossed salads. (Also refer to the *Tomato Bread Salad* recipe in the TOMATOES section.)

Combine the flour and salt, if desired, and work in enough cream to make a medium stiff dough. Knead a few times and roll out as thinly as possible on a floured board. Cut into small squares, circles, or triangles, and place close together on an ungreased cookie sheet. Prick with a fork to prevent curling. If desired, brush tops with egg yolk or lightly beaten whole egg and sprinkle with sesame or other seeds. Bake in a hot, 400°F oven for about 10 minutes until lightly browned. Cool on a rack. These are among the crispest, lightest homemade crackers.

*Sour Cream Crackers*   Mix ¼ teaspoon baking soda with the flour and use sour cream instead of sweet cream, for a more piquant flavor.

---

### Sour Cream Graham Crackers

(Makes 2– 3 dozen 2– 2½ inch squares.)

| | |
|---|---|
| 2 cups whole wheat flour (Refer to GRAHAM FLOUR at the beginning of the WHEAT section.) | ¼ teaspoon baking soda |
| | ¼ cup honey, or ¼ cup molasses, and 1 tablespoon sugar |
| 1 cup wheat germ, or an additional ¾ cup flour | 1 cup (about) sour cream |

Mix the flour, wheat germ, baking soda, and salt. If the soda is lumpy, press or sift it out. Work in the honey and sour cream adding enough sour cream to make a medium stiff dough. Roll out to about ⅛ inch thick. Cut into squares and place them close together on a very lightly oiled baking sheet. Bake in a hot, 400°F oven for about 10 minutes, till just beginning to brown. Cool on a rack. The best graham crackers ever!

---

# CRANBERRIES

EVERYONE IS FAMILIAR WITH CRANBERRY SAUCE FOR THE HOLIDAY turkey, and with the store bought bottles of clear red juice that list water and sugar ahead of cranberries in the contents. Not many are familiar with cranberry cultivation, as their growing requirements make them impractical for the family garden. Only those who live near cranberry bogs or places where they grow wild can harvest them. Northeastern American Indians and early settlers gathered them in huge quantities. As they keep better than most fruits they were carried on ships to prevent scurvy, and exported to Europe packed in barrels of water.

A few wild berries are enough like cranberries to be used in the same ways. Cranberry bush (or high bush cranberry) is well known

---

**CRACKER IDEAS,** *cont.*

**Pie Crust Crackers**   When making pie crust, roll out extra dough and cut in small shapes. Bake on an ungreased cookie sheet in the same oven as the pie, for 10 to 15 minutes.

**Cracker Crumbs**   Use cracker crumbs like fine dry bread crumbs, for such things as breading meat, topping casseroles. (Refer to USING DRIED BREAD, in the BREAD, YEAST section.) If a particular batch of crackers should prove unpopular, this is a good way to use them.

---

**OTHER CRACKER RECIPES**

Grandma Minnie's Onion Cookies, p.187
Potato Wafers, p.495
Sunflower Seed Crackers, p.620
Tortilla Chips, p.195

---

**STORAGE**

**Canning**   (Sweeten before canning for best color and flavor.)

**Whole Sauce**   Prepare *Extra Special Cranberry Sauce* (add oranges after opening), or use any sauce recipe. Pour boiling hot in jars, ½ in. headroom. Process in boiling water bath. Pints and quarts: 10 min.

**Jellied Sauce**   Cook 2 pounds berries in 1 quart water until popped. Put through strainer or food mill. Sweeten to taste, heat to boiling. Process as for WHOLE SAUCE. Refer to CANNING section and CANNING FRUIT JUICE AND SAUCE in FRUITS section.

and sometimes cultivated for fruit in far northern regions. A wild berry known variously as cowberry, foxberry, lingenberry, and rock cranberry is often gathered in northern Europe and used like cranberries.

## HANDLING CRANBERRIES

Cranberries are gathered in the fall, and can be kept in cold storage all winter. Where protected by snow they will sometimes stay in good condition on the plants through the winter. Extra cranberries are easy to can, dry, or freeze for year-round use. Home canned cranberry juice is excellent. Cranberries are high in pectin and jell readily when cooked with sweetening. (Refer to the PECTIN section.) Since cranberries are so tart they are good combined with sweet fruits. They blend especially well with sweet apples, sweet oranges, and raisins. (Refer to COMBINING SWEET AND TART FRUITS, in the FRUITS section.)

If cranberries are abundant, use them in recipes for other tart fruits. They will give their own special flavor to recipes for rhubarb, sour or crabapples, sour cherries, or currants and gooseberries.

## CRANBERRY RECIPES

### Extra Special Cranberry Sauce                    (Makes about 1 quart.)

¾ cup honey, or maple syrup
½ cup water
4 cups cranberries

1—2 oranges, peeled and
    chopped medium

Bring the honey or syrup and water to a boil. Add the cranberries and cook till they have popped, from 5 to 10 minutes. Cool completely, then mix in the chopped oranges. Let sit an hour or more before serving. This sauce can be made a day ahead.

### Cranberry Anadama Bread                          (Makes 2 loaves.)

⅔ cup whole grain cornmeal
    (Stoneground or home ground.)
2½ cups boiling water
3 tablespoons shortening
½ cup molasses
1½ teaspoon salt, optional
1½ cups coarsely chopped cranberries

1 tablespoon orange rind, grated
2 tablespoons honey or ½ cup
    sugar
2 tablespoons dry yeast dissolved
    in ½ cup warm water
7½ cups (about) flour. (Half
    whole wheat and half unbleached is good.)
1 tablespoon (about) milk

Very slowly add the cornmeal to the boiling water, stirring constantly. Cook till thickened, about 3 minutes. Remove from heat and

---

**STORAGE,** *cont.*

**Cold Storage**  (Very practical.) Raw berries keep for weeks refrigerated. To store for several months, wash well in cold water, let dry, or pat dry with clean towel. Pack in sterilized jars, seal with sterilized lids. Refrigerate or keep in other cold place. Refer to COLD STORAGE section and COLD WATER CANNING in same section.

**Drying**  Crack skins by dunking in boiling water 15—30 sec. Spread in single layer on trays and dry till hard. Or make fruit leather. Refer to DRYING FOODS section.

**Freezing**  Pack dry, clean raw berries in rigid containers to prevent crushed fruit. Seal and freeze. Prepared relish or sauce can also be frozen. Refer to FREEZING section.

1 POUND = 4 CUPS

---

### CRANBERRY IDEAS

**Raw Cranberry Relish**  Grind cranberries in a meat grinder or food chopper with such raw fruits as apples, oranges, and pineapple. Add ground or grated orange peel, raisins or other dried fruits, and honey to taste. For a mixture to go with beef or game meats, grind a small piece of horseradish root with the cranberries. When oranges are not used, a little lemon juice will be good.

**Cranberry Conserves** Cooked, sweetened mixtures of cranberries, chopped nuts, raisins, and perhaps an orange are an old and still delicious idea. The American Indians cooked cranberries with black walnuts and maple sugar or syrup to make a sauce for meats, or as a dessert. (Refer to *Fruit Conserves*, in the JAM AND JELLY section.) Half cranberries and half raisins are an old and respected pie filling.

mix in the shortening, molasses, and salt, if desired. Set aside till lukewarm.

Grind the cranberries coarsely in a meat grinder or other food chopper. Mix in the orange rind and sweetening, and add to the cornmeal mixture. Stir in the dissolved yeast. Work in enough flour to make a soft dough. Knead on a floured board for 5 to 10 minutes. Put in an oiled bowl, turning to oil all of the dough. Cover and let rise till doubled, about an hour. Punch down. Let rest 10 minutes. Shape into loaves and put in greased or oiled bread pans. Cover and let rise until almost doubled. Brush tops with milk.

Bake in a 375°F oven for 45 minutes, or till browned. Cool on racks. This festive bread is especially good toasted.

# CREAM

*C*ream! THE VERY WORD SUGGESTS THE BEST, THE RICH AND CHOICE, the part that rises to the top, the cream of the crop, and—in this health and weight conscious society—it also suggests a delicious excess, frowned on and often forbidden. Yet milk, including its cream, is a simple natural food produced routinely by the family cow or goat. The problem, if there is one, lies not with the cream or the animal that produced it, but with those who eat too much of it. In balanced amounts, cream is everything good the name suggests, while a glut of it is just as bad as it sounds.

When dairy animals, especially cows, are in full production there are apt to be large amounts of cream on hand. Some can be frozen, or made into butter and put by for leaner times. If there is still too much, it is better to fatten one's animals with it than to fatten oneself.

## HANDLING CREAM

***Separating Cream from Cow's Milk***  Because the fat globules in raw or pasteurized cow's milk are large, they rise naturally to the top to form a layer of cream. In homogenized milk the fat globules have been broken into tiny particles that do not rise and instead stay mixed throughout the milk. Homogenized milk drinkers have the convenience of never needing to mix in the cream, but they miss the luxury of taking a few spoonfuls from the top of the bottle of milk to use in some special way. It is no wonder old recipes so casually advise adding a little cream here and there. Before homogenization it was not necessary to buy cream in separate containers.

To collect cream for daily use, simply put fresh pasteurized milk in the refrigerator in wide mouthed containers. After a day a layer of

**CRANBERRY IDEAS,** *cont.*

**Cranberry Gravy**  Mix about ½ cup cranberry sauce with 2 cups chicken or turkey gravy. Jellied sauce will keep the texture of the gravy smooth, but whole cranberry sauce also tastes good. This is a festive way to serve up the leftovers of a roast chicken or turkey dinner.

**Cranberries in Baking**  Cut raw cranberries in half, or chop them very coarsely, and add to muffins, pancakes, or fruit breads. They can take the place of blueberries in muffins and pancakes.

**Cranberry Ice Cream or Sherbet**  Frozen desserts made with cranberries are outstanding. Use canned or freshly made sauce in *Fruit 'n Yogurt Ice Cream,* and use cranberry juice or puréed sauce to make sherbet. (Refer to the recipes in the ICE CREAM section.)

cream will be ready to be spooned or ladled out. For heavy cream, take only the very top portion of the cream, or wait 2 or 3 days, when the cream layer has become more stiff. For light cream or "top milk," the top portion of the milk can be poured off. It is nice to leave some cream to stir into the drinking milk, so it will not taste skimmed. In this way "You can have your cream and drink it too."

There are several ways to completely separate the cream, to leave only skim milk. One old method was to pour raw milk in shallow pans, protect it with a cloth, and set it in a cool place till a layer of stiff cream formed. The cream could be lifted off almost in one piece with a cream skimmer. A rich milk, like that from Jersey cows worked best. The slight acidity that developed as the milk sat helped stiffen the cream. This was also the first step for making both butter and cottage cheese. (Refer to SOURING OR RIPENING CREAM FOR BUTTER, in the BUTTER section.)

Another old and efficient method for separating larger amounts of cream is to put the milk in a straight sided bucket (called a shotgun can), and quickly chill it in ice water. Some shotgun cans had spigots on the bottom for drawing off the skim milk after the cream rose. Some also had a glass tube on the outside that showed the relative levels of cream and skim milk. Any container with a spigot on the bottom can be used in this way and placed in the refrigerator, but it must be made of a material that can be sterilized between uses.

The fastest, most efficient way to separate cream is with a mechanical separator which uses centrifugal force. However, even manually operated ones are quite expensive, and designed to separate several gallons of milk at once, so they are impractical for people with only one family cow.

**Separating Cream from Goat's Milk**  The fat globules in goat's milk are naturally small so the cream will not rise readily. The milk may sit for several days before any cream rises, and the separation is never as complete as with cow's milk. However, goat's milk varies, and cream rises more readily on the milk of some goats than on the milk of others. There seems to be a somewhat better separation if the milk has been pasteurized or frozen. For large amounts of goat's cream a mechanical separator will be necessary. Since these are expensive to buy and can be tedious to clean, people with only one or two milk goats may decide to forgo cream, and use their extra milk to make cheese. Fresh cheese is as easy to make as butter, if not easier, and is the traditional way to use extra goat's milk. (Refer to the CHEESE, FRESH section.)

**Storing Cream**  The only way to store fresh cream for long periods is to freeze it, but then its usefulness will be limited.

As frozen cream thaws, an oily fat separates from it that is unpleasant in hot drinks or hot soup. However, if heavy enough, it will whip, and can also be used in baking. If the cream is made into butter, cream cheese, or ice cream before freezing, the possibilities are greater. It can also be used in cooked and baked dishes that are to be frozen. (Refer to the BUTTER, ICE CREAM, and CHEESE sections.)

Cream keeps about a week in the refrigerator, and two weeks or so if made into cultured sour cream.

***Sour Cream***   Cream can be soured at home with a yogurt culture, or with cultured buttermilk, exactly like milk. It is heated to scald it, cooled to the proper temperature for adding the culture, and then held at a steady temperature until set. If a yogurt culture is used the procedures are the same as for making yogurt from milk. (Refer to SOURING OR RIPENING CREAM FOR BUTTER, in the BUTTER section, and MAKING YOGURT, in the YOGURT section.)

## CREAM RECIPES

### Cream Salad Dressing
(A rich dressing for most salads.)                    (Makes about 2 cups.)

*1 tablespoon dry mustard*
*1 teaspoon flour*
*½ teaspoon salt, optional*
*1 tablespoon honey or sugar*
*2 eggs*

*¾ cup vinegar (Homemade cider vinegar is nice.)*
*1 cup (about) medium to heavy cream*

Mix the mustard, flour, and salt, if desired. Stir in the sweetening and eggs. Add the vinegar. Cook in a double boiler, stirring constantly until the mixture thickens, about 10 minutes. Cool completely, then stir in enough cream for a smooth, creamy texture. If the cream is very heavy a little milk may also be necessary. This dressing is delicious both on salads and cooked vegetables. It is somewhat like mayonnaise, and can be used in the same ways. It will keep for a month or more when refrigerated.

### Whipped Cream Biscuits                    (Makes 12–18 biscuits.)

*2 cups whole wheat flour (Or a combination from the BREADS, QUICK section.)*

*2 teaspoons baking powder*
*1 cup heavy cream*

Sift together the flour and baking powder. Whip the cream till stiff. Mix the flour lightly into the cream with a fork. Turn out on a floured board and knead gently for 1 minute. Then pat the dough to ½ inch thick. Cut circles with a cookie or biscuit cutter, or a thin lipped glass. Put on an ungreased baking sheet and bake in a hot, 450°F oven for 12 minutes or till browned.

Instead of baking, these biscuits can be cooked on a hot griddle for about 5 minutes on each side. A superb way to use extra cream.

***Sour Cream Biscuits*** Use 1 teaspoon baking powder and ½ teaspoon baking soda instead of all baking powder. For a piquant flavor, use sour cream (without whipping) instead of sweet cream.

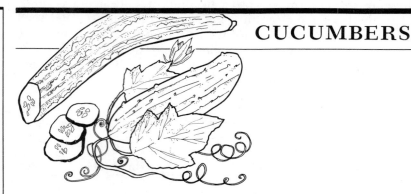

# CUCUMBERS

---

## STORAGE

**Canning** (Practical for pickles only.) See CUCUMBER RECIPES, below, and BASIC PICKLING RECIPES in PICKLING section.

**Cold Storage** Pack large, firm, unblemished cucumber with stem left on in damp sand or other protective material, and store in root cellar or similar condition. Storage life up to 2 mos. Refer to COLD STORAGE section. Also see *Kosher Dills,* below.

**Drying** Slice thinly or chop small. Dry till brittle. Use in soup or stew, or use crisp slices as chips with dips. Refer to DRYING FOODS section.

**Freezing** (Not acceptable raw except in a vinegar solution.) See VINEGARED CUCUMBERS, in IDEAS, below. Juice and cooked dishes may be frozen.

I BUSHEL RAW CUCUMBERS = 40 – 45 POUNDS = 14–24 QUARTS, PICKLED

---

CUCUMBER ARE ONE OF THE OLDEST KNOWN GARDEN VEGETABLES. They have been cultivated for over 3,000 years in parts of Asia and Africa, and there are seemingly over 3,000 uses for them. These include numerous ways to prepare them raw, to pickle them, and, less well known, to cook them.

All cucumbers do not look alike. The green, cylindrical varieties are the most common, but there are many others, ranging from the Apple or Lemon cucumber (which are shaped like the fruits), to the Sikkim variety grown in the Himalayas, which reach up to 15 inches long and 6 inches around. Also notable are the large, smooth skinned European and English cucumbers grown mostly in greenhouses, and the long, slender Chinese and Japanese varieties which are quite ridged and warty. The latter are easy to grow, and their mild flavor is excellent in salads, pickled, and cooked.

## HANDLING CUCUMBERS

Any cucumber over an inch long can be harvested, but they are usually allowed to grow to at least 3 or 4 inches. Often cucumbers are harvested small and immature for pickling, while medium sized ones are picked for salads. When full sized cucumbers are about to turn yellow they are excellent both cooked as a vegetable or pickled like fruit. (Refer to the *Spiced Pickled Fruit* recipe, in the PICKLING section.) Where garden space is limited, a single variety can be grown and picked at different stages for different purposes.

It is best to cut cucumbers leaving a short stem on each. Pulling may both injure the vine, and break the skin at the stem end where spoilage can start. Careful cutting is most important with whole pickling cucumbers and those to be kept in cold storage for some time. Home-grown cucumbers should not be peeled unless skins are tough, but waxed or sprayed store cucumbers must be peeled. Eating the skins is said to prevent gas and, of course, saves valuable nutrients. If the seeds are large, the cucumber's center can be scooped out and fed to chickens or livestock.

Under imperfect growing conditions the cucumbers' stem sections sometimes become bitter. If several slices are discarded from this end, the rest of the cucumber is usually good. A slight bitterness can be counteracted by vinegar dressings.

As cucumbers contain a lot of moisture they are sometimes sliced and pressed between two plates or small boards, with a weight on top to remove juice. A sprinkling of salt before pressing is often recommended to draw out liquid, but the salt can be avoided if slices are very thin. Another way to remove juice is to grate cucumbers or chop them small, and then squeeze them in a cloth. Pressed or squeezed cucumbers, being somewhat limp and dry, will absorb salad dressings instead of diluting them as do fresh slices. (See the grated salad and relish recipes below.) Cucumber juice is flavorful added to vegetable juice mixtures, aspics, and soups.

**Cooked Cucumbers**   Mature cucumbers are surprisingly delicious cooked. They are prepared much like summer squash or zucchini and can be used in the same recipes. However, their texture will be firmer and their flavor somewhat different. Even overripe, yellow cucumbers can be cooked if they are first peeled and seeded.

**Cucumber Pickles**   The best pickling cucumbers are immature, firm, small, and freshly harvested. If kept for even a day at room temperature they may later become hollow or shriveled after pickling. It is best to pick cucumbers on a dry day, as they will be waterlogged and less flavorful right after a heavy rain. For whole pickles, use unblemished cucumbers, cut to leave a small bit of stem, and remove any remnants of blossom. Less perfect cucumbers, if firm and fresh, are good for pickled slices, chunks, or relish, but must still be firm and fresh.

There are numerous cucumber pickle recipes, but only a few general types. Most often vinegar is the pickling agent, but a few depend on lactic acid (formed by natural fermentation) to preserve and flavor the cucumbers. In these salt is used to draw out the sugars and juice, providing the right conditions for fermentation. The process is like making sauerkraut. (Refer to MAKING FERMENTED PICKLES, in the PICKLING section.)

Pickles made with vinegar may be sweet or sour. The most nutritious are those made with a minimum of salt and sugar. (Refer to THE NUTRITIONAL VALUE OF PICKLES, in the PICKLING section.) The following pickle recipes are made with less salt and sugar than is usual.

# CUCUMBER RECIPES

### *Grated Cucumber Salad*      (Makes about 6 side servings.)

3 large cucumbers
1 small onion
horseradish root, small piece, or 1
   tablespoon (about) prepared
   horseradish, optional
3 tablespoons vinegar, or
   lemon juice

1 teaspoon honey or sugar
2–3 tablespoons dill or fennel
   leaves, or other fresh herbs,
   minced
pepper, optional

Grate the cucumbers coarsely into a cloth lined colander placed over a bowl. Gather up the ends of the cloth to make a bag, then tighten, twist, and squeeze to press out as much juice as possible. (Save the juice for a vegetable juice mixture or soup.) Grate the onion and horseradish, then combine with the cucumber. Mix in the sweetening and seasonings. Taste and adjust if necessary. This salad is especially good with fish or seafood.

    **Raw Cucumber Sauce**    Grate the cucumber more finely than for the salad, press well, and increase seasonings for a more piquant flavor. A little dry mustard instead of horseradish, and about ½ cup yogurt or sour cream can be added.

    This sauce will not store well and should be used soon after preparation. It is especially good with cold salmon.

### *Cucumber Stew*      (Makes about 6 side servings.)

3 large cucumbers
1 medium onion, sliced or
   chopped medium
¼ cup vinegar, or lemon
   juice

pepper, to taste
2 tablespoons butter, or several
   crisply fried slices bacon,
   crumbled

Peel and seed the cucumbers if necessary, then slice to taste, or chop them. They are nice sliced into ribbons. Carefully heat the cucumbers and onion in a dry saucepan, shaking or stirring them as they become hot. As soon as they cook and enough liquid comes out to prevent sticking, cover and simmer till tender, 10 to 15 minutes. If too much liquid collects, drain some off. Add vinegar or lemon juice, pepper, and butter, or bacon. Cook 2 or 3 minutes more and serve. This dish compares favorably with stewed summer squash. Many will prefer the cucumbers' firmer texture and more distinctive flavor. An excellent accompaniment for any meal.

    **Sautéed Cucumbers**    Steam the raw, prepared cucumbers for 5 to 10 minutes, depending on the thickness of the pieces, until they are partially cooked. Then sauté them in butter with the sliced or chopped onion. Season them to taste. A sprinkling of minced parsley or scallion makes a very pleasant addition.

### Stir-fried Cucumbers and Pork    (Makes about 6 side servings.)

2 large cucumbers
1 pound boneless pork
2½ tablespoons soy sauce
1 tablespoon sherry, or ½ teaspoon
    vinegar

1 teaspoon honey or sugar
1 tablespoon cornstarch
2 tablespoons water
2–3 tablespoons oil

If desired, remove seeds from the cucumbers and slice very thinly. Slice the pork very thinly, and cut into squares (about 1 inch). This is easiest to do if the pork is partially frozen. The cucumber and pork slices should be about the same size.

Mix the pork with 1½ tablespoons of the soy sauce, and the sherry or vinegar, honey or sugar, cornstarch, and water.

Heat 1½ tablespoons oil in a heavy frying pan or wok until it is very hot, but not smoking. Add the cucumbers and stir-fry 2 minutes, or until they are beginning to become limp. Remove from the pan. Add more oil, and when the pan is very hot put in the pork mixture. Sitr-fry about 2 minutes, or till the pork has changed color and cooked through. Return the cucumbers to the pan and add 1 tablespoon of soy sauce. Stir-fry over high heat for a minute to reheat and blend all ingredients. (Refer to the STIR-FRYING section.) Serve immediately with rice.

### Squeezed Cucumber Relish    (Makes 4 pints.)

12 (about) medium to large cucum-
    bers (Enough to make 2 quarts
    after squeezing.)
5–6 onions, grated or chopped small
2 cups vinegar

¼ cup honey, or ½ cup sugar
    (Increase for a sweeter
    relish.)
1 teaspoon turmeric
cayenne, or other hot pepper, to
    taste
1 teaspoon salt, optional

Grate the cucumbers, or chop them finely. Put them in a cloth lined colander over a bowl, and gather the ends of the cloth to make a bag. Tighten, twist, squeeze, and press the bag to remove as much juice as possible. (Reserve the juice for soups or juice mixtures.) In a large pot combine onions, vinegar, honey or sugar, tumeric, pepper, and salt, if desired, with the cucumber. Heat to a boil, uncovered, stirring frequently, and boil 5 minutes. Pour into clean hot jars, adjust lids and seal. Process in a boiling water bath for 10 minutes. (Refer to the CANNING section.)

---

### CUCUMBER IDEAS

**Cucumbers and Herbs**
Cucumbers are delicious with most fresh-from-the-garden herbs. Minced chives, scallions, dill leaves, fennel, basil, parsley, or summer savory are good individually or in combinations sprinkled over cucumber slices. They make a good salad without other seasoning, but a salad dressing or yogurt can be added.

**Vinegared Cucumbers**  For a cool, refreshing, summer side dish, marinate sliced or chopped cucumbers in vinegar for 15 minutes or longer. A mild homemade cider vinegar or wine vinegar is ideal. If harsher, stronger tasting vinegar must be used, dilute it half-and-half with water. Serve the cucumbers in the vinegar, or drain and sprinkle them with minced herbs, as described above.

Cucumbers can also be frozen in a half vinegar, half water mixture. When thawed and drained they can be added to salads.

**Cucumbers with Soy Sauce**
Sprinkle sliced cucumbers with soy sauce and perhaps sesame seeds, or with the Soy Sauce Dressing recipe, in the SALADS section. Or steam 5 to 10 minutes before adding soy sauce.

**Cucumber Sandwiches**
These are the coolest, crispest, quickest sandwiches of summer. They can be as simple as cucumber slices on buttered bread, or make a more elaborate combination with tomatoes, lettuce, and mayonnaise. Cucumber slices add a refreshing touch to tuna or egg salad sandwiches.

## CUCUMBER IDEAS, *cont.*

**Cucumber Soup**  Chopped cucumber is very good added to most vegetable and meat soups for the last 10 or 15 minutes of cooking. For an all cucumber soup, cook several chopped cucumbers in chicken, rabbit, or veal stock. Purée the mixture and enrich with milk and a little cream. Season with pepper, herbs, and salt, if desired. If a thickened soup is preferred, melt 2 tablespoons butter in the soup pot, stir in 2 tablespoons flour, then add the other ingredients.

**Cucumbers Replacing Summer Squash**  Cucumbers work well instead of zucchini and other summer squash in many recipes. They are good cooked with onions, tomatoes and herbs. Slices can be floured, breaded, or dipped in batter and sautéed 10 to 15 minutes. Or stuff cucumbers like zucchini. (Refer to the RECIPES, in the SQUASH, SUMMER section.)

**Honeyed Cucumber Spears**  For a unique and charming picnic dessert, follow the lead of some of Tolstoy's characters, and pass around crisp cucumber spears spread with honey.

### OTHER RECIPES FEATURING CUCUMBERS

## *German Style Dill Pickles*                                   (Makes 4 quarts.)

4 heads dill
4 cloves garlic, optional
4 small, hot red peppers, or pepper flakes to taste
4 quarts pickling cucumbers
8 grape leaves, optional
3 cups vinegar
6 cups water
2 tablespoons salt

Sterilize 4 quart jars and lids in boiling water. Put a head of dill, a peeled clove of garlic, and a whole pepper in each jar. Fill the jars with cucumbers without packing them too tightly. Put 2 grape leaves on top of each jar. Heat the vinegar, water, and salt to a full boil, then pour into the jars, filling them almost to the brim. Seal lids and let cool. Store in a cool place and wait a month before using them. Use within 3 or 4 months. If stored too long they may become soft. Their flavor is outstanding and well worth the limited storage life. (Refer to CANNING PICKLES, in the CANNING section.)

## *Kosher Dill Pickles*      (Makes ½–1 gallon, or more, as desired.)

several dozen small to medium pickling cucumbers
3–4 heads dill
3–4 cloves garlic, peeled
2–3 tablespoons pickling spices, optional (Try equal parts stick cinnamon, whole cloves, whole allspice, mace spears, mustard seeds, and bay leaf.)
brine made with ½ cup pickling salt to every 2 quarts water

Pack cucumbers, dill, peeled garlic, and pickling spices in a clean crock, gallon jar, or unchipped enameled pot. Pack the cucumbers closely but do not force and bruise them. Dissolve the salt in the water and pour over the cucumbers, making sure they are covered by about 2 inches of brine. (Refer to FERMENTED PICKLES, in the PICKLING section.) Put a plate or round wooden follower on the cucumbers, and weigh it down with a brick, a container of water, or other weight. It is important to be sure all of the cucumbers are well under the brine. (Refer to the KITCHEN UTENSILS section for how to arrange crocks or crock substitutes.)

Let sit for 3 days at room temperature, when fermentation should be well under way. Move to a cool place such as a cellar. The pickles can be eaten partially pickled after about a week. It takes a few weeks for them to pickle completely.

These pickles can be kept in the crock for several months if the crock is well covered, the cucumbers kept well under the brine, and the temperature cold enough, 35°F is ideal. With poor storage conditions the pickles soften and become strong tasting more quickly. (Refer to COLD STORAGE OF FOOD IN CROCKS, in the COLD STORAGE section.)

CURRANTS HAVE A COMPELLING, TART FLAVOR WHICH MAKES THEM extraordinary in jelly and preserves. Sauces made with red currant jelly or preserves are a popular accompaniment for ham and roast meat in England and France. One fancy red currant preserve is Bar-le-Duc, named after the French town where it originated. Each currant in it is pricked with a pin to absorb the syrup in which it is cooked so that it becomes plumply beautiful.

In the United States before the 1920's currants were a fairly common fruit. In the twenties most currants and gooseberries were uprooted, because they were found to be an alternate host for white pine blister rust, and white pine timber far overrode currants or gooseberries in importance. However, currants can still be grown or gathered wild in many places, and they remain both delicious and useful.

There are red, black, and white currant varieties. Because they are closely related to gooseberries they can be used in the same ways. Currants are a good source of vitamin C. Black currants, which have the most vitamin C, are also the most susceptible to white pine blister rust.

There is some confusion about dried currants. Those sold in stores are not actually currants, but a special kind of dried grapes. In recipes, "currants" often means the dried grapes rather than the true fresh currants. True currants are good dried, but as they dry hard they usually need soaking to reconstitute them.

## HANDLING CURRANTS

Currants will stay on the bush for 4 to 6 weeks after they change color or begin to ripen. As they hang, they become sweeter, and some varieties will become sweet enough to eat fresh. The black varieties are sweeter than the red. Pectin content is highest when currants are underripe or when they first ripen, so pick them early for jam or preserves. The red varieties contain the most pectin.

Pick currants on a dry day after the dew has evaporated. They can be picked one by one, removing the stem from each, or whole clusters can be broken off at once, or they can be stripped from the plant by holding a container under them and running a hand down each cluster. Though stripping damages the currants, it will not matter if the fruit is to be used immediately. Currants that are to be stored even for a few days should be picked more carefully, however,

***Stemming Currants*** If currants are to be cooked for juice or jelly their stems need not be removed. They can be strained out after cooking as they do not affect flavor. When it is necessary to remove stems, mix the currants with enough flour to coat them, then roll them gently between the palms of the hands till the stems come off. Then rinse away flour and stems together. The currants' little tails will rub off with the stems, but they are not noticeable if left on, even when eaten fresh or cooked whole. Even stems can be left on and eaten like the tails if the slight chewiness is not minded.

*Currant Juice*　Do not overlook this delicious specialty. Fresh, un-cooked juice is very good in punch, and for sherbet; the canned juice is good used like any tart juice. Currant wine used to be popular. (Refer to MAKING FRUIT JUICE AND SAUCE, in the FRUITS section, and to the ICE CREAM and WINE sections.)

# CURRANT RECIPES

### Fresh Currant Sauce for Meats　　　　　　(Makes 1–1½ cups)

⅓ cup fresh currants
3 tablespoons grated horseradish

1 cup beef or other red meat stock

Combine all ingredients in a saucepan and simmer for 15 minutes. Very good served with roast or boiled beef, or any other red meat.

### Three Currant Jelly Sauces for Meats

• Beat 1 cup currant jelly or preserves with a fork until smooth. Then mix in 2–4 tablespoons prepared mustard or horseradish. Serve with any red meat, whether hot or cold.

• Beat 1 cup currant jelly or preserves with a fork until smooth. Mix in 2 tablespoons grated orange rind and 2 tablespoons minced fresh mint leaves. Serve with lamb or chicken.

• Combine 1 cup currant jelly or preserves with 1 cup port wine and heat in a double boiler. Serve hot with game meat, poultry, or any dark meat.

### Red Currant Filled Pudding, American Indian Style　　　　　(Makes 6–10 servings.)

2 cups whole wheat flour
1 teaspoon baking powder
¾ cup cornmeal
½ cup butter, or shortening
1–1¼ cups boiling water

3–4 cups fresh currants
½ cup honey, or maple sugar
juice of ½ lemon, optional
(Depending on the tartness of the currants.)

Sift together the flour and baking powder, and mix in the corn-meal. Cut in the butter with a pastry cutter or two knives. Pour in part of the boiling water and mix quickly. Add more boiling water, stirring until a soft dough is formed. Butter a 1½–2 quart baking dish, then spread about ¾ of the dough over the bottom and sides to form a shell.

---

## CURRANT IDEAS

**Currants in Fruit Mixtures**
Combining currants with other fruits is an old and excellent idea. They go especially well with rasp-berries, but are also good with cherries, early apples, and other fruits that ripen around the same time. Such combinations make delicious juice and punch, jams and jellies, sherbet, ice cream, and pie or tart fillings. Currant-raspberry pie is exceptional.

**Fresh Currants in Baked Goods**　Use currants instead of blueberries in pancakes, muf-fins, and fruit breads, and add a little grated citrus fruit peel. Or use them in the Anadama bread recipe in the CRANBERRIES sec-tion instead of cranberries.

**Fresh Currants Over Ice**　Pick currants after they have become somewhat sweet. Spread them over a clear cube of ice in individ-ual bowls. According to one very old recipe book, "Of a sultry morning nothing is more refresh-ing."

Crush half of the currants with the honey or maple sugar, and stir till syrupy. Mix in the remaining whole currants, and lemon juice. Pour into the dough lined baking dish, then cover with the rest of the dough. Bake in a hot, 400°F oven for 35 to 40 minutes, or till the top is browned. Serve warm. This dessert is absolutely irresistible!

***Berry Filled Pudding***    Instead of currants use raspberries, blackberries, gooseberries, strawberries, or any other available berries.

# DANDELIONS

**OTHER RECIPES WITH CURRANTS**

Hot Fruit Soup, p.290
Recipes, and Ideas for Fruit p.290
Recipes for Jams and Jellies, p.361

**D**ANDELIONS CAN BE A DANDY VEGETABLE, BUT THEIR NAME ACtually comes from the French *dent-de-lion,* or tooth of a lion, describing the sharply indented leaf margins.

Dandelions are collected wild more often than cultivated, but some seed catalogs do carry seeds for big leaved varieties that do not get as bitter, or blossom as quickly, as the wild plants. The best wild dandelions for eating grow undisturbed in fields and open places. Though it may not seem so to those who strive for perfect lawns, mowed dandelions are somewhat stunted. The rage that some people feel towards dandelions in their lawns would be dissipated if they could discover the joys of eating them. They might even decide to stop mowing their lawns so the dandelions could reach their full potential!

## HANDLING DANDELIONS

Wild dandelion greens are harvested from early spring, when the first little leaves appear, till mid-spring when they begin to blossom. When the greens become too tough and bitter to enjoy, the blossoms can be harvested and used instead. The roots can be dug all year, depending on the way they are to be used. Starting with the crowns in spring, dandelions are practically a year-round vegetable. However, do not gather dandelions close to busy roads, because of contamination from car exhausts and winter treatments to remove ice.

***Dandelion Crowns***    In very early spring, when the first leaf tips begin to show, dig the plants and cut off the rosettes of beginning leaves and buds, or cut the plants an inch or two below the soil's surface

**STORAGE**

**Canning**    Cook young greens in minimum water till wilted. Cook older greens in large pot of boiling water 10 min., drain to remove bitterness. Pack, add boiling water, 1 in. headroom. Process 240°F, 11 pounds pressure. Pints: 1 hr. 10 min. Quarts: 1 hr. 30 min. Refer to CANNING section.

**Cold Storage**    *Roots* Refer to WINTER FORCING OF CHICORY ROOTS in CHICORY section.

**Drying**    To dry greens refer to SPINACH section. For tea refer to DRYING HERBS, in HERBS section. For roots refer to BREWING ROAST BEVERAGES in BEVERAGES section.

**Freezing**    Blanch tender leaves 1½–2 min. in steam or boiling water. Blanch tough leaves 5 min. in boiling water. Refer to FREEZING section.

2–3 POUNDS RAW GREENS = 1 QUART COOKED

with a sharp knife. They will be pale yellow or white with a crisp texture and mild flavor. They are delicious in salads. They can also be cooked quickly in a minimum of water, seasoned with butter and pepper, and served as a hot vegetable. Some like to cook the little, partially formed flower buds separately for a special treat.

Delicate, blanched leaves can be encouraged by piling soil over the plants, so that more leaves are blanched as they grow, or buckets can be turned upside-down over the plants to keep them in darkness. Roots forced in winter will also produce crisp, blanched leaves.

*Dandelion Greens*   The greens are the most prolific, useful part of the dandelion. Large amounts can be gathered, and canned or frozen for winter. Years ago they were salted down (salt cured) and stored, but that is the least nutritious way to handle them. Early spring greens are tender enough used raw for salads, or can be cooked in the water left on them from washing. Later in the season they become gradually more tough and bitter. Then they are best cooked in a large pot of boiling water for about 10 minutes and drained. This takes away some of the bitterness. Bitterness can also be handled as with their close relative, chicory greens. (Refer to the CHICORY section, and REMOVING BITTER TASTES FROM WILD FOODS, in the WILD FOODS section.)

Sand and dirt particles tend to collect in dandelion greens, and it is best to immerse them in several changes of cold water. Light bits of debris will float off, and the leaves can then be lifted out of the water, leaving sand and dirt behind. Picked greens wilt quickly, so refrigerate or prepare them without delay.

*Dandelion Blossoms*   Dandelion blossoms are good prepared like squash blossoms or elderberry flowers (refer to the SQUASH, SUMMER section), though they are best known for making dandelion wine. Gather the blossoms on a dry day and, most important, remove the stems and calyx (the outer ring of leaves around the blossoms). The inner green ring that holds the blossoms together can be left in place, though it does not matter if they fall apart. The blossoms can be pinched off the plant with the fingers, leaving stem and calyx behind, or picked and held by the stem while the blossoms are pinched or snipped off with scissors. If carefully picked from a clean place they will not need washing. (See RECIPES, below, for making punch and wine.)

*Dandelion Roots*   If dug in early spring, when the crowns are harvested, dandelion roots make a pleasant cooked vegetable. They should be peeled since the skin is very bitter. Slice the roots, and bring to a boil in plenty of water. Drain to remove any remaining bitterness, then cook and season like carrots, or other root vegetables.

Dandelion roots can also be roasted for a beverage, and forced in winter for their blanched leaves, as for chicory roots. (Refer to ROAST BEVERAGES, in the BEVERAGES section, and the CHICORY section.)

## DANDELION RECIPES

### Creamed Dandelion Greens

(Makes about 6 side servings.)

| | |
|---|---|
| 1 pound dandelion greens | 2 tablespoons butter, softened |
| 1 cup pearl onions, or a chopped onion | 2 tablespoons flour or cornmeal egg, hard-boiled and sliced, optional garnish |
| 1½ cups milk | |

Combine dandelion greens, onions, and milk in a saucepan. Heat to a simmer, and cook without boiling for about 15 minutes, or till the greens are tender. In a small bowl, work the butter and flour or cornmeal together to make a paste. Stir in some hot milk from the greens mixture, then add to the saucepan and stir to blend completely. Simmer about 10 minutes, stirring several times.

**Creamed Chicory Greens**   Use chicory greens instead of dandelions.

### Spicy Stir-fried Dandelion Greens

(Makes 6 small side servings, or appetizers for 6 to 10.)

| | |
|---|---|
| 1 tablespoon honey or sugar | ¼ teaspoon cayenne |
| 2 tablespoons vinegar | 2 tablespoons oil |
| 1 tablespoon soy sauce | 1 pound dandelion greens |

Combine the sweetening, vinegar, soy sauce, cayenne, and 1 tablespoon of the oil. Mix in the greens and marinate about 30 minutes. (The greens do not need chopping as they cook down enough to be handled with a fork or chop sticks.)

Drain the greens, saving the marinade. Heat a wok or heavy frying pan, and add the remaining tablespoon of oil. Stir-fry the greens 2 to 3 minutes. Add the marinade and heat quickly, stirring to combine thoroughly. This lively stir-fry is equally enticing served cold as an appetizer, or hot, with rice.

### Dandelion Blossom Punch

(Makes about 8 cups. Double amounts for a party.)

| | |
|---|---|
| 1 quart dandelion blossoms, stems and calyx removed | ½ cup honey, or 1 cup sugar |
| | 1 orange |
| 2 quarts boiling water | ½ lemon |

Pour the boiling water over the dandelion blossoms and let stand overnight. Strain out and discard the blossoms. Add the sweetening and bring to a boil. Thinly slice the orange and lemon with their peels. Pour the boiling blossom water over them, then let stand at room temperature for 3 days. Strain, pour over ice cubes or chill in the refrigerator, and enjoy. The flavor evokes a pleasantly herbal soft drink.

**Dandelion Wine**   Wine can be started in the same way as the above punch. The proportions are: 4 quarts blossoms, 4 quarts boiling

---

### DANDELION IDEAS

**Dandelion and other Greens**
Use dandelion greens in recipes for mustard greens, spinach, chicory, and other greens. They are delicious seasoned with minced ham, crisp crumbled bacon, vinegar, lemon juice, and sliced or chopped, hard-boiled eggs. Try mixing them with other spring greens, especially those with a bland flavor, such as comfrey.

**Dandelion Beet Salad**   Mix fresh, young dandelion greens or blanched crowns with cooked, sliced beets and pour a French or Italian dressing over them. Minced chives or scallions, and other salad greens or vegetables can be included.

**Dandelion and Pasta**   Mix hot, cooked dandelion greens with hot, cooked spaghetti or noodles. Toss with olive oil or butter, and Parmesan or another grated cheese. Serve immediately.

### OTHER RECIPES WITH DANDELIONS

Beans and Greens Soup, p.25
Braised Dandelion Greens, p.173
Dandelion and Bacon Salad, p.173
Dandelion Blossom Corn Cakes, p.602
Greens and Rice, p.519
Gumbo Z'Herbes, p.341
Hot Drinks (roots), p.42
Mix 'n Match Greens, p.688
Wild Salad Greens, p.532

water, 3 pounds (6 cups) sugar, 1 orange, 1 lemon, and ½ teaspoon yeast. Steep blossoms in the water as for the punch, and strain. Squeeze the orange and lemon, reserving juice and peels. Simmer blossom water, sugar, and peels together for 5 minutes. Cool to lukewarm and add reserved juice and yeast. Ferment as described in the WINE section.

# DRYING FOODS

IN A DRY CLIMATE IT IS DIRECT, SIMPLE, AND NATURAL TO DRY FOOD for storage. Even in humid climates the drying of certain foods, such as grains, mature beans, and herbs is taken for granted, and many other foods can be dried with some special attention. Primitive man learned very early that dry nuts, seeds, and fruits would keep all winter, and mankind has depended on dried foods ever since. Even with modern, mechanical refrigeration and freezing, and sophisticated canning techniques, there is a place for dried foods. Everyone depends on stored dry grains and flour, and dried fruits are widely used. In some parts of the world drying is an important means of storing vegetables, meat, and fish, as well. In China, huge quantities of vegetables and seafoods are dried, both commercially and in the home. These dried foods play an important and delicious part in Chinese cooking.

Anyone interested in food self-sufficiency is bound to consider drying as a method for storing at least some foods. It is a method with so many advantages that it cannot be ignored. It costs little or nothing and requires very little equipment, although specialized equipment is available. Dried foods are light, compact, and easy to store. Most can tolerate storage temperatures ranging from room temperature to way below freezing, so they can be stored anywhere if kept in protective containers or packages. Their quality is excellent for 6 months to a year or more, and they keep without spoiling almost indefinitely.

Still other advantages of dried foods are their flavor, nutritional excellence, and convenience. In dried fruits, for instance, natural sugars and nutrients, particularly minerals, are concentrated, making them an especially healthful, ready to eat sweet treat. The concentrated flavor of dried vegetables makes them outstanding when used as a seasoning. Dried vegetable shreds, flakes, or powder, kept handy on a kitchen shelf, can be added to soups, stews, or sauces in the same way as herbs. If desired, instant seasoning or soup mixtures can be prepared ahead. Dried mixtures which include meat are popular as hiking and camping foods, since they are easily carried and prepared.

Another virtue is that drying offers a different way to process familiar, plentiful foods. There is less monotony when foods, such as apples, are stored in a variety of ways. If some are stored in the root cellar, some canned, and some dried, they will be three times as enjoyable.

Home drying is experiencing a renaissance as a modern food storage method. Many new and old ideas for drying foods are surfacing, with many approaches, opinions, and sometimes disagreements to consider. Anyone who likes trying new things should enjoy experimenting with drying, using a variety of foods. There are probably plenty of interesting possibilities that have not been thought of yet.

## FOOD DRYING FACTORS

Food dries when warm, dry air circulates around it, so temperature, humidity, and ventilation or air movement must be considered, along with the type and preparation of the food to be dried.

Food can be dried at temperatures ranging from about 90 to 150°F. However, caution is necessary when temperatures are either very low or very high in this range. At 90°F, humidity must be low, and air circulation must be good, or the food will spoil before it can dry. Food will not dry outdoors in humid 90°F weather, but it will dry very well on a breezy 90°F day in the desert. To dry foods successfully in spite of high humidity, extra heat and good ventilation must be provided.

When drying at high temperatures, in the 130 to 150°F range, care must be taken that food does not cook, or form a crust that seals in moisture and prevents complete drying. Foods are most apt to cook or form a crust at the beginning of the drying process, when they are full of moisture. Directions for using electric food dryers usually advise beginning with temperatures around 120°F and increasing as drying progresses.

Different drying temperatures and techniques can affect the texture and flavor of the food dried. For instance, slices of zucchini, cucumber or banana dried quickly at a high temperature become crisp chips. Dried more slowly at a lower temperature, the zucchini or cucumber is papery rather than crisp and the banana is leathery and sweeter.

The ways in which dried foods will be used depends a great deal on their texture. If leathery but chewable, or crisp, they will probably be good eaten as is. If tough, or hard, or brittle, the food will need moistening or soaking, and probably cooking, before it is eaten. If hard foods can be ground to flakes or powders they may be very useful and versatile as seasoning ingredients.

## METHODS AND EQUIPMENT FOR DRYING FOOD

Food can be air dried, solar dried or dried with an artificial heat source. All home drying methods do essentially the same job, reducing the food's moisture to about 10 to 20% of the original content. Commercially, there are highly specialized dehydration methods that remove almost all the moisture, but these are not possible for use at home. Powdered milk, for instance, cannot be made at home.

The most practical home drying method changes with different circumstances, but one item of equipment is always useful. This is a movable drying tray or rack, or better yet, a set of them.

*Chinese bamboo drying rack*

***Drying Trays***   Conveniently sized trays or racks that will fit both outdoor and indoor drying situations are ideal. The same trays may then be used as shelves in dryers, or hung over a wood stove, or propped up in the sun on the south side of the house. The best trays have bottoms that allow air circulation. Wooden frames or old window screens with fiberglass or plastic screening are excellent. Do not use metal screens or hardware cloth as the metal may contaminate the food. Some drying trays have wooden slats or dowels placed ¼ to ½ inch apart, to hold the food. This wood should be a variety that will not flavor or stain the food. Cheesecloth or other cotton cloth can be laid on these trays if food is likely to drop through. Trays must always be positioned so that air can move under them.

***Outdoor Drying***   Nothing sounds easier than putting food outdoors and waiting for it to dry, and nothing is easier—if Mother Nature cooperates, the air is clean and dust free, the bugs and birds and rodents keep their distance, and the food itself is suitable for drying.

For outdoor air drying, warm, sunny, low-humidity weather is necessary. In some places, the entire summer is good for drying. In others, the requirements are a good weather forecast, luck, and a back-up system to finish drying food indoors. Anyone who has made hay in a humid climate knows the problems.

Food can be dried in either sun or shade, but generally fruit is sun dried and vegetables are protected from direct sunlight (see below). There are many ways to arrange food outdoors so that warm, dry air can reach it. It may be hung on clotheslines, threaded on strings and hung from eaves or under porch roofs, or it may be spread on racks or trays in the sun, or in an airy, shady place. The intense heat on a flat or gently sloping roof, or the reflected heat from a south facing wall, can sometimes be used to advantage. Screened enclosures are often used for protection from animals, and a light cloth cover will protect food from dust. Often it must be covered at night, or taken indoors away from night dampness and dew. When drying outdoors the best method must be worked out according to individual circumstances and the food to be dried.

In humid or cool climates a solar dryer can make the difference between the success and failure of outdoor drying.

***Solar Dryers***   Any enclosure that traps the sun's heat and allows good air circulation can be used as a solar dryer. Generally, achieving air circulation is a greater challenge than collecting heat. Enclosures heat quickly in the sun, as anyone knows who has climbed into a closed car on a sunny day.

Home built solar dryers range from finished cabinets with removable trays to temporary glass or plastic covered structures with sides open for air to circulate. Cold frames can be converted for summer use as solar dryers. They must be propped up so that air enters under the food and exits at the top, above the food. Old cars can be used if openings for air circulation can be made and covered with screen or cloth. Heat can be increased by painting a solar dryer flat black, and arranging a plastic or glass panel so it faces the sun. A thermometer that measures up to 200°F, like an oven or dairy thermometer, is an important aid.

Plans for building solar dryers are available from many sources. Ready-made dryers can also be purchased. (See REFERENCES at the end of this section.)

***Indoor Drying***   Most homes have warm, dry areas suitable for drying food. Attics are usually good places for drying herbs, nuts, and small quantities of grain. For foods that need more attention, the dry heat that radiates from wood burning stoves, furnaces, or appliances, such as refrigerators and hot water heaters, can be used. Do not, however, put food directly in the path of hot air from a furnace because of dust and possible contamination from fumes. In a pinch, food can be dried in a regular oven if the temperature can be set as low as 150°F and the oven door propped open for ventilation. Ovens are too expensive and inefficient to be used often for drying, but they may save a batch of food during rainy weather. Food can be dried in the heat left in the oven or warming oven of a wood or coal burning cookstove after the fire burns out, as long as it is moved when the fire is rebuilt.

The same trays used outdoors or in solar dryers can be hung or propped up over the indoor heat source. If the area is dusty, lay a light cotton cloth over the food.

The most carefree, though not the cheapest, way to dry food is with an electric dryer.

***Electric Dryers***   Home electric dryers are becoming more and more popular. Plans for making them are available from many sources, or they can be purchased ready to use. (See REFERENCES at the end of this section.) Units with built-in thermostats and controlled airflow take the guesswork out of food drying and ensure uniform results. They are, for many people, worth the expense.

## BASIC FOOD DRYING STEPS

• PREPARATION   Harvest food carefully, avoiding washing, if possible. If necessary, rinse quickly. Cut large pieces to a uniform size.

• SPREADING OUT TO DRY   Spread pieces of food in a thin layer on drying trays or racks, or hang or otherwise arrange so that air circulates freely around it. Begin drying as soon as possible after preparation and avoid interruptions in the drying process.

• REARRANGING WHILE DRYING   Stir, turn, or rearrange pieces of food to be sure they dry evenly. Change the position of drying trays if necessary. Check the temperature often, and adjust if required.

• TESTING FOR DRYNESS   When food appears dry, cool a few pieces. Cut or break leathery foods and squeeze. If moisture appears, drying is incomplete. Break hard or brittle pieces to see if they are dry inside. Check the larger pieces particularly. The pieces that dry first can be removed. Do not leave thoroughly dry food in a dryer at higher temperatures. It may scorch.

• OPTIONAL PASTEURIZATION   If contamination by insect eggs is a possibility, pasteurize the dried food by putting it, still spread out, in the oven at 175°F for 10 to 15 minutes according to the size of the food pieces. Another way to destroy insects and eggs is to freeze the dried food at 0°F for 3 to 4 days. Insect infestation is most likely on fruits dried outdoors.

• STORAGE   Cool dried food to room temperature before sealing in airtight containers. See STORING DRIED FOOD, below.

## PREPARATION FOR DRYING

Dried food of high quality results from properly prepared fresh food of high quality. Though preparation varies for different foods, generally small, uniform slices or pieces of food dry faster and better than large chunks. Mechanical slicers, choppers, and graters are helpful to achieve uniformity. (Refer to the KITCHEN UTENSILS section.)

Different sources recommend different predrying treatments for various foods. Most of these treatments are optional, and some are unnecessary where small batches of food can be quickly prepared and set to dry. However, there are other treatments which are very helpful. These are described with their pros and cons in the following pages. For more extensive information see the REFERENCES at the end of this section.

## DRYING FRUIT

(Also refer to the storage information in individual fruit sections elsewhere.)

Most fruits dry easily and well. Their acids and sugars help protect them from spoilage as they dry. Completely ripe or slightly overripe fruit makes the sweetest, most flavorful dried fruit.

Predrying treatments are seldom necessary if small batches of fruit are handled quickly. Anti-oxident and sulphur treatments prevent darkening of the fruit and, in some cases, minimize vitamin loss. Darkening is more likely with sun drying, but it does not affect flavor, so there is no real need to prevent it. If desired, however, darkening can be minimized by dipping the fruit in lemon juice, pineapple juice, or ascorbic acid just before drying. Occasionally blanching or precooking is suggested for fruit, but it is of no particular benefit, except to crack the skins of firm berries. If necessary, however, cooked fruit can be dried successfully.

Sun drying is the traditional method for drying fruit, and the results make delicious snacks. The sun seems to bring out sweetness and flavor, but fruit dried indoors or in the shade is also excellent.

Home dried fruit intended for long storage must be more leathery, or drier, than most commercially dried fruits. The latter are kept moist with preservatives and other controls that are neither available nor desirable for home use. (The extra moisture also means the fruit weighs more for sale by the pound.) Home dried fruit should feel tough, and no moisture should show if a piece is cut and squeezed. Berries and a few other fruits will be hard when dried, rather than leathery.

If fruit is dried quickly and in large pieces, it may need conditioning before it is stored. Conditioning ensures that all the fruit is evenly dried. Put the dried fruit in open containers in a dry, airy place at about room temperature for 10 days to 2 weeks. Stir the fruit every day. It can then be packaged and stored.

**Fruit Leather**  Drying puréed fruit to make a thin, pliable sheet of "leather" is a delicious way to preserve it for snacking. Apricot leather is the best known, but other fruits and fruit mixtures are also excellent.

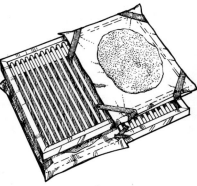

Purée spread on freezer wrap or heavy plastic taped to drying tray, ready for drying.

Leather is usually made from raw fruit, but cooked fruit, such as smooth applesauce, is also very good. Combinations of sweet and tart fruits, and variations that include ground or finely chopped nuts and seeds, are delicious. Honey or other sweetening may be added, as well as such spices as cinnamon or nutmeg. Thin purées, like those from juicy berries, are easier to dry if they are first thickened. One method is to combine chopped raw apple in a blender with the purée. Chia seeds and ground flax seeds are also good thickeners. The very thick pulp left from making fruit juices, particularly apple, can also be use. There are many possible combinations.

**Drying Fruit and Other Purées**  Spread purées in a layer about ¼ inch thick on a non-stick surface. A lightly oiled baking sheet, freezer wrap, or heavy plastic make convenient drying surfaces. Spread the purée as evenly as possible with a table knife or the back of a spoon. If using a dryer with several stacked shelves or trays, cover the right half of one tray, the left half of the next and so on. This allows air to circulate easily around the food. Sun drying is an excellent method for fruit leather.

Rolls of fruit leather ready to be sealed in waxed paper, and closed in a cannister.

Dry fruit purées until the top surface becomes less sticky and the sheet of fruit holds together in one piece. Then turn it over to dry the other side. Dry till leathery and somewhat tough. The sheet should be pliable, but not soft. Some fruit leathers may remain a little sticky even when dried. Purées other than fruit may become too crumbly for turning. These can just be loosened or crumbled and left till they are uniformly dry.

Store fruit leather and other dried purées in airtight containers. (See STORING DRIED FOOD, below.) Fruit leather may stick together when stored, so it is a good idea to put waxed paper between layers. If the leather is to be rolled, lay waxed paper on each sheet and roll them up together.

***Drying Apples, Melons, Pears, Persimmons, Quinces***   Core or remove seeds. Peeling is optional and depends on the toughness of the skins. They tend to become more tough or hard when dried. Slice the fruits about ¼ inch thick and lay on drying trays, preferably one layer deep. Turn slices once or twice during drying. Slices may also be threaded on strings and hung to dry. It may be necessary to use spacers, such as short sections of plastic straws, between slices to keep them from bunching. Another way to dry these fruits is to dice them for use like raisins. Dry till leathery and somewhat tough.

***Drying Stone Fruits***   Stone fruits are usually halved and pitted before drying, and large fruits like peaches must be pitted to dry properly. It is best not to peel stone fruits because skins are thin and tender, and they also hold in juices. Peaches can be rubbed to remove fuzz. Arrange pitted halves on drying trays, cut side up, so that juice collects in the hollows. Turn them when the cut side is dry enough not to stick to the drying tray. Stone fruits may also be cut in wedges or slices, or diced for drying. The smaller pieces dry fastest. Turn them several times during drying, and dry till leathery. Very sweet fruit may be sticky when dry, but it should not be soft inside or show moisture when squeezed.

***Drying Small, Firm Fruits such as Blueberries, Grapes, Rosehips, Cherry Tomatoes***   These fruits when whole have naturally waterproofed skins which slow the drying process. If the skins are cracked (checked), the fruits dry much more quickly, but this is optional. Each berry or fruit can be nicked with a knife, but it is much quicker to blanch them in boiling water to break the skins. (This is sometimes called "checking," because of the fine, often checkered, pattern of the breakage.) Put them in a strainer or colander in small batches and immerse in rapidly boiling water for 15 to 30 seconds, then dunk them in cold water and drain. Spread in a single layer on drying trays. If the fruit might fall through the trays, spread cheesecloth or any thin cotton cloth on the tray first.

Some of these fruits will become hard and others leathery when dry, but there should be no moisture inside when a fruit is broken open.

***Drying Soft Berries***   Soft berries are slow to dry and do not retain their original flavor. They are probably best dried as fruit leather. If dried whole they become hard, and can be ground for the fruit meal, described below, or used for tea. They are not especially good as snacks or cooked fruit.

If possible, avoid washing soft berries. Otherwise, rinse them very quickly. Spread in a single layer on drying trays. (Large strawberries should be cut in half.) Begin drying immediately and do not interrupt the drying process unless they are almost dry, as they spoil easily. Dry till hard, with no moisture showing when broken open.

## USING DRIED FRUIT

Often the kinds of fruit dried at home are less sweet than familiar commercially dried fruits, such as raisins, dates, figs and prunes. Most of the fruit varieties with an extra high sugar content, producing very sweet dried fruit, grow in warm climates. Dried sweet cherries are one of the sweetest dried fruits from a temperate climate. They also make delicious snacks, but some other dried fruits may be too tough or hard to enjoy as is. These fruits can be moisturized for snacking. They are also delightful additions to baked goods, or they can be soaked for a day or two to make "stewed fruit" without any stewing.

***Moisturizing Dried Fruits*** Dried fruit that is too tough or hard to chew can be softened in several ways. In a humid climate, it can simply be taken out of its container and exposed to the air for a few days. In a dry climate, a slice of raw apple can be added to the container. The dried fruit can also be covered with water, drained immediately, and kept in a closed container for a day.

***Fruit Meal*** Fruit that becomes hard when dry, such as rhubarb and most berries, can be ground in a mill or blender. This meal is excellent added to baked goods (refer to the COOKIES section for recipe), sprinkled on cereal or other foods, mixed with the *Granola* recipe in the CEREALS section, or made into herb tea (refer to the HERBS section). A quick jam or sauce can be made by mixing the meal with a little hot water, letting it sit a few minutes, and then mixing in honey to taste.

If dried fruit should accidentally have a browned, faintly scorched flavor because of drying too long at a high temperature, it can often be used as fruit meal. It may also be added to baked goods if chopped small but not ground.

## DRYING VEGETABLES

(Also refer to the storage information in individual vegetable sections elsewhere.)

The quality of most dried vegetables is best when dried away from direct sunlight, as the sun fades them and leaches out flavor. (If using an outdoor dryer designed to expose foods to sunlight shining through glass or plastic, cover the glass or plastic in a way that leaves ventilation holes open. Cloth or wood can be used.)

Small vegetables, or those that have been chopped, grated, or thinly sliced, dry more quickly with better quality than larger chunks. Small pieces are also more convenient because they need less soaking and cooking time. They can be easily added to soups, stews, and sauces. Flaked or powdered vegetables make an almost instant seasoning. The starchier, dried vegetables, such as potatoes, winter squash and mature beans and peas, can be ground and used as flour.

Blanching or cooking is recommended for many vegetables before drying. Raw, unblanched vegetables cut into small pieces dry well, but many lose flavor and vitamins after 6 months or so of storage. Precooked vegetables should retain quality for a year or more. In addition, precooking softens tissues, so vegetables dry faster and need less soaking and cooking time afterward. Vegetables used only for seasoning, such as onions, do not need blanching. With other vegetables, blanching is probably best unless they will be used within a few months.

Although called blanching, the cooking of vegetables before drying is much more complete than the quick blanching required before freezing. Generally, vegetables should be cooked through. Cooked, leftover vegetables can be dried successfully as long as they have not been mixed with butter or oil. Steaming is the best precooking method, because it removes fewer nutrients and is less apt to add unwanted water.

**Drying Root Vegetables, Tubers, Winter Squash**   These solid, non-watery vegetables dry very well. They taste like the fresh vegetable after soaking and cooking. Soaking and cooking times vary according to the size and toughness of the pieces. Large, tough pieces may need to soak an hour or longer, and cook a half hour or longer. Use the same water for soaking and cooking, and save for later use. If grated, finely chopped, or very thinly sliced before drying, vegetables can be added to soups, stews, and sauces without soaking.

Precooking or blanching is optional, but flavor is retained longer in storage if it has been done.

It is often practical to store root vegetables and tubers in the root cellar till midwinter and then, when there is time, dry those that might not be used by spring. If dried root vegetables are left over when a new crop comes in, they can be roasted and ground for a beverage. (Refer to the BEVERAGES section.)

**Drying Onions, Sweet and Hot Peppers, Mushrooms**   These and other vegetables used primarily for seasoning do not need precooking or any other treatment before drying. Chop them small or slice very thinly, so they can be added directly to foods without soaking. If brittle when dried, they can be crushed to flakes as for hot peppers.

**Drying Asparagus, Green Beans, Sweet Corn, Eggplant, Okra, Summer Squash**   For these and most other vegetables, precooking or blanching is optional, but improves the quality; sweet corn must be precooked (refer to the CORN, SWEET section). Thin slicing or chopping of larger pieces will improve their quality.

Before using, these vegetables should be soaked in water to cover till they have swelled to their original size, then simmered till tender.

**Drying Leafy Greens**   (Also refer to DRYING HERBS, in the HERBS section.) Although some greens, especially cabbage and Chinese cabbage, are dried and used in large quantities, drying is not most people's choice for storing greens. Freezing generally preserves their fresh flavor best, but some do well in cold storage and some are good canned. If greens must be dried, their color and flavor are best preserved by first steam blanching. Where necessary, prepare greens by cutting out heavy midribs and stems. Cut large leaves in half. Some greens may be shredded. Put small batches loosely in a steaming basket and steam till wilted, about 5 minutes for tender greens, longer for coarse or thick leaves. Spread on drying trays, with a minimum of overlapping. Most greens will be crumbly when dried.

Reconstitute dried leafy greens by pouring boiling water over them in a saucepan and simmering till tender, usually about 10 minutes.

## USING DRIED VEGETABLES FOR SOUP

Dried vegetables are ideal for making soup. They have been precut to a small size before drying, so no preparation is necessary, except perhaps a few minutes of soaking. Drying intensifies the flavor of most vegetables, improving the soup. A mixture of dried vegetables can be kept handy for quick soups of all kinds. If dried vegetables are ground to a powder, they make an almost instant vegetable broth.

*Dried, Chopped Vegetable Soup Combinations*   Vegetables must be dried separately and mixed after drying. A vegetable combination that is good fresh, such as onion, celery, carrot, and green pepper, is also good dried. Dried herbs, and vegetables such as mushrooms, okra, or tomato can be included to taste.

Dried vegetables in a soup mixture should be about the same size so they cook in the same amount of time. Vegetables which require a long soaking time, such as dried sweet corn, should not be included. They can be soaked separately and added to soup. A soup combination made of vegetables chopped small or grated requires a short cooking time. Add 1 to 2 tablespoons dried vegetables to each cup of cold water, soup stock or other liquid. Heat and simmer about 10 minutes, and the soup is ready.

Some strongly flavored vegetables, such as chopped, dried asparagus, make delicious soups, but are not good in combinations, except with a few vegetables, such as onion or potato.

*Vegetable Soup Powder*   Any dried vegetable soup mixture can be ground to a powder in a blender, grain mill or other grinder, as long as the vegetables have been completely dried till brittle or crumbly. If they are at all pliable, they will gum up the grinder. A few vegetables, such as onions, may be brittle when dried but absorb enough moisture later to become pliable again. These can be dried briefly in a low oven or food dryer just before grinding. Store the powder in an airtight container and try to use within 6 months, as it loses flavor with time.

Mix vegetable soup powder with water or soup stock, heat to a boil, and it is ready. The powder can also be added to hot water or soup stock and simmered briefly.

## DRYING MEAT

Drying large amounts of meat without salt for home storage is uncommon in the modern world, and there are no directions for doing it.

Rather, there are directions for drying meat for snacking and descriptions of old methods, taken mostly from the North American Indians, who used plain dried meat as a staple food. Anyone interested in drying as a means of preserving large quantities would have to learn from experience, taking, of course, basic precautions such as quick, thorough drying, and storage that prevents reabsorption of moisture. One thing is certain—it would be much healthier to depend on plain, dried meat as a staple than on salted meat. (Refer to the SALT CURING section.)

Current guidelines recommend that meat be dried cooked (see DRYING COOKED FOODS, below). Raw meat can be dried safely only if the temperature of the meat at the end of drying reaches 150°F. This is to ensure that bacteria that could cause illness have been killed. It is especially important that the meat be clean, fresh, and from a healthy animal. It must be handled with care, and protected from flies and dirt through all the stages of preparation, drying, and storage.

Only lean meat can be dried. Fat kept at normal temperatures turns rancid unless it has been rendered. (Refer to the LARD section.) American Indians got the nourishment from both by mixing dried lean meat with rendered fat to make PEMMICAN, below. Meats that dry well are lean beef, venison, and other lean game meats, rabbit, and poultry with the skin and all fat removed. Meat such as pork, or beef marbled with fat, cannot be successfully dried.

Meat to be dried must be cut in thin strips of ½ inch thick or less. It is then spread on drying trays or hung, on racks, and dried without delay or interruption. Outdoor air drying should not be attempted unless climatic conditions are perfect: low humidity day and night, clean air, and moderately warm, sunny, windy weather as in the mountainous regions of the western North America. In other climates the meat is likely to spoil before it dries and must be dried in a solar or indoor dryer, or hung on racks over the coals of a campfire, as was done by many American Indians. If a fire is used, it must be cool enough and the meat must be far enough away so it does not cook and drip juice instead of drying. It usually take 6 to 24 hours to dry meat, depending on its density and the drying temperature.

*For safe storage, meat must be very thoroughly dried.* It should look shrivelled and darkened, and the strips should be hard or brittle when cool. They can be broken to check that they are dry throughout. Strips of meat warm from a dryer may be somewhat pliable, but only till they have cooled. *Airtight, moisture-proof packaging is important for storing dried meat. In humid climates this is absolutely essential.* If dried meat should reabsorb moisture from the air, it could spoil or become unsafe to eat. Dried meats can also be stored refrigerated or frozen.

**Jerky** There are a great many versions of jerky, or jerked meat. The name comes from the Spanish *charqui,* describing the strips of dried or cured meat. Jerky can mean plain, unseasoned dried meat, or it can mean meat strips seasoned and then dried, or it can mean salt cured and smoked meat strips. Generally, jerky is eaten as a snack, but it can be cut up and used in stews or other dishes.

Meat for jerking is usually cut with the grain of the meat, not across it, so that the strips hold together while drying. If the meat is to be used for pemmican, it can be cut across the grain.

Following are some ways to season meat for jerky. (For a salted and smoked version, refer to the recipe for *Jim's Smoked Venison,* in the VENISON section.)

**Spiced Jerky**  Flavor meat strips with a sprinkling of salt, using about 1 teaspoon salt to 1 pound of meat. Mix herbs and other seasonings to taste and sprinkle on the meat. Rub or pound lightly to work the seasonings into the meat. Start drying immediately. A good seasoning combination is ¼ teaspoon black or red pepper, 1 tablespoon onion juice, and 1 teaspoon celery seed per pound of meat.

**Soy Sauced Jerky**  Sprinkle meat strips with soy sauce, using about ¼ cup per pound of meat. The soy sauce will give the meat a somewhat smoked taste when dried.

**Wine Marinated Jerky**  Marinate strips of meat in the refrigerator for several days in wine or beer seasoned with pepper, bay leaf, garlic, salt if desired, and other herbs to taste. Other favorite marinades can also be used. Drain the meat and, when it has stopped dripping, spread it out to dry. Drying can be started on a baking sheet, transferring the meat to a rack or drying tray when the surface wetness is gone.

**Brined Jerky**  Soak meat strips in a cool place overnight in brine made with 4½ tablespoons salt to 1 quart of water. In the morning pat the meat dry with cloth or paper towels, and roll it in coarsely ground black pepper. The pepper discourages flies, as well as adding flavor. If the jerky is too peppery for some tastes it can be rinsed before it is eaten. This type of jerky was made most often by early settlers in the dryer regions of western North America. The rich meaty flavor of venison is particularly striking when jerked in this way. It makes a memorable snack.

**Pemmican**  The name is Cree, but many North American Indians made this compact, nourishing, easily carried food.

To make pemmican begin by grinding or pounding unseasoned, dried meat to a powder. If the meat strips are cut across the grain before drying it is easier to pulverize. Mix dried blueberries or other dried berries, or raisins, with the meat powder. Large berries should be crushed, and raisins chopped small. A little maple sugar can also be added. To this mixture, add enough warm, rendered fat to make a stiff dough. Lard or beef tallow, or any good tasting fat, can be used. (Refer to the LARD section for rendering instructions.) Proportions are a matter of taste, but a good ratio is 1 pound of dried meat, 2 cups rendered fat, ½ cup dried berries, and 1 or 2 tablespoons of maple sugar. Shape the pemmican into small loaves and wrap each one in airtight, moisture-proof packaging.

Another way to prepare and package pemmican is to put the dried

*Cutting meat for beef jerky*

Cutting strips with the grain of the meat.

MUSCLE FIBER

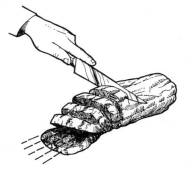

Cutting strips across the grain of the meat.

meat, berry, and sugar mixture in containers, such as small freezer boxes. Pour melted, rendered fat, into each container, slowly enough so the fat can soak in. Add just enough fat to hold the mixture together, but avoid a layer of fat on top. When cool, the containers can be sealed and stored.

## DRYING FISH AND SHELLFISH

It is not possible to dry raw fish or shellfish without salt in home situations. Some very lean kinds of fish are air dried by Alaskan and northwestern Canadian Indians, but the conditions that make it possible do not exist elsewhere. (For drying with salt, refer to SALTING FISH, in the FISH section.) Following is a dried fish snack that uses soy sauce for the salt. Fish meal from cooked fish scraps can be dried for animal feed. (Refer to FISH MEAL, in the FISH section.)

*Soy Sauced Fish*   Cut raw fish in small pieces of about ½ inch thick. Skinless fillets of large fish should be cut in 1 inch squares ½ inch thick. Small fish, such as smelt, can be cleaned, heads removed, and split down the middle. Minnow sized fish need only to be cleaned with heads removed if desired. Small bones can be chewed after drying so there is no need to remove them.

Dip fish pieces in soy sauce or sprinkle them with sauce so they are well coated. Begin drying on a plastic covered drying tray or on a baking sheet. When the surface wetness is gone, remove the plastic. Do not dry in direct sun, as it causes loss of color and flavor. Dry at a temperature below 90°F for the first 2 hours, and then at 200°F until it is finished, to avoid microbial contamination. The fish should become quite hard when dry. Store in an airtight container, in darkness.

These fish pieces have a pleasant, almost smoky, taste and a crunchy or chewy texture.

## DRYING COOKED FOODS

Cooked foods that are low in fat or oil can usually be dried successfully. They must be either in small, uniform pieces, or puréed. Wet or juicy foods must be drained or thickened before drying. Most cooked foods are best dried away from direct sunlight. Among the best for drying are: cooked vegetables and fruit; lean, thinly sliced, cooked meat; and such mixtures as stews and thick soups. Since most cooked foods spoil quickly, drying must be started as soon as they are prepared, and continued with as little interruption as possible till they are completely dry.

Puréed, cooked foods are dried as for fruit leather. In fact, any non-fatty food that can be spread in a thin layer can be dried this way. Try thick bean or pea soup, puréed vegetables, grain that has been sprouted and ground, puréed cooked meat, or puréed cottage cheese. The texture of these purées when dry is usually papery or crisp, rather than leathery. (See DRYING FRUIT AND OTHER PURÉES, above.)

Dried, cooked foods can be reconstituted with water and used like the original food, but some are tasty as dried snacks. Most of these dried foods are convenient and easily carried for camping and hiking trips.

## STORING DRIED FOOD

The key to safe storage of dried food is first making sure the food is completely dried, then protecting it so it cannot reabsorb moisture. Foods dry enough for storage have a characteristic look and feel. Some will be hard or brittle, some crumbly or papery, and some leathery or tough. If in doubt about a food's dryness, continue drying till there is no doubt. If food is dried in large or thick pieces, break open a few to check the inside for moistness. Dried food should be cool when packaged, as it can sweat if enclosed while still warm. If moisture should collect inside storage jars of dried food, open them and spread out the food to dry a while longer. With experience it becomes easier to tell when a food is thoroughly dry.

Where the climate is humid, it is essential to keep dried foods in airtight, moisture-proof containers. Even in dry climates, sealed containers are best to keep out insects and rodents. Jars or cans with tight lids are best. Containers with loose lids can be used if waxed paper is laid over the container's mouth and pressed down with the lid to seal it.

Some dried foods fade and lose flavor when exposed to light, so opaque containers or a dark storage area are recommended. Cool, dry storage areas are best, but most dried foods can tolerate ordinary room temperatures, and good packaging can protect them from high humidity.

Damage is sometimes caused by insects or eggs that get on dried food before it is packaged. If this is a problem, they can be destroyed by pasteurizing the dried food. (See BASIC FOOD DRYING STEPS, earlier in this section.)

Moist or partially dried fruit can be stored in the freezer as a handy snack, but it is more economical to dry the fruit completely, store it in the regular way, and then moisten it for eating. (See MOISTURIZING DRIED FRUITS, earlier in this section.)

Dried foods retain their quality for 6 months to a year or even several years, depending on the food type and its preparation.

## REFERENCES FOR DRYING

DeLong, Deanna, *How To Dry Foods*, 1979, H.P. Books. (A new edition is expected in 1988.)

Hertzberg, Ruth, *Putting Food By,* The Stephen Greene Press, 1982.

MacManiman, Gen, *Dry It, You'll Like It,* 1975, Living Foods Dehydrators, P.O. Box 546, Fall City, Washington, 980024. (This booklet includes plans for building an electric dryer.)

USDA Farmer's Bulletin, No. 984, *Farm and Home Drying of Fruits and Vegetables.*

---

### STORAGE

**Canning**   Remove fatty skin and as much other fat as possible. To can, refer to CHICKEN section.

**Freezing**   Remove loose fat including excess fat in the body cavity. Wrap whole, or cut in sections and wrap. Quality retained 6–9 mos. Refer to FREEZING section.

# DUCK

RAISING DUCKS FOR MEAT AND EGGS CAN BE AS PRACTICAL AS RAISING chickens, if conditions are right. The best egg laying breeds of ducks lay as dependably as chickens, and the meat breeds gain weight quickly for butchering as ducklings. Duck eggs are about half again as large as chicken eggs. They have a somewhat different taste, but can be used in all the same ways. They are excellent for baking and noodle making. (Refer to the EGGS section.)

Duck is a rich and delicious meat, wonderful for special occasions, and at the same time, it is versatile and can be cooked in many different ways. It enriches any dish in which it is used, from hash to spaghetti sauce. The different species and breeds of ducks vary considerably in size, and the meat varies in fattiness and flavor, so adjustments in cooking methods must sometimes be made to suit the individual duck. All ducks, domestic and wild, are good to eat except the mergansers and other fish eaters. (Even these can be eaten in an emergency, but do not invite friends to dinner!)

## HANDLING DUCK

In most respect, ducks are killed and cleaned like chickens (refer to the CHICKEN section). The main difference is in the plucking, but cooking methods also differ because of their greater fattiness and distinctive flavor.

*Plucking Ducks*   Dry picking a duck is tedious work that can be avoided unless the down is to be saved, in which case it must be picked or plucked dry before the feathers are treated in any way. Plain scalding water does not loosen duck feathers as it does chicken feathers, because duck feathers are naturally oiled and water cannot penetrate them. The easiest way to cut the oil is to add detergent to the scalding water. A paraffin coating also works. Some people combine methods, scalding to remove larger feathers and dipping in paraffin to finish the job. Some of the biggest feathers can be plucked before scalding or dipping. As well, wing tips can be cut off at the joint, removing the biggest wing feathers.

To scald with detergent, heat a big pot of water almost to a boil, 180–200°F, and add a few drops of dish washing detergent or shampoo. Swish the duck up and down in the pot to get water into the feathers. After 4 or 5 seconds, try to pull a few feathers to see if they have loosened. If not, continue swishing for a few more seconds. After the duck is plucked it will probably need singeing to remove pin feathers. Rinsing in several changes of cold water will remove traces of detergent as well as chilling the bird.

To make a paraffin dip, melt about 2 pounds of paraffin in a big pot of water. There will be a layer of paraffin floating on top. Heat to about 160°F. If it becomes too hot the paraffin will not stick. Dip the duck in the pot, lift it out, and let the paraffin harden. Repeat once or twice for a complete coating. When the paraffin is set, pull or rub it off. The feathers, pin feathers, and down should come off with it. The paraffin can be reused if it is put back in the hot water till melted again, strained through a sieve, or a piece of old screen to remove feathers, then cooled till the paraffin hardens on top of the water.

This old fashioned method will work with less heavily feathered ducks. Soak the duck in cold water for a few minutes, getting it thoroughly wet. Then roll it in a towel and put it in a pan. Pour boiling water over it and wait three or four minutes. Unwrap, and pluck.

Cut out the oil sac at the base of the tail.

**Oil Sac**  It is especially important when cleaning ducks to cut out the oil sac at the base of the tail. It is prominent and more apt to cause a bad taste than in chickens.

**Duck Feet, Neck, Head, and Giblets**  All of these parts can be used like those of chickens. (Refer to the CHICKEN section.) They make delicious duck soup. The liver is good fried plain, or it can be used like chicken liver. In China, duck feet are dried and used for making soup stock. The Chinese make a specialty of cured duck liver wrapped in a duck's foot and dried. For eating, this is soaked, chopped, and then steamed, usually with pork.

**Duck Fat**  It is well worth collecting and rendering duck fat. (For instructions, refer to the CHICKEN section.) The fatty skin can be cut in pieces and rendered with the fat to make cracklings. (Refer to CRACKLINGS, in the GOOSE section.)

Duck fat is excellent used like lard for frying and baking. It can even be spread on bread instead of butter. If from domestic duck, its flavor is mild and not as distinctive as chicken fat.

**Cooking Methods for Duck**  Domestic duck is a rich, fatty meat, so cooking methods must provide a way to remove excess fat. Most often, ducks are roasted on a rack so fat can drip off, but they can also be broiled or even fried as long as excess fat is poured off. Fat must be skimmed off soups, stews, and pan drippings.

Duck is often roasted without stuffing but, if it is to be stuffed, it should first be roasted for 15 minutes in a very hot, 500°F oven.

Pricking the breast and thighs will help to release the fat. Collected fat can then be poured off. Fruit stuffings are delicious in duck. It is also good cooked with tart fruits, fruit juice, or sauerkraut.

Wild duck can be cooked like other game birds, or like domestic duck, except that the steps for removing excess fat are seldom necessary. Young, wild ducks or dark meated, young, domestic ducks can be served rare after a brief hot roasting. Ducks that weigh 1½ to 2½ pounds after dressing take only 20 to 30 minutes at 500°F. They are done when well browned on the outside. Apples, grapes, or celery can be put inside the duck before roasting to draw out any strong flavors. These are discarded before serving. Very small, wild ducks can be roasted like other small birds. (Refer to the BIRDS, SMALL section.)

## DUCK RECIPES

### Simmered Orange Duck                 (Makes 6–8 servings.)

| | |
|---|---|
| 1 duck (2–4 pounds), cut in serving pieces | 1 tablespoon orange rind, grated |
| 1 onion, chopped | pepper, salt, optional |
| 1 stalk celery, chopped, optional | parsley, chopped, for garnish |
| juice of 2 oranges, or ½–1 cup of juice | |

Rub a large, heavy frying pan with a piece of duck fat or render enough fat in the pan to coat it. Fry the pieces of duck slowly in the pan. When enough fat has collected to prevent sticking, add and lightly brown the onions and celery with the duck. Pour off excess fat. Add the orange juice and rind. Season with pepper and salt, if desired. Cover and simmer over very low heat till the duck is tender, about 1 hour for young duck. If more convenient, this can be transferred to a casserole and cooked in the oven. Add a little water if the duck should dry out during cooking. Sprinkle with parsley before serving. This is delicious with rice or another cooked grain.

### Orange Pheasant, Raccoon, or other Game Birds or Animals
Replace duck with game meat, using butter or other fat for browning the meat. Extend cooking time as necessary.

### Baked Duck with Sauerkraut              (Makes 6–12 servings.)

| | |
|---|---|
| 1 duck (2–5 pounds) (May be young, or for stewing.) | 1 teaspoon grated orange or lemon rind |
| 1 quart sauerkraut, drained | water |
| 1 tablespoon honey | |

Preheat the oven to 450°F. Put the duck, breast down, on a rack over a roasting pan. Roast in the hot oven for 15 minutes. Lower heat to 350°F. Turn the duck breast side up and cook 20 minutes. Pour off the fat that has collected in the pan and remove the rack. Put the duck breast side down in the pan, and arrange the sauerkraut around it. Drip the honey over the sauerkraut and sprinkle with the grated rind. Add about ⅔ cup water. Bake young duck about 45 minutes at 350°F. Bake older, tougher duck till it is tender. Add more water to the pan if necessary. Remove from the oven, stir the sauerkraut, and turn the duck breast side up. Raise the temperature to 450°F, and bake till the skin is browned or about 15 to 20 minutes. The flavors of duck and sauerkraut enrich each other when they are cooked together.

**Small Birds or Goose Parts with Sauerkraut**    Instead of duck, use several small birds (refer to the BIRDS, SMALL section), or the breast, legs, or other parts of a goose. If the birds are lean, the preroasting in a hot oven should be omitted, and slices of bacon can be laid over the birds for the final few minutes of baking. Cooking times should be adjusted to suit the toughness of the meat.

---

**Duck Soup, Chinese Style**      (Makes 8–12 bowls.)

| | |
|---|---|
| 1 small stewing duck, or the feet, necks, gizzards, and hearts from 2 ducks | 6–8 mushrooms, sliced (May be fresh or dried and soaked.) |
| ¼–½ pound chunk of ham | 2–3 slices fresh ginger root, optional |
| ½ cup bamboo shoots, sliced | Chinese cabbage, optional |
| | scallion, minced, for garnish |

Put the duck in a large pot with about 2 quarts of water. Bring to a boil and skim off froth and fat. Add the ham, bamboo shoots, mushrooms, and ginger root. Bring to a boil again and let simmer, covered, till the duck is tender. It can take from 1½ to 3 hours, depending on the toughness of the meat. If Chinese cabbage is used, cut it in 1 inch strips and add during the last half-hour of cooking.

When done, strain off the broth and keep it hot. Slice the ham and the duck meat, or gizzards and hearts. Discard bones and feet. To serve, first put the vegetables in soup bowls. Then arrange slices of ham and duck on them, and fill the bowls with hot broth. Sprinkle with minced scallions.

---

**DUCK IDEAS,** *cont.*

**Sloppy Duck**   Grind raw or cooked duck meat. Sauté seasoning vegetables, such as onion, green pepper, celery, and garlic. Add and cook the duck meat when the vegetables are partly done. Stir often. Add tomato sauce to make a medium-thick mixture. Season and let simmer a few more minutes. Serve on toast or hamburger rolls.

---

**OTHER RECIPES WITH DUCK**

Basic Egg Noodles (with duck eggs), p.430
Duck and Apple or Rhubarb Stew, p.167
Gooseberry Sauce for Meat, p.311
Hot Water Pastry with Poultry Fat, p.386
Kitchen Smoked Chicken or Other Poultry, p.572
Poultry Risotto, p.520
Roast Duckling with Stuffing, p.307

---

---

**Page 238**

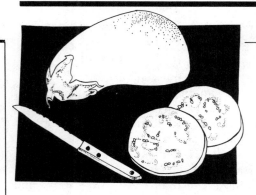

# EGGPLANT

## STORAGE

**Canning** (Not attractive, so best in mixed dishes.) Slice, or cube. Salt lightly, cover with cold water. Soak 45 min., drain. Boil in fresh water 5 min. Drain, pack, add boiling cooking water, 1 in. headroom. Process, 240°F, 11 pounds pressure. Pints: 30 min. Quarts: 40 min. Refer to CANNING section.

**Cold Storage** Harvest before frost. Keep in root cellar or refrigerator up to 2 mo. Refer to COLD STORAGE section.

**Drying** (Quality is good.) Slice ⅛ to ¼ in. thick. Cooking till tender, 5–10 min. in boiling water with 6 tbsp. vinegar or 4 tbsp. lemon juice added per gal. Dry till brittle. Refer to DRYING section.

**Freezing** (Tends to be soggy when thawed.) *Slices or Cubes* Blanch 4 min. in boiling water with ½ c. lemon juice or vinegar added per gal. May separate slices to be used for frying (refer to FREEZING SLICES in FREEZING section). Refer to FREEZING section generally. Also refer to FREEZING in CASSEROLES section.

I POUND = ABOUT 3 CUPS DICED RAW; 2 MEDIUM EGGPLANTS = ABOUT I QUART COOKED

THERE IS A NOVELTY VARIETY OF EGGPLANT WHOSE SMALL CREAMY white fruits look like hen's eggs, but the most familiar varieties look more like purple-black ostrich eggs. In between are many shapes and colors including a long, thin, almost snake-like variety, and another with stripes. In the Mediterranean region, the most popular are small and elongated, like a small zucchini squash. In spite of such variations, all eggplants respond to cooking in much the same ways.

Eggplant is a challenging vegetable. On its own it whets no one's appetite, but in the hands of a good cook it can be transformed into extraordinary dishes, some so renowned as to be legendary. Imam Bayildi is the eggplant dish that made the Imam faint—whether from shock at the cost of the olive oil it soaked up, or from delight at its flavor is not known. Moussaka is claimed by both the Greeks and the Turks, and is enjoyed throughout the Middle East. In France, Ratatouille is a classic vegetable stew, and Caponata and Eggplant Parmigiana are two of many superb eggplant dishes from Italy. Excellent but unheralded eggplant dishes come also from India and the Far East, and from the southern United States. Wherever eggplant is grown, there is a way to make it taste delicious.

Aubergine is the French and British name for eggplant, and some cookbooks use that term.

## HANDLING EGGPLANT

Eggplant can be harvested as soon as its skin becomes glossy. Young eggplants of about ⅓ to ½ their full grown size are especially tender and delicious. If left too long before picking, eggplants become seedy, often tough and bitter as well. Bitterness may also occur if picked before the skins become glossy, or when stunted from poor growing conditions.

Eggplant is not well suited for long-term storage. Although it can be canned, dried, and frozen, it is not as useful after processing as most other vegetables. It loses its special texture and may change flavor slightly. The best ways to preserve it are dried plain, or frozen in such dishes as vegetable stews and casseroles that contain a minimum of oil or fat. It freezes well in tomato mixtures. Otherwise, it is best enjoyed as a summer vegetable, and as late into the fall as it will keep in the refrigerator or root cellar.

Eggplant is virtually always cooked before it is eaten. Cooking methods range from frying through stewing, stuffing, mashing and charcoal broiling whole. If the eggplant is to be sliced or cut before cooking, delay cutting till the last minute to prevent darkening.

***Removing Bitterness from Eggplant***   The ideal approach to bitterness is to avoid it by using only young, freshly harvested eggplants. There are, however, several ways to remove bitterness should it occur. Halves, slices, or cubes of eggplant can be blanched for 3 or 4 minutes in boiling water with a little vinegar added, then patted dry with a towel. (This is similar to preparing it for freezing or drying. Refer to the food storage information above.) Another method is pressing or squeezing out the bitter juices. If very thinly sliced or chopped small, eggplant can be pressed under a plate or a small board weighed down with something heavy, such as a rock or container of nails. Moisture will collect on the pieces in about an hour, and can be removed by patting them dry with a towel. Grated or minced eggplant can be squeezed in a towel like grated cucumber to remove juice. (Refer to the CUCUMBERS section)

For very bitter eggplant, the most effective treatment is sprinkling the cut pieces with salt and draining them for an hour. They can be weighted down for quicker draining. (Salting vegetables is usually an objectionable practice because it causes loss of vitamins and minerals, but as eggplant is poor in these, the loss is minimal.) After draining, rinse the pieces in cool water, squeeze gently, and pat dry with a towel.

These treatments also make eggplant more pliable and cause it to soak up less oil when cooked, often desirable even when no bitterness is present.

## EGGPLANT RECIPES

### Eggplant Shellfish Casserole, Southern Style        (Makes about 6 dinner servings.)

2 medium eggplants, precooked and
   diced
1 large onion, chopped medium
several scallions, chopped medium
1 clove garlic, minced
½ cup parsley, minced
several tablespoons butter, or bacon
   fat for frying
½ teaspoon thyme
salt, optional (Omit if using
   canned shellfish.)

red pepper to taste
2 eggs, slightly beaten
1½ cups bread crumbs, soaked
   in water and squeezed dry
½–1 pound cooked shellfish
   meat (Shrimp, crab,
   crayfish, and clams are all
   good. They may be
   canned.)
¼–½ cup fine bread crumbs
1 tablespoon (about) butter, for
   topping

Sauté the onions, scallions, garlic, and parsley in butter or bacon fat for about 5 minutes, till soft but not brown. Add the eggplant, thyme, pepper, and salt, if desired, and stir to combine. Remove from heat and mix in the eggs and soaked bread crumbs. (If canned shellfish are used, the bread crumbs can be soaked in their liquid.) Fold in the shellfish. Fill a greased casserole with the mixture. Sprinkle top with bread crumbs and dot with butter. Bake at 350°F for about 30 minutes or till set. Eggplant and shellfish seem to have a natural affinity, no matter how they are combined.

*Stuffed Eggplant, Creole Style*   Steam or boil whole eggplants until tender, about 30 minutes. Cut in half lengthwise and hollow out the shells carefully leaving ¼ to ½ inch of flesh. Add the chopped center pulp to the casserole mixture above. Half a chopped sweet pepper can be included with the onions. When the shellfish are added, also add 2 or 3 tablespoons minced or ground ham. Mound the stuffing in the shells and bake as above.

### *Ratatouille* (Makes 6–10 side servings.)

4–6 tablespoons olive oil
2 large onions, chopped
1–3 cloves garlic, crushed or chopped
1 medium eggplant, diced
2 green peppers, cut in thin strips
2–3 small zucchini, sliced, optional
1 head fennel, sliced, optional

½ pound mushrooms, thinly sliced, optional
1 quart tomatoes, canned or fresh chopped
2 teaspoons mixed dried herbs or 1–2 tablespoons fresh herbs, minced (Basil, oregano and parsley are good.)
pepper, salt, optional

Heat 2–3 tablespoons of olive oil in a deep frying pan. Add and sauté the onions and garlic till limp. Add eggplant, green peppers, and optional vegetables. Sauté over low heat for 15 or 20 minutes or till soft but not browned, adding more oil as needed. Add tomatoes, herbs, pepper, and salt, if desired. Cover and simmer about 45 minutes, till it is fairly thick. Cook uncovered for the last few minutes, if necessary, to thicken it. Serve hot or cold.

*Caponata or Eggplant Relish*   Cook as above, omitting green peppers and optional vegetables, and adding instead 2 stalks diced celery. Reduce tomatoes to 2 cups and add with them 2 to 3 tablespoons vinegar and 2 to 3 tablespoons honey or sugar, adjusting for taste as it cooks. Simmer uncovered till it thickens, usually about 20 minutes. Optional additions are several tablespoons each of capers, pine nuts, chopped or halved green olives, and raisins, to be added with the tomatoes.

This make 1 to 2 quarts of relish and will keep 2 weeks or so, refrigerated. For a more piquant relish that keeps longer, increase amounts of vinegar and honey or sugar.

*Summer Garden Stew*   Follow the ratatouille recipe, but add or substitute whatever vegetables the garden is offering, ready to harvest. Green beans, sliced cucumbers, summer squash, and okra are all good. Sweet corn can be cut raw from the cob and added with the tomatoes, without sautéing.

### *Imam Bayildi* (One of many versions.)        (Makes 6 side servings.)

| | |
|---|---|
| 6 small eggplants | 2–3 cloves garlic, crushed |
| salt, optional | ¼ cup parsley, minced |
| Filling: | 4 medium tomatoes, chopped |
|   4 medium onions, thinly sliced | olive oil, to taste |
|   4 tablespoons olive oil | juice of 1 lemon |

To prepare the eggplants for salting and stuffing, cut off the stalks, and peel off lengthwise strips of skin, leaving alternating stripes of flesh and shiny peel. Make one deep lengthwise slit in each eggplant without cutting all the way through, and leaving about half an inch intact on each end. Sprinkle the eggplants with salt and drain in a colander while preparing the filling. (The salting makes them pliable enough for stuffing. Or halve the eggplants lengthwise and hollow them slightly for filling. This avoids salting, but the seasonings will not penetrate as well, and the appearance will be less interesting.)

Sauté the onions in oil till soft but not brown. Add garlic and cook a minute or so longer. Remove from heat and mix in the parsley and tomatoes.

Rinse salt off the eggplants and pat dry with paper or cloth towels. Push the filling into the slits in the eggplants. Lay them side by side in a large pan or pot, and put extra stuffing around them. Pour olive oil and lemon juice over them and add enough water to about cover them. (The amount of olive oil can vary according to taste. They can be covered entirely, or several tablespoons to ½ cup can be used.) Simmer covered over low heat for about an hour, or cook in a slow, 325°F oven. Serve at room temperature. A perfect first course for a meal celebrating a special occasion.

### *Moussaka*
(A middle eastern eggplant casserole.)        (Makes 6–10 dinner servings.)

| | |
|---|---|
| 2 medium eggplants | 1 medium tomato, chopped, |
| oil or butter |   and 2 tablespoons tomato |
| Meat Sauce: |   paste, or 1 cup tomato |
|   1 onion, thinly sliced |   sauce |
|   oil or butter for frying | 3 tablespoons parsley, minced |
|   1 pound ground beef or lamb | White sauce: |
|   pepper, to taste |   2 tablespoons butter |
|   salt, optional |   2 tablespoons flour |
|   ½ teaspoon allspice or cinnamon, |   1 cup milk |
|     optional |   pepper, salt, optional |
| |   1 egg yolk, beaten |

Slice eggplants thinly and press under a weight while making the meat sauce. (If eggplant is very bitter, the slices can be sprinkled

---

### EGGPLANT IDEAS

**Small Eggplant, Roasted Whole**  Select one small, unblemished eggplant per person. Roast the eggplants on a rack in a moderate oven till the stem end feels soft, about 45 minutes. Feel them rather than puncturing to test for doneness. They swell up while roasting, and it is more fun to let everyone do his own puncturing. Have butter or olive oil and lemon wedges on the table when the eggplant is served. Minced parsley and garlic or onion can also be on hand.

**Eggplant Cakes**  Finely mince raw eggplant together with a little onion. Squeeze out as much moisture as possible by hand, or by twisting in clean cloth. The volume will be considerably decreased. Mix eggplant with 1 or 2 lightly beaten eggs and enough flour to hold the mixture together. Season with pepper, and such herbs as parsley or celery leaves. Cook as thin patties in a well oiled frying pan, turning once to brown both sides.

**Mashed Eggplant**  Cook the eggplant whole by steaming, boiling, baking, or charcoal broiling till soft. Instead of broiling over charcoal, the eggplant can be set directly on top of a moderately hot wood burning stove, and turned often, till the skin on all sides is blackened and the inside is soft. Peel, pull, or rub off the skin. Mash the eggplant with a fork, or in a food mill or blender. Season and serve as a side dish, or mix with bread crumbs, egg, and seasonings and fry as patties.

## EGGPLANT IDEAS, *cont.*

**Eggplant Dip**  Mash cooked eggplant as above and beat in a little olive oil, lemon juice, crushed garlic, and salt, to taste. Yogurt can also be included. Serve the dip sprinkled with minced parsley. The flavor is especially good when the eggplant is charcoal broiled or cooked on the stovetop as described above.

This Middle Eastern favorite goes well with flat, Middle Eastern style bread. It is also delicious as a raw vegetable dip.

**Eggplant in Summer Squash Recipes**  Eggplant can be substituted for squash in many summer squash recipes, but it generally takes longer to cook. It can be stuffed as in the recipes in the SQUASH, SUMMER section, but should be precooked before stuffing.

with salt. Refer to REMOVING BITTERNESS FROM EGGPLANT, above.)

*Meat Sauce*  Sauté onions in oil or butter till golden. Add ground meat and sauté till browned. Season with allspice or cinnamon, pepper, and salt, if desired. Add tomato and parsley, and simmer about 15 minutes. If overly dry, add a little water but do not let the mixture become too wet.

Rinse eggplant slices in water and pat dry with a paper or cloth towel, and sauté in butter or oil till slightly browned. Drain on absorbent paper. In a large, deep baking dish, alternate layers of eggplant and meat sauce, starting and ending with eggplant. If desired, these steps can be done a day ahead, and the moussaka refrigerated for completion the next day.

*White Sauce*  Prepare by melting the butter in a saucepan, adding the flour, and stirring to mix completely. Add milk gradually, over low heat, stirring constantly. Simmer about 10 minutes, stirring very often, to thicken the sauce. Season with pepper and salt, if desired. Remove from heat and mix a little of the sauce into the beaten egg yolk. Add to the rest of the sauce, stirring while pouring. Spread the white sauce over the moussaka. Bake uncovered in a moderate, 375°F oven for 45 minutes, or till a brown crust has formed and the layers have cooked together. Cook a few minutes longer if the eggplant was prepared a day ahead and is cold when it goes in the oven.

### Masato's Mother's Japanese Eggplant                    (Makes 6–8 small side servings.)

| | |
|---|---|
| 2–3 small, slender eggplants, or 1 medium eggplant | 2 tablespoons soy sauce |
| | 1½ tablespoons honey, or sugar |
| 4–6 tablespoons vegetable oil | ¼ cup soup stock, or water |

Wash eggplants and pull off stalks. With the fingers, tear the eggplant into shreds lengthwise. Start tearing at the stalk end, through peel and all. By following the natural fibers, make shreds or strips about ½ inch wide and several inches long. The jagged edges soak up flavor especially well and give a special texture.

Heat the oil in a heavy frying pan or wok till quite hot. Stir-fry the eggplant over high heat for 3 to 5 minutes, till limp and lightly browned. It will soak up the oil and look dry, but no more oil is needed unless it is actually sticking. Add soy sauce, honey or sugar, and soup stock or water. These can be mixed ahead of time to be at hand for adding quickly. Cover and simmer over medium low heat till the eggplant is tender, 10 to 15 minutes. Stir once or twice.

This is good served hot with rice, or cold as a snack.

*Gobo, Japanese Style*  Cut gobo (refer to BURDOCK ROOTS in the HERB ROOTS section) into slivers or slices, and cook like eggplant, but use less oil. Slivered gobo will cook a little more quickly than would slices.

### OTHER RECIPES WITH EGGPLANT

Dried Vegetable Stew, p.601
Eggplant Sautéed in Batter (or Parmigiana), p.599
Marinated Eggplant, p.601
Vegetable and Rice Casserole, p.116
Vegetable Pie Casserole, p.116
Vegetable Recipes and Ideas, p.669

AN EGG IS A SINGLE FEMALE REPRODUCTIVE CELL. THIS CELL, WHEN produced by a bird, reptile, or fish, reaches a size so gigantic (for a cell), that it becomes a food in itself. Birds' eggs are eaten most often but, fish eggs or roe, and reptile eggs, especially from turtles and crocodiles, are excellent foods. Primitive man ate any kind of egg he could find, including insect eggs. By comparison, modern egg eating is limited and unadventurous.

The favorite eggs worldwide are, as might be expected, chicken eggs. Duck and goose eggs are next, and then eggs from other domestic fowl. Roe, particularly caviar, is much appreciated. (Refer to the ROE AND MILT section.) Emu and ostrich eggs are valued for food in their native countries, and in turtle recipes, their eggs are often called for. (Refer to the TURTLE section.) Eggs containing partially developed embryos are a specialty food in many Asian countries. They are incubated for about half the normal hatching time, and are usually served boiled.

Eggs deserve to be an important and popular food. They are almost perfect as a source of protein because their amino acid pattern is close to ideal for the human body. Eggs are also rich in vitamins and minerals, though the vitamin content in particular is affected by diet. Chickens that eat greens, bugs, and other natural foods produce eggs with a full, rich flavor and deep yellow-orange yolks, indicating a high vitamin A content. The exceptional quality of such eggs makes small-scale chicken raising very rewarding. Anyone used to eating eggs from chickens with a varied, natural diet will find commercially produced eggs hard to stomach.

***Fertile and Infertile Eggs*** The relative merits of fertile and infertile eggs are often discussed. Fertile eggs are laid by hens kept with a rooster, and are usually home produced. Ordinary store bought eggs are infertile. There is no discernible difference in the eating quality of fertile and infertile eggs when the hens are identically fed and housed. Variation is due more to differences in management between home flocks and commercial egg businesses. Beliefs that fertile eggs are more nutritious, or that infertile eggs keep better, are unfounded. The blood spots occasionally found in eggs do not indicate fertility, as is often thought. Rather, they indicate stress in the hen, and occur more often in commercial, infertile eggs than in eggs from contented, home raised hens. There is a difference in the nuclei of fertile and infertile eggs, which in no way affects eating quality.

## HANDLING EGGS

The goal of most people who keep small flocks is to have fresh eggs year-round. Success is much more likely today than it was a generation ago. There are more available breeds of chickens and ducks that are capable of laying all year, and their feed and management are bet-

---

### STORAGE

**Canning**  See PICKLED EGGS, below.

**Cold Storage**  (Preferred method for about 1–3 mo. storage.) See COLD STORAGE OF EGGS, and WATERGLASSING AND OTHER OLD METHODS FOR PRESERVING EGGS, below.

**Drying**  Though possible, quality tends to be poor because of a brown color caused by the egg's sugar content. Dried egg noodles are an excellent alternative. Refer to the NOODLES section.

**Freezing**  (Excellent for scrambled eggs, omelets, baked goods, and other cooked dishes, but not for using raw.) See FREEZING EGGS, below.

---

### EGG STATISTICS

**Average Weight for**

Bantam eggs = about ⅔ oz. (20 gr.)
Chicken eggs = about 2 oz. (60 gr.)
Duck eggs = about 3 oz. (80 gr.)
Goose eggs = about 8 oz. (200 gr.)
Ostrich eggs = about 3 lbs. (1,500 gr.)

**When Substituting**

3 bantam eggs = 1 chicken egg
1 duck egg = 1 large or 2 small chicken eggs
1 goose egg = 3–4 chicken eggs
1 ostrich egg = 22–25 chicken eggs

**Measurements for Average Chicken Eggs**

5–6 eggs = 1 cup
8–10 egg whites = 1 cup
12–14 egg yolks = 1 cup
2 tablespoons whites + 4 teaspoons yolk = 1 average whole egg

ter understood. With young, healthy hens, good housing and feed, and perhaps artificial light when days are short, there may be no need for egg storage. However, many people will want to store eggs when they are plentiful, in case of scarcity later. Freezing is most common, but simple refrigeration is often practical for several months. For storing without electricity, eggs can be preserved by an old fashioned method (see below). Eggs do not dry well using home processes, because the sugar that turns them brown cannot be removed. Another alternative is to make storable egg preparations, such as noodles, in large quantities. (Refer to the NOODLES section.)

Eggs that have been stored by any method must be cooked for use. They are neither safe nor practical for mayonnaise, eggnog, or desserts that require raw eggs. Stored eggs are best in mixed dishes, but they can also be scrambled. Only very fresh eggs should be stored.

***Checking Egg Freshness***   Home raised eggs sometimes need to be checked for freshness. They may be laid in the wrong place or in hidden nests, or a hen can hold back an egg when she has had a shock, so it is not fresh when it is laid. A simple precaution is to crack each egg separately in a small dish. Spoilage will be obvious in appearance and smell. If the egg is good it is slipped into the pan or bowl where it is wanted. Eggs with cracked or chipped shells should be used only in recipes which will be thoroughly cooked.

Another test is to put eggs in water to see if they float. As eggs get older, they lose moisture and become lighter. Fresh eggs will sink. If an egg floats high in the water it is no good. An egg that hangs suspended, neither sinking nor floating, is probably all right, but crack it in a separate dish to make sure.

The most reliable way to check eggs is to candle them to see what is inside. Candling is done by holding an egg against an egg sized hole in some opaque material, such as cardboard, with a lightbulb (or candle) behind it. This procedure is used when eggs are incubating to check the development of the embryo, so that infertile, dead, or spoiled eggs can be removed. The shells of brown eggs are often too dense to see through till their seventh or eighth day.

***Freezing Eggs***   Eggs cannot be frozen whole because the shells crack and the yolks coagulate. They must be broken, and the separated yolks, or the yolks and whites together, must be mixed with salt or sweetening to prevent coagulation. Egg whites can be frozen separately without additions. The salt or sweetening must be mixed in gently with a fork so that air is not beaten into the eggs. Use the following ratios:

For 1 cup egg yolks or 1 dozen whole eggs
Add ½ teaspoon salt or 1 tablespoon honey or sugar

Whether to add salt or sweetening depends on the way the eggs will be used. Label the packages to show which was added, and adjust recipes accordingly. Freeze the eggs in convenient amounts, because once thawed they spoil rapidly and cannot be kept. For this reason, they must be cooked for use.

It is usually most convenient to freeze eggs in ice cube trays or muffin tins in amounts equalling 1 or 2 eggs. After freezing, the cubes are transferred to plastic bags for storage. If 24 whole eggs are mixed with salt or sweetening, then divided into the twelve cups of a muffin tin, each cup will contain 2 eggs. To loosen frozen egg cubes from a muffin tin, run water over the tin's bottom and catch the cubes as they fall out.

Eggs will thaw in several hours at room temperature, or overnight in the refrigerator. Quality is retained 8 to 12 months. Whites and yolks frozen separately tend to retain quality longer than whole eggs. Four teaspoons yolk and two tablespoons whites equal one average size, whole egg.

***Cold Storage of Eggs*** Fresh eggs with clean, perfect shells will keep in prime condition in cold storage for a month, and will remain usable for several months. With time, however, the whites will become thin and runny, the yolks will break easily, and flavor will deteriorate. The refrigerator and the root cellar are both good storage places. Any area that stays cool without freezing can be used, though a constant temperature near 32°F is best.

Do not wash eggs before storage because this removes their natural protective coating. They can be wiped with a dry cloth. If that does not clean them, do not attempt to keep them long in cold storage. Pack the eggs, small end down, in egg cartons or other packing that will protect them from air currents but still allow some ventilation. When placed small end down, the yolks are less apt to stick to the shell. Protection from air currents slows evaporation of moisture from the egg and minimizes absorption of airborne contaminants and odors. If egg cartons are not available, the eggs can be packed in a dry material, such as oatmeal, bran, sawdust, or fine peat moss. Put several inches of the material in a container, set the eggs into it so they are well separated, and add more dry material to cover them completely. Another layer or two of eggs can be added, but more layers increases the risk of damage. Keep in a cold place. Before using, check each egg by cracking in a separate dish.

***Waterglassing and Other Old Preserving Methods*** The following cold storage methods work by sealing or clogging the pores in the egg's shell so that air is kept out and moisture is kept in. The eggs do lose quality, but they keep for a surprisingly long time, often for six months and sometimes even a year.

One method used to seal eggs was to coat the shells with grease or oil. Vaseline was found to be the best coating, but mineral oil, lard, and other fats and oils were also somewhat successful. Each egg had to be completely coated, then wiped clean before use. Another old approach was to immerse eggs in a protective liquid. Of the liquids used, a waterglass solution was most successful. Slaked limed or salt solutions gave the eggs a bad taste. Waterglassing is the only one of these methods still in use today. It is suggested only as a last resort, and other storage methods that do not require use of a non-food solution are preferred.

Waterglass is the common name for sodium silicate. Drugstores and building supply stores sell it, usually in the form of a syrup that tastes like washing soda. A pure grade should be used because an inferior grade can give eggs a bad taste. To make a waterglass solution for eggs, mix 1 part waterglass with 10 parts water that has been boiled and cooled. Put fresh, clean but unwashed eggs in a crock or food-safe plastic container. Set them small end down as much as possible. Pour the waterglass solution over them, to 2 inches above the top eggs. More eggs and waterglass solution can be added later. Cover the container tightly to prevent evaporation, and store in a cool place.

Eggs to be preserved this way should be only 1 or 2 days old. Much older and they will not keep well. Infertile eggs are recommended, but very fresh, fertile eggs can also be successfully preserved.

When the eggs are wanted, remove them from the solution and wash well. Because of changes in texture and flavor during storage, the eggs are best used in baking and other cooking. The egg whites, with time, lose their viscosity and cannot be beaten stiff, and the yolks break very easily. The shells may become too thin for boiling. If they can be boiled, a hole should be pricked in the rounded end to keep the egg from popping.

## COOKING EGGS

Most people have strong opinions about the way they prefer their eggs cooked. Eggs are liked the way they are liked, and no amount of cookbook advice will change that. However, some general cooking information can be useful.

***Room Temperature***  Eggs at room temperature are better for most cooking than cold eggs. At room temperature, the whites can be beaten stiff more easily and the yolks mix more readily with liquids. Recipes are usually designed with room temperature eggs in mind. Freshly laid eggs need not be refrigerated if used within a few days. If refrigerated, they should be taken out to warm up for a few hours before use in recipes requiring beating and mixing.

***Egg Cooking Temperatures***  Long cooking at high temperatures, especially when frying or baking, makes egg whites tough or rubbery, and indigestible, so eggs should be cooked with low or moderate heat. Baked egg mixtures and egg sauces will have poor textures if the heat is too high. An exception is the quick cooking of a thin sheet of egg at a fairly high temperature, as in EGG THREADS, below, and HERB SCRAMBLED EGGS, in the HERBS section.

***Peeling Hard-Boiled Eggs***  It seems that no cooking problem has generated more solutions than that of peeling hard-boiled eggs. The shells slip easily off some eggs, and must be picked bit by bit from others, or to save time, the egg may be scooped out of the shell with a spoon. Of particular interest to the chicken raiser is the fact that very fresh eggs are especially hard to peel. If possible, use eggs that are over 3 days old for boiling. An almost "sure-peel" cooking method is as follows: Have the eggs at room temperature. Lower them gently into boiling water and simmer about 15 minutes. Drain and shake them in the pot till the shells are cracked. Rinse in cold water and peel. Another method is to poke a pinhole in the air sack (rounded end), of each egg before boiling. This lets a little water seep in between the shell and the egg, making cracking unlikely and peeling easy.

   *Avoid Eating Raw Egg White*   Raw egg white can cause a deficiency in biotin (one of the B vitamins) when eaten regularly. This deficiency can be especially serious in children. Do not make eggnog or desserts using raw egg white except perhaps for special occasions.

## EGG RECIPES

*Baked Eggs Fantastic*                     (Makes 6–8 dinner servings.)

| | |
|---|---|
| 9–10 eggs | black pepper, to taste |
| 1½ cups cooked ham, ground or chopped small | cheese, thinly sliced or grated (Swiss or cheddar are excellent.) |
| ¼ cup green pepper, minced | |
| 1 cup mushrooms, thinly sliced (May be canned or fresh and precooked.) | paprika |

Break 3 of the eggs in a bowl and beat lightly with a fork. Pour half the beaten egg into an ungreased 1 or 1½ quart baking dish. The egg should just cover the bottom of the dish. Add a layer of half the ham, then half the green pepper and half the mushrooms. Sprinkle with pepper. Crack 3 or 4 eggs carefully, without breaking the yolks, and lay them on top of the mushrooms. It is easiest to breach each egg in a small dish, then slide it into place in the baking dish. Cover the eggs with a layer of cheese. Start over again with the rest of the beaten egg and layer the other ingredients, ending with cheese. Sprinkle with paprika. Cover and bake in a very low, 275° to 300°F oven, for about 2 hours or till the eggs are set. When done, a spoon will stand upright in the center of the dish.

   *Baked Eggs with Artichoke Hearts or Asparagus Spears*   Omit the green peppers and mushrooms and use instead about a cup of cooked, thinly sliced artichoke hearts or cooked chopped asparagus spears.

*Egg Pilau*                              (Makes about 6 servings.)

| | |
|---|---|
| 2 cups rice | 6 eggs |
| 4–4½ cups chicken stock, or other light soup stock | 4 tablespoons butter |
| | pepper, salt, optional |

Cook the rice in the soup stock as for the *Plainly Cooked Rice* recipe, in the RICE section. Meanwhile, stir the eggs in a bowl with a fork till mixed. Remove rice from the heat and mix in the butter and eggs. Stir quickly and steadily for a minute or two. The butter will melt and the eggs will cook, making a creamy texture. Season, if desired, and serve immediately without reheating. This dish is deliciously smooth and mild, and goes well with stronger, more distinctively flavored salads and vegetable dishes.

### Scots Eggs (Makes 6 eggs.)

6 eggs, hard-boiled, shelled (Medium or small eggs are easier to handle.)
⅔ cup bread crumbs
⅓ cup milk
½ teaspoon dry mustard
¼ teaspoon cayenne, or other pepper
1 cup lean ham, ground
1 raw egg
fat or oil for deep frying

Warm the bread crumbs in the milk till they can be mashed to a smooth paste with the back of a spoon. Remove from heat and work in the mustard, cayenne, and ham. Add the raw egg and mix well. Divide into 6 equal parts. With clean hands press the ham mixture around each of the hard-boiled eggs to coat completely.

Fry the coated eggs in deep fat or oil till browned on all sides. These are usually eaten cold as a snack. They are very attractive cut in half lengthwise and arranged on a bed of parsley.

**Scots Eggs in Sausage** Make a sausage "crust" by mixing 1 pound sausage meat with ½ cup bread crumbs and 1 raw egg. Omit the other ingredients. Press around the hard-boiled eggs and fry as above. These are delicious hot, with tomato sauce or gravy, or they can be eaten cold.

## Omelets

Omelets can vary from light, fluffy and fragile to hearty one-dish meals. The eggs should always be at room temperature. Below are some interesting and unusual omelets. For more omelet recipes, see the list at the end of this section.

### Korean Omelet (Makes 6–8 slices.)

6 eggs
1 teaspoon soy sauce
pinch sugar
2–3 scallions, minced
1 clove garlic, minced
1 tablespoon fresh ginger root, minced, optional
2 tablespoons sesame seeds or a few drops of sesame oil, optional
several tablespoons ground beef, or cooked, minced shrimp or ham, optional
oil for frying

Beat eggs lightly with a fork till white and yolks are mixed. Stir in soy sauce and sugar.

Heat a large, heavy frying pan, preferably 12 inch. Add enough oil to coat the bottom of the pan. Add the scallions, garlic, ginger root, and sesame. Stir for half a minute over moderately high heat. Add the beef, shrimp, or ham, if used, and fry, stirring constantly, about a minute. Mix the contents of the frying pan into the eggs. Add more oil to the pan, if necessary, and pour in the egg mixture. Tip the pan to spread the egg evenly. Cook over moderate heat without stirring till the egg is set and almost cooked through. The top of the omelet can be baked briefly under the broiler, or the whole omelet can be loosened with a slotted spatula and turned over in the frying pan. The omelet should be quite dry when done.

Turn out the omelet onto a cutting board or other flat surface and let it cool for about a minute. Roll it up as tightly as possible. Turn it seam side down to keep it from unrolling and cut into slices 1 to 2 inches wide. It is usually cooled before it is eaten. Since it is dry, it can be included in bag lunches, or taken on picnics. Korean children sometimes find a slice in their school lunch.

### Friar's Omelet (Makes about 6 moderate servings.)

| | |
|---|---|
| 2 slices bread, cut in cubes | ½ teaspoon dried herbs, or 1 |
| 3–4 tablespoons butter | teaspoon fresh herbs, minced |
| 2 tomatoes, chopped, or 1 cup | (Chives, thyme, basil, or |
| stewed tomatoes | tarragon are good.) |
| 6 eggs | pepper, salt, optional |
| 1 tablespoon parsley, minced | |

Lightly brown the bread cubes in butter in a large omelet or frying pan. Add the tomatoes, and heat to simmering. Meanwhile, lightly beat the eggs with salt if desired, pepper, parsley, and herbs. Pour the eggs into the pan and stir just enough to mix ingredients. Cook over low heat till the eggs are almost set. Fold the omelet in half and serve. If preferred, the omelet can be stirred like scrambled eggs and served without folding.

### The Foolproof Omelet (Makes about 6 moderate servings.)

| | |
|---|---|
| 4 eggs, separated | ¼ cup milk |
| ¾ cup cottage cheese, or other | 3 tablespoons onion, chopped |
| fresh cheese | 1 tablespoon butter |
| ⅛ teaspoon pepper | 2 tablespoons light cooking oil |

Use a blender to mix egg yolks, cottage cheese, pepper, milk, and onion. Blend till the mixture is thick and creamy, and pour into a bowl. Beat the egg whites till stiff and fold them into the yolk mixture. Heat the butter and oil in a large, heavy skillet till moderately hot. Add the egg mixture and cook over low heat till set. Use an insulating ring, if necessary, to keep the heat low after the egg is added, so the bottom does not burn. Brown the top of the omelet under the

## EGG IDEAS, cont.

egg and tilt the pan so it spreads into a thin sheet. Cook till set, which should take less than a minute. Turn out the cooked egg, and add more raw egg. Repeat till all the egg has been used. Cut into thin strips. An easy way to do this is to stack the egg sheets on top of each other, then roll them. Cut across the roll in very narrow slices.

Egg threads can be made ahead of time and stored in a closed container in the refrigerator for a few days.

**Creamed Egg Pie** Prebake a single pastry crust, or line a pie dish with thinly sliced bread. Fill with sliced, hard-boiled eggs and pour a well seasoned cream sauce over all. (Refer to the *Cream Sauce* recipe, in the MILK section.) Minced parsley and onion are good additions to the sauce. Sprinkle with bread crumbs and dots of butter, and bake in a moderate, 350°F oven till lightly browned, about 20 minutes.

**Eggs Poached in Stewed Vegetables** Eggs can be poached in any vegetable that makes a soft bed when cooked. Spinach and other greens, grated summer squash, peas, and many grated or chopped vegetable mixtures are delicious done this way. Stew the vegetables till almost cooked in a wide, shallow saucepan that has a lid. They can be stewed in soup stock, tomato juice, or water, but should not be too wet. Use the back of a spoon to make hollows in the vegetable for the eggs. The vegetable should be boiling gently. Crack each egg into a sauce dish and slide it into a hollow. A bit of butter or bacon fat, and pepper can be added. Cover and simmer till the eggs are set, 5 to 10 minutes. Serve on toast, or with potatoes, or a cooked grain for a quick and attractive lunch or supper dish. (Or try the recipe for *Eggs Nestled in Peas*, in the PEAS section.)

broiler for about 5 minutes. Have ready a warm platter, knife and slotted spatula. Carefully slide the omelet onto the platter and use the warm knife and spatula for serving. This handsome omelet is called foolproof, because it holds its shape well even while lifting and cutting. Its smooth flavor always pleases.

### Pickled Eggs, Two Ways

*1 dozen eggs, hard-boiled and shelled*
*Garlic Pickle:*
    *2 – 3 cups cider vinegar*
    *5 tablespoons honey, or ½ cup*
      *sugar*
    *2 – 3 cloves garlic, crushed*
    *1 ½ teaspoons mixed pickling*
      *spices*
    *½ teaspoon salt, optional*

*Spiced Pickle:*
    *2 – 3 cups vinegar*
    *1 small hot pepper minced, or*
      *1 teaspoon hot red pepper*
      *flakes*
    *10 whole allspice*
    *6 whole cloves*
    *12 coriander seeds*
    *2 bay leaves*
    *1 tablespoon honey, or sugar*
    *½ teaspoon salt, optional*

Put the eggs in hot, sterilized jars that have tight sealing lids. Put the pickling ingredients for either version in a saucepan, heat to a boil, and simmer 5 minutes. The amount of vinegar needed depends on the size of the eggs. Use the full 3 cups for large eggs.

Pour the boiling hot pickling liquid over the eggs in the jars, making sure the eggs are covered completely. The liquid can come almost to the jar rim. Seal the jars, cool, and store in a cool place. These will keep for several months. (Refer to STORING PICKLES, in the PICKLING section.)

**Eggs in Leftover Pickle Juice**   If the liquid left from other pickles has a good flavor, it can be used to pickle hard-boiled eggs. Marinate the eggs in the liquid for a day or two before eating them. These pickled eggs are milder and cannot be kept for long periods, like eggs pickled in straight vinegar. The liquid from the *Pickled Beets* recipe, in the BEETS section, or the *Spiced Pickled Cabbage* recipe, in the CABBAGE section makes a very attractive, pink pickled egg.

M OST SPECIES OF ELDERBERRIES DO NOT TASTE PARTICULARLY good raw, but they improve greatly when cooked. They are truly delectable if dried and then cooked, and are also appreciated for their juice, which is delicious canned, or can be made into jelly and wine. (Refer to the JAM AND JELLY and the WINE sections.)

Elderberry flowers are also edible, and are sometimes called elder blow. Fresh elderflowers can be added to pancakes and muffins, or dipped in batter and fried as fritters. Dried flowers can be used like an herb for tea or for flavoring. Fresh or dried, they are known as a flavoring in vinegar and as an ingredient in homemade cosmetics.

Wild elderberries are common in many places and can be harvested in large quantities. (Refer to the WILD FOODS section.) They are also easily cultivated. This easy availability plus their remarkably high vitamin C content makes elderberries a valuable fruit, well worth including in any family's food supply.

## ELDERBERRY RECIPES

### Dried Elderberry Chutney    (Makes about 4 pints.)

    2 cups cider vinegar
    ½ cup honey
    3 cups dried elderberries
    1 large onion, minced
    1 clove garlic, pressed or minced
    ½ lemon, finely sliced with peel
    1 teaspoon ginger powder, or minced fresh root
    ¼ teaspoon cayenne, or other hot pepper
    1 tablespoon mixed pickling spices

Heat the vinegar, honey, and 1 cup of water to make a syrup. Add the elderberries, onion, garlic, lemon, ginger, and cayenne. Tie the pickling spices in a small square of cheesecloth and add to the pot. Simmer, uncovered, stirring often to prevent sticking, till the mixture has cooked down and thickened. Remove the cheesecloth bag, and pour into hot canning jars. Process 10 minutes in a BOILING WATER BATH, as described in the CANNING section.

**Fresh Elderberry Chutney**   Omit the cup of water and use 2 pounds of fresh instead of dried berries. The elderberries can be mashed before they are added to the pot.

### Elderflower Face Cream
(From "The Farmers Weekly," Countrywise Books, 1966.)

"Melt 1 lb. pure lard in saucepan and add as many handfuls of elderflowers (stripped from stalks) as lard will cover. Simmer gently for about 1 hour. Strain through fine sieve or muslin. Before pouring into small screw-top jars, add a few drops of oil of lavender or other good scent. Use when cold. I make this face cream every year; my

## STORAGE

**Canning**   Caution! Add 2 tablespoons lemon juice or ½ teaspoon citric acid to every quart of juice, sauce, or whole berries before processing to increase acidity. For whole berries refer to BLUEBERRIES section. Also CANNING FRUIT JUICE AND SAUCE in FRUITS section, and Dried Elderberry Chutney, below.

**Drying**   (Excellent. The flavor improves with drying.) Blanch briefly to crack skins (optional). Spread on trays and dry till hard. Refer to DRYING FOODS section. For elder flowers refer to DRYING HERBS in HERBS section.

**Freezing**   Dry-pack plain raw elderberries in containers, or make sauce or juice. Refer to FREEZING section.

## ELDERBERRY IDEAS

**Elderberry and Tart Fruit Combinations**   Elderberries combine exceedingly well with tart, sour, or even astringent fruits. Those maturing around the same time as elderberries (crabapples, sour grapes, wild plums) are ideal, but rhubarb or cranberries that have been canned, frozen, or dried are also excellent. The proportions can be half and half, or to taste. Try making juice, jam and jelly, and pie. (Refer to COMBINING SWEET AND TART FRUITS, in the FRUITS section.)

**Elderberry Rob**   Spiced elderberry juice, or rob, is both healthful and delicious. Heat elderberry juice with honey to taste, a stick of cinnamon, and a few cloves. Allspice, nutmeg, and mace can also be added. Add lemon juice or vinegar to taste, or one of the above tart fruit juice combinations.

This makes a soothing, vitamin C-packed hot drink for people with colds, and can also be diluted for a cool drink.

grandmother—and no doubt many other people's grandmothers—used it lavishly, for they found it unfailingly good." *Miss A. Williams, Cardiganshire*

Other versions say to add a few drops of turpentine instead of lavender, or to use vaseline or cocoa butter instead of lard.

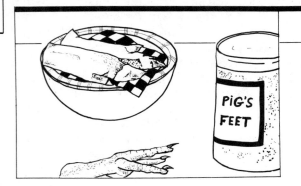

# FEET

THE FEET OF HOOFED ANIMALS AND POULTRY ARE ALL TOO OFTEN overlooked as food. Since feet are the best animal parts for making jelled soup stock, the waste is unfortunate. Calves' feet are the most often listed in old cookbooks for making gelatine or soup, but the feet of cows, bulls, lambs, sheep, goats, and deer can all be used. As a dish, pigs' feet are eaten the most frequently. They are meaty and are excellent in fancy stews as well as pickled. The feet of the different hoofed animals are interchangeable in recipes, as long as allowance is made for the size differences. Cows' and calves' feet are sometimes called "heels," and pigs' and sheep's feet are often called "trotters," especially in England. The feet of chickens, ducks, and other poultry can be used for making soup. (Refer to the CHICKEN and DUCK sections.)

it is not common and not often practical, but it is possible to use the feet of all edible animals. In the past, in the Yukon, even beaver and bear paws were pickled in much the same way as pigs' feet.

## CLEANING AND PREPARING
## THE FEET OF HOOFED ANIMALS

Cut off the animal's feet at the first joint above the hoof, or saw to a convenient size. In some animals, the bone to the first joint is too long for cooking pots, so sawing is necessary.

There are several ways to clean hooves and remove hair. With large or mature animals, except pigs, the hide is usually skinned and the outer layer, or shell, of the hoof is removed. The hooves must be boiled for about 15 minutes to loosen the outer shell. It can then be peeled or pulled off. The leg section can be skinned before or after boiling. Discard the boiling water. To finish cleaning the feet, cut them in half lengthwise, starting between the toes. Remove any dirt or bits of hide. If there is a gland between the toes, cut it out. Rinse well, and the feet are ready for use. An alternate cleaning method (used mainly for young animals) is to shave the hair from the legs, then clean the skin and hooves with vinegar. Bring them to a boil in plenty of water, drain and rinse, and they are ready to be cooked in fresh water.

The hide is almost always left on pigs' and baby lambs' feet. Pigs' feet are cleaned when the whole pig is scalded and scraped. As soon as the pig is taken from the scalding water, the toenails and dew claws are pulled off, and the leg hair is twisted off, using a tight grip with both hands. (Refer to the PORK section.) The hair on lambs' feet should be pulled or plucked. If necessary, they can be scalded to loosen hair. They are then singed like chickens to burn off stray hairs. (Refer to the CHICKEN section.) Kids' feet can be handled like lambs' feet or like those of larger animals.

Feet are usually cooked by simmering in water or other liquid for several hours, or till the bones pull out easily. The tender, gelatinous meat and cartilage can be eaten. The cooking liquid will set into a firm gelatine when cooled. (Refer to the GELATINE section.)

## FEET RECIPES

### *Pickled Pig's Feet, Soul Food Style*   (Makes about 6 dinner servings.)

| | |
|---|---|
| 4 pig's feet, cleaned and cut in half lengthwise | ½ pound mushrooms, sliced if large, optional |
| 2 cups cider vinegar | 1 tablespoon dried rosemary |
| 3 12 oz. bottles of beer | 1–2 cloves garlic, crushed |
| 2 onions, halved | 2–3 slices lemon with peel |
| 1½ cups celery, coarsely chopped | pepper, salt, optional |

Use a Dutch oven or other heavy pot with a tight lid. Put the pig's feet in the pot and add the vinegar, beer, onions, celery, mushrooms, rosemary, garlic, and lemon. Bring to a rapid boil, then cover and reduce heat. Simmer for 2 hours, or till the meat is tender but not mushy. After 1 hour season with pepper and salt, if desired. When done, there should be about an inch of liquid left in the pot.

These can be served hot with the vegetables and juice, or the juice can be strained to remove vegetables and poured over the pig's feet, then chilled for a jelled dish. An especially flavorful version of this familiar food.

**Barbecued Pig's Feet**   Pickle the pig's feet as above. Remove from the liquid to a shallow baking dish. Pour barbecue sauce made as follows over them, and bake 30 minutes in a moderate oven.

To make the sauce, combine in a saucepan 1 quart tomato purée, 3 tablespoons minced onion, 2 tablespoons honey or brown sugar, ¼ teaspoon pepper and 2 tablespoons Worcestershire or soy sauce. Simmer 45 minutes, uncovered, to blend flavors and thicken.

**Pickled Pig's Ears and Tail**   Scrape and wash pig's ears and tail and pickle as for feet. The ears can be cut in half or in strips. If 4 feet, 2 ears, and a tail are to be pickled together, increase pickling ingredients by half (3 cups vinegar, 4½ bottles of beer, and so on).

### Feet Aspic, Polish Style
(Makes 6–12 side servings.)

| | |
|---|---|
| 4 calf's feet, or another hoofed animal's feet (Use 6–8 feet if small.) | 1 leek, chopped |
| | 1 bay leaf |
| | 10 peppercorns |
| 2–4 pig's feet | dash each of marjoram, thyme, and nutmeg |
| 2 onions, chopped | |
| 2–3 carrots, diced | pepper, salt, optional |
| 1 parsley root, diced, or a bunch parsley, chopped | 2 egg whites and shells, crushed, optional |
| ½ celeriac, diced, or several stalks celery, chopped | lemon slices, optional |

Put the calf's and pig's feet in a large pot. Add the onions, carrots, parsley root, celeriac, leek, bay leaf, peppercorns, marjoram, thyme, and nutmeg. Add water to come about an inch above all ingredients. Bring to a boil and skim off froth. Cover and simmer 3 to 4 hours, or till the meat has fallen off the bones. Season with pepper and salt, if desired.

Strain the stock, removing any fat on it, and clear it if desired. (It tastes as good uncleared but does not look as appealing.) To clear, add the egg whites and shells, bring to a boil without stirring and let sit a few minutes. Remove the material that rises to the top and strain through cloth. Set aside.

Remove bones, and dice the meat and soft gelatinous cartilage. Lay this in a mold large enough to hold it with a little room to spare. The cooked, diced vegetables can also be added. Pour the stock into the mold and chill till set. Unmold and serve with lemon slices, or with olive oil and vinegar.

## STORAGE

**Canning**  Select firm but ripe fruit. Do not peel or remove stems. Pour boiling water over, simmer 5 min. *Caution!* Lemon juice or citric acid must be added when processed in a boiling water bath. Drain, pack, add 1 tablespoon lemon juice per pint; 2 tablespoons per quart. If using citric acid, add ½ teaspoon per

# FIGS

FIGS WERE ONE OF THE FIRST CULTIVATED TREE FRUITS. THEY WERE grown in the Mediterranean area in ancient times, and were important in the lives and mythology of the early Greeks and Romans. In the story of the founding of Rome, a fig tree overshadowed the wolf's cave where the twins, Romulus and Remus, were raised. The tree symbolized the future prosperity of the race.

In North America, figs are grown commercially in California and Texas, and in home gardens in most of the southern United States. If given special care and protection, they will grow in regions with moderately cold winters. Fresh, tree ripened figs are delicious, but as they do not keep well people who live outside their growing area can seldom enjoy them. Dried figs, however, are available and appreciated everywhere. Where figs are called for in recipes, dried figs are almost always what is meant.

Figs have a reputation as an herbal medicine. When fresh, they can be made into a poultice for boils and infections. They are also taken for insomnia, and as a laxative. The sap of unripe figs will curdle milk, so it is sometimes listed as a vegetable rennet for making cheese.

## HANDLING FIGS

The time for havesting figs depends on the variety and the intended use. Some varieties bear fruit twice a year. Figs grown in a marginally cool climate must be harvested before they are completely ripe because they sour if left on the tree. Figs for drying are often left to fall off the tree by themselves.

Figs can be canned or frozen, and are delicious pickled, or in jams and preserves, but drying is the primary preservation and storage method.

***Drying Figs***   Figs from the family tree in a marginal growing area should be picked when ripe, and dried like any other fruit. Small figs can be dried whole, but large one should be cut in half and dried like peach halves. (Refer to the DRYING section.) Whole figs can be blanched in boiling water for 30 to 45 seconds before drying to crack the skin and make them dry faster.

In warm, dry areas where figs are abundant, they are left on the tree till they are partially dry and fall to the ground. The ground is mowed or cleared ahead of time for easy gathering. They must be gathered every 2 or 3 days to prevent molding and insect infestation. Commercial figs are often sulfured or fumigated at this point, but such questionable treatments can be omitted by the home grower.

The partially dried figs are spread on racks or trays to finish drying. In some Mediterranean regions they are spread on a bed of rushes. Drying in the shade is recommended for some varieties, because the sun will toughen the skin. Figs are dried till firm and leathery, and no juice should show when they are squeezed. Keep dried figs in airtight packaging, like any other dried fruits.

In Lebanon, anise seed is used to ward off insects. After drying, each fig is individually dipped in a pan of boiling water containing a spoonful of anise seed. The figs are then spread out and redried before packaging.

**FIG IDEAS**

**Dried Figs in Fruit Juice**   Soak dried figs in orange, apple, or other fruit juice for several hours, or overnight. Serve like stewed fruit. A quicker method is to soak for a few minutes, then simmer over low heat till tender. For stuffed figs, drain the soaked figs, make a slit in each, and stuff with nutmeats. Roll in coconut or finely chopped nuts. Serve the rich soaking juice as a beverage.

**Fig Ice Cream**   Mash fresh figs and use in the *Fruit 'n Yogurt Ice Cream* recipe in the ICE CREAM section. Dried figs soaked as above also make delicious ice cream.

**FIG IDEAS,** *cont.*

For a fig parfait, chop or slice fresh figs and arrange in layers in a mold or dish, with sweetened whipped cream. Sherry, rum, or another liquor can be sprinkled over the figs or added to the whipped cream for flavoring. Freeze till solid and unmold for serving. Instead of whipped cream, softened vanilla ice cream can be used, then refrozen.

**Dried Figs in Baked Goods**
Chop dried figs, or cut them in pieces with scissors. Use in bread, muffins, and cookies instead of raisins.

**A Figgy Pudding**   Use chopped, dried figs in any steamed pudding. (Refer to the recipes in the STEAM COOKING section.) Try chopped, fresh figs instead of blackberries in the pudding recipe in the BLACK-BERRIES section.

---

**OTHER RECIPES
WITH FIGS**

## FIG RECIPES

*Fig Squares*                    (Makes about 3 dozen small squares.)

Filling:
2 cups dried figs, chopped
1 cup boiling water
rind of 1 lemon, grated, optional
¼ cup nuts, finely chopped,
    optional

Dough:
½ cup shortening or butter,
    softened
1 egg
¼ cup honey or sugar,
    optional
1 cup whole wheat flour
1 teaspoon baking powder
2 cups rolled oats

To make the filling, put figs in a saucepan and add the boiling water. Simmer uncovered, stirring often, till soft and jam-like, about 1 hour. Add more water if necessary. Add the lemon rind and nuts, and let cool while mixing dough.

Combine the shortening, egg, and sweetening. Sift together the flour and baking powder, and add with the rolled oats to make a stiff dough. Press half the dough in a shallow, ungreased baking pan. Spread the fig filling over it as evenly as possible. Spread the rest of the dough on top and pat smooth. Bake at 350°F for 30 minutes. Cut in squares while hot and let cool in the pan.

*Fig Bars*   Prepared fig filling as above. Make a plain cookie dough that can be rolled out. (The *Coasting Cookies* recipe in the COOKIES section can be used, omitting the spices.) Roll out the dough to ¼ inch or less, and cut into 3 inch squares. Put a small spoonful of fig filling on one side of each square. Fold the dough and pinch the edges together into a rectangular bar. Bake in a moderate, 350°F oven for 20 minutes or till browned.

*Dried Fruit Squares or Bars*   Use any dried fruit instead of figs to make the above filling. If dates are used, omit sweetening in the dough. Other dried fruits, such as peaches, pears or apricots, may need sweetening and extra water.

---

# FISH

FISH ARE THE SUBJECTS OF TALL TALES, FAIRY TALES, MYTHS, legends, and works of art. They also are, and have been through the ages, a primary protein food for people living in coastal areas. Though people living inland do not generally depend on fish as a staple, they, too, should enjoy it as often as possible, as it is an exceptionally healthful and delicious food. Anyone interested in food self-sufficiency, whether living inland or on the coast, will want to take full advantage of the locally available fish.

Fish culture (raising fish in small pools or ponds) is becoming both more popular and practical. As techniques continue to improve, fish are likely to become a standard homestead crop. Meanwhile, most of our food fish are still "wild." There are waterways nearly everywhere with edible fish in them, and most families have members who like to go fishing. Taking full advantage of fish caught for fun can bring considerable valuable food into a household.

Often, the most common, easy-to-catch fishes are ignored for food, because they are considered too hard to clean, too bony, or too troublesome in some other way. With practice and perhaps a new idea or two, most such problems can be overcome. Not only can most species be eaten they can be made to taste delicious as well. Before any fish are eaten, however, make sure they come from clean, unpolluted waters. Local fish and wildlife services can usually provide this information.

There are thousands of species of fish with many more localized variations, and the same species from different environments can taste quite different. Flavors change because of climate, the fishes' foods, the water they swim in. It is well worth experimenting to find the best ways to use common local varieties.

### STORAGE

**Canning** Procedures differ for different species. Refer to CANNING FISH, SHELLFISH AND ROE, and REFERENCES in CANNING section.

**Cold Storage** See BRINE CURING FISH and PICKLING FISH, below.

**Drying** Refer to DRYING FISH AND SHELLFISH, in DRYING FOODS section.

**Freezing** (The preferred home storage method.) See FREEZING FISH, below.

**Salt Curing** (Quite practical for home storage.) See SALTING FISH, below.

## HANDLING FISH

The one rule applying to all fish is that they be cared for immediately after they are caught. The absolute best tasting fish are caught, cleaned, cooked, and eaten within the hour, but such perfection is seldom possible. If instead, the fish are kept damp and cool after they are caught, and then cleaned and eaten, or refrigerated or otherwise stored without delay, they will be very good. They should be kept in the water at the fishing spot, or covered with something damp and kept shaded. It is best to clean fish when they are caught, but many people wait till they get home to do this job. While the taste of some varieties does not seem to be much affected by delayed cleaning, others are noticeably better if cleaned immediately. If uncleaned fish must be kept overnight, wrap them in a damp towel, put them in a plastic bag, and refrigerate them.

Fish caught from cool water in the spring, fall, and winter often taste better than fish caught from warm water in summer. This is probably at least partly due to the difficulty of cleaning and chilling fish quickly enough in warm weather to prevent the breakdown of flavor and texture that precedes spoilage. Extra diligence in caring for fish is necessary during the summer.

The ideal place to clean fish is outdoors, where fish scales can fly and a little mess will not matter. If there is a stream or running water nearby for rinsing the fish, all the better. The first step for cleaning most fish is scaling, though some fish will need skinning, while still others need neither.

It is always helpful to watch an experienced person clean a particular kind of fish, as there are often special tricks to be learned. Some basic procedures follow.

***Scaling Fish***   Fish must be damp when they are scaled, as dry scales will not come off. If a fish has dried out it can be soaked in water a few minutes before scaling, though it is best to keep it damp all along.

*Using a fish scaler*

Use the dull side of a knife, a saw toothed knife, or a fish scaler to scrape off the scales. A fish scaler is a small hand tool with little teeth that pick up the scales easily. If fish are to be scaled regularly it is worth getting one. Hold the scaler vertically against the fish, at a slight angle, not directly crosswise to the fish. Scrape starting from the tail and move towards the head. Once the scales have started to lift and come loose a few strokes will take off most of them on one side. A little extra attention close to the head and fins, and the fish can be turned over to scale the other side.

With a little practice scaling can be done very quickly. It takes longer to describe it than to do it.

***Removing Entrails and Trimming Fish***   To remove the fish's entrails, cut open the belly from vent to head. Clean out everything, including the red, kidney-like material along the backbone. If there are eggs set them aside for use. The male glands (milt) can also be saved. (Refer to the ROE AND MILT section.) The entrails can be fed to chickens or other animals, or they can be buried in the compost pile or garden. If the head is to be left on the fish, pull out the gills.

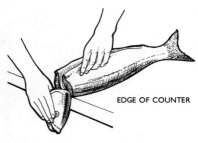

EDGE OF COUNTER

*Snapping a fish's backbone to remove the head.*

Whether to cut off the head, tail, and fins will depend on the kind of fish and the way it is to be used. Whole fish with head and tail on are very nice for steaming or baking. They seem to hold their flavor better if they are not cut apart, and there is a delicate morsel of meat in the cheek to be enjoyed. However, limited space in the pan or freezer may make it necessary to cut off heads and tails. When cutting off the head follow the line of the gills instead of cutting straight across, so as to lose less meat. For a bigger fish with a backbone that cannot be cut through, cut along the gills on both sides of the head up to the backbone. Hold the fish on its back, with the head over the edge of a counter or cutting board, and break the backbone by snapping the head downward.

Save the heads, tails, fins, and bones for making soup stock. (Refer to FISH AND SHELLFISH STOCK, in the SOUP section.) The Chinese dry shark's fins for later use in soups.

*Fish with head, tail, and fins removed*

***Removing Fins***   It is not always necessary to remove the fins. Do not bother with them if they are soft and not too noticeable, or if the fish is to be filleted. Remove the prominent, spiny fins along the center of the back and on the belly between the vent and the tail, including the bones that extend from the fin into the meat. There will be about as much bone going into the fish as there is on the outside in the fins. Never cut fins off next to the body because this will leave a loose row of sharp bones. Instead, use a thin bladed sharp knife to cut a slit on each side of the fin, then pull it out taking all of the bones. If the fin does not pull out fairly easily, the cuts may have to be made deeper. The paired fins on the belly between the head and vent are often cut away when the entrails are removed, and the paired fins next to the gills are usually cut off with the head.

***Skinning Fish*** Fish with tough skins and no scales, like catfish and eels, are best skinned. As exception would be eels for smoking, but even their skins are peeled off and discarded when the meat is eaten. Fish with scales may also be skinned, and the skin can usually be pulled off easily without special methods.

The kinds of fish that must be skinned often stay alive a long time out of water, and must be killed to avoid "skinning them alive." Stab catfish or bullheads in the head with a sharp knife to kill them, or kill them with a well placed blow to the head, using a hammer or heavy stick. Though eels are sometimes put in a container of salt to deslime and kill them, it is faster to stun or kill them with a blow to the head.

Skinning a tough skinned fish is basically a matter of anchoring the head firmly in one spot, cutting through the skin around the neck and pulling it off. Ways to hold the head immobile include nailing it to a board, putting a noose around its neck and hanging it, or, if the fish is small, holding the head in one hand and pulling off the skin with pliers.

After skinning remove the entrails, pull out the fins, and cut off head and tail. Usually the skin of these kinds of fish is discarded with the entrails because it is too oily or strong flavored for soup stock.

***Cutting Fish Fillets and Steaks*** Usually one fillet is cut from each side of a fish after it has been scaled or skinned and cleaned. A fish with special characteristics, such as a peculiar shape may have to be handled differently.

To cut regular fillets use a sharp, thin bladed knife such as a boning knife. Make a cut along one side of the backbone from the head to the tail, cutting down to and along the rib cage. Then lift the fillet enough to slice the meat away from the rib cage. If a fish is small and there is very little meat over the ribs, cut the fillet off where the ribs begin. Then turn the fish over, and cut the fillet from the other side. Tender skin can be left on fillets. However, to skin it, hold the fillet skin side down on a cutting board while cutting between the meat and the skin. The leftover bones make excellent soup stock.

Large fish are often cut crosswise into inch thick steaks, with the skin left on to hold he meat together. Long narrow fish whose shape does not lend itself to filleting can be cut crosswise into 2 or 3 inch chunks.

***Fish Liver*** The livers of large fish can be used, but they can only be eaten in small quantities and not more often than once a week, because the levels of vitamins A and D in them can be toxic. It is be-

*Skinning a catfish*

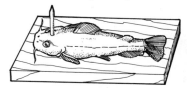

Impale a catfish on a big nail driven through a board with the sharp end sticking up several inches. Cut the skin around the neck and pull it off.

*Skinning a bullhead*

A small bullhead held to avoid poisonous spines. Cut a "T" across the neck and down one side of the back fin to make two flaps of skin for pulling with pliers. When most of the skin is off, pull out the back fin with the pliers. Turn the fish over to finish skinning, cleaning, and trimming.

*Skinning an eel*

Hang eel. Make a cut through the skin around the neck, about 3″ below the head. This avoids the gall bladder which is near the head, just below the skin's surface. Pull the skin off in one piece.

cause of these levels that fish liver oil is used as an A and D vitamin supplement.

One way to use fish livers is for a paté. (Refer to the *Liver Paté* recipe, in the SAUSAGE section.) In Scotland a "muggie" or fish's stomach is stuffed with a fish liver and oatmeal mixture to make a "hagga muggie," something like the *Haggis* recipe, in the LAMB AND MUTTON section. Sometimes cleaned fish heads are used as casings for the liver stuffing instead of the stomachs.

***Fish Meal for Animal Feed***   Parts of fish that might otherwise be wasted can be made into meal to use as a food supplement for dogs or chickens. The following instructions come from THE SMALL-HOLDER, a Canadian country people's newsletter.

"When we clean fish only the guts go into the compost. We keep the fillets for our use and the heads either for fish soup or baked for the dog. The back bones with all of the meat left on after filleting, fins and tails are baked in the oven until done (meat parts flaky). They are then removed to fresh pans and dried for a couple of days, turning the pieces over at least once a day. Then the whole works are ground up in a food chopper into a fairly fine meal. The meal is set in shallow pans (cake tins) in a warm place until thoroughly dried. It is stored in airtight jars." (Refer to DRYING FOODS section.)

## FREEZING FISH

Freezing is the best way to preserve fish, and quality will be excellent, especially for lean fish, if it is well packaged. Fish is quite subject to drying and freezer burn if not well protected. Always clean and trim fish ready for cooking before freezing it. Fatty fish will retain full quality for about 3 months, and lean fish for 6 months or longer.

There are several good ways to package fish for the freezer. Whole fish, both large and small, steaks, and large chunks or roasts of fish can be covered with water and frozen solid. Put enough small fish for a meal in a container suitable for freezing and cover with water, leaving some headroom. Large fish can be fitted into clean milk cartons and covered with water. Or, if containers are not available, fish can be covered with water in a bread pan, then removed from the pan after it is frozen solid and wrapped well for the freezer. Another way to store a large fish is to glaze it with ice. First the fish is frozen solid. Then it is dipped in cold water and returned to the freezer until a thin coating of ice forms. It is then dipped and frozen several more times to thicken the coating. The ice must be thick enough to withstand handling. It must then be wrapped well for storage. Fish that were frozen in a block of ice should be thawed in a strainer over the sink, or over another container to prevent soaking in water while they thaw. As fish do not keep well after thawing they should be cooked right away.

Frozen fish fillets and steaks seem to retain their flavor and texture best when they have been dipped in lemon juice or an ascorbic acid solution. Use undiluted lemon juice, or make a solution of 2 teaspoons crystalline ascorbic acid per quart cold water. Double wrap the dipped fillets or steaks. Individual slices can be separated with freezer wrap or waxed paper. Very thin fillets and steaks can be cooked without thawing if 2 to 5 minutes is added to the cooking time.

Precooked fish and prepared fish dishes can also be frozen. (Refer to the FREEZING section.)

## SALTING FISH

Fish spoils very quickly. If it cannot either be eaten, refrigerated or frozen very soon after it is caught, salting is an excellent alternative. It is the traditional method for preserving fish. Some nutrients are lost as in any salting procedure, but the protein is still there and the flavor is good. A light salting right after catching and cleaning will preserve fish for 24 hours or longer without refrigeration, while a complete salt curing will preserve them for long-term storage.

## BLAWN FISH (WINDBLOWN FISH)

### A traditional Scottish Method

"Obtain the fish—whiting, haddock or other white fish—as fresh as possible, clean and skin them, take out the eyes, cover the fish over with salt, immediately after which take them out and shake off the superfluous salt, pass a string through the eye-holes, and hang them up to dry in a passage, or some place where there is a current of air; the next morning take them off, just roll them lightly in a little flour, broil them gently over a slow fire, and serve hot, with a small piece of fresh butter rubbed over each, or serve quite dry if preferable." Marian McNeill, *The Scot's Kitchen*, Mayflower Books Ltd., England, 1974.

*Lightly Salting Fish for Temporary Storage* As soon as the fish are caught, scale, clean, and rinse them. Remove the gills but leave on the heads, tails, and fins. Rub the insides of the fish with plain or pickling salt and sprinkle over the outsides, about 4 teaspoons of salt per pound of fish. If the flavor is appreciated, a little pepper can be mixed with the salt before it is rubbed in. To keep unrefrigerated for up to 24 hours, pack the salted fish in a container in green leaves, or cover them with something damp. Damp burlap can be laid over the container as long as it does not touch the fish. Keep in the coolest place possible. The catch from an extended fishing trip can be handled in this way. Be sure to rinse the fish well before cooking or freezing them, to prevent excessive saltiness.

Fish will keep up to 10 days if rolled in salt till coated inside and out, and then packed in a container, but they must be soaked for a day in the refrigerator or other cold place in several changes of fresh water to remove excess salt before they are cooked. Packing in salt can be a preliminary step to pickling or smoking the fish. (See below, in this section.)

***Salt Curing Fish for Long Storage***    There are two methods of salting fish for long storage: dry salting and brine curing. Dry salted fish, especiall if fatty, keep longer than brine cured ones. Dry salting is also more dependable in warm climates since brined fish are wet and therefore more susceptible to spoilage if temperatures are too high during the cure, or when stored. Fish are cleaned in the same way for either method. Scale or skin as necessary, and clean out all trace of entrails and gills. When removing heads, leave collar bones in place to hold the fish together. This is especially important if the fish are to be hung for drying. Large fish may be filleted, and small ones split down the middle from the belly side, so that they lie flat with the back skin holding the two halves together. (Also refer to the SALT CURING section.)

***Dry Salting Fish***    For this method, fish are first cured in salt and then dried. To begin, coat the prepared fish with salt and stack them in layers with salt under, between, and over the fish. The usual ratio is 1 pound plain or pickling salt to 4 pounds of fish, but a little more salt may be necessary for very fatty fish. The salt draws out considerable liquid so the fish must be stacked in a way that allows them to drain, such as on a board or table top tilted for drainage. Large quantities can be stacked outdoors, but they must be protected from direct sunlight, rain, and dew. Leave the fish in the salt for 2 days to a week, depending on the size of the fish and the temperature range. Small fish in warm weather require the shortest salting time, but it does not hurt them to remain in the salt for an extra few days. If the fish are to be dried outdoors and weather conditions are damp and poor for drying, they can be left for a day or two while waiting for better weather.

Next, to prepare the fish for drying, scrub them in lightly salted water till no salt shows. Then drain and lay them on racks or hang them up to dry. If dried outdoors they should be shaded, as direct sunlight will cause them to turn unattractively rust colored. Dry until hard, so that no impressions show when the thickest parts are squeezed between thumb and forefinger. Store in airtight containers, in a cool, dry place. Unless the fish is very dry, it should be refrigerated or frozen after drying to prevent spoilage. (For further details about drying, refer to the DRYING FOODS section.)

***Brine Curing Fish***    First remove all traces of blood from the prepared fish by soaking them for 30 minutes in brine, ½ cup salt per gallon of water. Then coat them in salt, and pack them in a crock, using about 1 pound salt per 3 pounds of fish. Put a weight on them so that brine forms and covers them. (For details refer to CROCKS, in the KITCHEN UTENSILS section.) Small lean fish will cure in about 48 hours, while large, fatty fish take from 7 to 10 days. To store them after curing, scrub the fish in fresh brine and repack with a very light sprinkling of salt. Then press them down, and cover with saturated brine, made by stirring salt into the required amount of water until no more will dissolve. Store in a cool dark place. (For more detailed information, refer to the references, at the end of the SALT CURING section.)

***Using Salt Cured Fish***   Plain salt cured fish is a basic food that can be freshened and cooked in a variety of ways. Dry salt cod is the best known. Before mechanical refrigeration, it was a very common food because it kept indefinitely. Salt cod recipes appear in most old North American cookbooks, in some modern ones, and also in some Italian and other European ones. These recipes can be used for any variety of salt cured fish.

The first step is to freshen the fish by removing excess salt. Soak it in several changes of water, for anywhere from a few hours to 48 hours, depending on the size of the fish, its dryness and saltiness. This should be done in a cold place (below 45°F) such as the refrigerator. An overnight soaking is the most common. To shorten this time to an hour or less, the fish can be pulled into shreds and held under running water, or soaked in water that is changed every 5 or 10 minutes. Shreds of fish may also be simmered in water (to be discarded later), as in the *Salt Fish Cakes* recipe, below.

Freshened fish is best if steamed or stewed till done, flaked to remove bones, then combined with a sauce or used in recipes for pre-cooked fish.

## PICKLING FISH

Pickling is an excellent way to prepare and preserve all lean fish, (especially those with many fine bones, as the acid will soften the bones and make them edible). Pickled fish will keep for months in a cool (below 45°F) place if the pickling solution is at least half vinegar.

Salting is a necessary first step to pickling fish, as the salt firms the meat and helps prevent spoilage. Whole cleaned fish are usually packed in layers of salt in a crock to cure, while fillets or slices, which contain less moisture, are cured in brine. After salting, the fish is rinsed or soaked in fresh water, trimmed or if necessary cut in pieces, and packed in jars. A pickling mixture made with vinegar and spices is poured over it, and it is refrigerated till eaten. (See the *Light Pickled Fish* recipe, below.)

## SMOKING FISH

Though fish can be smoked for flavor without a salt cure, they will not keep any longer than cooked fish. (Refer to KITCHEN SMOKED FISH, in the SMOKING section.) For long storage they must first be salt cured, then smoked. Unlike other meats, fish can first be frozen, then thawed and smoked.

There are many methods for preparing, salting, and smoking different kinds of fish, often developed regionally for local fishes. Fish can usually be brine cured as described above, except that they are left for only 1 to 12 hours in the crock. The time will vary with the thickness of the meat, the weather, and the length of time they are to be stored. After the fish are taken from the salt and rinsed they are air dried in the shade for about 3 hours so that a "skin" forms on them. They will not smoke well otherwise. Smoking temperatures are kept below 90°F. The smoking time may vary from 24 hours to about 5 days or even longer. For more detailed information refer to COLD SMOKING, and the references in the SMOKING section.

## COOKING FISH

Timing is the most critical aspect of fish cookery. Whether a fish is steamed, stewed, broiled, sautéed or baked, it should be cooked only until done, never overdone. Undercooked fish will have an unpleasant texture and little flavor while overcooked fish will become dry and tough. Cooking time varies with the kind of fish and the cooking methods, so always check for doneness by poking the flesh with a fork in its thickest part. If well done it will separate into flakes, and the color will be opaque rather than translucent. If the flesh is light colored it will turn very white when done. With a whole fish, the color change can sometimes be seen by looking into its cavity along the ribs and backbone, making it unnecessary to damage its appearance with a fork.

A really fresh fish cooked with a minimum of handling and very little seasoning is beyond compare. More complicated and highly seasoned fish recipes are best saved for frozen fish or fish that has been refrigerated for a day or two. A few kinds of fish require a marinade to improve flavor. Dogfish, which may have an ammonia taste, and other strong tasting fish can be improved by soaking for several hours or overnight in the following solution: ½ tablespoon lemon juice, or 1 tablespoon vinegar per pound of fish, with water to cover.

Special pans for steaming or poaching fish can be bought with an elongated oval shape to fit a whole fish. Lacking one of these, fish may be trimmed or cut in pieces to fit available pans. One old recipe for steaming suggests securing "the tail of the fish in its mouth." If a way can be devised to do this, an inconveniently long fish will fit in a round pot or a square pan.

***Dealing with Boniness***   Many times the biggest hindrance to enjoying fish is the presence of fine bones running through the meat. Carefully picking them out when eating is one way to handle them. With some fish it helps to completely remove the fins. (See REMOVING FINS, above.) Some large fish may be deboned. Shad fillets for instance can be bent to expose the ends of the "Y" shaped bones, then these can be gripped with a cloth or dish towel and pulled out. Quite another approach is to cook the fish and flake it with the finger tips, removing bones in the process. Such fish is excellent in salads and many other dishes.

Small, bony fish are best handled by making the bones edible. Salting, smoking, and pickling all tend to soften bones enough so that they can be eaten. Cooking fish in an acidic liquid such as tomato, lemon juice, or vinegar dissolves bones if the cooking time is long enough, but this will also soften the meat. Another alternative is to remove the backbone and large rib bones and grind, mince very finely, or blenderize the meat. This can be used for special recipes, such as the *Gefilte Fish*, and FRESH FISH BURGERS, below. Eating the bones has the advantage of adding calcium to the diet.

## SOME COMMON FRESHWATER FISH

**Carp** In North America carp is regularly ignored as a food fish, but in Asia and parts of Europe it is considered a delicacy. In some places special varieties are raised in ponds as a food crop. It is likely that carp in America got a bad name because it can thrive in very dirty water. Though they should not, of course, be eaten if they come from polluted water, they can be taken from muddy water as long as the mud is clean. There are several ways to remove a muddy or strong taste:

• Keep carp from muddy water in fresh running water for about a week before eating them.

• Eat only the white meat. The dark meat is biochemically different from the white meat, so that only it will hold any strong flavors. For fillets of white meat, skin the carp and cut off the white meat only. As the skin is tough carp is often skinned in any case.

• Smoke or pickle carp. Smoked carp is especially good.

• For a good flavor of both white and dark meat rub the cleaned skinned fish, with the following dry marinade:

### Dry Marinade for Carp

| | |
|---|---|
| ¼ cup salt | 1 tablespoon vinegar |
| ¼ cup onion, ground, grated, or blenderized | ½ teaspoon black pepper |
| | 3 pounds (about) carp |

Mix all ingredients (adjust amounts for larger fish) and rub on the outside and in the cavity of the cleaned and skinned carp. Set aside and let sit 1 hour. Then wash off the marinade and rinse thoroughly. Use like any other fresh fish.

**Catfish and Bullheads** One or another of the many species of catfish and bullheads can be caught in most parts of the United States and many places in Canada. In the South catfish grow quite large and are sometimes raised commercially. As all sizes have an excellent flavor and few bones most people like them immediately. Their meat is dense and even the small bullheads have thick bodies, so they take longer to cook than most fish.

The main problem with these fish is getting them off the hook and skinning them without receiving a painful, bee-like sting from the spines in their fins. Wear heavy gloves for handling them or hold them without touching the fins. Catfish and bullheads must be skinned and the heads, tails, and fins must be removed. (See SKIN-NING FISH, above.)

***Bluegills, Sunfish, Sunnies, Gillies, and Pumpkinseeds*** All of these names belong to the same little easy-to-catch fish. It is the first fish many children catch, but it is rarely the first fish they eat. The frequent waste of these fish is quite unnecessary. They are an excellent pan fish, and can be cooked in many other ways as well. Their only shortcoming is their size. It does take a little longer to prepare enough of them for a meal than it would a larger fish, but the results are well worth it. Scale them and cut out the fins including the bones that go into the meat, as described in REMOVING FINS, above. Clean out entrails, cut off heads and tails, rinse, and they are ready for cooking. With a little practice this takes only 2 or 3 minutes per fish.

Bluegills can also be scaled, cleaned, and filleted. The tiny fillets are good steamed for 3 minutes, or dropped in boiling water for 2 minutes, chilled, and eaten with cocktail sauce like shrimp. They can also be stir-fried, or dipped in batter and deep fried.

***Eels*** In spite of their snake-like appearance eels are fish. They can be caught in large numbers in many rivers in the eastern United States and Canada, but are much more appreciated in Europe and Japan. Their life cycle is the reverse of the salmon. They hatch in the ocean, travel to fresh water to grow and develop, and then return to the ocean to spawn and die. Conger eels are large eels almost ready to return to the ocean. Small eels just coming into fresh water are sometimes called elvers.

Except when they are to be smoked, eels are best skinned. As their meat is rich and oily, with a higher fat content than most other fish, they are not usually fried. They excel when stewed, baked or broiled.

## FISH RECIPES

These recipes demonstrate many ways to cook fish; they are alike in that they do not call for a specific fish. The fish that are locally available are the ones to try.

### *Chinese Steamed Fish* (Makes 6–8 servings.)

2 *pounds fish, prepared for cooking*
    (May be one whole fish, several
    small fish, or fillets, or steaks.)
3 *tablespoons soy sauce*
¾ *teaspoon honey, or sugar*

1 *teaspoon salad oil*
3 *slices fresh ginger root,*
    *minced, optional*
2–3 *scallions, cut in ½ inch*
    *sections*

Select a shallow, heat-proof dish that will hold the fish and fit on a rack in a pot with a tight lid. (Refer to the STEAM COOKING section.) An oval dish with a whole fish in it will look elegant, but a round bowl with pieces of fish in it will taste just as good.

Arrange the fish in the dish. Mix the soy sauce, sweetening, oil, and ginger root, and pour over the fish. Sprinkle with scallions. Put about an inch of hot water in the pot, place the rack in it, set the dish of fish on the rack, and put on the lid. (The fish itself is not covered.) Start timing when the water boils. Steam 15 minutes for small fish, fillets or steaks, and 30 minutes for a whole large fish.

The fish is served in the dish in which it was steamed. A garnish of minced scallions or parsley can be sprinkled on after cooking if wished.

### Sally Katz' Jewish Style
### Fish Cakes (Gefilte Fish)               (Makes 2–3 quarts.)

| | |
|---|---|
| 6 pounds (about) fresh fish, before cleaning (Traditionally 2 pounds each of whitefish, pike, and carp, but any kind can be substituted. A combination is best.) | 2–3 carrots |
| | 1–2 teaspoons salt, optional |
| | 1½ teaspoons pepper |
| | 3 eggs |
| | ¾ cup (about) ice water |
| | 1 cup matzoh meal, cracker crumbs, or fine bread crumbs |
| 2–3 onions | |

Prepare the fish by scaling, cleaning, removing gills and filleting. (If any very fine bones are left in the fillets it will not matter as they will be chopped to bits.) Carefully skin the fillets and cut the skin into 1 to 2 inch wide strips, 4 or 5 inches long. (Or the fish can be skinned before filleting.) Set the strips of skin aside. Put the fish heads and bones in a large pot with a tight lid. Set aside one small onion, or a piece of a large onion. Cut the remainder into chunks and add them to the pot. Cut the carrots into thick, 2 inch long slices and add to the pot. Arrange the fish parts, onions, and carrots to make a flat layer in the bottom of the pot. Add half of the pepper, and a little salt, if desired. Add water to just cover these ingredients. Set aside.

Chop the small onion and the fish fillets into small pieces. (They can be coarsely ground in a meat grinder, but for best texture hand chop them. Or, if a grinder is used, finish chopping by hand.) Continue chopping, working in the eggs, one at a time. Sprinkle with ice water now and then, and add the matzoh meal or crumbs, a little at a time, along with the remaining pepper and salt. The ice water makes the mixture lighter and softer as it is absorbed. Chop till ingredients are blended and the texture very fine.

With dampened hands, shape the mixture into small oval or oblong patties. Wrap or fold a strip of fish skin around the middle of each. (If there are too few strips, some can be left plain.) Set the cakes close together in the pot on top of the layer of heads, bones, and vegetables, making two layers or more. They will feel soft and ready to fall apart, but they become firm as they cook. Cover, bring to a boil, and simmer 1 hour, or a little longer if several layers deep.

When done, uncover and let cool for 10 minutes. Take out the fish cakes one by one with a slotted spoon, and put them in a bowl or wide mouthed jars. Arrange slices of cooked carrot among the cakes. Then strain the stock and pour it over the gefilte fish. Chill in the refrigerator to form a firm gelatine. If it does not jell, pour it off, add a little dry gelatine, and warm the mixture to dissolve the granules. Then pour it back over the cakes, and return to the refrigerator.

Gefilte fish is traditionally eaten cold with fresh grated horseradish, or a horseradish relish. (Refer to HORSERADISH, in the HERB ROOTS section, and the BEETS section.) It makes a good first course for a festive meal, and a fine snack or light lunch.

### *Elizabethan Stuffed Fish*                          Makes 6–8 dinner servings.)

| | |
|---|---|
| *1 whole large fish, 3–5 pounds, scaled, cleaned, gills removed* | *2 raw egg yolks, or 1 egg* |
| *pepper, salt, optional* | *¼ teaspoon salt* |
| *2 cups cooked beets, beet greens, spinach, or a mixture of these* | *¼ teaspoon cinnamon* |
| *2 yolks of hard-boiled eggs, or 1 whole hard-boiled egg* | *¼ teaspoon sugar* |
| *2 tablespoons currants, or raisins* | *1 cup white wine, or 2–3 tablespoons vinegar in water to make 1 cup* |
| *¼ cup bread crumbs* | *3 tablespoons butter* |
| | *1 slice toast per serving* |

Sprinkle the inside of the fish with pepper and salt, if desired. Chop the vegetables, hard-boiled egg, and currants or raisins, and hard-boiled egg till fairly fine. Mix in the bread crumbs, raw egg, salt, cinnamon, and sugar. Fill the fish with this stuffing and close with skewers or sew it shut. Set in a roasting pan, then pour the wine or vinegar mixture over it. Dot generously with butter. Bake uncovered in a hot, 400°F oven, until the fish is cooked, usually 50 minutes to an hour. Baste every 15 to 20 minutes with the juices in the pan.

For each serving put a portion of fish and some stuffing on a slice of toast and spoon juice from the pan over all. The unique blend of vegetable and fruit in this filling goes very well with fish.

**Layered Fish Casserole**   Butter a baking dish and lay one large or several small fish fillets in it. Add the above stuffing in a layer and cover with fish fillets. Pour over the wine, dot with butter, and bake. Check for doneness after about 30 minutes. If the fillets are skinless cover the casserole for all but the last few minutes of the baking time.

### *Finnish Fish Pudding*                             (Makes 6–8 dinner servings.)

| | |
|---|---|
| *3–4 cups potatoes, cooked and mashed* | *1 onion, grated or minced* |
| *2 eggs, slightly beaten* | *2 anchovies, minced, or salt to taste, optional* |
| *1 cup milk* | |

2 tablespoons butter, softened or
  melted
2 teaspoons dill leaves or chives,
  minced
2–3 cups fish, cooked, boned,
  and flaked

2 cups peas, cooked (May be
  frozen.)
1 cup (about) fine dry bread
  crumbs
butter, for top

Combine the mashed potatoes, eggs, milk, onion, anchovies or salt, butter, and dill or chives. Gently stir in the fish and peas without mashing them. Butter a baking dish about 2½ quart size, and sprinkle bread crumbs in it. Put in the fish mixture and sprinkle bread crumbs on top. Dot with butter and bake in a moderate, 325–350°F oven for 30 to 40 minutes, or till set and lightly browned on top.

### Cold Portuguese Fish Vinaigrette   (Makes 6–10 small side servings.)

1½ pounds fish, ready to cook
  (Preferably a lean fish that
  flakes easily.)
2 onions, sliced
oil for frying (Preferably olive oil.)
6 cloves garlic, crushed (Or
  more, to taste.)
2 medium carrots, grated

1 small bunch parsley, minced
6 peppercorns
1 teaspoon paprika
1 bay leaf
4 tablespoons vinegar (Wine
  vinegar or homemade cider
  vinegar are nice.)
½ teaspoon salt

Steam or otherwise cook the fish till done. Cool, then flake with the fingers, removing skin and bones.

Sauté the onions in oil till they are golden. Remove the pan from the heat and immediately add garlic, carrots, parsley, peppercorns, paprika, bay leaf, vinegar and salt. Stir together and cool in a bowl. Mix in the fish gently without mashing the flakes. Cover and chill for 24 hours. Serve cold. It is especially good with hot baked or boiled potatoes.

### Fish and Greens, Amerindian Style   (Makes 10–12 soup bowlfuls.)

2 large potatoes, or 4 burdock roots
  (Refer to BURDOCK, in the
  HERB ROOTS section.)
1 onion, quartered
6 peppercorns
10 juniper berries, optional
1½–2 quarts fish stock, or water

1½ pounds (about) boned fish
  (Fresh, frozen, or cooked
  leftovers.)
1 pound greens, cut in bite sized
  pieces (Spinach, Swiss
  chard, wild greens, or
  others.)
sprig of fresh mint, or ½
  teaspoon dried
salt, optional

Cut potatoes or burdock into medium pieces and cook in a pot with the onion, peppercorns, juniper berries, and fish stock or water till tender, about 40 minutes. Mash the vegetables, peppercorns, and juniper berries against the side of the pot with a fork or the back of a spoon. Or put the mixture through a food mill. Reheat if necessary, then add the fish. If fish is raw cook the mixture about 10 minutes, then flake the fish with a fork. (Cook precooked flaked fish only enough to heat it.) Then add the greens, mint, salt if desired, and cook 5 minutes more. Serve in bowls as a hearty soup for lunch or supper.

### Old-fashioned Salt Fish Cakes (Makes 4–6 servings.)

*¼ pound dry salt cured fish* (Usually
   salt cod, but other home cured
   fish are just as good.)
*2–3 cups potatoes, diced*
*1 egg, lightly beaten*

*dash of pepper*
*dash of nutmeg, optional*
*several tablespoons oil, or but-
   ter, for frying*

Pull the fish into shreds or pieces with the fingers, removing any skin and bones. Cover with plenty of cold water and let soak from 5 minutes to an hour, depending on the saltiness. Drain after soaking and squeeze out extra moisture. Put the fish and potatoes in a sauce pan and cover with water. Cover, bring to a boil, then simmer about 15 minutes, till the potatoes are done. Drain. Beat with a fork until the mixture is fluffy. Mix in the egg, pepper, and nutmeg.

Heat a little oil or butter in a frying pan and drop forkfuls of the fish mixture into it to make small patties. These stay lighter if they are dropped in loosely rather than molded into even shapes. Fry until golden brown on both sides.

### Pickled Fish for Cold Storage

(One quart prepared fish makes about 1 quart pickled.)

*fish* (Enough to make 1 or more
   quarts prepared.)
*brine: ⅝ cup plain or pickling salt
   per quart water*
*onions, thinly sliced, to tase*
   (Can use almost as much
   onion as fish.)

Pickling mixture for about 1
   quart:
   *1½ tablespoons mixed pick-
      ling spices* (May include
      bay leaves, mustard
      seed, red pepper flakes,
      peppercorns, whole
      allspice and whole
      cloves.)
   *2 cups white or wine vinegar*
   *2 cups water*
   *⅓ cup honey, or sugar, op-
      tional*

Clean the fish and cut crosswise into ¼–½ inch thick slices, or, if the fish are small, cut fillets. If very large, the fish can be filleted and then sliced crosswise. (Fine bones will be softened by the vinegar so do not remove them) Mix salt and water to make enough brine to generously cover the fish. To find out how much is needed, cover the fish with plain water, then drain and measure the water used. Leave the fish in the brine at a cold temperature (below 45°F) for about 24 hours. Rinse well in plenty of fresh water. Make layers of the fish and slices of onion in a crock or glass jars.

Meanwhile prepare the same amount of pickling mixture as was made of brine. Combine the pickling spices, vinegar, water, and sweetening in a pot, and heat to a full boil. Cool to room temperature. Pour over the fish and onion and cover the crock or jars. Keep in a cool place (below 45°F) or refrigerate for about a week before eating. This fish will keep for several months if refrigerated. Pickled fish is an excellent appetizer or snack food, and can be enjoyed like any other pickle.

**Pickled Herring**   River herring (alewives) are good pickled this way as well as true herring. Other species can also be pickled like this, but they will not have the same taste or texture as herring.

Scale and clean the fish, cutting off heads and tails. Pack them in plain or pickling salt in a crock or other non-corrosive container. Put salt under, between layers, and over the fish. Leave about 5 days. Add a day or two if the fish are big or they are kept in a very cool place. Remove fish, rinse off salt, and soak overnight in fresh water in the refrigerator or other cold place. Drain and cut in 1½ inch thick chunks across the body or fillet and roll tightly to make "rollmops". If a fillet is too big for one roll, cut it in half lengthwise for two. Pack in a crock or jars. Rolls can be packed seam side down, or secured with toothpicks.

Prepare the pickling liquid, pour over the herring, cover, and store as for PICKLED FISH, above. If a very long storage period is expected increase ratio of vinegar to water to 4 cups vinegar per 2 cups of water. Herring can also be pickled in undiluted vinegar omitting the salt curing, but the flavor will be very strong. Refrigerate.

**Fish Pickled in Sour Cream**   Salt cure and freshen fish in one of the ways described above. Cut pieces 1 inch thick or less. For each 2 cups prepared fish, mix the following: 1 cup sour cream, 2 tablespoons cider vinegar, 2 teaspoons peppercorns, 2 teaspoons mustard seed, 1 teaspoon sugar and 3 bay leaves. The milt (reproductive glands) of male herring can be mashed with sugar, strained through a sieve to remove membranes and also mixed in. (Refer to the ROE AND MILT section.)

Stir the fish and a thinly sliced onion to taste, gently into the sour cream mixture. Let sit in the refrigerator for a day before using. This will keep for a week to ten days in the refrigerator. Serve as an appetizer or snack.

---

**FISH IDEAS,** *cont.*

**Fish in Gelatine**   Flaked cooked fish is very good in gelatines and aspics using vegetable juice or fish stock. If a concentrated stock is made from fish heads, bones, and skin it will jell by itself. (Refer to JELLED STOCK, in the GELATINE section.) Otherwise fish stock or vegetable juice can be jelled with powdered gelatine. Some especially good vegetables in fish gelatines are cucumbers, celery, cabbage, and green peppers. Minced fresh herbs, such as dill leaves, parsley or chervil, capers, chopped pickles or pickle relish, lemon juice or vinegar, pimientos and olives are also good additions.

---

**OTHER RECIPES FEATURING FISH**

Cabbage and Fish Salad, 91
Fish and Shellfish Stock, p.577
Fish and Vegetable Loaf, p.670
Fish Kedgeree, p.518
Gooseberry Sauce for Meat or
   Fish, p.311
Green Soybean and Fish Salad,
   p.587
Kitchen Smoked Fish, p.572
Lemon Butter (for fish), p.86
Red Wine Sauce with Fish, p.339
Roe or Milt Stuffing for Baked
   Fish, p.522
Seafood Risotto, p.519
Soy Sauced Fish, p.232
Tuna Stuffing for Summer
   Squash, p.600
Turnip and Fish Soup, p.658

Most natural foods have attractive and appetizing colors. Drops of artificial coloring cannot, for example, improve the warm tan and brown tones of whole grain baked goods, or the rich and subtle shades of pure fruit juice gelatines. The use of artificial color may relieve the blank non-color of highly processed and refined foods, but it would be much better to avoid the foods themselves, thereby solving the problem of making them look good. The use of blatant artificial colors is a favorite commercial method for making some of the least healthful foods attractive to children. There is also a continuing, niggling doubt about the colorings safety. The majority are chemical dyes after all—not foods, and eating them is not a necessity. Happily, neither is it necessary to give up the fun and fancy of changing and enhancing the colors of foods, as there are many natural ways to do so. Some natural food coloring may even make the food taste better.

## YELLOW

*Carrots*   Deep orange colored carrots can be juiced or puréed and added to such foods as puddings and baked goods to color them yellow. One old recipe suggests coloring butter by heating grated carrot in a little milk and straining it into the cream.

*Flower Petals*   Many old books suggest marigolds or pot marigolds (a variety of calendula) as sources of yellow coloring. Both marigold and calendula blossoms are edible and usually yellow or orange, but most modern varieties do not contain enough pigmentation to markedly change the color of other foods. If an old, intensely colored strain of pot marigold can be found, the color can be extracted by steeping the petals in water, milk, or another liquid, then straining for use in soups, baking, and many desserts.

All edible flower petals add a cheerful glint of color when mixed into salads and some cooked dishes, or they can be used as a garnish. For yellow tones, try dandelion, squash, and nasturtium blossoms, as well as marigold and calendula. (Refer to the DANDELIONS, SQUASH, SUMMER, and HERBS sections.) Flower petals can also be dried like herbs and stored for later use.

*Egg Yolks*   The yolks of eggs from chickens that eat a lot of greens are intensely yellow-orange. An extra yolk or two in custards, breads, and other foods will add a pleasing golden glow.

*Turmeric and Saffron*   These spices will color foods a bright yellow. They also add their own particular flavors, of course.

## GREEN

*Spinach, Other Greens, and Herbs*   Any leafy green can be puréed to add a green color to food. Raw spinach or other dark greens puréed in a blender with a little stock or water will color soups and sauces. Pale, creamed mixtures show the color best. Sauces blended with parsley, basil, or other fresh herbs are pleasingly green as well as flavorful. Mayonnaise can be tinted green in this way. Cooked puréed spinach or juice squeezed from cooked spinach can also be used. Cooked puréed spinach will make anything from mashed potatoes to muffins green, but it is best known for making green noodles (described in the NOODLES section). One old Scottish recipe calls for spinach juice in a citron pudding "to make it a fine green." For another spinach green dessert idea, refer to GELATINE EASTER EGGS, in the GELATINE section.

## RED AND PINK

*Beets*    Sliced or puréed beets, and beet cooking water are all excellent for coloring foods any shade from pinkish lavender to beet red. A small amount will add a lot of color. Horseradish is often turned dark red by adding grated beets, and eggs "pickled pink" with the addition of a beet slice, or the leftover juice from pickled beets. A few tablespoons of beet cooking water will tint most light colored foods pink or lavender.

*Berries*    Many kinds of berries will color foods red. The diluted juice of such dark berries as blackberries and blueberries will be red or pink. Berry juice makes a pretty red gelatine, pink ice cream, and pink lemonade, and works well with many fruit flavored mixtures, like the GELATINE EASTER EGGS, in the GELATINE section.

*Lobster Coral and Shellfish Shells*    The coral (unfertilized eggs) of a female lobster turn bright red with cooking. They can be pressed through a sieve or blenderized, then added to sauces and creamed soups for both flavor and color. The red color in cooked shells of lobster and shellfish can be extracted and used in several ways. The shells can be crushed and cooked in wine or diluted vinegar until the liquid is half reduced and red. After straining, this extract can be used for both flavor and color, as in the CORAL BUTTER idea, in the SHELLFISH section.

## BROWN

*Pan Scrapings and Browned Flour*    Much brown coloring comes from foods that have been roasted or fried. Generally, their flavor is pleasant if the food has not been burned. Pan scrapings from fried and roast meats are what give many gravies, soups, and stews both a rich brown color and a good flavor. They should never be wasted. A similar brown coloring is made by stirring a few tablespoons of flour with a few tablespoons of fat or oil over low heat until the mixture browns. Liquid is then added to make a brown sauce or roux.

*Roasted Roots, Grains, and Seeds*    Coffee substitutes made from roasted ingredients are excellent for darkening baked goods.

Pumpernickel and other dark breads are colored in this way. 2–4 tablespoons, finely ground, are enough for 1 loaf. Commercial substitutes like Postum and Inca, and homemade mixtures work equally well. (Refer to ROAST BEVERAGES, in the BEVERAGES section.)

**Dried Onions**   Onions that have been dried until they darken will give clear soups a golden brown color when simmered together for a few minutes. They make a beautiful French onion soup. The dry skins of some onions, if steeped in liquid, will also give a golden brown color.

**Dark Syrups**   Caramel coloring (or syrup) is sometimes made by melting and browning sugar, but its safety as a food has been questioned so it is best avoided. Molasses safely adds a similar deep brown color. Many other syrups give a beige to brown color to foods. Try dark maple syrup, dark honey, birch syrup (described in the MAPLE SYRUP section), watermelon syrup (in the WATERMELON section), and cider syrup (in the APPLES section).

# FREEZING FOODS

RUNNING A HOME FREEZER THROUGHOUT THE YEAR IS THE MOST modern way to preserve food, but freezing foods for later use is as ancient as the presence of humankind in cold climates. Primitive peoples almost certainly kept meat frozen in outdoor caches during the winter, and a few millennia later a nineteenth century cookbook gives directions for the proper thawing of meat stored outdoors in below freezing weather. The advent of the home freezer has changed freezing from an occasionally useful practice to a highly effective year-round storage method.

There are drawbacks to the use of a home freezer, but they have little to do with the way it preserves food. Freezing is the best way to retain the freshness of meat, fish, many vegetables, and a wide assortment of other foods. It is, instead, the expense of operation, the possibility of mechanical failure, and the dependance on outside power that limits the home freezer's usefulness. In sharp contrast to canned and dried foods which keep without special attention once processing is complete, frozen foods are always vulnerable. Something as minor as an accidentally unplugged electrical cord can spoil a year's food supply, while such major problems as power outages are entirely beyond individual control. While these are not reasons to avoid using a freezer, they are reasons for limiting use by storing part of the household's supply in a more self-reliant way. In deciding which method to use it makes sense to save the freezer for foods that lose quality or are difficult to process when stored in other ways. Green vegetables and meats should, for instance, have priority over fruits that are just as good or better canned, dried or root cellared.

## FROZEN FOOD QUALITY

The quality of the food coming out of the freezer can only be as good as the quality of what goes into it. If fresh food at its peak in flavor and ripeness is prepared, packaged, frozen, and thawed according to directions its quality will be excellent. If directions are ignored and food is simply tossed into the freezer it will not necessarily spoil—it might even taste good for a month or so—but then drying, freezer burn, or enzyme action begin to take their toll.

Other vital requirements for quality in frozen food are a properly functioning freezer, and good protective packaging to exclude air and retain moisture. Within these bounds there is room for experimenting and trying new ideas.

**Freezer Types and Temperatures**  For highest quality and longest storage life, food should be frozen quickly, and stored at 0°F or below. Food remains edible as long as it stays frozen, but it loses flavor and texture faster as the temperature gets higher. A food that retains full quality for a year when stored at 0°F, might taste good for only a month or two stored at 30°F. It is prudent to keep a thermometer in the freezer.

The best freezers are those in which temperature does not vary. A chest type is better than an upright because less warm air will get in when it is opened. A freezer without an automatic defroster is better than one with a defroster, because the warming of the freezer walls during the defrosting cycle may gradually reduce quality.

## PACKAGING FOODS FOR THE FREEZER

Packaging for freezing must be airtight and moisture-proof, with as little air space as possible around the food inside the package. Pack rigid containers closely to exclude air. Wrappings should press tightly against the food, and all packaging must have airtight lids or seals. Double wrapping is one way to insure a tight seal. Whole packages, including rigid containers, can be sealed inside plastic bags or another layer of wrapping. Watch packages in the freezer for punctures or lids that do not stay sealed. Any questionable ones should be re-wrapped.

**Rigid Freezer Containers**  For freezing soft and liquid foods use rigid containers. The best ones are the special freezer cartons sold in many stores, or glass jars with flared or straight sides. Containers with "shoulders" can break from the pressure of food expanding as it freezes. Glass jars with two-piece canning lids that will bulge to accommodate expanding food are excellent, but recycled food jars with good lids can also be used. Plastic containers should have lids that snap into place to make an airtight seal. If they do not seal tightly

*Rigid freezer containers*

Loose dry pack. No air space required.

*Broccoli*

Tight dry pack in straight sided container. ¼ inch (about) air space.

*Blueberries*

Liquid in flared pint container. ½ inch (about) air space.

*Fruit Juice*

Liquid in flared quart container. 1 inch (about) air space.

*Soup*

Liquid in straight sided quart container. 1½ inch (about) air space.

*Vegetables in tomato juice*

*Butcher wrap*

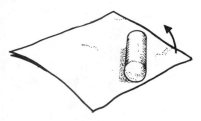

Start roll at corner of paper, tucking in tip.

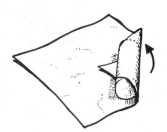

Roll to half way, fold in sides tightly.

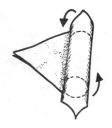

Fold new sides in.

Roll to end. Seal all edges with tape.

press a strip of freezer tape along the edge of the lid. Plastic containers that once held cottage cheese or ice cream can be recycled for freezer use if seals are checked. It is also possible to use rigid containers without lids by fitting plastic bags in them and filling and sealing the bags. Square or rectangular plastic containers take less freezer space than round containers.

Always leave an airspace in rigid containers to allow for food expansion while it is freezing. The space needed will depend on the liquidity of the food and the shape and size of the container.

***Plastic Freezer Storage Bags*** There is considerable concern among scientists about the safety of certain plastics made flexible with a chemical called phthalate or DEHP, as it is highly carcinogenic in animals. As a precaution, until more conclusive research results are publicized, the thinner more flexible plastic bags and food wrappings are not listed for food storage in this book. The heavy, freezer-strength plastic bags, however, are very convenient for packaging non-liquid foods. Their big advantage is that air can be more completely removed from them, giving better protection to odd shaped pieces of food, so these are included here. It is important to remove air before sealing them.

Though plastic bags cannot usually be reused in the freezer, they can be tested for leaks by blowing them up like a balloon, pinching them closed, and watching for escaping air. If reusing the good ones, it is best to use two, one inside the other.

***Freezer Wrap*** Firm chunks of food, especially meats, can be wrapped in special freezer paper and sealed with freezer tape. Use only tough moisture-proof wrapping. (Neither waxed paper, nor thin plastic, nor aluminum foil give adequate protection.) The wrappings must press against the food and be neatly and tightly folded to exclude air. Use a "butcher wrap" or "drugstore fold," or any method that folds the seams over twice to make an airtight seal. Though freezer tape that sticks at below zero temperature is best for sealing, cheap masking tape will usually hold if the strips go completely around the package and overlap. At spots where sharp bones push against the wrappings add extra tape to prevent punctures.

## SPECIAL FREEZING TECHNIQUES

***Freezing Slices*** It is often helpful to be able to separate frozen food slices without thawing them. They will thaw more quickly, or where appropriate, they may be cooked without thawing. For a separator, put a piece of freezer paper or waxed paper between each slice before it is frozen. Meat cut in steaks or chops, and any food sliced ready for frying, can be handled in this way.

***Freezing Before Wrapping*** Some foods freeze best spread on trays in a single layer with each piece separated. When frozen solid they are quickly packaged and returned to the freezer. As they do not stick together they can be taken out in any quantity, large or small, to use as needed. Some foods to handle this way are dollops of whipped cream, slices of tomato, and other vegetable and fruit pieces.

***Freezing Food Cubes*** Foods to be used in small amounts are very convenient frozen in ice cube trays or muffin tins. The solidly frozen cubes are then packaged and returned to the freezer. Later, one cube at a time can be removed for use. A muffin tin cup holds about twice as much as an ice cube tray section. If it is difficult to remove frozen cubes from a muffin tin run water on the bottom of the tin, loosening one or two cubes at a time, and catching them as they fall. Baby foods, eggs, and minced herbs can be conveniently frozen in cubes. (Refer to the EGGS and HERBS sections.)

***Concentrated Juice*** It is possible to make concentrated juice or syrup by partially freezing fruit juice or maple sap, draining off the liquid, and discarding the almost clear ice that remains. Repeat the freezing, draining, and discarding of ice several times or until the desired concentration is reached. It does take considerable time and attention to make a strong concentration with this method, but it has been used successfully both at home and commercially. Grape juice concentrated in this way retains the fruit's good, fresh flavor.

As the degree of freezing and draining time will vary under different conditions those who want to try this approach must experiment for themselves. To avoid waste, only discard those ice crystals which are quite clear and tasteless.

*Note:* For glazing or encasing food in ice, refer to FREEZING FISH, in the FISH section.

## FREEZING VEGETABLES

Freezing is the preferred way to preserve most green vegetables, as with this method they generally taste best and retain nutrients best. If stored at 0°F, they keep their high quality about 1 year. Most root vegetables and white or yellow vegetables are just as good or better canned or kept in a root cellar. Potatoes and cabbage do not freeze well in the home freezer, as ice crystals will form and break down their texture.

Wash and trim vegetables for freezing in the same way as for cooking. Cut large vegetables into uniform serving sized pieces. A quick precooking or blanching is recommended for vegetables before they are frozen.

***Blanching Vegetables*** Blanching is necessary to stop enzyme activity. Without it the vegetables gradually lose flavor and color and may also become tough. Anyone can discover that this is so by freezing a few test packages of raw vegetables, waiting six months, and then trying to eat them.

Vegetables must be blanched quickly at a temperature as near boiling as possible, using boiling water, steam, or as an experiment, a mi-

*Blanching*

crowave oven. (For the microwave, it is important to have even heating.) Steam blanching is often recommended because there is less leaching of nutrients into the blanching water, but it is harder to reach and maintain the necessary high temperature with steam. A good steamer with a tight lid is essential, and it is better to use boiling water than to make do with an inadequate steamer. (Refer to the STEAM COOKING section.)

Blanch vegetables in small batches of 1 to 2 pounds in plenty of boiling water or in a shallow layer in the steamer. An overload will slow down the blanching process and reduce quality. Generally blanching is complete when the vegetable changes color or turns a brighter green. Start timing only when the water has returned to a boil after the vegetables have been added. Steam blanching will take a minute or two longer than boiling water. (Blanching times are given in the storage information in each vegetable section.)

Once the vegetables are blanched, chill them quickly by dunking them in icy cold water for a minute or so to stop them cooking. This is most important for those green vegetables that overcook easily. Then drain, package and freeze them at the coldest temperature possible. If ice water is not available, vegetables can also be cooled fairly well by spreading them out in a single layer on a clean cloth or other surface.

Frozen vegetables tend to taste best if cooked. Drop them, solidly frozen, into a small amount of boiling water in a saucepan, cover them and cook just enough to heat them so they will not be overcooked.

***Freezing Leafy Greens*** Greens which require from 10 to 15 minutes of cooking are better frozen than the very quick cooking greens, as they will withstand the rigors of both blanching for freezing and cooking again for serving. Such wild greens as dandelion and lamb's quarters are excellent for freezing, as well as kale, Swiss chard, and spinach, but Chinese cabbage, lettuce, and other delicate greens will lose texture and become mushy.

Blanch greens in boiling water, or cook them till wilted in just the water left on them from washing, rather than steaming them. (In a steamer leaves tend to mat down into a solid layer, so that the steam cannot penetrate.) After cooking, spread the greens out to cool. If desired, chop them on a cutting board before freezing. Also freeze any liquid left from cooking greens, or use it in another way.

## FREEZING GARDEN VEGETABLES IN SOUP STOCK

Fresh garden vegetables frozen in stock make a very good base for all kinds of soups, bringing summer's flavors into winter meals.

Gather an assortment of vegetables, starting with such hearty ones as sweet corn, shelled green beans, and root vegetables. Add, perhaps, leafy greens, tomatoes, and onions, scallions or chives. Include fresh herbs like basil or summer savory. Heat soup stock to a boil while cleaning, chopping or otherwise preparing the vegetables. Use a minimum of stock for the quantity of vegetables. More liquid can be added once the soup mixture has been thawed. Put the slowest cooking vegetables in the boiling stock first. When it returns to a boil add the quick cooking vegetables and herbs, but do not add any other seasonings. Bring again to a boil, then chill quickly by setting the pot in a pan of cold water. When cool put the mixture in containers, label with the kind of stock and the primary vegetables used, and freeze. When thawed, other ingredients such as cooked chopped meat, cooked rice or noodles and seasonings can be added. To save their garden fresh flavor, do not cook the vegetables any longer than necessary when making the soup.

(For precise freezing instructions also refer to the storage boxes in each specific vegetable section in the book.)

## FREEZING FRUITS

Freezing is the best way to preserve the fresh taste of most kinds of berries, but other fruits are usually just as good canned, dried, or, in some cases, root cellared. Ice crystals form in many kinds of fruit when they are frozen, breaking them down and making them mushy when thawed. To avoid this, frozen fruits can be eaten only partly thawed.

Fruits may be packed plain for freezing, or covered with fruit juice or another liquid. Fruits that darken easily are usually covered with an acidic juice or with an ascorbic acid solution. Some fruits will be good made into fresh juice for freezing. (Refer to FRESH FRUIT JUICE, in the FRUITS section.) There is seldom any point in cooking and then freezing fruit. If fruit is to be cooked it is much more practical to can it for storage.

(For precise freezing instructions also refer to the storage boxes in each specific fruit section in the book.)

## LIQUIDS IN WHICH TO FREEZE FRUIT

**Fruit Juice**   Use juice made from the fruit to be frozen or use any complementary fruit juice. If the fruit darkens easily use an acidic juice like orange, grapefruit, pineapple, or water flavored with lemon juice. (Refer to COMBINING SWEET AND TART FRUITS, in the FRUITS section.)

**Pectin**   Thin or diluted homemade pectin has a good flavor and a smooth pleasant texture. It will add healthful sweetness to the fruit and help prevent darkening as well. (Refer to the PECTIN section.)

**Ascorbic Acid Solution**   An ascorbic acid solution is often recommended to prevent darkening. Unlike other liquids it does not add flavor. Proportions for the solution vary from ¼ to ¾ teaspoon crystalline ascorbic acid dissolved in one quart of water. Use the larger amount for the fruits most subject to darkening.

*Syrup* For a very light syrup heat 2–3 tablespoons honey, or maple syrup, or sugar in a quart of water. Bring to a boil, then cool completely. For a light syrup use ⅓ cup honey or maple syrup, or ½ cup sugar per quart of water.

*Note:* If the fruit floats in the liquid, crumple a piece of freezer wrap and put it on top of the fruit in the container to hold the fruit down. Otherwise the top pieces may darken.

## FREEZING MEAT AND POULTRY

Freezing is the ideal way to preserve meat and poultry because cooking methods are unaffected and flavor is the same when thawed as when fresh. All types and cuts of meat, including game meats, variety meats, wild birds, fish, and shellfish, are very good frozen, making it possible to enjoy home raised meat or game all year long. Before home freezers were available many people depended on such salt cured meats as ham, bacon, and corned beef, resulting in an overly salty diet.

Prepare meat and poultry as for cooking, including trimming and cutting or grinding. Chill home butchered meat or game meat from 12 to 24 hours before putting it in the freezer. As freezing has a tenderizing affect the aging recommended for some meats can be omitted. (Refer to AGING, in the MEAT section.)

Meat and poultry are subject to drying or freezer burn if not well wrapped and sealed. Double wrapping is best, especially if longer than a month or two storage is expected. Reinforce places where sharp bones push against the wrappings to prevent punctures, and put extra freezer tape on the outside of the package where there are bony points.

Storage life for meat and poultry at 0°F varies greatly depending on the kind of meat. Fatty meats, ground meat, and meat mixtures like sausage retain full quality from 3 to 6 months. Plain lean meats will keep their quality for a year or more, but it is generally not economical to leave food in the freezer for more than a year.

Most meat tastes better if it has been completely thawed before it is cooked. Roasts and large whole poultry must be thawed if the inside is to cook by the time the outside is done. Slow thawing inside the wrappings and in the refrigerator or other cool place is best, especially for large cuts, because thawing is more even and less juice is lost. It can take from 24 hours up to severals days to thaw a large roast or a turkey. Smaller cuts can be taken out of the freezer in the morning, and thawed at room temperature if they are to be cooked that evening. After thawing always cook meat without delay, as thawed meat will spoil much more quickly than fresh meat that was never frozen. Never re-freeze raw meat after it has thawed completely, as its quality will be poor, and it is possible for spoilage to begin if the meat has been above refrigerator temperature. It can be cooked and then frozen again.

(For precise freezing instructions refer also to the storage box in each specific meat or poultry section.)

## FREEZING COOKED FOODS

Bread and other baked goods and many kinds of precooked mixed dishes are excellent frozen. Most people experiment to find out which dishes in what amounts are most practical for them.

For some it works well to make extra baked goods and cooked dishes to put in the freezer in the winter and early spring. These can replace the vegetables and meats that were frozen during fall harvesting and butchering as they are used. The baked goods and cooked dishes can then be used during the busy late spring and summer months, making new space in the freezer for the season's harvests.

## FREEZING CAUTIONS

• Remember that foods that have been frozen and thawed will spoil much more quickly than fresh raw food. Most spoilage organisms are not killed by freezing, but merely held in an inactive state. Once thawed, the organisms can quickly spoil food tissues already broken down by ice crystals during the freezing process.

• Keep a close eye on the freezer and be prepared to take action if it should stop for any reason. A generator might be used during a prolonged power outage, or use dry ice to keep the food frozen. Avoid opening the freezer when there are problems. Another alternative during freezing weather is moving the food outdoors in animal-proof containers. If the food does begin to thaw, can or dry as much as possible. Some of it can also be salted. The rest must be cooked and eaten, or perhaps cooked and returned to the freezer when it is again in operation. (If food is only partly thawed, with ice crystals still showing in it, it can safely be refrozen, but quality may be noticeably lessened.) If foods are above refrigerator temperature, only the frozen fruits or other acid foods should be used or refrozen. Spoilage of fruit will show as fermentation or other quality loss. Cooked combination dishes or meats or poultry which show signs of spoilage must always be discarded.

• Keep the freezer as full as possible, as it takes less power to operate a full freezer. Empty and unplug a freezer with very little in it till it is needed again.

• Be aware that the flavors of some foods, especially seasonings, can change while they are stored in a freezer. Onions and salt lose strength over time. Others, such as pepper, cloves, garlic, celery, and sweet pepper may become strong or bitter tasting. Do not store highly seasoned foods for too long, and if possible plan to add seasonings when the food is cooked.

• Purées made in a blender or any device that whips air into them will lose quality faster in the freezer than sauces or purées made with a food mill or any method that mashes rather than whips. Cooking will drive the air out of blenderized foods, but then the fresh raw flavor will be lost.

# FROGS

**STORAGE**

**Canning**  To process, refer to canning directions in the CHICKEN section.

**Freezing**  Handle like meat or poultry. Refer to FREEZING FOODS section.

ALLOW 2–3 LARGE LEGS, OR 3–6 PAIRS OF SMALL LEGS PER SERVING

T HE DELICATE FLAVOR OF FROG'S LEGS MAKE THEM A GOURMET FOOD in many parts of the world. The hind legs of large bullfrogs are the frog's legs most often eaten, but the legs of small frogs also taste very good. In various parts of North America leopard frogs, green frogs, and pickerel frogs are also used for food.

Since most of the meat on a frog is on the hind legs the rest of the frog is usually discarded. However, it is possible to use the front legs, body, and liver for making a delicate soup.

## HANDLING FROGS

Frogs are hunted in many different ways with everything from sling shots, nets and hands, to spears and .22 rifles. Once a frog is killed its legs are very easy to prepare. Cut the hind legs off the body at the hip joint, pull off the skin, rinse, and they are ready to cook. The skin will come off very easily. Cutting off the feet is optional. For small frogs the legs can be cut off in one piece connected at the "waist". Removing the skin from the connected legs is like taking off a tiny pair of pants. Some people are disturbed by the legs twitching when they are skinned. To prevent this chill them first, before skinning them.

If the bony parts of the frog will be used for soup, cut off the head, then skin the rest. Discard the skin as it can sometimes be toxic. Clean out the innards, saving the liver (which looks like a very small chicken liver) and cut off the hind legs to use separately. Cook the body, front legs, and liver to make stock, which can be used for making a sauce to go with the hind legs.

Frog's legs are usually sautéed or fried, but they can also be broiled or stewed. Though they are often cooked like chicken, the best seasonings are those used with veal or rabbit which compliment the delicate white meat. (Try them in recipes from the VEAL and RABBIT sections.) Frog's legs usually take a little longer to cook than frying chickens or rabbits. The meat should be well done.

## FROG RECIPES

The following old recipe shows the care and respect with which frog's legs should be cooked. Some " sweet" herbs that go well with the meat are thyme, marjoram, parsley and tarragon.

### *A White Fricassy of Frogs, from Mr. Ganeau*

"Cut off the Hinder Legs, strip them of the Skin, and cut off the Feet, and boil them tender in a little Veal Broth, with whole Pepper and a little Salt, with a Bunch of Sweet Herbs and some Lemon-peel. Stew these with a Shallot, till the Flesh is a little tender; strain off the Liquor, and thicken it with Cream and Butter; Serve them hot with Mushrooms pickled, tossed up with the Sauce. They make a very good Dish, and their Bones being of a very fine Texture, are better to be eaten than those of Larks."

*In The Kitchen*, Elizabeth S. Miller, 1875.

### *Frog Soup, Italian Style*      (Makes 6–10 bowls.)

| | |
|---|---|
| *bodies, front legs, and livers from at least 1 dozen frogs* | *parsley and basil, a sprig each, minced* |
| 3 tablespoons olive oil | 1 tomato, chopped medium |
| 1 clove garlic, minced | 2–3 mushrooms, chopped |
| 1 small onion, minced | frogs' back legs, optional |
| 1 small carrot, minced | pepper, salt, optional |
| ½ stalk celery, minced | 2 tablespoons fine bread crumbs |

Heat the olive oil in a soup pot and sauté the garlic, onion, carrot, celery, parsley,and basil in it till their color brightens. Add the frog parts, tomato, mushroom, and 1½ quarts of water. Cover, and simmer about 1 hour. Take out and discard the frog's bony parts.

If using the back legs, add them and simmer till tender, 20–30 minutes. Season with pepper, and salt, if desired, and just before serving, sprinkle with bread crumbs. Toasted bread crumbs are nice, or use triangles of toast. Serve the back legs either in the soup, or separately.

---

**ANOTHER RECIPE FOR FROG**

Fried Frog's Legs, p.502

---

**STORAGE**

**Canning**   Refer to CANNING section, and see CANNING FRUIT JUICE AND SAUCE below.

**Cold Storage**   Refer to COLD STORAGE section.

**Drying**   Refer to DRYING FOODS section.

**Freezing**   Refer to FREEZING section, and see FREEZING FRUIT JUICE AND SAUCE below.

---

# FRUITS

THE ULTIMATE IN FOOD ENJOYMENT IS SURELY THE SAVORING OF ripe, freshly picked fruit. No instruction book can improve the taste of a juicy, sun-warmed strawberry or a crisp apple picked on a cool fall day! Recipes, and ideas for cooking, storing, and otherwise using fruit become helpful only after everyone has enjoyed as much as they want of the fresh fruit.

# SEMI-TROPICAL FRUITS

These fruits grow only in limited areas of the southern United States, but as they ship well, they are seen in stores in many places.

*Avocado*    There are two main types of avocados that grow in North America—large avocados with rough or bumpy seeds from Florida, and smaller ones with smooth seeds from California and Hawaii. Avocados are not sweet, but are oil rich, containing unsaturated fatty acids and Vitamins A and E. The fruits are not ripe until they feel soft when pressed. Firm fruits will ripen if kept at room temperature for several days to a week, or longer. When ripe, the stiff outer rinds peel off easily. Avocadoes are usually eaten raw and are delightful additions to salads with orange or grapefruit segments, or tomatoes. Mashed avocado is good in everything from soup to ice cream, but is best known as Guacamole (avocado sauce), a versatile Mexican sauce. Mashed avocado can be frozen if 2 teaspoons of lemon juice are mixed with every cupful. To keep avocadoes after they have been cut open, leave the seed in the part to be stored, squeeze the cut part with lemon or lime juice, wrap it well and refrigerate. (See the *Guacamole* and *Guatamalan Fruit Cup* recipes, below, and the AVOCADO ICE CREAM variation in the ICE CREAM section.)

*Citrus Fruits*    Most people think of citrus fruits as oranges, grapefruits, lemons and limes, but there are many others. One is the kumquat, a distinctive fruit that looks like a miniature orange and is eaten in entirety, both rind and fruit. A large fruit called variously, shaddock, pompelmous, or pummelo, is probably the parent of grapefruit. The most ancient of the citrus fruits is citron. Only its rind is edible, candied or pickled. (The citron melon whose rind is pickled is not related.)

Fresh, frozen, and canned citrus fruits and juice are shipped almost everywhere in North America, and are very familiar. Despite this, however, many have never tasted citrus fruits as their best—as fresh, tree ripened fruit. Eating these, or drinking their freshly squeezed juice is a heady experience, particularly the first time. If there is ever an opportunity to obtain them through special ordering, or during a trip to a citrus growing region, the experience is well worth extra effort and expense.

*Dried Citrus Peel*    Most dried peels make a flavorful seasoning for a variety of foods. Though used in the same ways as fresh grated rind only one third as much is needed. Since most commercial citrus fruits have been heavily sprayed with chemicals, their peels cannot be recommended for eating. Whenever a source of unsprayed fruit becomes available, dry as much peel as possible for future use. When dwarf lemon, lime, or orange trees are grown as house plants, the peel of their fruits can be dried. Such peels generally taste good even if the fruit itself does not.

To prepare peels for drying, scrape or pull of any remaining fruit. Cut them in strips or any convenient size, and spread them out in a warm, airy place. A food dryer works well, but the peels will dry at room temperature also. Once they are hard or brittle, store them in an airtight container. They can be gorund in a blender or other grinder as needed, or they can be ground and then stored. However, if pre-ground they lose flavor faster. The different kinds of citrus peel can substitute for each other in recipes; though the flavor varies, the results are all good. As well, a teaspoon of dried citrus peel instead of a teaspoon of vanilla in baked goods, puddings, and other desserts is a surprisingly delicious substitution.

For another way to preserve citrus fruit peels see the *Candied Fruit and Citrus Peel* recipe, below.

**Kiwi** This well-travelled fruit originated in China, then moved to New Zealand where an unimaginative name, Chinese Gooseberry, was changed to the catchier kiwi to make it more marketable, and now it is taking the U.S. and Canada by storm. The fuzzy brown-skinned fruit, with its attractive lime-green flesh and soft edible black seeds, is becoming familiar in grocery stores everywhere. The brown-skinned variety grows only in mild climates, but a new green-skinned, northern-hardy variety is now available from some plant nurseries. The plants are vines which grow much like grape vines.

Brown-skinned kiwis must be peeled before use. Press them to determine ripeness, as the skins always look the same. Their sweet-tart flavor is at its best when they are firm, yet not hard. If they soften too much they become bland and flavorless. Smooth, green-skinned kiwis do not need peeling, and are smaller and somewhat sweeter. Kiwi fruit is very high in Vitamin C and potassium.

Kiwis are most often used sliced, to take advantage of the stunning color contrast between green fruit and black seeds, but they can also be eaten whole, halved, or chopped. They make a perfect addition to most fruit cups and salads, and can be cooked like any tart fruit. Slices are easily dried to make a delightfully tart snack. No doubt they can also be frozen and canned successfully, but officially tested methods are not yet available.

**Olives** Though olive trees will grow in many locations across the southern United States, they bear fruit only in certain areas of California and Arizona. To be productive they must have dry hot summers and cool winters. Olive oil is the most important olive product, and has often replaced butter and animal fat. Pressing olives for oil is similar to pressing apples for cider. Fully ripe olives are picked in winter when they contain the most oil, then ground, seeds and all, pressed, then reground, and pressed a few times more. The first pressing produces virgin olive oil, and later pressings a denser, greener oil with a stronger olive flavor. Many prefer the flavor of the later pressings.

The familiar, canned, green and black olives are picked when underripe, then processed in lye or salt to remove bitterness. The shriveled black olives, often called Greek olives, are picked after frosts, when they are no longer bitter. They are usually salt cured and stored in olive oil.

*Pomegranates*   The name means apple with many grains. They are also known as Chinese apples. Pomegranates are eaten fresh, or pressed for juice. To open, cut off the crown and slice through the rind from top to bottom in strips, without cutting into the red, juicy "seeds." The fruit can then be pulled apart along its natural divisions. It is refreshingly tart eaten as is. The seeds can also be added to salads, and sprinkled on foods for garnish. Fresh pomegranate juice is excellent. Separate the red seeds from the white pith before pressing, and do not press hard enough to crush the seed's kernel, which will give an off flavor. The seeds can also be cooked and strained to make juice. Grenadine, a sweet syrup used to flavor beverages, is usually made from pomegranates.

## INSECTICIDES IN FRUIT

Most commercial fruits are treated with insecticides or other toxic chemicals at some time during growth and storage. Traces of them inevitably get inside the fruit where they cannot be washed or peeled off. It is well worthwhile, therefore, to raise or buy organically grown fruit, and to use wild fruit and fruit from neglected trees. If, however, the choice is between commercially raised fruit and no fruit at all, it seems best to eat and enjoy commercial fruit. However, processed fruit products that contain refined sugar or artificial sweeteners, preservatives, and artificial colorings and flavorings should certainly be avoided.

Insecticides on fruit skins are more successfully removed by washing in water containing a little vinegar or a few drops of detergent than by washing in plain water. Thorough rinsing is, of course, necessary. Peeling is another option, but this means the loss of vitamins, minerals, and flavor, which are often concentrated in or near the skin.

Fruit does not have to look perfect to taste delicious. Unsprayed or wild fruit may have superficial blemishes that can be trimmed off, or ignored. Seriously blemished or damaged fruit can often be trimmed and made into juice or sauce.

## COMBINING SWEET AND TART FRUITS

The range among fruit flavors is very broad, but most fruits can, nevertheless, be categorized as either sweet or bland, or tart or sour. Flavor-enhancing combinations can then be suggested to make sweet or bland fruits more piquant, and tart or sour fruits more mellow and sweet. A common example is the lemon juice so often sprinkled on sweet fruits to enhance their flavor.

Mellowing combinations are particularly valuable for very sour fruits. Often, sour fruit is considered unusable except in heavily sweetened mixtures, such as jams, jellies, pies and other desserts. Occasional treats of this kind are delicious, but there are less sugary ways to use sour fruit. Combining with sweet, bland fruits is ideal, since both flavors are improved and less additional sweetening is used. Fresh, dried, and canned fruits can be used, as well as juices and sauces. Very tart juices, from rhubarb, sour apple, or sour wild fruit, are useful when home canned in small jars for mixing with sweeter juices, and for adding to tea and other dishes instead of lemon juice.

## SWEET-TART FRUIT COMBINATIONS

combined with

| Sweet or Bland | Tart or Sour |
|---|---|
| (The possibilities are infinite.) | |
| Sweet Apples | Sour Apples |
| Bananas | Sour Cherries |
| Domestic Blueberries | Most Citrus Fruits |
| Sweet Cherries | Crabapples |
| Elderberries | Cranberries |
| Melons | Currants |
| Mulberries | Kiwi |
| Some Peaches | Gooseberries |
| Pears | Rhubarb |
| Persimmons | Sour Grapes |
| Rose Hips | Some Plums |
| Some Dried Fruits | Pomegranates |
|    (especially prunes, | Quince |
|    raisins, figs, | Many Wild Fruits |
|    and dates) |    and Berries |

## MAKING FRUIT JUICE AND SAUCE

Juice can be extracted from most fruits, and sauce can be made from any pulpy fruit. Berry juice is delicious, and stone fruits like peaches, apricots, and plums make good juice or sauce. Juice is always popular, and it is amazing how much a family can drink when the supply is plentiful. Fruit juice can also be used in gelatines, see the *Fruit Juice Pudding* recipe in this section, and in many other mixtures.

There are two approaches to making both juice and sauce. One is to use raw fruit, and the other is to extract the juice or make sauce from cooked fruit. For fruits other than citrus, the second approach is easier, but fresh juice and sauce are delicious and worth some extra effort.

*Fresh Fruit Juice*   Juice is easily squeezed from oranges and other citrus fruits. Most soft, raw fruit can be pressed through a sieve or food mill, or whirled in a blender and squeezed in a cloth to extract juice. If the fruit is very juicy, the purée may be thin enough to drink without straining. Peeling fruit before juicing is usually unnecessary but large pits or seeds should be removed, and some chopping may be required. The small seeds in berries or grapes are removed when a food mill, squeezing strainer or fine mesh sieve or cloth is used for straining. (Refer to SEEDINESS IN BLACKBERRIES in the BLACKBERRIES section, and UTENSILS FOR PURÉEING, in the KITCHEN UTENSILS section.)

Special equipment is needed to make juice from firm, raw fruits. They require chopping or grinding, then heavy pressure. Centrifugal juicers (best known for making carrot juice) will make juice in small quantities from most firm, raw fruits, but they are expensive and must be used almost every day to be worthwhile. Small quantities of juice can also be made by grinding firm fruit in a food chopper or processor and pressing it in a cloth bag under a heavy weight, or with an old fashioned fruit and lard press. (Refer to the KITCHEN UTENSILS section.) The equipment for making apple cider can be used for making juice from some other firm fruits. (Refer to the APPLES section.)

***Juice from Cooked Fruit***   When fruit is cooked till soft, the juice can be easily drained off or pressed out. The necessary equipment is a large cooking pot, and a big strainer or colander. If juice is made often, it would be worthwhile to purchase a steam juicer for extracting juice from fruit. Steam cooking can retain more of the fresh fruit flavor than boiling. A spigot or hose on the steamer drains off the juice when it is ready. (Refer to the illustration in the STEAM COOKING section.)

Peeling and seeding are generally unnecessary when cooking fruit for juice, since it will be strained later. Large fruits may be cut in pieces, and large pits may be taken out, if desired. A few peach or apricot pits can be left in for added flavor. Some water must usually be added, and the fruit must be stirred occasionally to help it cook evenly without sticking. Dry fruits may need to be covered with water. Fruits with tough skins, such as firm berries and grapes, should be mashed with a potato masher or similar tool to break the skins as they begin to cook. The flavor of some fruit juices is best if the cooking is kept at a simmer rather than a boil. (Refer to MAKING GRAPE JUICE in the GRAPES section.)

To make clear juice strain through a cloth, allowing the juice to drip without squeezing the pulp. Juice strained through a sieve will be cloudy, but heartier in flavor. (Refer to STRAINING ARRANGEMENTS FOR LIQUIDS in the KITCHEN UTENSILS section.) For a thick juice or nectar, some pulp should be pressed through the sieve with the liquid.

Homemade fruit juice is quite concentrated if made with a minimum of water and a long cooking time. Berries and wild fruits, in particular, make strong-flavored juices. These can be diluted for drinking, or used full strength to flavor gelatines, sherbets, and other dishes.

***Pulp from Making Fruit Juice***   There is a dryish pulp left when juice is extracted from raw or cooked fruit, which can be quite flavorful. A quick taste will determine whether it is worth saving. Spent pulp can be fed to livestock, or put in the compost pile. Pomace from making apple cider can be used for making pectin. (Refer to the PEC-TIN section.)

Most leftover pulp has enough flavor to make a second infusion of juice. Cover the pulp with water, heat to a boil, and strain. This juice can be mixed with the first batch, or used separately. Some very strong-flavored pulp can even be used for a third infusion. This diluted juice can be chilled, or poured over ice for a cool drink.

Other uses for fruit pulp are for making fruit sauce, butter, or leather, or fermenting it for vinegar. When a smooth-textured pulp is necessary, a strainer or food mill can be used to remove seeds, peels, and fibers. Thick, smooth pulp is ideal for making fruit butter, (refer to the JAM AND JELLY section), and fruit leather (refer to the DRYING section). The pulp from raw fruit is best for vinegar. (Refer to the VINEGAR section, and to USING APPLE PEELS AND CORES in the APPLES section.)

***Fruit Sauce***   Most kinds of fruit make good sauces. Like juice, they can be made from either raw or cooked fruit. Soft, raw fruits can be mashed through a sieve, food mill, or food press. (Refer to the KITCHEN UTENSILS section.) Other fruits can be peeled and cored or pitted as necessary, and puréed in a blender or food processor. Fresh fruit sauce should be eaten immediately since it darkens and loses flavor quickly.

Cooked fruit sauce can be made in several ways. Some fruits break down to a sauce when cooked, while others must be mashed or puréed. Most fruits can be "sauced" like apples. (Refer to the APPLES section.)

***Canning Fruit Juice and Sauce***   Acidic juices and sauces are among the easiest foods to can. (If a fruit's acidity is doubtful it is noted under CANNING in the box at the beginning of that section.) The juice or sauce should be heated to a boil, and poured into hot canning jars, leaving ¼ inch headroom for juice and ½ inch headroom for sauce. All modern canning guides require processing both pints and quarts for 10 minutes in a boiling water bath. (Refer to the CANNING section.) However, large quantities of acidic fruit juices are successfully home canned every year using the open kettle method. (Refer to OPEN KETTLE CANNING in the CANNING section.) Thick sauces and purées should be processed in a boiling water bath, since it is hard to know if a thick sauce is heated to 212°F throughout, and hard to keep it very hot while pouring and sealing. All blenderized purées or sauces should be cooked uncovered for several minutes before canning to drive out the air bubbles whipped into them by the blender.

The quality of a few fruit juices, including grape juice and some berry juice, is best if it is never boiled. These juices should be heated to a simmer rather. than a boil, or to about 190°F, before they are poured into jars. They must then be processed in a boiling water bath at 190°F for 30 minutes.

*Freezing Fruit Juice and Sauce*    Freezing is not as practical as canning for the majority of fruit juices and sauces. The quality of juice or sauce from cooked fruit is just as good or better canned, and no thawing is required before use. The flavor of some fresh, raw juices and sauces is quite special, and these may be frozen. It is also possible to make a concentrated fresh juice for freezing. (Refer to CONCENTRATED JUICE in the FREEZING section.)

Sauces intended for freezing should be made by mashing the fruit, or pushing it through a sieve or food mill. Blender sauces and purées have had air whipped into them, and enzymes have been released that make them lose quality quickly. It is better to freeze fruit whole or in slices, then put it in the blender when it is removed from the freezer. Some fruits make delicious frozen desserts if puréed in a blender or food processor while frozen, and eaten immediately. (Refer to the *Fruit Sherbet* recipes in the ICE CREAM section, and the FROZEN PERSIMMON DESSERTS idea in the PERSIMMONS section.)

## FRUIT RECIPES

### Wintertime Hot Fruit Soup                        (Makes 8–12 bowls.)

½ cup rice or barley, or ¼ cup tapioca
1 cup mixed dried fruit, chopped as necessary
2 cups (about) canned gooseberries, currants, sour cherries, or other unsweetened fruit

2–3 cups grapefruit juice, or other tart juice
honey, to taste, optional
2 tablespoons (about) cornstarch, or potato starch (Refer to the POTATOES section.)

In a pot combine the rice, barley, or tapioca with dried fruit and 2 quarts of water. Cover and cook about 30 minutes, or till the fruit is soft, and the rice or barley is almost cooked. Add the gooseberries or other fruit, and the grapefruit juice. Add honey to taste. It should be only slightly sweet. Heat, then simmer for a few minutes to blend flavors. Mix the cornstarch or potato starch in a little cold water and stir into the soup, adding enough for a smooth, slightly thickened texture. If tapioca is used, less starch will be needed.

This is an energizing hot soup for lunch or supper, or an after-school snack on a cold day. A spoonful of yogurt or sour cream can be floated on each soup bowl.

### Guatamalan Fruit Cup                              (Makes 6–8 cups.)

4–6 large oranges, peaches, or other fresh fruit
3 tablespoons parsley, minced
2 tablespoons chives, scallions, or sweet onions, minced

2 tablespoons pimiento, cut in thin strips
1–2 avocadoes, cut in bite sized pieces, optional
honey, or other sweetening, optional

If using oranges, cut them in half and remove segments with a small spoon or knife, working over a bowl to catch the juice. Cut peaches or other fruit into bite sized pieces, peeling if necessary. Combine the fruit and juice with the parsley, chives, scallions or onion, pimiento, and avocado, if desired. If tart, add sweetening, but do not let the mixture get too sweet. Serve in individual dishes, or scrape out orange peels and fill one for each serving. They make a delightful appetizer.

## *Fruit Curry*                    (Makes about 6 medium servings.)

2 tablespoons butter, or
   1 tablespoon oil
3–4 medium onions, sliced medium
2 medium apples, chopped medium
1 tablespoon curry powder, or to taste
hot red pepper, to taste
2 cups water, or light soup stock
½ teaspoon ginger root, minced, optional
1 bay leaf
1 teaspoon thyme, or marjoram
1 tablespoon honey

½ cup shredded, unsweetened coconut
½ cup raisins, or dried apricots, chopped
1 banana, sliced
1–2 cups fresh peaches, canteloupe, or other fruit, chopped, optional
lemon juice, to taste
almonds, slivered or chopped for garnish, optional

Heat the butter and oil in a heavy, deep frying pan or Dutch oven. Slowly sauté the onion and apple till the onion is limp. Stir in the curry powder and red pepper. Add the water or soup stock, ginger root, bay leaf, thyme or marjoram, honey, coconut, and raisins or dried apricots. Cover, and simmer 30 minutes. Add the banana and other fresh fruit. Cover and simmer till the fruit is barely cooked, about 5 to 10 minutes. Add lemon juice to taste. Set the almonds on the table in a dish so that people can help themselves. Serve with rice and yogurt, or a mildly seasoned raita. (Refer to the YOGURT section.)

## *Fruit Tempura*
(Japanese Fruit Fritters.)                    (Makes snacks for 6–8 people.)

Batter:
   1 teaspoon honey, or sugar
   1 egg, separated
   1 cup (about) flour (Half whole wheat and half unbleached is good.)
Fruits (Use one or several, or try other firm fruits.):
   apples, cored and sliced into ¼ inch thick wedges

pears, cored and sliced into ¼ inch thick wedges
bananas, sliced diagonally ½ to 1 inch thick
pineapple, canned or fresh, in chunks about 1 inch thick
oil or fat for deep frying (One that does not burn easily.)
1–2 tablespoons sesame oil, optional

To make the batter, mix the sweetening and egg yolk in a bowl, using a fork or wire whisk. Slowly add 1 cup of cold water, stirring constantly. Gradually add enough flour to make a batter of pancake consistency. Do not over-mix—the batter can be a bit lumpy. (This much can be done ahead of time and refrigerated for an hour or so.) Beat the egg white till stiff and fold into the batter.

Heat the oil or fat, including sesame oil if it is used, in a deep-fat fryer or wok to between 350° and 375°F. To test the temperature, drop in a bit of batter. It should sink, then rise immediately. Dip pieces of fruit in the batter one at a time and fry, turning once to brown evenly. They should cook in 3 to 5 minutes. Drain on a wire rack or paper and serve hot.

*Vegetable Tempura* Cut vegetables into easily handled pieces, steam to precook and chill completely. Deep-fry as for fruit, using the same batter.

### *Layered Bread and Fruit Pudding*  (Makes about 6 dessert servings.)

| | |
|---|---|
| 2 cups whole grain bread crumbs | ¼ cup honey, or other sweetening, to taste |
| ¼ cup wheat germ, optional | |
| 2 tablespoons butter, or other fat, melted | lemon juice and grated rind, to taste |
| 3 cups fresh prepared fruit, drained canned fruit, or soaked dried fruit (Apples, rhubarb or berries are all good. Pears spiced with ginger are a classic.) | spices to taste (Crushed herb seeds like anise, coriander or caraway are good.) |
| | ¼ cup (about) fruit juice or water |

Mix the bread crumbs, wheat germ, and melted butter or fat. In another bowl mix the fruit with the sweetening, lemon juice and rind, adjusting amounts according to the fruit's tartness.

Grease a 1½−2 quart baking dish, and spread a third of the bread crumb mixture in the bottom. Add half the fruit and sprinkle with spices. Add fruit juice or water as necessary to moisten the drier kinds of fruit. If dried fruit is used, use the soaking water. Spread on another third of the bread crumb mixture, then the rest of the fruit and spices. Top with the last third of the bread crumbs. Cover and bake in a moderate, 350°F oven, for 45 minutes, removing the cover after 30 minutes.

Serve warm or cold with milk or cream, or with one of the *Sauces for Steamed Puddings* in the STEAM COOKING section.

### *Fruit Juice Pudding*                              (Makes about 6 dessert servings.)

| | |
|---|---|
| 4 cups strongly flavored fruit juice such as berry or grape, or juice from wild fruits | 5−6 tablespoons potato starch (refer to the POTATOES section), cornstarch, or other thickener |
| | honey, or sugar, to taste |

Add about a cup of cool fruit juice to the starch and mix well. In a saucepan heat the rest of the juice and the sweetening to a boil. Pour in the juice and starch mixture very slowly, stirring constantly. Simmer over very low heat, stirring often, for about 5 minutes. Pour into a serving dish or individual dishes to cool.

This pudding is delicious with yogurt or unsweetened whipped cream, and perhaps sprinkled with chopped nuts.

### FRUIT IDEAS

**Mulled Fruit Juice** To mull means to heat and spice a beverage. Mulled cider is traditional, but most fruit juices are also excellent mulled. Heat the juice slowly with a cinnamon stick, a few whole cloves and other whole spices, if desired. Thin slices of orange or lemon can be added. Strong juice can be diluted with water or blander juice. If it is tart, add honey. Heat slowly to blend flavors, then remove it from the stove before it boils.

For a festive occasion, homemade wine can be mulled. Mix it with juice for a mulled punch.

## Guacamole
(Makes 1½–3 cups.)

2 large or 3 small ripe avocadoes, peeled, seeded, and mashed
1 tomato, chopped, or 1 tablespoon lemon juice
1 tablespoon onion, minced, optional
1 clove garlic, minced, optional
½ cup celery, minced, optional
fresh coriander leaves, minced, optional
1 tablespoon fresh hot pepper, minced, or dried flakes to taste
salt, optional

Combine all ingredients. Avocado darkens quickly, so it should be mixed just before serving. If that is not possible, put an avocado seed in the middle of the guacamole and cover closely to keep out oxygen.

Guacamole can be a salad dressing, a sandwich spread, a vegetable or chip dip, or a sauce for tacos and other Mexican foods.

## Candied Fruit and Citrus Peel

(Home candied fruits and peels are excellent in fruit cake and other baked goods. They are dryer than most commercial ones. Since they do not contain artificial colorings, flavorings, and preservatives they are far healthier and safer to use.)

For each pound of trimmed citrus fruit peel, pitted cherries, cubed pineapple, or other prepared fruit, use 2 cups honey or maple syrup, or a syrup made from 1½ cups water and 3 cups sugar.

If using citrus peel, cut it in strips or squares, then cover with water, cook till tender, drain and taste. If it still tastes strong and bitter, cover again with water, bring to a boil, and drain. Repeat as necessary to remove bitterness. (The flavor of some peels will be much stronger than others, depending on the kind of fruit and its season. Peels are strongest when the fruit first ripens.)

Cherries, pineapple, and other fruits do not need precooking. Put them, or the debittered peel, in a pot with the sweetener. Simmer, uncovered, over very low heat till the fruit or peel appears translucent and the liquid has almost disappeared. This will take from 40 to 60 minutes. Stir often towards the end of the cooking time to prevent burning. The fruit or peels will be sticky when removed from heat, especially when using honey. They can be spread on waxed paper in a food dryer, or on a baking sheet in a very low oven, 200°F or less, until most of the stickiness is gone.

*Candied Ginger Root*   Slice fresh ginger root, precook as for citrus peel, then proceed as described above. The water drained off cooked ginger root can be used for the *Gingerade* recipe in the BEVERAGES section.

## GARLIC

GARLIC IS RENOWNED AS A SEASONING AND A MEDICINAL HERB. Since ancient times it has been credited with preventing or curing numerous disorders. Authorities on folk remedies and herbal or natural medicines praise it highly, and modern scientific investigators find it as remarkable as did their ancestors. However, it is garlic as a vegetable and a food seasoning that is most interesting to cooks and those for whom they cook.

There are, it seems, two kinds of people in the world: those who love and those who hate garlic. But no one should consider himself or herself among the haters without first tasting the best quality fresh garlic prepared in as many ways as possible. The unpleasantly harsh or bitter taste of very old or long-frozen garlic may be the cause of an initial dislike. (Another source of bitterness may be the use of chemical fertilizers during cultivation.) The best garlic is home grown and no more than a year old. Its peeled cloves are firm and almost white, neither limp nor turning yellow or brown, and its flavor is comparatively mild.

There are several plants besides regular garlic which have a mild garlic flavor. Elephant garlic, with its very large cloves, is mild and can be added to foods as liberally as onions. Garlic chives, or Chinese leeks, have a mild garlic flavor. Like regular chives, the tops are minced and used for garnishes, as in salads and cottage cheese. Wild garlic tops can be minced and similarly used when they first come up in the spring. The seed stalks that sometimes grow from garlic plants also have a mild garlic flavor. They can be cut and cooked as a vegetable. (See GARLIC IDEAS below.)

### HANDLING GARLIC

Pull or dig up garlic when the tops begin to wither and die. In moderate climates this happens in mid-summer. It should be harvested before the tops die back entirely when the bulbs are easy to locate. Garlic must cure, or dry, in an airy place. It can be left outdoors for a few days in the shade or in the field with the tops covering the bulbs, but should not be left in direct sunlight.

One way to store garlic is to trim the heads, leaving about 1 inch of the tops and ½ an inch of the roots, and keep them like onions in net bags or other porous containers. Another method is to tie the garlic tops in bunches, or to braid them for hanging. This must be done while the tops are still green enough to be flexible.

Hang the braids in a cool corner of the kitchen, in the attic, a spare room, or the pantry. A braid of garlic makes an irresistible gift from the garden. Such braids can even be saved and given as Christmas presents.

***Peeling Garlic*** Garlic's thin, papery peel generally has to be removed before use. When only one or two cloves are needed, it is easy enough to pull off the peels. Pressing each clove firmly with the side of a knife blade loosens the peels. To quickly peel a larger number, blanch the separated cloves by dropping them in boiling water for 2 minutes, then drain them. This loosens the peels so they will easily slip off.

Garlic can be added unpeeled to soups or sauces that are to be strained before serving. It is also possible to mash garlic unpeeled through a garlic press, but there will be more waste than with peeled cloves.

***Crushing Garlic*** When crushed or mashed, garlic releases a strong flavor that seasons food quickly. A garlic press is often used to force the garlic clove through little holes in the press, making a kind of purée. Other ways to crush garlic are to hit it with a mallet or knife handle, or to press it with the flat of a knife blade. Another method is to mince the garlic, then mash it with the back of a spoon in a small cup or bowl, or with a mortar and pestle. A little salt is sometimes mashed with it, helping to remove bitterness.

***Garlic's Changing Flavor*** Garlic's strength and flavor changes dramatically with different methods of preparation. Garlic cloves used whole or sliced or minced are milder than crushed garlic. When cooked gently till well done, garlic is surprisingly mild and much different in flavor from either raw garlic or garlic sautéed quickly at high heat. Often, people do not even recognize the garlic taste when it has been simmered a while with other ingredients. Instead, they only notice an exceptionally good flavor. A garlic purée (see recipe below) will bring such a subtle flavor to many dishes.

Even raw garlic does not have to be overwhelming. It can be mixed with fresh parsley to modify and complement its taste. These two are so compatible that the very best remedy for garlic breath is to eat a bunch of fresh parsley. In fact, whenever raw garlic is used fresh parsley is sure to taste good as well.

There is a distinctive flavor and aroma to sautéed, lightly browned garlic. Some expert cooks say never to brown garlic, but there are also delicious dishes that depend on the browned garlic flavor, so it is in the end a matter of personal choice. Many Chinese stir-fried dishes begin with browning a minced garlic clove. (Refer to the STIR-FRYING section.)

*Braiding garlic*

To begin braid, twist or tie three plants together.

Add new plants at even intervals during braiding.

Tie knot to finish braid.

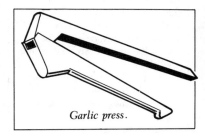

*Garlic press.*

# GARLIC RECIPES

The following recipes demonstrate many of the different ways in which garlic can be used.

### Raw Garlic and Parsley Relish                              (Make ¼ – ½ cup.)

*several cloves garlic*                                    *small bunch of fresh parsley*

Peel, chop, then mince garlic and parsley together till they are well mixed and rather fine textured. Sprinkle this relish on meat or vegetables when serving. Especially good sprinkled generously on a steak just before eating.

### Garlic Purée                                                        (Makes ½ – 1 cup.)

*5 heads of garlic* (They should be        *salt, optional*
    firm, not sprouting. Home              *1 tablespoon oil, preferably olive*
    grown are best.)

Wrap the garlic heads together in aluminum foil and bake in a hot, 400°F, oven till soft, from 50 to 60 minutes. Test by poking through a clove with a thin-bladed knife. Unwrap and let the garlic cool till it can be handled. Pull off enough of the peels and root attachment to separate the cloves. Set a fine mesh sieve in a bowl and squeeze each clove over it so the soft center is forced out from the root end and into the sieve. Discard the skins and press the cloves through the sieve with the back of a spoon. Mix with a dash of salt, if desired, and the oil. This purée will keep for a month or more if packed in a small jar and refrigerated with a thin layer of oil poured over the surface.

Add this purée to soups, stews, mashed or puréed vegetables, and salad dressings. It can even be mixed with butter and spread on bread for an hors d'oeuvre or snack. For those who like the purée, 20 or 25 heads can be puréed at once and stored in the refrigerator.

### A Garlicky Stuffing for Vegetables                  (Makes about 2 cups.)

*2 cups cooked dry beans*                   *½ cup parsley, minced*
*2 cups cooked rice*                        *1 tablespoon sesame seeds,*
*2 tablespoons garlic purée or several*         *toasted, optional*
    *cloves garlic, minced and lightly*     *pepper, salt, optional*
    *browned in butter or oil*              *2 tablespoons (about) butter or*
                                                *oil*

Partly mash the beans with a spoon or fork and mix with the rice, garlic, parsley, sesame seeds, pepper, and salt, if desired. Use to stuff green peppers, hollowed out tomatoes, zucchini or other summer squash, cabbage leaves, or other vegetables. Except for tomatoes, vegetables should first be steamed for about 10 minutes before stuffing. (Refer to the various vegetables RECIPES sections.)

Next, butter or oil a baking dish and arrange the stuffed vegetables

---

## GARLIC IDEAS

**Stewed Garlic Seed Stalks**
Cut seed stalks as soon as they appear in growing garlic plants. They are most tender then, and will also interfere with bulb formation if allowed to grow. Stew these stalks in a few tablespoons of water with a pat of butter or a little oil for about 10 minutes, and add a sprinkle of pepper, if desired. If there are too few stalks for a separate dish, they can be sliced and cooked with such vegetables as peas or green beans.

**Garlic Spaghetti**   Mince several garlic cloves and sauté till lightly browned in several tablespoons of oil or butter. Mince a small bunch of parsley. Toss hot spaghetti with the parsley, garlic, and oil or butter. If desired, season with pepper and salt, and serve immediately.

**Garlic Bread**   There are versions using garlic salt or garlic flavored oil or butter, but none are as good as home grown garlic with home baked bread. Sourdough bread is especially good for this. Slice the bread part way through, leaving the loaf attached at the bottom. Spread a little butter and a bit of mashed garlic on the slices. A garlic press is handy for mashing the garlic. Season with salt if desired, and bake for 15 to 20 minutes, or till the butter melts and the bread browns slightly.

For a variation, use olive oil instead of butter, and add a sprinkling of parmesan cheese or paprika.

in it. Dot with the butter or sprinkle with oil. Put several tablespoons of water in the baking dish. Bake uncovered 30 to 40 minutes in a moderate oven.

**Stuffed Vegetables in Tomato Sauce**  Prepare and stuff the vegetables as above. Omit water, and pour tomato sauce or stewed tomatoes over and around them. Bake as above.

## Garlic Soups

There are many ways to make garlic soup, but most include bread or toast. The very simplest are made with garlic, bread, olive oil, and water. A spoonful of garlic purée can be added to almost any soup to make it deliciously garlicky. Below are two Mediterranean recipes.

### Garlic Soup, Spanish Style                    (Makes about 6 bowls.)

| | |
|---|---|
| 5 cloves garlic | 2 slices whole wheat bread |
| ½ teaspoon salt, or to taste | 1 teaspoon paprika |
| 2 cups stewed tomatoes | 2 tablespoons oil |
| 1 green pepper, chopped | |

Mince the garlic, then mash it with salt to make a paste. Purée the tomatoes, green pepper, and bread in the blender, adding about 2 cups of water, or enough to make a thick soup. (Traditionally, all ingredients would be puréed with a mortar and pestle. It is also possible to put the garlic in the blender with the other ingredients, but this may make its flavor overly strong.)

Mix the oil and paprika in a soup pot and add the garlic and tomato mixtures. Bring to a boil, then simmer over low heat for 10 minutes. Stir several times to prevent sticking.

### Garlic Soup, Italian Style                    (Makes 6 bowls.)

| | |
|---|---|
| 6 cloves garlic, sliced | 6 slices bread, toasted |
| 6 tablespoons butter or olive oil | 6 tablespoons grated cheese |
| 6 cups chicken broth or other soup stock | parsley, minced |

In the soup pot, over low heat, gently sauté the garlic in butter or oil till soft but not brown. Add the chicken broth or stock and simmer 20 minutes. Put a slice of toast in each bowl and pour soup over it. Sprinkle cheese and parsley on top.

---

### GARLIC IDEAS, *cont.*

**Garlic and Potatoes**  Garlic combines well with many different styles of potatoes. A little garlic purée mixed with mashed potatoes tastes very good, and sliced or minced garlic can be fried with potatoes.

A Spanish recipe (*El Ajo de la Mano* or The Garlic of the Hand) combines them as follows: Boil potatoes in water with 1 or 2 dried hot peppers. Drain and slice the potatoes. Mash several cloves of garlic with a little paprika, salt, a few drops of vinegar, and a few teaspoons of oil. Mix with the potatoes and reheat before serving.

---

### OTHER RECIPES FEATURING GARLIC

Black-eyed Peas and Peppers, p.26
Garlic Herb Vinegar, p.677
Garlic Mayonnaise, p.534
Garlicky Bean Soup, p.24
Herb Sauce Marinade for Broiled Meat, p.340
Kimchi, p.176
Lamb Shanks with Garlic, p.380
Marinated Summer Squash, p.601
Pesto, Herb–Garlic Sauce, p.340
Portuguese Fish Vinaigrette, p.269
Veal Roasted Catalan Style, p.666

## STORAGE

**Canning** *Jelled stock* Can like soup stock (refer to SOUP section).

**Freezing** Cut stiffly jelled stock in chunks, wrap individually or pour warm stock in containers, cool before freezing. Must be warmed to melt before use. Do not freeze finished gelatines or aspics. (They will crack, form ice crystals, or weep when thawed.) Refer to FREEZING section.

GELATINE IS A PROTEIN EXTRACTED FROM THE BONES, CONNECTIVE tissue, sinews, and skin of animals, including poultry and fish. The dry, unflavored gelatine granules sold in stores are a purified form of this protein. It is not possible to make dry gelatine at home, but it is both possible and practical to extract it from animals' bony parts and scraps by boiling them in water. This sort of gelatine is familiar to everyone who has seen the way juice from roasted meat jells when it cools, or how some soup stocks jell when cold.

A bland, stiffly jelled stock can be used as a base for many delicious fruit, vegetable, or meat gelatines. Commercial unflavored powdered gelatine can be used to make fruit juice gelatines and other jelled dishes. Those unfortunate packaged gelatine dessert mixtures, with their sugar overload and artificial coloring and flavoring, should be avoided.

Gelatine is not nutritionally valuable as a protein because it lacks too many of the essential amino acids. Its value lies in its ability to mix with and jell warm liquids when they are chilled. This attribute makes it possible to create interesting new dishes from ordinary liquids—dishes which can be very nutritious with well-chosen ingredients.

Several substances besides gelatine will jell liquids. Agar agar acts like dry gelatine and can be substituted for it in recipes. It is derived from seaweed and is popular with those who wish to avoid gelatine from animal sources. There are also several kinds of seaweed that can be collected and used to make jelled foods. (Refer to the SEAWEED section.) Pectin, which occurs in some fruits is another substance that causes liquids to jell, but as it acts only when sugar and acid are present it is not a good gelatine substitute. (Refer to the PECTIN section.) Gelatine will jell any liquid except uncooked pineapple or papaya juice. These contain an enzyme that digests the gelatine protein. Cooked pineapple and papaya juices can be jelled because the enzyme is destroyed by heat.

Aspics are meat, vegetable, or tomato flavored gelatines, which are often quite elaborate and decorative. The word aspic has the same origin as the word asp, a kind of snake, apparently with the idea that the many colors of an aspic are like the many colors of a snake. In old cookbooks, gelatine dishes are generally called jellies. *Nineteenth Century Calf's Foot Jelly* (see RECIPES, below) was once a popular wine gelatine dessert.

## JELLED STOCK

Gelatines made from jelled stock have a remarkably delicate texture and subtle yet rich flavor. Almost all the bony parts of most animals can be used for making jelled stock, but the feet of hooved animals are the very best. They make an almost flavorless, stiffly jelled stock that is an ideal base for gelatine desserts and other gelatine dishes. Veal and pork bones and connective tissue make a stiff, bland jell that is also very good. Stock from rabbit bones is bland, but does not always jell stiffly enough. The feet of chickens and other poultry make a stiff jell, but will have a noticeable meat flavor. The heads, tails, and meatier parts of many animals make a stock that jells, but also with a meaty flavor. Fish heads, bones and skin make a stiff, fish-flavored jelled stock.

Though fruit gelatines require a base of bland or unflavored jelled stock, some outstanding vegetable and meat gelatines or aspics can be made with flavorful jelled stocks. For example, a fish-flavored gelatine is part of the Sally Katz *Gefilte Fish* recipe in the FISH section, and of the gelatine glazes described below. Both should be made from strongly flavored stocks.

A jelled stock is made the same way as an unseasoned concentrated soup stock. (Refer to the SOUP section.) If using hooved feet, refer to the FEET section. For cleaning chicken feet refer to the CHICKEN section, and for using bones refer to the BONES section. put the feet, bones, and other scrap parts in a non-aluminum pot. (Aluminum can cause cloudiness in the gelatine.) Add enough water to cover and a little above. Do not add any seasoning. Bring to a boil and skim. Cover, then simmer till the water is reduced by half or more. Large feet and bones should cook for at least 6 hours. Poultry feet and bones, and the bones of rabbits or other small animals should cook from 2 to 4 hours. Fish heads and bones should be just barely covered with water and simmered for not more than an hour. Longer cooking can give fish stock an unpleasant taste.

When the pot liquid is sufficiently reduced, strain it through a cloth and put it in a cold place overnight or till firmly set. Remove any congealed fat from the top. Turn the jelled stock out of its container and scrape off any sediment that is attached underneath. The jelled stock can be used as is or it can be clarified in the same way as soup stock. (Refer to the SOUP section, or see the recipe for *Nineteenth Century Calf's Foot Jelly* below.)

The best jelled stock is stiff to the point of being rubbery, because it can be diluted with a considerable amount of fruit juice or other liquid and still solidify when chilled. A soft jell can be stiffened by adding powdered gelatine as described below.

Stock gelatines differ in a few ways from those made with dry gelatine. Jelled stock takes longer to set, so prepare it 5 or 6 hours ahead of time. Also, as it softens or melts at room temperature, it must be kept chilled till served. Similarly, unmolded gelatines or aspics are apt to lose their shape if left in a warm room. However, they can be set on crushed ice if they are to be left out as part of a buffet.

**Fruit Gelatine from Stock**   To make fruit gelatines, warm a stiff, bland jelled stock till melted, and add a strongly flavored fruit juice. Sweeten with honey or sugar, if necessary. Chopped or sliced fruit, celery, or nuts can also be included. Then pour the mixture into one serving dish, or individual dessert dishes, and chill to reset.

It is not possible to give exact proportions of jelled stock to fruit juice because the jell's stiffness will vary. A very stiff jell can usually be mixed with half the amount of fruit juice, or 1 cup of fruit juice to 2 cups of jelled stock. A medium jell may allow only ¼ to ½ cup of juice with 2 cups of jelled stock. With practice the right proportions can be predicted quite accurately. If a gelatine becomes too diluted to set, it can be rescued by soaking a little powdered gelatine in cold water or juice, heating it till dissolved, and adding it to the gelatine mixture. (See USING COMMERCIAL POWDERED GELATINE below.)

Some good juices for flavoring jelled stock are lemon, rhubarb, frozen juice concentrates, such as orange or grape, and strongly flavored home canned juices from berries and wild fruits. See the *Fruit Juice Gelatine* recipe below.

**Vegetable or Meat Aspics from Stock**  Any jelled stock, including those with a strong meat or fish flavor, combines well with vegetables and the meat or fish that was used for making the stock.

First the melted jell is seasoned to taste. If it is already flavorful, very little seasoning will be needed. If bland, lemon juice or vinegar may be added for a tart taste. Tomato juice and a little onion juice are also good. Raw or cooked vegetables cut in attractive shapes may be mixed in, along with minced, fresh herbs, such as parsley, chervil, and scallions. Chopped or flaked meat, or fish, as appropriate, can be added, or slices may be set into the still soft gelatine. Often, ingredients are arranged in layers in the molded gelatine and unmolded on a bed of lettuce or parsley. See GELATINE MOLDS below.

**Gelatine Glazes**  A stiff, jelled stock can be used to glaze cold meats and other foods. The glaze keeps the food fresh and moist and is decorative, as well.

The juice or stock left from cooking the food to be glazed is often used, but any complementary flavored jell can be used. If it does not jell well, it should be stiffened by adding powdered gelatine. (See proportions below.) The food to be glazed must be quite cold and the gelatine at the point where it is just beginning to thicken, so that it will set almost as soon as it touches the food.

To glaze a larger piece of food, spoon or pour the gelatine over it; smaller pieces can be dipped into the gelatine. Very small pieces can be speared with a toothpick and dipped. A thick glaze can be achieved by coating the food once, chilling it to set the glaze completely, then coatinng it again. Sometimes a whole chicken or fish is glazed and decorated with vegetables slices or hard-boiled egg slices dipped in glaze and stuck against it. The vegetables can first be blanched, or cooked briefly to make them pliable.

Some extraordinary food displays can be created in this way, but they take time and patience. The busy homemaker might enjoy thinking about them more than actually doing them!

# USING COMMERCIAL POWDERED GELATINE ✓
## Proportions of Powder to Liquid

For a stiff jell: 1 tablespoon dry gelatine per 1¼ to 1½ cups liquid

For an average jell: 1 tablespoon dry gelatine per 2 cups liquid

For a soft jell: 1 tablespoon dry gelatine per 2¼ to 2½ cups liquid

To stiffen a soft jell use about 1 teaspoon dry gelatine per 2 cups of soft jelled liquid.

Any liquid can be jelled with dry gelatine, except uncooked pineapple or papaya juices which contain a protein-digesting enzyme. However, the cooked juices will jell. To use dry gelatine, simply soak it in a cool liquid till it swells, warm it till it dissolves, and chill till set. There are several ways to go about this. One practical method is to sprinkle 1 tablespoon gelatine over ½ cup of cold liquid in a small pan. Soak 5 minutes or till the gelatine swells, then warm the mixture slowly over very low heat, stirring constantly till the gelatine is dissolved. This takes just two minutes and the mixture will only be moderately warm. Look closely at the liquid coating the spoon to see if any undissolved granules show. When it is completely smooth, combine with the rest of the liquid to be jelled. The gelatine should set in about an hour in a refrigerator or similarly cold place.

Another method is to soak the powder for 5 minutes in ¼ cup cold liquid, then add 1 cup of boiling hot liquid. Stir till dissolved, then add the rest of the cold liquid. To speed the setting process add 8 to 10 large ice cubes, instead of the cold liquid, and stir till they are melted. If the gelatine starts to set before the cubes are completely melted, discard the remaining bits of ice. Adding ice cubes is, of course, adding water, so they can only be used if there is to be water in the recipe.

## GELATINE MOLDS

Nothing is more exotic than a mold of clear gelatine with an arrangement of colorful foods shimmering within it. The mold may be made with fruits for desserts, with vegetables or meats for a salad, or a whole fish or bird may be molded in gelatine for a main course. The historical recipe for pigeons in a mold of jelly at the beginning of the BIRDS, SMALL section describes an especially dramatic dish.

All gelatine molds are put together in the same way. The foods to be used in the mold must be well chilled. The mold container must have flared sides for easy unmolding, and it, too, must be chilled. The gelatine should be cooled till it has a slightly thickened texture like raw egg whites. If it becomes too thick to pour, it should be set in a pan of warm water to keep it softened.

To begin, rinse the mold with cold water and pour in enough gelatine to make a layer ½ to 1 inch thick. If using only one kind of gela-

---

**GELATINE IDEAS**

**Gelatine Fillings for Fruits and Vegetables** Any fruit or vegetable with a hollow space can be filled with a complementary flavored gelatine. Peach halves or melon halves are delicious with fruit gelatine. Green peppers or tomatoes can be cut in half, centers removed, and filled with vegetable or meat gelatine. The gelatine can be poured in when just ready to set, or a finished gelatine can be cubed and piled into the hollows. They both look and taste very good.

**Cottage Cheese, Cream Cheese, or Sour Cream Gelatines** A rich fruit or vegetable gelatine can be made by mixing ½ to 1 cup of small curd cottage cheese, cream cheese, or sour cream into about 1½ cups of gelatine before it sets. This mixture is good when filling fruits or vegetables as described above.

**GELATINE IDEAS,** *cont.*

**Milk Gelatines** Gelatine desserts can be made with a variety of flavored milk mixtures. A simple but delicious version is made by dissolving a tablespoon of gelatine powder in ½ cup of milk (See USING COMMERCIAL POWEDERED GELATINE, above), adding 4 tablespoons of honey, ¼ teaspoon vanilla or almond extract, and 1½ cups cold milk. For a special touch, sprinkle with carob powder and chopped nuts after the mixture has set.

**Gelatine Easter Eggs** To empty egg shells, make a ½ inch hole in one end of each egg by picking at it with a skewer, or other sharp tool. (This is easily done with thick-shelled, home-raised eggs, but a gentle touch is needed with thin-shelled eggs.) Stir the egg contents to break them and pour them out. Rinse the egg shells and set them in an egg carton with the open end up. To fill them with gelatine, use a small funnel, pouring slowing to avoid air bubbles. Chill till firm and peel them carefully.

One old cookbook suggests making a "nest" for these eggs by tinting some gelatine yellow with saffron and, after it is set, breaking it in pieces to arrange in a nest shape. Candied lemon peel cut in thin, straw-like strips can then be sprinkled over the nest. For some pretty, pastel colored eggs, use the milk gelatine (above) leaving some of it white, tinting some pink with berry juice, and some green with spinach juice. (For more about colorings refer to the FOOD COLORING section.)

tine, tilt the mold to coat the sides. Put the mold in the refrigerator for about 10 minutes or briefly in the freezer to set the gelatine. (Jelled stock will take longer to set than a powdered gelatine mixture.) Then, arrange the cold food on the gelatine. If small pieces will not stay in place, dip them in soft gelatine first. Next, pour in gelatine to surround and cover the food and chill till set. If the mold is in layers of different colors or flavors, chill after each layer. Remember when filling the mold that it will be turned upside down for unmolding and the ingredients will appear in reverse order.

To unmold, loosen the edges in several places with a thin knife. Rinse a platter in cold water, center it upside down over the mold, and turn both over together. The rinsing allows the gelatine to slide around a little if it fails to land in the right place. If the gelatine does not slip out immediately, dip a towel in hot water, wring it, and wrap it around the mold for a minute or so. Repeat this a second time if the gelatine will still not unmold.

A garnish of lettuce leaves, parsley, mayonnaise, or for a fruit mold, fresh fruit, is attractive. Keep chilled till serving time. This is especially important for jelled stock, which melts quite easily.

## GELATINE RECIPES

### Nineteenth Century
### Calf's Foot Jelly　　　　　　(Makes 6–8 dessert servings.)

| | |
|---|---|
| 4 calves' feet, or 3–4 pounds feet of deer or other hooved animals, or veal or pork bones | peel of 4 lemons, pared like an apple |
| 2 cups wine | juice of 4 lemons |
| ¾ cup honey, or 1 cup sugar | 4 egg whites, slightly beaten |
| | 4 egg shells, crushed |

(Refer to the FEET section for cleaning and preparing the feet.)

Put the feet in a pot with 4 quarts of cold water. Heat to a boil and skim. Simmer gently till water is reduced by half, from 6 to 8 hours. Strain the broth through a damp cloth laid in a colander, and set in a cold place till the next day. Remove all fat from the surface and measure 4 cups of the clear jelly. (Reserve extra gelatine for other uses.) In a pot, melt the gelatine and mix with wine, sweetener, lemon peel, juice and egg whites and shells to clarify the liquid. Boil, uncovered, for 15 minutes without stirring. Remove the thick froth, which will have most of the lemon peel and egg shell in it. Simmer 15 minutes more without stirring, skimming again if necessary. Add 1 cup cold water and boil 3 or 4 minutes more. Strain through a sieve or colander lined with a damp cloth. Pour into a serving dish or pretty individual dishes, and chill till set.

**Fruit Juice Gelatine** Instead of wine, add 2 cups of wild fruit juice, such as plum or blackberry. Sweeten to taste. Lemon peel and juice are optional, depending on the flavor of the juice. The egg whites and shells are also optional.

*Yogurt Chiffon Gelatine*          (Makes 4–6 dessert servings.)

| | |
|---|---|
| 1 tablespoon powdered gelatine | ¼ cup honey, or sugar, optional |
| 1 ½ cups fruit juice, or 2 cups canned fruit with juice | 1 cup yogurt, or buttermilk |

In a small saucepan, soak the gelatine with ½ cup of juice for 5 minutes. Warm over very low heat, stirring till the gelatine dissolves. Stir in sweetener, if desired. Combine with the rest of the juice, or fruit and juice, then with the yogurt or buttermilk. Pour into a large serving dish or individual bowls and chill till set, about an hour.

*Layered Fruit Gelatine*   Make about equal amounts of the above *Yogurt Chiffon Gelatine* and a fruit gelatine, with compatible flavor. For example, a canned peach yogurt chiffon is delicious with a grape juice gelatine. When both gelatine mixtures are nearly set, alternate layers of them in glass dishes or a large mold, chilling briefly after each layer. (See GELATINE MOLDS above.) Layers of fresh fruits, shredded coconut or chopped nuts can also be included. This colorful dessert can be crowned with a dollop of whipped cream or yogurt.

*Vegetable Chiffon Gelatine*   Use a flavorful vegetable juice or soup stock instead of fruit juice, or a stiffly jelled homemade stock. Add raw or cooked, chopped vegetables to taste. For additional flavor, ¼ cup mayonnaise can be mixed with ¾ cup yogurt or buttermilk.

Fancy layered versions can be created using different colored vegetables and hard-boiled egg slices. Beet or tomato juice gelatine will give a good color contrast.

> **OTHER GELATINE RECIPES**
>
> Butter Extended with Gelatine, p. 87
> Chicken Gelatine, p. 166
> Feet Recipes, p. 253
> Fish in Gelatine, p. 271
> Fresh Spinach Gelatine, p. 590
> Head Cheese, p. 327
> Lavender Delight, p. 321
> Red Beet Aspic, p. 39
> Sally Katz' Jewish Style Fish Cakes (Gefilte Fish), p. 267
> Tomato Aspic, p. 643
> Uncooked Jam and Jelly, p. 360

# GOOSE

ROAST GOOSE MAKES A SPLENDID ENTRÉE FOR A FESTIVE MEAL, AND IT is only one of many marvelous goose dishes. Goose meat can be a staple for anyone with suitable pasture. It can be served in hearty stews, casseroles, and many other dishes, and specialties can be made from such parts as the liver or neck skins, which are stuffed. Other bonuses for the goose raiser are goose down and eggs. The eggs are especially good for baking and noodle making. (Refer to the EGGS section.)

Wild geese are popular game birds with very good meat. (In some northeastern parts of the United States, the numbers of Canadian geese are increasing, so they may begin to appear more often on the dinner table. They can be cooked like domestic geese if allowance is made for their drier, less fatty flesh, or they can be cooked like other game birds. (Refer to WILD MEATS in the WILD FOODS section.)

> **STORAGE**
>
> **Canning**   Remove fatty skin and as much fat as possible. Remove large bones (or debone completely), and cut in conveniently sized pieces. Can like chicken. Refer to CHICKEN section.
>
> **Cold Storage**   Refer to PRESERVING MEAT IN RENDERED FAT in MEAT section.
>
> **Freezing**   Remove as much fat as possible. Wrap whole, or wrap parts separately in meal-sized portions. Quality retained 6–9 months. Refer to FREEZING section.

# HANDLING GEESE

Geese are killed like all other poultry. (Refer to BUTCHERING in the CHICKEN section.) If special care is taken to bleed them completely, their meat will both taste and keep better. The blood can be collected and saved for various uses. (Refer to the BLOOD section.) Wild geese should also be bled as soon as possible after they are shot. The jugular vein in the neck should be cut and they should be allowed to drain for a few minutes.

***Down and Feathers*** If the down is to be saved, it should be plucked dry, after the goose is killed and while it is still warm. The down can be put into a cheesecloth bag or a bag made from other light cloth. The bags can then be washed in warm, soapy water and hung in the shade to dry. If any skin sticks to the down remove it, because it could spoil the rest.

The soft, feathery parts of large feathers can be cut off the quills with scissors and included with the down. Though plucking the down is slow work, the quilts, pillows, and clothing made from it will last a lifetime, so it is time well spent.

If their down is not to be saved, pluck geese like ducks. (Refer to the DUCK section.) The first method described, which uses detergent in scalding water, is the most practical for geese. For a large goose, the second method would require too much paraffin.

Clean or draw geese like chickens. (Refer to DRAWING CHICKENS in the CHICKEN section.) The best young geese are often kept whole for roasting. It is a good idea to cut all other geese into their various parts, so that each can be prepared in the most suitable way, much like the various cuts of a large meat animal. Where geese are used as a common food there are always special recipes for goose legs, goose breast, goose liver, and others.

***Age*** The best geese for roasting are 10 months old or less. Older geese should be stewed or steamed for part of the cooking time. If a goose is just a little over 10 months old it may be practical to roast the breast, and cook the other parts separately. Geese older than 3 years are apt to become so tough and stringy that they are only good for soup. (Refer to the MEAT section, USING TOUGH MEAT.)

If a goose is not home raised it may be difficult to determine its age. A young goose should have tender skin, and easily separated joints. (Refer to DETERMINING THE ANIMAL'S AGE, in the WILD FOODS section.) But a 3 year old goose will seem very much like a 15 year old goose, so with some birds guesswork will be unavoidable.

***The Liver*** Goose livers, whether domestic or wild, are delicious. Take care when removing them not to break the attached green sac of gall; cut or pull it off carefully. Goose liver can be prepared like chicken liver, and the two are interchangeable in recipes. (Refer to CHICKEN LIVER, in the CHICKEN section.)

Goose liver used to make the fame *paté de foie gras* is not ordinary liver. *Foie gras* is French for fat liver—a very accurate description. Geese are force fed for months to make them and their livers as fat as possible. An ordinary goose liver weighs around 4 ounces while a *foie gras* can weigh as much as 3 pounds. Force feeding geese is outlawed in many countries because of its cruelty. It is also doubtful whether any meat should be eaten from an animal so grossly fat and, therefore, in poor health.

**Stuffing Goose Neck Skins**    When a goose's neck skin is removed in one long, tubular piece it makes an excellent casing for many kinds of stuffings. For the longest possible skin, cut the neck of the goose close to the head when killing it. After the goose is plucked and cleaned, cut through the skin around the neck as close to the body as possible. If the goose is to be cut in pieces, cut off the wings first and then cut through the skin from wing hole to wing hole. To peel off the skin, start on the wide or body end, and pull as if removing a glove. The skin will be inside out. Wash and turn it right side out. Tie or sew the small (head) end closed, stuff the skin, then tie or sew shut the other end.

*Stuffed goose neck skin*

Any poultry stuffing tastes good cooked in a goose neck skin, as do traditional goose neck stuffings. The stuffed skin can be either baked or stewed. It is usually served sliced crosswise, like a sausage.

**Stuffings and Cooking Methods**    A convenient way to prepare a neck skin is to fill it with the stuffing used for the roast goose, then roast it on the rack beside the goose for the last hour.

Another way is to use the raw meat trimmed from the goose's back, wings, and neck. Grind or mince it, and stuff the skin to make another meaty piece, like a leg or thigh, for stewing with vegetables. It should simmer without boiling for an hour or so, as boiling can cause it to burst.

Neck skins also make good casings for sausage or other seasoned meat mixtures, especially when using the liver or blood. (Refer to the recipe for *Liver Paté* in the SAUSAGE section and GOOSE BLOOD PUDDING in the BLOOD section.) Simmer these sausages from 25 to 30 minutes in water or goose broth. Do not allow it to boil or the skin might burst.

**Goose Fat**    It is well worth rendering goose fat in the same way as chicken fat. (Refer to the CHICKEN section.) Goose fat is excellent and delicious for frying potatoes, vegetables, and eggs. It can be used like lard in baking and can replace butter for flavoring casseroles, pastas, and soups. It also serves as a spread for bread, and, when there is enough of it, a way to preserve goose meat. (Refer to PRESERVING MEAT IN RENDERED FAT in the MEAT section.) Cracklings with the texture of crisp bacon can also be made from goose skin, when goose fat is rendered.

**Cracklings from Skin**    To make these crisp and crunchy snacks while rendering goose fat, cut fatty skin into 2 inch pieces, uniformly sized so that all will render in the same amount of time. Cracklings can be made from breast skin cut with the skin on one side, a layer of fat, and a thin layer of breast meat on the other side. Slash the meat-side in one or two places so that it will not curl. When breast skin is used for cracklings, the skin from the neck can be wrapped around the breast as a replacement.

Put the pieces of fatty skin in a deep pot and barely cover with water. Cook slowly, uncovered, till the water has evaporated, and the fat is rendered. When the cracklings start to brown, stir often to prevent burning. The heat can be increased to brown them, but they must be closely watched. When nicely browned, drain them, and save the fat. If they seem too greasy, they can be squeezed or pressed to remove more fat, or put on a rack in a low oven for a few minutes to drain further. (Refer to RENDERING FAT in the LARD section.)

**Goose Broth**  Parts of a goose not otherwise used make a good broth or soup stock. The feet are outstanding used in this way. Scald them in very hot water to loosen the outside skin which can then be peeled off. Another way to loosen the skin is to hold the feet in a flame or over coals, turning them until the skin blisters. Other parts to use for broth are the bones, the neck, back, gizzard, and heart if these are not to be used for something else.

To make the broth, simmer the feet, bones, and other parts in water for several hours like any soup stock. Use it as the liquid in recipes for goose as well as for soups. (Refer to SOUP STOCK, in the SOUP section.)

## GOOSE RECIPES

### *Roast Goose with Stuffing*                    (Makes 10–12 dinner servings.)

*1 young domestic or wild goose, 10 to 12 pounds, dressed.* (Halve this recipe for a small goose.)
Stuffing:
*giblets* (Gizzard and heart, liver optional.)
*2 medium onions, chopped*
*4 cups bread crumbs* (Cornbread crumbs are very good.)
*4 stalks celery, chopped*

*2 cups cranberries, gooseberries, or other tart fruit*
*½ pound mushrooms, chopped*
*1 pound prunes, cooked and pitted*
*juice from the cooked prunes*
*½ teaspoon pepper*
*½ teaspoon savory or thyme*
*salt, optional*
*sherry or apple cider for basting, optional*

For the stuffing, first simmer the giblets in a quart of water until tender, about 40 minutes. Chop the giblets small. Mix them and their cooking water with the onions, bread crumbs, celery, cranberries or other fruit, mushrooms, prunes with their juice, pepper, savory or thyme, and salt, if desired.

Stuff the goose and close the openings with skewers or by sewing them. Set on a rack over a dripping pan. If the goose is fat prick the skin well, especially around legs and wings. Roast in a 350°F oven till done, about 4 hours, or 20 to 25 minutes per pound. If a special flavor is desired, baste every few minutes with sherry or apple cider. During cooking, the fat that accumulate in the dripping pan can be poured off. The oven can be turned up for the last 10 minutes of roasting to make the skin browner and more crisp. (Whether this is necessary will depend on the oven.)

If the goose is very fat it can be pre-roasted like duck for 15 to 20 minutes to remove excess fat, and then stuffed. (Refer to the DUCK section.) The neck skin can be filled with extra stuffing and roasted with the goose for an hour. (See STUFFING GOOSE NECK SKINS above.)

***Roast Duckling with Stuffing***   Make a half recipe of stuffing for a large duck. Roast as for goose.

***Fruit Casserole***   Mix the above stuffing, omitting giblets. Add soup stock or fruit juice if it needs moistening. Add several tablespoons of softened butter, bacon fat, or another fat. Bake in a covered casserole for 1 hour.

This is a good side dish with pork and other meats. Chopped oranges are very good as the fruit instead of cranberries.

### *Stewed Goose with a Choice of Sauces*   (Makes 6–8 dinner servings.)

| | |
|---|---|
| 5 pounds (about) goose parts, or small goose cut in pieces (May be domestic or wild.) | 1 tablespoon honey |
| | 1 tablespoon vinegar (Preferably wine vinegar) |
| water | 2 teaspoons olive oil, or butter |
| Apicius' Sauce (Adapted from a recipe in *The Roman Cookery of Apicius*, by J. Edwards.) | 1 cup (about) goose broth |
| | Sweet and Sour Sauce with Apple: |
| ½ teaspoon pepper | 1 cup goose broth |
| ¼ teaspoon caraway seeds | 2 tablespoons (about) vinegar |
| 1 teaspoon cumin seeds | 1 tablespoon (about) honey, or sugar |
| 1 teaspoon celery seeds | 1 teaspoon prepared mustard, or a pinch powder |
| ½ teaspoon thyme | |
| ½ teaspoon ginger | ½ teaspoon pepper |
| ¼ cup hazelnuts, almonds, or sunflower seeds | 2½ cups apples, chopped |

Put the goose pieces in a pot and just cover them with water. Bring to a boil and skim off any foam that rises. Then cover and simmer over low heat.

For the Apicius Sauce, simmer the goose until the meat is just beginning to become tender, usually from 2 to 2½ hours. Drain off the broth, let sit till the fat rises and skim. Put the pepper, caraway, cumin and celery seeds, thyme, ginger, nuts or sunflower seeds, honey, vinegar, oil or butter, and 1 cup goose broth in a blender and blend until smooth. (Or use a mortar to grind the herb seeds and spices, then finely chop or grate the nuts, and combine with the rest of the sauce ingredients.) Pour this sauce over the goose in the pot and simmer another hour, or till the meat is quite tender. Turn the pieces several times so that all sides are flavored by the sauce and add a little more goose broth if it becomes dry.

For the Sweet and Sour Sauce with Apple, cook the goose till completely tender, from 3 to 4 hours. Drain off the broth and keep the meat warm. Skim the fat off of the broth after it rises. Heat a cup of the broth with the vinegar, honey or sugar, mustard, and pepper. When it boils add the apples and cook, uncovered, for 20 minutes more. Taste and adjust amounts of vinegar and sweetener for a pleasantly sweet and sour flavor. Amounts can vary considerably depending on the apples' tartness. Serve the sauce hot with the goose.

Stewed goose is very distinctively flavored using either of these sauces, so use plain accompaniments, such as rice, noodles, or potatoes, and plain cooked greens.

***Stewed Game Meat with Sauces***   Dark-meated game birds, venison, and other wild meats are excellent with either of these sauces.

---

### *Fricasseed Goose Parts*                              (Makes 6—8 dinner servings.)

| | |
|---|---|
| goose wings, neck, and back, cut in serving size pieces | 1 piece celeriac or a celery stalk |
| gizzard and heart, optional | 2 tablespoons goose fat |
| ginger, powdered, or a piece of ginger root, minced | 2 tablespoons flour |
| | 2 cups goose broth |
| 1—2 cloves garlic, crushed | 2 tablespoons parsley, minced |
| pepper, salt | |
| 1 onion | dumplings, optional (Any favorite recipe, using 1½—2 cups flour.) |

The evening before serving, rub the pieces of goose with ginger, garlic, pepper, and salt. Let stand overnight in a cool place. In the morning put them in a pot and cover with boiling water. Simmer covered over low heat for 1½ hours. Add the onion, and celeriac or celery. Simmer for another hour, or till the meat is tender. Altogether, parts from an old goose may take 3 or 4 hours. When done remove the meat and strain the broth. Skim the fat off of the broth.

Before mealtime, heat the goose fat in a pot and stir in the flour. Add about 2 cups of broth and stir over low heat until thickened. Taste and adjust seasonings. Add the parsley and pieces of goose and simmer until reheated. If duplings are included they can be cooked in the pot with the fricassee.

---

### GOOSE IDEAS

**Goose with Tart Accompaniments**   Goose, because of its richness and fattiness, is delicious with tart or pickled accompaniments. Some good choices are sauerkraut, pickled red cabbage, and tart fruits, such as in a cranberry sauce, citrus fruit mixtures, or the currant sauces for meat recipes. (Refer to the appropriate food sections for recipes.)

**Goose and Beef Stew**   Include a part of a goose such as a leg, the wings or the neck, when making stew with beef and vegetables. The flavors blend especially well.

### Goose Legs with Barley and Beans (Makes 6–8 dinner servings.)

*1 cup whole barley*
*1 cup dry small white beans*
*1 small onion, chopped*
*1 small kohlrabi, or turnip, chopped*
*1 carrot, sliced*
*1 small parsnip, sliced*

*goose legs and thighs* (If goose is large use the drumsticks alone.)
*2 tablespoons goose fat, or other fat, optional*
*1 teaspoon paprika*
*1 clove garlic, crushed*
*pepper, salt, optional*

Mix the barley and beans and soak them in water overnight. In the morning put them with their soaking water in a big pot, together with the legs and thighs, onion, kohlrabi or turnip, carrot, parsnip, fat, paprika, and garlic. (Omit the fat if legs and thighs are fatty.) Add water to cover all ingredients. Cover and simmer over low heat until beans and goose are both tender—usually from 3 to 5 hours. Stir once in a while and add hot water if the dish should start to dry out. This dish can also be cooked covered in a low oven if more convenient. If desired, season with pepper, and salt towards the end of the cooking time.

***Turkey Legs with Barley and Beans*** Use turkey legs or legs and thighs instead of goose legs.

### Goose Liver Pilaf (Makes about 6 dinner servings.)

*6 tablespoons goose fat, or butter*
*¾ pound goose livers, sliced*
*½ cup scallions, minced*
*pepper, salt, optional*
*½ teaspoon allspice, optional*
*1 onion, minced*
*1 tablespoon pine nuts, or sunflower seeds*

*2 cups raw rice, brown or white*
*1 tablespoon raisins*
*½ teaspoon honey, or sugar*
*½ cup tomato sauce, or 1 large tomato, chopped*
*4 tablespoons fresh dill leaves, or parsley, minced*

Heat 2 tablespoons of the fat or butter in a pan over moderate heat. Add the sliced liver and stir constantly until it has just changed color. Remove the slices to a dish. Sauté the scallions briefly in the same pan till they are limp. Add them to the liver. Gently mix in the allspice, pepper, and salt, if desired, and set aside.

Heat the remaining fat or butter in a Dutch oven or heavy pot, and sauté the onion until golden. Add the pine nuts or sunflower seeds and the rice. Stir over moderate heat for about 5 minutes or until the rice is evenly coated with fat. Add 4 cups of water, raisins, honey or sugar, and the tomato. Cover, bring to a boil and simmer till the rice is just cooked and the water absorbed, from 30 to 40 minutes for brown rice, less for white. Gently stir in the liver mixture and dill or parsley. Cover tightly and simmer over the lowest possible heat for 20 minutes to blend flavors.

***Chicken Liver Pilaf*** Use chicken livers and chicken fat instead of goose livers and fat.

**GOOSE IDEAS,** *cont.*

**Marinated Goose Breast**
Marinate the goose breast whole, or skin and bone it with the halves separated. Use the barbecue sauce from the CHEVON section, or any favorite marinade. Immerse several hours or overnight and broil, turning as necessary, until cooked through. If the skin has been removed the breast can be brushed with butter or oil. A small breast in two pieces will be done in about 20 minutes while a large whole breast may take twice as long. To avoid stringiness, slice the meat thinly across the grain when serving.

**Goose Stroganoff** Chop leftover cooked goose meat into bite-sized pieces. Sauté a cup of sliced mushrooms in goose fat, stir in 2 tablespoons flour and then 2 cups goose broth. Stir until thickened, then add the meat and a generous cup of sour cream or yogurt. Season with paprika, parsley, pepper, and salt. Heat gently without letting it boil, and serve with rice or potatoes.

**Goose Hash** Chop finely or grind leftover cooked goose meat and combine with potatoes and seasonings to make hash. (Refer to the *Browned Potato Hash* recipe in the POTATOES section.) Use goose fat for the frying if it is available. Chopped onion, celery, and parsley or dill work well as seasonings.

# GOOSEBERRIES

**Canning**  Trim tops, tails.
**Hot Pack Unsweetened**
Barely cover kettle bottom with cold water. Add berries. Bring to simmer, low heat. To prevent sticking, shake pot, do not stir. When hot through, fill jars, ½ in. headroom. Process, 212°F, boiling water bath. Pint: 15 min. Quart: 20 min.

**Sweetened**  Add ¼ — ½ cup honey or sugar per qt. Bring to simmer as above, omitting water. When cooked, let sit covered 2 — 3 hours to plump up berries. Fill jars; process as above, but start with warm instead of boiling water in canner.

**Cold Pack**  Put ½ cup hot syrup in each jar. (Refer to LIQ-UIDS FOR CANNING FRUIT in the CANNING section.) Fill with berries then syrup, ½ in. headroom. Process as above. Refer to CANNING section; also CANNING FRUIT JUICE AND SAUCE in FRUITS section, and *Gooseberry Chutney* below.

**Cold Storage**  See COLD WATER CANNING, COLD STORAGE section.

**Drying**  Trim tops, tails or winnow after dried. Dry until hard. Refer to DRYING section.

**Freezing**  Trip tops, tails. Package dry and plain, or cover with syrup or other liquid. Refer to FREEZING section.

ABOUT 2 POUNDS (5–8) CUPS FRESH BERRIES = 1 QUART CANNED OR FROZEN

GOOSEBERRIES ARE A PASSION FOR SOME PEOPLE; THEIR DISTINCT and special flavor is like no other. They are closely related to currants, but this is apparent not so much in taste as in appearance, growth habits, and the berry bush's unfortunate hosting of white pine blister rust. (Refer to the CURRANTS section.)

The British are particularly partial to the gooseberry and are responsible for such classics as *Gooseberry Fool* and GOOSEBERRY SAUCE WITH MACKEREL (see below). The particular varieties of gooseberries cultivated in Great Britain and northern Europe do not generally grow well in North America because of climatic differences and their susceptibility to mildew. However, native varieties can be cultivated in most of the cooler regions of the continent. Though these do not grow as large or become as sweet as the European gooseberries, they are delicious, nonetheless. Wild gooseberries are well worth picking when they can be found.

## HANDLING GOOSEBERRIES

Gooseberries are picked at different stages of ripeness for their various uses. They are most useful for cooking and making preserves when they are full sized, yet still green, firm, and very tart. At this stage they are high in pectin and as acidic as lemons or rhubarb, so they can be used in much the same ways. (Refer to COMBINING SWEET AND TART FRUIT in the FRUITS section.) This is also the best time to store them by cold water canning. (Refer to the COLD STORAGE section.) As they ripen they become sweeter, a few varieties becoming sweet enough to eat raw. If left too long, however, they are apt to become mushy, or, in some locations, wormy. The sweetest varieties become reddish or purple when fully ripe, while other varieties turn yellow or a paler green. Sweet gooseberries are very good in fruit cups and salads. They can be soaked in muscatel or another sweet wine to make a festive dessert.

Some gooseberry bushes are so dense and thorny that the berries are difficult to pick. Such bushes are most easily harvested by wearing sturdy leather gloves and stripping the berries from the branches into a basket or other container set under them. The leaves, twigs, and other debris that comes off can also be partly removed by rolling the berries down a slightly tilted "ramp" into another container. As the leaves and twigs do not roll easily, most of them will be left behind. A final sorting can be done when the gooseberries are topped and tailed. (Refer to GATHERING FRUITS, in the WILD FOODS section.)

***Removing Tops and Tails from Gooseberries***  The tops or stems and tails or remnants of blossoms that cling to gooseberries do not always have to be removed by hand. If used in a juice or a strained sauce, they will be strained out during processing. Otherwise, each berry can be trimmed with scissors or by pulling off the tops and tails with the fingers. This is fairly easy to do when the gooseberries are large, but tedious if the berries are small. The tops and tails of small wild gooseberries are usually not very noticeable and can simply be ignored.

## GOOSEBERRY RECIPES

### Gooseberry Fool

(Makes about 6 dessert servings.)

| | |
|---|---|
| 1 quart gooseberries | ½ cup heavy cream, whipped, or |
| 4 tablespoons butter | 1 ½ cups CUSTARD SAUCE, |
| honey, or sugar, to taste | unsweetened (Refer to the MILK section.) |

Put the gooseberries and butter in a heavy saucepan, cover, and simmer over low heat until the berries are just cooked through. Crush with a fork or purée with a food mill. Sweeten to taste with honey or sugar. Mix gently with the whipped cream or completely cooled custard sauce. Serve chilled. Macaroons are often served with this dessert.

**Gooseberry Ice Cream** This gooseberry fool mixture can be frozen to make ice cream. (The texture is best if the gooseberries are puréed.) For a different flavor, a cup of yogurt can be added. (Refer to *Fruit 'n Yogurt Ice Cream*, in the ICE CREAM section.)

**Berry Fool** Use strawberries, raspberries, or blackberries instead of gooseberries. A little grated lemon rind can be added with the sugar or honey.

**Gooseberry Sauce for Meat or Fish** Use half of the fool recipe ingredients, omit the sweetening, and puree the gooseberries while warm. Heat unwhipped cream (light may be used) and add with several tablespoons of the pan juices from cooking the meat or fish with which the sauce is to be served. (If added when cold, the cream might be curdled by acid in the berries.)

This sauce is good with mackerel or other fish, and with such fatty meats as pork, duck, or goose.

### Gooseberry Chutney

(Makes 5–6 pints canned.)

| | |
|---|---|
| 3 pounds tart gooseberries, topped and tailed | 2 cups vinegar |
| 1 pound raisins | ¼ cup mustard seeds |
| 3–4 medium onions, chopped | ½ teaspoon cayenne or other hot pepper |
| 2–3 garlic cloves, minced | ¼ teaspoon turmeric |
| 1–2 cups honey or sugar | |

Put all ingredients in a pot, bring to a boil, and simmer uncovered for about 2 hours. Stir often. Taste when almost done, and if necessary, adjust sweetening and vinegar. The mixture should be fairly thick.

---

## GOOSEBERRY IDEAS

**Gooseberry Tarts** Line muffin tins or other small pans with pastry dough. Put some fresh gooseberries in each. A single layer of large gooseberries pushed close together is about right. Mix milk, egg, and honey as for a custard (refer to recipe in MILK section), and fill the tart shells with it. Bake about 15 minutes in a 400°F oven, or until the custard is set.

**Elderflower or Mint Gooseberry Jelly** Use the juice of tart green gooseberries to make *Fruit Jelly with Honey* (recipe in JAM AND JELLY section), or any other standard jelly. For the last 5 to 10 minutes of cooking add a sprig of mint or head of elderflowers. Remove the herb before bottling the jelly. The elderflowers can be enclosed in a cheesecloth to keep them from disintegrating.

As green gooseberries are rich in pectin they should jell readily.

**Gooseberries Instead of Rhubarb** Use green, tart gooseberries in chopped rhubarb recipes, including rhubarb pie. (refer to the RHUBARB section, RECIPES and IDEAS.)

---

## OTHER RECIPES WITH GOOSEBERRIES

Blackberry Roll, p. 52
Fruit Casserole, p. 307
Hot Fruit Soup, p. 290
Hot Water Crust for Raised Pies, p. 385
Red Currant Dessert, p. 216
Roast Goose, p. 306
Also refer to Fruit Recipes and Ideas, p. 290

Ladle boiling hot chutney into jars and process in a boiling water bath for 10 minutes. (Refer to the CANNING section.)

**Rhubarb Chutney**   Use chopped, fresh rhubarb instead of gooseberries. The turmeric can be omitted.

# GRAINS

GRAINS OF ONE KIND OR ANOTHER SERVE AS A BASIC, LIFE-sustaining food for most of the world's peoples. In Asian countries rice is said to "give life." In the majority of Western countries wheat, in the form of bread, is the "staff of life." Corn is the basic grain in parts of both North and South America, while barley and oats have sustained life in places where other grains will not grow. Dependance on grain goes back to the beginnings of civilization. It was the growing and storing of grain that allowed primitive man to abandon nomadic life and settle to form communities.

Until fifty or a hundred years ago, most country people had an inherent sense of the importance of grain for human survival: it had to be grown to feed both the family, and the livestock that fed the family. Without stored grain winter would be a bleak and hungry prospect, and people made it their business to know how to grow, harvest, and store it. In the present affluent society with a more than ample food supply as near as the nearest grocery store, this knowledge has been dying out. Yet the desire to grow their own still remains with some people. Like the little red hen of storybook fame, who plants her seed and tends it, harvests her grain and grinds it, bakes her bread and then eats it herself, there are still those who want to do the whole thing themselves.

Some gardeners and modern homesteaders are successfully raising their own grain crops, and at the same time coming very close to food self sufficiency. The benefits are many. Grain can be grown, free of most chemical contamination; storage conditions can be controlled; the whole grain can be used including bran and germ; and flour and meal can be ground fresh, as needed. Those who cannot raise their own grain are finding it worthwhile to buy whole grain in bulk for home storage and grinding.

## HANDLING GRAIN

Reaping, threshing, and winnowing are the three steps necessary for harvesting most grain crops. Reaping is cutting the plants when the seeds are mature; threshing is beating the plants or seed heads to loosen the grain; and winnowing is separating the grain or seeds from the straw and chaff.

When harvested by hand, grain is reaped with a sickle, scythe, or grain cradle, threshed with a flail, and winnowed by tossing in a gentle wind to blow away the lighter straw and chaff. The tools, skill, and knowledge to do all this were developed over many centuries.

To instruct the modern small scale grower who wants to harvest grain in the time honored way, there are some older people who re-member how to do it and some younger people who have revived this nearly forgotten knowledge. There are also some very helpful books. (See REFERENCE SOURCES at end of this section.) The gardener who wants to havest a small patch of grain can do so as with any other seeds. (See HARVESTING in the HERB SEEDS section, THRESHING AND WINNOWING, in the SEEDS section, and also specific grains.)

***Eating Animal Feed Grains*** There is no reason why clean, high quality grains intended for animal feed should not be eaten by people. Feed corn for instance makes excellent cornmeal. (Refer to HARVEST-ING, in the CORN, DRY section.) Wheat and rye are also good, as long as they are clean. Some grains like oats and barley have hulls too tight to be removed by threshing or winnowing. Animals eat them whole, but for human consumption they must be hulled.

***Hulling Difficult Grains*** Though there is machinery to remove hulls from grains, it is usually not appropriate for those with only a small quantity to hull. There is, however, an assortment of methods and ideas that have been found to work in certain circumstances. Ex-perimentation is necessary to discover which methods might be practi-cal for a particular grain or a particular situation. Four approaches to the problem follow:

• Dry the grain thoroughly so that the hulls become brittle and can easily be cracked. The grain can be dried by baking in a low oven. 1½ hours at 180°F is recommended for oats, and can also be tried with other grains. When dry, put the grain through a grain mill at a very coarse setting, or whirl it briefly in a blender, or batter or bruise it in some other way. This is to knock loose the hulls, leaving the grain whole or cracked, but still unpulverized. Then it can be shaken through a sieve leaving the hulls behind, or it can be winnowed by pouring from one container to another in a breeze. Another alterna-tive is to cover it with water to float off the hulls. If water is used the grain must either be cooked right away, or redried.

• An old Scottish method for removing oat and barley hulls begins with stirring the grain in a pot over a hot fire until the kernels burst, like popping corn. This loosens the hulls which are then removed by putting the grain through a sieve. The grain is then ground into flour for baking or for making a gruel to drink. An equal mixture of barley and oats treated in this way was called "burstin."

• Wild grains are sometimes parched in an open flame to burn off hulls and chaff. A screen container of some kind is devised, the grain is put in it and then moved through the fire several times. If it is kept moving the hulls should burn off without the grain itself burning.

• Sprouting can make unhulled grains useable in several ways. Malt can be made from them (refer to MALTED BARLEY in the BARLEY section), and shoots can be cut to eat as greens (refer to SPROUTING GRAINS in the SPROUTS section). Occasionally also, sprouting may swell some grains enough to split the hulls so they can be rinsed off.

## GRINDING

Grain should be stored (cured) in a dry place for at least a month after harvesting and before it is ground. If too fresh it may gum up the grain mill and also be too difficult to handle for baking.

There are many devices for grinding grain at home. They range from two porous stones used like a mortar and pestle, to a streamlined appliance for the kitchen counter. Though blenders and food processors can be used for grinding small batches, they generally cannot stand up to the work of grinding a family's supply of bread flour. A meat grinder can be used only when grinding pre-soaked grains. (See SOAKED GRAIN CEREALS, under IDEAS, below.) For grinding meal and flour on a regular basis, a grain mill is a necessity.

***Grain Mills***    Small grain mills of many different styles and prices are now available. The cheapest hand turned models which clamp onto work surfaces are good only for small jobs. While useful for grinding a cup or two of grain, coffee beans, or dried root vegetables, they are not up to grinding the family's supply of bread flour. It would take at least an hour of really hard work to grind several pounds of flour for a batch of bread, and then the flour would probably be quite coarse. Though the better, more expensive hand turned mills do a faster and finer job, turning out large amounts of flour remains a lot of work. Converting the mill with a bicycle arrangement is one way to make the work easier. A good mill hitched to pedal power can grind 15 pounds of flour in an hour. An electric grain mill designed for home use should grind about 40 pounds in an hour. Either of these mills makes it completely practical to home grind all cereals and flour.

Most grain mills cannot grind dry soy beans because they are too oily. However, a small proportion of soy beans can be well mixed with the grain before grinding to make a nutritious blended cereal or flour.

***Meal or Grits and Flour***    Grain mills adjust from coarse to fine grinds, but the flour's final texture will depend on the kind of grain and the mill's efficiency. Some mills cannot grind finely enough for pastry flour, but can produce a good bread flour. Usually the flour will be finer if ground twice, first to meal and then to flour. Sometimes it is most practical to make cereal and flour at the same time by grinding and then sifting, using the coarser meal or grits as cereal and

## WHOLE GRAIN IDEAS

**Whole Grains in Soups and Stews**   Most grains are very good cooked whole in soups and stews. Some may need prior soaking or a long cooking time, but their pleasant, slightly chewy textures and good flavors make them worth the trouble. Two recipes that use grain in this way are *Rye and Split Peas or Beans*, in the RYE section, and *Ferique*, in the WHEAT section. Different whole grains can be substituted for each other in such recipes, as long as soaking and cooking times are adjusted.

**Mixing Grains Before Grinding** When one recipe calls for several kinds of flour the grains can be mixed before grinding. Cornbread, for example, can be made by combining wheat, corn, and perhaps some soybeans and grinding them together as needed. In this way the flour will be fresh without two separate grindings. Grain measurements must allow for their increased volume after grinding: ⅔ cup of wheat and ¾ cup of corn mixed and ground would equal 1 cup of whole wheat flour combined with 1 cup of cornmeal. The amount of grain to make a cup of flour is shown at the beginning of each grain section.

*A grain mill converted to run on pedal power.*

**Soaked Grain Cereals** Whole grains can be soaked for 12 to 24 hours or till they begin to sprout (refer to the SPROUTS section) and then used for cereal. Some eat such grains without cooking, but it is more practical and usually preferred if they are first ground and dried, then cooked as needed. To do this, drain after the soaking, and grind them in a food processor, meat grinder, or other device, and dry them in flat sheets. (Refer to the DRYING section for DRYING FRUIT AND OTHER PURÉES.) Break these in pieces and store in airtight containers. These pieces can then be covered with water and cooked for only 20 to 30 minutes as a breakfast cereal or a side dish with other meals. This is a very satisfactory method which does not require the use of a grain mill. The soaked grain can also be ground in a blender to a smooth mash, and the dried pieces enjoyed like crackers.

A very good variation is to soak combinations of whole grains, seeds, nuts, and dried fruits. Five or ten different grains and seeds can be combined. Good proportions such as: 2 cups of grains such as wheat, rice, barley, rye, corn, and millet; ½ cup of seeds, including alfalfa, flax, sunflower and sesame seeds; ¼ cup of mixed nuts or raw peanuts; and ¼ cup of mixed dried fruits. These can all be soaked together before the grinding and drying.

the finer for flour. Cereal that was not sifted may have too much fine powder mixed with it, making its cooked texture unpleasantly sticky. Note that the volume of a grain increases when it is ground. The amount of whole grain necessary to make a cup of flour is given at the beginning of each specific grain section.

## STORING GRAINS

Grains keep well if protected from insects and rodents, and if kept dry enough to prevent mold. They should keep a year or more in any dry place. Cool storage temperatures are best as they discourage insect activity.

If a grain is not thoroughly dry, either because of early harvesting or because it was caught in the rain after harvest, it should be spread out to dry in a dry, airy place. Metal or glass storage containers with tight lids provide the best protection from rodents. Where quantities are not too great metal garbage cans make excellent containers. Insects are not necessarily always a problem. Corn, for instance, is seldom infested by insects and the occasional, unnoticed egg or dormant insect are not harmful. Grains stored outside in cold weather and used before the warm weather will not need insect protection. When insect activity is great enough to cause problems, however, there are several ways to deal with them.

*Preventing Insect Damage*   Storage in clean, airtight containers will prevent insect damage where no insects or insect eggs were in the grain to begin with. Some people put a few bay leaves or other strong herbs in the grain to discourage stray insects. Cold storage, or refrigeration at 40°F or less, will prevent insect activity. To ensure safe storage and kill all insect eggs, grain can be heated for half an hour at 140°F. Though freezing at 0°F for 3 or 4 days is also supposed to kill eggs, this, too, is only practical for small amounts of grain.

Dry ice has been used to release carbon dioxide as a fumigant in containers of grain. With this method glass containers should not be used because of the risk of explosion. Instead, put two plastic bags one inside the other in a metal garbage can or similar metal container. Pour in enough grain to cover the bottom and put in a small, nut sized lump of dry ice. Fill the bag with grain and tie the top loosely, so that air can escape as the carbon dioxide gas rises. Leave overnight, then seal tightly and close the can lid.

Another method of control is to mix 1 cup diatomaceous earth, the powdery shells and skeletons of diatoms, with each 25 pounds of grain. They must be well mixed. Diatomaceous earth, harmless to humans, penetrates insects bodies, dehydrating and killing them. It is most often used when large amounts of grain are stored in bins in a barn.

*Storing Flour*   A big advantage of a home grain mill is that flour need not be stored, but can be freshly ground when wanted. Whole grain flour will deteriorate much more quickly than intact whole grains. This is because breaking up the grain exposes the oil in the germ to air causing rancidity. Home ground or stone ground grain is the most vulnerable since it has not been heated or otherwise processed. If natural whole grain flour must be stored, it should be kept in a cold place, such as the refrigerator or freezer.

Commercially produced flour usually keeps well stored in airtight containers as for grain.

---

## OTHER BASIC GRAIN PREPARATIONS

# REFERENCE SOURCES OF INFORMATION ABOUT GRAIN

Logsden, Gene, *Small Scale Grain Raising,* Rodale Press, 1977.
Seymour, John, *The Guide to Self-Sufficiency,* Popular Mechanics Books, 1976.

THE EARLIEST RECORDED CULTIVATION OF GRAPES WAS SO LONG AGO that it seems as if humankind has always grown them. The Bible says that Noah planted a vineyard, and there are mosaics of grape and wine production in Egypt dating back to 2400 B.C. Grapes were important in ancient Greece and Rome and continue to be important today in all temperate regions of the world. Through the centuries hundreds of distinctively different varieties of grapes have been developed to suit different climates and for different purposes. There are table grapes, raisin grapes, sweet juice grapes, and most specialized of all, wine grapes.

Home gardeners are restricted to varieties of grapes that suit their local climate, and there are likely to be limitations to the use of these varieties. The sweetest table grapes, for instance, do not make the best juice, and seedy grapes that are superb for juice will not make good raisins. Though wine grapes tend to make good juice and may also be good to eat fresh, growing them for vintage wines is beyond the scope of most gardeners. (Refer to the WINE section.)

There is no such thing as an all-purpose grape, nor is there ever likely to be one. However, new varieties are constantly being developed, and it is likely that gardeners in most areas will eventually have the choice of varieties suitable for most purposes.

The fruit is not the only edible part of the vine. The leaves are delicious stuffed or wrapped around meats while they cook, and a few can be laid on top of vegetables when they are pickled to make them crisp. In some cookbooks they are called vine leaves. (See USING GRAPE LEAVES, below.) Grape seeds are used as a coating for a special French cheese, and have been pressed commercially for their oil. Even the tartaric acid crystals that form in grape juice have a use: they are refined to make cream of tartar.

Some mention must also be made of wild grapes, as they can be picked in large quantities in some places. While some are sweet enough to eat raw, they are usually best made into juice and wild grape jelly.

## HANDLING GRAPES

The Encyclopedia Britannica says truthfully that "a grape is ripe when it has reached the stage best suited for the use to which it is to be put." For eating raw and making sweet juice, grapes should remain on the vine until fully ripe but still firm. If to be dried for raisins, they can be left on the vine until they begin to wither. For a tart juice or jelly they should be picked while still a little green, as they contain the most pectin then. Even grapes so green that their seeds are still soft can be used in an old fashioned sour grape pie.

*Seedy Grapes* Though grape seeds are perfectly safe to eat, they are a little hard to chew. It is easy enough to spit them out when

---

### STORAGE

**Canning** See CANNING GRAPE JUICE, below. For whole seedless or seeded grapes:

**Hot Pack** Bring grapes to boil in water or syrup. Drain, pack in jars, cover with same boiling hot liquid, ½ in. headroom. Process 212°F, boiling water bath. Pints: 15 min. Quarts: 20 min.

**Raw Pack** Fill jars without crushing. Add boiling water or syrup, ½ in. headroom. Process as above. Refer to CANNING section.

**Cold Storage** Catawbas, Tokays, Concords keep best. Pick when cool. Hold at 50°F until stems shrivel slightly. Arrange in shallow layers, or pack in straw. Will keep 1–2 months in root cellar. Best separated from other foods. Refer to COLD STORAGE section.

**Drying** See MAKING RAISINS, below.

**Freezing** (Seedless or seeded grapes only.) Remove stems. Dry pack or cover with juice or other liquid. Refer to FREEZING section, and FREEZING FRUIT JUICE AND SAUCE in the FRUITS section.

Note: See also PRESERVING GRAPE LEAVES IN SALT, PICKLED GRAPES, and BRANDIED GRAPES, below.

4 POUNDS FRESH GRAPES IN CLUSTERS = I QUART CANNED OR FROZEN OR ½ POUND RAISINS

eating grapes, but this is impossible with raisins. For drying, canning whole, or freezing, seedless grapes are almost a necessity. In juice-making, seeds are not a problem—in fact, the most flavorful juice grapes are seedy.

It is possible to cut open each grape and pick out the seeds, but this is a tedious process. One old cookbook suggests using a goose feather or a toothpick. Seeding a few grapes for a special salad or fruit cup in this way is not hard, but it is not practical for larger amounts. However, grapes with skins that slip off easily when squeezed can be seeded in the following way:

Separate the grape skins from the pulp and seeds by squeezing the grapes so that the pulp drops into a saucepan. They can be squeezed quickly, two at a time, one in each hand. Set the skins aside. Cook the juicy pulp until soft, then push through a sieve to remove the seeds. A food mill with a fine screen works very well. Mix this purée with the grape skins. If they are tough, the skins can be chopped. Do not discard them as most of the color and a lot of the flavor is in the grape's skin. This skin and pulp mixture will make many kinds of desserts, jams, and fruit leathers.

## MAKING GRAPE JUICE
(Refer also to MAKING FRUIT JUICE AND SAUCE
in the FRUITS section.)

Grapes are among the best kinds of fruit for juice-making, most families will drink as much grape juice over the winter as they can store. Because of their full, distinctive flavor, Concord type grapes are most popular for juice, but other somewhat tart varieties are also good. An overly sweet and bland juice can be combined with sour grape juice or another sour fruit juice for a pleasant combination. (Refer to COMBINING SWEET AND TART FRUITS, in the FRUITS section.)

Grape juice is best if prepared without boiling. Concord grape juice is acceptable after boiling, but loses its fresh flavor. The juice of other varieties will become completely flat and flavorless if boiled. Temperatures around 170°F are recommended. Cooking and canning temperatures should never exceed 200°F.

Fresh grapes are often crushed and pressed or squeezed to extract their juice. The squeezing strainer illustrated in the KITCHEN UTENSILS section has a special spiral grape part that makes an excellent, somewhat thick or pulpy juice. Some small apple cider presses can be adapted for making grape juice. (Refer to MAKING APPLE CIDER, in the APPLES section.) When grapes are pressed like apples there is no need to remove the stems; they will not flavor the juice and may even help in the pressing.

Where pressing equipment is not available it is most practical to cook the grapes before extracting the juice. First, remove the stems, which add a harsh flavor when cooked, and put the grapes in a heavy kettle with just enough water to prevent sticking. Heat to a low simmer, being careful not to let the fruit boil, and stir often. To speed up the release of juice, as the grapes begin to simmer, mash them with a potato masher or kitchen mallet. When cooked through, about 30 minutes, or longer if amounts are large, strain off the juice. For a clear juice, allow to drip through a cloth without squeezing. Juice made in this way will be quite concentrated and can be diluted before it is used.

Other ways to make grape juice are with a steam juicer, like the one in the STEAM COOKING section, and by the quick canning method described below. These methods make a more diluted juice, requiring more storage space, but the juice's flavor is still quite good.

The pulp (or pomace) left from making grape juice can be used either for a second infusion of juice or in several other ways. (Refer to PULP FROM MAKING FRUIT JUICE, in the FRUITS section.)

A peculiarity of grape juice is that tartaric acid crystals and sediment form after it sits for a while. Though harmless, these spoil the look of the juice. To get rid of the sediment, let the juice sit for 24 hours in a cool place, then pour or siphon off the clear juice without disturbing the bottom. If grape juice has been canned without taking this step, the juice can still be poured off carefully when the jar is opened, leaving the sediment behind.

Generally, canning is the most practical way to store grape juice, but it is nice to also freeze some uncooked if there is enough freezer space. (Refer to FREEZING FRUIT JUICE OR SAUCE, in the FRUITS section.)

**Canning Grape Juice**   Because boiling spoils the flavor, grape juice is processed in a boiling water bath canner at a temperature of 190°F. (Refer to the CANNING section.) Use a dairy thermometer or other thermometer to check the temperature and make sure it never goes over 200°F.

Fill hot canning jars with the hot grape juice, leaving ¼ inch headroom. For both pints and quarts process at 190°F for 30 minutes.

**Quick Canned Grape Juice**   This method is best used with strongly flavored, tart grapes such as Concord or wild grapes. More canning jars are needed since the juice is not concentrated, but the flavor will be good. Fill the jars about half full with clean, stemmed grapes. Optional: add 1 or 2 tablespoons honey or sugar to each jar. Fill with boiling water, leaving ¼ inch headroom. Process both pints and quarts in a boiling water bath at 190°F for 30 minutes, or at 212°F for 15 minutes. (Refer to the CANNING section.) Wait at least a month before opening, giving the water time to soak up the grape flavor.

Some people use the grapes as well as the juice. To remove seeds put them through a food mill or strainer.

## MAKING RAISINS

Raisins are exceedingly useful and popular dried fruits, and many who raise grapes are interested in making them. Most of North America's raisins come from parts of California where the climate is favorable for both growing and drying. However, grapes can be dried wherever they are grown, using the same methods used for drying other firm berries. (Refer to DRYING FRUIT, in the DRYING section.) What really curtails raisin making is the requirement of a sweet, seedless variety of grape; these do not grow everywhere. Seedy grapes can be dried, of course, but the seeds will become harder and more prominent, so that the raisins are not much fun to eat. They can, however, be soaked for their juice.

There is not, as yet, any handy home device for seeding grapes. Instead there are new efforts directed towards developing sweet, seedless grape varieties adapted to most climates. In the meantime, some kinds of seedy grapes can be made into fruit leather. (See SEEDY GRAPES, above, and refer to *Fruit Leather,* in the DRYING section.)

Before they are picked for drying, grapes should ripen completely to fully develop their sugar content. Their sweetness will not increase after picking. In California grapes are usually sundried in clusters. They are rather slow to dry, taking an average of 3 weeks in the sun. When small quantities are dried they can be stemmed and blanched to check (crack) skins, which will speed up drying. (Refer to DRYING FRUIT in the DRYING section.)

Sun dried raisins are dark in color, while those dried in the shade are lighter. Their quality is excellent either way. The very light colored store-bought raisins have usually been lye dipped and sulfur treated to bleach them. The sultana variety of seedless grape is often bleached and dried. The dried "currants" sold in stores are actually a variety of small grape, specially raised for drying. Wine grapes are occasionally dried, then later soaked and the juice used for making wine. This juice has a brownish rather than a red or purplish hue.

## USING GRAPE LEAVES

Grape leaves, also called vine leaves, add an unusual, slightly tart flavor to the foods with which they are cooked. They are widely used as cooked wrappings. Stuffed grape leaves (or "dolmas") are wonderful little cigar shaped rolls made everywhere in the Middle East. Grape leaves are also delicious wrapped around small game birds before cooking them. A grape leaf is often put in a jar of pickles, not for flavor, but to keep the pickles crisp. (See the *Dolmas* recipe, below, and the *German Style Dill Pickles* recipe, in the CUCUMBERS section.)

Grape leaves are best picked when they are about full sized, yet still young enough to be tender, usually in June. (Though they can be used later in the season, they may be a little tough.) First, cut the stems off the grape leaves to be used as wrappings, then blanch them in boiling water for 2 or 3 minutes or until they are limp. If the leaves are to be salted to preserve them, they will only need rinsing before they are used.

*Preserving Grape Leaves in Salt*    The easiest way to preserve grape leaves is to pack them in salt in a jar or crock. Place the fresh, dry leaves one at a time in the container, sprinkling each leaf with plain or pickling salt. Cover and store, preferably in a cool place. Before use, rinse each leaf very thoroughly with cold water to remove the salt. The leaves will keep indefinitely.

## GRAPE RECIPES

### *Grape Catsup*                    (Makes 2–3 pints.)

| | |
|---|---|
| 3 pounds grapes, stemmed | 1½ teaspoons pepper, cayenne or |
| ½–1½ cups honey or sugar | black |
| 1½ teaspoons cloves | 1½ teaspoons allspice |
| 1½ teaspoons cinnamon | ½ teaspoon salt, or to taste |
| | 1 cup vinegar |

Put grapes in a non-aluminum pot and partially crush with a potato masher to release some juice. Cover and simmer 10 minutes. Put through a sieve or food mill to purée and remove seeds. (If they are seedless, raw grapes can be used and puréed in a blender.) Mix the purée with the honey or sugar, using a lesser amount if the grapes are sweet. Add cloves, cinnamon, pepper, allspice, salt, and vinegar. Simmer uncovered until the mixture has thickened to a sauce—about 20 minutes. Pour while boiling hot into hot jars, adjust lids, and process pints or quarts 10 minutes in a boiling water bath. (Refer to the CANNING section.)

This spicy catsup is especially good with meat, meat loaf, and vegetable loaf. It can also be used as a tart marmalade.

### *Lavender Delight*              (Makes about 6 dessert servings.)

| | |
|---|---|
| 2 teaspoons powdered gelatine | 1 cup grape juice |
| ½ cup mild honey | |

Put the gelatine to soak in a mixing bowl with 2 tablespoons of water.

Mix the honey with ½ cup water in a saucepan. Boil 3 minutes, watching closely and stirring when necessary to prevent overflowing. Pour the hot honey syrup over the gelatine in the bowl. Beat about 5 minutes or till it becomes white and marshmallowy. Now beat in the grape juice. Chill in the refrigerator or freezer, just until the gelatine begins to set. Beat again until evenly foamy. Chill in the refrigerator and serve as a gelatine, or freeze until firm and serve as sherbet.

## GRAPE IDEAS

**Pickled Grapes**   Firm, perfect grapes with stems removed, will keep indefinitely if placed in jars and completely covered with vinegar. (Jars with ordinary lids are fine, and refrigeration is unnecessary.) Their flavor will be strong, and they are best used sparingly as a garnish for potato or meat salads, or with meats. For a milder pickle put a little sugar or honey in the jar with the grapes.

Grapes can also be spiced and pickled like other fruits. (Refer to the *Spiced Pickled Fruit* recipe in the PICKLING section.)

**Grapes in Salads**   Seedless grapes or grapes that have been sliced and seeded bring a pleasant flavor to tossed salads. Try a mixture of sliced grapes, sliced cucumbers, and such minced fresh herbs as mint, parsley, and chives in an oil and vinegar dressing.

**Frosted Grape Clusters**   For a special dessert, cut a bunch of grapes into small clusters of several grapes each. Dip the grapes into warm syrup; half honey and half water warmed together can be used. Then sprinkle with some flavorful powdery or finely chopped mixture, such as finely chopped nuts, carob powder, crisply dried bananas pulverized in a blender, or any combination of these.

Let the coated grapes dry on a rack from a few minutes to several hours before eating them. They can be refrigerated overnight, but will not keep much longer.

### GRAPE IDEAS, *cont.*

**Brandied Grapes**  Put perfect grapes, stems removed, in small jars. Cover with brandy or another liquor, cover, and store for 2 or 3 months. Both grapes and liquor improve in flavor. They can be used like brandied cherries. Grapes are also very good used instead of peaches in TUTTI FRUTTI. (Refer to PEACH IDEAS in the PEACHES section.)

*Stuffing, folding, and rolling a dolma*

***Fruit Juice Delight***   Use any strongly flavored juice in place of grape.

### Stuffed Grape Leaves or Dolmas    (Makes about 6 side servings.)

| | |
|---|---|
| 25–30 grape leaves (See USING GRAPE LEAVES, above.) | ¼ cup parsley leaves, minced |
| small bunch parsley stalks | 1–2 scallions, minced |
| several rhubarb stalks or tomato slices, optional | 1 teaspoon dill leaves, minced |
| ½ cup raw rice | 1 teaspoon mint leaves, minced |
| ½ cup cooked chick peas, or other beans, mashed, optional | pepper, salt, optional |
| | ¼ cup oil, preferably olive |
| | juice of 1–2 lemons |

Remove stems and blanch the grape leaves if they are fresh. If salted, rinse thoroughly. Put parsley stalks and rhubarb stalks or tomato slices (rhubarb in spring, tomato in fall, either flavor blends well) on the bottom of a large cooking pot, enough to cover the bottom. Intertwine them so that the dolmas will not sit directly on the bottom.

Make the stuffing by combining the rice, mashed beans, parsley, scallions, dill, mint, pepper and salt, if desired. Put a teaspoon of stuffing in the center of the veined (underside) of each leaf. Make rolls by folding the lower (wide) part of the leaf over the stuffing, folding in the sides as if making an envelope, and rolling to the shape of a small cigar, as illustrated. Set the rolls, loose side down, close together in the pot on top of the intertwined vegetables. When one layer is complete arrange the next layer crosswise over the first. Mix the oil and lemon juice, with about ½ cup water, and pour over the rolls. Set a small plate on top of them so they will not unroll. Cover and simmer gently over low heat for 2 hours. From time to time, add a little more water as needed. Allow to cool in the pan, and serve cold.

***Dolmas with Meat***   Omitting the beans, mix ½ pound ground lamb or other ground meat with the above stuffing ingredients. If available, lamb bones, or chicken wings or necks can be spread on the bottom of the pot with the parsley stalks. Omit the oil in the liquid that is poured over the rolls. These dolmas are usually served hot, but are also good cold.

***Stuffed Chard Leaves***   Cut large Swiss chard leaves in half or in thirds. Cut out the heavy part of the stalk. Blanch leaves briefly in boiling water to make them flexible. Stuff, roll, and cook as above.

<table>
<tbody>
</tbody>
</table>

| STORAGE |
|---|

**Canning**  *Not recommended!* The fat may deteriorate the sealing compound on canning lids, or cause strongly flavored meat.

**Cold Storage**  Use for old style, fully cured ham and bacon only. (See MODERN AND OLD STYLE CURES below.) When properly wrapped, or otherwise protected, will keep up to a year.

**Freezing**  Essential method for long storage of moist, mildly cured pork. Quality retained: ham 5–7 months; bacon, 3 months. Refer to the FREEZING FOODS section.

T HE BEST HOME CURED HAMS AND BACONS ARE AS FLAVORFUL AND finely textured as the fanciest gourmet cured meats. In quality, they far exceed their everyday grocery store equivalents. The necessary home curing skills were developed almost to an art form over the many centuries when salt curing was the only practical way to preserve pork. Many regional delicacies were created, such as prosciutto ham from Italy, and Smithfield Virginia hams from the southern U.S. Modernity has, however, brought change. Freezing is now the most practical way to preserve pork in most circumstances, and a new awareness of the hazards of a high salt diet has relegated ham and bacon to a minor dietary role. These cured meats may be enjoyed as a special treat, and used in small amounts to season other dishes. On occasion, salt curing may serve as an emergency food storage technique, but ham and bacon are not advisable basic food items.

Some general information about curing and using ham and bacon follows. For detailed curing instructions, consult the references at the end of this section.

## HANDLING HAM AND BACON

*Modern and Old Style Cures*  Modern cures for ham and bacon, whether home or commercial, are quite different from the traditional old farm cures. Modern hams and bacons have a short curing time, a mild flavor, and a moist, soft texture. The cure is not designed to prepare them for storage anywhere except in the refrigerator or freezer. Old style cures had to produce a drier, saltier meat that would keep through winter and into spring without mechanical refrigeration. They also produced the full flavor and firm texture that many prefer over the moist, mild modern cures.

The procedures for modern and old style home cures are much the same, except for the length of the curing time and concentration of salt and nitrates. (Refer to the SALT CURING section.) The main ingredients are plain or pickling salt, sugar or another sweetener, and usually nitrates (saltpeter). The sugar improves flavor and texture, and the meat is likely to become quite hard without it. Nitrates are controversial as a food ingredient, but they do give ham its characteristic pink color, and, more important, ensure safety from botulism toxin. Pork can be safely cured without nitrates, but care must be taken to keep it constantly chilled during processing and storage. It would be foolish to try an old style cure for unrefrigerated storage without high salt and nitrates. (Refer to USING NITRATES OR SALTPETER IN CURING MEATS, in the SALT CURING section.) Many curing mixtures also include artificial smoke flavoring, but it cannot match the flavor of a true smoke treatment. (Refer to the SMOKING section.) Spices and other seasonings are optional ingredients in cures.

*It is important to note that all home cured ham remains raw pork and must be thoroughly cooked before eating.* (Refer to UNDERSTANDING TRICHINOSIS, in the PORK section.) In contrast, most commercial hams are pre-cooked and can be eaten without further attention.

***Minimizing Salt Intake from Ham and Bacon***　　There are two approaches to the enjoyment of ham and bacon without eating excessive quantities of salt. One is to consider them a salt seasoning like anchovies or soy sauce, and use them in small amounts instead of salt or other salty ingredients. The other is to "freshen" the meats by soaking them in water, then draining to remove salt.

Chopped or ground ham, and chopped or fried and crumbled bacon make tasty seasonings for a wide variety of foods, ranging from sandwich fillings, stews and meat loaves, to vegetable dishes and salads. Several tablespoons will nicely flavor most family-sized recipes. Firm, old style ham sliced paper thin makes an exquisite seasoning. (There is an old saying to the effect that a cold boiled ham should be cut so thin as to cover an acre.) A paper thin slice adds up to very little salt, but it complements beautifully such bland foods as unsalted cottage cheese, and such fresh fruits as cantaloupe and other melons.

Freshening will remove salt from even the saltiest cured meats, leaving them edible and still rich in protein value. Old style ham and bacon is always freshened, unless used only for seasoning, and home cured meats often need considerable freshening, because oversalting is frequent and preferable to having a ham or serveral slabs of bacon spoil due to an inadequate cure. Mildly cured meats can also be freshened, but the soaking time should be very short as they quickly lose flavor.

Large hams are freshened by soaking from 12 to 24 hours in plenty of cold water, and ham and bacon slices by soaking from a few minutes to an hour. If the meat is very salty, change the soaking water several times. Another way to freshen slices is to heat them almost to a boil in water, drain, then taste to see if sufficient salt has been removed. If not, repeat the procedure. Hams and chunks of bacon will need pre-soaking in cold water to desalt evenly, and then more salt can be removed by heating them to a simmer in fresh water and draining. A raw potato can be included to absorb salt. It is possible to freshen ham and bacon till no salt at all can be tasted, but the flavor is best if some is left in the meat. After freshening, cook the meat as usual. Ham and bacon slices can be fried or broiled. If home cured, whole hams must be precooked before baking them or eating them cold.

*Precooking Home Cured (Raw) Hams*   Wash the ham and soak if necessary to remove salt. If it had an old style cure, scrubbing with a brush or scraping may be necessary to remove harmless surface mold. Bring a pot of water almost to a boil and put in the ham. Simmer, covered, allowing 20 to 30 minutes per pound. A small ham takes longer per pound than a large one. The meat is done when a thermometer inserted in the center reaches 165°F.

When done, drain and remove the skin. Trim fat if desired. The ham can now be baked or used in any ham recipe. Remember that it is perishable, and for storage, must be refrigerated as soon as it cools. (To make use of the cooking water, refer to IDEAS below.)

*Salt Pork*   The back and shoulder fat of a pig is cured like bacon to make salt pork. Refrigerate or freeze for storage, and use in small amounts for seasoning. It can be freshened to remove excess salt like the ham or bacon slices above.

## HAM AND BACON RECIPES

**Greens Stuffed Ham**        (Makes 6–10 dinner servings.)

(If ham is served just once a year, this is the way to prepare it.)

Stuffing for a 5 to 6 pound ham
(adjust for other sizes):
- 2–3 *pounds kale, collard greens, or cabbage* (Mixture is good.)
- 1½ *pounds (about) mustard greens, cress, or other greens*
- 4–5 *stalks celery with leaves, chopped small*
- 1 *green pepper, chopped small*
- 1 *tablespoon hot red pepper flakes, or to taste*
- 1 *teaspoon black pepper*
- 1 *tablespoon mustard seeds*
- 1 *tablespoon celery seeds*
- 1 *ham* (If home cured, freshen if necessary, and precook.)

Chop kale, collards or cabbage, and mustard or other greens into 1 inch pieces. Blanch briefly in a large pot of boiling water. When limp, drain well and mix in the celery, green pepper, red and black pepper, and mustard and celery seeds.

Prepare the ham for stuffing by cutting several 2-inch slits completely through it. Arrange the slits so that one does not slit open into another. For a large ham, it works well to make a lengthwise row of 3 slits, then an offset row of 2 slits and another row of 3 slits. If the ham is small, cut the slits to suit its contours, or alternatively remove the bone and stuff the cavity.

By hand, push the stuffing into the slits as far as possible from one side, then turn the ham over and finish filling from the other side. This will only use part of the stuffing. Set the ham in a baking dish and press the rest of the stuffing around and over it. Cover with a lid or aluminum foil, and bake 15 minutes per pound (1½ hours for a 6 pound ham), in a moderate, 350°F, oven. Serve hot or cold.

## HAM AND BACON IDEAS

**Ham or Bacon Biscuits**   Mix ½ cup minced or ground cooked ham, or crumbled, fried bacon with the dry ingredients of a batch of biscuits just after working in the shortening. Omit salt. Finish and bake as usual.

For a main course dish, serve with creamed hard boiled eggs. (Mix the chopped eggs into the *Cream Sauce*, page 416.)

**Using Ham Stock**   The stock left from boiling a ham is full of flavor, and can be used for stewing other meats, such as an old stewing rabbit or hen, or tough game meat. Simmer without boiling for several hours, or till the meat is tender. Do not add salt, and taste before adding other seasonings as they may not be needed. Such vegetables as potatoes, carrots, and cabbage make excellent additions.

**Quick-Barbecued Ham Slices** Brown thin slices of cooked ham lightly on butter, or other fat. For 6 slices, mix 1 tablespoon vinegar, ¼ teaspoon dry mustard and a dash of pepper. Pour over the ham and cook another minute or two. Serve very hot with unsalted rice, potatoes, or noodles.

**Ham Cooked in Hay**   An old French way to cook a whole ham was to tie it in cloth, set in on a bed of sweet hay in a big pot, surround and cover it with more hay, cover all with water, and boil until cooked through. The hay gives a special fragrance to the ham. Puréed split peas were often served with it.

*Potted Ham*                                        (Makes about 4 cups.)

| | |
|---|---|
| *4 cups (about) cooked ham* (Include some fat.) | *½ teaspoon nutmeg* |
| *1 teaspoon mace* | *½ teaspoon pepper* |
| *1 teaspoon allspice* | *lard or clarified butter to seal top, optional* |

Dice the ham and mix with the mace, allspice, nutmeg and pepper. Grind, then taste, and adjust seasonings if necessary, thoroughly mixing in any additions. Grind once or twice more to make a paste. Pack tightly into small jars. A thin layer of melted lard or clarified butter poured on top will help preserve the potted ham. Cover and store in the refrigerator. This keeps a month or more. Spread sparingly on whole grain bread or crackers for a zesty snack or hors d'oeuvre.

## REFERENCE SOURCES FOR HAM AND BACON

Ashbrook, Frank G., *Butchering, Processing and Preservation of Meat,* Van Nostrand Reinhold Co., New York, 1955. (Includes complete instructions for curing ham, bacon, and sausages, as well as much other valuable meat handling information.)

Eastman, Wilbur F., *Canning, Freezing, Curing and Smoking of Meat, Fish, and Game.* Garden Way Publishing Co., Vt., 1975.

*A Complete Guide to Home Meat Curing,* Morton Salt Company, P.O. Box 355, Argo, Ill. 60501. (Limited, because it deals only with Morton's own curing mixtures, but descriptions of procedures are clear and helpful.)

# HEADS

THE HEAD OF ANY MEAT ANIMAL, YOUNG OR OLD, DOMESTIC OR WILD, is a valuable source of food, so a killing method that spares the head is an appreciable saving. The bony parts make extraordinarily good soup. Both meat and stock have a flavor unmatched by those from other animal parts. The brains and tongue, usually cooked separately from the bony parts, are also great delicacies.

The heads of small animals, poultry, and fish are always worth adding to the soup pot, but most special dishes are made from the heads of large animals. Hogs' heads, cows' heads which are also called ox heads, and calves' heads are the most commonly used. Specialties are also made from particular parts, such as ox cheek, ox muzzle, pig's snout, and pig's ears. Lambs', sheep's and goats' heads, and the heads of the larger game animals like deer are also good, though less meaty.

## HANDLING LARGE ANIMALS' HEADS

A reason often given for not using an animal's head is that it is too difficult to clean. If considered in stages, however, cleaning a head is no more difficult than other butchering chores. First, it must be either skinned, or scalded and scraped to remove the hair. Pigs' heads are scalded and scraped with the rest of the animal, then cut away from the carcass. The heads of other animals are usually cut off and skinned, though they can also be scalded or singed and scraped. The head can then be cooked with the skin on. Long ago sheep's heads were taken to the local blacksmith to have the wool burned off.

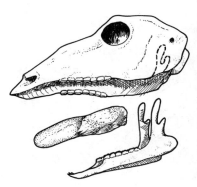

Skinned head, lower jaw and tongue removed.

The head is skinned like the rest of the animal. (Refer to skinning directions in the LAMB AND MUTTON and RABBIT sections.) A sharp knife is essential, and the skin is cut and pulled as necessary to remove it. A young animal's skin will come off more easily than that of an old one. The ears are cut off from the inside, next to the skull. Trimming around the lips, nose, and eyes is usually necessary. The eyes are removed by cutting around them, and pulling or prying them out. Next, the lower jaw is removed by cutting back from the corners of the mouth, and pulling or twisting till the joints can be found and unhinged. The tongue can then be cut out easily at the roots.

The head will now sit flat and can be sawed or split in half. Sawing will cause less damage to the brains and it will not create splinters. When sawed in half lengthwise, the nasal passages are exposed for easy cleaning. The brains can be lifted out neatly in two pieces. A very large head can be cut in four pieces for easire handling. (Refer to the BRAINS and TONGUE sections for using those parts.)

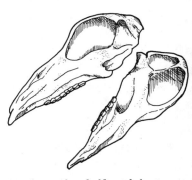

Head sawed in half, with brains removed.

Wash the pieces of head thoroughly in cool water, using a stiff brush around the teeth and nose. If the head is bloody, soak it in cold water for an hour or even overnight. If a head is especially hard to clean, it can be covered with water, brought to a boil, and drained before use in a recipe. No harm is done, however, if traces of blood remain when cooking begins. When boiling is called for, a careful skimming as it comes to a boil will also remove impurities that might cloud the finished dish.

Most recipes for heads begin with boiling them, but the heads of young animals are sometimes halved and baked or broiled, and whole heads are occasionally barbecued in outdoor pits.

## RECIPES FOR HEADS

### Head Cheese

There are many, many versions of this cold lunch meat. All begin in the same basic way, with simmering a head till the meat is tender and the stock is ready to jell when cooled. (Refer to the GELATINE section.) Differences lie in the kind of head used, and whether other animal parts are included, the seasonings or vegetables used, and the

*Stacked loaf pans of head cheese*

amount of jelled stock. The flavor of head meat and stock is so superior that some of the best head cheese is made simply from them, pepper, and salt. The ingredients in the three versions below can be adjusted to suit personal tastes.

> *1 head, cut in half or quartered, with brains and tongue removed* (Pig's, cow's or calf's heads are preferred. If a sheep's or other smaller head is used, feet or a knuckle bone should be included.)
>
> *pepper, salt, to taste* (Salt can be omitted, but a little enhances flavor.)
>
> Optional additions:
> *seasoning vegetables, such as chunks of celery, onion, carrot*
> *herbs and spices, such as parsley, thyme, marjoram, savory, sage, bay leaf, coriander, mace spears, whole cloves, or red pepper*

Trim as much fat as possible from the head and any other animal parts. Put in a large pot with seasoning vegetables, if used. Cover with water, bring to a boil, and skim well. Simmer, covered, till the meat is tender and ready to fall from the bones, usually 3 hours or longer. When done, drain off the cooking stock, and let sit till the fat rises and can be skimmed off completely. Let the head cool enough to handle, then take the meat off the bones. Use the meat and stock to make one of the following versions of head cheese.

***Head Cheese I (Packed Meat)***    Chop, or grind the meat coarsely, and season to taste with pepper and salt. If desired, minced fresh herbs can be mixed in, and are especially good in calf's head cheese. Pack the meat as firmly as possible into loaf pans. Stack the pans on top of each other, with a piece of waxed paper between each pan. Put a weight on the top pan to press them all, and refrigerate or leave in a cool place overnight. Next day, take the loaves out of the pans, wrap well, and refrigerate or freeze. This version freezes better than the others because extra jellied stock is not added. If the loaves should be too crumbly to slice, the meat can be heated to a boil with a little jelled stock, and returned to the loaf pans to set again.

Another method is to put the head cheese in a cloth bag, and hang it in a cool pantry or spare room till set. To make a bag, lay a large square of heavy cheesecloth, or other cotton cloth in a bowl. Put in the head cheese, gather the corners of the cloth together, and tie for hanging. (Extra stock can be used for making soup, or the *Scrapple*, below.)

***Head Cheese II (Meat in Gelatine)***    Pick the meat from the bones in small pieces, or dice it. Put it in a pot with enough stock to cover. Add pepper, salt, and any optional desired seasonings. Simmer, uncovered, for 30 minutes. Pour into molds. Cooked, sliced tongue can be arranged in a layer in the mold. Pressing is not necessary, but if loaf pans are used, they can be stacked and pressed as described above. Set the stack of pans in a larger pan to catch overflowing juices. Chill till set. Unmold, wrap, and refrigerate. This version can

## IDEAS FOR HEADS

### Roast Lambs' or Kids' Heads

Skin, trim, and clean the heads of young animals, removing lower jaw and tongue. Saw the heads in half lengthwise, leaving the brains in place. Set the halves in a shallow baking dish, cut side up, so each forms a dish holding the brains. Sprinkle with oregano, pepper, salt, lemon juice, and olive oil. Roast in a hot oven for 30 to 40 minutes, or till the brains are cooked through. Baste several times with the pan juice. Serve one half head per person. Though the brains are featured in this delicacy, the bits of meat clinging to the head are also very good. Nice served as a first course, or with salad for a fancy lunch.

be frozen, but the gelatine may crack or form ice crystals.

For long storage, the meat and stock mixture can be pressure canned. Seasonings should be added and the final cooking done when the jars are opened. Fill hot canning jars with boiling hot meat and stock, leaving 1 inch headroom. Pressure process at 240°F with 11 pounds of pressure. Process pints for 75 minutes, and quarts for 90 minutes. (Refer to the CANNING section.)

*Head Cheese III (Spicy Jelled Meat)*   (Scots Brawn is made in this way, using a cow's head and a foot to ensure a stiff jell.) After the meat is removed from the bones, refrigerate it, or reserve in a cool place. Return the bones to the pot with the stock. Add the water if necessary to cover the bones. Add pepper, salt, seasoning vegetables, herbs, and spices as desired. This can be made quite spicy with red pepper. Simmer, uncovered, for 2 or 3 hours. Strain off the stock and chill till it jells, usually overnight. Carefully remove all fat. Chop the reserved meat coarsely and put it in a pot with the jelled stock. Heat, taste, and adjust seasonings if necessary. Simmer for 15 minutes and pour into molds that have been rinsed in cold water. Chill till set, unmold, and wrap well. For long storage, pressure can as for HEAD CHEESE II, above. Herbs and spices are best omitted, and added after the jars are opened. Increase cooking time after opening to 30 minutes.

## Scrapple
(Also known by the Pennsylvania Dutch
names of Ponhaws or Pan Haas.)                      (Makes about 3 loaves.)

| | |
|---|---|
| 3 *quarts stock from cooking a head* (One large head, or 5–6 skinned rabbit heads can be used.) | 1 *teaspoon sage* |
| | 1 *teaspoon marjoram* |
| | ½ *teaspoon pepper* |
| | 1 *teaspoon (about) salt, optional* |
| 2 *cups or more cooked meat, ground or chopped small* (May be from heart, kidneys, liver, or tongue, as well as from the head.) | 2 *cups (about) cornmeal* |
| | 2 *cups whole wheat, or buckwheat flour, optional* (Can be reduced, or omitted and replaced with cornmeal.) |

Be sure all fat is removed from the stock. Mix the cornmeal with enough cool stock to moisten it. This will prevent lumps. Heat the rest of the stock with the meat, sage, marjoram, pepper and salt, if desired. When boiling, stir in the dampened cornmeal and, stirring constantly, add the flour. Cook slowly for 30 minutes to an hour, preferably in a double boiler. Otherwise, it will need almost constant stirring to avoid sticking and scorching. Long cooking improves the texture. When partly cooked, taste, and adjust seasonings if necessary. After it has thickened, pour into greased loaf pans and cool overnight, or till firmly set.

**IDEAS FOR HEADS,** *cont.*

**Head Soup**   Cook the bony parts of a head or several heads in water as for soup stock. Add root vegetables, seasonings, and other ingredients to taste. Sheep's head soup made with barley, dry peas, carrots, turnips, onions, and parsley is a Scottish favorite called Powsowdie. An early American favorite was a calf's head soup, cooked with a piece of ham or ham bone, seasoned with parsley, turnip or mustard green or other green herbs, mace, allspice, and cloves, and thickened with flour browned in butter. A clear head soup is good with the *Brain Balls* recipe in the BRAINS section, made from the same head.

**Pit Barbecued Head**   One large, absolutely fresh head with the hair and skin on and the eyes removed is the only ingredient. A cow's or calf's head, or the heads of moose or deer, are suitable.

Dig a large pit 3 feet deep and line it with stones. Light a large hardwood fire and burn it down to a deep bed of coals. Wrap the head in 3 layers of clean, water-soaked burlap, and tie with wire, leaving a long loop for a handle. Make a hollow in the coals, and bury the head with the wire handle sticking out. Cover the pit with damp newspaper or burlap, sealing the edges with dirt. Let cook 8 to 12 hours.

Pull out the head, using the wire handle. Unwrap it and remove the skin, which will come off easily. Slice the head meat, tongue, and brains. Serve with watercress, garlic butter, and corn-on-the cob, or other picnic favorites.

Turn the scrapple out of the pans and slice ¼ to ½ inch thick. If sticky, dust the slices with flour. Fry in fat or oil till browned on both sides. Serve hot with catsup, relish, or maple syrup. This makes a delicious breakfast dish.

Scrapple loaves will keep about a week in the refrigerator. For long storage, slice and freeze. The slices can be fried without thawing. (Refer to FREEZING SLICES in the FREEZING section.)

*Oatmeal Scrapple*   Use slow-cooking rolled oats or coarsely ground oats instead of cornmeal and flour. Less cooking time is required.

*Other Scraps Scrapple*   Any poultry or meat soup stock with leftover cooked meat can be made into scrapple. Stock from cooking a roast turkey or chicken carcass, and the leftover meat, gravy, and stuffing can all be combined and thickened with cornmeal for an excellent scrapple. Minced onions and parsley add flavor, especially when using a bland stock.

### STORAGE

**Canning**   Trim, removing all fat, and cut into chunks or slices. Pressure process like stewing beef. Refer to BEEF section.

**Freezing**   Trim, wrap whole, or cut in sections. Quality retained 1 year. Refer to FREEZING section.

#### AVERAGE WEIGHT

BEEF HEARTS: 4–6 POUNDS;   CALF AND PORK HEARTS: ABOUT ½ POUND;   LAMB HEARTS: ABOUT ¼ POUND

# HEART

AS THE HEART IS A MUSCLE, IT IS NO SURPRISE THAT THE MEAT TASTES like a muscle meat with an exceptionally compact texture. Most people like heart the first time they try it; or they would if it were cooked gently enough to keep it moist and tender. Besides its fine flavor heart has the virtue of being easy to clean and prepare. One could almost wish that an animal had more than one heart so that the meat could be enjoyed more often!

## HANDLING HEARTS

Trim off the valves or tubes, gristle, and as much fat as possible from around the top of the heart. Wash in cold water and the heart is ready for cooking. The fat surrounding the heart is hard and will not cook well, so set it aside for animal feed or discard it. Any fat needed for cooking with heart meat should be taken from another part of the animal.

The most important requirement for cooking heart is low heat, except when an initial quick searing to seal in juices is called for. Because of the lean, dense nature of the meat, it will become dry and tough if cooked too long with high heat. (Refer to LEAN MEAT, in the MEAT section.) Also because of its density, heart should be sliced thinly across the grain, either before cooking or before serving it. A raw heart is most easily sliced if cut in half and set flat side down on the cutting board.

Heart meat will make very good hamburger if ground with pork or beef fat, but it will lose its distinctive and interesting texture.

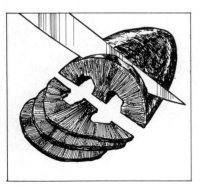

*Slicing heart*

Heart from various large animals, including game animals like deer, is interchangeable in recipes with cooking times adjusted for the heart's size and the age of the animal. A whole large beef heart takes from 3 or 4 hours to cook, while whole calf, pork, or lamb hearts take from 1½ to 2½ hours. Hearts from poultry and small animals like rabbits can also be used in heart recipes if enough can be collected. Use them whole in recipes calling for sliced heart meat. Otherwise, include them with other parts of the bird or animal in mixed dishes or in soups.

## HEART RECIPES

### Wine Simmered Heart     (Makes about 6 dinner servings.)

2 pounds (about) heart meat (Several small hearts, or part of a large one.)
2 – 3 tablespoons butter, or other fat, for frying
1 onion, chopped medium

1 clove garlic, minced, optional
parsley, several teaspoons, minced
½ – 1 cup dry red wine
pepper, salt, optional

Before slicing, quarter a large heart the long way, or cut smaller hearts in half. Then cut the meat across the grain into many thin, about ¼ inch, slices.

Melt the butter or fat in a large, heavy frying pan. Add the onion, garlic, and parsley and sauté over low heat for a minute or two. Add the heart slices and sauté gently over low heat, stirring often, till the meat has lost its red color; usually from 5 to 10 minutes. Add enough red wine to about half cover the meat. Season with pepper, and salt, if desired. Simmer uncovered, stirring now and then, for about 20 minutes, or till the meat is cooked through and the wine reduced to a sauce. Never let it boil.

Serve with noodles or rice, or over toast to absorb the sauce. This is an excellent way to prepare heart when trying it for the first time—the flavor is irresistible!

**Wine Simmered Kidneys**   Prepare and slice kidneys to use instead of heart. They will take about half as long to cook.

**Wine Simmered Liver**   Dust slices of liver with flour seasoned with black pepper and paprika. Use instead of heart, turning slices to brown lightly on both sides. Then simmer in wine from 10 to 15 minutes. Instead of wine, ½ cup wine vinegar, with water as needed, can also be used.

### English Mock Goose, or Stuffed Heart     (Makes 8 – 10 dinner servings.)

1 beef heart, or several smaller hearts
2 bay leaves
4 whole cloves
1 – 2 quarts beef soup stock, or water

2 – 3 cups bread crumbs
½ cup suet, pork fat, or fatty bacon, finely chopped
1 egg

---

**HEART IDEAS**

**Pickled Heart**   Pre-cook heart by simmering in water or soup stock, without boiling, till tender. Onion, bay leaf, or other herbs such as sage or rosemary can be included. Let the heart cool in the cooking stock, then drain, and slice thinly across the grain. Marinate the slices for several hours or overnight in a mixture of half vinegar and half water. A clove of garlic, a slice of raw onion, or other seasonings such as a few peppercorns, and a dash of salt, can be added. This dish keeps for about a week in the refrigerator.

Goose hearts or other small hearts can be pickled whole in this way.

**Stir-Fried Heart**   Very thinly sliced heart meat will be delicious stir-fried with vegetables in any combination that is good with beef. For an all-heart stir-fry, mix about a pound of thinly sliced heart with a tablespoon each of soy sauce, sherry, if desired, and water or soup stock. Add ½ tablespoon each, cornstarch and honey or sugar, and a scallion cut in 1 inch sections. A little minced fresh ginger root adds a nice flavor. Stir-fry for 3 minutes over very high heat and serve. (Refer to the STIR-FRYING section.)

*8 to 10 fresh sage leaves, minced, or 1 teaspoon dried sage*          *pepper, to taste*
*several slices bacon, or salt pork*

A day ahead of final preparation pre-cook the heart as follows. Trim, wash it and put it in a pot with the bay leaves and cloves. Cover with beef stock or water. Simmer covered over low heat till tender. Never let it boil. A beef heart will take from 3 to 5 hours. Smaller hearts may take as little as 1½ hours. Let the heart sit in the stock overnight in a cool place. Next day remove fat from the stock and take the heart out to drain.

Mix bread crumbs, suet or other fat, egg, sage, and pepper, and add enough of the stock from cooking the heart to make a fairly moist stuffing. Push some of the stuffing into the opening in the top of the heart, close with skewers, and set in a baking pan. Shape the rest of the stuffing into balls and arrange around the heart. Lay salt pork or bacon over all and bake in a hot, 400°F oven, for 30 minutes. To serve, slice the meat thinly across the grain. For a gravy, to serve with the meat, thicken and season some of the leftover stock. Mock goose is sometimes served for Christmas dinner instead of real goose, as the two meats have a similar texture.

# HERBS

## STORAGE

**Drying**  (Preferred method for most leafy herbs.) See DRYING HERBS, below.

**Freezing**  (Best for herbs that lose flavor if dried.) See FREEZING HERBS, below.

**Live Storage**  Maintain in garden, and as potted plants for a constant fresh supply. Note: See also PRESERVING HERBS IN VINEGAR, OIL, OR SALT, below.

I TEASPOON DRIED HERBS = 2–3 TEASPOONS MINCED FRESH HERBS

H ERBS HOLD THE SAME FASCINATION FOR PEOPLE TODAY AS THEY have through the ages. Old folk remedies for both physical and mental ills depended largely on medicinal herbs, and culinary herbs have been appreciated and explored as food seasoners over the centuries. These two herbal uses have, for the most part, remained quite distinct from each other, but there is now beginning to be a joining together of the two pathways. Though herbs are ostensibly regarded as food seasonings, we now ask more of them; they are to be an aid and a comfort in the constant battle waged by so many people against modern dietary excesses. Once it is understood that the affluent western world's diet is too rich in fats and sugar, too salty, and too full of artificial additives, a resolution is usually made to change to healthier fare. Then, eating habits of a lifetime must be broken, and in the process an empty, negative, and let-down feeling may arise. It is at this point that herbs come to the rescue. They can be more than a substitute for the flavors of sugar, salt, or anything else, and can fill flavor gaps in healthful and interesting ways. As well, herbs offer a delightfully positive way to be preoccupied about food. One can explore the diversity of flavors, aromas, medicinal benefits, and other delights of the world of herbs and, while doing so, leave behind the seemingly endless struggle against the urge to eat from the surrounding glut of unhealthful foods.

Tastes in herbs are personal. When specific directions are given for using herbs, they should be taken as suggestions, and when flat statements of their characteristics are made, they should be taken as opinions. There is no single right or wrong way to use an herb, instead there is the fun of trying many ways, learning perhaps, from others' suggestions and opinions, but in the end deciding for oneself. In any case, herb flavors will vary with their variety, the place they were grown, the season, and whether they are fresh or dried. The only way to understand a particular herb in a particular place at a particular time is to try it.

Gardeners are doubly blessed, as they have both the pleasure of growing herbs and the opportunity to explore their special qualities at a leisurely pace. Each can be tried alone while fresh, at different stages of growth, as well as dried, and in combination with other herbs and seasonings.

## HANDLING HERBS

Herbs freshly gathered when needed are the nicest. Herbs growing near the kitchen door, and pots of herbs on the windowsill will provide some fresh herbs throughout the year, but some will still need to be dried or perhaps frozen. Though drying is the best way to preserve most leafy herbs, there are a few that will lose or change flavor, notably chives, tarragon, basil, dill, and parsley. These can be frozen quite successfully for use in cooking, but as they become limp after thawing their usefulness in salads or as garnishes is limited.

***Drying Herbs*** Gather leafy green herbs when they are most flavorful, just before they bloom. The best time is in the morning of a dry day after the dew has evaporated. If they are cut or picked neatly they should not need washing. But if they are dusty, rinse them quickly in cool water and then shake or pat them dry with a towel. Then put them in an airy, shady place to dry. Sunlight fades them and destroys flavor so shaded drying is essential. Herbs can be tied in bunches by the stems, or put loosely in net bags and hung in an airy attic, shed, or porch for drying. Take them down and store them as soon as they are dry, as they tend to lose flavor and collect dust if left hanging. If using a food dryer, never let temperatures go above 100°F, as higher temperatures destroy flavor.

***Storing Dried Herbs*** To store, rub or crumble the leaves off the twigs or stems and close them in airtight containers. As a precaution, especially in damp climates, check inside the containers after a few days to see if any moisture has collected. If so, spread the herbs out to dry a few more days. If using clear glass containers, store them in a dark place to retain full color and flavor. (Refer to the DRYING section for details.)

As the flavor of dried herbs gradually diminishes during storage, it is best to renew the supply once a year. Leaf pieces or crumbled leaves retain flavor longer than powder. Powder small amounts as needed, using a blender or mortar and pestle. Do not discard the herbs' dry stems and twigs as they create a nice pleasant scent when burned. Use them to put on the coals when food is charcoal broiling or put them in the fireplace.

***Freezing Herbs*** Though sometimes herbs are blanched like vegetables before freezing, it is easier and just as good to make packets of a few sprigs each in amounts to be used at one time, and then freeze them. Use small freezer bags for these small portions, and freeze them in one large container. However, the best way to preserve the flavor of herbs in the freezer is to freeze them in cubes of ice. Chop or mince the herb and pack ice cube tray sections with it. Then add water to fill the tray, and freeze. When solid remove the cubes and store them in freezer bags. A cube will be just right for adding to soups and stews, and the flavor will be as good as fresh. Such cubes can also be thawed in a strainer, letting the water drain off, so that the herbs can be used in salads or cottage cheese. Favorite herb combinations can be minced together and frozen for a very convenient seasoning. For instance mixed celery leaf, parsley, and scallion cubes are very nice for adding to all sorts of dishes. See BOUQUET GARNI and FINES HERBES, under HERB IDEAS, for examples of some herb combinations, and refer to the FREEZING section for freezing details.

***Preserving Herbs in Vinegar or Oil*** Herb leaves covered with either of these will keep for months. Herbs like basil and tarragon which do not respond well to drying can be preserved in this way. Pack herb leaves loosely in jars, cover them with vinegar or oil, and store in a cool place. The basil flavor is best preserved if the vinegar is heated to a boil before it is added. Do not use cold pressed oils from health food stores because they become rancid too easily. As the herb will flavor the vinegar or oil, they too will be valuable for flavoring foods. Use the vinegar like any herb vinegar. (For suggestions, refer to the VINEGAR section.)

***Cooking With Herbs*** Herbs are surprisingly interchangeable in foods, considering the distinct differences in their flavors. Substitutions may not be appreciated when a particular herb is closely associated with a food, like oregano on pizzas and sage in breakfast sausages, but otherwise the possibilities are almost unlimited. Many different herbs and herb combinations will give zest and interest when cooked with foods as diverse as appetizers, main courses, vegetables, and even desserts. There is great fun in growing an unfamiliar garden herb to try in ordinary and unexpected ways. Get to know it first by adding it to simple dishes, such as scrambled eggs or a plain broth, then combine it with other herbs and seasonings in various sauces, stews, casseroles, breads, and whatever else imagination dictates.

Herbs blend in best and will yield the most flavor if added for about the last 20 minutes of a food's cooking time. (Except for a few strong herbs, like bay leaf and sage, which can be cooked for several hours and still add flavor.) To introduce distinct and separate flavors rather than blending them into foods, add them in the last 5 minutes of cooking, or just before serving.

## HERBS FROM THE GARDEN

(Also see the HERB ROOTS and HERB SEEDS sections.)

The following herbs and blossoms for seasoning are easily grown in most gardens, and are included in recipes throughout this book.

*Basil*   Basil tastes best fresh. It has much less flavor after drying, but can be frozen or preserved in oil or vinegar. Its flavor in vinegar is retained best if it is heated enough to wilt the leaves. Fresh basil is delicious in salads, especially in tomato salads, and used fresh or preserved as a seasoning for cooked tomato mixtures. Put a leaf or small sprig in each jar when canning tomatoes. Minced basil leaves with butter are very good on peas, green beans, and other green vegetables. They are also an excellent seasoning to add to soups, to dried bean dishes, and sprinkled on most fish fillets and steaks just before serving. For recipes featuring basil see the *Pesto, Herb-Garlic Sauce,* below, and the *Tomato Bread Salad* recipe, in the TOMATOES section.

*Bay and Bayberry Leaves*   Bay leaves come from the bay tree, a variety of laurel, native to the Mediterranean region. It must be distinguished from the American laurel which is poisonous. Though bay trees are not winter hardy in most of North America, they can be grown in tubs and brought indoors during cold weather.

Bayberry bush leaves, which grow wild along many North American coasts, can be used as a seasoning instead of bay leaves. Their flavor is different, but they complement many of the same foods. Both bay and bayberry leaves are easy to dry and store. Bayberry adds an especially nice aroma and flavor to shellfish dishes. Try 1 or 2 leaves in the *Shellfish Bisque* recipe, in the SHELLFISH section.

*Borage*   Tiny, newly formed borage leaves, minced and added to salads, give a delicate cucumber flavor. Add larger leaves to sauces for fish for the same effect. The young leaves can also be cooked and served like spinach or used in greens mixtures. (Refer to the WILD

FOODS section for ideas.) Float the brilliant blue borage flowers on cool summer drinks or sprinkle them on salads for a startling touch of color.

*Camomile*   The yellow center of the camomile blossom is the prized part of the plant. Gather the flowers when they are in full bloom and dry them for making a soothing and flavorful tea. (See *Herb Teas,* below.) Should there be too much camomile to drink, take a nice soothing bath in it, as recommended by early herbalists.

*Celery Leaves, Celeriac Leaves, Lovage*   All of these have a strong, fresh celery flavor excellent for seasoning all kinds of soup, stews and salads, especially potato salad. Lovage is also known as smallage or milage. The leaves and thin stalks of all of these plants dry very well. (Refer to the CELERY and CELERIAC sections, and for seeds, to the HERB SEEDS section.)

*Chervil*   Chervil can be used in about the same ways as parsley. Its flavor is mild and pleasant, so add generous amounts to foods. It is best fresh. It does not dry well, but can be frozen. When cooking, add it at the last minute because its flavor quickly disappears. It enhances the flavor of other herbs, which makes it important in *Fines Herbes* and other herb mixtures. (See the *Green Chervil Sauce,* below, and refer to the *Chicken Pie* recipe in the CHICKEN section.) Chervil roots are good cooked like carrots.

*Chives, Scallions, Other Onion Greens*   Though these related plants all differ in flavor their light onion taste makes them welcome in the same kinds of foods. They are best fresh, but they can also be frozen. Chives can be grown in pots on the window sill for winter use. Scallions or onion tops can also be grown indoors. (Refer to the ONIONS section.) Freshly chopped chives or scallions are a perfect garnish for potatoes, eggs, fresh cheeses, soups, and salads. For garlic chives or Chinese leeks and wild garlic, refer to the GARLIC section.

*Comfrey*   Refer to the COMFREY section.

*Coriander (Chinese Parsley, Cilantro)*   Coriander leaves are used like parsley in many parts of the world. In Mexico and the Caribbean this herb is called cilantro. It is also popular in the Middle East, India, China (hence Chinese parsley), and other far Eastern countries. The flavor of the fresh leaves is distinctive and strong, so try them cautiously at first. Float a leaf in soup, or mince a leaf or two and use as a garnish on stir-fried meat or chicken dishes. Then try the leaves in the *Herb Sauce Marinade for Broiled Meat,* below, or the FRESH TOMATO SAUCE, in the TOMATOES section. Coriander does not dry well, but can be frozen. The seeds are milder than the leaves. (Refer to the HERB SEEDS section.)

*Dill*   Fresh, feathery young dill leaves, sometimes called dill weed, are delicious in salads, and with potatoes, eggs, or fish. As the plant matures the leaves become tougher and less flavorful, but by then the flower umbels are forming so use them instead. An umbel or dill head is the classic flavoring for pickled cucumbers or other pickled vegetables. Use them before they reach full maturity and begin to dry out.

For a constant supply of dill leaves and umbels through summer and fall resow the seeds several times. In winter use the seeds for flavorings. Some recipes featuring dill are: DILL DEVILED EGGS, in the EGGS section, the CELERY SOUP variation in the ASPARAGUS section, *Finnish Fish Pudding,* in the FISH section, and *Three Bean Salad,* in the BEANS, FRESH section. Also refer to DILL SEEDS, in the HERB SEEDS section.

*Elder Flowers* Refer to the ELDERBERRIES section.

*Fennel* Fresh fennel leaves have a light, licorice flavor well known as a seasoning for fish, but they are also good used in the same ways as dill. Try them in the above, or in *Grated Cucumber Salad,* in the CUCUMBER section. Florence fennel, called finnochio in Italy, has thick bulbous stalks, and is a delicious vegetable either fresh or cooked. (Refer to the *Ratatouille* recipe, in the EGGPLANT section.) Fennel leaves can be frozen. The seeds can be used like anise seeds. (Refer to ANISE SEEDS, in the HERB SEEDS section.)

*Marjoram and Oregano* These two herbs are closely related. Oregano is sometimes called wild marjoram, and it has the stronger flavor. It is often used alone, while marjoram works well blended with other herbs, especially thyme. Both are most familiar dried, but they are also very good when used fresh. They are excellent in the popular Italian style tomato sauces, and very good with all meats, especially dark meated game birds, lamb, poultry, and fish, and they enhance as well, bean dishes, soups, and salads of all kinds. They are often suggested seasonings throughout this book. Some examples are SHAKER STYLE FISH SAUCE, in the FISH section, *Tomato Sauce for Pasta,* in the TOMATOES section, *Roast Lamb, Syrian Style,* in the LAMB section, *Ratatouille,* in the EGGPLANT section, and *Herbed Tomato Juice Cocktail,* in the TOMATOES section.

*Mint* There are many different kinds of mint, but peppermint and spearmint are the ones most often grown in the garden. Wild mint is widespread and varies greatly in flavor. Try samples from different locations to see which tastes best. The flavor of mint is strongest before it blooms, so cut it back occasionally to make new growth. In spring the tender new leaves are delicious in salads and fruit cups. Later the leaves become rougher and should be minced for eating fresh, or used in mixtures made in the blender. Dried mint is most often used for teas, but can be substituted for fresh mint in most recipes. Mint is good in herb combinations, and with meats and vegetables, as well as in drinks and desserts. (Refer to *Plum Mint Sauce,* in the PLUM section, *Tabbouleh, a Middle Eastern Salad,* in the WHEAT section, PEAR MINT SHERBET, in the ICE CREAM section, and *Fish and Greens, Amerindian Style,* in the FISH section.

*Nasturtium* The nasturtium is more than a pretty flower. It is an excellent herb with a brisk, peppery flavor. The leaves, buds, blossoms and seed pods are all edible. Use fresh leaves chopped into salads, or minced to add to cottage cheese or cream cheese. Add them just before serving, since they can develop a bitter taste. The dried leaves can also be used as a peppery seasoning.

The blossoms provide a lovely splash of color floated in soups, or garnishing salads, appetizers, and desserts. Both buds and seed pods can be pickled to use like capers, but the pods have a firmer texture than the buds. The dry seeds can be made into a sort of mustard. (Refer to the MUSTARD section.)

*Parsley*   Refer to the PARSLEY section.

*Rose Petals*   Refer to the ROSES section.

*Rosemary*   Rosemary is an interesting and versatile herb, equally good fresh or dried. It can be grown in the garden in summer, then kept in a pot in a cool place indoors during freezing weather. Used in the same way as sage and thyme, it is outstanding with light meats like rabbit, chicken, veal, lamb, or pork. A few twigs or leaves sprinkled on the coals when charcoal broiling one of these will add an exceedingly pleasant aroma and flavor. Some recipes featuring rosemary are: the Spanish version of BROILED OR GRILLED RABBIT under RABBIT IDEAS, in the RABBIT section, *Tripe, Italian Style,* in the TRIPE section, *Risotto,* in the RICE section, VEAL MEATBALLS WITH HERBS, in the VEAL section, and *Creamed Apple Soup,* in the APPLES section.

*Sage*   As sage is strong flavored it should be used with restraint. Mix parsley with it to tone down and complement its flavor. When dried its flavor is quite familiar, as the expected seasoning for poultry stuffings and breakfast sausage. Fresh sage has a somewhat different, milder yet delicious flavor. Mince tiny bits of it to add to eggs, cottage cheese, green beans, and eggplant and tomato dishes. Some recipes featuring sage are: *Savory Snap Bean Stew,* in the BEANS, FRESH section, *Breakfast Sausage,* in the SAUSAGE section, *Herb Bread,* in the BREAD, YEAST section, and *Saltimbocca, Veal with Ham Italian Style,* in the VEAL section

*Savory*   The two savories, summer and winter, differ somewhat in flavor, but can be used interchangeably. Winter savory has the strongest flavor. Both can be used fresh or dried. Summer savor is known for its affinity with green beans, but it goes well with many vegetables. Cabbage, Brussels sprouts, summer squash, and most vegetable mixtures taste very good seasoned with either savory. This herb also goes well with most meats and can be used instead of thyme. Try it in any of the recipes in the VEGETABLES section, in the *Pre-Mixed Oil and Lemon or Vinegar Dressing,* in the SALADS section, and in *Breakfast Sausage,* in the SAUSAGE section, and in *Herbed Pea Pod Soup,* in the PEAS section.

*Tarragon*   While Russian tarragon is easier to grow, French tarragon is the most flavorful variety. In some recipes, tarragon is called by its French name, estragon. Use it fresh or frozen since drying changes its flavor. It is very good with cucumber pickles instead of dill, and is a common flavoring in vinegar. Try it with chicken, seafood, vegetables, and in salads. Some recipes featuring it are: *Herb*

*Vinegar,* in the VINEGAR section, *Tomato Aspic* in the TOMATOES section, SEASONED SAUERKRAUT, in the SAUERKRAUT section, and *Friar's Omelet,* in the EGGS section.

**Thyme**    The strong yet pleasant flavor of thyme is good both fresh and dried. It enhances so many foods, and complements so many herb and spice mixtures, that enumeration is difficult. For a start, however, try it in meat and vegetable stuffings, stews, and casseroles, and put some fresh sprigs on the table for nibbling with meals. (See FRESH HERBS WITH MEALS, under HERB IDEAS, below.) When adventuring with herbs thyme is a must. Some recipes featuring it are: *Eggplant Shellfish Casserole,* in the EGGPLANT section, *Veal Roasted Catalan Style,* in the VEAL section, *Creole Cabbage Stuffing,* in the CABBAGE section, and *Small Birds Baked in Grape Leaves,* in the BIRDS, SMALL section.

## HERB RECIPES

These recipes can be the starting point for some interesting herbal adventures. The first five are sauces in which many different herbs and herb combinations can be tried. Have fun!

---

### Red Wine Herb Sauce                              (Makes about 1 cup.)

2 tablespoons oil, preferably olive
2 tablespoons flour
2 teaspoons basil, parsley, or celery
   leaves, minced
2 tablespoons chives, scallions, or
   onion, minced

1 teaspoon fresh oregano, marjoram or thyme, minced, or ½
   teaspoon dried
½ cup dry, red wine
½ cup (about) chicken or other
   light stock

Heat the oil in a saucepan and stir in the flour. Add the herbs, wine, and stock, and simmer uncovered, stirring often, till blended and thickened, about 10 minutes. If too thick, add a little more stock.

Pour over stuffed vegetables, fish, meat loaf or casseroles before baking them, or serve hot with these and other dishes. For a quick lunch, pour over sliced hard boiled eggs on toast or rice.

**Red Wine Sauce with Fish**    Lay mackerel, carp fillets, or other fresh, or frozen and thawed, fish in an oiled baking dish. Arrange tomato slices on top and sprinkle with pepper, and salt, if desired. Pour over the red wine sauce. Bake at 350°F, till the fish is done, from 30 to 40 minutes. This fish sauce is especially good made with basil.

---

### Green Chervil Sauce                              (Makes about 1 cup.)

This white wine sauce (from *Roman Cookery* by John Edwards, Hartley and Marks) makes an interesting contrast with the red wine sauce above.

¼ teaspoon coriander (seeds)
1 tablespoon chopped onion
2 sprigs fresh chervil, finely chopped
1 sprig lovage or celery leaves, finely
    chopped
1 fresh mint leaf

½ cup white wine
½ cup vegetable or chicken stock
1 teaspoon white wine vinegar
1 teaspoon honey
flour

In a saucepan, combine coriander and onion with fresh, chopped herbs. Combine with wine, stock, vinegar, and honey. Gently bring to a boil, then simmer over low heat for 10 minutes. Thicken with flour, and serve with fish, meat, or with cabbage rolls.

Care must be taken to assert the chervil's subtle flavor in the face of the other seasonings. This is a very fine sauce used with poached or baked fish. You may wish to reduce the quantity of lovage if this beautiful herb is new to your cuisine. Lovage can also be strewn decoratively atop the fish, like a coronet of parsley.

### Pesto, Herb-Garlic Sauce                                    (Makes ½ – ¾ cup.)

4 or more cloves garlic
⅓ cup (about) oil, preferably olive
1 packed cup fresh herb leaves
    (Though basil or parsley are
    traditionally Italian, many leafy
    herbs, including celery and sor-
    rel are very good.)

2 – 3 tablespoons Parmesan or
    Romano cheese, grated
2 – 3 tablespoons pine or
    pistachio nuts or 1 tablespoon
    sunflower seeds, optional

Whirl the garlic and oil in the blender till smooth, then blend in the herb leaves, cheese, and nuts, if desired, to make a thick sauce. The nuts give a richer, more distinctive flavor, but the pesto is excellent without them. A little more oil may be needed if they are used.

Stir the sauce into hot, freshly cooked spaghetti, or other pasta or noodles, and serve immediately with grated cheese. Or add to taste to chicken soup or other broths.

Pesto keeps for about a week in the refrigerator, and can be frozen for 1 to 2 months, but after that the garlic flavor will become too harsh.

### Herb Sauce Marinade for Broiled Meats   (For 2 – 4 pounds of meat.)

3 – 6 cloves garlic, crushed
2 tablespoons black pepper, freshly
    ground
2 tablespoons lemon juice
¼ teaspoon salt, optional

5 – 6 sprigs fresh herbs, minced
    (For a South-of-the-border
    flavor use coriander leaves,
    or try equal parts rosemary
    and thyme, or marjoram,
    sage and thyme.)

Mix the garlic, pepper, lemon juice, and salt, if desired, together.

Mix in the herbs, and mash the mixture in a dish with the back of a spoon, or use a mortar and pestle, to make a smooth paste.

Cut chicken, rabbit, pork, or other meat into pieces for broiling and rub the paste into them. Cover and refrigerate several hours or overnight. Broil over charcoal or in the oven.

### *Gumbo Z'Herbes* (Makes sauce for 6–8 rice servings.)

This sauce came from the Congo to New Orleans, where it was modified according to the available greens and herbs. Almost any assortment of greens and herbs can be used.

*1 pound salt pork*
*2–3 pounds fresh greens, mixed*
   *(Try mustard, spinach, lettuce,*
   *radish or turnip tops, beet tops,*
   *chard, watercress, endive,*
   *chicory, or dandelion.)*
*1–2 pounds cabbage, or bunch of*
   *kale or collard greens, chopped in*
   *large pieces*

*bunch of fresh herbs, mixed*
   *(Dill, tarragon, chives,*
   *thyme, parsley, fennel,*
   *celery leaves, or sage.)*
*3 tablespoons lard, or other fat*
*3 tablespoons flour*
*2 large onions, chopped*
*4 cloves garlic, minced*
*hot red pepper, fresh or dried, to*
   *taste*
*2 tablespoons (about) vinegar*

Cover the salt pork with water and cook it till tender, about 20 minutes. Drain and chop it into small cubes. Set aside.

Put the greens and cabbage, kale, or collards in a big pot and add enough water to just cover them. Cook until all are tender, about 20 minutes. Drain, and save the cooking water. While the greens are cooking remove any tough stems or stalks from the herbs. Mix herbs and cooked vegetables. Purée together in a blender, adding reserved cooking water, if necessary.

Heat the lard or fat in a pot and add the flour. Cook very slowly over low heat, stirring constantly, till the flour is browned, as for a roux. This takes about 20 mintues. Add the onions and garlic, and cook, stirring for several minutes. Mix in the salt pork cubes and the puréed greens with herbs. Heat, stirring, for 5 or 10 minutes or till everything is mixed and hot. Add some of the reserved cooking water if necessary to make the texture of a sauce or gravy. Season with pepper and vinegar, and serve over rice or noodles.

This delectable sauce makes it possible to eat large quantities of greens without having to feel virtuous!

## *HERB TEAS*

### *Some Suggested Herb Tea Combinations*

(To begin with use equal parts of each ingredient, then adjust to taste. For further experimentation, whole spices, such as a piece of cinamon bark or a clove, can be included.)

leaf, thyme, basil, savory, rosemary, and celery or lovage leaves. Parsley, bay leaf, and thyme are often used together, but any herbs can be used in any combination.

**Fines Herbes or Herb Seasoning for the Table** Throw out the salt shaker, and instead, have ready an herb mixture for seasoning food just before it is eaten. Fines herbes can be a mixture of finely minced fresh herbs or a mixture of crushed or powdered dried herbs. Though these can be sprinkled on foods in the last few seconds of cooking, there is something special about adding them at the table. A classic French mixture is parsley, chervil, chives, and tarragon. Other herbs that are good in such mixtures are basil, thyme, rosemary, oregano, marjoram, sage, and fennel. Combine them in roughly equal amounts, or adjust proportions to taste.

**Pickled Nasturtium Buds and Seed Pods** Nasturtium buds and pods can be pickled by simply pouring vinegar over them, and keeping them in a cool place for a few weeks. For a more flavorful pickle, pick seed pods on a dry day and dry them in the sun, or in very low heat in a food dryer till they are firm to the touch. It may take one to several days. For the pickling liquid, heat 2 cups of vinegar with 2 bay leaves, and 6 peppercorns. Bring to a boil, then remove from heat and let cool completely. Pack the seed pods in a jar, cover with the vinegar, seal, and store in a cool place for 3 or 4 weeks before using. The leftover liquid can be saved until more seed pods are collected and ready to pickle.

Mint with rosehip, rhubarb, or sour apple.
Celery, parsley, and comfrey.
Raspberry or strawberry leaves, with orange peel.

Sage with alfalfa, or clover.
Rose petals with parsley.
Camomile, alfalfa leaves, and comfrey.
Elder flowers with mint.

Proportions:

½–1 teaspoon dried herbs or about 2 teaspoons fresh herbs to 1 cup boiling water (Refer to WATER QUALITY, in the BEVERAGES section.)

Some common herb tea ingredients: (Separately or in combinations.)

Alfalfa leaves, dried
Camomile, dried
Celery leaves, dried
Citrus peel, dried (especially orange)
Comfrey leaves, fresh or dried
Clover blossoms, fresh or dried

Elder flowers, dried
Mint, fresh or dried
Parsley leaves, dried
Raspberry or strawberry leaves, dried
Rose petals, fresh or dried
Sage, fresh or dried

Ingredients to add tartness:

Berries, dried
→ Rhubarb stalks, chopped, fresh or dried

Rose hips, fresh or dried and crushed
Sour apple slices, dried

There are several satisfactory ways to brew herb teas. Which to use will depend on personal preference and the characteristics of the ingredients used.

For delicately flavored teas, warm the teapot and put the herbs in it. Bring water to a boil and pour it over them. Let steep from 5 to 10 minutes, or according to taste.

For stronger herb teas, heat water in a non-aluminum pot or saucepan, and when it boils take it off the heat, add the herbs, cover, and steep. If a very strong flavor is wanted or the ingredients are in large pieces the pot can be kept on very low heat while it steeps and the time can be as long as 20 to 30 minutes. If necessary, use an insulating ring under the pot to prevent boiling. If one of the ingredients for tartness is used, it can be put in the saucepan with the cold water and brought to a boil before adding the herb leaves. Pour the tea into cups through a strainer, or simply let ingredients settle to the bottom before drinking.

***Iced Herb Tea*** A strong infusion of any herb tea can be cooled and iced, or herb tea can be used instead of water when making lemonade. Iced mint tea is very refreshing.

## Green Drink (Makes 4–6 very small glasses.)

fresh herb leaves (Try mildly flavored herbs such as comfrey or parsley with stronger flavors like mint, sage, scallion, or chives.)

vegetable cooking water or juice, fruit juice, or water
vinegar, lemon juice, or small amount of a tart fruit
honey, or a sweet fruit

Remove any tough stems or stalks from the herbs and chop large leaves into small pieces. Put enough leaves loosely in a blender to almost fill it. Add vegetable cooking water or other liquid to about half fill the blender. Add vinegar or other tart flavor, and honey or other sweet flavor to taste. Blend till smooth. Taste and adjust seasonings, if desired. Serve immediately.

Change the ingredients in this drink with the seasons. In spring include wild greens, such as chickweed, wild onion, or wild mustard. It is as healthful and invigorating as a beverage can be.

## REFERENCES FOR GROWING AND COOKING WITH HERBS

Boxer, A., and Back, P., *The Herb Book,* Octopus Books Ltd. London, 1987. (A complete reference on herbs for the kitchen.)

Edwards, John, *Roman Cookery.* Hartley & Marks, Point Roberts, WA, 1986. (Historical herbal recipes adapted for today.)

Stuart, M., *The Encyclopedia of Herbs and Herbalism,* Crescent Books, New York, 1979.

---

# HERB ROOTS

Many roots and tubers are valuable as seasonings. The large roots of some herbs, like chervil and parsley, are flavorful but mild enough to eat as a vegetable. There are also root vegetables, like carrots and celeriac, that are regularly included in mixed dishes as seasonings, and there are ginger and horseradish, whose seasoning powers are well known. When the root or tuber of any plant is used for its distinctive flavor it is, at least on these pages, an herb root.

*Burdock Roots* These delectable roots are also known by their Japanese name, gobo, and are considered extraordinarily healthful in Japan. Their flavor is unique, but not overpowering, and they blend deliciously into meat, fish, and vegetable dishes. They are also good cooked alone. Burdock is biennial, and it is important, when gathering wild roots, to choose only the first year plants, which are without seed stalks. The roots of second year plants are tough and woody. Cultivated burdock has very long, tender roots. They are easily grown, but hard to dig up, because they break so easily. One solution is to grow them in high beds with wooden sides that can be removed for harvesting. Seeds are available from many seed catalogs.

Flavor any meat, fish or vegetable stew with burdock root slices. (Refer to *Fish and Greens, Amerindian Style,* in the FISH section.) Japanese style all-gobo dishes are made by cutting the roots into slices or slivers, then stewing them in stock or water with soy sauce for sea-

**STORAGE**

**Cold Storage** Most keep well in root cellars, or in similar conditions. (Optional: pack in damp sand or other damp material.) (Refer to COLD STORAGE section.)

**Drying** Slice or shred, then dry till hard. Some are best powdered for use. (Refer to DRYING VEGETABLES, in the DRYING section.)

**Freezing** Cook if practical, or package raw. Quality varies for different roots. (Refer to FREEZING FOODS section.)

soning. To cut these slivers hold a root by the top end and pare off thin strips from the other end, turning the root while cutting as if sharpening a large pencil. To prevent darkening, the roots are slivered into a pot of water and left to soak till they are drained just before cooking. However, as nutrients are lost with the water, and the burdock will darken anyway if soy sauce is added, the soaking can be omitted. Gobo cooks in 10 to 30 minutes, depending on the size of the pieces. (For a recipe, refer to the gobo variation of the *Japanese Eggplant* recipe, in the EGGPLANT section.)

**Ginger Root**   Powdered ginger can be made from dried ginger roots, but the fresh roots are more versatile and flavorful. Fresh ginger root is important in Chinese and other Asian cuisines. It can also be grated or finely minced to use in gingerbread, cookies, and cooked with fruits or fruit preserves. It is especially good with pears. For candying ginger, refer to the variation to *Candied Fruit and Peel,* in the FRUITS section, and for *Gingerade,* to the BEVERAGES section.

Ginger roots are actually tubers that are grown like potatoes, but they require a very long growing season. It is possible to plant the tuber in a large pot, keeping it outdoors in summer and bringing it in when the weather gets cold, but it needs space, sunlight and careful tending in order to produce new tubers. Fresh ginger roots are now sold in many grocery stores. They will keep for months in damp sand in a cool place, but they spoil quickly if left in a plastic bag and refrigerated. They are better off uncovered at room temperature, and can be used even after they are quite shriveled. They can also be frozen and grated as needed without thawing.

**Horseradish**   Horseradish roots do not gain their distinctively hot taste and pungent smell till after they are grated. Their hotness is caused by a reaction between two separate chemicals which must be freed by grating. Freshly grated horseradish is hottest and best, so leave the roots in the ground and dig as needed or store them in a root cellar where they will keep all winter. (Refer to the COLD STORAGE section.) Horseradish can be preserved by drying and powdering, by grating and freezing, or by grating and covering it with vinegar and then refrigerating it. Though it will gradually lose hotness stored in any of these ways, it retains some flavor for 2 to 3 months. The young leaves are good cooked like spinach, while the cooked root has a bland flavor.

While it is being grated, horseradish is a tear-jerker, with fumes that are much stronger than those from chopping onions. Among the many suggestions for avoiding the tears, are to grate the roots outdoors, letting a breeze blow away the fumes; to grate them near a hot stove so the heat carries the fumes upwards out of the way, or to let several people take turns grating, and when one succumbs let another take over. If using a blender or food processor do not lift the lid and inhale at the same time. A blender will cut the horseradish into separate little flakes that are good for freezing and can be taken out a spoon at a time without thawing. By adding vinegar to the horseradish in the blender a quick relish is made.

Grated horseradish is very good in many sauces, dips, and salad dressings. Mixed half and half with catsup it makes a popular seafood sauce. Mixed sparingly with softened butter it becomes a sandwich spread, and mixed with applesauce or other fruit sauces or preserves it becomes a relish for meats. For some examples, refer to the YOGURT HORSERADISH SAUCE FOR VEGETABLES, in the YOGURT section, the BEET AND HORSERADISH RELISH, in the BEETS section, and the *Fresh Currant Sauce for Meat,* in the CURRANTS section.

### Frozen Horseradish Cream

Grate a small to medium horseradish root and 2 to 3 medium apples, by hand or in a blender. Mix in 2 tablespoons honey and 2 cups yogurt. Freeze till mushy, stir with a fork, and freeze till solid. Just before use, let it soften enough to scoop out in balls. Serve with cold meats, fish, or fruit. For a salad, or an attractive side dish, put scoops of horseradish cream on peach halves or sliced persimmons, or decorate a platter of cold, sliced turkey or other meat with them.

# HERB SEEDS

M OST HERB SEEDS DRY AS THEY MATURE, AND NEED NO SPECIAL processing for storage. Many retain their flavor in a closed container for several years.

The complete spice cabinet always includes an array of flavorful seeds for seasoning foods. Most of those can be home raised or gathered wild, and can to a surprising extent replace imported spices like cinamon and cloves. Though the various seeds will not duplicate the specific flavors of imported spices, they offer a range of sharp, spicy, aromatic flavors which are intriguing to use in all kinds of dishes. The delight of desserts spiced with coriander, caraway or anise seeds; the vim of vegetables seasoned with dill, or fennel seeds, or with juniper berries; the zest of sauces made with celery or mustard seeds—Who can resist them?!

## HARVESTING HERB SEEDS

The first concern when harvesting small herb seeds is choosing the best time, which is after they are fully formed but before the seed pods are so dry that they shatter and scatter the seeds. Cut or pick the stalks or seed heads while they are still slightly green, and finish drying them on racks or trays in an airy place, preferably indoors, away from birds and rodents. If the seeds are very small, spread a cloth under them to catch any that fall. Another way to dry herb seeds is to tie a paper bag over the tops of a bunch of stalks, and hang them upside down so that the seeds will fall into the bag. It also sometimes works to tie a paper bag or cloth over the seed heads right on the plants in the garden, which will, at the same time, protect them from birds. If the plant is one whose seeds mature gradually, this way also catches the early seeds while waiting for the later ones. Some dry seed pods must be rubbed or crushed to loosen the seeds, and then winnowed to remove chaff and debris. (Refer to THRESHING AND WINNOWING, in the SEEDS section.)

If herb seeds are to be crushed to release more flavor, it is best to do so just before using them, otherwise the flavors dissipate. Seeds can be crushed with the back of a spoon against the side of a rounded cup, but a mortar and pestle is more effective. Seeds can be powdered in a blender, producing a texture which makes them especially good to use as spices in baked goods.

One to two cups of most kinds of herb seeds is enough for a year's supply of seasoning. If more seeds are gathered they make a gift that friends will appreciate.

## HERB SEEDS TO GROW AND GATHER

*Anise*   The lightly licorice flavor of anise seeds is delicious in cooked apple desserts, sauerkraut, and other fruit and vegetable dishes, and with fish and meats, as well. Add a pinch to cooked carrots or cabbage, to stews or soups with vegetables, and to meat or fish dishes. The crushed or powdered seeds make a good spice in cookies and fruit breads. A pleasant tea can be made by boiling them for 5 minutes in water. A sort of anisette can be made by steeping anise seeds in brandy for 6 weeks. Anise leaves are also flavorful. Try a few minced in fruit salads or green salads.

Star-anise, which is associated mostly with Chinese cooking, comes from an entirely different plant, and has a considerably stronger flavor. Small amounts are good used like anise seeds. For recipes with anise seeds, refer to the *Coleslaw* recipe in the CABBAGE section, and *Honey Rye Cookies* in the HONEY section.

*Caraway*   Rye bread with caraway seeds is a classic, but it is only one of many ways to use these versatile seeds. They are good whole in various kinds of cheese, soup, vegetable, and meat dishes. Try a few crushed in a potato salad. When crushed and used in baked desserts they have a delightful spicy flavor that is hard to identify. Mix some crushed caraway seeds with a little milk and honey and brush on loaves of raisin bread about 15 minutes before they come out of the oven, and everyone will be both delighted and mystified by the flavor. Some recipes with caraway are: *Coasting Cookies,* in the COOKIES section, SEASONED SAUERKRAUT, in the SAUERKRAUT section, *Herb Bread,* in the BREAD, YEAST section, *Braised Apples and Cabbage,* in the AP-

PLES section, and *Mutton Stew, Hungarian Style,* in the LAMB section.

*Celery, Celeriac, and Lovage* Commercially sold celery seeds for seasoning come from a wild, particularly strong tasting celery, but the seeds of cultivated celery, celeriac, and lovage are all worth collecting for their considerable celery flavor. The seeds are as versatile as the leaves, blending well with many other herbs and seasonings in all kinds of foods. They are very good in meat stews and sauces, crushed in salad dressings, and added to some breads and baked goods. Add a few to biscuit dough, or add some to creamed tuna served over biscuits. Some recipes featuring celery seeds are: *Herb Bread,* in the BREAD, YEAST section, *Greens Stuffed Ham,* in the HAM AND BACON section, SAVORY WHITE SAUCE, in the MILK section.

*Coriander* In contrast to the overwhelming flavor of the leaves, the seeds are pleasantly spicy, and growing coriander is very worthwhile for the seeds alone. Ground or powdered coriander seeds are excellent in gingerbread and pumpkin pie and can replace cinnamon or cloves in most recipes. They are often used ground in sausages. Some recipes featuring coriander seeds are: *Boerewors Sausage* and *Bologna,* in the SAUSAGE section, *Honey Rye Cookies,* in the HONEY section, *Lamb Stew, Middle Eastern Style,* in the LAMB section, *Spiced Pickled Eggs,* in the EGGS section, and *Green Chervil Sauce,* in the HERBS section.

*Dill* As the pleasantly haunting dill flavor tends to dominate in mixtures, these seeds become the primary seasoning. The flavor and texture are excellent in most hearty salads, including egg, potato, beet, seafood, and bean, and in most cooked fish, egg, and cabbage or sauerkraut dishes. They can often be used instead of celery or caraway seeds in recipes. Crush them just before use, for a richer flavor.

Some recipes featuring dill are: *Sauerkraut in a Silk Dress* in the SAUERKRAUT section, *Pickled Beets* in the BEETS section, and *Three Bean Salad,* in the BEANS, FRESH section.

*Fenugreek* Fenugreek is a legume resembling sweet clover. The seeds are slightly bitter, with a distinct curry aroma. (They are an ingredient in most curry powders). They blend well with oregano, thyme and other herbal seasonings for meat and vegetable stews, and soups. Crushing before use releases their flavor, and is important when brewing fenugreek tea. (Brew like the anise tea, above.) Fenugreek sprouts are unique and delicious, with an interesting taste eaten alone, or in salads and sandwiches. (Refer to the SPROUTS section.) Try the seeds in *Pot Au Feu,* in the BEEF section, or *Vegetable Hot Pot,* in the VEGETABLES section.

*Juniper Berries* These are fruits, but there is so little flesh around the seeds that they are used as seeds. If at all soft when gathered dry them in an airy place before storing them. Juniper trees and shrubs are found almost everywhere. All their berries are edible, but as some have a stronger flavor than others taste them to judge the amount to use. The berries are good for seasoning meat and fish stews and cooked cabbage. They are often included in marinades for meat. They are also used for flavoring gin. Bruise the berries and the smell of gin is recognizable. Some recipes featuring juniper berries are: *Fish and Greens, Amerindian Style,* in the FISH section, CABBAGE SEASONINGS, under IDEAS, in the CABBAGE section.

*Mustard*   Refer to the MUSTARD GREENS AND SEEDS section.
*Poppy*   Refer to the SEEDS section.
*Sesame*   Refer to the SEEDS section.

# HONEY

H ONEY IS UNIQUE AMONG FOODS, BOTH IN TASTE AND ORIGIN, SINCE an insect makes it, by a process that people can neither duplicate nor completely understand. The beekeeper's role is to study the habits of bees, and to arrange hives to suit their needs and his own. There is no making friends with bees—gaining their trust, scratching behind an ear or smoothing a feather, or any of the intimacy involved in caring for other family livestock. Bees go about their business and make honey with no response to humans, except to avoid flying into them, or to sting if one seems a threat. Bees would be unaffected if humankind disappeared, but people would certainly miss bees for their honey, and, more drastically, in their role as crop pollinators, when they are introduced after spraying and other factors have killed off all other insects.

Keeping a few beehives is practical in most rural and some urban locations, and honey can easily replace sugar as the only concentrated sweet food a family uses. Natural, raw honey tastes much better than the usual heated, purified, and sometimes adulterated store bought honey, which may be the product of feeding sugar water to bees when nectar is scarce. Raw honey retains the heady aroma and flavor of the

### STORAGE

Keeps well without special treatment. See GRANULATION OF HONEY DURING STORAGE, below.

1 POUND = 1½ CUPS

original nectar, and is generally believed to be more healthful than honey processed to remove or destroy enzymes, pollen, and other so-called impurities. In addition, raw honey may give one protection from allergies caused by local pollens.

Honey is a delightful food, but some caution is necessary in its use. It is a concentrated sweetener composed mostly of sugars, so eating too much will have the same bad effects as eating too much white sugar. Also, honey should never be given to a baby less than a year old. According to current research, botulism spores which often occur in honey can cause infant botulism poisoning. These spores are dangerous to babies even if the honey is cooked. (Refer to BOTULISM POISONING in the CANNING section.) After a year, a child's digestive system is thought mature enough to prevent toxin development, and honey is considered absolutely safe for everyone except small babies.

## EXTRACTING HONEY

Honey in the comb is fun to eat in small amounts, but for everyday use the honey must be exracted. A mechanical extractor is essential when many frames of honey are taken from a standard hive. It is possible, however, to extract honey by hand from a wild hive, or from one or two frames. The honey is sealed in the comb with wax covers (cappings), which must be removed before arranging the comb in a warm place, perhaps near a stove, so the honey can drip out. A temperature of 90°F, or a little more is necessary to make the honey flow, and care must be taken not to heat the comb enough to melt the wax, as such high temperatures seriously damage the honey's flavor, making it good only for cooking.

To extract honey from the irregularly shaped comb of a wild hive, break the comb into pieces so it is all opened, and put them in a cheescloth or net bag. Hang the bag, or set it on a rack over a large bowl to catch the honey as it drips. Leave in a warm, about 90°F, place for several hours or all day, turning several times. After dripping has stopped there will still be some honey stuck to the comb. This can be retrieved for cooking by heating it till the wax melts, letting it cool, and removing the wax in a hard cake. It is best to use an old pot saved just for that purpose since beeswax is hard to remove completely. A double boiler arrangement is safest, because wax catches fire easily.

To drain honey from a standard frame, cut off the cappings on one side with a hot knife, or break them open with a fork. Set two sticks across the top of a large roasting pan, and lay the frame on them so the honey drips into the pan. After several hours, remove or open the rest of the cappings and turn the frame over. If the cappings were cut off, put them in a strainer to drip. Finally, the wax can be melted as above to retrieve cooking honey. (Also see the *Mead from Cappings and Comb* recipe, below.)

After extraction, honey needs straining to remove bits of wax and dead bees. Fine debris that goes through the strainer will rise to the top of the honey container after a few days and can be skimmed off. The honey can then be stored. It may not be completely clear, because of traces of pollen or wax, but these are not harmful and may be healthful.

Mechanical honey extractors whirl uncapped frames, flinging the honey out by centrifugal force. Even the cheapest, hand-turned models are expensive, so it is a good item to share with another beekeeper. Mechanical extractors can also be built, and plans are available in some publications. Detailed directions for using extractors and handling honey are given in all beekeeping publications. (See the REFERENCES at the end of this section.)

*Cleaning Beeswax*   After the honey has been extracted, and the cappings and broken comb melted to separate them from the cooking honey, a cake of beeswax is left. It will need cleaning before it can be used for making candles or waxed thread. Scrape off and discard the layer of grainy material, sometimes called slumgum, stuck to the bottom of the cakes. Put the cake in a pot saved just for this purpose, or a smooth-sided tin can. Add 1 cup vinegar and ½ cup water, set in a larger pan of water for a double boiler, and heat very slowly till the wax has melted and mixed with the liquid. It may take several hours. Strain through a clean piece of old screen or several layers of cheesecloth into another old pot or tin can. Let cool and scrape as necessary. If there is still dirt in the wax, melt it again in plain water, strain, cool, and scrape again.

*Honey Granulation During Storage*   Some honey will granulate after it has been stored awhile. Some kinds of honey are much more susceptible than others. Commercial honey is heated and purified to prevent granulation, but flavor is lost. Large crystals may still form in honey after heating, but a fine, smooth granulation occurs only in raw honey.

Granulation is rarely a problem or a cause for concern. The honey still tastes delicious and can be used in the same ways. If desired, it can be liquified by setting the container in a pot of warm 120°F, water for several hours. The container can also be put in a black plastic bag and set in the sun for a few hours.

Granulated honey is a little more prone to fermenting than liquid honey, but this seldom happens if the bees finished and capped it before it was extracted. If stored honey should begin to bubble or show other signs of fermentation, heat it to 140°F to stop the process. Honey can be stored in any convenient place for a year or more, but it does gradually lose fragrance and flavor.

## COOKING WITH HONEY

Most foods that taste good sweetened with sugar taste as good or better sweetened with honey. Its flavor goes particularly well with whole grain cereals and flour, with tart, strong-flavored fruits, and with yogurt and buttermilk. As the recipes in this book emphasize such healthful ingredients, honey is the most often called for sweetener.

The best way to substitute honey for sugar is by taste. As it is sweeter than sugar and has its own flavor, less is normally used. A light, mild honey, such as clover, is preferred for general sweetening, but a dark, flavorful honey, such as buckwheat, is excellent in whole grained baked goods and anywhere molasses might be used. Baked goods made with honey stay moist longer than those made with sugar. They burn more easily while baking, however, so temperatures should be kept moderate. Honey is not a successful substitute for sugar in heavily sugared, white flour cakes and cookies. The best solution is to switch to healthier, less sweet recipes made with whole grain flour and moderate amounts of honey. (Refer to LIMITING SUGAR IN QUICK BREADS, in the BREAD section.)

Honey has a rather high acid content which is masked by its sweet taste. Mixed with fruit, it helps to keep the fruit from discoloring. In baked goods, baking soda is sometimes added to neutralize the acid.

When considerable honey is substituted for sugar in recipes, it may be necessary to reduce the amount of liquid called for. The basic recommendation is to omit ¼ cup liquid when 1 cup of honey is substituted for sugar.

## HONEY RECIPES

***Honey Rye Cookies***        (Makes about 5–6 dozen medium cookies.)

| | |
|---|---|
| 3 tablespoons butter | 1 teaspoon coriander, powdered |
| 1–2 tablespoons orange or lemon peel, grated | 3 cups rye flour, sifted |
| 2 cups honey | 1 teaspoon baking soda |
| 3 tablespoons rum, or other liquor | ¼–½ cup fine dry bread crumbs, or rye cracker crumbs |
| 1 teaspoon anise, crushed | |

Heat the butter in a small pan and sauté the orange or lemon peel for about 10 minutes, till the peel is translucent.

Combine the honey and rum in another pan and warm over low heat, stirring often, till they blend and become runny. Add the butter and peel, anise and coriander.

Stir the rye flour in a dry, heavy, frying pan, over medium heat, stirring constantly, till it browns to just a shade darker. Do not let it scorch. Mix the flour and baking soda in a bowl. If there are lumps in the soda, first put it through a sieve. Gradually pour the warm honey mixture into the flour, stirring constantly. Beat for 10 to 15 minutes. The batter thickens as it cools, finally becoming almost too stiff to beat.

Sprinkle buttered cookie sheets liberally with the crumbs. Put small spoonfuls of the batter on the sheets, and bake in a low oven, about 275°F, for 15 to 20 minutes, or till firm to the touch.

## HONEY IDEAS

**Honey Confection** Mix 1 part
honey with 1 part peanut butter,
sesame butter, or any kind of
ground nuts or seeds. Add
chopped, dried fruit, shredded
coconut, granola, chopped nuts,
or any combination of these, to
taste. Thicken to make a stiff
dough, using rolled oats pulverized in a blender, dry powdered milk, or carob powder.
Mold into small balls or bars, or
make one long, sausage-shaped
roll. Chill and slice the roll into
disks. Coat with carob powder,
coconut, or chopped nuts, if
desired. Keep this confection in
the refrigerator and use within a
week or two. This mixture can
also be used to stuff prunes,
dried apricots, or other dried
fruits.

**Honey Drizzled Muffins**
After the muffin batter is in the
tins, drizzle a little honey from a
spoon onto each one. While
baking, some of the honey blends
into the muffin and some stays on
top. A dash of coriander, or another spice, can be added with
the honey. Other baked goods,
such as fruit breads or coffee
cake, are also good this way, as
long as the baking temperature is
not high enough to burn the
honey.

These cookies have an unusual, spicy flavor, and a firm, chewy
texture. They will keep for months in an airtight container.

*Honey Rye Cake* Prepare the honey and flour mixtures as for the
cookies, but do not combine. Separate 3–4 eggs. Beat the yolks into
the honey mixture. Add the flour and stir to combine well. Long beating is not needed. Beat the egg whites till stiff, and fold into the batter. Butter a shallow cake pan, about 9 or 10 inches square, dust it
well with crumbs. Pour in the batter and bake in a moderate, 350°F,
oven for 30 minutes. This cake keeps better than most, without becoming stale.

*Mead*                                                        (Makes about 1 gallon.)

Mead is one of the most ancient alcoholic beverages. This recipe is
only one of many versions, and honey can be used instead of sugar for
many homemade wines. (Refer to the WINE section.)

*1 gallon water*                          *2 lemons, sliced with peel, or 1*
*4 pounds honey*                         *quart tart berries or currants,*
*several whole cloves, optional*      *optional*
*stick of cinnamon, optional*         *1 teaspoon dry yeast*

Combine the water, honey, cloves, cinnamon, and lemons or berries in a large pot. Heat to a boil, then simmer 30 minutes. Strain
into a crock or other large, non-metallic container. When cooled to
lukewarm, sprinkle in the dry yeast. Cover, ferment, and bottle according to the directions in the WINE section.

*Mead from Cappings and Comb* A thrifty way to make the honey
and water mixture for mead is to use the cappings and any comb that
cannot be reused after the honey has been extracted. Bring them to a
boil in a gallon of water, cool, and remove the cake of wax. Estimate
the sweetness of the liquid by taste, which should be "tolerably" sweet
according to some old directions, or weigh the cappings and comb before putting them in water and weigh the cake of wax that is removed. The difference will be the weight of the honey in the water.
Add more honey or water as needed.


## REFERENCE FOR BEEKEEPING

Dadant, ed., *The Hive and the Honey Bee,* Scribner, 1978. (The complete and definitive book on the subject.)

# ICE CREAM, SHERBET, AND POPSICLES

THE HOME FREEZER WAS NOT INVENTED WITH ICE CREAM IN MIND, but it has made that once special Sunday and holiday treat into an everyday dessert and snack. Unfortunately, most of the frozen treats found in stores are overly sweet, and artificially colored and flavored. Pospsicles for children, made of nothing but colored and flavored sugar water, are particularly objectionable and should be avoided. Happily, they are easily outclassed by the delicious ice creams, sherbets, and popsicles that can be made at home from healthful ingredients. Most are quick and simple to make, but it is also fun to recapture the old time holiday magic by making ice cream or sherbet with a hand-cranked ice cream churn. This family project makes the smoothest, best-tasting ice cream and can become a wonderful family tradition.

There are many names for various frozen desserts. Hard ice cream means ordinary ice cream, as distinguished from the commercially sold soft ice cream. Cumbersome machinery is necessary for making soft ice cream, so it is not practical for the home. Parfaits, mousses, and bombes are rich ice cream dishes, frozen in molds without stirring or churning. Sherbet, or *sorbet* in French, is made with fruit juice or purée, without cream. Simple sherbets are sometimes called ices, and fancy versions are frappés. Popsicles are frozen suckers made from fruit juice, or any sherbet or ice cream mix.

## MAKING ICE CREAM AND SHERBET

Ideally, ice cream and sherbet are constantly stirred or churned as they freeze to whip air into them, making them light, and preventing the formation of large ice crystals. Almost any liquid mixture will freeze smoothly in an ice cream churn. In a standard freezer, where steady churning is not possible, recipe adjustments can be made to ensure a smooth texture.

*Using a Freezer*  Instead of churning, ice creams and sherbets should be taken out of the freezer, and beaten or stirred several times while they freeze, but other steps are also necessary for a smooth, frozen dessert.

Cream and other whippable ingredients should be whipped separately and folded in. A small amount of added gelatine will help prevent the formation of large ice crystals. Using yogurt or buttermilk instead of milk will also give a smoother texture. When purées are used, mixing them in a blender beats in more air. Banana puréed in a blender is especially good for adding smoothness to both ice cream and sherbet. Beaten egg whites are called for in many sherbet recipes, but these cannot be recommended. (Refer to AVOID EATING RAW EGG WHITE, in the EGGS section.) If ice cream or sherbet should be icy in spite of precautions it can be whirled in a blender or food processor

*Ice cream churn*

till smooth, and eaten immediately as slush, or quickly refrozen. If it should thaw completely it will not refreeze well. A little water, juice, or milk may be needed for the blender to function.

The least cold area in a freezer is best for freezing ice cream or sherbet. They should take several hours to freeze, as faster freezing makes ice crystal formation more likely. In a refrigerator that has an ice cube section instead of a separate freezer section the coldest setting should be used.

***Using an Ice Cream Churn***　　Both old-fashioned, hand-cranked ice cream churns and electric models are sold in appliance and specialty stores. They have two main parts—an inside container with paddles and a lid to hold the ice cream or sherbet, and an outside container to hold a mixture of ice and salt. The salt lowers the melting point of the ice so it can freeze the dessert. A drainage hole lets melting ice water run off, so more ice and salt can be added. The crank or electric motor clamps over the top and turns the paddles.

To use a churn, pour in the ice cream or sherbet mixture, filling the container only from ½ to ⅔ full to allow for expansion. Set the paddles, cover, and crank in place, and add ice and salt. The cheapest rock salt can be used, and the ice should be crushed or chopped, using a ratio of 1 cup of salt for 3 to 6 quarts of ice. Churn very slowly at first, since it is possible to turn cream to butter by excess churning. As freezing begins and resistance is felt, churn more quickly.

After half an hour or so, churning will become so difficult that the crank can hardly be turned. Remove the crank, wipe away all traces of ice and salt around the lid, open the container, take out the paddles, and enjoy a taste. Scrape the ice cream back into the churn. Replace the lid, plugging the hole in it, and add more ice and salt. Wrap the whole churn with newspaper, burlap bags or other insulating material, and let it sit for 1 to 3 hours so the ice cream can set and mellow (ripen) in flavor. An alternative is to remove the ice cream and let it set and ripen in the freezer.

It is possible to keep ice cream frozen in the churn for another day by packing it with more ice and salt in the evening, using plenty of wrapping for insulation, and keeping it in a cool place.

***Using a Homemade Churn***　　A simple churn can be made using a large bucket for the outer container and a tall, narrow container, such as a one-gallon milk can, to hold the ice cream or sherbet. There should be about a 3-inch space between the inner and outer containers and the inner container must be higher than the bucket rim to keep ice and salt from entering. Put a layer of ice and salt in the bucket, set the ice cream container on it, and pack more ice and salt around the container. A large wooden spoon can be used for constant churning instead of the churn paddles. Pour out ice water and add more ice and salt when necessary. This is not as convenient or efficient as a proper churn, but it will produce delicious, smooth ice cream or sherbet.

***Using Snow in a Churn***   Snow can be used with salt instead of ice. The snow must be tamped well down into the churn to begin with, using a stick, and then tamped often while churning. The drainage hole must be watched and kept open, as snow can block it. It will probably take a little longer to freeze than when ice is used.

## MAKING POPSICLES

Homemade popsicles are a cool, refreshing, and healthful hot weather snack. They are likely to be eaten by both children and adults as fast as they can be made.

Special popsicle molds are sold with fitted handles, or plastic cups or ice cube trays can be used for molds. Handles can be devised from sticks, tongue depressors, or plastic spoons or forks. Mini-popsicles can be made in ice cube trays with small sections, using toothpicks for handles. To keep the handles centered in the molds, lay waxed paper over the molds after they are filled and cut a small slit to put the handle through.

If the popsicles do not slip out of the molds easily, run a little cool water on the outside. If a mold is wanted for reuse, popsicles can be individually wrapped and stored in the freezer.

## STORING ICE CREAM AND SHERBET

The richest ice creams begin to lose quality after 1 month in the freezer. Sherbet and less rich ice creams keep their quality for 2 months or longer. For long keeping, protect them from air. Fill containers (refer to RIGID CONTAINERS in the FREEZING FOODS section) full, with no air space, and when ice cream or sherbet is removed, press a piece of freezer or waxed paper against the surface to exclude air.

## ICE CREAM, SHERBET, AND POPSICLE RECIPES

These recipes are especially for those who like to experiment and create their own flavors.

***Fruit 'n Yogurt Ice Cream***   (Makes 1½ – 2 quarts.)

*1 – 2 cups fruit, crushed or puréed (May be fresh or cooked.)*
*honey, or other sweetener, to taste*
*juice of 1 lemon (Omit if fruit is tart.)*

*1 teaspoon gelatine, soaked in 2 tablespoons cold water till swelled, optional (Omit if using a churn.)*
*1 cup yogurt*
*1 cup heavy cream, or chilled evaporated milk*

Mix the fruit and honey till the honey is dissolved. Warm the honey a little for mixing, if necessary. Add lemon juice. Taste, and adjust amounts of honey and lemon juice for a strong, fairly sweet flavor. If using gelatine, warm it with the honey after it has soaked, or dissolve it till swelled in 2 tablespoons hot water and add to the fruit. Add the yogurt, and cream or milk. If NOT using a churn, whip the cream or evaporated milk and fold it in last. Stir well, or beat several times while it is freezing. (See USING A FREEZER, above.)

***Avocado, Mincemeat, Carob, and Other Ice Cream Flavors*** Any sauce or purée that goes well with yogurt can be used instead of fruit. Mashed avocado with lime instead of lemon juice is unusually delightful. A pint of the *Green Tomato Mincemeat* recipe in the TOMATOES, GREEN section goes very well. A banana puréed in the blender, with half the *Carob Syrup* recipe in the CAROB section, instead of honey make a tasty combination.

***Jam or Jelly Ice Cream*** Any kind of jam, jelly, or fruit preserves can be used instead of both fruit and honey. Just add to taste. For a ripple effect, fold jam or preserves into partly frozen ice cream. The amount of yogurt and cream should be increased to 1½ cups each, with about 1 cup preserves, to make 1½ to 2 quarts of ice cream.

### ICE CREAM, SHERBET, AND POPSICLE IDEAS

**Non-Dairy Ice Cream** Soy yogurt (refer to SOY MILK, in the SOYBEANS section) can be used as a base for some delicious, pudding-like frozen desserts. Put 1 or 2 cups in a blender, add 1 tablespoon vegetable oil for creaminess, and any flavorings desired. Blend till smooth, and freeze. If the texture become icy, return to the blender and beat again. Banana adds smoothness, and, mixed with *Carob Syrup* from the recipe in the CAROB section, is especially good. Several tablespoons of frozen orange juice concentrate and a little honey is also an excellent combination. These can also be frozen in molds for popsicles.

**Snow Ice Cream or Sherbet** Mound fresh, clean snow in a bowl, pour something sweet and flavorful over it, and eat immediately. For an ice cream taste, use cream mixed with a little honey or maple syrup, and any desired flavorings. For sherbet, use sweetened fruit juice, or fruit syrup.

### Mix-a-Flavor Ice Cream                    (Makes 1½ – 2 quarts.)

1 – 2 cups of any of the following:
　CUSTARD SAUCE (Refer to the MILK section.)
　PUMPKIN PURÉE (Refer to the SQUASH, WINTER AND PUMPKIN section.)
　CHESTNUT PURÉE, *made by simmering in milk* (Refer to the CHESTNUT section.)
　½ *cup (about) almonds, coconut, or other nuts puréed in a cup of milk in the blender*
　¼ *cup cooked rice simmered in 1½ cups milk until very soft.*
　½ *cup honey or maple syrup, or other sweet syrup, to taste*
　1 *teaspoon gelatine, soaked till swelled in 2 tablespoons cold milk or water, optional* (Omit if using a churn.)
　2 *cups heavy cream, or chilled, evaporated milk* (With the milk, flavoring must be strong to mask its taste.)
Any of the following, to taste:
　ROSE WATER (Refer to the ROSES section.)

*nutmeg, cinnamon, or other spices*
*rum, kirsch, or other liquors*
*chopped nuts*
*chopped, dried fruit, or candied fruit* (Refer to the FRUITS section.)
*cookie crumbs, especially crumbled Peanut Macaroons* (Refer to the PEANUTS section.)
*brown bread crumbs, or pumpernickle bread crumbs*
*rolled oats dried in a slow oven till crunchy and slightly browned*
*candied ginger root* (refer to *Candied Fruit* in the FRUITS section) *or chopped, fresh ginger root simmered with ¼ cup water and the honey or syrup called for above*
*crushed peppermint candy, other candy chips*

Sweeten the milk, sauce, or purée with honey or syrup, and add liquid flavorings. If gelatine is used, it can be dissolved in a warm sauce or purée, or in 2 tablespoons hot water and mixed with other ingredients. Nuts, dried fruit, crumbs, oats, or candy can be folded in when the ice cream is partly frozen. If NOT using a churn, whip the cream or canned milk separately and fold it in. Stir well, or beat several times while it is freezing. (See USING A FREEZER, above.)

### *Fruit Sherbet*               (Makes 1—1½ quarts.)

| | |
|---|---|
| *3—4 cups fruit juice, or thin fruit purée* | *juice of 1 lemon, optional* |
| *1—2 tablespoons honey, or other sweetening, optional* | *1 teaspoon gelatine soaked till swelled in 2 tablespoons cold fruit juice or water, optional* |
| *1—2 bananas, puréed in blender, optional* | *(Omit if churn is used.)* |

Combine the fruit juice or purée, honey, banana, and lemon juice to taste. The flavor should be neither too strong nor too sweet. The most refreshing sherbets are cool and light, and a little tart. If gelatine is used dissolve it, after it has soaked, in several tablespoons of hot fruit juice or water, then add to the other ingredients. Freeze in an ice cream churn, or take it out of the freezer and beat well several times while it freezes.

If the sherbet should form ice crystals, put it in a blender while frozen and beat till smooth, adding a little juice or water, if necessary, to make the blender function. Eat immediately, or return the sherbet to the freezer. Most sherbets taste best when somewhat soft rather than frozen solid.

*Milk, Buttermilk, or Yogurt Sherbet*   Use 2 cups fruit juice or purée and from 1 to 2 cups milk, yogurt, or buttermilk, and make sherbet as above. Curdling may occur, but does not hurt flavor or texture.

*Popsicles*   Any sherbet mixture can be frozen in popsicle molds. (See MAKING POPSICLES, above.) Versions with banana and yogurt are especially good.

*Apple Cider Ice, Sassafras Tea Ice, and Other Ices*   Freeze apple cider, fruit juice, sassafras tea, or other herb tea as for sherbet without adding other ingredients. These are very refreshing when served partly frozen, or just slushy. The juice or tea can be frozen in ice cube trays, and the cubes put in a blender or food processor to "slush" them just before serving.

*Melon, Pear-Mint, and Other Fresh Fruit Sherbets*   Most fresh fruits are excellent puréed and frozen for sherbet with few added ingredients. Plain cantaloupe or watermelon sherbet is delicious. Remove seeds and cut off rinds before puréeing. Melon pieces can be frozen, then puréed in a little orange or other fruit juice, and served immediately. Make pear-mint sherbet by puréeing cored, chopped pear with lemon juice and a little mint jelly or strongly flavored mint tea and honey. Fruits that darken easily should be mixed with lemon, another acidic juice, or yogurt, to keep their color fresh.

---

### ICE CREAM, SHERBET, AND POPSICLE IDEAS, *cont.*

**Vegetable Sherbets**   Puréed vegetables or vegetable juice can be frozen to eat as an appetizer before dinner, or instead of a salad or vegetable dish during hot weather. Such vegetables as carrots and zucchini are very good puréed in fruit juice with a little honey for a dessert sherbet, or for popsicles. Raw vegetables can be puréed in a blender, or cooked and then puréed.

A tomato sherbet cocktail can be made from any well seasoned tomato juice or sauce. Fresh tomatoes, a scallion, and a little fresh mint, basil, or other herbs, all puréed in a blender, make a refreshing sherbet. Purée carrots, raw or cooked, in orange juice for a carrot salad sherbet. Stir in a few raisins when partly frozen. For a unique frozen condiment refer to the *Frozen Horse-radish Cream* recipe, in the HERB ROOTS section.

---

### OTHER ICE CREAM, SHERBET, AND POPSICLE RECIPES

# JAM AND JELLY

TRADITIONAL FRUIT JAMS, JELLIES AND OTHER PRESERVES WERE almost always highly sweetened. There are now also many low-sugar fruit spreads, which were developed in response to current awareness of the harm caused by eating too much sugar. Some of the most delicious of these depend entirely on the natural fruit for sweetness, but they tend to resemble sauces and gelatines rather than old-fashioned jams and jellies. Other new spreads rely on artificial sweeteners, and sometimes preservatives as well, and cannot be recommended.

A great deal can be said in praise of both natural spreads made from sweet fruits, and the traditional jams and jellies which are often made from fruit so sour it is mouth-puckering. Well made sour fruit jams and jellies have a wonderful, sweet-sour intensity that can only be described as mouth-watering, and, since a scant teaspoon is enough to transform an ordinary slice of toast into a feast for the gods, even the most calorie conscious will find little to worry about.

## MAKING JAM, JELLY, AND OTHER FRUIT SPREADS

Making a perfect, old-fashioned jelly takes careful attention to detail, while jams, fruit butters, preserves, conserves, and marmalades can be handled more casually, though they also have painstaking variations. Fruit, and sugar or another sweetener are the basic ingredients. Mild-flavored honey is excellent instead of sugar in some kinds of jelly, and in most of the other fruit spreads. Maple syrup is delicious in some preserves.

Pectin, which occurs naturally in some fruits, is essential for jelling jelly, and a help for setting or thickening other fruit spreads. For pectin contents and directions for making pectin, refer to the PEC-TIN section. The methods and recipes included here depend on fruits' natural pectin, or on the addition of homemade pectin. The pectin sold in stores requires different procedures and comes with its own instructions. Jams and jellies made with it will have a higher sugar content, unless labeled otherwise and there is a higher yield from a given amount of fruit. The flavor is less full and not as intense as that of old-style jam and jelly. A special low-methoxyl pectin, sold in some health food stores, jells without added sweeteners. It cannot be homemade, and, in sour fruit preparations at least, little is gained as sweetening is often necessary for palatability.

***Making Jelly***    Tart, strongly flavored fruits, such as wild berries and grapes, are best for traditional jelly. For a clear, sparkling jelly, the fruit juice must be strained from cooked fruit through cloth with no squeezing or pressing. The cloth can be tied or sewn into a bag and hung to drip overnight. (Refer to JUICE FROM COOKED FRUIT, in the FRUITS section.)

Before it will jell, fruit juice must contain acid, pectin, and sugar. Lemon juice, or another acidic juice, and homemade pectin can be added where needed. Another alternative is to combine fruits low in acid or pectin with fruits high in these. Apples are good in combinations because they are high in pectin and not too pronounced in flavor.

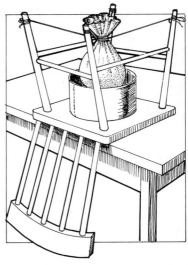

*One way to strain fruit juice for jelly*

When ready, the juice is boiled with a measured amount of sugar till it reaches the jelly stage. The proportions necessary for jelling are from ¾ to 1¼ cup of sugar per cup of juice. To jell properly, jelly must be made in small amounts. A good batch size is 4 cups of juice or less.

If using a jelly or candy thermometer to test for jelling the temperature should be about 220°F near sea level, and 8°F above the boiling point for water at higher altitudes. The jelly stage is usually reached after 10 to 20 minutes of boiling.

The classic test is made by spooning up a little of the boiling jelly, holding it well above the pot for a moment to cool, then pouring it off. if the last drops fall in two slow, separate drips, it is almost done. If the last drops slide off in one sheet, the jelly is done and should be poured immediately into jars or glasses. Another way to test it is to put a little jelly on a cool saucer and set it in the freezer for a minute to see if it jells.

If it has not jelled after 30 minutes of boiling, the mixture probably lacks pectin, acid, or sugar. The flavor can be damaged by too much boiling, so it is best to take the pot off the stove after half an hour and enjoy fruit syrup instead of jelly.

Jelly can be sealed in canning jars by the open kettle canning method (refer to the CANNING section), or it can be poured in glasses, cooled till it sets, and covered with a thin layer of melted paraffin. It should NOT be processed in a boiling water bath, as continued cooking in a closed container will prevent a proper jell.

***Making Jams and Fruit Butters***    These are made by simply cooking fruit with a sweetener till thickened. Jam is made from chopped or mashed fruit, and butter is made from a smooth sauce or purée. The pulp left from making fruit juice can also sometimes be used. (Refer to PULP FROM MAKING FRUIT JUICE in the FRUITS section.) The amount of added sweetening can be judged by taste. Some fruits need very little. The *Apple Cider Butter* recipe in the APPLES section can be made without any sugar at all. Fruits that are juicy and not likely to thicken in a reasonable time can be mixed with chopped apple or applesauce, homemade pectin, or powdered gelatine (refer to the GELATINE section) to make them set. Dry fruits may need the addition of water or fruit juice when cooked.

Jam and fruit butter must be stirred almost constantly while cooking to keep them from sticking and burning. Using a pot with a heavy bottom, moderate heat, and perhaps an insulating ring to diffuse heat will also help prevent burning.

Jams and fruit butters that are sweetened to taste may contain too little sugar to keep if sealed with paraffin, and should be canned by processing in a boiling water bath for 10 minutes, or else frozen.

**Making Preserves, Conserves, and Marmalades**   These are made of fruit cooked in syrup till the fruit is translucent and the syrup has reached the jelly stage. Preserves are usually made of large pieces of one kind of fruit. Conserves are a mixture of fruits, often with raisins and nuts added. Marmalade has shreds of citrus fruit peel cooked into it.

There are several ways to make these spreads. Fruits and sweetening can be mixed and cooked like jam, forming their own syrup. Fruit and sugar can be layered in a pot and left several hours or overnight, till juice is drawn out to form a syrup, and then it can be cooked. Syrup can also be made separately, with the fruit added to it and cooked. Citrus fruit peel for marmalade is usually cooked in water till tender, then both peel and cooking water are used. The peel can be grated or ground before cooking, or the orange, lemon or other citrus fruit can be cooked whole and thinly sliced.

Considerable sweetening is necessary to give the fruit in preserves, conserves, and marmalade their traditional appearance and flavor. The standard ratio is ¼ to ½ cup of honey or ½ to ¾ cup of sugar per cup of fruit. With this in mind, however, new versions can be adapted to taste.

If the syrup should thicken before the fruit is cooked, a little fruit juice or water can be added. If the fruit is done and the syrup remains too runny, the syrup can be drained and boiled separately as for jelly, and mixed with the fruit when it is almost done. These spreads should be canned rather than sealed with paraffin, unless they have been cooked to the jelly stage.

**Uncooked Jam and Jelly**   Fresh, raw fruit can be mashed or puréed, sweetened, and set with gelatine. A squeezing strainer will remove seeds and peels from many fruits while puréeing. (Refer to the KITCHEN UTENSILS section.) Fresh fruit juice (refer to the FRUITS section) can also be jelled with gelatine. Sweetening is optional. (Refer to USING COMMERCIAL POWDERED GELATINE, in the

GELATINE section.) Uncooked jams and jellies can also be made with commercial pectin according to the package directions, but large amounts of sugar or artificial sweeteners are required, whereas gelatine works without either. Natural or homemade pectin must be cooked with fruit before it can set.

Uncooked jams and jellies made with about equal parts fruit and sweetening will keep about 3 weeks in the refrigerator. Without sugar, they will keep about a week. For long storage they must be frozen.

## RECIPES FOR JAMS AND JELLIES

These recipes feature sweeteners other than refined sugar, and are best made with fruit too sour to enjoy unsweetened. Their flavor intensity makes them satisfying eaten in very small amounts.

### *Fruit Jelly with Honey*                    (Makes 4–5 half pints.)

3 cups tart, pectin-rich fruit juice, or       2 cups mild honey
    2 cups juice and 1 cup homemade
    pectin (Refer to the PECTIN
    section.)

Boil the juice and honey in a deep pot, as they may boil over in a shallow pot. Skim off froth as it appears. When the jelly stage is reached, pour into glasses or jars and seal. (See MAKING JELLY, above.)

Strongly flavored fruits, especially wild fruits, are best for honey jelly. The jelly will not be as clear and bright as when made with sugar, but the flavor will be superb.

### *Maple Fruit Preserves*                     (Makes 3–4 half pints.)

1 cup maple syrup                              1 apple, chopped, optional
3–4 cups berries, pitted cherries,
    sliced peaches, plums, or other
    fruit

Heat the maple syrup to a boil, then add the fruit. Simmer, uncovered, till the fruit has cooked through and appears translucent, 20–30 minutes. If the syrup is still very thin, strain it off and boil it separately for a few minutes, then add the fruit and boil again. Pour into jars and process in a boiling water bath for 10 minutes. (Refer to the CANNING section.) If the fruit is low in pectin, the apple will help thicken it.

---

**JAM AND JELLY IDEAS**

**Freezing Fruit for Jam and Jelly** If there is freezer space, it is often convenient to freeze berries or other fresh fruit in the summer, for making jam or jelly in the winter. The fruit should be packaged in the amounts needed for making one batch of jam or jelly. There will be more time for cooking it in the winter, and the heat from the stove will be welcome, rather than stifling.

**Last Minute Jam** Make a quick jam in the blender using fresh, canned, or frozen fruit. Add raw apple pieces, or banana for thickening, and sweeten, if desired. Enjoy right away on toast or waffles, or make really special peanut butter and jam sandwiches.

**Jelly Melt Cereal** For a change from the usual, put a spoonful of jelly on a bowl of hot cereal and let it melt before "digging in". Yogurt instead of milk goes very well.

---

**OTHER JAM AND JELLY RECIPES**

Apple Cider Butter, p. 8
Blueberry (or Raspberry) Marmalade, p. 57
Cranberry Conserves, p. 206
Elderflower or Mint Gooseberry Jelly, p. 311
Raisin Stuffed Rose Hips (preserves), p. 526
Watermelon Conserve, p. 680

### OTHER RECIPES WITH JAM OR JELLY

Flavored Yogurt, p.706
Fresh Currant Sauces for Meats
　　(II, III, and IV), p.216
Jam or Jelly Ice Cubes, p.356
Jam, Jelly or Marmalade Sauce,
　　p.612

*Fruit and Nut Conserves*　　　　　　　　　(Makes 4–5 pints.)

2 quarts tart berries, grapes, or other fruit, seeded and chopped as necessary

2 cups honey, or add sweetening to taste

½ cup raisins, or chopped figs or prunes

½ cup nuts, chopped, or ¼ cup sunflower seeds

spices, grated lemon peel, or other flavorings, to taste, optional

Combine all ingredients in a large pot, and heat slowly, stirring constantly to prevent sticking. When juice has collected, increase the heat and stir occasionally. Maintain at a slow boil till the fruit is well cooked and the mixture has thickened, about 20–30 minutes. Pour into jars and process in a boiling water bath for 10 minutes. (Refer to the CANNING section.)

# JERUSALEM ARTICHOKES

T HE JERUSALEM ARTICHOKE IS A NATIVE AMERICAN PLANT BELONG- ing to the sunflower family. Its abundant tubers were a common food among Indians in the eastern half of the continent, and so early settlers soon learned to appreciate them as well. Eventually, they became popular in Europe, where they were given the implausible name of Jerusalem artichokes. "Jerusalem" may have been derived from *girasole,* the Italian name for sunflower. The vegetable is also occasionally called sunchoke, and is sometimes listed under artichokes in gardening books and cookbooks. If there is any confusion with globe artichokes, the description, or directions for preparation will clarify which is meant.

Jerusalem artichokes are easily grown where the climate is not too dry, and are found wild in many places. The tubers somewhat resemble small, knobby potatoes, and can be mistaken for fresh ginger roots. This versatile vegetable is crisp with a mild, earthy flavor when eaten raw, and tender, with an unobtrusive root vegetable taste, when cooked. To go with their improbable name, Jerusalem artichokes are improbably delicious prepared in the same ways as cucumbers, both raw and cooked. A more descriptive name would have been cucumber-rooted sunflower.

## HANDLING JERUSALEM ARTICHOKES

The Jerusalem artichoke tuber is a cold weather vegetable that is not ready to eat till after autumn frosts. It does not keep well after digging, which limits its commercial value, but makes it practical for

### STORAGE

**Canning**　Pickled only. See *Jerusalem Artichoke Pickles,* below.

**Cold Storage**　Will keep refrigerated 1–2 weeks only. Packed in damp material in root cellar will keep about 1 month. Refer to COLD STORAGE section.

**Drying**　Slice to uniform size. Optional: Steam till tender, 5–10 min. Dry till hard. Refer to DRYING section.

**Freezing**　Cut to uniform size. Blanch in boiling water with 1 or teaspoons vinegar. Large chunks: 3 min.; sliced or diced: 1 min. Refer to FREEZING section.

**Live Storage**　Leave in ground. Dig up in fall, winter, and early spring.

the home gardener who can dig tubers as needed in the fall, during winter thaws, and in the spring before growth starts. Though very good when dried, frozen, or pickled for storage, they are most appreciated in winter and early spring when few other fresh home-grown vegetables are available. Dried slices, after being reconstituted by soaking, can be used in most recipes that require cooking. Both dried and fresh Jerusalem artichokes are especially good in stir-fried dishes.

People who feel compelled to peel Jerusalem artichokes are bound to dislike them because the job is so tedious. There is no reason the peels cannot be eaten. The tubers can be broken apart, scrubbed with a brush if necessary, then used. An alternative is to blanch them in boiling water, drain them, and rub the peels off. The tubers from newer hybrids are smoother and easier to clean than those from old strains or wild plants.

Steaming or boiling for 10 to 20 minutes is the basic cooking method for Jerusalem artichokes, but they can also be baked or sautéed. They have one peculiarity. If they are cooked much longer than is required to soften them, they will toughen or become hard again.

# JERUSALEM ARTICHOKE RECIPES

## *Jerusalem Artichoke Salad*   (Makes about 6 side servings.)

1 pound Jerusalem artichokes, diced
2 tablespoons onion, minced, or 2 scallions, chopped
¼ cup vegetable oil
¼ cup vinegar
1 teaspoon honey

1 tablespoon fresh herbs, minced, or 1 teaspoon dried herbs (Mint is especially good, but parsley, thyme, and rosemary are also excellent.)
lettuce, or other salad greens

Mix the Jerusalem artichokes, onion or scallion, oil, vinegar, honey, and herbs in a bowl. Let marinate at room temperature for an hour. Add greens and toss.

## *Jerusalem Artichoke Pie*   (Makes about 6 side servings.)

2 pounds Jerusalem artichokes, sliced or diced
soup stock, or water
2 cups frozen peas, green beans, or other green vegetable
2 tablespoons butter
2 tablespoons flour

parsley, or other herbs, minced, optional
pepper, salt, optional
1½–2 cups mashed potatoes
bread crumbs, for topping
grated cheese, or dots of butter

Cook the Jerusalem artichokes in a pot with enough soup stock or water to cover for about 15 minutes, or till just tender. If using frozen peas or green beans, stir them in and reheat. If using another green vegetable, add it, allowing time for it to cook through without

---

### JERUSALEM ARTICHOKE IDEAS

**Jerusalem Artichokes Simmered in Stock**   Cover chunks or thick slices of Jerusalem artichoke with chicken stock or another soup stock, and simmer till tender, with most of the stock absorbed, 20 to 30 minutes. Do not overcook, or they will toughen. Serve with a lump of butter, a sprinkle of lemon juice or vinegar, and parsley for garnish.

**Grated Jerusalem Artichoke in Soup or Salad**   Grated Jerusalem artichoke is a good addition to most meat or vegetable soups, about 5 minutes before they are done. For salads, sprinkle grated Jerusalem artichoke with lemon juice or vinegar immediately after grating to keep it from discoloring.

**Tomato Sauced Jerusalem Artichokes**   Cut Jerusalem artichokes in chunks or slices and cook about 20 minutes in any well-seasoned tomato sauce. Serve separately, with noodles or other pasta.

**Jerusalem Artichokes in Cucumber Recipes**   Jerusalem artichokes do not taste anything like cucumbers, but they appreciate the same seasonings and can be prepared in the same ways. For instance, slice them raw and marinate in a vinegar mixture. (Refer to the *Vinegared Cucumbers* recipe, and try them in other recipes in the CUCUMBER section.)

overcooking the artichokes. Drain, saving the cooking liquid.

Melt the butter in a saucepan and stir in the flour. Then gradually stir in about 2 cups of the cooking liquid, or enough to make a creamy sauce. If there is not enough liquid, add soup stock, milk, or water. Season to taste with parsley or other herbs, pepper, and salt, if desired.

Line the bottom and sides of a shallow casserole or deep pie dish with mashed potatoes. Add the mixed vegetables. Pour the sauce over them, and sprinkle with bread crumbs, and cheese or dots of butter. Bake in a hot 425°F, oven, till the top is lightly browned, about 15 minutes.

**Rutabaga, Kohlrabi, or Salsify Pie**  Use diced rutabaga or kohlrabi, or sliced salsify instead of Jerusalem artichoke. Since kohlrabi is often in season with peas, they can be fresh instead of frozen.

### Jerusalem Artichoke Pickles   (Makes 4 quarts, or 8 pints, canned.)

5 cups vinegar (Refer to **PICKLING VINEGAR** in the PICKLING section.)

5 cups water

½ cup honey

1 teaspoon salt, optional

1 tablespoon turmeric, optional (It gives a golden color.)

3 tablespoons pickling spices, tied in a cloth (Refer to the PICKLING section.)

4 quarts Jerusalem artichokes, cut in chunks or sliced

4 cloves garlic, optional

Heat the vinegar, water, honey, salt, turmeric, and pickling spices to a boil and simmer 15 minutes. Take out the pickling spices.

Meanwhile, pack the Jerusalem artichokes in clean, hot canning jars, leaving ½ inch headroom. If using garlic, put a whole clove in each quart jar, or a half clove in pints. Pour the boiling hot vinegar mixture into each jar, leaving ½ inch headroom. Adjust lids and process in a boiling water bath for 15 minutes. (Refer to the CANNING section.)

# KALE

T HE HANDSOME, DARK GREEN LEAVES OF KALE ARE LIKELY TO BE THE last green crop in the garden. As the cold deepens, their flavor sweetens, and kale comes into its own as the most delectable of winter vegetables.

Kale belongs to the cabbage family and is very closely related to collard (refer to the COLLARDS section), but it is individual in taste.

Sea kale, considered to be a gourmet's vegetable, is another plant entirely. It grows wild along British and European Atlantic coasts.

## HANDLING KALE

The kale season begins after autumn frosts, so never judge this vegetable by its flavor in warmer weather. If well mulched, kale can be harvested in very cold weather, and may even last till spring. The early leaves that grow on overwintered plants are tender and delicious in salads. Otherwise, kale is best cooked. When preparing it, discard the tough stalks of large leaves. Leafy parts can be chopped, or torn with the fingers. Kale needs a longer cooking time than most greens, and should be steamed or boiled for about 20 minutes. If cooked with meat or potatoes, or a grain, such as oats or barley, simmer it from 30 to 40 minutes to mingle flavors.

## KALE RECIPES

### Kale Soup, Scottish Style                    (Makes 8–12 medium bowls.)

beef soup bone
1 cup barley
large bunch kale

2–3 leeks, sliced, optional
pepper, salt, to taste

Put the soup bone in a pot with 3 quarts of water and add the barley. Bring to a boil and skim well. Let simmer about 3 hours. Tear the kale leaves into small pieces, discarding tough stalks. Add kale, leeks, pepper and salt to the soup, and simmer 20 to 30 minutes. Serve with the *Oatcakes* recipe in the OATS section, for a traditional Scottish combination.

### Kale Cakes                                    (Makes about 6 servings.)

2 pounds kale, heavy stalks removed
1 cup cottage cheese, or other fresh
    cheese
2 tablespoons flour
⅓ cup cheese, grated
2 eggs

2 tablespoons parsley, minced,
    or 1 teaspoon dried herbs
    (Such as marjoram, thyme,
    or savory.)
1 teaspoon fennel or dill seeds,
    crushed
pepper, salt, optional
2–4 tablespoons butter and oil,
    combined for frying

Cook the kale in a minimum of water for about 15 minutes. Chop finely on a board, or purée in a blender or food mill. If large curd cottage cheese is used, mash it through a sieve, or purée with the kale. Mix the kale, cottage cheese, flour, grated cheese, eggs, parsley, fen-

---

### STORAGE, *cont.*

**Drying**   Refer to DRYING LEAFY GREENS, in DRYING section.

**Freezing**   Cut into pieces, removing heavy stalks. Blanch in boiling water for 2 min. Refer to FREEZING section.

2–3 POUNDS = 1 QUART COOKED

---

### KALE IDEAS

**Kale and Potatoes**   Put cubed potatoes in the bottom of a big pot and just cover with water. Pile plenty of chopped kale on top, cover, and cook 20 to 30 minutes, or till both kale and potaotes are done. Serve with the *Cheese Sauce* recipe in the MILK section.

**Kale and Sausage Soup**   Arrange kale and potatoes as in recipe above, add chopped onions and parsley, and then slices of a spicy sausage such as pepperoni, Spanish chorizo, or Portuguese chourico. Add soup stock or water, adjusting the amount according to the desired thickness, and cook 30 to 40 minutes, till all ingredients are done. If desired, other vegetables and pre-cooked, dried beans can be included.

**Kale and Meat Stew**   Kale is good stewed with most meats. Simmer ham, beef, or other stewing meat in water to cover, till almost tender, add a large bunch of chopped kale, and cook another 30 to 40 minutes. A stewing rabbit cut into pieces and cooked with a small chunk of ham or ham bone is especially delicious with kale.

**Crispy Fried Kale**   Heat several tablespoons of oil or other fat in a large frying pan or wok, and add crushed garlic and shredded or chopped kale. Fry, stirring often, over fairly high heat. Serve when crisp, in about 10 minutes.

nel or dill seeds, pepper, and salt, if desired. Heat a generous amount of butter and oil in a large frying pan. Drop in spoonfuls of the batter and brown on both sides. The cakes should be from 2 to 3 inches in diameter. Serve for breakfast, lunch, or supper.

**Greens Cakes**   Use another green instead of kale. The outer leaves of cabbage or cauliflower are good. If spinach or other, more delicate greens are used, precook them 3 to 5 minutes instead of 15 minutes.

# KIDNEYS

CAREFULLY COOKED KIDNEYS ARE AS TENDER AND JUICY A MORSEL AS could be desired. Their mild, delicate flavor will please the most finicky eater. Carelessly cooked kidneys, however, are tough, dry, and strong tasting. To avoid this misfortune, start with absolutely fresh kidneys, clean them well, keep the cooking heat low to moderate, do not overcook them—and enjoy. Since most of the world's cuisines include special dishes made with kidneys, there are many wonderful ways to prepare them. Kidneys from different animals can be interchanged in recipes where slicing or dicing is required. When whole or halved kidneys are called for, those from any young animal will be suitable.

People who raise their own meat animals, or who kill game animals, are fortunate because they can enjoy kidneys they know to be fresh, carefully handled, and from healthy animals. Store-bought kidneys from unknown sources are questionable, as they tend to store chemical feed additives and other ingested contaminents.

## CLEANING AND PREPARATION

Kidneys, which come in pairs, lie embedded in fat against the middle part of an animal's back. They can easily be pulled out of the fat. A thin membrane covers them, which is also easily pulled off. In the center of each kidney, there is a core of white, fatty-looking material. Cut this core out entirely before washing the kidneys, as all bad odors and tastes are in this core, and water can spread them to the meat. Removing the core before washing is especially important with older animals where odors and tastes are stronger. The kidneys of very young animals have little core, and flavors are so mild that coring is not always necessary.

Most kidneys are oval, and can be cored with a small pair of scissors. Fingernail scissors work well because of the curved blade. If kidneys are to be cut in half lengthwise, coring is easier. Beef kidneys are composed of a series of rounded segments, and have a large, prominent white core. With them it is best to cut off the kidney meat in slices or pieces, leaving the core behind. A little meat must be left on the core because of the difficulty of following segments while avoiding the white part, but the meat obtained will be untainted. The kidneys of rabbits and other small animals do not have to be cored.

If desired, after the core is removed, the kidneys of older animals can be rinsed in water with a little vinegar added. This neutralizes any lingering odor. Rinse again in fresh water.

The secrets of cooking kidneys are keeping the heat low to moderate, and not cooking them too long. They can be given a quick searing, as for stir-frying, but this must be brief. The kidneys of young animals, such as lamb and veal, are often broiled, or threaded on a skewer and cooked like shish kebab. Beef and pork kidneys are most often sautéed, but can also be cooked by baking, stir-frying, and other methods. Cooking times vary from 3 minutes for stir-frying, up to 20 minutes for large pieces on low heat. The kidneys of big game animals like deer are excellent and should be used.

**Kidney Fat** The fat surrounding the kidneys is the purest of any animal fat. It should be rendered and used for frying, or used as suet. (Refer to LEAF FAT, in the LARD section.)

## KIDNEY RECIPES

*Steak and Kidney Pie*                    (Makes about 6 dinner servings.)

| | |
|---|---|
| 1 beef kidney, or kidneys from another animal (Venison kidneys are excellent.) | ½ pound mushrooms, sliced thickly, optional |
| 1 pound beef steak, or steak from the animal whose kidneys are used | 1 tablespoon flour |
| lard, or butter, for frying | 1 cup beef or other soup stock, or water |
| 1 onion, sliced | pepper, salt, optional |
| | pastry dough for a double crust pie, or biscuit dough for a single crust |

Cut the kidney into cubes, being sure to remove all of the white core. Cube the steak. Heat the lard or butter in a large frying pan and toss the onion in it. Add the kidneys and steak and sauté over moderate heat, stirring till the meat has lost its red color. Add the mushrooms, and stir to coat with fat. Stir in the flour. Add the soup stock, pepper, and salt, if desired, and let simmer, uncovered, stirring often, till the meat is just cooked through, about 15 minutes. Do not let it boil. Cool while preparing pastry or biscuit dough.

If using pastry dough, line a deep pie dish or a similarly sized baking dish with dough, fill with the steak and kidneys and add the top crust. If using biscuit dough, put the steak and kidneys in a baking dish or casserole. Cut small biscuits from the dough and set them on top so that they just touch, to cover the whole pie. Bake in a hot oven till the crust or biscuit is lightly browned, 20 to 30 minutes.

## KIDNEY IDEAS

**Kidney Omelet** Lightly sauté sliced kidneys in butter. Season to taste. A little dry wine over the kidneys is excellent. Prepare omelet and fold kidneys in the center, or pour them over it as a sauce before serving. (Refer to the EGGS section.)

**Breaded Kidney Slices** Dip kidney slices in lightly beaten egg, then in a mixture of fine, dry breadcrumbs and flour seasoned to taste. Sauté over medium heat till both sides are browned, about 5 minutes on each side. Serve with lemon slices, or a piquant sauce.

**Kidneys Baked in Their Own Fat** Use veal kidneys, or kidneys from another young animal with good tasting fat. Trim the kidneys, leaving a layer of the fat surrounding them. If they are from a baby animal, coring can be omitted. Otherwise snip out the cores with a small pair of scissors. Bake on a rack in a low, 300°F, oven. A ½ pound veal kidney will cook in about 1 hour.

## OTHER RECIPES
## WITH KIDNEYS

Faggots, p. 592
Kidneys Simmered in Wine, p. 331
Scrapple, p. 329

## *Perfect Broiled Kidneys*  (Makes 6–8 lunch servings.)

*2 veal kidneys, 4 lamb kidneys, or
   kidneys from another young
   animal
juice of 1 lemon
2 tablespoons olive oil*

*pepper, salt, optional
bacon, several slices, optional
toast, slices, optional
parsley for garnish, optional*

Pull off membranes, cut kidneys in half lengthwise, and cut out the cores. Cut each half veal kidney into 2 or 3 strips. Lamb kidneys can be left as halves. Rinse in cold water and pat dry with a towel. Rub or toss kidneys with lemon juice, then with olive oil. Sprinkle with pepper and salt, or omit salt if using bacon.

Broil the kidneys on a rack, turning to cook both sides, or thread them on a skewer, alternating kidney with small pieces of bacon, and broil over hot coals. Another method is to wrap each piece of kidney in bacon and broil on a rack or skewer. Cook 5 or 6 minutes on each side, or till the kidneys are just cooked. They should still be juicy and pink inside. They are delicious served on toast with parsley sprigs.

## *Stir-fried Kidneys*  (Makes about 6 dinner servings.)

*1 beef kidney, 4 pork kidneys, or kid-
   neys from another animal (About
   1 pound meat after slicing.)
2 teaspoons sherry, or dry white wine
   (Or use 1 teaspoon vinegar and
   ½ teaspoon sugar in 2 tablespoons water.)*

*2 scallions, cut in 1 inch pieces,
   or a small onion, thinly sliced
2 tablespoons soy sauce
1 tablespoon cornstarch
½ cup soup stock, or water
3 tablespoons lard*

Cut the kidneys into thin slices, carefully removing all bits of white core. Rinse the slices in cold water, then mix with the sherry or wine, and the scallions or onion. In another dish, mix the soy sauce, cornstarch, and soup stock or water.

Heat the lard till quite hot in a wok or heavy frying pan. Stir-fry the kidney mixture for 3 minutes. Add the soy sauce mixture, and stir-fry ½ minute, or till the sauce thickens. (Refer to the STIR-FRYING section.) Serve immediately. This dish does not reheat well.

# KITCHEN UTENSILS

T HE COUNTRY KITCHEN IS A WORKSHOP, AND KITCHEN UTENSILS ARE the tools of a trade. Like other tools, good kitchen utensils save time, energy, and contribute to a better product. They are also personal, and must suit the needs of the user. For some people and some purposes, a good quality electric utensil is the right choice. For others, a sturdy, well-designed hand tool is more appropriate. Following are some basic, but sometimes overlooked utensils that are helpful in a country kitchen. Specialized tools for a particular food are described in that food's section.

## CAST IRONWARE

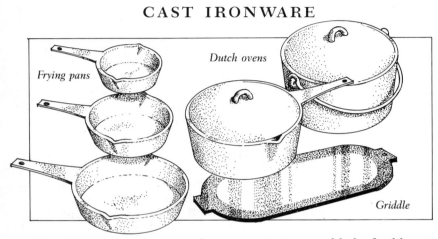

*Frying pans*  
*Dutch ovens*  
*Griddle*

Cast iron spreads heat evenly, to sauté, stew, and bake food beautifully. It lasts almost forever if well cared for. Cast iron utensils should be heated for a few minutes on the stove before food is added. If they are well seasoned, food will not stick to them. To season new cast ironware or reseason older ware, rub with oil or unsalted fat and put in a low, 250 to 300°F, oven for 2 to 3 hours. If rusted, remove the rust with a very fine steel wool before seasoning. If encrusted with old grease and food residues, scrape and then use steel wool, or, in extreme cases, burn clean in an outdoor fire. Repeated frying will also season ironware. To clean cast iron, wash it quickly and dry immediately. It should never be soaked. If not well seasoned, rub a thin layer of oil over utensils after washing. Frying pans can often be wiped clean with a paper towel without washing.

The only real objection to cast iron pots and pans is their heaviness. Using them is good for developing the wrists.

## TALL POTS, TINY PANS

Extra tall pots are useful for foods that boil over easily, foods that cook down a lot, such as greens, and "tall" foods, such as soup bones and asparagus. Handy sizes are a 6 inch diameter pot about 7 inches high, an 8 inch diameter pot about 8 inches high, and perhaps a restaurant sized pot about 12 inches high. Tiny pans are valuable for small amounts—melting butter, rendering fat from one chicken, heating one serving, and making quick sauces.

***Avoiding Aluminum***   Aluminum pots and pans are cheap and they

*Crocks and crock substitutes.*

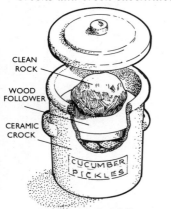

Crock with wooden follower cut to fit, and a clean stone as a weight to hold down food.

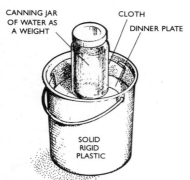

*Sturdy* plastic containers designed for foods. (Other plastic containers may release toxic chemicals.) Use cloth over the food, a dinner plate follower, and jar of water as weight.

Stainless steel or unchipped enamel pot. Heavy platter follower.

conduct heat well. However, there are questions about their safety. Acid foods absorb traces of aluminum from cooking pots, and it is not yet known how serious a problem this is. Never slow-cook or store acid foods in aluminum, or use pitted or badly discolored aluminum pots.

Enameled and stainless steel pots and pans are recommended. Stainless steel does not conduct heat well, but stainless steel pots with copper or aluminum outside bottoms remedy this problem.

## CROCKS AND CROCK SUBSTITUTES

Various arrangements of crocks and substitute containers can be used for pickling or storing foods in a liquid. The container should have a disc-shaped follower that fits its inside diameter well enough to hold down small food pieces, and should weigh enough to prevent floating.

## KNIVES

It is astonishing how often otherwise well equipped kitchens are knife poor. Well-sharpened knives of various styles and sizes are essential for safe, accurate cutting. Nothing is more dangerous than a dull, poor quality knife, too small or too big for the task at hand. Much more effort is required, accuracy is impaired, and painful cuts are much more likely. Shown here are some special knife styles, highly useful in the kitchen.

*Hunting knife.* (For tough kitchen jobs.)

*Cleaver*

*Bread knife*

*Boning knives*

## UTENSILS FOR PURÉEING, OR MAKING SAUCE

The three devices illustrated are all used for making purées by forcing soft foods through a sieve or strainer, while removing small seeds, skins, and other rough material from foods. This gives them an advantage over blenders and food processors, which must pulverize all parts of a food to make a purée. The hand tools also work without whipping air into foods—an advantage when canning or freezing.

The squeezing strainer is intended for large jobs, such as making tomato sauce, and puréeing berries or pumpkin for canning or freez-

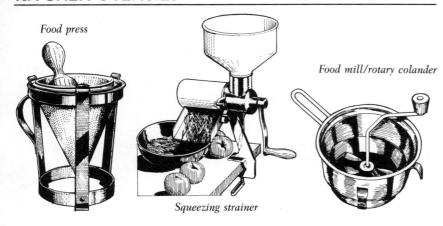

Food press

Squeezing strainer

Food mill/rotary colander

ing. There will be less waste if the rough material is put through a second time. The food mill and food press are slower, but can be used for big or small jobs. They are most convenient for puréeing soups and sauces in day-to-day cooking. A good quality food mill or rotary colander with a strong spring is more efficient than a food press.

## SLICERS AND GRATERS

There are numerous styles of food slicers and graters. Most important are the sharpness of their cutting edges, handling convenience, and safety. The cabbage cutter pictured here is ideal for big jobs. It can be used for slicing potatoes, onions, and other bulky vegetables, as well as for shredding cabbage.

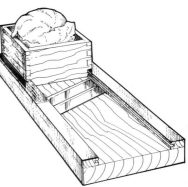

For slicing potatoes, onions, bulky vegetables, and for shredding cabbage.

## STRAINING ARRANGEMENTS
## FOR LIQUIDS

Strainer and funnel for narrow necked bottle.

Strainer, wide mouth funnel for jar.

Colander with rack above large container.

For clearer liquids, a cloth should be laid inside the strainer or colander. (Refer to MAKING JELLY, in the JAM AND JELLY section.)

# FRUIT AND LARD PRESS

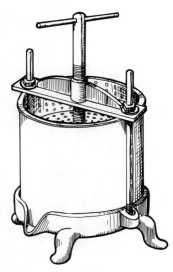

*Old fashioned fruit and lard press*

This old fashioned food press has many uses in a modern country kitchen, especially pressing juice from chopped, ground, or cooked fruit, and pressing out the last of the melted lard when fat is rendered. Some models have a sausage stuffing attachment as well. In some cases, a cloth liner fitted into the press is helpful to prevent food particles from squeezing out with the liquid. Some old style country stores and catalogs sell fruit and lard presses, or they can sometimes be found in antique stores and at auctions.

## OTHER SPECIALIZED KITCHEN UTENSILS

Apple peelers and corers, in the APPLES section
Bean slicers or frenchers, and bean or pea shellers, in the BEANS section
Cheese molds and presses, in the CHEESE, AGED section
Cherry pitters, in the CHERRIES section
Cider presses, in the APPLES section
Corn cutters, in the CORN, SWEET section
Corn shellers, in the CORN, DRY section
Dough mixers, in the BREAD, YEAST section
Garlic press, in the GARLIC section
Grain mills, in the GRAINS section
Meat grinder, in the MEAT section
Noodle maker, in the NOODLES section
Pressure cooker, in the STEAM COOKING section
Rotary cheese or nut grater, in the CHEESE, AGED section
Vegetable juice extractors, in the VEGETABLES section

# KOHLRABI

THE KOHLRABI PLANT HAS ITS OWN SPECIAL WAY OF BEING A VEGE-table. Its stem enlarges just above the ground to form a round, firm bulb with a tuft of small leaves growing out of the top, and larger leaves here and there around the sides. The bulb tastes similar to the inner stalks of its close relatives, cauliflower and broccoli, but is crisper and sweeter. Kohlrabi is delicious raw ("I eat 'em like apples," says one enthusiastic admirer), and it is delicious cooked. Even the leaves are tasty cooked like cabbage.

It is surprising that kohrabies are not better known, since they are easy to grow and store, as well as being easy to enjoy in many different ways. Their name is German, taken from the Italian *caroli rape,* cabbage turnip.

## HANDLING KOHLRABI

Harvest kohlrabies when small, between 2 and 4 inches in diameter. If they grow much larger, they become woody and strongly flavored. In close plantings they should be cut, since pulling disturbs the roots of adjacent plants. Plant kohlrabies intended for winter storage in summer, so that they are not overly large when harvested. Light frosts will not hurt them, but they must be pulled before heavy frosts.

Very small, tender kohlrabies do not need peeling. Peel medium sized bulbs, and save the leaves of all for greens. Raw kohlrabi is delicious sliced, chopped, or shredded in salads, or cut into sticks and eaten like carrot sticks. Small kohlrabies can be steamed or boiled whole, while larger ones are most often sliced or diced before cooking.

## KOHLRABI RECIPES

### Green and White Kohlrabi          (Makes about 6 side servings.)

6–8 small, or 3–4 medium
  kohlrabies, including leaves, or
  use cabbage leaves
2 cups milk, or kohlrabi cooking
  water

2 tablespoons butter
2 tablespoons flour
pepper, salt, to taste

Cut off the kohlrabi leaves, and cook in a small amount of water till tender. Chop small and set aside.

Trim the kohlrabi bulbs and peel if necessary. Leave small bulbs whole, but slice, or dice larger ones. Simmer in a saucepan with the milk or soup stock till tender, 10 to 15 minutes. In a separate pan, melt the butter and stir in the flour. Add the milk or cooking water, and simmer, stirring, till it thickens. Season with pepper and salt, if desired. Add the kohlrabies and reheat. Serve with the greens arranged in a ring around the edge of the serving dish, or simply mix the two parts together.

### Shellfish Stuffed Kohlrabi          (Makes about 6 side servings.)

6–8 medium kohlrabies
½ pound (about) shrimp, crayfish, or
  another shellfish, peeled and
  chopped
1 tablespoon butter, softened (Or
  use the CORAL BUTTER idea in
  the SHELLFISH section.)

1 egg, slightly beaten
3 tablespoons dry breadcrumbs
1 tablespoon dill leaves, or
  parsley, minced
pepper, salt, optional

## KOHLRABI IDEAS

**Kohlrabi with Dips**  Cut crisp, raw kohlrabies into sticks or slices and serve with vegetable dips. On an assorted platter, they are likely to be the most popular raw vegetable.

**Sautéed Kohlrabi**  Slice kohlrabies thickly and steam till tender, or use cooked leftovers, or precooked, frozen and thawed slices. Sauté in butter or olive oil till golden brown. A half clove of garlic can be sautéed with them and removed, or add minced onion and curry powder to the butter or oil before the kohlrabi slices. Intense seasoning flavors blend well with this vegetable without overwhelming it.

**Kohlrabi in Cauliflower Recipes**  Styles of preparing and seasoning cauliflower, both raw and cooked, work well for kohlrabies. (Refer to the CAULIFLOWER section.)

**Kohlrabi Greens**  The kohlrabi leaves are tender and delicious, and are worth cooking separately as greens. Season them like cabbage or collard greens. (Refer to CABBAGE and COLLARDS sections.) Small, tender leaves add a delicate, cabbagy flavor to salads.

**OTHER RECIPES
WITH KOHLRABI**

Kohlrabi Pie, p.364
Pickled Kohlrabi Sticks, p.120
Vegetable Recipes and Ideas,
    p.669

Peel the kohlrabies and cut in half lengthwise. Scoop out the centers to make a hollow in each half. (Save the centers for use below, or slice them to add to salads or vegetable mixtures.) To make the stuffing, mix together the shellfish, butter, egg, breadcrumbs, dill or parsley, pepper, and salt, if desired. (If canned salted shellfish is used, omit salt. If heavily salted it can be rinsed before use.) Press a mound of stuffing into each kohlrabi half. Set them in a casserole, baking dish, or Dutch oven. The kohlrabi centers can be tucked in around the stuffed halves. Add half an inch of water and cover. Bake 30 minutes, or till tender, in a moderate oven, or simmer over low heat on top of the stove.

Instead of shellfish stuffing, use any stuffing that goes well with vegetables. (Try the summer squash stuffing recipes in the SQUASH, SUMMER section.)

# LAMB (AND MUTTON)

*The mountain sheep are sweeter,
But the valley sheep are fatter.
We therefore deemed it meeter
To carry off the latter.*

Thomas Love Peacock

**STORAGE**

**Canning**   Trim off all fat, then can as for beef (see BEEF section).

**Cold Storage**   See AGING MEAT, in MEAT section.

**Drying**   Must be lean (no fat running through it). See DRYING MEAT, in DRYING section.

**Freezing**   (Only method to preserve lamb's special character.) Quality retained 12 months. Refer to FREEZING section.

**Salt Curing**   (Cures easily, but flavor tends to be strong. Considered a delicacy by some.) Legs and shoulders cured like ham (see HAM AND BACON section). Breast and shank corned like beef, see CORNED CHEVON, LAMB OR VENISON, in BEEF section.

LAMB IS THE MEAT OF A YOUNG SHEEP, WHILE MUTTON IS THAT OF A mature sheep. The exact age when lamb becomes mutton is not agreed upon, but the change has definitely occurred by one year. In practice, lambs are usually butchered in late fall, taking advantage of summer and fall pasture while avoiding the problems of winter feeding. At that time, they will be 8 to 10 months old.

Sheep are seldom raised for mutton, since its distinctive flavor is not always appreciated. However, mutton can be delicious and some prefer it to lamb. In Scotland, it was once common practice to keep wethers (castrated males) on pasture for two or three years like beef cattle because their mutton was so well liked. At the other extreme, unweaned lambs and goats are commonly butchered in spring in the

Mediterranean region. (Refer to the CHEVON section.) Sheep are dairy animals in some parts of the world. Their milk is used like goat's milk and cheeses made from it are renowned. (Refer to the MILK section.)

Modern homesteaders who raise sheep are perpetuating an ancient way of life. Archeological evidence suggests that sheep were the first domesticated animals. Their use for wool, meat and milk goes back to the beginnings of civilization. Sheep raising has also left a less material heritage, namely, the ideal of a good shepherd guarding his flock and gathering in lambs that have gone astray. Conversely, there are also black sheep, wolves in sheep's clothing, and the sheep that must be counted before sleep comes.

## HANDLING LAMB AND MUTTON

The killing, skinning, and cutting up of carcasses is basically the same for most meat animals. Differences are due more to the animal's size and weight than its species. Butchering a baby lamb is much the same as butchering a rabbit or other small animal (refer to the CHEVON section), while butchering a full sized sheep is comparable to handling a calf or deer. Inexperienced people can kill, skin, and cut up a lamb or sheep successfully without special equipment, but would probably need help handling an animal as heavy as a pig or a cow.

The lamb or sheep must be killed without too much preliminary stress, then skinned and cleaned without soiling the meat. The carcass must be cut into pieces without undue waste, and the useable parts set aside. The following describes one butchering method. For other methods and more detailed directions, see the REFERENCES at the end of this section.

*Killing and Skinning Lambs and Sheep*   Killing is the least pleasant but also the quickest part of butchering. Those who raise and butcher their own meat animals have the satisfaction of knowing the animals have had good food, good treatment, and a quick, humane death.

A lamb or sheep is usually killed by cutting through the arteries and veins in its throat, then pulling back its head to break the neck. They can also be shot with a .22 caliber gun from a few inches behind the head, or stunned with a blow to the back of the head, but the throat must still be cut immediately so that they are bled out completely. This is important if the meat is to keep well and look its best. (Refer to USING BLOODY OR BRUISED MEAT in the MEAT section, and to the BLOOD section.) The disadvantage of shooting is that it ruins the head, brains, and tongue for use.

After active bleeding has stopped, the animal must be skinned. A sharp, sturdy knife is essential. The legs are skinned first. A cut is made through the hide, up the inside of each leg. A cut across the breast connects the cuts on the front legs, and another just in front of the anus connects the cuts on the back legs. The hide can then be

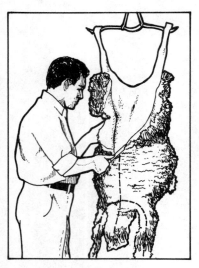

*Removing the hide*

pulled away from the legs and the feet can be cut off at the first joint. Large lambs or sheep should be hung at this stage, using meat hooks or a rop threaded between the tendons and bone of the hind legs. A stick can be used to keep the hind legs well separated. A small lamb can be skinned on its back on a table, but the job is easier if it too is hung.

Have warm water and a cloth available for wiping off the meat and washing hands, if necessary. The hide is cut open down the belly and removed in one piece. It is always peeled back away from the meat, like taking off a coat inside out. The wool must not touch the meat, because it will stick and soil it. Care should also be taken not to cut into the fell, which is the layer of membrane and fat covering the meat under the hide. However, the meat will be useable even if the skinning job is not perfect, as long as it is kept clean. The best method is to push with the fist between the hide and meat to loosen the hide, using a knife only when "fisting" is not possible, to reduce the chance of nicking the fell or meat.

Once the hide has been pushed away from the hind legs, a cut should be made completely around the anus so that 10 or 12 inches of the colon can be pulled out of the body cavity. The end of the colon should be tied with a cord to keep the contents from spilling out, then dropped back into the body cavity. The hide can then be skinned from the rest of the body and neck, and the head cut off, by disjointing it at the base of the skull. (To use it, refer to the HEADS section.)

To eviscerate the carcass the belly should be cut down the center to the breastbone. When the first opening is made, one hand can hold back the intestines while the cut is finished. It is important not to cut into the intestines. Take the insides out carefully, separating useable parts. (See the list of parts below.) The organ meats of lambs are especially choice. Cut or pull away the gall bladder carefully from the the liver as soon as possible so it does not break. Wash all organ meats well in cold water and refrigerate them.

The rib cage can be cut open to remove the heart and lungs, and to cool the carcass quickly. If the animal is over a year old, a saw will be needed as well as a knife. The carcass should be chilled quickly. It should not be cut till it is completely cold, as it then keeps better, and handles more easily. If the weather is cool, it can be hung in a shed or anywhere outdoors that is protected from pets and other animals. Otherwise, it should be put into a cooler, or refrigerated. Large lambs and mutton are improved by aging in a cool place for 10 days to two weeks unless the meat is to be frozen. Spring lamb needs no aging. (Refer to AGING in the MEAT section, page 403–404.)

## THE PARTS OF A LAMB
## OR MUTTON CARCASS

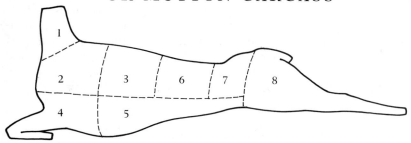

*Lamb parts*

1. NECK (STEW)
2. SHOULDER (STEW, CHOPS, ROAST)
3. RACK (CHOPS, CROWN ROAST)
4. SHANK (STEW, BARBECUE)
5. BREAST (STEW, BARBEQUE)
6. LOIN (CHOPS, ROAST)
7. SIRLOIN (ROAST, PART OF LEG)
8. LEG (ROAST, CHOPS)

*To clean, prepare, and use, refer to the appropriate sections:* BLOOD; BONES; GELATINE; SOUP; LARD AND OTHER FATS; FEET; HEAD; BRAINS; TONGUE; HEART; KIDNEYS; LIVER; LUNGS; SPLEEN; TRIPE, CHITTERLINGS, AND PAUNCH.

For the stomach of unweaned lamb, refer to the RENNET section. For the thymus and pancreas, refer to the SWEETBREADS section. For an undocked tail, refer to the TAILS section. For trimmings and scraps, refer to the MEAT section. For testicles, from castrating as well as from butchering, refer to the TESTICLES section. For intestines, refer to SAUSAGE CASINGS, in the SAUSAGE section.

***Cutting Lamb or Mutton Carcasses*** Large carcasses are easier to handle if they are split down the backbone into two halves. When the carcass is small, chops are sometimes cut across the backbone, making a butterfly shape. The shoulder section is usually cut off between the fifth and sixth ribs, though the third and fourth rib can also be used. Whether to cut the different parts of the carcass into roasts, chops, stew meat, or meat for grinding depends on the size and age of the animal, and on personal preferences. With common sense, a good knife, and a meat saw or hacksaw, useable pieces can be obtained. If some do not look like those from the butcher shop, it will not affect the flavor. See the REFERENCES at the end of the section, some of which include detailed diagrams and instructions for cutting.

***Cooking Lamb and Mutton*** If one's only experience with eating lamb has been lamb chops or a leg of lamb, many delightful lamb dishes await discovery. There are stews of all kinds, patties and meatballs from ground lamb, and marinated, broiled lamb. Mutton is also outstanding in stews, curries, and sausage. The original mincemeat was probably made with mutton. Recipes for stewing lamb can use mutton, increasing the cooking time as necessary, and perhaps increasing the amount of seasoning. Recipes for venison and other game meat are also good for mutton. (Refer to the VENISON section. Also refer to USING TOUGH MEAT, in the MEAT section.)

The most bothersome part of cooking lamb or mutton is the fat. Sheep fat is hard, and tends to coat the mouth when eaten. In an older animal, it can also be strong flavored. As much fat as possible should be trimmed off older lamb and mutton, and if fat is needed for cooking, use another kind. Recipes for lamb or mutton often include tomatoes, wine, or fruit to cut the fat and moderate its effect. Rendered sheep fat or tallow is usually used for making soap or candles, rather than food. The extra fat can be rendered and poured around well-seasoned, cooked meat to preserve it. (Refer to PRESERVING MEAT IN RENDERED FAT, in the MEAT section.)

## LAMB AND MUTTON RECIPES

### *Lamb Stew, Middle Eastern Style*    (Makes 4–6 dinner servings.)

2 tablespoons oil or butter, or a mixture of oil and butter
1 pound lamb, boned and cut into small cubes
1 onion, chopped
1 clove garlic, minced, optional

1 pound green beans, spinach, or other green vegetable
½ teaspoon coriander, nutmeg, or cinnamon
salt, optional
juice of ½ lemon

Heat the oil or butter in a heavy pot and lightly brown the lamb, onion, and garlic in it. Add 1 cup of water, cover tightly, and simmer over very low heat till the lamb is almost tender. Depending on the toughness of the meat, the cooking time could be from 20 minutes to an hour.

Snap the green beans in pieces, or cut other vegetables to bite size. When the lamb is ready, add the vegetable, coriander or other spice, and salt, if desired. Cover and cook 15 minutes, or till the vegetable is done. Add the lemon juice. Delicious served with rice, bulghur wheat, or the *Syrian Bread,* from the BREAD, YEAST section.

***Middle Eastern Lamb with Okra, Eggplant, or Zucchini***  Lightly brown the lamb, onion, and garlic as above, but add about 1 cup tomato sauce or juice, or fresh chopped tomatoes, instead of water. In another pan, lightly brown the chopped okra, eggplant, or zucchini in oil and add instead of the green beans or other green vegetable. Finish cooking as above.

### *Mutton Stew, Hungarian Style*    (Makes 6–10 dinner servings.)

5 pounds mutton or lamb ribs, or stewing meat with bones
1 large onion, minced
1 tablespoon lard, or bacon fat
2 teaspoons paprika
1 teaspoon cayenne, or to taste
½ cup water
¼ teaspoon caraway seeds

2 cloves garlic, crushed
1 teaspoon salt, or to taste
5 medium potatoes, diced
2 green peppers, diced
2 medium tomatoes, diced or 1 cup stewed tomatoes
1 recipe Little Dumplings (See below.)

Cut ribs or stewing meat into 1 inch pieces. Other cuts can be left in larger pieces. Heat the lard or bacon fat in a Dutch oven or heavy pot and brown the onion in it. Remove from heat, stir in the paprika and cayenne, and immediately add ½ cup water. Return to heat and add the ribs or stewing meat and bones, caraway seeds, garlic, and salt. Cover and cook over very low heat to barely simmering, till the meat becomes tender, usually about 2 hours. With a tight lid no extra water will be needed, but if it should dry out, add a few tablespoons of water.

When the mutton or lamb is about done, add potatoes, green peppers, tomatoes, and another ½ cup water. Cover and cook 30 minutes or till the vegetables are done. Add the dumplings, cook 2 or 3 more minutes and serve.

***Little Dumplings*** Thoroughly mix 2 eggs and 6 tablespoons of flour. If necessary, add a little more flour to make a stiff batter. Drop tiny ¼ teaspoon-sized bits of dough into the simmering stew, and cook from 2 to 3 minutes.

### *Lamb Meatballs* (Makes about 6 dinner servings.)

| | |
|---|---|
| 1½ pounds lamb | 2 tablespoons (about) flour, optional |
| 6 carrots | |
| 1 onion | fat, or oil, for frying |
| 1 egg | 2 cups lamb broth, optional |
| pepper, salt, optional | |

With a meat grinder, grind the lamb, carrots, and onion together. Or if the lamb is already ground, grate the carrots and onion and mix them with it. Mix in the egg, pepper, and salt, if desired. Shape into small balls or patties. Dust with flour if desired and fry till browned on all sides. Add ½ cup water or lamb broth, cover, and simmer for 10 minutes, or till the meat is cooked through. Serve plain, or with the following sauce.

***Sauce*** Drain the liquid from the meatballs into a saucepan. Add three tablespoons of flour and stir till smooth. Then add 1½ cups lamb broth and stir over moderate heat till thickened. Taste and adjust seasonings. Mix the sauce with the meatballs and serve with potatoes, rice, or noodles.

### *Barbecued Lamb Breast, Chinese Style* (Makes about 6 picnic servings.)

| | |
|---|---|
| 2–3 pounds lamb breast | 1 clove garlic, crushed |
| 4 tablespoons soy sauce | 2 teaspoons honey |

Cut the lamb breast into individual ribs. Combine the soy sauce, garlic, and honey and mix it with the ribs. Let marinate for at least a ½ hour, but 2 or 3 hours will develop a better flavor. Turn the meat several times while it marinates. Broil in the oven or over coals, allowing from 5 to 10 minutes for each side, depending on the thickness of the pieces.

These are best eaten with the fingers and are perfect for cookouts and picnics.

**Barbecued Spare Ribs Chevon Breast, Veal Breast, or Beef Slices**   All these can be marinated and broiled in this way.

### Lamb Shanks with Garlic

2–3 pounds lamb shanks
½ teaspoon salt
3 tablespoons oil, preferably olive
15–20 cloves garlic, unpeeled

½ teaspoon mixed dried herbs
(Thyme, marjoram, and
sage blend well.)
½ cup dry, white wine
pepper, freshly ground, to taste

Trim all fat from the shanks and sprinkle them with salt. Heat the oil in a Dutch oven or heavy pot with a tight lid. It should hold the shanks without much extra space. Lightly brown them in the oil, turning them often. Add the garlic, cover, and simmer over very low heat, allowing the meat to slowly stew in its own juices. If after 30 minutes or so the natural juices evaporate, add a spoonful of water from time to time to keep a little liquid in the bottom of the pot. After an hour add the herbs and cook till the meat is tender, about 30 minutes more.

Then, remove the lid and let all moisture evaporate till the shanks are sizzling in fat. Take out the meat and set it aside. Pour off excess fat. Leave the garlic in the pot and add the wine. Stir to dissolve the meat scrapings. Purée the garlic and wine using a sieve or food mill. Return the purée to the pot and simmer a few minutes till reduced to a small amount of sauce. Return the shanks to the pot and turn them, allowing the sauce to glaze them. Sprinkle with pepper and serve. The garlic flavor will be mellow, almost mild in spite of the quantity used and freshly ground pepper add character. Serve with bread or potatoes and unadorned green vegetables.

### Roast Lamb, Syrian Style          (Makes 8–12 dinner servings.)

5 pounds (about) lamb roast
1 tablespoon olive oil
2 cloves garlic, minced
¼ teaspoon pepper
¼ teaspoon bay leaf, crushed

¼ teaspoon each of marjoram,
sage, thyme, and powdered
ginger
1 teaspoon salt, optional

Cut small gashes here and there on the surface of the roast. Combine the olive oil, garlic, pepper, bay leaf, other herbs, and a little salt, if desired. Rub the mixture all over the roast, pressing it into the gashes. Roast on a rack from 1½ to 2 hours. Sear the meat in a 500°F oven for 15 minutes to retain juices and then roast at 350°F till done, or roast at 350°F the whole time. This is an impressive main course for any festive meal.

---

### LAMB AND MUTTON IDEAS

**Lamb Pie**   Grind leftover cooked lamb and mix it with minced onion, parsley, and such herbs as oregano and sage. Moisten with tomatoes, lamb broth, or leftover gravy to make a pie filling. Or fry raw ground lamb and season it. Less moisture will be needed. Several small pies can be made instead of one large pie. Cut a hole in the center of the top crusts and bake 30 minutes in a hot, about 400°F, oven. If the pies are dry when done carefully pour a little hot gravy into the hole in the crust. The *Hot Water Crust* recipe in the LARD section is good for these.

For Shepherd's Pie put the filling in a shallow baking dish or a deep pie dish and spread a layer of mashed potatoes on top for the crust.

*Welsh Mutton Soup*                    (Makes 6—8 medium bowls.)

2 pounds (about) mutton, or lamb      2—4 leeks, whole
   neck in one piece               2 tablespoons parsley, chopped
¼ cup barley                          pepper, salt, optional
1 large carrot, sliced                marigold flowers, optional
¼ cup turnip, or rutabaga, diced
4 medium potatoes, diced

Put the meat in a deep pot and cover with water. Bring to a boil, skim off the foam, and add the barley, carrot, turnip, or rutabaga, potatoes, and half of the leeks. Simmer about 2 hours or till the meat is tender. Take out the meat, separate it into smaller pieces and return to the soup. Take out and discard the spent leeks.

Clean and slice the rest of the leeks, discarding the coarsest green part. Add them to the soup with the parsley, pepper and salt, if desired, and cook 5 minutes. The leek should stay crisp. Serve in wide soup bowls. For a fanciful Welsh touch a small marigold flower can be floated in each bowl.

*Haggis*                    (Will make 10 or more servings, depending on the sheep's size.)

Haggis is like a steamed pudding or big sausage using the paunch (stomach) of a sheep as the casing, and a hash of oatmeal and the sheep's organ meats for stuffing. Though known as a Scottish dish, many other cultures, including the Greeks and Romans, have had their own versions. Variations can be made according to ingredients on hand and the whim of the cook.

1 sheep's paunch (The first           1 cup coarse oatmeal (Or rolled
   stomach or rumen. Refer to the       oats whirled briefly in the
   TRIPE section.)                       blender.)
1 pair sheep's lungs                  ½ teaspoon pepper, or to taste
1 sheep's heart                          (May include some cayenne.)
½ a sheep liver                       2—3 tablespoons vinegar, or
3 onions                                 lemon juice, optional
½ pound beef or sheep suet            1 teaspoon salt, optional

Take the paunch out of the sheep when it is slaughtered, empty it, and wash well in cold water. Turn it inside out and scald for one minute by immersing it in boiling water. Scrape off the loose lining and rinse. Soak the paunch for several hours or overnight in cold water, with about 1 tablespoon salt in 2 quarts. Leave the paunch inside out for stuffing.

Put the lungs, heart, and liver in a pot and cover them with cold water. For cleaning them refer to the LUNGS, HEART, and LIVER sections. Bring to a boil and simmer for about an hour till they are all well done. The wind pipe can be left attached to the lungs and hung over the side of the pot, with the idea of releasing impurities from the lungs while they cook. Take out the lungs, heart, and liver when

---

**Mutton and Prune-Apple Pie**
Cut leftover cooked mutton or lamb in small pieces. Line a deep pie dish with pastry and put a layer of meat on it. Cut several pitted prunes in pieces and put them here and there in the meat. Cover with a layer of sliced tart apples. Sprinkle with a little honey or sugar. Add another layer of meat and prunes and one of apple slices. Put on the top crust, seal the edges and prick with a fork or cut a hole in the center. Bake in a hot, 375—400°F oven for about 40 minutes.

**Shish Kebab**   Cut lamb from the leg or shoulder into 1 or 2 inch chunks and marinate them for several hours. For a marinade, try the sauce for *Barbecued Chevon*, in the CHEVON section, the soy sauce mixture for the *Barbecued Lamb Breast* recipe above, or a mixture of yougurt, grated onion, pepper and salt. Thread the meat on skewers. It can be alternated with chunks of tomato, green pepper and cucumber, or with small onions and mushrooms. Broil over hot coals or in the broiler. Brush with marinade several times while it broils, and turn till brown on all sides.

done and let cool. Save the cooking broth. Grind the lungs, heart, liver, onions, and suet in a meat grinder, or for a better texture finely chop the lungs, heart, onions, and suet and grate the liver, using any food grater. (When cooked, grating is easier than chopping.)

Toast the oatmeal in a low 200–300°F oven, or heavy pan on top of the stove, till lightly browned and very dry. Add it to the meat mixture along with the pepper, vinegar or lemon juice, and salt. Add enough of the cooking broth to moisten the mixture to a thick mush's consistency. With it fill the paunch about ⅔ full, leaving space for expansion. Sew the paunch closed with coarse thread and a large needle. Press out air before taking the last few stitches.

Heat enough water to a boil in a large pot to later cover the haggis. (Extra broth or soup stock can be used instead of water.) Put in the haggis. When it starts to swell, prick it several times with a needle to keep it from bursting. Boil for 3 hours, uncovered, adding more boiling water if necessary. Do not interrupt the cooking with cold water.

To serve, take out the thread and dish out the haggis with a spoon. The paunch is also good to eat. As accompaniments, try relishes and spicy sauces that go well with ordinary hash or meat loaf.

***Haggis Without a Paunch***   Make the stuffing mixture as above and steam it in a mold for 3 hours. (Refer to STEAM COOKING PUDDINGS, in the STEAM COOKING section.) Or put the stuffing in a baking dish, cover it tightly, and bake in a moderate, 350°F oven for about an hour.

***Deer or Calf Haggis***   Use the paunch, lungs, heart, and liver of a deer or a calf in the above recipe.

## REFERENCES FOR BUTCHERING LAMB

Ashbrook, Frank G., *Butchering, Processing and Preservation of Meat*, Van Nostrand Reinhold, Co., N.Y. (Includes complete directions for killing, as well as the cutting and processing of the meat. Illustrated with photographs.)

*A Complete Guide to Home Meat Curing*, Morton Salt Company, P.O. Box 355, Argo, Ill. 60501 (Excellent for cutting the carcass, but not helpful otherwise.)

# LARD AND OTHER FATS

THE FAT ON ANIMAL AND POULTRY CARCASSES IS WELL WORTH saving. Besides its value as a food, it can be made into useful items such as soap, candles, skin cream, or grease for shoes and leather. It can also be used in pet foods and for feeding birds in winter. Fat keeps much longer without becoming rancid, and is more useful if it has been rendered by heating it until it is melted. This process is also known as trying or trying out fat.

Lard (rendered pork fat), is well known for its excellence in frying and baking, but other soft fats are also good for these purposes. Some early American settlers used bear fat for all of their cooking, and in some places goose and other poultry fats are used much more than lard.

Fresh hard fats are called suet, and after rendering they are called tallow. Though tallow is prized for making candles because of its hardness, it is not as nice as lard for cooking. Suet is sometimes chopped or ground to use in steamed puddings and mincemeat, giving them richness and their characteristic texture.

Animal fats are much maligned as a food, yet they have considerable nutritional value. They are not as high in the fatty acids needed by the human body as vegetable oils, but they do contain some, and some fat soluble vitamins, such as A and E as well, and they supply body energy and heat. They become a nutritional problem only when eaten in excessive amounts. A well balanced diet can reasonably include some animal fat, as well as some vegetable oil. (Refer also to the introduction to the BUTTER section.)

Fat from home raised animals fed chemical-free diets is particularly desirable, as fat collects more toxins from feed additives than does muscle meat and can be unhealthful for that reason.

## VARIETIES OF FAT

*Leaf Fat*   The fat inside an animal's ribs and around its kidneys is the leaf fat, and is the best quality of fat. When rendered it makes the purest and whitest lard or tallow possible. The best suet is fresh leaf fat, usually from beef, but it can also come from sheep or deer leaf fat.

*Back or Shoulder Fat*   Pigs have large amounts of back and shoulder fat. Salt pork is cured from it. It is also rendered for a good lard, often together with the leaf fat. Other animals have much less back and shoulder fat, but what there is can be rendered or used as suet.

*Caul and Ruffle Fats*   The caul is the thin sheet of membrane and fat extending from the stomach over the intestines. When butchering pigs, cows, and calves, the caul is separated from the stomach and intestines, washed in cold water and hung to dry. Pieces of the caul can be wrapped around lean meat to baste it with fat during roasting or broiling. The ruffle fat is entwined with the intestines, and is pulled away from them while they are still warm. This is the first step in preparing intestines for use as sausage casings. (Refer to the SAUSAGE section.) The ruffle fat should be washed and hung like the caul.

Lard or tallow rendered from caul and ruffle fat is darker, with a less bland taste than leaf, back, and shoulder fat, so it is usually used for making such things as soap, rather than for cooking.

---

### STORAGE

**Freezing**  (The only way to store fresh fat.) Wrap chunks of fresh fat as for meat. Quality retained 6–12 months. See STORING LARD AND OTHER RENDERED FATS, below, and FREEZING section.

**Cold Storage**  Rendered fat only! See STORING LARD AND OTHER RENDERED FATS, below.

Some soft fats:
  Pork (Lard when
    rendered)
  Chicken
  Duck
  Goose
  Rabbit
  Bear
Some hard fats:
  Beef
  Lamb and
    mutton
  Venison
  (All suet
    when fresh,
    tallow when
    rendered.)

## RENDERING FAT FOR LARD OR TALLOW

Rendering is a simple process, but it must be done carefully if the resulting lard or tallow is to be pure in taste and appearance.

*Preparing the Fat*   Pull or trim the fat off the animal's carcass as soon as possible after butchering and cooling. If the fat cannot be rendered immediately, keep it refrigerated or chilled and render it within a few days. If longer storage is necessary, freeze it.

Do not mix fats from different animal species because the rendering time is likely to be different. Fat from different parts of the same animal can be rendered in one batch. Lard can be made from a combination of fat trimmings and leaf, back, and shoulder fat. Pork skin can be cut up and rendered with pork fat, but every bit of meat must be trimmed off. Meat scorches easily and a small piece can ruin the taste and appearance of a whole batch of lard or tallow.

Cut the fat into small, evenly sized pieces, or grind it coarsely before rendering. Grinding is more practical except when cracklings (see below) are wanted or when the batch is quite small.

*Cooking the Fat*   Put the prepared fat in an extra large, heavy bottomed pot that will catch splatters, prevent boiling over, and distribute heat evenly. (Keep children and pets away from the stove while the fat is cooking.) If using an electric stove that concentrates heat in one spot, an insulating mat will help to prevent scorching. It is possible to avoid problems with scorching by rendering the fat in a slow oven for 12 to 24 hours, but lard made in the oven must be frozen for storage, since there may still be moisture in it. Begin rendering in a cold pot over low heat. A little water can be added to keep pieces of fat from sticking and burning before they melt, or a handful of the fat can be heated in the pot until some has melted and then the rest of the fat can be added. Stir almost constantly as rendering begins and frequently throughout.

When enough fat has melted so that the whole potful can be easily stirred, increase the heat to moderate. The fat will start boiling and sputtering as water evaporates. When most of the water is gone the temperature will gradually rise above 212°F and the boiling will stop. When it reaches 255°F on a deep frying thermometer the rendering is complete. Continued cooking will scorch the lard or tallow. The bits of membrane (cracklings) in the melted fat will show when rendering is complete. Watch closely when the cracklings begin to float. Rendering can be stopped when the floating cracklings turn light brown, though some moisture may remain in the fat. However, when the browned cracklings begin to sink slowly to the bottom of the pot it is time to take the fat off the fire. Do not continue cooking as the cracklings or the sediment on the bottom will burn.

Let the pot of rendered fat sit off the stove for a few minutes, till all the sediment has settled. Dip the clear fat on top into containers, and strain the rest through a cloth lined colander, or, if easier, strain the whole amount. With a large batch the cloth may become clogged and need changing. After it is strained a raw, peeled potato is sometimes stirred in hot lard to pick up any remaining impurities and whiten it. The cracklings and sediment can be pressed in a fruit and lard press (refer to the KITCHEN UTENSILS section) or squeezed in the straining cloth to collect more fat. If using ground fat rather than chopped, pressing will not be necessary.

Pour the hot, clear lard or tallow into containers, filling them to the brim. Cool quickly to obtain a finer texture. When cool, close the containers with tight lids.

***Storing Lard and Other Rendered Fats***  For keeping for several months without freezing, remove all moisture from the lard or other fat during the rendering. Moisture will cause a sour taste to develop during storage. It must also be protected from air and light which cause rancidity. To prevent exposure to air, fill containers leaving as little air space as possible, and keep them sealed. Best are small containers that will be emptied fairly quickly. When taking out some of the lard or fat, leave a flat surface in the container rather than a gouged hole as there is less surface exposed to air. If using glass containers, store them in a dark place. With these precautions lard and other rendered fat will keep in a cool place for months, but during hot summer weather they should be refrigerated. Once fat becomes rancid, it cannot be revived. It is both unhealthful and unappetizing.

If any moisture remains in lard, freeze it. It can go into the freezer in containers. Or pour the hot lard into a large pan or mold to cool. When solidified, cut it in chunks and wrap it for the freezer.

## CRACKLINGS

Pork cracklings are a popular snack in some places, and can be added to cornbread batter and used in cooking in the same ways as crisp, fried bacon. Pork skin makes the best pork cracklings, but pieces of any crisp membrane left from rendering are also very good. For cracklings left from rendering goose and duck fat refer to CRACKLINGS, in the GOOSE section.

Cut pork skin into rectangles. A good size is about ½ inch wide, ½ inch thick, and 1–2 inches long. Render till the cracklings float and are nicely browned. Bubbles can be seen in them when they are done. Scoop them out with a perforated spoon or sieve, and let them drain in a colander or on paper towels. They can also be put on a rack in a low, 200–300°F oven to drain and become still crisper.

## LARD RECIPE

### *Hot Water Crust for Raised Pies*

"Raised" means that the pie crust's sides rise and stand without a pie pan to hold them. Though raised pies usually have meat fillings, they are also good filled with fruit. Gooseberry raised pies are traditional in some parts of England. (For lamb and mutton fillings, refer to IDEAS in the LAMB AND MUTTON section.)

3 ½ cups (about) flour (Preferably whole wheat.)
½ teaspoon salt, optional
¾ cup lard
¾ cup water

Mix the flour, and salt, if desired, in a bowl, and make a well in the center. Heat the lard and water in a saucepan, and, when boiling, pour them into the well. Stir with a wooden spoon starting in the center, and gradually bringing in flour from the sides. When cool enough to handle, knead the dough till it forms a smooth ball. Add a little more flour if the dough is sticky, but do not let it get too stiff. It should still be warm when the crust is shaped.

Reserve about ⅓ of the dough for the top crust. Pat the rest into a flattened ball. Push down in the center with a fist to make a depression, and set a large jar in it. The jar should be 4 to 5 inches or more in diameter. Shape or "raise" the dough around the jar, pressing by hand to form an even casing. The sides can rise from 4 to 5 inches. The jar can be turned upside down for some of the shaping, and turned on its side and gently rolled to smooth the dough casing. When formed, cut a strip of brown paper a little narrower than the height of the casing and wrap it around the outside. Tie loosely in place with a string. When cool, the dough should hold its shape well. Work out the jar and set the casing with the paper wrapper on a baking sheet. Roll out the top crust.

Fill the casing with any pie filling. Dampen the edges, add the top crust, and pinch together. Cut a hole in the center for steam to escape. Bake from 1 to 1½ hours, in a moderate, 350°F oven, till browned. Leave the paper tied around the crust till the pie has cooled.

Several small crusts instead of a large one can be made by shaping smaller amounts of dough around smaller jars.

***Hot Water Pastry with Poultry Fat***   Use rendered chicken, duck, or goose fat instead of lard in this recipe.

# LEAVENS

A LEAVEN IS ANYTHING THAT WILL MAKE A BATTER OR DOUGH LIGHT. Baking soda, baking powder, and yeast are leavens that work by forming tiny bubbles of carbon dioxide throughout the batter or dough making it rise. A leavening action also results from moisture changing to steam during cooking, from air beaten into batters, and from the addition of beaten egg whites, or other whipped ingredients. The heat of cooking then sets the batter or dough in the desired expanded state.

Yeast causes the gradual release of carbon dioxide into the dough through a process of fermentation. (Refer to the YEAST section.) Baking soda and baking powder depend on the quick reaction between an alkaline (base) substance and an acid, triggered by adding moisture. This reaction creates many tiny carbon dioxide bubbles, much like the classic grade school experiment, in which vinegar and baking soda are mixed causing furious bubbling and foaming.

## BAKING SODA AND BAKING POWDER

Baking soda is sodium bicarbonate, or bicarbonate of soda, or, in some old cookbooks, saleratus. It is the alkaline or base material in most quick leavening actions. When used in batters along with an acid ingredient like sour milk, sourdough, or molasses it makes them rise and at the same time it neutralizes any strong acid tastes. Baked goods made in this way have an especially light and tender texture.

Baking powder is a mixture containing both baking soda and one or more acidic powders. These react with each other when mixed with any liquid. To prevent the absorption of moisture while in storage, cornstarch or another anti-moisture ingredient is also included in the mixtures.

Various different baking powder formulas have been used through the years. The modern double acting baking powders are almost fool proof to use, but there are objections to some of their ingredients. As the aluminum compounds used are generally unhealthful, health stores supply aluminum-free baking powders. People on low-sodium diets may wish to avoid baking soda, and sodium-free baking powders are also available, using potassium bicarbonate (potash) as the alkaline ingredient.

Earlier baking powders used cream of tartar (potassium bitartrate) as the acid ingredient. It was single acting (reacting once), giving off carbon dioxide bubbles as soon as moisture touched it. Double acting baking powder reacts twice, first when moistened and again when heated. ("Double acting" does not mean the power to raise twice as much batter, and the measurements called for in recipes are the same for all types of baking powder.) The advantages of double action are that batter or dough can be refrigerated or frozen before being baked, and the order of mixing ingredients can be casual. If using single acting baking powder, combine ingredients quickly, and put them immediately in a pre-heated oven. Double acting baking powder takes the punch out of the old jokes about cakes falling if someone jumps on the floor or opens the oven door.

**Home Mixed Baking Powder**  Single acting baking powder is easily made by mixing 2 parts cream of tartar, 1 part baking soda, and 1 part cornstarch. It must be stored in airtight containers. It may be easier simply to sift ½ teaspoon cream of tartar and ¼ teaspoon baking soda with the dry ingredients for every teaspoon of baking powder called for.

**Interchanging Baking Powder and Baking Soda**  These two leavens can sometimes be substituted for each other. When recipes calling for baking soda are enhanced with high protein ingredients like wheat germ, powdered milk, and nutritional yeast, baking powder can be used instead of baking soda. The extra protein neutralizes the acid in the ingredients making baking soda unnecessary. Substitute 1 teaspoon of baking powder for every ½ teaspoon of baking soda.

Baking soda can be used in recipes calling for baking powder, if there is some acid present in the ingredients, or if substitutions of acidic for non-acidic ingredients can be made. For instance, honey and molasses are acidic and can be used instead of sugar, or sour milk or yogurt can be used instead of sweet milk. Use half as much baking soda as is required of baking powder.

## LEAVENS AT HIGH ALTITUDES

High altitudes cause the carbon dioxide bubbles produced by the leavening action to expand faster than at low altitudes. Consequently, yeast dough tends to rise more quickly, and less baking soda and baking powder are needed for the same leavening action. At altitudes over 5,000 feet, decrease amounts of baking soda and baking powder ⅛ to ¼ teaspoon, per teaspoon called for. There are recipes specifically designed for high altitude baking in mountainous areas. (Contact local or state agricultural agents for information.)

## UNUSUAL LEAVENS

***Snow for Leavening***  Using very fresh snow for the liquid in the batter is an old time way to make cornbread light. One old recipe suggests mixing 1 cup of cornmeal with 2 cups of light dry snow, or 1 cup wet snow, but as much as 4 cups may be needed if the snow is very dry. Mix outdoors, or in a cool place. Mound the batter up in the baking pan and put immediately into a very hot, 400°F–450°F, oven, as it must set quickly before the snow melts and its lightness is lost. Only new fallen snow will make the bread light.

***Leavening with Ashes***  In colonial times, preparations from hardwood ashes or corncob ashes were sometimes used like baking soda. The ashes were mixed with boiling water and left to sit until they settled. Two or three spoonfuls of the clear liquid on top were then added to batters or dough to make it rise.

This is the same method used for making a lye solution for hominy (refer to the CORN, DRY section) or for making soap. Such solutions can be strong and should be used with caution.

The American Indians added small amounts of different kinds of wood ashes to food for leavening and for flavor.

***Sourdough***  Use this leaven like yeast, or like sour milk to react with baking soda. (Refer to the SOURDOUGH section.)

## STORAGE

For CANNING, DRYING, and FREEZING refer to ONIONS section, but COLD STORAGE (following) is the preferred method.

**Cold Storage**   Pull, and pack upright in damp sand or soil in root cellar, or in any cool, dark place, or mulch in garden through winter. Refer to COLD STORAGE section.

LEEKS ARE CLOSELY RELATED TO ONIONS, WITH AN ONION-LIKE smell and taste. However, they are not merely another kind of onion, but have a distinctive quality that makes them as beloved as a vegetable can be by those who know them well. Leeks are delicious cooked plainly to be eaten every day of the week, and they are equally delicious in fancy dishes. Simple leek and potato soups have been satisfying daily fare in countless European homes for centuries, while Vichyssoise, a chilled leek soup so rich it has been called leek ice cream, is on the menu in the most elegant restaurants. There have been disputes for a century or two about the ingredients in the Scottish leek soup, Cock-a-leekie. While some may question the presence of prunes, most agree that the soup must be thick with leeks.

Growing the largest thick, white-stalked leeks is a gardening challenge, and in Wales there are leek growing contests. However, ordinary, even scrawny leeks keep well, have excellent flavor, and are easily grown in most gardens. Wild leeks are among the best tasting wild onions. Where plentiful they can be used in recipes instead of cultivated leeks.

## HANDLING LEEKS

Leeks are planted in early spring for a fall and winter crop and are rarely harvested before the first frosts. Where winters are not too severe, leeks can be mulched and left in the garden to be pulled as needed. The also keep very well in a root cellar or any cool dark place if replanted in containers of sand or soil and kept slightly damp.

The lower white and light green part of the leek is the most tender, and is the part called for in recipes. The coarser, upper leaves are often cut off and discarded, but they are very flavorful, so save them for making soup stock. (Refer to the SOUP section.) Or chop them small to add to soups and stews.

After the outside leaves are pulled off and the top leaves and roots trimmed, carefully wash the leeks. Dirt becomes embedded in the folds of the leaves as they grow and will not easily rinse out. If the leeks are to be sliced, rinse them after slicing, with special attention to the section where the leaves start. If the leeks are to be used

*Preparing a leek*

whole, make a slit, from just below the beginning of the leaves up to the top, so the leaves can be spread apart and rinsed.

Though leeks are almost always cooked, small amounts are good minced and added raw to salads.

## LEEK RECIPES

### Everyday Leek Soup　　　　　　　(Makes 8–12 medium bowls.)

| | |
|---|---|
| *1 pound (about) leeks, trimmed, thinly sliced* | *1–3 tablespoons butter* |
| | *salt, optional* |
| *1 pound (about) potatoes, quartered, thinly sliced* | *1 small slice dried bread or toast per serving, optional* |

Heat about 2 quarts of water to a boil, and add leeks and potatoes. Cook 30 minutes or till the vegetables are tender. Add salt, if desired, and a little butter, or spread butter on the dry bread or toast, and put a slice in each soup bowl. Ladle the hot soup over it. The result is a soup that is well flavored and fully satisfying, despite its simplicity.

***Cream of Leek Soup***　　Sauté the leeks, potatoes, and a chopped onion in the butter, and add 5 to 6 cups chicken stock or other soup stock. Cook till the vegetables are very soft and add 2 to 3 cups milk. For a richer flavor include some top milk or light cream. Heat to blend flavors, season to taste. If a smoother texture is desired, the vegetables can be puréed before adding the milk.

***Vichyssoise***　　Add a cup of heavy cream to cooked Cream of Leek Soup. Chill and serve cold, garnished with minced chives or scallions.

***Hearty Meat and Leek Soup***　　Make *Everyday Leek Soup* using beef, venison, or other dark stock instead of water. Chopped carrots, celery, parsley, and a bay leaf can also be included. Add the cooked, chopped meat to make a hearty meal. The leek flavor blends especially well with venison.

***Leek and Jerusalem Artichoke Soup***　　Replace potatoes with Jerusalem artichokes in any of the above versions and reduce cooking time to about 20 minutes.

### Cock-a-leekie

(Makes 8–12 medium bowls soup and usually 6 or more dinner servings chicken meat.)

| | |
|---|---|
| *3 (about) pounds leeks* | *1 pound prunes, pitted* |
| *1 stewing chicken, cut in pieces* | *pepper, salt, optional* |
| *beef soup bone (optional)* | |

Cut the green tops off the leeks. Reserve the leeks and tie the tops in a bundle with string. If tops are unavailable, use several whole cleaned leeks. Put the leek tops, chicken, and beef bone in a soup pot and cover with water. Bring slowly to a boil, uncovered, and skim off any foam. Simmer, covered, till the chicken is tender, about 2 hours. Take out and discard the spent leek tops and beef bone, and set aside the chicken. Skim excess fat off the broth or soak it up with paper napkins or paper towels.

Meanwhile, cut the reserved leeks into 1 inch sections and rinse well. Put them and the prunes in the soup broth. Season with a generous amount of pepper, and salt if desired. Simmer 20 minutes or till leeks and prunes are done. Add small pieces of boned chicken or reserve the meat for another use.

### *Leek Meatballs in Lemon Sauce*
*(from Greece)*                                    (Makes 4–6 dinner servings.)

| | |
|---|---|
| *2 pounds leeks* | *1–2 tablespoons oil for frying,* |
| *1 pound ground beef* | *preferably olive oil* |
| *1 cup fine dry breadcrumbs* | *juice of two lemons* |
| *2 eggs* | *1 tablespoon butter* |
| *pepper, salt, optional* | *¾ cup water* |

Clean the leeks and steam them for 20 minutes or till tender, then chop small. Mix with the ground beef, breadcrumbs, eggs, and seasonings. When thoroughly mixed shape into small balls and fry in oil till lightly browned. Drain on paper towels.

Put the lemon juice, butter, and ¾ cup water in a frying pan with a lid, or in a large, shallow saucepan. Bring to a boil, add the meatballs, cover, and simmer over low heat for 15 to 20 minutes. Shake the pan or stir carefully several times to turn the meatballs without breaking them. If they start to dry out, add a little more water. There will be only a little sauce when they are done.

***Swiss Chard Meatballs in Lemon Sauce***   Cook 1 to 1½ pounds Swiss chard in a minimum of water till tender. Mince or grind, and use in the meatballs instead of leeks.

---

# LETTUCE

LETTUCE COMES IN SEVERAL DIFFERENT TYPES: HEAD (OR CABBAGE) lettuce, loose leaf lettuce, Bibb (or butterhead) which forms a soft loose head, cos (or romain) which forms a loose, oblong head, and stem lettuce (or celtuce) with thick stems and narrow leaves. These all have noticeably different flavors and textures, but can be prepared in the same ways and are freely interchangeable in salads. Endive, escarole, and chicory are sometimes called lettuce, but they are a different plant. (Refer to the CHICORY section.)

To have a salad made with homegrown lettuce every day of the year would be ideal, but it is not easy. There is no practical way to store fresh lettuce except for short periods of refrigeration, so a constant

---

### LEEK IDEAS *cont.*

**Leek Fritters**   Cut leeks into 2 inch sections and steam till just tender. Cool, dip in batter, and deep fry. (Refer to the VEGETABLE TEMPURA variation in the FRUITS section.) Or marinate the cooked leek pieces in a dressing as for the Leek Salads above, drain a few minutes, then dip in batter and fry. Serve alone as an appetizer, or as part of a mixed tempura platter.

**Leeks Stewed in Butter**   Melt butter in a saucepan with a tight lid. Add chopped or thinly sliced leeks. Cover and simmer over very low heat till leeks are tender, about 15 minutes. Season with pepper and a squeeze of lemon juice or dash of vinegar. For a sweet and sour flavor add a little honey to the butter in which the leeks are cooked.

### OTHER RECIPES WITH LEEKS

Kale Soup, Scottish Style, p.365
Pease Porridge, p.465
Pot au Feu, p.34
Quince and Leek Stew, p.496
Recipes and Ideas for Vegetables, p.669
Vegetable Hot Pot (and variations), p.669
Welsh Mutton Soup, p.381

### STORAGE

**Cold Storage**   Solid heads keep refrigerated about 1 month. Loose heads, leaves keep a few days to 2 weeks. See CLEANING AND CRISPING LETTUCE, below. *Note:* Refer also to SAUERKRAUT section.

supply depends on the cleverness of the gardener. The choice of varieties, timing of plantings, and the use of cooling shade in summer, and window sills, cold frames and green houses in winter all help extend the lettuce season, but there may still be lettuceless times. Fortunately, there are alternatives other than buying tasteless lettuce from the store. (Refer to the SALADS section for these, and for discussion of the nutritional values of fresh salads.)

## HANDLING LETTUCE

Pick lettuce when it is cool in the garden, and during hot sunny weather pick in the morning before the day's heat drains out its crispness. Properly handled, it will stay crisp for several days. Limp lettuce will sometimes revive if handled in the same way.

***Cleaning and Crisping Lettuce*** Wash lettuce soon after picking. If it is nearly clean, a quick rinsing in cold water is enough. If there is dirt between the leaves, separate them and put them in a big pan of cool water. Swish around gently and lift the lettuce out of the water, leaving the dirt behind. Repeat if necessary, using fresh water. If dirt still clings, rinse the leaves individually.

There are various ways to dry lettuce, from shaking the leaves, or patting them dry with a towel, to using a special cage-like device that spins lettuce making the water fly off it. For handy home-style lettuce spinning, put the wet lettuce on a big, cloth dish towel. Gather the corners of the towel to make a "bag," take it outdoors, hold firmly and swing the bag around several times in a full circle so that the water flies out. If the lettuce will be made into salad immediately, other leafy ingredients can be rinsed and swung in the towel with it.

To crisp limp lettuce, or to store it, leave the damp towel around it, and put the whole bundle in a big plastic bag in the refrigerator. The lettuce will be crisp after several hours, and should keep several days to a week wrapped in this way.

Though lettuce is most important as a raw vegetable, there are some very good ways to cook it. These are useful when it is most plentiful and threatening to go to seed in the garden. As well, firm varieties can be fermented for sauerkraut. (Refer to the SAUERKRAUT section.)

## LETTUCE RECIPES

***Korean Style Lettuce Bundles***                    (Makes 6—8 snack servings.)

1 scallion, minced
½ teaspoon paprika
⅛ teaspoon hot red pepper or a few drops tabasco sauce
1 tablespoon soy sauce
1 tablespoon sesame seeds, raw or toasted

½ teaspoon sesame or other oil
12—16 medium-sized lettuce leaves
1—2 cups leftover cold cooked rice

Mix the scallion, paprika, hot pepper, soy sauce, sesame seeds, and oil in a small dish to make a sauce. Amounts of ingredients can be adjusted to taste.

Put the lettuce leaves, rice, and sauce on the table. Each person can then make bundles by taking a lettuce leaf, putting a spoon of rice on it, adding some sauce and rolling it up. A very nice snack or quick lunch.

### Braised Lettuce                          (Makes about 6 side servings.)

1 bunch or medium head of lettuce,
    cut in sections or wedges
2 (about) tablespoons butter
¾ cup bread crumbs

1½ tablespoons cheese, grated,
    optional (Cheddar, swiss,
    Parmesan, and most
    others.)
pepper, to taste

Steam the lettuce for about 5 minutes or cook it in the water left on it after washing. It will wilt and turn a brighter shade of green. Butter a shallow baking dish and arrange the lettuce in it. Dot with more butter. Sprinkle with bread crumbs or with the cheese and bread crumbs mixed. Season with pepper. Bake in a hot, 450°F oven for about 15 minutes.

**Braised Chinese Cabbage**   Replace lettuce with Chinese cabbage in this recipe.

### Lettuce Soup                              (About 6 medium bowls.)

2 large bunches or heads of lettuce,
    or outside leaves from 3 or 4
    bunches
2 cups chicken stock, or other light
    soup stock

2 cups milk
¼ teaspoon nutmeg, or to taste
1 teaspoon honey or sugar
pepper, salt, optional
1–2 tablespoons butter or cream

Shred the lettuce and put it in a pan with the soup stock. Simmer gently till the lettuce is soft. Purée in a blender or with a food mill. Return to the pan, add the milk, and season with nutmeg, honey or sugar, pepper, and salt, if desired. Heat without boiling. Just before serving stir in a little butter or cream.

This delicate soup is said to have a soothing or tranquilizing effect.

---

## LETTUCE IDEAS

**Old Fashioned Lettuce Salad**   Toss crisp lettuce and minced scallion or onion together with the *Cream Salad Dressing* recipe in the CREAM section. In the past, this combination was commonly enjoyed when cream was plentiful and salad oil unavailable.

**Squeezed Lettuce Salad** When there is extra lettuce, shred a large amount, then squeeze it hard, a handful at a time. Let the water that comes out drain away. Mix with oil and vinegar or any other dressing. Much more lettuce than usual will be used, and the dressing will be absorbed more completely. Though everyone generally likes this salad, few can guess how it was made.

## OTHER RECIPES FEATURING LETTUCE

Fall Vegetable Salads p.533
Making Sauerkraut, p.540
Potherb Pie, p.590
Spring Salads, p.532

---

# LIVER

LIVER HAS TO LIVE WITH ITS REPUTATION. EVERYONE KNOWS THAT IT is full of vitamins and minerals, and is "good for you," but there is also a widespread feeling that it does not taste good and is to be eaten only from a sense of duty. Often those who dislike liver have had it overcooked and dry, with a flavor too strong to be disguised by any amount of onions, bacon, and catsup. Fresh, carefully cooked liver is tender, juicy, and mild flavored and needs absolutely no disguise. Its freshness is all important, and the only way to ensure this is to raise meat animals, hunt them, or buy directly from someone else who raises them.

Many country families take for granted that there will be liver for dinner the day an animal is butchered, and everyone looks forward to a delicious meal. The next day liver also tastes good, but from then on the flavor gets gradually stronger. Very few livers make their way into a plastic package in the meat section of a grocery store soon enough to be really good. There is also the likelihood that store-bought liver contains more than its share of the additives fed to commercially raised animals. One function of the liver is to detoxify drugs and other harmful substances, which may then be stored in it. When animals are home raised such additives can be avoided or at least carefully controlled.

## HANDLING LIVER

*Cleaning*  The livers of all sizes and species of animals, whether domestic or wild, are cleaned and cooked in the same basic ways. Though calf's liver is considered choice, beef, lamb, and pork livers are all very good, too. Livers from game animals are generally excellent, and without any gamey flavors. The livers of domestic and wild rabbits, and other small animals like racoons, woodchucks, opossoms, and porcupines are mild flavored, tender, and always worth saving. Poultry liver has its own special qualities, and many recipes have been created for it. (For poultry and fish livers, refer to the CHICKEN, GOOSE, and FISH sections, respectively.)

When taking the liver out of an animal's carcass it is important to immediately find the gall bladder, and carefully cut or pull it off. It is the small sac attached to the liver, containing the greenish liquid called bile or gall. Bile gives a bitter taste to any meat it touches. There are pioneer American stories telling of the use of buffalo gall for seasoning meat, but nowadays few would enjoy the taste. If the gall bladder should break, trim off the area touched and wash the liver immediately in plenty of cold water. If bitterness remains, use the meat as pet food. As deer do not have gall bladders, their livers are easier to clean.

Wash the fresh liver in cold water, and trim off any noticeable veins or blood vessels. Refrigerate or chill immediately. Do not soak in water as is sometimes recommended, as this will leech out flavor and nutrients. Some livers have a thin membrane covering them which can be pulled off before the liver is cooked or frozen. Wait to slice liver till just before cooking, as it loses juice and develops a stronger flavor more quickly if it sits sliced for hours (or days in the store). It is especially important not to slice liver before freezing it. (That is the main cause of dissatisfaction with frozen liver.) In any case, it is easier to slice later when it is partly thawed. A large liver can be frozen in meal-sized chunks.

If liver will not be used within 2 days of butchering an animal, freeze it as soon as it has lost its body heat.

***Cooking***   Cook liver for a short time only, using low to medium heat, except when an initial quick searing is required. Both overcooking and using high heat will make it dry and tough. (Refer to the LEAN MEAT instructions on page 407.) Livers from different animals can usually substitue for each other in recipes, but cooking times may have to be adjusted according to the animal's age, and the size of the liver. Liver from young animals is the most tender and mildly flavored, and is especialy good sautéed or broiled. Very thin slices can be cooked in 1 or 2 minutes per side, while thick slices may take about 5 minutes per side. Livers from older animals are especially good if stewed or baked with flavorful sauces and seasonings.

The taste of strong flavored liver can be improved by soaking it for 30 minutes in milk, buttermilk, or a favorite marinade. The liquid will take on a bitter taste and should be discarded.

Livers range in color from dark purple to reddish black to beige brown. These shades are all normal varying with the feed and the season, and are equally healthful. However, a misshapen liver, or one that has many white bumps or lesions, is diseased and should be thrown out. If there are one or two small white bumps they can be trimmed off before using the rest of the liver.

## LIVER RECIPES

### *Farmer's Liver Loaf*                           (Makes 8–12 dinner servings.)

| | |
|---|---|
| 2 *pounds liver* | 1 – 2 *teaspoons dried herbs* (Try |
| 2 *slices bacon, or a slice of salt pork,* |     thyme, marjoram, savory, |
|     *pork fat, or other fat* |     sage, celery leaves.) |
| 1 *onion, or leek* | ¼ *cup (about) parsley, minced* |
| 1 *carrot* | 2 *eggs* |
| 1 *potato, optional* | 1 *cup fine dry breadcrumbs or* |
| ½ *stalk celery, optional* |     *ground oatmeal* (Or rolled |
| ½ *green pepper, optional* |     oats whirled in a blender.) |
| ½ *cup tomato sauce, or catsup* | *pepper, to taste* |
| 1 *teaspoon paprika, optional* | *salt, to taste* (Omit if using salt |
| |     pork.) |

In a meat grinder or food processor, grind together the liver, bacon or other fat, onion or leek, carrot, potato, celery, and green pepper. Add the tomato sauce or catsup, paprika, herbs, parsley, eggs, and breadcrumbs or oatmeal, pepper, and salt, if desired, and mix well. Grease 1 large or 2 small loaf pans and pack in the liver mixture. Bake uncovered in a low oven, 300°F, for about an hour. The loaf should pull away from the sides and be firm in the middle when done. Slice and serve hot with relish, gravy, or a spicy sauce. Irresistible!

---

### LIVER IDEAS

**Liver Soup**   Cut raw liver in small pieces, in shreds, or grind it. Just before serving add it to boiling soup, take the pot off the stove, wait about 2 minutes, and serve. To make shreds, slice the liver very thinly and then cut the slices into thin strips. Cutting is easiest when the liver is partly frozen. Any vegetable soup can be enriched this way.

For a Chinese variation, mix liver shreds with a little soy sauce. Cut spinach leaves or other greens into pieces. If desired, slice a few mushrooms and mince some ginger root. Heat several cups of water or soup stock to a boil and add the liver, spinach, and any other ingredients. Let stay on the stove 2 minutes and then serve.

**Skewered Liver Variations**
Cubes of seasoned liver coated with fat or oil are good threaded on skewers and broiled. A small strip of bacon wrapped around each piece of liver is one way to add necessary fat. Pieces of onion, green pepper, or other vegetables can alternate on the skewer with the liver. A bay leaf can be threaded on here and there for a different flavor.

A recipe from Tuscany rolls cubes of pork liver in fennel seeds, adds a sprinkle of pepper and salt, and wraps a piece of rete or caul from a lamb around each cube. (Refer to CAUL FAT, in the LARD section.) A Middle Eastern recipe spreads a paste of garlic crushed with salt on cubes of liver, then sprinkles the cubes with olive oil, pepper, and crushed, dried mint. This marinates for 30 minutes and is served with a squeeze of lemon juice after it is broiled.

Skewered liver cooks in about 10 minutes. Do not overcook it.

### LIVER IDEAS, *cont.*

**Savory Liver Tomato Sauce**

Heat tomato sauce and season it with parsley, pepper, and any other favorite seasonings, such as garlic, hot red pepper, basil or oregano. In a separate pan heat oil and sauté a chopped onion till limp. Add chopped or diced liver and cook 5 minutes, stirring often. Add the hot tomato sauce, and simmer uncovered, without boiling, for about 20 minutes. Very good served over noodles, spaghetti, or rice. This makes even strong flavored and tough liver quite enjoyable.

---

### OTHER RECIPES WITH LIVER

Also see recipes using chicken livers, in the CHICKEN section.

---

Leftover slices are delicious browned on both sides in a frying pan.

***Farmer's Meat Loaf***  Instead of liver use any red meat. A mixture of beef and pork is good. If the meat contains fat, omit bacon or other fat. If it is already ground, grate or mince the vegetables to go in it. Wheat germ can replace some of the breadcrumbs if desired. If the mixture is too dry add extra tomato sauce or water.

### Sally's Knishes                                    (Makes 6–8 servings.)

| | |
|---|---|
| 2 cups flour | ¼ teaspoon pepper |
| 1 teaspoon baking powder | ½ cup mashed potatoes |
| 3 tablespoons fat | 1–2 teaspoons minced onion, |
| 2 eggs |    optional |
| 2 cups liver, cooked and ground | ½ teaspoon salt, optional |

Sift the flour with baking powder and cut in 1 tablespoon fat. Beat the eggs with 2 tablespoons water, add them to the flour mixture, and work together to make a smooth dough. Roll out on a lightly floured board in a thin sheet. Cut to make 8 to 12 squares of dough.

Mix the ground liver with the pepper, potatoes, onion, and salt, if desired. Divide the mixture to make a mound of filling on each square of dough. Moisten the edges of the dough with water and fold them over to make a triangular shape. Press the edges together firmly. Melt the remaining 2 tablespoons of fat in a shallow baking pan. Set the knishes in it and bake in a moderate, 350°F oven for about 45 minutes, or till the crust is nicely browned. Serve these tasty liver pastries for lunch or supper or inbetween, with green salad.

### Liver Stroganoff                          (Makes about 6 dinner servings.)

| | |
|---|---|
| ¼ pound bacon, sliced | ½ cup sour cream |
| 1 onion, sliced | ½ cup milk |
| ¼ pound mushrooms, sliced if large | ½ teaspoon thyme |
| 1 pound liver, cut in small cubes | a few drops tabasco, or dash of |
| 2 tablespoons flour |    hot red pepper |

In a large frying pan, fry the bacon until crisp. Take it out, crumble it, and set aside. In the remaining bacon fat, sauté the onion and mushrooms till tender, then take them out and set aside. Toss the liver in the flour to coat it. Mix extra flour that did not stick to the liver with the sour cream, milk, thyme, and tabasco or hot pepper.

Sauté the liver cubes in the same bacon fat over moderate heat, turning to cook all sides briefly. As soon as the liver's raw color is gone, add the sour cream mixture. Simmer over low heat till the sauce has thickened, from 5 to 10 minutes. Stir often, and do not let it boil. Add the reserved bacon, onion, and mushrooms, stir to combine and heat for a minute or two more. Delicious served over rice, it is best when first made, and will not reheat well.

***Heart Stroganoff*** Cut leftover cooked heart meat into small cubes, and use instead of the liver. But do not toss the heart in flour, and add just 1½ tablespoons flour to the sour cream mixture. The heart needs only to be heated in the bacon fat before the sour cream mixture is added.

# LUNGS

Lungs, or lights, as they are called in many old recipes, are a lightweight food—literally and gustatorily. Their taste is bland and their texture soft. They can be the main ingredient in a well seasoned stew or soup, but more often they are prepared in mixtures with other organ meats from the same animal. They act as fillers or extenders, without adding any distinctive taste of their own.

## HANDLING LUNGS

Lungs are easily recognized and removed from an animal's carcass. Often a piece of the windpipe is still attached, which must be cut off before they are thoroughly washed. If the lungs have blood in them they can be cleaned by running cold water into them till they are full and the water runs through them. However, it is not worth trying to clean lungs from game animals shot in the lungs. Use them for pet food instead.

Cook lungs whole, and then chop or grind them, or cut them into bite-sized pieces before cooking. Lungs from older animals will take from 1½ to 2 hours to cook, while those from young animals take about 30 minutes. Lungs are apt to make a sighing or wheezing noise when first heated, which is most noticeable when they are cooked whole.

## LUNG RECIPES

***Lungs and Beans with Basil*** (Makes about 6 dinner servings.)

2 tablespoons oil
3 tablespoons salt pork, or fatty bacon, minced
1 stalk celery, chopped medium
1 small onion, sliced
1 sprig parsley, minced
1 small clove garlic, minced
1 pound lungs, cut in small cubes

¼ cup dry red wine, optional
1 cup canned tomatoes, or fresh tomatoes, chopped
pepper, to taste
2½ cups cooked kidney beans, undrained
2 teaspoons (about) fresh basil, minced

### LUNG IDEAS

**Sheep's Pluck/Pig's Haslet**
"Pluck" and "haslet" are old-time names for organ meats, particularly lungs, liver, and heart. Many delectable peasant style dishes can be made with various combinations of these meats. For an old fashioned sheep's pluck casserole, layer thinly sliced lamb or sheep lungs and liver with sliced potatoes and onions, in a greased baking dish. Season with pepper, and such fresh minced herbs as sage, parsley, thyme, and celery leaves. Cover with bacon slices, or thin slices of beef, or lamb suet, and bake in a slow, about 325°F, oven, from 1½ to 2 hours. This mixture can also be stewed over low heat.

For traditional pig's haslet to roast over an open fire, make a hash-like mixture of chopped pig's lungs, liver, heart, sweetbreads (optional), and a little fat and lean pork. Season with minced onion, pepper, salt, if desired, and herbs, as for the pluck. Wrap the mixture in a caul (refer to caul fat in the LARD section), and fasten with needle and thread. Tie with a string for hanging over a fire, or roast on a rack over charcoal. Keep the fire low and cook for about two hours.

## LUNG IDEAS, *cont.*

**Calf's Lungs and Heart** Put the lungs and heart in a big pot with such soup vegetables as onion, leek, celeriac, and carrot. Cover with cold water, bring to a boil, and simmer 1½ hours. Drain, reserving stock. Chop the lungs and heart into small pieces. Make a gravy by melting 2 tablespoons butter, stirring in 2 tablespoons flour, and adding about 2 cups of the reserved stock. Season with a little vinegar, some nutmeg, pepper, and salt, if desired. Add the lungs and heart, simmer 30 minutes, and serve over noodles or with potatoes. The lungs and heart of young animals other than calves can be used to make this foolproof and always enjoyable dish.

Heat the oil in a Dutch oven or other heavy pot. Add the salt pork or bacon, celery, onion, parsley, and garlic, and sauté till the vegetables are lightly browned. Add the lungs and continue to sauté till they are lightly browned. Stir very often and add a tablespoon or so of water if they begin to stick. Add the wine, and stir till evaporated. Add the tomatoes and pepper and simmer uncovered for 20 minutes. Add the beans, cover, and simmer till the lungs are tender, about 1 hour if they are from a mature animal. Check and add more water if needed. Add the basil just before serving. This hearty stew goes well with rice, noodles, or potatoes.

*Tripe and Beans* Use tripe that has been pre-cooked until almost tender instead of lungs. (Refer to the TRIPE, CHITTERLINGS AND PAUNCH section.) Do not brown the tripe, but add it with the tomatoes, and omit the wine.

### Chinese Lung Soup                    (Makes 8–12 medium bowls.)

| | |
|---|---|
| ½ pig's lungs, *in bite sized pieces* (Or substitute another animal's lungs.) | ¼ *cup dried mushrooms, soaked, or 1 cup fresh mushrooms, sliced* |
| 6 *cups water* | 1 *tablespoon sherry, optional* |
| ½ *cup barley* | 3–4 *slices ginger root* *pepper, salt, optional* |

Put the lungs in a dry frying pan and stir over low heat till the water has evaporated from them. Then put them in a soup pot with 6 cups of water, and the barley, mushrooms, sherry, and ginger root. Simmer over low heat for 2 hours. If desired, season with pepper and salt when done. The lungs and barley give this soup texture and the mushrooms and seasonings give it flavor.

## OTHER RECIPES WITH LUNGS

Faggots, p. 592
Haggis, p. 381
Soup Stock, p. 575

# MAPLE SYRUP

## STORAGE

**Canning** See CANNING MAPLE SYRUP, below.

1 CUP MAPLE SYRUP = ABOUT 1 CUP HONEY OR 1½ CUPS GRANULATED SUGAR; 1 CUP MAPLE SUGAR, GRATED AND LOOSE WITHOUT PACKING = 1 CUP BROWN OR GRANULATED SUGAR

**I**N EARLY SPRING, WHEN THE SUN SHINES WARMLY DURING THE DAY but the nights revert to the cold of winter, the sap rises in maple trees and it is time to harvest the first and sweetest crop of the year. Maple sap when it is fresh from the tree tastes like cool spring water with a hint of sweetness. It is good simply to drink, and wonderful for making tea, diluting frozen orange juice, and making sourdough bread. But it is the syrup that is the important product of this harvest. Syrup making is an exhilerating family project for ending winter's doldrums. Everyone can help collect sap, gather wood, and keep the fire going, and, of course, everyone must taste from time to time to see if the sap has become syrup yet.

## MAKING MAPLE SYRUP

A family that can make a year's supply of maple syrup will not need any other concentrated sweet. Sugar can be made from the syrup and, as was done by North American Indians and early settlers, the syrup or the sugar can be used to sweeten fruits and desserts, and to flavor all kinds of meat and vegetable mixtures. To do so it is not necessary to live in the range of the sugar maple tree, as any species of large maple tree gives sap that can be boiled down to syrup. The flavor of the syrup will be the same, though the sap of some trees may have a lower sugar content, requiring lengthier boiling. Sugar content depends on the health and location of the tree as well as on the variety. A box elder, which is a strain of maple, or a red or silver maple with a full crown in a sunny location might have sweeter sap than a poorly situated sugar maple.

As maple syrup is made throughout the spring, there will be different grades or flavors of syrup. Cool weather syrup is light colored and mild flavored. It is good used like a mild honey as a sweetener. Warm weather syrup is darker and more strongly maple flavored. It is ideal for making such desserts as maple ice cream, and many prefer its full flavor over the lighter kind for pancakes. Sap should not be collected after tree buds begin to swell because the syrup will have an unpleasant "buddy" taste.

*Collecting Sap*   Any small tube can be fitted into a hole drilled into a maple tree trunk, with a container hung under it to collect dripping sap. There are, however, advantages to buying special spiles and containers. The spiles have a hook attached for holding the container, and the best containers are covered to keep out rain, dirt, and most insects. There are some very efficient sap bags made of durable, reusable plastic.

To tap a tree, drill a hole low on the trunk for the spile (tube) to fit into. The hole should be 2 to 3 feet above the ground, about ½ inch in diameter, and from 2 to 2½ inches deep, with a very slight slant for the sap to run down. Sap that is flowing well will start dripping as soon as the hole is cleared of shavings and the spile tapped into place. On the best days a good tree can fill gallon containers several times per day. Collect sap at least once a day, whether containers are full or not, then store it in a cold place till it can be boiled down. When the flow stops, remove the spiles and leave the hole unplugged, as then the tree will heal itself most quickly.

*Storing Sap*   If it can be kept cold, below 40°F, sap can be collected and kept up to a week before it is boiled. If the sap warms enough for microorganisms to become active in it the syrup will have an unpleasant, "greenish" taste. Often this taste has been blamed on late collection of sap, after buds have formed, when in fact it was due to the sap being kept too warm.

It is practical to keep sap outdoors in a shady place as long as nights are cold, and if the sap freezes the ice will keep it cool during the day. Towards the end of the season, when the weather is warmer, a colder storage place must be found or the sap must be boiled without delay. New garbage cans made of food grade plastic make good storage containers.

Take any floating ice out of the sap and discard it before boiling, since there is very little sugar in it. In fact, it is possible to make syrup by repeatedly freezing sap and removing the ice, but this is impractical except with very small amounts. (Refer to CONCENTRATED JUICE, in the FREEZING section.)

***Boiling Down Sap for Syrup***   From 25 to 40 gallons of maple sap must be boiled for each gallon of syrup. It is the variation in sugar content of the sap from different trees that accounts for this range. Even at best there is still a lot of boiling to be done, so do most of it over an outdoor fire. So much steam would be hard on the house's interior, and the expense becomes too great if an electric or gas stove is used.

The sap for six or seven gallons of syrup, enough for many families for a year, can be boiled down over a camp fire. A bigger operation will require a sugar house with equipment such as special evaporation pans. Large, shallow pans are best for boiling sap, to provide a large surface for evaporation. People with welding equipment can devise excellent evaporation pans, often by cutting some large metal container in half. Use several canning kettles or other large pots if nothing better is available. The largest deep, enameled roasting pans with lids work well, and the lid can also be used if it sits flat.

There is no harm in mixing batches of sap at different stages of evaporation, or adding fresh sap to partly boiled sap, and boiling can be interrupted for the night and begun again the next day. All of these things are likely when using makeshift containers over a camp fire.

Once sap has boiled down to a thin syrup, take it indoors and finish it where it can be watched more closely. Strain out any bits of debris through a cloth lined colander. A wood heating stove is most economical for continued cooking, and can be used even if not hot enough to maintain a full boil. Declare the syrup done when it tastes right, or when a thermometer reaches 7°F above the boiling point of water. At sea level this means the syrup will be 219°F. Continued boiling will make a sweeter, thicker syrup, and eventually bring it to the maple sugar stage.

***Clearing Maple Syrup***   Maple syrup often contains a harmless, grainy substance called sugar sand. There are years when so little sand is present that it can be ignored, while in other years the syrup will be clouded with it. In big operations syrup is filtered but this is difficult in the home kitchen, because the syrup tends to cool and sit above the filter without going through. There are other ways to clear the syrup. It can be set aside for 2 or 3 days, allowing the sand to settle to the bottom. The clear syrup can then be carefully poured off, and the remaining cloudy syrup used in cooking or for maple sugar.

Syrup can also be cleared like soup stock by using egg whites. To do so, let the syrup cool, then mix in one beaten egg white for each gallon of syrup. Heat without stirring. (If the syrup is stirred while it heats this procedure will not succeed.) Once it boils, a foam will form. Skim this off and a clear syrup will remain.

*Canning Maple Syrup*   Canning is the best way to store homemade maple syrup, as without canning mold is likely to develop over time. Though it is possible to remove spots of mold, and then to bring the syrup to a boil to prevent more mold forming, invisible traces of mold may remain, and there is evidence that this can be harmful to health. If the syrup is canned and the jars are refrigerated after opening, mold will never be a problem.

Syrup is easily canned by heating it to 212°F (almost to a boil) and sealing it in jars as in open kettle canning. (Refer to the CANNING section). Use regular canning jars or recycled jars with lids that vacuum seal. Sometimes syrup hotter than 212°F will bubble out around the lids when they are sealed. If this happens, remove and rinse the lids in boiling water, wipe the jar rim and seal again. The syrup should be cool enough to seal properly this time.

*Syrup from Black Birch and other Trees*   Several kinds of trees can be tapped like maples to collect their spring sap. Sycamores, black walnut, butternut, hickory, and yellow and white birch can be tapped as well as black birch. All have a clear sap that is good to drink. Though it can be boiled down in hopes of making syrup, the only consistently successful kind is black birch.

The black birch tree is also called sweet birch and cherry birch. Black birch sap rises just after the maple syrup season is over, so the same equipment can be used for both. Procedures for tapping and evaporating are the same, but black birch sap takes about twice as long as maple to boil down to syrup. It makes a very dark syrup which tastes like sorghum or blackstrap molasses. It is used like molasses. Try the *Coasting Cookies* recipe at the beginning of the COOKIES section, using birch syrup. Incidentally, black birch twigs and inner bark have the flavor of wintergreen and can be used for making tea.

## MAKING MAPLE SUGAR

To make maple sugar, maple syrup is boiled till the sugar content becomes high enough for it to solidify when cooled. Use a candy thermometer or the familiar soft, medium, and hard ball candy test to check for sugar content. To make plain maple sugar for cooking use syrup alone, but many kinds of fancy maple candy can be made using other ingredients. Recipes for these are included in books and pamphlets on maple syrup production.

For plain maple sugar, boil the syrup till it reaches 28–30°F above the boiling point of water (242°F at sea level), or till a hard ball forms when a little is dropped in ice water. Watch the syrup closely to prevent burning or boiling over. If it threatens to boil over add a tiny bit

---

### MAPLE IDEAS

**Jack Wax**   To make this traditional treat, boil maple sap till it reaches the soft ball stage, or till it is about 20°F above the local boiling point of water. Then, pour it boiling hot on clean snow or crushed ice. Scoop it up with a fork and eat it right away. Some people like this with dill pickles.

**Maple Sugar Pinwheels**   Roll out biscuit dough to make a sheet about ¼ to ½ inch thick. Spread with melted butter and sprinkle with maple sugar shavings. Add chopped nuts or seeds, raisins or other dried fruits, and spices, if they are liked. Make a roll starting with the long side of the rectangle of dough. Turn the roll so that the seam side is down, and slice across it to make ½ inch thick pinwheel biscuits. Put them on an ungreased baking sheet, and bake like regular biscuits.

### MAPLE IDEAS, *cont.*

**Maple Syrup as a Sweet Sauce**

Maple syrup is delicious over cereals, puddings, ice cream and fresh fruits. Try a little on hot cereal for breakfast, or over steamed puddings, or bread pudding. It goes well with most kinds of fresh berries, sliced peaches, and many other fruits. Try marinating strawberries in maple syrup for a few hours. They are a real treat.

For an especially rich, warm sauce, melt a few tablespoons of butter in hot maple syrup and add some chopped nuts. Together with pancakes this makes a superb Sunday breakfast.

of butter to calm it down. When it has boiled enough, take the syrup off the stove and let it sit for a few minutes, till it cools to about 155°F. Then beat it with a wooden spoon till it begins to thicken. Have ready a buttered, shallow dish or other mold and immediately pour in the maple sugar, before it can set in the pot. For many small pieces of sugar, use buttered muffin tins for molds, and take the sugar out when it is hard. If it sticks, heat the bottom of the mold slightly to loosen it.

Store maple sugar in airtight containers, as it can absorb moisture from the air and ferment or mold if left exposed. For extended storage it can be refrigerated or frozen.

This maple sugar will be very hard, and must be grated or crushed for most uses. Small amounts can be shaved off with a knife.

## MAPLE RECIPES

### Nasty Pudding
(Makes about 6 dessert servings.)

2 cups wholewheat flour
2 teaspoons baking powder
1 cup (about) milk
½ cup butter, melted

¼ – ½ cup raisins, chopped nuts, or seeds, optional
1 cup maple syrup

Mix the flour and baking powder. Stir in the milk and melted butter, adding a little more milk if necessary to make a smooth, thick batter. Spread in an 8 or 9 inch square or round buttered baking pan. Sprinkle with raisins, nuts, or seeds, if desired. Bring the maple syrup and ½ cup water to a boil and pour over the pudding batter. Bake in a medium oven, 350°F, for 35 to 40 minutes. Dish out with a spoon (as it's too nasty to slice!) and serve with milk or cream.

### Maple Wine
(Makes about 1 gallon)

1 gallon plus 1¼ cups maple sap
1 quart plus 2 tablespoons maple syrup

1 teaspoon baking yeast
2 oranges and 2 lemons, or 4 oranges

Bring 1¼ cups sap to a boil and add 2 tablespoons syrup. Cool to lukewarm and add the yeast. Put in a clean bottle, plug the top with cotton, and let sit 24 hours.

Next day squeeze the oranges and lemons, reserving the juice. Boil the peels in the gallon of sap for 20 minutes. Pour in a crock or other container, along with the maple syrup. Cool to room temperature and add the reserved juice and the yeast mixture. Ferment and finish the wine according to the directions in the WINE section.

"I F IT IS NOT IN YOUR POWER TO KEEP MEAT IN AN ICE HOUSE, IN summer, keep it in a cool dark cellar, wrapped around with wet cloths, on top of which lay boughs of elderberry. The evaporation from the cloth will keep the meat cool and the elderberry will keep off insects.

If you should unfortunately be obliged to use stale meat or poultry rub it in and out with soda before washing it."

*Housekeeping in Old Virginia,* Marion Cabell Tyree, 1879

In the last hundred years enormous changes have taken place in meat storing techniques. With refrigerators and freezers storage is easier and retention of quality is better for meats than for most other fresh foods. Modern worries are not about keeping meat fresh, but about the feed and additives used to raise commercial meat animals, and about the processing of meat before it reaches the store. In addition, there is concern about how much meat is appropriate for a healthful diet.

Meat is an excellent, high quality, protein food, containing vitamins and minerals not easily available from other sources. However, there can be too much of a good thing, and it is possible to get in the habit of eating too much meat. If a person's stomach is always full of meat there is not room for enough whole grains, vegetables, and other essential foods, and the diet becomes unbalanced.

Though this is not the place to assess modern methods for raising and processing meat, the fact is many people believe that meat sold in stores rarely tastes as good as meat from animals home raised on natural feeds. Anyone who has had the good fortune to eat naturally raised beef, pork, or chicken cannot doubt its better flavor and texture, and the difference is often startling. The meat of one hundred years ago, kept fresh with wet cloths and elderberry boughs, may well have been better tasting than most of the meat sold today.

Some people are finding it practical to raise their own meat animals. Others buy meat from people who raise animals with as much home grown or natural feed as possible. Hunting is another way to obtain some excellent meat. (Refer to WILD MEATS, in the WILD FOODS section.) For information on butchering and cutting meat refer to sections on specific meat animals, particularly the CHICKEN, LAMB, and RABBIT sections.

## HANDLING MEAT

*Aging* Beef, older lamb or mutton, venison, and a few other meats are improved by a period of seasoning or aging. Pork, veal, young lamb, and meat from any other young animal will not need aging, but will be ready to eat as soon as the carcass has cooled after the animal

---

**STORAGE**

**Canning** Refer to CANNING section, and the FOOD STORAGE sections for specific meats.

**Cold Storage** See AGING MEAT, MEAT STORED IN FAT, and MINCEMEAT, below.

**Drying** Refer to DRYING section.

**Freezing** Refer to FREEZING section.

**Salt Curing** Refer to SALT CURING, and see HAM AND BACON section.

is slaughtered. Meats that benefit from aging become more tender and juicy, and darker in color, and their flavor improves due to the natural action of enzymes and other ripening agents. (However, not all like the flavor of aged meat.)

Modern innovations have made the aging of meat less important than it once was. Aging will not be necessary if meat is to be frozen, since after a month in the freezer there is no discernible difference between aged meat and meat frozen the day after butchering. (Meat can also be tenderized with the enzyme papain.)

***Naturally Aged Meat*** Sides or quarters of beef, older lamb, mutton, and venison should be neatly trimmed. Whole, cleaned deer can be aged with the hide on. Avoid making gashes or cuts in the meat. Never wash the meat because contact with water promotes spoilage. Hang the meat in a meat cooler or other cool place. If the animal is butchered in cool, fall weather the meat can be hung in an outbuilding, but changes in temperature must be watched. Ideally, the temperature should be 34 to 36°F, but above freezing and below 40°F will be adequate. Even a few days' aging improves meat, but 10 days to 2 weeks is still better. Beef can be aged for as long as 6 weeks.

Before mechanical refrigeration, aging was a way of preserving fresh meat for a few extra weeks as well as for improving its flavor. If a quarter or side of lean meat was hung in a dry, cool airy place for long enough, it would develop a leathery rind that protected it up to 6 weeks, possibly longer. The meat for each meal would be cut off when it was needed and the quarter or side rehung. The leathery rind would be trimmed off and fed to the dog, while the family would enjoy the tender, well aged meat. In a humid climate, an unheated attic might be dry and cool enough to allow a rind to form. If not, the meat would become slimy or moldy on the outside, yet it still might be trimmed down to good meat underneath.

***Aging Game Birds*** There is a tradition of aging game birds to achieve a "high" flavor, much appreciated by some. The birds are not plucked or cleaned, but simply hung by the head or the feet in the same kind of cool place used for aging other meat. They are left hanging until just before they begin to spoil, for up to 10 days, and then are plucked, and cleaned for cooking.

## PRESERVING MEAT IN RENDERED FAT

An old but effective way to preserve meat is to cook it and pack it in crocks, surrounded and covered with rendered fat. The covered crocks are kept in a cellar, or other cool place (below 45°F). Fatty meats like pork are most often kept in this way, since fat can be rendered from the same animal that supplied the meat. In places where geese are force fed to fatten them, their meat is often preserved in their fat. In the Middle East, sheep are sometimes force fed to fatten them for the same purpose. In India the same principle is used with olive oil instead of fat covering cooked, highly seasoned meats of several kinds. Often the meat is deep fried in the same fat used for storing it.

For this method to succeed, the meat must be cooked till well done, and the fat rendered completely with no moisture remaining in it. (Refer to RENDERING FAT, in the LARD section.) The crock must be tightly and carefully packed, to exclude air or oxygen. If prepared in the fall, and kept at temperatures below 45°F, the meat should keep until spring.

***Preserving Meat in Lard*** Cook any meat as it would be cooked for serving, making sure that it is well done. Pork chops, sausage patties, and even roasts can be prepared this way. Scald a crock with boiling water and let it dry completely. Put in a layer of hot, cooked meat without packing it too tightly. The lard must be able to run into all of the spaces around the meat. Pour in hot, melted lard, add another layer of meat, and more lard, until the crock is full. There must be enough lard to completely cover all of the meat with a layer of pure lard on top. Cover the crock tightly, and store at a temperature between freezing and 45°F. A sheet of aluminum foil could be tied or rubber banded in place under the crock lid. If stored in a root cellar or other damp place the cover must keep out moisture. For substitutes for crocks refer to the KITCHEN UTENSILS section.

When taking a portion of meat out of the crock, cover the remainder well with lard. If necessary, melt more lard to be poured in.

## USING BLOODY OR BRUISED MEAT

Meat that is bloody or bruised because of a bullet wound or rough handling during the slaughter, and meat with a blood residue from incomplete bleeding is useable. Cut out any areas showing old bruises, and partly healed wounds, and discard them.

Bloody and bruised meat spoils sooner and looks less appealing than ordinary meat, but there is nothing wrong with its food value, as the blood adds nutrients. Grinding the meat for hamburger lets the extra redness improve the appearance, and is a good way to use it. Cut the meat into pieces, and wash it in cold water, checking for bone fragments if it comes from the area of a bullet wound. Grind and freeze it immediately, or refrigerate it for use in the next day or so. This ground meat will taste as good as any other.

Another way to handle bloody meat is to soak it for several hours or overnight in several changes of cold water. While this will remove blood, it also removes flavor and nutrients. Because of the contact with water this meat must also be cooked or frozen without delay.

## USING TOUGH MEAT

When animals are home raised there will be tough meat to cook from time to time, usually from older, culled animals. Hunters may also bring in older animals with tough meat. Tough meat can be recognized when the carcass is cut by its firmness, by hard to separate joints, and by noticeable sinew and gristle that is hard to cut through. As well, the cross sections of bone in an older animal are white and flinty, while in a young animal they are red and porous.

Tough meat does have some advantages. It is more flavorful and makes better soups or stews than tender meat. In stews, or canned, it will hold its shape and texture. It cannot, however, be successfully roasted with dry heat, or fried, or broiled, unless it has first been ground or pounded. Tough meat is best cooked at low temperatures, since high heat causes it to shrink and become stringy and dry. Pressure cooking is sometimes recommended to tenderize tough meat. The high heat first toughens the meat even more, and then, with continued cooking, softens it. In the process the meat shrinks, and may stay stringy even after it has softened. If a comparison is made, most people find they prefer the flavor and texture of meat stewed slowly at a temperature below a boil for many hours over the same meat pressure cooked.

### Dealing with Moderately Tough Meat
• Slice very thinly across the grain. This cuts through long fibers, making them less noticeable. Raw meat can be thinly sliced as for stir-frying, or cooked meat can be thinly sliced as when serving roasts or pot roasts.
• Before cooking, pound steaks or chops with a mallet, or with the blunt edge of a heavy knife, to break up and tenderize fibers.
• Marinate the meat for several hours before cooking it. A marinade containing vinegar, wine, or another acidic ingredient is the most effective.
• Steam or stew the meat over low heat for part of the cooking time. Steaks and chops can be quickly seared at high heat, and then simmered, covered with a few tablespoons of liquid, until tender, keeping the temperature below a boil.
• Grind the meat for hamburger or sausage.

### Measures for Very Tough Meat
• Simmer, stew, or pot roast all day, or as long as is necessary, keeping the temperature below a boil. 180°F is ideal. Use a trivet or an insulated pad if necessary to control the heat. The top of a wood burning heating stove is often practical for this kind of cooking. Including tomatoes or another acidic ingredient will help tenderize the meat.
• When meat remains tough or stringy even after long cooking, grind it or mince it, cutting across the grain and use in casseroles, hash, and sausage type mixtures.
• Marinate meat from 24 hours up to several days in a mixture including vinegar, or wine, or another acidic ingredient. Keep in a cool place and turn the meat every so often. (Refer to the MARINADE FOR TOUGH MEAT, in the *Barbecued Chevon* recipe, in the CHEVON section.)
• If meat from an old and scrawny animal remains tough and stringy

in spite of all treatments, treat it as if it were a soup bone, and use it in soup stock. The dog might enjoy wrestling the leathery left-overs.

## GRINDING MEAT

It is quite possible to chop or mince meat for hamburger by hand. The meat's texture will be excellent, but most people have neither the time nor the patience for this approach. Both hand-turned and electric meat grinders will grind good textured meat if they have a sharp blade or cutting knife, and a chopper plate with sharp-edged holes. If these parts are dull the meat will be pushed through by the auger, coming out in strings, with the juice crushed out, and the meat is likely to be dry, stringy, or tough after cooking. New blades and plates can be ordered for meat grinders of standard makes and sizes. It is helpful to have several plates, with holes of different sizes for grinding coarsely or more finely. Coarsely ground meat will have a loose texture, while finely ground meat will be more dense and compact.

Raw meat grinds most easily when cold. For a fine texture it is best to grind the meat first with a coarse blade, and then again with a fine blade, but grinding several times with a coarse blade will also make a reasonably fine texture. If the meat warms up very much during the first grinding chill it before grinding it again.

Take apart and clean the meat grinder immediately after using it, so that bits of meat do not harden and stick in difficult to reach places. Make sure that the parts are completely dry before putting them away, as otherwise they may rust. Setting them on the warm top of a wood burning stove for a few minutes is one sure way to dry them.

## COOKING MEAT

Cooking store bought meat which is often quite fatty and tender to the point of bland, watery mushiness, is not the same as cooking the firmer, leaner, more flavorful meat of home raised animals. Store bought meats seem best when cooked quickly at a fairly high temperature, perhaps because this seals in whatever flavor is present. Home raised meats benefit from longer cooking at lower temperatures. If the meat is lean a low temperature is essential.

***Lean Meat*** Without the protection and insulation of fat around and through it, lean meat cooks faster than fatty meat and cannot withstand high temperatures. If cooked too long, or with high heat, lean meat will dry out and toughen no matter how tender it may have been.

To remain tender, very lean, delicate meats like liver and kidneys must be cooked briefly and at low temperatures. Other very lean meats, like rabbit and meat from baby animals, may be cooked longer but still at low temperatures. An exception is when quickly searing the outside of the meat over high heat but then care must be taken to lower the heat or remove the meat from the fire before it overcooks. Actual cooking time will vary with the meat's thickness. Thinly sliced, lean, tender meat can be stir-fried in as little as one minute. Sautéeing or broiling medium thick slices may take from 2 to 5 minutes per side, while stewing or roasting larger chunks may take from 30 to 60 minutes. Lean, tough meat can be stewed for as long as necessary to make it tender, at about 180°F.

Another way to handle lean meat is to add fat to it, but then the advantages of a nutritious low fat food are lost. Bacon, salt pork, caul fat or other fat can be laid over lean meat or wrapped around it before it is cooked. Or it can be larded by poking strips of fat into slits in the meat or running through it with a larding needle. The meat can then be cooked at normal temperature.

## MEAT RECIPES

**Chinese Master Sauce for**
**Red-Cooking Meat**                              (Makes about 2½ quarts.)

This master sauce is a soy sauce mixture used for stewing varioius meats. It is saved and reused again and again, becoming richer and more delicious with each use. Any kind of meat can be stewed in it, whether it is tough, tender, lean, or fatty, including organ meats, and wild game, as well as beef, lamb, pork, and poultry.

After red-cooking, the meat can be served hot or cold, or used in stir-fries, fried rice (refer to the STIR-FRYING and RICE sections) and in school lunch sandwiches. Kids love it!

*1 cup soy sauce*
*2 quarts (about) water*
*Optional flavorings:*
   *1 cup sherry, or white wine*
   *2−4 tablespoons honey, or*
     *other sweetening*
   *2 scallions, in pieces*
   *1 or more cloves garlic, crushed*

*1−2 slices fresh ginger root*
*1 teaspoon whole peppercorns*
*½ teaspoon anise seeds, or*
   *star anise*
*meat, up to 4 pounds* (One large chunk, or in serving size pieces.)

To start the master sauce, combine the soy sauce, water, and optional flavorings in a large pot. Bring to a boil, then add meat. If the liquid does not cover the meat, add extra water, as needed. Cover and simmer, turning the meat occasionally to flavor and color it evenly. Cook till tender. The time will vary from about 30 minutes to 2 or more hours, depending on toughness. Remove the meat and serve immediately, or cool and use in Western or Chinese dishes.

To save the sauce, strain, chill, and remove any congealed fat. Store in the refrigerator and use about once a week, or freeze for less frequent use. Add water, as necessary, when using it, and after every second or third use, or when the sauce appears weak, add ¼ cup soy sauce, and optional flavorings, to taste.

### Old Fashioned Mincemeat (Makes 8–10 quarts.)

Old fashioned mincemeat will keep for months in crocks or jars in a cool place, because of its large sugar and acidic content. The brandy also helps. There are many variations, but basically mincemeats are made up of about equal weights of lean meat and dried or candied fruit, together with ¾ the meat's weight in sugar, and ¼ to ½ its weight in suet. Chopped apples equal to the weight of the meat are often added as well. Apple cider, a little vinegar, molasses, and orange or lemon rind and juice, may be added as flavorings, and the mixture may be spiced with cinnamon, cloves, allspice, and nutmeg. Brandy, and sometimes whiskey or sherry are added at the end. If the basic proportions are followed, mincemeat can be made to suit personal tastes, using any readily available ingredients. If it should become too strongly flavored, mix in chopped apple before cooking it. (For a meatless version, refer to the *Green Tomato Mincemeat* recipe in the TOMATOES, GREEN section.)

As well as a filling for pies, mincemeat is very good added to cookies and muffins, used as stuffing for baked apples, and substituted for fruit in any appropriate dessert. This mincemeat recipe is a rich version that has to be stored for several weeks before reaching its full flavor. Traditionally, it was made around Thanksgiving to be used in Christmas pies.

2 *pounds lean meat* (Beef, beef heart, beef tongue, or any red meat.)
½ *pound suet, minced or coarsely ground*
2 *pounds apples, cored, and minced without peeling*
1½ *pounds raisins*
1 *pound currants*
½ *pound candied fruit* (Citron, orange and lemon peel are good, preferable homemade. Refer to *Candied Peel* in the FRUITS section.)

1½ *pounds brown sugar*
1½ *teaspoons each cloves, allspice, mace, and nutmeg*
1 *tablespoon cinnamon*
1½ *teaspoons salt, optional*
1 *orange, juice and grated rind*
2 *cups apple cider boiled down from 4 cups, or 2 cups sherry*
2 *cups brandy*

The day before making the mincemeat, cook the meat in water to cover till it is tender. (Reserve the broth for another use.) Cool the meat and chop or grind it coarsely. It can be chopped or ground with the suet. Mix all ingredients well, except the sherry if used and the brandy. Pack in a crock or similar container, and pour sherry and brandy on top. Close the crock tightly and store in a cold place, below 40°F. Wait 3 to 4 weeks before using, and use up within 2 to 3 months.

Serve pies, desserts and baked goods made from mincemeat warm so the suet is melted.

***Mincemeat in Jars*** Use cider or other fruit juice instead of sherry,

## OTHER BASIC MEAT PREPARATIONS

Bones for Flavoring, p. 58
Browned Potato Hash, p. 494
Gelatine Glazes, p. 300
Farmer's Meat Loaf, p. 396
Preparing Meat for Stir-frying, p. 613
Sausage Recipes, p. 551
Salt Curing Meat, Poultry, and Fish, p. 538

and replace brown sugar with honey, or another sweetener, if desired. Combine the cooked, ground meat and all other ingredients, except brandy, in a large pot. Simmer, uncovered, 1–1½ hours, stirring often. Pour boiling hot in sterilized, hot jars, add 2 or 3 tablespoons brandy to each jar, then close tightly. Keep the jars in a cold place, at about 40°F, and use within 3 or 4 months.

This version is ideal for distinctively flavored meats, such as mutton, venison, and other game meats, as the additional cooking blends flavors more completely. If the meat has a very strong flavor, add ½ cup vinegar to the ingredients. Suet from these meats can be used instead of beef suet if its taste is mild.

Both mincemeat versions can be used in the same ways. Do not miss trying them in tarts, or in muffins instead of raisins.

# MELONS

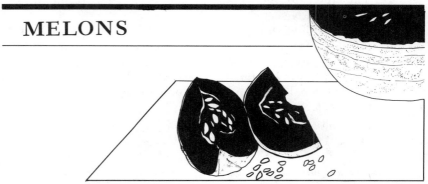

D OWN THROUGH THE CENTURIES THERE HAVE BEEN SO MANY varieties and variations of varieties of melons that it would be impossible even to begin to evaluate them all. The melons best known in western countries are sweet fruits, delicious eaten fresh, but in China and other Asian countries, some melons are prepared as a vegetable, and a few varieties are grown for their seeds which are dried and eaten like nuts. Melons that are used as vegetables may be cut in pieces and stir-fried, or added to soups and stews. They taste something like cucumber or the white part of watermelon rind.

Sweet melons can be loosely divided into three groups: cantaloupes and muskmelons; honeydews, Persians, and casabas (sometimes called winter melons because they keep well); and watermelons. As watermelons have a different structure from other melons they are used somewhat differently. (Refer to the WATERMELON section.)

## HANDLING MELONS

Do not pick melons until they are completely ripe, as they do not gain sweetness after harvest. It is easy to tell when cantaloupes and muskmelons are ripe because they slip or separate from their stems by themselves. When a crack shows around the stem where it connects

## STORAGE

**Canning**   Not feasible unless pickled. (Refer to *Spiced Pickled Fruit*, in PICKLING section.)

**Cold Storage**   Honeydews, Persians, casabas only. Storage life 1–2 months in root cellar. (Refer to COLD STORAGE section.)

**Drying**   Slice thinly. Dry to leathery. (Refer to DRYING section.)

**Freezing**   Cut slices, cubes, or balls. Package plain, or in juice or syrup. Best eaten when partly thawed. (Refer to FREEZING section.)

to the fruit the melon can be picked. Melons that do not separate can be judged for their ripeness by their color, their smell, and a slight softness when pressed at their stem end. Once picked, melons will develop a richer flavor if kept for a day or two in a warm place, and afterwards will keep best in a cool, humid place. Cantaloupes and muskmelons should be eaten within a week or so. Others may keep from several weeks up to 2 months. However, melons are best as a fresh fruit, and something is lost when they are preserved for long storage, no matter which method is used. After freezing they will lose texture and are best eaten before they thaw completely. Dried melon has a sweet, odd flavor that only some people like. Melon juice and purée is best when mixed with lemon juice or another tart juice. (Refer to COMBINING SWEET AND TART FRUITS, in the FRUITS section.) Use melons caught by the weather before they ripen completely for pickling. (Refer to the *Spiced Pickled Fruit* recipe, in the PICKLING section.)

**Melon Seeds** Melon seeds are as nutritious and flavorful as pumpkin or sunflower seeds, but are too small to shell successfully. Some, which have very thin shells, can be dried or roasted, shells and all, and eaten as a snack. Otherwise, the seeds can be ground with water, then strained to make a "milk" to be used like coconut milk, or see the *Melon Seed Drink* recipe below.


## MELON RECIPES

**Marinated Melon Salad**     (Makes about 6 side servings.)

1 honeydew, large cantaloupe, or
    other melon, seeded, peeled and
    sliced medium
2–3 tablespoons parsley, minced
1 scallion, or small onion, minced
6 tablespoons oil (Olive, or a nut
    oil, such as walnut, are su-
    perb.)
3 tablespoons lemon juice
½ teaspoon prepared mustard, or
    crushed mustard seeds
½ teaspoon freshly ground black
    pepper, or to taste (It should
    taste peppery.)
½ teaspoon fresh herbs, minced
    (Try savory, tarragon,
    rosemary, thyme.)
¼ teaspoon salt, optional
lettuce leaves, as needed to line
    bowls

Mix the melon slices with the parsley and onion. Combine the oil, lemon juice, mustard, pepper, herbs, and salt, if desired, in a jar, shake well, and pour over the melon. Cover and let marinate in a cool place for several hours. Stir once or twice. Arrange lettuce leaves in a large bowl, or in individual salad bowls, and add the melon. A little minced parsley or other garnish can be sprinkled on top, if desired.

**Cantaloupe Cucumber Salad** Instead of one melon, use a medium cantaloup and a cucumber to make this salad. The color combination is very attractive.

## MELON IDEAS

**Melon Appetizers** A section of melon with a sprinkle of lemon or lime juice makes a refreshing appetizer or first course. If a paper thin slice of ham is laid on the melon it is deliciously elegant as well.

**Melon Mixers** Though fresh, ripe melon is perfectly delicious unenhanced, it is fun to mix with other fruits and flavorings. Cherries, or chopped orange, grapefruit, or pineapple intermingle pleasantly. Add a sprinkle of minced mint leaf, nutmeg, powdered coriander seed, or grated fresh ginger for distinction. Some find that a dash of sweet wine or liqueur makes the mixture irresistible.

## STORAGE

**Cold Storage** Refer to CHEESE, AGED section.

**Freezing** Pasteurized skim milk is best. Flakes separate from cream and do not remix. Quality retained 4–5 months. (Refer to FREEZING section.)

## *Curried Cantaloupe*                    (Makes about 6 side servings.)

| | |
|---|---|
| 2 tablespoons oil | 1–2 teaspoons curry powder |
| 1 small onion, minced | 3 cups cantaloupe or other |
| 1 fresh, hot pepper, minced, or other | melon, cut in cubes or balls |
| hot pepper, to taste | juice of 1 lemon |
| ½ teaspoon fresh ginger root, | 1 tablespoon honey |
| minced, optional | |

Heat a heavy pan or wok and add the oil. Fry the onion, pepper, and ginger root for about 5 minutes, stirring often. Stir in the curry powder. Put on high heat and add the cantaloupe. Stir-fry for 1 minute. Reduce heat and add the lemon juice and honey. Cover and simmer for 2 or 3 minutes, till the cantaloupe is heated through. Amounts of lemon juice and honey can be adjusted to taste.

This curry is very good served hot with rice or as a cold side dish.

*Cantaloupe Curry with Yogurt* When the curry has cooled stir in ½ to 1 cup yogurt. Serve cold as a refreshing summer soup or side dish.

## *Melon Seed Drink*                    (Makes 4–5 glasses.)

| | |
|---|---|
| 1 cup melon seeds, separated from | tiny sliver of rind from a lemon |
| pulp and fibers | or lime |
| 2 tablespoons honey, or to taste | a few almonds, optional |

Put all ingredients in a blender with a cup or so of water, and blend till smooth. Add 4 to 5 cups of water to the seed purée and let sit for half a day. Strain into a bowl through a damp cloth. Gather the edges of the cloth and twist and squeeze to get as much milk out of the seeds as possible. Chill, or serve over ice. The smooth, mysterious, almost haunting quality of this beverage (with or without a hint of almond), makes it a summertime favorite with young and old.

# MILK

## MILK PRODUCTS IN OTHER SECTIONS

```
                        MILK
        ┌───────────────┼───────────────┐
   COLOSTRUM                          YOGURT
        ┌───────┴───────┐       ┌───────┴───────┐
      Curds          WHEY    Skim Milk        CREAM
        ┌───────┬───────┐               ┌───────┴───────┐
CHEESE, AGED  CHEESE, FRESH          BUTTER        Buttermilk
```

I N MANY AREAS OF THE WORLD, MILK IS CONSIDERED STRICTLY A FOOD for babies. In fact, among racial groups whose heritage does not include the keeping of dairy animals, most individuals cannot digest milk after childhood because their systems lack the necessary enzymes. In North America and much of Europe, however, milk is an accepted, important food for people of all ages. It is the only reliable source of calcium in many peopole's diets, and a good source of protein and vitamins as well.

To the general public, "milk" means cow's milk, but to those who raise their own dairy animals milk is just as apt to mean goat's milk. In various far-flung places sheep, reindeer, water buffalo, camels, and mares are also valued for their milk. No doubt, the milk of any mammal would be a good food if it could be easily obtained.

The milk from animals of different species differs in composition. There are even differences in the milk of individual animals of the same breed, but the basic ways of using milk will be the same. The difference between milk straight from a healthy dairy animal and milk from plasticized store cartons is very great. Those with a milk cow or with milk goats share the satisfaction of drinking truly good, truly fresh milk. Those who cannot keep a dairy animal of their own can (where sales are not restricted) obtain milk from someone who does, and have a share of the goodness.

## COW'S AND GOAT'S MILK COMPARED

Comparing the flavors of cow's and goat's milk can quickly lead to disagreement. Some will argue that there is no difference, others will say that one or the other is better, and somone may unfairly berate goat's milk because he or she once had some that was strong tasting. Though it is true that goat's milk can taste strong in some circumstances, cow's milk can too, if the cow has been eating the wrong weeds. A strong taste is less likely in cow's milk, partly because the breeding and raising of dairy cows, and the handling of the milk is so standardized. However, anyone can have good tasting goat's milk by following reliable guides for keeping goats and handling their milk.

The main difference between cow's and goat's milk is in the cream. Cream in cow's milk occurs in large particles or fat globules that rise to the surface after the milk sits for awhile. The cream in goat's milk occurs in small particles which do not readily rise. (Refer to the instructions for separating cream from milk, in the CREAM section.)

When being made into yogurt, cheese, or custard, goat's milk will usually not set or clabber as quickly or firmly as cow's milk. To counter this, goat's milk can be left to incubate longer when a culture is mixed with it, and an extra egg can be added to custards.

## MILK: RAW AND PASTEURIZED

Raw milk is milk fresh from the dairy animal, unheated and untreated. Pasteurized milk has been heated to a temperature high enough to kill any harmful bacteria in it. Milk is easily pasteurized at home, and must be done, according to recent findings, even where there is no doubt about the healthfulness of the dairy animal or the cleanliness of the milk. Cream will rise on pasteurized cow's milk exactly as it does on raw milk. Homogenization breaks up the fat globules in the milk, creating tiny particles that remain evenly distributed instead of rising. Goat's milk has been described as naturally homogenized.

Milk cannot be homogenized at home, nor is there any reason for doing it. Most people with their own cow's milk find it a luxury to be able to skim off a little cream or top milk whenever they are needed.

## ENSURING SAFE, HIGH QUALITY
## HOME PRODUCED MILK

If the following safeguards are followed, the resulting milk should be safe to use.
• Make sure dairy animals are healthy.
• When milking, have scrupulously clean hands and clean milking utensils. Wash the dairy animal's udder before milking, preferably with one of the commercial disinfectant preparations intended for that purpose.
• Discard the first squirt of milk from a teat in case it is not completely clean.
• As soon as milking is finished, strain the milk through a commercial filter for this purpose, and chill as quickly as possible. The fastest method is to set containers of milk in a large pan of ice cold water, stirring occasionally, and changing the water when it begins to warm. A cold spring or stream will serve instead of the pan if one is close by. Refrigerate the milk as soon as it is cool. A small quantity of milk may cool quickly enough if put in the refrigerator immediately, or put milk in the freezer for half an hour, and then transfer it to the refrigerator.
• Before washing them in hot or scalding water, rinse milk buckets and other utensils in cold water, as soon as possible after milking. Hot water can harden milk deposits in difficult to reach places where they will be almost impossible to remove.
• Be especially strict with cleanliness during hot weather, when spoilage organisms are rampant.
• If milk is stored in glass containers, keep them out of the light, as light destroys riboflavin (Vitamin B2).
• Those who use home produced milk should consider supplements of Vitamin D, especially for children during the winter months. It is necessary for the body's absorption of calcium, and added to all commercially produced milk.

# HANDLING MILK

***Using Raw Milk***   Many prefer the taste of raw milk to that of pasteurized milk, find it far superior to homogenized milk, and, where dairy animals are healthy and high standards of cleanliness are maintained, have used it for a lifetime in perfect health. However, serious consideration must be given to recent studies holding raw milk responsible for assorted bacterial infections. Also, new bacteria may be introduced into the dairy animals and cause illness. The young and old are especially susceptible, and their symptoms may be more serious. Often, people who drink raw milk regularly are immune to these infections, but they also carry the pathogens and may unwittingly transfer them, causing illness in others. For this reason, some raw milk devotees have, reluctantly, begun pasteurizing home raised milk. The taste is still very good, and there is still the pleasure of cooking with raw milk for the special, full flavor it gives to custards, cream sauces, creamed soups, and other milk dishes. The important nutritional values of milk are not changed when milk is pasteurized.

If raw milk is to be stored, it must be quickly chilled after milking and then kept cold. It will soon spoil if alternately warmed and chilled, as when taken out of the refrigerator for use and not promptly returned. When carefully chilled and refrigerated it will stay fresh for up to a week. However, some raw goat's milk may develop a strong taste after only 3 or 4 days and should either be used or pasteurized within that time.

***Pasteurizing Milk***   (Cream is pasteurized in the same way as whole and skim milk.) There are two procedures for pasteurizing milk. Either heat the milk to 145°F, and hold it there for 30 minutes, or heat it to 166°F, then uncover and chill. For best flavor chill the milk quickly after either procedure. Milk for drinking is usually pasteurized the first way, with the lower temperature. Special pasteurizers can be purchased to do the job automatically. If pasteurizing in a pot on the stove with a dairy thermometer, it is much easier to bring the milk to 166°F than to maintain the lower temperature for 30 minutes. Use a heavy pot over low even heat or a double boiler. Or set the pot with the milk in it in another larger pot of hot water, if a regular double boiler is not available. Stir the milk often so that it heats evenly, and does not stick to the pot. The quickest way to chill milk after pasteurizing is to set it in a large container of ice cold water, changing the water when it warms up.

After pasteurizing, refrigerated milk should keep from 1 week to 10 days. For sour milk a culture must be added. (Refer to the BUTTER and the YOGURT sections.)

***Scalding Milk***   Like pasteurizing, scalding destroys unwanted organisms in milk, but a thermometer is not necessary. To scald, heat the milk till it steams, showing tiny bubbles around the edge of the pan, which happens between 180° and 200°F. Raw milk can be scalded for use in cooking, and before making yogurt or some kinds of cheeses, but is not as good for drinking as is carefully pasteurized milk, because of its flat, cooked taste.

***Souring Milk***   To make pasteurized milk pleasantly sour, a culture must be added. Pasteurized milk left at room temperature will spoil rather than clabber like raw milk, since the necessary bacteria are destroyed by the high heat. The missing bacteria can be replaced by buttermilk (¼ to ½ cup cultured buttermilk per quart). Or a yogurt culture (about 2 tablespoons of fresh yogurt per quart, or dried yogurt culture according to directions) can be used. The best temperature range for the milk is 85 to 100°F. Milk can also be soured by adding 1 tablespoon of lemon juice or vinegar to one cup (minus 1 tablespoon) of milk, but this will give a different kind of sour flavor. As it sours, the milk will thicken, and some clear whey may separate from it. The cream from whole cow's milk will rise and form a thick layer on top that can be lifted off to use as sour cream in cooking or for making butter. The sour skimmed milk can be made into cottage cheese. (Refer to SOURING OR RIPENING CREAM FOR BUTTER, in the BUTTER section.) Lightly soured milk was once a popular dessert. (Refer to *Bonny-Clabber,* at the beginning of the CHEESE, FRESH section.)

## LONG TERM MILK STORAGE

People who keep a cow, or one or two goats for milk for themselves are likely sometimes to have too much milk, and not enough at other times. However, there are few practical ways to preserve extra milk. Home canning does not yield satisfactory results. Making powdered milk at home is not possible. Milk can be frozen for drinking later, though, and best quality will be obtained if 1 quart quantities are used, so freezing is quick. (Refer to EVAPORATING MILK, below.) In the end, the best ways to use up extra milk are still the traditional ones: making aged cheeses, or butter and fresh cheeses, both of which can be frozen, or feeding it to livestock.

## MILK RECIPES

These are all basic recipes from which many other interesting dishes can be created.

***Cream Sauce***                                                              (Makes about 2 cups.)

A cream or white sauce, is the base for all kinds of flavorful sauces, creamed dishes, and creamed soups. The variations below show some of the possibilities.

*3 tablespoons butter, oil, or other fat*  
*3–4 tablespoons flour* (Unbleached, whole wheat, rice or oat flour are all good.)

*2 cups (about) milk*  
*pepper, salt, optional*

Melt the butter or oil in a heavy saucepan over low heat. Stir in the flour and cook, stirring, for 3 or 4 minutes. Add the milk gradually, stirring constantly till it thickens. Simmer uncovered, stirring often, for 5 to 10 minutes, and season to taste.

The thickness of the sauce will depend on the kind and amount of flour and the amount of milk added. Add more milk if the sauce is too thick, but the flavor will be off if more flour is added in an attempt to make it thicker.

**Savory White Sauce**   Mince a small onion and small amounts of other vegetables, to taste, such as green pepper, celery, and parsley. Sauté the vegetables for 2 or 3 minutes in the butter or oil before adding the flour. When the milk is added, also add some celery seeds, or other herb seeds and herbs to taste.

**Brown Sauce (Roux)**   Add flour to butter or oil, as for the cream sauce, but continue cooking the mixture over low heat, stirring almost constantly till it turns a rich brown color. Cook slowly, for 10 to 15 minutes to avoid a burned taste. A little minced onion can be sautéed in the butter or oil before the flour is added, if desired. Soup stock or water can be used instead of part or all of the milk. A gravy can be made in this way when pan drippings are not available.

**Cheese Sauce**   Prepare cream sauce or savory white sauce, omitting salt. When it has simmered for 5 minutes, add 1 cup diced or grated cheese. Remove pan from the stove and stir till the cheese has melted and is completely blended in. Use immediately. Very good over toast, potatoes, and many kinds of steamed vegetables.

### Smooth Milk Pudding   (Makes about 6 dessert servings.)

| | |
|---|---|
| 6 level tablespoons wholewheat, pastry or unbleached flour, cornstarch, potato starch, rice flour or other flour | 2 eggs |
| | 4 cups milk |
| | 1 teaspoon vanilla, or other flavoring, to taste, optional |
| ¼ cup (about) honey, maple syrup, or other sweetener | small lump of butter, optional |

In a heavy saucepan or top of a double boiler, combine the flour or starch, honey or other sweetening, eggs, and about ¼ cup of the milk. Use just enough milk to make an easily stirred mixture. Stir or beat till completely smooth, without lumps or bumps. Stir in the rest of the milk. Put the pot on low to medium heat, or cook in the double boiler. Stir constantly, especially as it begins to cook. After about 15 minutes, when thick and smooth, remove from stove, and stir in the vanilla and butter. Pour into serving dishes or small individual dishes and let cool. This pudding becomes thicker as it sits, and is so full bodied it could make packaged pudding mixes obsolete.

**Extra Light Pudding**   Have eggs at room temperature. Separate the yolks and mix them, instead of whole eggs, with the flour or starch and the other ingredients. Beat the whites till stiff. Cook the pudding as above and fold in the whites when it is removed from the stove.

## MILK IDEAS

**Spiced Milk**   Heat milk with a piece of cinnamon stick and 1 or 2 whole cloves in it, or add other spices to taste. Crushed anise seeds are very nice. Sweeten with honey or maple syrup, or heat some raisins in the milk with the spices. Strain if desired, and serve hot or cold.

**Hot Honey Egg-Nog**   Beat 1 egg and 1 teaspoon honey together till light. Heat about a cup of milk till almost boiling, and pour into the egg mixture. Stir and pour in a mug. Sprinkle with nutmeg, if desired. This is more nutritious than cold versions with raw egg, because the egg has been cooked by the hot milk. (Refer to AVOID EATING RAW EGG WHITE in the EGGS section.)

**Dad's Graveyard Stew**   Half fill a glass or mug with dry, whole grain bread broken in pieces. Add a small dab of butter. Sweetening is optional. Heat milk to scalding and pour it over the bread to fill the glass or mug. Drink the milk and eat the soaked bread with a spoon. Crumbled crackers can be used instead of bread.

**Evaporating Milk**   To reduce the bulk of whole or skim milk, making it more practical for freezing, heat to a boil, then simmer very slowly, uncovered, till it is reduced by half. To prevent scorching use a large double boiler or an insulating pad, leaving enough space to avoid accidental boiling over. The flavor will be stronger than that of commercially canned evaporated milk, so it is best used in cooking. (Home pressure canning is not recommended because quality is poor and processing directions are not available.)

Sweetened condensed milk is excessively sweet and should be used sparingly. It is made by simmering 2 parts milk with 1 part sugar, stirring often till thickened (about 2 hours). It will keep several months if refrigerated.

## MILK IDEAS, *cont.*

**Milk Atole** The Mexican version of this drink is made with masa harina. (Refer to the CORN, DRIED section.) For 6 cupfuls, put ½ cup masa harina in a large saucepan and stir in 2½ cups water. Add a cinnamon stick, and a vanilla bean or a few drops of vanilla extract. Heat, stirring often, and simmer till thickened, as for a sauce. Remove from heat, and add several tablespoons of honey or sugar, and 3 cups of milk. Reheat, stirring often, but do not boil. Serve when quite hot.

Atole is very good made with whole wheat flour, finely ground oatmeal, or other whole grain flours instead of masa harina. For one large mugful use 2 tablespoons flour, ½ cup water, 1 cup milk, and 1 teaspoon honey.

On a cold day, this nourishing, smoothly creamy drink makes a perfect replacement for the traditional, but not particularly healthful, cup of hot cocoa.

---

### OTHER RECIPES FEATURING MILK

---

Butter should either be omitted or added before the whites. When eggs are plentiful, 1 or 2 extra can be used, for a richer pudding.

*Carob Pudding* Mix 6 tablespoons carob powder with the flour or starch and proceed for *Smooth Milk Pudding,* above. More than ¼ cup of milk will be needed to make the first mixture smooth.

For an attractive effect, make the extra light variation above, but do not fold in the egg whites completely, so that white foam will appear here and there in the dark pudding.

*Nut Pudding* Stir about ½ cup chopped or ground nuts into the pudding with the flavoring and butter. For a very nutty pudding use a nut milk (refer to the NUTS section), instead of some or all of the milk in the pudding.

*Banana Pudding* Stir mashed banana into any version of this pudding after it has cooked and thickened.

### Real Country Custard

(Makes 6–8 dessert servings, or one large pie filling.)

> 4–6 chicken eggs, 3–4 duck eggs, or 1–2 goose eggs, beaten lightly
> 3 cups milk (Raw milk is especially good.)
>
> ¼ cup (about) honey, or maple syrup
> nutmeg, vanilla, or other flavoring, to taste, optional

If using one large baking dish, beat the eggs in it then mix in the other ingredients. Or, for individual custard cups, mix in a bowl and fill them afterwards. Set the baking dish or custard cups in a shallow pan with a little water in it. Bake in a low, about 300°F oven till set. Cups will take about 30 minutes; a large baking dish 40 minutes or longer. Slow baking is important for a good texture. To test for doneness, make a small cut in the custard with a knife. If the blade comes out clean the custard is done. It will set more firmly as it cools. A true country dish, a classic way to use up extra eggs, and a safe way to appreciate raw milk's deliciousness.

*Bread, Rice, or Noodle Pudding* Add stale bread cut in cubes, or cold cooked rice, or noodles, to the custard mixture. Add any amount up to 3 cups. Increase sweetening and flavoring to taste. Raisins or chopped dried fruit make a pleasant addition.

Or, for a main course, omit sweetening, dessert flavorings, and dried fruit. Instead, season with such minced vegetables as onion and green pepper, such herbs as parsley, celery leaves or seeds, sage, and thyme, and hot pepper, if desired.

*Popcorn Pudding* Soak 4 cups unseasoned popcorn in the milk overnight. The next day, add eggs, sweetening, and flavoring, and bake as above.

*Pumpkin or Chestnut Pudding* Add up to 3 cups puréed pumpkin, winter squash, or chestnuts to the custard mixture. Light cream or undiluted evaporated milk can be substituted for all or part of the plain milk. Increase sweetening to taste. Molasses and pumpkin pie spices are very good with the pumpkin or squash.

*Custard Pies*   Make single pastry crusts, then prick and bake them at 450°F for 10 minutes. As soon as they are done, pour a plain custard mixture (or any variation) into it, and bake at 325°F till set. The basic custard recipe makes one large pie. For a 9 inch pie use 2 cups milk and about 3 eggs. The above variations make two large or three small pies.

*Custard Sauce*   Mix the custard ingredients in a heavy saucepan, then cook 5 to 10 minutes over moderate heat, stirring constantly till thickened and smooth. Use as a dessert topping, or chill in individual dishes for a quick custard pudding.

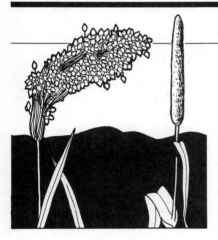

# MILLET

MILLET IS SELDOM THE FEATURED ATTRACTION WHEN FOOD GRAINS are reviewed, yet it has many superior characteristics. Among these are its high quality protein and its easy digestibility. Most grains form acid in the stomach as they are digested, but millet has a high mineral content which counteracts acidity. The bland flavor, and somewhat dry, coarse texture of plain, cooked millet may not appeal to everyone, but these very characteristics make it a good mixer. It complements other flavors and textures, and tastes delicious mixed with meat, vegetables, or other, smoother grains. Millet flour is excellent, especially for making flatbread and crackers.

Millet is the basic food for many peoples in parts of Asia and Africa too dry and hot for other grains to grow well. It is among the foods that have been acclaimed because they are eaten by the long-lived Hunza people. Millet is a grain with good potential for growing on a small scale for home use, and for feeding poultry and other livestock. (Refer to the GRAINS section.)

## COOKING MILLET

Whole millet cooks more quickly than most whole grains, taking

### MILLET IDEAS

**Herbed Millet Chapatis**   Follow the recipe for *Basic Flatbread* in the BREAD, QUICK section, using ¾ cup whole wheat flour, and about 2 cups millet flour, and working ½ cup finely minced, fresh herbs into the dough. One good mixture is parsley and chives or scallions, with a touch of thyme, savory, or basil. Use coriander leaves instead of parsley, if their stronger flavor is enjoyed. If fresh herbs are not available, use a tablespoon of dried herbs, although the effect will not be quite as good.

## MILLET IDEAS, *cont.*

**Millet Soufflé**   Cooked millet is delicious made into a soufflé by mixing it with milk, beaten egg yolks, and seasonings, and then folding in stiffly beaten egg whites, and baking until set. Good proportions are: 2 cups cooked millet, 1 cup milk, and 4 eggs. Pepper and grated cheese are the traditional seasonings. Crushed herb seeds, like dill or caraway and minced onion will add extra zest. For another variation, make the SPOONBREAD FROM LEFTOVERS, in IDEAS in the CEREALS section, using millet.

**Millet Meal Replacing Cornmeal**   Coarsely ground millet meal acts like cornmeal in baked goods and can be substituted for it in bread and muffins. As millet's flavoring is less distinctive, special seasonings add a nice touch. Minced, fresh, or dried herbs are especially good.

**Millet Crackers**   Millet flour is very good in most cracker recipes instead of wheat flour. Try it in the RECIPES, in the CRACKERS section.

### OTHER RECIPES WITH MILLET

Basic Hot Cooked Cereal, p. 127
Cereal Ideas (Breakfast), p. 127
Ideas for Grain, p. 314
Sourdough Muffins (with millet flour), p. 583

Refer also to the REFERENCE SOURCES at the end of the GRAINS section for further information about millet.

only 15 to 30 minutes, depending on the type. It does not need soaking. For cereal add 1 part millet to 2 parts boiling water. (Refer to the *Basic Hot Cooked Cereal* recipe in the CEREALS section.) The flavor of millet cereal can be enhanced by lightly toasting the raw grains in a dry frying pan over medium heat. Stir to brown the grains lightly and evenly. For a richer flavor brown the raw millet in a little oil or other fat, and cook in a soup stock or whey instead of plain water.

Millet grinds easily into meal or flour. Millet meal and flour are especially versatile, and can be used instead of wheat flour in most recipes that are not leavened with yeasts. (It lacks the gluten necessary for rising. Refer to BREAD FLOUR in the BREAD, YEAST section.) When baking powder is called for, millet flour can be substituted for ⅓ of the wheat flour, or use all millet flour and twice as much baking powder.

## MILLET RECIPES

### *Millet with Onion*                    (Makes about 6 side servings.)

| | |
|---|---|
| *1 cup millet* | *oil or fat, for frying* |
| *1 large onion, chopped* | *pepper, salt, optional* |

Heat the millet in a dry frying pan, stirring very often, till the grains are just lightly browned. At the same time bring 2¼ cups of water to a boil. Add the toasted millet to the boiling water gradually. (It bubbles up suddenly on contact.) Cover, and cook over low heat, without stirring until it is done, about 20 minutes.

While the millet is cooking, gently sauté the onion in oil or fat till limp and translucent, but not browned. Mix the millet and onion, season with pepper and salt, if desired.

This simple but delicious dish is likely to change the mind of anyone who had thought they did not like millet.

### *Shepherd's Millet, Hungarian Style*              (Makes about 6 dinner servings.)

| | |
|---|---|
| *1 pound stewing lamb, or other stew meat, in ½ inch pieces* | *½ teaspoon marjoram or oregano* |
| *1 whole carrot, optional* | *1 tablespoon paprika* |
| *1 whole parsnip, optional* | *½ teaspoon cayenne, or to taste* |
| *1–2 tablespoons oil or lard* | *salt, optional* |
| *2 onions, chopped medium* | *1½ cups millet* |
| *1–2 cloves garlic, crushed* | |

Put the meat, carrot, and parsnip in a pot, and add about 6 cups of water. Bring to a boil, and simmer, covered, for an hour or till the meat is tender. Drain, saving the broth. The carrot and parsnip can be discarded, or chopped and used with the meat.

Heat the oil or lard in a heavy pot, and gently sauté the onions in it until limp. Add the meat, garlic, marjoram or oregano, paprika, and cayenne. Stir over moderate heat for a minute. Add the reserved broth (there should be about 4 cups, or add water if necessary), salt if desired, and the millet. Cover, and simmer over low heat for about 20 minutes, or till the millet is done.

*Millet Peanut Butter Cookies*     (Makes about 4 dozen small cookies.)

| | |
|---|---|
| ¼ *cup butter, or lard* | 1 *egg* |
| ½ *cup peanut butter* | 1 ½ *cups millet flour* |
| ½ *cup honey* | 2 *teaspoons baking powder* |

Cream together the butter or lard, peanut butter, honey, and egg. Mix well or sift the millet flour and baking powder, and add to the creamed mixture. Stir to combine well, then put small spoonfuls on a lightly oiled cookie sheet. Bake at 375°F for 8 to 10 minutes, or till lightly browned. Watch closely, as they burn easily. The slightly sandy quality of the flour is very pleasant in cookies.

   *Rice, or Sorghum Peanut Butter Cookies*   Instead of millet flour use rice flour or grain sorghum flour to make these cookies.

# MULBERRIES

MULBERRIES ARE OFTEN IGNORED AND LEFT UNUSED, YET THEY CAN be quite delicious. There are two kinds, red and white. Red mulberries, which are a dark, reddish purple or "mulberry" color when ripe, taste very good and can be eaten fresh like other soft berries or used in the same recipes as blackberries. White mulberries, which can be pale pale green to almost beige in color, are very sweet and can be eaten out of hand, though they tend to be dry, and somewhat bland. They are excellent dried and ground into a meal to use in baking. White mulberry meal is a common food in Afghanistan. Since many mulberry trees are wild there is considerable variation in the quality of the fruit. With luck and persistent tasting it is possible to find a mulberry tree with exceptionally good fruit.

## HANDLING MULBERRIES

To gather mulberries in quantity, it is usually easiest to spread an old sheet or large drop cloth under the tree, and shake the branches

---

### MULBERRY STORAGE

**Canning**   Not practical except for red mulberry juice. Add 1–2 tablespoons lemon juice per quart. (Refer to CANNING FRUIT JUICE AND SAUCE, in FRUITS section.)

**Drying**   Best for white mulberries. Dry until hard. Grind to meal. (Refer to DRYING section.)

**Freezing**   Acceptable for red mulberries. (Refer to BLACKBERRIES section.)

### MULBERRY IDEAS

**Mulberry Bread Pudding** Sweeten red mulberry juice with honey, and pour over slices of dry bread arranged in a bowl. Let sit in a cool place for 24 hours, so that the bread completely absorbs the juice. Cover with a layer of a milk pudding or custard sauce. (Refer to recipes in the MILK section.) Or serve simply with milk.

**Mulberry-Ade**   In the Middle East, red mulberry syrup is mixed into ice water to make a delicious, cool drink for hot weather. For a concentrated syrup, boil 1 part mulberry juice with 1 part honey, or 1½ parts sugar, adding lemon juice, if desired. One tablespoon of this will flavor a glassful of ice water. Or make mulberry-ade by simply mixing mulberry juice, lemon juice, water, and then sweetening to taste.

**Mulberry Meal**   Grind a mixture of dried white mulberries

**MULBERRY IDEAS,** *cont.*

and other dried fruits and nuts in a meat grinder, or knead mulberry meal into the ground dried fruit and nut mixture to make a stiff dough. Shape the dough into small balls and roll them in mulberry meal. They make a nutritious, sweet snack.

## OTHER RECIPES
## WITH MULBERRIES

over it. If the tree is too big to shake, spread the cloth, weighted down with a few rocks, and leave it there to catch the berries as they fall by themselves. Then collect the berries once a day.

Red mulberries to be eaten fresh need no preparation, except a quick rinsing if dusty. Their small stems can be removed, but that is optional. Where people object to the axis or core that goes part way into each berry, try making them into juice. Red mulberry juice is delicious. Make from fresh berries by mashing and straining them, or by squeezing them in a cloth. (Refer to MAKING FRUIT JUICE AND SAUCE, in the FRUITS section.) A little lemon juice brings out the flavor, or try mixing it with the tart juices. (Refer to COMBINING SWEET AND TART FRUITS, in the FRUITS section.)

Do not wash white mulberries collected for drying unless really necessary. If they require washing, do it just before the drying starts, as they turn brown and spoil quickly once they become wet. The dried mulberries are easily ground to meal in a blender, grain mill, or other grinder. This meal is quite sweet with a delicate flavor, so can be added to most baked goods for sweetening. (Refer to USING DRIED FRUIT, in the FRUITS section.)

# MUSHROOMS

To THE SCIENTIST THE MUSHROOM IS A FLESHY FUNGUS; TO the epicure it is a gastronomic delight. To the country dweller it is a delicious food, expensive to buy but practical to grow and gather wild.

The mushroom most often home grown is *agaricus campestris,* the same variety sold fresh in stores. The spawn (fragments of mycelia) is available from many garden catalogs and there are publications which give growing directions. Another cultivated variety, common in Japan, is grown from plugs planted in holes drilled in logs, but information about them is hard to find.

Before edible wild mushrooms can be safely gathered it is essential to learn to identify the different kinds, but it is not necessary to become a mycological expert. A few delicious wild mushrooms are easy to identify, once their characteristics are learned. The more confusing and potentially dangerous ones can be avoided, even though some among them may be good to eat.

Truffles, which are subterranean fungi, are a relative of mushrooms, and are used in very small amounts for flavoring the same kinds of foods that go well with mushrooms. Most come from Europe and are available only at very high prices. The various dried mushrooms and wood fungus found in Chinese grocery stores and other specialty shops are interesting and much less expensive.

## HANDLING MUSHROOMS

When gathering mushrooms, whether cultivated or wild, brush off loose soil and trim the stem end before putting them in a container. Soil clinging to one mushroom can stick here and there to others, making the whole batch hard to clean. If carefully gathered, wiping with a damp cloth may be all that is required. If they must be washed, do so quickly, in cool water, and pat dry with a towel. If allowed to soak, they become soggy and easily spoil. For large or mature mushrooms it is best to separate the caps and stems, as the stems tend to be tougher and slower cooking than the caps. Use them for adding flavor to sauces. Use the caps whole or sliced in dishes ranging from salads and appetizers to main courses.

The different wild mushrooms vary greatly in taste and in the way they respond to cooking, and simple directions are impossible. Those who like to experiment should enjoy trying them in different ways.

Generally, drying is the best way to preserve mushrooms, and the flavor of some varieties is even enhanced by drying. When canned or frozen, they tend to lose flavor, and may lose texture as well. The canned, *Pickled Mushrooms* recipe below is an exception.

**Drying Mushrooms** There are two approaches to drying mushrooms. One is to dry them whole or in thick slices, for reconstituting as a featured ingredient in various dishes. The other is to chop them small before drying, or to grind them after drying, both for use as seasoning in sauces, soups, and other dishes. It is often most practical to dry the caps whole and chop the stems. Dry the stems of large mushrooms separately, in any case, since they dry more slowly than the caps.

If mushrooms are to be dried whole or in slices, trim them and wipe them clean with a damp cloth. It is best not to wash them. Sometimes soil that sticks when they are fresh will brush off after a day of drying. Wash off any remaining soil just before soaking the mushrooms to reconstitute them. They usually need about 30 minutes of soaking in warm water. Soil settled in the soaking water will be left behind when the clear part is poured off. Dried mushrooms and wood fungus from Chinese groceries usually need washing and trimming when they are soaked.

Mushrooms dried for seasoning may have to be washed, since they will be used without pre-soaking. If chopped small before drying, they will need only a few minutes of cooking. If ground in a mill or flaked in a blender they can be added just before a dish is served. (Refer to USING DRIED VEGETABLES FOR SOUP, in the DRYING section.)

Mushrooms will dry easily in any dry, airy place, whether in the sun or shade. Use drying trays or string them on a thread and hang

---

### STORAGE

**Canning** Pressure can only! Trim, wash, cut to uniform size. Blanch 4 min. in boiling water. Optional: To prevent darkening, add 1 tablespoon vinegar per quart blanching water, or add ⅛ teaspoon ascorbic acid to each pint jar, and 1/16 teaspoon to half pints. Pack in jars, add fresh boiling water, ½ in. headroom. Process 240°F, 11 pounds pressure. Both pints and half pints: 40 min. (Refer to CANNING section.) See also *Pickled Mushrooms*, below.

**Drying** See DRYING MUSHROOMS, below.

**Freezing** Trim, clean with damp cloth. May be quartered or sliced. Sauté, and pack in cooking juices, or steam blanch in single layer, 3–5 min. Quality retained 8–10 months. (Refer to FREEZING section.)

1 POUND FRESH MUSHROOMS = 4–5 CUPS SLICED (1–1½ CUPS COOKED); 1 POUND FRESH = ABOUT 3 OUNCES DRIED

them up to dry. Once they are hard or brittle store them in airtight containers.

# MUSHROOM RECIPES

## Mushrooms in Yogurt   (Makes about 6 side servings.)

4 tablespoons butter
2 tablespoons onion, grated
1 pound mushrooms, sliced
pepper, salt, optional
sprinkle of nutmeg, optional
1 tablespoon flour

1 cup goat's milk yogurt or Stabilized Cow's Milk Yogurt (Recipe in the YOGURT section.)
parsley, minced, for garnish

Heat butter in a heavy frying pan, and sauté the onion in it for about 3 minutes. Add the mushrooms, nutmeg, pepper, and salt, if desired. Sauté over medium heat, stirring often. The butter will quickly be absorbed and the mushrooms will look dry, but there is no need to add more butter. After a few minutes the mushrooms shrink, releasing fat. Let them brown lightly and cook till any moisture in the pan has evaporated. Stir in the flour and cook for a minute, or till flour and fat are blended. Remove from heat and stir in the yogurt. Return to low heat and cook, stirring, for 2 or 3 minutes, till the sauce thickens. Serve sprinkled with parsley as a side or lunch dish. It goes well with meat, or with such cooked green vegetables as broccoli.

**Mushrooms in Sour Cream**  Omit flour and add sour cream instead of yogurt. Do not boil after the sour cream is added.

**Creamed Mushrooms**  Increase butter to 5 tablespoons, and increase flour to 3 tablespoons. Replace yogurt with about 2 cups of milk. Simmer 5 to 10 minutes after it is added. Adjust seasonings. Serve on toast or with potatoes or other starchy foods.

**Cream of Mushroom Soup**  A tablespoon or two of minced celery or other seasoning vegetables can be sautéed with the onion if desired. The amount of mushrooms can be reduced to ½ or ¼ pound, and chopped stems used. Increase flour to 2 tablespoons, and add 2 or 3 cups chicken stock, or other soup stock, instead of yogurt. Cover, and simmer about 20 minutes. Purée in a blender or food mill, if desired. Add 1 or 2 cups milk or light cream and reheat. Adjust seasonings, and serve.

This version beats most canned mushroom soups by a country mile, and can be used instead in recipes calling for the canned soup.

## Stuffed Mushrooms, Italian Style   (Makes 6 side servings.)

12 large mushrooms
3 tablespoons (about) olive oil, or butter
1 small onion, minced

1 small clove garlic, minced
4 anchovy filets, or salt, to taste
1 tablespoon parsley, minced
½ teaspoon pepper

| 1 slice bread (preferably whole grain), soaked in water and squeezed dry | 1 egg, slightly beaten<br>2 tablespoons dry, fine bread crumbs |

Gently pull the mushroom stems away from the caps. Wipe the caps clean with a damp cloth. If necessary, quickly rinse and dry the stems, then mince them. Heat about 2 tablespoons oil or butter in a pan, then gently sauté the chopped stems, onion, and garlic in it for about 5 minutes. Add the anchovies or salt, parsley, and pepper, and cook another 5 minutes over higher heat. Remove from stove, then add the softened, soaked bread and the egg, and mix well.

Use this mixture to stuff the raw mushroom caps, shaping it into a mound in each cap. Put stuffed caps in an oiled or buttered shallow baking dish. Sprinkle with the dry breadcrumbs, and then with olive oil or put a dot of butter on each. Bake in a hot, 400°F, oven, for 20 minutes

### MUSHROOM IDEAS, *cont.*

**Dried Mushrooms in Wine**
Soak dried mushrooms in white wine for about an hour, then add to soups, sauces, and meat dishes, including any wine that has not soaked in. For an easy sauce to go on rice or cooked vegetables, sauté chopped scallion or onion in butter, stir in a little flour for thickening, and add the wine soaked mushrooms with some broth, vegetable stock, or water. Simmer about 20 minutes, till the mushrooms are cooked, and season to taste. Freshly ground black pepper adds a nice finishing touch.

### *Stewed Mushroom Soup*     (Makes 6—8 medium bowls.)

| 1—1½ cups strongly flavored dried mushrooms<br>3 thin slices fresh ginger root, optional<br>2 scallions in 1—2 inch pieces, or 1 small onion, thinly sliced<br>6 cups chicken stock, or other light soup stock | 1 tablespoon rendered chicken fat, or butter<br>2 teaspoons dry sherry, or ½ teaspoon homemade cider or wine vinegar<br>1 teaspoon honey, or sugar |

Soak the mushrooms in water till swelled, usually 30 to 60 minutes. Drain, then trim stems as necessary. (Add the soaking water to the soup, or discard it if cloudy.) Combine all ingredients in a pot, cover, and simmer gently for about 30 minutes. Though Chinese in character, this soup will complement any meal.

### *Pickled Mushrooms, Syrian Style*     (Makes 4 pints, canned.)

| 4 pounds small mushrooms (Wild coral mushrooms are good.)<br>½ teaspoon salt, optional<br>1 tablespoon peppercorns, cracked or coarsely ground | 1 cup salad oil, optional<br>4 cups vinegar<br>mace blades or whole cloves<br>sprigs fresh thyme or dried thyme |

Clean and trim mushrooms, and put them, with salt, if desired, into a pan and cover with cold water. Heat to a boil, covered, then simmer 5 minutes over low heat. Drain and pat dry with a towel. (Reserve cooking water for soup or other uses.) Pack the mushrooms into sterilized jars, sprinkle with peppercorns, and put a blade of mace or a whole clove, and a sprig of thyme or pinch of dried thyme in each jar.

Heat the oil and vinegar to a boil. If not using oil, use 4 cups

### OTHER RECIPES FEATURING MUSHROOMS

Baked Eggs Fantastic, p. 247
Celery Stir-fried with Mushrooms, p. 123
Fruit Casserole, p. 307
Liver Stroganoff, p. 396
Roast Goose with Stuffing, p. 306
Shish Kebab, p. 381
Tofu Stir-fried with Mushrooms, p. 634

vinegar and 1 cup water. Heat to boiling, then pour boiling hot over mushrooms. Seal with canning lids, leaving the rings in place after the jars cool. Store in a cool dark place, and wait several weeks before using. (Refer to CANNING PICKLES in the CANNING section.) These are excellent alone, as well as in antipastos and salads.

---

**STORAGE**

To preserve mustard greens refer to SPINACH section.

Mature dry mustard seeds keep indefinitely in closed containers.

---

# MUSTARD  (GREENS AND SEEDS)

THE MUSTARD PLANT GOT ITS NAME FROM A CONDIMENT MADE BY mixing must, which is wine in the first stages of fermentation, with the powdered seeds of the plant. Most gardeners cultivate mustard for its greens, not its seeds, but both are valuable. The lightly hot taste of mustard greens distinguishes them from blander greens, making them a favorite with many. Mustard seeds make a good seasoning used whole or powdered, and home prepared mustard is excellent. The seeds are easy to collect from wild plants, so it may be more practical to gather them than to grow them. Wild mustard greens are good in early spring, but their season is short compared to cultivated greens.

Most varieties of mustard can be grown for both greens and seeds. Black mustard is an ancient variety still cultivated for both. It is also the most common wild variety. White mustard is often cultivated for its large white or yellow seeds but the greens are also good. Chinese or Indian mustard is mild flavored and is grown primarily for its greens. The greens and seeds of many mustard relatives can be used like mustard. Radish tops and turnip greens can be cooked like mustard greens, and their seeds, as well as Chinese cabbage seeds, can be used for seasoning. Rocket, or garden rocket, is a relative of mustard whose leaves are used as a fresh herb. Their strong and distinctive taste goes well with fresh tomatoes.

## HANDLING MUSTARD

Mustard greens are cool weather vegetables that grow very quickly. In the South they are a winter crop. Further north they are welcomed as the first spring crop harvested from a spring planting. The early small leaves are very good in salads, but larger leaves are best cooked. If mustard plants are left to go to seed, the flower buds and flowers can be eaten, but these are usually saved to develop seeds. Gather seed pods before they are dry enough to split open and scatter seeds. Seed stalks can be picked when the lowest pods have begun to split, or pick pods individually. Lay stalks or pods on cloth or plastic to finish drying. They can then be crushed and winnowed to separate the seeds. (Refer to THRESHING AND WINNOWING in the SEEDS section.)

Whole mustard seeds are good for seasoning pickles and meat marinades, and they can be sprouted. (Refer to the SPROUTS section.) Crushed or powdered, the seeds can be added to stews, sauces, and salad dressings.

**Prepared Mustard from Seeds** Dry, powdered mustard is made by pulverizing mustard seeds. The powder can then be made into a creamy, prepared mustard.

The simplest preparations combine powdered mustard with vinegar or another liquid. Seasonings such as tarragon and turmeric may be added. Turmeric intensifies the yellow color. For less hot preparations, flour or another bland ingredient is added. The flour can be lightly browned to take away the raw taste. If vinegar is used the prepared mustard will keep indefinitely.

Other kinds of edible seeds with a hot, peppery flavor can also be made into a condiment like mustard. Dry nasturtium seeds and Chinese cabbage seeds have been used in this way.

# MUSTARD GREENS AND SEEDS RECIPES

**Eggs Mustard**   (Makes about 6 side or lunch servings.)

6 eggs, hard-boiled, shelled
4 tablespoons oil
3 tablespoons prepared mustard

1½ teaspons paprika
1 teaspoon turmeric
2 pounds (about) mustard greens

Put the oil in a heavy sauce pan and set the eggs close together in one layer in it. Mix the mustard, paprika, and turmeric with ¼ cup water. Pour over the eggs, cover, and simmer over very low heat for 40 minutes. If the heat is too high the eggs will toughen. Use an insulating pad if necessary. Turn the eggs several times, and add a little water, if it evaporates.

Meanwhile, cook the mustard greens till tender in the water left on them after washing. Arrange a bed of the greens in a serving dish, and put the eggs and their sauce on top. Eye-pleasing and brisk, but not startling in flavor, most like Eggs Mustard immediately.

**Prepared Mustard**   (Makes about 1 cup.)

¾ cup (about) vinegar
Optional seasonings: (May use 1 alone, or any combination.)
  slice of onion
  sprig of tarragon, or ½ teaspoon dried
  ½ teaspoon celery or lovage seeds
  1 clove garlic, crushed

4 tablespoons powdered mustard
1 tablespoon flour, lightly browned in a dry frying pan
½ teaspoon pepper
½ teaspoon turmeric
½ teaspoon salt, optional
1 tablespoon honey or sugar
1 tablespoon oil

Mix the vinegar with any optional seasonings used, and let sit overnight.

The next day combine the mustard powder, flour, pepper, turmeric, and salt, if desired, in a bowl. Heat the vinegar, seasonings and honey or sugar to a boil, then strain out and discard seasonings. Pour boiling hot into the bowl, stirring while pouring. If too thick, heat and add a little more vinegar. Mix the oil into the prepared mustard and store in a jar in the refrigerator. This keeps indefinitely. A doubled recipe can be made. Flavor will vary with seed varieties. Most are excellent used like commercial prepared mustards.

### *Sunflower Mustard Butter*                          (Makes about 1 cup.)

½ *cup sunflower seeds*          2 *tablespoons oil*
1 *tablespoon mustard seeds*     *dash of salt, optional*

Mix the sunflower and mustard seeds and cover them with water. Let them soak several hours or till swollen. Put them in a blender with their soaking water. Add oil, and salt, if desired, and blend until smooth and thick. If necesary, add a little more water to make the blender function. Very good with vegetables, or spread on crackers, or in sandwiches.

---

**STORAGE**

**Canning**  *Soup* Boil noodles in plenty of stock till done. Pour hot in jars, ½ in. headroom. Process, 240°F, 11 pounds pressure. Pints: 50 min. Quarts: 60 min. (Refer to CANNING section.)

**Drying**  Spread freshly cut strands in single layer, or hang on broom handle sized rack in warm, dry place. Dry till brittle. Stored in airtight containers, will keep for months. (Refer to DRYING section.)

**Freezing**  After cutting, pack loosely in containers in meal sized portions. To cook, drop while frozen into boiling water or soup. Quality retained 8–10 months. (Refer to FREEZING section.)

# NOODLES

Pasta is the general name for all of the various dough mixtures that are rolled and cut or otherwise shaped for cooking in boiling water or soups. Spaghetti and macaroni are the two seen most prominently on store shelves. Egg noodles are the most practical kind for making at home. Pasta can be homemade without eggs, as it often is in Italy and some Asian countries, but it presents problems if the right flour and the right equipment are not available. In Italy, a special high gluten, durum wheat flour is used to provide the necessary cohesiveness. Eggs provide it where ordinary flour is used. Special tools can be purchased for making rounded spaghetti strands and other special shapes.

Egg noodles are easy to make in any kitchen, and provide a practical, delicious way to use extra eggs. As they keep well either dried or frozen, large amounts can be made and stored when eggs are plentiful. Special noodle making machines are available in specialty stores or by mail order, that save time rolling out and cutting the dough. They adjust to make strands of different widths.

## NOODLE INGREDIENTS

*Flour* Finely ground, high gluten wheat flour, of the kind used for making bread, makes the most manageable dough. Noodles made with it have a good texture, and hold together well during handling, cooking, and storage. However, any medium to finely ground wheat flour can be used. Unbleached white flour makes smooth, golden yellow noodles. Whole wheat flour makes noodles with an excellent flavor. Their thinness and smoothness will depend on the fineness of the grind. Other kinds of flour such as buckwheat or soy, makes noodles with good flavor, but the dough is very difficult to roll and cut long strands. When dried, the noodles are sure to break into small pieces, but they will still be very good in soups. Using half unbleached white flour with non-wheat flours will improve their manageability.

The amount of flour called for in noodle recipes is always an approximation. Flour's moisture content is variable, and this changes the amount of liquid it will absorb. Also, egg sizes vary. Use the amount of flour that makes a stiff but workable dough.

*Eggs* Most noodles are made with whole eggs, but either yolks or whites can be used alone. Yolks make very rich noodles. Egg whites have little effect on color or flavor.

Duck eggs and goose eggs are prized for noodle making, because of their extra cohesiveness and good flavor. To substitute them in recipes calling for chicken eggs, refer to EGG STATISTICS, in the EGGS section.

*Other Ingredients* Nothing besides flour and eggs is needed for good noodles, but the addition of a little water and a little oil or cream will make the dough easier to work, ensuring smooth, evenly thin noodles. Though salt is often added, there is no need for it. Sometimes milk is added instead of water or oil. This will make a soft noodle, without the "al dente" or firm quality required in Italian pasta recipes. They are good in chicken noodle soup. Different colors and flavors of noodles can be created by adding different, puréed vegetables. See the GREEN NOODLES and RAINBOW NOODLES recipe variations below.

## COOKING NOODLES AND OTHER PASTA

For the best textured noodles and pasta, cook them in a big pot with plenty of water so they are not crowded. Bring the water to a full boil and add them gradually, keeping the water almost boiling. Tasting is the best way to test for doneness. Thin, fresh noodles can take as little as 3 minutes, while thick, dried ones may take 10 minutes, or longer. When done, lift them out of the water with tongs and a slotted spoon. When lifted out, each strand has a slight coating of water that will keep it separate and improve its texture. When drained in a colander they tend to mat down and stick together.

# NOODLE RECIPES

### *Basic Egg Noodles*       (Makes 8 or more average dinner servings.)

| | |
|---|---|
| 4 *(about) cups flour* | 2 *teaspoons oil or cream, op-* |
| 4 *chicken eggs, or 1 goose egg, or* | *tional* |
| 2−3 *duck eggs* | 2 *teaspoons water, optional* |

Put 3½ cups flour into a large mixing bowl, and make a well in the center of it. Put the eggs, oil or cream, and water into the well. Mix, starting in the center, using a fork to break the egg yolks and bring in the flour nearest to the center. When most of the flour is mixed in, use a spoon or clean hands to make a stiff but workable dough, adding more flour as necessary. Turn out on a floured board and knead into a smooth ball of dough. This may take up to 10 minutes. If it becomes too stiff or crumbles apart, add a sprinkle of water. If it is too soft, work in more flour. When smooth, cover the ball of dough with the upside-down mixing bowl, and let it rest for ½ to 1 hour. This will make the dough easier to roll out and improve the noodle's texture.

Divide the dough into 3 or 4 balls and roll out each ball to make a thin sheet. For paper thin noodles, divide the dough into 5 or 6 balls to make it easier to handle. Let the sheets dry until they have lost all traces of stickiness before cutting the noodles. Lay them on a floured cloth on a table, or hang them over a broom handle held up between the backs of two chairs. The drying time will depend on the humidity of the room, as well as on the texture of the dough. In a dry climate the sheets might be ready to cut almost immediately, while it might take more than an hour where the humidity is high. If the dough begins to crack around the edges it is too dry. If this should happen, trim off the edges and use them in soups.

For wide noodles, stack the sheets of dough on top of one another, and cut them into long strips with a sharp knife. Separate the layers of noodles after cutting. For narrow noodles roll the sheets of dough into a cylinder and cut across in narrow slices. Each slice will make a long noodle coiled up like a jelly roll. Shake out the coiled noodles. Some of the batch can be cut narrow for soup noodles, and wider for main course recipes.

Noodles can be cooked as soon as they are cut, or they can be left to dry a little longer to make sure they will not stick together. Keep them in the refrigerator for 1 or 2 days, or freeze them for longer storage. Also they can be dried completely for storage. Air tight containers are best. If frozen they will keep their freshness, making them nice for main course dishes. For soups they are handiest dried.

### *Milk and Egg Noodles*   Make noodles using ½ cup milk and 2 eggs with about 4 cups of flour. Omit oil or cream, and water. These soft noodles are very good in a hearty soup.

### *Green Noodles*   Make spinach purée and drain well so it is not at all watery. Use ½ cup spinach purée and 2 eggs with about 4 cups of flour. Use the 2 teaspoons oil or cream, but omit water. Any kind of

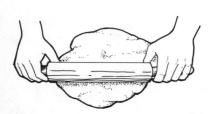

*Slicing rolled noodle dough*

cooked, puréed greens can be used instead of spinach. Lamb's quarter noodles are outstanding.

***Rainbow Noodles*** Make noodles of different colors using differently colored puréed vegetables in the same way green noodles are made. Carrot purée makes yellow-orange noodles, and beet purée makes pinkish-red noodles. Colors can be intensified by using egg yolks instead of whole eggs in carrot noodles, and egg whites in beet noodles. For a rainbow dish of noodles, prepare separate batches of green, orange, red, and plain egg noodles, and cook a combination of them.

***Fresh Herb Noodle Squares*** Gather about a cup of herb leaves from the garden. Some to try are parsley, basil, dandelion leaves, rocket, purslane, thyme, and savory. Purée these in a blender with just enough water to make it function, or chop and then crush them with a mortar and pestle. Make noodles using the herb purée, 2 eggs, and about 4 cups flour. The dough will be a little softer than regular noodle dough. Cut in 1 to 1½ inch squares. Before cooking the noodles add a tablespoon of oil to the boiling water to keep them from sticking together. These are delicious served simply with butter, or with butter and cheese. They must be frozen for storage rather than dried.

## Eggless Noodles, or Plain Pasta

(Makes 4–6 average dinner servings.)

3 cups (about) flour (Preferably high gluten wheat flour, but any fine textured wheat flour will do.)

1 cup warm water
2–3 tablespoons oil

Mix flour and water, using enough flour to make a stiff but workable dough. Knead vigorously till the dough is pliable, about 10 minutes. Divide into 3 smooth balls. Put oil in a bowl and roll the balls of dough in it to coat them completely. Leave the balls in the bowl, and cover with a large plate. Let rest in a warm place for 2 hours. Wipe the oil off the dough with a towel. Roll out each ball to paper thinness. Cut, store, and cook like egg noodles.

## Trickled Soup Noodles

(Makes enough for 1–2 quarts soup or stew.)

These noodles can be made and added in the last few minutes before serving, to enliven and enrich soups and thin stews.

2 eggs

½ cup (about) flour (Whole wheat, rice, buckwheat, and many others.)

Put the eggs in a bowl with 2 tablespoons of water and stir with a fork to blend. Mix in enough flour to make a thick, pancake-like batter. Select a funnel with a small opening, and rinse it with hot water to help the batter slide through. Put a finger over the opening and fill

## NOODLE IDEAS

**Leftover Fried Noodles** Use a heavy frying pan that will hold the leftover cooked noodles in a layer no more than an inch deep. Heat oil or another fat in the frying pan, then press the noodles into it in an even layer. Fry over medium heat, without stirring, until the bottom is lightly browned and crisp. Turn over the whole layer with a spatula, if possible in one piece. Let brown on the other side. The noodles should be crisp on the outside and soft on the inside. Serve with Chinese stir-fried dishes as in chow mein, or serve with spaghetti sauce.

All kinds of pasta, including leftover cooked spaghetti, are good fried in this way.

**Noodle Omelets** Mix cold, cooked noodles with lightly beaten eggs and season to taste. Melt a little butter in a heavy frying pan and spread the omelet evenly in it. Cook over very low heat till set on the bottom, then brown the top under the broiler. Or finish by sliding the omelet onto a plate, then turning it back into the pan upside down for another minute or two.

For a chicken noodle omelet, Middle Eastern style, include some chopped chicken meat seasoned with crushed cardamom seeds. Serve cut in wedges and garnished with parsley.

**Homemade Noodles Instead of Commercial Pasta** The sauces and seasonings that are good with spaghetti, macaroni, and other pastas are just as good with homemade noodles. These noodles, in fact, are higher in protein because of the eggs in them, making them a better main meal dish.

the funnel with batter, hold it over boiling soup or stew, then remove the finger, letting the batter trickle into the soup. Be sure to hold it so the batter trickles into liquid, not onto solid ingredients. Simmer about 5 minutes before serving.

### *Classic Green Lasagna*                          (Makes 6–8 dinner servings.)

| | |
|---|---|
| ½ recipe Green Noodles, above, rolled very thin, 1 inch wide | ½ celery stalk, chopped small |
| 1 cup cream sauce (Refer to recipe in the MILK section.) | ¼ pound ground beef |
| Meat sauce: | 1 cup tomato sauce |
| 2–3 tablespoons oil, preferably olive | 1 cup soup stock, or ½ cup stock and ½ cup white wine |
| 1 small onion, chopped small | pepper, salt, optional |
| 1 small carrot, chopped small | Parmesan or other hard cheese, grated |

Pre-cook the noodles and spread them out on a damp cloth to keep them from sticking together. Prepare the cream and meat sauces. For the meat sauce, heat the oil in a frying pan, then lightly brown the onion, carrot, and celery over medium heat. Add the meat, and also brown it lightly. Add the tomato sauce, soup stock or soup stock and wine, pepper, and salt, if desired. Simmer, uncovered, over very low heat till the vegetables are very soft and all flavors blended, from 30 to 40 minutes.

To assemble, oil a shallow, about 8 by 10–12 inch baking dish, and put a layer of noodles in the bottom. Spread with a thin layer of meat sauce, a thin layer of white sauce, and a sprinkling of grated cheese. Repeat the layers till the dish is filled, ending with the sauces. Sprinkle cheese on top, then bake in a hot, 375°F, oven for about 30 minutes, till the top is browned.

This is a superb lasagna, close in flavor to its northern Italian origins.

---

### OTHER RECIPES WITH NOODLES

---

### STORAGE

**Canning** Dry hot pack only! Spread nut meats in a shallow layer, bake at 250°F for 30 min. or till hot, dry, but not brown. Pack hot, in pints or half pints only. Process, 228°F, 5 pounds pressure, 10 min. or boiling water bath, 20 min. Keep water level below jar rims or jars may float. (Refer to CANNING section.)

# NUTS

Nuts are rich in flavor and rich in protein, fat, and b vitamins. They have been a highly valued food since the beginnings of the human race, and the gathering and storing of nuts for winter was essential for survival for many primitive people. In the modern world, nuts are valued more as a luxury than as a necessity, but they are still an excellent food to gather and store.

Just about everywhere in the United States and southern Canada there are kinds of nuts that can be cultivated or gathered from wild trees and shrubs. The uses of the different varieties are generally the same in spite of their assorted sizes, shapes, and flavors. Notable exceptions are chestnuts, which are starchy rather than oily, and peanuts, which are legumes rather than true nuts. (Refer to the CHESTNUTS and PEANUTS sections.)

## SOME NORTH AMERICAN NUTS

*Acorns*  Oak trees of many species are common in eastern North America, and several species also grow in the west. The acorns from different species vary considerably in taste. Some are sweet enough to eat raw, but many kinds are too bitter to eat unless the tannin has been leeched out of them. (Refer to REMOVING BITTERNESS in the WILD FOODS section.) Tasting is the best way to tell whether acorns from a particular tree will need treatment.

Acorns are easier to peel if soaked overnight in water to make the shells split. The nut meats can be roasted, then ground to make a dark meal or flour for baking. They can also be roasted and brewed for a beverage. (Refer to the BEVERAGES section.)

*Almonds*  Almond trees are cultivated in the warmer areas of the Pacific coast. Besides the familiar, sweet almonds there is a bitter variety used in small amounts for flavoring some almond pastes and ground mixtures. Soft, immature (green) almonds are good to eat, as well as the mature dry nuts. There is a botanical relationship between almonds and the stone fruits that can be tasted in the slightly bitter almond flavor of the kernels inside the pits of apricots, peaches, and plums. (Refer to the APRICOTS section.) Sometimes the kernels of those fruits are used to replace almonds in paste and other preparations.

*Beech Nuts*  Beech trees grow throughout the eastern United States and southern Canada, but they produce more and larger nuts in the northern part of their range. Beech nuts are thin shelled, small, and triangular in shape with a sweet, pleasant flavor.

*Black Walnuts*  Black walnut trees grow throughout the eastern United States, but they are becoming scarce because so many have been harvested for their valuable wood. The nuts fall from the trees with thick green hulls around them which later blacken. They must be crushed and removed before the hard shells are cracked and the nutmeats picked out. In spite of these difficulties, black walnuts are prized for their rich flavor. They are especially good in baking.

*Butternuts (White Walnuts)*  Like black walnuts, these also grow wild in North America, with about the same range. Butternuts are difficult to shell, but their flavor is excellent. They can be used like regular walnuts or like black walnuts.

*Cashews*  Cashews can be cultivated only in the warmest regions of the United States. The trees are evergreen, related to poison ivy. The

| STORAGE, *cont.* |
| --- |

**Cold Storage**  See STORING NUTS, below.

**Drying**  See CURING NUTS, below.

**Freezing**  Leave in shells or shell, and freeze whole, chopped or ground. Package airtight. Quality retained 1–2 years. (Refer to FREEZING section.) Also see PICKLING WALNUTS AND BUTTERNUTS, below.

I POUND NUTS IN SHELLS = ABOUT ½ POUND SHELLED = 1½–2 CUPS NUTMEATS

ACORN

ALMOND

BEECH NUT

BLACK WALNUT

BUTTERNUT

CASHEW

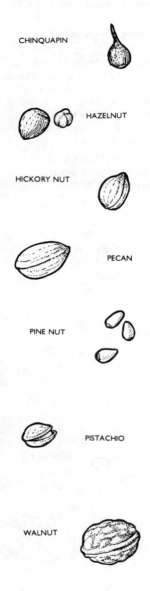

CHINQUAPIN

HAZELNUT

HICKORY NUT

PECAN

PINE NUT

PISTACHIO

WALNUT

nuts must be roasted before they are shelled to dispel the irritating oil that surrounds them. Cashew butter is as flavorful and as versatile as peanut butter, though not as well known.

*Chinquapins*  This name is applies to several different trees or shrubs that grow in various locations, primarily in the southern half of the United States. Their nuts are good tasting but are used only locally. There is also a chinquapin oak whose acorns are quite bitter.

*Hazelnuts or Filberts*  Native American hazelnuts are smaller than European filberts, but they taste the same. Hazelnuts grow on shrubs rather than trees in scattered locations throughout the United States. Filberts can be cultivated in the same range as peaches, but they excel along the Pacific coast.

*Hickory Nuts*  Most species of hickory trees bear good tasing nuts. There is, however, the Bitter Hickory tree, whose nuts are inedible. The nuts of the pignut hickory are reputed to be bitter, yet often they taste quite good. The best test is to taste the nuts of individual trees. Most hickories grow in the eastern United States and southeastern Canada.

*Pecans*  Pecans are the largest and meatiest of the hickory nuts. They are cultivated and also found growing wild in the southeastern United States.

*Pine Nuts*  Several species of nut pines produce nuts large enough to eat. The piñon pine is probably the best known. Usually the pine cones are gathered and then roasted to loosen the nuts, so that they fall out or are easily removed. As their flavor is unique, they are not usually interchangeable with other nuts in recipes. Pine nuts are often used as garnish or for flavoring in Middle Eastern and Mediterranean cooking.

*Pistachios*  In North America these nuts can be cultivated only in some interior California valleys. They are set apart by the unusual green color of their kernels, and their special, rich flavor. Their shells are sometimes dyed red for a decorative effect, but they seem to taste best in their natural beige shells.

*Walnuts*  English walnuts, the most familiar kind, are cultivated in the southern United States and along the Pacific coast. One variety, the Carpathian walnut, can stand colder temperatures, so family orchards farther north sometimes include them. Walnuts can be used in salads or in cooking when they first fall from the tree, but cured walnuts are most familiar, as curing is necessary for them to keep well. (See below.) Immature walnuts are very good pickled.

## HANDLING NUTS

Nuts should be allowed to fall naturally from the tree when they become mature. They should not be picked, or hit to knock them loose, but branches can be shaken, if low enough to reach, so that mature nuts fall. Gather nuts from the ground soon after they fall so that squirrels, worms, and mold do not take too large a toll. People have been known to gather nuts before dawn to beat the squirrels to those that fell during the night.

*Hulling Nuts*  Many kinds of nuts grow surrounded by a thick hull or husk. Usually these split open when mature, and the nuts fall out or easily separate. The hulls of black walnuts are an exception. They must be crushed or broken to free the nuts. Suggestions for doing this range from grinding each nut under the hell of one's boot to driving a car back and forth over them. If a wooden trough is made to fit the car's tire it will hold the nuts and they will not spin out from under the wheel.

Remove hulls from nuts when they are gathered or soon afterwards to prevent them from staining the nuts or giving them a bitter flavor. Walnut hulls are used for making a fabric dye, and they will also dye the hands of anyone who handles them. Such stains are almost impossible to wash off, so wear gloves when gathering and hulling.

After nuts are hulled put them in a container of water to separate any that are diseased or rotten. These will float and can be discarded. Drain the good nuts and immediately spread them out to dry.

*Curing Nuts*  Most freshly gathered nuts taste better and keep better if cured (dried in their shells) for several weeks to a month before being eaten or stored. For curing, spread them out in a dry, airy, shaded place. Old window screens make good curing trays. If the nuts are piled up more than two nuts deep, stir or rearrange them every few days to make sure they cure evenly. Screened porches or well ventilated attics make good drying places. Of course, squirrels and other rodents must be kept out.

To check if the nuts have cured long enough, crack one and inspect the nutmeats. Any green or bitter taste should be gone, and the kernels should be brittle enough to snap when bitten or broken.

*Storing Nuts*  Cured nuts keep best in their shells unless they are to be canned or frozen. Some varieties, particularly walnuts, pecans, filberts, and hickory nuts, will keep as long as a year in a cool storage place. Containers should allow some ventilation for moisture to escape, otherwise mildew or mold may develop. Dry peat moss can be packed around nuts to absorb moisture.

Shelled nut meats become rancid rather quickly when exposed to air and light. They will keep several months in the refrigerator, but for longer storage they should be canned or frozen.

*Shelling Nuts*  Some nuts have shells so thin they can easily be cracked with teeth or fingers and some are so tough they can resist a sharp blow with a hammer. Nuts are most easily cracked, and the nut meats will come out in larger pieces, if the nuts are placed in the nutcracker the long way, or held upright and hit on their most pointed end. Once the shell is broken, a nut pick can be used to pry out hard to reach nut meats, but it may be easier to crack the shell again. Place halves (or quarters, if need be) the long way in the nut cracker or hold them upright as when cracking whole nuts. Shrivelled and dark looking nut meats are usually bitter and best discarded.

## CRACKING THE TOUGHEST NUTS

• Soften nut shells by pouring boiling water over them, then let them sit 15 to 20 minutes. Drain and shell.

• Freeze nuts to make the shells brittle. Remove only a few at a time from the freezer, and crack them before they start to thaw.

• Use a vise to crack the nuts. Position the nuts the long way and tighten the vise slowly so that it cracks without mashing them.

• Try roasting the nuts in the shell in a low oven for 20 to 30 minutes before cracking. This makes some nuts easier to crack.

• As a last resort smash nuts and shells together, then cook in plenty of water, till oil and nutmeats rise and shells sink. Skim off oil and nuts for use. The liquid can be strained through cloth to make nut milk. See NUT OIL, NUT MILK, and NUT FLOUR, below.

***Blanching Nut Meats***   Nut meats are blanched by pouring boiling water over them, waiting 1 minute, then draining them. This loosens their thin, dark skins so they can be peeled or rubbed off. Nuts are blanched for their white appearance, but the procedure is not otherwise desirable, since the skins add flavor and nutritional value.

## BASIC NUT PREPARATIONS

Nuts are so good plain that it is easy to eat a great many just as they come from the shell. However, there are several worthwhile nut preparations that offer variety, and can be the basis of some very delicious dishes.

***Nut Butter***   When nuts are ground in a way that crushes them the result is smooth nut butter. Only the oiliest nuts will turn to butter in a blender without added oil. (Add oil as for making peanut butter. Refer to the PEANUTS section.) A meat grinder can be used to make butter from most kinds of nuts without adding oil. It will take 2 or 3 grindings. To store, refrigerate in a closed container.

Use nut butters like peanut butter or regular butter. They are very delicious mixed with hot, cooked vegetables. A mixture of nut butter and maple syrup or honey is very good on bread.

***Nut Meal***   Nuts can be grated, flaked, or finely chopped to make meal. Most kinds can be flaked in a blender if they are done in small batches, a few tablespoons at a time. Some meat grinders have grating attachments that can be used to make nut meal, or the small hand-turned rotary graters for hard cheese can be used. (Refer to the illustration in the CHEESE, AGED section.) Nuts can also be grated, one at a time, on a vegetable grater, or chopped finely with a knife, but these methods are very slow.

Use nut meal instead of some of the flour in baked goods. It is delicious in pancake batter and pie crusts. Nut meal is also good sprinkled over foods or used as a coating for sticky, dried fruit, dough-nuts, or any food that might otherwise be rolled in powdered sugar.

*Nut Milk*    A purée of nuts and water is a nut milk that can be used in many ways, often instead of regular milk. If a perfectly smooth nut milk is wanted, strain through cloth. To make nut milk in a blender, first pulverize the nuts, then add water, and blend till smooth. For a fairly thick milk, pulverize ½ cup nuts and add 1 cup of water. If the milk is strained, use the leftover nut pulp in baked goods, puddings, and vegetable loaves or patties.

*Cooking Nuts for Oil, Milk, and Flour*    Nuts were often made into oil, milk, and flour by the eastern American Indians. It is possible to make all three from the same batch of nuts.

Grind or chop the nuts, then add 4 or 5 times their volume of water. Cook till the nut oil rises, then pour through a sieve into a tall, wide-mouthed jar. This will make it easier to skim the nut oil off the top with a spoon. Some kinds of nuts may have very little oil. Use nut oils in salad dressings, or for seasoning cooked vegetables and other hot foods. Use the cooking liquid like milk in baked goods, desserts, and fruit flavored beverages. To make nut flour, dry the sediment or bits of nut left after the milk is strained off. When completely dry, grind to a fine texture in a blender or a grain mill. Once their oil has been removed, the nuts will not clog a mill.

*Pickling Walnuts or Butternuts*    An old-fashioned, strong-flavored pickle can be made from walnuts or butternuts picked in early sum-mer, when the nuts are almost full size and tender enough for a needle to go through them easily. The nuts are pickled hulls and all, and can be eaten about a month after they are finished though they are said to improve in flavor if kept 1 or 2 years. They are a unique treat and, like other pickles, good for snacking, or to accompany bland foods.

Both recipes below come from *Housekeeping In Old Virginia,* 1875. The walnut catsup was also made from immature walnuts, and butternuts.

### *Walnut Pickle*                              (For about 100 walnuts.)

"Pour boiling salt water on [4 pounds pickling salt to 1 gallon water], and let them [the nuts] be covered with it nine days, changing it every third day. [Drain.] Put them on dishes to air, until they are black [2–3 days], then soak out the salt and put them in weak vinegar for a day or two, put into the jar, and pour on hot the following pick-led vinegar: 7 ounces ginger (root), 7 ounces of garlic, 7 ounces of salt, 7 ounces of horseradish, ½ ounce red pepper, ½ ounce of orange peel, ½ ounce of mace, ½ ounce of cloves, 1 ounce black pepper, all boiled in 1 gallon strong vinegar."

---

### NUTTY IDEAS

**Roasted Nuts**    Freshly roasted nuts make the ultimate snack food. For plain roasted nuts spread them on a baking sheet, and roast in a moderate, 350°F, oven for about 10 minutes or till lightly browned. Stir once or twice, and watch closely to pre-vent burning. For salted nuts, mix a teaspoon of oil with each cup of nuts, and sprinkle with salt before roasting. For an al-most smoky flavor, mix 1 tea-spoon soy sauce and 1 teaspoon oil with each cup of nuts before roasting. A stove top version can be made by using any nuts in the BEER NUTS recipe in the PEANUTS section.

**Seasoned Nuts and Grains**    Cook a grain such as rice, bulghur wheat, or barley, in soup stock instead of water. When done and the liquid is absorbed, stir in chopped nuts, minced parsley, and other herbs and seasonings to taste. This makes a nutritious side dish or main course. It is also a delicious stuffing for vegetables such as green peppers or squash.

**Nut Shakes**  Pulverize 1 or 2 tablespoons of nuts in a blender, add about a cup of milk or water, an ice cube, and fresh or canned fruit and honey to taste. Blend till smooth. The nuts thicken and enrich this classic beverage.

**Nut Soup**  Pulverize ½ to 1 cup nuts in a blender, and add soup stock to make a purée. Include 1 or 2 cloves garlic, if desired. Mix in more soup stock as needed for a thin, creamy texture. Heat to a boil and season to taste. Freshly ground black pepper and a little milk or cream are very nice. Serve with a sprinkle of minced parsley, or a dash of paprika for color. Slivered nuts are also an attractive garnish.

**Nut Meal Vegetable Topping**  Mix 1 cup nut meal or finely chopped nuts with about 2 tablespoons melted butter. Sprinkle over vegetable casseroles, stuffed vegetables, and anywhere that a bread crumb topping might have been used.

**Maple Nuts**  Heat about a cup of maple syrup in a saucepan. When it boils, remove from heat and drop in some walnut halves, acorns, hazelnuts, or what have you. Dried fruits can also be included. Stir to coat all ingredients, then lift them out with a slotted spoon. Eat right away. Great as a sticky treat for unexpected company! Leftover syrup can be saved for cooking or another sticky treat.

For canning, soak the blackened nuts in water for several hours to remove salt, drain, and pack in canning jars. Boil the vinegar and seasonings, omitting the salt, and pour boiling hot over the nuts. Seal and store in a cool place. (Refer to CANNING PICKLES in the CANNING section.)

### Walnut Catsup

"Take forty black walnuts that you can stick a pin through; mash and put them in a gallon of vinegar, boil it down to three quarts and strain it. Then add a few cloves of garlic or onion with any kind of spice you like, and salt. When cool bottle it. Have good corks."

Use this strongly flavored sauce sparingly with meats and in mixed dishes. It makes a good substitute for Worcestershire sauce.

## NUT RECIPES

### Stir-fried Nuts and Green Vegetables  (Makes about 6 side servings.)

| | |
|---|---|
| 3 tablespoons soy sauce | 2 slices fresh ginger root, minced, optional |
| 1 tablespoon sherry, or 1 teaspoon vinegar | 2 — 3 onions, cut in eighths, separated |
| 1 teaspoon honey, or sugar | 1 pound green vegetable, 2 cups (about) cut in small sections (Try broccoli, green beans, Swiss chard.) |
| ¾ cup soup stock, or water | |
| 1 tablespoon cornstarch | |
| 3 (about) tablespoons oil | |
| 1 cup nuts, halved or very coarsely chopped (Almonds, cashews, or hazelnuts are excellent.) | ½ cup Jerusalem artichoke, burdock, or other root vegetable, sliced, optional |

Mix the soy sauce, sherry or vinegar, honey or sugar, and stock or water in a little dish. In another small dish mix the cornstarch with 2 tablespoons water. Prepare other ingredients and have them ready.

Heat a wok or heavy frying pan and add the oil. Add the nuts and stir-fry 1—2 minutes or till lightly browned. Remove and set aside, leaving as much oil in the pan as possible. If necessary, add oil to make about 1 tablespoon. With the heat high stir-fry the ginger root for several seconds, then add the onion and stir-fry for about a minute. Add the green vegetable and Jerusalem artichoke or root vegetable, and stir-fry for 2—3 minutes or till the green of the vegetable has brightened. Add the soy sauce mixture, cover, and cook over moderate heat for 2—3 minutes. Uncover, push the vegetables to one side, and add the cornstarch. Stir till sauce thickens, about 1 minute. Mix in the nuts and serve with noodles or rice. (Refer to the STIR-FRYING section.)

## Vegetable Nut Loaf                    (Makes about 6 dinner servings.)

1 cup walnuts or other nuts, grated (Or pulverized in blender in small batches.)

1 cup carrots, parsnips, zucchini, or other vegetables, grated

1 small onion, grated

2 cups fresh bread crumbs, or mashed potatoes

1 cup milk, soup stock, tomato juice, or water

1 teaspoon paprika

¼ teaspoon cayenne, optional

2 tablespoons parsley, minced

2 teaspoons honey

2 tablespoons soy sauce

1 egg, beaten

Thoroughly mix all ingredients and press into a well oiled loaf pan. Bake in a moderate, 350°F, oven for 30 to 40 minutes, or till the loaf is set and lightly browned. Serve from the pan, or unmold on a platter. Very satisfying with relish or chutney.

**Peanut Butter Vegetable Loaf**  Omit nuts and use ½ cup peanut butter instead. A clove of minced or crushed garlic is a tasty addition, as the peanut flavor is strong, and needs an equally strong seasoning.

## Triple Nut Torte                      (Makes 8–10 dessert servings.)

½ cup walnuts

½ cup almonds

2 tablespoons pine nuts, or cashews

3 tablespoons fine dry bread crumbs

6 eggs, separated (Must be at room temperature.)

3 tablespoons honey, or ⅓ cup sugar

tart fruit jam or jelly, optional

Grate the walnuts, almonds, and pine nuts or cashews to make a fine meal. Or pulverize them in the blender in very small batches so that they will not pack down. Mix in 2 tablespoons of the bread crumbs.

Beat together the egg yolks and the honey or sugar till light. Fold in the nut mixture. Then, beat the egg whites until stiff and fold them in. Prepare a shallow cake pan by buttering it and dusting it with the other tablespoon of crumbs. Pour in the batter and bake in a 300°F oven for 25 to 30 minutes. To test for doneness press gently with a finger. If done it will spring back, if not a dent will remain.

Take out of pan and spread with jam or jelly if desired. This is richer than most cakes, so a little goes a long way.

---

**OTHER RECIPES FEATURING NUTS**

Almond Lake, p.559
Bread Crumb Filling, p.8
Brussels Sprouts with Nuts, p.78
Cheese Nut Patties, p.145
Corn with Nuts or Seeds, p.197
Corn Mohawk from H. R. Mills, p.202
Fresh Beans and Nuts, p.31
Honey Confection, p.352
Mulberry Meal, p.421
Nut Butter Salad Dressing, p.533
Nutty Baked Peaches, p.455
Nut Pudding, p.418
Nut Topping for Pumpkin Pie, p.607
Nutty Lemon Butter Sauce, p.87
Parsnip Nut Cakes, p.452
Persimmons and Nuts, p.476
Prune Sweetmeats, p.484
Roast Turkey with Pecan Stuffing, p.654
Steeped Apricot Nut Sauce, p.11
Waldorf Salad, p.124

---

# OATS

ROLLED OATS ARE FAMILIAR TO EVERYONE. THEY ARE ONE OF THE best products offered by the grocery store, for they are plain, unadulterated, and healthful, as well as economical. However, they are only one of many possibilities. Whole oats, oat groats, oatmeal, and

## STORAGE

Note: Refer to STORING GRAIN in GRAINS section.

ABOUT ⅔ CUP WHOLE OATS = I CUP OATMEAL OR FLOUR;  I CUP ROLLED OATS = I CUP OAT FLOUR

oat flour are as versatile and useful as other whole grain kernels, and ground meals and flours. In Scotland, where oats are a basic food, many kinds of breads, sausage-like stuffings, desserts, and even beverages are made from oatmeal and oat flour. Some grocery stores sell Scottish style oatmeal, and health food stores usually sell oat groats or steel cut oats. (Steel cutting makes sharp edged pieces for a chewier texture after cooking.) Any of these, or rolled oats, can be ground to flour or a fine meal at home in a blender.

Oats are often grown on small farms and homesteads to feed livestock, but the thin, scratchy little hull clinging to each oat grain is objectionable to people, though animals do not mind it. The machinery for hulling oats on a large scale is not practical for small quantities, so other methods must be devised. Though there is a hull-less or naked oat variety, it is grown mostly in mountainous parts of Asia, and is almost impossible to obtain in North America.

## HANDLING OATS

Oats are reaped, threshed, and winnowed like other grains, but unlike wheat or rye, oats are still in their hulls after threshing. To remove hulls refer to the GRAINS section. Hulled oats are easily ground in a grain mill or blender to make meal and flour, as described in the GRAINS section. Oatmeal can be used like cornmeal in baking and for thickening. The oatmeal flavor and texture are mild and smooth, blending well in all kinds of combinations. Oat flour is superb for coating foods before frying, and excellent for thickening soups and gravies. The flour from rolled oats is just as useful for these purposes as flour from whole oats, but the texture of meal from rolled oats is different from whole oatmeal and cannot always be substituted for it in recipes.

Hulls removed from oats at home can also be used. In the past, in Scotland, oat hulls were mixed with water and fermented. The sediment, called sowans, was made into various kinds of porridge and bread. Sowans were valued as a health food as well as for flavor. Today, oat hulls are processed commercially to make a solvent used in paint remover, among other things.

An unusual way to use oats with hulls is to sprout them and eat the shoots. (Refer to the SPROUTS section.)

***Rolling Oats***   Rolling is a way of flattening grain kernels, producing the characteristic shape and texture, and making them quicker cooking. It is possible, though not generally practical, to make rolled oats at home. Commercially, oats are steamed to soften them, flattened with heavy rollers, then dried. Quick cooking rolled oats are made by cutting the oat grains into several smaller pieces before rolling them. As a home project, whole oats can be cooked in about twice their volume of water till the water is absorbed, then flattened with a heavy rolling pin, and dried in a food dryer or very low oven. The difficult part is flattening them sufficiently with a rolling pin and one's muscles instead of heavy rollers.

## OAT IDEAS

**Oatade**   To make 2 glassfuls of this smooth and nourishing cool drink, put a tablespoon of oat flour (made from rolled oats in a blender) in a saucepan with 1 to 2 tablespoons each of honey and lemon juice. Mix in enough cold water to moisten the flour. Add 2 cups boiling water, stirring while pouring, simmer 2 or 3 minutes, then chill. Adjust amounts of honey and lemon juice to taste or, for another flavor, use *Raspberry Shrub* (refer to RASPBERRIES section) instead of lemon juice.

Hot oatades are also good. A hot drink known as sherry posset can be made using several tablespoons of sherry instead of lemon juice, together with grated nutmeg and a few whole cloves.

If rolled oats are made from unhulled oats, the hulls will loosen during the process. They can then be floated off by covering the rolled oats with water, but the oats must then be cooked immediately, and cannot be used in recipes calling for dry rolled oats.

Rolled oats are good to eat without cooking since they were pre-cooked when softened for rolling. (Refer to the *Muesli* recipe in the CEREALS section.)

## OAT RECIPES

### Steamed Oat Pudding          (Makes about 6 dinner servings.)

2 cups oatmeal (Scottish style, not *small bunch parsley, minced,*
   from rolled oats.)                     *and other herbes to taste* (Try
1 egg, lightly beaten, optional      sage, marjoram, or savory.)
2 onions, minced                        2 tablespoons oat flour, or other
½ teaspoon pepper                      flour
½ teaspoon salt, optional
¼ cup suet, minced, or lard, or other
   fat

Mix the oatmeal, egg if used, onion, pepper, salt, if desired, suet or fat, and parsley. The texture will be crumbly. Make a bag for the pudding by laying a square of tightly woven, cotton cloth in a bowl large enough to hold the pudding mixture. Rub or dust the flour over the cloth and put in the pudding. Gather the sides of the cloth and tie them, leaving a little space in the bag for expansion. (Refer to the steamed pudding recipes, in the STEAM COOKING section.)

Have ready a large pot of boiling water, and drop the pudding into it. Cover and boil for three hours. If necessary, add more boiling water, and turn the pudding over once or twice. When it is done, un-wrap, and put it in a serving dish. The outside will be a little sticky, and the inside will have a nice, grainy texture. Serve for dinner in-stead of potatoes or rice.

### Oatcakes
(Scottish flatbread.)          (Makes 8 medium wedge-shaped flatbreads.)

2½ (about) cups fine oatmeal or oat    2 tablespoons fat, melted, or oil
   flour (May use rolled oat flour.)       (Chicken or goose fat is ex-
¼ teaspoon salt, optional               cellent.)
                                            hot water

Mix 2 cups oatmeal in a bowl with the salt, if desired. Make a hol-low in the center, and pour in the fat or oil and about ⅓ cup hot water. Mix to make a stiff but workable dough, adding a little more hot water, if necessary. Shape the dough into two balls, and roll out each on a surface well sprinkled with oatmeal or oat flour. Roll as thinly as possible, about ⅛ inch, using oatmeal or flour to keep the dough from sticking. The edges of the flattened dough can be

---

**OAT IDEAS,** *cont.*

**Rich Oat Wafers**  In a frying pan melt ¼ cup butter and ¼ cup honey. Stir in 2 cups rolled oats, then fry over medium heat, stir-ring often, till nicely browned. To form wafers, remove from stove, and at once firmly press spoonfuls into the bottom of muf-fin tin cups. Let cool completely before taking out of the muffin tins. These are a sweet treat everyone loves.

**Toasted Oats**  Spread rolled oats on a dry baking sheet, and lightly brown in a moderate oven, stirring often. They should brown evenly without becoming dark. Add these toasted oats to soups instead of noodles or rice, sprinkle them on foods as a crunchy garnish, or incorporate them into desserts as in the next Idea. The oats taste best freshly toasted. If they are to be stored, refrigerate them in a closed con-tainer.

**Toasted Oat Desserts**  Mix toasted oats with yogurt, honey, and fruit, or with yogurt and a fruit syrup, jam or jelly, for a quick pudding. To make Scottish Cream Croudie, use whipped cream instead of yogurt and add raspberries or other fresh ber-ries.

Also refer to BREAKFAST CEREAL IDEAS, in the CEREALS section.

trimmed to make neat circles, if desired. Cut the circles into quarters or smaller wedges. As the dough falls apart easily, use a spatula when moving the wedges to the griddle.

Cook the oatcakes on an ungreased griddle or heavy frying pan over moderately high heat. Let one side cook till the edges start to curl slightly, then turn to cook the other side. Each side takes 3 to 4 minutes.

Hot oatcakes are very good for breakfast with butter and marmalade, and also good as crackers. They are served traditionally with the *Kale Soup,* in the KALE section.

# OKRA

O KRA EVOKES LOVE OFTEN, DISLIKE SOMETIMES, BUT INDIFFERence? Never! This vegetable belongs to the mallow family which in general has the mucilaginous, sticky texture that cannot be ignored. (Another member is the marsh mallow, from which the original marshmallows were made.)

Okra is best known and best loved in the southeastern United States where it is highly productive. Southern varieties do not do well in the North because they require a long warm growing season, but now the development of some excellent short season varieties is extending its range and popularity. In the South another name for okra is gumbo. This can be confusing to the non-Southerner, since gumbos are also stews or soups thickened with okra, or filé (powdered, dried sassafras leaves).

## HANDLING OKRA

Only okra pods picked when very young will be tender—pick them within a few days of the time the blossoms fall, as the pods quickly become woody if left on the plant. To keep the plants producing, pods must be picked every second or third day. As canned, dried, and frozen okra are all excellent, the choice of storage depends on individual preferences. It is handy, however, to have a supply of thinly sliced dried okra or dried, powdered okra that can be quickly added to stews and soups to thicken and flavor them.

Powdered okra can be added to foods at the last minute before serving, or put it on the table in a shaker for people to add as they wish. Filé, a similar thickener, is made of dried, powdered sassafras leaves, with powdered okra and spices sometimes included. A chewed sassafras leaf has the same mucilaginous quality as okra.

Fresh okra will take from 15 to 30 minutes to cook, depending on the size of the pods and the cooking method. If it is pre-cooked in boiling water or steam, the pods should be left whole with the caps on. Cutting into the seed chamber before cooking will cause the loss of juice and flavor. When cooked, the caps can be trimmed off and the okra sliced, if desired.

A quite different way to use okra is to cook the seeds like peas. They have a distinctive, interesting flavor. Mature, dry seeds can be roasted and brewed for beverages. (Refer to the BEVERAGES section.)

## OKRA RECIPES

### Okra Stuffed Tomatoes                (Makes 6–8 side servings.)

| | |
|---|---|
| 6–8 tomatoes | ½ cup onion, minced |
| 4 tablespoons butter | 1 clove garlic, minced |
| 1 pound okra, sliced medium | 1½ cups cooked rice |
| 2 tablespoons parsley, minced | pepper, salt, optional |

Hollow out the tomatoes, reserving the pulp. Melt the butter and sauté the okra, parsley, onion, and garlic in it. Stir often, till the onions and okra are soft, about 20 minutes. Then add the tomato pulp, rice, pepper, and salt, if desired, and cook another 5 minutes. Stuff the tomatoes with this mixture and place them close together in a buttered baking dish. Bake for 10 minutes in a 400°F oven. The tomato and okra flavors go very well together.

### Okra Soup                (Makes 6–8 medium bowls.)

| | |
|---|---|
| ¼ pound salt pork, or bacon, chopped fine, or several tablespoons oil | 1 large tomato, chopped, or 1 cup stewed tomatoes |
| 2 cups okra, thinly sliced | 4 cups chicken stock, other soup stock, or water |
| 1 small green pepper, chopped medium | 1 teaspoon honey, or brown sugar |
| 1 cup celery, chopped medium | ½ teaspoon paprika |

Heat the salt pork or bacon till fat is rendered from it, or heat the oil. Add the okra, green pepper, and celery, and fry slowly, stirring often, till the vegetables are soft. Heat the soup stock or water to a boil, then add the fried vegetable mixture, tomato, honey or brown sugar, and paprika. Simmer for about 30 minutes. The okra gives a smooth, delicious texture to this soup.

*Dried Okra Soup*   Add about ½ cup thinly sliced dried okra to the soup stock or water when it is cold, and heat them together. Dried green pepper and dried celery can also be used, and frying the vegetables omitted. In this case, crisply fried crumbled bacon makes a nice garnish.

---

### OKRA IDEAS

**Southern Fried Okra**   Trim the caps off the okra pods. Leave small pods whole, and cut large pods in several pieces. Roll or shake in cornmeal or flour seasoned with pepper and salt, if desired. Fry in oil or fat over medium heat, turning as necessary, till the okra is golden brown and soft. Watch the heat because okra burns easily.

As a variation, mash the trimmed okra pods with cornmeal and fry as small patties.

**Okra Salads**   Steam whole okra pods till tender. Trim off caps, then dress with a little vinegar, pepper, and salt, if desired, while still hot. Cool and serve as a simple side dish, or a salad to go with meat. Steamed okra is also very good marinated in an oil and vinegar dressing, or any favorite salad dressing, for half an hour or so, and tossed with salad greens. Raw, sliced or chopped okra can be added in small amounts to any salad.

### *Chicken Okra Gumbo, Creole Style* (Makes about 6 dinner servings.)

*2 pounds (about) chicken cut in serv-
    ing pieces (A small fryer or part
    of a stewing hen.)*
*oil, bacon drippings, or chicken fat,
    for frying*
*1½ pounds okra, sliced medium*
*1 large onion, chopped medium*
*2 tablespoons flour*
*1 fresh tomato, chopped, or 1 cup
    canned tomatoes*

*small bunch parsley, chopped*
*1 bay leaf*
*small ham bone or several
    tablespoons chopped ham, op-
    tional*
*salt, optional (Omit if using
    bacon drippings or ham.)*
*hot red pepper, to taste (Fresh
    minced, dry flakes, or pow-
    der.)*

Heat the oil or fat in a Dutch oven or other heavy pan, and fry the chicken pieces in it till browned on all sides. Take out the chicken, then fry the okra and onion in the same fat over low heat till lightly browned. Take them out also.

Reserve 2 tablespoons of the fat, and discard the rest. Mix in the flour and stir constantly over very low heat for 10–15 minutes to make a nicely browned roux. Then return the chicken, okra, and onions to the pan, and add the tomato, parsley, bay leaf, and ham or ham bone. Add hot water to just cover the ingredients, and season with red pepper and salt, if desired. Cover and simmer over low heat from 1 to 2 hours, or till the chicken is done. Very good served with rice.

# ONIONS

EVERYWHERE IN THE WORLD, HUMANKIND EATS ONIONS, AND onions are called for in recipes more often than any other vegetable. They are eaten raw and cooked in every style, using every method ever devised. They are also as delicious tossed into the coals of a campfire and roasted, as they are mingled with the rarest ingredients in the haughtiest cuisines. In addition, onions are credited with most of the same medicinal values as garlic, though in a milder way, and are eaten to maintain health and prevent disease. And last but not least, they are said to repel both insects and witches.

Onions come in many forms and varieties. Most familiar are the mature, papery skinned bulbs. These range anywhere from marble sized to grapefruit sized, and they may be any color from white-beige-yellow-brown to purplish-red. Their flavors and aromas may range from sweet and mild to harsh and tear jerking. Next most common are slender, young, green scallions. All young onions with green tops may be called scallions, no matter what they will be like at maturity. The bunching types of onions, and the multiplier (Egyptian) onions never produce large bulbs. These are valuable because they can overwinter in the garden and provide scallions in very early spring and late fall. Shallots are close relatives of onions, grown like garlic but eaten like onions. Their special flavor is prized by many cooks. (For other onion relatives refer to CHIVES, SCALLIONS and GREEN ONIONS, in the HERBS section, and to the LEEKS section.)

Many kinds of wild onions are worth gathering, and there is one species or another growing over most of North America. Some are so strong they can be used only for seasoning, but others can be used like cultivated onions.

## STORAGE

**Canning** (Resulting texture or color may be poor.) Small (about 1 in. diameter) preferred. Trim, peel, push large needle or ice pick into root end to help hold shape. Boil 5 min. Pack hot in jars, add boiling cooking water, ½ in. headroom. Pressure process, 240°F, 11 pounds pressure. Pints: 25 min. Quarts: 30 min. (Refer to CANNING section.)

**Cold Storage** See CURING AND STORING MATURE ONIONS, below.

**Drying** See DRYING ONIONS, below.

**Freezing** *Mature Onions* Blanch 3–7 min. (Texture poor. Best used to flavor cooked dishes.) (Refer to FREEZING section.) *Greens and Scallions* (Refer to FREEZING HERBS in HERB section.)

I POUND ONIONS = ABOUT 3½ CUPS, CHOPPED

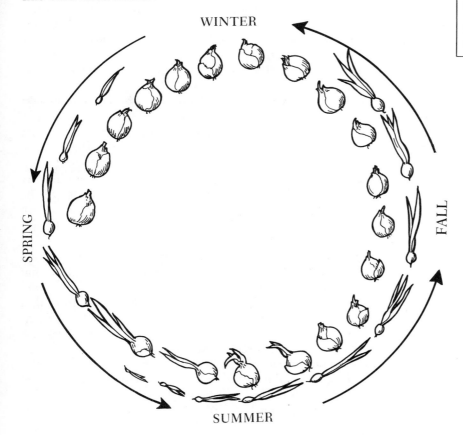

*The onion year*

# HANDLING ONIONS

It would be ideal to always have a supply of homegrown onions in the store room, and a stand of small, green onions ready to pull in the garden, but in most places, this is difficult to achieve. It is not so difficult, however, to have homegrown onions of one kind or the other on hand throughout the year. Recipes can then be adjusted to suit the available onions, with no need to purchase any.

***Green Onions (Scallions)*** To be good these almost have to be fresh. If dried they are tasteless. They may retain their flavor when frozen, but their texture will be poor. The longer they can be maintained in the garden, the better.

The earliest green onions of the season are likely to come from overwintered multiplier or bunching onions. These can be pulled as scallions, or the greens can be cut off at ground level to use like chives, leaving the bulbs to produce more greens. Later in the season, scallions will come from the thinnings of onions grown from sets or seeds. In winter, it is possible to grow onion greens by planting sets in pots on the window sill. Sets collected from the tops of multiplier onions in the summer can be used.

When green onions are not available for the table, a slice of mature onion can be minced and used instead. Conversely, green onions, including their tops, can be chopped and used in cooking instead of mature onions. As they cook quickly, it is best to add them towards the end of the cooking time. They are excellent in soups and stews. If fried the cooking time should be very brief.

***Curing and Storing Mature Onions*** Onions are ready to harvest when the tops have stopped growing and have fallen over. After pulling or digging them, spread the onions out in a single layer in a dry airy place to cure for about a week. If the weather is dry they can be left outdoors on the ground, with their tops flopped over them to protect them from the sun. Otherwise they can be spread out in any sheltered, well ventilated place. When cured the onion tops will be dry and shrunken at the neck of the bulb. Set aside any onions with thick necks to be used first, as they will not keep long. Cut the dry leaves off about an inch above the bulbs.

Store onions in net bags, or in well ventilated boxes in a dry, cool place. A root cellar is too damp. They are better off in a dry place that is too warm than in a cool, damp place. An unheated attic or a spare room that stays above freezing is excellent. The length of time that cured onions will keep depends on their variety as well as storage conditions. Many varieties will keep 2 to 3 months. Only the long keeping, winter varieties can be stored till spring.

Check stored onions ocasionally for softness, spoilage, or sprouting. The sprouts can be used like scallions. Dry any which show signs of sprouting or spoiling before they can be used.

Onions can be braided and hung like garlic (refer to the GARLIC section for directions), but they are not likely to keep as well as those cured and stored as above.

***Drying Onions*** Drying mature onions is easy, and they are convenient to use. For drying, simply slice them thinly and evenly and spread them on drying trays. Dry till hard or brittle. Onions do not need blanching. So that all slices are uniform it is best to use a vegetable slicer. (Refer to the KITCHEN UTENSILS section.) With varying thicknesses extra thin slices may turn brown before thicker slices have dried completely. Onions may also turn brown if they are dried in heat over about 130°F. However, this coloring is not necessarily a bad thing, and brown onions can give color and flavor to some soups, gravies, and meat stews. (Refer to the FOOD COLORING section.)

Dried onions can be added directly to any liquid mixtures as long as they are allowed about 20 minutes of cooking time. For instant seasoning, bring them first to meal or powder in a blender or other grinder, but they must be completely hard or brittle. Sometimes during storage onions become somewhat limp or leathery, and though they will continue to keep, they must be heated briefly to make them brittle again before grinding.

***Peeling and Preparing Onions*** Though onions taste good roasted, steamed, or boiled in their skins and peeled when done, they must be peeled before being cooked in mixtures. Peeling a few onions for immediate use is easy, but when preparing many onions time can be saved if they are blanched in boiling water for about half a minute, then dunked in cold water to chill them. This will loosen the skins so that they slip off easily.

When cooking whole onions, cut a small X in their stem ends, or poke a hole in them with a large needle, or ice pick. This will cause the inside to cook almost at the same speed as the outside, making the splitting off of the outside layers or the pushing out of inner layers less likely.

To chop onions quickly, first cut them in half the long way, through the root and stem end, then lay the halves flat on the cutting board. Make several cuts the long way, leaving the root end intact to keep layers from sliding apart. Then, slice across the grain, starting at the stem end. To mince, make the long cuts closer together and slice more thinly.

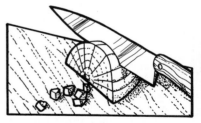

*Chopping or mincing onions*

The fumes that rise when peeling and slicing the stronger types of onions cause many harmless tears. The best preventive is probably a very sharp knife that will cut without crushing and releasing fumes, but relief can be found in other ways as well. If onions are cold, they will give off fewer fumes and cause fewer tears. When they are stored in a cold place, leave them there till just before preparing them. Other suggestions are, keeping a piece of bread in one's mouth, using a fan to blow fumes away, and peeling them under the cold water faucet. Or the more drastic measures in the HORSERADISH section can be tried.

***Onion Juice*** Occasionally onion juice is wanted as a flavoring. A pulpy juice can be made by grating onions with a fine grater. Juice can also be pressed from a cut onion half using the reamer style of juicer. For just a little juice, scrape the cut side of an onion with a teaspoon, or press a small piece of onion in a garlic press.

As onion juice loses its flavor quickly, do not make it till ready to use it.

***Cooking Onions*** Onions cooked quickly, at higher temperatures will have a sharper taste than those cooked more slowly. High heat also causes a strong onion odor that many people find objectionable. Onions are usually preferred cooked slowly over low to moderate heat. Prepared this way, they become soft, translucent, and almost sweet-tasting, without browning. They also taste delicious cooked very slowly till brown and reduced almost to a purée.

## ONION RECIPES

### *Bewitched Onion Stew*                    (Makes about 6 side servings.)

| | |
|---|---|
| 3 *tablespoons butter, or oil* | *1 cup soup stock, or water* |
| 3 – 4 *medium onions, chopped small* | *1 tablespoon (about) lemon* |
| 2 *cups small onions, peeled* | *juice, or vinegar* |
| 2 *cups carrots, cut to the size of the* | *pepper, salt, optional* |
| *small onions* | *parsley, minced* |

Heat the butter or oil, then sauté the chopped onions in it over low heat till they brown lightly and become very soft. This will take 30 to 40 minutes. Stir the onions often, especially when they begin to brown.

Poke a hole in the stem end of each small onion with a large needle or the point of a knife, and put them in a pot with the carrots and soup stock or water. Cook, covered, till onions and carrots are tender, about 30 minutes. Combine with the sautéed onions and season with lemon juice or vinegar, pepper and salt, if desired. Place on a serving dish and garnish with parsley.

This makes a colorful, flavorful Halloween vegetable dish.

### *Onion Pudding*                          (Makes about 6 side servings.)

| | |
|---|---|
| 2 *cups onions, halved and thinly* | ¼ *cup cheese, grated, optional* |
| *sliced* | *(Swiss is excellent.)* |
| 2 *tablespoons butter* | ¼ *cup flour* |
| 2 *eggs, lightly beaten* | *pepper, salt, optional* |
| 1 *cup milk* | |

Melt the butter in a sauce pan. Add the onions, then cover and stew them over very low heat for 30 minutes. They should become soft and translucent, but not brown. Let cool for a few minutes.

Mix the eggs, milk, cheese, flour, pepper, and salt, if desired. Stir in the onions. Pour in a buttered baking dish and bake in a hot, 450°F oven for 20 to 25 minutes, or till the pudding puffs up and browns lightly. The pudding falls as it cools, but its flavor remains full.

---

### ONION IDEAS

**Onions Stewed in Fruit Juice**

To make a side dish that goes especially well with roast meats, put peeled onions, whole or quartered, in a saucepan; add a dab of butter or other fat; and pour in enough apple cider, orange juice, or another fruit juice to about half cover them. Simmer covered till the onions are tender, from 30 to 40 minutes. Season to taste with mint or thyme, and perhaps a little grated lemon peel.

For a sauce texture, chop the onions, then stew them only 10 to 15 minutes. If thickening is needed, add fine, dry bread crumbs, a spoonful at a time, till it is thick enough. Try with hamburgers as a change from catsup.

**Onions Roasted Over Coals**

Put whole, unpeeled onions into the coals around the edge of a camp fire, or a fireplace fire, or put them on the rack of a charcoal broiler. Turn them often, roasting them slowly till they are charred on the outside and very soft and brown on the inside. Large onions may take an hour and a half. They are delicious by themselves, with no added seasonings. The American Indians often cooked wild onions in this way.

### Stuffed Onion Rings

3 medium onions, sliced ½ inch thick

½ pound ground meat, or 1 medium can (about 1 cup) tuna, or other fish

4 slices whole grain bread, soaked in water and squeezed dry

2 teaspoons sesame seeds, or chopped sunflower seeds

1 scallion, minced, or 2 tablespoons onion centers, minced

1 clove garlic, minced

pepper, salt, optional (Omit salt if using canned fish.)

¼ cup (about) flour

2 eggs, slightly beaten

3–4 tablespoons oil

Slice the onions ½ inch thick and separate into rings. There should be from 15 to 20 rings. Set centers and ends aside for other uses. Steam the rings about 3 minutes or till limp.

Mix the ground meat or fish, bread, seeds, scallions or minced onion, garlic, pepper and salt, if desired, for the stuffing. Press stuffing into each onion ring. Dip the stuffed rings into flour, then into the egg, and sauté in oil in a frying pan. Turn to brown on both sides, allowing about 5 minutes per side.

These make a very good appetizer if the rings are small. For a main course they can be served with tomato sauce, or another favorite sauce.

### Andalusian Onion Omelet (Makes 3 large or 6 moderate servings.)

6 tablespoons (about) oil, preferably olive

9–10 cups onions, finely chopped

6 eggs, at room temperature

Heat the oil in a Dutch oven or large frying pan with a lid. Add the onions, cover, and cook for 20 minutes over medium heat without stirring. Uncover and cook another 30 to 40 minutes, stirring to keep the onions from sticking. When almost done they will need stirring more often. When reduced to a soft, brown purée, remove the onions from the pan, leaving behind as much oil as possible, and let them cool a few minutes. They can be cooked several hours ahead of time, if preferred.

Beat the eggs till light, then mix in the onions. Reheat the pan used for cooking the onions, adding a little more oil if necessary. When it is quite hot, pour in ⅓ of the omelet mixture. After a moment shake the pan, or use a spatula to loosen the omelet around the edges, keeping it free in the pan. When the omelet is almost firm turn it over in one piece in the pan. This can be done by sliding it onto a plate, putting the pan upside down over the plate and turning both plate and pan over together. Shake as the second side browns, and serve immediately. Divide the rest of the omelet mixture in half and cook the second and third omelets in the same way, adding a little

## PARSLEY IDEAS

**Parsley Bouquet**    To keep a bunch of parsley fresh for several days after it is picked, put it in a glass of water as if it were a bouquet of flowers. For extra long keeping put it, glass and all, in the refrigerator. Sometimes wilted parsley will revive in a glass of water.

**All-purpose Parsley**    Use fresh parsely as a substitute for other fresh herbs when they are not available. Such herbs as basil, mint, and dill leaves can be replaced with parsley in most recipes. Though the flavor will be entirely different, it will usually still be very good.

**Parsley Tea**    Dry extra parsley leaves and stems for making herb tea. Though not parsleyish, their flavor will be mild and pleasant, and will blend well with stronger flavors. Second year parsley plants that are tough and almost ready to go to seed are good dried for tea. (Refer to the HERBS section.)

**Parsley Stems**    These have a nice flavor. Chop them small and use them in salads and in cooking along with the tops.

**Parsley and Garlic**    Recipes that include one of these are likely to taste good if the other is added as well. (Refer to THE CHANGING FLAVOR OF GARLIC, in the GARLIC section.)

more oil to the pan for each. The first person served will surely envy the cook, who gets the last serving and can savor the last few bites after everyone else has finished.

# PARSLEY

A GOOD FIRST STEP WHEN PREPARING A MEAL IS INTO THE GARDEN TO gather a bunch of fresh parsley, as there is sure to be a need for it at some point. Parsley is the most useful fresh herb anyone can grow. It goes well with virtually every kind of main course, side dish, and salad—sometimes as an ingredient, sometimes as a garnish and sometimes both. Besides color and flavor, it adds nutritional value, thanks to its rich vitamin and mineral content.

There are three types of parsley: curly leaf, plain leaf or Italian, and turnip rooted or Hamburg. Curly leafed parsley has a mild taste and looks pretty in salads and as a garnish. Plain leafed parsley is more flavorful, and is the best kind to use in cooking. It is often chopped or minced for salads and for sprinkling on foods as a garnish, as well as for cooking in mixed dishes. The large roots of turnip-rooted parsley are cooked and eaten like other root vegetables. (Refer to the CELERIAC section for ideas.) Its leaves are good used like plain leafed parsley. (Sometimes fresh coriander leaves are called Chinese parsley, but they are an entirely different plant with a different stronger flavor.)

## PARSLEY RECIPES

### Parsley Salad                                      (Makes 4–6 servings.)

large bunch parsley, minced
1–2 scallions, minced
small clove galic, minced, optional
2 tablespoons oil

1 tablespoon lemon juice, or
    cider or wine vinegar
pinch of rosemary, optional
pepper, salt, to taste
lettuce leaves, optional

Mix the parsley, scallions, garlic, oil, lemon juice or vinegar, rosemary, pepper, and salt. Adjust seasonings to taste. If desired, arrange spoonfuls on lettuce leaves to serve as individual salads. Mincing improves the parsley texture so that the flavor can be enjoyed in quantity.

*Spanish Parsley Sauce*                         (Makes 1–1½ cups.)

| | |
|---|---|
| 1 small clove garlic | 1 tablespoon wine or cider |
| 1 small potato, boiled | vinegar |
| medium bunch parsley | pepper, salt, optional |
| 2 tablespoons oil (Preferably olive.) | |

Combine all ingredients in a blender. Add a few tablespoons of water to make the blender work, and blend till smooth. This sauce can also be made with a mortar and pestle, first mashing the garlic, potato, and parsley, and then adding the other ingredients.

Serve as a sauce for fish or hot vegetables, or used as a dip for raw vegetables. It also makes an attractive salad dressing.

---

**OTHER RECIPES FEATURING PARSLEY**

Garlicky Bean Soup, p.24
Garlicky Stuffing for Vegetables, p.296
Greens and Rice, p.519
Pesto, Herb-Garlic Sauce, p.340
Potherb Pie, p.590
Raw Garlic and Parsley Relish, p.296
Recipes and Ideas for Herbs, p.339
Tabbouleh, a Middle Eastern Salad, p.684

---

# PARSNIPS

THE PARSNIP IS AN OLD FASHIONED VEGETABLE THAT LOST IMPORtance when modern storage methods were developed. Few now appreciate the value of a vegetable that can stay frozen in the ground all winter and still be sweet and ready to eat with the first spring thaws. Today's parsnip eaters can only appreciate parsnips for their fine sweet flavor when fried or mashed, for the delicious way they blend into beef stews and boiled vegetable dishes, and for the delicious way they soak up meat juices when cooked in the roasting pan.

## HANDLING PARSNIPS

Parsnips are not worth eating till after a few weeks of near freezing or below freezing fall weather. The cold turns the starch in the roots to sugar, giving them their typically sweet flavor. Store bought parsnips often have a poor flavor compared to home grown ones, which suggests that some store parsnips may be harvested too early. When home grown it is not usually necessary to harvest parsnips in large numbers for storage, since they can be dug a few at a time as needed in the fall and spring. If digging them in winter is not practical, some can be kept in a root cellar or another cool place.

Clean parsnips by washing and scrubbing with a vegetable brush. Avoid paring or scraping off skin since it contains nutrients. If parsnips are to be precooked, steam them whole, and trim off the top and root ends, and slice them only after they are cooked. Less flavor is lost in this way. Never boil parsnips in water that is later discarded, as some old recipes advise. The sugars that give parsnips their special

---

**STORAGE**

**Canning**  Slice or dice, boil 5 min., pack hot. Cover with boiling cooking water, ½ in. headroom. Process, 240°F, 11 pounds pressure. Pints: 30 min. Quarts: 35 min. (Refer to CANNING section.)

**Cold Storage**  Pack in damp material. Will keep all winter in root cellar, or similar place. (Refer to COLD STORAGE section.)

**STORAGE,** *cont.*

**Drying**  Slice, or shred raw. May steam whole till tender, then trim, slice. Dry to hard or brittle. (Refer to DRYING section.) See also ROAST BEVERAGES, in BEVERAGES section.

**Freezing**  Slice across, or lengthwise. Blanch in boiling water 2–3 min. (Refer to FREEZING section.)

**Live Storage**  (Easiest, most practical storage method.) Leave in ground, mulched. Dig up during fall, winter thaws, and early spring.

flavor are dissolved and lost in the cooking water, along with water soluble vitamins and minerals.

Sometimes a fibrous or woody core develops in parsnips, and this must be removed, but gardeners seldom have this problem with home grown roots. If necessary, the cores can be cut out of raw parsnips after they are cut in halves or quarters the long way. Whole parsnips can be steamed till tender, split open the long way, and the cores lifted out in one piece.

## PARSNIP RECIPES

### *Old Fashioned Fried Parsnips*     (Makes about 6 side servings.)

*4–6 parsnips*
*3 tablespoons (about) butter, or meat drippings*

*3 tablespoons (about) flour*

Clean the parsnips and steam them whole till tender, about 30 minutes. When done, trim, and cut small ones in half the long way. Cut large ones in ½ inch thick slices, the long way. Melt butter or drippings in a frying pan, dip each parsnip slice in it, then roll it in flour. (Use meat drippings from the meat with which the parsnips will be served.) When all of the slices are floured, heat the frying pan, adding more butter or drippings if necessary. Fry the parsnips till they are a delicate brown on both sides.

### *Parsnip Nut Cakes*     (Makes about 6 side servings.)

*3 cups cooked, mashed parsnips*
*¼ cup nuts, chopped small*
*3 tablespoons flour*

*3 tablespoons milk*
*pepper, salt, optional*
*butter or oil, for frying*

Mix the parsnips, nuts, flour, milk, pepper, and salt, if desired. Fry spoonfuls in butter or oil in a frying pan. If the batter is too thick to spread into a small pancake shape, pat it out with the back of the spoon. Turn to brown both sides. They are very good for breakfast, as well as for lunch or dinner.

### *Curried Parsnip Soup*     (Makes 6–8 medium bowls.)

*4 tablespoons butter*
*2–3 cups parsnips, diced medium*
*½ cup onion, chopped medium*
*1 clove garlic, crushed*
*1 tablespoon flour*
*1–2 teaspoons curry powder, or to taste*

*4 cups beef stock, or other soup stock*
*½ cup light cream*
*pepper, salt, optional*
*chives or scallions, minced, optional*

Melt the butter in a pot and add the parsnips, onion, and garlic. Cover and cook over low heat for about 10 minutes. The vegetables should soften but not brown. Stir in the flour and curry powder and cook about a minute. Heat the soup stock in a separate pan, then add it slowly, while stirring. Simmer together, covered, for 20 minutes. If desired, purée the soup with a food mill or blender. Season to taste, and stir in the cream. Reheat as necessary, but do not boil. Sprinkle the chives or scallions on individual bowls of soup.

### Soy Glazed Parsnips

(Makes about 6 side servings.)

4–6 medium parsnips
2 tablespoons oil or other fat
4 tablespoons soy sauce

2 tablespoons honey
¼ teaspoon dry mustard, optional

Steam whole parsnips till tender, about 30 minutes. Trim and slice. Heat the oil, honey, soy sauce, and mustard in a large frying pan. Add the parsnips and cook over low heat for about 10 minutes, stirring often. The parsnips will become glazed with the soy sauce mixture and any extra liquid will evaporate.

**Orange Glazed Parsnip**  Instead of soy sauce use 2 tablespoons of frozen orange juice concentrate and 2 tablespoons water to make the glaze.

**Glazed Carrots or Onions**  Pre-cook carrots or small whole onions and prepare them like parsnips, using either the soy sauce or orange glaze. Mixtures of all three vegetables or of any two can be glazed in this way.

### Parsnip Wine

(Makes about 1 gallon.)

4 pounds parsnips, grated
4 oranges, sliced with peel

3½ pounds sugar or honey
1 tablespoon dry baking yeast

Heat the grated parsnips in 3 quarts of water. When they boil skim off all material that rises and cook 5 minutes. Strain, then add the oranges and half the sugar. Cool to lukewarm and add the yeast. Put in a crock or other non-corrosive container, cover, and set in a warm place to ferment for 10 days.

Strain the must (wine mixture) through a cloth. Heat the other half of the sugar to a boil in two quarts of water, or the honey in one quart. Let cool to room temperature and add to the must. Put into a gallon jug with a fermentation lock, and let sit several months, or till fermentation has stopped. When clear, siphon into bottles, seal, and let it age. It is best after a year. Parsnip wine, after a year of aging, tastes more like whiskey or hard liquor than like wine. For more detailed directions, refer to the WINE section.

---

**PARSNIP IDEAS**

**Parsnip Salad**  Steam parsnips till tender. Cool, trim, slice, and mix with mayonnaise or another salad dressing. Serve on lettuce leaves, garnished with parsley and a dash of paprika, or mix with other salad vegetables. A good use for plain leftover parsnips.

**Parsnips in Carrot Recipes** Parsnips are good instead of carrots in most cooked recipes. They can be sliced and stewed or fried, or grated raw and used in recipes for vegetable and meat loaves, carrot cakes, and other baked goods.

**Puréed Parsnips**  Steam or boil parsnips in a minimum of water and purée them with a food mill, press, or blender. Use the purée as a side dish, or like pumpkin purée in desserts and bread.

For a thicker purée to serve like mashed potatoes, cook a potato with the parsnips and mash with a potato masher. Another way to thicken the purée is to make a thick cream sauce (refer to the MILK section), using 1 tablespoon butter, 1 tablespoon flour, and ½ cup milk or parsnip cooking water. Mix with the parsnip purée and cook about 5 minutes.

---

**OTHER RECIPES WITH PARSNIPS**

Parsnip or Asparagus Soufflé, p.658
Pot Au Feu, p.34
Recipes and Ideas for Vegetables, p.669
Roast Beverages, p.42
Vegetable Hot Pot, p.669
Vegetable or Fruit Quick Bread, p.64

# PEACHES

Peaches are universally popular. Their sweet juiciness when fresh, and their excellence when canned, dried, and frozen, make them a "peach" of a fruit. They probably originated in China since they are mentioned about 2,000 years ago in Chinese writing, and from there they spread throughout the world. Peaches were one of the first fresh fruits brought to America by colonists, and they adapted so well that they now grow wild in some parts of the southern United States. They can be cultivated through most of the United States and parts of southern Canada.

Nectarines are, in these pages, included with peaches. Though sometimes described as crosses between plums and peaches, botanically they are the same as peaches. There is only the minor difference of the nectarine's smooth and the peach's fuzzy skin. They both come in yellow and white varieties, and can be either cling or freestone. Both yellow varieties are high in Vitamin A, while the white varieties are low in it. Nectarines grow more successfully in western North America than in the East. Generally they are not as satisfactory as peaches when canned, dried, or frozen, but they are handled in the same ways, and can be used in the same recipes.

## HANDLING PEACHES

Usually peaches are picked after they have started to ripen and before they become soft, but those with their own trees can wait until the peaches are fully ripe and eat or process them immediately after picking. Peaches picked when soft bruise easily and do not keep long. If picked green they never ripen properly. Pick them gently by tilting and twisting them off their stems. If grabbed at and yanked they are sure to be bruised.

***Peeling Peaches*** Peaches can be eaten fuzz, peel, and all, or the fuzz can be gently rubbed off with a towel, but many people like their peaches peeled. When the fruit is very ripe the peels pull off easily. If just underripe, blanch in boiling water for 30 to 60 seconds, then dip in cold water. The peels will slip off easily. Nectarines are almost never peeled since their skin is smooth. (See PEACH SKIN JUICE, below.)

***Pitting Peaches*** The pits, or stones, easily come out of freestone peaches and nectarines when the fruit is cut in half. The flesh of clingstone fruits is firmly attached to the pits, as the name implies.

There are special sharp-edged pitting spoons that can be pushed in, starting at the stem end of the fruit, and going to the bottom of the pit to free it. If a pitting spoon is not available, cut completely around the peach or nectarine along its crease, making sure to cut down to the pit all the way around. Then hold the fruit with both hands and twist the halves in opposite directions. If the pit still does not come loose, cut around it as closely as possible with a small sharp knife. Hold the fruit over a bowl while pitting, to catch the dripping juice.

There are red fibers in the cavities of some types of peaches that turn brown and unattractive when cooked. To avoid this, the fibers can be scraped out with a spoon when the peaches are pitted.

A few peach pits or the kernels inside the pits are often cooked with peaches because they add flavor. There are warnings not to eat the kernels because of the prussic acid (hydrogen cyanide) in them. However, the pits are used for flavoring without harmful effects. (Refer to USING APRICOT PITS in the APRICOTS section.)

## PEACH RECIPES

### Nutty Baked Peaches (Makes about 6 dessert servings.)

6 fresh peaches or 12 peach halves (about), canned
¼ cup honey, or maple syrup
3 tablespoons butter, softened

¾ cup nuts, grated, or 1 cup fine dry coconut, unsweetened
¼ cup flour
1 egg

If fresh, peel the peaches, halve them and remove the pits. With a small spoon scoop out some of the center of each peach half to enlarge the hollow. Leave a shell ¼ to ½ inch thick. Make a filling by mashing the scooped peach pulp with a fork, and mixing in the honey or maple syrup, butter, nuts or coconut, flour, and egg. Spoon this filling into the shells, dividing it evenly. Set the filled peaches close together in a shallow, buttered baking dish. Bake about 30 minutes at 375°F, or till lightly browned.

### Peach Cake in a Pie Pan (Makes 6–8 dessert servings.)

3–4 pounds fresh peaches, peeled and sliced
2 teaspoons lemon juice
⅓ cup honey
1½ tablespoons tapioca
1 teaspoon cinnamon
2½ cups (about) flour (Preferably whole grain.)

1 teaspoon baking powder
2 tablespoons butter
1 egg, beaten
2 tablespoons honey
½ cup milk
1 teaspoon vanilla, optional
1 tablespoon (about) butter, for top

Combine the sliced peaches, lemon juice, honey, tapioca, and cinnamon, and set aside.

Sift the flour and baking powder, then work 2 tablespoons of butter into it, using fingers or a pastry cutter. Mix the eggs, honey, milk and

**Peach Skin Juice** When peeling large numbers of peaches for canning or freezing, collect the skins in a saucepan as they are removed. Cover them with water, heat, and simmer about 10 minutes. Strain through cloth. This juice can be used as the liquid for canning or freezing the peaches, but it is more fun to drink it as peachade. (This is not, of course, recommended if the peaches have been sprayed with insecticides.)

**Peach Bloom** Make a sauce by mixing lemon juice and a little warm water with strawberry jam or preserves, or another berry preserve. Peel fresh peaches and put one whole in each dish (or use halves if the peaches are large). Pour some sauce over each, sprinkle with slivered almonds, and chill before serving. Add other embellishments if desired. A scoop of ice cream on a peach half with the sauce on top makes a peach Melba.

**Tutti Frutti** Marinating fresh peaches in alcoholic beverages has occurred to many people in many places. Brandied peaches are best known, but wines from champagne to homemade dandelion, and liquors from corn whiskey in the South during prohibition to tequila in Mexico have been used. The marination can last only a few hours or for months or years. It is tutti frutti when sliced fresh peaches are packed in a large jar or crock, covered with the chosen beverage and left for at least 2 weeks; 2 months is better. Both peaches and beverage take a new, exotic flavor.

For a fruitier version a mixture of fruits can by used. Pears, cherries, and all kinds of berries are good. Rum goes well where cherries are used. Berries are best strained out and discarded or used in another way, because they get overly soft.

## OTHER RECIPES WITH PEACHES

Baked Apricots, p.11
Guatemalan Fruit Cup, p.290
Maple Fruit Preserves, p.361
Maple Syrup as a Sweet Sauce,
    p.402
Recipes and Ideas for Fruit,
    p.290
Spiced Pickled Fruit, p.480

vanilla, and add to the flour mixture. Stir to make a stiff dough, then roll out a bottom crust for a large, deep pie dish. The crust will be cookie-like, and fairly thick. Make a decorative arrangement of peach slices on the crust, including all their juice. Put small dabs of butter here and there. Then bake in a moderate, 350°F oven, till peaches are done and crust is lightly browned, from 30—40 minutes. Serve warm or cold.

# PEANUTS

T HE PEANUT IS WELL NAMED—"PEA" BECAUSE THE PEANUT PLANT IS a legume which grows like the pea, except that the pods form underground, and "nut" because the seeds in the pods are nut-like. The peanut's big advantage over true nuts is that a crop can be planted and harvested in the same season, while nut trees must grow for years before they come to bearing age.

Peanuts are native to tropical America, but they have become an important crop in such far flung places as India, China, and West Africa. Large quantities are also grown in the southeastern United States. Gardeners in moderate climates farther north can grow short season varieties very successfully.

In the South peanuts are sometimes called goobers, and elsewhere in the world they are known variously as groundnuts, groundpeas, and earthnuts. The two best known varieties are the small round Spanish peanuts, and the larger more oval shaped Virginia peanuts. These are somewhat different in flavor, but are handled and used in the same ways. All peanuts are rich in oil and vitamins, and, in combination with cooked grains or whole grain bread, make a very high quality protein food.

## HANDLING PEANUTS

Peanuts are harvested in the fall when the seeds are fully formed, and the veins inside the shells are darkening. The whole plant is dug or pulled with peanuts attached. Most peanuts are cured (dried) before use, but they can also be boiled and eaten fresh.

***Curing Peanuts*** Cure peanuts for about 2 months in a dry airy place that is not too warm. If too hot they dry too quickly and their flavor will be poor. They can be cured in an airy shed, or a well ventilated attic. In cooler climates an attic is best. Dryness and good ventilation are important to prevent development of aflatoxin, a carcinogenic mold. Peanut plants can be stacked or hung, and the

## STORAGE

**Canning**   See MAKING PEANUT BUTTER, below. Pack in hot half pint or pint jars, 1 in. headroom. Process, boiling water bath. Hold temperature at 190°F, 60 min., both half pints and pints. (Refer to CANNING and NUTS sections.)

**Cold Storage**   Keep refrigerated, or in a cold place after shelling to prevent rancidity. (Refer to STORING NUTS, in NUTS section.)

**Drying**   See CURING PEANUTS, below.

**Freezing**   Mature, green (not cured) peanuts in shells: blanch 10 min. in boiling water. Drain, chill, package. Also may freeze raw or roasted, shelled or unshelled peanuts, and peanut butter. (Refer to FREEZING section.)

I POUND IN THE SHELL = ABOUT 2¼ CUPS, SHELLED = ABOUT 1½ CUPS PEANUT BUTTER

peanuts picked off after curing, or they can be picked off when they are harvested, and spread on screens or trays for curing.

Cured peanuts used without roasting are called raw peanuts. They are very good in many cooked dishes, but their roasted flavor is the most familiar.

***Roasting Peanuts*** Though usually roasted in their shells, peanuts taste just as good if roasted after shelling. However, they keep best in their shells. Spread peanuts in a single layer on baking sheets in a 300°F oven till they are just barely browned, from 20 to 30 minutes for peanuts in the shell and 10 to 15 minutes for raw shelled peanuts. Shake the sheets, or stir several times to brown them evenly. Taste to test for doneness. A light roasting saves nutrients, especially the B vitamins, and their flavor will be excellent.

***Making Peanut Butter*** Peanut butter is simply roasted, ground peanuts. Raw peanuts can also be ground for a butter, but the flavor will not be of a typical peanut butter. Though the thin skins covering each peanut are sometimes removed before grinding, this is unnecessary. Skins add flavor and nutrients, and are not noticeable after grinding. Adding salt is optional, with up to ½ teaspoon per cup as the usual amount.

Peanuts can be ground to butter by putting them through a meat grinder several times. The first grinding will be difficult, but subsequent ones will be easy. Blenders and food processors will also grind peanut butter. If using a blender, add 1½ to 3 tablespoons of oil per cup. Begin by flaking the nuts in the blender. Then gradually add the oil, and continue blending till the texture is right. For chunky peanut butter, set aside some peanuts after the first grinding with a meat grinder, or some chopped in the blender, then mix into the smooth butter.

To store homemade peanut butter, always refrigerate, can, or freeze it. It will become rancid more easily than most commercial peanut butters, because the germ (heart) of the nut is not removed, and because it is not treated to retard rancidity. If freshly roasted peanuts are used, homemade peanut butter is far more delicious than any that can be purchased, including most health food store offerings.

***Peanut Oil and Flour*** Large quantities of commercially grown peanuts are pressed for oil and the residue made into flour. Too much heavy equipment is involved to make this a practical pursuit for homesteaders, and, though small amounts of oil can be collected from peanuts ground in a meat grinder, this leaves a very dry peanut butter.

To make peanut meal like flour for use in baking, grate peanuts or whirl them in a blender in very small batches. This meal is rich, but very flavorful.

***Blanching and Peeling Peanuts*** To change their appearance, shelled peanuts are sometimes blanched to loosen and peel off the thin, dark, inner skin covering each nut. However, this is an unnecessary and undesirable procedure. The flavorful skins contain nutrients, and are too thin to be troublesome when eaten. They are blanched by dropping them in boiling water for 3 minutes. After draining and chilling the skins are easily rubbed off.

## PEANUT RECIPES

(See also MAKING PEANUT BUTTER, above.)

### *West African Groundpea Stew*          (Makes 6–8 dinner servings.)

| | |
|---|---|
| 3 *pounds (about) stewing chicken, cut in serving pieces* | *black pepper, to taste* |
| 2 *large onions, thickly sliced* | *salt, optional (Omit of using salted peanut butter.)* |
| 4 *hardboiled whole eggs, peeled* | 1 ¼ *cups shelled, freshly roasted* |
| ½-1 *cup mushrooms, sliced, optional (Fresh or canned.)* | *peanuts, or* ⅔ *cup peanut butter* |

Put the chicken and onion in a pot with just enough water to cover. Bring to a boil, skim, and simmer about 1 hour, or till the chicken is half done. Remove extra fat, and set aside 2 cups chicken stock. To the pot, add the eggs, mushroom, pepper, and salt, if desired. Chop or flake the roasted peanuts. If using a blender, blend in 3 or 4 batches. Purée the peanuts and the chicken stock in the blender till smooth. If using chunky peanut butter, purée it also with stock. Smooth peanut butter can simply be mixed with the stock. (Fresh roasted peanuts give the best flavor.) Pour the peanut purée into the pot with the chicken and other ingredients, then continue simmering covered, till the chicken is tender, from ½ to 1 hour. Halve the eggs just before serving. The peanuts make the sauce deliciously creamy and rich—perfect over rice.

### *Peanut Macaroons*          (Makes about 2 dozen medium cookies.)

| | |
|---|---|
| 1 *cup raw peanuts* | ¼ *cup honey, or maple syrup* |
| 2 *tablespoons flour* | *peanut halves for garnish, optional* |
| 2 *egg whites* | |

Grate the peanuts to a fine meal. This is easily done in 4 or 5 batches in the blender. Mix the meal with the flour.

Beat the egg whites till stiff. If using honey, warm it just enough to make it run easily. Fold the honey or maple syrup into the egg whites, then fold in the peanut meal mixture. Have ready a greased and floured cookie sheet. Drop on the batter, a teaspoon at a time, leaving space for the macaroons to spread. Put a peanut half on each and bake about 10 minutes in a low, 300°F, oven. They should just brown lightly. Remove them from the pans as soon as they come from the oven, as they tend to stick. They are especially delicate in flavor and texture.

---

### PEANUT IDEAS

**Peanut Accompaniment**  Set a bowl of chopped peanuts on the table when serving bean, rice, or grain dishes, and let everyone sprinkle them on for themselves. The peanuts add protein as well as a crunchy texture. They go especially well with chili beans and with curries. A dish of chopped raw scallions or onions is nice for sprinkling along with the peanuts.

**Peanuts in Salads**  Toss some roasted and chopped peanuts with lettuce or shredded cabbage salads. Finish with a tangy dressing of oil and lemon juice, with a few crushed mustard seeds, and a drop of honey.

**Beer Nuts**  Heat a cast iron or other heavy frying pan till quite hot, and fry 2 cups raw peanuts in about a teaspoon of oil for 5 to 10 minutes till golden brown. Meanwhile mix 2 tablespoons honey, 1 teaspoon soy sauce, and ¼ teaspoon cayenne pepper. Remove the pan from the stove, and immediately put in the honey mixture. Stir till peanuts are well coated. They will stick together in a clump when hot, but will easily break apart after cooling. A very good snack with or without beer.

*Indonesian Peanut Sauce*                    (Makes about 2 cups.)

| | |
|---|---|
| 1 tablespoon oil | 1 cup coconut milk, or water |
| 1 medium onion, minced | 1 teaspoon honey |
| 1 clove garlic, minced | 2 teaspoons soy sauce |
| 1 slice ginger root, minced, optional | 1 tablespoon lemon juice |
| 1 small hot pepper, minced, or ½–1 teaspoon hot pepper flakes or powder | ½ cup peanut butter |

Heat the oil in a saucepan and add the onion, garlic, ginger root, and hot pepper. Sauté over medium heat, stirring, till the onion is soft but not brown.

In a bowl, mix together the coconut milk or water, honey, soy sauce, lemon juice, and peanut butter. Stir into the onion mixture and simmer for 5 to 10 mintues. Watch closely and stir often, because it easily sticks and burns.

It is delicious used as a dip with raw vegetables, or mixed with hot cooked vegetables. It is very good with green beans, or cabbage, cauliflower, or carrots, and served with rice.

---

### OTHER RECIPES WITH PEANUTS

Fresh Beans with Nuts, p.31
Honey Confection, p.352
Nut Butter Salad Dressing, p.533
Peanut Butter Carob Squares, p.111
Peanut Butter Vegetable Loaf, p.439
Recipes and Ideas for Nuts, p.438

---

# PEARS

P EARS ARE GOOD MIXERS. THEY LIKE ALL KINDS OF SPICES AND flavorings, and they fit into every kind of fruit situation, from beverages and compotes to baked desserts. They are also favorites for eating plain whether fresh, canned, or dried. In fact, in temperate climates, they rate just after apples as the second most popular fruit.

There are many pear varieties, and some that excel for a particular purpose, such as anjous for winter storage, or sekels for pickling and stewing. Most make good juice and sauce. Several varieties of pear trees are likely to be included in even a small home orchard.

## HANDLING PEARS

Most kinds of pears have a better texture and keep better if picked when they show the very earliest signs of ripening—when their skins turn a lighter shade of green, and the stems separate easily from the fruiting spurs as the pears are lifted. If pears must be pulled from the tree, it is best to wait a little longer to harvest them. Pears left unpicked till fully ripe are more apt to turn brown in their center, or to form stony granules in their flesh, and they will not keep long in cold storage.

***Peeling and Coring Pears*** Most pear skins are thin and not troublesome to eat so peeling is not necessary. Even canned pears

---

### STORAGE

**Canning**  Peel (optional—see below), halve, and core. Optional: Add flavoring to each jar. (Refer to PEAR FLAVORINGS under IDEAS, below.)

**Raw Pack**  Halves, quarters, slices. Add boiling juice, syrup, or water, ½ in. headroom. Process boiling water bath. Pints: 25 min. Quarts: 30 min.

**Hot Pack**  Cook halves or quarters in boiling syrup, juice, or water for 2 min. Drain, pack, add boiling cooking liquid, ½ in. headroom. Process boiling water bath. Pints: 20 min. Quarts: 25 min. Refer to CANNING section. See also CANNING FRUIT JUICE AND SAUCE in FRUITS section. *Caution:* If fruit is overripe, add 2 teaspoons lemon juice per pint, 4 teaspoons per quart. See also *Pear Relish,* below, *Spiced Pickled Fruit* in PICKLING section, and CANNING FRUIT JUICE AND SAUCE in FRUITS section.

**Cold Storage**  Winter varieties. Pick green and hard. Cure 1 week in airy place no warmer than 70°F. Store like apples. (Refer to APPLES section.) Storage life 2–7 mos. depending on variety. Ripen for several days at room temperature before eating. (Refer to COLD STORAGE section.)

**Drying**  Use ripe, but still firm pears. Halve, core, set on tray cut side up, or for fast drying, slice thinly, and core (optional). May separate outside skin-covered slices, which dry more slowly. Dry to leathery. Also purée for leather. Refer to DRYING section.

**Freezing**  Use ripe, but firm pears. Halve, or quarter, core. Cook several at a time, 1–2 minutes in liquid, lift out, cool, pack. Cover with cooled cooking liquid. (Pre-cooking improves texture.) (Refer to FREEZING section.) Also refer to FREEZING FRUIT JUICE AND SAUCE in FRUITS section.

2–2½ POUNDS FRESH = 1 QUART CANNED OR FROZEN;  1 BUSHEL = 20–25 QUARTS CANNED OR FROZEN

taste good with the peels on, but many do not like their appearance. Pears can be pared like apples, or blanched in boiling water from 1 to 3 minutes to loosen the skins, then peeled. Blanching time depends on the variety of pear. Though the skins do not slip off as easily as do blanched peach skins, it is faster than paring.

Pear cores can be eaten since they are soft enough to be chewable, but most people do not enjoy them. Cores, and the fibrous veins that go from the stem to the core, are easily cut or scooped out after the pears are cut in half.

As pears darken quickly after they are peeled or halved, they can be sprinkled with lemon juice, or dipped in an ascorbic acid solution, made by dissolving 1 teaspoon crystalline ascorbic acid in 1 cup water. However, this can be omitted if the pears are prepared quickly, in small batches.

## PEAR RECIPES

### Pears and Potatoes

(Makes 6–8 side servings.)

2 tablespoons fat or oil
1 onion, chopped small
2 tablespoons flour
1½ cups light stock, or water
1 tablespoon honey, or brown sugar
½ teaspoon salt, optional
6 medium pears
4–5 medium potatoes

Heat the fat or oil in a heavy saucepan. Add the onion, and stir to coat it with oil. Add the flour, and cook over low heat, stirring often, till well browned, 10 to 15 minutes. Add the stock or water, sweetening, and salt, and cook over moderate heat, stirring often, to make a smooth brown sauce.

Meanwhile, cut the pears into quarters and core them. Do not peel them. Cut the potatoes into chunks about the same size as the pieces of pear. (Peeling optional.) There should be about an equal amount of pears and potatoes. Put them in the brown sauce, cover, and cook over medium low heat till both are done, about 30 minutes. Stir once or twice while they cook. If they should start to dry out and stick, add a little water, but do not make the sauce thin. Serve as a very tasty and unusual alternative to plain potatoes.

### Piquant Pear Relish

(Makes 4–5 pints.)

3 quarts (about) hard green pears (Windfalls are excellent.)
2 medium onions
4–6 sweet red or green peppers
1 fresh hot pepper, or dry flakes, or powder, to taste
4 tablespoons mustard seed, or mustard powder (Seeds are milder.)
4 tablespoons flour
1 tablespoon cumin seeds
1 tablespoon turmeric, optional (For color.)
½ teaspoon salt, optional
3½ cups vinegar
½ cup honey

Grate the pears, onions, and sweet and hot peppers, or grind them with a meat grinder or food processor. (If using dry flakes or powder, add to the following mustard mixture.)

Mix the mustard, flour, cumin, turmeric, and salt, if desired, in a large pot. Moisten with enough of the vinegar to make a paste. Then add the rest of the vinegar and the honey, and heat, stirring often. Simmer about 5 minutes, till the mixture thickens. Add the pear mixture, and bring to a boil, stirring to prevent sticking. Pour into hot canning jars, leaving ½ inch headroom. Process in a boiling water bath, 10 minutes. (Refer to CANNING section.)

This distinctive relish improves with several months of storage.

## PEAR IDEAS

*Pear Flavorings*   Stewed pears and baked pear desserts are greatly enhanced with distinctive flavorings, such as mint leaves, ginger root slices, twists or gratings of citrus peel, and whole cloves, coriander seeds, or other spices. Lemon juice goes well with any of these. Use it when adding flavorings to jars of pears before canning.

*Grated Pears*   Firm or hard pears can be grated and used in many ways. Add them to salads along with crisp vegetables like grated carrots or cabbage. Use them in fruit breads, muffins, and other baking and with vegetables in raw or cooked relishes, like the ones in the CUCUMBERS section.

*Perry*   When pears are plentiful, try crushing and pressing some for juice, using equipment for making apple cider. The fresh juice is good and sweet, but it is not "perry" till after it has fermented like hard cider. (Refer to MAKING APPLE CIDER in the APPLES section.)

*Pears in Wine or Cider*   Firm pears, and especially sekel pears are good stewed in port, or another kind of wine, or in apple cider. They are attractive peeled whole, carefully leaving the stem in place, but larger pear halves are also good. Cover the pears with the wine or cider in a saucepan, adding a twist of lemon or orange peel, a stick of cinnamon, or other whole spice, and a little sweetening, if desired. Simmer gently till the pears are soft. If there is too much juice left, take out the pears and boil the juice down to a syrup. Pour it over the pears and chill. If using canned pears, simmer the canning liquid with wine and flavorings till considerably reduced, then add the pears and simmer briefly.

Pears can also be baked in wine or cider in a very low oven. One old recipe suggests layering pears with grape leaves in an "earthen pot," covering them with cider and cooking them all night in a very low oven. The grape leaves add an interesting tartness to this dish.

*Steamed Pear Cups*   Prepare 1 pear per person. Cut the top off each pear, about 1 inch down, leaving the stem on for a handle. Scoop out the core with a small spoon or apple corer, without cutting through the bottom of the pear. Put a spoon of honey in the hole and cover with the pear top. Set each pear upright in an individual cup, such as a custard cup. Put the cups on a rack in a pot over boiling water, and steam till tender. They will take 15 to 30 minutes to cook depending on their size and ripeness. (Refer to the STEAM COOKING section.) Serve warm in the cups.

This Chinese recipe is said to be good for coughs and colds.

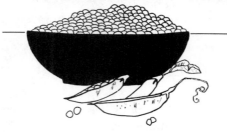

# PEAS

F RESH SHELLED GREEN PEAS ARE A DELICACY KNOWN ONLY TO THOSE who have them growing in the garden. Eaten right out of the pod when picked, there is no tastier raw vegetable. Any sensible child soon finds his or her way to the pea patch to shell and eat some on the spot. Adults would be well advised to do the same. After everyone has had a fresh snack, peas can be picked for cooking, freezing, or canning. Peas were among the first vegetables to be canned when the process was invented, and later among the first to be frozen. They are still among the best for either purpose.

Two other types of peas can be grown in the garden: edible podded peas and mature dry peas. The edible, podded snow peas that come from China and other Asian countries are picked while the pods are flat, tender, and crisp. Snap or sugar snap peas are a new edible, podded variety that remain tender even after the peas are fully developed in the pods. Dry peas, to be shelled and used like dry beans, can be collected from any variety of pea by leaving the pods to dry on the vine, or a split pea variety can be grown.

Chick peas, cow peas, and black-eyed peas are all beans rather than peas. (Refer to the BEANS, DRY section.)

## HANDLING PEAS

***Green Peas*** Pick green or garden peas, also called English peas, after the peas are swollen in the pods but before the pods lighten in color. If picking is delayed too long they will become hard and bitter. However, such peas can be left on the vine to mature and then harvested as dry peas.

Eat or process fresh peas as soon after picking as possible. If they must be kept for any length of time, refrigerate them. The sugar in the peas rapidly turns to starch after they are picked and they lose sweetness. Shelling is the only preparation peas need. Small batches are easily shelled by hand, but preparing large batches for freezing or canning becomes tedious. Pea shelling can be a family project with everyone helping, or a bean or pea sheller can be purchased. There are manually and electrically operated models that shell both fresh beans and peas quickly. (Refer to the BEANS, FRESH section.)

Freshly shelled peas need not be washed if hands and utensils are clean. The pod protects the peas so well that they are likely to be cleaner without washing.

Home grown green peas are ideal for freezing. If picked at their prime and quickly processed and frozen, they will be far sweeter and more tender than commercially sold frozen peas. Canned peas are also good, but they cannot match the fresh flavor of frozen peas.

Green pea pods are lined with a membrane that is too stiff to eat, but the fleshy part of the pod has a good flavor. Take advantage of this by using pea pods when making soup stock and then straining them out. (See *Herbed Pea Pod Soup,* below.) The pods can also be dried for later use.

**Edible Podded Peas**   Both snow peas and snap or sugar snap peas can be harvested over a longer season than green peas, providing they are consistently picked and not allowed to mature on the vine. Snow peas must be picked while the pods are still flat. They become too tough and stringy to enjoy when they fill out. Snap or sugar snap peas remain tender till the pods are swollen and the peas have reached full size. As much of their flavor is in the pods, they do not compare with the green peas when shelled.

Both types of edible podded peas are best fresh since freezing is the only practical way to store them, and then they lose the crispness that makes them so delightful to eat. Snap peas are really salad vegetables, and some should be picked every day or two for eating raw as a snack or adding to salads. Snow peas are known for their excellence when stir-fried, but they are also delicious raw. Steam both snap and snow peas for 2 or 3 minutes for eating as a hot vegetable, or add them to soup for the last minute or two of cooking. If cooked longer they will lose both texture and flavor.

There are strings along the seams of edible podded peas that are hardly noticeable if the peas are raw, but they can become bothersome after cooking. To remove the strings, break off the tip of the pod and pull. The strings will come off with the tip.

Edible podded peas are practical both as early pods to be picked for eating raw, and later (when many other garden vegetables are available) to mature for a crop of dry peas.

**Dry Peas**   Dry peas, also called soup peas, make good soup or stew no matter what their variety. Cooked larger dried peas are very much like beans. Split peas are a special variety listed in seed catalogs and intended only for dried use. Dry peas are picked, shelled, and stored like dry beans. (Refer to SHELLING AND STORING DRY BEANS, in the BEANS section.)

Pea flour can be made by grinding dry peas in a grain mill. It can be used for making quick pea soup or small amounts can be used for some baking. (The pea flavor is strong, and may not be appreciated in more delicate baked goods.) It is also possible to sprout dry peas and use them like bean sprouts, but they are not as easy to sprout as smaller sized seeds. (Refer to the SPROUTS section.)

## PEA IDEAS

### Steamed Snap Pea Salad

String snap peas and steam them for about 2 minutes, just till they change color. Toss with oil and vinegar, or another favorite salad dressing while they are warm. Cool and add any preferred salad vegetables and seasonings. Chopped scallion, parsley, sweet pepper, and celery are very good. The steamed snap peas are also delicious added to potato or egg salads. They add color and flavor.

### Peas with Herbs
Fresh herbs make perfect seasonings for hot peas. While the peas are cooking, mince some fresh basil, savory, mint, fennel, or parsley, and put it in the serving dish with a pat of butter or a spoon of oil. Put the hot peas in the dish, stir, and serve. Dried herbs can be used if fresh are not available.

### Peas' Special Greenness

When cooked just enough to brighten them, both shelled and edible podded peas have an intense, fresh green color guaranteed to make any dish containing them look more appetizing. Add snow or snap peas to soups, especially clear ones, a minute or two before serving time. Mix fresh, cooked, shelled peas, or frozen peas, cooked just enough to thaw them, with hot cooked potatoes, macaroni, onions, or any root vegetable. Layer peas in casseroles, or add them to stews, or stuffings, or cooked grains. They will add flavor as bright as their color.

## PEA RECIPES

### Eggs Nestled in Peas
(Makes 4 lunch or breakfast servings.)

| | |
|---|---|
| 1 tablespoon butter, or olive oil | 4 – 5 eggs |
| 2 cups shelled peas, fresh or frozen | 6 tablespoons light cream, optional |
| ¼ teaspoon each nutmeg, mace, and black pepper | |

Use a saucepan or casserole that can double as a serving dish. Heat ¼ cup water together with butter or oil. Add the peas and seasonings. Cover and cook till the peas are half done, 5 to 7 minutes. Frozen peas need only be thawed and heated. Taste and adjust seasonings if necessary. Make four depressions in the peas with the back of a spoon. Then break each egg in a dish, and slide it into a depression. Cover and simmer till the eggs are set and the peas tender, from 5 to 10 minutes. Serve plain, or make the following topping.

Beat the fifth egg with the cream. Pour this over the peas and eggs, as soon as they are done, and put under the broiler till bubbly, 1 – 2 minutes.

### Herbed Pea Pod Soup
(Makes about 6 medium bowls.)

| | |
|---|---|
| pods from shelling 2 or more pounds peas | ½ – 1 cup peas, optional |
| 4 tablespoons butter | sprig mint or savory, minced |
| 2 – 3 scallions, chopped | ⅓ cup milk, or cream, optional |
| 2 tablespoons flour | pepper, salt, optional |

Put the pea pods in a pot and add about a quart of water. The water should cover only half of the pods. Cover and cook 30 to 40 minutes, till the pods are very soft. Stir several times. Put through a food mill or strainer to remove membranes and strings.

Melt the butter in the soup pot and sauté the scallion in it till limp. Stir in the flour till completely blended, then add the liquid from the pea pods, the peas, and the mint or savory. Heat and simmer, stirring often, till the soup is smooth and slightly thickened. Remove from heat, stir in the milk or cream, and season if desired. Though this delicately flavored soup can be reheated, do not let it boil.

*Pease Porridge*                                    (Makes 8–12 bowls.)

2 cups dry peas
1 quart vegetable or meat stock
2 onions, or leeks, chopped
2 carrots, diced

2 stalks celery, diced
1 turnip, diced
pepper, salt, optional

Soak the peas in water overnight. Cook the peas, their soaking water, and the soup stock over low heat till the peas are almost soft, about 2 hours. Add the onions or leeks, carrots, celery, turnip, and seasonings. Cook for another half hour or till the vegetables are done.

This porridge is very good served like a stew or a soup. If desired, purée it with a food mill or blender for a smooth texture. It makes a hearty dish that goes well with rye bread or rye crackers.

**OTHER RECIPES WITH PEAS**

Finnish Fish Pudding, p. 268
Jerusalem Artichoke Pie, p. 363
Recipes and Ideas for Vegetables, p. 669
Risi e Bisi, p. 520
Roast Beverages (dried peas), p. 44
Rye and Split Peas, p. 529
Simple Soup, East Asian Style, p. 577
Split Pea or Mung Bean Kedgeree, p. 518
Sweet Potato Nests for Green Vegetables, p. 624
Turnip Cups with Peas, p. 659

# PECTIN

Pectin is the substance in fruit that causes it to jell. For jelling to occur, cooking is necessary to extract or activate pectin. Other requirements are the presence of acid, which most fruits contain naturally, and the addition of a true sugar or other concentrated sweetener. Apples and quinces are especially high in pectin, and a liquid pectin can be easily extracted from raw apples, apple peels and cores, or apple pomace by boiling them in water. (Pomace is the pulp left from making apple cider. Refer to the APPLES section.)

Homemade pectin is most often used to make jelly and other preserves from low-pectin fruits, but it is also valuable in other ways. Its smooth texture and flavor blends well with more intense fruit juices. It is the ideal liquid in which to freeze fresh fruit, helping to prevent darkening of the fruit and improving texture and flavor. When made from apple parts that would otherwise be wasted, pectin exemplifies the proverbial "something from nothing."

A special kind of pectin, low methoxyl, is extracted from citrus fruits by a process impossible to duplicate at home. It jells when certain calcium compounds are present. Since sugar is not necessary for jelling, it will be of interest to those who want to make sugarless or low-sugar preserves. Low-methoxyl pectin and directions for its use are available from some health food stores and mail-order catalogs. Directions for making preserves with homemade pectin, and a discussion of other jelling agents are in the JAM AND JELLY section.

**STORAGE**

**Canning** *Homemade* (below): Pour boiling hot into hot jars. Seal as for OPEN KETTLE CANNING in CANNING section, or process in a boiling water bath, 10 min. (Refer to CANNING section generally.)

**Freezing** *Homemade* (below): Cool, pour into containers, leave air space. (Refer to FREEZING section.)

# THE PECTIN CONTENT OF FRUITS

Fruits contain varying amounts of pectin, depending on their variety and ripeness. As fruit ripens its pectin content diminishes, so that overripe fruits have very little. Skins and cores contain more pectin than the pulp.

Pectin can be extracted from any high-pectin fruit by boiling it in water. Apples are the most popular because their flavor does not overwhelm, and because cores and peels, or pomace from making cider are often available in large amounts.

### High Pectin Fruits

Apples, sour, and crabapples
Blackberries, sour
Cranberries
Red currants
Gooseberries
Eastern concord grapes
Lemons and the white part of citrus peel
Loganberries
Plums, except prune plums
Quince

### Moderate Pectin Fruits

(A few sour apples can be cooked with these to ensure jelling.)
Ripe apples
Ripe blackberries
Sour cherries
Chokecherries
Grapefruit
California grapes
Oranges

### Low Pectin Fruits

(An acidic juice, such as lemon, as well as pectin, maybe needed to jell some of these.)
Apricots
Blueberries
Figs
Western concord grapes
Peaches
Pears
Prune plums
Raspberries
Strawberries
Rhubarb
Sweet cherries
Overripe fruit

High-pectin fruits and juices may be mixed with low-pectin fruits and juices to obtain jelling combinations. Often the flavor is improved as well. (Refer to COMBINING SWEET AND TART FRUITS in the FRUITS section.)

## MAKING PECTIN

Pectin is usually made from fresh apples or apple leftovers, but dried apple can be used if it was dried raw without blanching. When whole apples, such as windfalls, are used, they should be sliced with peels and cores retained. Underripe quince or another high-pectin fruit can be used instead of apple, but the flavor is usually too strong for most blends.

To make pectin, put the apple pieces or pomace in a pot and cover with cold water. Bring to a boil and simmer for 20 to 30 minutes, or till the fruit is soft. Strain through cloth till it stops dripping. If the pectin is to be used for jelly, do not press or squeeze the cloth, as that causes cloudy jelly. Otherwise pressing saves time. Return the fruit pulp to the pot, add more water and cook another 10 to 15 minutes. Strain through cloth again, and let it drain overnight, or press, if cloudiness does not matter. Combine the juice from both strainings.

The next step is to boil down the juice to make a concentrate. For most uses it should be reduced to half its original volume, when it will have a smooth and somewhat slick, or slippery, texture. It should jell low-pectin juices if mixed half and half. When boiled down to about ⅙ or ⅛ of its original volume, it becomes a ropy syrup that should jell in a ratio of ½ to ¾ cup pectin per 4 cups of fruit juice. For storage, can or freeze pectin at the preferred concentration.

It is possible to test fruit juices or mixtures of juice and homemade pectin for jelling, as below. Juice must be cooked before testing. If the test shows a lack of pectin, more can be added before the jelly is made.

***Pectin Test with Alcohol***   Measure 1 teaspoon of the fruit juice or juice and pectin mixture. Add 1 tablespoon of standard, 70% rubbing alcohol. If this forms into one clot, enough pectin is present for jelling. If several small dabs form, more pectin is needed. Do not taste this! The alcohol is poison.

***Pectin Test with Magnesium Sulfate (Epsom salts)***   Measure 2 tablespoons of the juice or juice and pectin mixture. Stir in 1 tablespoon magnesium sulfate, then stir in 2 teaspoons sugar. Set aside for 20 minutes. If the mixture jells, there is enough pectin for making jelly.

(Refer to the JAM AND JELLY section for other requirements and procedures.)

---

### HOMEMADE PECTIN IDEAS

**Pectin Pack for Freezing Fruit**
Use pectin that has been boiled down to half its original volume as the covering liquid for fresh fruits to be frozen. It is especially good with fruits that darken easily, such as peaches, pears, apricots, sweet cherries, and figs. (Refer to the FREEZING section.)

**Pectin with Fruit Juice**   Dilute strong-flavored fruit juices and frozen juice concentrates with thin pectin instead of water for a smoother, sweeter drink. (Refer to the RHUBARB ideas section for RHUBARB PUNCH.)

**Sour Fruit Cooked in Pectin**
Use thin pectin as the liquid for cooking rhubarb and other very sour fruits. Pectin adds smoothness and sweetness so that less sweetening is needed. Tart fruits can also be canned in pectin.

**Pectin Syrup**   Boil down homemade pectin to a thin syrup. Add honey or sugar to taste, and cook to blend. Very little sweetening is needed. Such flavorings as a cinnamon stick, a slice of ginger root, or a sprig of mint can be included.

**Hair Setting Liquid**   Comb thinnish homemade pectin into hair, and set as usual.

# PEPPERS, HOT

THERE ARE PEOPLE WHO LOVE FOOD SEASONED TILL IT IS FIERY hot with peppers, while others can tolerate only a hint of hotness. These are heartfelt differences, so neither type is likely to change preference. They must agree to disagree, and the family cook must pepper foods to suit family tastes. In any case, the required hot peppers—whether few and mild, or many and fiery—can be grown and processed at home. Fresh hot peppers can be used in many recipes, and they can also be dried and ground for pepper flakes or powder, pickled, or made into hot sauce. For those who prefer to grow their own seasonings, hot pepper flakes and powder can be used instead of imported black or white pepper. The flavor is not quite the same, but the results are good.

There are many varieties of hot peppers, with many levels of intensity. Some that grow well in temperate climates are the relatively mild Hungarian Hot Wax, the red-hot Cayenne, which is thin-fleshed and easily dried, and the very hot, green Jalapeño. Jalapeños are thick fleshed, with a hotness that does not manifest itself immediately after tasting. Their heat builds and spread gradually, lasting a long time. The initial mildness may fool the unsuspecting into taking a large bite and suffering the fiery consequences.

Chili peppers are often thought to be a variety of hot pepper, which leads to some confusion. In Mexico, chile is the general name for peppers, while the different kinds are known by such names as chile pequin, chile poblano. Mexican recipes will specify whether a hot or a sweet pepper is required, and often call for a particular variety. If American recipes call for chili peppers, any hot pepper can be used, though specific varieties are intended in some regions. (To make chili powder, which is a blend of many ingredients, refer to the PEPPERS, SWEET section, following this section. For Chili Sauce, which is not generally very hot, refer to the *Tomato Catsup* recipe in the TOMATOES section.)

## HANDLING HOT PEPPERS

Hot peppers can be picked and used as soon as they reach a reasonable size, but they are hottest when fully mature. Red and yellow varieties are mature when they have lost all green coloring and become completely red or yellow. The hotness of homegrown peppers can be erratic. In the same garden, and even on the same plant, one pepper can be considerably hotter than another that looks the same. The hotness evens out once they are dried and ground, or pickled.

Thin-fleshed varieties of hot peppers are usually preserved by drying. Fleshy varieties can be dried, but they are also excellent pickled, or canned, or frozen as for sweet peppers.

***Drying Hot Peppers*** The thin-fleshed peppers, like cayenne or tabasco, are dried whole. They can be spread on trays, or threaded through their stems and hung for drying. The whole pepper plant can also be pulled and hung in a warm, dry place. When the peppers are completely dry and hard, they can be stored whole in airtight containers, or they can be flaked, or powdered. If stored whole, pieces can be broken off or crumbled as needed. The stems are discarded but the fiery seeds are usually retained.

Thick-fleshed peppers are usually sliced or chopped, and spread on trays for drying. They can be flaked or ground for seasoning.

Be sure that dried peppers are brittle before grinding. If still leathery, they will gum up the grinder or blender. For flakes, grind peppers coarsely in a grain mill, or whirl briefly in a blender. Grind finely or pulverize for powder. Seal in airtight containers. Powder will cake if exposed to air in a humid climate.

Hot pepper flakes and powder gradually lose flavor so replace the supply each year. For blends that sometimes include hot pepper, refer to the PEPPERS, SWEET section. (Also refer to the DRYING section.)

## HOT PEPPER CAUTIONS

• To prevent burning skin when handling batches of fresh hot peppers, wear rubber gloves, or rub hands with oil. The gloves or oil may not be necessary when chopping just one hot pepper. Anyone who rubs his or her eyes, or puts in contact lenses after handling peppers is going to be very miserable for a while. Burning hands can be soothed by rubbing them with salt. eyes should be rinsed with a lot of cool water.

• When flaking or pulverizing dried hot peppers in a blender, keep the lid on till the dust has settled in the container. Otherwise, the dust is likely to cause an attack of sneezing and crying.

• Cook large batches of hot peppers in a well-ventilated room to avoid a build-up of irritating fumes.

## HOT PEPPER RECIPES

***Red Hot Sauce***      (Yields vary widely with the peppers' fleshiness.)

*hot, red peppers* (The hotter the better.)
*1 or more garlic cloves, optional*

*vinegar* (Amount to equal the measure of puréed peppers.)

Trim the stems off the peppers. Cut large peppers in pieces. Cook with the garlic in just enough water to prevent sticking for about 10 minutes, or till the peppers are soft. Put through a food mill or sieve

---

### HOT PEPPER IDEAS

**Hot Peppers and Cheese** Fresh or pickled hot peppers are delicious with most kinds of cheese. Put slivers of hot pepper in cheese sandwiches, or with cheese on crackers. Add minced hot peppers to cottage cheese and other fresh cheeses, or add them to cheese sauce, or the *Old English Herbed Cheese Spread* recipe in the CHEESE, AGED section. All of these are "pepper uppers."

**Jalapeño Hot Dogs** Arrange a circle of frankurters upright around the sides of a wide-mouth jar. Put hot pickled peppers in the center. Fill the jar with pickling liquid from the peppers, adding vinegar if more liquid is needed. Cover the jar and refrigerate for about 6 weeks before using. Cut the frankfurters in slices and spear them with toothpicks for hors d'oeuvres, or put slices between crackers for truly hot "dogs."

**Peppers in Sherry** Pack whole fresh cayenne, or other thin-fleshed hot peppers, in a jar, and cover with sherry. This preserves the peppers and flavors the sherry. Both can be added to sauces and stews, or try using the sherry when some is called for in stir-fried dishes.

with a fine screen, or purée in a blender. Sieving removes seeds, producing a slightly better flavor. Measure the pepper purée. Put an equal amount of vinegar in a saucepan and heat just to a boil. Combine the hot vinegar with the purée. Cool and seal in bottles. Store in a cool, dark place. The color fades if kept in the light.

### Hot Pepper Pickle

| | |
|---|---|
| *Jalapeños, red cherry peppers, or other fleshy peppers* | *bay leaves* |
| | *whole cloves* |
| *vinegar* (Refer to PICKLING section.) | *onion slices, or tiny, whole onions* |
| Optional ingredients: | *carrots, sliced thickly* |
| *garlic cloves* | *salt* |

Put whole peppers with stems into hot, sterilized jars. If desired, a garlic clove, a bay leaf, and a few whole cloves can be put in each jar, and onion and carrot slices can be included among the peppers. Leave about 1 inch headroom. Heat a mixture of half vinegar, half water, and a little salt, if desired. Prepare 1 cup vinegar, 1 cup water, and ¼ teaspoon salt per quart jar. Pour the boiling hot vinegar mixture over the peppers, filling the jars almost to the rims. Seal immediately. Cool and store. (Refer to the CANNING section, and CANNING PICKLES in that section.)

Hot pickled peppers are excellent minced and added to cooked dishes, and mixtures of all kinds. Many enjoy them plain for snacking, or as an accompaniment with meals.

## PEPPERS, SWEET

### STORAGE

**Canning** Hot pack only. Cut out stems, cores. Halved or sliced, optional. Cook 3 min. in boiling water. Optional: Dip in cold water and peel. Pack in hot jars, 1 in. headroom. Add 1 tablespoon vinegar to pints, 2 tablespoons to quarts. (Note: A standard vinegar is necessary for safety.) Add boiling cooking water; ½ in. headroom. Process, 240°F, 11 pounds pressure. Pints: 35 min. Quarts: 45 min. (Refer to CANNING section.) See also *Sweet Pepper Relish,* and PIMIENTOS, below.

THANKS TO COLUMBUS, WHO OSTENSIBLY TASTED A HOT VEGETABLE in the New World and called it pepper, there are two completely unrelated plants with the same common name. One is the tropical pepper tree, which is the source of both black and white peppercorns, and the other is the plant that produces the fleshy green, red, and yellow peppers grown in gardens almost everywhere. The fleshy peppers remain a confusing group even after they have been distinguished from black and white peppercorns.

There are at least a hundred varieties and, since they cross-pollinate readily, endless variations are possible. If sweet and hot peppers are grown in the same garden, cross-pollination is likely to cause unpicked sweet pepper seeds saved for planting to produce hot tasting peppers, no matter how sweet they look.

Peppers can be green, red, or yellow when mature, and they vary from large, globular, thick-fleshed types to small, narrow, thin-fleshed types. Green peppers usually refer to large, sweet peppers, while red peppers usually mean small, hot peppers. Yet there are many mild, sweet peppers that are red, and some of the hottest peppers imaginable are green. In countries like Mexico and Hungary, which use peppers extensively, the different varieties are used with great discrimination. Though there are said to be 61 named varieties in Mexico, according to one source, 9 varieties are as many as most cooks need. Elsewhere, 2 or 3 are usually enough; a large, sweet one for salads and vegetable dishes, a hot one for drying, pickling, and making spicy dishes, and perhaps a pimiento for preserving and for making paprika, or a medium-hot kind for peppery but not burning hot fried peppers. As hot peppers are handled quite differently from sweet peppers, they are discussed in a separate section. (Refer to PEPPERS, HOT.)

## HANDLING SWEET PEPPERS

Sweet peppers can be harvested as soon as they become firm, glossy, and heavy, or they can be left on the plant till they turn red or yellow. Most green varieties eventually change color if left on the plant. Red, sweet peppers are especially high in vitamin C, while green peppers are lower in C, but higher in vitamin A. Both are exceptionally healthful.

Peppers should be cut rather than pulled, leaving part of the stem on the plant, otherwise whole branches may break off with the pepper. When frost threatens, pick all peppers, including the very small ones. Those that are almost mature will continue to ripen for a while after picking. Small, immature peppers can be cored, seeded, and chopped, then dried, or frozen. They are good as seasoning for tomato sauces, vegetable stews, and other dishes. The cores and seeds of sweet peppers should always be removed because they have a strong and sometimes hot flavor.

*Peeling Peppers*   Most peppers are eaten without peeling, which takes advantage of the skin's vitamin content, but peeled peppers are sometimes preferred. The peels will slip off easily if whole peppers are blanched in boiling water for 4 to 5 minutes, then dunked in cold water. They can also be roasted 5 minutes in a very hot oven and peeled when cool enough to handle. The most interesting peeling method is to char the skins, then rinse them off in cold water. This will add a special flavor that is espceially good for the PIMIENTOS and *Chiles Rellenos*, below.

To char peppers, hold them on a fork or skewer over hot coals or in a flame, turning constantly till completely blackened. Or lay the peppers directly on the top of a hot wood- or coal-burning stove, then turn till charred on all sides. Run cold water over them, or put them in a pan of cold water and rub to remove the skins.

---

**STORAGE,** *cont.*

**Cold Storage**   Ideal temperature 45–50°F with high humidity. Will keep 2–4 weeks in refrigerator vegetable bin.

**Drying**   Cut out stems, cores. Chop and dry raw for seasoning. Steam quarters, or large pieces 10–12 min. Dry till hard, or brittle, and reconstutute as vegetable. (Refer to DRYING section.) See also PAPRIKA, below.

**Freezing**   Cut out stems, cores. Cut rings, strips, or dice. Pack dry. Optional: Blanch halves 3 min. to render limp for packing. (Refer to FREEZING section.) See also PIMIENTOS, below.

3 AVERAGE PEPPERS = ABOUT 1 PINT CANNED OR FROZEN; 1 POUND PEPPERS = ABOUT 3 CUPS, CHOPPED

***Pimientos***   Pimiento pepper varieties are thick fleshed, red, very sweet, and usually medium sized. They require a longer growing season than some other varieties, but can be garden grown in most moderate climates. Home preserving is an excellent alternative to the small, expensive jars of commercially prepared pimientos. In addition, any sweet pepper that becomes completely red when ripe can be preserved and used like pimientos.

Pimientos are prepared by cooking, peeling, and removing stems, cores, and seeds. The heat necessary for peeling them should make them limp enough for freezing, canning, or packing in oil. They have a wonderful, smoky flavor when charred and peeled as described above. The peeled and cored pimiento can be left whole, cut into large pieces, or into strips. Freezing is the easiest preserving method, and it best retains color and flavor. Wrap small portions of prepared pimiento in freezer wrap or foil and pack them in a freezer container. The wrapping makes it possible to separate small portions as needed. If used in cooking, the pimiento can be added frozen. For salads and garnish, it must be thawed for about half an hour.

To can, pack the prepared pimiento in hot, half-pint or pint jars, leaving ½ inch headroom. Add 1½ teaspoons vinegar to half pints, and 1 tablespoon vinegar to pints. Do not add any other liquid. Process at 240°F, 11 pounds of pressure, for 20 minutes for half pints and pints. (Refer to the CANNING section.)

To preserve in oil, first put the prepared pimientos in a bowl and cover with vinegar. Cover the bowl and refrigerate for 2 days. Drain completely. (The vinegar will have a pleasing flavor and can be used for salads and cooking.) Pack the pimientos in jars and cover with oil. Olive oil is excellent, but any oil will do, except cold pressed oils that easily become rancid. Close the jars tightly and refrigerate or keep in a cool, dark place. These will keep all winter. They taste delicious, but the color is not as good as when frozen. The oil can also be used.

***Paprika***   There are at least six named blends or flavors of Hungarian paprika, ranging from mild and delicate to hot, so why not create a special, homestead blend. Any sweet pepper varieties that have ripened to a full, red color can be dried and ground for paprika. Pimiento varieties are excellent. Stems, cores, and seeds should be removed before drying, and the pepper pieces must be brittle, not leathery, when ground in a mill, or pulverized in a blender. Seal tightly in jars to prevent the paprika from caking during storage. For a hotter paprika, add ground, hot, red pepper to taste.

***Chili Powder***   As sold in stores, chili powder is a blend of powdered sweet and hot peppers, with the addition of other herbs and spices. These usually include cumin, oregano, coriander, cloves, and garlic powder. Other possibilities are allspice and turmeric. A basic formula is: 3 tablespoons sweet paprika, ¼ teaspoon hot pepper, 1 teaspoon cumin and 2 teaspoons other herbs and spices mixed. This can be premixed, or the various seasonings can be added to taste during cooking. In Mexico, premixed chili powder is not used.

## SWEET PEPPER RECIPES

### Stuffed Peppers, Middle Eastern Style    (Makes 6 medium, or 4 large servings.)

| | |
|---|---|
| 6 medium, or 4 large sweet peppers | 2 tablespoons parsley, finely chopped |
| 1 onion, chopped small | |
| 2 tablespoons oil | ¼ teaspoon cinnamon, or allspice |
| ½ pound ground lamb, beef, or other lean meat | |
| | pepper, salt, optional |
| ½ cup raw rice | raisins, pine nuts, optional |
| 1 tomato, chopped, or ½ cup stewed tomatoes | potato and onion slices, optional |
| | ½ cup tomato sauce, or water |

Cut around the stem of each pepper and lift out the top. Reserve the tops for lids. Remove cores and seeds.

Sauté the onions in oil till soft, using a large frying pan over low heat. Add the meat, and cook gently till it changes color. Add the rice, tomato, parsley, cinnamon or allspice, pepper, and salt, if desired. Include a few raisins, or raisins and pine nuts, for an enticing variation. Add 1 cup water and simmer uncovered for 15 minutes, or till the rice is half cooked. Fill the peppers loosely with this mixture, then replace the tops. Set in an oiled baking dish. Slices of potato and onion can be tucked around and between the peppers. Pour tomato sauce or water into the baking dish, cover, then bake 40 minutes in a moderate, 375°F oven. Uncover, add a little water if the dish is dry, and bake another 20 minutes.

**Stuffed Peppers and Tomatoes**   Use 3 medium peppers and 3 medium tomatoes. Cut out and reserve the tops of the tomatoes, scrape out the centers, and stuff like the peppers. Use the centers for the chopped tomato in the stuffing. Alternate stuffed peppers and tomatoes in the baking dish.

### Chiles Rellenos (Mexican Stuffed Peppers)   (Makes 6 dinner or 12 side dish servings.)

| | |
|---|---|
| 12 medium, narrow, elongated peppers (Try Banana or Hungarian Wax types. Can be mildly hot.) | Bean stuffing: 3 cups cooked beans, mashed (Try kidney or pinto beans.) |
| Cheese stuffing: 3 cups cheese, shredded (Mild cheddar or American are good.) | Garnish: sour cream or yogurt |
| Garnish: 2 cups tomato sauce, seasoned with oregano, onion, and garlic | 4 eggs, room temperature flour lard, or oil |

Char the outside of the peppers by turning them over hot coals or under a broiler. (See PEELING PEPPERS, above). As soon as they have blackened, wrap the peppers in a damp towel for 30 minutes to steam

---

### SWEET PEPPER IDEAS

**Stuffed Pepper Salads**  Hearty salads, such as tuna, chicken, potato, or egg salad are delicious in green pepper halves. Cut the peppers lengthwise, and remove stems and cores. Fill with the salad, and set on lettuce leaves. Gelatine fillings (refer to the GELATINE section) are also good.

For an eye-catching salad, cut the top and core out of a large green pepper, and pack cottage cheese into it. Chill for an hour or more in the refrigerator, then cut into slices ½ to 1 inch thick. This makes pepper rings filled with cottage cheese. Arrange the rings on lettuce, and garnish with minced scallion, parsley, or other fresh herbs, and a dusting of paprika. Add some slices of tomato or sweet onion for color and flavor.

### SWEET PEPPER
IDEAS, *cont.*

**Corn Peppers** Cut peppers in half lengthwise, and remove stems and cores. Fill the halves with a mixture of cooked corn and grated cheese, then bake about 20 minutes in a moderate oven. Put 2 or 3 tablespoons of water in the pan around the peppers. 1 cup corn mixed with ½ cup cheese fills 2 to 3 large pepper halves. Minced onion and a dash of hot pepper can be added to the corn mixture if desired, or a succotash mixture (from the BEANS, FRESH section) can be used. If very soft peppers are preferred, steam the pepper halves about 5 minutes before filling them.

**Stuffings for Sweet Peppers**
Most mixtures made with beans, bread crumbs, meat, or vegetables are tasty in sweet peppers. Try the CELERY BREAD CRUMB STUFFING in the CELERY section, *A Garlicky Stuffing for Vegetables* in the GARLIC section, the SEASONED NUTS AND GRAINS idea in the NUTS section, and the vegetable loaf mixture in the VEGETABLES section. If the stuffings do not require long cooking, the peppers can be precooked by steaming or roasting for 5–10 minutes, then baked without lids.

For small portions, cut peppers in half lengthwise and core them to make 2 shells.

### OTHER RECIPES
### FEATURING SWEET
### PEPPERS

Black-eyed Peas and Peppers, p.26
Cheese and Pepper Pie, p.134
Corn Mohawk, p.202
Pimiento Lunch Loaf, p.555
Recipes and Ideas for Vegetables, p.669
Shish Kebab, p.381

in their own heat. When done, peel the skin. Make a lengthwise slit in each pepper, and remove the stem and core. Stuff with either the cheese or the beans. Toothpicks can be used to hold the peppers together, but should not be necessary with careful handling. If cheese stuffing is used, heat the tomato sauce and let it simmer gently, uncovered, till it becomes somewhat thick.

Separate the eggs. Beat the whites till stiff. Beat the yolks till stiff in another bowl, then fold the whites into the yolks. Roll each stuffed pepper in flour, dip it in the egg, and fry in lard or oil till golden brown. (The peppers can also be deep fried.) When done drain the excess fat from the pepper, and put them in a serving dish. Pour on tomato sauce if the chiles rellenos have a cheese stuffing. If they have a bean stuffing, spread them with sour cream or yogurt.

### Sweet Peppers and Sausage, Hungarian Style
(Makes about 6 dinner servings.)

| | |
|---|---|
| 1 teaspoon bacon drippings, lard, or other fat | 3 cups (about) sweet peppers, sliced |
| 1 medium onion, minced | 1 pound smoked sausage |
| 1 teaspoon paprika | 4 eggs, hard-boiled |
| ¼ cup tomato sauce | |

Heat the bacon drippings or fat in a frying pan, add the onion, and stir to coat it with fat. Add the paprika and ¼ cup water. Cook, stirring often, till the water has evaporated and only fat remains. Add the tomato sauce and peppers and stir together. Lay the sausage on top, cover the pan, and cook over low heat for about 20 minutes. Take out and slice the sausage.

Spread half the pepper mixture in a baking dish, then arrange the sausage on it. Slice the eggs and lay them on the sausage. Cover with the rest of the pepper mixture. Bake in a moderate, 375°F, oven for about 10 minutes, and serve.

Another way to finish this dish is to stir the sliced sausage into the pepper mixture, and put this in a serving dish. Arrange the egg slices on top.

### Herbed Sweet Pepper Relish
(Makes 5–6 pints, canned.)

| | |
|---|---|
| 2 quarts chopped green peppers (about 12 peppers) | 1 tablespoon fresh lovage, or celery leaves, minced, or 1 teaspoon dried |
| 2 quarts chopped red peppers (about 12 peppers) | 1 tablespoon fresh tarragon, minced (If unavailable, double lovage or celery.) |
| 1 quart chopped onions (6–8 onions) | |
| 1 hot pepper, seeded and minced, or hot pepper flakes, optional | 1 tablespoon fresh savory, minced, or 1 teaspoon dried |
| ¾ cup honey, or brown sugar | 1 teaspoon salt, optional |
| | 3 cups vinegar |

Combine all ingredients, bring to a boil, and simmer uncovered for 30 minutes, or till well blended and slightly thickened. Ladle hot into hot canning jars and process in a boiling water bath for 10 minutes for both pints and quarts. (Refer to the CANNING section.) This attractive relish has an intriguing flavor that goes with anything. It is excellent, for example, with hamburgers, hard-boiled eggs, and raw vegetables, and does great things for sandwiches.

# PERSIMMONS

## STORAGE

**Canning** Purée, and add 2 tablespoons lemon juice per quart. Heat, pour in jars, ½ in. headroom. Process boiling water bath. 30 min. for both half pints and pints. (Refer to CANNING section.)

**Drying** (Excellent, very sweet.) Halve or slice, remove seeds. Dry whole if small, or purée for leather. (Refer to DRYING section.)

**Freezing** Pack whole, or purée, with lemon juice to taste, or ⅛ teaspoon crystalline ascorbic acid per quart. (Refer to FREEZING section.)

THE PERSIMMON DESERVES MORE ATTENTION THAN IT USUALLY receives. A soft, sweet fruit with a remarkable orange color, it is delicious fresh, and exceptionally good dried or frozen. There are two basic types, the native American, or wild, persimmon, and the cultivated Japanese or Chinese varieties. Both may be used in the same ways.

The American persimmon tree grows wild in moderate parts of the eastern and midwestern United States, where it is also cultivated. Its fruits are small, about an inch in diameter, but they can usually be gathered in large quantities. As the quality of the wild fruits varies, it is wise to taste samples from different trees to find the best. Sometimes trees bear unpollinated, almost seedless fruits. However, the flavor of seedy fruit is just as good. The Japanese and Chinese persimmon trees grown in the south of the United States produce tomato-shaped fruits.

Persimmons are an excellent source of vitamins C and A. They have been known to occasionally cause the buildup of a ball of indigestible fiber in the stomach, but this has only occurred with regular consumption of large amounts over a number of years, and should not discourage anyone from enjoying them in reasonable amounts.

## HANDLING PERSIMMONS

Persimmons are ready to eat in the fall, as soon as they become soft. This may happen before or after frosts. Because they ripen slowly, and may stay on the tree into mid-winter, it is often mistakenly thought that frosts are necessary for ripening. Fully mature persimmons tend to become squashed when picked, or smashed if they fall to the ground, but they can be picked when just beginning to soften, and kept in a warm room to finish ripening. Wild persimmons can be gathered by spreading a large sheet under the tree and shaking the branches to make the almost-ripe fruit fall. Such underripe persimmons are so mouth-puckering that it is hard to believe they will ever taste good.

## PERSIMMON IDEAS

**Frozen Persimmon Desserts**
Freeze whole, ripe persimmons till solid. Just before serving, grate them into individual dishes. Garnish with shredded coconut, chopped nuts, mint leaves, or a sprinkling of lemon juice and grated rind. Serve the persimmon while it is still icy.

The frozen persimmons can also be thinly sliced and arranged with orange slices, or other fruits. This is wonderful with *Frozen Horse-radish Cream* (refer to the HERB ROOTS section), or with yogurt.

**Persimmon Cheese Balls**   Mix puréed persimmon that is not too juicy with cream cheese or smooth cottage cheese. Shape into balls, or use a scoop, and serve with fruit salads or fruit desserts. The color is as enticing as the flavor.

**Dried Persimmons and Nuts**
Open whole, dried persimmons, remove the seeds, and replace them with nuts. If large, the stuffed persimmons can be sliced. Alternatively, dried persimmon halves or slices can be wrapped around nuts for a similar effect.

## OTHER RECIPES WITH PERSIMMON

Roast Beverages (Seeds), p.44
Fruit 'n Yogurt Ice Cream, p.355
Fruit Recipes and Ideas, p.290

Persimmons lend themselves naturally to freezing, as they do not lose texture or flavor, as do so many fruits. In fact, frozen persimmons picked from wild trees in mid-winter can be perfectly ripe and delicious when thawed. Dried persimmons are almost as sweet as figs or dates, and can be substituted for either in recipes.

It is not necessary to peel persimmons, since the skins are thin. However, if peeling is preferred, first rub the skins with the dull side of the knife to loosen them. Persimmons are excellent with yogurt, with acidic fruits like oranges and grapefruit, or simply sprinkled with lemon juice. Their amazing color and sweetness make them welcome in fruit mixtures. (Refer to the FRUITS section for combinations.)

Soft, fresh persimmons are easily puréed, and many recipes call for them in that form. Use a sieve or food mill, as blenders whip in too much air. (Refer to FRUIT SAUCE in the FRUITS section.)

## PERSIMMON RECIPE

*Persimmon Pudding*                          (Makes about 6 dessert servings.)

| | |
|---|---|
| *1 cup persimmon purée* | *1 cup milk* |
| *¼ cup butter, melted* | *1 cup flour* |
| *¼ cup honey or brown sugar,* | *1 teaspoon baking powder* |
| *optional* | *¼ cup nuts, chopped, optional* |

Mix the persimmon with the butter, sweetening, and milk. If stiff honey is used, warm it along with the butter. Sift the flour and baking powder together, and stir into the wet ingredients. Add the nuts. Pour the batter into a greased baking dish. Bake at 325°F for 1 hour, or till the pudding is set and pulls away from the side of the dish. Serve warm or cold, and add milk, cream, or a pudding sauce from the STEAM COOKING section.

*Fruit Sauce Pudding*   Instead of persimmon purée, use any fresh or canned fruit sauce or purée. Such spices as cinnamon and nutmeg can be added, to taste.

# PICKLING

## STORAGE

**Canning**   (Refer to CANNING PICKLES, in CANNING section.)
**Cold Storage**   See STORING PICKLES, below.

PICKLING IS A METHOD OF FLAVORING AND PRESERVING FOODS IN acidic solutions. The use of salt solutions for preserving foods is sometimes also known as pickling, but the foods so preserved are salted, or salt cured. They are not pickled according to most people's understanding of the word, and they are not called "pickles." (For the use of salt solutions refer to the SALT CURING section.) There are two basic ways to pickle foods with acidic solutions. The most com-

mon method requires the use of vinegar, which contains acetic acid. The other is by a process of natural fermentation that produces lactic acid. Sauerkraut (made from cabbage) is the best-known fermented pickle, but other vegetables can also be fermented. Many vegetables can be pickled in either way, and occasionally pickling is begun by fermentation, with vinegar added later as a preservative. Meats, fish, and fruits are virtually always pickled with vinegar. Meats and fish tend to spoil rather than ferment in a favorable way, and fruits can, of course, be fermented, but the result is an alocholic beverage or vinegar, not a pickle.

## THE NUTRITIONAL VALUE OF PICKLES

Pickled foods can be nutritious, but often they are not. Water soluble vitamins and minerals are leached out and discarded with the soaking water or pickling liquid. Excessive amounts of salt and sugar are often used, and commercially pickled foods may contain questionable additives. Such defects are often dismissed as insignificant because pickles are seldom eaten in quantity. However, since foods can be pickled at home, using methods that avoid unhealthful ingredients, why not make pickles that can be enjoyed without reservations?

The large amounts of salt and sugar in some pickles are their most serious nutritional defect. Neither salt nor sugar is necessary to the process of making vinegar pickles, as the food is preserved by the vinegar. Salt can simply be omitted from many vinegared pickle recipes, while the amount of sweetener in most sweet pickle recipes can be reduced. To obtain a pleasant sweet-sour flavor use moderate amounts of honey or sugar. Very sweet pickles will taste cloying to anyone used to a more piquant flavor.

Some salt is necessary for making most fermented pickles, as it draws out moisture and sugars from vegetables, allowing fermentation to begin. However, the amount of salt ingested per serving is small. Sugar is not necessary in fermented pickles, and the lactic acid in them has been recommended for its healthfulness.

***Relish and Chutney***   Most relishes are spicy blends of chopped or ground vegetables, pickled with vinegar. Chutneys are similar mixtures of fruit or vegetables spiced for an East Indian flavor. Relishes and chutneys can be exceptionally healthful pickled foods when made with fresh, unsoaked vegetables and fruits, and little or no salt and sweetening. Since there is no liquid to discard, no nutrients are lost. Relish and chutney are exceptionally good substitutes for fatty sauces and gravies, or excessively salty or sweet condiments. In colonial times, large quantities of different relishes were put by every fall, to accompany meals all winter. It would be very worthwhile to revive this practice.

## MAKING FERMENTED PICKLES

Fermenting vegetables to make pickles can have its ups and downs, because it depends on the action of naturally present lactic acid producing bacteria. Conditions must be arranged to suit the bacteria. Vegetables are usually sliced or shredded, and mixed with enough salt to draw out moisture and natural sugars. Approximately 3 tablespoons salt to 5 pounds vegetables are required. If the vegetables are too dry to produce their own moisture, or if making large pickles, use a solution of salt water, about 3 to 4 tablespoons of salt per quart of water. It is possible to use less salt, but the chances for spoilage or a mushy texture increase as the proportion of salt is decreased. On the other hand, if too much salt is added, the necessary bacteria may not grow.

The best temperature for fermentation is between 60 and 70°F. At higher temperatures the vegetables may become soft, or spoil. (Fermented pickles are seldom successful in hot summer weather unless there is a cool basement in which to keep them.) At temperatures below 60°F the fermentation process becomes very slow. Also essential is the use of pure salt, pure water, and high quality vegetables. See the requirements for vinegared pickles, below. There are helpful basic directions for making any fermented pickles in the SAUERKRAUT section. (Also see OTHER RECIPES at the end of this section.)

## MAKING VINEGARED PICKLES

The basic requirements for successful pickling with vinegar are as follows.

***Vegetables and Fruits***  Use only fresh vegetables and fruits of high quality. If produce is bruised, overripe, or overgrown, the pickles are apt to be either mushy or woody. A spot of mold can affect the flavor of a whole batch of pickles, even after being cooked to kill bacteria. Misshapen or blemished but fresh, firm vegetables can be trimmed and used for sliced or chunked pickles, or for relish.

***Water***  Water that contains such minerals as iron or sulphur can darken pickles, calcium can shrivel them, other impurities can affect the flavor. Pure, soft water is best. (Refer to WATER in the BEVERAGES section.)

***Salt***  Ordinary table salt can darken pickles because it contains iodine and other additives. However, this problem is minimal when pickles are made with very little salt. Sea salt and kosher salt are excellent, as well as plain and pickling salt.

*Vinegar* All modern vinegared pickle recipes are designed for vinegar with 4% to 5% acetic acid. Commercial vinegars are standardized at that level. Homemade vinegar is not generally recommended for pickling because its acid content is unknown, and its flavor is too distinctive. As well, it is likely to cause cloudy or dark pickles. For a few specific uses, refer to the VINEGAR section. Use white vinegar when a clear pickling liquid is desired. Cider or wine vinegar can be used whenever their flavor is compatible.

*Sweeteners* Because it adds neither color nor flavor, white sugar is often used, but sweet pickles taste just as good made with mild honey. Dark honey, or brown sugar will add more flavor. As honey should not be boiled for a long time, add it near the end of the pickle's cooking time. In many pickle recipes the sweetening can be reduced by half and still give a pleasant, sweet-sour flavor.

*Herbs and Spices* The most common pickling herb for vegetables is dill. Heads of dill give the best flavor, but seeds can also be used. Other good seasonings are garlic, horseradish, hot pepper, bay leaf, tarragon, mustard seed, celery seed, coriander seed, whole cloves, whole allspice, cinnamon bark, and mace spears (pieces). Blends of various herbs and spices are used for some pickles. These can be bought already mixed, or added to taste. Powdered spices are seldom used because they cloud the pickling liquid and dull the flavor.

*Risks with Additives for Crispness* Alum and calcium chloride are used to make pickles more crisp. However, even a speck too much of one of these can give food a bitter taste, and larger amounts of alum can cause stomach upsets, so they are best avoided. They are not necessary if the foods to be pickled are fresh and of high quality. The use of grape leaves is a traditional way to add crispness. A layer of grape leaves in the bottom of the pickling crock, and another on top of the pickles, or one or two grape leaves in each jar of pickles is all that is needed.

*Utensils* Use only enamel, stainless steel, or other non-corrosive pots for cooking pickles or pickling mixtures. Aluminum reacts with the acid. Glass jars, stoneware, or pottery crocks are best for storing pickles. If plastic containers are used they will smell like pickles from then on.

## STORING PICKLES

In the past, pickled foods were packed in crocks and stored in the cellar for the winter. Most pickles are now canned, with a boiling water bath, and stored like other canned foods. Canning is the best way to store pickles that require cooking to prepare, but some pickled foods, including most fermented pickles, have a better texture and flavor if kept raw. Some vegetables can be pickled by packing them raw in jars, pouring a boiling hot vinegar solution over them, and

## IDEAS FOR USING THE LIQUID FROM VINEGARED PICKLES

(The pickle liquid can be strained through cloth to clarify it and make it more attractive.)

**Eggs or Beets Marinated in Pickle Liquid**  If the pickling liquid has a good flavor, pour it over shelled, hardboiled eggs, or cooked, sliced beets. Unsweetened pickle liquid is ideal for beets. Marinate from several hours to several days in the refrigerator before serving. (Refer to the *Pickled Eggs* recipe in the EGGS section.)

**Pickle Liquid Salad Dressings**
If pickle liquid is strongly flavored, mix it with oil, or add to mayonnaise for salad dressings. These dressings go well with hearty salads, such as potato, egg, or chicken. (Refer to the QUICK POTATO SALAD idea, in the POTATOES section.)

**Spiced Fruit Pickle Beverages**
Strain and dilute the liquid from spiced, pickled fruit to make a delicious hot or cold drink.

**Pickle Liquid Sauce**  If the flavor is pleasant, pickle liquid can be poured over rice, or other cooked grains for a Middle Eastern touch.

**Flavored Vinegar from Pickling**  When full-strength vinegar has been used for pickling, it can be drained off and used like an herb vinegar. (Refer to the VINEGAR section.) It will have the flavor of the fruit or vegetable it covered.

**Dried Vegetable Pickles**
Reconstitute dried vegetables by soaking them in pickle liquid for a few hours, or overnight. If the vegetables were dried raw, they may taste best cooked in the liquid for few minutes after soaking. Refrigerate them, and use within a few weeks. This is a surprisingly delicious way to use any dried vegetable that pickles well, such as beets, green beans, and some kinds of dried mushrooms.

sealing without further processing. (Refer to CANNING PICKLES in the CANNING section, and, for recipes, to *German Style Dill Pickles,* in the CUCUMBERS section, and HOT PEPPER PICKLES, in the PEPPERS, HOT section.)

Pickled eggs and meats, and some raw pickles and relishes must be made in small amounts and refrigerated for use within days, or at most a month or two. For keeping all winter, pickled foods must be quite acidic, carefully packed, and kept where the temperature stays between freezing and 40°F. Full strength vinegar will preserve pickles packed in crocks better than the half-vinegar, half-water blend used for many canned pickles. Plenty of liquid must be used, and the food must be kept well below its surface so it is never exposed to air. Crocks and other containers must be tightly covered to keep out dust and other contaminants, and to protect them from high humidity. It is also necessary to inspect them frequently to remove any mold that begins to grow on the surface. (Refer to the directions for using crocks, in the KITCHEN UTENSILS and COLD STORAGE sections. For fermented pickles refer to KEEPING SAUERKRAUT IN COLD STORAGE, in the SAUERKRAUT section.)

## BASIC PICKLE RECIPES

### *Spiced Pickled Fruit*                                      (Makes 6–7 pints, canned.)

*8–12 pounds fruit, about 4 quarts prepared* (Use any fruit. Firm or slightly underripe give the best texture.)

*1 quart vinegar* (Can be homemade; refer to VINEGAR section.)

*1 cup (about) honey, or 1½ cups sugar, or to taste*

*3 tablespoons mixed, whole pickling spices* (Or, 1 tablespoon each, stick cinnamon and cloves, and ½ tablespoon each allspice and mace spears.)

Small fruits for pickling whole should be unblemished. Larger fruits can be trimmed and cut into chunks or slices.

To make the pickling liquid, put the vinegar, sweetening, spices, and about 1 quart water in a pot. If the fruit is very juicy, use less water. Tie the spices in a cloth bag to be removed just before the pickling liquid is poured in the canning jars, or add them loose. Heat the pickling liquid to a boil, and proceed as described below for the different fruits. For fruits not listed, especially slices or chunks, cook and can as follows.

Add a small portion of fruit to the boiling liquid. Cook just till the fuit is heated through, then dip it out with a sieve or slotted spoon, and put into hot canning jars. Add more fruit to the liquid and repeat. When all the fruit is in the jars, heat the liquid to a full boil and pour over the fruit, leaving ½ inch headroom. Process in a boiling water bath for 20 minutes, both pints and quarts. (Refer to the CANNING section.)

*Small Whole Peaches, Sekel Pears, or other Small Pears*   Among peaches, clingstones are best. Peel peaches. Blanching will make them easier to peel. Peel pears carefully, leaving stems on for handles, or omit peeling. A slice of ginger root can be included with the spices. Heat the liquid to a boil, and cook the peaches or pears a few at a time for 2 or 3 minutes, or till heated. Lift out fruit with a sieve or slotted spoon, and put it into a bowl or pot. Pour the boiling liquid over it, then let stand overnight. Pack fruit in hot canning jars. Bring the pickling liquid to a boil and pour over fruit in jars. Process as above.

*Crabapples, Whole Plums*   Leave stems on crabapples for handles. Pierce each crabapple or plum deeply with a needle to help prevent bursting. Heat the pickling liquid, then let it cool. Add the fruit and heat to a boil. Remove from heat and let sit overnight. Reheat the next day, and process as above.

*Watermelon Rind, Melon, Cherries*   Trim outer skin from watermelon rind or melon, and cut in slices or chunks. Leave cherries whole and unpitted, with stems on. Heat the pickling liquid to a boil, and pour over the fruit. Let sit overnight. Next day, drain off the liquid, heat it to a boil, and pour over the fruit. Repeat these steps the third day. On the fourth day, heat the fruit and liquid together and can as above. This procedure improves texture, preventing soft or mushy pickles.

*Spiced Cucumber Pickles*   Although not a fruit, cucumbers can be pickled like the watermelon rind, above. (Use standard 4% or 5% vinegar, rather than homemade.) Slice the cucumbers without peeling. Overly ripe cucumbers can be seeded, cut in chunks, and pickled in this way also.

## Old Virginia Relish   (Makes about 2 pints, canned.)

Many old fashioned mixed vegetable relishes can be made in the fall from common garden extras. Piccalilli and Chow Chow are similar, but Piccalilli is often unsweetened, and Chow Chow is usually made in a mustard sauce.

| | |
|---|---|
| *1 quart cabbage, chopped* | *½ teaspoon cinnamon* |
| *2 cups green tomatoes, chopped* | *½ teaspoon cloves* |
| *1 green pepper, chopped* | *2 teaspoons celery seeds* |
| *2 medium onions, chopped* | *1 tablespoon turmeric* |
| *1 tablespoon whole mustard seeds* | *½ cup honey, or 1 cup sugar* |
| *1 slice ginger root, minced, or 1½* | *2 cups vinegar* |
| *   teaspoons powdered dry ginger* | |

Chop vegetables coarsely for a full texture, or chop finely or grind for a smooth relish. Mix all ingredients in a large pot, heat to a boil, then simmer about 20 minutes, or till well blended. Ladle hot into hot canning jars. Process in a boiling water bath, 10 minutes, for both pints and quarts. (Refer to the CANNING section.)

### OTHER PICKLE RECIPES

*Fermented Pickles*
Kimchi, p.176
Kosher Dill Pickles, p.214
Making Sauerkraut, p.540
Pickled Cauliflower Stalks, p.120

*Vinegar Pickled Vegetables*
Dilly Green Beans, p.32
Dilly Green Tomatoes, p.645
German Style Dill Pickles, p.214
Hot Pepper Pickles, p.470 •
Pickled Beets, p.41
Pickled Mushrooms, Syrian Style, p.425
Pickled Nasturtium Buds and Seed Pods, p.342
Spiced Pickled Cabbage for Canning, p.95

*Relish and Chutney Recipes*
Apricot Chutney, p.12
Canned Corn Relish, Shaker or Yankee Style, p.202
Caponata or Eggplant Relish, p.240
Dried Elderberry Chutney, p.251
Gooseberry Chutney, p.311
Grape Catsup, p.321
Herbed Sweet Pepper Relish, p.474
Mushroom Extract, p.424
Pear Relish, p.460
Raw Cranberry Relish, p.206
Raw Garlic and Parsley Relish, p.296
Squeezed Cucumber Relish, p.213
Tomato Apple Catsup, p.639

# PLUMS

**Canning**  Leave whole, pierced with needle to prevent bursting, or halve and pit.

**Hot Pack**  Cook fruit 2 min. in boiling syrup, juice, or water. Let stand 20–30 min. Drain, pack, add boiling cooking liquid, ½ in. headroom. Process boiling water bath. Pints: 20 min. Quarts: 25 min.

**Raw Pack**  Add boiling syrup, juice, or water, ½ in. headroom. Process as for HOT PACK. (Refer to CANNING section. Refer also to CANNING FRUIT JUICE AND SAUCE in FRUITS section.)

**Drying**  See PRUNES, below.

**Freezing**  Whole, or halved and pitted. Pack dry, or cover with liquid. (Refer to FREEZING section. Refer also to FREEZING FRUIT JUICE AND SAUCE in FRUITS section.)

2–2½ POUNDS = 1 QUART CANNED OR FROZEN

1 BUSHEL = 20–30 QUARTS, CANNED OR FROZEN

PLUMS ARE GROWN IN MORE PLACES IN THE WORLD THAN ANY other stone fruit, resulting in a wide and interesting array of plum recipes. There is someone, somewhere, who will know a good way to use every kind of plum, whatever its size, shape, color, or flavor. Strange as it seems, however, that most traditional of plum dishes, the Christmas plum pudding, does not contain a single plum.

Several distinctly different kinds of stone fruits are called plums. European plum varieties are the best known and most widely cultivated. They include prune plums and all the common fresh and canned varieties. Japanese and Chinese varieties are gaining acceptance. They are very good fresh or canned, but less good dried. The various small, tart tasting plum varieties are excellent for making juice or preserves, but not sweet enough to enjoy as fresh fruit. Most wild plums fall into this group, as do damson plums, which are most appreciated in Europe for making all kinds of preserves.

## HANDLING PLUMS

Pick plums for canning and freezing while they are still firm and a little tart, as these retain the best texture and flavor after processing. Fully ripe plums are quite soft and sweet, very good for eating fresh, making sauce, and drying.

Plums are easy to prepare. They never need peeling and can often be used unpitted. Flavor is lost if they are peeled. When cooking plums whole, pierce them with a needle to help prevent bursting. Though the skins will still crack, they will not curl off. Freestone varieties are easily separated from their pits after they are cut open. It is easier to cook clingstone varieties and pick out the pits afterwards, or the flesh can be sliced off fresh plums in several pieces. The pits will still have fruit on them and can be used for making juice. To do so, cover them with water, cook a few minutes, and strain off juice. Drink it as plumade, or use as the liquid for canned or frozen plums.

***Prunes***  The word "prune" usually refers to the dried fruit, but it can also mean a fresh plum intended for drying whole. Dried prunes were once a winter staple, used in all kinds of dishes, from main courses to desserts and snacks. Because of modern freezing and canning methods, prunes are no longer of vital importance, but they are still among the best tasting and sweetest dried fruits.

Prune plums are not a specific plum variety, but any kind of plum with a sugar content high enough to allow drying without pitting. When sugar content is too low, whole plums are likely to ferment rather than dry. Such plums can be cut in half, pitted, and dried like a peach. They will taste good, but they will not be prunes. (Refer to the DRYING section.)

Most prune plums will hang on the tree and continue to sweeten even after they are completely ripe and soft. The best prunes come from plums left to drop from the tree by themselves. They must be gathered from the ground every day or two, or, for easy gathering, a sheet can be laid on the ground, and the tree shaken over it to make loose plums drop. The plums can be spread immediately on trays for drying in the sun or in a dryer, or they can be treated first to crack or check the skins so as to speed the drying process. Though lye treatments have been used, there are more agreeable home methods. One is to simply nick each plum with a knife, so that the skin is broken. Another method is to soak the plums for 20 minutes in hot water to soften the skins. This will speed drying without breaking the skins. Plums can also be blanched briefly in boiling water to check their skins, but this may cause pieces of skin to curl off. Before blanching the whole batch, test a few plums to see how it works.

In a hot, dry climate prunes are dried for 4 to 5 days in the sun, and then moved to an airy, shaded place to finish drying. Each prune is turned over after 2 or 3 days in the sun. It takes from 12 to 24 hours to dry them in a mechanical dryer. The prunes will be leathery when finished. (Refer to the DRYING section.)

Old fashioned, home-dried prunes are quite different from most of those now sold in grocery stores. Commercial prunes are usually "moisturized," which means, among other things, less prunes per pound and less flavor per prune. Home-dried prunes are harder and drier, with a fuller flavor. Children enjoy chewing them for a snack but their jaws will get more exercise than usual. (Refer to MOISTENING DRIED FRUIT in the DRYING section.) Very dry prunes will need soaking for several hours or overnight before they are cooked.

## PLUM AND PRUNE RECIPES

### Hungarian Plum Dumplings    (Makes about 8 dessert servings.)

1½ pounds potatoes, 3 cups (about) riced
1 egg
5 tablespoons (about) butter
1½ cups (about) flour
16 ripe plums (Usually prune plums.)

3 tablespoons (about) honey, or sugar
1 teaspoon (about) cinnamon
½ cup fine bread crumbs, or ground nuts

Boil the potatoes in their skins. Peel and rice them, or push them through a sieve or food mill while they are warm. Let cool, then mix them with the egg and 1 tablespoon of melted butter. Add enough flour for a workable dough, and knead well on a floured surface. Roll or pat out the dough ¼ to ½ inch thick. Cut it into 16 squares.

Slit each plum open on one side to remove the pit, keeping it in one piece. Put about a half teaspoon of sweetening and a dash of cinnamon inside each plum, and set one on each square of dough. Shape

### PLUM AND PRUNE IDEAS

**Plum and Wine Gelatine**
Drain and reserve the juice from canned or stewed plums. Pit the plums, and put them in a mold or serving dish. Measure the juice, and mix in and soak 1 tablespoon powdered gelatine per cup. Heat to dissolve the gelatine. Add ½ cup wine for each cup of juice, sweeten, if necessary, and pour over the plums. Sweet wines are excellent in this. White wine is attractive with green or yellow plums, and red wine with red or purple plums. Chill to set the gelatine. Very pleasant as a side dish with a meal, as well as for dessert.

**Plum Soup** Flavor puréed plums with lemon juice and grated rind. If too tart, add a little honey. Mix a tablespoon of tapioca or cornstarch into each quart of the purée. Heat gradually, stirring often, till thickened. Serve hot, with a spoon of yogurt in each bowl, as a smooth, satisfying cold weather treat.

## PLUM AND PRUNE IDEAS, cont.

### Unstewed "Stewed" Prunes

Soak prunes in water to cover and set in a cool place for several days, or till they are plump and the juice is dark and thick. (Refer to USING DRIED FRUITS in the FRUITS section.) Home dried prunes are much better for this than commercial moisturized prunes. For a fancy dish soak the prunes in sweet wine instead of water.

### Prune Bits Instead of Raisins

Cut up prunes with scissors or a knife, and use like raisins in baked goods, salads, and snack mixtures.

### Prune Sweetmeats

If prunes are very dry, soak to moisten them. Then cut a slit in each prune, take out the pit, and put in a nut, such as a walnut half or an almond. If the prunes are sticky, roll them in finely chopped nuts or fine, dry coconut. Let sit a few hours before serving, to moisten the nuts and blend flavors.

### Tea Prunes

Pour boiling hot tea over prunes to cover. Let sit overnight and serve like stewed prunes. Regular tea or an herb tea with a compatible flavor are all good. Replace pits with nuts before adding tea for a delightful dessert.

the dough to form a complete casing around the plums and pinch or press it closed. If the dough is at all sticky, roll the completed dumplings gently in flour.

Have about 3 quarts of water boiling in a large pot. With a spoon or sieve, lower the dumplings gently into the water. Nudge them gently so they do not stick to the pot. Keep the heat high and the water boiling. After about 10 minutes the dumplings will rise to the surface. Cook them for 5 minutes after they rise, then take them out with a slotted spoon or sieve.

If bread crumbs are to be used, brown them gently in about 4 tablespoons of butter. If using nuts, mix them with melted butter. Roll the hot dumplings in the bread crumb or nut mixture till they are coated all over. They make a delicious yet not overly rich dessert.

### Steamed Pork and Plums, Chinese Style

(Makes about 6 side servings.)

| | |
|---|---|
| 2 pounds spare ribs, or 1 pound lean pork | 1 tablespoon honey (Or to taste depending on sweetness of plums.) |
| 1 pound fresh plums, pitted, or 1 pint canned plums, drained and pitted | 2 tablespoons soy sauce |
| 1 tablespoon oil | 1 teaspoon cider vinegar, or 2 tablespoons sherry |
| 1 slice ginger root, minced | 1 tablespoon cornstarch |

Cut spare ribs in 1½ inch sections or cut pork into ½ to 1 inch squares. Halve or quarter larger plums.

Heat the oil till quite hot in a wok or frying pan. Stir the ginger root briefly in it, then add the pork, and stir-fry over high heat for 4 or 5 minutes. Put it in a dish that will fit in a steamer. (Refer to the STEAM COOKING section.) Mix the plums with the pork. In another dish, mix the honey, soy sauce, vinegar or sherry, and cornstarch. Pour this over the pork and plums and steam for 30 minutes. Serve in the steaming dish.

### Plum Mint Sauce for Meats

(Makes 2–3 cups.)

| | |
|---|---|
| 3 cups pitted plums (Windfalls can be used.) | ¼ cup (about) honey, or sugar, optional |
| 1 cup cider or wine vinegar | 1 tablespoon fresh mint leaves, minced |

Stew the plums in the vinegar till they are soft. If the flavor is sour, add honey or sugar to balance it. The taste should be more tart than sweet. If a smooth texture is preferred, purée the mixture. Just before serving, heat the sauce and add the mint. Serve hot with meat or fish.

This recipe can be increased for canning, but do not add the mint till it is heated for serving.

*Prune Porridge*                           (Makes 10–12 large bowls.)

(This old Scottish recipe is thought to be a forerunner of Christmas plum pudding, from a time when the pudding actually had plums or prunes in it.)

2 *quarts beef or other meat soup stock*
2 *cups (about) bread crumbs*
1 *cup pitted prunes, soaked if necessary*
2 *cups mixed dried fruits, soaked if hard* (Try raisins, dried apricots, dried apples.)

¼ *teaspoon each pepper, mace, nutmeg*
1 *cup (about) cooked meat, bite size pieces, optional* (Usually beef or another red meat.)

Warm the beef stock, and remove from heat. Add enough bread crumbs to thicken it, and let soak for a few minutes. Beat to make a smooth mixture, or push through a sieve or food mill. Add the prunes, dried fruits, spices, and meat. (Include soaking water if there is any.) Heat to a boil, then simmer, covered, till the fruit is soft, about 30 minutes. Stir often to prevent sticking.

This porridge reheats well, and is deliciously satisfying for breakfast, lunch, or supper.

---

**OTHER RECIPES FEATURING PLUMS**

Baked Apricots, p.11
Baked Fruit Pudding, p.74
Fruit Juice Delight, p.322
Moroccan Stew with Prunes, p.497
Recipes and Ideas for Fruit, p.290
Roast Goose with Stuffing p.306
Spiced Pickled Fruit, Whole Plums, p.480
Stewed Chestnuts with Vegetables or Fruit, p.150

---

# PORK

PIG, HOG, AND SWINE ALL DESCRIBE THE SAME ANIMAL, AND CAN be used interchangeably to mean both domestic and wild species. In the United States, hog is also used to mean large, young, domesticated pigs, or the pork producing animals, specifically.

In countries with dense populations and limited pasture, hogs are the most practical of the large animals to raise for meat. They produce more edible meat on less feed than any other large domestic animal, and they eat a great variety of feeds, including much that would otherwise be wasted. For these reasons pork is the principle meat in countries as diverse as Mexico, China, and Hungary.

If allowed, pigs could easily be raised in suburban back yards, and much of their feed could be kitchen scraps. In wartime England "pig-keeping" was common in some populated areas. People had shares in pigs, and there were pig bins on street corners where people could deposit clean kitchen wastes. In this way excellent meat was produced with very little expense. Today homesteaders raise hogs for the same practical reasons as everyone else. They need little space, and part of their feed can be homestead extras like garden produce, milk,

---

**STORAGE**

**Canning** Trim off fat. Can as for beef. (Refer to BEEF section.)

**Cold Storage** (Refer to PRESERVING MEAT IN RENDERED FAT in MEAT section.)

**Drying** Not feasible. Fat becomes rancid.

**Freezing** Cut. Wrap. Quality retained 6–8 mos. (Refer to FREEZING section.)

**Salt Curing** (Refer to HAM AND BACON section.)

and kitchen scraps. Another dividend is the high quality of home raised pork, compared to the commercial variety. It is so good that the first taste is a delicious surprise, even to someone prepared for a difference.

Pork is richer in B vitamins than any other meat, and is a good source of minerals, as well. And since modern breeding practices are producing leaner pigs, even the disadvantage of a high fat content is diminishing. Pork is a valuable nutritious food and has a place in well balanced diets.

## HANDLING PORK

Though pork usually comes from young hogs, pigs can be butchered and used at any age. Suckling pigs sometimes are butchered as early as three weeks of age. When tough old sows must be culled, their meat is usually ground for sausage. Old boars have a poor reputation as meat animals. Some sources suggest castrating them, then butchering them after the wound heals, because this improves the meat's flavor. Wild pigs ("boar" in the southeastern, and "peccary" or "javelina" in the southwestern United States), are sometimes hunted. Young wild boar tastes like exceptionally good pork. Older wild boar and peccary require long slow cooking like any tough meat.

Butchering hogs is within the capabilities of most homesteads, though it takes two people and some extra equipment to do the job. The hog must be killed, bled, dunked in scalding water to loosen hair or bristles, and scraped. Hogs can be skinned rather than scraped, but valuable rind and fat are lost when this is done. After scraping the hog is hung and entrails and head are removed, saving useful parts. The carcass is cut in half and cooled completely. Since pork does not benefit by aging, the meat can be cut and used, or processed for storage after 24 to 48 hours of cooling. For detailed information on butchering and cutting pork, refer to the reference sources listed at the end of the HAM AND BACON section.

Suckling pigs are scalded like large pigs, or like chickens, in hot water, 140 to 150°F, and scraped to remove hair. They are cleaned like rabbits (refer to the RABBIT section) if small, or like lambs (refer to the LAMB AND MUTTON section), if larger. The head is left on and cleaned well around the ears, snout, and mouth. The eyes are removed.

## PARTS OF A HOG CARCASS

*To clean and prepare:*

Blood, refer to BLOOD section.

Bones, sinew, gristle, refer to BONES section, GELATINE, and SOUP sections.

Fat, refer to LARD section. For salt pork, refer to HAM AND BACON section.

Feet, refer to FEET section.

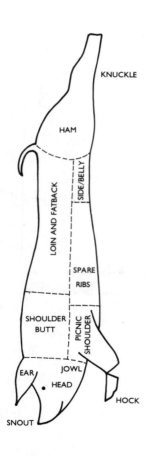

*Parts of a hog carcass*

Head, refer to HEAD, BRAINS, and TONGUE sections.

Heart, refer to HEART section.

Intestines, refer to SAUSAGE CASINGS, pages 548–50, and CAUL, AND RUFFLE FAT, page 383, and the TRIPE, CHITTERLINGS, AND PAUNCH section.

Kidneys, refer to KIDNEYS section.

Liver, refer to LIVER section.

Lungs, refer to LUNGS section.

Rind or skin, refer to CRACKLINGS, page 385.

Spleen, refer to SPLEEN section.

Stomach, refer to TRIPE, CHITTERLINGS, AND PAUNCH section.

Sweetbreads, refer to SWEETBREADS section.

Trimmings and Scraps, refer to GRINDING MEAT, page 407, BLOODY OR BRUISED MEAT, page 405.

Tail, refer to TAILS section.

Testicles, refer to TESTICLES section.

For salt curing all meaty and fatty parts refer to HAM AND BACON section. Also refer to the MEAT and SAUSAGE sections.

## UNDERSTANDING TRICHINOSIS

Though trichinosis is not a common disease, it is so closely associated with pork that it should be understood by anyone who raises hogs. Trichinosis is contracted by eating infected and undercooked or raw pork. The disease is caused by a parasitic round worm, *Trichinella spiralis*. The trichinae larvae develop in the intestines of the animal or human host, and eventually a new generation of larvae penetrates into the host's muscle fibers, forming cysts that may contain live organisms for many years. When such infected muscle meat is eaten by a susceptible animal, a new cycle begins. Bear meat as well as pork can cause trichinosis. Dogs, cats, and rats can also get the disease, but these are not a threat for humans, unless a pig should eat an infected dead animal.

Light cases of trichinosis can easily go unnoticed. Even in serious cases the symptoms are like those of many other ailments, making diagnosis difficult. Prevention, however, is easy. Trichinae larvae are killed by temperatures above 137°F, so cooking pork till no pinkness shows or till a meat thermometer reads about 160°F will make it completely safe to eat. There is not much danger of infection from fresh pork, since it is always cooked, but cured pork products are a greater threat, since some may be eaten raw. In North America, most commercially cured pork is precooked. In Europe some kinds of ham and sausage are customarily eaten raw, but the hog carcasses are routinely inspected microscopically to ensure the meat is free of trichinae larvae.

Those who raise their own hogs can reduce the risk of trichinosis by cooking all meat scraps used as feed. If pork is to be home-cured, and the ham or sausage is intended for eating raw, freeze these products before use. When subjected to a temperature of 5°F or less for 20 to 30 days, trichinae larvae will be killed.

If these precautionary steps are carefully followed, there will be no reason to worry about trichinosis.

## PORK RECIPES

### *Marinated Roast Suckling Pig*    (Makes about 1 serving per pound.)

(Large suckling pigs are roasted on a spit, over coals. A small pig can be roasted either in the oven or on a spit.)

| | |
|---|---|
| *1 suckling pig, 10 to 15 pounds, cleaned* (Increase ingredients proportionately for larger pigs.) | *4 cloves garlic, crushed* |
| | *1 teaspoon thyme, or oregano* |
| | *⅛ teaspoon cumin seed* |
| *juice of 1 large orange* | *⅛ teaspoon saffron, optional* |
| *juice of ½ lemon, or lime* | *1 teaspoon salt, optional* |
| *1 teaspoon pepper* | |

Score the pig lightly through the skin on all sides. Combine the orange and lemon or lime juice. Rub the pig with about half of the juice, both outside and in the cavity. Mix the rest of the juice with the pepper, garlic, thyme or oregano, cumin, saffron, and salt, if desired. The mixture can be puréed in the blender. Rub the pig again, inside and out, with the seasoned juice mixture. Reserve extra juice for basting. Wrap or cover the pig and leave it in the refrigerator, or another cool place, overnight or up to 24 hours.

If roasted on a rack in the oven, the pig will take 2½ to 3 hours at 325°F. The meat should reach about 180°F on a meat thermometer. If roasted on a spit over hot coals it may take longer, and a large pig will take 5 hours or more. Cut into the pig at a joint to make sure the meat is done. Whether oven or spit roasted, baste occasionally with the extra juice and seasoning mixture.

To carve, remove front and back legs, and cut down the center of the back along the backbone. Then cut slices across each half. Some crackly skin and a rib can be included in each slice, or the meat can be cut away from the ribs.

**Roast Pork**    Prepare pork roast like the suckling pig, adjusting amounts of juice and seasonings to size. Allow 30 to 35 minutes per pound of meat, or roast till it reaches 180°F on a meat thermometer.

**Stuffed Suckling Pig**    Use a pig small enough to roast in the oven. Omit the scoring and juice and seasonings. Stuff the pig with any bread crumb poultry stuffing. Stuffings containing fruit, like the stuffing recipe in the GOOSE section, are especially good. Skewer or stitch closed the opening in the pig. Put a piece of wood or a corncob in its mouth during roasting to keep the mouth open, so as to replace it with an apple when done. Truss with the legs close under the body, and cover the ears and tail with aluminum foil. Roast allowing 30 minutes per pound. The roasting time will be about twice as long for the stuffed pig as for an unstuffed one.

---

### PORK IDEAS

**Pork Seasoned Vegetables**

Shreds, or thin, bite-sized slices of pork make an ideal vegetable seasoning. Their fattiness enhances flavor, and they make a tasty, salt-free replacement for bacon or ham seasonings. Stir-fried vegetables with pork is a Chinese classic (refer to the STIR-FRYING section), but all styles of cooked vegetables will benefit. Sauté raw pork shreds or slices in pork fat, oil, or butter till cooked through and lightly browned, or briefly heat and brown cooked leftover bits. Toss with hot cooked vegetables and serve. Such green vegetables as green beans, chopped broccoli, and spinach are delicious prepared this way. Very little pork will season a large dish of vegetables, and other seasonings are not needed, except, perhaps, a small accent of lemon juice or vinegar. Pork bits are also very good in creamed vegetables, vegetable soups, and stews. It is well worth freezing small portions of pork for these purposes.

### Quebec Pork Ragout

(Makes 10–15 dinner servings.)

| | |
|---|---|
| 1 pork tongue | 6 whole cloves |
| 1 pork heart, in large cubes | 1 bay leaf |
| 2 pounds beef, in large cubes | pepper, salt, optional |
| 2 pig's legs with feet, knuckles, hocks | flour to thicken |
| 2 onions, sliced | |

Cut the pig's legs into 4 or more pieces. Boil the tongue 5 minutes, peel off the skin, and cut it into large cubes. Put the legs, tongue, heart, and beef in a large pot and add the onions, cloves, bay leaf, pepper, and salt, if desired. Add water to cover. Bring to a boil and skim well. Simmer, covered, till the meat is done, for about 2 hours. Thicken by mixing several spoons of flour with cold water, and stirring it in. Adjust seasonings and simmer till thickened. A grand feast, for anyone who helped with the butchering of the pig!

**Pasta or Dumpling Ragout** Omit flour, and add any kind of pasta or dumplings and cook about 15 minutes.

### Meat Balls with Dipping Sauce, Japanese Style

(Makes about 6 side or snack servings.)

| | |
|---|---|
| 1 pound lean pork, ground | Dipping Sauce: |
| ¼ cup mushrooms, minced (Fresh or dried and soaked.) | ⅓ cup light soy sauce |
| | 3 tablespoons vinegar |
| 1 egg | 1 tablespoon honey or sugar |
| 2 scallions, or a small onion, minced | ⅓ cup sake or white wine, optional |
| ¼ cup fine bread crumbs | ¼ cup chicken or fish stock, optional |
| 1 tablespoon soy sauce | |
| ½ teaspoon honey or sugar | |
| 3 tablespoons (about) oil | |

Mix together the pork, mushrooms, egg, scallions, bread crumbs, soy sauce, and honey or sugar. Shape into 1 inch balls. Heat the oil in a frying pan, and sauté the balls, turning them often, till they are cooked through and well browned.

Mix the dipping sauce ingredients.

Serve each person with a small dish of cool dipping sauce. Pick up a hot meat ball with fork or chop sticks, dip it in the sauce, and eat it.

### Puaa (Hawaiian Pork)

(Makes 4–6 servings.)

| | |
|---|---|
| 1 teaspoon oil | 1 bay leaf |
| 2 cloves garlic, crushed | pepper, salt, optional |
| 2 pounds lean stewing pork, in 2 inch cubes | 3–4 scallions, cut in 1 inch sections |
| ¼ cup vinegar | |

---

## PORK IDEAS, *cont.*

**Pork with Herbs** Herb seasonings go very well with pork. These can be rubbed on the meat before frying or broiling, pressed into slits in roasts, or added to gravy, sauces, and stuffings. Try rosemary, thyme, sage, and bay leaves. Caraway, fennel, or celery seeds are also very good.

**Lemoned Pork Chops** Trim as much fat as possible from pork chops or steaks, and rub them with lemon juice. Let sit 1 to 2 hours. If desired, sprinkle the meat with pepper, salt, and caraway seeds, or some of the other herbs mentioned above. Dust with flour and fry, starting with fairly high heat to brown them, and reducing heat to cook through.

---

## OTHER RECIPES FEATURING PORK

Heat the oil in a heavy pot and lightly brown the garlic in it. Add the pork, vinegar, bay leaf, pepper, and salt, if desired. Cover, and cook over very low heat at barely a simmer, for 1 to 2 hours, or till the meat is very tender. With a tight lid there should be no need to add extra liquid. When done, remove the lid and increase heat to evaporate any remaining liquid. Keep the heat high, and quickly brown the meat, stirring to keep it from sticking. Then add 2 tablespoons of water and the scallions, and stir for about a minute. Excellent with rice and green vegetables.

***Wild Meat, Hawaiian Style*** Cook meat from fairly young, wild animals in this way. Opossom, raccoon, and woodchuck are some to try. Turtle meat is another possibility. For very lean meat, increase oil to 2 tablespoons.

## STORAGE

**Canning** (Small new potatoes best.) Rub or scrape off skins. Leave whole, or dice.

**Hot Pack** Pour boiling water over, boil 10 min. Drain, pack in jars, add boiling cooking water, ½ in. headroom. Process, 240°F, 11 pounds pressure. *Whole Potatoes* Pints: 30 min., Quarts: 40 min. (Refer to CANNING section.) *Diced potatoes* (because of denser pack) Pints: 35 min., Quarts: 40 min. (Refer to CANNING section.)

**Cold Storage** See KEEPING POTATOES IN COLD STORAGE, below.

**Drying** See DRYING POTATOES, below.

**Freezing** (Quality poor if raw.) May bake, cool and wrap; or french fry to light color, cool and wrap; or cook in mixtures. (Refer to FREEZING section.)

I POUND RAW = 2 CUPS MASHED; 2½–3 POUNDS RAW = I QUART CANNED

# POTATOES

PEOPLE CAN STAY HEALTHY ON A DIET OF WHITE OR IRISH POTA-toes and very little else, if they eat enough of them. Many of the poor of Europe have done so. According to one estimate, it takes two pounds of potatoes to make a nutritious meal for one person. The Irish were eating an average of eight pounds per person, per day, before the disastrous famine of 1845 and 1846 when their potato crops were destroyed by a blight. Though the famine illustrated all too graphically the danger of depending entirely on one food crop, it also demonstrates the potato's exceptional food value. A whole people could never have come to depend on them so completely had they not been so nutritious.

Besides starch, potatoes contain vitamins, minerals, and some high quality protein. There is not very much of any of these in one potato, but when many are eaten the cumulative amounts are significant. Their Vitamin C and protein are especially important whenever potatoes are a major part of the diet. Contrary to some opinion, they are not a high calorie food, and eating a potato is about as fattening as eating an apple. Their bad reputation comes from the gravy, butter, and cream that so often accompany them.

Potatoes are a good crop for homestead gardeners. They are productive in a small space, require no special equipment for growing and harvesting, and are easily stored for winter. They are more productive per acre than grains, even when calculated by their dry weight. Mature potatoes will keep in any dark place for several months, and long keeping varieties will last into spring in a root cellar.

Potatoes were first cultivated by the Incas in the Andes Mountains of Peru and Bolivia, and many unique potato varieties are still grown by Indians living there. The early Spanish explorers of South America took potatoes back to Europe where they spread rapidly, and early settlers brought them to North America. Most present day American and European varieties came from the same beginnings and are basically alike. A few seed companies do sell distinctive sets, like the yellow fingerling potatoes that make such good potato salads, and the blue-fleshed novelty varieties, but otherwise potatoes are white fleshed with similar flavors. The different varieties bred to suit particular climates and to resist diseases have not changed the basic character of the vegetable.

Sweet potatoes and yams are from an entirely different plant. (Refer to the SWEET POTATOES section.)

## HANDLING POTATOES

Potatoes that are harvested early, soon after the plant's blossoms form, are called new potatoes. They are thin skinned, delicately flavored, and can be as small as one inch in diameter. As new potatoes do not keep well, they are usually gathered a batch at a time from around the potato plants, leaving the rest of the crop to continue growing. For long storage, they can be canned.

Mature potatoes can be dug as soon as most of the plant tops have turned yellow. If the weather is cool and dry, they can be left in the ground till the first frosts. Potatoes keep so well in any cool, dark place that other methods for preserving them are unnecessary. Most varieties can be stored for two or three months, and long keeping varieties will last till late spring in a root cellar.

If they are cooked and dried, potato quality is good, while it is acceptable if they are cooked and frozen. Raw potatoes do not freeze well in home freezers because ice crystals form, rupturing the flesh and causing a watery texture when thawed. Commercially frozen potatoes are more successful because extreme low temperatures are used, bypassing the crystal stage.

***Keeping Potatoes in Cold Storage*** Before they are stored, potatoes need about 2 weeks of conditioning at 60 to 70°F. This allows skins to toughen and any scraped places to heal. Spread potatoes out in a spare room or shed—anywhere away from sun and wind. Set imperfect potatoes aside to use first. Conditioning is less important for potatoes left in the ground for a month or 6 weeks after their tops died back, but that is not possible in damp or warm weather.

When ready, pack the potatoes in boxes, bins, or other containers, allowing for some air circulation, and put them in the cold storage area. Ideal conditions are 40°F, with a humidity of 80–90%, as in a root cellar, but they will keep in outdoor pits, or cool, dark basements. Keep them in the dark to prevent them turning green, and protect them from freezing. A brown ring will show inside frozen potatoes when they are cut open, and they soon turn watery, blacken, and spoil. If the temperature stays between freezing and 35°F for very long, the starch in the potatoes begins to turn to sugar, and they become hard and difficult to cook. This can be corrected by holding the potatoes at room temperature for 1 or 2 weeks before cooking them. The sugar will then turn back into starch.

Break the sprouts off potatoes as soon as they appear. If they are left to grow the potatoes will soon wither, but if they are removed the potatoes will often be good to eat for several more months. It may be necessary to go through stored potatoes several times in late winter or spring to remove sprouts.

Always store potatoes and apples separately. If stored together the potatoes will make the apples musty. (Refer to the APPLES and COLD STORAGE sections.)

If there are more potatoes in cold storage than can be used, dry, or cook and freeze the extras. If cooked, extra and damaged potatoes make excellent chicken and livestock feed.

**Drying Potatoes**   Potatoes must be cooked before they are dried, unless being dried for flour. Steam or boil them (unpeeled) till they are cooked through but not mushy. For slices, peel and cut them about ¼ inch thick. Spread on drying trays and dry till hard. To reconstitute, put the slices in a saucepan, pour boiling water over them, and simmer over low heat till they are expanded and heated through. Add extra water if necessary.

Riced dried potatoes are very useful. After the potatoes are cooked, spread them out in a pan or colander, in a cool, airy place for a day or two so that they will be light and fluffy when riced, rather than sticky. Peel the potatoes just before ricing. Push them through a ricer or food mill, and let them fall directly onto drying trays, lined if necessary. (Refer to DRYING FRUIT AND OTHER PURÉES in the DRYING section.) Move the ricer or food mill around over the tray for a loose, even layer. Do not press or push the potato around after it is on the tray, as this will make it mat or stick together. Dry to a crumbly meal. To use for mashed potatoes, pour hot water or hot milk over the meal to cover, and let sit over very low heat till the liquid is absorbed. If too thick add a little more liquid. Potato meal is also good for making potato soup or for thickening soups and stews.

Raw potatoes can be sliced or grated, then dried, and ground for flour. They are likely to discolor while drying, even when treated with an ascorbic acid solution, and the flour will have a greyish appearance.

**Making Potato Starch**   Pure white potato starch can be extracted from raw potatoes and dried to use for thickening like cornstarch or arrowroot starch. Grate several pounds of potatoes as finely as possible. Add about twice their volume of cold water and stir well. Pour through a fine sieve, or a cloth lined colander, using cloth that is not tightly woven. After the water has sat for a few minutes, the starch will settle to the bottom, and the water can be poured off. To obtain as much starch as possible, stir fresh, cold water into the potato gratings, let sit, and drain several times more.

After collecting and draining all the starch, rinse it by adding more cold water, mixing, then letting it settle again. Pour off the clear water. The starch will remain as a damp, caked paste in the container. Spread it in a shallow pan, or on a lined drying tray, and dry it in a food dryer or in the sun. If the starch is lumpy after it is dry, sift it or roll over it with a rolling pin. It will keep indefinitely in a closed container. A pound of potatoes yields from ¼ to ½ cup of starch. The potato gratings can be cooked for soup or for feeding livestock.

Potato starch is popular in many northern European countries for thickening fruit purée, or for juice to make puddings. (Refer to the *Fruit Juice Pudding* recipe in the FRUITS section.)

***Saving Potatoes' Nutrients***   Peeling potatoes is the classic before dinner chore. It is also the way to throw out the most nutritious part of the potato, since most of the vitamins and minerals are concentrated immediately under the skin. Peeling raw potatoes cuts most of these away, even when parings are thin. If peeling is delayed till after potatoes are cooked, the skins will slip off without taking any flesh, and most nutrients are saved. Another alternative is to eat the peel with the potatoes. If potatoes were scrubbed with a brush and well rinsed, they can be sliced and fried, and cooked in most other ways, without peeling. As the skins do not have much flavor after they are cooked, it is largely the habit of seeing completely white potatoes that makes peeling seem necessary.

Damaged skin or green areas should be cut off. The green, caused by too much exposure to light, contains a toxic substance (solanine), and should not be eaten. Once green areas are cut away the rest of the potato can be eaten.

Another common practice that removes potato nutrients is soaking them, and then throwing out the soaking water, with its water soluble vitamins and minerals. Soaking to prevent discoloration is not necessary if potatoes are prepared just before they are cooked. To avoid losing nutrients in discarded potato cooking water, steam the potatoes, or boil them in a minimum of water, and then use the water as a cooking ingredient. It is excellent in bread dough, or sour dough, or added to soups and stews.

## POTATO RECIPES

### *Potato Pancakes, Jewish Style*                    (Makes about 6 servings.)

6 *medium potatoes* (About 6 cups after grating.)
3 *eggs, well beaten*
2 *tablespoons fine cracker crumbs, or flour*

*salt, optional*
2–3 *tablespoons fat for frying* (Chicken fat is excellent.)
*apple sauce* (To accompany.)

Grate the potatoes finely. If a lot of liquid collects around them pour off most of it. (Save for another use.) Mix the potato with the eggs, crumbs or flour, and salt, if desired. Heat the fat in a frying

---

### POTATO IDEAS

**Baked or Boiled Potatoes with Yogurt**   Instead of bathing baked or boiled potatoes in butter, gravy, or other rich accompaniments, serve them with dishes of yogurt and minced onion or scallion. Each person can then mash a potato, and add yogurt and onion or scallion to taste. Minced parsley or some other herbs like fresh dill, tarragon, or fennel, can also be included.

**Oven Browned Potatoes**
Scrub potatoes and cut them in uniform pieces. They can be large or small, diced, sliced, or cut in sticks. Rub or toss them with oil to coat all cut surfaces. Spread in a baking pan, and bake in a moderate oven till evenly browned. This may take 30 to 60 minutes, depending on the size of the pieces. Shake the pan, or stir the potatoes several times, for even browning. If desired, sprinkle with paprika when done. These are convenient to make when the oven is to be used for other baking for the same meal, and their browned flavor is pleasant and satisfying without butter or rich gravy.

**Seasoning Potatoes for Mashing**   Potatoes for mashing can be made more flavorful by adding seasonings to their cooking water. Cook any of the following with the potatoes: a small onion, a cut clove of garlic, a bay leaf, a sprig of celery leaves, or other herbs. Remove the seasonings before mashing the potatoes.

**POTATO IDEAS,** *cont.*

**Leftover Potato Patties**  Mix leftover mashed potatoes with egg and seasonings to taste. Shape into patties, and sauté till brown on both sides. Minced onion, leftover cooked, chopped vegetables or meat, or any kind of canned or cooked fish, or shellfish are very good in these patties. For a quick lunch or supper, serve potato patties with homemade relish or catsup.

**Quick Potato Salad**  Mix diced, leftover potatoes with liquid from dill pickles, or with a prepared Italian or French salad dressing, and add vegetables, herbs, and garnishes to taste.

**Mashed Potato Crust**  Oil a pie pan or shallow baking dish. Press mashed potato evenly against the bottom and sides. If the mashed potato is too stiff to be workable, mix a little milk into it. Bake in a hot, 375–425°F oven till the crust is browned, then fill it with creamed vegetables, creamed tuna, or other mixtures. Serve immediately, or sprinkle with bread crumbs and dots of butter and brown under the broiler. (Or refer to the *Jerusalem Artichoke Pie* recipe, in the JERUSALEM ARTICHOKES section.)

---

### OTHER RECIPES FEATURING POTATOES

pan. Put in spoonfuls of the potato mixture and flatten them to make a small pancake. Brown slowly, about 10 minutes per side to make the edges crispy, and serve hot with applesauce for breakfast, lunch, or supper.

### *Italian Potato Soup*                                (Makes 6–8 medium bowls.)

| | |
|---|---|
| 1½ *pounds (about 3 cups) potatoes, diced* | 2 *cloves garlic, minced* |
| 2 *cups milk* | *bunch parsley, minced* |
| 1 *egg, lightly beaten* | 1–2 *slices lean bacon, or small piece ham, finely chopped* |
| 1–2 *tablespoons oil* | *parmesan cheese* |
| 1 *medium onion, finely chopped* | *croutons, optional* |
| 1 *medium carrot, finely chopped* | |
| 1 *celery stick, finely chopped* | |

Cook the potatoes in 1 cup of water and 1 cup of the milk. When soft, mash or beat them till smooth. Mix the other cup of milk with the egg and stir into the potato. Reheat, stirring often, without letting it boil.

Meanwhile, heat the oil, and sauté the onion, carrot, celery, garlic, parsley, and bacon or ham over low heat till the vegetables are soft, but not brown. Stir into the soup.

Sprinkle cheese on the soup after it is in the bowls, and add croutons, if desired.

### *Potato Hash, Plain Browned, or Herbed*                     (Makes 1 or more servings.)

| | |
|---|---|
| *potatoes, grated raw, or cooked, diced small* | *herbs, fresh minced, or dried, to taste* (Try parsley, thyme, sage, rosemary.) |
| *oil or fat, for frying* | *cooked meat, chopped small or ground* (Up to ½ the quantity potatoes.) |
| *vegetables, grated raw, or cooked and diced small* (About ½ the amount of potatoes. Try onion, celery, carrot, parsnip, other root vegetables.) | *pepper, to taste* |
| | *salt, optional* |

For plain hash, heat the oil or fat in a frying pan and spread an even, fairly thin layer of potatoes in it, pressing down as necessary with a spatula. (Cook large quantities in batches.) Brown one side, then turn in one piece, and brown the other. Raw grated potatoes are easiest to turn, and make an especially crisp hash.

For a fancy hash, combine the potatoes, vegetables, herbs, and meat, if desired. Fry like plain hash, except turn in smaller sections, or stir to brown here and there.

Sprinkle either version with pepper, and salt, if desired.

**Red Flannel Hash**  Make the hash of ½ part cooked potato, ¼ part cooked and ground beef, and ¼ part cooked diced beets. Corned beef instead of plain cooked beef makes still another good variation.

### *Crisp Potato Wafers*                    (Makes about 4 dozen.)

*1 cup cooked potatoes, mashed*      *1 egg yolk, beaten lightly*
*½ cup butter, softened*             *1 tablespoon milk, or water*
*1 cup whole wheat flour*            *caraway seeds, salt, optional*

Mix the potato, butter, and flour, and work with a spoon or knead
to make a smooth dough. Chill for about 30 minutes. Roll out ⅛ inch
thick, and put on ungreased baking sheets. The dough can be rolled
directly on the sheets if they are lightly floured. Mix the egg yolk and
milk, and brush it on the dough. Sprinkle with caraway seeds and
salt, if desired. Before putting in the oven, cut through the dough to
make 1 by 3 inch strips. Bake at about 375°F till delicately brown and
crisp. Delicious with soup, or eaten like any other crackers.

**OTHER RECIPES,** *cont.*
Kale and Potatoes, p.365
Pears and Potatoes, p.460
Potato Raita, p.706
Recipes and Ideas for Vegetables,
    p.669
Soybean Patties, p.588
Swiss Chard with Potatoes and
    Garbanzo Beans, p.626

# QUINCES

T HE QUINCE IS AN ANCIENT FRUIT EATEN IN THE MEDITERRANEAN
area at least since the time of the early Greeks. It was brought to
America by early settlers who valued it highly for making jelly and
preserves. In the last half century it has, regrettably, lost much of its
popularity. Many have never heard of it, and the fruit on many old
quince bushes or trees goes unused because no one knows how to enjoy it. Most varieties are too hard and astringent to eat raw. They require long cooking to soften them and to bring out their delicate flavor
and color. They are delightful fruits when well prepared, and deserve
to be rediscovered.

Quinces grow on small, bush-like trees. The fruit is greenish yellow to yellow, with the look of a lumpy apple or pear. When fully
ripe, the flesh is cream to apricot colored. Quince trees grow like
other fruit trees, but take less space. They are an attractive and practical addition to any garden.

### STORAGE

**Canning**   Cook whole in water to
soften, about 20 min. Slice or
chunk, removing cores. Pack,
cover with boiling syrup made from
cooking water, ½ in. headroom.
Process boiling water bath. Pints
and quarts: 60 min. (Refer to
CANNING section. See also CAN-
NING FRUIT JUICE AND SAUCE, in
FRUITS section.)

**Cold Storage**   Pick before fully
ripe. Store like apples. Will keep
2–3 mos. (Refer to KEEPING AP-
PLES IN COLD STORAGE in APPLES
section.)

**Drying**   Handling easier if cooked
whole till soft. Slice, core, dry to
hard. Thick cooked sauce makes
good leather. (Refer to DRYING
section.)

**Freezing**   Must be precooked.
(Refer to FREEZING FRUIT JUICE
AND SAUCE in FRUITS section.)

## HANDLING QUINCES

Quinces can be left on the tree till after the first fall frost, to be picked as needed. For long keeping in a root cellar or other cool place, harvest them a few weeks before frosts while they are still a little underripe. They are best used like tart cooking apples, and can be stewed, baked, and made into sauce or juice. The slight fuzz on their skins can be rubbed off with a cloth before they are cooked. Peeling is not necessary. If the quince are very hard, and difficult to core, cook them first, and then core them. As quince skins and cores are flavorful, and rich in pectin, do not discard them but cook them in water and strain them for juice. This juice can be made into jelly, or mixed with bland, low pectin fruits. (Refer to the PECTIN and the JAM AND JELLY sections.)

When quinces are too hard to be easily cored or sliced, they can be precooked to soften them. Cover whole quinces with boiling water and leave them standing a few minutes, or boil or steam them till soft, when they can be cored and sliced. Always save the cooking water to use with the fruit, or for juice. Quinces hold their shape even after they are tender. Traditionally, they were tested for doneness by poking with a straw to see if it would penetrate completely. Some varieties turn a pretty, rosy red color when completely done, which usually takes from 40 minutes to an hour.

## QUINCE RECIPES

### QUINCE IDEAS

**Baked Quince** Rub the fuzz off the quince with a cloth, and cut out the core as for baked apples. Precooking makes coring easier. Put a spoon of honey and a dab of butter in each quince, and set them close together in a baking dish. Sprinkle with ginger, or pepper, or other spices if desired. Add water to the baking dish half way up the quince and bake in a hot, 375–400°F oven for about an hour if raw, 30 minutes if precooked.

**Quince in Apple Recipes** Quinces are often a delicious replacement for apples in cooked recipes. A longer cooking time will be necessary, unless the quinces are precooked. Quince sauce is a very good substitute for applesauce. (Refer to recipes in the APPLES section.)

*Quince Compote*     (Makes about 6 dessert servings.)

  *2 pounds (about) quince*     *lemon juice and grated rind to*
  *¼ cup honey, or to taste*        *taste, optional*

Rub fuzz off the quince, cover with boiling water, and simmer about 30 minutes, till softened. Drain, saving the cooking water. Peel, remove cores and slice. Simmer the slices in the cooking water for about 30 minutes more. If there is too much juice, boil it uncovered till reduced. Add honey and lemon, and bring to a boil to blend flavors. Chill before serving.

*Orange or Mulberry Quince Compote*  Cook the sliced quince in orange juice, or red mulberry juice (refer to the MULBERRIES section), instead of their cooking water. Omit lemon juice, and add a stick of cinnamon bark, or any other spice, to taste.

*Quince and Leek Stew*  Quarter the cooked quince, rather than slicing them, and stew them with a cup of sliced leeks, a tablespoon butter or olive oil, the honey, and quince liquid to cover. A little white wine can be added instead of lemon juice, if desired. Makes an unusual and very agreeable side dish with roast pork, ham, and other rich meats.

## Moroccan Stew with Quince    (Makes 4–6 dinner servings.)

2 pounds (about) stewing lamb or
    chicken, cut in pieces
2 onions, chopped fine
bunch fresh parsley, or coriander
    leaves, minced
½ teaspoon powdered ginger
⅛ teapoon each black pepper,
    cayenne, and paprika

salt, optional
1 pound (about) quince,
    quartered, cored, not peeled
    (Or precook, core, and use
    cooking water in stew.)

Put the lamb or chicken, half the onion, the parsley or coriander,
ginger, 3 kinds of pepper, and salt, if desired, in a stewing pot. Add
water to cover, heat, and simmer till the meat is tender, usually about
an hour. Add the other half of the onion, and the quince, and cook
till the quince is just tender, about 30 minutes. Do not overcook.
Very good served with rice.

**Apples, Pears, Prunes, or Raisins and Meat Stew**    Use any of these
fruits instead of quince to make this stew. Use ¼ pound raisins or
prunes or the dish will be too sweet. If the prunes are very dry, presoak them and add them with their soaking water.

**OTHER RECIPES
WITH QUINCE**

Cabbage and Quince Sauerkraut,
    p. 542
Recipes and Ideas for Fruit,
    p. 290
Vegetable or Fruit Quick Bread,
    p. 64

# RABBIT

THERE SEEMS TO BE QUITE AN UNREASONABLE DEGREE OF PREJU-
dice against eating rabbit, because people conceive of them as
docile, cuddly pets. In fact, rabbits are meat animals as much as
lambs, pigs, and calves, and they are not always docile or cuddly.
They are well known for their quickness ("like a bunny"), and for
their powerful hind legs which can deliver the ultimate in "rabbit
punches".

Rabbits are very practical animals for families to raise for their own
meat supply. They can be kept under circumstances that would be
unsuitable for any other domestic animal, including chickens. They

**STORAGE**

**Canning**    Cut in pieces (boning
optional). Handle and process like
chicken. (Refer to CHICKEN section.)

**Drying**    Practical because meat is
so lean. (Refer to DRYING MEAT in
DRYING section.)

**Freezing**    Leave whole, or cut in
pieces. Quality retained for 1 year.
(Refer to FREEZING section.)

**Live Storage**    Breed, then
butcher as needed, avoiding the
time and expense of canning or
freezing.

take very little space, they are clean, and they do not make loud noises. They are also easy to care for, easy to butcher, and their meat is low in fat, high in protein, and versatile to use. As well, it is possible to raise rabbits entirely on homegrown and wild feed. For centuries, poor people all over the world have raised rabbits in order to have meat at no cost except labor. When meat was scarce during the world wars, many people in the southern United States raised rabbits on whatever feed they could find.

Most modern rabbit producers depend on commercial feeds, because more rabbits can be raised to butchering size in less time. However, rabbits raised primarily on garden extras (grass, hay, wild greens, oats) can be healthy and reasonably productive. Some prefer the meat of the naturally fed animals because questionable feed additives are avoided, and because they find the flavor is better.

Wild rabbits and hare, which are closely related, are as good to eat as domestic rabbits. They are widespread, and taken by hunters more often than any other game animal. Though they have a more distinctive flavor than domestic rabbit, they taste more delicate and milder than most game meats. In recipes, domestic rabbit, wild rabbit, and hare can be considered interchangeable. Very young wild rabbit or hare can be tender enough for frying. Test the ears to find out their age. If the animal is young, they will be tender and tear easily. (Also refer to DETERMINING THE ANIMAL'S AGE in the WILD FOODS section.)

## HANDLING RABBIT

Domestic rabbits are easy and fast to skin and clean. Plucking and cleaning chickens takes considerably longer. Some experienced people can kill, skin, and clean as many as 100 rabbits in an hour. Most can handle 4 or 5 an hour with a minimum of practice.

*Killing Rabbits*    For the beginner, the hardest part of butchering is killing the animal. The scream of a rabbit in distress is most unnerving, and anyone who has caused the sound will want to butcher properly to avoid hearing it again. Rabbits must be stunned quickly so that there is no struggle or suffering, and the throat must be cut or the head cut off right away for complete bleeding. There are several ways to do this.

The professional way to stun a rabbit is to dislocate its neck. Hold the rabbit by its hind legs with one hand, and its head with the other, with the thumb on its neck behind the ears, and the fingers under its chin. Stretch the rabbit out, press the thumb down, and raise the head with a jerk. This must be done as one quick motion which dislocates the neck, making the rabbit unconscious. It takes hand and arm strength, and must be done correctly. Another method that may be easier for some is to stun the rabbit with a sharp blow to its head. Hold it by the loins, and hit it either just behind or just in front of the ears with a strong, heavy stick, such as the handle from an old hammer. While doing so, hold the rabbit in the air with the head down, or on a firm surface, such as a chopping block.

The rabbit's blood can be caught for use when the throat is cut (refer to the BLOOD section), and the head saved for making soup stock.

***Skinning Rabbits*** There is more than one way to skin a rabbit. Domestic rabbits are skinned before being cleaned, while wild rabbits are usually cleaned in the field and brought home for skinning. If the rabbit is young, with skin that separates easily, the skin can be pulled off in any way that keeps the meat clean. It will ruin the skin for tanning, and is slower than a planned method, but it does work.

To skin a rabbit quickly before cleaning, hang it by one hind leg, using a hook or a piece of cord between the tendon and the leg bone next to the first or ankle joint. Cut off the other three feet at the ankle joint, cut off the tail, and then the head, if still attached. Cut through the skin around the leg used for hanging. Cut just below the hook or cord, being careful not to cut through the tendon or into the meat. Next cut through the skin of each hind leg from the ankle to the base of the tail. Peel the skin off the hind legs, and pull it down so it peels off the body inside out, like taking off a glove. Usually, the rabbit is cleaned before it is taken down and the remaining foot cut off.

Two people can quickly skin a rabbit without hanging it, if one holds the hind feet and the other pulls off the hide. The head can be skinned by simply pulling the skin and cutting as necessary to free it. Cut off the ears next to the skull, after pulling back the skin around them. It is possible to use the head even if it was hit to stun the rabbit. (Refer to BLOODY OR BRUISED MEAT in the MEAT section.)

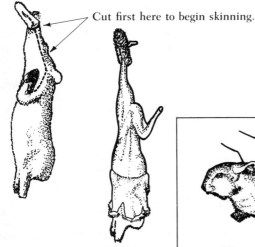

Cut first here to begin skinning.

*Skinning a domestic rabbit before cleaning.*

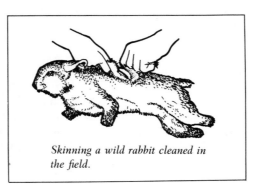

*Skinning a wild rabbit cleaned in the field.*

*Parts of a rabbit*

LIVER

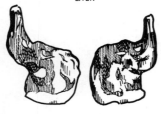

FRONT LEGS AND SHOULDER

NECK AND RIBS

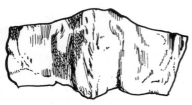

SADDLE

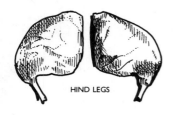

HIND LEGS

A rabbit cut into its basic parts.

To skin a wild rabbit that has already been cleaned, first cut off all four feet. Then cut a slit through the skin across the center of the back. Put the fingers of both hands in the slit and pull in opposite directions. The skin will come off in two pieces. The tail and head can be cut off either before or after skinning. If any hair or dirt should stick to the meat, wipe it off with a cloth dipped in hot water.

**Cleaning Rabbits**　　The cleaning procedure is the same whether the carcass is hanging, or lying on a flat surface.

Cut through the abdominal wall from the rib cage to the anus, and most of the entrails will fall or pull out easily. Watch for the bladder, which if full, looks like a small water filled balloon, and remove it without breaking or squeezing it. Separate the liver, and cut off the small green sac (gall bladder) attached to it. It will make the liver bitter and inedible if it breaks or stays against the liver for very long. Break the membrane separating the chest cavity from the stomach, and take out the heart and lungs. Both can be used. The kidneys, which are against the back with fat around them, can also be used.

To make cleaning easier, the rib cage can be cut open and the small bone protecting the anus can be cut. Thoroughly rinse the carcass and all of the useable parts in cold water, but do not soak them as is sometimes directed. The meat will absorb water and might absorb "off" flavors, if soaked. Chill thoroughly before cooking or freezing.

### Using Rabbit Parts

*Blood*　　Rabbit blood is most often used in sauces to accompany the meat, but it can be used like any animal's blood. (Refer to the BLOOD section, and see RECIPES, below.)

*Head, Heart, Kidneys, Lungs, Bones, Scraps*　　All these parts together make a good, mild, light colored soup stock. (Refer to the HEADS section, especially the *Scrapple* recipe.)

*Liver*　　Be sure to save the rabbit's liver. It is mild flavored and very good in all kinds of liver recipes. (Refer to the LIVER section. An Italian favorite is the RABBIT LIVER TOMATO SAUCE in the TOMATOES section.)

*Fat*　　Rabbit fat is very soft. Some over-fed domestic rabbits have layers of fat that can be pulled away from the carcass and rendered for shortening or lard. (Refer to the LARD AND OTHER FATS section.)

## COOKING RABBIT

There are so many different ways to cook rabbit that it can be a family's primary meat, and be no more repetitive than beef or pork. Those who ignore the uniqueness of rabbit cookery with the advice to "cook it like chicken" are on the wrong track. Rabbit meat may look something like chicken, but it has a different flavor, and it does not respond in the same way to the various cooking methods or blend in the same way with seasonings. If rabbit must be compared to another kind of meat, veal is the most likely choice. Both are lean, white, and delicately flavored, and they go well with the same seasonings, particularly such herbs as rosemary, sage, and thyme. Often veal recipes can be adapted to suit rabbit.

Rabbit is leaner than most other meats. Even when a rabbit has body fat, when the fat is pulled away from the meat it leaves no fattiness in the flesh. Low cooking temperatures are necessary to prevent dryness or stringiness, unless fat is cooked with it. (Refer to COOKING LEAN MEAT, in the MEAT section.) With this in mind rabbit can be fried, stir-fried, stewed, baked, stuffed and roasted, or boned and ground.

The saddle and hind legs of a rabbit are the meatiest parts, and can be cooked separately from the bonier ribs, shoulders, and front legs, especially if the rabbit is large. One possibility is to cut off both the front and hind legs, and stuff the body section to make a meat roll for roasting. More often the whole rabbit is stuffed and roasted. In some countries it is customary to leave on the head as well.

When boneless meat is wanted for stir-frying or grinding, it is easiest to bone just the saddle and back legs. One way to use the front section is to cook it in water till the meat is tender, and then to pick it away from the bones to use in salads, sandwiches, or hash. The bones along with the head and other scraps, can be returned to the cooking water, and cooked long enough to make soup stock. (Refer to the SOUP section.) If cooked down sufficiently, rabbit stock makes a mild, fairly stiff gelatine that can be flavored in many different ways. (Refer to the GELATINE section.)

## RABBIT RECIPES

### Katie's Fried Rabbit

(From 6–10 servings, on rabbit's size.)

1 young rabbit
flour, or fine dry bread crumbs, or a
    combination
pepper, salt, optional
pinch ginger, optional

2 eggs, lightly beaten
3 tablespoons (about) oil
3 tablespoons (about) butter
lemon wedges

Cut the rabbit into pieces, no piece bigger than the size of an egg. Where necessary cut through bone with poultry shears, a meat cleaver, or a heavy knife. Rinse the pieces and pat them dry.

Season the flour or bread crumbs with pepper, salt and ginger, if desired. Dip the meat first into egg, then into the flour or bread crumbs. Fry in half oil and half butter in a heavy frying pan. Do not crowd the pan. If necessary, fry in several batches. Use medium to high heat and turn the pieces often. When well browned drain on absorbent paper.

The pieces' small size, and the frequent turning allows them to cook through in about 20 minutes, without becoming dry. Very good served hot or cold, with wedges of lemon for squeezing over the meat. Terrific to take on picnics.

***Fried Frog's Legs***   Fry frog's legs in the same way, omitting ginger. Leave them full size if small or joint them if large. They may take longer to cook than the rabbit.

### Lapin au Sauce Piquant
(French "Country" Rabbit.)                (Makes 8–10 dinner servings.)

*1 large stewing rabbit, cut in serving*
*    pieces*
*hot red pepper, to taste* (Tradition-
    ally very hot.)
*salt, optional*
*2–3 tablespoons lard, oil, or other*
*    fat*
*2 cups onions, chopped medium*

*1 cup parsley, minced* (Or
    parsley with mixed green
    onion tops.)
*1 tablespoon garlic, minced*
*2 cups tomato sauce*
*1 can tomato paste, optional*
    (Use if the sauce is thin.)
*1 cup white wine, or water*

Season the rabbit with red pepper and salt, if desired. Heat the fat in a large, heavy frying pan with a lid (or transfer to a stewing pot after frying). Brown the rabbit in the fat, turning often. Add the onions, parsley, garlic, tomato sauce, tomato paste, and wine or water. Cover, heat to a boil, then reduce heat, and simmer without boiling for 1½ to 2 hours, till the rabbit is tender. Use low heat to keep the meat juicy. This rabbit is delicious served with rice.

***Chicken in a Piquant Sauce***   Instead of a rabbit, use a stewing hen cut in pieces, and add 1 to 2 cups chopped celery with the onion.

### Baked Rabbit in Ale
                                       (Makes about 6 dinner servings.)

*3 ounce piece (about) salt pork*
*1 tablespoon oil, or drippings*
*4 medium onions, sliced*
*1 young rabbit, cut in serving pieces*
*2 teaspoons honey, or sugar*
*pepper, to taste*

*2–3 slices bread, preferably*
*    French or Italian*
*prepared mustard, preferably*
*    Dijon*
*1 bottle (about) mild ale, or beer*

Simmer the salt pork in water for 20 minutes. Drain, and chop it in about ¼ inch cubes. Heat oil in a large frying pan, and slowly fry the salt pork and onions in it. Fat will be rendered from the salt pork, and the onions should be lightly browned. Stir often. When done, scoop out salt pork and onions with a slotted spoon and set them aside. Pat the rabbit pieces dry, and fry them in the fat in the pan over low heat, turning the meat often, till lightly browned. (Do not crowd the pan, but fry in two batches, if necessary.)

Put the rabbit pieces close together in one layer in a baking dish. Spread the salt pork and onions over the rabbit, and sprinkle with honey or sugar, and pepper. Spread the bread slices with mustard and set them on top, mustard side up, to cover the top. Add ale or beer just to the level of the bread. Cover, and bake in a moderate, 325°–350°F, oven for 40 to 60 minutes, or till the rabbit is very tender. Uncover for the last 15 minutes of baking to brown the top.

Serve with simple accompaniments—a plain green salad or unseasoned cooked vegetables—so as not to overshadow this dish's exquisitely delicate flavor.

### *Jim's Rabbit with Oyster Dressing* (Makes 8–12 dinner servings.)

2–3 small wild rabbits, or 1 large
    domestic rabbit
1 stalk celery, chopped medium
1 onion, chopped medium
1 tablespoon fat, or oil
5 cups (about) bread crumbs
small bunch parsley, chopped fine
1 teaspoon sage

1–1½ cups oysters with liquid
    (Canned or fresh, whole or
    chopped.)
pepper, to taste
1 cup or more rabbit or oyster
    broth
6 (about) bacon slices

Sauté the celery and onion in the fat till limp. Mix with the bread crumbs, parsley, sage, oysters, and pepper. Moisten with broth to make a stuffing that holds together without being soggy. The amount of liquid will vary with the dryness of the crumbs.

Stuff the rabbits, filling them so that the stuffing is mounded up along the opening. They are baked open, not stitched shut. Oil a baking dish, and spread the rest of the stuffing in it. Set the rabbits on it, backs down, stuffed side up. The baking dish should hold them without much extra space. Lay slices of bacon over all, and bake in a moderate, 350°F oven for 1½ hours, or till the meat is tender. Great for holidays and special occasions!

### *Sandy's Rolled Rabbit Pastry* (Makes about 6 dinner servings.)

2 tablespoons butter
1 medium onion, finely chopped
¼ cup celery, finely chopped
1 tablespoon flour
½ cup milk
1 teaspoon aromatic bitters, or finely
    grated lemon rind

2 cups cooked rabbit meat,
    chopped small
¼ teaspoon salt, optional
pastry for a single pie crust (Try
    a dash of poultry seasoning
    in the flour.)

Melt the butter in a saucepan, and cook the onion and celery in it till the onion is golden. Stir the flour in well. Add the milk and cook till thickened, stirring constantly. Remove from heat, then stir in the aromatic bitters, rabbit meat, and salt, if desired. Let cool while preparing the pastry.

Roll out the pastry dough in a 10 by 10 inch square. Spread the rabbit mixture over the dough leaving only a small margin. Roll up tightly and place seam side down on an oiled baking sheet. Brush with

---

### RABBIT IDEAS

**Rabbit Pot Pie** Cooked rabbit with gravy or sauce makes a very good pot pie. Use leftover rabbit stew, or make a cream sauce or gravy to go with any kind of leftover cooked rabbit meat. Put the heated rabbit and sauce in a deep pie dish, or shallow baking dish. Cover with a pastry crust, or a batch of biscuits set close together for a crust. Bake 15 to 20 minutes in a hot, 400°F, oven, till the crust is lightly browned.

**Broiled or Grilled Rabbit**
Young, tender rabbit can be broiled or grilled, if protected with some kind of fat so that it will not dry out. Lay slices of bacon over the meat, or wrap bacon around each piece, or rub it with butter or oil before cooking, and baste while it cooks. Keep it far enough from the heat to keep it from cooking too fast.

A Spanish way to broil rabbit is to coat it wih garlic flavored mayonnaise (refer to the recipe in the SALADS section). The meat may also be basted with mayonnaise and some served as a dip to eat with the rabbit. Rosemary is sometimes sprinkled on the meat, or rosemary twigs are put on the hot coals while it broils.

**Little Rabbit Legs** Cook the front legs of 8 or 10 rabbits separately. Their small size makes an interesting dish, rather like small frog's legs. Collect the legs in the freezer till there are enough for a meal. They should all be from rabbits of the same age in order to cook in the same length of time. They can be fried, stewed, or baked, and are very good in the *Baked Rabbit in Ale* recipe, in this section.

### RABBIT IDEAS, *cont.*

**Ground Rabbit**   Ground rabbit meat makes an excellent replacement for ground veal. It can also replace ground pork, if adjustments are made for its leanness. Always cook over low heat and not too long, to prevent drying, or include pork fat, or another kind of fat when grinding it. Make rabbit burgers, or use it in the MEAT LOAF variation in the LIVER section or in *Breakfast Sausage* in the SAUSAGE section.

### OTHER RECIPES
### WITH RABBIT

Herb Sauce Marinade for Broiled
   Meats, p.340
Kale with Meat, p.365
Scrapple, p.329
Tomato Meat Sauce, p.641
Using Ham Stock, p.325

milk, and bake in a hot, 400°F, oven till golden brown, about 35 minutes. Serve hot. This is very good with a mushroom sauce. (Refer to the MUSHROOMS section for recipes.)

## Stewed Rabbit, with Liver or Blood Sauce               (Makes 6–10 dinner servings.)

*1 cup tomato sauce*
*2–4 cups soup stock, or water*
*1 rabbit, fryer or stewer, cut in serv-*
   *ing pieces*
*1 bay leaf*
*1 clove garlic, minced*
*1 small onion, minced*

*1 small carrot, minced*
*½ stalk celery, minced*
*1 tablespoon parsley, minced*
*pepper, salt, optional*
*blood from 1 rabbit, or 1 rabbit*
   *liver*

In a stew pot, heat the tomato sauce with enough soup stock or water to about cover the rabbit. When just boiling, add the rabbit pieces, bay leaf, and garlic. If necessary, add more stock or water. Bring again to a boil, then reduce heat and simmer very slowly, till the meat is becoming a little tender, about 30 minutes for a fryer and 1 to 1½ hours for a stewer. Add the onion, carrot, celery, parsley, pepper, and salt, if desired. Simmer for another 30 to 40 minutes or till the meat is very tender.

Meanwhile prepare the liver or the blood. If using blood stir it with a little vinegar as soon as it is collected to keep it from coagulating. (Refer to the BLOOD section.) If liver is used, grind or purée it, or chop very small. Stir the blood or liver into the stewed rabbit about 5 minutes before serving it. It may be kept hot on the stove, but do not let it boil again. The blood or liver will thicken and enrich the sauce. Very good with noodles, potatoes, rice, and other cooked grains.

# RADISHES

Round, red, raw radishes are a familiar and delightfully crisp nibble, and a salad favorite, but they are an embellishment rather than a food staple. It is the large winter radishes commonly grown in East Asian countries, and in some places in Europe, that are a basic vegetable crop. They are similar to turnips, and used in many Chinese and Japanese dishes. They are practical to grow because they can be started late in summer as a second planting, after the harvest of some other crop, and because they can be stored through the winter. There are many shapes and colors of winter radishes, but all of them are large in size. Roots weighing one or two pounds are com-

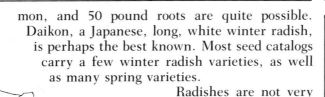

mon, and 50 pound roots are quite possible. Daikon, a Japanese, long, white winter radish, is perhaps the best known. Most seed catalogs carry a few winter radish varieties, as well as many spring varieties.

Radishes are not very high in nutrients, but as there is an old belief that they are good for digestion, they may have hidden virtues. Radish leaves are also good to eat, and are more nutritious than the roots. They make a good cooked vegetable, like their close relatives, turnip tops and mustard greens. Radish seed pods, picked while young and tender, make a surprisingly good, if peppery, vegetable for eating raw, and for cooking, or pickling. The pods which form on radish plants after they flower look like small, pointy-ended green beans. If left to mature and dry, their seeds can be collected for sprouting, or for a seasoning like mustard seeds. (Refer to THRESHING AND WINNOWING in the SEEDS section, and to the SPROUTS and MUSTARD sections.)

## HANDLING RADISHES

The fastest growing radishes taste best. Pull spring radishes as soon as they reach a reasonable size. Those that stay in the ground too long will become hot, and may turn pithy or woody. Some can be left growing to produce pods or seeds for gathering during the summer. Winter radishes can withstand light frosts, but should be pulled before hard freezes.

The only preparation small radishes need is washing and trimming. If the tops are attractive, leave them on as a handle, and include the radishes with other vegetables for dipping. Do not soak radishes in cold water, because they will lose flavor. Keep them crisp by putting them in a closed container in the refrigerator. Large radishes are usually sliced or shredded.

Small, young radish leaves are good raw in salads. Chop finely and they will lose their scratchy quality. Large or mature tops are best cooked.

***Using Very Hot Radishes*** To tone down the taste of radishes that are too hot or peppery, marinate them for a few minutes in vinegar, soy sauce, or any salad dressing. (See the recipe for *Marinated Salad Radishes*, below.) Fermenting them like pickles will also tame them. (Refer to the SAUERKRAUT section and the recipe for *Kimchi* in the CHINESE CABBAGE section.) A way to take advantage of their hotness is to dry and grind them, or grate them finely before drying, for a

## RADISH IDEAS

**Radish Sandwiches** Finely grate spring or winter radishes. Add seasonings to taste, such as a minced scallion, dill leaves, and parsley, and moisten with yogurt, sour cream, or mayonnaise. Spread on rye or pumpernickle bread. A squeeze of lemon juice adds a nice touch, especially if the radish is hot.

For a quick canapé, spread small squares of dark bread with butter, and put a slice of radish on each.

**Marinated Salad Radishes** To prepare extra hot radishes for use in salads, slice and marinate them in vinegar for 2 to 3 hours, using about ½ cup vinegar for 2 cups radishes. The drained slices will pep up green salads, potato, egg and tuna salads, and even some fruit salads. Use leftover vinegar in salad dressings, or for the next batch of radishes.

**Radish Seed Pods** Let a few radish plants grow in an out-of-the-way corner of the garden till they flower and produce seed pods. Or use the pods of radishes planted with beans to discourage bean beetles. Pick the pods while they are young and still crisp enough to snap apart like green beans. Add them raw to salads or cook them with vegetable mixtures. Their crisp, bright pepperiness suits stir-fried dishes especially well.

## OTHER RECIPES WITH RADISHES

peppery seasoning to sprinkle on salads, soups, and other dishes.

Radishes that become tough or woody as well as hot are difficult to use except for making soup stock.

## RADISH RECIPES

### Sweet and Sour Red Radishes        (Makes 1½ to 2 cups.)

| | |
|---|---|
| *large bunch (a dozen or more) red radishes* | *1½ tablespoons vinegar* |
| *radish greens, optional* | *1½ teaspoons honey, or sugar* |
| *1 teaspoon (about) salt* (Omit if not using greens.) | *2 teaspoons (about) oil* |
| *1 tablespoon soy sauce* | *1 teaspoon sesame seeds, or a few drops sesame oil, optional* |

Wash and trim the radishes. If using the greens, rinse and shred them. Sprinkle with salt and let sit to draw out juices while preparing the radishes.

Partly crush each radish by hitting it lightly with a mallet, or pressing it with the side of a heavy knife. They should have cracks and openings, but be in one piece. Mix the soy sauce, vinegar, honey or sugar, oil, and sesame seeds or oil. Toss with the radishes.

Squeeze the radish greens hard with the hands, to thoroughly crush the leaves and squeeze out the juice. Add the greens to the radish mixture. A little more oil can be added, if desired. (The squeezing will take away the scratchiness of the leaves and make them absorb the sauce, and much of the salt will be removed with the juice.)

**Sweet and Sour Winter Radish** Grate 1 to 2 cups of winter radish, or cut to matchstick size, or slice thinly. Marinate in the above soy sauce mixture for several hours. A pinch of turmeric can be added for color, and a garnish of minced scallion, chives, or parsley is very nice.

### Beef and Winter Radish Soup      (Makes 8–10 medium bowls.)

| | |
|---|---|
| *6 cups beef soup stock* | *several fresh mushrooms, sliced or soaked, dried mushrooms, sliced, with soaking water* |
| *3 cups winter radish, thinly sliced (Halve or quarter large radish before slicing.)* | |
| *1 onion, sliced thin* | *4 teaspoons soy sauce, or to taste* |
| *1–2 cloves garlic, minced* | *¼–½ pound lean, ground beef, or very thin, inch-square beef steak slices* |

Heat stock to a boil, then add the radish, onion, garlic, mushrooms, and soy sauce. Reduce heat and simmer 30 minutes. Add the beef, stirring to separate the pieces, then remove from stove. Wait about a minute before serving. The meat will be cooked almost instantly by the soup's heat, without ever simmering or boiling, which keeps it very tender. The radish, mushroom, and beef flavors make a perfect marriage.

***Turnip and Meat Soup***    Use turnips instead of winter radish for making this soup. Other kinds of soup stock and meat can be used instead of beef. Pork and venison are especially good.

# RASPBERRIES

N OTHING TASTES BETTER ON A SUMMER DAY THAN A BOWL OF freshly picked raspberries, but the raspberry aroma, flavor, and color are just as welcome in winter. Sparkling raspberry juice, and rich, red raspberry sauce are winter luxuries known only to those who freeze and can their own.

Red raspberries are the most familiar, but there are black, purple, white, and yellow varieties. All berries are raspberries that separate from their cores when picked, leaving their centers hollow. Some wild, black raspberries are called "black caps," because picking them is like taking tiny caps off very tiny heads. In some places, wild raspberries, especially the red varieties, are so abundant and easy to pick that there is no need to cultivate them. All raspberries are hardy and well suited to northern climates.

## HANDLING RASPBERRIES

Raspberries are ripe and ready to pick when they come off their cores with a gentle touch. If pressing and pulling is necessary, they are not ready. As ripe raspberries are soft, pick them into shallow containers to keep them from packing down and crushing each other. (Immediately use any raspberries that are crushed for sauce or juice.) While picking, remove and discard any moldy berries on the plants, because the mold can quickly spread to other berries, spoiling them for later picking. This is worthwhile even for wild berries, if one intends to return to pick the same spot again.

Washing is not necessary for raspberries growing in a clean, dust free place. If they must be washed, do not do so till just before using them, as the water and handling make them spoil quickly. Wash them gently, by putting them in a large pan of cool water, swishing them around by hand, then lifting them out into a colander to drain.

Some kinds of wild raspberries are very seedy but still make good juice or sauce. (Refer to SEEDINESS IN BLACKBERRIES in the BLACK-BERRIES section.)

---

### STORAGE

**Canning**   Berries become very soft, juice is excellent. Pour about ½ cup boiling water, juice, or syrup in jars, fill with berries, shake to pack, add more boiling liquid, ½ in. headroom. Process boiling water bath. Pints: 10 min. Quarts: 15 min. (Refer to CANNING section. Refer also to CANNING FRUIT JUICE AND SAUCE in FRUITS section.)

**Drying**   (Refer to DRYING SOFT BERRIES in DRYING section.) Leaves for herb tea: Refer to DRYING HERBS in HERBS section.

**Freezing**   Pack dry, unsweetened, or spread in shallow layer; sprinkle with about ¼ cup sugar or honey per quart, pack gently. Or pack and cover with liquid. (Refer to LIQUIDS IN WHICH TO FREEZE FRUIT in FREEZING section.)

5–8 CUPS FRESH = I QUART CANNED, OR FROZEN

---

### RASPBERRY IDEAS

**Raspberry-Orange**   This flavor combination is always a winner. Fresh raspberry and diced orange fruit cup, chilled and sprinkled with coconut or chopped nuts, is superb. Half raspberry and half orange juice is delightful to drink and makes an outstanding gelatine, to say nothing of its sherbet and ice cream possibilities. When the raspberry supply is limited, there is no better way to extend it.

### RASPBERRY IDEAS, *cont.*

**Raspberry Orange Sauce**
Cook raspberries with very thin slices of orange with the rind, and sweeten with a little honey or maple syrup. For a stronger orange flavor add extra orange juice, especially concentrated frozen juice. Simmer over moderate heat for 10 to 15 minutes, stirring often as it heats up to prevent sticking. This sauce is very nice with meats, or enjoy it with breakfast or for dessert. To can, pour hot in jars and process for 10 minutes in a boiling water bath. (Refer to the CANNING section.)

**Raspberry Juice Blends**  Raspberry juice blends deliciously with apple, currant, peach, and other fruit juices, as well as orange juice. As good for gelatines, sherbets, and jelly-making as for beverages.

---

### OTHER RECIPES WITH RASPBERRIES

---

### STORAGE

Note: See MAKING RENNET FROM LAMB'S, CALF'S, OR KID'S STOMACHS for preservation methods.

3 JUNKET RENNET TABLETS OR ABOUT ¼ HANSEN'S RENNET TABLET COAGULATES 1–2 GALLONS MILK TO MAKE CHEESE, OR ABOUT 6 CUPS MILK FOR JUNKET PUDDING

---

## RASPBERRY RECIPE

### *Raspberry Shrub*

This old-fashioned beverage retains the heady aroma of raspberries on a hot summer day better than any other raspberry preparation.

*raspberries, freshly picked* (Washed, if necessary.)　　*vinegar* (Preferably homemade, or raw cider vinegar.)

Pack the raspberries into a jar and add vinegar to fill it. Run a knife around the sides of the jar to release air bubbles. The vinegar must fill all spaces between berries. Close or cover the jar, and keep it in a dark place at room temperature for a month. Then strain through cloth and pour the raspberry vinegar into sterile bottles for storage. Store in a cool, dark place.

To make a refreshing glass of raspberry shrub, put several spoonfuls of the raspberry vinegar in the glass, and add cold water. Sweeten, if desired.

For another raspberry shrub beverage refer to the OATADE idea in the OATS section.

**Blackberry or Strawberry Shrub**  Use either of these instead of raspberries.

---

# RENNET

RENNET IS A SUBSTANCE ADDED TO MILK TO CAUSE IT TO COAGUlate for making cheese or a custard-like pudding called junket. Most rennets contain the enzyme rennin, which is extracted from the stomach of a nursing baby animal, but there are also rennets from plant sources. Both rennets have been used since ancient times, and both can be made at home.

Using homemade rennet requires some experimentation, since, unlike commercial rennets, strength cannot be calculated precisely, but homemade animal rennet is completely dependable once one is accustomed to using it. Homemade vegetable rennets are less predictable. Problems may occur, such as poor quality curd, whey that fails to drain off as it should, and intrusive flavors from the vegetable. To begin with, try homemade vegetable rennets cautiously with only small amounts of milk.

Commercial rennet is usually sold in tablet form, though liquid rennet is sometimes also available. Rennet sold for making cheese works just as well for making junket pudding. Though the junket rennet tablets sold in grocery stores can be used for cottage cheese, they are not as good for other kinds of cheeses. Vegetable rennet is sold by some mail order companies. For companies that sell rennet, refer to the REFERENCES FOR MAKING CHEESE at the end of the CHEESE, AGED section.

## MAKING RENNET FROM LAMB'S, CALF'S OR KID'S STOMACHS

The calf, lamb, or kid (baby goat) used for obtaining rennet must be so young that it has never eaten anything but milk. Rennin, the enzyme in the baby animal's stomach that coagulates milk, gradually disappears after the animal starts to eat solid food. When the baby animal is butchered, the largest of the four stomach compartments, which usually contains milk curds, is removed for making rennet. The stomach lining, and sometimes the curds, are preserved to use for rennet as needed. The following preservation methods are from old-time sources and require salting or drying. Because enzymes are destroyed by heat, temperatures above 100°F must be avoided.

Freezing is a possible storage method, though it is no more convenient than salt curing or drying, and there is no availabe information on the freezer life of the rennin enzyme. However, cold temperatures do not usually harm enzymes, and freezing avoids the use of salt. As an experiment, spread 1 to 2 inch pieces of stomach on a tray to keep them separated, then freeze, and package them. To use, soak a piece of stomach 12 or more hours in a minimum of water, then use the liquid for coagulating the milk. To preserve stomachs in wine, see *Junket from Wine-Preserved Rennet* below.

***Preserving Rennet in Brine***   Clean and wash the stomach inside and out. In a large jar, crock, or other container, make a strong brine by mixing plain or pickling salt into warm water till no more salt will dissolve. A little salt should settle to the bottom. About 6 tablespoons of salt dissolve in 1 quart of water. For a lamb's or kid's stomach make about a quart of brine. For a calf's stomach make 2 quarts.

Cool the brine to room temperature, then immerse the stomach in it. Cover and store in a cool place. After 3 or 4 days the solution can be used. From 1 to 2 teaspoons should coagulate 2 gallons of milk for making cheese. Leave the stomach in the solution during storage, taking out liquid as needed. It will keep indefinitely. One lamb's or calf's stomach can make over 100 pounds of cheese.

***Dry Salting Rennet***   This method was common in the early days in North America. Clean the stomach inside and out and rub it well all over with plain or pickling salt. Then dry it in an airy place. It can be cut open to lie flat on a drying rack, but do not use a food dryer if there is any chance of the temperature rising above 100°F. One old way was to stretch out the stomach over a stick, and prop it up where air could circulate.

When the stomach is dry, cut it into about 1 inch pieces and store in a tightly closed jar. For use, put a piece in slightly warm water to cover, and soak it all day or overnight. Pour this liquid into the milk. It should coagulate several gallons.

***Rennet Coated in Wood Ashes and Dried***   Take the whole stomach from the baby animal without removing the curds inside. Roll it immediately in clean hardwood ashes till well coated, then hang it in a dry, airy place. The lye in the wood ashes will keep the stomach from spoiling as it dries. When completely dried, remove the curds to use as rennet, and discard the stomach lining. The curds should be powdery, and may need grinding to get rid of lumps. Store the powder in a tightly sealed jar in a cool place. To use, put ⅛ teaspoon of the powder in a cup, and add one drop of water at a time, mixing after each drop till a thick paste is formed. Then add enough water to dissolve the powder completely. Add this liquid to milk to make cheese. The ⅛ teaspoon, in solution, should be enough to coagulate 8 to 12 gallons of milk.

## MAKING RENNET FROM PLANTS

Quite a few different plants have been described as having the ability to coagulate milk. Among them are stinging nettles, fig juice, the Cardus species of sunflower, sorrel, and giant purple thistles. Directions for making plant rennets are hard to find and often vague, so expect to learn through experimentation. At best, vegetable rennets are likely to set less dense curd and require longer to work than animal rennets.

***Nettles for Rennet***   Boil a bunch of nettles for 20 to 30 minutes in just enough water to cover them, and strain off the liquid. Usually as much plain or pickling salt as will dissolve is stirred into the liquid while it is still warm. The salt preserves the liquid, but it may also add more salt to the cheese than is desirable, and may inhibit the ripening of the curd. Freezing ½ cup portions of unsalted liquid is another possibility. The amount of liquid needed for successful coagulation vary considerably, but ½ cup per gallon of milk is a reasonable amount to try.

***Giant Purple Thistles for Rennet***   Gather thistle florets after the heads have turned brown, before the down appears, and dry them in an airy, shady place. To prepare enough for about a gallon of milk, pulverize 1 to 2 tablespoonfuls with a mortar and pestle. Add just enough warm water to cover the powder and soak for 5 minutes. Pound this mixture in the mortar, and let sit for another 5 minutes. Repeat several times, till a brown liquid forms. Strain through cloth. This step is essential for removing the tiny, irritating hairs that would otherwise get into the cheese. Use a teaspoon or slightly more of the liquid for each quart of milk to be coagulated. If too much is used it may give the cheese an unpleasant taste, and might even cause indigestion.

# RENNET RECIPES (JUNKET)

Junket is an exquisitely delicate, custard-like dessert made with rennet and milk. As it takes only seconds to mix, it is as "instant" as most advertized instant puddings. Junket made with wine or another liquor, and fresh home produced milk, is an out-of-this-world kind of treat. Below are old-fashioned and modern versions of wine junket.

### *Junket from*
### *Wine-Preserved Rennet*        (Makes about 6 dessert servings.)

(From *In The Kitchen,* by Elizabeth S. Miller, 1875.)

"Cut a fresh or dried rennet [The largest stomach of a lamb, kid, or calf as described above.] in strips two inches long and half an inch wide; if a dried rennet is used it must be soaked until it has no taste of the salt which was used in drying. Put the pieces in a quart bottle and fill it with sherry; in two or three days it will be ready to use. When the wine is exhausted the bottle may be filled again and again.

Warm to about blood-heat a quart of fresh milk with a gill [½ cup] of fine sugar; have ready in a cup two tablespoonsfuls of the rennet wine (see above rule) and a teaspoonful of vanilla; pour the milk in the dish in which it is to be served; place the thermometer it it, and when it has fallen to 94° pour in the rennet and stir gently to mix it; then leave it, and it will stiffen in a few minutes, when it may be placed on ice until wanted. If preferred, it may be poured in cups with a little nutmeg grated over the top. After a little experience the thermometer may be dispensed with, and the temperature of the milk tested by the finger."

### *Wine Junket, Modern Style*     (Makes about 6 dessert servings.)

*1½ junket tablets, or ⅛ Hansen's*     *3 cups milk*
   *cheese rennet tablet*               *4 tablespoons honey*
*6 tablespoons sherry, homemade*    *nutmeg*
   *wine, or another liquor*

Dissolve the junket or rennet tablets in the sherry. (Extra amounts can be made and stored indefinitely.) Mix the milk and honey, and heat to lukewarm, 90° to 100°F. If a single, large dish is to be used, pour the milk and honey in it and stir in the sherry-rennet mixture. If making individual servings, stir the sherry mixture into the milk and honey, then pour immediately into the small dessert dishes. Let the junket sit without disturbance for about 15 minutes, or till it sets. Sprinkle with nutmeg and refrigerate. (Stirring the junket for too long, or moving the dishes before the junket has set, may prevent setting.)

---

**OTHER RECIPES
WITH RENNET**

Refer to the recipes for fresh cheese, p.143

# RHUBARB

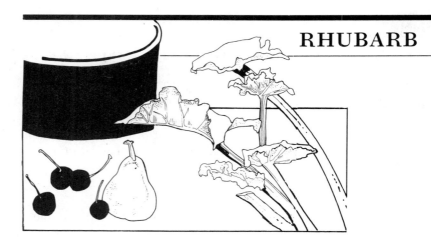

## STORAGE

**Canning**   Cut ½–1 in. slices, mix in 3–4 tablespoons honey, or ⅓ cup sugar per quart. Let stand 3–4 hours to draw out juice. Bring slowly to boil, then boil ½ min. Ladle into jars, ½ in. headroom. Process boiling water bath. Pints and quarts: 10 min. (Refer to CANNING section. Refer also to CANNING FRUIT JUICE AND SAUCE in FRUITS section.)

**Cold Storage**   (Refer to COLD WATER CANNING in COLD STORAGE section.)

**Drying**   Slice or chop, dry to hard. Good in *Herb Teas* (refer to HERBS section). Or grind for FRUIT MEAL or purée for FRUIT LEATHER. (Refer to DRYING section.)

**Freezing**   Slice. Optional: Blanch 1 min. in boiling water to set color and flavor. Pack dry or cover with liquid. (Refer to LIQUIDS IN WHICH TO FREEZE FRUIT in FREEZING section, and FREEZING section generally.)

**Winter Forcing**   Dig roots in late fall, replant in containers. Leave outside till frozen solid. (Freezing is required for new growth to begin.) Bring into cellar, or other cool, humid place. Harvest new stalks as they grow.

2 POUNDS FRESH = ABOUT 1 QUART CANNED OR FROZEN

RHUBARB—THE FRUIT THAT IS NOT A FRUIT—IS ACTUALLY THE STALK of a plant related to buckwheat. It grows best in the North where winters are cold. Among its many advantages are its permanence in the garden (once established it is always there), and its earliness. It can be harvested long before any true fruits mature. An old name for rhubarb is pieplant, which describes one popular use, but there are many other ways to prepare it.

Rhubarb's one disadvantage is the large amount of sweetening commonly added to counter its tartness, but even this tartness can be turned to advantage. Rhubarb or its juice can be used like lemon to enliven the flavor of bland, sweet fruits, or used like tomato to perk up meat stews or soups. Rhubarb, onion, and beef flavors, for instance, go surprisingly well together. Why not grow a rhubarb plant near the kitchen door, beside the patch of herbs to inspire such uses?

Only the stalks of rhubarb plants are edible. The leaves contain enough oxalic acid to be poisonous and sometimes fatal. Do not confuse rhubarb leaves with rhubarb chard, which is a red-stalked variety of Swiss chard, and quite safe to eat.

## HANDLING RHUBARB

Rhubarb stalks should be pulled rather than cut, as cutting leaves the stalk's base in the ground to rot. Grasp the stalks near the base and pull with a slight twisting motion. Cut the leaves off outdoors. A brisk whack with a knife works best, and the leaves can go directly onto the compost pile. The bottom of the stalks can also be trimmed outdoors. Rinsing and slicing is the only other preparation necessary before cooking. Do not peel rhubarb stalks. Many old cookbooks advise it, but as the newer varieties are less stringy, as well as redder and sweeter, this advice no longer applies.

Rhubarb is most tender and sweet in spring and early summer, so these are the best times to can or freeze it. As rhubarb contains a lot of water, add only a tiny bit in the bottom of the pot when stewing it, to keep it from sticking as it begins to cook. Rhubarb can also be baked in a covered dish in the oven without adding water. Or it can be mixed with a little honey or sugar after it is sliced, and left sitting till enough juice has collected for cooking it.

*Reducing the Sweetening*  Rhubarb recipes usually call for ½ cup or more of sugar per quart of chopped fruit. Reduce this amount to 3 to 4 tablespoons honey or ⅓ cup sugar for a flavor that is still pleasantly sweet and sour. The reddest, sweetest varieties can be tried with even less sweetening. Add a dab of butter to mask some of the acidity.

An excellent way to reduce the amount of sweetening is to cook it with sweet fruits. Use dried fruits like raisins, figs or dates. A mixture with berries is often very good. Such juice combinations as rhubarb and bland wild berry juice, rhubarb-sweet cherry juice, or rhubarb-pear juice, can all be extraordinarily delicious. (Refer to COMBINING SWEET AND TART FRUITS in the FRUITS section for ideas.)

## RHUBARB RECIPES

*Crumbly Topped Rhubarb*      (Makes about 6 dessert servings.)

4 cups rhubarb, slice thinly
1 tablespoon whole wheat flour
¼ cup honey or ⅓ cup sugar
1 teaspoon fresh ginger root, minced, optional
½ teaspoon powdered coriander, or other spices to taste

Topping:
6 tablespoons butter, softened or melted
½ cup whole wheat flour
½ cup rolled oats
¼ cup wheat germ
¼ cup maple sugar or brown sugar

Combine the rhubarb, the tablespoon of flour, honey or sugar, ginger root, and coriander. Spread in a buttered or oiled deep pie dish, or shallow baking dish. Mix the butter, the half cup of flour, rolled oats, wheat germ, and maple or brown sugar. Spread over the rhubarb mixture as a topping. Bake in a moderate, 350°F, oven for 40 minutes, or till the rhubarb is tender, and the top browned. Serve warm or cold with milk or cream.

*Crumbly Topped Rhubarb Conserve*  To the rhubarb add 1 cup raisins and ¼ cup sunflower seeds or ½ cup chopped nuts. Reduce sweetening to 3 tablespoons honey or 4–5 tablespoons sugar, and prepare as above.

For a date version, add chopped dates to the rhubarb instead of raisins. The rhubarb sweetening can be further reduced or eliminated, if desired, but the brown or maple sugar in the topping is still needed.

---

**RHUBARB IDEAS**

**Rhubarb-Fresh Fruit Cocktail** Enliven canned rhubarb by mixing it with fresh fruits to taste. Chopped apple, diced orange, pineapple, strawberries or other fresh berries are all good. Add a finely minced mint leaf for a special flavor. Serve chilled as an appetizer or dessert.

**Rhubarb Punch**  Dilute rhubarb juice with water or with sweet, bland apple juice, or another mild juice. Thin apple pectin (refer to the PECTIN section) gives a smooth flavor. Add white wine or ginger ale to taste, and ice to chill.

**Rhubarb Date (or Fig) Pie**  Mix chopped rhubarb with an equal amount of chopped dates or dried figs for a pie filling. The dried fruit will thicken as well as sweeten the rhubarb, making other ingredients unnecessary. Dots of butter can be put on the fruit before the top crust is added.

### Rhubarb Meat Sauce for Rice or Noodles

(Makes sauce for about 6 dinner servings.)

| | |
|---|---|
| 1 onion, finely chopped | 2 tablespoons honey |
| 2 tablespoons oil or butter | red pepper, to taste |
| 2 cups rhubarb, chopped | salt, optional |
| 1–2 cloves garlic, minced | 2–3 cups cooked meat, diced |
| ½ cup tomato sauce | (Try beef, pork, lamb, or chicken.) |

Lightly brown the onion in the oil or butter. Add rhubarb and garlic and stir to coat with fat. Stir in tomato sauce, honey, pepper, and salt, if desired. Simmer, uncovered, about 15 minutes, till the rhubarb is soft. Add the meat and simmer about 5 minutes, or till it is heated through. Taste and adjust seasonings. The flavor should be tart more than sweet, and quite spicy. Serve over hot rice or noodles.

**Green Tomato Meat Sauce for Rice or Noodles**    Use chopped green tomatoes instead of rhubarb to make this sauce.

## STORAGE

*Note:* Refer to STORING GRAIN in GRAINS section.

⅞ CUP RICE = ABOUT 1 CUP RICE FLOUR

# RICE

FOR THE MAJORITY OF NORTH AMERICANS RICE IS ENJOYED AS a change of pace from potatoes and bread, but it is not a mainstay in people's diets. For a large percentage of the rest of the world's population, the reverse is true, and rice is the most important food. Because people from so many different cultures depend on rice, there are an extraordinary number of ways to prepare and eat it. In the Far East rice is most often cooked plain, but its accompaniments are diverse. The mixed rice dishes favored in other parts of the world are as various as the people who developed them. The names alone are intriguing: jambalaya, which is Creole, paella from Spain, risotto from Italy, kedgeree, which originated in India and spread throughout the British Empire, pilau (or pilav or pilaf), which came from India, but was changed in both spelling and composition by those who adopted it. Rice has so much to offer, from its plain practicality to its round-the-world versatility, that anyone can find numerous ways to enjoy it.

Few North American gardeners think of growing rice on a small scale for themselves, but it is quite possible, and it is the way it is grown in most Asian countries. Neither a warm, humid climate nor a rice paddy are essential. The Japanese have developed rice varieties suited to fairly cool climates, and there are the so-called upland varieties that grow like wheat and do not need to be submerged in water. Upland rice, however, is not nearly as productive as rice grown

in water. (For information about growing rice refer to the REFER-
ENCES at the end of the GRAINS section.)

Wild rice is not botanically related to other rices except in that all
are grasses. Wild rice was so named because of the coincidental fact
that it grows in water. Anyone lucky enough to be able to gather wild
rice will have no trouble finding ways to use it. It is cooked like any
grain, often without seasonings, since it is so flavorful by itself.

## HANDLING RICE

As rice paddies are dry at harvest time, the steps for harvesting rice
are the same as for harvesting other grains. Like oats, rice has hulls
(husks) that cling to the kernels after threshing. Some hitting or rubbing action is necessary to loosen them before winnowing. In Japan
there are small hand powered machines for milling small quantities of
rice. The old way was to put the grain in a hollow stump and pound
it with a wooden mallet. (Refer to the GRAINS section.)

The different kinds of rice are usually classified according to the
shape of the grain: short, medium, or long. All can be cooked in the
same ways, but one may be preferred over another for a particular
dish. Long grain rice is sometimes considered more elegant, perhaps
because it is a little easier to cook without stickiness. Short and medium grained rice have a moist, tender texture that is often preferred
for everyday eating. The distinction between brown and white rice is
a more important one, much like the distinction between wholewheat
and white flour. "Brown rice" is the whole grain, complete with bran
and germ, and with vitamins, minerals, fiber, fat, protein, and starch
intact. White rice has been polished to remove bran and germ,
which, in effect, removes all nutrients except the protein and starch.
Even when enriched or converted to increase vitamin content it does
not match brown rice in nutritional quality. Brown rice generally has
a richer flavor and chewier texture than white rice. Least flavorful
(and least nutritious) is quick cooking or minute white rice, which
has a flat, bland taste.

*Rice Flour*    Brown rice makes excellent flour for many uses, and is
easily ground at home in a grain mill. (Refer to the GRAINS section.)
Rice flour gives a light, pleasantly grainy texture to muffins and
cookies. When finely ground, it is one of the best thickenings for
puddings, sauces, and soups, making them smooth without any
starchy taste. It is a favorite with the many people who are allergic to
wheat.

*Cooking Rice*    The cooking of rice can be a controversial subject,
and disagreements are likely to begin with the question of whether
rice should be rinsed or not. This is easily answered for brown rice,
where rinsing is unnecessary. When white rice is rinsed to remove
surface starch, sometimes vitamins which were added as enrichment
are also washed away. Brown rice need only be rinsed if chaff or
debris is mixed with it, as it has no surface starch. A quick rinsing

will not affect nutrients. To retain the nutrients in soaked rice, cook it in its soaking water. Many people have favorite methods of rice cooking that they swear by, all of which are fine, except those requiring a large amount of water to be discarded, together with most vitamins and minerals.

When cooking rice in a pre-measured amount of water to be completely absorbed by the time it is done, adjustments may be needed for different batches of rice. Newly harvested rice, for instance, has a high moisture content, requiring less cooking water than rice that has dried in storage. As well, tastes will vary. Some prefer the soft, moist texture of rice made with a little extra water, while others like firm textured rice made with a minimum of water. Cooking times may also need adjustment, especially when using brown rice in recipes intended for white rice. Brown rice takes 30 to 45 minutes to cook, depending on type, as compared to 20 minutes for white rice.

The *Plainly Cooked Rice* recipe that follows is a basic Oriental cooking method. It is excellent for both brown and white rice, if cooking times and quantities of water are adjusted, and is never salted because it accompanies highly seasoned foods. When done, the grains of rice should be distinct and never mushy, yet they should stick together just a little. A slight stickiness seems to enhance the flavor, and certainly makes the rice easier to pick up with chopsticks or a fork.

## RICE RECIPES

### *Plainly Cooked Rice*           (Makes 5−7 cups.)

*2 cups rice*

*2¼ to 4 cups water, usually*
(The amount can vary from 2¼ to over 4 cups with the type of rice. See COOKING RICE, above.)

If desired, rinse and drain rice. Put the rice and cold water in a pot with a tight lid. Put the pot on high heat and bring it to a full rolling boil. After 5 minutes reduce heat to medium and cook 10 to 15 minutes. Then reduce heat to low and simmer till the rice is done. Altogether, brown rice takes 30−45 minutes, and white rice about 20 minutes. Do not stir or lift the lid unnecessarily, as that gives a mushy texture. When the rice is done all water should be absorbed. Taste a few grains to test for doneness. After the rice is cooked its texture will improve if it sits for 5 to 10 minutes, covered but off the heat.

To reheat leftover rice without adding water or changing its texture, steam in a bowl or in individual bowls. (Refer to the STEAM COOKING section.)

## Paella
(Makes 6—10 dinner servings.)

1 small frying chicken, or about 2 pounds chicken wings
3—4 tablespoons oil, preferably olive
¼ pound lean pork, cubed, optional
2 cups raw rice
1 medium tomato, chopped, or ½ cup canned tomatoes
2 cloves garlic, minced
½ teaspoon paprika
5 cups chicken stock, light soup stock, or water

⅛ teaspoon saffron or ½ teaspoon turmeric
1 cup green peas, fresh or frozen
½ pound (about) shellfish, cleaned as necessary (Can be shrimp, crayfish, squid, or clams and mussels in the shell.)
pimiento strips, for garnish, optional

Cut the chicken into small serving pieces. Heat the oil in a large, heavy frying pan till almost smoking, then brown the chicken and pork in it. Add the rice and fry, stirring often, for about 5 minutes, till its color turns brighter (or darker). Mix in the tomato, garlic, and paprika. If the frying pan does not have a tight lid, transfer the mixture to a Dutch oven or casserole. Heat stock or water to a boil, and add it and the saffron or turmeric. Cover and cook over high heat for 5 minutes, then reduce heat and simmer till the rice is almost done, about 30 minutes for brown rice or 15 minutes for white. Stir in the peas and shellfish, or if using clams or mussels in the shell, set them on top. Cover and simmer over low heat, or bake in a moderate, 350°F oven till rice, peas, and shellfish are done, about 10 minutes. Let rest off the heat for about 10 minutes before serving. Garnish with pimiento, if desired.

Paella is memorable for its striking color contrasts—saffron yellow rice, bright green peas, red pimiento—and for its distinctive blend of seasoning, chicken, and shellfish flavors.

## Jambalaya
(Makes 6—8 dinner servings.)

1 tablespoon lard, oil, or other fat
2 onions, chopped small
½ green pepper, chopped small
1 pound ham, or smoked sausage, in ½ inch cubes (Or ½ pound of each.)
2 cloves garlic, minced
2 tablespoons parsley, minced
½ teaspoon thyme
2 bay leaves
½ teaspoon cloves, powdered

2—3 tomatoes, chopped, or 1½ cups canned tomatoes, or sauce
1—2 cups cooked shrimp, crab, or other shellfish
2 cups (about) soup stock, or water
2 cups raw rice
1 teaspoon cayenne or other hot pepper, or to taste

Heat the lard in a Dutch oven, or other heavy pot. Sauté the onion and green pepper in it over medium heat for about 5 minutes. Add the ham, or sausage, and garlic, and brown lightly. Stir in the parsley, thyme, bay leaves, and cloves, and sauté for a minute or two. Add the tomato, shrimp or crab, and soup stock, and bring to a boil. Add the rice and hot pepper, stir once, and cook covered, without stirring, till the rice is done, 30 to 40 minutes for brown rice, or 20 minutes for white. Though cooked on top of the stove, Jambalaya has the versatility and convenience of a good casserole recipe.

***Leftovers Jambalaya*** Instead of ham or sausage, use any kind of cooked leftover meat or poultry. Chicken or turkey jambalaya are very good. The shellfish can be omitted and vegetables and herbs changed to taste.

## Kedgeree, East Indian Style
(Makes 6–8 side servings.)

| | |
|---|---|
| *1 cup rice* | *¼ teaspoon cumin seeds, optional* |
| *1 cup lentils* | *tional* |
| *2 tablespoons butter* | *2–3 slices fresh ginger root,* |
| *2 tablespoons oil* | *minced, optional* |
| *2 onions, halved, and thinly sliced* | *pepper, salt, optional* |
| *2 bay leaves* | |

Soak the rice and lentils in 4 cups water for about an hour. Drain, reserving the soaking water. Meanwhile, heat the butter and oil in a heavy pot, and sauté the onions over low heat till golden but not browned. Take out the onions, pressing them to leave as much butter and oil in the pot as possible, and set them aside. Add the drained rice and lentils and sauté, stirring often, about 10 minutes till the fat is absorbed. Add the bay leaves, cumin seeds, ginger root, pepper, and salt, if desired. Stir about a minute, then add the reserved soaking water. Bring to a boil over high heat, then reduce heat, cover, and simmer about 30 minutes, or till most of the water has been absorbed. Turn heat to the lowest possible level, just enough to keep the pot hot, and let sit 20 to 30 minutes. Just before serving mix in the onions.

***Split Pea or Mung Bean Kedgeree*** Use split peas or mung beans instead of lentils. The peas or beans and rice can be cooked in their soaking water without first sautéeing them, if desired. The butter and oil can be added with the onions at serving time.

## Fish Kedgeree
(Makes 4–6 lunch or supper servings.)

| | |
|---|---|
| *2–3 cups cooked rice* | *salt, optional* (Omit if using |
| *1 cup (about) cooked fish, deboned,* | salty canned fish.) |
| *flaked* (Try canned tuna or | *2 eggs, lightly beaten, or 2* |
| other canned fish.) | *hardboiled* |
| *3–4 tablespoons butter* | *parsley, optional* |
| *cayenne or black pepper, to taste* | |

Mix together the rice and fish. Melt the butter in a heavy pot or in the top of a double boiler. Add the rice and fish, and heat, stirring often. Add pepper, nutmeg, and salt, if desired. If using lightly beaten eggs, stir them into the hot mixture and let sit a minute or two, till they set. If using hardboiled eggs, dice the whites and mix them in. Crumble or grate the yolks over the top. Garnish with parsley, and serve for an excellent quick lunch or supper.

### Dirty Rice, Cajun Style

(Makes about 6 dinner servings.)

4 cups (about) chicken stock, or
  water
4–6 chicken livers
4–6 chicken gizzards
4–6 chicken hearts
1½ cups raw rice
1 large onion, chopped small
4 stalks celery, chopped small
1 large green pepper, chopped small

2 cloves garlic, minced, optional
4 tablespoons chicken fat, or
  other fat
hot red pepper, to taste
salt, optional
½ cup scallions, minced
½ cup parsley, minced

Heat the chicken stock or water, and cook the livers, gizzards, and hearts in it. Take the livers out when they are cooked through, after about 20 minutes. The gizzards and hearts will take about an hour. Remove them when done and reserve the stock. Mash the livers with a fork and mix with about a cup of the reserved stock, or purée them in a blender. Cook the rice in the remaining stock, adding water if necessary to make 2½ to 3 cups stock.

Meanwhile, finely chop the gizzards and heart, and sauté them with the onion, celery, green pepper, and garlic, in the chicken fat. When the vegetables are limp, add the mashed liver mixture, red pepper, and salt, if desired. Simmer over low heat for about 30 minutes. Then combine with the cooked rice, and garnish with the scallions and parsley. The rice will look "dirty" but taste delicious.

### Risotto

(Makes about 6 dinner servings.)

4 tablepsoons butter, or oil
1 small onion, minced
½ stalk celery, minced, optional
small clove garlic, minced, optional
1 or more mushrooms, chopped, optional
2 cups raw rice

3–4 tablespoons dry white wine,
  or sherry
5 cups light soup stock, heated
1 teaspoon fresh rosemary,
  minced, or ½ teaspoon dried
pepper, to taste
¼ cup (about) Parmesan or similar hard cheese, grated

Heat the butter or oil in a heavy pot with a tight lid. Lightly brown the onion, celery, garlic, and mushrooms in it. Add the rice and cook, stirring often, till it has a slightly translucent or golden look, about 10 minutes. Add the wine and cook, stirring, for a minute, or till it stops steaming and the moisture is evaporated. Add the hot soup stock and rosemary. When the mixture comes to a boil stir in about a

## RICE IDEAS, cont.

**Congee** This is a thin rice porridge or gruel often made in China for breakfast or a midnight snack. Make it by cooking a small amount of rice in considerable water till the rice is very soft and the water has thickened a little. Leftover cooked rice, the scrapings stuck to the rice pot, or raw rice can all be used. Make the congee thin enough to drink or thick enough to eat with a spoon, according to taste. Using ¼ cup raw brown rice cooked in 3 cups of water for about 2 hours will make a thin congee. Or add vegetables, meat and seasonings for a soup.

**Greens and Rice** Make the *Plainly Cooked Rice* recipe, above. As soon as it is soft and all the water is absorbed, stir in about 2 cups of chopped, fresh greens. Cover the pot and let sit 10 minutes, to let the heat of the rice cook the greens. Spinach, wild greens, Swiss chard, mustard greens are some that can be used. Minced parsley leaves or a mixture of parsley and greens is also good. Serve the greens and rice plain, with butter, or with the same sauces that go well with plain rice. For an elegant touch add 2–3 tablespoons sherry or white wine to the rice cooking water.

**Browned Brown Rice** For a nice nutty flavor, lightly brown raw rice in a dry pot or frying pan before cooking it as usual. The browning takes 5 minutes or a little longer over fairly high heat. Stir to prevent scorching. A pleasant change from plain cooked rice.

tablespoon of the cheese. Reduce heat, then simmer covered till the rice is tender and all the liquid is absorbed. Several times as it cooks stir more cheese, adding 2 to 3 tablespoons altogether. Cooking time will vary from 30 to 50 minutes, according to the kind of rice. Serve with more grated cheese, if desired.

**Risi e Bise**   When the risotto is about half done, cook 2 cups of fresh or frozen peas in a separate pot. Mix them into the risotto just before serving.

**Meat, Poultry, or Seafood Risotto**   Add cooked chopped meat, poultry, or seafood to the risotto about 5 minutes before it is done. Choose the stock to agree with the addition. For instance, a risotto made with duck broth and duck meat is very good, and fish stock is excellent with fish or shellfish.

### Mat's Fried Rice, Homestead Style

(Makes about 6 side servings.)

*1–2 eggs*
*2 tablespoons (about) oil, for frying*
*1 clove garlic, minced*
*1–2 slices fresh ginger root, minced, optional*
*1–2 cups homestead vegetables, chopped small (Perhaps onion or scallion, carrot, cabbage, Chinese cabbage, broccoli, greens, green pepper, sprouts.)*

*½ cup (about) cooked meat or shrimp, chopped small, optional*
*2–3 cups cooked rice (Preferably a day old.)*
*2–3 tablespoons soy sauce*

Have all ingredients prepared and ready. Stir the eggs with a fork just enough to mix them. Crumble the rice apart if it is in clumps. Then, heat a large heavy frying pan till quite hot. Add about a tablespoon of oil and tip the pan to spread it out. Add the egg, then tip the pan again so that it spreads out and cooks almost immediately. Turn the egg over to cook the top briefly, then put it on a dish. (The serving dish can be used.) Quickly break or cut it into pieces with the spatula. Add a little more oil to the frying pan, and stir-fry the garlic and ginger root for half a minute. Add the vegetables, and stir-fry for 2 or 3 minutes, till their colors brighten. Then put them in the dish with the egg. If meat, shrimp, or sausage are used, stir-fry them briefly, then put them with the vegetables and egg. If the pan is dry, add a little more oil, and add the rice. Stir constantly till the rice is slightly browned. Lastly, stir in the soy sauce, and mix in the egg, vegetables, and meat or shrimp. Reheat for about a minute.

This dish takes longer to explain than to make, and requires no special Chinese ingredients or materials.

THE ROE ARE THE TWO LONG EGG FILLED SACS FOUND INside the female fish before it spawns. These eggs are a delicacy well worth saving. The best known roe preparation is caviar—fish eggs removed from the sac and preserved in salt. However, roe fresh from the fish is just as special, and much more versatile, since it can be cooked in many different ways.

Milt are the two long, whitish fluid-filled sacs or glands found inside the male fish before it breeds. These are sometimes called "white roe" or "soft roe," and then the eggs sacs are called "hard roe." A milter is a ready to breed male fish. While the word milt is occasionally used to mean spleen, the context generally makes the meaning clear. Sometimes the egg masses of lobster, sea urchin, and other shellfish are called roe. (Refer to the SHELLFISH section.)

Though most roe and milt are edible, there are a few toxic kinds. Most of these come from southern waters. Do not, for instance, eat the roe of gar, barracuda, carbezon, or puffers. The roe from carp, shad, herring, river herring, salmon, cod, mackerel, and mullet are widely eaten. These fish often contain roe in large amounts, but roe from bass, trout, bluegills or sunfish, and other easily caught fresh water fish make a delicious tidbit. Shad, herring, and smelt milt are often eaten, and are considered choice. Some fishes' milts are too small to be useful.

## HANDLING ROE AND MILT

When cleaning fish, take out the roe and milt carefully, trying not to break the sacs. (Refer to REMOVING ENTRAILS AND TRIMMING FISH in the FISH section.) Rinse gently in cold water. If the roe should break, rinse it in a fine meshed sieve to keep the eggs from washing away. If the milt breaks and the fluid is lost there will be nothing to save. It is best to use or freeze roe and milt within a day of catching the fish. If necessary they can be refrigerated for 2 days, but they quickly lose flavor and texture. Roe can also be preserved in salt (see HOMESTEAD CAVIAR, below). Milt is not practical for salting.

Whole or unbroken roe and milt are cooked much like sweetbreads or brains, and can be used in some of the same recipes. To firm them for easier handling, they are often precooked by simmering in water or stock for 5 to 20 minutes, depending on size. Prick large roe with a tough membrane several times with a needle to keep it from bursting while cooking. A very low cooking temperature will also help prevent bursting. Any tough membranes or fibers appearing after precooking should be peeled off. Salmon milt has a vein that should be removed.

The texture of roe is best when the eggs are at a medium stage of development. Immature roe is very small and compact, while fully ripe roe tends to be too firm, or rubbery. In comparison with the graininess of roe, milt has a smooth, creamy texture. It can be mashed in a sieve, and the fluid collected to add to sauces.

## SALT CURING ROE

Roe can be salted very successfully, but milt is not practical for salting.

**Homestead Caviar**   Classic caviar is made from sturgeon eggs with painstaking, almost mystical, care. A more ordinary but very good tasting caviar can be made at home from the roe of any kind of fish, as long as the individual eggs are fairly well developed and big enough to show up separately.

Begin by separating the eggs from the sac in which they come. Rinse and then break whole roe into pieces in a wide mesh (about ¼ inch) sieve. The holes must be big enough to let individual eggs go through. Stir gently by hand till all the eggs have fallen through, leaving membranes behind. Measure the eggs and prepare double their amount of very salty brine. Use 1⅛ cup plain or pickling salt to a quart of cold water. Soak the eggs in the brine for 10 to 20 minutes. (Larger eggs need the longer soaking time.) Put the eggs to drain in a fine mesh sieve for an hour, in the refrigerator or another cool place (below 45°F). Pack in jars, filling them to the brim leaving almost no air space. Refrigerate for 1 to 2 months and drain before using. For longer storage drain, repack, and freeze them.

If desired, this caviar can be soaked in fresh water for a few minutes and drained, to remove salt just before it is used. However, it will still be quite salty and should be eaten sparingly, with unsalted accompaniments. It is excellent mixed with the *Lemon Butter* from the BUTTER section, made with unsalted butter. Serve this caviar butter with fish or vegetables.

## ROE AND MILT RECIPES

### *Roe and Milt Ramekins, Polish Style*       (Makes about 4–6 servings.)

| | |
|---|---|
| 1 pound (about) roe and milt, mixed (Fish livers can also be included.) | 2 tablespoons flour |
| vegetable stock, or water | ⅔ cup sour cream |
| 1 medium onion, minced | pepper, salt, optional |
| 2 tablespoons (about) oil, or butter | ¼ cup (about) fine bread crumbs |

Cover the roe and milt with vegetable stock, or water. Heat and simmer for 5 to 10 minutes, till they are cooked through. Drain, reserving stock. Remove any noticeable membranes. Dice or chop coarsely.

---

## ROE AND MILT IDEAS

**Roe or Milt Salad**   Simmer roe or milt in water or soup stock till cooked through. Drain, cool, and remove noticeable membranes. Cut cubes or slices, and marinate in French dressing or other salad dressing for a few minutes. Add diced cucumber or other salad vegetables to taste, and arrange on a bed of lettuce or watercress. If desired, add mayonnaise.

**Roe Scrambled Eggs**   This is a good way to use accidentally broken roe, and a good use for small amounts. Break the roe, then beat with regular eggs, using a fork. Scramble as usual. Garnish with minced parsley, if desired. The roe add texture and a lightly pleasant fish flavor.

**Quick Fresh Caviar**   Separate fresh roe into individual eggs, as in the directions for HOME-STEAD CAVIAR. Season with freshly ground pepper, finely minced onion or onion juice (refer to the ONIONS section), salt, to taste, and a little brandy, if desired. To serve, spread on buttered toast or bread, and eat at once, as raw roe will not keep long.

**Roe or Milt Stuffings for Baked Fish**   Simmer roe in water till firm and remove membranes. The milt can be pre-cooked with the roe or pressed in a sieve and the fluid collected to add to the stuffing. For each cup of prepared roe and milt add ½ cup soft breadcrumbs, 2 tablespoons softened butter or other fat, and seasonings, to taste. Pepper, such fresh minced herbs as basil, tarragon, and savory are all good. Stuff the fish and bake in a hot oven till well done. White wine or melted buter are very good for basting. Shad is especially good prepared this way. For preparing and baking the fish, refer to the *Elizabethan Stuffed Fish* recipe, in the FISH section.

Sauté the onion in the oil or butter till limp. Stir in the flour, then add ¼ cup of the reserved stock, stirring constantly till it thickens. Remove from heat and stir in the sour cream, and pepper and salt, if desired. Fill 4 to 6 custard cups or ramekins with the mixture. Brown the bread crumbs in a little butter or oil, then sprinkle on top. Bake in a hot, about 400°F, oven for 10 minutes.

### *Roe with Herb Sauce*  (Makes about 6 small appetizer or side servings.)

| | |
|---|---|
| 1 pound (about) roe<br>flour, for dusting<br>pepper, salt, optional<br>4 tablespoons butter<br>3 teaspoons lemon juice | 1 teaspoon chives or scallions,<br>  minced<br>1 teaspoon fresh basil, chervil,<br>  or parsley, minced, or ¼<br>  teaspoon dried thyme or<br>  savory |

Prick large roe with a needle several times and simmer in water over very low heat till firm. Drain and dust the roe with flour seasoned with pepper and salt, if desired. Dust small roe with flour without precooking.

Heat the butter in a heavy frying pan, and sauté the roe over low heat till golden brown on both sides. Remove them to a serving dish and keep warm. Heat the butter left in the pan till it begins to brown slightly. Add the lemon juice and herbs. Cook over low heat for a minute, stirring. Pour over the roe and serve immediately. To fully appreciate the delicate flavor and interesting texture, serve alone as an appetizer or first course.

***Roe Hors d'Oeuvres***  Fry small roe as above. Put a toothpick in each and serve with lemon wedges or a sprinkling of lemon juice, omitting herbs.

**ROE AND MILT
IDEAS,** *cont.*

**Milt Cream Sauce**  Press the milt in a sieve to remove membranes and extract fluid. Add this to the *Cream Sauce* in the MILK section, and serve with fish, vegetables, or potatoes. The milt adds smoothness and a delicate, faintly fishy flavor.

**ANOTHER RECIPE
WITH ROE AND MILT**

Fish Pickled in Sour Cream (with milt), p.271

# ROSES

Aᴿᴼˢᴱ ɪs ᴍᴏʀᴇ ᴛʜᴀɴ ᴀ ᴘʀᴇᴛᴛʏ ꜰʟᴏᴡᴇʀ. ɪᴛ ɪs ᴛʜᴇ ʙʟᴏssᴏᴍ ᴏꜰ the rose hip—a highly respected fruit, and its petals can be an exotic flavoring in food. Particularly useful are wild roses and some old or standard rose varieties. Most modern hybrids have too little fragrance to be used for flavoring, and they produce no fruits. Those who wish to eat their roses as well as look at them must find some wild ones, or else plant varieties known to produce rose hips, or known for their scent. *Rosa rugosa* is a variety often advertized for its hips. Damask roses are famous for their scent, but are rarely found in

**STORAGE**

**Canning**  Rose hip juice or purée (Refer to ᴄᴀɴɴɪɴɢ ꜰʀᴜɪᴛ ᴊᴜɪᴄᴇ ᴀɴᴅ sᴀᴜᴄᴇ in FRUITS section.) *Caution:* Add 2 tablespoons lemon juice to each pint to increase acidity. See also *Rose Petal Syrup,* below.

**STORAGE,** *cont.*

**Drying**  *Rose Hips* Spread out, dry till brittle or hard. Optional: Blanch briefly or nick with knife to crack skins and speed drying. Crush or grind if for teas. *Rose Petals* Trim off base of petals (see below). Dry till papery. Use for tea or flavoring. (Refer to DRYING section.)

**Freezing**  *Rose Hips* May trim blossom and stem ends. Package dry. *Rose Water* (see below) freeze as ice cubes. (Refer to FREEZING section.)

nurseries or garden catalogs. They are used to make rose attar, a perfume or fragrant oil. The rose geranium is known for its scent, but it is not botanically related to roses.

Since the discovery of rose hips' high vitamin C content, they have often been regarded as vitamin supplements to take dutifully rather than fruits to be enjoyed. Yet rose hips were enjoyed long before anyone ever heard of vitamins. In Scandinavian countries they have always been a favorite fruit. The American Indians always appreciated them, as did the early American colonists, and they can be just as enjoyable today. Well prepared rosehips are both a taste treat and a nutritional bonus.

Besides the petals and hips, the rose plant has other edible parts. Its first spring leaves, and the blossom can be added to salads. The leaves, both fresh and dried, can be made into herb teas, and the roots can be slivered and dried for rose root tea. The flavor of all of these will be mild and pleasant without any distinctive rose taste.

## HANDLING ROSES

Gather only those rose petals and hips that have not been sprayed with insecticides. Wild roses growing along roadways, and ornamental roses are often heavily sprayed.

*Gathering and Preparing Rose Petals*  Gather the petals from strongly scented roses on a dry morning, before the heat of the day has dissipated their fragrance. Choose blossoms in full bloom. The white or yellow area at the bottom of each petal must be trimmed off, as it is bitter tasting. This is easy to do while picking the petals. Pick a "pinch" of petals at a time, snip off the bottoms with scissors, and put them in a container. Or hold the petals with the fingers of one hand and twist off the bottoms with the other. (There is no need to trim petals for sachets.)

If the petals come from a clean location and are picked neatly washing will not be necessary. If they must be washed, put them in a colander and lower them into a pan of cool water. Swish them gently, lift them out, and let them drain. They are then ready for drying or using in one of the recipes below, or for making into rose water.

***Making Rose Water***   Rose water is an intensely rose flavored liquid used like vanilla to flavor desserts, beverages, and other foods. True rose water is distilled from rose petals, but flavorful imitations can be made by simmering trimmed, crushed rose petals in a small amount of water, then straining through cloth to remove the spent petals. The temperature must stay below a boil or the flavor will be dissipated. Another possibility is to put 2 parts rose petals with 1 part hot water in a blender, liquify, and strain through cloth.

A sort of kitchen drip still for rose petals can be made as shown in the diagram. It takes about a pound of trimmed rose petals to make a cup of rose water. Place a rack in the bottom of a large pot and bring a quart of water to a boil in it. Then add the rose petals. Put in the bowl with the ice cube, being sure it is centered on the rack. Place the lid on upside down and put ice cubes in it. Keep the heat fairly high. The rose flavored steam will hit the cold lid, condense, run down to the center of the concave lid and drip into the bowl. The ice cube in the bowl keeps the collected rose water from re-evaporating. Stop when there is about a cup of rose water, because after that the flavor becomes too weak.

Rose water kept in a tightly closed bottle in the refrigerator will last for months. It can also be frozen in small cubes of 2 or 3 tablespoons each, adding a cube to flavor a food. Rose water is widely used in middle eastern recipes.

***Gathering and Preparing Rose Hips***   One or two rose hips can be nibbled fresh, but as they are too dry and seedy to enjoy raw in large quantities they are best cooked in some way or dried for making tea. Rose hips have their best flavor and highest Vitamin C content in the fall when they are fully colored and fully ripe. They are usually picked after the first frost. If they shrivel on the plant before they are picked, the fibers around the seeds become scratchy. This will not affect teas or juices, but for purées they should be picked earlier.

Rose hips picked in a clean place can be dried or made into juice without washing or other preparation. Loose bits of the blossom end and stems are harmless. If the hips must be washed, put them in plenty of cool water, and rub them between the hands to remove bits of blossom and stem. Float off as much debris as possible, then lift the hips out of the water, leaving heavier dirt behind.

To make juice or purée, cover the hips with water and cook them till soft. Strain through cloth or a fine sieve for juice. Purée them by pushing them through a sieve or other device to remove seeds. (Refer to MAKING FRUIT JUICE AND SAUCE in the FRUITS section.) Rose hip juice and purée are good in combinations with tart fruits.

Rose hips vary in size from smaller than a pea to almost as large as a plum, and it is best to dry tiny hips for tea or to use them for juice, so as to avoid tedious trimming. Large fleshy hips can be stewed or

*Making rose water with a still*

Lid upside down with ice cubes in it.

Rack

Boiling water with rose petals in it.

Bowl with 1 ice cube in it.

made into preserves. For these, trim the blossom and stem ends, then slit them open on one side to scrape out the seeds.

## ROSE RECIPES

### *Rose Petal Syrup* (Makes about 1 pint.)

| | |
|---|---|
| *1 cup rhubarb juice, or ½ cup lemon juice* | *1 cup honey, or 1½ cups sugar* <br> *1 cup rose petals, trimmed (See above.)* |

Put the rhubarb juice and 1 cup water, or the lemon juice and 1½ cups water, in a saucepan with the sweetening. Heat to a boil, then simmer, uncovered, for 10 minutes. Add the rose petals and simmer without boiling for another 10 minutes. Strain to remove the rose petals, if desired, or they can be left in the syrup.

To can, pour hot into jars, and seal as in open kettle canning, or process in a boiling water bath for 5 minutes. (Refer to the CANNING section.)

**Rose Beverages** For a roseade, put several spoons of rose petal syrup in a glass, add ice water, and stir. For a rose milk drink, add cold milk to the syrup. These can also be made with hot water or hot milk.

### *Rose Hip Soup* (Makes 5–6 medium bowls.)

| | |
|---|---|
| *1 quart rose hip juice or purée (fresh or canned)* <br> *2–4 tablespoons honey* <br> *1–3 tablespoons lemon juice or homemade cider vinegar, optional (Omit if using canned juice or purée.)* | *1 tablespoon potato starch, cornstarch, or tapioca granules* <br> *6 (about) tablespoons sour cream or yogurt, optional* |

Heat the rose hip juice or purée, honey, and lemon juice or vinegar. Adjust amounts of honey and lemon juice or vinegar to give a lively sweet tart flavor. Mix the starch or tapioca in enough cold water to moisten it, and stir it in. Cook till the soup thickens slightly and clears. Float a spoon of sour cream or yogurt in each bowl of soup when it is served.

**Dried Rose Hip Soup** Soak ½ cup dried rose hips in a quart of water for a few minutes, then cook till soft. Mash with a fork and strain, reserving liquid. Add another cup of water to the pulp, heat to a boil, then strain. Combine the juice from both strainings and use for making the soup.

**Rose Hip Pudding** Add honey to taste, and increase starch or tapioca to 5–6 tablespoons. After it has thickened pour the pudding into individual dishes or into a serving dish to cool. The flavor is brisk and very fruity.

---

### ROSE IDEAS

**Rose Hip Apple Sauce** Cook apples for making sauce in rose hip juice, or cook rose hips and apples together and purée them using a sieve or other straining device to remove the seeds.

**Raisin Stuffed Rose Hips** Use large, fleshy rose hips. Trim the blossom and stem end and slit the hips open on one side to scrape out the seedy centers. Put in several raisins. Eat as a fresh snack, or cook gently in a little water to make stewed fruit. For preserves, cook the stuffed hips in a syrup. (Refer to the JAM AND JELLY section.)

**Rose Custard** Make a plain custard, and flavor it with 2–3 teaspoons rose water, or add a handful of fresh or dried, trimmed rose petals. The bread, rice, and noodle variations of the *Real Country Custard* recipe in the MILK section are also good with rose flavoring.

**Rose Vinegar or Brandy** Fill a bottle with fresh, trimmed rose petals. Add vinegar or brandy to cover, close the bottle, and steep. After a month, strain off the vinegar or brandy and rebottle.

---

### OTHER RECIPES WITH ROSES

Herb Tea, p. 341
Mix-a-Flavor Ice Cream, p. 356

# RUTABAGAS

Rutabagas are a vegetable of the north. They grow best and are most appreciated in the Scandiniavian countries, Russia, Scotland, Canada, and other northern locations. They do not grow well in warm climates, even as a winter vegetable.

Rutabagas are sometimes confused with ordinary, summer turnips, but the confusion is in the name and not in the taste. Rutabagas are also known as Swedish turnips, Swedes, Canadian turnips, and winter or yellow turnips. In Canada they are often just called turnips. Though both rutabagas and turnips are members of the cabbage family, they are different species. Rutabagas have edible cabbage-like leaves and look like cabbage plants until their roots start to swell, while turnip leaves look and taste like mustard greens. Rutabagas have a sweeter taste and denser texture than turnips. They are very good eaten raw and are, in fact, as versatile as carrots. They can very often be substituted for carrots, turnips, and other root vegetables in recipes.

**Canning** Not recommended. (They discolor and develop a strong taste.)

**Cold Storing** (Excellent, the preferred storage method.) Trim tops to 1 in. Lay in bins in root cellar, or pack in damp sand or other damp material in any cool place. Will keep all winter. (Refer to COLD STORAGE section.)

**Drying** Slice thinly, or grate. Steam to pre-cook (optional). Dry till hard. Refer to DRYING section.

**Freezing** Cut in cubes, blanch 2 min. in boiling water, or cook, and mash. (Refer to FREEZING section.)

## HANDLING RUTABAGAS

Do not harvest rutabagas until after fall frosts, as before frost they have a hot, strong flavor. When harvested for storage in a root cellar or similar place, trim the tops but leave the roots as they are, and do not wash them. There will be no need for the paraffin or wax coating that is sometimes used commercially if the rutabagas are stored in a humid place or are packed in a damp material.

Before use, scrub rutabagas with a vegetable brush to clean them. Peeling is unnecessary, unless the skin is blemished or has been waxed. Often rutabagas are too big to eat at one time, but cut sections keep very well covered in the refrigerator.

**Rutabaga in Salads** Raw rutabaga is an excellent salad ingredient when thinly sliced or grated. A mixture of grated rutabaga, grated apple, and alfalfa sprouts makes a delicious winter salad. Raw rutabaga slices are also good to eat like carrot sticks, and go well with vegetable dips. In winter a rutabaga in the refrigerator is a boon for salad makers to add here and there, as needed.

**Sautéed Rutabaga Slices** Cut ½ inch thick slices of rutabaga and steam them for 3—4 minutes. Then sauté them in butter or another fat. They will be very good sautéed in the fat of the meat with which they are served.

**Neep Purry** This is Scottish style mashed rutabaga. Cut the rutabaga in pieces, then cook and mash it like potatoes. Season with butter, pepper, powdered ginger, and salt, if desired. Make plenty, as everyone will want a second helping.

## RUTABAGA RECIPES

### Finnish Rutabaga Pudding
(Makes about 6 side servings.)

| | |
|---|---|
| ¼ cup fine bread crumbs | ⅛ teaspoon nutmeg |
| ¼ cup milk | pepper, salt, optional |
| 2 eggs | 2 teaspoons molasses, or honey |
| 4 cups mashed rutabaga | 1 tablespoon (about) butter |

Soak the bread crumbs in the milk for a few minutes. Then beat in the eggs with a fork. Add the rutabaga, pepper, salt, if desired, and molasses or honey. Mix well and pour into a buttered baking dish. Dot with butter, then bake uncovered for an hour in a moderate,

350°F, oven. The pudding will set and should be lightly browned. Serve as a side dish instead of potatoes, or as a light supper, or lunch.

### Rutabagas Stewed with Bacon          (Makes about 6 side servings.)

2—3 *thick slices bacon, chopped*          *pepper, to taste*
6 *cups (about) rutabaga, sliced*
    *medium*

Put about a third of the bacon in the bottom of a heavy saucepan. Cover with a layer of rutabagas, a sprinkle of pepper, and more bacon. Add the rest of the ingredients in layers. Then add ¼ cup water, cover tightly, and put over medium heat. To prevent sticking, shake the pot several times as cooking begins. Simmer from 20 to 30 minutes, till the rutabagas are soft. This simple, zestful stew goes well with plainly cooked green vegetables.

# RYE

RYE SEEMS TO DRAW MORE PRAISE FOR ITS ABILITY TO GROW ON poor soil in very cold weather than it does for its flavor, yet it has a very special taste. According to the Encyclopedia Brittanica rye is grown for only three purposes, rye whiskey, rye bread, and animal feed. Rye bread is delicious and rye whiskey has its appeal, but there are many other ways for people to eat rye, among them, rye breakfast cereals, rye crackers, sprouted rye, and whole grain rye dishes. These all become specialties because they have the distinctive, down-to-earth flavor of rye.

Rye is as practical for homesteaders to grow and harvest on a small scale as any other grain except, perhaps, corn. Those who grow rye as green manure might like to let a patch mature and try their hand at harvesting the grain.

## HANDLING RYE

Rye is harvested like wheat. The hulls easily fall off the kernel when it is threshed, and the grain is ready to use after winnowing.

To make rye meal and rye flour, refer to GRINDING GRAIN FOR CEREAL AND FLOUR in the GRAINS section.

Besides wheat, rye flour is the only flour that works with yeast to make bread rise, but as the reaction is small, one hundred percent rye bread is very heavy. For this reason rye bread is almost always made partly with wheat flour. (Refer to BREAD FLOUR in the BREAD, YEAST section.) Baking powder or baking soda will successfully raise rye flour baked goods, but more leavening than is usual for wheat flour may be required. Rye flour works very well in sourdough starters. (Refer to the SOURDOUGH section.) Some stores sell rolled rye flakes, which are like rolled oats and can be used in the same ways, except that they require longer cooking. They can also be whirled briefly in the blender to make rye meal. It is not practical to make rolled rye at home.

## RYE RECIPES

### Rye and Split Peas                    (Makes 6–8 side servings.)

| | |
|---|---|
| 1 cup whole rye | 3 tablespoons lard, oil, or bacon |
| 5 cups (about) soup stock, or water | fat |
| 1 cup split peas | herbs, to taste (Try sage, |
| 1 bay leaf | thyme, and parsley.) |
| 1 onion, chopped medium | pepper, salt, optional |
| 1–2 carrots, chopped medium | ¼ to 1 cup or more cooked meat, |
| 1 stalk celery, or part of a celeriac, | chopped, or 1-3 fried, |
| chopped medium | crumbled bacon slices, op- |
| | tional |

Soak the rye in the stock or water overnight. If using stock, keep in a cool place while soaking. The next day add the split peas and bay leaf, then simmer over low heat till tender, about 2 hours. Add more stock or water, if necessary.

Sauté the onion, carrots, and celery or celeriac in the lard or fat till limp. Add with the herbs, seasonings, and meat or bacon to the rye and split peas. Simmer about 15 minutes and serve. One taste, and most will agree that the rye and split peas are a perfect combination.

**Rye and Beans**  Soak a cup of dry beans overnight with the rye, omitting the split peas.

### Rye Drops (For soups or salads.)          (Makes 2–3 dozen.)

| | |
|---|---|
| ¾ cup rye meal (Or rye flakes | 1 tablespoons molasses, or honey |
| whirled briefly in blender.) | 1 egg, slightly beaten |
| ¾ cup rye flour | ½ cup milk |
| 1 teaspoon baking powder | fat, or oil, for frying |
| ¼ teaspoon salt, optional | |

Mix the rye meal, flour, baking powder, and salt, if desired. Add the molasses, egg, and milk, and stir together to make a fairly thick

## RYE IDEAS

**Sprouted Rye in Baked Goods**
Sprout rye (refer to the SPROUTS section) till the shoot is about as long as the rye kernel. Add to baked goods like adding nuts and seeds, for chewiness and flavor. Sprouted rye is excellent in the SOURDOUGH RYE variation of the *Rye Bread* recipe in the BREAD, YEAST section, or for any baking which includes rye flour.

**Rye Bread or Rye Cracker Crumbs**  Try rye crumbs when bread or cracker crumbs are called for. They add a flavorful heartiness mixed into or sprinkled on casseroles, and are very good in desserts with fruit, especially apples. For a special treat make the *Layered Bread and Fruit Pudding* in the FRUITS section, using rye crumbs and apples.

**Rye for Breakfast**  Some excellent hot rye breakfast cereals can be made with cracked rye or rye meal, rolled rye flakes, and the RYE, BULGHUR STYLE in the WHEAT section. (Refer to *Basic Hot Cooked Cereal* in the CEREALS section.) Cooked whole rye is also good made the day before for reheating in the morning. Even a homemade, ready-to-eat cereal is possible if the *Grape Nuts* in the CEREALS section are made with rye flour.

## OTHER RECIPES
## WITH RYE

batter. Drop by small teaspoonfuls into ¼ to ½ inch of hot fat or into a generous amount of hot oil or fat in a frying pan. Turn as necessary to brown on all sides. Drain on paper. Especially good with bean, pea, and other hearty soups, or with green or bean salads.

### *Fermented Rye Liquid for Flavoring Soups* (Makes enough liquid to flavor from 2–3 pots.)

*½ cup sourdough* (Refer to SOUR-DOUGH section.)     *2 (about) cups rye flour*

Add enough rye flour and water to the sourdough to make 2 or 3 cups of rather stiff dough. Put the dough in a 2 quart jar or similar container, cover loosely, and keep at room temperature till it becomes light and bubbly, usually overnight. Add about 3 cups cold water, then let stand till the liquid becomes clear. If the room is cool, this may take several days. Carefully pour off the liquid, which will have a clean, pleasantly sour flavor. Use in the rye soup recipe below, or in any soup to replace tomato, lemon juice, or other tart ingredients. It is especially good in sweet and sour mixtures.

For more fermented rye liquid, add another 3–4 cups of cold water to the same jar, then let sit another day or so. It will be weaker than the first batch, but still flavorful. A third, very weak batch is also possible. Fermented rye liquid will keep about a week in the refrigerator.

It offers an unusual way to take advantage of the special, tart flavor typical of such naturally fermented foods as sauerkraut, fermented pickles, and sourdough.

### *Fermented Rye Soup* (Makes 8–10 medium bowls.)

*2 cups (about) fermented rye liquid* (See previous recipe.), *or sauerkraut juice*

*4 cups (about) soup stock* (Beef, game meat, or other strongly flavored stock are especially good.)

*several mushrooms, sliced* (Dried mushrooms, soaked, sliced, added with soaking water are excellent.)

*cooked meat (½–2 cups), diced* (Or meat from making the soup stock.)

*1 cup whole cooked rye, optional*
*pepper, salt, optional*
*3 tablespoons butter*
*3 tablespoons flour*
*boiled potatoes (8–10 pieces), optional*

Combine the rye liquid or sauerkraut juice, soup stock, mushrooms, meat, whole rye, pepper, and salt, if desired, in a pot and heat. Adjust the proportions of rye liquid and soup stock to make a pleasant tartness. In a small, heavy frying pan melt the butter, add the flour, and cook, stirring, till it browns. Then stir in a few tablespoons of the hot soup. When it thickens, mix it into the rest of the soup. Simmer about 10 minutes. Put a piece of boiled potato in each soup bowl and pour the soup over it, or serve the soup plain.

# SALADS AND SALAD DRESSINGS

THE VALUE OF FRESH SALADS IN THE DIET CANNOT BE OVERSTATED. Besides fresh fruits, they contain the only raw foods that most people eat. The good health that comes from eating salads every day seems greater than the sum of their vitamins, minerals, other nutrients, and fiber, perhaps because they complement meaty and starchy foods so well. A heavy meat and potatoes meal can be transformed to a lighter, more balanced, and digestible one with the simple addition of a big green salad.

Salads made with home raised ingredients are inevitably seasonal, as raw salad ingredients cannot be stored for long, except for some root cellared vegetables and fruits. Salad greens are best harvested day to day, or at least week to week. Raising them to have on hand throughout the year offers both challenge and reward. The challenge, which is greatest in winter, can be met in many ways. There is the sprouting of seeds, especially alfalfa (refer to the SPROUTS section), the use of cold frames, window sill pots, and greenhouses for growing winter greens, and the forcing of roots in winter (refer to the CHICORY section). The rewards are many, and home grown salads always taste fresh and alive, never limp and tired like so many grocery store offerings.

With the change of seasons, there is an intriguing variety in salads. The delicate crispness of early spring greens gradually gives way to the full, rich flavors of summer ripe tomatoes, cucumbers, and green vegetables. The fall brings a bountiful array of cool weather vegetables and greens to be replaced, as they fade, by the tender sprouts, carefully nurtured greens, and stored cabbages, root vegetables, and fruits of winter. The greatest reward of all, for those who grow their own salad ingredients and eat salads regularly, will be a family in the best of health.

Lettuce is the first salad ingredient to come to mind, but it is only one of hundreds of possibilities. For variety, and when lettuce is not available, many other kinds of greens, raw vegetables, and raw fruits can be the basis for a salad. If salad making prospects seem bleak, look through the RECIPES and IDEAS for the vegetables and fruits on hand. There may be the makings of a salad among them. Salad recipes need not be followed precisely. Most salads are put together casually from available ingredients according to family tastes. Some salads are good undressed, but most often a dressing adds the finishing touch. Favorite salad dressings go with many combinations of ingredients and can be used through the four seasons. For these reasons the recipes given here are for dressings rather than salad combinations. For complete salad recipes, and the preparation of specific ingredients, refer to the sections for individual vegetables and fruits. For the preparation of leafy greens for salads, refer to the LETTUCE section.

**Hearty Salads**   Salads of cooked ingredients, such as meat, fish, eggs, or potatoes, do not take the place of raw salads unless made with a large proportion of raw ingredients. Hearty salads of cooked ingredients are delicious as the meal's main course, with a green salad as an accompaniment.

## SALAD DRESSING RECIPES

### Oil and Vinegar Tossed Salad

| | |
|---|---|
| 2 measures oil (Olive, safflower, or another pleasantly flavored oil.) | salt, optional |
| pepper, to taste | 1 measure vinegar (Preferably raw cider or wine vinegar.) |

The quality and flavor of the oil and vinegar must be good for a good salad. Never use flat, flavorless oil or harsh tasting vinegar.

Have salad ingredients ready in a large bowl. They should be dry, without droplets of water on them. Use a large spoon and fork for tossing. Measure the oil by pouring it into the spoon, add it to the salad, and toss till all ingredients are coated with oil. Then add seasonings and vinegar. If salt is used, dissolve it first in vinegar by setting the spoon on the salad, putting the salt and pepper in it, and pouring in some vinegar. Stir with the fork to mix, then add to the salad. If added directly, the salt grains stick to the salad ingredients and cannot be tasted. Toss the salad well. A large green salad usually takes about 3 tablespoons oil and 1½ tablespoons vinegar. Amounts can be adjusted, to taste.

### Pre-Mixed Oil and Lemon or Vinegar Dressing                    (Makes about ½ cup.)

| | |
|---|---|
| 4 tablespoons oil | 2 tablespoons catsup, or concentrated frozen orange juice |
| 2 tablespoons lemon juice, or 3–4 tablespoons vinegar | fresh herbs, minced, or dried herbs (Or try Herb Vinegar in the VINEGAR section.) |
| Optional: | crushed herb seeds (Especially celery, savory, or dill.) |
| ½ teaspoon honey | garlic, whole clove, or crushed, or minced |
| ½ teaspoon dry, or 1 teaspoon prepared mustard | |
| ½ teaspoon paprika | |
| dash cayenne, or black pepper | |
| ¼ teaspoon salt | |

---

## SEASONAL SALAD IDEAS

**Wild Spring Salad Greens**   In early spring wild greens are mild and tender, while later they tend to become too strong flavored or too tough to eat raw. It is impossible to make a complete list of wild salad plants since they vary so much with location; a few common ones are dandelion crowns, chickweed, watercress, and such wild herbs as mint, and wild onion or garlic tops. Fresh wild greens are delicious in combination with the last of the root cellar vegetables, alfalfa sprouts, or the first garden lettuce, spinach, or mustard greens.

**Tossed Spring Salads**   As spring salad greens, wild or cultivated, are delicate and wilt easily, do not add salad dressings till the last minute before serving. Light dressings, like the Oil and Vinegar Tossed Salad dressing recipe, are best. Rinse, dry, and keep the greens refrigerated like lettuce.

**Herbed Summer Salad Platter**
Gather summer vegetables fresh from the garden and arrange them attractively on a platter. Slices or wedges of tomato, slices of cucumber, zucchini or other summer squash, strips of green and red sweet pepper, green and yellow snap beans, and sugar snap peas are some possibilities. Mince a combination of fresh herbs, such as scallions, parsley, and basil, and sprinkle these over the vegetables. This is very good served without any other seasoning, but a sprinkle of pepper or a salad dressing can be added.

Put the oil and lemon juice or vinegar in a small jar and add any desired optional ingredients. Cover the jar and shake, till ingredients are completely blended. Taste and adjust seasonings. If using a whole garlic clove, make the dressing a day ahead, and remove the garlic before using the dressing. If using fresh herbs, add them just before the dressing is used, or they may become overly strong. Keep refrigerated.

### *Soy Sauce Dressing* (Makes about ¼ cup.)

| | |
|---|---|
| 2 tablespoons soy sauce | ½ *clove garlic, crushed* |
| 2 teaspoons vinegar | ½ *teaspoon fresh ginger root,* |
| 2 teaspoons honey | *grated or minced* |
| Optional: | *pinch cayenne, or other hot* |
| *1 teaspoon sesame seeds, or* | *pepper* |
| *sesame oil* | |

Mix soy sauce, vinegar, honey, and any optional ingredients, making sure the honey is blended in completely. This is enough dressing for one large salad or several small ones. It will give unusual zest and interest to even the most ordinary salad, and makes a flavorful dip for raw vegetables, as well.

### *Nut Butter Salad Dressing* (Makes ½– ¾ cup.)

| | |
|---|---|
| ¼ *cup nut butter* (For blending nut butter refer to the NUTS section.) | ¼ *teaspoon cayenne, or other hot pepper, optional* |
| *1 teaspoon honey* | ½ *clove garlic, or small piece onion, optional* |
| *1 tablespoon vinegar* | |
| *1 teaspoon soy sauce, or ¼ teaspoon salt* | |

Mix all ingredients thoroughly with about ¼ cup water. This can be done in a blender. If not using a blender, crush the garlic or onion with a garlic press. Adjust the amount of water to make a creamy dressing that pours. Adjust seasonings to taste.

This dressing is especially good with salads containing fruit.

### *Homemade Mayonnaise* (Makes 1¼–1¾ cups.)

| | |
|---|---|
| *2–3 egg yolks, or 1 whole egg* | *1 tablespoon prepared, or ½ teaspoon dry mustard, optional* |
| *1 tablespoon (about) vinegar, or lemon juice* | *1–1 ½ cups oil* (Best are corn, peanut, olive, or another high quality vegetable oil.) |
| ¼ *teaspoon salt, optional* | |

Have the ingredients at room temperature. The mayonnaise can be made with an electric mixer, a blender, a wire whisk, or an egg beater. If using an egg beater, it is nice to have a second person to pour the oil.

**SEASONAL SALAD IDEAS,** *cont.*

**Marinated Summer Salads** Strongly flavored summer vegetables are often very good marinated in a salad dressing for an hour or so. Dressings with vinegar will modify strong tastes in radishes, cucumbers, onions, and other vegetables, and flavors blend pleasantly while they marinate.

**Fall Vegetable Salads** A touch of frost improves the flavor of many fall vegetables for eating raw. Cabbage and cabbage family vegetables become sweeter and more crisp. Root vegetables like carrots also become sweeter and better tasting. Salads combining the last of the warm weather vegetables, like tomatoes, and the first of the cool weather vegetables, like cabbage and fall lettuce, are possible at no other time of the year. Mayonnaise, yogurt salad dressings, or other thick, flavorful dressings are especially good on these salads.

**Alfalfa Sprout Winter Salads** In winter salads, alfalfa sprouts can take the place of lettuce. (For sprouting the seeds refer to the SPROUTS section.) Alfalfa sprouts are good in all kinds of salads, but they blend particularly well with coarsely grated root vegetables like carrots and rutabagas, and coarsely grated fruits like apple or pear. The grated shreds and sprouts are about the same size and will toss together very nicely. A salad of about ½ sprouts, ¼ grated root vegetable, and ¼ grated apple with a touch of minced onion and parsley is invariably delicious. The *Pre-Mixed Oil and Lemon or Vinegar Dressing*, above, goes well with it.

Put the egg, and a few drops of the vinegar or lemon juice, and salt, if desired, in a blender or mixing bowl. (If using a blender, check instruction book for the proper setting and procedure. A low speed is usual.) Add the mustard and mix ingredients together. Begin to beat the mixture, adding oil a few drops at a time. Beat continuously, all the while slowly adding oil. After about ⅓ cup of oil has been added the mixture will start to thicken. Now add the oil a little faster, pouring it in a thin stream. Add a few more drops of vinegar or lemon juice as beating continues. the mixture will look and taste like mayonnaise after about 1 cup of oil has been added. More oil will make it lighter and milder. When the mayonnnaise is about done, taste and add vinegar or lemon juice and other seasonings as desired.

Make this mayonnaise in small batches, as needed. Homemade mayonnaise has an excellent flavor, but will not keep like similar commercial dressings. Refrigerate and use it within a day or two of making it. Salads or sandwiches made with homemade mayonnaise must also be refrigerated, or kept in a cooler. This is especially important when preparing such foods for warm weather picnics. The raw egg in this mayonnaise makes it a good medium for the development of food poisoning organisms.

***Garlic Mayonnaise*** Purée 2 or more cloves of garlic in the blender with the egg. If not using a blender it must be crushed before it is added and the mixture is beaten. Serve this garlic mayonnaise as a delicious sauce for fish, meat, and vegetables, as well as with salads.

A thinner, and very garlicky mayonnaise can be made by omitting the egg and using 6 to 8 cloves of garlic instead.

***Rescuing Separated Mayonnaise*** Put an egg yolk in a mixing bowl or blender and gradually beat the separated mayonnaise into it. (It is said that mayonnaise made in a thunderstorm will not bind, so use this treatment after the storm has passed.)

# SALSIFY (OYSTER PLANT)

S ALSIFY IS PRIMARILY A ROOT VEGETABLE, THOUGH ITS LEAVES and flower stalks are also good to eat. The roots have a distinctive, oyster-like flavor which accounts for its other names, oyster plant and vegetable oyster. A century ago salsify was well known and quite popular in North America. It has lost importance probably because it is not a good market crop, since the roots shrivel after a few days in the open air. It is ideal, however, for gardeners who want to extend their gardening season. Salsify is dug late in fall and early in spring

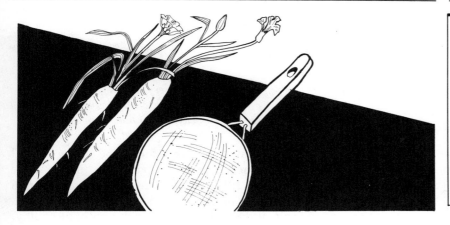

when there is little else to harvest, and the roots will keep well if protected.

There are several varieties of salsify. In the past, the white rooted kinds were most common in North America, but many seed catalogs now carry Scorzonera (black salsify). From Northern Europe, it has black skinned roots and is more flavorful than the white varieties. Wild salsify, also called goatsbeard, is as good to eat as the cultivated plant. It is most common in areas with somewhat dry climates. All of the salsifies can be prepared in the same ways.

## HANDLING SALSIFY

Salsify roots have a richer, more oystery taste after heavy frosts. Their best season is probably early spring, before they sprout. Use the roots soon after they are dug, or pack them in damp sand, peat moss, or another damp material to keep them from shrivelling.

Young salsify leaves are very good in salads, and, if cut before the buds begin to open, the flower stalks are good prepared like asparagus. As the plant is a biennial, the flower stalks do not appear till the second year. Since the roots are harvested the first year, the stalks are seldom cultivated, but they can be gathered from wild plants. Salsify has a milky sap that can be allowed to congeal for chewing like chewing gum.

Clean salsify roots by scrubbing with a brush instead of peeling them, unless the skins are very rough. They discolor quickly after they are scraped or pared. Though directions often say to put them in water with a little vinegar in it after cleaning them, this can be avoided if they are prepared quickly and cooking is begun immediately. Salsify roots are rich in minerals, and soaking removes some of them as well as some of the flavor of the vegetable. Another way to handle them is to steam them whole, peeling and slicing them after they are done.

### SALSIFY IDEAS, *cont.*

**Salsify Fritters**   Steam and trim the roots, then cut in thick slices 2 or 3 inches long. Sprinkle with oil and lemon juice, and let sit for a few minutes. Then dip the pieces in batter and deep fry till golden brown. (Refer to the VEGETABLE TEMPURA variation in the FRUITS section.)

### OTHER RECIPES WITH SALSIFY

Recipes and Ideas for Vegetables, p.669
Salsify Pie, p.364
Scalloped Salsify, p.119

## SALSIFY RECIPE

**Mock Oyster Chowder**                          (Makes 6–8 medium bowls.)

2–3 *pounds salsify roots*
2 *cups (about) milk*
2 *tablespoons butter*

1 *teaspoon celery seeds, dried celery leaves, or 1 tablespoon fresh celery leaves, minced*
*cayenne or black pepper, to taste*
*salt, optional*

Wash, trim, and scrape the roots. At the same time, bring several cups of water to a boil. Slice the salsify into a pot, then quickly cover it with boiling water. Simmer till tender, 15 to 20 minutes. Stir in enough milk to make a chowder texture, and add butter, celery seeds or leaves, pepper, and salt, if desired. Reheat slowly, without boiling. Flavor will be best if the chowder is kept covered over very low heat from 30 to 60 minutes before it is served.

# SALT CURING

S ALT CURING CANNOT BE RECOMMENDED AS A NUTRITIOUS WAY to preserve food, but it may, on occasion, be valuable as a backup method to save foods when other storage methods are not possible. Situations may arise where canning, cold storage, and freezing facilities are not available, and where drying is not practical, leaving only salt curing.

The use of salt to preserve food is as old as recorded history. Meat, fish, and vegetables can be preserved entirely with salt, and salt is a factor in the keeping of many foods. Salted butter keeps its flavor longer than unsalted. Salt is important in the aging and preserving of cheeses, and plays a part in the making of fermented pickles, and sauerkraut for storage. However, modern storage methods, particularly canning and freezing, have made dependance on salt alone much less common than it once was. Today, when foods are treated with salt, it is usually a light cure to add flavor, rather than a complete preservation method. Unfortunately, light cures are not more nutritious. They are just as likely to add unhealthful amounts of salt to the diet as fully cured foods, because they are eaten "as is," while fully cured foods are freshened (soaked in water to remove excess salt) before they are eaten.

Another disadvantage of both light and full salt cures is the vitamin and mineral loss they cause. The salt draws out natural juices which are eventually discarded, and any remaining water soluble vitamins and minerals are likely to be lost when foods are soaked in water dur-

### CURING RATIOS

*Note:* Use pure or pickling salt only!

**Ratio for 10% or Standard Brine**   (Enough to float a fresh egg.) 1 pound salt to 9 pints water; or 1½ cups salt to 1 gallon water; or 6 tablespoons salt to 1 quart water

**Ratio for Dry Salt that Preserves Most Foods**   1 pound salt to 4 pounds food (Pack in shallow layers in non-corrosive container, beginning with ½ in. salt and ending with salt. Extra salt has no effect, but too little can mean spoilage.)

ing processing, or freshened. Vegetables in particular will retain very few nutrients after salt curing. Since proteins are not affected, salt cured meats, poultry, and fish will remain valuable high protein foods.

It is important to eat salt cured foods only in moderation, and to make allowance for their saltiness by omitting salt from accompanying foods. Also, be sure to serve fresh vegetables or other vitamin and mineral rich foods with them.

## BASIC SALT CURING PROCEDURES

(For how-to directions see the lists of recipes and references at the end of this section.)

*The Various Salts for Curing Foods* The salts used for curing foods must be pure without additives. Table salt cannot be used because its additives can sometimes cause discoloration and "off" flavors. Any food grade salt labeled as plain, dairy, or for pickling can be used. Sea salt, which is refined from sea water, and kosher salt, which is sea salt in larger flakes or crystals, can also be used. As kosher salt is less dense than other salt, it must be measured by weight rather than volume. The rock salts sold for clearing ice from roads are not pure enough to use. When old recipes call for rock salt they refer to a clean variety that is no longer available. Some English recipes call for bay salt which is a pure rock salt.

*Dry Salting and Brining* There are two basic methods for salt curing foods. One is dry salting, in which the food is coated with or packed in salt. The other is brining or brine curing, in which the food is soaked in a solution of salt and liquid known as brine. The brine may be a mixture of salt and water, or may be formed from juices drawn out of foods when they are salted.

The necessary ratio of salt to food, whether dry or in brine, will vary with the type of food and the way it is cured. A ratio of 1 pound salt to 4 pounds food will preserve almost anything. Less salt is necessary when other methods of preservation are used along with the salting. A food might, for instance, be dried as well as salted, or fermented with salt to make it acidic, or it might be kept in cold storage to help preserve it.

The standard, approved brine for salt curing is a 10% salt solution, the same brine required when an old recipe calls for adding salt to water till it floats a fresh egg or a potato. (See the ratios of salt to water in the storage box at the beginning of this section.) When foods contain a lot of moisture, more salt, about ¾ cup to a quart of water, may be required, to achieve a 10% final solution.

Dry salted foods must be stored in a dry place, or they must be packaged to protect them from moisture. A cool storage place is best. Brined foods can be drained and dried after curing and stored like dry salted foods, or left in the brine and stored in a cool place. (Refer to COLD STORAGE OF FOOD IN CROCKS in the COLD STORAGE section.)

# SALT CURING MEAT, POULTRY, AND FISH

All meats, poultry or fish can be preserved with a salt cure. These foods are often also smoked after being cured, to add flavor and to help preserve them, by drying them and repelling insects, but it is an optional treatment. (Refer to the SMOKING section.) The vital factor in their preservation is the complete penetration of the flesh by a strong concentration of salt. Many factors affect the rate of penetration, among them the size and density of the pieces of meat or fish, the temperature during the curing time, and the curing methods used. Ways to cope with these variables are explained in specific salt curing recipes. Another consideration is the composition of the cure. Fish and many other foods are cured in salt alone. Meat and poultry cures often include sugar or other sweeteners, herbs, and spices to improve flavor and texture, and often also specify a lower than standard ratio of salt to meat. When this is the case, saltpeter is commonly added to ensure safety, and because it improves color and flavor. However, the use of saltpeter is controversial for health reasons.

***Using Nitrates or Saltpeter***　Saltpeter is potassium nitrate, but occasionally sodium nitrate is also meant. Both nitrates are used in about the same ways in meat cures. Saltpeter, added in very small amounts, gives a pleasant flavor and an attractive pinkish or reddish color. Without it the cured meat looks greyish. However, its most important function is to inhibit the development of botulism toxins.

For centuries saltpeter was used in meat cures with no known bad effects. Then it was discovered that nitrates turn to nitrites in the meat, which in some circumstances react with amines to form nitrosamines. Nitrosamines are well known carcinogens, and some research indicates that nitrites alone may be carcinogenic.

The next question, to which there is no simple answer, is whether meat and poultry can be salt cured without saltpeter, and still be safe to eat and pleasantly flavored. It has been proved that saltpeter inhibits the growth of the botulinum spores which produce toxins, and meats cured without it have caused cases of botulism poisoning. Whether other safeguards can replace saltpeter will often depend on circumstances.

In low acid canned foods botulism poisoning is prevented by killing the toxin producing spores with a processing temperature of 240°F. (Refer to the paragraphs on BOTULISM POISONING in the CANNING section.) However, such high temperatures would ruin the quality of most cured meats. Instead, cured meats must be made safe by inhibiting the spores' ability to grow and produce toxins. This is achieved by a combination of factors working together to keep the meat safe. Among these are the salt concentration, the meat's dryness, the temperature at which it is stored, and the presence of saltpeter. When saltpeter is not used, other substances or conditions must be substituted to positively inhibit spore growth. Inhibiting factors and their application to the home curing of meat, poultry and fish are explained below.

***Salt Concentrations for Cured Foods*** A concentration of 10% salt for brine cured foods, and a ratio of 1 pound salt to 4 pounds food for dry salting, will completely prevent the development of botulinum toxins without the use of saltpeter. However, the concentration of salt in hams, bacon, corned beef, and sausages like salami, usually ranges between only 2% and 4%. While this amount of salt will help, other inhibitors are necessary, and saltpeter has traditionally been used to ensure the safety of these meats. If saltpeter is not used, careful temperature control is a possible safety measure for home curing.

***Controlled Temperatures When Salt Curing*** Toxin cannot develop from botulinum spores at temperatures below 38°F (3.3°C). Frozen foods is, of course, completely safe. Maintaining temperatures at, or below, 38°F during the meat's curing and storage will keep it safe. If it can be managed, this is an attractive way to ensure the safety of home cured meat. However, if the storage place is subject to changes in temperature, or if the meat is to be smoked, this method is not safe and should not be used.

***Drying When Salt Curing*** Botulinum toxins cannot develop in foods without moisture. To keep them safe, many foods can be dried in conjunction with salting, as for example, dry salted fish and some kinds of jerky. To remain safe, these foods must be stored in a dry place, or sealed in airtight packaging to prevent the reabsorption of moisture, especially if the climate is humid. The relative dryness of old style country hams, and some types of salt cured hard sausage, helps inhibit development of toxins, but as they still contain some moisture, saltpeter is also required. At the present time, there is no known way to safely duplicate their special flavor and texture without it.

***Acidity When Salt Curing*** Botulinum spores cannot develop in foods when their pH level is 4.6 or less. Most salt cured meats do not contain enough acid to be useful, but there are a few kinds of fermented or pickled sausages that are protected by their acidity.

***Sugar When Salt Curing*** A 50% sugar level in foods will prevent the development of botulinum spores. Although cures for meat often include sugar, its level is too low to contribute to the meat's safety.

*Note:* The greatest danger of botulism poisoning is from the cured meats that are eaten raw, such as hard salamis and some hams. Saltpeter must always be used in cures for these.

All meats must be handled in a sanitary way, and utensils and cutting boards must be scrupulously clean, to minimize the chances of picking up botulinum spores. However, it must be assumed that the meat may be contaminated with botulinum spores.

***Freshening*** This is a way to remove excess salt from cured foods by soaking them in water till the salt has dissolved and can be discarded. All heavily salted cured foods must be freshened before they are eaten, except when used in very small amounts for seasoning. Large, very salty chunks will require several changes of water, and sometimes overnight soaking as well, while small, thin pieces will need only 15 to 30 minutes.

If soaked long enough, it is possible to remove all the discernible salt flavor from foods. However, most prefer to retain a lightly salted flavor. (Refer to MINIMIZING SALT INTAKE FROM HAM AND BACON in the HAM AND BACON section, and USING SALT CURED FISH in the FISH section.)

## REFERENCE SOURCES FOR SALT CURING

Ashbrook, Frank G., *Butchering, Processing and Preservation of Meat,* Van Nostrand Reinhold Co., 1955. (For meat and fish.)

Hertzberg, Ruth, *Putting Food By,* Stephen Greene Press, 1982. (For vegetables.)

# SAUERKRAUT

CABBAGE IS KNOWN AS THE SAUERKRAUT VEGETABLE, BUT SAUER-kraut made from other vegetables is equally delicious. All result from a natural fermentation process in which the vegetable's sugars are changed to lactic acid through the action of naturally occurring bacteria. The shredding or slicing, and the addition of salt draws out vegetable juices which the bacteria then act upon. Fermented pickles are made in a similar way. (Refer to MAKING FERMENTED PICKLES in the PICKLING section.)

There is lactic acid in sour or fermented milk products and in good quality silage used for feeding livestock, as well as in sauerkraut and fermented pickles. Foods containing it are exceedingly healthful, especially when eaten uncooked. Fresh, homemade sauerkraut can be as beneficial as yogurt, and should receive more praise than it normally does. It should be noted, however, that made in the standard way, it contains considerable salt, and salt from other sources should be avoided when eating it. (Low and no salt versions are possible [see below], but many find their texture, if not their flavor, unacceptable.) Sauerkraut juice is delicious in juice mixtures, and is as beneficial as the sauerkraut itself. Both are known for improving digestion.

## MAKING SAUERKRAUT

To make sauerkraut, use cabbage, savoy cabbage, Chinese cabbage, collard greens, kale, firm lettuce, white or winter radish, rutabaga or

## STORAGE

**Canning**   Excellent for cabbage sauerkraut or firm textured krauts. See CANNING SAUERKRAUT and SAUERKRAUT MADE IN CANNING JARS, below.

**Cold Storage**   Excellent. See KEEPING SAUERKRAUT IN COLD STORAGE, below.

*Vegetables Suitable for Sauerkraut:* All cabbages, including savoy. (Red cabbage fades; is least attractive.) Chinese cabbage, collard greens, kale, lettuce (firm), radish (white or winter), rutabaga, turnip (when fermented called "Sauer Rüben").

5 POUNDS VEGETABLES MAKES ABOUT 2½ QUARTS SAUERKRAUT

turnip. Weigh the vegetables after they are ready for use, and measure 3 tablespoons plain, pickling, or sea salt for each 5 pounds of vegetables. (2½% salt measured by weight. For a low salt version, see LOW SALT SAUERKRAUT, below.)

Prepare leafy vegetables by cutting out the cores or heavy stalks and slicing them thinly into shreds. Root vegetables must be very thinly sliced. If large, cut the roots into fourths or eighths before slicing. A vegetable slicer or cabbage cutter (refer to the KITCHEN UTENSILS section) helps to quickly make even slices or shreds.

Have ready a crock, large jar, or other non-porous container which is large enough to leave room above the vegetable for the brine to rise. Mix together the vegetable and salt, put it in the container, and tamp it down. If making a large amount, mix 5 pounds of the vegetable with 3 tablespoons of salt in the container, then tamp it down to make the first layer. Mix the required amount of salt with the rest of the vegetable and also tamp it down in layers. Letting the vegetable and salt mixture sit a few minutes before tamping will make it easier to handle. Firm vegetables, like cabbage, must be tamped hard enough to start juices flowing. More delicate vegetables, like Chinese cabbage or lettuce, must be tamped only gently. Use a wooden mallet or a jar bottom for tamping. A sturdy mallet can be made with a piece of wood the size of a baseball bat with the tip cut off to make a flat surface.

MALLET

*Tamping in sauerkraut vegetables*

When all of the vegetable and salt have been tamped into the container, cover with a clean cloth tucked in around the edges. (Dip the cloth in boiling water to clean it.) Set a plate or wooden follower on the cloth. The follower should fit the container without much room to spare. Put a weight such as a large jar of water or a clean rock on the follower. (Refer to CROCKS AND CROCK SUBSTITUTES in the KITCHEN UTENSILS section.)

After 24 hours enough juice or brine will come out of the vegetable to completely cover it. If there is not enough brine, add cold water to cover.

Keep the sauerkraut container where the temperature will go no higher than 72°F. It is likely to turn soft and may spoil rather than ferment, if temperatures are too high. If the temperature is near 70°F, fermentation will take from about 10 days to 2 weeks. If it is below 60°F, fermentation may take as long as 4 to 6 weeks. Some prefer the flavor of slowly fermented sauerkraut, but it tastes very good either way.

Check the fermenting sauerkraut every day or two. Skim off any scum that forms, and replace the cloth with a clean one. Clean or scald the follower and weight before replacing them. Some directions advise changing the cloth every day, but unless problems develop, it is not necessary. While it ferments, bubbles will show in the sauerkraut, and the level of the brine may rise. If the container is filled too full it may overflow. There will also be a strong sauerkraut aroma, which some people enjoy, while others do not.

Partly fermented sauerkraut is quite delicious. Some can be removed to eat when the cloth is changed, making sure the surface is leveled to allow the brine to completely cover it. When all fermentation activity ends, or when the sauerkraut tastes pleasantly tart, it can be prepared for cold storage or canned.

***Low Salt Sauerkraut***   Proceed as above, using 1½ to 2 teaspoons salt per 5 pounds of prepared vegetables. The finished texture tends to be overly soft, but the flavor will be pleasantly tart. To store, refrigerate it for a month or so, or can it like regular sauerkraut (see CANNING SAUERKRAUT, below). It is not recommended for keeping long term in cold storage.

Cabbage can also be fermented without the use of salt, but most find both flavor and texture poor and failures frequent.

***Seasoned Sauerkraut***   Many kinds of flavorings, such as herb seeds and herbs, are good in sauerkraut. They can be mixed in with the salt or sprinkled between the layers as they are tamped down. Caraway, dill, or celery seeds each add an excellent flavor. Other good seasonings are bay leaf, peppercorns, tarragon sprigs, garlic, onion rings, and shreds of horseradish root. For interest and an agreeable flavor, a layer of grape leaves can also be included.

***Cabbage and Apple or Quince Sauerkraut***   Thinly slice 1 or 2 tart apples or quince for every 5 pounds of cabbage and mix them in. If making a large quantity of sauerkraut a few whole apples can be distributed through it. The apples are deliciously flavored as well as the sauerkraut.

***Keeping Sauerkraut in Cold Storage***   Some people believe that fresh, uncooked sauerkraut is more nutritious than cooked sauerkraut because of its beneficial bacteria and enzymes, and so prefer to keep it in cold storage. When cold storage is not possible, canning retains an excellent flavor and the sauerkraut is still nutritious. To prepare for storage, take the cloth off the sauerkraut. Clean or scald the follower and return it to hold the sauerkraut under the brine. A weight will no longer be needed. Close the container tightly. Cover with aluminum foil if there is no lid. Store in a cool place between freezing and 45°F, check frequently, and remove any surface film or mold.

***Canning Sauerkraut***   For canning, sauerkraut made from firm vegetables is best. (Lettuce or Chinese cabbage sauerkraut will become soft.) Heat the sauerkraut and its juice in a pot till almost boiling. Pack it into hot jars leaving ½ inch headroom. The sauerkraut can be drained and packed, and the juice brought to a boil and added, or tongs or a slotted spoon can be used to lift the sauerkraut out of the pot and directly into the jars, and then the juice added to fill them. If there is not enough juice add a little boiling water. Process in a boiling water bath. Pints: 11 minutes. Quarts: 16 minutes. (Refer to the CANNING section.)

***Sauerkraut Made in Canning Jars***   Mix shredded cabbage with salt as described above, and let sit for a few minutes till wilted, for easier packing. Press firmly into clean canning jars, leaving 1 inch head-room. Make a weak brine of 1 teaspoon salt to 1 quart water, and add to fill jars to ½ inch headroom. Close with canning lids and rings, but do not tighten. Set jars in a pan to catch any overflow and leave to ferment as above. Check often to make sure cabbage is covered with brine, and add more, if necessary. Fermentation may take from 2 to 4 weeks. When it stops and the cabbage looks, smells, and tastes like sauerkraut, remove jar lids and rings and boil them in water for 5 minutes to soften the sealing compound. Clean jar rims, seal jars, and process as described above. Since the jars are cold, put them in hot rather than boiling water and time from when the water starts boiling.

## HINTS FOR SUCCESSFUL SAUERKRAUT

• Use only fresh, firm vegetables. Using old, wilted, or woody vegetables results in poor texture or flavor.
• Use pure water. Water containing chlorine, calcium salts, or other salts or minerals may interfere with the fermentation process. (Refer to WATER QUALITY in the BEVERAGES section.)
• Make sure the salt/vegetable ratio is right and that they are well mixed. If the sauerkraut becomes too soft there may not be enough salt. Softness can also be caused by high temperatures, air pockets, and uneven salt distribution. Too much salt, or its uneven distribution, can cause unwelcome yeasts to grow which will turn the sauerkraut pink and inedible.
• Make sure the vegetable stays covered with brine. If not properly covered or weighted down, it can turn pink, turn dark, or even rot on the surface, and must then be discarded.

## USING HOMEMADE SAUERKRAUT

The tartness of sauerkraut will vary considerably with different batches and with fermentation time. Partly fermented sauerkraut is mild, and very good as a fresh condiment with meals, or as a snack. Any partly fermented sauerkraut is good used like the Chinese Cabbage variation of the *Kimchi* recipe in the CHINESE CABBAGE section. Mild sauerkraut will not need rinsing, and its juice can be used in recipes. If sauerkraut is very tart it may be necessary to drain it, rinse it in cold water, then drain again. If possible use the juice. (See the *Sauerkraut Soup,* and SAUERKRAUT TOMATO JUICE, below.)

As often as possible eat sauerkraut fresh rather than cooked.

## SAUERKRAUT RECIPES

When using sauerkraut made with standard salt/vegetable ratios, be sure to serve these recipes with unsalted accompaniments.

### Sauerkraut Salad with Three Dressings  (Makes 6–8 side servings.)

1 quart sauerkraut, preferably fresh
1 apple, grated or chopped, optional
1 teaspoon onion, minced, optional
2–3 tablespoons raisins, optional
Dressing I:
   4 tablespoons salad oil
   ½ teaspoon paprika
   ¼ teaspoon dry mustard, optional

Dressing II:
   ¼–½ cup yogurt, or sour
     cream
   1–3 tablespoons parsley,
     minced, optional
Dressing III:
   ½ cup thick tomato sauce, or
     homemade catsup
   1 teaspoon paprika
   juice from ½ lemon

Drain the sauerkraut. If very tart, rinse it in cold water, then drain again. Mix with the apple, onion, and raisins. Combine the ingredients of the preferred salad dressing and toss with the salad.

### Sauerkraut in a Silk Dress  (Makes about 6 dinner servings.)

2–4 cups sauerkraut
½ teaspoon peppercorns
1 bay leaf
1 tablespoon caraway or dill seeds
1–2 onion, sliced medium

1 apple, sliced medium
1–2 pounds spare ribs, pork
   shoulder, or meaty pork bones
1 medium potato, grated finely

If the sauerkraut is mild, put it in a large pot with its juice. If it is very tart, drain it first. Mix in the peppercorns, bay leaf, caraway or dill seeds, onions, and apple. Add water to just cover the sauerkraut, and set the spare ribs or other pork on top. Cover the pot, and bring slowly to a boil. Simmer over low heat 1 to 1½ hours, till the pork is done. Take it out, and stir the grated potato into the sauerkraut mixture. Simmer about 15 minutes more, or till the juice has thickened. Serve the pork separately or return it to the pot for five minutes to reheat it. If using pork bones, pick off the meat, return it to the pot, and discard the bones.

**Wild Meat with Sauerkraut**   Any of the fattier wild or game meats can be cooked with sauerkraut instead of pork. Raccoon, wood chuck, opossum, or bear meat are all possibilities.

**Beef with Sauerkraut**   Cook brisket of beef, or other stewing beef, with the sauerkraut instead of pork, omitting the apple. A cup of tomato sauce can be added instead.

### Sauerkraut Sautéed with Onions  (Makes about 6 side servings.)

2–4 onions, sliced thinly
¼ cup lard, or oil

1 quart sauerkraut, drained
red or black pepper, to taste

In a frying pan, sauté the onions gently in the lard or oil for about 5 minutes, till limp. Add the sauerkraut, and continue over medium heat, turning often till lightly browned. Season with pepper. This is a very good side dish with most meats.

**Sauerkraut and Onions Stewed**   Sauté the sauerkraut and onions as above, but in a pot. When they are browned, add 1 cup of mild sauerkraut juice or soup stock, and seasonings, to taste. Caraway, dill, or celery seeds add a distinctive flavor. Cover, and simmer over low heat for 30 minutes.

**Sauerkraut Stuffed Onion Rolls or Loaves**   Sauté sauerkraut and onions, as above, to use as a filling for bread or biscuit dough. For pinwheel rolls, roll out either kind of dough into a rectangular shape. Spread on the filling and roll, starting with the long side to make a long narrow cylinder. If using biscuit dough, cut across the cylinder to make ½ inch thick slices and bake like biscuits. If using bread dough, cut the cylinder into 1 inch slices, put them in muffin tin cups or on a baking sheet, let rise, and bake like yeast rolls. For a loaf, use bread dough rolled out to a rectangle, spread with filling, and roll up from the short side. Set in a bread pan, seam side down, let rise, and bake like bread.

### Beans and Sauerkraut, Hungarian Style                  (Makes 8–10 dinner servings.)

| | |
|---|---|
| 2 cups pinto or kidney beans | 1 quart sauerkraut |
| ½–1 pound smoked pork, or other smoked meat (Sliced, or 1 piece.) | 2 cups tomato sauce |
| | ½ cup sour cream |

Soak the beans overnight. In the morning put the beans, their soaking water, and the smoked meat in a large pot. Add water to cover, if needed. Cook over very low heat till the beans are done, usually for several hours. If the sauerkraut is very tart, drain it. In a separate pot, heat it with the tomato sauce, and simmer about 10 minutes. Then add to the beans and meat, and simmer another 10 minutes. Remove from the heat, then stir in the sour cream. Do not boil again after the sour cream is added. A peasant dish fit for kings!

### Sauerkraut Soup                    (Makes 10–12 medium bowls.)

| | |
|---|---|
| 2 tablespoons bacon fat, or lard | ½ cup tomato sauce |
| 2 tablespoons flour | 1 cup (about) cooked rice, optional |
| 1 small onion, minced | |
| 1 tablespoon paprika | small piece smoked sausage, sliced, optional |
| 1 quart sauerkraut with juice, or 1 quart juice only | 10–12 tablespoons yogurt or sour cream, optional |
| 1 quart soup stock | |

In a soup pot, heat the bacon fat or lard, then stir in the flour. Lightly brown the flour, stirring, over low heat about 5 minutes. Add the onion, and cook another 5 minutes. Stir in the paprika, then add the sauerkraut, soup stock, and tomato sauce. Heat and simmer 10 to

---

**SAUERKRAUT IDEAS**

**Sauerkraut Sandwiches** Drain sauerkraut well. Fresh sauerkraut is outstanding, but canned is also good. For a simply delicious sandwich, spread rye bread with butter or mayonnaise, add sauerkraut, and that is it! Sauerkraut is excellent in sandwiches with roast beef and other leftover cooked meats. Try it with homemade bologna (refer to the SAUSAGE section).

**Sauerkraut in Mixed Salads** Small quantities of drained, fresh sauerkraut add a very nice flavor to tossed green salads and vegetable salads, especially to bean salads. Reduce the amount of vinegar or lemon juice in the dressing and omit salt when adding sauerkraut.

**Sauerkraut-Tomato Juice and Other Mixtures** Half sauerkraut juice with half tomato juice make a very good beverage. Sauerkraut juice combines very well with many vegetable juice mixtures.

**OTHER RECIPES
WITH SAUERKRAUT**

Baked Duck with Sauerkraut,
　　p.236
Fermented Rye Soup, p.530
Sauerkraut Bean Salad, p.30

## STORAGE

**Canning**　*Breakfast Sausage Patties* (See below, but make them without sage, which turns bitter when canned.) Process like *Lean Chopped Meat* (Refer to BEEF STORAGE section.) See also CANNING BOLOGNA, below.

**Cold Storage**　For sausage patties, refer to PRESERVING MEAT IN LARD in MEAT section. *Salt Cured Dry Sausage* (see below) keeps 6 mos.–1 yr. in a cool, dry place.

**Freezing**　Wrap like meat. Quality retained 2–6 mos. Sausage seasonings may change in flavor after about 2 mos. (Refer to FREEZING CAUTIONS in FREEZING section.)

15 minutes. If using them, add the rice and sausage, and simmer 5 minutes more. Put a spoon of yogurt or sour cream on each bowl of soup when serving it.

The sauerkraut adds welcome tartness to this soup, and can also be added to other soups that need perking up.

# SAUSAGE

Whoever first thought of chopping meat into little bits before eating it should be credited with the invention of the sausage. After all, once the meat was chopped, it was only natural to add seasonings and then put everything back together again in new shapes, patting it into patties, pressing it into molds, or stuffing it into casings.

Sausages are so appealing that every culture since the ancient Greeks, and probably many before them, has tried its hand at making them. An astonishing variety of sausages has been created, and a book can only describe a sampling. To simplify the subject, sausages are here divided into three general types: fresh sausage, from raw, ground meats, such as breakfast sausage; precooked sausage, for eating cold or reheating, including lunch meats, patés, and loaf or pudding type sausages, intended for slicing and frying; and salt cured, dry sausages, such as salami. Excellent fresh and precooked sausages are easily made at home by anyone with a meat grinder or the patience to chop meat by hand. Salt cured, dry sausages can be made at home, but require more know-how, attention, and equipment than the others.

## HANDLING SAUSAGE

To produce chopped or ground meat with a good texture and without stringiness, use a meat grinder with a sharp blade and plate. Different plates for a coarse and a fine grind are helpful. (Refer to GRINDING MEAT, in the MEAT section.)

Sausage making options include the addition of ingredients other than meat, the use of different kinds of seasonings, and a choice of sausage shapes. Most fresh and precooked sausage can be made without stuffing into casings, but it is fun and not difficult to stuff sausages, and the resulting taste is quite special. (See PREPARING CASINGS AND STUFFING SAUSAGES, below.)

*Fresh Sausage*　Most beginners first try fresh, bulk sausage, or sausage patties. The process is the same as making hamburger, except that pork with fat is usually used, rather than beef, and special seasonings are added. Many other meats make good, fresh sausage if

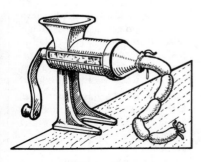

*Meat grinder.*

enough fat is added, but without fat the sausage will become dry and hard after being cooked. Typical proportions are 2–3 parts lean meat to 1 part fat. Beef and other red meats can be mixed with pork and pork fat for fresh sausage. Any fresh sausage mixture can be shaped into patties for frying or broiling, used loose in recipes, or stuffed into casings to make links or a long coil.

A great advantage to making fresh sausage at home is that the amount of salt can be limited. It can be added, to taste, to season, not to preserve the meat. Fresh sausage must, of course, be handled like any fresh meat, and must be refrigerated before and after grinding, and after stuffing in casings. When preparing large amounts, refrigerate the portions not being handled so that the meat will not warm up between grindings, or between grinding and stuffing. Use the sausage soon after it is made, or else freeze it or preserve it in another way.

*Precooked Sausage*   The most popular precooked sausages are wieners, also known as frankfurters or hot dogs, and bologna or baloney. It is not possible to duplicate the smooth texture of the commercial versions at home. Their meats are liquified in high speed choppers and forced into casings under high pressure. Homemade bologna is somewhat coarse or crumbly in texture, but excellent in flavor. Anyone can try making wieners by stuffing a bologna mixture into narrow casings, but hot dog lovers may not be satisfied with the results.

Sausage mixtures can be precooked in several ways. They can be baked in loaf pans, steamed in molds, or stuffed in casings and simmered in water, till they are cooked through. The meat can also be cooked before grinding and then stuffed into casings. A liver sausage mixture can, for instance, be stuffed into casings, and cooked to make liverwurst. If it is smoked before cooking it becomes Braunschweiger sausage. If steamed in a small pot, it is a paté.

There are no clearcut definitions as to what is and what is not a sausage among precooked meat loaf and hash type mixtures. Blood pudding and head cheese are likely to be classed as sausage, while scrapple, haggis, and others are borderline.

*Salt Cured Dry Sausage*   Modern practice does not recommend trying salt cured sausage at home unless it is to be stored refrigerated. The difficulty, when curing and drying sausage at home, is finding a place with the necessary low temperature and controlled humidity. Most cellars are too damp, and basements are too warm. Under the wrong conditions the sausage will mold or spoil before it has had time to cure and dry.

In cured, dry sausage it is important to use saltpeter to protect against botulism poisoning. The word botulism was derived from "botulus," the Latin word for sausage. The connection is all too obvious. (Refer to USING NITRATES OR SALTPETER, in the SALT CURING section.) If cured sausage containing pork is to be eaten uncooked, it must be frozen for a month to ensure that no trichinae larvae are present. (Refer to UNDERSTANDING TRICHINOSIS, in the PORK section.) For detailed instructions and recipes, consult the REFERENCE SOURCES at the end of the HAM AND BACON section.

## PREPARING CASINGS AND STUFFING SAUSAGE

There is something especially good about sausages stuffed in casings. They are more moist, mellower in flavor, and more fun to eat. Any sausages that are to be smoked or salt cured and dried must be stuffed in casings.

There are several kinds of natural and synthetic casing. Casings can be made at home from animal intestines and muslin. Both natural and synthetic casings can be purchased from mail order catalogs for butcher supplies. Butchers who make their own sausage may also be willing to sell casings.

***Synthetic Casings***   These are made from collagen, which is animal protein, or from wood fiber or cellulose. Collagen casings are edible and are usually used for small sausages. They do not hold up well when boiled. Wood fiber or cellulose casings are used for large sized sausages, and must be removed before the sausage is eaten.

***Muslin Casings***   Clean muslin, a sturdy, plainly woven cotton cloth, can be sewn into tubes or bags, which are stuffed to make large sized sausages. A strip of cloth 8 inches wide and 18 inches long will make a sausage 2 to 2½ inches in diameter and 15 inches long. A 13 to 14 inch wide strip will make a 4 inch diameter casing, which could be from 24 to 30 inches long. Make these casings with ½ inch seams and sew or tie one end shut with string. The other end can then be tied after stuffing. Before stuffing dip the bag in water and wring it out, or dip it in melted lard, to make it easier to remove when the sausage is eaten.

***Sausage Casings from Intestines***   The small intestines from hogs and sheep are used more often than any others. Hog intestines will make sausages the size of Polish or Italian sausage, while sheep intestines make small sausages the size of breakfast links. Beef intestines, also known as rounds, can be used for large sausages. Hog bungs (colons) are also used for large sausages. The intestines of goats and animals of a similar size can be used like sheep intestines. All can be cleaned and preserved in the same ways.

***Cleaning Intestines***   Intestines will be easier to clean if the animal is not fed, except for water, for 24 hours before butchering. The animal should also be well wormed, or the intestines may have too many worm holes to be useable.

When cleaning the animal, separate the small intestine. Cut it off next to the stomach and where it connects to the large intestine. While it is still warm, pull away fat and membranes (refer to RUFFLE FAT, in the LARD section), and empty it by stripping between two fingers, or thumb and fingers. (One end of the intestine can be tied shut to avoid mess before the fat is pulled off.) If cleaning cannot be finished immediately, rinse the intestine and keep it immersed in salt water.

Next, turn the intestine inside out, scrape, and wash it. The easiest way to turn it is to fold up one end to make a sort of cuff, and then run water into the cuff. The resulting pressure will turn it inside out. This procedure is easiest with two people, one to hold the "cuff" and the other to feed in the intestine as it is turned. If it should tear or a hole should appear, cut that piece off and start again with a new section.

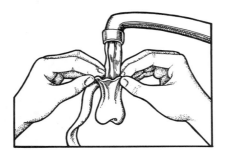

Turning an intestine inside out.

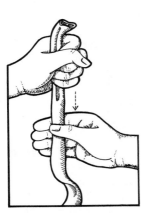

Stripping an intestine.

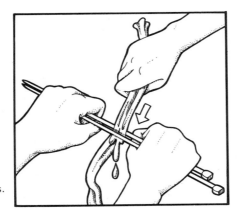

Scraping mucous from intestines.
(End resting in a basin.)

After turning, the intestine will have a mucousy coating which must be scraped off. One way is to put it in a bucket of water and set a smooth 30 inch by 3 inch board in the bucket, so that the intestine can lie against it as it is scraped. For a scraper use a smooth piece of wood, sharp on one side for scraping and rounded on the other for a handle. The wood must be completely smooth to prevent snagging and tearing. Scrape with one hand, wrapping the cleaned intestine around the other hand as it is done to keep it out of the way. Another way to clean intestines is to have one person hold two knitting needles or other smooth rods together while another person pulls the intestines between them. Two scrapings are usually needed to get off all the mucous. Rinse again, and the casings are ready to use. Or, if they retain an intestinal odor, they can be rinsed or soaked briefly in water mixed with a little baking soda (about 1½ teaspoons per gallon), then rinsed in fresh water.

If the casings are not going to be used immediately, pack them in salt or freeze them. Packing in salt may be more convenient, since the wanted length is easily taken out later. Use plenty of salt and coat the casings completely in it. (Refer to the SALT CURING section.) Salted casings must be soaked in water for a few minutes and well rinsed before they are stuffed. (For other uses for intestines, refer to the TRIPE, CHITTERLINGS AND PAUNCH section.)

## STUFFING SAUSAGE

*Sausage stuffing horn.*

Large sausages can be stuffed by simply pressing the sausage mixture into the casing with thumbs and fingers or a spoon. A funnel, or a horn (stuffing spout) will be necessary for stuffing small or narrow sausages. Stuffing horns come in different sizes. Small horns can be used to stuff fairly large sausages, but not the reverse. Horns are available from stores and catalogs selling country kitchen equipment and supplies. Stuff all sausages tightly to prevent air pockets.

***Using a Funnel or Stuffing Horn***    A stuffing horn for filling sausages by hand is just a funnel with an especially long, narrow end, and an opening to suit the size of the sausage being stuffed. There are stuffing horns to fit meat grinders, so the auger can force the sausage mixture into the casings. The casing is put on the horn in the same way whether it is to be filled by hand or with the meat grinder. Almost the whole length of the casing, which must be soft and pliable, is bunched up on the narrow part of the horn and the end of the casing is tied or twisted and held shut. As the sausage mixture is pushed into the casing it will slide off the horn. When stuffing by hand, poke through the stuffing horn with a skewer to remove air pockets. To prevent air pockets when using a meat grinder with a stuffing horn, hold the casing as it fills at a sightly upward angle with one hand, and crank with the other hand if the meat grinder is manual. The grinder blade can be removed when the grinder is used for stuffing.

For ring sausages fill 15 inch lengths of casing and tie the ends together. A string loop can be made for hanging the sausage. A ring is a convenient shape for smoking because sections of the sausage cannot touch or stick to each other.

To make links, twist the casing shut at desired intervals. When first learning to make links stop the stuffing while making each link. With practice each link can be twisted as it comes along without interruption. The links are less apt to unwind if one sausage is twisted in one direction and the next in the opposite direction. When stuffing by hand, the sausage horn can be turned instead of the sausage.

If a casing breaks during stuffing, tie it off before the break and start again with the remaining casing. Stuffing too tightly can cause the casings to burst, so a happy medium between too loose, with air holes, and too tight, must be found.

## SAUSAGE MAKING SAFEGUARDS

- Use only fresh, high quality meat and fat.
- Chill the meat for easier grinding, and to keep it better. If preparing large amounts, the grinder's friction may warm the meat, so re-chill between grindings, and between grinding and stuffing. This is especialy important in hot weather.
- Use fresh spices and herbs, and plain or sea salt.
- Keep all utensils absolutely clean. Scald wooden cutting boards and wooden utensils with boiling water.
- Refrigerate or freeze the sausages till they are used.

## SAUSAGE RECIPES

Increase ingredients proportionately to freeze or can these recipes in large quantities.

### Breakfast Sausage      (Makes 16–20 side servings.)

3 *pounds lean pork, or other white meat*
1 *pound pork fat*
4 *teaspoons sage, ground*
2 *teaspoons black pepper, ground*
2 *teaspoons salt, or less, to taste*

Optional seasonings:
½ *teaspoon red pepper*
½ *teaspoon cloves, nutmeg, allspice, or ginger*
1 *teaspoon sugar* (Do not use for long storing.)
1 *teaspoon thyme, marjoram, summer savory, or other herbs*

Cut the meat and fat into evenly sized, small pieces. Mix together sage, black pepper, salt, and any other seasonings used. Then mix the seasonings evenly into the meat and fat. Grind coarsely or finely, according to taste. (Breakfast sausage is usually ground coarsely.)

Fry a small piece and taste for seasoning. The flavor should be strong because they will mellow after the sausage sits for a while. If adding more seasonings, sprinkle them evenly over the meat and work them in thoroughly.

This sausage mixture can be shaped into patties, packed into molds to slice for patties, or stuffed into casings. If using casings, stuff them immediately after the sausage is made, as it will stiffen and become difficult to work. If the sausage is to be packed in molds, knead cold water into it, ½ cup of water to every 4 pounds of sausage. The water will prevent crumbling when slicing. Pack the mixture tightly into pans or molds, and chill thoroughly before slicing. The sausage can be shaped into a roll for later slicing. Molded loaves or rolls can be frozen, and then sliced when they come out of the freezer.

**Sausage Extenders**   The most familiar way to extend fresh sausage is with bread crumbs. Soak the crumbs in water and squeeze dry before adding them. Cooked cereal grains or cooked and ground soy beans can also be used. (Refer to SOY PROTEIN, in the SOYBEANS section.) How much extender to add will depend very much on personal tastes. Several cups might be tried in this recipe.

**Chicken or Turkey Sausage**   Use boned raw chicken or turkey meat, and the bird's skin and fat. The ground skin will add flavor and moisture. If not enough chicken or turkey fat is available, use pork fat. Use the seasonings above, or try pepper, allspice, ground coriander seeds, and salt. Mix and grind like regular sausage, and for juiciness, work in ½ cup cold water per four pounds of sausage before making patties, packing in molds, or stuffing in casings.

Do not overcook or use high heat with chicken or turkey sausage, as it dries out more easily than pork.

**Beef or Game Meat and Pork Sausage**   Make sausage as above, using 2 pounds beef, venison, moose, elk, antelope, or other red meat, with 1–2 pounds lean pork, and 1 pound pork fat. Grind twice to improve the texture of the red meat.

## Spanish Chorizo and Italian Sausage                 (Makes 15 to 20 dinner servings.)

3 ½ pounds lean pork, in small cubes
1 ½ pounds pork fat, in small cubes

casings (Usually 3–3½ yards pig intestines.)

Spanish sausage:
1 tablespoon coriander seeds; lightly dry pan roasted, ground
3 tablespoons paprika
2 tablespoons garlic, minced
1 teaspoon black pepper, freshly ground

½ teaspoon hot, red pepper flakes
½ teaspoon cumin, ground
2 teaspoons oregano, crushed
¼ teaspoon cloves, ground
3 teaspoons salt, or less, to taste
3 tablespoons red wine vinegar

Italian seasonings:
1 ½–2 teaspoons fennel seeds
pepper, to taste

2 teaspoons salt, or less to taste

Spicy Italian:

1 small onion, minced
1 clove garlic, minced
1 tablespoon peppercorns, crushed or
    coarsely ground
1½ teaspoons fennel seeds
½ teaspoon bay leaf, crushed
¼ teaspoon thyme
¼ teaspoon coriander seeds, ground

2 teaspoons salt, or less, to taste
¾ cup red wine
1–4 tablespoons hot red pepper
    flakes, optional (Omit, or
    only a little for sweet
    sausage.)
2 teaspoons paprika, optional
    (Omit for sweet sausage.)

Mix together pork, pork fat, and the chosen seasonings. Distribute the seasonings evenly—easiest if mixing by hand. Grind with a coarse blade. Test fry a small piece, and adjust seasonings if necessary, remembering that flavors will mellow after a while.

Stuff the sausage mixture into casings, and make 5 to 6 inch links. (Patties, though atypical, can also be made.) If freezing the sausages, use them within 2 months, especially if they contain garlic, which develops a harsh taste with long storage.

### *Boerewors, South African Sausage* (Makes 12 to 16 dinner servings.)

1 pound mutton, in small pieces
1 pound pork, in small pieces
1 pound beef, in small pieces
1 teaspoon pepper
1 tablespoon coriander seeds, ground
¼ teaspoon cloves, ground
1 teaspoon allspice, ground

1 teaspoon salt, or to taste
2 teaspoons vinegar
1 pound pork fat, or ½ pound
    pork fat and ½ pound mutton
    tail fat, in tiny cubes
casings (3 to 4 yards pig in-
    testines)

Mix together the mutton, pork, beef, pepper, coriander, cloves, allspice, and salt. Distribute the spices evenly. Grind twice. Mix in the vinegar and cubes of fat. Stuff into casings, making long coiled sections.

To cook the boerewors, first steam the coils, or simmer them in water without letting them boil, for 15 to 20 minutes. Then broil or grill over charcoal till nicely browned.

### *Bologna Style Sausage* (Makes about 12 pounds.)

Though this sausage is most often salt cured and smoked, it is quite possible to omit these procedures, and reduce the amount of salt to taste. Without curing and smoking, its flavor will be more like that of the fresh sausages, above.

10 pounds beef, in small pieces
¼ pound plain salt, if to be salt
    cured (2 tablespoons or less, to
    taste, if not.)
1¼ teaspoons crystalline ascorbic
    acid, optional (To hold color.)
2½ pounds pork, in small pieces
2–3 tablespoons black pepper

1–2 tablespoons coriander
    seeds, ground
onion or garlic, minced
3–4 cups cold water
muslin casings or beef casings or
    rounds (See SAUSAGE
    CASINGS FROM INTESTINES,
    above.)

For salt curing, mix the beef with the ¼ pound salt, and ascorbic acid if desired. Grind with the coarse plate of a meat grinder. Refrigerate or set in a cool place (below 45°F) to cure for 48 hours. Then grind again with a fine plate.

When the beef is ready, prepare the pork by mixing it with the black pepper, coriander, and onion or garlic, and grinding it. Then thoroughly mix the beef and pork, and grind once more through the fine plate. Add the water, and mix or knead together by hand, till the whole mass is sticky or doughy.

Stuff the bologna mixture into the casings as tightly as possible. Use short casings to fit an available cooking pot, or tie long casings in convenient lengths. Hang the Bologna overnight in a cold place (below 45°F) or refrigerate it uncovered, allowing air to circulate around it. Smoke at a cool temperature, 60 to 70°F, for 2 to 3 hours, till the color is rich and brown. (Refer to the SMOKING section.)

As soon as smoking is complete, put the Bologna in hot, not boiling water, 175 to 200°F. Cook till it floats, or squeaks when pinched and suddenly released, 20 to 30 minutes. Put in cold water to chill, then hang or set in a cold, airy place for an hour or so to dry the surface. Refrigerate till used, or for long storage, can or freeze it. As it will lose flavor if frozen for longer than 2 months, canning may be preferred.

To make bologna without salt curing, grind the unsalted beef, using a coarse and then a fine plate. Immediately mix in the pork and seasonings, including salt to taste. Grind again, and proceed as above, except do not smoke.

***Canning Bologna***    Bologna style sausage must be hot packed and processed at 15 pounds pressure. If possible, can immediately after the Bologna is cooked, using the cooking water. Otherwise, reheat it in a bland soup stock for 10 to 20 minutes without boiling. While hot, cut into sections to fit canning jars, removing muslin casings. Pack in jars leaving 1 inch headroom. Add boiling cooking water or stock, maintaining 1 inch headroom. Pressure process at 250°F, 15 pounds pressure (10 pounds pressure for a weighted gauge). Pints: 75 minutes. Quarts: 90 minutes. (Refer to the CANNING section.)

***Venison or Chevon Bologna***    Instead of beef, use venison or chevon from a mature goat. Coriander is sometimes omitted with these.

***Bologna Lunch Loaf***    Combine Bologna ingredients and grind several times, omitting curing and smoking steps. Amounts can be reduced to 2½ pounds beef, ½ pound pork, salt and other seasonings to taste, and about ¾ cup water. This makes one large or 2 small loaves. The mixture can be puréed in a food processor or a blender, 4 tablespoons at a time with enough cold water to make the blender function. The purée will be the consistency of peanut butter. Any excess water will come out of the loaf as it bakes, and can be poured off to use for soup stock.

Press the Bologna mixture firmly into loaf pans to remove air holes. Wax paper can be laid on top while pressing. Bake at 275°F for about

2 hours, or till a meat thermometer shows 160°F. Chill quickly when done by setting the pan on ice or in ice water, then unmold and slice thinly for lunch meat. Refrigerate for short term storage, and freeze any that will not be used within a week.

*Pimiento Lunch Loaf* For a special treat, prepare the bologna lunch loaf as above. After grinding, add, for a large loaf, ½ cup pimientos, drained and chopped, ½ cup pickle relish, drained, and, if desired, chopped green or black olives. Instead of coriander, try a mixture of oregano and paprika.

## *Liver Paté/*
## *Sandwich Spread*   (Makes about 10 side servings or 20 appetizers.)

| | |
|---|---|
| ½ *pound meat, raw, or cooked* (Poultry, rabbit, veal, pork, or a game animal.) | *pinch thyme, or other herbs, to taste* |
| ½ *pound liver, raw or cooked* | ¼ *teaspoon pepper, or to taste* |
| ¼ *pound fatty pork, bacon, or salt pork* | *salt, optional* (Omit if using bacon or salt pork.) |
| 2 – 3 *tablespoons parsley, minced* | *1 egg, slightly beaten* |
| *1 small onion, minced* | *1 – 2 tablespoons cognac, sherry, or ½ teaspoon wine vinegar* |

Cut the meats and fatty pork, bacon, or salt pork into small pieces. Mix with the parsley, onion, thyme, pepper, and salt, if desired, distributing ingredients evenly. Grind twice with the meat grinder. Mix in the egg and cognac, sherry, or vinegar. Check the seasonings by frying a small piece and tasting. Flavors should be strong, since they mellow after cooking and sitting.

Pack into 1 or 2 molds, small baking dishes or crocks. If using 2 molds, one can be frozen. Tightly cover the molds with lids, or aluminum foil tied in place. Steam on a rack in a pot of water, or bake in a shallow pan of water in a low, about 325°F oven. Cook for 1 to 1½ hours. It is done when a toothpick or straw comes out clean, or when the paté floats in its own fat. Refrigerate. A weight, such as a small jar of water, can be put on the paté while it cools to compact it.

Unsalted patés keep about a week in the refrigerator if well covered. Salted versions will keep up to 2 weeks and sometimes longer.

---

### OTHER RECIPES FOR MAKING SAUSAGE

### RECIPES FEATURING SAUSAGE

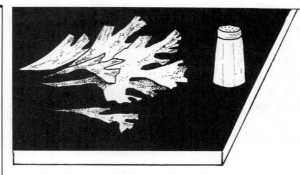

Seaweed is amazingly flavorful, as well as nutritionally valuable. Important vitamins, minerals, and protein in seaweed have brought it to the attention of the health conscious, but in North America it has often been swallowed in pill form or choked down in powdered form, when it could so easily be enjoyed as a tasty vegetable. In Hawaii, limu (seaweed) is a favorite food, and the Japanese and many other Asian peoples know how to appreciate seaweed as a food. Anyone who has had the good fortune to eat some of the Japanese snacks and vegetable dishes using it will know why, as they are delicious. Scotland is another country with a long seaweed eating tradition, complete with tasty traditional recipes. During colonial times New Englanders and other East coast North Americans made use of seaweed, but then it gradually lost its importance. The current revival of interest in seaweed foods is sure to last once people discover what an excellent vegetable it is.

In primitive times all coastal people gathered and ate seaweed, and some inland people made journeys to the coast to gather a year's supply. Gathering one's own is still the best way to obtain a supply of seaweed. It is sold in some health food and Asian food stores but the price may be prohibitively high. Since there is abundant, free, edible seaweed growing along both North American coasts, inlanders might take a hint from their ancestors, and make seaweed foraging a part of a seaside vacation. It could easily become the most memorable part of the trip!

## COMMON EDIBLE SEAWEEDS

(For the identification and use of less common, regional varieties, see the reference sources at the end of this section.)

**Dulse** This reddish seaweed is common along the New England coast and around the maritime provinces of Canada. Though most often dried and chewed as a snack, it is also good in cooked dishes. When fresh its flavor is not as good as it is after drying.

**Irish Moss or Carrageen** This is an exceedingly useful seaweed. Many additives for emulsifying, thickening, and stabilizing processed foods are derived from it. It can be gathered and used fresh or dried to make aspics and desserts. Though it is often left outdoors to bleach

DULSE

IRISH MOSS

in sun and rain before use, this removes its flavor as well as its color. In most dishes, the sea tang of unbleached Irish moss is quite pleasant. Though Irish moss can be cooked and served as a vegetable, usually the stock or liquid extracted from it by boiling in water and straining is preferred. This liquid will set like gelatine when cooked, though with a less rubbery texture. Irish moss is very much like agar agar, which comes from a similar kind of seaweed. (See the *Seashore Blancmange* recipe, below.)

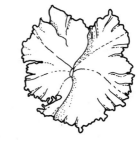

LAVER

**Laver**  Many kinds of laver are eaten around the world. Nori, a Japanese variety, is cultivated in bays and inlets, and made into thin sheets that can be used for food wrappings or toasted for a snack. Laver is generally tender enough to be nibbled raw, and is one of the best seaweeds to cook as a vegetable. Dried fronds of laver can be stuffed like cabbage leaves. They may need a brief blanching in boiling water to make them pliable. The "sloke" used to make the *Sloke Jelly*, below, is a kind of laver.

**Kelp**  There are many edible kinds of kelp. The Japanese call them "kombu." They generally take longer to cook than other seaweeds. Dried and powdered kelp makes a good seasoning, or the base for a seaweed soup. When dried and shredded it also makes a good vegetable dish.

KELP

## HANDLING SEAWEED

Some seaweeds can be gathered when they wash ashore, but others must be cut or pulled from underwater. Cutting is best as it leaves the roots to continue growing, especially where large quantities are harvested.

Seaweed is generally dried to preserve it, though it can also be frozen. If it is dried, it will usually need soaking for a few minutes to an hour before it is cooked. Most seaweeds can be substituted for each other in recipes, if soaking and cooking times are adjusted. Seaweeds of all kinds, as well as Irish moss, become gelatinous when cooked, making them good for thickening and flavoring soups and stews. The seaweed flavor goes well with onions, and is usually improved by the addition of lemon or orange juice, or another tart flavor.

## SEAWEED RECIPES

The following instructions from *The Scot's Kitchen* for preparing sloke, a kind of laver, can also be used for other seaweeds.

### Sloke Jelly

"The weed is brought home from the rocky pools and carefully washed to remove all sand and dirt. It is then steeped for a few hours in cold water, sometimes with a little salt, sometimes with a little bicarbonate of soda, which is said to remove bitterness. [Drain and rinse after steeping.]

Put the prepared sloke into a thick-bottomed pot with water to cover and boil gently to a jelly, stirring constantly with a wooden spoon. When thoroughly cooked, it becomes a dark green. Let it cool, then store in earthenware jars. It will keep good for two or three weeks. [In the refrigerator or another cool place.]

The jelly was often spread on bread. The Caithness fishermen used to take a supply of it with them when they went to sea, and ate it with oatcakes.

*Sloke Sauce* Prepare the sloke as for jelly, and add pepper and lemon juice to taste. The juice of a bitter orange goes excellently with sloke, as with carrageen. Serve very hot. It is especially good with roast mutton."

### Seaweed 'n Beans (Makes about 6 dinner servings.)

| | |
|---|---|
| 1½ cups dry beans (All kinds are good.) | 2 large onions, sliced medium |
| 1 cup (about) dried seaweed, bite sized pieces | 2 carrots, sliced medium |
| | soy sauce, or sea salt, optional |
| | vinegar, or lemon juice, to taste |

Soak the beans overnight. In the morning start them cooking. At the same time start the seaweed soaking in water. In about an hour, when the beans are about half done, add the seaweed with its soaking water, and the onions and carrots. Simmer over low heat till all ingredients are tender, about another 1½ hours. Stir from time to time. If desired, season with soy sauce or salt, and vinegar or lemon juice. The seaweed is said to prevent the beans from causing gas.

### Seashore Blancmange (Makes about 6 dessert servings.)

(Blancmange was originally set with Irish moss.)

| | |
|---|---|
| ½ ounce dried Irish moss, or 3–4 tablespoons agar agar | 2 tablespoons honey or sugar, or to taste |
| 1 quart milk | 1 egg, well beaten |
| strip lemon rind, or other flavoring, optional (Try rose water from the ROSES section.) | |

Soak the Irish moss in water to cover in a saucepan for ½ to one hour. If using agar agar, soak it in about a cup of water for 5 minutes. Add the milk and lemon rind. (If using unbleached Irish moss, its flavor will make the lemon rind unnecessary.) Heat slowly to a boil, then simmer, stirring often, till thick and smooth, about 20 minutes. Add the sweetening and stir to dissolve. Remove from the heat and stir a little of the pudding into the beaten egg. Then stir the egg mixture into the rest of the pudding. Return to low heat for another second or two, stirring constantly, then pour through a strainer or colander into a mold dampened by rinsing it with cold water. Use

---

### SEAWEED IDEAS

**Seaweed Salads** Very tender seaweeds are good chopped raw and added to salads. Tougher varieties can be cooked, then chopped for salads. A mixture of lettuce, chopped radishes, scallion, oranges, and seaweed, with a little orange juice poured over for a dressing makes a good salad. Another good mixture is cucumber, cooked flaked fish or shellfish, and chopped seaweed. The *Soy Sauce Dressing* in the SALADS section is very good on this mixture.

**Seaweed Soup** Seaweed broth makes a good soup all by itself, as well as being a base for heartier soups. For the broth, soak dried seaweed, cut it in pieces, and simmer till the water is thickened slightly and the seaweed is tender. Onion adds a nice flavor simmered with the seaweed. Straining is optional. Powdered seaweed can also be used in this way. Good seasonings for the broth are pepper, and lemon juice or vinegar. For a creamed version, make a strong seaweed broth and add milk, or milk with a little cream, to thin it. A Korean version calls for seaweed broth with shredded beef, garlic, scallions, and soy sauce. A hearty vegetable soup can be made by adding chopped vegetables and cooked rice and beans.

**Toasted Seaweed Garnish** Dried dulse or sheets of nori can be toasted by putting them briefly on the top of a hot wood burning stove or close under the oven broiler. They are done when they change color. Crumble them on salads, cooked vegetables, potatoes, eggs, and over cooked rice. Immediately after toasting, these seaweeds also are a delicious snack.

any dish with flared sides for a mold. (If using powdered agar agar straining will not be necessary.)

Chill the blancmange till set, then turn it out of the mold. If desired, serve with cream or sour cream.

*Almond Lake*   Instead of dairy milk, use only 2 cups of almond milk (refer to NUT MILK, in the NUTS section) strained through cloth. The reduced amount of liquid is necessary for a stiff set. Omit the lemon rind, honey, and egg. After the mixture has cooked, pour it into a shallow pan to set. The almond milk should be about ½ inch deep. After it jells, cut it into small cubes and serve them in a "lake" of syrup from canned fruit, or mixed with canned fruit in plenty of juice. Peach or apricot nectar sweetened with maple syrup or honey also makes a good "lake." This is adapted from a popular Chinese dessert.

<table>
<tr><td>**ANOTHER RECIPE<br>WITH SEAWEED**</td></tr>
<tr><td>Garlicky Bean Soup, p.24</td></tr>
</table>

## EDIBLE SEAWEED REFERENCES

Guberlet, Muriel Lewin, *Seaweeds at Ebb-Tide,* University of Washington Press, 1971. (For identifying Pacific Coast seaweeds.)

Hilson, C. J., *Seaweeds,* Pennsylvania State University Press, 1977. (For identifying Atlantic Coast seaweeds.)

# SEEDS

<table>
<tr><td>**STORAGE**</td></tr>
<tr><td>*Note:* If mature and dry, most seeds can be stored a year or more in any dry place.</td></tr>
</table>

T HERE ARE EDIBLE SEEDS SO UNIQUE IN CHARACTER THAT THEY cannot be classed with grains or nuts or other groups of seeds. These special seeds are all high in food value as well as pleasing in taste. They merit attention in the kitchen and, when possible, space in the garden. Some notable seeds are described below.

*Alfalfa Seeds*   Alfalfa is a good food for people as well as for livestock. Its tender shoots and leafy tips can be added to salads or cooked with mixed greens, and the leaves can be dried for making herb tea, but the seeds are the most valuable part. They are easily sprouted at home for a vegetable that rivals lettuce in its versatility. For many people alfalfa sprouts serve as a basic winter salad and sandwich green. They can be sprouted regularly and a fresh, crisp, raw home-grown vegetable will always be on hand. (Refer to the SPROUTS section.)

Alfalfa seeds can be harvested on a small scale from wild plants, or from cultivated alfalfa that is allowed to mature. They are also economical to buy, considering the quantity of sprouts they produce. Only 1 to 2 pounds of seeds will keep the average family well supplied with sprouts for a whole winter. Be sure to buy only seeds intended for sprouting, as those for planting may have been treated with chemicals.

***Amaranth Seeds*** Amaranth, also known as pigweed or redroot when it grows wild, is a native American food plant, once cultivated for its seeds by the Indians in many parts of North, Central, and South America. Cooked amaranth leaves are popular in southern Asia, Africa, and the West Indies, while in North America there is increasing interest in both its seed and its green crop. Several seed catalogs offer two varieties, one primarily for greens and the other for seeds.

Growing and harvesting amaranth seeds on a small scale is easier than raising most grains, and the seeds are immediately likeable in cooked cereals. (Refer to AMARANTH CEREAL, in the CEREALS, BREAKFAST section.) They are also good ground into flour, for breads and other baked goods. Use ¼ to ⅓ part amaranth flour in yeast breads, fruit breads, pancakes, and muffins. For a nutty flavor, roast the seeds, or pop them in a dry frying pan. They can also be sprouted.

Wild amaranth is widespread all over North America. Its young greens can be eaten, and later the seeds can be gathered and used like the cultivated varieties.

***Chia Seeds*** Chia grows wild in the Southwest, in the dry parts of California and in Mexico, where the Indians collect them in large quantities. They are often roasted or parched and ground into meal to mix with wheat flour or cornmeal, for mush or bread. When crushed or soaked in water, the seeds become mucilagenous. In Mexico a smooth, slightly thickened drink is made by soaking them in water, and then flavoring it like lemonade and chilling it. Chia seeds can also be sprouted. (Refer to the SPROUTS section.)

***Flax Seeds*** Flax is a plant with many uses. The fibers are made into linen and the pressed seeds yield linseed oil. The seeds can also be added to cereal, or sprouted. (Refer to the SPROUTS section.) Like chia, flax seeds become mucilagenous when soaked in water. To make a healthy drink from them, put some in boiling water and leave for about 3 hours. Drink hot or cold. Soaked flax seeds are a very good natural laxative.

***Poppy Seeds*** Seed varieties of poppies will grow in most gardens, but because they are similar to, and sometimes the same as, opium varieties, their cultivation is illegal in North America. However, the seed never contains opium, which occurs only in the immature fruits.

Poppy seeds are good sprinkled on bread and other baked goods, and mixed into dough or batter. Crushing them before cooking brings out the poppy seed flavor. A very special and delicious filling for cookies and pastries can be made from them. (See the *Poppy Seed Filling* recipe, below.)

***Pumpkin Seeds*** Refer to the SQUASH, WINTER AND PUMPKIN section.

***Sesame Seeds*** Sesame needs a long, warm growing season, but otherwise it is easy to grow. The seed pods are harvested in the fall, before they become dry enough to shatter, and are then spread out on trays or screens to finish drying. The seeds still have thin hulls after they are separated from the pods, but as they taste good with hulls left on, there is no need to try to hull them. They are sold both un-hulled and hulled. Unhulled seeds are especially flavorful if toasted in a dry frying pan for a few minutes. Ground sesame seeds make a smooth butter known as Tahini, that can be used like peanut butter or other nut butters. It is common in Middle Eastern cooking. (Refer to the PEANUTS and NUTS sections for ideas.)

*Sunflower Seeds*   Refer to the SUNFLOWERS section.

## HANDLING SEEDS

*Harvesting*   When small plots of seed plants are grown in the garden they can be harvested like herb seeds. (Refer to HARVESTING, in the HERB SEEDS section.) With larger plantings the seed stalks or heads are usually cut or reaped like grain. Some kinds of seeds fall out of their pods by themselves as soon as they are thoroughly dry. Others must be crushed or threshed to release the seeds.

*Threshing and Winnowing*   Seed heads must be completely dry before they are threshed. Some kinds can be left to dry on the plant in the field or garden. Others must be cut slightly green, before the seeds fall out, then dried on trays in the sun, or in another dry airy place.

There are quite a few different ways to thresh seed heads, and different methods can be tried to find out what works best for a particular plant. Sometimes the seed stalks can be laid on a firm surface and hit with a heavy stick or flail, as in threshing grain. Or a bunch of seed stalks can be hit against the inside of a bucket or other container, causing the seeds to fall into the container. It may be possible to bend the tops of the seed plants over the edge of a bucket without cutting them and then hitting them with a stick to knock off the seeds. Seed pods which are separated from the stalks can be crushed to release the seeds by rolling over them with a rolling pin or by tamping them in a bucket using a mallet or heavy stick. Be careful not to hit so hard that seeds are damaged.

After they are loosened from the pods the seeds will usually still be mixed with bits of chaff, and stems. Winnowing is a way of blowing off this light debris. Do this outdoors on a breezy day, or set up a fan to provide the breeze. Pour the seeds slowly from one container to another, and the heavier seeds will fall straight down into the container, while the lighter debris is blown away. The containers must be wide topped and deep enough to catch bouncing seeds. After pouring the seeds back and forth 5 or 6 times the light debris should be gone. It is best to begin pouring cautiously to be sure the breeze is not strong enough to blow away seeds as well as chaff. Traditionally seeds have also been tossed in the air and caught instead of being poured.

If any heavier debris still remains, shake the seeds through a screen or sieve with mesh of just the right size to let the seeds through and catch any sticks, or lumps of dirt. If the seeds are then still not clean, just before using them, cover them with water, so that they sink, while the debris floats and can be poured off.

*Threshing seed heads*

*Winnowing seeds.*

Bend seed plant tops into bucket.
Use stick for threshing.

## SEED RECIPES

***Poppy Seed Filling***                                              (Makes about 2 cups.)

1 cup poppy seeds
1 cup milk
2 tablespoons butter
2 tablespoons molasses, or honey
¼ – ½ cup raisins, or pitted,
    chopped prunes

½ teaspoon lemon rind, grated,
    optional
¼ cup almonds, grated or
    ground, optional

Grind the poppy seeds, or bruise them by whirling them in a blender. Put them in a saucepan with the rest of the ingredients, and cook, stirring often, till the mixture blends and thickens. Very good used instead of figs as filling for the FIG BARS, in the FIGS section, or as a pastry filling.

*Hamantaschen, or Three Cornered Hats*  Roll out small balls of bread dough to make 4–5 inch diameter circles. Put a spoon of poppy seed filling on each circle, then fold up the sides to make 3 corners. Pinch the seams well to keep the filling from running out. Set on oiled baking sheets, brush with warm honey, if desired. Let rise about 20 minutes, then bake in a moderate, 350°F oven till lightly browned. These are traditional for the Jewish holiday of Purim. An enticing pastry, and less rich than most.

**OTHER BASIC
SEED PREPARATIONS**

Harvesting Herb Seeds, p.561
Hot Cereals, p.126

*Hummus (Chick Pea Tahini Dip),
Middle Eastern Style*                            (Makes about 1 quart.)

| | |
|---|---|
| *1 cup sesame Tahini* (sesame butter) | *2 cups cooked chick peas* (Or |
| *½ cup cold water* | *garbanzo beans.*) |
| *juice of 3 lemons* | *1 tablespoon olive oil* |
| *1 clove garlic, crushed* | *parsley, minced* (For garnish.) |
| *½ teaspoon salt, optional* | *paprika* (For garnish.) |

If oil has separated from the Tahini, stir it in till smooth. Then stir in the water, which thickens it dramatically. Then stir in the lemon juice, which will thin the mixture to a butter texture again. Mix in the garlic, and salt, if desired. Mash the chick peas through a sieve or food mill, and mix them in, stirring till smooth. Spread in an attractive shallow dish, such as a pie pan. Dribble oil over the surface. Arrange the parsley around the edge in a ring, and in any interesting pattern over the middle, like decorating a cake. Sprinkle lightly with paprika.

Serve as a dip with raw vegetables, or with pieces of the *Syrian Bread,* in the BREAD, YEAST section, or flatbread. Tear the bread, rather than cutting it, as the ragged edges seem to taste best.

# SHELLFISH

Certain shellfish, such as oysters, clams, lobsters, shrimp, and crabs are universally appreciated and need no introduction, but other equally delicious shellfish are commonly overlooked. Mussels and snails, for instance, are delicious and easily gathered on many sheashores. Crayfish, also known as crawdads or crawfish, are widely distributed in inland waters, and are as good to eat as any saltwater shellfish.

Most shellfish are wild foods that anyone in the right place at the right time can gather or catch, within the limits of the law. Many of the less well known kinds are so abundant that there are no regula-

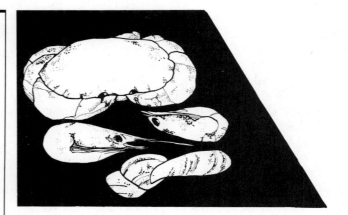

tions for harvesting them. The happy alternative to paying high prices for shellfish from the store is to go out and gather them for oneself.

## SOME EDIBLE SHELLFISH

*Mollusks*   Clams, many varieties, including some fresh water; cockles; oysters; mussels; scallops. Snails, including whelks, abalone, periwinkles, and some land snails. Squid and octopus.

*Crustaceans*   Crab; crayfish, crawdads, crawfish; lobster; shrimp.

*Other*   Sea urchins. (Only the roe or gonads are eaten.)

## HANDLING SHELLFISH

Every kind of shellfish has its own distinctive characteristics and unique flavor, but the basic handling of this class of food is the same for all. Shellfish must come from clean, unpolluted water. This is absolutely essential if they are to be eaten raw. Sand and mud can be cleaned out of some shellfish by soaking them in water for a few hours, or for a day or two in several changes of water, but this will not necessarily remove serious pollutants, such as the organisms that cause hepatitis. If there is any doubt, cook the shellfish till well done before eating them.

Shellfish must be alive when they are shelled or cooked, with the exception of shrimp and squid. Any that die after they are gathered or caught must be discarded, as they spoil very quickly. Most shellfish can be kept alive in the refrigerator for a day or two in a dry container, as long as they have never been exposed to fresh water. A few, such as oysters, will live a week or more in a cool place.

General procedures for cleaning and preparing the different kinds of shellfish follow. For more detailed information see the REFERENCES at the end of this section.

***Preparing Clams, Oysters, Mussels, Scallops, and Other Bivalves***
There are numerous edible bivalves—shellfish with two shells hinged

on one side. The first step in their preparation is sorting and washing them. If alive, their shells will be clamped tightly shut or will shut tightly when tapped. If they do not shut, discard them, as they are dead. Some shellfish require only a quick rinsing, or are clean enough to use without washing. Others, like mussels, need scrubbing with a brush. Mussels have a "beard" sticking out of their shells which must be yanked or cut off. Oysters may have rocks or smaller oysters attached to them which can be broken off.

Bivalved shellfish are either pried open while alive, or cooked in the shell which causes them to open. Cooking in the shell is easier, but the pleasures of eating them raw are lost. Some kinds of clams, oysters, and scallops are delectable raw, but others, including mussels, taste better cooked. To catch their juices, cook these bivalves with one half of the shell deeper than the other, with the deep side down.

There is a technique for shucking (prying) bivalves open. A knife is forced between the two shells and pushed along the inside to cut through the muscle that holds the shell closed. Oysters are the most difficult to open. Breaking off the edge or lip of the shell makes it easier to see where to insert the knife. The knife should slide along the flattest side of the shell. There are helpful short, sturdy oyster knives for this task. This technique is easiest to learn by watching someone with experience.

Catch the juice when opening shellfish, or save the cooking water, as both are flavorful and good for making broths, soups, or for adding to seafood recipes. If necessary, strain through cloth to remove bits of shell. (Refer to FISH AND SHELLFISH STOCK, in the SOUPS section.)

Freshwater clams can be eaten cooked, if they come from a clean source, but they have less flavor than the saltwater clams.

***Preparing Crabs, Crayfish, Lobsters, and Shrimp*** The usual way to cook crustaceans is to drop them alive into boiling water and cook them till they turn bright red. (Shrimp are cooked in the same way, but not alive.) Cooking time will depend on their size, and on the time it takes to return the water to a boil. As flavor is better and it is more humane when they cook quickly, they should not be crowded in the pot of water, causing a slower return to a boil. Small sizes will cook in 3 or 4 minutes, and larger ones in 10 minutes or so. The use of boiling seawater will improve crab and lobster flavor. When done, crack the shells and pick out the meat. Most of the meat is in the claws and the tails of lobsters and crayfish.

Crustacean meat is always cooked before it is eaten, but some recipes do require raw lobster or crayfish meat initially. For these, the lobster or crayfish can be stabbed in the thorax, at the base of the neck where it joins the body, or cut in half at that point. Another way to kill the animal is to put it in a container, pour boiling water over it, wait about 3 minutes, then chill it in ice water. This will leave the meat essentially raw.

The red shells of all these crustaceans and the eggs of lobsters, also known as roe or coral, can be used for coloring and flavoring food. (Refer to LOBSTER CORAL AND SHELLFISH SHELLS, in the FOOD COLORING section, CORAL BUTTER, below, and FISH AND SHELLFISH STOCK, in the SOUPS section.)

***Using Crayfish*** Crayfish look like lobsters, their meat has a seafood flavor, and they are especially prized because they are common inland. Even small, 3 to 4 inch long, crayfish can be used. The meat in their tail is the size of a small shrimp. There is usually a vein of mud running through the tail meat that should be removed, like cleaning a shrimp. It may no longer be noticeable if the crayfish are kept in fresh running water for several days before they are cooked. It is also possible to eviscerate live crayfish just before cooking, by pulling off the middle tail fin with a quick twist, so that the vein and stomach come off with it. The main meat of the crayfish is in the tail, but if the claws are large they can also be cracked for meat.

Crayfish can be caught with a fish line or string using raw fish, meat, or bacon rind for bait. When the crayfish grabs the bait it is pulled in slowly, then scooped up with a net. Small crayfish can be scooped up with a kitchen sieve. In some places, special traps and other devices are used to catch crayfish in large numbers.

***Preparing Squid and Octopus*** These two similar mollusks have rudimentary or undeveloped shells. The squid has ten tentacles while the octopus has eight. Octopus are caught or speared along the southern part of both the East and West coasts. Though not many people catch squid for themselves, it is possible to do so from a boat, using feathered hooks (mackerel jigs), by attracting them at night with a light, and scooping them up with dip nets. The body sacs, tentacles, and sometimes the ink are all eaten. Clean them by cutting the viscera out of the body sacs. Turning them inside out will help. They can be cut in pieces for cooking, or the body sacs can be stuffed, and the ink collected from the ink sacs to use like blood for making sauces. The meat from large octopus may need pounding to tenderize it. Handle it like the snail meat below.

***Preparing Snails*** There are many species of edible sea and land snails. Abalone are the best known and prized sea snails, and as a result, have become scarce in most places. Other varieties are common, easily collected, and equally good. Whelks of different kinds, for instance, are common on both Atlantic and Pacific coasts.

The edible part of the snail is the foot. The viscera and the operculum (the stiff membrane that seals off the opening of the shell) are to be discarded. There are two ways to get the snail meat out of the shell. One way is to drop them alive in boiling water, and cook till they push out of their shells. After they are drained the meat can easily be picked out. The other way is to break the shell of the live snail with a hammer and take out the meat.

Snail meat is often tough or rubbery, and there are various methods to tenderize it. The raw meat of large snails can be sliced into ½ inch thick steaks, and pounded lightly with a wooden mallet or similar tool.

Abalone is treated in this way. The steak can then be rolled in flour or breaded and fried. Another way to use tough snail meat is to grind it and make patties for frying or use it in any recipe for minced or chopped shellfish meat. Snail meat can also be tenderized by pickling, as in the PICKLED SNAILS idea, below.

*Land Snails*   The edible land snails have an operculum (foot membrane) that seals them in tightly when they hibernate. These snails are always kept alive for a time after they are collected to clean mud or dirt out of their systems, and to get rid of anything toxic to humans they may have eaten. They are sometimes starved as long as 10 days, then fed for a few days before they are cooked. Keep them in a screen covered container or cover them in another way that gives them plenty of air. Without a lid they will crawl out, and very likely up the walls. See the recipe for *Land Snails, Roman Style*, below, for one way to feed them. Once they are cleaned, cook land snails like other snails.

*Using Shellfish Shells*   The shells of all kinds of shellfish can be crushed to supply calcium for chickens, to add to the compost pile, or to sprinkle in the garden. Hard mollusk shells can be crushed with a sledge hammer, if no faster system is available. Or put large shells in the garden or on garden paths to disintegrate slowly over the years.

To use crustacean shells see PREPARING CRABS, CRAYFISH, LOBSTERS, AND SHRIMP, above.

## SHELLFISH RECIPES

(These recipes feature common but often ignored shellfish varieties.)

### Steamed Mussels                    (Makes 4–6 side servings.)

    4–5 pounds mussels, in shells        1 cup dry white wine, or water
    1 medium onion, chopped medium       3 tablespoons oil, optional
    2 cloves garlic or more, chopped     ¼ cup parsley
        medium

Scrub mussels, pull off the beards, and rinse well. Put the onion and garlic in the bottom of a pot and set the mussels on them. Add the wine, oil, and half of the parsley. Cover and bring quickly to a boil. Steam about 5 minutes, just till the mussels open. Do not overcook. Discard any whose shells do not open.

Serve the mussels in their shells on a large shallow dish with their broth poured over them, and the rest of the parsley sprinkled on top.

*Leftover Mussels in Tomato Sauce*   Take steamed mussels out of their shells and set them aside. Strain the remaining broth and cook it, uncovered, with tomato sauce or fresh chopped tomatoes, till it thickens, about 30 minutes. (If considerable broth is left save some for soup.) Season with thyme, pepper, and other herbs to taste. Add the mussels just before serving. This is very good over spaghetti or other pastas, on toast, or with the GARLIC BREAD, in the GARLIC section.

---

**SHELLFISH IDEAS**

**Shellfish Patties**   Mince or grind cooked or raw shellfish meat. Add about twice as much mashed potato or soft bread crumbs as shellfish. If bread crumbs are dry, moisten them with shellfish broth. Mix in one or two beaten eggs, and season with minced dill leaves, celery seed, or other herbs, pepper, and salt, if desired. Shape into patties and sauté gently in butter or oil, till lightly browned on both sides. This is a good way to use tough snail or clam meat, as the grinding tenderizes it.

## SHELLFISH IDEAS, *cont.*

**Pickled Snails**  Boil snails, and take them from their shells. If large, cut into bite sized pieces. Put such pickling spices as bay leaf, garlic, peppercorns, and whole spices in jars. Add the snail meat. Bring vinegar to a boil and pour it full strength over the snails to fill the jar. Seal jars and keep in a cool place. Wait several weeks before trying these. (Refer to CANNING PICKLES, in the CANNING section.) Other cooked shellfish meats can also be pickled in this way.

**Crustacean Cocktail**  Any pieces of cooked shellfish meat are as good as shrimp served as an appetizer. A deluxe version of a favorite cocktail sauce is made by mixing freshly grated horseradish into homemade tomato catsup. Add the horseradish gradually, tasting to find the preferred hotness. Half and half will be very hot.

**Coral Butter**  Crush the red shells left from boiling crustaceans and put them in a saucepan with butter, about ½ pound butter for shells from 4 to 5 pounds shellfish. Simmer over low heat, or in a double boiler, for 30 minutes. Add about a cup of liquid from cooking the shellfish, or a cup of water, and heat to a simmer. Either skim off the butter as it rises, or pour through a fine mesh sieve and take off the butter after it hardens. Store, tightly covered in the refrigerator. The butter will have the flavor of the shellfish and an attractive coral pink color. Use it when butter is called for in seafood recipes, and for flavoring cream sauces and vegetable dishes.

**Mollusks Steamed with Grain**  Cook rice or another whole grain in the amount of water the kernels can absorb while cooking, selecting a pot with extra space. When the grain is tender, set clams, mussels, or other mol-

### Land Snails, Roman Style                    (Makes about 6 side servings.)

4 pounds (about) live land snails
4 slices bread, soaked in water
several cups vinegar (For baths.)
4 tablespoons, or more, salt (For baths.)
3 tablespoons olive oil

2 cloves garlic, sliced
1 anchovy filet, or salt, to taste
1 quart cooked tomatoes
1 sprig mint
hot red pepper, to taste

Put the snails in a large container covered with screen, or another lid with many air holes, and leave them for several days to a week. Then rinse them well, return them to the container along with the soaked bread, and leave for another 2 days. Make a cleansing bath for them, using 1 cup vinegar, 2 tablespoons salt, and a cup or two of water. Put in the snails and mix well by hand. This will make a lot of foam. Drain and repeat with fresh baths of vinegar, salt, and water till there is no more foam. Rinse well in fresh water. Put the snails in a pot with fresh, cold water to cover. Put over low heat and bring slowly to a boil. When the snails begin to push out of the shells, turn heat high and boil 10 minutes. Drain, chill in cold water, and drain again.

Heat the oil in a large pot and lightly brown the garlic. If using an anchovy, also add and brown it. Add tomatoes, then cook, uncovered, for 15 minutes. Add mint, red pepper, and salt, if desired. Put in the snails still in their shells, and simmer 30 minutes.

Serve with oyster forks or nutpick so that everyone can take their own snails out of the shells. A special treat to be savored, and well worth the lengthy preparation time.

### Boiled Crayfish                              (Makes 4–6 side servings.)

4 pounds (about) live crayfish
2 stalks celery with leaves
1 onion, quartered
6 bay leaves
1 sprig thyme, or 1 teaspoon dried thyme

2 cloves garlic
½ teaspoon cayenne
1 teaspoon salt
parsley sprigs, optional

Wash crayfish in 5 or 6 changes of water, till the water stays clear.

Heat 2–3 quarts of water. When it boils add the celery, onion, bay leaves, thyme, garlic, cayenne, and salt. Boil about 10 minutes, then put in the crayfish one by one so that the water keeps boiling. Boil 5 to 7 minutes after the last one is added. They will turn bright red. Remove from heat and let the crayfish cool in their cooking water.

Serve while still a little warm or chill completely. Garnish with parsley. An arrangement of the red crayfish and green parsley on crushed ice makes a very attractive first course. Everyone picks their own meat out of the shells.

Strain the cooking broth and use it with the discarded shells to make the bisque below, or use in another way.

*Boiled Shrimp or Crab*   Use shrimp or crab instead of crayfish in this recipe.

### Shellfish Bisque

(Makes 6–10 medium bowls.)

2 tablespoons butter
1 large carrot, diced
1 small onion, chopped medium
shells and clean boiled crustacean
    leftovers
½ cup white wine, or 1 teaspoon
    lemon juice or cider vinegar
1½ quarts (about) shellfish or fish
    broth, or other very light stock

herbs to taste (Fresh dill,
    parsley, chervil, and
    bayberry leaves are good.)
½ cup raw rice
½ cup cream
¼ cup brandy, optional
black pepper, cayenne, to taste
salt, optional
bits of shellfish meat, optional
parsley or scallion, minced, for
    garnish

Heat the butter in a soup pot, and sauté the carrot and onion in it, till the onion is golden. Crush the larger pieces of shell. Add shells and leftovers, wine, broth or soup stock, herbs, and rice. Simmer, covered, till the rice is soft, 30 to 40 minutes. Push through a sieve or food mill to purée and remove shells. Return the purée to the pot and add cream, brandy, pepper, and salt, if desired. Reheat, but do not boil. If desired, add bits of shellfish meat just before serving, and garnish with parsley.

### SHELLFISH REFERENCES

Gibbons, Euell, *Stalking the Blue-eyed Scallop*, David McKay Co. Inc., N.Y., 1964.

**SHELLFISH IDEAS,** *cont.*

lusks in the shell on top of the grain. Cover tightly and let sit over very low heat till the steam from the grain has cooked the mollusks and caused the shells to open. The mollusks' juice will flavor the grain deliciously. Such other seasonings as garlic, onion, bay leaf and pepper can be added, if desired.

**OTHER RECIPES
FEATURING
SHELLFISH**

Bird and Oyster Pie, p.50
Boiled Turkey (with oysters),
    p.655
Chinese Cabbage and Shrimp,
    Stir-fried, p.176
Eggplant Shellfish Casserole,
    Southern Style, p.239
Horseradish Seafood Sauce
    (under Horseradish), p.344
Jambalaya, p.517
Jim's Rabbit with Oyster
    Dressing, p.503
Lobster Coral and Shellfish
    Shells (for food coloring),
    p.273
Paella, p.517
Seafood Risotto, p.520
Seaweed Salad, p.558
Shellfish Stuffed Kohlrabi, p.373
Tomato Seafood Sauce, p.641

# SMOKING

WHEN A FOOD IS COOKED BY HOLDING IT OVER AN OPEN FIRE, SMOKE flavoring is the inevitable result. The first cave people who learned to cook rather than to eat meat raw would also have been the first to enjoy smoked foods. Smoke was, more than likely, the first flavoring agent ever added to meat, and an appreciation of its taste has persisted through the ages. Perhaps the present universal enjoyment of smoked foods reflects some primeval response in human taste buds to the wonderful discovery that fire could be controlled and used to cook food.

Modern research suggests that eating smoked foods is not healthful, as there are coal-tar derivatives in smoke that can cause cancer. It seems to be the fate of modern affluent people always to be faced with a choice. Should one follow one's primitive urges and eat what tastes good, or should one heed up-to-date advice and avoid every suspect food? Probably the best answer, at least with regard to smoked foods, is moderation: Enjoy a little, but avoid a lot.

Meat, poultry, sausage, fish, and cheese are the foods most often smoked. The two basic approaches to smoking foods are hot smoking and cold smoking. Hot smoking cooks and smokes foods at the same time, or else it adds a quick smoke flavoring to precooked foods. Cold smoking makes use of smoke at a relatively cool temperature over a long period of time to flavor and dry foods. Cold smoked foods may stay in the smoker for hours, days, or even weeks, and after smoking they will still be essentially raw. This is why most foods are heavily salted or salt cured before they are smoked, as without the salt the food would spoil before the smoking was completed. (Refer to the SALT CURING section.) Ham, dry cured sausage, and whole smoked cheeses are all cold smoked foods.

***Hot Smoking***    Food cooked over a smoking camp fire is hot smoked, but that is only one way of achieving the desired results. Any arrangement can be used that surrounds food with a light haze of smoke, at a temperature high enough to cook it. A temperature of 250°F or so is necessary. A barbecue grill can be enclosed to hold in the smoke, and damp or green hardwood chips, or herb twigs and leaves can be sprinkled on the coals to make a flavorful smoke. About half as many coals as usual will be needed, since the heat is held in. It is important to use a drip pan or another arrangement to keep fat from dripping into the fire, as the burnt fat smoke adds a bad flavor. To prevent this happening the fire can also be made on one side of the barbecue grill and the food set on the other side. Most sporting goods stores and catalogs sell smoke cookers that come with directions for their use.

The Chinese have a way of smoking cooked foods quickly to flavor them, which can be easily adapted for use on the kitchen stove. For this use a cast iron frying pan or another pot that can stand dry heat. Fit aluminum foil into the pan, using long sheets that can later be sealed around a rack with food on it. (To make an extra large sheet of

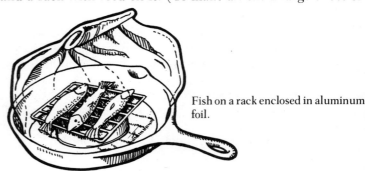

Fish on a rack enclosed in aluminum foil.

*Kitchen smoker*

aluminum foil, overlap the long edges of two sheets and fold together to make an airtight seal.) To make the smoke, sprinkle brown sugar, sometimes with spices like anise or cinnamon, on the aluminum foil. Put the food on a perforated dish or rack and prop it up over the brown sugar. An aluminum foil pan with holes punched in it can be used for the dish, with a tuna fish can with both ends removed for the prop. Wrap the aluminum foil sheets around all of this and seal airtight. Use moderately high heat and smoke the food from 3 to 10 minutes, depending on the size of the pieces of food. To check for smoke formation, make a tiny hole in the foil. When smoke comes out, pinch the hole shut, and begin timing. When the time is up the pan can be taken outside for opening, which keeps the smoke out of the kitchen. See RECIPES FOR HOT SMOKING, below.

*Cold Smoking* Successful cold smoking relies on the use of a temperature controlled smoker. The heat must never go over 120°F, and the results are usually best if it is kept between 70 and 90°F. A damper, or a way to close off the air supply to the fire, is important to keep the fire smoldering instead of bursting into hot flames. Often the fire is built several yards away from the smoker, allowing the smoke to cool in the pipe carrying it to the smoker. There are designs for building both temporary and permanent smokers and smoke houses in many publications. See the SMOKING REFERENCES at the end of this section.

If using a smoker for the first time, make a test fire using a thermometer to practice maintaining a light haze of smoke at an even temperature. The type of fuel, weather conditions, and the sizes and kinds of food to be smoked are some of the factors to consider. It is best to aim for a light smoking at first, as the food can be returned to a smoker for an increased smoke flavor, but nothing can be done once the taste gets too strong.

*Fuels for Smoking* Hickory wood is a favorite fuel for making smoke, but many other woods also give a good flavor. Some that have been used successfully are oak, maple, ash, birch, pecan, apple, cherry, choke cherry and other fruit woods, grape vine wood, peeled willow and peeled alder. The dry cobs from field corn (not sweet corn) also make a good fuel. Soft evergreen woods, such as pine, must not be used. They give a bad taste which some people compare to the taste of turpentine.

Green or unseasoned wood chips can be used, or dry wood chips or sawdust can be soaked in water to dampen them before use. Dry knots from trees and punky (partly decayed) wood are sometimes recommended because they smoulder for a long time.

*Preparations for Cold Smoking* A salt cure is necessary before meat, poultry or fish can be cold smoked. (Refer to the SALT CURING section.) For recipes for salt cured foods that can be smoked see the OTHER BASIC PREPARATIONS FOR SMOKING list at the end of this section.

After the salt cure, meat, poultry, and fish are rinsed or soaked for a time in water to remove surface salt, and then hung till they stop dripping. This may take a few hours or overnight. In the smoker, foods must hang without touching either each other or the side walls. After smoking they must be cooled completely before they are wrapped or otherwise enclosed for storage.

## RECIPES FOR HOT SMOKING

### *Kitchen Smoked Fish*          (Makes 10 or more appetizer servings.)

*3 – 4 pounds fish*               *oil* (For frying.)
*3 tablespoons salt, optional*     *3 tablespoons brown sugar*

If the fish are small, clean them, but leave them whole. If they are large, cut them in 3 to 4 inch sections. If a salted flavor is desired, sprinkle the fish inside and out with the salt, and let them sit in a cool place for 24 hours. Then rinse in cold water and let drain an hour or more, till the skin is fairly dry. Fry the fish (plain or salted) in oil to just cook through, about 5 minutes on each side.

Set up the kitchen smoker (see HOT SMOKING, above) and sprinkle the brown sugar on the aluminum foil. Put in the fish propped up on its rack, seal the foil wrapper, and set over moderately high heat. Smoke 3 minutes after the smoke forms. Serve cold as a snack, or appetizer, with raw vegetables, pickles, and other antipasto favorites. This keeps only a few days to a week refrigerated, but can be frozen for longer storage.

### *Kitchen Smoked Chicken,*
### *or Other Poultry*                        (Makes 6 – 10 side servings.)

*1 chicken, or 3 pounds (about) other*     *4 tablespoons brown sugar*
*poultry, precooked* (Stewed or       *1 – 2 teaspoons sesame oil, or*
*steamed.*)                              *other oil, optional*
*1 teaspoon salt, optional*

The bird can be whole or cut in pieces. Drain well, dry the meat with paper towels, and rub inside and out with salt, if desired.

Arrange the kitchen smoker (see HOT SMOKING, above), sprinkle the brown sugar on the aluminum foil, arrange the chicken as explained above, and seal. Put over moderately high heat. If cut in pieces, smoke 5 minutes. If whole, smoke 10 minutes. Then remove from heat, but leave sealed 10 more minutes. If desired, rub the meat with the oil after removing from smoker. Serve warm or cold as the "pièce de résistance" of a holiday luncheon or supper.

### *Chinese Smoked Beef*          (Makes 8 – 12 appetizer servings.)

*1 ½ pounds lean beef*            *½ cup brown sugar*
*¼ cup soy sauce*                 *2 teaspoons cinnamon*
*¼ cup sherry*                    *2 teaspoons anise*
*1 teaspoon sugar*                *2 teaspoons cloves*

Cut the beef in strips ¼ inch thick, 1 inch wide, and 2 inches long. Mix together the beef, soy sauce, sherry, and sugar. Let sit 1 hour, turning occasionally. Put in saucepan, cover, and cook over medium heat till tender, about 40 minutes. Drain well.

Arrange a kitchen smoker (see HOT SMOKING, above), and sprinkle the brown sugar, cinnamon, anise, and cloves on the aluminum foil. Put in the beef on a rack as described, seal, and smoke from 5 to 7 minutes. The smoke from the spices adds a very special flavor. Serve hot or cold for snacking or hors d'oeuvres.

## SMOKING REFERENCES

Ashbrook, Frank G., *Butchering, Processing and Preservation of Meat*, Van Nostrand Reinhold Company, N.Y., 1955.

**OTHER BASIC PREPARATIONS FOR SMOKING**

Bologna Lunch Loaf, p.554
Dried Chip Beef, p.37
Jim's Smoked Venison, p.673
Smoked Mozarella, p.142

# SORGHUM

**STORAGE**

**Syrup** Will keep a year or longer in closed containers.
**Grain** Refer to STORING GRAIN in the GRAINS section.

WHEN SORGHUM IS MENTIONED, MOST PEOPLE THINK OF THE SWEET molasses-like syrup. There are, however, two distinct edible kinds of sorghum: sweet sorghum grown for the sweet juice in its stalks to be made into syrup, and grain sorghum, which is often grown as livestock feed but can also be enjoyed by people. Broomcorn is another variety whose seed heads are made into brooms.

A century ago sorghum syrup was the main sweetener used in sorghum growing areas. It was made by farm families for their own use, and today it still offers a way for homesteaders to be sweetly self-sufficient.

Grain sorghum, also known as milo, durra, feterita, and kaffir, is the most important cereal grain in some parts of Africa. In its food value it is comparable to corn, but in a dry climate it is more productive. It grows well in the southwestern United States, and could be grown in many other parts of North America. It is possible to harvest grain on a small scale from the same sweet sorghum plants used for making syrup.

## HANDLING SORGHUM

*Grain Sorghum* The seed heads of grain sorghum and sweet sorghum are harvested, stored, and used in the same way, except that sweet sorghum is usually harvested earlier and the seed heads hung or spread out to dry thoroughly before they are threshed. The grain is threshed and winnowed as easily as wheat, and can be stored and ground like other grains. (Refer to the GRAINS section.)

Whole sorghum kernels taste best if soaked half a day or overnight, and then cooked about 30 minutes, till soft. Use them like barley or any other whole cooked grain. Sorghum meal and flour are very much like millet meal and flour, and can almost always be interchanged in recipes. (Refer to the MILLET section.)

*Sweet Sorghum*   Sorghum stalks contain the most juice when the seeds are at the tough, doughy stage. At harvest time, the stalks are cut close to the ground, the seed heads are cut off for drying, and the leaves stripped off and fed to the livestock. The stalks are then crushed and pressed for juice.

At one time, in most farm communities there were small sorghum mills that extracted juice from the stalks people brought, but there are few mills left, especially in the more northern sorghum areas. Where there is no mill it will take homestead ingenuity to devise a home juice extraction system. Some have managed to obtain juice by hand chopping the stalks or putting them through a leaf shredder, and then pressing them in a cider press, but heavier presses would be better.

*Making Sorghum Syrup or Molasses*   Boiling down and evaporating sorghum juice is basically the same as boiling maple sap for syrup. (Refer to the MAPLE SYRUP section.) However, sorghum juice takes less time to boil down, and the foam that rises on the juice must be skimmed off continuously through the whole evaporation process. If this is not done the syrup will have a bitter taste. The syrup has boiled enough when it "strings" off a spoon like jelly that is almost done, and the temperature on a candy thermometer is between 226 and 230°F.

Strain the syrup through cloth as soon as it is done. Its quality will be best if it is cooled quickly. In the past sorghum syrup was often made near a cool spring for convenient, quick cooling. The bottled syrup will keep for a year or more in a cool place. Sorghum syrup can be used in place of molasses in all recipes. Some recipes calling for molasses are referring to sorghum, not sugar cane molasses. (For more detailed sorghum information, refer to the list at the end of the GRAINS section.)

## SORGHUM RECIPES

*Sorghum Meat Loaf*                              (Makes 4–6 dinner servings.)

| | |
|---|---|
| 1 pound ground beef, or other meat | ½ green pepper, minced or ground |
| 1 ½ cups cooked sorghum kernels | herbs, to taste (Try parsley, celery leaves, sage, thyme.) |
| ½ cup tomato sauce or juice | black or red pepper, to taste |
| 1 small onion, minced or ground | salt, optional |

Mix all ingredients thoroughly. Press into a lightly oiled loaf pan or shape into a rounded loaf in a shallow pan. Bake about 40 minutes in a moderate, 350°F oven. The sorghum gives a hearty grainy flavor and texture.

---

### SORGHUM IDEAS

**Sorghum Kernels in Stews and Soups**   Soak and precook sorghum kernels. Then add them to stew or soup in place of rice, barley, or other starchy ingredients. To blend flavors cook them a half hour or so in the stew or soup. A chicken sorghum soup, or a beef stew with sorghum instead of potatoes are both excellent.

**Sugar from Sorghum Syrup**
Old directions describe how to make granulated sugar from sorghum. The syrup is boiled till thick, poured into open pans to cook. then kept in a warm , over 80°F, place for about 10 days, till it granulates. It is then put in a sieve or another perforated container which lets the molasses drain off, leaving the sugar.

### Sorghum Sourdough Muffins  (Makes 12 standard sized muffins.)

1 ½ cups sorghum flour
½ teaspoon baking soda
¼ cup powdered milk
¼ cup shortening, softened, or oil
2 eggs

¼ cup sorghum syrup
1 cup (about) sourdough (Refer
  to the SOURDOUGH sec-
  tion.)
½ cup cooked sorghum kernels,
  optional

Sift together the sorghum flour and baking soda, and mix in the powdered milk. In a separate bowl, mix the shortening or oil, eggs, and sorghum syrup. Then mix in the sourdough and sorghum kernels. Stir this mixture into the flour mixture, to make a fairly thick batter. If it is too stiff, add a little more sourdough or a little water or milk, and stir only enough to mix well. Put in greased or oiled muffin tins, and bake at 350°F for 25 minutes, till nicely browned. This is a way to enjoy both grain and sweet sorghum at the same time.

**OTHER RECIPES
WITH SORGHUM**

Coasting Cookies, p. 187
Dark Syrups, p. 274
Roast Beverages, p. 44
Millet and Grain Sorghum, p. 126
Sorghum Peanut Butter Cookies,
  p. 421

# SOUPS

O RDINARY SOUP, AS DEFINED BY THE DICTIONARY, IS A LIQUID FOOD prepared from meat, fish, or vegetable stock, but the most wonderful soup, according to legend, was made from a stone. It is easy to make fine soup from fine ingredients, but the soups that inspire awe are those made with love and the odds and ends on hand, meager though they may be.

Wonderful soups can be made entirely from parts of animals, poultry, fish, and vegetables that cannot be used in other ways. No food is more economical, more nutritious, or more delicious than soup.

## SOUP STOCKS AND THEIR INGREDIENTS

Stock is the liquid base for most soups, and is made by cooking various foodstuffs in water to draw out their flavor. Sometimes the liquid is strained and the spent solids discarded, and sometimes the solid ingredients become part of the soup. Strained and seasoned stock is known variously a broth, consommé, and bouillon. Creamed or milk soups are usually made with a mixture of stock and milk. A flavorful stock can be used as the liquid ingredient in many preparations besides soup to enhance all kinds of sauces, gravies, and meat and vegetable dishes. It is often practical to make large quantities of stock when ingredients are available, freezing or canning the extra. (Refer also to USING JELLED STOCK, in the GELATINE section.) Most of the

**STORAGE**

**Canning**  *Soup Stock* Heat to boil, fill jars, 1 in. headroom. Process 240°F, 11 pounds pressure. Pints: 20 min. Quarts: 25 min. *Mixed Soups* Pressure process only! Use time for ingredient requiring longest processing. (Refer to CANNING section.)

**Drying**  Refer to DRIED VEGETABLE SOUP COMBINATIONS, and for drying thick puréed soups, DRYING COOKED FOODS in DRYING section.

**Freezing**  Cool, leaving airspace in containers. Or freeze stock as ice cubes. *Quality retained:* Unseasoned stock: 1 yr.; seasoned mixtures: 4 to 6 mos. (Refer to FREEZING section. Also to FREEZING GARDEN FRESH VEGETABLES IN SOUP STOCK in same section.)

ingredients described below are wonderful for making soup stock, but difficult to use in other ways.

***Bones*** All bones, not just knuckle or "soup" bones, from all animals, poultry, and fish are worth using for soup stock. To obtain the most flavor from large bones crack or saw them in pieces. Bones left over from cooked meats and poultry also make good stock. For preparation of bones and bony parts see the BONES, FEET, HEADS, and TAILS sections and the CHICKEN section.

***Scraps from Butchering*** Pieces of tendon, fiber, skin, and any other clean scraps not otherwise useful are welcome in the stock pot.

***Organ Meats*** There are usually other, more interesting ways to use these meats, but when they are not liked, or the amount is too small to cook separately, use them for soup stock. (Refer to the specific organ meat sections for their preparation.)

***Very Tough Meat*** Meat too tough for other uses can be made into soup stock. (Refer to USING TOUGH MEAT, in the MEAT section.)

***Root Vegetables*** Fibrous, tough, or misshapen root vegetables are excellent for making stock. Strain them out and discard them when they have lost their flavor. Among the most flavorful are carrot, celeriac, and parsley root.

***Onion*** Onion flavor is welcome in all soup stocks. Use their green tops, seed stalks, and wild onions, too. A few onion skins can be added to color stock brown, but too many will create a bitter flavor.

***Vegetable Trimmings*** The stalks, outer leaves, and skins of most green vegetables add valuable flavor to soup stock. Exceptions are cabbage and cabbage family vegetables, whose flavor can become unpleasantly strong in soups. The vegetable trimmings are best chopped and added about 30 minutes before the stock is done, and then strained out. Longer cooking impairs their flavor and destroys vitamins.

***Herbs*** Herb stems, stalks, and plants that are going to seed can be added with vegetable trimmings to flavor stock.

***Tomato or Vinegar*** An acidic ingredient cooked with bones is valuable for making soup stock, because it dissolves the calcium in the bones, making it available in the soup. The tomato flavor is usually liked, or a tablespoon or two of vinegar can be used for a light or clear stock.

***Salt*** A small amount of salt cooked with bones and other ingredients will draw out flavor and some nutrients. Use only ½ to 1 teaspoon for a large pot of stock. Too much salt at the beginning can result in oversalted soup after long cooking has concentrated the stock. (Of course, the salt is optional and can be omitted.)

## MAKING SOUP STOCK

Use a heavy pot with a good lid. Avoid aluminum which can make the stock cloudy. Put bones and meaty ingredients in the pot and cover with plenty of cold water. Pure, soft water makes the best stock. Bring to a boil and skim well when foam rises. If left in the soup, the scum settles back into the stock, affecting both flavor and appearance. After skimming, add root vegetables, onion, tomato or vinegar, and salt, if desired. Cover and simmer for as many hours as necessary to extract flavor from the ingredients. (Approximate cooking times are given below for the different types of stock.) Add vegetable trimmings and herbs, and cook another half hour over moderately high heat. Strain through cloth or a fine mesh strainer. If the stock is to be used immediately, skim off fat with a spoon, or soak it up by laying a paper towel gently on the surface and lifting it off when it fills with fat. If for later use, chill it and lift off the fat after it solidifies. Stock for freezing or canning can be boiled down in an open pot to concentrate it, saving containers and storage space.

*Dark Stock* Stock made from the bones and meat of beef and other red meated animals is darker and heartier than stock from white meated animals and poultry. To emphasize this dark color and to add flavor, the bones and meat scraps can be browned in fat in the bottom of the soup pot before adding water. When using small bones or bone pieces, simmer 4 to 6 hours. Longer, very slow simmering for up to 12 hours, is necessary to extract all the flavor from such large, dense bones as beef. Wood burning heating stoves are ideal for this. If the stove is too hot for simmering use a metal ring or put the pot on two bricks to moderate the heat.

*Light Stock* Bones and scraps from chicken, veal, rabbit, and other light meated poultry and animals make a light stock that combines well with a great many flavors. Stock made from poultry carcasses left from roasts is darker than stock from raw bones. For the most flavor, crack bones with a meat cleaver to expose the marrow before making the stock. Always strain the stock through cloth to remove bone slivers. To extract the flavor, simmer raw bones from 4 to 6 hours. Simmer carcasses from roast poultry for only 1 or 2 hours, or else the stock will have a musty taste.

*Fish and Shellfish Stock* Use well rinsed fish bones, heads, tails, skins, and trimmings to make fish stock. Shellfish stock can be made from the shells of boiled lobster, crab, crayfish, and shrimp. Put the fish parts or shells in the soup pot with chopped vegetables and herbs. Add water, bring to a boil, skim, and then simmer only 20 to 30 minutes, as longer cooking may cause a strong taste to develop. Always strain through cloth.

*Vegetable Stock* An excellent flavorful stock can be made entirely from vegetables. Cook root vegetables, onions, and tomatoes, if desired, for an hour or so, then add green vegetable trimmings and herbs. Cook another 30 minutes and strain. If a puréed soup is wanted, push through a strainer or food mill to remove coarse fibers.

*The Continuous Stock Pot* A pot of soup stock simmering continuously on a wood burning heater or cook stove is an institution in some households. Bones, and meat and vegetable scraps go into the pot as they occur. Stock is ladled out as it is wanted, more water is added, and the process can continue as long as the flavor remains

---

## SOUP IDEAS

**Simple Soup, East Asian Style** Heat lightly seasoned soup stock to a boil. While it is heating, put soup ingredients that require little or no cooking in individual soup bowls. Chopped scallions, bean or other sprouts, pieces of spinach, watercress, or other greens, and snow or snap peas are all good choices. Pour boiling stock over the vegetables in each bowl and serve immediately. The greens will brighten in color yet still be crisp, and the soup will be cooled to a perfect temperature for eating. If a more filling soup is wanted, put a few bite sized pieces of tofu (refer to the TOFU section) in each bowl with the greens, or put in some cooked leftover rice or noodles.

**Stewing Foods in the Stock Pot** When making soup stock, it is quite practical to stew meat, poultry, or large vegetables in the same pot. After the stock is simmering add pot roasts, tongue, oxtails, whole sausages, stewing hens, or odd whole root vegetables such as celeriac, carrots, potatoes. Remove meats or vegetables as soon as they are tender, and let the stock continue cooking. Unlike the handling of bones and other stock ingredients, foods for stewing must not be started in cold stock because this will take too much flavor out of them. The stock will, nevertheless, be enriched by the stewed foods and no nutrients will be discarded in the cooking water.

## SOUP IDEAS, *cont.*

Often it is convenient to start stock in the morning, and then add meat and vegetables at the right times to have them ready for dinner. In the evening the stock can be strained and chilled in the refrigerator overnight for removing fat the next morning.

**Stock or Broth as a Beverage**
A lightly seasoned cup of hot, homemade soup stock is as good and as nourishing as a hot beverage can be. In China a cup of light broth is often served as an accompaniment to meals, and throughout the world soup is known as an ideal beverage for those who are sick or convalescent.

good. The only limitation to the ingredients is at the discretion of the cook. Bones left on dinner plates can be rinsed and added, along with trimmings of all kinds. Should the stock in the pot take on an unwanted flavor, it can be emptied and the process can begin again.

## CLARIFYING SOUP STOCK

Stock will be clear enough for most purposes if well skimmed when it first boils up and carefully strained when done. However, a sparkling clear stock is possible, using egg whites and shells as clarifying agents. The stock must be at room temperature with all fat removed. For each quart of stock stir in 1 slightly beaten egg white and 1 crumpled egg shell. Put on low heat and bring slowly to a simmer. Do not stir and do not boil hard, as either will prevent clarification. A heavy crust of foam will form as the stock heats. Push this gently aside to leave an open space and watch to see that the stock does not boil. Hold just below a boil for 10 to 15 minutes. Take the pot off the stove, then gently lift off the main part of the foam with a spatula or slotted spoon, without disturbing the remaining stock. Let stand 30 minutes. Then line a colander with a damp cloth and gently ladle the stock into it. (Pouring might force sediments through the cloth.) Cool the cleared stock uncovered.

## USING SOUP STOCK

There are recipes using soup stock in most cookbooks. If these call for canned broth, consommé, or bouillon cubes with water, homemade stock can be used instead. It will probably be an improvement. However, soup recipes are not very helpful for ideas when creating a soup using homemade stock and the leftovers and odds and ends on hand.

***Creating an Original Soup***　　The first step in creating a soup is tasting the stock to see if it needs perking up or toning down. A bland stock can be enriched by adding lightly sautéed onions and other chopped vegetables. For quick enhancement, add seasonings like soy sauce, garlic mashed through a garlic press, fresh minced or dried herbs, kelp powder, or a dash of red pepper or Tobasco sauce, and a garnish, such as grated cheese.

A strong flavored stock is good for making a thick, hearty soup. Large amounts of cooked leftover vegetables, potatoes, and beans, can be added, and other less common thickeners, such as stale bread or bread crumbs, and nut or sunflower seed meal, are also excellent. If desired, the soup can be puréed with a food mill or blender. Strong stock can also be diluted with vegetable cooking water, tomatoes, or tomato juice, milk, or another liquid.

S OURDOUGH IS UNIQUE AMONG LEAVENS, GIVING BAKED GOODS A special flavor and texture as well as making them light. Once a sourdough starter is established it can be continued indefinitely, and good ones are treasured and handed down from one generation to the next along with an innate sense of their workings. There are many systems for maintaining sourdough, many ways to use it, and many opinions about it, so to the uninitiated it is often a puzzlement and even a mystique. A reputable bread cookbook may advise against bothering with it because it is a disappointment, while an advocate may advise caring for it as if it were a loved family pet. Its most devoted champions, the people who grew up in "sourdough" households, will advise everyone to adopt a starter and begin eating the best hot cakes, waffles, and bread in the world.

## HANDLING SOURDOUGH

A sourdough starter is a small amount of dough, alive with the beneficial yeasts and bacteria that cause fermentation. The starter is increased for use by the addition of flour and water. Once the new dough is active—fermenting, bubbling, and smelling refreshingly sour—a new starter is reserved from it, and the rest of the dough is used for baking. Sourdough improves with use. If a starter is not used, the life in it will gradually die out and it will spoil.

A nice way to begin with sourdough is to get a starter from a relative or a friend. If that is not possible, a dry sourdough starter can be bought from a specialty store or mail order catalog, or it can be started from scratch. It will take a month or so of frequent use to bring a newly made starter to a lively, flavorful state. After that it will be the same as an established starter, and its goodness will depend on the way it is handled.

***Beginning a Sourdough Starter*** Starters are begun by making a simple batter or dough, then keeping it in a warm place till natural yeasts and bacteria cause it to ferment. Mix together 1½ cups of flour, 1 tablespoon honey or sugar, and about 1½ cups water. Add enough water for the texture of a thick pancake batter. Potato cooking water is excellent instead of plain water, or milk can be used, and a sprinkling of a dry baking yeast can be added to speed fermentation. Put the batter in a crock or large wide mouth jar, leaving plenty of room for expansion. Cover with cloth or screen to keep out insects yet let in air, and let sit at a warm room temperature. Stir once a day. After 3 or 4 days the dough should begin to bubble and smell sour.

When the starter is working well, stir in a cup of flour and a cup of water. The next day take out 1½ to 2 cups of sourdough to use for baking, leaving about a cup as the continuing starter. After another day or two, add flour and water again, and continue using the starter often.

If the flour and water mixture does not ferment after 3 or 4 days, look for conditions that may be inhibiting or stopping fermentation, such as very high or very low temperatures, or chlorine in the water or any other substance that would stop bacterial and yeast activity. It is usually easiest to succeed in warm summer weather, when there are more wild yeasts and bacteria around.

***Using a Sourdough Starter***   The character or quality of sourdough will change according to how the starter is managed. What suits one person and one situation may not suit another. Starters kept at room temperature and used every day or two will become light and bubbly, and only mildly sour. Starters used every 3 or 4 days and kept in a cool, unrefrigerated place will also be lively and not too sour. Such starters are good for making sourdough bread or rolls without the use of yeast or another leaven. They are also good in sourdough recipes calling for baking soda. (See the recipes below.) Starters used once a week or less often must be refrigerated between times and will tend to become less lively and more sour. They are good for hot cakes and other baking that calls for baking soda. Baking soda neutralizes the acid taste while combining with the acid to make the dough light. (Refer to the LEAVENS section.) If a sour, inactive starter is used for making bread, yeast must be added to make sure the bread rises. Baking soda can be worked into overly sour bread dough to make it rise, but yeast is the healthier choice.

There are systems using a starter that require a proofing box or another means of holding the starter and the dough made from it at 85°F while they work. Such a starter must be refrigerated between uses. In this way the starter is made to work like an old fashioned liquid yeast (refer to the YEAST section), but it will lose the distinctive sourdough flavor.

***Sourdough Containers***   Old time prospectors sometimes used wooden containers, and even hollowed out logs to hold their sourdough, but eventually crocks became the accepted containers. A 2 quart jar can be used instead. The starter remains in the crock or jar. In the evening, flour and water are mixed with the starter in the crock, the amount of flour depending on the amount of sourdough wanted. In the morning, the sourdough is poured into a mixing bowl, leaving about a cup in the crock as the continuing starter. In dry climates, this can go on for months without the necessity of emptying and washing the crock. In a humid climate, mold or other spoilage may occur on the sides of the crock, and it must be emptied and washed every few weeks before the starter can be returned to it.

Another way to manage is to keep the sourdough starter in a quart sized jar. Then put the starter in a bowl for mixing with flour and water. After the dough has worked, take a cupful out and put it in a clean jar as the starter for next time. A new starter must always be taken out before any other ingredients are mixed with the dough, or else that strain of sourdough will be lost forever. It is also possible to take all of the starter out of the jar except 1 or 2 tablespoons, and then add enough flour and water to it to build it back up to a cup of starter.

***Storing Sourdough Starters*** Though the only sure way to perpetuate a particular starter is to keep using it often, there may be times when this is not possible. Starters can usually be revived after 3 to 4 weeks in the refrigerator, but they will be very sour and inactive for the next use or two. Sometimes, but not always, starters can be frozen successfully. The longer a starter stays in the freezer the less the chance of reviving it. There are records of starters revived from the dried scrapings on the insides of sourdough crocks that have not been used for months, but this is likely only in a dry climate.

The old way to keep sourdough while travelling was to mix enough flour into the starter to make a stiff ball of dough, and put it inside the flour sack. This was not for long storage, however. The sourdough would be used for making camp bread every few days, or as it was needed. People on camping trips might like to try this system.

***Reviving Inactive Starters*** When a starter has not been used for a while it becomes very sour, and a layer of clear darkish liquid forms on it. Though there is no harm in the liquid, it is usually poured off because of its sourness. Under certain conditions it is possible for this liquid to develop a high alcoholic content. It is the "hootch" drunk in gold rush days. A starter that molds or smells rotten should be thrown out.

Though a starter can be revived by using it again in the regular way, the process will be faster if the starter is kept at room temperature and "fed" for a week or two. Every other day during this time, stir 2 or 3 tablespoons of flour and the same amount of water into the starter. Potato cooking water instead of plain water also encourages fermentation. Gradually the starter will become light and bubbly again.

## SOURDOUGH'S LIKES AND DISLIKES

• Sourdough likes pure, fresh, soft water, potato cooking water, and the spring sap of maple trees. It dislikes hard, mineralized water which tends to suppress its activity, and it hates chlorinated water, which kills it.

• Sourdough likes whole wheat flour, unbleached flour, rye flour, buckwheat flour, and small amounts of potato flour. It also likes a change of flour from time to time. It dislikes soy flour and any other bean and pea flours. Try rice flour, corn flour, and other grain flours cautiously to test the response.

• Sourdough likes above all else to be used often and dislikes neglect.

## SOURDOUGH RECIPES

***Sourdough Hot Cakes***                    (Makes 6–8 breakfast servings.)

1 cup (about) sourdough starter
2–4 cups flour
2–4 cups water
1–2 eggs
1–2 tablespoons oil, melted butter,
    or other fat
1 tablespoon honey, molasses, or
    other sweetener

¼ cup powdered milk, optional
½ teaspoon (about) baking soda
½ cup (about) nut meal, op-
    tional
1–2 cups blueberries, other ber-
    ries, chopped apple, other
    chopped fruit, or mashed
    banana, optional

In the evening mix the starter with flour and water to a fairly thick pancake batter consistency. Place the batter in a container large enough to allow it to triple its volume. A lively starter can cause an overflow in a too small container. Cover, and let sit overnight at room temperature. If the room temperature is cool, mix early in the evening to allow plenty of time for it to work. In hot weather mix it last thing in the evening, so that it will not rise and then fall again before morning. If it should rise and fall, however, no real harm is done. The baking soda in the recipe will cause it to rise again when it bakes.

In the morning reserve about 1 cup of the batter for the starter for next time. Into the rest mix the eggs, oil or butter, sweetener, and powdered milk, if desired. Fold in the baking soda. (If lumpy, push the soda through a small mesh sieve before adding it.) If the starter is unusually sour, the baking soda can be increased slightly to neutralize the taste. Fold in nuts and fruit, if any are used.

Pour the batter onto a hot, greased griddle, making large or small hot cakes according to taste. Bake till browned on one side, then turn and brown the other. Serve them while hot, and be prepared never to be able to appreciate an ordinary pancake again. Save leftovers. They are surprisingly good cold.

***Sourdough Waffles or Extra Light Hot Cakes***   Use 2 or 3 eggs and separate them. Add the yolks to the batter along with the oil or butter and the sweetening. Beat the whites till stiff, then fold them in after all other ingredients have been added. Omit berries or other fruit from waffles as they tend to stick to the waffle iron.

***Yukon Style Sourdough Bannock***        (Makes 25–30 small, biscuit sized bannocks.)

½ cup sourdough starter
1 cup lukewarm water
2 cups (about) whole wheat flour
1 teaspoon baking powder
¼ teaspoon baking soda

½ teaspoon salt, optional
½ cup corn flour (fine corn-
    meal), or ½ cup whole wheat
    flour

Mix the starter, water, and 1 cup of the whole wheat flour, and let sit till bubbly, about 8 hours, in a warm place. Mix it in the evening for baking next morning, or in the morning to bake for supper.

Spread a cup of flour on a bread board or work surface and pour the sourdough mixture onto it. Combine the baking powder, baking soda, and salt, if desired, making sure there are no lumps, and mix with the remaining ½ cup corn or wheat flour. Sprinkle over the dough. Mix the dough and flour together by hand and knead lightly. Shape it into a ball and roll out about ½ inch thick. Cut with a round cutter, as for biscuits. Put the rounds close together on a baking sheet or in shallow pans. Let rise about 30 minutes, then bake in a hot, 375°F oven for 30 to 35 minutes.

### Sourdough Muffins (Makes 1 dozen.)

1 ½ cups flour (Try rice flour, cornmeal, millet flour, whole wheat.)
½ teaspoon (about) baking soda
¼ cup powdered milk, optional
¼ – ½ cup chopped nuts, shredded coconut, sunflower seeds, optional
1 cup raisins (Or other dried fruit, chopped, or berries, chopped apples.), optional

¼ cup oil, butter, or other fat, melted
2 – 4 tablespoons honey, molasses, or other sweetener
2 eggs
1 cup (about) sourdough starter

Mix or sift flour and baking soda in a large bowl. If the sourdough starter is very sour increase the amount of baking soda slightly to neutralize the acid taste. Mix in the powdered milk, nuts or seeds, and fruit, if used.

In a separate bowl mix the oil or butter, sweetener, eggs, and sourdough starter. Stir into the dry ingredients to make a fairly thick batter. Add more sourdough, or a little water or milk, if the batter is too stiff. Do not beat after the ingredients are well mixed. Put in greased muffin tins and bake in a medium hot, 375°F oven for 25 minutes, till the muffins are browned and firm to the touch. Wait a minute or two before removing these from the tins and they are less apt to stick.

Sourdough muffins retain their flavor and texture longer than other muffins, and are as delicious 2 or 3 days later, either cold or reheated, as when freshly baked.

### Sourdough Carob Cake (Makes about 16 small squares.)

2 cups flour
½ cup carob powder
1 teaspoon coriander powder or cinnamon, optional
1 teaspoon baking soda

3 eggs, beaten
⅓ cup oil, or butter, melted
½ cup honey
1 cup sourdough

Sift together the flour, carob powder, coriander or cinnamon, and baking soda. In another bowl, beat the eggs and then add the oil or butter, honey, and sourdough. (If the honey is stiff warm it slightly.) Stir into the flour mixture. If the sourdough is thick it may be necessary to add a few tablespoons of water, but the batter should be stiffer than ordinary cake batter. Pour into a buttered 8 inch square cake pan, or any other similar sized pan. Bake at 350°F for 35 to 40 minutes, till a toothpick comes out clean. This moist cake keeps well, and provides an unusually nutritious and tasty sweet treat.

### *Sourdough Bread*                      (Makes 4 long, thin loaves.)

A lively, mildly sour starter is best for bread. See USING A SOURDOUGH STARTER, above.

*1 cup sourdough starter*
*6—9 cups flour, whole wheat or unbleached*
*4 cups (about) potato cooking water, or plain water*
*Optional:*
  *1—3 teaspoons dry yeast, dissolved in warm water* (Necessary if starter is inactive.)

*1—2 tablespoons oil or fat, melted*
*1—2 tablespoons honey, or other sweetener*
*1—2 eggs, lightly beaten*
*1 cup wheat germ*
*1 cup powdered milk*
*1 teaspoon salt, or to taste*

In the evening mix together the sourdough starter, 4 cups flour, and enough water to make a medium batter. Cover, and keep at room temperature overnight. If the temperature is a little cool it will work more slowly, but it will still work.

In the morning take out a cup of dough for the continuing starter. Then mix in optional ingredients. Work in enough flour to make an easily kneaded bread dough. Knead 5 minutes or so, and let rise in a warm place. (Refer to the BREAD, YEAST section for detailed directions.) Without yeast, it will take from 2 to 3 hours to rise. Shape into loaves. Long, thin French-style loaves are very nice. Let rise from 30 to 40 minutes. It need not be double in bulk because it will rise further in the oven. Bake in a moderately hot, 375°F oven, for 30 to 50 minutes. Time will vary with the shape of the loaves, but sourdough bread takes a little longer to bake than ordinary yeast bread.

# SOYBEANS

SOYBEANS ARE WELL KNOWN FOR THEIR HIGH PROTEIN CONTENT. Their composition also differs from all other beans in its higher fat and lower carbohydrate content. Though dry soybeans can be cooked like other dry beans, their flavor and texture are quite different, and the usual bean seasonings do not suit them. In North America the tendency has been to prepare them like other dry beans, and then to reject them because they are not as good as expected. In Asian countries, where soybeans have been an important food for many, many centuries, special preparations are made from them, totally unlike western bean dishes. A few of these, like soy sauce and tofu (soybean curd), are gaining acceptance everywhere, and the soybean may eventually be appreciated in all of its ramifications in the West as it is in the Far East.

Soybeans are easily grown as a garden crop in most climates. They can be harvested as fresh, shelled, green soybeans, or as mature, dry soybeans, and used in all kinds of savory ways.

Soybeans are also known as soya beans, and the products made from them are named accordingly.

---

### STORAGE

**Canning** *Fresh, green* Shell (see below). Cover with boiling water, boil 1 min. Drain, pack in jars, add boiling cooking water, 1 in. headroom. Process 240°F, 11 pounds pressure. Pints: 55 min. Quarts: 65 min. Refer to CANNING section.

**Drying** *Fresh, green* Steam in pods 10 min. Shell (see below). Dry till hard or brittle. Refer to DRYING FOODS section. For mature soybeans, refer to HANDLING DRIED BEANS in BEANS, DRY section.

**Freezing** *Fresh, green* Blanch in boiling water 5 min. Shell (see below), or freeze in pod for snack (see below). Package dry. (Refer to FREEZING section.)

⅞ CUP DRY SOYBEANS = ABOUT 1 CUP FLOUR

---

## SOYBEAN PREPARATIONS

**Miso**   Miso is the Japanese name for a flavorful, fermented soybean paste. It is usually made from a mixture of soybeans, grain, and salt. There are also Chinese versions. Miso is often used as a base for soups, and as a seasoning for meat, fish, and vegetables. It is possible, but difficult, to make miso at home. (See REFERENCES at the end of this section.)

**Soybean Sprouts**   Soybeans germinate easily, but conditions must be just right to grow larger, tender sprouts from them. (Refer to the SPROUTS section.)

**Soy Flour**   The flour made by grinding dry soybeans is useful for making soy milk, and as a nutritious addition to baked goods, and pasta. Because of their oil content it is not always possible to grind them in a home grain mill. However, a mill that cannot grind them alone will grind them if they are mixed with two or three times their quantity of wheat or another grain. (Refer to the GRAINS and the BREAD, QUICK sections.)

The flour ground at home will be whole or full fat soy flour. Health food stores often sell low fat soy flour or other soy powders intended for special purposes, such as making low fat soy milk. It is not possible to make these at home.

**Soy Grits**   Coarsely ground soybeans can be used in baked goods, breakfast cereals, and meat or vegetable dishes to add a chewy or nutty texture. Few enjoy their flavor alone, but they blend well in mixtures. Often soy grits are added precooked, but this is not necessary in moist mixtures to be cooked 30 minutes or longer.

***Soy Milk***    Soy milk can be made from soy flour or from whole, dry soybeans. Making milk from dry soybeans is the first step when making tofu. (Refer to the TOFU section.) To make milk from soy flour, mix the flour with enough warm water to make a paste, then stir in more water, and cook over low heat for about 15 minutes, stirring very often. A good mix is 1 cup soy flour to 6 cups water, but this can be varied to taste. Strain the milk through cloth for complete smoothness.

Soy milk can be substituted for dairy milk in many recipes and milk mixtures. It can be made into yogurt in exactly the same way as dairy milk, using a dairy starter. (Follow the directions for making yogurt in the YOGURT section, and try it in the NON-DAIRY ICE CREAM, in the ICE CREAM section.) Instant soy milk powders are available in some stores. Though soy milk is not a tasty beverage by itself, it is excellent in mixtures.

***Soy Nuts***    Whole dry soybeans can be soaked, cooked, and then roasted to eat as a crunchy, nut-like snack.

***Soy Oil***    The oil pressed from soybeans is among the best vegetable oils for use in cooking and for salads. Unfortunately it is not possible to press the beans at home.

***Soy Protein***    This is a commercial concentrate made from soybeans, often used as an extender for sausage and other ground meat preparations such as hamburger patties and meat loaf. It cannot be duplicated at home, and the additives in it make its use questionable in any case. Cooked, ground soybeans can be made at home and used as meat extenders in most of the same ways.

***Soy Sauce***    Natural soy sauce, without chemicals, is pressed from a fermented mixture of soybean, wheat, and salt. It might possibly be made at home, but could take as long as 2 years—an impractical endeavor for most people.

When buying soy sauce look at the ingredients on the label. If made with chemicals the label will list acid hydrolyzed vegetable protein, sweeteners, and caramel coloring. Naturally fermented soy sauce contains only soybeans, wheat or another grain, and salt. Tamari is one natural soy sauce sold in many health food stores. Low-salt, naturally fermented soy sauce is also available in some places.

***Tempeh***    Tempeh is an Indonesian food made from soybeans. The soybeans are cooked, and then inoculated with a starter of special mold spores. They are then held at a temperature of 90°F for several days while mycelium grow from the spores, binding the beans together into a sort of cake. This can be cooked and eaten in a variety of ways. Most people like the flavor the first time they try it. Tempeh is easily made at home, if an incubator can be arranged to hold the temperature at 90°F. Mold starters are available from several mail order sources. (See REFERENCES at the end of this section.)

***Tofu***    Tofu is the Japanese name for soybean curd. It is also made in China and other far eastern countries. (Refer to the TOFU section for detailed information.)

## HANDLING SOYBEANS

While seed catalogs sell separate strains of soybeans for shelling green and for maturing to dry beans, in a small garden it works quite well to plant only one variety and harvest some green, leaving the rest to mature.

*Harvesting and Shelling Green Soybeans* Pick soybean pods after the beans have formed in them, and before they begin to lose their green color. As it is very difficult to shell raw green soybeans, blanch them in boiling water or steam them for about 5 minutes. This will make the pods open easily for shelling. Squeeze them over a dish and the beans will pop out into it, or shell them directly into freezer containers. Green soybeans cooked in the pod are a common snack in Japan. (See SOYBEAN IDEAS, below.)

*Harvesting and Using Mature Soybeans* Gather mature soybeans after the pods have turned yellow, but before they have dried enough to shatter and scatter the beans. If the pods are not completely dry, spread them out to dry in an airy place. Shell and store like regular dry beans. (Refer to the BEANS, DRY section.)

To be digestible, soybeans must be well cooked before they are eaten. Dry soybeans can be ground into flour or grits and then cooked in various ways, or whole beans can be soaked in water and cooked. This is the first step for many different dishes. Soaking and cooking times will vary according to the strain and age of beans, but overnight soaking and several hours cooking is usually necessary. Some sources suggest cooking them from 7 to 8 hours to make them as soft as possible. They can be pressure cooked, adding a teaspoon of oil for each cup of beans to prevent them from clogging the steam escape valve, but they are as good or better when slow cooked. If the soaking water from soybeans is discarded and they are cooked in fresh water, they are less apt to cause gas when eaten.

## SOYBEAN RECIPES

### *Green Soybean and Fish Salad* (Makes about 6 side servings.)

1½ cups (about) cooked, shelled, green soybeans
1 cup (about) cooked, flaked fish, or 1 can tuna
1 cucumber, chopped
1–2 scallions, minced
small bunch lettuce, or other salad greens
¼ cup feta or other cheese, in small pieces, optional
¼ cup croutons, or toasted bread cubes, optional
2 hard-boiled eggs, sliced, optional
1 recipe Pre-Mixed Oil and Lemon or Vinegar Dressing with herbs (Refer to the SALADS section.), or any favorite dressing

Cut or tear the lettuce or salad greens in bite sized pieces. Toss together all the salad ingredients, then toss with the salad dressing. The soybeans add delightful color and texture.

## SOYBEAN IDEAS

**Brown Soybeans** Add several tablespoons soy sauce to dry beans' soaking water. Soak overnight. Next day cook the beans in the soaking water. When they are tender, remove the lid and cook till the water is absorbed, and all of the soy sauce flavor and color is in the soybeans. Serve cold as a snack, add to salads, or use instead of plain soybeans for patties or other dishes.

**Green Soybean Snack** Cook green soybeans in the pod in plenty of well salted boiling water for about 10 to 15 minutes, till the pods start to open slightly. Drain and eat hot or cooled. Everyone shells their own soybeans by putting the pods in their mouths and sucking out the beans. This Japanese snack is for both young and old. The salt can be omitted.

Green soybeans frozen in the pod can be dropped in boiling water while still frozen for a quick snack.

**Green Soybean Succotash** Green shelled soybeans are very good cooked with corn, instead of ordinary fresh shelled beans, to make succotash. (Refer to *Succotash,* in the BEANS, FRESH section.) In the winter use dried or frozen green soybeans and sweet corn to make the dish.

### *Soybean Patties*  (Makes about 6 dinner servings.)

3 cups cooked soybeans, drained, and mashed or ground

2 eggs
3–4 tablespoons oil or butter

Variation 1:
1 cup cooked rice
1 cup bread crumbs
1 clove garlic, minced
2 tablespoons parsley, minced

1 teaspoon dill leaves, or other herbs, minced
2 tablespoons soy sauce
dash pepper

Variation 2:
2 cups mashed potatoes
1 small onion, minced

1 cup raw vegetables, grated, minced, or ground (Try carrot, green pepper, or celery.)
pepper, salt, optional

Combine the soybeans, eggs, and the ingredients for the chosen variation. Shape into patties. Sauté them in the oil or butter, turning to brown on both sides, or set them on a greased baking sheet with a dot of butter on each, and bake in a moderate, 350°F oven for about 20 minutes.

Patties made with rice and bread crumbs are very good served with a cream or cheese sauce, and those made with potato are good with tomato sauce. Either one is delicious served with homemade relish instead of a sauce.

### *Yellow Soybean Curry*  (Makes about 6 dinner servings.)

2 stalks celery, chopped medium
1 onion, chopped medium
1 carrot, chopped medium
1 green pepper, chopped medium
1 clove garlic, minced

⅓ cup (about) oil
3 cups cooked soybeans, with their cooking water
2 teaspoons curry powder, or to taste

Sauté the celery, onion, carrot, green pepper, and garlic in the oil in a pot till lightly browned. Add the soybeans and cooking water. If the mixture seems dry, add a little plain water. Cover, and simmer 20 minutes. Add the curry powder and simmer another 5 minutes.

Serve with rice or noodles and a chutney.

## REFERENCES FOR SOYBEAN PREPARATIONS

Shurtleff, William, and Aoyagi, Akiko, *The Book of Tofu* (1975), *The Book of Miso* (1976), and *The Book of Tempeh* (1979), Autumn Press, Kanagawa-ken, Japan.

# SPINACH

**STORAGE**

**Canning** Trim stems, midribs. Cook till wilted in minimal water (see below). Pack hot, add boiling water, 1 in. headroom. Process, 240°F, 11 pounds pressure. Pints: 1 hr. 10 min. Quarts: 1 hr. 30 min. (Refer to CANNING section.)

**Drying** Trim coarse stems, midribs. Optional: Steam blanch 4–6 min. to wilt. Spread on trays with minimal overlap. Dry till crumbly. (Refer to DRYING section.)

**Freezing** (Best storage method.) Trim, blanch 2 min. in boiling water. Chill, package. (Refer to FREEZING section.)

2–3 POUNDS FRESH = 1 QUART CANNED OR FROZEN

S PINACH IS THE PROTOTYPE OF POTHERBS—THE GREENS TO WHICH all other greens are compared. When Popeye, the cartoon sailorman, began swallowing it by the canful to give himself amazing strength, he made spinach interesting to modern children, but it was respected and cultivated for many centuries before that. It dates back to 8th century China, to Persia even earlier, and only became known in Europe in the 12th century.

Most gardeners raise spinach, or similar greens, of which there are many. New Zealand spinach is a valuable one because it grows well in hot weather when regular spinach goes to seed. Lamb's quarters, which grow wild in many gardens, taste so much like spinach that they almost make its cultivation unnecessary.

## HANDLING SPINACH

Spinach can be harvested by cutting the whole plant, but often in home gardens only the outside leaves are gathered, leaving the plant to produce more leaves. If soil is caught in the creases the spinach leaves will need thorough washing. It is best to wash spinach just before use, so that water does not stand on the leaves, making it spoil more quickly. If it must be washed ahead of time, dry it immediately as lettuce is dried.

Rinse spinach leaves individually under running water or put a bunch in a large pan of water, swish it around vigorously, and lift it out. It may take several changes of water to clean it completely. Never leave spinach soaking in water, allowing water soluble vitamins and minerals to be lost.

*Cooking Spinach* Spinach must be cooked quickly to retain its many vitamins and minerals. Steaming is not an efficient way, because the leaves mat down and the steam fails to penetrate. The best simple, quick way to cook it is in a pot with only the water that clings to the leaves after they are washed. Put the damp spinach in a pot, cover, and set it over moderately high heat. After 2 or 3 minutes, when the bottom leaves have wilted, and steam is coming up around the edges, turn over the whole mass of spinach using forks or a small spatula. Cover, and continue cooking another 2 or 3 minutes, till the spinach is limp and soft, but still bright green. Serve hot with seasonings, or use in recipes calling for precooked spinach. If there are a few tablespoons of cooking water left in the pot, use them with the spinach or in any vegetable mixture, or drink them to give strength to the cook.

*Oxalic Acid in Spinach* When cooked spinach has a harsh taste with a teeth-on-edge quality, it is because it contains a lot of oxalic acid. This taste does not occur in raw spinach, and its intensity can vary considerably in different batches. The presence of oxalic acid is unfortunate, as it ties up the calcium in the spinach, so that it cannot be used. (The many other vitamins and minerals in spinach are not affected.)

There are several ways to neutralize this unpleasant taste. Cooking it with high protein foods like milk, eggs, or cheese works well. A sprinkling of lemon juice also works, because of the lemon's high calcium content.

## SPINACH RECIPES

### Stir-fried Spinach                        (Makes 4–6 side servings.)

*2 pounds spinach*                       ¼ *teaspoon salt, optional*
*3 tablespoons vegetable oil or fat*

Leave the spinach leaves whole, but separate them if they are in bunches. Shake off as much water as possible after washing, or pat dry with a towel. Heat the oil or fat in a wok or heavy frying pan till it is very hot. Put in the spinach all at once, and, if using it, immediately sprinkle the salt on top. Stir-fry for about 3 minutes, till the spinach is wilted but still bright in color. (Refer to the STIR-FRYING section.)

### Potherb Pie                              (Makes about 6 side servings.)

*1 pound spinach*                        *2 eggs, beaten*
*1 pound lettuce leaves*                 *1 cup top milk, or light cream*
*large bunch parsley, stems removed*     *pepper, to taste*
*small bunch beet tops, or Swiss chard*  ¼ *teaspoon salt, optional*
*small bunch cress or mustard greens*    *single crust for top of pie* (Use
*few comfrey and/or borage leaves,*          pastry or bread dough.)
*   optional*

Cook all of the greens together in a large pot in just the water left on from washing them. When completely wilted, take out the greens and chop them small, squeezing out excess juice in the process. (Save juice for another purpose.) Mix the greens with the eggs, milk or cream, pepper, and salt, if desired. Put in a deep pie dish or shallow baking dish and cover the top with the crust. Bake in a moderately hot, 375°F oven for about 20 minutes, till browned. An ideal dish for the gardener who has a little of this and a little of that, but not enough of any one green to feed the family. Other greens combinations can also be delicious.

**Spinach and Cheese Pie**  Use 2 pounds spinach and omit the other greens. Cook several chopped scallions or a small onion with the spinach. Mix 1½–2 cups crumbled feta or other cheese with the chopped spinach. Omit eggs, cream, and salt. Add minced dill leaves, mint, or

---

## SPINACH IDEAS

**Spinach in Salads**  Raw spinach torn in bite sized pieces is excellent in salads in place of some of the lettuce. Its dark green color and rich flavor contrast nicely with the lighter milder lettuce. Raw sliced mushrooms go especially well with spinach in salads.

**Spinach and Orange**  As a change from spinach with lemon, try sprinkling hot cooked spinach with orange juice and garnishing it with thin slices of orange.

**Spinach Pancakes**  For supper, add chopped, cooked spinach to pancake batter and cook as usual. Serve the pancakes with the *Cream Sauce* or CHEESE SAUCE, in the MILK section.

**Spinach with Herbs**  Herbs beautifully complement the spinach flavor, whether cooked with plain spinach or added to mixed spinach dishes. Parsley, rosemary, basil, tarragon, and mint go especially well.

**Cold Spinach and Yogurt**  Chop leftover cooked spinach and mix it with yogurt. Season with crushed garlic and pepper to taste. Serve as a cooling side dish with curries, chili beans, or other hot spicy dishes.

**Fresh Spinach Gelatine**  Flavor stock for jelling (refer to JELLED STOCK, in the GELATINE section) with lemon juice or vinegar, and pepper or paprika, if desired. Mix in raw chopped spinach, and some minced scallion, celery, and fresh herbs. Then stir in small curd cottage cheese. Chill till set. Serve on lettuce leaves, or, for a change, spinach leaves, with a dollop of mayonnaise on top.

rosemary if desired. The crust can be brushed with olive oil, or oil can be sprinkled over the spinach and cheese.

### *Schav*

(Or Spinach Soup with Sorrel.)　　　　　(Makes 8–10 medium bowls.)

*1 pound spinach, chopped medium*
*½ pound sorrel or sour grass,*
*trimmed and chopped* (If unavailable, use 1½ pounds spinach,
with added lemon juice to
taste.)
*juice of 1 lemon*
*4 scallions or 1 onion, chopped*
*medium*

*1 medium potato, peeled*
*2 tablespoons honey or sugar, or*
*to taste*
*¼ teaspoon salt, optional*
*2 eggs, lightly beaten*
*sour cream, or yogurt, 1 spoon*
*per bowl, optional*

**OTHER RECIPES
WITH SPINACH**

Baked Brains and Spinach, p.61
Beans and Greens Soup, p.25
Casserole Marinara, p.117
Endive or Escarole with Spinach,
　p.173
Fish and Greens, Amerindian
　Style, p.269
Greens and Rice, p.519
Greens Cakes, p.366
Green Noodles, p.430
Lamb Stew, Middle Eastern
　Style, p.378
Spinach, Other Greens, and
　Herbs (for food coloring),
　p.272

Cook the spinach, sorrel, lemon juice, scallions or onion, potato, honey or sugar, and salt, if desired, in about 2 quarts of water. After they have cooked for about 30 minutes, taste and adjust the amounts of lemon juice and sweetener for a sweet-sour flavor. Cook another 10 minutes, or till the potato is soft. Mash the potato with a fork, and mix it into the soup.

Take the soup off the stove and add several spoonfuls to the eggs in a separate dish, stirring it in a spoonful at a time. Then stir the egg into the the rest of the soup. This procedure will prevent curdling. If the soup is reheated, do not let it boil. If desired put a spoon of sour cream or yogurt in each bowl before the soup is served. Schav, of northern European origin, has a hearty, almost haunting, flavor which many find irresistible.

# SPLEEN

THE SPLEEN IS AN ORGAN OR GLAND LOCATED JUST BELOW THE DIA-
phragm. In meat animals it is also called the milt or melt. It con-
sists of pulpy red and white tissue which functions as a blood filter. Though spleen is not a favorite meat, it is quite edible. It is almost al-
ways cooked with other glandular meats, such as lungs, heart, and liver, and used in stews and hashes. When from a pig, all of these organs cooked together are sometimes called "pig's fry."

Wash the spleen well in cold water as soon as it is taken out of the carcass, and keep it in a cold place till it is used.

**ANOTHER RECIPE
WITH SPLEEN**

Son-of-a-bitch Stew, p.666

## SPLEEN RECIPE

**Faggots**
(Or English Style Hash Balls.)                    (Makes 4–6 servings.)

*1 pound pig's fry* (Pieces of pig's spleen, lungs, liver, heart, kidneys, sweetbreads, or as many as possible.)
*1 large onion, chopped medium*
*¼ cup bread crumbs*

*¼ teaspoon each pepper, ginger, sage, paprika*
*1 teaspoon salt, optional*
*1 pig's caul* (Refer to CAUL FAT, in the LARD section.)

Put the pig's fry and onion in a pot, cover with water, and cook till tender. Drain and mix a few tablespoons of the broth with the bread crumbs. (Save the rest of the broth for making gravy, or another use.) Grind or chop fine the pig's fry and onion, and mix with the bread crumbs, pepper, ginger, sage, paprika, and salt, if desired.

Cut the caul in 4 inch squares. Shape the pig's fry mixture into balls, then wrap a piece of caul around each. Set on a baking sheet and brown quickly in a hot, 425°F oven. If wrapping is difficult, set the balls on the baking sheet and lay a piece of caul over each. If desired, serve with brown gravy, made from the extra broth. These are very tasty and can be compared to *Haggis*, in the LAMB AND MUTTON section, or to any hash made with organ meats.

**STORAGE**

*Note:* Long storage is counter to the purpose of sprouting. For a constant, fresh supply, start sprouts weekly.

**Canning**  No tested methods for home canning available.

**Drying**  Spread on trays. Dry till hard or papery. (Texture varies with type of sprout.) May grind to powder for soups. (Refer to DRYING section.)

**Freezing**  Steam blanch 3 min. Chill. Package. (Will be limp when thawed.) (Refer to FREEZING section.)

# SPROUTS

SPROUTING SEEDS IS A PHENOMENALLY EASY WAY TO GROW FRESH vegetables in winter. This method of cultivation requires no soil, no sun, no growing lights, no greenhouse, not even a south facing window sill. All that is necessary are seeds, a jar or other container that can be drained, and a room temperature place to keep them. Some seeds, particularly bean seeds, need an even temperature round the clock to sprout well, but others, like alfalfa seeds, sprout perfectly well in a room that is warm in the daytime and cool at night. Alfalfa sprouts will grow in the usual temperature differences of homes heated with wood burning stoves.

The sprouting of seeds is not a new idea. For centuries mung beans and soybeans have been sprouted in China, and lentils have been sprouted in India. Sprouting oats for winter feed for chickens is an old farm practice, and sprouting is the first step for making barley malt. Alfalfa sprouts are, however, an innovation, and they make fresh, home grown winter salads possible for everyone at negligible expense. Only one or two pounds of alfalfa seeds will keep an average family in salads throughout an entire winter.

Along with their other virtues, sprouted seeds are very nutritious. Dormant seeds already have a high food value, and when sprouted their value increases, particularly in their vitamin content.

## HANDLING SPROUTS

Sprouts from plain, untreated seeds of the majority of food plants can be eaten, but there are exceptions. Do not eat sprouted potato, tomato, sorghum, Sudan grass, castorbean, apple, or stone fruit seeds, because they can be toxic. Also do not sprout seeds purchased for planting in the garden, as they may have been chemically treated in some way that does not show either on the seed or on the label. The best sources of sprouting seeds are health food stores and seed catalogs selling seeds intended specifically for sprouting, and of course, seeds collected from one's own garden. For harvesting seeds see pages 561–62.

## SPROUTING ARRANGEMENTS

Most seeds sprout best in darkness, to mimic natural growing conditions. Their container must allow good water drainage, and they must be kept damp while they grow by frequent watering or rinsing. They are ready to eat in 3 days to a week. An uncommon approach to sprouting is the planting of seeds in a thin layer of soil to be tended like seedlings for the garden. This is possible only for the larger seeds—beans, grain, or sunflower seeds. Such sprouts are often difficult to use because of the tangle of roots and dirt. Sometimes the shoots are cut for use and the root section discarded.

***Sprouting Jars*** Any wide mouthed glass jar of quart size or larger can be used for sprouting. A cover is needed that will let in air and retain the seeds when the jar is tipped and drained. A piece of a nylon stocking, nylon netting, or plastic screening can be used. If using a canning jar, the covering can be held in place with a canning lid ring. Otherwise use a rubber band. Another possibility is to punch many small holes in a regular lid. The seeds are soaked in the jar, drained, rinsed and drained again, and then put in a dark place, such as a cupboard or unused oven to begin to grow. To keep the seeds moist, the jar is filled with water and drained several times a day. Between rinsings, the jar should be propped on its side so that moisture can drain out. If the seeds sit in water they will rot.

*Alfalfa sprouts in jar.*

***Opaque Sprouting Containers*** New clay flower pots, or boxes made of plain, untreated wood, with small holes drilled in the bottom make good sprouting containers. With a lid to keep them dark inside, they can be kept in plain view on the sink drainboard for convenience in watering. Clay pots must be soaked in water for an hour, and wooden boxes for a few minutes, before the seeds go in. The moisture held by the clay or wood will help keep the seeds evenly damp. The hole in the clay pot must be covered with plastic screen or cloth. These sprouters must be scalded with boiling water or left in the sun for a while between uses to clean them.

A set of wooden sprouting boxes that stack one above the other can be made. Each box should be 3 inches deep to give the sprouts growing space. The whole stack can be watered at once by filling the top box, then letting the water trickle down through the other boxes. A different kind of sprout can be grown in each box.

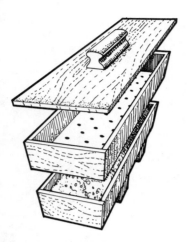

*Set of stacked sprouting boxes.*

**Sprouting Trays**   A baking pan or plastic container of shoebox-size can be made into a sprouter by punching or drilling holes in the bottom and propping it over a drainage pan. For the first day or two of sprouting, a damp paper towel can be kept on the bottom of the container to hold moisture. However, if left too long, the paper may promote spoilage, especially in damp climates. Cover with cloth or a piece of wood. If transparent, keep the tray in a dark place. Pour water over the sprouts as needed to keep them damp, and empty the drainage tray every day. In this kind of sprouter the seeds are undisturbed as they grow. They will look like a dense miniature forest by the time they are ready for use.

## BASIC STEPS OF SEED SPROUTING

• Measure an amount of seeds that will not crowd the sprouting container. For an average sized sprouter, such as a quart jar, use 2 tablespoons of tiny seeds like alfalfa or radish, ¼ cup of medium seeds, like grains or small beans, or ½ cup large seeds like sunflower or large beans.

• Cover the seeds with plenty of lukewarm water and soak about 8 hours, or overnight. Drain the seeds, rinse them in lukewarm water, and drain again. (Use the soaking water for watering house plants, as it contains beneficial nutrients.) Spread the seeds out in their sprouter, then keep them in the dark at room temperature, ideally 70°F, but many kinds of seeds will sprout even when nighttime temperatures are considerably lower. Excessively warm temperatures, however, encourage mold or other spoilage.

• Rinse or water the seeds 3 or 4 times a day. Water more frequently when the seeds are just beginning to germinate, especially where humidity is low. Use room temperature water, as icy water will discourage growth. Make sure the sprouter's drainage is good.

• When the sprouts are big enough to use, some kinds are improved if uncovered or put in the light for a day to make their leaves turn green.

• Wash the sprouts in a large pan of cool water to remove loose seed coverings. The coverings will float and can be poured off. Any seed coverings that stick will not impair the taste of the sprouts. Lift the sprouts out of the wash water, leaving unsprouted seeds behind. Drain well and store in a closed container in the refrigerator. They will keep about a week.

## SEEDS FOR SPROUTING

The seeds described below can all be home grown and harvested.

*Sprouting Alfalfa, Red Clover, and Fenugreek*   The seeds of these three legumes are easily sprouted, taking 4 to 7 days. Cool night temperatures slow their growth, but do not affect their taste. They are ready to eat when tiny leaves appear. Their flavor and vitamin content is improved if they are kept in the light for a day to turn the leaves green. Red clover sprouts are smaller than alfalfa, and fenugreek sprouts are larger. All are delicious raw in salads and sandwiches.

*Sprouting Radish, Mustard, and Cress*   The sprouts of radish, mustard and cress are all peppery in flavor, and are liked more as garnishes or flavorings than as main salad ingredients. As these seeds sprout in about the same time as alfalfa, a few can be mixed in with alfalfa seeds to be sprouted together for a slightly peppery salad mixture.

*Sprouting Chia and Flax*   These seeds become sticky or gelatinous when soaked. To keep them from sticking together in a clump, start them soaking by sprinkling them over water in a dish. Many prefer the taste of chia sprouts when very small, about ¼ inch. Grow flax sprouts till leaves appear. They can be left in the light to turn the leaves green.

*Sprouting Mung Beans and Lentils*   The familiar sprouts found in Chinese cooking are mung bean sprouts. Mung beans and lentils are easy to sprout if there is a place to keep them that stays near 70°F. If it is too cool, they will grow slowly and have a woody, uncooked, bean taste. When they grow as they should, the sprouts burst out of their seed coverings, and these are easily floated off when washing the sprouts. These sprouts are tender and taste very good raw. They will be 1 or 2 inches long and have two tiny leaves in 4 to 5 days. They taste especially good if kept in the light for a day to turn the leaves green. Once they turn green, mung bean sprouts do not look like typical Chinese bean sprouts, but they will be excellent used in the same ways.

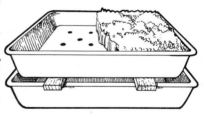

*Mung sprouts ready to use.*

*Sprouting Soybeans*   Soybeans germinate easily if the seeds are less than a year old, but it is difficult to grow them to fullsized, tender sprouts, like those sold in Chinese grocery stores. Black soybeans are best for sprouting. To prevent mold, commercially sprouted soybeans are often watered with a very mild solution of chlorinated lime. For the best chances of success without using chemicals, keep the soybeans at an even 70°F and keep them evenly moist. Large batches of sprouts will generate their own heat after 2 or 3 days, and must be cooled down with ice water to prevent rot. They take 6 to 8 days to grow and become 2 to 3 inches long. A brief blanching before they are eaten will improve their flavor.

*Sprouting Dry Beans*   All bean seeds make better sprouts if kept near 70°F while sprouting. After they have soaked, discard any seeds that float, as they will not sprout. Small sized beans make sprouts that can be used like mung bean sprouts. They usually are ready in 3 to 5 days, when they are about an inch long. Use large sized bean sprouts when the sprout is only as long as the seed it grows from, as the sprouts begin to taste bitter if grown longer. Large sprouted beans must be cooked before they are eaten. They are very good added to soups, stews, and vegetable dishes.

*Sprouting Grains* All grains can be sprouted, except sorghum, whose sprouts are toxic. Grains with tight hulls, like barley, must be sprouted unhulled. There are two basic approaches to sprouting grains. One is to sprout them like other seeds in a sprouter, till the shoots are only as long as the original seed. These can be used in baking for their pleasant, chewy taste. They can also be dried and ground, as for MALTED BARLEY (refer to the BARLEY section). The other way is to cover the grain seeds with a thin layer of soil, and grow them in a sunny window for their grassy green tops. Cut the tops when they are 2 or 3 inches high, then mince them for salads. Chew them for their sweet flavor, but the "cud" must be spat out.

It will take 2 to 5 days for grains to sprout till the shoot reaches the length of the seed. Grains generally sprout very well regardless of differences in day and night temperatures.

*Sprouting Sunflower Seeds* Use only unhulled seeds. If grown in a sprouter, use the sprouts as soon as the shells have split open, when they can be easily removed. Perhaps the best way to enjoy sprouted sunflowers is to grow them in about ½ inch of soil in a sunny window, and cut the shoots when they are 2 or 3 inches tall, with two green leaves. The shoots are sometimes called sunflower lettuce and are very good in salads.

## SPROUTS RECIPES

**Essene Bread**                                              (Makes 6 thick or 12 thin patties.)

The Essenes were an ancient Jewish sect, whose asceticism precluded all but the purest and simplest foods, as exemplified by this bread.

2 *cups whole grain, for sprouting*
  (Rye, wheat, triticale or a mixture of these is excellent.)
¼ *teaspoon caraway or other herb*
  *seeds, optional* (Refer to the
  HERB SEEDS section.)

¼ *cup dried fruit, soaked,*
  *drained and chopped if neces-*
  *sary, optional*
*oil for baking sheets, or several*
  *tablespoons sesame seeds*

Sprout the grain till the shoots are about the same length as the kernels. If noticeably damp, let the sprouted grain sit exposed to the air for a few hours, till no wetness shows. Grind to a dough in a meat grinder or food processor. If using caraway or other herb seeds, grind them along with the grain. Dried fruit can also be ground in, or it can be chopped small and worked into the dough after grinding. Knead the dough to distribute herb seeds or fruit evenly throughout.

Shape the dough into 6 large, inch-thick patties or make twice as many thin patties. Lightly oil baking sheets, or sprinkle them with sesame seeds, and set the patties on them. Let dry in the sun, in a food dryer, or in another warm, airy place, such as near a stove, till the tops of the patties are dry to the touch. This usually takes about 1 hour. Then turn them over and bake them in a very low, 250°F oven for about an hour. Thin patties will take less time than thick ones. The bread will rise slightly and darken in color. (It is also possible to put the dough in small, oiled baking dishes or loaf pans and bake it for several hours in a very low, 250°F oven, but the texture will tend to be more pudding-like than bread-like.)

This bread has a somewhat sweet flavor and a moist, dense texture. It tastes very good by itself, or with butter or other toppings. Keep it a week to 10 days in the refrigerator, or freeze it for long storage.

---

**OTHER RECIPES WITH SPROUTS**

Alfalfa Sprout Winter Salads, p.533
Cookie Leather, p.188
Mat's Fried Rice, Homestead Style, p.520
Simple Soup, East Asian Style, p.577
Sprouted Rye in Baked Goods, p.530

---

### Buttered Sprouts, East Indian Style
(Makes about 6 side servings.)

2 tablespoons butter
1–2 tablespoons fresh herbs, or onion, minced (Try parsley or coriander leaves, and chives or scallions.)

black pepper
1 quart lentil or mung bean sprouts, or similar sized sprouts
1 tablespoon soup stock, or water
lemon juice, optional

Melt the butter in a saucepan and stir the herbs and pepper into it. Add the sprouts, and turn them over several times to coat them wih butter. Add the stock or water, cover with a tight lid and steam over fairly high heat for 2 or 3 minutes. The sprouts will settle in the pot and become bright in color. They should still be crisp when served. If desired, sprinkle them with lemon juice. These make a delightfully different vegetable side dish.

---

# SQUASH, SUMMER

---

SUMMER SQUASH IS ANY SQUASH EATEN YOUNG, WHILE THE SKIN IS tender, and the seeds undeveloped. Zucchini is the all-round favorite, but yellow straightneck and crookneck, and patty pan or scallop squash are also popular. Winter squash varieties make good summer squash if picked when very small. All varieties can be prepared in the same ways, though there will be differences in flavor and texture.

A well known characteristic of most summer squash is their ten-

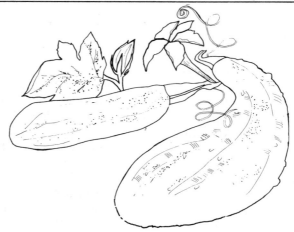

dency towards bursts of rampant productivity. When weather and growing conditions are right, a great many squash can appear in a very short time. Though an overwhelming supply has been known to dampen enthusiasm for eating them, it need not do so. Summer squash are an excellent summertime staple, and there are so many good ways to prepare them that they can be eaten every day of their growing season, yet still be missed when the season ends. There are also good ways to put them by for winter, though they will not retain the delicate crispness of raw squash, or the firm bite of freshly cooked squash.

Marrow or vegetable marrow is a large, oval summer squash, best known in England, though a few North American seed catalogs do include it. The cymling or simlin, sometimes mentioned in old cookbooks, is patty pan squash. Courgettes, the French name for small summer squash, is also seen in some English language cookbooks.

## HANDLING SQUASH

Summer squash can be harvested at any size, from fingerling with blossom attached to quite large, as long as the skin is still tender. Even the occasional overgrown squash hidden under its leaves can be used, though it will lack the good flavor and texture of the small ones.

Nothing is easier to prepare than summer squash. All they need is a rinse to take off dust or dirt. (Peeling would remove so much flavor and color that little of value would remain.) Only an overly mature squash will need seeding.

*Squash Blossoms* The blossoms of both summer and winter squash are very good to eat. They can be gathered from different varieties, and used together in one dish. However, note the difference between male and female blossoms. Usually, only the male blossoms are gathered since they do not affect yield. (A few are left for pollination.) When a female blossom is picked, the result is one less squash. These are meatier than the male blossoms and quite delicious fried in batter, so try them if they can be spared. See the recipes below for ways to prepare blossoms.

## SUMMER SQUASH RECIPES

### Summer Squash Sautéed in Batter                    (Makes about 6 side servings.)

| | |
|---|---|
| 1 cup flour | 1 pound (about) summer squash |
| pepper, salt, optional | 2−3 tablespoons oil or fat |
| 2 eggs | |

Put the flour, pepper, and salt, if desired, in a bowl, then stir in enough water to make a stiff batter. Beat in the eggs with a fork to make the consistency of pancake batter. Let sit while preparing the squash.

Slice the squash about ¼ inch thick. Slice small narrow squash diagonally to make larger slices. Heat oil or fat in a large frying pan. Drop the slices in the batter and sauté them over medium heat, turning once. Test with a fork to be sure they are cooked through before serving. These are quick and delicious—a favorite with children as well as adults.

**Summer Squash Parmigiana**   In a casserole or baking dish, make layers of the above summer squash sautéed in batter, a well seasoned tomato sauce, such as the one for pasta in the TOMATOES section, and parmesan, or another grated cheese. If desired, include some slices of mozarella. Top with grated cheese and bake about 30 minutes in a moderate, 375°F, oven.

**Eggplant Sautéed in Batter, or Eggplant Parmigiana**   Use eggplant instead of summer squash in the above ways.

**Squash Blossoms Sautéed in Batter**   Dip squash blossoms in batter and fry as above. The meaty female blossoms are especially good this way.

### Patty-cake Squash                    (Makes about 6 side servings.)

| | |
|---|---|
| 4 cups summer squash, grated | 2 tablespoons (about) fine dry |
| 1 small onion, grated | bread crumbs |
| 2 eggs, lightly beaten | 2−3 tablespoons butter, or oil, |
| ¼ cup flour | for frying |
| pepper, to taste | yogurt, to taste |
| ¼ teaspoon salt, optional | |

Put the grated squash and onion in a strainer and press out extra liquid. Then mix with eggs, flour, pepper, and salt, if desired. Add bread crumbs as needed for a medium thick batter. Heat butter or oil in a frying pan, then put in large spoonfuls of the squash mixture. Flatten with a spoon to make pancake thickness. Brown lightly on both sides, and serve the patty-cakes with yogurt. They are good for breakfast, lunch, or dinner.

*Ways to stuff squash.*

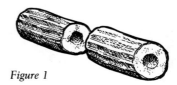

Figure 1

Cut zucchini or other cylindrical squashes in 3 to 5 inch sections, and hollow them out with an apple corer.

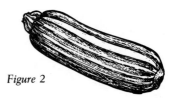

Figure 2

Steam small zucchini till softened, then slit deeply to make a space for stuffing.

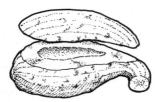

*Figure 3*

For large squash cut off a "lid" and hollow the centers for stuffing. If desired, set the lids on top of the stuffing.

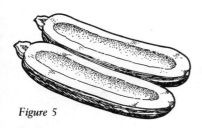

*Figure 4*

Cut large cylindrical squash in thick slices, cut out centers for stuffing.

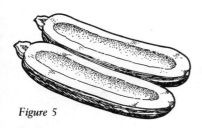

*Figure 5*

Cut overgrown zucchini or other squash in half, and remove center for stuffing.

## STUFFED SUMMER SQUASH

There are many ways to prepare the different varieties of summer squash for stuffing, and a great many stuffings to put in them. Below are some possibilities. (Squash prepared as in Figures 1, 2, and 4 can be steam blanched 5 minutes and frozen. Thaw before use.)

### I Cheese and Ham, or Salami Stuffing

*slices or sticks of cheese* (Swiss or mozarella are very good.)

*chunks or slices of ham or salami
tomato sauce, seasoned to taste*

Prepare squash as in Figures 1 or 4. Prepare, to fit into the centers of the squash sections, either sticks of cheese wrapped in thin slices of ham or salami, or ham or salami sticks, wrapped in thin slices of cheese. Stuff a wrapped stick into the center of each squash section. Put the stuffed squash close together in an oiled baking dish. Pour tomato sauce over them and bake 30 to 40 minutes in a moderate, 350°F oven.

### II Middle Eastern Stuffing          (Makes about 6 dinner servings.)

*1 cup raw rice
1 ½ pounds ground lamb
½ cup tomatoes, fresh chopped or canned
pepper, salt, optional
3 cups (about) goat milk yogurt, or stabilized yogurt* (Recipe in the YOGURT section.)

*1–3 cloves garlic, crushed or minced
1 teaspoon fresh mint leaves, minced, or ¼ teaspoon dried
2 tablespoons butter*

Prepare 2 to 3 pounds squash as in Figures 1, 2, or 4. Mix the rice, lamb, tomato, pepper, and salt, if desired, and stuff the squash, leaving room for the rice to swell. Put in a Dutch oven, or other heavy pot with a tight lid. Add 2 cups water and simmer, covered, 20 minutes, till the rice has swelled. Add the yogurt, cover, and simmer 20 more minutes. Keep the heat very low. Sauté the garlic and mint in the butter and pour over just before serving. The garlic and mint add an unusual finishing touch to this very tasty dish.

### III Tuna Stuffing          (Makes about 6 dinner servings.)

*4–6 slices bread, soaked in water, squeezed dry
2 tablespoons oil
2 tablespoons parsley, minced
1 large can (1½–2 cups) tuna
2 cups (about) tomato sauce, seasoned to taste* (Or mix tomato sauce and soup stock.)

*2 tablespoons capers,* PICKLED NASTURTIUM BUDS (Refer to the HERBS section.), *or relish, drained
dash of pepper*

Prepare 2 to 3 pounds squash in any of the ways shown above. combine all ingredients except tomato sauce, and put the mix in the squash, mounding it up somewhat where appropriate. Put the squash in an oiled baking pan or dish, then pour the sauce around it. Bake in a moderate, 375°F oven, for about 45 minutes, till the zucchini is tender when poked with a fork.

For other stuffings refer to the *Versatile Vegetable Loaf* mixtures, in the VEGETABLES section, and SEASONED NUTS AND GRAINS, in the NUTS section.

### Summer Squash Stew, Mexican Style

(Makes about 6 side servings.)

| | |
|---|---|
| 1 quart stewed summer squash and tomato (Frozen, canned, or freshly cooked.) | ½ teaspoon cayenne, or other hot pepper |
| 1 cup whole kernel corn (Frozen, canned, or fresh.) | ¼ teaspoon coriander seed, powdered |
| 2 tablespoons oil | 1 teaspoon fresh mint leaves, minced, or ½ teaspoon dried |
| 1 small onion, chopped medium | salt, optional |
| 1 clove garlic, minced | 1–2 cups milk, or soup stock |

Thaw the summer squash and tomato with the corn in a pot if necessary. Heat the oil in a pan and sauté the onion and garlic till the onion is transparent. Add to the summer squash mixture along with the cayenne, coriander, mint, and salt, if desired. Add enough milk or soup stock to just cover the vegetables. Simmer, covered, for an hour.

**Dried Vegetable Stew**   Soak 1 cup dried summer squash or dried eggplant, 1 cup dried tomato, and ¼ cup dried sweet corn in water to cover, for several hours, or till the vegetables swell. Use to make the stew above.

### Marinated Summer Squash

(Makes about 1 quart.)

| | |
|---|---|
| 2 medium summer squash (About 12 inch zucchini are good.) | 1 tablespoon oregano, or other herbs, such as basil or thyme |
| 1 cup cider vinegar | pepper, salt, optional |
| 2 cups water | 2 cups (about) olive oil or other oil |
| 6 cloves garlic, crushed | |

Cut squash in ¼ inch slices. If squash are thick, cut in halves or fourths before slicing. Put the slices in a saucepan with the vinegar and water. Bring to a boil, then simmer 5 minutes. Drain squash well, and let cool.

Put a layer of the squash slices in a wide mouth jar or crock. Sprinkle with garlic, oregano, or other herbs, pepper, and salt, if desired. Add more layers of squash and seasonings till all ingredients are used. Cover with oil, and keep in a cool, preferably not refrigerated, place for one week before using. It will keep for months in a cool place. When the squash has been eaten reuse the oil for another batch, or use it for salad dressing. A delightful snack or appetizer.

**Marinated Eggplant**   Slice and marinate like the squash.

---

**SUMMER SQUASH IDEAS**

**Steamed Fingerling Squash**
Pick very small (2–5 inch) summer squash when they are plentiful. (If blossoms are still attached, separate them and fry them in batter.) Steam the squash about 5 minutes, long enough to brighten their color but not long enough to soften them. These are exquisite eaten plain without any seasonings, or cooled and seasoned with olive oil, a sprinkling of minced fresh herbs, such as scallions and basil, and pepper, and salt, if desired.

**Yellow Squash and Onions**
Slice the yellow squash, and then slice about half as much onion. Simmer these 10–15 minutes in just enough water to keep them from sticking, till both are tender. Stir once or twice. Season with pepper and butter, and serve hot.

**Stir-fried Summer Squash**
Slice the squash thinly, ⅛ inch if possible. In a wok or heavy frying pan, heat 1 or 2 tablespoons lard or oil, then stir-fry minced garlic and ginger root (optional) in it briefly. Over high heat add and stir-fry the squash about 2 minutes. Add a little soy sauce or water and a dash of pepper. Cover and cook over moderate heat about 5 minutes.

## Zucchini Dill Pickles                    (Makes 6 pints, canned.)

| | |
|---|---|
| 6 heads of dill | 6 grape leaves, optional |
| 6 cloves garlic | 4 cups vinegar |
| 5 pounds (about) zucchini, in chunks or slices | salt, optional |
| | 5 cups water |

Put 1 dill head and 1 whole clove of garlic in each of 6 hot pint canning jars. Fill with zucchini, leaving ½ inch headroom. If desired, put a grape leaf on top for flavor, and to help keep pickles crisp.

Heat the vinegar, water, and salt, if desired, to a full boil, then pour into jars to just cover ingredients. Run a thin knife around the inside of the jars to remove air bubbles, and, if necessary, add more vinegar solution. Adjust lids and process in a boiling water bath canner for 10 minutes. Wait 6 weeks before using the pickles. They are as good as, or better than, most canned dill cucumber pickles.

## Squash Blossom Corn Cakes        (Makes about 2 dozen small cakes, or 1 dozen muffins.)

| | |
|---|---|
| 1 cup whole corn meal | 2 eggs |
| 2 tablespoons honey, or sugar | 1 cup squash blossoms, coarsely chopped (See above.) |
| salt, optional | |
| 1 cup boiling water | 1 cup flour |
| ½ cup butter, or oil | 1½ teaspoons baking powder |
| ¾ cup milk | |

Put the cornmeal, honey or sugar, and salt, if desired, in a heatproof bowl and stir in the boiling water. Add the butter or oil and stir till melted or mixed. Then mix in the milk, eggs, and squash blossoms. Mix or sift together the flour and baking powder, and add to the batter. Drop by spoonfuls on a hot greased griddle and bake, turning to brown both sides, or bake in muffin tins in the oven for about 20 minutes. Either way these are delicious. Have them for breakfast or any other meal.

**Dandelion Blossom or Elderflower Corn Cakes** Instead of squash blossoms use either dandelion blossoms or elderflowers. For the dandelion blossoms, take off the green part at the base of the blossoms letting the petals fall free. The elderflowers must be stripped from their stems.

## Squash Blossom Soup              (Makes about 6 medium bowls.)

| | |
|---|---|
| 2 tablespoons butter | 1 quart chicken stock, or other light soup stock |
| 1 small onion, finely chopped | |
| 1–2 cups squash blossoms, coarsely chopped (See above.) | pepper, salt, optional |

Heat the butter in a pot and sauté the onion in it till limp. Add the blossoms, and sauté till they too are limp, about 5 minutes. Add the chicken stock, heat, season to taste, and simmer 5 minutes. This soup has a bright cheerful color as well as a lovely flavor.

Winter squash and pumpkins are somewhat different botanically, but they are quite alike as foods. Some, wanting the best of both, choose to eat winter squash and call it pumpkin. The flesh of pumpkins is apt to be more watery and stringy than that of winter squash, but the name pumpkin or "punkin" has a friendlier, more toothsome sound. The best pumpkin pies are made of winter squash. The range in size, shape, and skin color of different kinds of winter squash is remarkable, yet the flesh inside all of them is pumpkin colored. Its yellow to orange color indicates high vitamin A content. Japanese varieties of winter squash are becoming well known and popular. They have dense, dry, flavorful flesh that is excellent in pumpkin recipes. As their skin is quite thin, it can be eaten with the flesh, but this thinness means they may spoil sooner when stored. Squash and pumpkins are widely valued as winter food because they are so easily grown in quantity for long storage.

## HANDLING WINTER SQUASH

Winter squash and pumpkins are harvested in fall, around the time of the first frosts. Hard shelled varieties are not damaged by light frosts, but thinner skinned varieties must be protected or brought in before the first frost. Winter squash and pumpkins keep so well in a cool, dry, storage place that no other storage methods are necessary for fall and winter use. Any extra squash in storage can be canned or frozen during late fall or winter, when there is spare time. They also dry well, but their quality will be best if they are dried as soon as they are harvested.

Immature winter squash and pumpkin can be prepared like summer squash, and their blossoms used together with summer squash blossoms. (Refer to the recipes in the SQUASH, SUMMER section.)

***Curing and Storing Winter Squash and Pumpkins***  For long storage use only completely mature winter squash and pumpkins that were harvested with their stems on, and that are free of bruises and scrapes. Set aside any with broken stems or other damage for early use. (Butternuts are an exception in that they will keep without stems.)

After harvesting, cure winter squash and pumpkins from 10 days to 2 weeks to toughen their skins. They can be left outdoors in dry sunny weather, but must be covered at night to protect them from frosts. Or they can be cured indoors, at room temperature. If thick skinned varieties are washed in a solution of about a tablespoon of chlorine bleach to a gallon of water, their skins will be disinfected, discouraging mold or rot. Dry them immediately after doing this, as lingering dampness can also cause spoilage.

A dry, airy storage place with a temperature between 45 and 60°F will be needed. (Root cellars are too damp.) Use an attic, spare room,

---

### STORAGE

**Canning**  Peel, cut in 1 in. cubes. Bring to boil in water to cover. Drain, pack, add boiling cooking water, ½ in. headroom. Process 240°F, 11 pounds pressure. Pints: 55 min. Quarts: 1 hr. 30 min. *Purée* (See below.) Heat to simmer, stirring. Fill jars, ½ in. headroom. Process, 240°F, 11 pounds pressure. Pints: 65 min. Quarts: 80 min. (Refer to CANNING section.)

**Cold Storage**  See CURING AND STORING WINTER SQUASH AND PUMPKIN, below

**Drying**  (Solid fleshed varieties best.) Peel, slice, or grate. Optional: Steam blanch, 6 min. Spread on trays, or slice thick rings and hang. Dry till leathery or brittle. Dry purée as for fruit leather. (Refer to DRYING FOODS section.)

**Freezing**  Purée (see below.) Fill containers, leaving airspace. (Refer to FREEZING section.)

ABOUT 3 POUNDS WHOLE RAW = 1 QUART CANNED OR FROZEN

or a cool bedroom. Storage at temperatures above 60°F will make squash and pumpkins stringy. Spread out the squash in the storage place so that they do not touch each other. Check them occasionally for mold, and wipe them with vegetable oil if any is found, to remove it and seal that spot.

Most winter squash and pumpkins will keep from 3 to 4 months in a good storage place. A few, like Hubbard squash, will keep for 6 months.

**Pumpkin Seeds**  The seeds of all pumpkins and mature squash have a nice, nut-like flavor, but their shells can be a problem. There is, however, a naked seeded pumpkin called "Lady Godiva" that is grown for its seeds alone. Its flesh is too watery and stringy to enjoy. Ordinary squash and pumpkin seeds can be eaten in spite of their shells. Roast them like nuts (see the NUTS section), and eat them shell and all. They can be boiled about 15 minutes to soften shells before roasting. Some people become adept at shelling the seeds with their teeth, eating the nutty part and spitting out the shell. Other possibilities are to grind seeds and shells to use in baking, or to experiment with shelling them like sunflower seeds. (Refer to the SUNFLOWERS section.) As the seeds of different kinds of squash and pumpkin vary in size and toughness of shell, a system that works poorly for one may do very well for another. The seeds are too good to be tossed to the chickens without first giving people a chance to try them.

For an easy way to separate seeds from the fibers and pulp around them, scrape out the centers of the squash, put them in a bucket or pan, cover them with warm water and let them sit at room temperature for several days. As they begin to ferment, the pulpy parts will rise and float and the seeds will sink. Pour off the pulp and drain and dry the seeds. Spread them out in a warm, airy place so that they dry quickly, or use a food dryer.

Use naked pumpkin seeds or shelled seeds in the same ways as sunflower seeds or nuts. They are delicious in muffins, cookies, and breads.

**Winter Squash and Pumpkin Purée**  Before it is puréed, squash or pumpkin must be cooked by baking, steaming, or stewing. To bake, cut the squash or pumpkins in half, scoop out the seedy centers, and set the halves, cut side down, on an oiled baking sheet. Bake in a moderate, 350°F oven till soft. The time will vary with the thickness of the flesh, taking from 30 to 60 minutes. Test with a fork for doneness. When cool enough to handle, scrape out the flesh, discarding the peel. To steam or stew, cut the squash or pumpkin in pieces and slice off the peel. Steam on a rack, or stew in a minimum of water till soft. If watery after stewing, continue to cook uncovered to evaporate moisture. The cooked flesh can be mashed like potatoes, but the texture will not be smooth. For smoothness, put it through a sieve or food mill. (Refer to the KITCHEN UTENSILS section.)

**Spaghetti Squash**  This unusual squash makes a virtue of stringiness, as its long, spaghetti-like strands are its claim to fame. Boil or steam it whole, or cut the long way, and steam half, saving the other half for another meal. When soft, scrape the flesh out of the skin. It will come out in long strands that can be seasoned and served immediately while they are hot. They can be served with spaghetti sauce, but in spite of the name, they may be better liked with vegetable seasonings. (See the HERB TOSSED SPAGHETTI SQUASH idea, below.)

# WINTER SQUASH AND PUMPKIN RECIPES

### *Tafifa, or Pumpkin Stew, Middle Eastern Style*                        (Makes 4–6 dinner servings.)

| | |
|---|---|
| 2 tablespoons oil | 3 pounds (about) pumpkin or |
| 1–2 cups cooked meat, coarsely | winter squash, in peeled 2 |
| chopped | inch chunks |
| 1 clove garlic, crushed | 2 cups cabbage, shredded |
| 6 shallots, peeled, or 1–2 onions, in | pepper, salt, optional |
| chunks | |

Heat the oil in a stew pot and sauté the meat, garlic, and shallots or onions in it for about 5 minutes. Add the pumpkin, cabbage, pepper, and salt, if desired. Cover tightly, then simmer over very low heat for about 1½ hours. Check from time to time and, if necessary, add a little water to prevent sticking. This will vary according to the moisture content of the vegetables. A wonderful way to combine cabbage and pumpkin—two often stored winter vegetables.

### *Stuffed Winter Squash*                                (Makes 6–8 side servings.)

2 large acorn squash (Or any
   squash, adjusting stuffing
   amount if necessary.)
Corn Stuffing:

| | |
|---|---|
| 2 cups sweet corn kernels, canned or | 2 onions, chopped medium |
| frozen | ¼ cup (about) soy sauce or miso |
| 1 sweet pepper, chopped medium | (Fermented soy bean paste.) |

Apple Stuffing:

| | |
|---|---|
| 2 large apples, chopped medium | ½ cup raisins, optional |
| 2 onions, chopped medium | honey, or maple syrup, optional |
| ½ teaspoon cloves, or ginger | bacon slices, optional |

Cut the squash in half and remove the seedy centers. Scoop out half or more of the flesh, leaving shells ¼ to ½ inch thick. Put ¼ cup water in each shell, then bake at 400°F till soft, from 30 to 40 minutes.

Meanwhile put the scooped out pieces of squash in a pan with a minimum of water, and cook till softened. Add the chosen stuffing ingredients, except for the honey or maple syrup and bacon for the ap-

---

## WINTER SQUASH AND PUMPKIN IDEAS

**Seasonings for Baked Chunks** Cut serving sized chunks of winter squash or pumpkin and set them in a baking pan. Sprinkle with pepper, and dot with butter, or cover with a slice of bacon. Or, dribble with honey, molasses, or maple syrup, and dot with butter. Or, spread with a mixture of orange juice concentrate, adding a little honey, and dots of butter or bacon slices, if desired. Put a few tablespoons of water in the pan around the squash or pumpkin and bake till tender, usually 40 minutes to an hour.

**Sautéed Winter Squash or Pumpkin** Slice peeled squash or pumpkin thinly, and sauté slowly in butter or another fat. Sliced onion, minced garlic, or other sliced vegetables can also be sautéed with it. Season with pepper, and such minced herbs as parsley and mint. If a sauce is wanted, add apple cider or a little light cream for the last few minutes of cooking.

**Herb Tossed Spaghetti Squash**   While the spaghetti squash is cooking (see above), mix minced fresh chervil or parsley, or dried herbs, such as thyme, mint or celery leaves, with melted butter, oil or with bacon fat and crisp, crumbled bacon. Toss the mixture with hot strands of spaghetti squash and serve immediately. If oil was used the leftovers will be good later as a salad or cold vegetable dish. As a variation, chopped onion, celery, carrot shreds, and other vegetables can be sautéed in the fat and tossed with the spaghetti squash and herbs.

**Squash Cornmeal Mush**   In a heavy saucepan or double boiler, mix about 2 cups thin puréed winter squash or pumpkin, ½ cup cornmeal, and 1 tablespoon butter. Cook together slowly, stirring often, until very thick. It will take from 30 to 40 minutes. Stir in about ½ cup diced mild cheese. Serve hot, like mashed potatoes, or cool in a mold, slice, and sauté the slices.

**Winter Squash for Summer**
When winter squash forms too late in the season to have a chance to mature, pick them tiny, 2 to 3 inches, and steam them whole. Season to taste. A dish of tiny, recognizable squash shapes, such as acorn or butternut, has a whimsical look as well as a fine flavor.

**After the Jack-O-Lantern**
Enjoy the glow of the jack-o-lantern for a day or two, then cut the pumpkin in pieces, trimming off smoky or waxy portions. Prepare in a favorite way and enjoy the jack-o-lantern a second time.

ple stuffing. Cook about 10 minutes, till heated through. Fill the baked shells with stuffing. For the apple stuffing, honey or maple syrup can be drizzled on top and bacon slices laid over all. Bake from 10 to 15 minutes in a hot, 400°F oven.

***Pumpkin and Corn or Apple Casserole***   Mix about 3 cups of puréed squash or pumpkin with the stuffing ingredients, then bake in a hot oven for about 40 minutes.

### *Pumpkin or Squash Soup*   (Makes 10–12 medium bowls.)

| | |
|---|---|
| 4 *tablespoons butter, or other fat* | 6 *cups chicken stock, other soup* |
| 3–4 *large onions, thinly sliced, or* | *stock, or water* |
| *chopped medium* | 1 *stalk celery, chopped medium* |
| 4 *cloves garlic, crushed* | *pepper, salt, optional* |
| 2½–3 *pounds winter squash or* | *lemon juice, to taste, optional* |
| *pumpkin, in peeled pieces* | |

Melt the butter or fat in a soup pot, then gently sauté the onions and garlic till the onions are limp. Add the squash or pumpkin and sauté gently for another 10 minutes, stirring often. Add the stock or water, celery, pepper, and salt, if desired. Cover, bring to a boil, then simmer till the squash or pumpkin is soft, about 40 minutes.

Purée the soup with a food mill, blender, or other device. Reheat, adjust seasonings, and add lemon juice to taste. A smooth, rich tasting soup, without overly rich ingredients.

***Curried Pumpkin Soup***   After sautéeing the squash or pumpkin, stir in 2 to 3 teaspoons curry powder. Then proceed as above. The curry picks up and complements the pumpkin or squash flavor.

### *Out-of-This-World Pumpkin Pie*   (Makes one 9–10 inch pie.)

| | |
|---|---|
| 2 *cups puréed winter squash* | 1¼ *cups light cream, or evapo-* |
| ½ *cup honey, or ¾ cup brown sugar* | *rated milk* |
| 2 *tablespoons molasses* | 3 *eggs and 1 yolk, lightly beaten* |
| 1 *teaspoon cinnamon* | 1 *egg white, lightly beaten* |
| 1 *teaspoon ginger* | *single 9–10 inch pie shell* |
| ½ *teaspoon cloves* | 1 *nut topping recipe, below* |
| ½ *teaspoon nutmeg* | |
| ¼ *cup bourbon whiskey, rum, or* | |
| *brandy* | |

Mix the puréed squash, honey or sugar, molasses, spices, whiskey or other liquor, and the 3 eggs and yolk. Beat till smooth. Brush the bottom and sides of the pie shell with the egg white. Pour in the pie filling. Put in a hot, 450°F oven and bake 10 minutes. Then reduce heat to 325°F, and bake from 30 to 40 minutes more, till the pie has set. Make a small slit with a knife to test for firmness.

Let the pie cool completely, then add the following topping.

Nut Topping:

⅔ cup brown or grated maple sugar     ½ cup pecans, walnuts, hickory
3 tablespoons butter, melted             nuts, or butternuts, chopped
1 tablespoon heavy cream               nut halves, optional (For gar-
                                        nish.)

> **OTHER RECIPES
> FEATURING WINTER
> SQUASH OR PUMPKIN**
>
> Mix-a-Flavor Ice Cream, p.356
> Pumpkin Pudding, p.418
> Recipes, and Ideas for
>    Vegetables, p.669
> Squash Blossom Corn Cakes,
>    p.602
> Squash Blossom Soup, p.602
> Squash Blossoms Sautéed in
>    Batter, p.599
> Vegetable Hot Pot, p.669
> Winter Squash, Japanese Style,
>    p.624

Mix all topping ingredients, except nut halves. Spread the mixture on the cold pie. Arrange the nut halves on top. Put under a broiler, about 3 inches from the heat. Broil till the topping is bubbly and lightly browned, about 2 or 3 minutes. Watch closely because it will easily burn. (If the phone rings do not answer it!) Serve in small slices—it is very rich.

**Sweet Potato Pie**   Use mashed sweet potato instead of winter squash. Because sweet potato is sweeter than squash, reduce sweetening to ⅓ cup honey or ½ cup brown sugar. Spices are optional.

**Pumpkin Ice Cream**   Mix all the pie filling ingredients except the eggs, and freeze like other frozen desserts. (Refer to the ICE CREAM section.)

# STEAM COOKING

STEAMING IS HIGHLY RECOMMENDED AS A NUTRITIOUS WAY TO COOK foods, especially vegetables, but it is not always as highly esteemed for its flavorful results. The difficulty lies not with the method itself, but with its implementation. If steamed foods seem dull, flavorless, or unimaginative, then the potential of steam cooking has not been realized.

In some parts of the world, ovens are not common and steam cooking replaces baking as a basic way to prepare food. Steamed breads and puddings replace baked bread, and meat, poultry, and fish are steamed rather than roasted. The moist, tender goodness of foods perfectly cooked with steam need only be tried to be enjoyed.

**Steaming Under Pressure**   Though pressure cookers use steam for cooking, they function at such high temperatures that the gentleness of regular steam cooking is lost. These high temperatures are essential for canning low-acid foods, but otherwise, the main advantage of pressure cooking is speed. The flavor and texture of meats and most other foods are better with the use of conventional methods. (Refer to USING TOUGH MEAT, in the MEAT section.) Since most vegetables cook quickly, there is a tendency to overcook them in a pressure cooker, and in any case, little time is saved. A pressure cooker does make a good utensil for steaming vegetables when used with the vent open.

*Arrangements for steaming green vegetables, potatoes, root vegetables, and some kinds of meat and fish.*

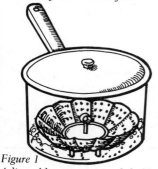

Figure 1
Adjustable steaming rack holds food above boiling water.

Colander set on tuna-sized can with both ends removed serves as steaming rack.

Figure 2
Large steamer, for steaming large quantities of vegetables for freezing or drying, and for steaming shellfish.

This section will deal with steam cooking without pressure. (However, when pressure is used it is important to carefully follow the manufacturer's instructions, especially those concerning safety.)

There are several different ways to use steam for cooking. Foods can be set on a rack directly over boiling water, or place in a dish or mold, and set on a stand in a pot with boiling water. Old time bag puddings are made by tying the pudding mixture in a cloth and either placing it in, or suspending it over, boiling water. Another way to use steam (which is not always known as steaming) is to cook foods, especially vegetables, with only a little water in a pot with a tight lid. The water turns to steam when heated, and the steam cooks the food.

## STEAM COOKING VEGETABLES

Vegetables retain more of their vitamins and minerals when steamed than when they are boiled, as boiling water leaches out most water soluble nutrients. Although the water in a steamer may collect some food value and flavor from the vegetables, it is not as valuable to save for soup and other cooking as the water from boiled vegetables. Both flavor and food value of most green and root vegetables are better when they are steamed rather than boiled—with a few exceptions. Such leafy greens as spinach mat down in a steamer and do not cook efficiently. (Refer to COOKING SPINACH, in the SPINACH section.) Green vegetables requiring a quick, high cooking heat may cook too slowly if the steamer is not hot enough, or if it is too crowded. Green beans, for instance, taste better cooked quickly in plenty of boiling water than they do cooked in most steamers. If steamed, they should be cooked in small batches over plenty of boiling water for quick, hot steam, in a steaming pot with a tight lid.

## STEAM COOKING PUDDINGS

"Puddings should be
Full of currants for me:
Boiled in a pail,
Tied in the tail
Of an old bleached shirt:
So hot that they hurt."

Richard Hughes, from *Poets, Painters, Puddings*

When electric and gas cookstoves moved into North American kitchens, steamed puddings, for the most part, moved out. It is neither practical nor pleasant to have big pots of water, with puddings in them, boiling on electric or gas ranges for hours and hours at a time. The return of wood stoves could bring back the steamed pudding, at least to some households. A pot of water is a necessity on a wood heating stove to increase humidity, so why not put a pudding in the pot!

Steamed puddings can range from rich, sweet desserts, to simple breads and main course meat dishes. In older cookbooks, the distinction between steamed, cereal type sausages and steamed puddings is very slight. Fruit mixtures might be steamed in sausage casings or tripe skins, and meat mixtures in fancy molds. Since all are cooked in the same way they are all puddings. The following directions apply equally to *Haggis* (in the LAMB AND MUTTON section) and CHRIST-MAS PLUM PUDDING, below.

Pudding mixtures can be packed in molds, tied in pudding cloths, or stuffed in such casings as an animal's cleaned stomach or large intestine.

***Steaming in Molds*** A mold is any closed container used to hold a pudding mixture while it steams. Its sides should be straight or flared for easy unmolding. Tin cans without grooves with aluminum foil or greased paper lids tightly tied in place make good molds. (See Figure 6, below.) There are also commercial molds for steaming, some of them with very decorative shapes. In England, crockery pudding basins are used with the approximate shape of a flower pot. The lid for a mold must be tight, and must extend over the edge of the mold to keep water from seeping in. When aluminum foil is tied on to make a lid, a string handle can be added for lifting the mold out of the steaming pot.

Butter or grease pudding molds, and fill them about ¾ full, to leave room for the pudding to expand. Seal them and put them on a rack in the steaming pot. Add boiling water up to about ⅔ of the mold. More water may make it float, or may boil up and under the lid. Add more boiling water as necessary while the pudding cooks. As the heat is gentle it will take hours for a pudding to cook, and overcooking is not really a possibility. Never open a pudding mold during cooking, as the pudding may fall, or water may get in. Pint sized puddings will cook in about 1 hour. Large puddings can take 4 hours or longer.

To unmold, take off the lid when the pudding is done and let sit a couple of minutes. Then run a knife around the edge and turn out on a plate. If the mold was a tin can, the bottom can be cut out with a can opener and the pudding pushed out.

***Steaming in Pudding Cloths or Bags*** Puddings tied in cloths can be set on racks over boiling water, or hung over the side of the pot; most often they are dropped right into the boiling water. When this is done they are also called "boiled puddings." (See Figure 7, below.)

A pudding cloth or bag must be made of strong, tightly woven cotton cloth. If washed with detergent rinse it separately to remove all traces. Prepare the cloth or bag for the pudding mixture by dipping it in boiling water, then lay it out in a large bowl and rub flour over it to help keep the pudding from sticking later on. The flour will become damp and make a sort of paste covering the cloth. After adding the pudding mixture, tie the bag securely, leaving some airspace for the pudding to expand. If cooking the pudding in boiling water, keep the water at a full boil, and at a level always high enough to cover the

*Arrangements for steaming fish and meat, Chinese style (see recipes listed at end of this section), or for reheating lefovers, especially cooked rice and other cooked grains.*

Figure 3
Bowl of food on rack in 1–2 inches boiling water.

Individual bowls of food set on canning rings or a rack in 1–2 inches boiling water.

Figure 4

Chinese tiered steamer, using a wok with bamboo racks, and a lid. Steams several foods at once to make a meal, with the food requiring longest, hottest cooking on the bottom tier.

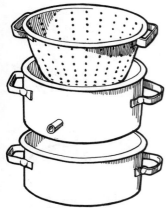

*Figure 5*
Steam juicer. (The original is the Finnish Mehu-Maija.) Fruits or vegetables go in the perforated section. A raised opening in the middle section lets in steam, which cooks the food, releasing the juice for collection from the spigot.

*Figure 6*
Tin can "molds" with aluminum foil lids tied in place. For steaming breads and puddings.

*Figure 7*
Bag pudding cooking in boiling water. For fruit puddings, breads, and meat and grain puddings.

pudding, or the pudding may become soggy. When taking the pudding out of the boiling water, dunk it in cold water to make the cloth easier to remove. The texture of the puddings will be like dumplings, damp, or slightly sticky on the outside and dry inside.

In the past steamed fruit puddings were often left in their bags after cooking, and hung in a cool place for several weeks or longer. They were reheated by returning them to boiling water—for at least an hour if the pudding was large. Some people used to make "hen and chicks" puddings. The hen was a large pudding which stayed in the boiling water several hours longer than the chicks, which were several small puddings. The chicks were for every day and the hen was saved for some special occasion.

## STEAM COOKING FOODS IN OPEN DISHES

For this Chinese steam cooking method, put fish, meat, vegetables or mixtures of these in uncovered dishes, and set them on a rack in boiling water. (See Figure 3, above.) The moisture that collects in them will make a flavorful sauce for the food, which is served in its steaming dish. It is best to use heat resistant dishes, but ordinary serving dishes will suffice if they are protected from sudden temperature changes. Warm them before putting them in the steamer, or put them in before the water in the steamer starts boiling. Start timing when the water can be heard boiling or when steam comes out around the lid. Never open the steaming pot during the cooking time. Tongs can be used to lift the dishes out of the steamer. (See OTHER STEAM COOKED RECIPES at the end of this section for examples of this steaming method.)

## STEAM COOKING CAUTIONS

• Pots used for steaming must have close fitting lids to hold in the steam. Do not lift the lid unnecessarily during the steaming because heat will be lost.

• Do not mistake a cloud of water vapor for steam. Vapor often rises from hot, but not boiling, water. Foods will not cook properly if the water is not heard or seen boiling. Start counting time only when the water is visibly boiling.

• When steam cooking foods for long periods of time, occasionally check the level of the water and add more boiling water as needed. Never add cold water because it will interrupt the cooking.

• Keep face and hands away from the steam that pours out when opening a steamer, and tilt the lid to direct the steam away from people. The steam will dissipate in a minute or so, when the food can be removed from the steamer. Tongs are handy for lifting out racks or containers of food.

## STEAM COOKING RECIPES

***Whole Grain Boston Brown Bread***

(Makes 1 large or several small breads.)

1 cup whole rye flour or meal
1 cup cornmeal
1 cup whole wheat flour
¾ teaspoon baking soda
½ teaspoon salt, optional

¾ cup molasses
2 cups sour milk, buttermilk, or
   1 cup sourdough and 1 cup
   sweet milk

Thoroughly mix the rye flour, cornmeal, whole wheat flour, baking soda, and salt. If the soda is lumpy it can be sifted with the flour. Add the molasses and sour milk, buttermilk, or sourdough mixture. Butter a large mold or several smaller molds. Smooth sided tin cans work well. Pour the batter into the mold or molds, filling them about ¾ full. Cover the tops tightly, then steam on a rack over boiling water. (See STEAMING IN MOLDS, above.) A large mold will take 2½ hours, and small molds 1½ hours. If tin cans were used for molds, slice the bread into neat, round slices.

This bread is traditional served with baked beans, but it is equally good with butter for breakfast, or with other vegetable dishes.

***Vermont Brown Bread***    Use ½ cup maple syrup instead of the molasses to make this bread. Raisins or other dried fruits can be included.

***Steamed Suet Pudding,***
***Plain or Fancy***

(Makes 1 large or several small puddings.)

Many suet pudding variations are possible, from very plain, to serve with a meal like bread, to a very fancy, rich dessert.

3 cups bread crumbs, or 1½ cups
   crumbs and 1½ cups whole grain
   flour
1 cup suet, ground or finely chopped
   (Beef fat or another hard fat.
   Refer to the LARD AND
   OTHER FATS section.)
½ cup molasses, honey, or other
   sweetening, optional
1–2 teaspoons spices, optional (Try
   cinnamon, cloves, nutmeg.)

2–6 eggs, separated (The more
   eggs, the richer the pudding.)
¾ cup (about) milk, sour milk,
   fruit juice, or juice from
   Spiced Pickled Fruit in the
   PICKLING section
1–4 cups dried fruit, chopped if
   necessary, optional
½–1 cup nuts, chopped, optional

Mix the bread crumbs or bread crumbs and flour with the suet. Add the sweetening and spices if either are used. Mix in the egg yolks, and enough milk or other liquid to make a medium thick batter. Less liquid is needed when more egg yolks are included. Mix in dried fruit and nuts if using them. Beat egg whites till stiff, and fold them in. Pour into 1 or more buttered molds, or use well floured pudding

---

**STEAM COOKING IDEAS**

**Fried Steamed Pudding**   One way to use leftover steamed pudding is to slice it and brown the slices on both sides in oil, lard, or butter. Surprisingly good for steamed fruit puddings, as well as for meat puddings, and a good, quick breakfast or lunch if the pudding is not too rich.

**Bedfordshire Clanger**   This idea originated among English working women long before such short cuts as frozen dinners were possible. The clanger would be put on to steam in the morning and served as both main course and dessert at dinner.

   Pastry or biscuit dough (using minced suet instead of lard or other shortening) is rolled out in a big rectangle. A strip of dough is cut from the long side and laid down the center, dividing the dough the long way. One half is spread with ground beef, minced onion, and seasonings. The other half is spread with jam or other preserves. The dough is dampened around the edges and rolled up, keeping the divider in place. The whole thing is then tied in a well floured pudding cloth and steamed in a pot of boiling water for several hours.

cloths. (See above.) Steam 4 hours or more for 1 large pudding, and 1½ to 2 hours for smaller ones. Serve the pudding warm, as the suet will not taste good cold. If desired, serve the pudding with one of the sauces listed below.

***Christmas Plum Pudding***   Make suet pudding using the larger amounts given for all optional ingredients. Use 6 eggs. Mix in several tablespoons of rum, brandy, or sherry before folding in the egg whites. The richest of all—keep the servings small!

### Sauces for Steamed Puddings

***Creamy Sauce***   Make ½ recipe of the *Smooth Milk Pudding* (in the MILK section), but use more milk, 2½ to 3 cups, for a thin consistency.

***Fruit Sauce***   Use apple sauce, or any puréed fruit. Puréed prunes thinned with orange juice are especially good.

***Jam, Jelly, or Marmalade Sauce***   Thin any sweet fruit preserves with very hot water to make sauce.

***Tutti Frutti Sauce***   Use the TUTTI FRUTTI idea in the PEACHES section as is, or mash the fruit for a saucier texture.

***Sour Cream Fruit Sauce***   Mix sweetened, strong flavored fruit juice with sour cream for a sweet, tangy sauce. Cherry, berry, or cranberry juice are all very good.

# STIR-FRYING

STIR-FRYING IS THE CHINESE WAY TO QUICKLY COOK ALL KINDS OF vegetables, meats, poultry, and fish. The foods are cut small (preparation takes considerably longer than cooking), then stirred over high heat in a minimum of fat or oil. The average cooking time for stir-fried dishes is only 5 minutes. Because of this quick cooking, foods retain fresh flavor, texture, color, and a high nutritional value.

Although stir-frying is a Chinese cooking method, vegetables stir-fried with plain seasonings go very well as side dishes with western style meals. There are in fact some western recipes, particularly from the Mediterranean area, that use the same principle as stir-frying. Thinly sliced meats or vegetables are sautéed quickly in very hot olive oil, seasoned, and served immediately.

Stir-frying is a valuable cooking technique for everyday use. It is a way to give familiar, sometimes boring, vegetables a new look and a new flavor. It is a way to stretch small amounts of meat with large amounts of vegetables to make nourishing family meals. It is also a very good way to ensure satisfied after dinner smiles all around the table.

All ingredients for stir-frying must be prepared and set out ready to use before cooking begins. Stir-frying is too quick to allow time for chopping last minute ingredients or hunting for last minute seasonings. One Chinese cookbook calls the procedure "blitz cooking." Usually, all ingredients for a particular stir-fried dish are cut in the same approximate size and shape. If the meat is in small, thin slices, the vegetables are also thinly sliced. If the meat is shredded, then so are the vegetables. Chinese stir-frying is done in a wok, but a large frying pan that holds heat well can be used instead.

***Stir-frying with a Wok***  The wok is a unique Chinese cooking pan. Ideal for stir-frying, it can also be used for steaming (Figure 4, in the STEAM COOKING section) and deep fat frying. Woks are shaped as if cut from a sphere. Their shallow, curved shape has many advantages. Less oil or fat is needed in stir-frying or deep frying than in western utensils. The curved sides of the wok transfer heat along with the bottom, creating a large, hot surface area, that cooks the foods faster. Foods are easily stirred and turned in the curved shape. Woks also fit nicely into the openings of old fashioned wood or coal burning cookstoves when a stove lid is removed. For use with gas or electric stoves, woks come with a metal ring to support them over the burner. Gas works better than electricity when cooking with a wok, because gas heat adjusts more quickly.

*Long-handled wok.*

The best woks are made from thin tempered iron. They must be seasoned and cared for like cast iron cookware. (Refer to the KITCHEN UTENSILS section.) Avoid stainless steel and aluminum woks because they do not heat as hot or as evenly. There are woks with one long handle which are easier to move around when hot than those with a small handle on each side. A large sized wok is most practical, since it can be used to cook both small and large amounts. Woks are sold in many stores carrying kitchen utensils. Lids and spatulas with a curved edge to fit the wok often go with them. Though a spatula is nice to have, it is not essential, and any large lid will work as well as a wok lid.

***Preparing Meat for Stir-frying***  Any reasonably tender meat will be good stir-fried. Pork and chicken are frequently used, but beef, other poultry, rabbit, fish, shellfish, and game meats can also be very good.

Thin slicing is the main chore when preparing the meat. A Chinese housewife can slice meat as thin as $1/16$ inch, but $1/8$ to $1/4$ inch slices are more realistic for the less experienced. A sharp knife is essential, and the slicing will be easier if the meat is partly frozen and firm. Always slice across the grain of the meat to prevent stringiness. Stir-fry no more than a pound of meat at one time, as too much meat cools the pan and slows the cooking.

Leftover cooked meat can be sliced or shredded and stir-fried. Add it after other ingredients and cook it just long enough to heat it.

***Preparing Vegetables for Stir-frying***  Most vegetables are very good stir-fried. Stir-fry slow cooking vegetables over high heat for a minute or two, then add a few tablespoons of liquid, cover and cook them for 3 to 5 minutes more. There are many different ways to cut vegetables depending on their size, shape, and texture, but thin slices are the most common. A vegetable slicer (refer to the KITCHEN UTENSILS section) can make slicing easier. When one part of a vegetable cooks more slowly than another, separate the parts. For instance, the stalks of Chinese cabbage are sliced separately to be cooked longer than the green, leafy parts.

It is best not to prepare vegetables too far ahead of time, because exposure to air after slicing causes loss of nutrients. If early preparation is necessary refrigerate them in the meantime.

***Fats and Oils for Stir-frying***  Lard or a good quality cooking oil is preferred for stir-frying. Peanut oil is often used. Lard rendered from a home raised pig is excellent. Home rendered fats such as chicken fat can also be used.

***Seasonings for Stir-fried Dishes***  Stir-fried dishes do not require particular or special seasonings. If served as part of a western style meal, pepper, herbs, and salt, if desired, do very well. The basic Chinese seasoning for stir-frying is soy sauce, but garlic, fresh ginger root, and dry sherry (as a substitute for Chinese rice wine) are all common. (Dry powdered ginger is not a good substitute for fresh ginger root, as the taste is quite different.)

Chinese recipes often call for both soy sauce and salt, but the salt should be omitted, because soy sauce is salty enough. Chinese stir-fried dishes are highly seasoned because they are eaten in relatively small amounts with a lot of (unsalted) rice. However, as westerners tend to eat more of the stir-fried dish and less rice, less seasoning will be needed in the stir-fry.

***Liquids and Thickeners for Stir-frying***  Several tablespoons to $1/2$ cup of liquid will be required for many stir-fried dishes. Though plain water can be used, soup stock or the soaking water from dried vegetables will add a better flavor. Soup stock (usually chicken stock) can be frozen in small containers or as ice cubes for use in stir-frying. Thaw and warm them before use, as cold liquids will slow down the cooking too much.

Cornstarch or another starch is often used to thicken the sauce around stir-fried foods. This thickening is optional, depending on personal preference, and on the wetness and type of ingredients in a particular dish. Arrowroot starch is preferred by some over cornstarch, as they consider it healthier. Homemade potato starch (see the POTATOES section) also works very well. Always mix the starch with water or another liquid before adding it. It can be mixed with soy sauce and other ingredients, or with water or stock and added last, just before the dish is served. But all the liquids and thickenings for a particular dish should be measured, mixed if necessary, and set out with other ingredients before cooking begins.

## BASIC STIR-FRYING STEPS

• Assemble and prepare all ingredients. If many different ones are included, arrange them in the order in which they will be added. Have in mind the procedures to be used. Long pauses to find ingredients or figure out the next step will lead to over-cooked foods. With practice the preparation will become second nature.

• Heat the wok or frying pan, add fat or oil, then heat it almost to smoking before adding anything else. If the pan is not hot enough foods may stick. Perfection depends on high heat.

• Add an ingredient and stir or toss it constantly, so that the heat sears the pieces on all sides, especially the cut edges. This step seals in juice and flavor. Minced garlic and ginger roots can be added first and stirred for a second or two, followed by a meat or vegetable.

• If an ingredient is to be stir-fried briefly and taken out of the wok or frying pan while another is added, have a dish ready to hold it. The serving dish can be used for this.

• When adding liquids, pour them in around the sides of the pan or clean a place in the center to pour them. They will heat faster if they contact the pan before the food. If the pan is to be covered, do it quickly after the liquid is added so that it does not steam away. Reduce the heat to medium while the pan is covered.

• Ideally, each ingredient in a stir-fry is cooked for the exact time it needs. The pace can be hectic when a real effort is made to do this, especially when learning. Eventually, though, a free-wheeling style develops that makes stir-frying fun and an invigorating way to cook. Fortunately, stir-fried foods almost always taste good, whether this ideal is met or not.

• To enjoy it at its best, everyone should be ready to eat as soon as the stir-fry is done. (A Chinese proverb says it is better for the diners to wait for the dish, than for the dish to wait for the diners.)

---

**STIR-FRYING
RECIPES**

*Note:* The suggested numbers of servings given with these recipes are for western style meals. If served Chinese style, the estimates can be raised because more rice will be eaten, and usually, more dishes of various kinds will be prepared.

THE HEADY FRAGRANCE OF A PATCH OF RIPE STRAWBERRIES ON A HOT summer afternoon is unforgettable. It lingers with every strawberry put by for winter, whether domestic or wild. The large, sweet strawberries cultivated in the garden are superb, and the tiny, intense strawberries gathered from their wild hiding places are superlative. Always for strawberries the larger question is not how to use them, but how to get enough of them.

## HANDLING STRAWBERRIES

Strawberries must be completely ripe when picked. Gather them on a dry day, and handle them gently, without squeezing or pinching. If carefully picked from a clean patch they can be used without washing. If they must be rinsed, do it just before they are hulled and used. Do not allow them to be hit with the full force of the water from the kitchen faucet, but dunk them in a pan of water, or pour water gently over them.

As strawberries keep best with hulls on, use them within a day if they are hulled as they are picked. Wild strawberries are easiest to hull as they are picked, and it is tedious in the extreme to go through the tiny berries later, hulling each one. If berries must be rinsed after hulling, do it quickly. Wild strawberries can be eaten without hulling, but they will have a scratchy texture. There is no need to hull strawberries when making juice or purée, as the hulls can be strained out.

## STRAWBERRY RECIPES

### Not-So-Rich
### Strawberry Shortcake
(Makes about 6 dessert servings.)

1 quart strawberries
½ cup maple syrup, honey, or another sweetener
1 recipe biscuit dough (Try the Whipped Cream Biscuits recipe in the CREAM section.)

1–2 teaspoons grated orange peel, optional
2 cups (about) yogurt

Slice the strawberries, then let them soak in the sweetener for an hour or more. (Warm stiff honey enough to liquify it.) A few perfect strawberries can be reserved for decoration.

Mix the biscuit dough and, if desired, add grated orange peel to the flour. Divide the dough in half, then roll out into two circles about 9 inches in diameter. Put one circle on top of the other for easy separation later on, then bake like biscuits till lightly browned. When done, separate the layers and use either warm or cool.

To assemble, place the bottom shortcake layer on a serving platter. Pour half of the sweetened strawberries and juice over it. Cover with yogurt, then put on the top shortcake layer. Slowly pour on the rest of the strawberries, letting the juice soak in. (If desired, the shortcake layer can be placed soft side up to hold juice.) Top with yogurt and any berries saved for decoration. Best when eaten as soon as it is put together.

### *Strawberry Butter*                                (Makes about 1 cup.)

½ cup strawberries, trimmed, fresh
   or frozen
½ cup butter

2 tablespoons honey, optional
   (Omit if berries are pre-
   sweetened.)

Put ingredients in a blender and blend till smooth, which will take several minutes. The delicate pink color and fresh flavor make this a very special spread for waffles, pancakes, or toast, or try a dollop on warm baked or steamed desserts.

## STRAWBERRY IDEAS

*Strawberry Juice*   Canned strawberry juice is an unbelievably precious luxury in winter. Damaged or misshapen strawberries are excellent for making juice—an excellent alternative to the usual highly sugared preserves. Strawberry juice makes very special gelatines and sherbets as well as fruit drinks.

*Strawberry Salad*   Arrange whole or halved strawberries on a bed of lettuce. For a dressing mix ¼ cup crushed strawberries, 1 tablespoon honey, and a cup of mayonnaise. The *Yogurt Fruit Salad Dressing,* in the YOGURT section, is also very good.

*Strawberries with Dips*   For a simple but elegant dessert or snack, serve whole, unhulled strawberries with a dip. Plain thick cream, yogurt, or the salad dressings immediately above are all very good. The strawberries are held by the hull, dipped, and eaten.

*Rescuing Bland or Dry Strawberries*   Strawberries that are too bland or dry (Not likely when home grown!) are greatly improved with a sprinkle of lemon juice or mild wine vinegar. These bring out flavor and add juiciness.

*Marinated Strawberries*   Strawberries combine pleasurably with many different alcoholic beverages. In Italy they are marinated in Marsala, or any red or white wine; in Mexico in Tequila; and in England they are traditional with claret. Sherry, champagne, and orange liqueurs are other favorites. The strawberries can be left whole or sliced, and can be marinated for just a few minutes or chilled in the liquor for several hours before they are served.

**OTHER RECIPES
WITH STRAWBERRIES**

# SUNFLOWERS

**STORAGE**

*Note:* With shells, store like grain. (Refer to STORING GRAIN in GRAINS section.)

**Cold Storage**  *Shelled seeds* Keep in closed container in refrigerator, or other cool place. Quality retained for mos. *Home pressed oil* Keeps 2–3 mos. refrigerated.

**Freezing**  *Shelled seeds* Quality retained 1 yr. or longer.

SUNFLOWERS ARE NATIVE TO NORTH AND SOUTH AMERICA AND HAVE always been appreciated by American Indians. The seeds are valued for their versatile nut-like meats and for the high quality oil that can be pressed from them. But though they are the most important part of the plant, all parts can be used: the sprouts or seedlings in salads, the buds as a cooked vegetable, the roasted shells steeped for a beverage, the leaves for livestock feed, the petals for dye, and the fibers in the stalks for making cords and ropes like those from hemp.

Sunflowers grow well in gardens everywhere. They are cultivated like corn, but they can be grown successfully farther north. They make a practical homesteader's crop once the problem of shelling the seeds has been solved. They are also the only cool climate crop suitable for pressing on a small scale to make vegetable oil.

## HANDLING SUNFLOWERS

It is best to harvest sunflower seed heads after the seeds are fully formed but before they are mature and completely dry. Too many things are likely to happen to seeds left on the plant. Birds may take an unfair share, or worms may get into them, or they may fall to the ground and be lost. As there is a lot of moisture in the seed heads when they are harvested early, they must be hung or spread out in a dry place. Do not stack or leave them in a damp place, or they will mold. If there are signs of worms, remove the seeds from the heads as soon as they are harvested, and dry them immediately in a food dryer or oven at its lowest setting, 150–200°F. If worm free, the seeds can be removed at any time after the heads are dry.

For a few sunflower heads, the seeds can be rubbed off by hand. Wear gloves to protect fingers, or use a stiff brush or similar tool. When there are many, rub the heads on ½ inch mesh hardware cloth laid over a box or wheelbarrow. Some use a wire brush attached to an electric motor to remove seeds. Bits of debris can be winnowed out (refer to the SEEDS section), or they can be removed later, with the shells.

## SHELLING SUNFLOWER SEEDS

For snacking, sunflower seeds can be shelled one by one. Some people are good at holding them on end between their teeth, cracking them, and spitting out the shells. For shelling larger quantities some ingenuity is required. (Hopefully someone will eventually market a handy shelling device for small scale use.) One way is to sort them according to size and then put them through a grain mill or grinder adjusted to crack the shells without crushing the meats. The seeds can be sorted for size by shaking them on ¼ inch mesh hardware cloth so that small seeds fall through. These seeds can be further sorted by putting two layers of ¼ inch hardware cloth together, but slightly offset to make smaller holes. To crack the shells a grain mill must be adjusted so that the space between the plates is just slightly smaller than the size of the seeds. Some mills adjust more easily than others so it is necessary to experiment. For some sizes of seeds, a meat chopper with the coarsest chopping plate might work. This system will only work if the sunflower seeds are thoroughly dry, so that the shells crack easily.

Small farm hammermills for grinding livestock feed have been used with screens removed to shell sunflower seeds. It is also possible that local feed mills might be willing to shell moderate amounts.

Once the shells are cracked they can be removed by winnowing, or by floating them off with water. Shelled sunflower seeds do not winnow as easily as most grains and seeds, because the seeds and shells are too close in weight; if the breeze is not just right the seeds will blow away with the shells. To float off the shells, put seeds and shells in a large container and fill with water. Stir to loosen any seeds stuck to shells and then let sit about 5 minutes till the seeds settle. Pour off the shells and drain the seeds. If necessary, repeat the procedure. Then spread out the seeds to dry completely before storing them. Shells from sunflower seeds can be roasted for a beverage. (Refer to ROASTING ROOTS, GRAINS, AND SEEDS FOR BEVERAGES in the BEVERAGES section.)

## PRESSING SUNFLOWER SEEDS FOR OIL

Oil seed sunflowers yield considerably more oil than the eating varieties, but both can be pressed. Oil varieties can be ground, shells and all, in a meat grinder or other grinder, and then pressed. Eating varieties must be shelled first and then ground. Though a fruit or lard press will remove some oil, a heavier press is necessary to obtain oil in practical quantities and to avoid waste. If a small press is used, try cooking the leftover material to recover more oil and perhaps milk and flour as well. (Refer to COOKING NUTS FOR OIL, MILK AND FLOUR, in the NUTS section.) Perhaps it will eventually be possible to buy the necessary equipment for small scale pressing.

Home pressed oil must be refrigerated for storage.

## SUNFLOWER SEED IDEAS

**Sunflower Seeds Instead of Nuts**   Use sunflower seeds in recipes instead of nuts. Since the seeds are small they can replace coarsely chopped nuts without any chopping. As sunflower seeds go further than most kinds of nuts less will be needed. When recipes call for ½ cup nuts, use 4 to 6 tablespoons sunflower seeds. For a nuttier taste, roast sunflower seeds for about 15 minutes in a moderate, 350°F oven, or shake them for 5 to 10 minutes in a hot, dry frying pan till lightly browned.

**Snack Mixes**   Mix sunflower seeds with raisins and other dried fruits, nuts, and coconut for snacking. When sunflower seeds and peanuts are combined, the protein value is especially high.

**Sunflower Seed Meal**   Grind sunflower seeds to a meal with a blender or food chopper. (They are too oily for a grain mill.) Use in place of about ¼ of the flour in baked goods, or add to vegetable loaves, patties, and stews. The meal enriches baked goods, and thickens stews without overwhelming other ingredients' flavors.

**Sunflower Peanut Butter**   When making peanut butter, use 1 part sunflower seeds (roasted, if desired) to 3 parts peanuts. (Refer to ROASTING PEANUTS and MAKING PEANUT BUTTER, in the PEANUTS section.) The blend makes a pleasant change from plain peanut butter, and the protein value is increased.

## OTHER RECIPES FEATURING SUNFLOWERS OR SUNFLOWER SEEDS

# SUNFLOWER SEED RECIPES

### Sunflower Seed Broth                    (Makes 5–6 medium bowls.)

| | |
|---|---|
| 1½ cups shelled sunflower seeds | pepper, salt, optional |
| 1 onion, chopped | chives, scallions, or dill leaves, |
| 1 quart light soup stock | minced |

Combine the sunflower seeds, onion, and soup stock in a saucepan, and simmer covered for 45 minutes. Season to taste, and serve with chives, scallions, or dill sprinkled on each bowlful. Few will guess that sunflower seeds are the main ingredient, but everyone will enjoy the full, almost creamy flavor.

### Sunflower Seed Cakes                    (Makes 18–24 small cakes.)

| | |
|---|---|
| 3 cups shelled sunflower seeds | 6 tablespoons (about) flour, or fine cornmeal |
| 2 teaspoons honey, or maple syrup | 2–4 tablespoons oil, for frying |

Put the seeds in a heavy saucepan with 3 cups of water, then simmer covered over low heat for 1 hour. If water remains, cook further, uncovered, to evaporate it. Grind the seeds, or press them through a food mill. Mix in the honey, or maple syrup, and work in flour or cornmeal, a spoon at a time, for a stiff dough. Shape into thin, about 3 inch diameter cakes, and brown in oil on both sides. Very good with plain apple or apricot sauce for breakfast. Or sweeten the sauce, add powdered coriander seed or other spices, and have them for dessert.

**Sunflower Seed Crackers**   Add 1 tablespoon of oil to the dough, along with the honey or syrup. Roll out thinly on a floured board, and cut into square or rectangular crackers. Bake 10–15 minutes on an oiled baking sheet, in a hot, 375°F oven till lightly browned. If the crackers are not crisp, dry them in a very low oven or food dryer till they are.

### Sunflower Dinner Loaf                    (Makes about 6 dinner servings.)

| | |
|---|---|
| ½ cup sunflower seeds | 2 eggs, lightly beaten |
| ¾ cup sunflower seed meal (Ground in food chopper or blender.) | ½ teaspoon paprika, or pepper |
| ½ cup fine bread crumbs | parsley, minced, and fresh or dried savory or thyme, to taste |
| 1 cup mashed potatoes, mashed cooked beans, or cooked rice | 1 tablespoon lemon juice or vinegar |
| 1 small onion or leek, minced | salt, optional |
| 1 cup celery, carrot, or green pepper, grated or minced, optional | ¼ cup (about) vegetable cooking water, optional |

Mix all ingredients thoroughly. If dry, add vegetable cooking water or plain water to moisten. Press into a greased loaf pan, then bake 45 minutes in a moderate 350°F oven.

Very tasty served with tomato sauce, or a homemade relish or chutney.

### REFERENCES FOR SUNFLOWERS

Organic Gardening Magazine, April 1979.

**OTHER RECIPES WITH SUNFLOWERS,** *cont.*

Sunflower Mustard Butter, p. 428
Sunflower Seeds or Meal (in hot cereals), p. 126

# SWEETBREADS

SWEETBREADS HAVE AN AURA OF MYSTERY ABOUT THEM. THEIR name gives no clue to their identity, and their reputation as a gourmet food is not revealing. They are glandular meats which have, when carefully cooked, a mild flavor and delicate texture. Several different glands are known as sweetbreads when used for food. The thymus and pancreas are the most often eaten but the salivary and lymphatic glands are sometimes included. All are cooked in the same ways and taste very similar. The thymus, known as the neck or throat sweetbread because of its location, is largest in young animals and most often comes from veal or lamb. The pancreas, located near the stomach, is known as the heart or stomach sweetbread. Though heart sweetbreads from veal and lamb are usually preferred, they can be taken from mutton, beef, venison, pork, and other large animals. Because sweetbreads from mature animals are not as delicate as those from young animals, they are often combined with other variety meats in meat loaves, patés, and hash type mixtures. As sweetbreads and brains are cooked in much the same ways, they can be interchanged in most recipes, but there are differences in flavor and texture. (Refer to the BRAINS section.)

### HANDLING SWEETBREADS

It is important to use sweetbreads while they are very fresh, as they spoil easily. If they cannot be eaten within 2 or 3 days of butchering they should be frozen. Wash sweetbreads in cold water as soon as they are taken from the animal's carcass. If they contain traces of blood, soak them in slightly salted water for an hour. Rinse, drain, and refrigerate. Sweetbreads are usually precooked to make them firm enough to handle.

*Precooking Sweetbreads*   After washing, put the sweetbreads in a saucepan and cover them with cold soup stock or water. Soup stock is best because the sweetbreads will contribute their flavor, which might otherwise be lost. Slowly heat the sweetbreads and liquid to a boil, then simmer without boiling till the sweetbreads are firm and white throughout. Cooking time will vary with the size of the sweetbreads.

**STORAGE**

**Freezing**   Handle like meat. (Refer to FREEZING section.) Quality retained about 4 mos.

Those from a small lamb will be done almost as soon as they reach a boil. Veal or other large sweetbreads will need about 20 minutes of simmering. When done, take out the sweetbreads and put them to chill in cold water for several minutes. Drain well, and trim off tubes, cartilage, and tough membranes. Leave the thin membranes that hold small sections together. At this stage the sweetbreads can be used in recipes that call for small pieces or chopped sweetbreads. When they are to be used whole or in thick slices, they are usually pressed. For pressing put them between two plates or small boards with several pounds of weight on top, then leave them in a cold place for several hours or overnight.

## SWEETBREAD RECIPES

### Italian Style Sweetbreads

(Makes about 6 appetizer or first course servings.)

| | |
|---|---|
| 1 pound sweetbreads, precooked and pressed (See above.) | 3 tablespoons ham, minced (Prosciutto is best.) |
| ¼ cup butter | 2 tablespoons sherry, or Marsala |
| 6 fresh sage leaves, or 1 teaspoon dried | |

Leave the sweetbreads whole, or cut them in thick slices. Heat the butter in a frying pan, then add the sweetbreads and sage. Turn the sweetbreads often, using moderate heat, till browned on all sides. Add the ham and cook 2 minutes, turning ingredients several times. Then add the sherry, or Marsala, and cook another 2 minutes, turning to flavor the sweetbreads on all sides. Serve immediately. They are delicious on toast or on bread fried in butter.

### Sweetbread Loaf

(Makes 6 dinner servings.)

| | |
|---|---|
| 1 pound sweetbreads, precooked, chopped | ¼ teaspoon pepper |
| 2 slices bread, soaked in water or milk, squeezed | Sauce for Loaf: |
| | 3 tablespoons butter |
| 3 eggs, separated | 3 tablespoons flour |
| 2 tablespoons butter, softened or melted | 2 cups sweetbread stock, from precooking |
| 1 tablespoon parsley, minced | pepper, salt, optional |
| ¼ teaspoon mace, or nutmeg | parsley or chervil, minced, optional (For garnish.) |

Mix the sweetbreads, soaked bread, egg yolks, butter, parsley, mace or nutmeg, and pepper. Beat the egg whites till stiff, then fold them in. Butter a baking dish and pour in the mixture. Set in a pan of water and bake in a moderate, 350°F oven, for 30 minutes, or till the loaf is set.

Meanwhile make the sauce. In a saucepan melt the butter and mix in the flour. Gradually add the stock, and stir till it thickens. Season with pepper and salt, if desired, and simmer about 5 minutes. Serve alongside the loaf or turn out the loaf on a platter, pour the sauce over it, and sprinkle with parsley or chervil.

# SWEET POTATOES

SWEET POTATOES ARE GOOD ANYTIME—WITH MEALS AND IN BE-tween. Their high nutritional value and sweetness make them an ideal snack food that provides staying power. A cold, cooked sweet potato carried in a spare pocket can mean energy for another few hours of work. Sweet potatoes, native to Central and South America, once were the basic life sustaining food for groups of American Indians. However, their worth is lost when they are candied in sugary syrups. It is hard to understand the compulsion to add quantities of sugar to a food that is naturally very sweet, especially when there are numerous and delicious ways to fix it.

Sweet potatoes grow as perennials in tropical climates, but they are easily cultivated as annuals in temperate regions with fairly long growing seasons. Sweet potato flesh ranges from creamy white and orange to a purplish color. Moist, orange fleshed sweet potatoes are often known as yams. True yams, however, are an entirely different tropical plant requiring a full 12 month growing season, and are seldom seen outside the tropics. Sweet potatoes are not related to white potatoes.

## HANDLING SWEET POTATOES

Sweet potatoes can be dug at any time after they are big enough to eat, but their main harvest is in the fall. In the South they are dug when the leaves turn yellow, while further north they are dug at about the time of the first frost. They will deteriorate if left in the ground after it turns cold. Sweet potatoes must be dug carefully, because the skins are tender and likely to rot if damaged. Before they are stored, sweet potatoes must be cured to toughen the skins and heal slight scrapes.

*Curing and Storing Sweet Potatoes* Sweet potatoes are cured by holding them between 80 and 85°F, and between 85 and 90% humidity, for 4 to 7 days. If cured longer than 7 days they will start to shrivel. Any warm place can be used for curing if they are loosely covered with plastic or another material to maintain humidity. After curing, store them where the temperature is between 55 and 60°F, with high humidity. If the temperature is too low the sweet potatoes

---

**STORAGE**

**Canning** Steam, or boil to half-cooked, about 20 min. Dunk in cold water, peel. If large, cut uniform pieces.

**Dry Pack** While hot, press close together in jars without mashing, 1 in. headroom. Add nothing. Process, 240°F, 11 pounds pressure. Pints: 1 hr. 5 min. Quarts: 1 hr. 35 min.

**Wet Pack** Fill jars without pressing, add boiling water, 1 in. headroom. Process 240°F, 11 pounds pressure. Pints: 55 min. Quarts: 1 hr. 35 min. (Refer to CANNING section.)

**Cold Storage** See CURING AND STORING SWEET POTATOES, below.

**Drying** Steam till cooked, 30–40 min. Peel, slice or shred, and dry till leathery, or brittle. Or slice raw, dry till hard, and grind to flour. (Refer to DRYING section.)

**Freezing** Cure (see below). Steam, boil, or bake till tender. Let cool at room temperature. Wrap individually, or peel, slice as desired, and pack. Or mash (optional), add 1 tablespoon lemon or orange juice per pint to prevent darkening. (Refer to FREEZING section.)

2–3 POUNDS FRESH = 1 QUART COOKED

## SWEET POTATO IDEAS

**Sweet Potatoes Ahead**  As there are so many ways to use cooked sweet potatoes, cook some extra when baking or steaming them for a meal. The extras can then be sliced or mashed for everything from salads to desserts. (See below.) Use mashed sweet potato in recipes for puréed pumpkin, and use sliced, cooked sweet potatoes for frying or scalloping like white potatoes.

**Broiled Sweet Potatoes**  This is a quick and delicious way to use whole, cooked sweet potatoes. Cut them in half the long way and make several shallow slashes on the cut side. Brush with butter or oil and season with pepper and salt, if desired. Put under a broiler for about 10 minutes, long enough to heat and slightly brown them.

**Sweet Potato Salads**  Dice or slice cooked sweet potatoes to use in vegetable or fruit salads. Make an old fashioned salad by mixing sliced, sweet potatoes with thinly sliced onion. For a dressing, make the *Old Fashioned Coleslaw Dressing* (in the CABBAGE section), omitting the sweetener. Pour it over the sweet potato and onion while it is hot. This salad is very good both warm and cool.

For a fruit salad, combine diced, cooked sweet potato, diced oranges, and chopped celery and green pepper. A half mayonnaise and half yogurt mixture makes a good dressing, or use any favorite dressing. If desired, include nuts and assorted chopped fruits.

**Sweet Potato Chips**  Slice raw sweet potatoes very thinly. Peeling is unnecessary. Soak in ice water for 15 minutes, drain thoroughly, and fry in deep, hot fat till lightly browned and crisp.

**Sweet Potato Desserts**
These potatoes' sweetness makes them ideal for naturally sweet desserts. Arrange cooked, sliced sweet potatoes in a shallow bak-

will blacken and rot. A basement or spare room may be a good storage place. The sweet potatoes can be loosely covered to increase humidity, but they need circulating air and should not be sealed in.

Sweet potatoes will become sweeter during storage as their starch gradually turns to sugar. If well cured and carefully stored, they may keep as long as 6 months, though 3 to 4 months is more common.

***Preparing Sweet Potatoes***  Raw sweet potatoes should never be peeled, as too many nutrients will be lost. The skins are thin and good to eat, so peeling is unnecessary. However, if desired, the peels can easily be removed after the sweet potatoes are cooked.

For slightly firm sweet potatoes, steam or bake them from 30 to 45 minutes, depending on size. With longer cooking they will become very soft and easy to mash.

Sweet potato tops can be cooked like spinach and eaten as greens.

## SWEET POTATO RECIPES

### Sweet Potatoes, Japanese Style                    (Makes 6–8 snack or small side servings.)

| | |
|---|---|
| *3–4 medium sweet potatoes, in 1 inch chunks* | *2 teaspoons soy sauce* |
| *1 cup (about) soup stock, or water* | *2 tablespoons sherry, or white wine* |
| *1 tablespoon honey* | |

Cook the sweet potato chunks in the soup stock or water till they are barely tender, about 10 minutes. Add honey, soy sauce, and sherry or white wine. Simmer, uncovered, till the liquid is reduced to a syrup and the sweet potatoes are soft, another 15 to 20 minutes. Taste and adjust seasonings, if necessary. An excellent snack and pick-me-up eaten warm or cold. Or serve them for dinner with rice and other Japanese or Chinese dishes.

***Winter Squash, Japanese Style***  Use a Japanese squash variety instead of sweet potatoes. This squash is thin skinned, and can be cut into cubes without peeling. The skins add a pleasant flavor to the dish.

### Sweet Potato Nests for Green Vegetables  (Makes 6 side servings.)

| | |
|---|---|
| *2–3 pounds sweet potatoes* | *3 cups (about) green beans, Brussels sprouts, peas, or another green vegetable* |
| *1 egg, beaten* | |
| *pepper, salt, optional* | *2 tablespoons butter, melted* |
| | *¼ cup nuts, chopped to taste* |

Steam or bake the sweet potatoes, then, while still hot, peel and mash them. Mix in the egg, and pepper, and salt, if desired, and spoon the still warm mixture into 6 nest-like shapes on an ungreased baking sheet.

Meanwhile, cook the green vegetable till just tender. Fill the nests with the vegetable, drizzle over each nest a teaspoon of butter and a sprinkling of nuts. Bake from 10 to 15 minutes in a moderate, 350°F oven. To serve, lift the nest with a pancake turner.

Using Brussels sprouts in the nest will give an amusing eggs in nest appearance.

### *Arkansas Spoon Bread*                    (Makes about 6 side servings.)

| | |
|---|---|
| 4 eggs, beaten slightly | 1 teaspoon lemon peel, grated |
| ¼ cup honey | 1 cup milk |
| ¼ cup oil | 1 teaspoon orange peel, grated |
| 4 – 5 cups sweet potato, grated raw with peel | ½ teaspoon nutmeg |

Combine eggs, honey, and oil. Mix in the grated sweet potato, milk, lemon and orange rind and nutmeg. Pour into a well oiled baking dish and bake at 325°F for 1 hour or till set.

Serve warm or cold with ham or chicken, or save for dessert.

---

## SWISS CHARD

---

SWISS CHARD IS A GARDENER'S DELIGHT. IT IS ONE OF THE FEW leafy greens that grows well over a long season, through both hot and cold weather. It seldom goes to seed, and no matter how often it is cut, it will soon grow a new set of leaves. One small planting of Swiss chard is enough to keep a family in greens for the entire gardening season. The catch may be that the cook is not as delighted with this constant supply as the gardener. When Swiss chard is merely cooked like any other green, the other greens are often preferred. The best recourse, then, is finding ways to make Swiss chard taste as good or better than other greens.

As Swiss chard has more body and does not cook down as much as most greens, it will hold its own better in mixed dishes. It is excellent combined with beans, grains, or meats. The thick stalks have a celery-like texture and are good prepared separately, while the leafy parts are very good in salads and other mixtures.

Swiss chard, also known simply as chard, is closely related to the beet, and rhubarb chard, a red stalked variety, looks very beet-like. Cooked beet greens and Swiss chard cooked without its stalks are virtually indistinguishable, and are interchangeable in recipes.

### SWEET POTATO IDEAS, *cont.*

ing dish with canned fruit and its juice. Sprinkle spices, bread crumbs, and dots of butter on top and bake for a few minutes in a hot oven. Crushed pineapple or sliced peaches are very good in this dessert. Puddings can be made from puréed sweet potato mixed with dried fruits and nuts. If the mixture is stiff, puréed fruit, fruit juice, or whipped cream can be mixed in. Add such spices as ginger, cinnamon, or nutmeg. If eggs and milk are included the mixture can be baked like a custard. Imagination and improvisation are the most important ingredients.

### OTHER RECIPES WITH SWEET POTATOES

Sweet Potato Pie, p.607
Wild Meat Baked with Sweet Potatoes, p.693

### STORAGE

*Note:* Often grown for a continual supply of fresh greens, rather than stored.

To store, handle like spinach. (Refer to SPINACH section.)

# HANDLING SWISS CHARD

Cut the outer leaves of growing Swiss chard without damaging the small inner leaves. Leaves can be harvested about once a week from an established plant, and it is best to harvest often to prevent the leaves from becoming coarse and overgrown. Chard's thick stalks and midribs take a little longer to cook than the green parts. When steaming or stewing, slice the stalks and put them in the bottom of the pot with green parts on top to give the stalks a little extra cooking time.

# SWISS CHARD RECIPES

### Swiss Chard with Potatoes and Garbanzo Beans
(Makes about 6 side servings.)

3 tablespoons lard, oil, or other fat
1 onion, minced
1 clove garlic, optional
½ teaspoon hot red pepper flakes, or to taste
1 cup tomato sauce, or 1 ½ cups fresh tomatoes, chopped

salt, optional
1 ½ pounds Swiss chard, cooked and chopped
2 − 3 medium potatoes, cooked, cut in cubes
1 ½ cups cooked garbanzo beans (Or chick peas.)
grated cheese, optional

Heat the lard or oil in a large frying pan, then sauté the onion and garlic in it till the onion is limp. Discard the garlic. Add the red pepper, tomato, and salt, if desired, and simmer, uncovered, for about 30 minutes, or till the sauce is somewhat thickened. Add the Swiss chard, potatoes, and garbanzo beans, and cook till they are all heated through, stirring often. Serve with grated cheese to sprinkle on top, if desired.

### Swiss Chard with Potatoes and Corn, or Black-eyed Peas, or Other Beans
Instead of garbanzo beans use cooked whole kernel corn, cooked black-eyed peas, or another kind of beans.

### Chard with Lentils and Lemon
(Makes about 6 medium bowls.)

2 cups cooked lentils
2 pounds Swiss chard leaves, chopped medium, stalks removed (See CHARD STALKS WITH SAUCE, below.)
1 medium onion, chopped medium
3 tablespoons oil

4 cloves garlic, crushed
½ teaspoon salt, optional
1 tablespoon fresh coriander leaves, or celery leaves, minced
½ cup lemon juice, or to taste
1 teaspoon flour

Heat the lentils, adding a little water if they are very thick. Stir in the chard greens, and simmer for 5 to 10 minutes.

In another pan sauté the onion in the oil till limp. Crush the garlic with the salt, if using it. (It can be crushed against the side of a cup with the back of a spoon.) Stir into the onion, then add to the lentils

---

## SWISS CHARD IDEAS

**Stir-fried Swiss Chard**  Separate the stalks and thick midribs from the leafy greens, and cut them diagonally into about 1 inch pieces. Cut the greens into larger, irregular pieces. Heat oil or fat, then stir-fry the stalks for about 1 minute. Add several tablespoons of water or soup stock, cover and let cook over medium heat about 5 minutes. Increase heat to high, uncover, and add the greens. Stir-fry about 2 minutes. Minced garlic and fresh ginger root can be included, if desired.

Swiss chard is good stir-fried in mixtures if the stalks and green parts are added separately. Meat goes especially well with it. (Refer to the STIR-FRYING section.)

**Swiss Chard Greens in Salads**  Tear or cut off the green parts of Swiss chard leaves to use in salads. (The greens taste better raw than the stalks.) A strongly flavored dressing is best, perhaps the *Pre-mixed Oil and Lemon or Vinegar Dressing*, in the SALADS section, with catsup or orange juice concentrate included.

and chard, along with the coriander or celery leaves. Mix the flour with the lemon juice and stir them in. Simmer another 5 minutes. Nice for lunch or supper served in individual bowls, like chili.

### Swiss Chard, Italian Style

(Makes about 6 side servings.)

1 large bunch Swiss chard
¼ cup oil (Preferably olive.)
2 medium onions, thinly sliced
2 cloves garlic, minced
2 tablespoons parsley, minced
¼ pound (about 1 cup) mushrooms,
    thinly sliced

3 – 4 eggs, beaten
½ teaspoon pepper
3 tablespoons grated Parmesan
    cheese
½ cup fine bread crumbs

Cut the stalks and thick midribs of the chard away from the leafy greens. Chop the greens, bite sized, and set them aside. Cut the stalks and midribs crosswise into shreds.

Heat the oil in a large frying pan, and gently sauté the shredded stalk and onions in it. When the onions are limp, add the parsley, garlic, and mushrooms, and sauté 2 or 3 minutes. Add the chopped chard greens and cook, stirring, about 5 minutes, till the greens are wilted. Remove from pan and let cool.

Combine the Swiss chard mixture with the eggs, pepper, and cheese. Oil a shallow baking dish, and sprinkle with half of the bread crumbs. Spread the Swiss chard and eggs mixture in the dish, then sprinkle the rest of the crumbs on top. Bake in a 375°F oven for about 20 minutes, till set. Let cool a few minutes before serving. Elegant and delicious warm or cold.

*Sautéed Chard*    Prepare and sauté chard, onions, garlic, and parsley, as above, and serve as the dinner vegetable. (Mushrooms are optional.)

---

**SWISS CHARD IDEAS,** *cont.*

**Chard Stalks with Sauce**   Cut Swiss chard stalks in pieces and steam them till tender, from 5 to 10 minutes. Serve with the *Cream Sauce*, in the MILK section, or mix with the EGGPLANT DIP, in the EGGPLANT section. They are also good with sauces made from Tahini (sesame butter, refer to SESAME SEEDS, in the SEEDS section).

---

**OTHER RECIPES WITH SWISS CHARD**

---

# TAILS

THE TAIL OF ANY MEAT ANIMAL CAN BE COOKED, IF IT IS BIG ENOUGH to bother with after it is skinned. Tails, which are mostly gelatinous cartilage and bone, are excellent for making stews and soups, and the small amount of meat on them is rich and flavorful. Oxtail, which is the popular name for the tail of any beef animal, is the tail best known for cooking. It can be prepared as a fancy gourmet dish — some go so far as to bone and stuff it — or it can be made into a simple stew. Pig's tails, calf's tails, kangaroo's tails, beaver's tails, and sheep's tails are also used as food in various places. There is a breed of sheep

---

**STORAGE**

**Freezing**   Prepare (see below), then package like meat. (Refer to FREEZING section.)

in South Africa whose tail is renowned as a source of cooking fat. The tail stores fat, and can weigh as much as 20 or 30 pounds. Kangaroo tail is prepared like oxtail and said to be equally good. Beaver's tails are favored by outdoor persons for roasting over camp fires. The roasting puffs up the hide which can then be peeled off, leaving the rich, gelatinous meat.

## HANDLING TAILS

The first step in preparing most tails is skinning. Usually, the skin or hide is pulled off when the rest of the carcass is skinned. After skinning, large tails are cut through the vertebrae into pieces for stewing. Tails from small animals are usually added whole to the soup pot. All kinds of tail can be used in oxtail recipes if cooking times are adjusted. Tails from young animals will cook in about half the time of the mature animal's tail, or in about half the time of an oxtail.

## TAIL RECIPES

**_Savory Oxtail Stew_**                                      (Makes 5–6 dinner servings.)

1 slice bacon, chopped
1 large oxtail, or 2–3 calf's tails
   (3–4 pounds), disjointed
1 onion, chopped medium
1 clove garlic, minced
1 carrot, diced
small bunch parsley, minced

½ teaspoon pepper, or to taste
¾ cup wine (Preferably dry red
   wine.)
½ cup tomato sauce, or 1 fresh
   tomato, chopped medium
3 stalks celery, cut in large pieces

Trim off fat and disjoint the tail to make serving size pieces. Heat the bacon slowly in a large frying pan, till some of its fat is rendered. Add the tail and sauté till the pieces begin to brown, turning them often. Add the onion, garlic, carrot, and parsley, and sauté for another 5 to 10 minutes to brown all ingredients. Add the pepper and wine, and cook uncovered till the wine evaporates. Add the tomato sauce, or chopped tomato, and cover tightly. If the frying pan does not have a lid transfer to a pot with a lid. Simmer over very low heat till the tail meat is tender. Oxtail may take as long as 4 hours, calf's tail about 2 hours. Add water if it begins to dry out. At the end, add the celery, and cook another 20 minutes, till the celery is just tender.

### Miss Grey's Lamb-tail Pie
From *Farmhouse Fare,* by Countrywise Books, England, 1946.

[Docked lamb's tails are recommended for this dish if they are large enough. Tails docked from very young lambs are too small to be useful.]
"Cut off the longest of the wool with scissors. Prepare the scald by putting 1 part cold to 3 parts of boiling water, and immerse the tails for a few minutes: then the wool will come off easily. Stew the tails in water with a carrot and onion, or in veal stock; they will want to stew for some time if they are fairly big—some farmers' wives roll each [cooked] tail in chopped parsley before putting into the pie-dish. Hard-boiled eggs may—or may not—be added. Cover with short crust, and bake. Brush with beaten egg when partly baked."

**OTHER RECIPES WITH TAILS**

Head Cheese, p.327
Pickled Pig's Ears and Tail, p.253
Stewing Foods in the Stock Pot, p.577

# TESTICLES

**STORAGE**

**Freezing** Prepare (see below), then package like meat. Quality retained about 4 mos. (Refer to FREEZING section.)

THE NAMES OF TESTICLES WHEN THEY ARE USED AS A FOOD ARE OFTEN euphemistic. Lamb's testicles are called "Rocky Mountain oysters," or just "mountain oysters," and pig's testicles are sometimes called "Texas strawberries." "Lamb's fries" and "calf's fries" are still others. Whatever name they go by, the testicles of young animals are a great delicacy, and there is no point in letting them go to waste because of a misplaced squeamishness.

Generally, testicles from young animals become available when the animals are castrated, by cutting to remove them. Testicles from mature animals are likely to be tough, and are best added to the soup pot.

## HANDLING TESTICLES

When testicles are enclosed in membrane or skin, cut through it and peel it away, leaving the soft inner tissue. Handle carefully, keeping the inner part in one round piece. Testicles can be precooked to firm them, and then used in recipes in the same way as brains or sweetbreads, but they can also be rolled in flour and sautéed without precooking. As they tend to pop and spatter when sautéed raw, use some kind of loose cover.

To precook testicles, put them in gently boiling water or soup stock, then simmer below a boil for 6 to 7 minutes. Take them out and chill them quickly as soon as they are done by dunking them in cold water. Cooking at high temperatures or for long periods of time will toughen them.

## TESTICLE RECIPE

*Sautéed Mountain Oysters*          (Quantities will vary with the number of animals castrated.)

*testicles from young animals*          *parsley or fresh tarragon, minced*
*butter*          *lemon juice*

Prepare and precook the testicles as described above. Then cut them into ½ inch slices. Heat the butter, then sauté the slices in it for about 3 minutes. Turn gently to keep from breaking them. Add the parsley or tarragon, and sauté for another 3 or 4 minutes. Sprinkle with lemon juice just before serving. These are as delicate and delicious as other glandular meats, and in no way resemble oysters.

---

### STORAGE

**Drying**   (Texture is changed; can be used in soup or stew.) Slice thinly, dry till hard. (Refer to DRYING section.)

**Freezing**   (Texture becomes firmer, drier, more crumbly, more absorbent.) Optional: Slice or cube. To thaw, cover with boiling water, let stand 15 to 20 min. Quality retained 6 mos. (Refer to FREEZING section.)

2 CUPS DRY SOYBEANS = 2 AVERAGE CAKES TOFU = 2½ – 3 POUNDS

---

# TOFU

"TOFU" IS THE JAPANESE NAME FOR SOYBEAN CURD OR SOYBEAN cheese. It has been a common food in the Far East for centuries, but for North Americans it is a new and interesting discovery. Besides its high protein value and easy digestibility, tofu has a bland flavor that goes as well with western style cooking as it does with far eastern cooking. Most people like it immediately and enjoy trying it in different ways.

Making tofu is as easy as making cottage cheese or yeast bread, so it is well within the capabilities of most households. When soybeans are home raised (refer to the SOYBEANS section), making tofu is one of the most practical and delicious ways to use them.

## MAKING TOFU

The preliminary step for making tofu is to make soy milk. The best tofu comes from milk made from whole, dry soybeans, but it is also possible to use milk made from soy flour. (Refer to SOY MILK, in the

SOYBEANS section.) Only one other ingredient besides soy milk is required—a solidifier to separate the tofu curds from the whey. Nigari, a by-product of the extraction of salt from sea water, is the preferred solidifier. (Bittern is its English but little used name.) Other solidifiers are fresh sea water, lemon or lime juice, vinegar, calcium sulfate or magnesium sulfate (Epsom salts). Nigari is available in many health food stores and by mail order from some natural foods catalogs.

Most kitchens have the necessary utensils for making tofu, except for a mold or box in which to drain and press it. A colander or a cheese mold can be substituted, but anyone who makes tofu regularly will appreciate having tofu molds. They can be homemade from untreated wood, such as maple. (Avoid pine, as it could give an unwanted flavor.) The cloth liner should be cotton with a somewhat coarse weave, to allow easy draining.

***Making Soy Milk from Dry Soybeans*** (The quantities of ingredients may be doubled or halved, as desired.) Soak 2 cups of dry soybeans in 2 quarts of water for about 10 hours. Increase soaking time if the temperature is much below 70°F, or decrease it if the temperature is much above 70°F. After soaking, drain the soybeans, rinse them, then drain again. If it is not possible to make the soy milk immediately, the drained soybeans can be refrigerated for about a day.

The next step is puréeing or grinding the soaked beans. If using a blender, add 6 cups of water to the soybeans and purée them in small batches that the blender can handle. Meanwhile start heating 2½ quarts of water in a large pot. If using a meat grinder, grind the soybeans twice using the finest blade, and heat 4 quarts of water.

Add the ground or puréed soybeans to the heated water. The blender or grinder parts can be rinsed with a little water and that too can be added. Heat to a boil, stirring often, and watch carefully, as it will foam up suddenly as it begins to boil.

Line a colander with a sturdy piece of cotton cloth and set it over a large container. (Refer to STRAINING ARRANGEMENTS FOR LIQUIDS, in the KITCHEN UTENSILS section.) When the soybean mixture boils, pour it into the cloth to strain off the milk. Pull the sides of the cloth together to form a bag and squeeze to remove as much milk as possible. Use a large spoon, potato masher, or other tool for pressing, since the bag will be too hot for the hands. The grainy material left in the cloth is known as okara. Put it into a container with a quart of warm water. Stir it, then pour it back into the cloth lined colander to strain off more milk. As this is less hot, it can be squeezed by hand to remove as much milk as possible. Combine the milk from the two squeezings. There will be 3 to 4 quarts. (See USING OKARA, below.)

***Making Tofu from Soy Milk*** Put soy milk in a large pot, and heat to simmering. Simmer from 5 to 7 minutes, stirring often and watching closely, as it will easily stick and burn. If using a thin bottomed pot or an electric burner with "hot spots," use an insulating ring under the pot to prevent scorching. Remove from heat after it has sim-

*Tofu box*

Follower to fit into box. Handles for easy removal.

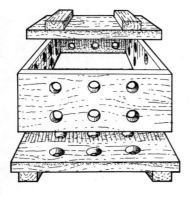

Box: Good dimensions are 8″ × 4″ × 3″. Can be changed for larger or smaller amounts.

Bottom board: A little larger than the box, with legs to raise it for drainage. Drainage holes about ⅜″ diameter.

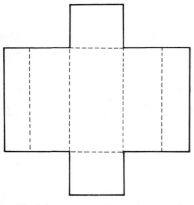

Cloth liner, cut to fit neatly into tofu box when the sides are folded up on dotted lines. The flaps must be long enough to fold over the top of the tofu.

mered, and have ready one of the following solidifiers:

2½ teaspoons dry nigari dissolved in 2 cups water, or

2 cups fresh sea water, or

5 tablespoons lemon or lime juice, with water to make 2 cups, or

4 tablespoons vinegar with water to make 2 cups, or

2½ teaspoons magnesium sulfate (Epsom salts) or calcium sulfate dissolved in 2 cups water.

Begin to stir the very hot soy milk and slowly pour in ⅔ cup of the solidifier. Stir 5 or 6 times, and hold the spoon still till the liquid stops moving. Remove the spoon and dribble another ⅔ cup of the solidifier into the soy milk without stirring. Cover the pot and wait 3 minutes. Then dribble the rest of the solidifier over the soy milk and stir just the top half inch for about 10 times around. Cover the pot again and wait 3 to 6 minutes. If clouds of white curds have not separated from the whey, stir the surface and they should appear. If the whey is milky looking, wait another minute, then stir again. If the whey still looks milky it will be necessary to mix another ⅔ cup of the solidifier and stir it in. When using magnesium sulfate for the solidifier, it takes longer and may be more difficult to make the curds separate. Sometimes with nigari the curds will separate before the full amount of solidifier has been added. If the whey is clear the remainder need not be used.

Line a tofu box or other mold with cotton cloth. Dip out a little of the whey from around the tofu curds, and pour it over the cloth to dampen it. Then use a ladle or cup to dip up the curds and whey mixture and pour it gently into the mold. If the mold fills up, wait a minute or two for it to drain, then add more curds and whey. The whey can be saved and used. (See USING WHEY FROM TOFU, below.)

When all of the curds are in the box and most of the whey has drained off, fold the cloth over the curds and set the follower in place. Set a 1–1½ pound weight, like a small jar of water, on the follower, and leave for about 15 minutes.

Slide the tofu, still wrapped in cloth, into a large container of cold water. Let cool for a couple of minutes, then gently unwrap the tofu while it is under water. If it is rectangular, cut it in half to make 2 square cakes while still immersed. Leave in the water a few more minutes to chill thoroughly. It will become firmer as it cools. Use the tofu right after taking it out of the cold water, or store it in the refrigerator for as long as a week. If stored, keep it in a container covered with cold water, and change the water every second day.

## USING TOFU

Tofu is excellent when seasoned and eaten cold (see *Fresh Tofu, Japanese Style,* below), and equally good sliced or cubed and cooked briefly in soups, stews, and stir-fried dishes. Its texture is delicate, and it will break or crumble if cooked longer than a couple of minutes. Because it is so bland, tofu combines well with all kinds of seasonings and flavorings. It has been incorporated into foods as divergent as eggplant parmigiana and ice cream.

As tofu is softer and crumbles more easily than the Chinese style bean curd intended for stir-fried dishes, it must be lifted and turned gently, rather than stirred. Bean curd from Chinese grocery stores is pressed into the shape of small, firm pillows, which can be sliced without easily falling apart. These require special molds and longer pressing.

## USING OKARA

Okara is the damp, solid material left after the milk has been squeezed out of puréed or ground soybeans. It can be used while still damp in vegetable or meat loaves, and patties, but it is more practical to use dried. It makes a light, fluffy meal not to be confused with soy grits, which are ground dry beans. (For grits refer to the SOYBEANS section.) Damp okara will keep only 2 or 3 days in the refrigerator, while dried okara will keep indefinitely, and can be used in all kinds of baked goods and cereals, as well as in vegetable or meat mixtures.

As okara stays loose without stickiness or cohesiveness when cooked, it is very good included in cereals like granola (refer to *Granola,* in the CEREALS, BREAKFAST section), but it cannot be used as a binder in sauces or patties. Because it has so little flavor it tastes best mixed with strongly flavored foods, and is not usually enjoyed by itself.

***Drying Okara*** Spread the damp okara on a lined drying tray and dry in a food dryer, or spread on baking sheets and dry in a very low oven. Turn often or stir to dry the okara evenly. When completely dry, cool, and store in tightly closed containers.

## USING WHEY FROM TOFU

The whey from tofu can be used as a cooking liquid, like the whey from dairy cheeses. (Refer to the WHEY section.) In Asian countries it is often used as a cleanser. It can be a shampoo and skin cleanser, a dishwashing liquid for greasy pots and pans and all dishes, and a woodwork cleaner.

Some animals, including dogs and horses, will drink this whey instead of water, and its nutrients benefit house plants when they are watered with it.

## TOFU RECIPES

### *Fresh Tofu, Japanese Style*

tofu, in ½–1 inch cubes
soy sauce
garnishes:
    scallions or chives, minced

fresh ginger root, grated, optional
toasted sesame seeds, optional

Arrange the tofu cubes in a serving dish, and dribble soy sauce over them. Sprinkle with scallions or chives, and ginger root, and sesame seeds, if desired. The color combination—white tofu, brown soy sauce, and green scallions or chives—is very attractive.

Serve as a snack, or as a side dish with a meal. The cubes are just right for picking up with chop sticks. The clean, fresh flavor of home-made tofu shows to perfection eaten in this way.

### *Tofu Scrambled Eggs* (Makes 4– 5 side servings.)

| | |
|---|---|
| 3 *eggs* | *½ pound (about 1 cup) tofu* |
| 3 *teaspoons soy sauce* | *oil, a few drops, optional* (For |
| 1 *teaspoon honey, or sugar* | pan.) |
| 1 *teaspoon fresh ginger root, minced,* | |
| *or ¼ teaspoon pepper* | |

Combine eggs, soy sauce, sweetener, and ginger root or pepper in a bowl, and stir with a fork till well mixed.

Put the tofu in a dry frying pan over medium heat, and cut or break it into small pieces with a spatula. Cook, stirring and turning, till the moisture that collects has evaporated. This usually takes about 2 minutes, but it will take longer if the tofu was freshly made. When it is dry and crumbly, pour in the egg mixture and scramble till set. (The flavor is best if the pan was not oiled, but if the tofu sticks excessively while drying, remove it, then clean and lightly oil the pan, then return it to the pan and add eggs. A well seasoned cast iron pan will prevent sticking.) Very good hot for breakfast or lunch, or as a cold snack.

### *Tofu Stir-fried with Mushrooms* (Makes 4– 6 side servings.)

| | |
|---|---|
| 3 – 4 *tablespoons oil, or lard* | 2 *cups (about) tofu, in 1 inch* |
| 3 – 4 *scallions, in 1 inch sections, or* | *cubes, or ½ inch slices* |
| 1 *onion, sliced* | 2 *tablespoons soy sauce* |
| ¼ *pound (about 1 cup) mushrooms,* | |
| *cut in ¼ inch slices* | |

Heat the oil or lard in a wok or heavy frying pan. Add the scallion or onion and stir-fry 1 or 2 *seconds*. Add the mushrooms and stir-fry about 2 minutes. Add the tofu, and stir and turn it very gently for about 2 minutes, trying not to break the pieces. (If it should crumble the dish will still taste good, but it will not look as nice.) Add the soy sauce and stir or turn gently for another minute. (Refer to the STIR-FRYING section.) Serve immediately.

*Tofu in Stir-frying* Tofu combines well with most vegetable or meat stir-fried dishes. Always add it towards the end of the stir-frying, turning it gently, as described above.

Tomatoes are ideal for a first taste of food self-sufficiency. Most beginning gardeners are immediately successful growing them, and many home canners learn this skill by canning them. When fresh-from-the-garden tomatoes are eaten all summer and fall, and home grown tomatoes are canned for the rest of the year, the bad old days of eating the expensive, lackluster store offerings quickly fade to nothing but an uneasy memory.

Botanically, the tomato is a fruit, but in practice it is a unique, much favored vegetable. Many gardeners grow several varieties at once for different purposes, including, perhaps, an early variety to extend the season, a large, sweet one for slicing, and a meaty Italian variety for sauce. Gardeners will enjoy especially good tomatoes if they raise their own seedlings, because then they can select the most flavorful varieties, rather than those bred to withstand mechanical harvesting and commercial storage conditions.

## HANDLING TOMATOES

Tomatoes reach their peak in flavor and nutritional value when fully ripe, full colored, and still somewhat firm. If left till overripe, they become soft, and lose both flavor and acidity. Those that are picked green and ripened indoors never attain the flavor of vine ripened fruits, but they are acceptable after frosts, when vine ripening is impossible.

Though canning is the most popular way to preserve tomatoes, drying is almost as practical. The quality of cooked frozen tomatoes is equal to that of canned tomatoes, but the thawing time makes them less convenient. Raw, frozen tomatoes turn mushy when thawed, but some like them for color in salads. They taste best partly thawed.

## PEELING TOMATOES

Peeling tomatoes is never a necessity, though it is sometimes preferred. Tomatoes eaten fresh are seldom peeled since skins are tender and flavorful. They are often peeled before canning to avoid curls of skin that separate during processing. An alternative to peeling before canning is to pick out bothersome curls of skin when the canned tomatoes are opened. There are differences of opinion about the flavor the peels contribute. If cooked with peels, tomatoes have a stronger, richer flavor. If cooked without, their flavor is sweeter and milder. Peeling is unnecessary when making sauce or juice, since peels are either strained out or puréed with the rest of the tomato, but some prefer the sweeter flavor of sauce made without peels.

---

### STORAGE

**Canning** (See THE ACIDITY OF TOMATOES FOR CANNING, below.) Leave whole if small or medium. Halve if large.

**Hot Pack only** To blanch, for about 4 cups boiling tomato juice, add 4–6 large halves, or more medium, or small tomatoes, return to boil, lift out with a slotted spoon or sieve. Optional: Slip off skins. Pack in jars. Blanch more tomatoes in same juice till jars filled. Add boiling cooking juice, ½ in. headroom. Process boiling water bath. Pints: 35 min. Quarts: 45 min. (Refer to CANNING section.) See also CANNING TOMATO SAUCE, PURÉE, OR JUICE, CANNING TOMATO PASTE and TOMATO RECIPES FOR CANNING, below.

**Cold Storage** If firm ripe, will keep refrigerated about 2 weeks. (Refer to WAYS TO RIPEN GREEN TOMATOES, in the TOMATOES, GREEN section.)

**Drying** See DRYING TOMATOES, below.

**Freezing** (Not as practical as canning or drying.) Pour cooled, stewed sauce, juice or uncooked purée, in containers. *Fresh, ripe* (Will be soft to mushy when thawed.) Put wedges or slices on trays, freeze solid, then package. *Paste* Pack in ice cube trays for convenient quantities. Unmold when solid and package. (Refer to FREEZING section.)

1⅓ CUPS CHOPPED FRESH = 1 CUP STEWED OR CANNED
1 BUSHEL FRESH = 15–20 QUARTS CANNED

Tomatoes are quick and easy to peel after they are scalded with boiling water. This loosens the skin enough to slip off almost in one piece. Dunk the tomatoes in boiling water 30 seconds, lift them out and let them cool. Or dip them in cold water to cool more quickly. Dunk only a few at a time in a large pot of boiling water, so that the boiling hardly stops. Another method is to put the tomatoes in a container, pour boiling water over them, wait about a minute, and then drain them, before peeling.

## DRYING TOMATOES

Both fresh tomatoes and tomato paste dry very well. Their flavor is excellent and they are convenient to use. (See DRYING TOMATO PASTE, below.)

Small sized, fresh, ripe tomatoes are best for drying. Large tomatoes must be sliced, causing loss of juice. Long or pear shaped tomatoes can be halved the long way and set on drying trays cut side up, which saves the juice. Peeling is not necessary. Small cherry tomatoes can be dried whole. Check their skins like those of firm berries (refer to the DRYING FOODS section) to make them dry faster, or they can be peeled completely, which is almost as easy. It takes several days to sun dry tomatoes, and about 24 hours to dry them in an electric dryer. Opinions differ, but many believe that sun drying gives tomatoes a sweeter, intense flavor.

Use dried tomatoes as a snack, like any dried fruit, or add them to soups, stews, and other cooked dishes. They can be soaked, and added with the soaking water, or they can be added to liquid mixtures without soaking if allowed to cook 30 minutes or longer.

## THE ACIDITY OF TOMATOES FOR CANNING

Tomatoes can vary considerably in acidity, depending on their variety and their growing conditions or location. In some circumstances, modern varieties may be borderline for canning safely by the boiling water bath method. (Refer to REQUIREMENTS FOR CANNING HIGH AND LOW ACID FOODS, in the CANNING section.)

## PRECAUTIONS FOR SAFE BOILING WATER BATH CANNING

• Avoid canning very low acid varieties, soft, overripe tomatoes with wrinkled skins, or those from dead vines. Tomatoes lose acidity as they ripen. Add lemon juice, or pure crystalline citric acid. The usual amounts per quart: 2 tablespoons lemon juice or ½ teaspoon citric acid. (Sour salt is another name for citric acid.)

• Can tomatoes by a hot pack method such as the one described in

STORAGE at the beginning of this section, or make sauce or juice (see below). Cooking before canning concentrates flavor and acidity, and ensures a better pack. Add tomato juice if more liquid is needed. (Salt may be omitted, as it has no effect on the safety of the tomatoes.)

• Mixtures of tomatoes and other vegetables such as zucchini or okra must always be pressure processed for the time required by the other vegetable. (Exceptions are tested recipes for such mixtures as catsup which include vinegar, increasing acidity to a safe level. It is safe to include one basil leaf, one clove of garlic, or a piece of hot pepper pod in the jar of canned tomatoes or tomato sauce, but larger quantities must not be added unless part of a tested recipe.)

## MAKING TOMATO SAUCE, PURÉE, OR JUICE

There are several different styles of tomato sauce and purée, and several different methods for making them. The choice will vary with personal preferences and intended uses. It may be practical to can more than one style for a greater variety of uses.

***Crushed Tomato Sauce*** Chop fresh, unpeeled tomatoes, or peel them first, and put them in the pot. Crush with a potato masher or any other tool to make plenty of juice. Heat to a boil, stirring often, then simmer, uncovered, till they are cooked through and thickened to taste. This may take from 15 minutes to an hour, or more.

***Smooth Tomato Sauce or Purée*** Italian or paste varieties of tomatoes make the thickest, most flavorful smooth sauce. The tomatoes can be cooked first and then put through a puréeing device, or they can be puréed while raw and then cooked. If the flavor of the peels is not especially wanted, it is easiest to purée them raw, as described below. (For puréeing tools, refer to the KITCHEN UTENSILS section.)

For the quickest way to prepare tomatoes for cooking before puréeing, wash and trim them as necessary, and then squeeze them by hand to break the skins to release their juice. Hold the tomatoes, one in each hand, over the cooking pot, squeeze, and drop them in. Children with clean hands are sure to enjoy helping with this chore. If squeezing is not appealing, the tomatoes can be quartered and dropped in the pot. Heat to a boil, stirring often, and cook uncovered, till the tomatoes are completely soft and juicy. Then put them through a sieve or strainer. A food mill works very well. For a thick sauce, cook the tomatoes down either before or after they are puréed, or strain off the thin juice to use in another way. However, the tomato flavor will be strongest if the sauce is thickened by cooking to evaporate extra moisture.

To make purée from raw tomatoes, a squeezing strainer, such as the one illustrated in the KITCHEN UTENSILS section, will be the fastest way to remove peels and seeds before cooking. To avoid waste, put the peels and seeds through the strainer a second time to remove more of the pulp. Even so, there is likely to be a smaller yield of sauce with this method as compared to cooking the tomatoes before purée-ing. However, those who prefer a sweet, mild tomato sauce will find a squeezing strainer well worth the investment. Avoid buying one that is made of aluminum. (Refer to AVOIDING ALUMINUM, in the KITCHEN UTENSILS section.) The raw purée must be heated to a boil before it is canned. It is usually simmered uncovered to thicken it before canning.

*Tomato Juice*  Tomato juice can be made in any of the ways smooth sauce or purée is made, except that it is not cooked down to thicken it. It is actually not necessary to make canned tomato juice as a separate project, since the canned sauce or purée can be diluted when it is opened to make juice.

*Canning Tomato Sauce, Purée or Juice*  (These should be plain full strength tomato without dilution of any sort.) Heat the sauce, purée or juice to a full boil, stir to be sure it is evenly thick, and pour in hot canning jars leaving ½ inch headroom. Process juice and thin sauce or purée in a boiling water bath, both pints and quarts—15 minutes. Process thick sauce or purée in half pint or pint jars only—30 minutes. (Refer to the CANNING section.)

## MAKING TOMATO PASTE

The first step for making tomato paste is to make a smooth sauce or purée by one of the above methods. This is then thickened, either by cooking uncovered to evaporate more moisture, or by draining through a cloth to remove juice. If it is to be cooked, keep the tomato sauce or purée over low heat and stir it often to prevent sticking and burning. An insulating ring under the pot is a help. Cook the paste till it is as thick as mashed potatoes. It should have an intensely concentrated tomato flavor.

Either raw tomato purée or cooked sauce can be thickened by putting it in a cloth bag and hanging it to drain, or by draining it in a cloth lined colander. Use the drained juice when canning whole tomatoes or add it to vegetable juice mixtures or cooked dishes. Tomato paste made in this way will be sweet and mild compared to the paste concentrated by cooking. If the paste is from raw tomatoes the flavor can be preserved by freezing it. Freeze it in ice cube trays, and then store the cubes in a freezer container, where they will be available in small quantities, as needed.

*Canning Tomato Paste*  If the tomato paste was concentrated by cooking, spoon it hot into hot half pint jars as soon as it is thick enough. If the paste was made by draining, heat it slowly, stirring often to keep it from sticking, then fill the jars, leaving ½ inch headroom. Process in a boiling water bath, in half pint jars for 45 minutes. (Refer to the CANNING section.)

*Drying Tomato Paste*  Dry tomato paste like fruit leather. (Refer to

DRYING FRUIT AND OTHER PURÉES, in the DRYING FOODS section.) Seasoning vegetables such as onion, garlic, celery, parsley, and other herbs can be cooked and puréed with the tomatoes to make the paste, but plain tomato paste will be more versatile. Tear or cut off pieces of tomato leather to add to soups, stews, or sauces, or roll the leather and slice small cross sections before storing it. The flavor is strong, so add sparingly. To reconstitute the leather as a paste, pour boiling water over it and let it sit about 30 minutes, till it softens.

## TOMATO RECIPES FOR CANNING

This catsup is much more nutritious than its commercial counterparts, since it contains considerably less sugar and salt. In fact, it is excellent without any salt at all.

### *Thirteen Seasonings Tomato Catsup* (Makes about 3 pints.)

| | |
|---|---|
| 4 quarts tomatoes, chopped or squeezed | 1½ teaspoons peppercorns |
| 4 onions, chopped | 1–2 bay leaves |
| 1 sweet red pepper, chopped, optional | 1 teaspoon mustard seed, or ¼ teaspoon dry mustard |
| 1 clove garlic, minced, optional | 1 tablespoon paprika, optional |
| 1½ teaspoons each whole cloves, allspice, mace | ½ teaspoon cayenne powder, optional |
| 1 small stick cinnamon | ¼–½ cup honey, or sugar |
| 1½ teaspoons celery seed (Or cook 1 stalk chopped celery with vegetables.) | 1 teaspoon salt, optional |
| | 1 cup (about) vinegar |

Cook together the tomatoes, onion, sweet pepper, and garlic, uncovered, till they are all soft, from 30 to 40 minutes. Put through the finest screen of a food mill or another strainer for a smooth purée. (If using a blender the flavor will not be as good, because of the pulverized peels and seeds.) Return the purée to the cooking pot. Tie the whole spices, seeds, and bay leaves in a cloth bag and add them to the pot. (Powdered spices will darken the catsup's color.) Add dry mustard, paprika, and cayenne, if desired. Stir in honey or sugar, and salt, if desired. Simmer, uncovered, over low heat till boiled down and thickened, stirring often to prevent sticking and burning. This may take 2 or more hours. Next, remove the spice bag and add the vinegar. Stir, taste, and adjust sweetener, vinegar, and any other seasonings. It should taste more piquant and less sweet than commercial catsups. (The flavor improves with age.)

Bring the catsup to a full boil, stir for even thickness, and pour in hot canning jars, ½ inch headroom. Process in a boiling water bath, for 10 minutes for both pints and quarts. (Refer to the CANNING section.)

**Tomato Apple Catsup** Use 2 quarts apples and 2 quarts tomatoes instead of all tomatoes. The apples must be chopped, but peeling and coring are optional, if puréed through a sieve. Excellent, especially when the tomato supply is limited. The apple does not change the flavor drastically, but does add a pleasant fruitiness.

*Chili Sauce*   Chili sauce is made like catsup with a rougher texture, and a spicier, more intensely sweet and sour flavor. Chop the tomatoes small. They can be peeled to avoid curls of skin. Grind the onions and other vegetables. Sweet peppers can be increased to 2 or 3. Cook to a sauce without puréeing. Ginger and nutmeg can be used instead of cinnamon and mace. Increase hot red pepper to 1 tablespoon, or to taste, and, if desired, increase amounts of sweetener and vinegar.

### *Herbed Tomato Juice Cocktail*          (Makes about 3 quarts.)

10 pounds firm, ripe tomatoes, chopped
8 whole cloves
2 bay leaves
½ teaspoon peppercorns, or ground pepper
1 teaspoon dill seed, or 1 head dill
several sprigs parsley
sprig basil
sprig fresh marjoram, or oregano, or 1 teaspoon dried
bunch chives, several scallions, or 1 small onion, chopped
1 tablespoon honey, or sugar
1 cup vinegar

Combine all ingredients, then cook, covered, 45 minutes, till the vegetables are soft. Purée through the fine screen of a food mill or another strainer. Taste and adjust seasonings, if desired.

Heat to a boil, stir for even thickness, and pour in hot canning jars, ½ inch headroom. Process in a boiling water bath for 10 minutes for both pints and quarts. (Refer to the CANNING section.)

*Hot Tomato Bouillon*   Heat tomato juice cocktail and pour it into bowls. Put a dab of butter in each bowl, and if desired, sprinkle with minced parsley. This makes a nice first course in cold weather.

## TOMATO RECIPES

The first two recipes are "from scratch" versions of common commercially canned tomato products. Since home canned tomato or tomato sauce is the ideal main ingredient in both, they are likely to be mainstays in households depending entirely on home grown tomatoes.

### *Tomato Sauce for Pasta*              (Makes 4–6 cups sauce.)

3 tablespoons oil, butter, or another fat (Half oil, half butter is excellent.)
1 onion, minced
1–2 cloves garlic, minced
¼ cup carrot, minced, or 1 tablespoon dried shreds
¼ cup celery, minced, or 1 tablespoon dried shreds
¼ cup green pepper, minced, or 1 tablespoon dried shreds

¼ cup mushrooms, chopped, or
   1 tablespoon dried slices, optional
1 – 1 ½ quarts tomato sauce, or
   purée
   fresh herbs, minced, or dried

herbs (Try parsley, basil,
   oregano, thyme, marjoram.)
pepper, to taste
salt, optional
2 cups stewed tomatoes or fresh
   tomatoes, chopped, optional

In a large saucepan or a frying pan heat the oil, butter, or other fat. Sauté the onion, garlic, and fresh carrot, celery, green pepper, and mushrooms, if they are used. When the onion is limp and golden, add the tomato sauce and any dried vegetables used. Simmer, uncovered, over very low heat, till thickened to taste, stirring from time to time. This may take from one to several hours. Add the herbs and pepper, and the salt and stewed or fresh tomatoes, if desired, about 20 to 30 minutes before the sauce is done. The stewed or fresh tomatoes add more texture and a fresh flavor that some people like.

This sauce is excellent with spaghetti, noodles, and other pasta, or with rice and other grains, or in Italian style dishes, such as lasagna or pizza.

**Tomato Meat Sauce**    About ¼ pound meat of any kind, raw or cooked, will flavor a batch of tomato sauce. Brown ground beef or other ground meat, or glandular meats such as liver cut in small pieces, in the oil or fat for a minute or two before adding the onion and other vegetables. The sauce is then completed as above. If using leftover cooked meat add it with the tomato sauce.

Rabbit liver tomato sauce is a favorite Italian specialty. One rabbit liver is just right for flavoring a batch of sauce. Traditionally rabbit liver tomato sauce is served with homemade egg noodles cut very wide. (Refer to the NOODLES section.) The livers of racoons, opossums, and other small wild animals are very good used in the same ways.

**Tomato Seafood Sauce**    Most kinds of fish or shellfish are delicious in tomato sauce, whether they are fresh or cooked leftovers, or canned. Add the seafood about 20 minutes before the sauce is to be served. If there is any broth with the seafood, add it earlier with the tomato sauce. Fresh shellfish such as clams, mussels, or whole crabs, can be washed well, then cooked in the tomato sauce, to retain every bit of their flavor. Often this is served shells and all, letting everyone pick out the shellfish meats for themselves.

### Cream of Tomato Soup     (Makes about 10 medium bowls.)

2 tablespoons onion, minced
2 tablespoons celery or lovage,
   minced
2 tablespoons butter
1 tablespoon flour
4 cups milk

4 cups canned tomatoes, puréed
   (Or 2 cups tomato sauce
   mixed with 2 cups water.)
¼ teaspoon baking soda (To
   prevent curdling. Omit if
   using goat's milk.)
pepper, salt, optional

---

**TOMATO IDEAS**

**Salad Stuffed Tomatoes**   Cut off the tops of large, firm, ripe tomatoes, and scoop out the centers with a spoon. Stuff the shells with a hearty salad mixture such as tuna, egg, potato, or macaroni. These are delicious and attractive set on a bed of greens.

**Broiled or Fried Tomato Slices**   Cut tomatoes into ½ – ¾ inch slices, and sauté them in oil or butter. When done they are good seasoned with pepper, minced parsley, a sprinkle of lemon juice, and salt, if desired. Before frying, the slices can also be dipped in cornmeal, fine, dry bread crumbs, or flour.

**Broiled Tomatoes with Cheese and Broccoli**   Put thick slices of tomato on a baking sheet, and top with slices of cheese or a layer of grated cheese.

Broil till the cheese is melted. Or broil this combination on toast. For a fancy broiled tomato treat, mix chopped, cooked broccoli, minced scallion or onion, and grated cheese, and spread on the tomato slices before broiling. Other cheese-vegetable mixtures can also be tried.

**Fresh Tomato Sauce**  Mince fresh, very ripe tomatoes with seasoning vegetables and herbs, such as sweet peppers, scallions or onion, parsley, and basil. The texture when chopped by hand in a wooden bowl is excellent, but a blender can also be used. Serve with meat, fish, cooked vegetables, or pasta. Chill to serve with cold meats and salads.

For a Mexican style sauce mince the tomatoes with hot peppers, onion, and fresh coriander leaves. This goes with tacos, tostadas, egg dishes, and many meat, poultry, and fish dishes.

**Whipped Tomato Cream**
Fold smooth, thick tomato sauce into an equal amount of stiffly whipped cream. Season with pepper and lemon juice. Use as salad dressing or as a dip for raw vegetables. It also adds a special touch to vegetable aspics, and cooked vegetable salads.

**Home Canned Tomato Sauce Instead of Paste or Juice**  It is not really necessary to can tomato purée in three thicknesses—thin for juice, medium for sauce, and thick for paste. Instead, dilute a medium sauce with water, vegetable juice, vegetable cooking water, or another liquid, such as the SAUERKRAUT TOMATO JUICE in the SAUERKRAUT section, to make juice. A rich tomato sauce can replace tomato paste in most recipes, by adding twice or three times as much sauce as the called for paste, and reducing the other liquids in the recipe proportionally.

Sauté the onion and celery in the butter in a soup pot, till the onion is transparent, then stir in the flour. Slowly add 1 cup of the milk, stirring constantly till it thickens. Then add the rest of the milk, and simmer over low heat for about 5 minutes.

In another pot, heat the tomato purée or tomato sauce and water. Add the baking soda and wait for foaming to stop. Pour the tomato mixture slowly into the milk mixture, stirring constantly. Season with pepper and salt, if desired, and serve immediately. If reheated do not boil, and if, in spite of all precautions, the soup should curdle, rename it "Tomato Cheese Soup." It will still be enjoyable, as curdling changes only the appearance and texture, not the flavor or nutritional value. An outstanding cream of tomato soup, either way.

### *Tomato Bread Salad*                         (Makes about 6 medium servings.)

| | |
|---|---|
| *2 – 3 large, ripe tomatoes, chopped small* (Save juice.) | *2 – 3 tablespoons oil* (Preferably olive.) |
| *1 scallion, minced* | *1 – 2 tablespoons vinegar* (Preferably wine vinegar or homemade cider vinegar.) |
| *parsley, minced* | |
| *several leaves rocket, cress, or basil, minced* | *pepper, salt, optional* |
| | *6 slices (or 1 per serving) hard dried whole grain bread* |

Combine the tomatoes, scallion, parsley, and rocket, cress, or basil. Toss with oil, then add vinegar, pepper, and salt, if desired. Let sit for 10 to 15 minutes before assembling the salads.

Dip the bread slices in water, or hold under the tap for a moment, just long enough to dampen them, and set one on each plate. Pile the tomato mixture on the bread, taking care to spoon some juice over each serving. This Italian style salad is sure to be a summertime favorite. If extra large servings are made, it is an excellent one-dish lunch.

*Friselli*  These dried bread rounds are especially made for this salad. Shape whole wheat bread dough or other whole grain dough into flat round shapes as if making hamburger rolls. When baked, cut through the rolls to make two round slices. Dry in a food dryer or very low oven, till hard and dry thoughout. Friselli will keep indefinitely in airtight containers.

### *Fran's Cold Tomato Soup*                         (Makes about 6 medium bowls.)

| | |
|---|---|
| *3 cups tomatoes, chopped* | *pepper, salt, optional* |
| *1 large or 2 small cucumbers, chopped* | *1 large cucumber, diced, for garnish* |
| *1 – 2 cloves garlic, chopped* | *vinegar to cover the cucumber* (Preferably cider or wine vinegar.) |
| *1½ tablespoons honey, or 2 tablespoons sugar* | |

Cook the tomatoes, cucumbers, garlic, and sweetener together about 45 minutes, till the vegetables are soft. Purée in a blender or food mill. Season with pepper, and salt, if desired, cool, then refrigerate till well chilled.

To make the garnish place diced cucumber in a small bowl and cover with vinegar. Let sit a few minutes.

To serve put an ice cube in each soup bowl, and ladle the tomato mixture over it. Pass the cucumber in vinegar so that each person can add them to taste. This is marvelously refreshing in hot weather.

**OTHER RECIPES
FEATURING TOMATOES**

Apple, Onion, and Tomato
 Savory, p.6
Celery and Tomato Casserole,
 p.124
Garlic Soup, Spanish Style,
 p.297
Gelatine Fillings for Fruits and
 Vegetables, p.301
Liver Tomato Sauce, p.396
Okra Stuffed Tomatoes, p.443
Recipes, and Ideas for
 Vegetables, p.669
Sauerkraut-Tomato Juice, p.545
Shish Kebab, p.381
Stuffed Peppers and Tomatoes,
 p.473
Vegetable Sherbets, p.357

### *Tomato Aspic*                          (Makes about 6 side servings.)

3 cups tomato juice, or 4 cups fresh
 tomatoes, chopped
1 small onion, chopped
4 stalks celery with leaves, chopped
sprig basil, tarragon, or other herbs
1 bay leaf
1 teaspoon paprika

2 tablespoons (about) lemon
 juice or vinegar
2 tablespoons dry gelatine, in ½
 cup cold water
1–2 cups raw vegetables, sliced,
 grated, or chopped, optional
 (Try cucumber, olives, carrot, green pepper, celery.)

Put the tomato juice or fresh tomatoes in a pot with the onion, celery, basil or tarragon, bay leaf, paprika, and lemon juice or vinegar. Cook covered 20 to 30 minutes and strain off the juice. (Serve the celery and onion separately, or add them to another dish.) Taste the juice and add more seasonings, or lemon juice or vinegar, if it is too bland. The flavor should be pronounced. Measure the juice, and, if necessary, add hot water to make 3½ cups. Add the soaked gelatine and stir till it is dissolved. Add any raw vegetables used. Pour into a large mold or into individual, cup sized molds, and chill till set.

Unmold the aspic, and, if desired, add mayonnaise or the WHIPPED TOMATO CREAM, under TOMATO IDEAS, and such garnishes as parsley and lettuce leaves.

# TOMATOES, GREEN

GREEN TOMATOES CAN BE COUNTED AS A CROP IN THEMSELVES WHEN large quantities are harvested just before fall frosts. There are many special ways to use them that transform them from something of a nuisance to an absolute delight.

Not all green tomatoes taste alike. Full sized, green tomatoes of the

**STORAGE**

**Canning**  See GREEN TOMATO RECIPES FOR CANNING, below.

**Cold Storage**  Keep in cool place 1–2 mos. See also WAYS TO RIPEN GREEN TOMATOES, below.

**Drying**  Possible. (Harsh flavor allows few uses.)

**Freezing**  Best for cooked mixtures. (Refer to FREEZING section.)

sweeter varieties are very good fried, stuffed, and added to mixed dishes. The less mature, more acidic green tomatoes taste too harsh to enjoy by themselves. They are best made into relishes, condiments and other spicy mixtures. Green tomatoes ripened indoors attain full color and a reasonably good taste, but they can never match vine ripened quality.

Mexican green tomatoes, or tomatillos, are a different plant from regular tomatoes. They are grown in the southwestern United States and are used often in Mexican cooking. Seeds are available from some catalogs, and some specialty stores sell them canned.

## HANDLING GREEN TOMATOES

After they have been picked green tomatoes should be sorted. Those beginning to change color can be set aside to ripen. The perfect, full sized green fruits can be stored in a cool place, either to be used later in green tomato recipes or for slow ripening. Small, misshapen, or very immature green tomatoes can be used in one of the canning recipes in the recipe section below.

## RIPENING GREEN TOMATOES

Green tomatoes will usually ripen if they are picked after their skins have become glossy. Remove stems, then wash and dry them, if necessary. Tomatoes ripen fastest if kept at room temperature. Though they often are put on a window sill, they can sit anywhere. Spread them out in a single layer so that ripe ones show up readily and check them every day or two. Some people find that keeping them in brown paper bags speeds ripening.

To delay ripening so that some fresh tomatoes will be available over a longer period of time, store the green tomatoes in a cool place, ideally 55–58°F. If kept below 50°F for more than a few days, they may never ripen properly. Each tomato can be wrapped in newspaper, or packed in dry leaves, hay or straw, but they keep about as well uncovered, and are much easier to check for signs of ripening or spoilage. Arrange them no deeper than two layers. Check once a week, and move those beginning to turn red to room temperature to finish ripening. Green tomatoes will keep from 4 to 8 weeks.

An easy way to store green tomatoes growing on small plants is to pull the whole plant, and hang it upside down in a cool place, such as a basement. Then pick the tomatoes off as they ripen. Another way to extend the fresh tomato season is to devise protection for the tomato plants in the garden, using hay, straw, plastic, or another material. This allows the tomatoes to continue to ripen after early frosts.

## CANNED GREEN TOMATO RECIPES

### *Green Tomato Hot Sauce*                    (Makes 8–9 half pints.)

3 quarts green tomatoes, chopped
    small, or ground
1 quart ripe tomatoes, chopped
    small, or ground
1 onion, chopped, or ground
1–2 cloves garlic, ground, or
    pressed, optional

1 cup fresh, hot peppers, minced
    or ground, or ¼ cup (about)
    hot pepper flakes
1 cup vinegar
1 teaspoon salt, optional

Combine all ingredients, and cook uncovered, stirring often, for about 20 minutes, or till thickened. Ladle into hot canning jars, ½ inch headroom, and process in a boiling water bath, for 10 minutes for both half pints or pints. (Refer to the CANNING section.) Serve with tacos and other Mexican foods, or as a hot, piquant sauce with other dishes.

### *Dilly Green Tomatoes*                        (Makes 5 quarts.)

5 cloves garlic
5 3"–4" pieces celery stalk
5 small hot peppers, or pepper flakes,
    to taste
5 heads dill

5 quarts small, perfect green
    tomatoes (Cherry tomatoes
    are excellent.)
1 quart vinegar
2 quarts water
1 teaspoon salt, optional

Boil jars and lids in water to cover for 5 minutes.

Put garlic, celery, hot pepper, and dill in each jar. Fill with green tomatoes, leaving ½ inch headroom. Combine the vinegar, water, and salt, if desired, in a saucepan, heat, and boil 5 minutes. Pour boiling hot over the tomatoes, filling the jars almost to the brim. Seal immediately. (Because of the green tomato's high acidity, the ratio of vinegar to water is lower than usual for this pickling method, and the pickles keep exceptionally well. Refer to CANNING PICKLES, in the CANNING section.) Wait at least a month before opening. They will be a favorite with those who like their pickles strong.

### *Green Tomato Mincemeat*                    (Makes about 6 pints.)

4 quarts green tomatoes, chopped
    small
2 quarts cored apples, chopped small
1 pound raisins (about 3 cups), or
    other dried fruit
¼ cup lemon, orange, or other citrus
    peel, grated or minced

1 tablespoon cinnamon
¼ teaspoon allspice
¼ teaspoon cloves
1 cup molasses
1 cup vinegar, or ¾ cup vinegar
    and ¼ cup lemon juice

## GREEN TOMATO IDEAS

**Green Tomatoes for Tartness**
Add a chopped green tomato to stews, casseroles, and soups where a touch of tartness would be welcome. Green tomatoes go especially well in curries.

**Green Tomato in Baked Goods**  Use chopped green tomatoes in muffins, fruit breads, and other baking instead of berries or other fruits. Grated lemon or orange peel and spices such as cinnamon, ginger, and powdered coriander seeds complement the green tomato flavor.

**Cornmeal Coated Green Tomato Slices**  Select large, green tomatoes of a sweet variety, and slice them about ½ inch thick. Season the cornmeal with pepper, and salt, if desired, and dip the slices in it, coating them completely. Sauté in oil or fat till nicely browned on both sides. As an extra touch, put a crushed clove of garlic in the oil or fat and stir it around once or twice, before adding the tomato slices.

**Green Tomato Parmigiana**
Sauté green tomato slices, as above, or dip them first in beaten egg, and then in cornmeal or flour. Set the sautéed slices next to each other in a shallow baking dish, or on a baking sheet. Spoon a well seasoned tomato sauce over them, put a slice of mozarella cheese on each, then sprinkle with Parmesan cheese. Bake 20 minutes at about 375°F, till hot and bubbly.

## OTHER RECIPES WITH GREEN TOMATOES

Green Tomato Meat Sauce for
   Rice or Noodles, p.514
Old Virginia Relish, p.481

Combine all ingredients in a big pot, then cook, covered, about 1 hour. If the mixture is too thin, remove the lid for the last few minutes of cooking. Ladle hot into hot jars, leaving ½ inch headroom, and process in a boiling water bath for 10 minutes, for both pints and quarts. (Refer to the CANNING section.)

Use this mincemeat like applesauce in dessert recipes or like regular mincemeat. Use in the *Green Tomato Cookies,* below, and for MINCEMEAT ICE CREAM, in the ICE CREAM section.

## GREEN TOMATO RECIPES

### *Home Fry Green Tomatoes*          (Makes about 6 side servings.)

| | |
|---|---|
| 2 tablespoons (*about*) butter, oil, or other fat | 1 clove garlic, minced, optional |
| 2 – 3 large green tomatoes, sliced thin (Use a sweet variety.) | ½ green pepper, sliced thin, optional |
| 1 onion, sliced thin | pepper, salt, optional |

Heat butter or oil in a large frying pan, and add the green tomato, onion, garlic, and green pepper. Fry slowly over low heat, turning often, till the tomatoes lose their shape and become a soft mass in the frying pan—about 30 minutes. Season to taste, then raise the heat for a couple of minutes for a slight brown glaze. These go especially well with beef or other red meat.

*Curried Green Tomatoes*  Fry a thinly sliced apple with the green tomatoes. When about half done, stir in 1 – 2 teaspoons curry powder, and add enough water or soup stock for a sauce consistency. Cover and simmer till ingredients are soft, and omit browning. Very good served with rice or any other cooked grain.

### *Green Tomato Cookies*     (Makes about 3 dozen medium cookies.)

| | |
|---|---|
| ½ cup butter, or lard | 2 cups whole wheat flour |
| ¼ – ¾ cup honey | 1 teaspoon baking powder |
| 2 eggs | ½ cup nuts, chopped, or ¼ cup sunflower seeds |
| 1 pint Green Tomato Mincemeat, above, or 1 ½ cups fresh green tomato, ground or minced | |

Mix together the butter or lard and honey. (Use the larger amount of honey with fresh green tomatoes.) If stiff, warm the mixture slightly to blend it. Stir in the eggs, one at a time, then the green tomato. Sift the flour and baking powder, and mix in the nuts or seeds. Combine the wet and dry ingredients. Drop by teaspoonfuls on a greased cookie sheet, then bake in a moderately hot, 375°F oven from 15 to 20 minutes, till lightly browned. Remove from pan and cool on a clean cloth.

THE TONGUE IS AS TASTY AS ANY PART OF A MEAT ANIMAL. IN THE early days when buffalo were slaughtered so wantonly on the Great Plains, some hunters killed the animals just for their tongues, leaving the rest of the carcass to rot. Times have, to some extent, reversed themselves, and many hunters of big game animals take the rest of the meat, including the liver and heart, and leave the tongue. The same is often true when domestic animals are slaughtered. This waste is small, compared to that of the old time "tongue" hunters, but it is still a waste, and one that is hard to explain, since tongues are as easy to prepare as any stew meat, and as easy to enjoy as any cut of meat.

## HANDLING TONGUE

Cut the tongue out of the head at the root or base, where it connects inside the mouth. This is most easily done if the lower jaw is removed first. (Refer to HANDLING LARGE ANIMAL'S HEADS, in the HEADS section.) Wash tongues thoroughly in cold water. If necessary to loosen dirt or blood, soak in cold water for a few minutes, then scrub clean with a brush. Rinse well.

All tongues, large and small, can be cooked in the same, basic ways. With adjustments in cooking times for the animals' different sizes and ages, they are all interchangeable in recipes.

*Precooking and Skinning Tongues*  The first step is to cook them in water till their skin covering has loosened and can be peeled off. They can be cooked till tender and then skinned, or simmered till they can be skinned, and then finished in another way.

Cover tongues with cold water and bring to a boil. Skim well, removing all of the foam that collects, then simmer over low heat. Large beef tongues can be peeled after about an hour of cooking, but it takes up to 4 hours of cooking to make them tender. Small tongues can be peeled after 15 to 20 minutes, and need from 1 to 2 hours of cooking to make them tender. Test with a fork for doneness. Tongues will peel most easily while warm, as their skins tend to stick when cold. Take them out of the cooking water, and leave them to sit till they are cool enough to handle. Or dip them in cold water to cool them quickly. Peel or pull off the rough whitish looking skin, and, at the same time, trim off any fat or tiny bones left at the root end of the tongue. Occasionally, the skin of the small tongues from young animals will stick, even if they are warm. When this happens the skin will usually be tender enough to eat, but it can also be pared off with a knife. To keep tongues moist that are to be eaten cold, cook them till tender, skin them, and then return them to the cooking water to cool completely.

To give the meat extra flavor, tongues can be cooked in soup stock,

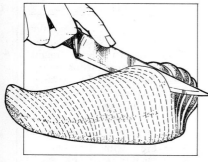

*Slicing beef tongue.*

## TONGUE IDEAS

**Tongue Sandwiches** Cooked sliced tongue makes outstanding sandwiches. It is excellent with mustard, mayonnaise, or relish for moisture and with watercress, lettuce, or sprouts for greenery.

**Quick Pickled Tongue** Marinate cooked, sliced tongue in a mixture of half vinegar and half water for several hours, or overnight. Add seasonings, such as peppercorns, bay leaf, and thin garlic or onion slices. Serve for lunch, as a snack, or hors d'oeuvre. It will keep about a week refrigerated, and is a good way to use a small tongue so that everyone has a taste. Heart meat can be pickled in the same way (refer to the HEART section), and the two can be combined to make one larger dish.

**Tongue Casserole** Make a bread crumb stuffing, using the broth from cooking the tongue or white wine or some of each to moisten it. The CELERY BREAD CRUMB STUFFING, in the CELERY section, is good. Butter a baking dish or casserole, then make alternate layers of stuffing and cooked, sliced tongue. Begin and end with stuffing. Dot the top with butter, or lay slices of bacon over it. Bake 30 to 40 minutes in a low, 325°F oven.

or the cooking water can be seasoned. Classic seasonings for a large tongue are half a lemon with peel, a stalk of celery with leaves, half an onion, a bay leaf, and sprigs of parsley and thyme. A clove of garlic is optional. Add seasonings after skinning.

Slice tongue across the grain at the base (wide end), and slice the tip diagonally to make bigger, better looking slices.

## TONGUE RECIPES

### Tongue, Yukon Style           (Makes 6–10 servings.)

| | |
|---|---|
| 1 tongue from moose, caribou, small cow, calf (Or several smaller animals' tongues.) | 1 onion, chopped medium |
| | 1 tablespoon flour |
| | 1 tablespoon lemon juice |
| 1 tablespoon onion juice, or minced onion | 1 tablespoon vinegar |
| | 2 tablespoons raisins |
| 1 sprig parsley | 2 tablespoons honey |
| 2 whole cloves | 1 bay leaf |
| 2 tablespoons butter | pepper, salt, optional |

Put the tongue in a pot and cover with water. Bring to a boil, skim as necessary, then add the onion juice, parsley, and cloves. Simmer till the meat is tender, 1 to 4 hours depending on size. Take out the tongue and skin it as soon as it is cool enough to handle. Slice the meat and strain the cooking broth.

Melt the butter in a frying pan, and gently sauté the onion in it for a minute or so. Add the flour, and brown it slowly, stirring constantly. Add 2 cups of the broth, lemon juice, vinegar, raisins, honey, bay leaf, pepper, and salt, if desired. Heat to a simmer, stirring, and add the sliced tongue. Cover and simmer over very low heat about 25 minutes. With its delicious sweet and sour sauce, this dish goes very well with homemade bread, or with rice.

### Cold Tongue Mexican Style       (Makes 8–12 side servings.)

| | |
|---|---|
| 2 pounds (about) cooked tongue (See PRECOOKING AND SKINNING TONGUE, above.) | ¼ cup wine vinegar, or homemade cider vinegar |
| | ¼ teaspoon salt, optional |
| 1 sweet onion, sliced paper thin | ½ teaspoon (about) black pepper, freshly ground |
| 1 orange with peel, sliced paper thin | |
| several olives, pitted, sliced | parsley, or coriander leaves, minced |
| ¾ cup olive oil | |

Cut the tongue in thin slices. Arrange with onion, orange, and olives in attractive layers in a shallow serving dish. Combine the oil, vinegar, pepper, and salt, if desired, to make a dressing and pour over the tongue arrangement. Refrigerate for 24 hours. Just before serving sprinkle with parsley or coriander. Excellent as an appetizer or the featured dish of a buffet.

*Pickled Lamb's Tongues*          (Makes about 2 quarts.)

| | |
|---|---|
| 4 pounds (about) lamb's tongues, or other small tongues | 12 peppercorns |
| | 6 whole cloves |
| 3 cups vinegar | 1 bay leaf |
| 1 onion | 1 teaspoon salt |

Put the tongues in a pot, add the vinegar, and then enough water to cover the tongues completely. Bring slowly to a boil and skim. Add the onion, peppercorns, cloves, bay leaf, and salt. Simmer slowly till the tongues are tender, from 1 to 2 hours. Take out the tongues, and, as soon as they can be handled, skin them. When cool, pack them in jars or a crock. Strain the cooking liquid, and pour it over them, adding vinegar if there is not enough to cover them. These tongues will keep several weeks or longer refrigerated. Serve as a snack, like other hearty pickled foods. They make superior picnic fare.

---

**OTHER RECIPES WITH TONGUE**

Head Cheese, p.327
Mincemeat in Jars, p.409
Quebec Pork Ragout, p.489
Salt Cured Tongue, p.37
Scrapple, p.329
Son-of-a-Bitch Stew, p.666

---

# TRIPE, CHITTERLINGS, AND PAUNCH

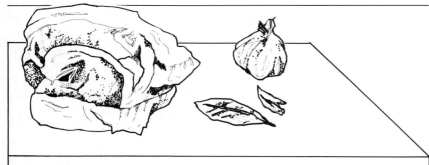

**STORAGE**

**Freezing** Clean and prepare (see below). Precook (optional). Wrap like meat. Quality retained about 4 mos. (Refer to FREEZING section.)

**Salt Curing** See PICKLED TRIPE, below.

---

TRIPE, CHITTERLINGS, AND PAUNCH ARE ALL WAYS OF PREPARING the stomachs and intestines of large meat animals. As they are all cleaned in about the same way, and can be cooked in the same ways, they are grouped together here.

"Tripe" commonly refers to the first and second stomachs of cows or calves, but sheep, pig, and game animal stomachs may also be called tripe. Honeycomb tripe comes from the cow's second stomach, and gets its name from the shape of its deep indentations. It is often considered the best kind of tripe, but smooth, regular tripe has just as much flavor. "Pocket tripe" is made from the end of a stomach which has a curved, pocket-like shape. Chitterlings, usually pronounced "chitlins" are made from a pig's stomach and intestines, which have been cleaned, cut in pieces, and are then cooked like tripe. Opinions differ as to which portions of the intestines and stomach can rightly be used as chitterlings. The stomachs of sheep, goats, deer, and pigs are known as paunches when they are removed, cleaned whole, and used as a casing for hash or sausage type mixtures. The first stomachs of cows are also sometimes called paunches even though used as tripe.

Tripe, chitterlings, and paunch are not high in nutritional value, but they are considered easy to digest, and they do have a special "something" about their flavor and texture that makes them taste very good. Haggis and Tripe à la Mode de Caen are renowned specialties from them. While such bland organ meats as lungs and spleen are often disguised in cooked mixtures, or eaten only to avoid wasting them, tripe, chitterlings, and paunch are widely sought after, and a favorite on many food lists.

## HANDLING TRIPE, CHITTERLINGS, AND PAUNCH

As soon as possible after slaughtering, remove the stomach from an animal's carcass, then empty it and wash it in cold water. If a paunch is wanted for stuffing, make a 4–5 inch slit in the stomach to empty it, and then turn it inside out for washing. A stomach for tripe or chitterlings can be cut open completely for easy cleaning. After the stomach is well washed, scald it to loosen the inside lining, and then scrape the lining off. If this cannot be done immediately, the washed stomach can be refrigerated, or kept in a cool place soaking in water with a little vinegar or salt added. But it must be taken care of during the next day.

*Scalding and Scraping Stomachs*   Heat a large pot of water almost to a boil, take it off the stove, then drop in the stomach. Paunches should be inside out. Keep a cow's stomach in the scalding water from 10–15 minutes to loosen the lining. A young animal's stomach will be ready to scrape in several minutes. The lining appears as a thin layer, slightly darker in color than the rest of the stomach. If the stomach is fairly smooth it scrapes off easily. However, scraping honeycomb tripe is slow work because of its indentations. Scrape it till it looks quite white. A dull edged knife makes a good scraping tool. A Chinese method for removing the lining is to rub the stomach on a rough stone. Rinse well after scraping.

Clean intestines for chitterlings like stomachs, except that they will not need scalding. Thin stomachs can be packed in salt and stored like intestines. They must be soaked to remove salt before use. (Refer to CLEANING INTESTINES, in the SAUSAGE section.)

*Precooking Tripe or Chitterlings*   Stomachs need long simmering to make them tender. Tripe and chitterlings can be precooked in water, with or without seasonings, and then used in various recipes. Cooking can take from several to 12 hours, depending on the age and toughness of the animal. It is possible to use a pressure cooker, but texture will be better with long, slow cooking. Soup bones can be cooked with tripe or chitterlings to make the cooking water into a flavorful stock. (Refer to the SOUP section.) Cut large tripe into convenient sized pieces before precooking. The fat on cow's tripe is most easily removed after precooking and chilling. (Precooked tripe can sometimes be bought in butcher shops and stores.)

Paunches are stuffed raw, then simmered long enough to tenderize them. As they are usually from younger animals they require only 2–3 hours of cooking. (Refer to the *Haggis* recipe, in the LAMB AND MUTTON section.)

*Pickled Tripe*   An old-time way to store tripe is to salt cure and pickle it. Precook tripe as above, till almost tender. For 10 pounds of tripe make a brine of 1 pound plain or pickling salt and 6½ cups water. Put the tripe in the brine, then weigh it down so it is entirely submerged. After 3 or 4 days, remove the tripe, rinse in fresh water, and put it in a crock or similar container. Cover with full strength vinegar and weigh it down so that it is completely submerged. (Refer to CROCKS AND CROCK SUBSTITUTES, in the KITCHEN UTENSILS section.) Store in a cool place. This tripe will keep for several months, or through the winter. To use, soak it in fresh water for several hours, and then drain it. It may take several changes of soaking water to remove the salt and vinegar taste. When freshened, use like ordinary precooked tripe.

# TRIPE, CHITTERLINGS, AND PAUNCH RECIPES

## *Tripe, Italian Style*   (Makes about 6 medium servings.)

- 2 tablespoons butter, or olive oil
- 2 tablespoons bacon, chopped, optional
- 1 onion, chopped
- 1 bay leaf
- 2 pounds tripe, precooked
- 1½ cups tomato sauce
- 1 clove garlic, minced
- 1 tablespoon parsley, minced
- 1 tablespoon rosemary, crushed dash pepper
- ¼ teaspoon salt, optional
- 1 cup (about) stock from cooking the tripe, or soup stock, or water

Heat the butter or oil in a large frying pan and add the bacon, onion and bay leaf. Sauté over low heat till the onion and bacon are browned. Cut the tripe in thin strips and add with the tomato, garlic, parsley, rosemary, pepper, and salt, if desired. Simmer over low heat from 1–2 hours, till the tripe is very tender, adding stock or water as needed to keep the mixture moist. It can be left quite thick to serve with rice or pasta, or it can be served in a bowl as a thin stew. This is a very good way to try the tripe for the first time. Rosemary suits tripe particularly well, making a dish most will like, or even love, immediately.

---

### TRIPE, CHITTERLINGS AND PAUNCH IDEAS

**Head Cheese in a Pig's Paunch**
Clean and scrape the paunch from a pig. Make a head cheese like the HEAD CHEESE I, in the HEADS section. Pack the mixture into the paunch, then stitch or tie it shut. Heat the stock left from cooking the head to a simmer. Do not let it boil. Put in the paunch to simmer till it floats, about 30 minutes. Hang it up to chill, or press it under a board and weight. The paunch will be too tough to eat and acts only as a casing. For a tender paunch, to be eaten as part of the head cheese, increase simmering time to about 2 hours. Always keep the heat below a boil to prevent bursting.

**TRIPE IDEAS,** *cont.*

**Tripe or Chitterlings in Stews and Soups**  Stew pieces of tripe or chitterlings with any slow cooking stew or soup meat. These enrich the gravy or stock and give it an especially good flavor. They go well with any of the vegetables and seasonings used in stews and soups.

**Marinated Tripe**  Precook tripe over low heat till very tender. Cut in strips and marinate for several hours up to several days in homemade cider vinegar or another fine flavored vinegar. Add thinly sliced onions, peppercorns, salt, if desired, and other seasonings to taste. A favorite salad dressing is another possible marinade. Any kind of tripe can be marinated—even moose tripe has been prepared in this way.

**Ground or Chopped Tripe, or Chitterlings**  Precook tripe or chitterlings till tender, then grind or chop it small. Include it in mixtures for hash, meat loaves, scrapple, or head cheese. It will add a special flavor to these mixtures, as well as extending them.

**OTHER RECIPES WITH TRIPE**

Haggis, p.381
Soup Stock (with Organ Meats), p.576
Tripe and Beans, p.398

## Tripe à la Mode de Caen  (Makes 6–8 dinner servings.)

There are many variations of this traditional French dish.

3 pounds (about) fresh tripe, in 1½ inch squares
½ calf's foot, or a slice of knuckle bone
3 onions, sliced medium
3 carrots, sliced medium
2 cloves of garlic
2 bay leaves
sprig parsley
sprig fresh thyme, or ½ teaspoon dried
celery leaves from 1 stalk
pepper, to taste
salt, optional
1 onion stuck with 2–3 cloves
2 cups (about) white wine

This dish is traditionally made in an earthenware pot, but a deep casserole with a lid or a bean pot works just as well. Make a layer of tripe around the calf's foot or knuckle bone in the bottom of the pot. Add a layer of onions and a layer of carrots. Add the garlic, bay leaves, parsley, thyme, and celery leaves. Or tie them in a cloth bag for removing later. Sprinkle with pepper and salt, if desired. Add the rest of the tripe, onions, and carrots in alternating layers, and season. Put the onion stuck with cloves on top. Mix the wine with 2 cups of water and pour over all. If necessary, add more water to cover ingredients. Cover tightly. Use several layers of aluminum foil tied tightly in place if the lid is not tight. Bake in a slow, 250°F oven from 8 to 12 hours.

Before serving remove the onion stuck with cloves, the bag of spent herbs, and the calf's foot or bone. Homemade sourdough or French bread is the perfect accompaniment.

## Chitlins, Soul Food Style  (Makes about 6 servings.)

5 pounds (about) cleaned chitterlings, in 2 inch pieces
2 red pepper pods, cut in several pieces
6 whole cloves
1 bay leaf
2 cloves garlic
1 large onion, whole
1 stalk celery, with leaves
1 teaspoon black pepper
¼ cup vinegar
salt, optional

Put the chitterlings, pepper pods, cloves, bay leaf, garlic, onion, celery, black pepper, and vinegar in a pot. Heat enough water to a boil to cover all ingredients, and add boiling hot, salting lightly, if desired. Simmer gently for about 3 hours, or till tender. Serve like a stew, with freshly baked cornbread to round out the meal.

*Fried Chitterlings or Tripe*  Cook chitterlings as in the recipe above and drain, or precook tripe till quite tender. Roll pieces in seasoned flour or cornmeal, or dip in beaten egg and then in fine dry bread crumbs, or dip in a batter, such as the VEGETABLE TEMPURA batter, in the FRUITS section. Sauté in butter or other fat in a frying pan, or deep fry till golden brown. Drain on paper. Very good with lemon juice squeezed on them, or with catsup or chili sauce.

BECAUSE THE TURKEY IS AN ALL-AMERICAN BIRD, "MUCH MORE respectable" than the bald eagle, Benjamin Franklin thought it should be the United States' national bird. He called the bald eagle "a Bird of Bad moral character." In any case, the turkey is and always has been an important food in the Americas. Wild turkeys were once so common over large parts of North and Central America that when wheat was scarce, slices of turkey breast were reportedly substituted for bread to make turkey sandwiches. (With turkey on the outside, the sandwich would indeed be hearty, and very tasty as well, especially with corn relish and lettuce on the inside.) In some areas wild turkeys are increasing and can be hunted in season. Their meat is juicier and less wild tasting than many other game meats. A young, wild turkey can be roasted like a domestic turkey, and older, tougher birds are excellent for stewing.

Modern domestic turkeys have an interesting origin. The Aztec Indians of Mexico had domesticated their local strain of wild turkey, and some of these birds were taken back to Spain by the conquistadors. From Spain they spread throughout Europe, and then early English colonists brought some birds to North America. These turkeys crossed with the local northeastern strain of wild turkey were the foundation stock for our present day domestic turkeys.

## HANDLING TURKEYS

Turkeys are killed, plucked, and cleaned like chickens. (Refer to the CHICKEN section.) If a large, heavy turkey is to be killed by cutting off its head, have two people do the job: one to hold the turkey and one to do the chopping. About a minute in scalding water will loosen turkey feathers as it does chicken feathers. Plucking will be easiest if the turkey is hung by its feet at a convenient height. A garbage can or other container can be set under the bird to catch the feathers.

Today turkeys are bred to be very meaty, with only small cavities for stuffing, and recipes in old cookbooks usually yield about twice as much dressing as will fit the recommended bird weight. Modern turkeys hold about ½ cup stuffing per 1 pound of dressed weight.

Roasting whole is just one of many possible ways to prepare turkey meat. When the turkey is cut and frozen as separate parts, the dark meat can be stewed or cooked according to game recipes, and the breast thinly sliced for cutlets or stir-frying. Turkey meat can be used in most chicken recipes. If the jointed pieces of a turkey are too large to cook like chicken, cut them smaller. Cut a drum stick in half the long way, bone it, then cut it to a convenient size. As turkey is likely to require longer cooking than a tender fryer, cooking times may need adjustment.

***Salt Cured and Smoked Turkey*** Most kinds of poultry are enjoyed when cured and smoked, and turkey is the favorite. Curing and smoking can also be a way to preserve turkey for 6 to 8 weeks after butchering. For longer storage it must be frozen. However, a very discouraging aspect of salt curing turkey and other poultry is the strong concentration of salt required—considerably stronger than the concentration used for ham and bacon. For this reason cured poultry should be eaten only sparingly. (For directions, refer to the references listed at the end of the SALT CURING section.)

For a delicious smoked flavor, turkey can be smoke cooked or hot smoked just before serving it. (Refer to the *Kitchen Smoked Chicken, or Other Poultry* recipe, in the SMOKING section.)

## TURKEY RECIPES

### *Roast Turkey with Pecan Stuffing*

(Makes 12 or more dinner servings.)

10 pound turkey, ready for stuffing
Stuffing (For a larger bird increase amounts proportionately):
1 tablespoon lard or butter
1 medium onion, minced
1 turkey liver, cooked, grated or minced
½ cup mushrooms, chopped fine
3 cups fine dry bread crumbs (Preferably whole grain.)
2 tablespoons butter, softened
½ teaspoon pepper

½ teaspoon celery seed
½ teaspoon thyme
1 tablespoon parsley, minced
¼ teaspoon nutmeg
⅛ teaspoon mace
½ teaspoon salt, optional
¼ cup turkey stock, or water
3 eggs, hard boiled
1 cup pecans, chopped medium fine (Or use walnuts, hickory nuts, or butternuts.)
¼ cup sherry

Have the turkey at room temperature when stuffing it, and put into the oven very soon after.

To make the stuffing, melt the lard or butter in a frying pan, then sauté the onion in it till limp. Add the liver and mushrooms, and sauté till becoming golden over low heat. Set aside to cool while preparing the rest of the stuffing.

Combine the bread crumbs, softened butter, pepper, celery seed, thyme, parsley, nutmeg, mace, and salt, if desired. Heat the stock or water to a boil, then mix thoroughly into the bread crumb mixture. Mince the egg whites or put them through a potato ricer. Rub the yolks against the side of a bowl with a spoon till smooth. Mix whites, yolks, pecans, sherry, and the liver and mushroom mixture into the stuffing.

Stuff both body and breast cavities. Fill them, but do not pack down the stuffing, as it will swell somewhat during roasting. Close the openings with skewers or a heavy needle and thread. Tie the wings and legs in place against the body. Set on a rack in a roasting pan. If desired, to seal in juices, put into a very hot, 450°F oven and turn down to 300°F immediately. Otherwise, roast between 300 and 325°F from the beginning. Either way, allow 30 minutes roasting time per pound for birds up to 10 pounds, and 15 to 20 minutes per

---

### TURKEY IDEAS

**Pressed Cold Turkey Loaf**

Make layers of sliced, cooked, light and dark turkey meat in a loaf pan. Press by setting another loaf pan of the same size on the meat, and putting something heavy into the second pan. Refrigerate till well chilled.

Meanwhile boil down turkey stock to make about 2 cups that are concentrated enough to jell, or else add dry gelatine. (Refer to

pound for heavier birds. If using a meat thermometer, insert it into the thigh next to the body, taking care that it does not touch bone. It should read about 190°F when the bird is done. Or test for doneness by wiggling the drumstick, which should be loose at the joint.

In some ovens the breast and wings of a turkey will burn or overcook before the rest of the bird is done. To prevent this, cover the breast with aluminum foil or a cloth rubbed with unsalted lard or another fat. Remove the cover for the last 30 minutes or so to crisp the skin. Another method for retaining moisture in the breast meat is roasting breast side down for the first half of the cooking time. However, it is difficult to turn over a large bird without damaging the skin and spoiling its appearance. When done, remove skewers, threads, and strings, and set it on a serving platter or board. Let it sit about 20 minutes before carving, and it will slice more smoothly. This stuffing has a delicious blend of flavors, and is almost as high in protein as the meat itself, so small servings are advisable.

*Roasting Wild or Very Lean Turkeys*   Rub unsalted lard or butter on the skin before the turkey goes in the oven to help prevent drying. Cornmeal can be sprinkled on the skin over the lard or butter, for still more protection.

*Turkey Soup from the Carcass*   The bones and scraps from a roast turkey make delicious soup. For the most flavor, break or crack large leg bones with a meat cleaver or poultry shears. Put the bones, scraps, seasoning vegetables, and herbs in a big pot, add water, then simmer about 1½ hours. Strain through cloth to remove slivers of bone and other debris. The stock can be enriched with pan drippings or leftover gravy, and soup ingredients can be added to taste. (Refer to the SOUP section.)

## Best Turkey Giblet Gravy

(Makes 2–3 cups.)

| | |
|---|---|
| 1 turkey neck, gizzard, and heart | 1 teaspoon peppercorns |
| 1 turkey liver, optional | pan juices and scrapings from a |
| 1 cup wine (Preferably dry, white.) | roast turkey, optional |
| 2–3 sprigs parsley | 1–2 tablespoons flour |
| 1–2 carrots, in thick slices | salt, optional |
| 1 onion stuck with 2 cloves | |

Put the neck, gizzard, heart, and the liver, if desired, in a pot. Add the wine and enough water to just cover the meats, or use plain water. Add the parsley, carrot, onion, and peppercorns. Bring to a boil and skim off any froth that rises. Cover, then simmer for about an hour, till the gizzard is tender when poked with a fork. Take out the gizzard, heart, and liver, chop small, then set aside. Continue to simmer the rest of the ingredients, uncovered, till the liquid has reduced to 1 or 2 cups. Strain, and discard the neck and vegetables.

Put the pan juices and scrapings in a small container, then skim off the fat when it rises. Mix with the stock made from the neck and giblets. Heat about 2 tablespoons of the fat collected from the pan juices (or use another fat), in a saucepan. Stir in the flour, moisten-

the GELATINE section.) Remove the weight from the turkey slices and pour stock over them till it comes almost to the top of the meat. Put the weight in place again, then chill till set. Turn the loaf out of pan, and slice cold like any luncheon meat. Chicken and chicken stock can be used instead of turkey.

**Boiled Turkey**   This is an old-time recipe for a bird that is a little too tough for roasting. Cook stuffed or unstuffed. Prepare the turkey as for roasting, then tie it in a cotton cloth to hold it in shape. Put it in a large kettle with enough warm water to cover it completely. Add 1 cup raw rice, and heat to a boil, then simmer till the meat is tender, about 3 hours. Take out the turkey, let it drain a few minutes, and unwrap it on a serving platter. (Save the cooking water and rice for soup.) Garnish with slices of lemon, or serve with the *Cream Sauce,* in the MILK section, or the *Lemon Butter,* in the BUTTER section.

Or fill the cavity of the boiled turkey with stewed oysters as soon as it is done, and make a sauce of oyster broth, butter, and herbs to go with it.

**Leftover Turkey Casserole**   Make layers of sliced or diced leftover turkey meat, leftover stuffing, and leftover gravy, in a baking dish. If there is no dressing, use seasoned bread crumbs, cooked macaroni, or another pasta. If there is no gravy use a *Cream Sauce,* in the MILK section, or CREAMED MUSHROOMS, in the MUSHROOMS section. Bake in a hot, 375°F oven for 25 minutes.

If using diced turkey, macaroni, and creamed mushrooms, and the top is sprinkled with bread crumbs, Parmesan cheese, and dribbles of olive oil, this becomes an Italian favorite known as Turkey Tetrazzini.

## TURKEY IDEAS, cont.

**Deviled Turkey** Butter a shallow baking dish and arrange thick slices of turkey in it. Spread a little soft butter on the turkey. In a separate dish mix a marinade of equal parts of lemon juice or wine vinegar, sherry, and prepared mustard. Add celery seed, mushroom catsup (refer to IDEAS, in the MUSHROOMS section), or other seasonings, to taste. Pour the marinade over the turkey and let sit for about an hour. Then bake in a moderate oven for 20 minutes.

## Turkey Breast for Stir-frying

Raw breast meat from a turkey is excellent used instead of chicken or another light meat in stir-fried dishes. Cut the breast into very thin slices, across the grain where possible, then cut the slices into small rectangles or shreds. Deboned turkey breast can be frozen in ½ to 1 pound chunks and sliced more easily when partly thawed. Try it in *Asparagus Stir-fried with Meat,* in the ASPARAGUS section. (Also refer to the STIR-FRYING section.)

ing it completely. Add the stock and juices and cook, stirring, till smooth and thickened, usually about 5 minutes. Add the chopped gizzard, heart, and liver, and simmer another couple of minutes. Taste, and adjust seasonings, adding salt if desired. (This gravy must be tasted to be appreciated.)

***Giblet Gravy from Chicken, Goose, or Other Poultry*** Gravy can be made in the same way from the neck, gizzard, heart, and liver of any poultry.

### Turkey Mole                     (Makes 8–12 dinner servings.)

This dish originated with the Aztec Indians of Mexico.

*1 small turkey, or ½ large (8–10 pounds), in serving pieces*
*4 tablespoons lard*
*1 hot red or green pepper, or add to taste (If dried, presoak to soften.)*
*2 onions, chopped*
*4 cloves of garlic, chopped*
*½ teaspoon anise seeds*
*2–3 sprigs fresh coriander, or parsley*
*4 tablespoons sesame seeds*
*1 tortilla, or 1 slice toast, broken in pieces*
*1 cup almonds*
*½ cup raisins*
*1½ cups stewed tomatoes, or 2 cups fresh tomatoes, chopped*
*½ teaspoon cloves*
*½ teaspoon cinnamon*
*½ teaspoon coriander seeds, ground*
*1½ squares (1½ ounces) unsweetened chocolate*
*2 cups (about) turkey stock (Reserved when meat is cooked.)*

Put the turkey pieces in a pot and cover them with water. Bring to a boil, then simmer 1 hour, till the meat is just tender. Drain, and reserve the stock. Dry the turkey on towels. Heat the lard in a frying pan and brown the meat. Transfer the browned pieces to a large baking dish.

Combine the hot pepper, onion, garlic, anise seeds, coriander or parsley, 2 tablespoons of the sesame seeds, tortilla or toast, almonds, raisins, and tomatoes. Put the mixture in a blender in several batches and purée coarsely. If too thick for the blender to handle, add a little of the reserved turkey stock. However, make the purée as thick as possible.

Put the purée in the same frying pan used for browning the turkey. Heat quickly and cook 5 minutes over high heat, stirring constantly. Reduce heat, then add the cloves, cinnamon, coriander seeds, and chocolate. Stir till the chocolate has melted. Then stir in enough of the reserved stock to make the sauce about as thick as heavy cream — usually about 2 cups.

Pour the sauce over the turkey in the baking dish. Cover and bake in a low, 325°F oven for 30 minutes. Just before serving sprinkle with the other 2 tablespoons of sesame seeds.

Goes well with rice, or serve it with rice, beans, and tortillas.

***Chicken Mole*** Use a large chicken instead of a turkey, halve the rest of the ingredients, and adjust the simmering time in the first step. A fryer will be tender in less than an hour, and a stewing hen will take longer.

Turnips are by reputation plain, unexciting, everyday fare, but their reputation does not do them justice. Turnips have been cultivated for centuries, during which time they have been food for livestock, for peasants, and the *pièce de resistance* on the tables of kings. They have often been boiled, but they have also been souffléed, gratinéed, stuffed with fruit, simmered in wine, and carved into elaborate shapes to grace fancy dishes. Today's turnip eaters are lucky, for this is a vegetable that is easy to grow, and very productive, and it comes with a legacy of interesting recipes handed down through centuries of worldwide turnip eating.

Turnip greens are as good to eat as the roots, and some varieties are grown just for their greens. They taste like mustard greens and can be prepared in the same ways. (Refer to the MUSTARD GREENS AND SEEDS section.) To differentiate between turnips and rutabagas refer to the RUTABAGA section.

## HANDLING TURNIPS

Spring planted turnips are best picked small, before the weather gets too hot, when they are crisp and mild enough to eat raw. The greens are also best when young. Turnips planted to mature in the fall can be left in the ground till after light frosts. If they are to be stored in a root cellar or outdoor pit, cut off the tops about an inch above the turnip. Do not wash them or trim the roots. Any turnips left in the root cellar in early spring can be re-planted for a very early crop of greens. Cut the greens before seed stalks develop. The tops that grow while the turnips are in storage are also good to eat.

Before cooking, trim and wash turnips, using a vegetable brush when necessary. They do not need peeling.

### STORAGE

**Canning** Not recommended for roots. (Tend to discolor and become strong flavored, except if fermented.) (Refer to CANNING SAUERKRAUT in SAUERKRAUT section.) *Greens* Can like spinach. (Refer to SPINACH section.)

**Cold Storage** *Roots* Plant to mature in fall. Pack in damp sand or other damp material. Keep 2–4 mos. in root cellar or similar conditions. Turnip odor affects fruit and penetrates living areas—outdoor storage preferred. (Refer to COLD STORAGE section.) Also refer to KEEPING SAUERKRAUT IN COLD STORAGE in SAUERKRAUT section.

**Drying** *Roots* Slice thinly, or shred. Optional: Steam to cook through. Dry to brittle or leathery. *Greens* Optional: Steam blanch 4–6 min. to wilt. Spread on trays with minimal overlap. Dry till crumbly. (Refer to DRYING section.)

**Freezing** *Roots* Dice or slice. Blanch in boiling water: 2 min. Steam: 2½ min. Or cook and mash. *Greens* Blanch in boiling water: 2 min. (Refer to FREEZING section.)

## TURNIP RECIPES

### Turnip Gratin                    (Makes 5–6 side servings.)

| | |
|---|---|
| *1–2 pounds turnips, thinly sliced* | *pepper, to taste* |
| *1 clove garlic, optional* | *½ cup milk, or light cream* |
| *3 tablespoons (about) butter* | *¼ cup cheese, grated* |
| *1 tablespoon parsley, minced* | *¼ cup bread crumbs* |

Steam the turnip slices for 3 or 4 minutes. Rub a shallow baking dish or deep pie dish with the garlic cut in half, or with garlic mashed in a garlic press. Then butter the dish. Make a layer of half of the turnips. Sprinkle with parsley and pepper. Add the rest of turnips in another layer. Pour the milk or cream over all. Sprinkle with the cheese and bread crumbs, and dot with shavings of butter. Bake in a hot, 375°F oven for 40 minutes, or till the turnip is tender. Good served hot or warm.

### Turnip Soufflé (Makes 4–6 servings.)

2 cups (about) turnips, cooked, mashed or puréed
2 tablespoons butter, melted

3 tablespoons light cream, or evaporated milk
4 eggs, separated
pepper, salt, optional

Combine the turnips, butter, cream or evaporated milk, and egg yolks. Beat till smooth. Season with pepper and salt, if desired. Beat the egg whites till stiff and fold them into the turnip mixture. Pour into a buttered baking dish, then bake at 450°F for about 20 minutes, till browned on top and set. Usually served immediately, because like any soufflé, it falls after a few minutes. However, it tastes just as delicious fallen, as long as it is still warm.

***Parsnip or Asparagus Soufflé, or Vegetable Purée Soufflé*** Cook and mash or purée parsnips, asparagus, or any other vegetable, and use instead of the turnips.

### Turnip Tzimmes (Makes about 6 dinner servings.)

2 pounds beef brisket, or another stew meat
1 onion, chopped
3 tablespoons (about) fat, or oil
2 pounds turnips, in 1 inch cubes

dash of nutmeg, optional
¼ cup honey, optional
pepper, salt, optional
2 tablespoons flour

In a pot, brown the meat and onion in about a tablespoon of fat or oil. Add the turnips and enough water to cover ingredients. Bring to a boil, and skim if necessary. Add nutmeg, honey, pepper and salt, if desired. Cover, then simmer till the meat is tender, which may take several hours. Turn the meat several times and add a little hot water if it begins to dry out. When done there should be 1 to 2 cups of broth in the pot.

Next, heat 2 tablespoons of fat or oil in a frying pan, add the flour, and brown slowly, stirring over low heat. Then gradually add about a cup of broth from the meat and turnips. Stir till thickened. Add to the meat and turnips and simmer, uncovered, till the turnips are glazed, another 15 to 20 minutes.

***Carrot Tzimmes*** Use carrot cut in 1 inch sections instead of turnips.

### Turnips in Cumin Sauce, Old Roman Style (Makes 4–6 side servings.)

Adapted from John Edwards' *The Roman Cookery of Apicius*, Hartley and Marks, 1985.

The turnip seasonings of rosemary, ginger, wine, and sweetening have the blessing of the ages, as they appear in this Roman recipe and in the centuries later Elizabethan recipe that follows.

---

## TURNIP IDEAS

**Raw Turnip Instead of Radishes** Turnips harvested in cool weather taste as crisp and good as radishes. They can be sliced or grated for salads, or sliced or cut into sticks to go with dips. Use them in the radish RECIPES and IDEAS, in the RADISHES section.

**Turnip Sculptures** Carve raw turnips into fanciful shapes. Use the "chips" in salads or cooking and use the sculpture for garnishes and decoration. Young people may enjoy this more than carving bars of soap or pieces of balsa wood since they can eat the results after showing them off.

**Turnip and Fish Soup** Grate some turnips and simmer in fish stock. Season to taste. For a Chinese flavor, add a few slices of fresh ginger root, a minced scallion, and a little sherry. This soup can be made with a fish head, gills removed. Brown the head, scallion, and ginger root in a little lard or oil in a soup pot. Add water and simmer half an hour. Then add the grated turnip and simmer for another 5 minutes. If desired, take the fish head out, or leave it in as a conversation piece.

½ cup white wine
1 pound turnips, cubed
½ teaspoon cumin seed
pinch of rosemary

¼ teaspoon ginger (Preferably
 the fresh root, minced.)
1 teaspoon honey
2 teaspoons olive oil
1 tablespoon (about) flour
 pepper

Simmer the wine in a small pan to reduce it to ¼ cup. Meanwhile, cook the turnips in 1½ cups water till they are half done, from 5 to 10 minutes. Drain, and reserve the cooking water.

Add the cumin, rosemary, ginger, honey, olive oil, and the reduced wine to the turnips, and add enough of the turnip cooking water to just cover them. Finish cooking them in this sauce. When done, thicken the sauce by mixing the flour with a little cool water and stirring some of the liquid from the turnips into it. Then add it to the pot, and stir till thickened. Sprinkle with pepper just before serving.

## Elizabethan Stuffed Turnips

(Makes 6 side servings.)

3 large turnips
1½ cups apple, minced
3 tablespoons raisins or currants
2 yolks of hard-boiled eggs, mashed
3 tablespoons fine, dry bread crumbs
½ teaspoon cinnamon

¼ teaspoon ginger (Preferably
 the fresh root, minced.)
¾ cup red wine or apple cider
1 tablespoon vinegar
1 tablespoon butter
¼ teaspoon rosemary
⅓ cup dates, chopped, or 2
 tablespoons (about) honey

Cut the turnips in half through their "equator," and cut a slice from the stem and root ends so that the halves will sit flat. With a paring knife, or the end of an apple corer, hollow out each half to make a cup. (Use the leftover centers in another way. See TURNIP IDEAS.)

Mix together the apple, raisins or currants, egg yolks, bread crumbs, cinnamon, and ginger. Fill the turnip cups with this mixture, mounding it up to use all of the stuffing. Put the cups in a wide pot or deep frying pan with a lid. They must fit in one layer. In a saucepan, heat the wine or cider, vinegar, butter, and rosemary with about a cup of water. When the butter has melted, pour carefully around the turnip cups. The level of the liquid must stay below the top of the turnips. Save any extra liquid to add after the turnips have cooked a while. Simmer, covered, without boiling till done, about 50 minutes. Add the dates or honey to the liquid around the turnip cups and simmer another 5 minutes.

Serve the turnip cups in small dishes with some of the sauce from cooking them spooned over each. They can be an elegant side dish with meat, a snack, or even a dessert.

---

### TURNIP IDEAS, cont.

**Mashed Turnips**  Steam turnips or stew them in a minimum of water till tender. Mash with a potato masher, ricer, or food mill. Season like mashed potatoes. Mixtures of half turnip and half potato, or turnips, apples, and potatoes are also very good mashed.

**Turnips with Sausage**  Dice turnips and stew them in a little butter in a tightly covered saucepan over low heat. When almost done add small pieces of smoked sausage.

**Turnip Cups with Peas**
Steam whole turnips till cooked through, but not too soft, from 30 to 50 minutes, depending on size. Cut a slice off the bottom of each turnip so that it will sit flat. Then cut off the top and hollow out the center for a cup. If the turnips are very large, cut them in half for two cups, one from the bottom and one from the top half. (The centers can be used for MASHED TURNIPS, above.) Season cooked peas with butter, pepper, and, if desired, diced ham. Fill the cups and serve immediately, or warm them a few minutes in the oven in a buttered pan.

---

### OTHER RECIPES WITH TURNIPS

Colcannon, p.91
Fermented Turnip, Rutabaga, or
 Winter Radish, p.177
Kimchi, p.176
Making Sauerkraut, p.540
Recipes, and Ideas for Mustard
 Greens (using turnip greens),
 p.427
Recipes, and Ideas for
 Vegetables, p.669
Turnip and Meat Soup, p.507

EVERY SPECIES OF TURTLE HAS PROBABLY BEEN EATEN AT ONE TIME or another. Most primitive people made extensive use of them, because they were easy to catch and their shells were useful, and certainly, no doubt, because their meat tasted so good.

In the eastern half of North America snapping turtles are eaten more often than any other species. They are common pests in farm ponds and slow moving streams, where they feed on small fish, ducklings, and goslings. (It is their habit to lurk under water and grab the baby birds by their feet and pull them under.) Terrapin, which include several kinds of small, freshwater turtles, are often used for food, especially in the southeastern United States, and some cookbooks list turtle recipes under that name. The diamond-back is the best known terrapin. Some other commonly eaten freshwater species are the Pacific pond turtle, the Mississippi, Mobile, and Suwanee turtles, and red-bellied, yellow-bellied, and chicken turtles. Different kinds of turtles can be used interchangeably in recipes. Though sea turtles are also well known for food, they are seldom available. To be safe for eating, freshwater turtles must be taken from clean, unpolluted waters. As many species are long lived, they may collect larger amounts of such toxins as PCBs than do fish. Care must also be taken not to harvest endangered species.

## HANDLING TURTLES

All parts of a turtle are edible except the shell, bones, gall bladder, and sand bag. The liver and eggs are considered delicacies. The intestines can be eaten, though that depends on personal tastes. In some localities, the intestines and sand bag are called the "dead man," and with such a name it is not surprising that both are discarded. There are six meaty pieces, the four legs, tail, and neck.

*Turtle Eggs*   Eggs found inside a female turtle are usually used along with the meat in soups and stews. Turtle eggs that are dug out of nests in the ground where they were laid can be cooked like chicken eggs. When boiled, the yolks of turtle eggs set, but the whites remain soft. The whites can be mashed into the hard cooked yolks to moisten them, and used in recipes such as the CREAMED TURTLE, below.

## KILLING AND CLEANING TURTLES

Large turtles can be killed by chopping off their heads or by shooting them in the head. Small turtles are often killed by dropping them alive in boiling water, but can be decapitated as well. Snapping turtles are the most difficult to deal with, because of their strong jaws, sharp claws, and mean dispositions. The following directions can, in general, be applied to other species, as well. For turtles whose heads retract completely into their shells, pressing down on the upper shell will make the head protrude so it can be chopped off.

*Killing Snapping Turtles*  The only safe way to pick up a live snapping turtle is by the tail. It is important to stay out of reach of the claws and head both before and after killing it. The turtle can be teased into snapping onto a long stick so that its head can be pulled out as far as possible for easy chopping. The stick also keeps the jaws occupied. As a turtle will continue to thrash around for a long time after the head is off, the claws are still dangerous. Some people chop off the claws with a hatchet right after chopping off the head, making the carcass safer to handle. The severed head can also continue to be dangerous for a while. A snapper's head has been known to clamp onto a curious dog's paw so tightly, that it was necessary to cut open the head at the jaws to release the paw. If a turtle is shot in the head to kill it, the head must still be cut off so that the carcass will bleed out completely.

After the head is cut off, hang the turtle by the tail for several hours or overnight while it bleeds, and also to let some of the movement stop. The carcass can continue to move for as long as 3 days after death, so it is likely that movement will be felt when it is cleaned and cut up. This after death reflex activity seems more pronounced when a turtle was beheaded than when it was shot.

*Cleaning Snapping Turtles*  A snapping turtle has two layers of skin, a thin blackish skin over a thick, tough hide. Scalding and rubbing will remove the black skin, so that the hide can be cooked with the meat. However, some prefer to skin off the hide when cleaning the turtle, making scalding unnecessary.

To scald, drop the turtle in boiling water for about a minute, or put it in a big kettle and pour boiling water over it. When the toenails loosen, take it out and rub off the skin. If left in the water too long the skin will tighten again.

The first step in cleaning the turtle is to set it on its back, and remove the under or lower shell, known as the star. Cut completely around the edge of the star and lift it off. The bridges or places where it connects to the upper shell may be too tough to cut with a knife. If so, set a hatchet or cleaver in position and tap with a hammer to cut through them. (The bridges in other species are harder and must usually be cut with a saw or hatchet.)

Once the star is removed the inside parts can be recognized by anyone who has cleaned chickens. Remove the green sac (gall bladder) from the liver as soon as it is located. Some cut out and remove the edible parts one by one. Others cut all the way around the shell, removing all of the contents together and then separating them. There are bony connections to the shell near the neck and near the tail, which usually require a hatchet or cleaver and hammer to cut through. Because turtle bones have an odd, unfamiliar shape, it may take extra probing to find the joints and disjoint them. All of the fat should be discarded because it has a strong, fishy taste. There are two fillets of meat inside the rib-like structure against the "backbone" of the shell that are taken out last. To get them out, cut the "ribs" with a hatchet, or a strong pruning shears. The empty shell can be hung in a tree for the birds to clean out, or given to the chickens to clean, and then used for a container or for decoration. (Dogs are likely to chew the shell to pieces if given the chance.)

Wash the turtle meat well, and refrigerate it till it is to be cooked or frozen. While old directions often advised soaking it in salted water overnight, or bringing it to a boil in water with baking soda, and then draining, rinsing, and cooking it in fresh water, these steps are not necessary with modern refrigeration.

*Cooking Snapping Turtles*  Snapping turtle meat is tough, requiring long, slow cooking. While ideal for soup, it is also good precooked till tender, and then fried, creamed, or used in any recipe for cooked meat. It is best to slice it thinly across the grain to minimize stringiness. (Refer to USING TOUGH MEAT, in the MEAT section.)

The meat's flavor is excellent. There are those who like it better than any other meat, and happily fill their freezers with it. It is variously described as tasting like chicken, beef, pork, seafood, and other meats, which seems to prove that its taste is unique.

*Boiling Small Turtles*  Drop live terrapins and other small sized turtles into plenty of boiling water and boil 10 minutes or so. Then take them out and rub the black skin off the head and legs. It may be necessary to pry out the head to get at it. (Some directions say to start the turtle in cold water and bring to a boil, which causes the head to protrude, but this method seems unnecessarily cruel. Another alternative is to cut off the head just before boiling, but it is doubtful whether this is any kinder to the turtle.) When the black skin is off and the turtle has been well rinsed, put it in a pot of fresh water and cook till tender, usually about 2 hours. Save the broth, which is delicious, and let the turtle cool on its back, so that juices collect in the shell. Then pry off the under shell, cut the gall bladder off the liver, and take out the sand bag, which is near the center against the upper shell. The intestines can be discarded, if desired. The meat, liver, and eggs can be taken out to use as ingredients in recipes, or they can be chopped and seasoned, for baking and serving in the shell.

*Snapping turtle hung for bleeding. Shows undershell, or star.*

## TURTLE RECIPES

### *Snapper Soup*                          (Makes 10–12 medium bowls.)

3–4 pounds snapping turtle meat
  (Preferably with hide.)
1 tablespoon vinegar
2 stalks celery, with leaves
2 medium carrots
1 large onion
2 bay leaves
1 clove garlic
sprig of parsley

sprig thyme, or 1 teaspoon dried
  thyme
pepper, salt, optional
4 tablespoons butter
2 tablespoons flour
½ cup sherry, optional
2–3 hard-boiled eggs, peeled,
  sliced (Or, if the turtle had
  eggs, use the hard-boiled
  yolks.)

Put the turtle meat, vinegar, celery, carrots, onion, bay leaf, garlic, parsley, and thyme in a soup pot, and cover with about 2 quarts water. Bring to a boil and skim. Reduce heat, then simmer covered till the meat is tender, from 2 to 3 hours. When done, strain, reserving the stock. When cool enough to handle pick the meat away from the bones, and discard bones, hide, and spent vegetables.

Cut the turtle meat into small pieces across the grain to prevent stringiness. Melt the butter in the soup pot, then brown the meat in it. Next, blend in the flour and add the reserved stock. Reheat and simmer a few minutes, stirring often. Add the sherry and egg slices just before serving, or serve garnished with the egg, and let everyone add sherry to suit themselves. Turtle excels for making soup, and this one is a classic.

### Turtle Soup, Creole Style

(Makes 10–14 medium bowls.)

| | |
|---|---|
| 3–4 pounds turtle meat | ¼ teaspoon cloves |
| 1 turtle liver, optional | ¼ teaspoon allspice |
| 1½ teaspoons oil | 2 fresh tomatoes, chopped, or 1 |
| 1½ teaspoons butter | cup stewed |
| 1 onion, minced | cayenne pepper, to taste |
| 2 tablespoons ham, minced | salt, optional |
| 1 clove garlic, minced | 2 chicken eggs, or the eggs from |
| 2 tablespoons flour | the turtle, hard-boiled, |
| 1 tablespoon parsley, minced | chopped |
| 1 teaspoon thyme | ½ cup white wine, or sherry |
| 1 bay leaf, crumbled | ½ of a lemon, sliced very thinly |

Simmer the turtle meat and liver in about 2 quarts water to cover till tender. Take the liver out in about 30 minutes. The turtle meat may take from 2–3 hours. Drain, reserving stock. Pick the meat off the bones, then chop it small across the grain. Chop the liver as well.

Heat the oil and butter in a soup pot, and slowly brown the turtle meat and liver in it. Add the ham and garlic, and sauté another minute or two. Stir in the flour, till completely moist. Add the reserved stock, parsley, thyme, bay leaf, cloves, allspice, and tomatoes. Heat, then simmer for about 30 minutes, till flavors are blended. Season with cayenne and salt, if desired. Just before serving add the chopped eggs, wine, and lemon slices. An elegant, full flavored soup.

## TURTLE IDEAS

### Thin Sliced Snapper on Toast

Slice raw snapper meat very thinly across the grain. Shake the slices in flour, then sauté them slowly in butter till lightly browned. Season with pepper, rosemary, or other herbs, to taste. Add soup stock, water or wine to half cover the meat. Cover with a tight lid, then simmer over very low heat till tender, about 1 hour. When done a little cream can be added, if desired. Delicious served on toast sprinkled with paprika and minced parsley.

### Creamed Turtle

Cooked, chopped turtle meat is very good heated in a cream sauce made partly with turtle stock. (Refer to the *Cream Sauce*, in the MILK section.) Cayenne or paprika, and a little lemon juice make good seasonings.

For a fancy version, heat 4 cups turtle meat in about a cup of stock or milk, then thicken with 5 yolks of hard-boiled eggs mashed with 2 tablespoons softened butter. Add a cup of light cream and the chopped whites of the hardboiled eggs. Season with cayenne pepper and sherry, then heat, but do not boil.

### Turtle Baked in the Shell

Scrub and rinse the turtle's shell after removing the contents, or use the shell from a whole boiled turtle. Fill the shell with cooked, chopped, seasoned turtle meat. Add cooking juice or stock for moisture, or use CREAMED TURTLE, above. Sprinkle with bread crumbs and dots of butter, then bake about 30 minutes in a moderate, 350°F oven.

# VEAL

Veal is the meat of a calf butchered while young enough to have the light delicacy of the suckling animal. Calves up to about 14 weeks are considered to be veal. From 15 weeks to 1 year the meat is often called baby beef. Most veal recipes require the lean, succulent meat of a very young animal for which baby beef is not suitable. (Baby beef is best when cooked and seasoned in the same manner as mature beef.)

The raising of veal calves is the subject of considerable controversy. Some calves are deliberately fed an iron deficient diet, and kept in a darkened place without exercise to keep their meat fashionably white and delicate. Antibiotics are a routine part of their feed to maintain their weakened bodies. As well as the question of the inhumanity of this practice, there is the question of whether it is wise to eat meat from an anemic animal in poor health. Eating home raised or naturally raised veal can be doubly satisfying—its flavor is superb, and there is the reassuring knowledge that the animal's life was normal and healthy, if short. Naturally raised veal is sometimes marketed as rose veal, to emphasize the meat's healthy, pink glow.

## HANDLING VEAL

Calves are first stunned, then stuck to kill and bleed them in the same way as mature cows. The general procedure for skinning and cutting up the carcass is the same as for other meat animals of a similar size. (Refer to KILLING AND SKINNING LAMBS AND SHEEP, in the LAMB AND MUTTON section.) As veal dries out quickly after the carcass is skinned, the hide can be left on till just before cutting up the meat. However, skinning is easiest while the animal is still warm. Sometimes the caul is draped over the hind quarters after they are skinned to help prevent drying. (Refer to CAUL AND RUFFLE FATS, in

### STORAGE

**Canning** Stewed or ground meat is best. Process like beef. (Refer to BEEF section.)

**Drying** Can be done as meat is very lean; other storage methods preferred. (Refer to DRYING MEAT in DRYING section.)

**Freezing** (Best storage method.) Quality retained 8–12 mos. (Refer to FREEZING section.)

the LARD section.) For more detailed directions refer to the REFER-
ENCE SOURCES at the end of the LAMB AND MUTTON section.

The sweetbreads, liver, heart, kidneys, tongue, and brains of a calf
are choice and should be carefully reserved. The testicles, whether
from butchering or castration, are also good. The feet and bones are
valuable for making a clear, bland, readily jelled stock. The list on
page 377 of useable parts of a lamb or mutton carcass and ways to use
them also applies to veal.

Veal is very lean, with a high moisture content, and must be
cooked either at a low temperature, or with fat. (Refer to LEAN
MEAT, in the MEAT section.)

*Cutting Veal Scallops*   Scallops (cutlets) are the very thin slices of
meat often called for in veal recipes. They are cut from the leg, but
instead of slicing crosswise, as for steaks, the meat is separated into
sections the long way, following the animal's natural muscular structure. Then thin slices are cut on the bias from these sections. Each
scallop should be in one piece with no seams showing. To flatten
them, the scallops are pounded lightly with the flat or broad side of a
cleaver, or heavy knife, or with a wooden mallet. The pounding must
be gentle, to prevent breaking the meat into pieces. Though crosswise
slices of veal can be used in place of bias cut scallops, they do not
handle as easily and their texture is less perfect.

## VEAL RECIPES

### Saltimbocca
(Italian style veal with ham.)            (Makes about 6 dinner servings.)

2 pounds (about) veal scallops (To slice, see above.)

sage, fresh or dried (One leaf per scallop.)

¼ pound (about) prosciutto, or an-other ham, sliced paper thin (One slice per scallop.)

2 tablespoons butter
1 tablespoon oil
pepper
2 tablespoons white wine, veal stock, or water
parsley, minced, for garnish

Pound the scallops very lightly to flatten them. Put a fresh sage
leaf or a sprinkle of dried sage on each scallop, then lay a slice of ham
on top. Pin together with a toothpick. Heat the butter and oil in a
large frying pan till quite hot. Put in the meat, sprinkle with pepper,
and sauté over fairly high heat for a short time on both sides, till the
veal is browned. Put the slices, ham side up, on a serving platter.
Add the wine, stock, or water to the frying pan and stir, scraping the
bottom and sides for a rich juice. Pour over the saltimbocca, sprinkle
with parsley and serve.

The simple perfection of this dish is best complemented by simple
accompaniments, especially new potatoes, and peas or another green
vegetable.

---

### VEAL IDEAS
**Veal Meatballs with Herbs**
More than most meats, veal is
well complemented by the flavor
of herbs. Rosemary is particularly good, but sage, bay leaf,
thyme, and others are also excellent. A good way to try different herbs is to add them to meatballs made from ground veal. Use
herbs fresh, minced, or dried.
Try meatballs like *Lamb Meatballs*
in the LAMB AND MUTTON section.

## VEAL IDEAS, *cont.*

**Veal Scaloppine with Vegetables** Cut veal scallops (cutlets) into 3 inch squares and pound lightly to flatten them. Sauté them slowly in olive oil or another fat till lightly browned. Then add enough sliced or chopped vegetables to equal or exceed the amount of veal. Some good choices are fresh celery, green pepper, shelled limas, green beans, tomatoes, peas, carrots, onions, and zucchini, or summer squash. Combinations of many vegetables or just one or two are equally delicious. Cover, then simmer very slowly till the vegetables are tender. Water will not be needed unless the vegetables are very dry. Season with pepper and herbs such as those mentioned above. The goodness of this dish depends on the full, fresh flavor of the vegetables. It is best when they are just gathered from the garden.

### *Veal Roasted Catalan Style*  (Makes about 6 dinner servings.)

| | |
|---|---|
| 2–3 *pound roast of veal* | 2 *cloves* |
| 2 *tablespoons lard, or oil* | 1 *bay leaf* |
| 1 *head garlic, unpeeled* (Separate cloves.) | *small stick cinnamon* |
| *sprig fresh thyme, or* ½ *teaspoon dried* | *pepper, salt, optional* |
| | ¾ *cup dry white wine* |
| 6 *peppercorns* | ¼ *cup dark rum* |

Use a Dutch oven or another heavy pot with a tight lid. Heat the fat or oil in it, then put in the roast, garlic, thyme, peppercorns, cloves, bay leaf, and cinnamon stick. Sauté, turning often, till the roast is evenly browned on all sides. Sprinkle with pepper, and salt, if desired, then pour the wine and rum over the meat. Cover and simmer over very low heat, about 2 hours, till the meat is tender. Turn occasionally, and if it begins to dry out, add a few tablespoons of water.

To serve, slice the meat and arrange it on a serving platter. Then strain the richly flavored sauce in the cooking pot and pour it over the slices. The meat will be very good reheated in the sauce the second day.

### *Son-of-a-Bitch Stew*  (Makes 12 or more dinner servings.)

This pioneer American stew has many variations, but all include the "marrow gut," a tube connecting the two stomachs of a suckling calf. This tube, containing partly digested milk that resembles marrow, gives the stew its distinctive flavor.

| | |
|---|---|
| 4–5 *small pieces suet* | 2–3 *pounds veal steak, cubed* (Usually from lean meat inside the ribs.) |
| ½ *calf's heart, cubed* | |
| 1 *calf's tongue, cubed* (Blanching and skinning, optional, refer to TONGUE section.) | 3 *feet marrow gut, in 1 inch pieces* |
| ½ *calf's spleen, cubed* | 1 *set calf's brains* |
| ¼ *calf's liver, cubed* | *pepper, salt, optional* |
| 1 *set calf's sweetbreads, cubed* | |

Put the suet in a big pot over a slow fire. When enough fat has melted, add the heart and tongue, and cook gently for a few minutes, stirring often. (As these are the slowest cooking parts, they are given a head start, while other parts are prepared.) Next, add the spleen, liver, sweetbreads, and steak. Add them in small quantities, and stir after each addition to coat the pieces with fat. Add the marrow gut, stir, and then add enough hot water to cover all ingredients. Simmer from 30 minutes to an hour, till all is tender. Precook the brains to firm them. (Refer to the BRAINS section.) Then, cube them and add them with pepper, and salt, if desired, just before eating the stew.

T HE WORD VEGETABLE IS SOMETIMES USED TO DESCRIBE A PERSON who leads "a monotonous, passive, or merely physical existence." Unfortunately, many vegetables intended for the table deserve the same description, though they should be one of the brightest, most enticing parts of a meal. It seems that monotonous vegetables are a North American tradition. Early American cookbooks, which are valuable sources of information on other subjects, usually recommend preparing fresh vegetables in ways that destroy flavor, texture, and nutritive value. Modern America carries on this tradition in another way. Agricultural and marketing techniques dictate the development of vegetable varieties suitable for machine cultivation and harvesting, for long distance shipping, and for long "shelf time" in grocery stores. Attributes such as tenderness, crispness, juiciness, and a sweet, delicate flavor have become either irrelevant or a hindrance. Because of this sad state of affairs, many people have never tasted really delicious vegetables, and cannot be blamed for not knowing the difference.

Anyone who doubts a difference in quality has only to taste an average store carrot, tomato, or cabbage, and then taste the same vegetable of a strain selected for its flavor, grown by organic methods, and picked fresh from the garden at its prime.

## HOW TO GET FULL FLAVOR AND NUTRITIONAL VALUE FROM GARDEN VEGETABLES

• Depend, as much as possible, on vegetables that are in season and fresh. Plan the garden for an extended season, including early spring and late fall vegetables.

• Pick vegetables just before they are to be eaten. An empty refrigerator vegetable compartment, and a quick trip to the garden just before mealtime is a winning combination. If delay is unavoidable, refrigerate or keep vegetables in another cool, dark place in the interim.

• Do as little peeling, paring, and trimming as possible. Remove only tough parts, blemishes, or damaged areas. Many vitamins and minerals are in or just under the vegetable's skin. The skin also contributes valuable flavor.

• Never soak vegetables to clean them or to prevent discoloring. Wash in cool water, scrub with a brush if necessary, and rinse quickly. Use the vegetables immediately after rinsing to avoid discoloration, or sprinkle them with lemon juice, vinegar, or an ascorbic acid solution. Soaking removes water soluble vitamins, minerals, and natural sugars and flavors as well.

• Except for some kinds of blanching, do not cook vegetables in a large amount of water that is to be discarded. (Refer to BLANCHING VEGETABLES, in the FREEZING section.) Steaming, stir-frying, and simmering in a minimum of water are good cooking methods. (Refer

| STORAGE | |
|---|---|
| **Canning** | Refer to CANNING section. |
| **Cold Storage** | Refer to COLD STORAGE section. |
| **Drying** | Refer to DRYING section. |
| **Freezing** | Refer to FREEZING section. |

to the STEAM COOKING and STIR-FRYING sections.) Use leftover cooking water in soups, or for the liquid in recipes.

• Avoid overcooking. Most vegetables taste best while still brightly colored and somewhat crisp or firm.

## VEGETABLE JUICE

Raw vegetable juice is a popular health drink. It can be made with most kinds of vegetables, but a modern juice extractor will be needed for hard or tough vegetables. Carrot juice is best known, and some people drink a small glass every day. (Larger amounts have been known to turn a person's skin yellow.) An electric centrifugal juice extractor is expensive and only practical for making small quantities of fresh juice to drink immediately. It will make juice from raw apples, and grapes, but the amounts produced at one time are too small to be worth canning or freezing. There are less costly manually operated juice extractors, but they are still a fairly expensive tool if not used regularly. Moist, raw vegetables, like cucumbers, can be made into juice in the same ways as soft fruits. (Refer to FRESH FRUIT JUICE, in the FRUITS section.)

Another way to make juice using raw, firm vegetables is to chop them, and then to put them in a blender or food processor with water, vegetable cooking water, or another liquid, and purée them. Healthful mixtures sometimes called "green drinks" are made in this way, using green vegetables, herbs, and seasonings. One advantage of juice mixtures made from the whole vegetable is the inclusion of the fiber, which is known to be important for a healthful diet. For ideas for vegetable juice mixtures see CARROT DRINKS, in the CARROTS section, and WILD GREEN DRINKS, in the WILD FOODS section.

The most common cold cooked vegetable juices are tomato and tomato vegetable blends (refer to TOMATO JUICE, in the TOMATOES section), but any thinly puréed vegetable, flavored perhaps with lemon juice, can be chilled for a beverage. Hot cooked vegetable juice mixtures are most highly appreciated, but go by a different name—soup!

## MAKING VEGETABLE SOUP

The quality of the vegetables used for making soups is very important. Poorly grown, or old, limp vegetables do not have enough flavor to give a good taste to their cooking water. However, clean vegetable trimmings and imperfectly shaped vegetables should certainly go in the soup pot, as long as they are fresh and home-grown for full flavor. European recipes calling for a carrot, a stalk of celery, and a sprig of parsley to flavor a whole big pot of soup, must be an enigma to anyone depending on American supermarket vegetables. Perhaps three or four times that quantity of depleted store vegetables will be needed to match their strength of flavor, and it will still not be as good. There is no way to replace missing natural sugars, aromatic oils, minerals, and vitamins. Regrettably the standard way to pep up the flavor is to add excess salt, MSG (monosodium glutamate), sugar, and artificial flavorings.

(Refer also to the SOUP section, and refer to individual vegetable sections for recipes.)

## VEGETABLE RECIPES

### *Vegetable Hot Pot*    (Makes about 6–8 side servings.)

6 cups (about) winter vegetables, in bite sized chunks (Try carrots, parsnips, rutabagas, turnips, Jerusalem artichokes, leeks, onions, celeriac, winter squash.)

3 tablespoons (about) butter, oil, or other fat

3 tablespoons flour
cayenne, or hot pepper, to taste
1 teaspoon fenugreek seeds, or other herb seeds, crushed, optional

Sauté the vegetables lightly in the butter or oil in a large pot, stirring often. Mix the flour with a little water to moisten it, then add a cup or so of water. Pour over the vegetables, and add more water as necessary to cover three quarters of the vegetables. Add cayenne, and fenugreek. Cover and simmer on top of the stove, or put in a covered casserole in a moderate, 350°F oven, and cook till the vegetables are tender, about 40 minutes.

The colors of the vegetables make this an attractive dish, and the fenugreek gives an unusual spiciness, but the flavor is also excellent without it. It reheats very well.

**Old Fashioned Vegetable Soup**  Cook a mixture of vegetables and seasonings as above, including parsley or other herbs, to taste. When done, purée with a food mill or blender. Return to the soup pot and add water for a medium thin consistency. Adjust seasonings to taste and reheat. A little cream can be stirred in just before the soup is served.

### *Versatile Vegetable Loaf*    (Makes 6–8 dinner servings.)

1–2 cups cooked vegetables, chopped or mashed (Leftover green vegetables, peas, carrots, potatoes, are excellent. Cabbage family vegetables may give a strong taste.)

1 cup raw vegetables, minced or grated (Try onion, celery, green pepper, carrot, summer squash.)

1–1½ cups cooked rice, other cooked grains, cooked, mashed beans, or a combination

1 cup bread crumbs
½–1 cup nuts, chopped or ground, or sunflower or other seeds
¼ cup oil, or softened butter
2 eggs, lightly beaten
herbs, to taste (Try parsley, savory and minced garlic.)
pepper, paprika, to taste
salt, optional
1–2 cups vegetable juice, or cooking water, stewed tomatoes, or another liquid

**VEGETABLE IDEAS**

**Uncommon Raw Vegetables and Dips**  Most vegetables that are good raw taste good with dips. Some of the less common ones are kohlrabi sticks, cabbage leaves or other stiff leaved greens, asparagus spears, very thin beet slices, sugar snap peas, and snap beans of different colors. Some dips to try are the *Guacamole* recipe in the FRUITS section, the FRESH CHEESE DIPS idea in the CHEESE, FRESH section, the *Spanish Parsley Sauce* recipe in the PARSLEY section, the *Indonesian Peanut Sauce* recipe in the PEANUTS section, and the *Whipped Tomato Cream* idea in the TOMATOES section.

Mix all ingredients, adding the vegetable juice or other liquid last.
Adjust the amount of liquid for a moist, not runny mixture. Press
into an oiled or buttered baking dish, or a large loaf pan. Bake from
40 to 60 minutes in a moderate, 350°F oven. Make a small cut in the
center to see if it is set, then serve with relish, chutney, or another
sauce. Leftovers are very good sliced or shaped into patties and fried.

***Fish and Vegetable Loaf*** Mix canned salmon, tuna, or other fish,
or leftover cooked and flaked fish, with the loaf ingredients, and bake
as above.

### Savory Vegetable Pie                    (Makes about 6 dinner servings.)

*pastry or biscuit dough*
*4−6 cups fresh vegetables, sliced*
    (Try tomatoes, onions, summer
    squash.)
*herbs, to taste* (Try basil with
    tomato, rosemary with onion,
    summer savory or thyme with
    summer squash.)

*pepper, to taste*
*1½ cups mayonnaise* (GARLIC
    MAYONNAISE, in the
    SALADS section, is ex-
    cellent.)
*1 cup cheese, grated*

Roll out the dough and line a deep pie dish with it. Fill with the
sliced vegetables and sprinkle with herbs and pepper. Mix the mayonnaise with the cheese, then spread over the top. Bake in a hot, 400°F
oven for about 40 minutes, or till the top is nicely browned and the
vegetables are cooked. (Vegetables like onion and squash will retain
some firmness of texture. If a soft texture is preferred, steam them
till half done before putting them in the pie dish.)

### Curried Vegetables                              (Makes about 6 servings.)

*2−3 onions, sliced*
*3 tablespoons butter*
*2 tablespoons flour*
*1 tablespoon curry powder, or to taste*
*hot pepper or paprika, to taste, op-*
    *tional*
*1½ cups (about) vegetable cooking*
    *water, milk, or soup stock*

*parsley, minced, or other herbs,*
    *to taste, optional*
*3 cups (about) cooked vegetables*
    (Frozen and thawed, or
    leftovers. Try cauliflower,
    green beans, carrots,
    potatoes, peas, or turnips,
    separately or mixed.)

Sauté the onions in butter till limp. Stir in the flour, curry powder, and hot pepper or paprika. Slowly add the cooking water or other
liquid, stirring constantly. Simmer 10 minutes, stirring often. Add
the parsley and vegetables, cover, and simmer another 5 to 10 minutes, till the vegetables are well heated. Excellent with rice or
potatoes.

***Curried Vegetable Soup*** Increase the liquid added to 4 or 5 cups.
The soup can be puréed after it is finished, or the vegetables can be
puréed before they are added.

DEER THRIVE ALMOST EVERYWHERE IN NORTH AMERICA, AND AS they are hunted more often than any animal except rabbits, they are a food source available to a great many people. Hunting may be an exciting sport, but it is not a complete and satisfying action till the hunter has met the moral obligation of making good use of his kill. This obligation is easy to fulfill when the meat is venison.

Venison is an extraordinarily delicious and healthful meat. It could be labeled "organically grown," since deer eat natural foods without the additives fed routinely to domestic meat animals. It is a fine textured, lean meat. Even when a deer is fat, the fat does not run through the meat and can be trimmed off. The flavor of venison is quite distinctive, but is not strong or gamey if the deer was bled, cleaned, and cooled as promptly and carefully as when butchering a domestic animal. Cookbooks are misguided if they imply that cooking venison is a complicated procedure whose purpose is to disguise the natural taste of the meat. Venison is quite as good when cooked simply as when cooked in elaborate, richly seasoned ways. It is as versatile as beef, and can easily be the principal meat in a family's diet.

The variety meats of a deer deserve special mention. They are excellent, with very little wild or gamey flavor. The liver, heart, kidneys, tongue, and brains can be used in any recipes calling for these parts from a domestic animal.

## HANDLING VENISON

The essentials of bleeding, cleaning, and skinning deer are the same as for butchering a similarly sized domestic animal. Differences are due mostly to the field conditions in which deer are killed. The throat must be cut as soon as possible to bleed them, unless they were shot in the lungs, causing them to bleed internally. Usually a deer is field dressed, that is, the stomach cavity is emptied right away, and the animal is skinned later, at home. The liver and heart can be left in the carcass if the deer is taken home within an hour or two. Otherwise, take them out immediately, and chill and carry them separately. As deer do not have gall bladders, there is no need to worry about breaking one. It is very important to cool the carcass quickly. If the weather is cold this presents no problem, but the deer must not be tied next to the hot engine of a car when taking it home. If the weather is warm, the body cavity must be emptied completely, and propped open with a stick. It may be best to skin the animal immediately since the hide will hold in body heat. The carcass should not be washed, since meat spoils more quickly after it gets wet, but any dirt or hair sticking to the meat can be wiped off with a cloth.

For general procedures for skinning and cutting up a deer, refer to the LAMB AND MUTTON section, and the REFERENCES at the end of

---

### STORAGE

**Canning** (Excellent, especially stewing meat.) Process like beef. (Refer to BEEF section.)

**Cold Storage** Refer to AGING and MINCEMEAT IN JARS in MEAT section.

**Drying** Dries well. (Refer to DRYING MEAT in DRYING section.)

**Freezing** (Excellent.) Cut ready for cooking. Quality retained 12 mos. (Refer to FREEZING section.)

**Salt Curing** Most often cured as JERKY. (Refer to BRINED JERKY in DRYING section. Also CORNED CHEVON, LAMB, OR VENISON in BEEF section. See *Jim's Smoked Venison,* below.)

it. To use variety meats and other special parts of a deer, refer to THE PARTS OF A LAMB OR MUTTON CARCASS, in the same section.

Venison will benefit from several weeks of aging unless it is to be put in the freezer when it is cut. Refer to AGING, in the MEAT section. Though venison fat is often discarded, it can be rendered and used as tallow. (Refer to the LARD section.) The flavor of the fat may or may not be strong, and the fat must be cooked and tasted to find out. To use meat that became bloody or bruised when an animal was killed, refer to USING BLOODY OR BRUISED MEAT, in the MEAT section.

*Cooking Venison*   As with any meat animal, the age of a deer makes a big difference in the way the meat is cooked. The meat of an old buck with a magnificent set of antlers is not going to be as tender as the meat of a one-year-old with insignificant horns. Tender venison from a young deer can be fried, stir-fried, and oven roasted. It is also excellent cooked rare, in spite of some opinions to the contrary. The meat from an old deer is best stewed, or otherwise cooked with moist heat, or it can be ground. (Refer to USING TOUGH MEAT, in the MEAT section.) Because of its leanness, venison must be cooked with low heat, or with fat added.

## VENISON RECIPES

### Rob Roy's Pleasure, or Scottish Venison Pot Roast       (Makes 6–10 dinner servings.)

2 onions stuck with 3 cloves, thickly sliced
2 carrots, thickly sliced
2 celery stalks, thickly sliced
several sprigs parsley
1 sprig fresh thyme, or ½ teaspoon dried
1 bay leaf
1 spear or piece of mace, optional

1–2 cups venison, or beef soup stock
salt, optional
3–4 pound haunch, or other roast of venison
1 cup claret, or dry red wine
cayenne pepper, to taste
brandy, optional

Arrange the onions, carrots, celery, parsley, thyme, bay leaf, and mace in the bottom of a Dutch oven or other heavy pot with a tight lid. Add enough soup stock to cover the vegetables. If desired, season with salt. Set the venison on top of the vegetables and cover tightly. Bring to a boil, then simmer over very low heat on top of the stove or in a moderate, 350°F oven. Cook till the meat is just becoming tender, usually 2–3 hours, basting several times with the juices in the pot while it cooks. Pour over the claret, sprinkle with cayenne, and cook about 30 minutes longer till very tender.

When done take out the venison and put it in a buttered serving dish. Pour several spoons of the cooking juice over it to keep it moist. Strain the rest of the juice, add a little brandy, if desired, and boil it till reduced to a flavorful sauce. Adjust seasonings if necessary, and pour over the roast just before serving.

*Jim's Smoked Venison*                    (Makes dozens of snack servings.)

2–5 pounds venison, in long strips
1½ cups salt dissolved in 1 gallon
    water (Enough salt to float a
    raw peeled potato.)

8 tablespoons honey
8 tablespoons maple syrup
8 tablespoons molasses

Cut the strips of venison with the grain of the meat, rather than across it, and they will hold together.

Put the brine in a pot and add the honey, maple syrup, and molasses. Amounts can be adjusted to taste. Heat just to a boil and dip in the strips of venison a few at a time. Leave them about a minute, or just till they change color. Then take them out, dip them in fresh, cold water to quickly chill them, and spread them out to let the moisture dry off. Then cold smoke for about 12 hours, using black birch, apple, or hickory wood. (Refer to the SMOKING section.) Will keep refrigerated for about a month; freeze for long storage.

**OTHER RECIPES
WITH VENISON**

Corned Venison, p. 36
Deer Haggis, p. 382
Game Meat and Pork Sausage,
    p. 552
Hearty Meat and Leek Soup,
    p. 390
Mincemeat in Jars, p. 409
Nineteenth Century Calf's Foot
    Jelly, p. 302
Polish Style Beets for Roast
    Meats, p. 40
Steak and Kidney Pie, p. 367
Stewed Game Meat with Sauces,
    p. 308
Sweet and Sour Venison, p. 155
Turnip and Meat Soup, p. 507
Venison Bologna, p. 554
Venison Sausage, Czech Style,
    p. 157
Venison Sukiyaki, p. 35

# VINEGAR

V INEGAR CAN BE AS SIMPLE OR AS COMPLICATED AS ANYONE WANTS to make it. Chemically it is nothing more than a dilute solution of acetic acid. White distilled vinegar, which is made from pure alcohol, is vinegar in its plainest form. Other common vinegars are cider vinegar made from apples, and wine vinegar from grape wine. Their distinctive flavors come from the fruit. Malt vinegar is made from malted barley. Many other kinds of fruits, grains, and even some starchy vegetables have been made into vinegar. In fact, any food that can be fermented to make alcohol can also be fermented to make vinegar. Homemade vinegar usually comes from fruit, because it is less complicated than making vinegar from grains or vegetables.

Since ancient times vinegar has been appreciated for its ability to preserve or pickle other foods, and raw vinegar has always been credited with medicinal value. It is certain also that raw, homemade apple cider vinegar tastes better than any standardized, pasteurized, store vinegar.

The usual home method for making vinegar is simply to set out a sweet, fruity liquid and wait for it to "turn." If the liquid is raw apple cider, containing no preservatives, success is almost guaranteed. Success with other fruit juices and liquids is less certain, but an understanding of the process will help to improve the odds.

## MAKING VINEGAR FROM FRUIT

The fermentation of a sweet liquid into vinegar occurs in two stages. First the sugar is converted to alcohol by yeasts, and then the

**STORAGE**

*Note:* If pasteurized, vinegar keeps indefinitely almost anywhere. See STORING HOMEMADE VINEGAR, below.

alcohol is converted to acetic acid by bacteria. When conditions are right, naturally occurring yeasts and bacteria do these jobs, but poor conditions can allow unfavorable organisms to interfere with the desired fermentation. The vinegar maker must see that conditions are right for the growth of the desirable yeasts and bacteria. Starters of yeast or acetic-acid-producing bacteria can be added to assist the process.

*The Alcoholic Fermentation*   A sweet, fruity liquid set in a warm place should begin to ferment on its own. Look for a bubbling and foaming, with accompanying alcoholic smells and tastes. Fermentation will start within a day or two and continue for a week or more. Once enough alcohol has been produced, the change to acetic acid begins.

The liquid to be fermented may be fresh raw fruit juice, or juicy mashed fruits, or fruit trimmings and culls, with water added. If the fruit is not very sweet, add sugar, molasses or another sweetener to give it a sweet, but not overly sweet, taste. Honey can also be used, but it must be pasteurized, because raw honey often contains unfavorable wild yeasts. To get fermentation off to a good start, a little baking yeast or wine yeast can be added. About ½ teaspoon dry yeast with 1 gallon of liquid is enough. To ferment cooked juice or fruit, a yeast starter will always be necessary, after which the process becomes the same as for making wine. (Refer to the WINE section.)

The ideal temperature for fermentation is between 80 to 85°F, but it can also occur successfully at somewhat lower temperatures, or in a place where temperatures fluctuate. A warm room temperature is usually satisfactory. Temperatures rising too much above 90°F may kill yeasts and bacteria and stop fermentation.

Cover the vinegar container loosely, so that air can get in, and leave room for the liquid to rise while it ferments. If using mashed fruits or fruit trimmings, stir them once a day for the first few days. After fermentation is well started, strain out the solid material, and return the liquid to the container.

*The Acetification*   Acetic-acid-producing bacteria are everywhere in the environment and will turn up when conditions are right—when enough alcohol has formed in a fermenting liquid for them to have something to work on. As they need air, use a wide mouthed container covered with a cloth to keep out dust and insects. They can work in a cool place, but their action will be slower, and it will take longer for the vinegar to form. The process may take from one month to several months, depending on circumstances.

As they work, the bacteria form a gelatinous surface layer on the vinegar which is called the "mother of vinegar." Push the "mother" aside to check on the progress of the vinegar, but do not stir it in. When acetification is complete, the mother of vinegar will sink to the bottom of the container. The vinegar may then be strained through cloth to remove the mother and any sediment that is present, and sealed in bottles. Any vinegar that already tastes good before the mother sinks is usable, but a new mother may form in it even after it has been strained and bottled.

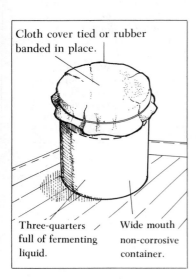

Cloth cover tied or rubber banded in place.

Three-quarters full of fermenting liquid.

Wide mouth non-corrosive container.

*Vinegar in the making.*

The mother from one batch of vinegar can be added as a starter to a new batch that has just finished alcoholic fermentation, but a little raw vinegar makes a better starter, since the acid in it will give some protection against any unfavorable organisms that might interfere with the desired process. Never use pasteurized vinegar as a starter, since there are no live bacteria in it.

Mother of vinegar is quite harmless and can be eaten. (Chickens love it.)

*Cider Vinegar* Raw freshly pressed apple juice without preservatives will easily turn to a pleasant vinegar without special attention. Anyone who has tried to keep hard cider hard will know how easily this can happen. It is well worth letting a gallon or so of apple cider turn to vinegar every year, in order to enjoy the good flavor of the raw vinegar for salad dressings and as a condiment.

Though many directions advise leaving cider in a cool place to ferment, fermentation will be faster and the vinegar will also be excellent if it is kept in a warm place.

*Wine Vinegar* Wine with an alcoholic content of 10% or more will not turn to vinegar and must first be diluted. (Too much alcohol will inactivate the acetic-acid-producing bacteria.) As alcohol content increases up to 10%, however, the strength of the resulting vinegar also increases. Many homemade wines will turn to vinegar if left where air can reach them. However, commercial wines almost always contain additives that prevent them from turning. The quality of wine vinegar tends to vary considerably, but a good flavored homemade wine is likely to make good vinegar.

The French and Italian wine vinegars with their superb flavors are homemade as an ongoing process in those countries, helped by the fact that untreated wine is routinely available. A permanent keg or jug is used, called a "vinaigrier" in France. It has a spigot at the bottom for drawing off vinegar, a place at the top for adding wine, and an opening for aeration. Vinegar making begins with wine and a starter of wine vinegar. Once vinegar has formed, some is taken out regularly from the bottom of the keg, and more wine is regularly added to the top.

Sometimes sweet, fresh, grape juice from ripe grapes will turn to vinegar as easily as apple cider, while at other times, the wrong kinds of organisms take over and results are poor. To guarantee success use pasteurized grape juice and proceed as for making wine.

*Vinegar from Mashed Fruit, Fruit Trimmings, and Culls* Clean, fresh leftovers of many fruits, including apples, grapes, pears, peaches, plums, apricots, pineapples, and berries can be used for making vinegar. Or use the trimmings left from canning. Put the peels, cores, whole mashed or chopped fruit, juice, or a mixture of these into a container. The scraps must be fresh without traces of mold or other spoilage. Add water to cover all, unless there is plenty of natural juice. Usually sugar or another sweetener must be added, and a sprinkle of dry yeast is a good idea. If, after a day or so, fermentation has not begun, add a little more sweetening or yeast. (If worst should come to worst, and the mixture spoils rather than ferments, very little is lost, since the trimmings would have gone into the compost pile anyway.)

Stir the fruit mixture every day for the first few days. After 4 or 5 days, when it is fermenting freely, strain it to remove solids. They can be pressed or squeezed to obtain as much juice as possible. Then return the juice to the vinegar container to continue its fermentation.

## STORING HOMEMADE VINEGAR

Homemade raw vinegar is less stable than pasteurized store vinegar, because a slight amount of bacterial activity may continue in it. Thin strands of mother of vinegar may form, or sediment may continue to settle. These in no way affect its quality. In fact, the flavor is likely to develop and improve during storage. If desired, strain the vinegar when it is to be used.

To minimize activity in the vinegar while it is stored, keep it in bottles filled as full as possible, leaving very little air space. A cool, dark storage place is best. After several months the vinegar can be strained through cloth, or carefully poured or siphoned out of the bottles, leaving sediment behind, and then rebottled.

Raw vinegar can be heated to about 160°F to pasteurize and stabilize it, in the same way that milk is pasteurized, but its special flavor and possible health benefits will be lost.

## THE ACIDITY OF HOMEMADE VINEGAR

Commercial vinegar is standardized at 4 to 5% acidity. Homemade vinegar may be either milder or stronger. This presents no problem for ordinary uses, because it can be added to taste. If it seems very strong or harsh it can be diluted with a little water before use. The uncertain acidity can be a problem, however, when making many kinds of pickles. Do not use homemade vinegar for pickling and canning vegetables or other low acid foods, unless its acidity has been tested and found to be 4% or more (see below).

***Some Pickling Uses for Homemade Vinegar*** Besides the uncertainty of its acidity, homemade vinegar may present problems because of its tendency to cloud or discolor pickles, and because its flavor may not go well with some pickle flavors. There are, however, some kinds of pickles in which it will always taste good, such as pickled fruits. As long as the fruit is acidic enough for safe boiling water bath canning, there is no danger from lower than standard acidity vinegar. The flavor of homemade vinegar goes well with most fruits, and the color of the fruit is usually dark enough not to be affected by the color of the vinegar. Use homemade vinegar in *Spiced Pickled Fruits* (refer to PICKLING section), and in fruit chutneys. Homemade vinegar can also be used to taste, for a quick pickled flavor, in pickled foods not intended for canning, such as meats marinated in vinegar. Refer to the OTHER

RECIPES list at the end of the PICKLING section for possibilities.

***Testing the Acidity of Homemade Vinegar***   One way to test the acidity of vinegar is to use an acid testing kit for wine, sold in winemakers' supply stores and winemaking mail order catalogs. If the kit is not new it should be tested on standard vinegar to check for accuracy. The vinegar can be diluted with a measured amount of water before testing so as to use up the test kit less quickly. (Those who are familiar with titration can, perhaps, devise a test of this kind for themselves.)

## VINEGAR RECIPES

*Herb Vinegar*                         (Makes 1–2 quarts.)

> *handful fresh herbs, crushed, or 3*    *1–2 quarts vinegar* (Homemade
> *tablespoons (about) dried herbs*      cider vinegar or any mild
> (Basil and tarragon best fresh.       flavored vinegar.)
> Others fresh or dried. Try
> elderflowers or celery leaves.)

Put the herbs in jars or another container, then warm the vinegar, pour it over them, and cover. Warm vinegar will more readily absorb the herb flavor. To retain the character of raw vinegar, warm it only slightly. Steep for about 3 weeks before using. The vinegar can be strained and rebottled, or attractive sprays of herbs can be left in the vinegar. Store in a cool dark place.

When an herb flavor is wanted right away, the herbs and vinegar can be heated to just a boil in a covered enamel or stainless steel pot, and left to cool. This vinegar can be used after several hours, but its flavor tends to be harsher than slowly steeped raw vinegar.

For ways to use herb vinegars, see the VINEGAR IDEAS. To use vinegar as a way to preserve herbs, refer to the HERBS section.

***Garlic Herb Vinegar***   Partly crush one or more cloves of unpeeled garlic. Steep the garlic in the vinegar for 24 hours, then remove it. The garlic can be added with the herbs and fished out the next day, or it can be put in and removed before adding the herbs. Basil and garlic are a very good combination. Garlic can also be used alone.

*Hay-time Molasses Switchel*
(A refreshing beverage.)                   (Makes 6–12 cups.)

> *1 cup cider vinegar* (Preferably    *1 teaspoon powdered ginger, or 1*
>    homemade or raw.)           *tablespoon grated ginger root*
> *½ cup (about) molasses*
> *½ cup (about) honey, or brown sugar*

Mix ingredients with 1 to 2 quarts cold water. Taste and adjust flavors, as desired. This refreshing old-time drink was used for relieving thirst and giving energy to people cutting hay on a hot day.

---

### VINEGAR IDEAS

**Vinegar as a Condiment**   A small bottle of vinegar on the table is as good with many foods as catsup or mustard. It can also replace the salt shaker, and add flavor to vegetables, cooked grains, potatoes (especially French fried), and salads. Try it instead of lemon juice on fish or meat. Homemade vinegar, herb vinegar, and wine vinegar will contribute an extra special flavor.

**Herb Vinegar Dressings and Marinades**   Instead of plain vinegar, use herb vinegar in salad dressings and marinades for meats and vegetables. It is very good for making the mayonnaise in the SALADS section. The herb flavors give extra zest wherever the vinegar is used.

**Unplanned Fruit Vinegar**   In hot weather, soft fruits like blackberries sometimes begin to ferment on their own, if they were left unrefrigerated after being picked. If this should happen, take advantage of the situation by putting the fruit in a wide mouthed container, and let it turn to vinegar like the VINEGAR FROM MASHED FRUIT discussed above. With such a good start it is quite likely to succeed.

---

### OTHER RECIPES FEATURING VINEGAR

Preserving Herbs in Vinegar, p. 334
Raspberry Shrub, p. 508
Recipes, and Ideas for Pickles, p. 480
Rose Vinegar, p. 526
Salad Dressing Recipes, p. 532

## STORAGE

**Live Storage** Keeps several weeks, or longer, with stems in water in a loose bouquet. (Often begins to grow.) Set in cool place inside, outside, or covered in the refrigerator. Change water every few days.

## WATERCRESS IDEAS

**Watercress Sandwiches** Plain watercress is good in bread and butter sandwiches, or try mincing it and mixing it with other ingredients for a special sandwich spread. It is sometimes mixed into cream cheese or softened butter, or included in hard-boiled egg mixtures to add a brisk, peppery flavor.

**Watercress in Salad Dressings** Minced watercress adds a nice peppery flavor and green color to mayonnaise, oil and vinegar dressings, or yogurt dressings. For a smooth texture, make oil and vinegar watercress dressings in the blender.

**Watercress Instead of Parsley** Sprigs of watercress can replace parsley as a garnish with many foods, including meats, molded salads, and potato dishes. Watercress also does well in most cooked recipes calling for parsley, and since it is available early in spring, before parsley can be grown, it is very handy to use then.

WATERCRESS, WITH ITS DELIGHTFULLY PEPPERY TASTE AND CRISP texture, is renowned as an herb, a salad green, and a green vegetable. There are several kinds of land cress with a similarly peppery taste, but their texture is more like other greens of the mustard family, to which cresses belong. (Refer to the MUSTARD GREENS AND SEEDS section.)

Wild watercress is widely distributed. It likes cool, shallow, slowly running water in a limestone region. It can often be started in springs and brooks where it does not already grow, or it can be grown as a garden crop if fresh, cold water can be provided daily.

## HANDLING WATERCRESS

As watercress picks up pollutants readily, it must come from clean water, especially if it is to be eaten raw. Treatments with water purifying tablets have been suggested, but as a survival technique rather than a way to have a delicious salad.

Watercress is at its best during cool weather. Cut or pinch it off at water level to gather it, or trim off the bottoms later, when using it. The green stems as well as the leaves are good to eat, but the underwater stems and roots are tough. Watercress seeds are good sprouted. (Refer to the SPROUTS section.)

## WATERCRESS RECIPE

### Watercress Soup
(Makes 10–12 medium bowls.)

2–3 handfuls (about 1 pound) watercress
2 tablespoons butter
1 onion, chopped small
1 clove garlic, minced
2 medium potatoes, diced

1½ quarts chicken stock, or other stock
pepper, salt, optional
1½ cups milk, buttermilk, yogurt (Cow's milk yogurt must be stabilized. Refer to the YOGURT section.)

Pick off a cup or so of watercress leaves and set them aside. Heat the butter in a soup pot, then sauté the onion and garlic in it over low heat till limp. Add the potatoes, and cook another 5 minutes or so, stirring. Add the stock and season with pepper and salt, if desired, unless the stock is already seasoned. Bring to a boil, then add the watercress, except for the reserved leaves. Simmer, covered, till the potatoes are very soft, from 20 to 30 minutes. Then purée the soup in a blender or with a food mill. Return it to the stove, add the milk, buttermilk or yogurt, and reheat without boiling. Add the reserved watercress leaves, and serve. Delicately flavored, and very attractively colored as well.

---

| OTHER RECIPES WITH WATERCRESS |
|---|
| Greens Stuffed Ham, p.325 |
| Gumbo Z'Herbes, p.341 |
| Potherb Pie, p.590 |
| Simple Soup, East Asian Style, p.577 |
| Wild Spring Salad Greens, p.532 |

# WATERMELONS

WATERMELONS HAVE BEEN IN EXISTENCE FOR SO LONG THAT THERE is a word for them in Sanskrit, and there are pictures of them in early Egyptian works of art. They are well named, since they are as thirst quenching as a cool drink of water and as sweet to eat as the very nicest of melons. Above all else, watermelons are a fruit for eating fresh. Recipes for their use do not make sense unless they are so plentiful that they cannot all be eaten fresh.

## HANDLING WATERMELONS

There are a great many ways to judge the ripeness of watermelons, but none seem to be foolproof. The novice can try several methods and pick the melon when all methods seem to indicate ripeness. With practice a sort of sixth sense develops, and then it does not matter which test is used, and the chosen watermelon will be ripe. There is one catch, however: watermelons must ripen in hot weather. Those caught by cool weather will never become as sweet and juicy as they should.

## TESTS FOR WATERMELON RIPENESS

• Knock on the melon with the knuckles. A hollow sound means it is ripe.
• Check the tendril nearest the melon. In most varieties it will die when the melon is ripe.
• Look at the underside of the melon. The light patch there will usually turn yellow and become slightly rough when ripe.
• Scratch the melon's skin with a fingernail. It becomes less tough and can be easily scraped when the melon is ripe.

| STORAGE |
|---|
| **Canning** *Juice* See WATERMELON SYRUP, below. *Rind* Refer to PICKLING WATERMELON RIND in PICKLING section. |
| **Drying** Possible, if peeled, sliced and seeded, but less useful than other dried fruits. |
| **Freezing** Cut 1 in. cubes or balls, seeds removed. Serve only partly thawed to avoid mushiness. Refer to FREEZING section. |

• Cut a wedge shaped plug out of the watermelon, and look or taste for ripeness. Replace the plug if underripe. (This has the obvious disadvantage of marring the fruit and making an entrance for ants.)

Watermelon will keep up to a week in the refrigerator after it is cut open if the exposed side is protected. The rinds and seeds are both edible, but it is difficult to find ways to use them. The white part of the rind can be made into pickles or preserves, but because considerable sweetening is required, only small amounts should be eaten. As a last resort, give them to chickens and other birds, who like the leftover rinds and seeds.

*Watermelon Molasses or Syrup*   To make an excellent natural sweetener from extra watermelons, cut off their rinds and white part, and make juice from the red flesh by crushing and pressing it, or by cooking and straining it. (Refer to MAKING FRUIT JUICE, in the FRUITS section.) Then boil the juice in an open kettle till it is concentrated to a syrup. It will look like molasses, and have a sweet, somewhat strong flavor. Towards the end of the boiling, watch closely and stir it often to prevent burning. Use instead of molasses or other kinds of syrup. To can, pour it boiling hot in hot jars and seal immediately. (Refer to OPEN KETTLE CANNING, in the CANNING section.)

*Watermelon Seeds*   The meats inside watermelon seeds are as good to eat as the insides of pumpkin or squash seeds, but they are so difficult to shell that this is usually impractical. Reportedly, there are less hard, dried watermelon seeds of some Chinese varieties that can be eaten, shells and all. If trying hard seeds, it is best to cook them in water for a short while to soften them before drying or roasting them. (Refer to PUMPKIN SEEDS, in the SQUASH, WINTER section.)

Some American Indian tribes used watermelon seeds to make a medicinal tea because it was thought to relieve high blood pressure and to expel worms.

## WATERMELON RECIPE

*Watermelon Cooler*                                 (Makes about 4–6 glasses.)

3 pounds (about) watermelon,           1 tablespoon (about) honey
  peeled, cut in chunks, seeded        mint leaves, optional
3–4 tablespoons yogurt

Put the watermelon, yogurt, and honey in a blender and blend till smooth. The amounts of yogurt and honey can be adjusted to taste. Pour over ice cubes in a glass, and, if desired, add a mint leaf or sprig of mint. Pale pink and very refreshing.

*Watermelon Popsicles*   Freeze this mixture in popsicle molds. These popsicles can also be made from watermelon purée without the yogurt, honey optional.

---

**WATERMELON IDEAS**

**Watermelon Wedges with Meals**   Trim off rind, then cut watermelon into small, easy to handle wedges, and put a plate of them on the table with a meal. They look nice on a bed of greens, and can take the place of a salad or a vegetable. A sprinkle of lemon or lime juice can be added for a sharper taste.

**Watermelon Conserve**   Dice or chop the white part of watermelon rind, or use parts with just a tinge of pink. Mix with chopped apple, thinly sliced, or chopped lemon or orange, with peel, and honey or sugar, for sweetening. Raisins and nuts can be included. To make the conserve, refer to *Fruit and Nut Conserves,* in the JAM AND JELLY section.

**Watermelon Lotion**   Collect the "water" when slicing a watermelon and use it as a face lotion. This is an old-time way to soothe the skin. It was also said to remove freckles, if applied often enough.

---

**OTHER RECIPES
WITH WATERMELON**

THE CULTIVATION OF WHEAT IS A VERY ANCIENT FORM OF AGRICULture and a "tried and true" way to ensure a year-round food supply. It goes back to at least 7,000 B.C. The homesteaders of today with an interest in raising wheat can draw upon 9,000 years of tradition and practical experience; and, in the same way, anyone who cooks with it can draw upon the experience of many centuries.

During the last century, the trend in North America has been to eat less wheat products and more meat and processed foods. Of the wheat eaten, a large proportion has been in the form of refined white flour made into white bread and other baked goods. Most recently, the pendulum has begun to swing away from white flour products and towards whole wheat and other whole grains. The health benefits of eating whole grains are well known, and this last change is a welcome one.

Grinding wheat into flour and making whole wheat bread is an outstanding way to use this grain, but it is only one of many possibilities. A number of them are described below, together with some other forms of wheat.

**Bran**   The outside layer of a kernel of wheat (and of other grains) is the bran. Wheat bran is often removed for separate use in cereals and for baking. It is valuable for the fiber it adds to the diet, and for its B vitamin and protein content. Sometimes bran can be separated from home ground flour by sifting. The fine flour goes through and the coarser bran is caught in the sifter. However, an efficient grinder will pulverize the bran along with the rest of the kernel, making separation impossible. Whole wheat flour always includes the bran.

**Bulghur Wheat**   This wheat is cooked, dried, and then coarsely ground. It is popular in the Middle East. There are many unusual and delicious ways to use it, and it can be made at home. (See BASIC WHEAT PREPARATIONS, below.)

**Couscous**   To make this North African food, the wheat is ground coarsely, then rubbed with a little fine flour to separate each grain. It is usually steamed in special pots over a stew or broth, not cooked in the liquid.

**Cracked Wheat**   Anyone with a grain mill can grind wheat coarsely to make cracked wheat. The texture will be improved if it is sifted to remove fine flour. (Refer to MEAL OR GRITS AND FLOUR, in the GRAINS section.)

**Cream of Wheat**   This well known breakfast cereal is finely cracked wheat, usually with the bran and germ removed.

**Durum Wheat**   Durum is a hardy variety of wheat, known for making the best spaghetti and other pastas.

**Gluten**   Gluten is the plant protein in wheat and other grains. A high gluten content is necessary in flours used for making yeast breads if the bread is to rise well. (Refer to BREAD FLOUR, in the BREAD, YEAST section.) Gluten can be separated from wheat flour to use as a meat substitute, and some vegetarian cookbooks give directions for doing this.

*Graham Flour*   For all practical purposes, graham flour and whole wheat flour are the same. Sometimes a particular grind or texture is labeled graham flour to distinguish it from another kind of whole wheat flour, but there is no standard rule for this. (The name comes from Sylvester Graham, who promoted whole wheat baked goods, especially graham crackers, during the 19th century.)

*Hard Red Wheat*   The best bread flour is ground from hard red varieties of wheat. (Hard red winter wheat is graded somewhat higher than hard red spring wheat. White wheat also makes good bread.) It is the wheat's high gluten content which causes yeast breads to rise well.

*Semolina*   Semolina is finely cracked durum wheat. Usually, it consists of the coarser particles left when the fine flour is sifted off for making pasta. It is like cream of wheat, and can be used in the same ways, but its texture is a little more distinctive.

*Soft Wheat*   Flour from soft varieties of wheat is ideal for many kinds of non-yeast baking. Whole wheat pastry flour is finely ground soft wheat.

*Unbleached White Flour*   This is flour with the bran and germ removed, but it has not been subjected to the final chemical bleaching process used for ordinary white flour. It is therefore a step above white flour in nutritional quality.

*Wheat Berries*   This is the name usually given whole kernels of wheat. Wheat berries are very good cooked whole as a grain dish. (See BASIC WHEAT PREPARATIONS, below.)

*Wheat Flakes*   Whole wheat kernels are sometimes steamed and rolled like oats to make wheat flakes. (Refer to ROLLING OATS, in the OATS section.) Wheat flakes are a little coarser in texture and slower cooking than rolled oats, but they are good used in the same ways.

*Wheat Germ*   The nucleus or germ of the wheat kernel is commonly available as a health food. It is a rich source of iron, vitamin E, and the B vitamins. It is not possible to separate it when grinding flour at home, but its benefits are incorporated into whole wheat flour. For improved nutritional value, small quantities of wheat germ can be added to baked goods and many other foods without changing their character. For a recipe featuring wheat germ, refer to the *Molasses Brownies* recipe, in the COOKIES section. Always store wheat germ in the refrigerator or freezer, because once separated from the whole grain, its oil is exposed to the air and quickly becomes rancid.

Wheat is relatively easy to harvest on a small scale. For general procedures, and instructions for grinding, and for storing of both the whole grain and the flour, refer to the GRAINS section.

## BASIC WHEAT PREPARATIONS

### *Cooked Wheat Berries*

The soaking and cooking times needed for making wheat berries soft, and the amount of water they absorb, will vary with the variety of wheat and its dryness. Adjust the following directions to suit the wheat berries used.

Soak 1 part berries in 2 parts water for several hours, or overnight. Then, using the soaking water, simmer covered till the berries are soft and the water is absorbed. This may take 1 hour or longer. If they dry out, a little water may be added during cooking, but all water should be absorbed when they are done so that nutrients are not lost with discarded cooking water. The pot can be uncovered for the last few minutes of cooking to let excess water evaporate.

Wheat berries are very good served instead of rice or another grain. They are also good added to soups, stews, casseroles and other mixed dishes. They have a pleasant, somewhat chewy texture.

### *Bulghur Wheat*

(Also bulgur, burghul, and burghol.)

Cook several cups of wheat berries as described above, making sure all cooking water is absorbed. Spread on drying trays or baking sheets, then leave in a food dryer or another dry, airy place till the kernels are completely dry and very hard. Stir several times so that they dry evenly. Grind coarsely in a grain mill. (These kernels are too hard for most blenders to handle.)

Because bulghur wheat is precooked, it will only need soaking to soften it for eating. It will soften most quickly in warm water. Home-made bulghur often requires a longer soaking time than store bought, especially if very coarsely ground. Use 1 part soaking water to 1 part bulghur, and most of the water will be absorbed. Any excess can be squeezed off by hand.

To make a hot breakfast cereal from bulghur wheat, put it in cold water, heat to a simmer, then cook 10 to 15 minutes.

**Rye, Bulghur Style** Whole rye berries can be cooked, dried, and ground like wheat berries, and used in the same ways.

## WHEAT RECIPES

### *Ferique, Egyptian Style*
### *Chicken with Wheat*          (Makes 6 or more dinner servings.)

½ pound (1¼ cups) wheat berries
1 chicken (3–4 pounds) for roasting
  or stewing, in pieces if desired

1 soup bone or calf's foot (Refer
  to the FEET section.)
6 eggs (In their shells.)
1–2 teaspoons turmeric
pepper, salt, optional

Cover the wheat berries with water, and soak several hours, or overnight.

Put the chicken, soup bone, and eggs in their shells in a pot. Rinse the eggs. Their shells must be perfect, as for hard-boiling. Add the wheat with its soaking water, the turmeric, pepper, and salt, if desired. Add 5 cups of water. Bring to a boil, then simmer, covered, till the chicken and wheat are tender. The meat should be falling from the bones. For a stewing hen this will take from 3 to 4 hours. Take out the eggs, shell them, then return them to the pot for 10 more minutes. The long cooking will give the eggs a creamy texture, and the turmeric turns them pale yellow.

Serve in individual bowls for an unusual and very tasty one dish meal.

***Rye Berries, or Other Whole Grains, with Chicken*** Use rye berries or another slow cooking whole grain instead of wheat berries.

### Tabbouleh, a Middle Eastern Salad (Makes about 6 side servings.)

| | |
|---|---|
| 1 cup bulghur wheat | ¼ – ½ cup mint leaves, minced |
| ½ – 1 cup scallions or onion, minced | 1 – 2 tomatoes, chopped small, |
| pepper, to taste | optional |
| salt, optional | ¼ – ½ cup olive oil |
| 1 – 1 ½ cups parsley, minced | ½ – 1 cup lemon juice |

Soak the bulghur for about ½ to 1 hour, in warm water, till it has softened and swelled. Warm water speeds the process. When soft, drain the wheat, then squeeze out extra water by hand. Mix the softened wheat with onions, pepper, and salt, if desired, then squeeze or press to spread the onion juice into the wheat. Add the parsley, mint, tomatoes, oil, and lemon juice. Adjust proportions to taste.

This salad can be piled on a platter and decorated with tomato slices, or such other vegetables as olives, cucumber, or green pepper slices. Traditionally, it is often eaten by scooping it up with lettuce or cabbage leaves, but no matter how it is served, it is always delicious.

### Kibbeh, Lamb and Bulghur Wheat, Middle Eastern Style (Makes about 6 servings.)

| | |
|---|---|
| 1 pound lamb, ground | 1 cup bulghur wheat, finely cracked |
| 1 large onion, ground, or grated | pepper, salt, optional |

Grind the lamb and onion together, or knead them together after they are ground. Put through the grinder several times, or knead thoroughly to make a soft, smooth texture. Work in several tablespoons cold water while grinding or kneading.

Rinse the bulghur wheat by running water through it in a fine strainer, then squeeze out extra water. Knead it into the lamb mixture adding pepper, and salt, if desired, or put through the grinder again. Cook the kibbeh like hamburger patties, or make fat, cigar shaped rolls, and broil or fry them. They are also good cooked like meatballs in vegetable stew.

*Raw Kibbeh*  If the lamb was home raised, or from a trustworthy source, this mixture is very good eaten raw, like steak tartare. For a traditional raw hors d'oeuvre, flatten the kibbeh on a round plate or pie dish. The top is usually scored or indented in a decorative pattern, and melted butter or lemon juice is sprinkled over it. It can be scooped up with lettuce leaves to eat it.

**OTHER RECIPES
FEATURING WHEAT**

Roast Beverages, p. 44
Sprouting Grains, p. 595
Whole Grain Ideas, p. 314

# WHEY

**STORAGE**

**Cold Storage**  *Whey Cheese,* see below. Well wrapped, keeps several months in a cool place

WHEN MILK SEPARATES INTO CURDS AND WHEY, THE CURDS BECOME cheese and the whey becomes a problem. Whey is too full of nutrients to throw out, as it contains most of the water soluble vitamins and minerals from the milk, considerable calcium and lactose (milk sugar), and some protein. Its flavor is too distinctive to add willy-nilly to every kind of food, and there is likely too much of it to use up where it does suit. Large quantities are most easily used in beverages or for making special whey cheeses. Other options are to feed it to farm animals and pets, or, least constructive, to water the garden with it.

The liquid left from making tofu (soybean curd) is also called whey, and also contains some nutrients. It can be used in many of the same ways as whey from milk. (Refer to USING WHEY FROM TOFU, in the TOFU section.)

## HANDLING WHEY

Whey can range from sweet, to slightly sour, to very sour, depending on the acidity of the milk when it is separated and the lapse of time before the whey is drained off. The sweetest whey comes from fresh milk set with rennet, without the addition of a culture. Whey is also quite sweet when rennet and a culture are added at the same time, and the whey is drained off soon after the curd sets.

Whey cheeses and most beverages taste best when sweet whey is used. Sour whey can be used instead of sour milk in most quick bread recipes, and also as the liquid in yeast breads, as long as the sour flavor is a pleasant one. Use sweet whey soon after it is collected. Sour whey can be refrigerated for a few days.

*Whey Cheeses* To make whey cheeses, the whey is boiled till reduced to a thick, creamy consistency. Then, as it cools, it solidifies. Ricotta is not a whey cheese, though it is sometimes called one because it is made using whey. (Refer to the *Ricotta* recipe, in the CHEESE, FRESH section.) The best known whey cheeses are made in the Scandinavian countries. Mysost is made from cow's milk whey, while gjetost is made from goat's milk whey. Gjetost is considered better than mysost. Primost and fløtost are cheeses made from whey with a little milk or cream added.

Whey cheeses, with their light brown color and smooth, dense texture, taste completely unlike ordinary cheese. Because milk sugar is concentrated in them they are very sweet. They are seldom made from sour whey because the flavor tends to be too harsh. Sometimes baking soda is added to neutralize acidity, but its taste, if discernible, is also unpleasant.

The directions for gjetost that follow can also be used with whey from other animals' milk.

## WHEY RECIPES

### Gjetost
(A sweet, dense, light brown cheese.)        (Makes 1–3 cups cheese.)

*3–4 quarts sweet goat's milk whey*        *½–1 cup whole milk, or cream, optional*

Bring the whey and milk or cream to a boil in a heavy pot. A wide pot is best, to allow for more evaporation. Simmer, uncovered, stirring often. When a solid albuminous material rises to the surface, skim it off with a sieve, and reserve it. When the whey has been reduced to about ¼ of its original volume and has begun to thicken, watch it closely, stirring most of the time to prevent burning. Use an insulating ring if necessary. Cook till it is creamy, light brown, and as thick as pudding. It should reach 240°F on a candy thermometer. Stir in the reserved albuminous material, then pour it into a bowl. Stir for a few minutes more to prevent sugar crystals forming, then pour into an oiled or greased mold. If the cheese begins to granulate or foam while it cooks, it has been left on the stove too long, and both texture and flavor will be poor. If removed a little too soon, it may not set firmly, but it will be a very good spread for bread or crackers.

When the cheese has cooled and become firm, cut it in convenient sized pieces, and wrap well in aluminum foil or another sturdy material. Store in a cool place, where it will keep several months. Thin slices of gjetost are very good on bread or crackers. Because gjetost and the other whey cheeses are so different from ordinary cheese, they may be an acquired taste. Once they are appreciated, however, the cook will find it hard to keep up with the demand.

## WHEY IDEAS

**Whey and Tomato or Vegetable Juice** Whey mixed half and half with tomato juice or purée makes a pleasant drink. The whey can be sweet or sour. Whey can also be used when making vegetable juices in the blender. (Refer to MAKING VEGETABLE JUICE, in the VEGETABLES section.)

**Sour Whey for Baking** When making biscuits, cornbread, and other quick breads calling for sour milk or buttermilk, use sour whey instead. Sour whey can also be used for making yeast breads, but begin with a small batch to be sure the flavor is liked.

**Vegetable Whey Soup** Use whey as the liquid or stock when making vegetable soup. It goes especially well with such strong flavors as onion.

*Wheyade* (Makes 6–8 large glasses.)

**OTHER RECIPES
WITH WHEY**

Basic Hot Cooked Cereal, p.127
Bonny-Clabber, p.136
Grape Nuts, p.127
Ricotta, p.142

Green whey, which is whey made from freshly milked milk set with rennet, is a refreshing cool drink without anything added. It was so much appreciated in Scotland at one time, that making it was a first priority and using up the curds was the problem. When making cheese, the whey's flavor may be less than perfect, and mixtures such as this wheyade are preferred.

*2 quarts sweet whey*
*½ cup (about) lemon juice, or an-
other strong flavored or concentrated fruit juice*

*honey or other sweetening, to
taste*

Combine the whey with lemon juice or other fruit juice and honey to taste. Pour over ice cubes or chill before drinking.

# WILD FOODS

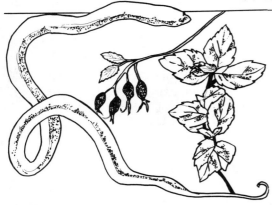

WILD FOODS OUGHT TO BE AN INTEGRAL PART OF EVERY COUNTRY person's diet. From edible weeds in the garden to wild nuts, berries, and other fruits in fields and fence rows, from fish in ponds and streams to small and big wild animals, wild things are a legitimate and practical source of food. Human beings who harvest wild foods, in a responsible way, fit just as comfortably, or more comfortably, into the ecological scheme of things, as those who remove wildlife from a plot of land in order to establish their own choice of food plants and animals. When a wild plant or animal is abundant, the species' health and circumstances are likely to be improved by judicious harvesting.

Those who gather wild foods in large quantities and store some for later use will gain in many ways. Wild foods are genuinely organically grown and very nutritious—except in a few special cases, such as plants which grow along highways polluted by car exhaust. The time it takes to hunt or gather wild foods can be less than the time needed to raise the same amount of food, whether it is plant or animal. Best of all, wild foods can be twice enjoyed, once during the gathering or hunting away from regular routines, and again when they are eaten.

Throughout this book, wild and domestically produced foods are given equal weight, and where appropriate, both the wild and domestic versions of each one are included. Widely distributed wild foods, such as dandelions and venison, are given separate sections and treated on the same basis as domestically produced foods.

Wild foods are not as uniform in quality, size, or taste as domestic foods. They can also vary considerably from region to region, from season to season, and even from one individual tree, animal, or group of plants to another. If an unfamiliar wild food does not meet expectations the first time it is tried, try the same food again from different locations and at different times of the year. In addition, try it with different methods of preparation.

Once a particular wild food has been enjoyed for a season or two its use become routine. When a good wild berry patch is discovered, for instance, and the ripening time is known, it is easy to return year after year for the harvest.

## HANDLING WILD PLANT FOODS

Before eating them, it is necessary to correctly identify unfamiliar wild vegetables and fruits. Sometimes an experienced friend or neighbor can help, and there are many good books that can be consulted. When a particular plant or a part of one is known to be edible, different methods of collection can be tried to discover which is most efficient.

***Gathering Soft Berries, Wild Greens, and Other Vegetables*** When gathering those wild foods that must be picked or collected one by one, it helps to do the job as neatly and cleanly as possible. It is tedious to have to remove leaves, stems, twigs, or bits of dirt later on. Even children can gather cleanly if they understand the reasons for it. Wild berries can be refrigerated or frozen as soon as they are brought home if stems and leaves were already removed. Wild greens that were trimmed before being put in a container will need only a quick rinsing before being cooked. If dirt is mixed with them and dry leaves and roots are still attached, it will take as long to clean them at home as it did to gather them.

***Gathering Fruits or Nuts from Trees and Bushes*** Picking firm bush and tree fruits, as well as nuts, one by one, may not always be the easiest way to harvest them. Try putting a large sheet on the ground, and then shake branches to make the fruit or nuts fall onto it. Sometimes the sheet can be left for a day or so, held in place with rocks to collect the harvest that falls of its own accord. When the sheet is picked up there will be leaves and other debris mixed in, and the methods for removing them will vary according to their size and other characteristics. The large ones can be separated by hand. Shake small fruits on hardware cloth, using a mesh that will let fruit fall through while retaining twigs and leaves. Remove light debris by winnowing in a breeze. (Refer to THRESHING AND WINNOWING, in the SEEDS section.) Some fruits sink in water, allowing debris to float off. It is best to do this at the time the fruit will be used, as most fruits spoil more quickly after they are washed. A method that works with small, round berries like wild blueberries is to roll them down a wide, slightly slanted board. Leaves and twigs will get stuck on the board, while the berries roll down and into a container placed at the bottom. Adjust the slant of the board by trial and error to find the best angle, and clean debris off the board every so often.

*Cleaning debris from small berries*

Guard rails keep berries from rolling off.

**Using Wild Berries** Wild berries of one kind or another are found everywhere and are often so abundant that they can entirely replace cultivated berries. Many people use them for preserves or jelly, but other less sugary ways can be found to use large quantities. Most kinds of berries freeze well. (Refer to FREEZING FRUITS, in the FREEZING section.) Canned berry juice becomes a real treasure during the winter months. (Refer to MAKING FRUIT JUICE AND SAUCE, in the FRUITS section.) Soft berries generally do not dry well, but firm ones can be quite good dried. A method used by northwestern Indians to dry saskatoons (a kind of Juneberry), and other small berries, is to cook them, and then shape them into small, flat patties. The cooking juice is saved, and as the patties dry, it is poured onto them a little at a time, to soak in and dry with them. Either the dried patties are eaten, or they are soaked to make a sauce. (For more about berries, refer to specific berry sections.)

**Using Wild Greens** Spring is the best season for wild greens, as most are more tender and mild flavored when young. Many can be eaten raw as well as cooked. Later in the season, some of the best wild greens are edible weeds from the garden. Lamb's quarters or purslane, for instance, can provide as much delicious food as the crops they invade.

*Lamb's quarters*

There are so many different wild greens, varying so much from locality to locality, that they cannot be adequately described here. However, it is very worthwhile to find out what is edible in any one area and to take advantage of it. For the basic preparation and storage of wild greens, refer to the SPINACH section. Also refer to such well known greens as chicory and watercress by name.

**Removing Bitterness** A bitter or harsh taste in a wild plant can often be removed by soaking or cooking in large amounts of water, then draining and discarding the water. If necessary, repeat this treatment several times, using fresh water each time.

Late spring dandelion greens, pokeweed shoots, and other very strong flavored greens can be put in a large pot of boiling water, cooked till tender, drained, and then served. It is unfortunate that

*Purslane*

water soluble nutrients are lost with the bitterness, but the green's flavor remains full and delicious, fuller in fact than that of many cultivated greens. If greens are only mildly bitter, cook them with milk, or season with vinegar or lemon juice to complement their flavor. (Refer to the CHICORY and DANDELIONS sections.) Most kinds of acorns must be shelled and then boiled in several changes of water to remove tannin before they become edible. (Refer to ACORNS, in the NUTS section.)

## HANDLING WILD MEATS

Most warm blooded animals and birds are edible, but most people prefer herbivores (those that live mostly on plants, seeds, and insects) over the carnivores (meat-eaters). Many wild cold blooded animals are also edible. (Refer to the FISH, FROGS, SHELLFISH, and TURTLE sections.)

*Gaminess* The notion that wild animals and birds always have a strong, unpleasant, gamey taste stops some people from trying them. Wild meats do have a richer flavor than most domestic meats, for the same reasons that chickens running free, eating wild foods will have more flavor than those eating only prepared feed. As well, the taste of wild meat can vary with the kind of food the animal has been eating. None of this results in an unpleasant or bad taste, however. If there is a bad taste, it is almost always due to the mishandling of the meat during or after the kill. If the word "gamey" is used to describe the rich flavor of wild meats, the connotations should be pleasant ones, and any gaminess associated with the taste of poorly handled meat can be prevented.

Wild animals and birds must be bled, the entrails removed, and the carcass cooled as soon after the kill as possible. If this is done there should be no bad tastes. Wild meats require the same care as home butchered domestic animals, with the same procedures, except that entrails are usually removed in the field, and skinning or plucking is done afterwards at home. The organ meats of wild animals and birds are excellent and should be saved. For cleaning wild birds, refer to the CHICKEN and BIRDS, SMALL sections. For small wild animals, refer to the RABBIT section, and for larger wild animals, refer to the LAMB AND MUTTON, and the VENISON sections. For using the organ meats, refer to the specific section for each.

Though directions for wild meats often suggest soaking in water with added salt or baking soda to improve flavor, this is not necessary with mechanical refrigeration, which prevents the taint due to keeping meat in warm weather. Many wild meats, especially the dark or red meats, are improved if refrigerated about 2 days before they are cooked or frozen. If there has been a problem in handling, such as the intestine's or stomach's contents getting on the meat, soaking in water with a little added vinegar is preferable to the use of salt or soda. An hour's soaking will usually be enough. For meat damaged by a bullet or by rough handling, refer to USING BLOODY OR BRUISED MEAT, in the MEAT section.

*Determining the Animal's Age*   To cook meat properly it is necessary to know how old and tough it is, and it is often difficult to tell the age of a wild animal. Some indications are size, and the appearance of the fur or feathers, and teeth. Young animals and birds will be easier to skin or pluck, and it is easier to cut through their sinews, to separate the joints, and the flesh will feel softer when pressed. The inside of a bone will show red tissue in a young animal or bird, and will look white or yellow in an old one. In young birds, the beaks or bills and spurs are softer or more pliable, and the claws are likely to be sharp. Pheasants and grouse can be tested by lifting them by the lower part of the bill. If it breaks the bird is young.

If indications remain inconclusive, the final test is to cook some meat to test it. If it is still tough after moderate cooking, the animal is more than likely an older one. If fried meat remains tough, cover it with water or another liquid and simmer it till it is tender. Note, however, that wild meat is very often lean, and lean, tender meat can be made tough by high temperatures and long cooking. (Refer to LEAN MEAT, in the MEAT section.)

With experience it becomes easier to accurately judge the age and toughness of wild meat. Tough meat is just as useful and delicious as tender meat, if properly cooked. In fact, tough meat from an animal in prime condition is likely to be better than tender meat from a young animal in poor condition. Certain game meats can be tenderized by aging. (Refer to the MEAT section.)

## LESS COMMON WILD MEATS

*Bear*   Bear meat is sometimes compared to pork because of its fattiness, and also because it can carry trichinosis. (Refer to UNDERSTANDING TRICHINOSIS, in the PORK section.) However, bear meat is dark and tastes quite unlike pork. Steaks from a young bear are tender enough to be fried, but they must be well done. Bear fat can be rendered to use for cooking.

*Beaver*   The dark, rich meat of beaver is usually well liked. When roasted over a campfire the tail becomes a choice part. (Refer to the TAILS section.)

*Big Game Animals*   When they can be taken, big game animals like moose, elk, caribou, and antelope provide large amounts of very good meat. They are bled, cleaned, and skinned like deer. The meat of each has its own characteristic flavor, but cooking methods are the same as for venison. (Refer to the VENISON section.)

*Birds*   For small, wild birds, refer to the BIRDS, SMALL section. For large, wild land birds, refer to the CHICKEN and TURKEY sections. For waterfowl, refer to the DUCK and the GOOSE sections.

***Muskrat*** After skinning, a muskrat's musk glands must be removed. They are located in the armpits of the front legs and at the small of the back on either side of the spine, and appear as small nodes or kernels of glandular material. All fat must be trimmed off. The meat is dark, and usually requires precooking, or long, slow cooking to make it tender.

***Opossum*** Opossum meat, which is light colored and mild flavored, can be cooked like rabbit. (Refer to the RABBIT section.) The liver has an excellent flavor.

***Raccoon*** Raccoon meat is dark, distinctively flavored, and quite good if carefully prepared. It is important to remove the small nodes or scent glands from the armpits of the front legs, and from the small of the back, on either side of the spine. If the glands cannot be found, this may be because the animal is young and they have not developed yet, or they may have been trimmed off with the hide. Every bit of fat must be trimmed away. The meat is best if it is refrigerated for 2 days before cooking. Long slow cooking is usually necessary.

***Rattlesnake*** When a rattlesnake is killed, the head must be carefully cut off, and then buried to avoid contact with the poison. The meat is white and delicate. Snakes continue to wriggle for a long time after they have been killed and can be difficult to skin. It can be nailed to a board or hung like catfish or eel (refer to SKINNING FISH, in the FISH section) for skinning and cleaning. The meat is very good dredged in seasoned flour and fried like chicken.

***Woodchuck/Groundhog*** These two names belong to the same animal. It is a menace in farm fields because of the holes it digs, and is often killed. It is a pity to waste the meat, because it is quite good—dark, but not strong flavored. After skinning, the scent glands must be removed as for muskrat, above. Woodchuck meat is good boned, ground, and prepared like hamburger. Some like it with a small proportion of pork added. Woodchuck is also very good when stewed like raccoon or another red meat. Refrigerate it for a day or two before using it.

***Squirrel, Gopher, and Other Small Rodents*** Most small rodents have been used for food at one time or another, but the eastern gray squirrel is probably liked the best. The meat is dark, not too tough, and has a good flavor. Squirrels can be skinned like wild rabbits after the entrails are removed (refer to the RABBIT section), or they can be skinned as follows. Cut through the tail at its base from underneath, so that the skin of the tail and the back are still attached. Step on the tail, and pull up slowly on the hind legs. The skin will come off the body, head, and front legs, but still be attached to the front feet. With one foot still on the tail, the skin on the hind legs can then be pulled up and off. Squirrels are very good stewed, or they can be cooked in any way that allows from 1 to 1½ hours cooking time.

Gophers are sometimes singed to remove hair rather than skinned. They usually take about twice as long to cook as gray squirrels.

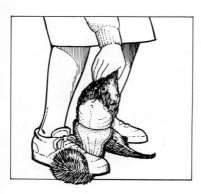

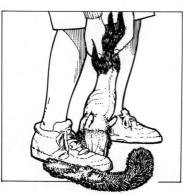

*Skinning a squirrel.*

## WILD MEAT RECIPES

### *William Zelt's Woodchuck Burgers*     (Makes about 9 pounds.)

*1 large woodchuck (groundhog),*
*boned and ground (About 5*
*pounds of meat.)*
*4 pounds lean pork, ground*

*1 ¼ teaspoons allspice*
*¼ teaspoon mace*
*2 teaspoons pepper*
*salt, optional*

Mix all ingredients thoroughly. Work in about 2 cups of cold water while mixing. Shape the meat into patties. (Freeze extra patties, with wax paper or freezer wrap between them, for easy separation when used.)

**Wild Meat Burgers**   All kinds of lean, wild meat are good ground with pork for burgers. Adjust proportions and seasonings to taste.

### *Wild Meat Baked*
### *with Sweet Potatoes*     (Makes 6 or more dinner servings.)

*1 raccoon, opossum, woodchuck,*
*several muskrats, or other small*
*wild animals, in serving size*
*pieces*
*2–3 tablespoons vinegar, optional*
*1 onion, quartered*
*1 stalk celery with leaves, in chunks*
*½ green pepper, in chunks*

*1–2 teaspoons cayenne pepper*
*1–2 cloves garlic*
*salt, optional*
*2–4 tablespoons lard or other fat*
*3–5 medium sweet potatoes,*
*quartered*
*2 tablespoons flour*

Be sure to remove glands after skinning the animal if it is necessary. (See RACCOON, above.) If desired, soak the meat in water with the vinegar added for about an hour, to modify its wild taste. Drain and discard the soaking water. Then put the meat in a pot with the onion, celery, green pepper, cayenne, garlic, and salt, if desired. Add enough hot water to just cover all ingredients. Heat to a simmer, and skim if necessary. Simmer, covered, without boiling, till the meat is almost tender. This may take from 1 to 4 hours, depending on the toughness of the meat. Drain the meat well, and strain the broth. If there are more than 2 cups of broth, boil it down, uncovered, to reduce it.

Heat the lard or fat in a large frying pan, and brown the pieces of meat on all sides. Then arrange meat and sweet potato in a large, wide baking dish.

Pour off any excess fat in the frying pan, leaving about 2 table-spoons. Stir the flour into the fat, then add the 2 cups of broth. Stir over low heat till thickened to a gravy. Taste and adjust seasonings. Pour the gravy over the meat and sweet potatoes, then bake in a moderate, 350°F oven for about 40 minutes, till both are quite tender.

---

**OTHER RECIPES**
**FEATURING**
**WILD FOODS**

*Wild Plant Foods*
Fruit Juice Gelatine, p. 302
Green Noodles, p. 430
Gumbo Z'Herbes, p. 341
Making Rennet from Plants,
   p. 510
Roast Beverages, p. 42
Syrup from Black Birch and
   Other Trees, p. 401
Wild Spring Salad Greens, p. 532

*Wild Meats*
Game Meat and Pork Sausage,
   p. 552
Game Meat Pie, p. 50
Stewed Game Meat with Sauces,
   p. 308
Tomato Meat Sauce (with livers
   from small animals), p. 641
Wild Meat with Sauerkraut,
   p. 544

IT IS REMARKABLY GRATIFYING, ON SPECIAL OCCASIONS, TO BE ABLE to open a bottle of wine homemade from extra fruits, root vegetables, flower blossoms, or herbs. There is a long tradition of making such wines in Great Britain and parts of Europe, and they were made routinely in many early American households. The necessary ingredients are on hand in most family gardens and kitchens. Table wines from grapes can also be homemade—many families with a Mediterranean heritage make them—but they require special skill, some special equipment, and many bushels of the right varieties of grapes. Wine grapes can be a study in themselves. For example, grapes for making dry wine must be high in acidity and moderate in sugar content, while grapes for sweet wines should be less acidic with a high sugar content. From here on the subtleties multiply, till finally the individuality of a special variety grown in a particular vineyard during a particular season becomes significant.

For a first try at wine making, the fruit, root, blossom, and herb wines are clearly the best choice. If both the wine making experience and the wine are enjoyed, the interest can be followed wherever it may lead.

## HANDLING WINE

In nature fermentation is happening all the time. Wild yeasts convert the sugars in sweet, juicy fruits or sweet liquids into alcohol whenever they get the chance. The difficulty, from the wine maker's point of view, is that nature does not always have human taste buds in mind. Some wild yeasts cause a bad flavor, or they produce too little alcohol and the wine turns to vinegar. (Refer to WINE VINEGAR, in the VINEGAR section.) The wine maker's aim is to control the natural fermentation process so that the results will always taste good. The controls usually include using a cultured yeast, and adding sugar to insure a high alcohol content. Other basic requirements are warmth, and a way to control exposure to air (a fermentation lock).

The first step in wine making is preparing the must—the sweet, flavorful liquid that is to be fermented. Next comes the stage of rapid fermentation, lasting about a week, followed by an extended period of slower fermentation. When this ends, there is the clearing, bottling, aging, and, of course, the drinking of the wine.

## THE MUST

About 5 quarts of must are needed to make 1 gallon of wine. The must is flavored by fruits, root vegetables, blossoms or herbs, and usually sugar, and a live yeast starter added. Sometimes an acidic ingredient is needed as well. Some wine makers also add yeast nutrients, a sulfite for sterilizing the must, and clearing agents. None of the latter are described here, as wine can be made without them. However, many wine makers do find them useful. They are sold in wine making supply stores, and wine making books always explain them.

*Sugar Content*    Too little sugar in the must will produce wine with a low alcohol content that does not keep well. Too much sugar may prevent the wine from fermenting properly, or it may make wine overly sweet. Dry wines result when almost all of the sugar in the must is changed to alcohol, and the trick is to add as much sugar as the yeast can use, but no more. When wines are made from root vegetables, blossoms, or herbs containing very little natural sugar, from 3½ to 4 pounds are needed per gallon of wine. For fruit wines, the sugar requirement will vary with the sweetness of the fruit. Very few fruits are sweet enough without the addition of some sweetening.

A sweetener can be added to the must in two or three batches, while it ferments, rather than all at once at the beginning. In this way, the yeast can make better use of it. Honey or maple syrup can be used instead of sugar, if desired. As they add their own flavor, they should be used only with flavors with which they blend well. Substitute honey at the rate of 1 pound honey for 1 pound sugar.

*Acidity*    When fruit is used to make wine, it will supply the necessary acid. When roots, blossoms, or herbs are used, oranges, lemons, or some of each must be included. They will make the wine ferment better and they improve its flavor. If the must is too acidic because of underripe or sour fruit, the wine is likely to be astringent or harsh.

*Wine Yeast*    With the exception of a few kinds of grape wine, wild yeasts are not dependable for making good wine. The likelihood of poor fermentation and a bad flavor is too great. Though baking yeast can be used, the best wine is made with special wine yeasts from wine making suppliers. Fruit wines, especially, will benefit from the use of wine yeast. Baking yeast tends to leave a yeasty taste in the wine, it is harder to clear, and the final alcoholic content is usually lower. If using baking yeast, it can be spread on a piece of rye bread and floated in the must, hopefully making a yeasty taste less likely.

Before adding the wine yeast, the water used for the must is boiled to destroy wild yeasts and bacteria. Sometimes all ingredients are boiled, and it is important to use clean utensils at all stages of wine making, so that wild yeasts and bacteria are not introduced.

Yeast works best when the must is kept consistently warm. A room temperature of 65–70°F is ideal. Big temperature changes, as from warm days to cool night, will interfere with the yeast's activity.

## THE WINE'S FERMENTATION

Put the must in a crock, a sturdy polyethylene plastic pail, or another non-corrosive container. Do not fill the container more than ⅔ full. Add a cover to keep out dust and insects, but which allows the

*First stage of fermentation (5–10 days).*

Plastic tied or rubber banded in place.

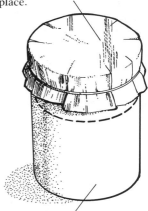

Non-corrosive container of must.

*Second stage of fermentation using simple lock.*

Tight stopper with tube through it.

Container kept full of water.

carbon dioxide gas that forms during fermentation to escape. Plastic, such as a large bag intended for use with food, will make a good cover because the carbon dioxide can easily escape, while there is little exposure to airborne contamination. Keep at an even room temperature. The must should begin to actively bubble and ferment within a day or two. After about a week the bubbling should subside.

When the must is bubbling only slightly, strain it through cloth to remove solids, then put it in a glass jug with a fermentation lock. The lock is a device that lets carbon dioxide escape while keeping air from entering. Fermentation locks that screw onto standard gallon jugs are available from wine making suppliers, but the illustrated arrangement works just as well. The tube through the stopper must be above the level of the must, and the level of the water in the small container must cover the end of the tube so that escaping carbon dioxide will go into the water and bubble out.

The second stage of fermentation lasts till all fermentation stops, usually 1 to 3 months. During this stage, the jug can be kept a little below room temperature, but it should not be kept in a cold place.

## CLEARING, BOTTLING, AND AGING

Sometimes wine will have cleared by itself by the time fermentation stops. If not, leave it another month or so to see if it improves, or siphon it into another jug, leaving sediment behind, and then let it sit. Some people report that adding a pinch of dry gelatine or a crumpled egg shell will help. Once the wine is clear, carefully siphon it into sterilized bottles and seal it airtight. Do not use old corks, because they may carry bad flavors or contamination. Plastic "corks" are available that are cheaper than genuine corks.

Some homemade wines taste good after only a month or two, and some are better aged from several months to a year. It is interesting to reserve bottles to open at different stages to see how the wine develops. Also, try using homemade wines at different temperatures, including well chilled and hot mulled, and use it in cooking. It enhances all kinds of mixed dishes. Dry wine is best in general cooking, and sweet wine is good in many old fashioned desserts. See the list alongside for recipes and ideas.

# WOODSTOVE COOKERY

COOKING ON AN OLD STYLE WOOD OR COAL BURNING COOKSTOVE IS A way of life that does not necessarily belong in the past. In the right circumstances, these old stoves have an economy and convenience that is not duplicated by any modern range, and they suit the needs of many country people as well now as they did in the past. With innovations, such as airtight fire boxes, and grates adjusting to different positions for winter and summer, they can be even more versatile.

An old style cookstove offers, with one batch of fuel, a hot oven, a warming oven or shelf, surfaces for frying and boiling, places for simmering or slow cooking, and places to cook very, very slowly. A busy person can be making soup stock, scalding milk for yogurt, keeping bread warm as it rises, baking a casserole for dinner, drying fruit, and, at the same time, heating the house and drying wet mittens. If there is a catch to this marvel, it is that it takes some expertise to operate it to live up to its full potential.

A wood cookstove must, to begin with, be properly installed with a chimney that draws well. The ashes and soot that build up inside the stove must be cleaned out regularly, especially in the spaces around and under the oven. Learning to adjust the drafts is essential for building quick fires and for controlling heat, including the oven heat. It is also useful to understand the burning characteristics of different kinds of wood, and to have an assortment of sizes and types of wood on hand. The help of someone who understands old style cookstoves, or a book describing in detail how to operate them will make it easier to get started. With time and experience, the operation of the stove becomes second nature, and there arises a satisfying warm glow from the stove, the cook, the family, and anyone passing by.

## WOODSTOVE COOKING
## IN HOT WEATHER

In summer the heat from an old style cookstove can be too much of a good thing. Here are some ways to alleviate the problem:

• As much as possible, cook early in the morning.

• Use a kind of wood that makes a quick, hot fire, and then burns out. It also helps to split the wood small.

• Some stoves have a grate that can be adjusted to a higher position in summer, allowing a smaller fire to be built for cooking. If the grate is not adjustable, it may be possible to devise a temporary grate for the same effect.

• Construct a vent above the stove to draw out heat. In the past, vents were sometimes made by installing a stove pipe from the ceiling directly over the fire box and out through the roof. A trap door in the ceiling could be opened to let out heat, and then closed when not needed. Add a cap to the stove pipe to keep out rain.

• Use a different stove in summer. An electric, gas, or camp stove can be used, but nicest of all is an outdoor summer kitchen. True wood stove lovers might have a second wood cookstove outdoors— ideally, under a roof, screened in, and with sink and work space alongside.

## COOKING WITH WOOD BURNING HEATERS

Any wood heating stove with a flat top can be used for some kinds of cooking. Soups, stews, steamed puddings, and other foods that need long cooking all do well. If low heat for simmering is wanted, a rack or two fire bricks can be put under the pot, as necessary. Some people have designed homemade stove top ovens that make baking possible as well. Also, the warm area around a wood burning stove can be useful for drying foods, keeping bread dough warm while it rises, and other activities.

---

### YIELD

I TABLESPOON DRY YEAST = I OUNCE CAKE OF YEAST = ½ CUP HOMEMADE YEAST (SEE BELOW) ⅔ OUNCE YEAST CAKE = 2 TEA-SPOONS DRY YEAST

# YEAST

A LONE "YEAST" IS A MICROSCOPIC, SINGLE CELLED PLANT OF THE fungus family. A tablespoon of yeast is a mass of billions of these cells. There are hundreds of yeast varieties, some useful and some troublesome. Wild, naturally occurring yeasts are sometimes useful, but at other times they can cause foods to spoil or they interfere with the action of cultured yeast or bacteria. Like any plant, a yeast is a valuable crop when there is a way to make use of it, and a weed when there is not. Most useful are yeast strains that have been isolated and cultured for special purposes, such as making bread, wine, or beer.

Yeast functions by converting carbohydrates to carbon dioxide and alcohol. When yeast bread is made, the carbon dioxide bubbles are

the desired product of the yeast's activity, because they make the bread rise. The tiny quantity of alcohol produced is eliminated during baking. When wine and beer are made, the alcohol is the desired product, and most of the carbon dioxide escapes into the air. Sometimes soda pop is made with yeast, by trapping carbon dioxide bubbles in the drink to make it fizzy.

## HANDLING YEAST

Today most live yeast is sold as dry granules that will keep for months if refrigerated. Dry yeast is so convenient and effective that it has supplanted other forms. Before it was developed, small, moist cakes of compressed yeast were generally available, but as these keep only a few weeks refrigerated, dry yeast is much more practical. Before the easy availability of any kind of yeast, housewives often kept yeast starters going, as in the recipes below. Long ago, before special baker's yeasts were isolated, bread was sometimes made using the barm (foam) that rises on fermenting beer.

*Conditions Affecting Live Yeasts*  All yeasts thrive in warm, moist conditions. They are active between about 50 and 100°F, with the greatest activity occurring in the middle of that range. Chilled or frozen yeast becomes inactive and then begins to work again when the temperature rises—unless it has died as a result of staying cold for too long. It will last about 2 months in the freezer. Yeast is killed by temperatures between about 140 and 190°F. One of the purposes of pasteurizing or scalding food is killing wild yeasts to prevent their activity. For more about live yeasts, refer to BREAD YEAST, in the BREAD, YEAST section, and WINE YEAST, in the WINE section.

## NUTRITIONAL YEAST

Dead, spent yeast is an important food supplement because of its high protein and B vitamin content. Brewer's yeast, a by-product of the brewing industry, is the best known among nutritional yeasts, but there are others grown specifically for use as food supplements. Live yeast should never be eaten, because it can remain active in the body and consume nutrients, rather than contributing them.

There is considerable variation in the taste of the different kinds of nutritional yeast. Some are mild in flavor and good added to all kinds of foods. They are often mixed with water or juice for drinking. Strong tasting nutritional yeasts can be used in the same ways, but the flavor may take some getting used to.

## RECIPES FOR MAKING YEAST

These recipes illustrate two ways to make old fashioned liquid yeast, preferred by some because its slow action gives breads such as rye and pumpernickel an especially good texture and flavor. The first recipe, which requires a yeast starter, is very dependable. It can be used to extend a limited supply of dry yeast. The second recipe is a way to capture and propagate wild yeasts—tricky, but interesting. Hops are called for to improve flavor, and in the hope of increasing the chances for an effective, non-sour yeast. (For sour starters, refer to the SOURDOUGH section.)

### *Liquid Yeast*                                    (Makes 5–6 cups.)

| | |
|---|---|
| *4 medium potatoes* | *3 tablespoons sugar* |
| *1 teaspoon salt* | *1 tablespoon dry yeast* |

Cook the potatoes in 1 quart of water. When done take them out, saving the cooking water, and put them through a potato ricer or food mill, or mash them well. (Peeling is optional.) Mix the potatoes, potato cooking water, salt, and sugar. Let cool to room temperature. Dissolve the yeast in ¼ cup lukewarm water, add it to the potato mixture, and put it in a large jar, or a crock. Let stand in a warm place, and every time it rises stir it down. After a day or so it will stop working. When it stops, put it in the refrigerator in a closed jar. Use ½ cup of this instead of 1 tablespoon dry yeast. When only ½ cup of the yeast remains, use it to make a new batch.

Eventually the liquid yeast will become weak and, perhaps, take on a bad odor. At this point, discontinue using this batch and start over again with more dry yeast.

**Liquid Yeast with Hops**   Cook the potatoes as above, then remove them from the water. Add 2 or 3 tablespoons hops to the water while it is hot. Let steep while the potatoes are being mashed, then strain, discarding the hops. Finish making the yeast as above. The hops help preserve the yeast, and give a special earthy flavor to breads raised with it.

## Mrs. Yarmol's Yeast
From *In the Kitchen,* by Elizabeth S. Miller, 1875.

**OTHER BASIC
YEAST PREPARATIONS**

Bread Yeast, p.67
Wine Yeast, p.695

"Three pounds of potatoes.

Half a pint of flour.

Half a pint of best brown sugar.

One pint of hops.

Two even teaspoonfuls of salt.

Two gallons of water.

Monday morning boil the hops in the water for half an hour, strain it in a crock, and let the liquid become milk-warm; add the salt and sugar, mix the flour smooth with some of the liquor, and then stir all well together. On Wednesday add the potatoes boiled and mashed, stir well, and let it stand till Thursday; then strain, and put it in stone jugs, but for the first day or two leave the corks quite loose; stir the yeast occasionally while making and keep near the fire. It should be made two weeks before using, and will keep any length of time, improving with age. Keep it in a cool place and shake the jug before pouring from it, but with the cork out, holding the palm of the hand over the mouth to prevent the escape of the yeast."

# YOGURT

**STORAGE**

**Cold Storage**  Keeps about 2 weeks refrigerated.

**Freezing**  Poor, loses texture when thawed. But excellent in frozen desserts. Refer to ICE CREAM section.

IT IS NATURAL FOR RAW MILK TO CLABBER, THAT IS TO THICKEN AND become sour when left sitting in a warm place. This clabbering is caused by the lactic-acid-producing bacteria naturally present in the milk or in the environment. There are many different lactic acid bacteria, which may be present in various circumstances, and the flavor of the clabbered milk will vary accordingly. Yogurt is one kind of clabbered milk that occurs naturally only in certain very warm climates where its particular bacteria are present. In order to make yogurt in other places, it is necessary first to heat the milk to destroy the natural bacteria and other organisms in it, then to add yogurt making bacteria and to keep the milk warm while they work.

For many centuries yogurt has been a well known and important food throughout the Balkans, the Middle East, and India. The name "yogurt" is Turkish. In many middle eastern countries it is known as laban. Since the successful isolation of the bacteria that produce yogurt, and the development of freeze dried cultures, yogurt has become well known and popular throughout the world. Many other kinds of clabbered milk are enjoyed in various places. Favorites have often been perpetuated for generations by saving a starter from one batch to add to the milk for the next batch. Several different kinds of "thick milk" are made in the Scandinavian countries. Kefir, which originated in the Caucasus, in Russia, contains, besides lactic acid bacteria, a lactose fermenting yeast which gives it a slight fizziness. Kumiss, also from Russia, is milk fermented with yeast rather than bacteria. It is said to have a very high alcoholic content when made from mare's milk. In North America in the early days, milk that clabbered naturally without a starter was eaten often and considered a delicacy. (Refer to BONNY-CLABBER, in the CHEESE, FRESH section.)

## HANDLING YOGURT

Homemade yogurt has a lighter, more delicate texture than most commercial brands. When store yogurt has a dense, pudding-like texture, stabilizers, such as gelatine or starch, have probably been added to it. Often there are no live or active bacteria in it, in which case it is merely a yogurt flavored product, and not yogurt, with beneficial live bacteria.

***Acidophilus Yogurt*** The bacteria most often used for making yogurt are L. bulgaricus, L. acidophilus, and Streptococcus thermophilus. All of these bacteria are helpful to the digestive system, but L. acidophilus is considered especially helpful, because it can become established in the digestive tract, and continue to be beneficial for long periods of time. As milk cultured only with L. acidophilus is more acid and thinner than yogurt made with a combination of bacteria, many people prefer the combination. The labels on yogurt and freeze dried yogurt cultures usually list the bacteria in them. Kefir also includes L. acidophilus. (See MAKING KEFIR, below.)

## MAKING YOGURT

The basic procedure for making yogurt is simple: warm milk is mixed with a starter, and then kept warm for several hours, till it clabbers—but there are many ways to go about doing this.

***The Milk*** Any kind of milk—whole, skim, partially skimmed, or light or heavy cream—from any dairy animal, as well as dry, powdered milk, or canned milk, can be made into yogurt. Even soy milk (refer to the SOYBEANS section) can be used. The only two requirements are that the milk be free of bacteria and other organisms that might interfere with the yogurt culture, and it be kept warm, between about 90 and 110°F. Scald fresh milk, or heat it to about 185°F to kill unwanted organisms. (Refer to SCALDING MILK, in the MILK section.) Then cool it till lukewarm, for adding the culture. If using a dairy thermometer cool to 115°F. (It can be cooled quickly by setting the pot of hot milk in a pan of cold water and stirring often.) Once the culture is stirred in, it will be just right for incubation. The temperature can also be tested without a thermometer by dripping milk on the wrist as when testing a baby's bottle, or by putting a finger in the milk and counting slowly to 10. If the heat is comfortable for that long the temperature is right.

When using powdered milk or canned milk, scalding will not be necessary, since they are already sterile. The powdered milk can be reconstituted with warm water, and the canned milk diluted with hot water for the right temperature.

If thick yogurt is preferred, add several tablespoons to ½ cup of powdered milk to each quart of milk before adding the culture. Or simmer the milk, uncovered, over very low heat till it is reduced by about ⅓, then cool, and then add the culture. This is often done in the Middle East. The milk must be watched carefully and stirred often to prevent burning.

***The Yogurt Culture***   Both fresh yogurt with live bacteria in it, and a freeze dried yogurt culture can be used as the starter for a new batch. Dried cultures are sold by most health food stores and through mail order catalogs. When using a dried culture, follow the directions that come with it.

Only some brands of plain yogurt can be used for a culture. If the label says that the cultures in the yogurt are live or active, that there are no odd ingredients such as stabilizers, flavorings, or preservatives, and it is fresh, then yogurt from the store makes an excellent starter. It is considerably cheaper than freeze dried cultures. After making the first batch of yogurt with a purchased starter, succeeding ones can be made with a starter saved from the batch before. About 2 tablespoons of fresh yogurt are needed for 1 quart of milk. To keep the process going, yogurt must be made every week or two.

When yogurt is made time after time with a starter from the previous batch, it may eventually lose flavor, change flavor, or refuse to set because of weakening or gradual changes in the culture. The cure is to start again with a fresh culture. Some suggest beginning with a fresh culture once a month, but many people find that their yogurt will taste good and set well for two months, and sometimes considerably longer. Strict cleanliness in handling milk and utensils will help yogurt cultures keep their good flavor longer.

***Yogurt Containers***   It is best to make yogurt in containers of a size to be used quickly, as it keeps best when unopened and undisturbed. If spoonfuls are taken out of a large container, whey will collect and spoilage organisms may get in. Cup or pint size glass jars are excellent. If using plastic containers, they should be smooth and without scratches. It is also helpful to scald them with boiling water.

***Yogurt Incubation***   While it is clabbering, yogurt must be incubated (kept warm) from 3 to 5 hours in a place where it will not be moved or disturbed. If there is a warm place with a steady temperature between 90 and 110°F, near a stove or heater, or in an oven with a pilot light, the yogurt can be incubated there. It should be kept in the dark as this will prevent loss of vitamin $B_2$. When a warm place is not handy, it is quite easy to insulate yogurt containers to hold in the heat for the necessary time. A large container can simply be wrapped in heavy towels or a blanket, or a thermos bottle can be used. Small containers can be kept in an insulated box, or in warm water as shown. Even in a cool room the yogurt will succeed, if well enough wrapped. Also, electric yogurt makers with controlled heat can be purchased.

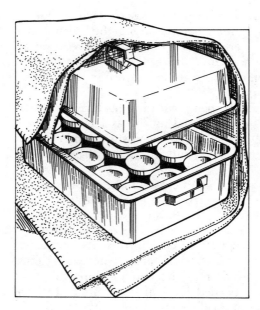

*Incubating yogurt.*

Wrap blanket or towels around pan.

Use a roasting pan with lid, or any large pot.

Yogurt in 1 cup sized jars, with lids.

Warm water, at about 110°F.

## YOGURT PROBLEMS

### *If Yogurt Does Not Set or Clabber:*
• The starter may not have been active (alive).
• The temperature may have been too high (above 115°F), killing the lactic-acid-producing bacteria.
• The temperature may have been too low (below 90°F), so that the bacteria worked too slowly. (In this case, the yogurt may still set, if given more time.)
• The yogurt may have been moved or disturbed during incubation.
• Traces of antibiotics or disinfectants in the milk or on utensils may have killed the lactic acid bacteria.
• Bacteriophage viruses may be destroying the yogurt bacteria. (This is not a common home problem. To get rid of the virus all cultures must be thrown out, and all utensils and work surfaces must be sterilized before a new culture can be started.)

### *If Yogurt Is Too Sour:*
• Incubation time may have been too long.
• Too much starter may have been used.

### *If Too Much Whey Collects:*
• The incubation time may have been too long.
• The temperature may have been just a little too high.

• Moving the yogurt during incubation may have caused curds and whey to separate.

*If the Yogurt Has an "Off" Taste, or Spoils:*
• The milk or the utensils may not have been clean.
• The culture may have been too old, or contaminated with spoilage organisms.

## COOKING WITH YOGURT

Cooked yogurt is not as nutritious as fresh, because it no longer has live bacteria in it. It does, however, have a nice, tart flavor that tastes good in all kinds of dishes. It can be used instead of buttermilk, sour milk, or sour cream in many recipes. In Middle Eastern cooking, it is used as the liquid in many kinds of meat or vegetable stews and soups. Goat's milk yogurt is easier to cook with than cow's milk yogurt, because it will not curdle. (See the *Stabilized Cow's Milk Yogurt* recipe, below.)

## MAKING KEFIR

After yogurt, kefir is probably the best known clabbered milk. Stores and mail order businesses which sell freeze dried yogurt cultures usually also sell kefir cultures. Kefir is made from milk in the same way as yogurt, except that it is incubated at room temperature, 65–75°F, for about 24 hours. Directions come with the culture. Many people prefer kefir, because of its unique fizzy taste, and because it can be made without special insulation, or a heat source to keep it warm.

Besides kefir made from the above yogurt-like culture, there is another kind made from small, curd-like particles called kefir grains. These are added to the milk to clabber it, and when they have done their work they are strained out and can be reused. They will last indefinitely if properly cared for. Kefir made from grains will be thinner and more like a beverage than kefir from a freeze dried culture. Live kefir grains are not readily available, but a few dairy products laboratories do carry them. They should not be confused with the dried kefir grains sometimes sold by health food stores as a nutritional supplement. Those are dead and cannot be used as a culture.

## YOGURT RECIPES

*Basic Yogurt*                                    (Makes about 1 quart.)

*1 quart milk*
*¼ – ½ cup dry powdered milk, optional (For thicker yogurt.)*

*2 – 3 tablespoons active yogurt (If using freeze dried culture, follow its directions.)*

Scald the milk, then cool to about 115°F. Stir in the powdered milk, if using it. Mix the active yogurt with a little of the warm milk and stir till smooth. If lumps persist put through a sieve. Mix the yogurt with the rest of the milk, then pour into containers. Keep warm, between 90 and 110°F, for 3 to 5 hours, till set. Open and tilt a container to check if the yogurt has set. When set, put it in the refrigerator to chill. The sooner it is chilled, the milder it will be.

**Flavored Yogurt**　Vanilla, honey, carob syrup (refer to the CAROB section), or other flavorings can be mixed with the milk before making it into yogurt, but it may be more practical to make plain yogurt, and add the desired flavorings when eating it. Fruits, which are a favorite addition, can be fresh, canned, or made into sauce and sweetened to taste. Or fruit jam or jelly can be used. Flavored yogurts make delicious sauces for puddings and fruit gelatines.

### Potato Raita
(A yogurt dish from India.)　　　　　　　　　　(Makes 4–6 side servings.)

| | |
|---|---|
| 2 cups yogurt | 1 teaspoon coriander seed, powdered |
| 2 medium cooked potatoes, chopped | |
| ½ teaspoon cayenne | ½ teaspoon cumin seed, powdered |

Put the yogurt in a bowl and stir till smooth. Add the potatoes, cayenne, coriander, and cumin. Chill well, and serve as a side dish with meals. Or serve with salad as a quick hot weather lunch or supper.

**Cucumber Raita**　Omit potatoes. Chop, or slice 1 or 2 cucumbers very thin. Salt very lightly, and then let drain in the refrigerator for about 2 hours. Mix the cucumber with the yogurt and use only cumin for seasoning. Or instead, season with garlic crushed with a garlic press, black pepper, and minced fresh mint or parsley leaves. Paprika can be sprinkled on top for color. A very pleasant salad in hot weather!

**Carrot, Onion, or Other Vegetable Raita**　Omit potatoes. Coarsely grate 2 or 3 carrots, and steam for about 3 minutes. Or thinly slice several onions and blanch them briefly in boiling water, or steam them. Or precook other vegetables to taste. Mix with yogurt, and season as for potato raita, or to taste in any other way. Serve as a vegetable side dish or relish.

### Yogurt Dressing for Vegetable Salads
(Makes 1–1¼ cups.)

| | |
|---|---|
| 1 cup yogurt | 1–2 tablespoons parsley, or other fresh herbs, minced |
| 1–2 tablespoons lemon juice | |
| 1–2 tablespoons scallions, chives, or onion, minced | pepper, paprika, salt, to taste |

Mix the yogurt with the other ingredients, adjusting amounts to taste. This dressing is delicious combined with leftover cooked vegetables, or on green salads, grated raw vegetable salads, egg salads, and many other mixtures.

### Yogurt Fruit Salad Dressing (Makes 1¼–1¾ cups.)

1 cup yogurt
¼ cup orange, pineapple, other fruit
    juice, or ½ cup tart applesauce
1 tablespoon honey, or to taste
1 teaspoon lemon juice, or to taste
½ teaspoon lemon or orange
    rind, grated, optional
½ teaspoon celery seed, crushed
    to bruise them, optional

Mix yogurt with fruit juice or applesauce, and flavor with honey, lemon juice, lemon or orange rind, and celery seed. Chill before pouring over the fruit salad. The citrus rind and celery seeds add an unexpected but very compatible piquancy to the dressing.

### Yogurt Cream Cheese (Makes 1–2 cups.)

1 quart yogurt (Or any convenient
    amount.)

Line a colander with a clean cloth and pour the yogurt into it. Leave in the colander as the whey drips off, or gather in the corners of the cloth to make a bag, then tie and hang it while it drains. Let drain all day or overnight, till a light creamy cheese forms in the cloth. Scrape the cheese into a container, cover, and refrigerate. It will keep from several days to a week.

Yogurt cream cheese is like regular cream cheese but a little more tart. It can be used in all the same ways.

**Yogurt Cheese Balls** Shape the yogurt cheese into small, round balls. If soft, let them sit covered overnight in the refrigerator. Then roll them in olive oil and sprinkle with paprika. They are sometimes served for breakfast in the Middle East, but are a nice snack any time, anywhere.

### Unbaked Yogurt Cheese Pie (Makes about 6 dessert servings.)

3 cups yogurt cream cheese (See
    preceding recipe.)
3 tablespoons honey
1 teaspoon vanilla, or grated
    orange peel
single 9 inch baked pie shell

Mix the yogurt cheese, honey, and vanilla or orange peel, and stir till completely smooth. Pour into the pie shell, then chill 24 hours before serving.

**Cream Cheese Pie** Make WHOLE MILK CREAM CHEESE (refer to the CHEESE, FRESH section) and use it instead of yogurt cream cheese to make the pie.

## YOGURT IDEA

**Yogurt Drinks** For a very simple and refreshing Middle Eastern style drink, mix 1 part yogurt with 1 part cold water. If desired, add some mint leaves and a dash of salt. This drink is especially light when mixed in a blender. Pour over ice cubes.

For yogurt shakes, use yogurt instead of milk with any favorite flavorings and blend till smooth in a blender. Yogurt makes excellent banana and other fruit shakes. (Buttermilk can also be used in these drinks instead of yogurt.)

*Yogurt Cheese Cake*                              (Makes about 6 dessert servings.)

2 cups yogurt cream cheese (See recipe above.)
3 eggs, separated
1 tablespoon lemon juice

1 teaspoon grated lemon rind
½ cup honey
single unbaked 9 inch graham cracker crumb crust

Mix the yogurt cream cheese, egg yolks, lemon juice, lemon rind, and honey till smooth. Beat the egg whites till stiff, then fold them in. Pour into the crust and bake in a low, 300°F oven for 40 minutes, till set. This cake is outstanding with fresh berries or other fruits.

*Cheese Cake* Use WHOLE MILK CREAM CHEESE (refer to the CHEESE, FRESH section) instead of yogurt cream cheese in this recipe.

*Stabilized Cow's Milk Yogurt*                              (Makes 5 cups.)

Cow's milk yogurt will curdle when cooked, unless stabilized in some way. (If using goat's milk yogurt which does not curdle, this procedure will be unnecessary.)

5 cups cow's milk yogurt

1 egg white, or 1 tablespoon cornstarch

Put the yogurt in a saucepan and beat till smooth. Next, if using egg white, beat it lightly. If using cornstarch, mix it with about 2 tablespoons of water. Then add the egg white or cornstarch to the yogurt. Heat slowly, stirring constantly in the same direction till it begins to simmer. Keep heat very low and simmer about 10 minutes, till thickened. Do not cover the pot, because condensed moisture dripping from the lid may ruin the yogurt. When thickened, the yogurt can be cooked with other ingredients, as desired.

*Yogurt Horseradish Sauce for Vegetables* Cook 2 cups yogurt with 1 tablespoon cornstarch, as described. When thickened to a sauce, remove from heat and mix in 1 to 2 tablespoons grated horseradish. Season with pepper, and salt, if desired. If more tartness is preferred, add about a teaspoon of vinegar. Pour over hot cooked vegetables and serve immediately. Especially good with Brussels sprouts and broccoli.

*Armenian Yogurt Soup*                              (Makes 9–12 medium bowls.)

2 eggs
5 cups yogurt
¼ pound noodles, or other pasta
pepper, salt, optional

1 large onion, minced
4 tablespoons (about) butter
3 tablespoons dried mint, or fresh mint, minced

Beat the eggs lightly in a pot, then add the yogurt and beat together till smooth. Put over low heat, then bring slowly to a boil, stirring constantly in the same direction. (This will prevent curdling of cow's milk yogurt.) When it boils, add 2 cups water, and the noodles or pasta. Return to a boil, then simmer till the noodles or pasta are done.

If too thick add water to taste. Season with pepper, and salt, if desired.

Meanwhile, sauté the onion in butter till golden. Then add mint and sauté another minute. To serve, ladle soup into bowls, and add some of the onion, mint and butter to each. As invigorating in winter as chilled yogurt dishes are refreshing in summer.

# SUBJECT INDEX

# INDEX OF RECIPES & FOOD IDEAS